THE
NEW BOOK
OF
KNOWLEDGE

THE
NEW BOOK
OF
KNOWLEDGE

Scholastic Library Publishing, Inc.
Danbury, Connecticut

VOLUME 12

M

M, the 13th letter in the English alphabet, was also the 13th letter in the ancient Hebrew and Phoenician alphabets and the twelfth letter in the classical Greek alphabet. The Hebrews and Phoenicians called it *mem.* The Greeks called it *mu.*

Many language scholars believe that the Phoenician word *mem* meant water and that the form of the letter was a simplified picture of waves. The letter *mem* looked like this: ↯.

The Greeks based their alphabet on that of the Phoenicians and borrowed the Phoenician letter M without changing its sound. The Greek *mu* looked like this: *M* .

Since the time of the Greeks, neither the consonant sound nor the shape of the letter has changed very much. The Romans learned the Greek alphabet from another ancient people, called the Etruscans. They wrote the letter as the Greeks had written it: M. It is this version that is used in the English alphabet today.

In English the sound of M, as in *mat*, is produced by pressing the lips together and making the sound while the air blocked by the lips passes through the nose. Unlike many other letters, the letter M is never silent except before N in a few words derived from the Greek language, such as *mnemonic.*

In Roman numerals, M is the symbol for 1,000. An M with a line above it ($\overline{\text{M}}$) denotes 1,000,000. M is also the abbreviation for Master in college degrees. A small m can stand for either mile or meter in measurements. It can also stand for married in genealogy. In Germany, M stands for mark, the basic unit of money.

M is found in many other abbreviations, among them mm, which stands for millimeter. In chemistry, Mg stands for the element magnesium. In French, M. stands for monsieur. In the U.S. Army, Maj. is the abbreviation for major, and MP stands for military police. In England, an M.P. is a member of Parliament.

Reviewed by MARIO PEI
Author, *The Story of Language*

See also ALPHABET.

MAASS, CLARA. See NEW JERSEY (Famous People).

SOME WAYS TO REPRESENT M:

The **manuscript** or printed forms of the letter (left) are highly readable. The **cursive** letters (right) are formed from slanted flowing strokes joining one letter to the next.

The **Manual Alphabet** (left) enables a deaf person to communicate by forming letters with the fingers of one hand. **Braille** (right) is a system by which a blind person can use fingertips to "read" raised dots that stand for letters.

The **International Code of Signals** is a special group of flags used to send and receive messages at sea. Each letter is represented by a different flag.

International Morse Code is used to send messages by radio signals. Each letter is expressed as a combination of dots (•) and dashes (– –).

MacARTHUR, DOUGLAS (1880–1964)

General Douglas MacArthur was one of the most brilliant and controversial American military leaders. He was born on January 26, 1880, in Little Rock, Arkansas. His father, Arthur MacArthur, was a famous general. Young MacArthur graduated from the U.S. Military Academy at West Point in 1903 at the head of his class. Years of service in various parts of the world followed.

During World War I, MacArthur commanded the 42nd (Rainbow) Division in France. He was wounded a number of times and cited for bravery seven times.

MacArthur returned to West Point as its superintendent in 1919. In 1930 he was appointed U.S. Army chief of staff—the youngest man ever to hold the post. In 1935, MacArthur became military adviser to the government of the Philippines. After the United States entered World War II in 1941, Japanese troops invaded the Philippines. MacArthur commanded the Filipino and American soldiers in a heroic but hopeless resistance. Ordered to Australia, he made his famous promise, "I shall return."

From Australia, MacArthur led the Allied campaign in the Southwest Pacific that brought him back victoriously to the Philippines and that helped defeat Japan. After the war ended in 1945, MacArthur was given command of the occupation forces in Japan. He introduced reforms, including a democratic constitution, that changed Japanese society.

When the Korean War broke out in 1950, MacArthur was named commander of the United Nations forces. His bold amphibious landing behind North Korean lines at Inchon seemed the decisive blow of the war. But the entry of Chinese troops into the war led to prolonged, bitter fighting. MacArthur wanted to strike at Chinese territory. Forbidden to do so, he publicly criticized U.S. government policy. In 1951, President Harry S. Truman angrily removed him from command. MacArthur returned to the United States, where many Americans greeted him as a hero.

MacArthur was mentioned as a possible Republican candidate for president in 1952 but failed to get the nomination. He died in Washington, D.C., on April 5, 1964.

Reviewed by JULES ARCHER
Author, *Front-Line General: Douglas MacArthur*

MACAULAY, DAVID. See CHILDREN'S LITERATURE (Profiles).
MACBETH. See SHAKESPEARE, WILLIAM.

MACDONALD, SIR JOHN A. (1815–1891)

Sir John A. Macdonald is rightly called the father of Canadian Confederation. It was his ability to persuade political opponents to cooperate and compromise that helped create the Dominion of Canada in 1867.

John Alexander Macdonald was born in Glasgow, Scotland, on January 11, 1815. He came as a boy to Kingston, Upper Canada, and grew up to become a successful lawyer. When the provinces of Upper and Lower Canada (now Ontario and Quebec) were united in 1841, Macdonald became active in politics. In 1844 he was elected to Parliament as a moderate Conservative. Two years later he became a cabinet member. Macdonald rose in his party and laid the foundation for the alliance of English Conservatives and French Liberals that came to power in 1854. In 1857 he became leader of the Conservatives.

The union of the two Canadas gave each equal power in Parliament. Because of this and because of religious and language differences, no party could get enough support to stay in office more than a few years. By 1864 the Canadian Parliament was deadlocked, and Macdonald was ready to consider some basic change in the constitution. The leader of the Liberals, George Brown, was an enemy of Macdonald's. Nevertheless, Brown offered to join with him to break the deadlock.

Later in 1864 Macdonald, Brown, and other leading Canadians visited a conference of statesmen from the Maritime colonies held at Charlottetown, Prince Edward Island. They persuaded them to consider a federation of all British North America. At a second conference, in Quebec City, terms were agreed on for a new federal constitution—the British North America Act. Macdonald led in these developments, and he became Canada's first prime minister when the Dominion was formed in 1867. He was knighted that same year.

Only the provinces of Nova Scotia, New Brunswick, Ontario, and Quebec joined the Confederation in 1867. But Macdonald worked to extend the new Dominion from the Atlantic to the Pacific. In 1869 the lands that are now the Prairie Provinces were bought from the Hudson's Bay Company. In 1870 British Columbia joined, and in 1873 Prince Edward Island was added.

British Columbia entered the Dominion because Macdonald had promised to build a transcontinental railroad. He won an election in 1872, but he was forced from office by his political enemies when it was learned that his party had accepted campaign funds from Hugh Allan, a shipowner who wanted the railroad contract. This incident is called the Pacific Scandal.

The Liberals held office from 1873 to 1878. But Macdonald easily won re-election in 1878 with promises to build the railroad and to help industry in eastern Canada by a "National Policy" of higher tariffs, or taxes, on foreign-made goods. With government help the Canadian Pacific Railway was completed in 1885. Macdonald's National Policy seemed so successful that it was carried on by later Liberal governments.

However, Macdonald faced problems that threatened to destroy his young country. Twice—in 1870 and 1885—Louis Riel led rebellions in the western territories against their inclusion in the Dominion. Riel's execution in 1885 for treason cost Macdonald the support of many French Canadians, who thought Riel was fighting for French Canadian rights. Macdonald was also opposed by some provinces who claimed that the federal government was too powerful. In 1891 Macdonald won his last election—a campaign to defend his National Policy. But the strain of the campaign led to a stroke and his death on June 6, 1891.

Throughout his life Macdonald suffered many family misfortunes, including the death of his first wife and one of their sons. Popular with everyone for his happy, carefree manner, John A., as he was called, was never a great orator. But his political strength came from his ability to talk with everyone and to win compromises even from his enemies.

JOHN S. MOIR
University of Toronto

MACDOWELL, EDWARD (1860–1908)

Edward MacDowell was one of the first American composers to win international recognition. He was born in New York City on December 18, 1860, and began his musical training there. Because of his exceptional talent, Edward's music teachers advised him to continue his musical education in Paris. Edward and his mother moved there in 1876.

For two years he studied piano at the Paris Conservatory. He then went to Germany to study piano and composition with some of the leading teachers of the time. The great Franz Liszt heard MacDowell, and in 1882 he arranged for him to play before an important international music society.

When MacDowell's formal studies were completed, he decided to stay in Germany. He earned a living teaching piano and giving concerts; he devoted his spare time to composition. One of his first piano pupils was an American, Marian Nevins, whom he married in 1884. Four years later they returned to the United States and settled in Boston.

MacDowell's reputation as a composer, concert pianist, and teacher grew steadily. In 1896, Columbia University appointed him its first professor of music, calling him "the greatest musical genius America has produced." Nine years later MacDowell developed a severe mental illness that ended his career. He died on January 23, 1908.

Although only 47 when he died, MacDowell had already achieved considerable fame. His two piano concertos and *Indian Suite* for orchestra are still played. Probably his best-known works are the short pieces for piano, *Woodland Sketches*, *Fireside Tales*, and *New England Idyls*.

After his death, MacDowell's admirers established the MacDowell Colony as a memorial to him. The colony, located in Peterborough, New Hampshire, offers young American artists an inexpensive place to work in quiet and inspiring surroundings.

Reviewed by MARGERY MORGAN LOWENS
Peabody Conservatory of Music

MACEDONIA

F.Y.R. Macedonia

Macedonia is a nation in southeastern Europe that was once a republic of the former nation of Yugoslavia. It is bordered by Bulgaria on the east, Greece on the south, Albania on the west, and Serbia and Montenegro on the north. Skopje, situated on the Vardar River, is the capital and largest city.

The name "Macedonia" also refers to a larger historical region of the Balkan Peninsula. Ancient Macedonia was the kingdom from which Alexander the Great conquered a vast empire.

People. About two-thirds of the population is ethnic Macedonian and one-quarter is Albanian. Turks and Serbs make up most of the remainder of the population. The official language is Macedonian, which belongs to the South Slavic group of languages. Most Macedonians are members of the Eastern Orthodox Church. The Turks and most of the Albanians practice Islam.

Land. Macedonia is mountainous and crossed by several valleys, notably the valley of the Vardar River. The highest peak, Mount Korab, rises 9,030 feet (2,752 meters) on the Albanian border. The climate is marked by hot summers and cold, snowy winters.

Economy. Macedonia is a poor nation, with an economy based chiefly on agricultural produce, including rice, tobacco, wheat, corn, millet, cotton, sesame, mulberry leaves, citrus, vegetables, and livestock.

History and Government. The historical region of Macedonia was ruled by the Ottoman Turks from the 1300's until the 1800's. Following the Balkan Wars of 1912–13, Macedonia was divided among Greece, Serbia, and Bulgaria. In 1918, Serbian Macedonia became part of the newly formed Yugoslavia.

Macedonia proclaimed its independence from Yugoslavia in 1991. A dispute with Greece over the name "Macedonia" delayed its entry into the United Nations until 1993, when it officially became the Former Yugoslav Republic of Macedonia. In 2001, NATO forces restored order after a growing self-government movement among Macedonia's ethnic Albanians led to armed rebellion.

Macedonia's government consists of an elected Assembly (the Sobranje), with a president as head of state. Boris Trajkovski, elected president in 1999, died in 2004. Social Democrat leader Branko Crvenkovski was elected to succeed him.

Reviewed by JANUSZ BUGAJSKI
Center for Strategic and International Studies

MACHIAVELLI, NICCOLÒ. See RENAISSANCE (Profiles).

MACHINES. See WORK, POWER, AND MACHINES.

MACKENZIE, ALEXANDER. See CANADA, GOVERNMENT OF (Profiles).

FACTS and figures

THE FORMER YUGOSLAV REPUBLIC OF MACEDONIA is the official name of the country.

LOCATION: Southeastern Europe.

AREA: 9,781 sq mi (25,333 km²).

POPULATION: 2,100,000 (estimate).

CAPITAL AND LARGEST CITY: Skopje.

MAJOR LANGUAGE: Macedonian.

MAJOR RELIGIOUS GROUP: Eastern Orthodox.

GOVERNMENT: Republic. **Head of state**—president. **Head of government**—prime minister. **Legislature**—Assembly (Sobranje).

CHIEF PRODUCTS: Agricultural—rice, tobacco, wheat, corn, millet, cotton, sesame, mulberry leaves, citrus, vegetables, livestock. **Manufactured**—textiles, wood products, tobacco products, processed foods. **Mineral**—coal, metallic chromium, lead, zinc, ferronickel.

MONETARY UNIT: Denar (1 denar = 100 deni).

MACKENZIE, SIR ALEXANDER (1764–1820)

The first white person to cross North America and reach the Pacific Ocean above Mexico was the explorer Alexander Mackenzie. Mackenzie was born in Scotland in 1764. When he was a child the family moved to New York. In 1778 young Mackenzie was sent to school in Montreal, but he soon left school to join a fur-trading company.

In 1784, Mackenzie's employers sent him to Fort Detroit on a trading and exploring expedition. But to his disappointment, he found that much of the area had already been explored, and he returned to Canada.

On June 3, 1789, Mackenzie started out on an expedition for the newly formed North West Company. With a small party of Canadians and Indians, he left Fort Chipewyan on the shores of Lake Athabasca in central Canada. For the next three weeks, the group sought an outlet from the frozen waters of Great Slave Lake to the Pacific Ocean. Finally they discovered a river—but it flowed north-west to the Arctic Ocean, instead of west to the Pacific. Mackenzie called it the Disappointment River, but the great stream now bears his name. In September the disgruntled party returned to the fort, traveling nearly 3,000 miles (4,800 kilometers) by canoe.

In 1793, Mackenzie set out on a new attempt to reach the Pacific Ocean. Starting on the Peace River, he led his small party westward. On July 22, 1793, after a slow and dangerous journey, the group finally caught sight of the Pacific Ocean, at Dean Channel in what is now British Columbia.

After this victory, Mackenzie turned to fur trading and became rich. Later he went to England, where he published a book about his explorations. In 1802 he was knighted by King George III. Sir Alexander returned to Canada and served for several years in the Legislative Assembly of Lower Canada. In 1808 he settled in Scotland, where he remained until his death on March 11, 1820.

Reviewed by NOEL B. GERSON
Author, *The Magnificent Adventures of Alexander Mackenzie*

MACKENZIE, WILLIAM LYON (1795–1861)

William Lyon Mackenzie, known as the "little rebel," was born on March 12, 1795, near Dundee, Scotland. In 1820 he immigrated to Canada. In 1824, in Queenston, he started a newspaper, the *Colonial Advocate*, which he soon moved to York. In 1822 he had married Isabel Baxter.

Mackenzie became deeply involved in politics as a Reformer. His criticism of the Family Compact, the small group that ran the colony of Upper Canada, led to an attack on his printing shop. But this only served to make him a popular hero.

In 1828 Mackenzie was elected to the Legislative Assembly. A fiery speaker, he was expelled from the Assembly five times for criticizing it. But each time he was re-elected. In 1835, when York became Toronto, Mackenzie became its first mayor. The following year he wrote most of the famous *Seventh Report of the Committee on Grievances*.

Mackenzie had said many harsh things against the government. But he never suggested rebellion until the lieutenant-governor, Sir Francis Bond Head, interfered in the elections of 1836 to defeat the Reformers. In December 1837, Mackenzie led a revolt in Toronto. It was poorly planned, and only a few hundred men joined him. The rebellion was easily put down, and Mackenzie escaped to Navy Island in the Niagara River. There he hoped Americans would help him make Upper Canada a republic. He received some support from American sympathizers, but the United States government sent him to prison for violating the neutrality laws.

After his release from prison, Mackenzie lived with his family in New York City until 1849, when he was allowed to return to Canada. From 1851 to 1858 he again sat in Parliament but had little influence. He died in Toronto on August 28, 1861.

JOHN S. MOIR
University of Toronto

MACLACHLAN, PATRICIA. See CHILDREN'S LITERATURE (Profiles).

MACMILLAN, HAROLD (1894–1986)

Harold Macmillan was a Conservative member of Parliament (1924–29; 1931–45; 1945–64) and prime minister of Great Britain (1957–63). Born Maurice Harold Macmillan in London on February 10, 1894, he was the grandson of the founder of the Macmillan publishing house. Educated at Oxford University, he fought in France during World War I and in 1916 was severely wounded at the Battle of the Somme. After marrying Lady Dorothy Cavendish in 1920, he entered the family publishing business. He was elected to Parliament for the first time in 1923 as a Conservative who favored progressive social reform.

During World War II Macmillan was sent to Allied Headquarters in North Africa to serve as Prime Minister Winston Churchill's political representative (1942–45). Later, as minister of housing (1951–54), he won a reputation as "the man who got things done." After brief terms as minister of defense (1954–55), foreign secretary (1955), and chancellor of the exchequer (1955), Macmillan succeeded the ailing Anthony Eden as prime minister on January 10, 1957. His quiet, confident style boosted Conservative morale and helped his party win an increased majority in the 1959 general election.

As prime minister, Macmillan's first priority was to strengthen Anglo-American relations, which had been strained by Great Britain's actions in the Suez Crisis of 1956. He also sought to ease tensions between the United States and the Soviet Union, first regarding the Berlin Wall (1961) and later during the Cuban Missile Crisis (1962). Another priority was to strengthen Britain's ties to Europe by having it join the European Economic Community (or Common Market), but Macmillan's attempts were rejected by the French president, Charles de Gaulle.

In 1963, a scandal broke out concerning the private life of John Profumo, Macmillan's minister for war. The media criticized Macmillan and charged that the "Profumo Affair" proved he was out of touch with his government. It was ill health, however, that forced him to resign in October 1963. He later published his memoirs in six volumes. On his 90th birthday he was created Earl of Stockton. He died on December 29, 1986.

ALAN PALMER
Author, *The Penguin Dictionary of Modern History*

MACON. See GEORGIA (Cities).

MACRAMÉ

Macramé, the art of decorative knotting, is a fascinating craft, and is not difficult to learn. Most macramé pieces are made by tying cord or yarn into just three different kinds of knots —the square knot, the double half hitch, and the overhand knot—and simple variations of these knots. If you can tie a shoelace, you can learn to make these knots.

You can use these knots to make many useful items—key chains, watch straps, necklaces, lamp shades, pillows, placemats, purses and book bags, and belts for every size and shape of person. You can also make purely decorative items such as wall hangings and holiday decorations. As your skill in macramé increases, more ideas will occur to you.

Macramé is a very old craft. In Spain and Italy during the 1400's, macramé lace was used to decorate items used in churches. Since that time, interest in macramé has faded and revived many times. In the mid-1800's, American and British sailors whiled away the hours during long voyages by knotting, and they became quite skilled. The most recent revival of interest in macramé began in the United States in the 1960's.

▶GETTING STARTED

To get started in macramé, you will need some tightly twisted cord or yarn; several long, sturdy pins ("T" pins); a pair of scissors; and a ruler or tape measure. You will also need a board about 12 by 18 inches (30 by 46 centimeters) on which to do your work. It should be firm, but soft enough for pins to be pushed into it.

The supplies are easily found. Sturdy pins are available wherever sewing supplies are sold. Craft shops carry cord that is specifically made for macramé. It comes in an assortment of lovely colors and is available in a number of weights or textures. Hardware stores also

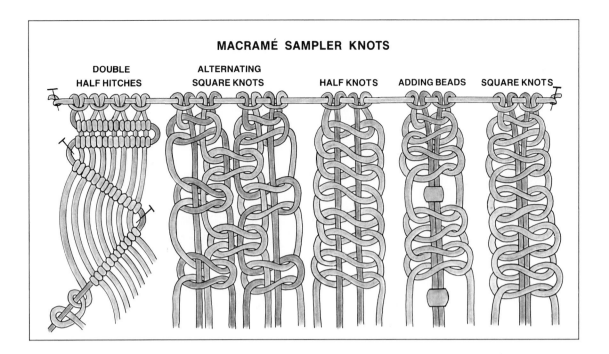

MACRAMÉ SAMPLER KNOTS

DOUBLE HALF HITCHES · ALTERNATING SQUARE KNOTS · HALF KNOTS · ADDING BEADS · SQUARE KNOTS

have cord that is excellent for knotting. It is called seine twine, chalk line, or mason line. It is often white or yellow and is made of either cotton or nylon. Cotton cord is easier than synthetics for a beginner to work with because it is less slippery. Good sizes for knotting are numbers 18 and 24.

A piece of insulating board or wallboard makes a good knotting board. You can also use a plastic foam pillow form or even a stack of cardboard or corrugated cardboard pieces, glued together at the edges.

That is all the equipment you need, but there are other items that are fun or helpful to have on hand. You may want some beads or bells with large holes, a few small dowels or sticks, or a key ring for your projects. Other useful items are rubber bands, for holding loose ends of cord, and a small crochet hook, to help pull the cords through the beads.

▶ HINTS FOR MAKING PROJECTS

Before starting on a project, practice your knotting technique. The best way to do this is to make a sampler. Complete instructions for a sampler appear in this article. The Macramé Sampler Knots Chart above and the Knotting Chart on page 7a will guide you in tying the basic knots from which your sampler and most other macramé pieces are formed.

When you are comfortable with the basic knots, you are ready to attempt your first projects. Here are some tips that will help you.

• It is hard to know how long each cord should be cut. Tightly knotted work requires more cord than open work. As a general rule, measure each cord eight times longer than your finished work will be. You will fold each cord in half when you mount it, so each knotting cord will be four times longer than the finished work.

• If the cords are very long, they will be difficult to work with. Shorten each one by rolling it into a neat bundle and fastening it with a rubber band.

• Use pins freely to anchor your work and to pull against while knotting.

• Before you tighten each knot, make sure it is in the place where you want it to be.

• Firmly knotted pieces tend to look neat and handsome.

• Knots look crisp and clear when tightly twisted cords are used. Other cords and yarns may be used, but the effect will be different.

As you become more skilled at the art of macramé, you may want to try other variations of the basic knots. If you look at books devoted to macramé, you will find pictures and ideas, as well as shortcuts and helpful hints.

▶ MAKING A SAMPLER

A good way to learn macramé is to make a sampler showing some basic kinds of knots. You will need about 50 feet (15 meters) of

KNOTTING CHART

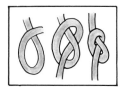

OVERHAND KNOT

Make a loop. Bring the end of the cord through the loop. Pull to tighten the knot.

LARK'S HEAD KNOT

Fold the cord in half. Place the loop in front of the dowel or knotting cord (A). Pull the loop behind the dowel (B). Pull the 2 ends of the cord through the loop (C). Tighten.

HALF KNOT/SQUARE KNOT

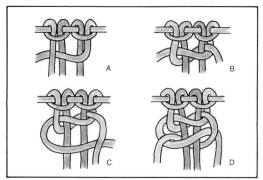

Put the right cord over the 2 center cords and under the left cord (A). Then pass the left cord under the 2 center cords and through the loop formed by the right cord (B). Steps A and B complete a half knot. To make a square knot, continue to diagram C, placing what is now the left cord over the 2 center cords and under the right cord. Then pass the right cord under the 2 center cords and through the loop formed by the left cord (D). Tighten.

HALF HITCH/DOUBLE HALF HITCH

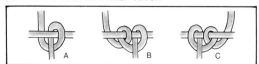

To make a half hitch, place the knotting cord behind the holding cord. Bring it under the holding cord, then up and over it, passing the end of the knotting cord through the loop (A). To form a double half hitch, continue by passing the knotting cord up and over the holding cord and pulling it through the loop (B). Tighten. Diagrams A and B show a half hitch worked from left to right across a holding cord. Diagram C shows the same knot worked from right to left.

HORIZONTAL DOUBLE HALF HITCH

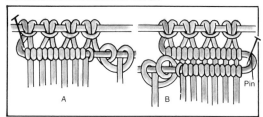

Place a pin as shown in diagram A to anchor your holding cord so you can keep it in a horizontal position across the other cords. Tie a double half hitch with the first cord at left. Repeat with each of the cords across the row (A). To reverse direction, move your pin to the right side and, using the same holding cord, position it in the opposite direction and tie a double half hitch with each cord, working from right to left (B).

ALTERNATING SQUARE KNOTS

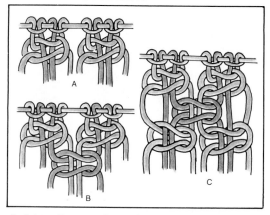

Begin by making a row of square knots with each group of 4 cords (A). Then for the next row, put the first 2 cords aside. Tie a square knot with 2 cords from the first knot of the previous row and 2 cords from the second knot of the previous row. Continue, using 2 cords from the second knot and 2 from the third, and so on. The last 2 cords will remain unused (B). The third row repeats the first row (C), the fourth row repeats the second row, and so on.

DIAGONAL DOUBLE HALF HITCHES

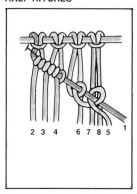 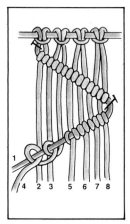

To make a line of diagonal double half hitches from upper left to lower right, place the pin between cords 1 and 2 and use the far left cord (1) as the knotting cord. Place it at the desired angle across the other cords and make a double half hitch with each cord (A). To reverse direction, place the pin to the right of cord 8. Position the holding cord at the desired angle across the other cords, and tie double half hitches, beginning with cord 8 as shown.

In order to clarify the knotting procedures, the holding cords appear slightly darker than the knotting cords in these diagrams.

cord and a few beads of a size that will slide onto the cord. You may wish to use different cord colors for each knot. Begin by cutting 13 cords, each 45 inches (115 centimeters) long. Cut another cord 14 inches (36 centimeters) long. This short cord will be your mounting cord; the others will be your knotting cords.

Make an **overhand knot** near each end of the short cord (see the Knotting Chart). Spread the cord on your knotting board. Push a strong pin through each knot and into the board to hold the mounting cord in place.

Now you are ready to attach your knotting cords to the mounting cord. Attach the first cord with a **lark's head knot** as shown in the Knotting Chart. Then take another cord and mount it to the left of the first one. You now have four cord ends with which to knot.

Square Knots. Your first piece of work will be a sennit, or row, of square knots. To make a square knot, follow the diagram in the Knotting Chart.

Continue making square knots until the sennit is about 4 inches (10 centimeters) long.

Adding Beads. Make another sennit that includes beads. Attach two more cords to the mounting cord and make two square knots. Then thread the core cords through the center of a bead. Push the bead up until it rests just below the last square knot. Make another square knot just below the bead, to hold it in place. Then continue making square knots, inserting beads wherever you please.

Half Knots. A spiral sennit will form if you make just the first half of the square knot and repeat that over and over again. Attach two more knotting cords and start making half square knots, one right under the other.

Alternating Square Knots. Alternating square knots form an interesting pattern. The procedure is shown in the Knotting Chart. Attach four knotting cords to your board so that you have eight free ends with which to knot. Make a square knot using the first four cords and another square knot using the last four cords. Then take the first two cords and the last two cords and pin them out of the way. Make a square knot using the four center cords. Release the cords you have set aside. Make square knots again—one from the first four cords and one from the last four cords. Repeat the above steps alternating between rows of one and two square knots until your sennit reaches the desired length.

Double Half Hitches. Your last sennit will be made up of double half hitches. See the Knotting Chart for instructions on how to form the knots. Again, attach four cords so that you have eight free ends with which to knot. Think of them as being numbered 1 through 8, from left to right. Put a pin just below the mounting cord, between cords 1 and 2. Then place cord 1 on top of all the other cords, just below the mounting cord. This cord will be your **knot-bearing cord**.

Tie a double half hitch with the first cord at the left (cord 2). Repeat with cords 3, 4, 5, 6, 7, and 8 to make a row of horizontal double half hitches. Then reverse directions. Put a pin between your last cord and the knot-bearing cord. Then bring the knot bearer all the way over to the left. It should be just under your first row of knots. Hold the knot bearer with your left hand. With your right hand, make another row. Follow the same steps, but start from the right, using cords 8, 7, 6, 5, 4, 3, and 2.

Next, use double half hitches to make angles, as shown in the Knotting Chart. Begin from the left. Place a pin between your knot-bearing cord and cord 2, and bring your knot bearer over to the right. Hold it at about a 45-degree angle to your last row of knots. (If you want your angles to be perfect, you can draw a 45-degree angle on your knotting board and use it as a guide.) Make a row of double half hitches all along the knot bearer from left to right. Then change directions. Bring the knot bearer back to the left at another 45-degree angle, pin it in place, and knot from right to left along it.

Continue to practice double half hitches by angling to the right again. Finish with two rows of horizontal double half hitches.

Finishing the Sampler. You will notice that some of the cords of your sampler are much longer than the others. The cords in the center of the square-knot sennits are longest because they stayed in place while the other cords made knots around them. To finish your sampler, trim the cords so that they are all the same length. Near the bottom of each cord, make an overhand knot. If your cords are slippery, make an overhand knot just below the last knot of your sampler, too. Your sampler is now complete.

HELENE BRESS
Author, *The Macramé Book*

MADAGASCAR

Madagascar is an island nation located in the Indian Ocean off the southeastern coast of Africa. It is the fourth largest island in the world, after Greenland, New Guinea, and Borneo. Its people, who are called Malagasy, have developed a unique mixture of Asian and African cultures. Formerly a French colony, Madagascar gained its independence in 1960.

▶THE PEOPLE

Some of the earliest inhabitants of Madagascar came from what is now Indonesia. Others were black Africans who crossed the Mozambique Channel from the African mainland. The descendants of the Indonesian settlers, known as the Merina, once ruled most of Madagascar. Today the Merina generally live in the interior near the capital city, Antananarivo. They are outnumbered by the var-

The marketplace in Antananarivo, the capital and largest city of Madagascar. The Rova, the royal estate of the old Merina kingdom, overlooks the city.

ious groups of black African descent, who live mostly along the coast.

There have been conflicts between the Merina and the descendants of the black Africans. But the two groups of people have been intermarrying for generations. Over the centuries they have developed a common language and have come to share a common culture.

Language and Religion. Malagasy, a language much like Indonesian, is spoken throughout the country. Both Malagasy and French are official languages. More than half of the people follow traditional religious beliefs based on ancestor worship. About 40 percent are Christians, and another 5 percent are Muslims.

Way of Life. In the larger towns and cities, people live in stone, cement, or brick houses that usually have steep, pointed roofs. Houses in the countryside are made of wood or mud and often have two or three stories. Most rural families live in lofts above the areas where their animals are kept.

A traditional garment worn by both Malagasy men and women is the *lamba,* a large white shawl usually made of unbleached muslin. City dwellers sometimes wear the *lamba* over European-style clothing.

▶THE LAND

Madagascar is an island of contrasts. Along the eastern and western coasts and in the north, the soil is fertile. Temperatures are warm. Annual rainfall is heaviest in the north and along the eastern coast. Less rain falls in the cooler, mountainous interior, and the south is hot and dry. The heart of the interior is the densely populated central plateau around Antananarivo. Many of the trees have been cut down, and the soil is badly eroded. The highest point in the country is Mount Maromokotro in the north, which rises to 9,436 feet (2,876 meters).

▶THE ECONOMY

Madagascar's economy is based primarily on agriculture. Most of the people make their living as subsistence farmers, growing food for their own use on small plots, or as animal herders. Cattle raising is important in the sparsely populated south. Coffee, sugarcane, vanilla beans, tobacco, sisal (a fiber used in making cord and twine), cloves, and cotton, grown on large plantations, are the leading commercial crops. Rice is the most important food crop, but some must be imported to meet the country's needs. What little industry exists is based largely on the processing of agricultural products, although some textiles, chemicals, and cement are manufactured.

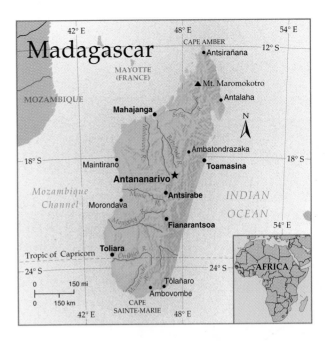

Madagascar

▶ MAJOR CITIES

Antananarivo, the capital and largest city of Madagascar, was also the capital of the Merina kingdom. A railroad links it with **Toamasina**, the nation's chief port.

▶ HISTORY AND GOVERNMENT

The Malagasy had already developed their distinctive language by the time Arab traders began to visit the area in the A.D. 900's. Europeans first sighted Madagascar in the early 1500's. The French established a permanent settlement in the mid-1600's.

After the 1780's the powerful Merina kingdom was able to unify almost all of the island. During this period, Britain and France were competing for control of the Indian Ocean. At first, European missionaries and traders were welcomed, but later Merina rulers often tried to drive them from the island. The European rivalry for influence in Madagascar ended in 1885, when Britain recognized a French pro-

---

FACTS and figures

REPUBLIC OF MADAGASCAR is the official name of the country.

LOCATION: Indian Ocean, southeast of Africa.

AREA: 226,657 sq mi (587,041 km²).

POPULATION: 14,900,000 (estimate).

CAPITAL AND LARGEST CITY: Antananarivo.

MAJOR LANGUAGES: Malagasy, French.

MAJOR RELIGIOUS GROUPS: Traditional, Christian, Muslim.

GOVERNMENT: Republic. **Head of state**—president. **Head of government**—prime minister. **Legislature**—Senate, National People's Assembly.

CHIEF PRODUCTS: Agricultural—rice, coffee, sugarcane, vanilla beans, tobacco, sisal, cloves, cotton, livestock. **Manufactured**—processed food, textiles, cement, soap. **Mineral**—chromite, graphite, mica.

MONETARY UNIT: Malagasy franc (1 franc = 100 centimes).

---

tectorate over the island. In 1896, Madagascar was made a colony of France.

Madagascar won full independence in 1960 as the Malagasy Republic. Its first president, Philibert Tsiranana, served until 1972, when he was forced to resign after a period of social unrest. The government was then led by a series of military officers. In 1975 the country's name was changed to Madagascar, and Didier Ratsiraka was elected president.

A multiparty constitution adopted by voters in 1992 reduced the powers of the president and created a two-house legislature with a directly elected lower house. The following year, Ratsiraka lost the presidential election to his rival Albert Zafy. But in 1996, Zafy was forced from office by the legislature after he tried to reduce its powers. Ratsiraka defeated Zafy in the 1997 election.

In 2001, Marc Ravalomanana challenged Ratsiraka for the presidency. Neither candidate won a majority, and a runoff election was scheduled. But violence erupted as Ravalomanana claimed he had been cheated of a clear victory. While awaiting a recount of votes, Ravalomanana established a parallel government and appointed his own cabinet members. The international community recognized Ravalomanana, and Ratsiraka fled to France.

EDWARD J. MILES
University of Vermont

MADISON. See WISCONSIN (Cities).

JAMES MADISON (1751-1836)

4th President of the United States

FACTS ABOUT MADISON

Birthplace: Port Conway, Virginia
Religion: Episcopalian
College Attended: College of New Jersey (now Princeton University), Princeton, New Jersey
Occupation: Lawyer
Married: Dolley Payne Todd
Children: None
Political Party: Democratic-Republican
Office Held Before Becoming President: Secretary of State
President Who Preceded Him: Thomas Jefferson
Age on Becoming President: 57
Years in the Presidency: 1809–1817
Vice President: George Clinton (1st term); Elbridge Gerry (2nd term)
President Who Succeeded Him: James Monroe
Age at Death: 85
Burial Place: Montpelier, Virginia

DURING MADISON'S PRESIDENCY

Louisiana was admitted to the Union (1812). *Left:* Single-ship naval battles were a feature of the War of 1812 (1812–14) between the United States and Britain. Francis Scott Key wrote the words for what became "The Star-Spangled Banner" (1814). *Below:* In Europe, an Allied victory against the French at the Battle of Waterloo (1815) marked the final defeat of Napoleon I. *Below left:* The stethoscope, a device for listening to the heart, was invented by the French physician René Laënnec (1816). Indiana was admitted to the Union (1816).

MADISON, JAMES. James Madison is perhaps best remembered as one of the founders of the United States and as the Father of the Constitution. This title refers to the leading part he played in framing the charter under which the American people have been governed since 1789. Madison was only 36 years old when that work was completed, but he had been in public life for eleven years and was unsurpassed in his knowledge of government. His long public career, which eventually spanned some forty years, included four terms in Congress and eight years as secretary of state, in addition to his two terms as president.

▶ EARLY YEARS

Madison was born on March 16, 1751, in Port Conway, Virginia, the eldest of twelve children. His great-great-grandfather, a ship carpenter, had emigrated from England in 1653 and become a tobacco farmer in the Virginia tidelands. James Madison's grandfa-ther and father built up a farm of more than 5,000 acres (2,000 hectares) in what is now Orange County, Virginia. This great farm, Montpelier (then spelled Montpellier), remained James Madison's home throughout his 85 years.

James was taught to read and write by his mother and grandmother. Soon after his 11th birthday he was sent to boarding school, where he studied English, mathematics, French, Spanish, and Latin. After two years of additional tutoring, the 18-year-old Madison entered the College of New Jersey (now Princeton University), where he completed the four-year course in two years, sleeping only five hours a night and considerably damaging his health. For five years after his graduation in 1771, he continued his extensive studies at home, which included training in the law. At the same time, he was teaching his younger brothers and sisters.

In 1774, as the Revolutionary War with Britain approached, Madison enlisted for military service. But he was forced to drop out, because of the physical strain, before his company was called to active duty. He turned, instead, to public service.

▶ ENTRY INTO POLITICS

Madison served on the Orange County Committee of Safety until 1776, when he was elected to the Virginia Revolutionary Convention. There he wrote the strong guarantee of religious freedom in the Virginia Declaration of Rights and helped pass a resolution asking the Continental Congress to issue the Declaration of Independence. Madison then served a 1-year term in the Virginia legislature but was defeated for re-election in 1777 because he refused to follow the custom of furnishing whiskey to the voters. He was immediately appointed to the governor's council, which managed the state's war efforts. In 1780 he was elected to the Continental Congress, where he quickly rose to a position of leadership, despite being one of its youngest members and boyish in appearance.

With the coming of peace in 1783, Madison devoted his efforts to strengthening the weak national government that had been set up under the Articles of Confederation. Elected again to the Virginia legislature, he persuaded his state to issue a call for a convention of the states to establish a more effective form of government. He attended the Annapolis Convention in 1786, and in 1787 he was sent as a delegate to the Constitutional Convention at Philadelphia.

▶ CONSTITUTIONAL CONVENTION

The essential problem facing the framers of the Constitution was to find a way to establish governmental authority and yet maintain liberty. Up to Madison's time, most scholars had assumed that small republics were freer than large ones. But Madison observed that the opposite was true in America. Tyrannical majorities often ruled in the smaller states, while in the larger ones, the greater diversity of interests prevented one faction, or interest group, from acquiring undue power.

Madison's plan, which became the basis for the government of the United States, called for a strong chief executive (the president), a legislature composed of two houses, and an independent judiciary, or court system. Each state would have control of its local affairs. The larger such a federal republic became, Madison reasoned, the more liberty it could safely enjoy, for the different interests of the various sections of the country would divide the factions that might otherwise produce tyranny.

After the Constitution was adopted, Madison joined Alexander Hamilton and John Jay in writing *The Federalist* papers, in order to secure its ratification by the states. Madison also led the supporters of the Constitution at the Virginia ratifying convention. See the article on the United States Constitution in Volume U-V. An article on *The Federalist* appears in Volume F.

▶ CONGRESSIONAL CAREER AND MARRIAGE

In 1789, Madison was elected to the House of Representatives in the First Congress of the United States. There he proposed and took a leading role in

Madison (the small figure seated at center) is almost lost among the numerous delegates at the Constitutional Convention, held in Philadelphia in 1787. But he played a leading role in framing the document under which the United States is governed.

the passage of the first ten amendments to the Constitution, known as the Bill of Rights. Madison may therefore be called the Father of the Bill of Rights as well as of the Constitution. See the article on the Bill of Rights in Volume B.

Madison at first strongly supported the administration of President George Washington. But he came to oppose the financial policies of Alexander Hamilton, Washington's secretary of the treasury, because he felt they favored commercial interests at the expense of the country's agriculture and gave special privileges to persons of wealth. As political parties began to form, Madison and Thomas Jefferson became leaders of the Republicans (later called Democratic-Republicans), who represented the interests of the ordinary people. They were the opposition to Hamilton's Federalists.

In 1794, Madison married Dolley Payne Todd, a 26-year-old widow. Dolley Madison was especially noted for her graciousness and charm as a hostess during her husband's years in the presidency.

Madison left Congress in 1797 and returned home, discouraged by his party's failure against the dominant Federalists. In 1798 he drafted the Virginia Resolutions in protest against the Alien and Sedition Acts, enacted during President John Adams' administration. See the article on John Adams (The Alien and Sedition Acts) in Volume A.

Dolley Madison was especially noted for her graciousness and charm as a hostess during James Madison's presidency.

▶ SECRETARY OF STATE

Madison served two more terms in the Virginia legislature. He was then appointed secretary of state by Thomas Jefferson, who had succeeded Adams as president in 1801. In this capacity, Madison helped promote the purchase of the vast Louisiana Territory from France in 1803. See the article on the Louisiana Purchase in Volume L.

His most vexing problems in foreign affairs arose from the hostilities between Britain and France during the Napoleonic Wars. Both countries, in the course of the war, interfered with U.S. trade, although Britain, with its more powerful fleet, was the greater offender. Public opinion in the United States was outraged, in particular, by the British practice of stopping American ships and impressing their seamen—that is, forcing them to serve in the British navy.

Madison strongly upheld the right of neutral countries like the United States to trade with nations at war, free from the threat of blockade or other interference. But all his protests were ignored. He supported Jefferson's attempt to preserve peace by passage of the Embargo Act in 1807, which forbade all exports and prohibited American ships from leaving port, but this proved unsuccessful and only served to damage U.S. trade.

▶ PRESIDENT

With Jefferson's support, Madison easily won election as president in 1808. He received 122 electoral votes to 47 for his Federalist opponent, Charles C. Pinckney.

Continuing Crisis. Madison's immediate concern on taking office in 1809 was the continuing crisis with Britain and France. Earlier that year, Congress had replaced the Embargo Act with the Non-Intercourse Act,

British troops captured Washington, D.C., in 1814, during the War of 1812. They burned parts of the city, including the Capitol and White House, forcing Madison and other members of the government to flee.

which permitted trade with all countries except Britain and France, but this was also a failure. In 1810, Congress repealed the remaining restrictions, but it authorized the president to again cut off trade with either country if the other agreed to end its oppressive practices. An agreement to do so by the French, which proved false, led to a commercial break with Britain in 1811 and to war in 1812.

Montpelier was the Madison family estate in Orange County, Virginia. It remained James Madison's home throughout his long life, both before and after his presidency.

A few months after the declaration of war, Madison was re-elected president, receiving 128 electoral votes. The Federalist candidate, DeWitt Clinton, received 89 votes.

War of 1812. With only a small army and navy, the United States was ill prepared for war. The navy won some brilliant battles at sea early in the conflict, but the raw American troops met with successive defeats. Washington, D.C., itself, was captured by the British in 1814. Part of the city, including the White House, was burned, and Madison was forced to flee with other members of the government. But eventually the American soldiers, gaining experience and discipline, were able to drive the veteran British troops from the battlefield, and a reasonable peace treaty was achieved in 1814.

Throughout the war, the Federalists of New England, which was severely affected by the collapse of trade, had opposed what they called "Mr. Madison's war." Amid the rejoicings over peace, the Federalist Party broke down and soon vanished from existence. For a complete account of the war, see the article on the War of 1812 in Volume W-X-Y-Z.

Domestic Measures. The years following the war were marked by a spirit of optimism, economic growth, and westward expansion. Responding to the nationalistic mood, Madison proposed an ambitious domestic program to Congress. Its measures included a rechartering of the national bank, the Bank of the United States; government support for the building of roads and canals to link the various parts of the nation; and a tariff, or tax on imports, to protect new industries.

▶ LATER YEARS

After leaving the presidency in 1817, Madison returned to Montpelier, where he engaged in scientific farming, originating methods of agriculture that did not become common until a century later. With his wife, Dolley, he welcomed visitors from all over the United States and Europe. Equally welcome were the children of relatives, for the Madisons had none of their own. After Jefferson's death in 1826, Madison succeeded his old friend as head of the new University of Virginia.

Madison died at Montpelier on June 28, 1836. His last thoughts were for the country he had so long served: "The advice nearest to my heart and deepest in my convictions," he wrote, "is that the Union of the States be cherished and perpetuated."

IRVING BRANT
Author, *James Madison*

MADONNA. See MARY, VIRGIN.

IMPORTANT DATES IN THE LIFE OF JAMES MADISON

1751	Born in Port Conway, Virginia, March 16.
1771	Graduated from the College of New Jersey (now Princeton University).
1776–77	Served in the Virginia legislature.
1778	Appointed to the Virginia governor's council.
1780–83	Served in the Continental Congress.
1784–86	Served again in the Virginia legislature.
1787	Attended the Constitutional Convention in Philadelphia.
1789–97	Served in the U.S. House of Representatives.
1799	Elected again to the Virginia legislature.
1801–09	Served as secretary of state.
1809–17	Served as fourth president of the United States.
1826	Succeeded Thomas Jefferson as head of the University of Virginia.
1836	Died at Montpelier, June 28.

MADRAS (CHENNAI)

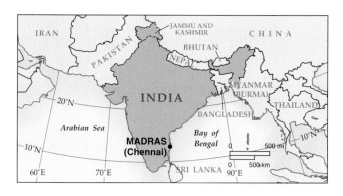

Madras, renamed Chennai in 1996, is India's fourth largest city. It is the capital of the state of Tamil Nadu ("home of the Tamils"), formerly known as Madras state, and is the cultural center for India's Tamil-speaking peoples. The city proper has a population of nearly 4 million. An additional 2 million people live in the metropolitan area.

The City. Madras, a leading port city, lies along India's southeast coast, on the Bay of Bengal. With its fine highways, railroads, rivers, canals, and an international airport, Madras is an important transportation terminal in the south.

Mount Road is the city's main thoroughfare. It passes through the central shopping and hotel areas before reaching the residential district in the south. An attractive city sight is the wide shore drive called the Marina. At one end of it is the Roman Catholic

George, the site of the original settlement. Additional attractions include the Horticultural Gardens, the National Art Gallery, and a beautiful array of Hindu temples.

Economic Activity. George Town is the main commercial district of Madras. Nearby are industrial areas where cotton textile and handloom industries flourish. The world-famous Madras plaid cloth is made there. Other local industries include engineering works, bicycle factories, iron foundries, and tanneries.

History. Madras was founded in 1639. At that time, an Indian rajah granted a strip of land to Francis Day, a British subject and chief agent of the East India Company. On this site, Fort Saint George was established. Between 1702 and 1801, the fort was captured in turn by the Moguls, Marathas (people of west and central India), and the French. It also was taken by the forces of Haidar Ali, the Muslim ruler of Mysore in southern India.

By 1801, most of the territory that presently makes up the state of Tamil Nadu had been ceded (given over) to the British by defeated Indian rulers. The city of Madras then became the capital of one of the largest administrative units of British India.

Madras, the capital of the state of Tamil Nadu, is among the largest cities in India. It is a leading center of commerce and transportation.

Cathedral of Saint Thomé, believed to be the burial place of the Apostle Thomas. Nearby is the early Portuguese settlement of Saint Thomé, established in 1504 and later incorporated into Madras. Between the cathedral and Madras' busy harbor are government buildings, Madras University, and Fort Saint

Reviewed by BALKRISHNA G. GOKHALE
Wake Forest University

MADRID

Madrid is located on a high, windswept plateau almost in the geographic center of Spain. With a population of more than 3,000,000, it is the largest city in Spain and one of the largest capital cities in Europe.

The Moors, a Muslim people who invaded Spain in the 8th century A.D., built a fortified village on the site of present-day Madrid. Conquered in 1083 by Alfonso VI, the king of Leon and Castile, it remained an unimportant place until 1561. In that year, King Philip II made Madrid the center of his vast empire. It has been the capital of Spain ever since, except for a brief period (1601–06) when the court was moved to Valladolid.

Much of the sprawling city was built during the 1600's and 1700's. This part, once surrounded by walls, is known as Old Madrid. Madrid has expanded rapidly in recent years by annexing nearby communities.

In the middle of Old Madrid is a plaza called the Puerta del Sol (Gate of the Sun). Streets fan out from the Puerta del Sol like the sun's rays. Those going west lead to the Opera House, the Plaza Mayor (Main Plaza), and the Royal Palace and Armory. The Plaza Mayor is another historic square. It was built in the 1600's as a kind of outdoor theater. From the balconies of the surrounding buildings, nobles and kings once watched festivals, bullfights, horse races, and ceremonies. The interiors of the huge stone Royal Palace are hung with fine silks and Flemish tapestries. The Royal Armory in the left wing of the Royal Palace houses one of the finest collections of weapons and armor in the world.

One of Madrid's best-known streets is the Paseo del Prado, a broad, parklike boulevard lined with museums, monuments, government buildings, and plazas. On the Paseo del Prado is the Prado, a world-famous art gallery housing paintings and sculptures collected by Spanish kings. Madrid has many other fine museums and libraries. Among the institutions of higher learning in the city is the University of Madrid, in University City.

The people of Madrid are called Madrileños. They are known for their love of night life. As in other parts of Spain, dinners and social gatherings start at about ten o'clock or even later. Movies, concerts, and plays often begin performances at the same hour.

Like all Spaniards, Madrileños love soccer, *pelota* (jai alai), and, of course, the bullfights at the Plaza de Toros. They often visit one of the largest of the city's many parks, the Retiro. It has playgrounds, gardens, bridle paths, lakes, a zoo, an outdoor theater, and café-restaurants where Madrileños enjoy eating and dancing. Restaurants in Madrid range from those serving typical Spanish dishes to those offering an international menu.

Madrid remains the political and cultural capital of Spain. It is also the center of Spanish printing, publishing, and moviemaking. And since the country developed a modern network of roads and railroads converging on the city, Madrid has become the leading manufacturing center of Spain.

Reviewed by RAFAEL MILLÁN
Former editor, *Aguilar* (Madrid)

See also PRADO.

The Avenida de José Antonio, or Gran Via, lies in the center of Madrid. It is one of the city's main avenues and is known for its fine shops and hotels.

There is a magazine for nearly every activity or interest. It is estimated that in North America alone, more than 65,000 different magazines are published.

MAGAZINES

The meaning of the word "magazine" is "storehouse" or "treasury"—and a magazine is truly a treasury of interesting material. Magazines give readers more specialized information than any other channel of mass communication, including newspapers, radio, and television. A magazine will tell you how to build a model plane or how to lose weight, which are the best jogging sneakers, or what your favorite celebrity eats for breakfast.

Magazines are sometimes called periodicals because they are published regularly at specific times. In the United States alone, there are 9,000 magazines that are published at least four times a year.

Magazines are divided into general- or special-interest magazines, sometimes called consumer magazines, and business magazines, sometimes called trade magazines. There are also scholarly journals, which report on research in various fields. A **business magazine** deals with the commercial and financial aspects of a particular business. **Special-interest** magazines, sometimes called hobby magazines, contain information on a specific subject—computers or horseback riding, for example. **General-interest** magazines are designed to appeal to a wide variety of readers. They include **newsweeklies,** which summarize the news, and **digests,** which reprint material from other publications. Some carry articles of interest to certain reader groups—men, women, or children, for example. **Intellectual** and **opinion** magazines analyze current events. General- and special-interest magazines are sold on newsstands or by subscription.

▶ **PRODUCING MAGAZINES**

The production of a magazine involves many steps before the final product is distributed to the newsstand or mailed to a subscriber's home. Story ideas are the backbone of every issue.

Suppose a writer has an idea for an article and sends a letter describing the idea to an editor of a general-interest magazine. The editor may have the title of science editor or entertainment editor, depending on what the article is about. If the editor likes the proposal, it is then discussed with other editors—perhaps the articles editor, managing editor, and editor in chief. If they all agree that the article would be of interest to their readers, the writer is given the assignment. The editors send a contract that states what the fee will be and when the article is due.

The author sends in the article at the deadline time, and it is read sometimes by as many as five editors. The author may be asked to make revisions or to make the article shorter or longer. Then the editors decide where it will be placed in the magazine and whether it will be illustrated with photographs or drawings. They also decide on a working title.

The editor in charge of the article sends copies to the picture editor, who will either assign a photographer to take pictures or have a researcher find appropriate pictures. If artwork is to be used, an artist will be commissioned to do drawings or paintings.

The next step is the design of a **page layout** —a mock-up of what the finished pages will look like. This is done by the art director. Suppose the story will take four pages and have five photographs. The art director must measure the length of the story and decide how large the illustrations will be. The art director also decides how much space to allow for a title, a blurb (a brief statement that tells readers something about the article), a byline (the author's name), and picture captions.

The layout is given to the editor, who must cut and edit the manuscript to fit it. Then the article is sent to a copy editor, who makes sure that it fits the magazine's style (its normal usage in punctuation and grammar). Many magazines have a fact checker who must verify every important fact, date, and name.

After the managing editor and the editor approve the copy, it is ready to be set in type by computer. The set copy comes out in long sheets called **galleys.** Then the printer makes a **mechanical,** cutting the galleys and pasting them up to fit the page layout. The mechanical is photographed to produce a negative, which is then exposed onto an **offset** plate. You will find more about the offset process in the article PRINTING in Volume P.

The four pages of the article are printed as part of a **signature**—a large sheet that when folded will form a section of the magazine. After all the signatures are printed, other machines fold them, bind them together, cut the pages free, and address copies to subscribers.

▶ **AMERICAN CHILDREN'S MAGAZINES**

Youth's Companion, founded in 1827, was the first magazine published especially for children. Its publishers, Nathaniel Willis and Asa Rand, wanted to encourage ''virtue and piety'' and ''to warn against the ways of transgression.'' In the 1850's *Youth's Com-* *panion* had the largest circulation of any American magazine.

Other magazines imitated *Youth's Companion. Student and Schoolmate,* begun in 1854, published travel articles, stories in serial form, sheet music, poems, and declamations. (Declamations were speeches or recitations with dramatic gestures.)

A similar magazine was *Our Young Folks,* popular from 1865 to 1873. Then came the magazine for children that was probably the most popular of all, *St. Nicholas.*

First issued in 1873 by Roswell Smith, *St. Nicholas* was edited for its first 32 years by Mary Mapes Dodge, author of *Hans Brinker, or, The Silver Skates.* Mrs. Dodge recruited well-known writers for her magazine. Mark Twain's *Tom Sawyer Abroad* first appeared in its pages. So did Frances Hodgson Burnett's *Little Lord Fauntleroy* and Rudyard Kipling's *Jungle Book* stories. Louisa May Alcott and Kate Douglas Wiggin were regular contributors.

Mrs. Dodge encouraged young readers to send in their own stories and poems. Budding writers whose work was published in *St. Nicholas* became members of the St. Nicholas League. Some of them later became famous. Edna St. Vincent Millay, Robert Benchley, Ring Lardner, William Faulkner, Rachel Field, and Stephen Vincent Benét all wrote for *St. Nicholas* when they were children.

St. Nicholas and *Youth's Companion* were the most popular youth magazines in the country when *American Boy* appeared in 1899. It had adventure and nature stories. Similar magazines followed—*Boy's Life* (1912), which is still published, and *Open Road* (1919), which published correspondence between young people in the United States and other countries.

After World War I the old favorites began to lose popularity. *Youth's Companion* survived until 1929, when it merged with *American Boy.* A year later *St. Nicholas* was sold to *Scholastic,* but it did not re-appear until 1935. *St. Nicholas* changed hands several times before it vanished finally in 1941. *American Boy* published its last issue in July, 1941.

Since that time many new children's magazines have come on the market to take the place of those that disappeared. Some of the most popular ones are listed on the following page.

SOME POPULAR MAGAZINES FOR CHILDREN

The following children's magazines are those with the highest home circulation in the United States and Canada. Included in the annotation are the year of first publication, the recommended age range for readership, the number of issues each year, and a brief description.

American Girl. 1992, 8–12, six issues. Magazine for girls contains stories, paper dolls, games, crafts, and contests.

Boy's Life. 1911, 8–14, monthly. Boy Scouts of America magazine contains fiction and nonfiction articles emphasizing outdoor life, sports, and recreation.

Children's Digest. 1950, 9–12, eight issues. Fiction, nonfiction, and activities are intended to enhance the well-being of children.

Cobblestone. 1980, 8–14, monthly. Each issue covers an aspect of American history, developed through both fiction and nonfiction.

Cricket. 1973, 6–12, monthly. High-quality literature includes fantasy, folklore and fairytales, realistic fiction, science and nature articles, poems, crafts, and puzzles.

Guideposts for Kids. 1992, 7–11, six issues. Contains Christian inspirational stories for children.

Highlights for Children. 1946, 2–12, eleven issues. An emphasis on creativity combined with puzzles and games helps children learn while having fun.

Humpty Dumpty's Magazine. 1952, 4–6, eight issues. Puzzles, crafts, and humorous stories are geared toward teaching better health habits.

Jack and Jill. 1938, 7–10, eight issues. Exciting and humorous stories emphasize health, safety, exercise, and nutrition.

Kids Discover. 1991, 6 & up, ten issues. Educational magazine; each issue covers a single topic on nature, science, geography, or man-made wonders.

Kids' Web World. 1996, 5–15, six issues. Introduction to the Internet offers reviews of Web sites for kids; how to use the Web to do school projects; scavenger hunts; and sports-related topics.

National Geographic World. 1975, 8–13, monthly. Features stories on outdoor adventure, natural history, sports, science, and history.

Nickelodeon Magazine. 1992, 8–14, ten issues. Humorous magazine contains articles on general-interest topics, as well as puzzles and quizzes, with an eight-page comic book in every issue.

Odyssey. 1978, 8–14, monthly. Space program updates, stargazing tips, science experiments, and puzzles assist the astronomy enthusiast.

OWL Magazine. 1976, 8–12, nine issues. A discovery magazine, it presents articles on science, nature, and technology (including the Internet).

Ranger Rick. 1967, 6–13, monthly. Teaches about natural history and the environment through stunning photos and lively text.

Sesame Street Magazine. 1971, 2–6, ten issues. Games, puzzles, and picture stories further the educational goals of the television show.

Teen. 1957, 12–19, monthly. Fashion and grooming tips are combined with other articles of interest to teenage girls.

3-2-1 Contact. 1979, 8–14, ten issues. Lively writing and attractive graphics characterize this science magazine.

Turtle Magazine for Preschool Kids. 1979, 2–5, eight issues. Stories, poems, and activities convey positive messages on health.

Yes Magazine. ("Youth Excited by Success") 1992, 13 & up, ten issues. Issues of interest to teenage African Americans include study habits, scholarships, health and fitness, careers, and business enterprises.

Your Big Backyard. 1979, 3–5, monthly. For the preschooler, this magazine helps young children discover the natural world.

Zillions for Kids by Consumer Reports. 1980, 8–14, bimonthly. A product-rating and consumer-advice source for young people.

The first magazine was a weekly, *The Review*. It was started in 1704 in London by Daniel Defoe, who wrote *Robinson Crusoe*. Defoe had strong opinions about the British Government's policies, and he wanted to publish his ideas so that people could read them. He published his periodical by himself until 1713.

Other magazines followed *The Review*. The most popular was *The Tatler*, published by Richard Steele in 1709. It was the first magazine to sell space to advertisers. In 1710 a scholar named Joseph Addison joined the magazine, and the two men wrote essays. *The Tatler* became famous for humorous essays on all subjects, from national and foreign affairs to London society and the theater. In 1711, Addison and Steele started another magazine, *The Spectator*. Essays from both magazines are considered to be the first literature of merit to come from magazines, and they are collected in many anthologies.

The first periodical to use the word "magazine" in its title was *The Gentleman's Magazine* (1731). It was a collection of articles and poems copied from newspapers and journals by Edward Cave, a London bookseller, who used the name Sylvanus Urban.

Benjamin Franklin and Andrew Bradford, two rival printers in Philadelphia, published the first American magazines. Franklin (who later became a distinguished statesman, writer, and philosopher) was publishing a newspaper, *The Pennsylvania Gazette*, as well as *Poor Richard's Almanack*. But he wanted to start another publication that would be read throughout the British colonies. He called his monthly magazine *The General Magazine, and Historical Chronicle, for All the British Plantations in America*. The first issue was 70 pages long and was dated January, 1741, although it did not actually go on sale until February 16.

Meanwhile, Bradford had learned of Franklin's idea and rushed to print his magazine. It was called *The American Magazine, or a Monthly View of the Political State of the British Colonies*. His publication went on sale on February 13, three days before Franklin's.

After six months, Franklin stopped his magazine. Bradford's lasted for only two issues. But there were more magazines to take their place. The aim of these magazines was to spread the idea of revolt against England. History gives credit to one magazine for doing more than all the rest to bring about the Revolutionary War. This was the *Pennsylvania Magazine*, published by Thomas Paine. In 1775 it carried Paine's famous essay "On Liberty."

Magazines were so numerous after the revolution that in 1824 the *Cincinnati Literary Gazette* published this verse:

This is the age of Magazines—
Even Skeptics must confess it:
Where is the town of much renown
That has not one to bless it?

The special-interest magazine was born in the 1800's. There were religious magazines, farm magazines, literary magazines, and magazines for doctors, teachers, bankers, druggists, homemakers, and children. The first popular children's magazine, *Youth's Companion*, started in 1827. The first women's magazine, *Godey's Ladies Book*, started in 1830. *Godey's* crusaded for women's education at a time when more than half the women in the United States could not read. For 68 years it influenced the manners and tastes of American families. During the 1800's, three other women's magazines were started, and they are still published. They are *Harper's Bazaar* (1867), *McCall's* (1870), and *Ladies' Home Journal* (1883).

Many famous American writers had their stories first published in magazines. Washington Irving, James Fenimore Cooper, Nathaniel Hawthorne, John Greenleaf Whittier, Oliver Wendell Holmes, and Henry Wadsworth Longfellow contributed to *The Knickerbocker*.

LISTS OF MAGAZINES

Ulrich's International Periodicals Directory lists the magazines of all countries, classified according to subject. *Ayer Directory of Publications* lists newspapers and magazines in the United States and Canada. *The Standard Periodical Directory* is the largest of the directories for U.S. and Canadian publications. It has information on more than 60,000 publications. *Consumer Magazine and Farm Publication Rates and Data* lists U.S. and international consumer magazines. Other sources are *Literary Market Place* and the *Readers' Guide to Periodical Literature*, which lists magazine articles by topic and author. Most libraries have at least some of these directories.

This magazine was the first really popular monthly and was published in New York from 1833 to 1865. Rival magazines soon sprang up, including *Graham's Magazine, The Saturday Evening Post, Harper's Magazine,* and *The Atlantic Monthly.*

By the 1900's the United States had improved transportation and mail services. Brand-name products were being distributed over a wide area. And advertisers wanted to promote their products in the pages of magazines. When publishers discovered that advertising could cover their expenses, they cut the prices for copies of their magazines. *McClure's Magazine, Munsey's Magazine,* and *Cosmopolitan* were lively, entertaining 10-cent monthlies. *The Saturday Evening Post* and its chief rival, *Collier's,* were the leading 5-cent weeklies.

Gradually, magazines that did not get enough advertising went out of business. Drawing many readers was not enough to guarantee success. For example, *Collier's* folded in 1956 with 4,000,000 readers.

The single largest category of magazines is women's magazines. *Ladies Home Journal* has been published for more than a century.

But there were always new magazines coming along. *The New Yorker,* started in 1925, became known for its excellent fiction. And in the 1920's, two new types of magazines appeared. The first was *The Reader's Digest,* which condensed longer articles that had appeared in other magazines. It was an overnight success. By 1935 its circulation had reached 1,000,000. Then it tripled and continued to multiply. Today it is one of the most popular general-interest magazines. It is published in 41 different editions, which are written and edited in 17 different languages.

The second new type was *Time,* a weekly newsmagazine that summed up important events around the world. Two young graduates of Yale University, Henry R. Luce and Briton Hadden, introduced the magazine in 1923. Time Incorporated soon became a publishing giant. In 1930 the company launched *Fortune,* a monthly for business executives. In 1936 a weekly picture magazine, *Life,* was started. It continued until 1972 and was revived as a monthly in 1978. Other magazines published by Time Incorporated include *Sports Illustrated* (1954); *Money* (1972); *People* (1974), a magazine of gossip and articles on celebrities; and *Discover* (1980), a science magazine.

Meanwhile, *Time*'s newsweekly format was so successful that it was copied. In 1933, *U.S. News & World Report* and *Newsweek* entered the market. All the newsweeklies have international editions. *National Geographic* and *Business Week* are two other important magazines that publish overseas editions.

Today magazines publish less fiction than they did in the early days. Special-interest magazines have become more and more popular. *TV Guide,* which carries television program listings, has one of the largest circulations of all magazines in the United States. Traditional women's magazines are still widely read, but the women's rights movement has given rise to such magazines as *Ms.* and *Working Woman. Ebony* and *Essence* were started for black readers. City and regional magazines have sprung up. *Sunset* reports on life in the West, and *Southern Living* on life in the South. And most major cities now have city magazines.

BARBARA BELFORD
Columbia Graduate School of Journalism

MAGELLAN (SPACECRAFT). See SPACE PROBES.

In 1520, Portuguese explorer Ferdinand Magellan found the narrow channel at the tip of South America that connects the Atlantic and Pacific oceans. Called the Strait of Magellan, it is 560 kilometers (about 350 miles) long.

MAGELLAN, FERDINAND (1480?–1521)

Ferdinand Magellan, the famous Portuguese navigator, was probably born in the former province of Entre-Douro-e-Minho, in northern Portugal, in 1480. Little is known of his early life, but when he was 25 he sailed to India, where the Portuguese were building an empire. In 1509 he traveled as far east as Malacca, near modern Singapore. The next year he helped conquer Goa in India. He became interested in the spice trade and learned that cloves, the costliest of all of the spices, grew mostly in the Molucca islands, east of Malacca. By this time an expert navigator, Magellan began to think about a possible route to reach the Moluccas from the west instead of by the usual route, around Africa and eastward across the Indian Ocean.

The Spaniards had found the New World. But they had not found the strait at the southern tip of South America, between the Atlantic and Pacific oceans. Magellan believed such a waterway existed. The best way to reach the Moluccas, he thought, would be to find this passage and sail west. Magellan and most other people thought that the Pacific would prove to be a small body of water.

By 1513, Magellan was back in Portugal from the East. He found that King Manuel had no interest in sending him to the Moluccas. In 1518 he decided to look to Spain for backing for his voyage. The Spanish king, Charles I, was interested at once. Magellan had little trouble in getting 5 ships and about 240 men. He did not intend to sail around the world but meant to find the Moluccas, load his ships with spices, and return by the same route.

The fleet left the Spanish port of Sanlúcar on September 20, 1519. Magellan sailed along the west coast of Africa and then crossed to Brazil and followed the South American coast to Patagonia, stopping for the winter in a desolate bay. There he crushed a mutiny led by Spanish officers who disliked sailing under a Portuguese. When warmer weather came, he pushed on. He found the strait now named for him and entered the Pacific Ocean. He called the ocean Pacific (peaceful) because it seemed very calm. He had only three ships left, for one had been wrecked near the strait and another had deserted.

What Magellan had thought would be a small ocean now proved enormous. He and his men ran out of food and fresh water. Many died of scurvy, a disease caused by a lack of vitamin C. They all might have died if they had not sighted the Ladrone Islands (now the Marianas). They took all the provisions they could find and sailed on to the Philippines. There, Magellan took sides in a war between two local chiefs, and he was killed in a battle on the island of Mactan on April 27, 1521. He had not sailed completely around the globe but had come very near to doing it.

After Magellan's death, his crews elected the Spaniard Juan Sebastian del Cano their leader. Cano found the Moluccas and loaded his one remaining ship, the *Victoria,* with spices and food. He decided to go home the shortest way—by completing the voyage around the world. There was again a shortage of food and much suffering. But Cano brought the *Victoria,* with 18 surviving crew members and a few East Indians aboard, back to Sanlúcar on September 6, 1522. The first voyage around the world had taken almost three years.

CHARLES E. NOWELL
Editor, *Magellan's Voyage Around the World*

Abracadabra! The woman seems to have been sawn in half. Only very experienced magicians can attempt this trick, here performed by Doug Henning.

MAGIC

Magic is the use of spells, charms, or tricks to produce certain effects. One who practices magic is a magician. In ancient days, magicians were believed to have extraordinary powers with which they could perform all sorts of marvelous acts. They supposedly could heal the sick, make rain fall, cast out evil spirits, and communicate with the dead. Naturally the ancient peoples held their magicians in awe.

Records going back more than 1,000 years show that magic was performed for entertainment in Egypt, China, and India. In Europe, magic flourished particularly during the Middle Ages. During that period (from about A.D. 500 to 1500), self-styled wizards traveled about, giving magic shows. They used the scientific discoveries of the day to perform their so-called magic, and they carefully guarded their secrets.

A trick they often did was called "Cups and Balls." It is one of the oldest tricks known, and magicians today still perform it. Three metal cups are set in a row, upside down. A small ball is placed underneath each cup. With a magic wand, the magician taps a cup and then raises it. The ball has disappeared. A second cup is tapped, then raised, and the magician finds two balls there. The balls seem to have jumped, invisibly, from cup to cup. Suddenly the magician tips over the cups, and there is now an orange, or some other large object, underneath each cup.

This trick is done by **sleight of hand,** which is the art of deceiving, or tricking, the eye by skillful movements of the hands. By the use of sleight of hand, small objects, such as balls, cards, or coins, can be made suddenly to appear or vanish or to "change" into something else.

▶ MODERN MAGICIANS

Modern magic as a form of entertainment started around the middle of the 19th century. One of the greatest magicians of that day was a Frenchman, Robert Houdin (1805–71), who is known as the father of modern magic. Houdin created a sensation in Paris.

The French Government sent him to Algeria to match his skill against that of the rebellious Marabouts, a group of Arabs who controlled the people with their acts of magic. Houdin announced that he had the power to take away the strength of the Arab leaders. He then performed one of his great tricks, in which he used the principle of electromagnetism to make light objects seem heavy.

On a floor rested a small wooden box with a metal bottom. Houdin called on a man from the audience to lift the box, which he did with ease. Pretending to take away the man's strength, Houdin dared him to lift the box again. At this point, Houdin's hidden assistant turned on a strong electromagnet concealed beneath the stage. This held the metal-bottomed box fast to the floor, and the man struggled in vain, unable to lift the box. The Arabs viewed this demonstration with awe and soon concluded that French magicians were more powerful than their own.

After Robert Houdin other magicians became famous as entertainers. The name of each was usually identified with a particular type of magic or with some outstanding trick or illusion. (In the language of magicians, an illusion is an elaborate trick in which a human being or animal is used.)

Harry Kellar (1849–1922) was one of the great magicians of the 20th century. He held audiences spellbound by his illusion "The Princess of Karnac." By supposedly hypnotic influence, he caused a "hypnotized" girl to rise slowly from a couch into mid-air. He then passed a solid hoop around her as she floated in space, seeming to prove that her body had no means of support.

Howard Thurston (1869–1936) was another famous illusionist. One of his illusions was sawing a woman in half. He placed a woman in a coffin-like box, her head sticking out at one end, her feet at the other. Using a large saw, Thurston then sawed through the box and the lady. When the separated halves were brought together again, the woman sprang up from the box, whole and sound.

Harry Houdini (1874–1926) achieved worldwide fame as an escape artist. His specialty was escaping from handcuffs, leg irons, and shackles, and he took chances few others would. One of his feature tricks was the "Milk Can Escape." Handcuffed, Houdini stepped into an airtight metal can filled with water.

The can's cover was then locked on from the outside with padlocks. Houdini made his escape from this dangerous enclosure within minutes, while the audience watched breathlessly. He was a master showman.

Ching Ling Foo (1854–1922) amazed audiences by producing from empty shawls large bowls of water filled with goldfish.

Joseph Dunninger (1896–1975) gained his reputation and fame as a "mentalist." He mystified millions of people with his performances on stage and television. Dunninger, who apparently read the minds of members of his audience, was a fascinating performer.

Other famous modern magicians are Herrmann the Great (1843–96), Harry Blackstone (1885–1965), Horace Goldin (1873–1939), The Great Leon (1876–1951), Jarrow (1876–1960), Cardini (1895–1973), Doug Henning (1947–   ), and David Copperfield (1956–   ).

▶ THE ART OF MAGIC

Magic appeals to everyone because people love to be mystified. The amateur magician who can entertain with a few clever tricks is always welcome in any social gathering.

Many of the most baffling tricks are extremely simple. Some are done by sleight of hand. Others are performed with the help of a cleverly constructed mechanical aid. A great many tricks require neither sleight of hand nor special equipment. They can be learned easily and can make one an effective magician.

Knowing how the tricks are done is one thing. Performing them so that they mystify and entertain is another. There are some important rules to follow, and one also has to know something of the psychology of deception, or trickery.

The Art of Misdirection. The old saying that "the hand is quicker than the eye" is supposed to sum up the art of the magician. This is false. The real secret of the magician's art lies in fooling the mind rather than the eye. The means by which this is done is called misdirection.

Misdirection is a form of mental suggestion. It is the art of transferring the attention of the audience to what the magician wants them to see and of drawing it away from all the secret actions so that they go unnoticed. For example, if you are the magician, you

"MYSTERY OF THE FOUR ACES"

1 Before beginning this trick, put the four aces facedown on top of the deck. Then place the deck facedown on the table and announce you will not touch the cards again until the trick is ended. Ask a helper to cut the deck in half, placing the upper half to the right of the lower half.

2 Ask your helper to cut the decks in half again, placing the upper halves below the lower halves to form a square (now the aces will be on top of Packet D).

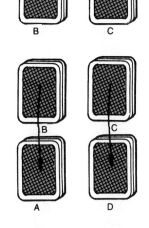

3 Ask your helper to pick up Packet A, remove the top three cards, and place them facedown on the space that Packet A just occupied.

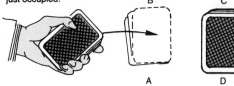

4 Now have your helper deal one card from Packet A to the top of each of the other packets, B, C, and D.

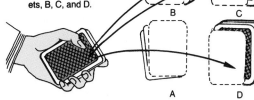

5 Finally, your helper must lay the balance of Packet A on top of the three cards that were first removed. Using Packets B, C, and D, your helper must repeat steps 3 to 5, placing the cards on the packets in clockwise order. When all four packets have been dealt, wave your hand over the packets and turn up the top cards to reveal four aces.

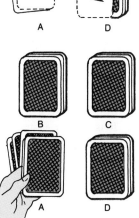

throw a small ball into the air with an upward motion of your hand. Every eye in the audience will follow the ball as it rises and falls. You also pointedly move your head and eyes to follow the course of the ball in flight. Repeating the action, this time you only pretend to throw the ball upward; actually you keep it in the palm of your hand. (This is known as palming.) Again you follow the imaginary flight of the ball with your head and eyes exactly as you did the first time, when the ball was in actual flight. Imitating you, the audience does the same thing. The magician's eyes peer upward for a moment. Then, with a look of surprise, they are turned to the audience, as if to ask, "What happened to the ball?" To the audience, it appears that the ball has vanished in mid-air.

Another method of controlling spectators' attention calls for entertaining talk by the performer. This diverting talk is called patter. It not only holds the audience's attention but it also makes the trick more enjoyable and helps hide the magician's secret moves from those watching.

Magicians' Rules. Here are some rules that good magicians carefully follow:

(1) Never tell the audience what trick you intend to perform; otherwise the element of surprise is lost, and the chance of detection is increased.

(2) Never perform the same trick twice on the same program. What the audience missed the first time it may discover upon seeing a trick the second time.

(3) Practice even the simplest tricks before attempting to perform them. Once you have gained some skill, you may broaden your knowledge. One way of doing this is to read good books on magic and get new ideas from them.

The following tricks will be a good start for you as a beginner magician. Although they are mystifying, they are easy to do.

▶ SPIRIT RING ON ROPE

In this baffling trick, your wrists are tied with a length of cord. You then take a solid ring, which has been examined, and turning your back for a few moments, you cause the ring to appear on the cord.

The secret is that, unknown to the audience, two rings are used. They may be plastic bracelets, alike in size and color, obtainable at any store selling novelty jewelry.

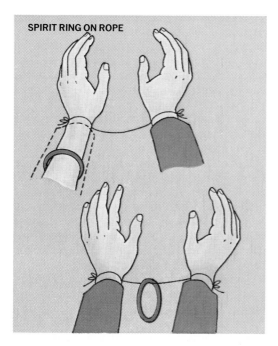

SPIRIT RING ON ROPE

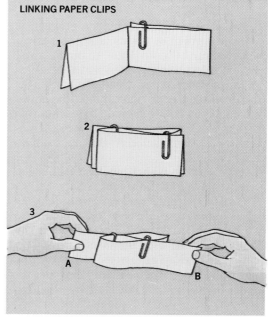

LINKING PAPER CLIPS

Beforehand, slip one of the rings over your left arm as far up as it will go, as shown in the illustration. It will be hidden by your sleeve. The pressure of your arm will hold it in place.

Have a friend tie a piece of cord fairly tight around your wrists, as shown. There should be about 30 centimeters (1 foot) of cord between the wrists. Hold your hands up while they are being tied, to prevent the ring on your arm from slipping down.

Next, hand out the duplicate ring for examination. When it is returned, turn your back and quickly put this ring into your shirt pocket or inside coat pocket, at the same time allowing the ring on your arm to slip down over the cord. Turn around and show the ring now hanging from the cord.

▶LINKING PAPER CLIPS

To do this easy but puzzling trick, fold in half, lengthwise, a rectangle of paper about 20 centimeters (8 inches) long and 8 centimeters (3 inches) wide, keeping the folded edge on top. Now fold the paper into three parts, accordion style. Place a paper clip over the middle and back folds. (Illustration 1.)

Place another paper clip over the front and middle folds. (Illustration 2.)

Grasp ends A and B firmly and pull the paper straight. (Illustration 3.) The two paper clips will fly off, mysteriously linked together.

▶THE DIGIT PROBLEM

Here is a mystifying mind-reading trick that you can perform for your friends at a party or some other gathering.

Ask two persons to assist you. Instruct them that when you turn your back and say "Ready," they must both hold up from one to five fingers and then call aloud the total of the two hands.

When this has been done, you immediately announce the number of fingers each of them is showing.

The secret is simple and ingenious. One of the two persons who participates is your secret assistant. The first time it is worked, your assistant must hold up two fingers. When the total is called, you simply subtract 2 and announce the number of fingers each of them has extended.

Contrary to the usual rule, you now offer to repeat the trick. This time your assistant must hold up the same number of fingers that the other person held up previously. Since you also know what that number is, you subtract it from the new total called and again announce the number of fingers each of them is showing. At each repetition it is your assistant's duty to hold up the same number of fingers as were last extended by the other person.

GEORGE G. KAPLAN
Author, *The Fine Art of Magic*

MAGNA CARTA

On June 15, 1215, King John of England met with a group of barons at Runnymede, a meadow near London. There he put his royal seal on a document, written in Latin, called the Magna Carta (Great Charter). The Magna Carta was the first attempt to limit the power of the king by law. John did not wish to sign the Magna Carta, but he had become so unpopular with his subjects that he had no choice.

Dissatisfaction with King John had begun many years before the signing of the Magna Carta. His subjects were angry with the King for his ruthlessness. He taxed them heavily so that he could carry on military campaigns in France. Often he used the taxes for his own selfish purposes. The barons had asked the King many times to agree to their demands for rights, but each time John refused. Stephen Langton, Archbishop of Canterbury, helped organize the barons' opposition to the King. In fact, it was Langton and the barons who drew up the Magna Carta. In the spring of 1215, the barons occupied London. King John finally realized that he had to give in to the barons' demands and agreed to the meeting at Runnymede.

The Magna Carta established the principle that certain customs and laws had more authority than the king and that if the king did not observe these laws, the people had the right to force him to do so. Many of the 63 articles in the Magna Carta dealt with specific problems of the times, such as payments of feudal dues and justice in the law courts. One of the articles guaranteed the freedom of the church. Other articles in the Magna Carta listed the barons' rights and privileges.

The most famous article, number 39, stated that "no freeman shall be arrested or imprisoned . . . except by the lawful judgment of his equals and according to the law of the land." It was later expanded to guarantee a jury trial for everyone. This was followed by article 40, which stated, "To no one will we sell, to no one will we refuse or delay right or justice." Another famous article was number 12, which stated that "no scutage [taxes] or aid shall be levied . . . unless by the common consent of our kingdom." During their fight for independence, American colonists extended this to mean "no taxation without representation."

At the time it was issued, the Magna Carta was not very effective. Civil war soon broke out between King John and the barons. It was still raging when John died on October 19, 1216. The charter was re-issued several times after his death. But only in the 1600's did the Magna Carta become a symbol of English liberty. Defenders of Parliament used the document to support their attempts to limit the power of King Charles I. By the end of the century, supreme authority rested in the hands of Parliament, as it does today.

In an attempt to simplify the laws of England, parts of the Magna Carta have been revised or repealed. But these changes have not destroyed or diminished the importance of this famous document. After more than 700 years, it remains a cornerstone of freedom in the Western world.

Reviewed by GOLDWIN SMITH
Author, *A History of England*

King John signed the Magna Carta reluctantly, since signing it was admitting that he was bound by the law.

MAGNESIUM

Magnesium is a silvery white metal that is very light in weight. It is the lightest of the engineering metals—the metals most often used in industry. Magnesium is also one of the easiest metals to shape with machine tools.

Like many other metals, magnesium is given added strength and durability when it is alloyed, or mixed, with other metals. The metals most commonly alloyed with magnesium are aluminum, manganese, and zinc.

Because they are light and strong, magnesium alloys are used in airplanes, missiles, rockets, and lightweight machine parts. They are also used in other products that need to be light, such as luggage, portable tools, hand trucks, and ladders.

Magnesium is one of several ingredients in chlorophyll, the green food-making substance in plants. Magnesium is also found in animals, where it is part of the chemical process in which sugar is broken down to provide energy. Beans, liver, nuts, and whole-grain cereals are foods that are rich in magnesium.

Magnesium compounds are used in several medicines. Epsom salts, for example, is actually magnesium sulfate. Milk of magnesia is a mixture of magnesium hydroxide and water.

When magnesium is powdered, or when it is shaped into thin ribbon or wire, it ignites easily and burns with an intense white flame. For this reason it is used in fireworks, signal flares, photographic flashbulbs, and incendiary bombs.

The printing industry uses large quantities of magnesium for making photoengraving plates because the metal can be etched very easily. Reproductions of drawings and photographs are etched on the plates, which are used for printing illustrations in books, magazines, and newspapers.

▶SOURCES OF MAGNESIUM

More than 60 minerals contain magnesium. The most important mineral sources of magnesium are dolomite and magnesite. No magnesium metal is found uncombined in nature.

Magnesium compounds were known and used for many years before the pure metal was extracted from them. The compounds were confused with lime (a chemical containing calcium) until 1755. In that year, the Scottish chemist Joseph Black proved that lime and magnesium compounds were different substances. He did this by showing that they react differently when treated with the same acids.

In 1808 the English chemist Sir Humphry Davy extracted a small amount of magnesium metal from a compound of magnesium by heating it with potassium and mercury. He called the metal magnium but later changed the name to magnesium. The name comes from an area in ancient Greece called Magnesia, where deposits of magnesium compounds were found.

One of the largest supplies of magnesium is found dissolved in seawater. The element makes up about 0.13 percent of seawater. The supply of magnesium is almost unlimited because there are methods for extracting the metal from seawater.

In 1833, electricity was first used by the English scientist Michael Faraday to extract magnesium metal from magnesium chloride. In this kind of process, called electrolysis, an electric current is used to break down a chemical compound into its elements.

This is the method now used to extract large quantities of magnesium from seawater. In huge tanks, seawater is treated with several chemicals to obtain magnesium chloride. Then an electric current is passed through the magnesium chloride, which breaks down into magnesium metal and chlorine gas. More than 1 kilogram (2.2 pounds) of magnesium can be obtained from each metric ton of seawater with this method.

Reviewed by WILLIAM S. WISE
University of California—Santa Barbara
See also METALS AND METALLURGY.

FACTS ABOUT MAGNESIUM

CHEMICAL SYMBOL: Mg.

ATOMIC WEIGHT: 24.312.

SPECIFIC GRAVITY: 1.74 (nearly 1¾ times as heavy as water).

COLOR: Silvery white.

PROPERTIES: Lightest structural metal produced in quantity; is easy to machine and to etch; ignites easily in powdered form or when shaped into wire; burns with an intense white flame.

OCCURRENCE: Sixth most abundant element on earth; third most abundant engineering metal (after aluminum and iron); occurs as carbonate or silicate, never as a native metal.

CHIEF SOURCES: Dolomite; magnesite; magnesium chloride extracted from seawater.

MAGNETS AND MAGNETISM

If ancient sailors came back from the past, they would be surprised by modern navigational instruments such as radar scopes and satellite receivers. Inside those instruments would be things that would not surprise them: magnets.

Magnets are as important today as they were hundreds of years ago when sailors used them as compasses to guide them on their voyages. In ancient times magnets were viewed as magical, with a mysterious ability to pull certain metals or be pulled in a certain direction. Today we understand that the magic of magnets is a basic force of nature, related to electricity and light.

Even though we understand the mystery, we still marvel at what modern magnetic machines can do. Because of our knowledge of magnets, we can create images of the organs inside the body and write encyclopedias on spots no larger than pinheads.

▶ **DISCOVERING MAGNETS**

Humans discovered magnets and magnetism thousands of years ago. Pieces of a certain kind of black stone exerted forces on each other and on objects made of iron. The stones became known as **magnets** and the force as **magnetism**. According to one story, those names came from a place called Magnesia in Asia Minor where magnetic rocks were first found. Another story credits the discovery of magnetism to a shepherd named

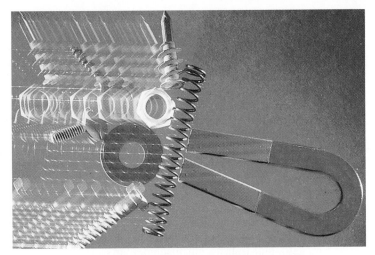

This horseshoe magnet exerts an invisible force that can attract certain metal objects containing iron, such as nuts, bolts, and springs.

Magnes, who stood on a large black rock and felt it pulling on the metal nails in his sandals.

Magnetic Poles

After some time, people discovered that long, thin magnets hanging from threads would always point in a north-south direction. The same end of the magnet would always point north. The opposite end would point south. These ends became known as the **poles** of the magnet, the north pole pointing north and the south pole pointing south. Soon sailors learned to use magnets to keep track of their direction on the open sea where there were no landmarks to guide them. The black rock then became known as **lodestone**, meaning "leading stone," because it enabled sailors to find their destination. The first magnetic device that humans ever made was the sailor's compass, which used a lodestone to measure the direction in which a ship was traveling.

Magnetic Fields and Lines of Force

If you put two magnets close to each other, you can feel forces between their poles. Two north poles or two south poles push each other away (or **repel**); a north and a south pole pull toward each other (**attract**). When an object experiences a push or pull through empty space, scientists describe the effect as a **field**.

Even though a magnetic field is invisible, you can imagine it as a pattern of lines that loop from one pole of a magnet to the oppo-

Lines of magnetic force stretch across two opposite poles, which attract one another. Lines of force from two like poles push away, or repel, one another.

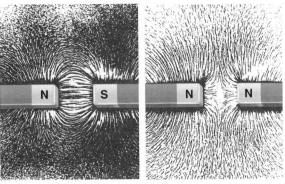

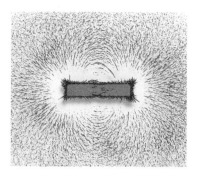

Iron filings sprinkled near a bar magnet reveal its lines of force. The area around the magnet is called a magnetic field.

site pole. You can see these lines if you put a magnet under a piece of cardboard and sprinkle iron filings on top. The filings will arrange themselves along the **lines of force**. The lines bunch together near the edges of the magnet by the poles, because that is where the field is strongest. If you put a north pole of one magnet near a south pole of another, the lines of force will connect the two poles. If two north poles or two south poles are close together, the lines follow paths that push away from one another.

Earth's Magnetic Field

A compass works because our planet has a magnetic field, with a north pole and a south pole. Earth's magnetic poles are not at exactly the same spots as the north and south geographic poles. The north magnetic pole, also known as magnetic north, is located in northern Canada. Compass needles point toward the north magnetic pole, not toward the north geographic pole, or true north. The difference between true north and magnetic north is known as the **magnetic deviation**. Knowing the deviation is important if you are using a compass to find your way in an area with few landmarks, such as a forest.

The direction of Earth's magnetic field is usually not perfectly horizontal. If you had a compass needle that could turn in any direction—north, south, east, west, up, or down—you would find that it would point generally northward but also somewhat upward or downward. The **magnetic dip** angle measures the amount that the field at a place points up or down. Together, magnetic deviation and magnetic dip describe the direction of the lines of force of Earth's magnetic field in your location.

Spectacular effects of Earth's magnetic field can be seen near the poles. Particles from the sun are drawn toward the poles and zip through the atmosphere, producing colorful **auroras** in the night sky.

The magnetized needle of a compass always points toward Earth's north magnetic pole. Hikers can use compasses to find out the direction in which they are traveling.

▶ MAGNETISM AND ELECTRICITY

As scientists in the 1700's and 1800's began to study magnetism and electricity, they discovered many similarities between the two. Just as magnets have north and south poles, electricity has positive and negative charges. Just as two north or two south magnetic poles repel each other, so do two positive or two negative electric charges. And just as a north and a south magnetic pole attract each other, so do a positive and a negative electric charge.

Scientists studied the strength of those attractive or repulsive forces and learned that it depends on the distance between the charges or poles. They also learned that the strength of those forces depends on the amount of charge or the closeness of the lines of force at the poles. For both electricity and magnetism, they came up with similar mathematical formulas to describe what they observed.

They found one important difference between electricity and magnetism. Positive and negative electrical charges can exist sepa-

Earth is surrounded by a magnetic field, with poles that are different from our planet's geographic poles. That difference is called magnetic deviation.

North geographic pole

North magnetic pole

Earth's magnetic field

The northern lights, or aurora borealis, occur when particles from the sun are drawn toward Earth's north magnetic pole and zip through the atmosphere.

rately. An object or particle can have a positive or a negative charge. Magnets, however, always have both a north and south pole. If you break a magnet in the middle, you will create two magnets. The half with the original north pole now has a south pole at its end of the break. The half with the original south pole now has a north pole at its end of the break. A large magnet is made up of many small magnets with their north and south poles aligned. A magnet is sometimes called a dipole ("di" is from the Greek word for "two") because it must have two poles. Scientists continue to look for isolated north or south poles, called **magnetic monopoles** ("mono" is from the Greek word for "one"). However, no monopoles have yet been found.

Electric Motors and Generators

In the early 1800's, scientists began applying their knowledge of the relationships be-tween electricity and magnetism to make useful devices. In 1820, Danish physicist Hans Christian Oersted discovered that an electric current passing through a wire near a compass would cause the compass needle to move. The current created a magnetic field that circled the wire. Soon after that, French scientist André Marie Ampère developed the first **electromagnet**—a magnet produced by electricity—by wrapping a current-carrying wire into a coil. In 1821, the English scientist Michael Faraday invented the electric motor. He used the magnetic force between a wire

---

See For Yourself

How to Make an Electromagnet

You can turn an ordinary nail into an electromagnet using only an iron nail, an insulated metal wire with exposed metal ends, and a household battery, such as a 9-volt battery (a type used in some transistor radios).

Step 1: Make sure the nail is unmagnetized by bringing its head and its point close to the north pole of a compass. If both ends attract the north pole, then you know the nail is not magnetized.

Step 2: Wrap the insulated metal wire around the nail in a spiral, and connect one of its exposed metal ends to the battery's positive terminal and the other to the negative terminal for a few seconds. As long as the current is flowing in it, the wire will be an electromagnet.

Step 3: Remove the wire's ends from the battery and slide the nail out of the coil. If you were successful in magnetizing the nail, one end of it will attract the north pole of the compass, and the other end will repel it.

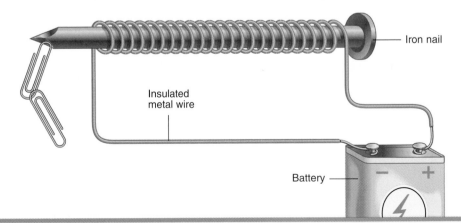

Iron nail

Insulated metal wire

Battery

carrying a current and a magnet to produce rotary motion. The motor turned electrical energy into mechanical energy.

In 1831, Faraday discovered a way to convert mechanical energy into electrical energy. He showed that moving a coil of wire

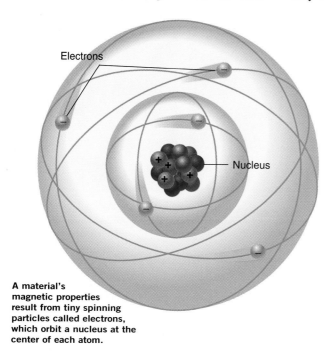

A material's magnetic properties result from tiny spinning particles called electrons, which orbit a nucleus at the center of each atom.

through a magnetic field would cause an electric current to flow through the wire. That discovery paved the way for the invention of the electric generator. (You can learn more by reading the articles ELECTRIC MOTORS and ELECTRIC GENERATORS in Volume E.)

Magnetism and Light

In 1865, Scottish physicist James Clerk Maxwell made a momentous discovery about the relationship between electricity and magnetism. He produced a new set of equations describing the two forces as one force called **electromagnetism**. Maxwell's equations predicted the existence of waves of energy called **electromagnetic waves** that would travel through empty space at a particular speed. When he compared that predicted speed with the measured speed of light, they were nearly the same. Could light be an electromagnetic wave? Maxwell said yes. Furthermore, he said, many other electromagnetic waves would exist. Maxwell's prediction was correct.

▶ MAGNETISM AND MATTER

By the end of the 1800's, scientists understood the basic relationships between electricity and magnetism, but they did not know where the forces came from. From chemistry, they knew that matter was made up of tiny particles called **atoms**. However, in the late 1800's and early 1900's, they discovered that atoms were made up of even tinier particles. Furthermore, these particles appeared to have certain magnetic and electric properties.

Magnetism of Atoms

Scientists soon discovered that the magnetism of a substance comes mainly from particles called **electrons**. Inside a substance's atoms, negatively charged electrons orbit positively charged centers called **nuclei** (singular: nucleus). Orbiting electrons produce a very weak "orbital" magnetism, just as an electrical current in a wire produces a magnetic field. Orbiting electrons also act as if they were tiny spinning balls of negative charge, creating a stronger type of magnetism called **spin**. Each orbit can be occupied by no more than two electrons, one with its spin in the same direction as the orbital magnetism and one with its spin in the opposite direction. In most atoms, electrons pair off, leaving little magnetism overall. In certain atoms, such as iron, a few orbits have only one electron. These unpaired electrons make the atoms magnetic.

The atoms of most solid materials are arranged in a repeating pattern called a crystal. Even if the atoms are magnetic, the crystal may not be. The atoms may line up so that the magnetism of one atom is opposite to its neighbor's. However, when the atoms tend to align with one another, the material is powerfully magnetic.

Magnetic Domains

A magnetic material does not always show its magnetism. Sometimes you have to study it very closely. Then you will discover it is made up of many small regions, called **domains**, where the magnetic fields of the atoms point in the same direction. However, not all some living creatures can detect and use Earth's magnetic field to survive? Some migratory birds have small magnetically sensitive structures in their heads. Scientists believe these structures help the birds find their way between their winter and summer homes. Certain bacteria produce needle-shaped crystals of **magnetite**, a magnetic form of iron oxide, within their bodies. Those crystals enable them to follow magnetic lines of force through the mud to find the nutrients they need for life. Similar, but much smaller, crystals of magnetite have been found in a meteorite that most scientists believe was once part of the planet Mars. Those crystals and

other findings within the extraterrestrial rock have led some scientists to believe that bacteria once lived—and may still live—on Mars.

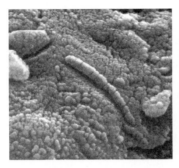

Left: A Martian meteorite was found to contain magnetite crystals, perhaps produced by what appear to be fossilized bacteria. *Right:* Snow geese may sense Earth's magnetic field to guide them during migration.

a material's domains have their fields pointing in the same direction. Often, the magnetism of one domain cancels out the magnetism of another, and the material is said to be unmagnetized. By putting the material in a strong external magnetic field, you can magnetize it. Magnetizing makes the different magnetisms of a material's domains line up with the external field.

Unmagnetized metals have tiny areas, called domains, whose magnetic fields point in many directions. A strong magnet magnetizes a metal by making these fields line up.

Unmagnetized metal

Magnetized metal

▶ **TYPES OF MAGNETS**

Magnets and magnetic materials are often divided into two classes: **permanent magnets** and **electromagnets**. Permanent magnets are made from materials that remain magnetized even after they are removed from a magnetic field. Although iron is the best-known type of permanent magnet, many other substances can be magnetic. The most powerful magnetic substance known is a chemical compound combining the element neodymium with iron and the very light element boron. The compound produces a magnetic field hundreds of times stronger than a similar piece of magnetic iron.

Electromagnets are coils of wire that become magnetic when electricity passes through them. Sometimes the coils are wrapped around the easily magnetized core of a permanent magnet to increase their strength. Electromagnets are particularly useful because the shape and strength of their magnetic fields can be easily controlled.

To create a very strong field, a very large current is required. Unfortunately, in a coil of normal wire, a large current uses a great amount of energy and produces a lot of heat. To eliminate that problem, the most powerful electromagnets—and the most powerful magnets of any kind—use coils made of a **superconductor**. A superconductor is a material that carries electricity without any loss of energy. All known superconductors work only at extremely low temperatures, so superconducting coils must be kept chilled in frigid fluids such as liquid helium.

▶ MODERN MAGNETIC DEVICES

Magnets and magnetic materials are used in many modern devices. Although high magnetic field strength can be very desirable, sometimes less strength is needed. Refrigerator magnets, which are usually made of a magnetic substance called ferrite embedded in plastic, must have a strong enough field to stick to the steel of a refrigerator door but not so strong that you cannot remove them. To store a sound or television picture, a magnetic audiotape or videotape must be made of a material that can have its magnetization changed easily by passing close to a small electromagnet, called the recording head.

One of the most important modern magnetic devices is the disk drive used to store information in a computer. The surface of the disk is coated with a special magnetic material that can have microscopic domains. The information is stored as a pattern of magnetic field directions in those domains. A nearly microscopic electromagnet is used to "write," or create, that pattern, and an even smaller magnetically sensitive device is used to "read," or detect, a pattern that was previously written. New magnetic information storage materials are constantly being developed. Some have domains so tiny that the entire set of *The New Book of Knowledge* could be stored on a spot no larger than a pinhead.

Another very important modern device is the **magnetic resonance imaging** (**MRI**) machine. It has improved medical care by creating detailed images of organs and structures inside the human body, especially the brain. These images would be difficult or impossible to obtain with X rays, and MRI does not damage body cells as X rays can in high doses. MRI uses the magnetic properties of the nuclei of atoms in the body.

▶ MAGNETISM IN THE FUTURE

In some parts of the world, **magnetic levitation** (**maglev**) trains float above their rails,

This maglev train in Sydney, Australia, uses very powerful electromagnets to levitate, or float, above its track and travel smoothly.

lifted by the force between electromagnets in the train and electromagnets below the tracks. Some of these trains use superconducting magnets; others use powerful normal electromagnets. These trains can travel smoothly at speeds up to 300 miles (about 480 kilometers) per hour—half the usual speed of a jet plane.

Maglev trains may be an important part of our transportation future. Since they can travel to the heart of a downtown area, just as regular trains do, people may find maglev travel ultimately quicker and more convenient than taking a plane.

In every other area where magnets and magnetism are important today, advances in technology will make them even more important in the future. Those ancient sailors would be astonished to see all the places magnetism will take us—and so, no doubt, will we.

ALFRED B. (FRED) BORTZ
Author, science books for children

See also ATOMS; COMPUTERS; EARTH; ELECTRIC GENERATORS; ELECTRICITY; ELECTRIC MOTORS; IMAGING, DIAGNOSTIC; LIGHT; MATERIALS SCIENCE; SOUND RECORDING; VIDEO RECORDING.

MAHLER, GUSTAV (1860–1911)

Gustav Mahler, the great Austrian composer and conductor, was born on July 7, 1860, in Kalischt, Bohemia (now Kaliste, Czech Republic). At the age of 15, he was enrolled at the Vienna Conservatory, where he studied piano and composition.

In 1880, Mahler began to conduct at small opera houses. Gradually he moved on to important positions at larger theaters in Prague, Budapest, and Hamburg. In 1897 he became artistic director of the Imperial Opera in Vienna. There he brought about needed reforms in the preparation and staging of operas. The Imperial Opera gained international prominence under his direction. During summers in Vienna, when the opera house was closed, Mahler worked on his own compositions. He wrote song cycles and symphonies. Gradually he was recognized as an important composer for the way he combined songs and symphonies and created new instrumental combinations. He was known especially for expanding the traditional form of the symphony and for using many performers. His Eighth Symphony has been described as a "symphony of a thousand." It requires a large chorus, many soloists, and a huge orchestra.

Mahler was a very demanding conductor, and his occasional fits of temper made him enemies. In 1907 he resigned from the Imperial Opera and accepted a position with the Metropolitan Opera in New York City, where he remained for three seasons (1908–10). His conducting of the operas of Mozart and Wagner account for some of the finest performances in the history of the Metropolitan. He also conducted the New York Philharmonic Orchestra.

Mahler's last three years were marred by ill health. He spent as much time as he could composing because he hoped to leave behind works of lasting importance. Some of his best-known works—the symphonic cycle *Song of the Earth*, the Ninth Symphony, and the unfinished Tenth Symphony—were composed during his last years. He died in Vienna on May 18, 1911. Mahler's fame grew after his death. Today he is regarded as one of the greatest composers of his generation.

WILLIAM ASHBROOK
Philadelphia College of the Performing Arts

MAIL ORDER

Mail-order shopping, a form of direct marketing, is a convenient and popular way to make purchases from home. In recent years a wide variety of goods have become available through this method of shopping, and more and more people are making use of it.

All forms of direct marketing use advertising to offer goods and services directly to people. Direct mail, using the postal system, is one type of advertising used in direct marketing. Mail order is a type of direct mail that allows people to order products from their homes or offices.

▶DIRECT MARKETING

The means of communication used in direct marketing may be catalogs or letters, magazine or newspaper advertisements, radio or television commercials, or the telephone. Whatever method is used, people are asked to respond directly by mail or phone.

Direct marketing is a very efficient way to sell and deliver goods—it does not necessarily require a store or in-person sales calls. For this reason it is used by many types of businesses—magazine and newspaper circulation departments, credit card companies, book and record companies, financial services, and insurance companies. Some businesses that use direct marketing, such as catalog and other mail-order firms, have no stores. Others use direct marketing along with other selling methods. Even retail stores sell merchandise through the mail or by telephone. Direct marketing is also used by colleges and universities and by most fund-raising groups.

▶HOW MAIL ORDER WORKS

Mail order is basically a simple process. A business selects a product or a group of products to offer to you and mails an advertisement or a catalog to your home. There is usually an order form for you to fill in and mail if you wish to buy something. Or there may be a telephone number, so that you can call and place your order personally. Payment is usually mailed with the order (or separately, if the order was placed by telephone.) Many mailers allow customers to charge purchases. Some allow payment on delivery.

After the company receives your order, it packs the product and ships it. Sometimes, in the United States, the merchandise is sent through the U.S. Postal Service. Sometimes other carriers, such as United Parcel Service, are used. Mail-order firms usually allow customers to exchange or return most items.

But mail order involves more than just assembling a list of products and sending out mail describing them. The products themselves must be selected wisely. The offer must be presented in a bright, original way, to show the customer its interest and value. And the seller must fill orders promptly.

Direct mail advertisements must reach the right people—people who are likely to be interested in the product being offered. Mailing lists help the seller reach these people. They are drawn up according to information on income, education, interests, home ownership, marital status, and other factors. Thus a firm that wanted to sell a lawn sprinkler through the mail, for example, would probably look for a list of homeowners.

▶ THE GROWTH OF MAIL ORDER

Mail-order shopping began to grow in the late 1800's, in the American Midwest. It filled the important role of providing goods to rural families who did not live near stores. These families had little means of getting the products they needed in their daily lives. In time such early mail-order companies as Montgomery Ward (which started in 1872) and Sears (1886) grew to become huge marketers of general merchandise, providing household, personal, and even automotive products to a vast number of shoppers.

Today mail order is a big business, generating $85 billion in catalog sales a year and growing at a steady rate. There are several reasons why mail order has grown in recent years. One is the variety of merchandise available. You can purchase almost any kind of product through the mail, from telephones to personal computers.

Another reason is the convenience of shopping at any hour of the day or night from the comfort of home. This is especially helpful to working people who have busy schedules.

A large mail-order operation looks more like an office than a store. The incoming orders are entered into a computer, which makes it possible to handle a large number of accounts efficiently and accurately.

These people have little time to shop in stores, but they must still feed and clothe themselves and their families and furnish their homes. Older people also use mail order because they find shopping at home safe and easy.

As personal computer use has become widespread, it is common for people to shop at home over the Internet. Today many companies sell goods and services through their own Web sites and advertise on other sites they think potential customers will visit. Customers fill out electronic order forms, and products are delivered to their homes. Shopping this way is simple and fast. However, some people do not feel secure exchanging personal information electronically and prefer traditional mail order shopping.

Mail order and other methods of direct marketing are efficient and economical ways to do business. In recent years they have changed the way many people in the United States shop. It is likely that mail order will continue to grow because it fills the needs of so many different kinds of people.

ROBERT F. DeLAY
Direct Marketing Association

See also SALES AND MARKETING.

MAINE

Maine's name may come from the fact that early explorers and colonists referred to the area's "mainland," or "main," to distinguish it from the many islands along the coast.

The state's vast forests, many of them pines and other evergreens, have given rise to its nickname, the Pine Tree State. New Englanders have long referred to Maine as Down East. This is because ships traveling from Boston must sail east and downwind to get to Maine. Maine is also called Vacationland. Its scenic lakes and mountains, great forests, and rugged coastline notched with many snug harbors make a delightful setting for year-round recreation.

Maine is the easternmost of all the fifty states—the first to greet the morning sun. West Quoddy Head, on the Atlantic coast near the Canadian border, lies farther east than any other point in the United States. Maine's location in the northeastern corner of the nation gives it an international flavor: It borders on only one other state, New Hampshire, but on two Canadian provinces, Quebec and New Brunswick. The people of Maine share much in common with their neighbors to the north.

Once dependent on resource-based industries—forestry, farming, and fishing—and later on manufacturing, Maine's economy is now based largely on service industries. Still, the state remains famous for products of land and sea: potatoes, blueberries, and lobsters.

Maine did not become a state until 1820, but it has a long history. Its first inhabitants, Paleo-Indians, arrived about 10,000 B.C. and were followed by several other prehistoric Native American peoples. The first European known to have visited the Maine coast was explorer Giovanni da Verrazano, who came in 1524. By the early 1600's, European fishermen were frequent visitors to the Maine coast. Between 1625 and 1640, several colonial settlements were established along the coast. Today, forts, blockhouses, monuments, and historic buildings are reminders of Maine's proud, eventful past.

▶ **LAND**

Maine is the largest of the New England states. It is almost as large as all the others

State flag

combined. The 45th parallel of latitude runs near the center of Maine. Several towns on this line of latitude can boast that they lie midway between the North Pole and the equator.

Land Regions

The rugged surface of Maine is an ancient, worn-down land. The mountains of the present day are only the stumps of mountains that once were very high. During the Ice Age, all of the area that is now Maine was covered by glaciers. The great weight of the ice pushed the land down, submerging much of the coastal area. Today the land rises toward the northwest in a series of three steps. These steps divide the state into three distinct land regions: the Seaboard Lowland, the New England Upland, and the White Mountains region.

The Seaboard Lowland is the name given to the sloping coastal border of New England. In Maine this region extends inland for distances ranging from about 20 to 60 miles (30 to 95 kilometers). In general it is lower than the adjoining upland. But the Seaboard Lowland is broken in places by hills.

Along the coast southwest of Casco Bay, there are numerous sandy beaches and tidal

Opposite page, clockwise from left: **A bull moose browses in a secluded Maine pond. Cross-country skiers pause to view Mount Katahdin, the state's highest peak. Maine's deeply indented coast is dotted with picturesque coves and harbors.**

State flower:
Eastern white pinecone and tassel

State tree:
Eastern white pine

FACTS AND FIGURES

Location: Northeast corner of the United States; bordered on the west by New Hampshire; on the northwest by Quebec, Canada; on the north and east by New Brunswick, Canada; and on the south by the Atlantic Ocean.

Area: 33,741 sq mi (87,388 km²); rank, 39th.

Population: 1,274,923 (2000 census); rank, 40th.

Elevation: *Highest*—Mount Katahdin, 5,267 ft (1,605 m); *lowest*—sea level, along the Atlantic coast.

Capital: Augusta.

Statehood: March 15, 1820; 23rd state.

State Motto: *Dirigo* ("I lead").

State Song: "State of Maine Song."

Nicknames: Pine Tree State; Vacationland.

Abbreviations: ME; Me.

State bird:
Chickadee

Above: The rocky cliffs of Mount Desert Island typify the rugged beauty of Maine's coastline. This and other scenic sections of the island are preserved as part of Acadia National Park. *Opposite page:* An autumn view of Moosehead Lake; located in west central Maine, it is the largest of the state's many lakes.

marshlands. The rest of Maine's coastline is rugged and deeply indented—the true "rock-bound coast of Maine." It was formed by the submergence of parallel rows of old, worn-down mountains and hills. The tops of these mountains extend into the sea, some as rocky peninsulas and others as islands. Mount Desert Island is the largest of the more than 1,000 islands. At 1,532 feet (467 meters), Cadillac Mountain on this island is the highest point on the Atlantic Coast of North America.

The New England Upland is a rolling area, averaging between 300 and 1,000 feet (90 and 300 meters) in elevation. Rivers have cut deeply into the land. Towns and cities are lo-cated in the river valleys. The upland slopes are forested. The central basin, which includes Augusta and Bangor, and the northern Aroostook basin are the state's chief agricultural areas.

The White Mountains region extends into Maine from New Hampshire. In Maine this region averages above 3,000 feet (1,000 meters) in elevation. It has a plateaulike surface with groups of mountains rising abruptly above the surrounding land. Maine's highest peak, Mount Katahdin, is in the White Mountains region.

Rivers, Lakes, and Coastal Waters

The St. John River forms part of Maine's northern boundary with the Canadian province of New Brunswick. The St. John and its tributaries, the Aroostook and the Allagash, drain the northern part of the state. The chief rivers of southern Maine are the Piscataqua, Saco, Androscoggin, Kennebec, Penobscot, and St. Croix. The Androscoggin joins the Kennebec below Augusta to form Merrymeeting Bay. The St. Croix forms Maine's eastern boundary.

Maine has more than 2,000 lakes and ponds, connected by a wide network of brooks, streams, and rivers. Rock basins, scoured out by the glaciers, filled with water to create the largest lakes in the state. Moosehead Lake, southwest of Mount Katahdin, is one of the nation's largest freshwater lakes entirely within a state's borders. Five of the six Rangeley Lakes are in Maine. (The other is on the border between Maine and New Hampshire.) The Belgrade Lakes form another chain. Artificial lakes, such as Wyman and Flagstaff, help to control the rivers.

Maine's general coastline measures 228 miles (367 kilometers). But the total shoreline, counting all the inlets and bays, is 3,478 miles (5,596 kilometers) long.

Climate

Maine's cool, moist climate is one of its attractions. Summer temperatures are usually not extremely high, with average July temperatures of 62°F (17°C) in the northern interior and 64°F (18°C) on the coast. Furthermore, even the warmest summer days are invariably followed by cool nights. January temperatures along the coast are well below freezing, averaging 27°F (–3°C), while to the

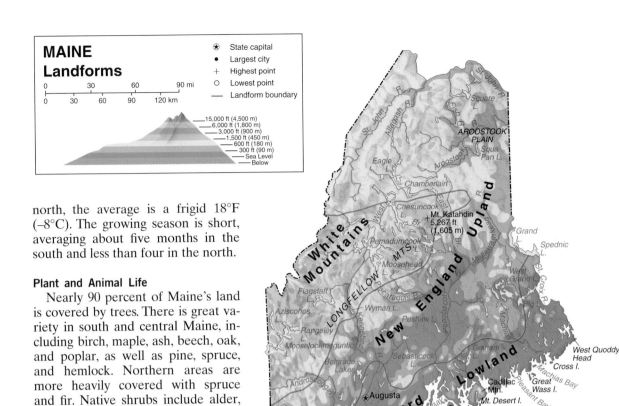

north, the average is a frigid 18°F (–8°C). The growing season is short, averaging about five months in the south and less than four in the north.

Plant and Animal Life

Nearly 90 percent of Maine's land is covered by trees. There is great variety in south and central Maine, including birch, maple, ash, beech, oak, and poplar, as well as pine, spruce, and hemlock. Northern areas are more heavily covered with spruce and fir. Native shrubs include alder, witch hazel, sumac, chokecherries, and gooseberries. The most common wildflowers are black-eyed Susans, buttercups, goldenrod, dandelions, field daisies, mayflowers, Queen Anne's lace, and wild roses. Also found in Maine's woods are fiddlehead ferns, a delicacy harvested in the spring, with many canned for local and out-of-state markets.

Moose are probably Maine's most famous animals; they share the woods and countryside with deer, bears, coyotes, squirrels, rabbits, and other smaller creatures. Inland and coastal birds include eagles, owls, hawks, grouse, turkeys, ducks, and a great variety of

including tourmaline, rose quartz, and aquamarine, have been mined in western Maine.

Maine has strong environmental laws to conserve its resources and to control how land is developed and water resources are used. The state's Land Use Regulation Commission is responsible for the use of wild forested lands; the Department of Environmental Protection oversees the development of land and the use of shorelines in the more populated parts of the state.

▶ PEOPLE

Most of the people live in the southwestern part of the state. The northern and northwestern parts are sparsely populated. Maine's northernmost county, Aroostook, is larger

songbirds. The deep woods of Maine are famous for their blackflies and mosquitos.

Maine lakes and streams contain salmon, trout, bass, sunfish, perch, pickerel, and eels. Recently introduced in some lakes, northern pike is becoming increasingly common. Offshore, seals and whales abound, as well as cod, haddock, halibut, mackerel, tuna, herring, and sharks.

Natural Resources

In addition to its forests and wildlife, Maine's natural resources include water, soils, and minerals.

Numerous waterfalls and whitewater rapids cascade down Maine's rugged landscape. The force of falling water was used to turn the waterwheels that powered early sawmills and gristmills. Today waterpower is used to generate electricity. The thousands of lakes and streams within the state also are important, as sources of water and as recreational sites.

The clay loams of central Maine and Aroostook County are excellent for farming. Elsewhere the soils generally are thin and not very fertile.

Maine has a variety of metallic minerals, but efforts to mine them economically have failed. The chief minerals are sand and gravel, brick clay, peat, and small quantities of granite and slate. Some semiprecious gemstones,

Above: Fly-fishing in a Maine river is one of many outdoor activities enjoyed by residents and visitors alike. The state abounds in areas of unspoiled natural beauty. *Below right:* Bowdoin College, founded in Brunswick in 1794, is Maine's oldest college.

than Connecticut and Rhode Island together, but only 8 percent of the state's people live there. Maine's population is about 45 percent urban and 55 percent rural, although it should be noted that many so-called urban areas are fairly small communities.

Descendants of the Native Americans who greeted the first Europeans still live in the state. Two tribes, the Passamaquoddys and the Penobscots, now inhabit reservations. Members of two other groups, the Micmacs and Maliceets, also live in Maine but not on reservations.

The earliest European settlers were English or Scotch-Irish, some of whom came to Maine from Massachusetts. Today people of British ancestry make up the state's largest population group. People of French ancestry make up the next largest group. Some are descended from French Canadians who immigrated to Maine in the late 1800's to work in the mills. Others trace their origins to an earlier group, the Acadians, who were driven from Nova Scotia in the 1750's when they refused to swear allegiance to England. Newcomers continue to settle in Maine, but nearly all residents were born in the United States.

Education

An education law passed in 1789 required all towns of at least 50 families to provide six months of schooling. Towns of 200 families or more were required to support a grammar school.

Even before this, many communities were supporting small grammar schools, and by the late 1700's, an increasing number of towns were setting up private academies. In 1821, Portland opened Maine's first—and the nation's second—free public high school.

Bowdoin College, established in 1794 in Brunswick, was the first college in Maine. Maine has since seen the establishment of 18 more private colleges, including Colby College in Waterville (1813) and Bates College in Lewiston (1864).

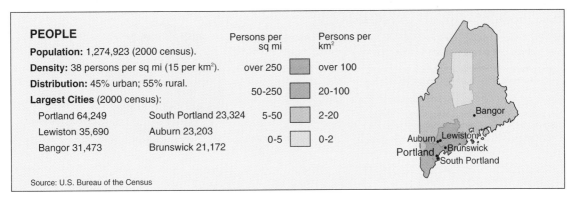

PEOPLE

Population: 1,274,923 (2000 census).

Density: 38 persons per sq mi (15 per km²).

Distribution: 45% urban; 55% rural.

Largest Cities (2000 census):

Portland 64,249	South Portland 23,324
Lewiston 35,690	Auburn 23,203
Bangor 31,473	Brunswick 21,172

Persons per sq mi		Persons per km²
over 250		over 100
50-250		20-100
5-50		2-20
0-5		0-2

Source: U.S. Bureau of the Census

Above: Wood products, paper products, and lumber contribute heavily to Maine's economy. *Right:* The Bath Iron Works is a center of shipbuilding and ship repair.

The University of Maine was established at Orono in 1865. Today, in addition to the Orono campus, the university has branches in Augusta, Farmington, Fort Kent, Machias, and Presque Isle. The University of Southern Maine, in Portland, along with its law school, is also a major part of the state system. The state supports two-year vocational and technical institutes in Auburn, Bangor, Aroostook, and South Portland and the Maine Maritime Academy in Castine.

Libraries, Museums, and the Arts

A public library was organized in Falmouth (now Portland) in the 1760's. It was burned during the British bombardment in 1775, but it was rebuilt, and it has become one of the best libraries in the Northeast. Bangor also has an especially well equipped library. Besides these two major repositories, there are about 250 other public libraries in cities and towns across the state. The state library, organized in Augusta in 1836, has a large collection of state-related material.

The Maine State Museum in Augusta has exhibits on Maine's natural and human history. Excellent historical exhibitions can be seen at the Maine Historical Society in Portland, York Institute in Saco, Brick Store Museum in Kennebunk, and the York Historical Association in York. Several significant art museums are located in the state, including the Portland Museum of Art in Portland, the William A. Farnsworth Library and Art Museum in Rockland, and the art museums at Bowdoin and Colby colleges and at the University of Maine at Orono. The Penobscot Marine Museum in Searsport and Maine Maritime Museum in Bath provide major exhibitions on Maine maritime history. Museums focusing on Maine's prehistory and ethnohistory include the Anthropology Museum

PRODUCTS AND INDUSTRIES

Manufacturing: Pulp and paper products, transportation equipment, wood products, leather products, electronics and electrical equipment, food products, plastic goods, fabricated metal products, textiles.

Agriculture: Potatoes, dairy products, apples, blueberries, maple sugar and syrup.

Minerals: Sand and gravel, semi-precious gemstones.

Services: Wholesale and retail trade; finance, insurance, and real estate; business, social, and personal services; transportation, communication, and utilities; government.

*Gross state product is the total value of goods and services produced in a year.

Percentage of Gross State Product* by Industry

- Agriculture 2%
- Construction 4%
- Transportation, communication, and utilities 8%
- Business, social, and personal services 19%
- Government 14%
- Manufacturing 18%
- Wholesale and retail trade 17%
- Finance, insurance, and real estate 18%

Source: U.S. Bureau of Economic Analysis

at the University of Maine and the Abbe Museum at Bar Harbor.

Portland and Bangor have symphony orchestras. Throughout the state there are summer music camps. Lakewood, near Skowhegan, is the oldest summer playhouse in the nation.

▶ ECONOMY

Maine's economy has undergone dramatic changes over the past several decades, shifting steadily from manufacturing and resource-based industries to services.

Services

Service industries account for more than 75 percent of Maine's gross state product (GSP)—the total value of goods and services produced in a year. Business, social, and personal services make up the largest sector. These include, for example, automotive repair, legal and medical services, and services related to Maine's long-established recreation and tourist industry. Finance, insurance, and real estate rank second among the service industries.

Wholesale and retail trade is both active and vital. Portland, Lewiston-Auburn, and Bangor are the state's leading trade centers. Many small local businesses are disappearing as larger national operations move in. On the other hand, a number of small specialty firms, such as the outdoor clothing company L.L. Bean, have developed national markets for their wares.

Government—including public schools, hospitals, and military bases—and transportation, communication, and utilities are Maine's other service industries.

Manufacturing

Although contributing less than 20 percent of the GSP, manufacturing remains important. Maine's forests provide the raw material for the state's leading manufacture, pulp and paper products. Large paper mills operate in Millinocket, Rumford, Jay, Skowhegan, and other locations across the state.

Transportation equipment is the second most important manufacture. Shipbuilding and ship repair employ large workforces at the Bath Iron Works establishments in Bath and Portland. Wood products rank third in importance: Sawmills cut substantial quantities of lumber, and shops and small factories create a variety of products ranging from furniture to toothpicks.

Other manufactures include shoes and other leather goods, electronic and electrical equipment, food products, and textiles.

Agriculture and Fishing

Once a mainstay of Maine's economy, farming has declined dramatically. Increasingly, Maine farmers have focused on serving specialized markets. Fresh milk, eggs, and, to a lesser degree, vegetables are aimed at local and regional markets. Apples from central Maine, blueberries from the northeast coastal region, and potatoes from Aroostook County

Maine is famous for products of land and sea.
Left: Lobstering remains an important activity; the annual catch is the nation's highest.
Below: Maine is a leading potato-growing state.

Places of Interest

Wadsworth-Longfellow House, Portland

Portland Head Light, Cape Elizabeth

Old Gaol Museum, York Village

Acadia National Park

Acadia National Park is located on parts of Mount Desert Island, Isle au Haut, and Schoodic Peninsula. Scenic drives and hiking trails provide access to many of the park's natural features, including the summit of Cadillac Mountain, the highest point on the Atlantic Coast of North America.

Allagash Wilderness Waterway, along the Allagash River in northern Maine, preserves one of the nation's few remaining wilderness rivers. The area, which attracts canoeists, campers, and fishermen, was established through federal-state cooperation.

Black Mansion, in Ellsworth, was built about 1820. It is often called Maine's Mount Vernon because it resembles George Washington's Virginia home. Features include collections of china and furniture, a formal garden, and a carriage house.

Fort Western, in Augusta, is one of the few remaining French and Indian War forts still standing in the United States. Established in 1754, it served first as a fort, then as a trading post, and finally as a residence. Benedict Arnold stopped there on his 1775 march to capture Quebec.

Maine Beaches. Beautiful sand beaches stretch from Ogunquit to Wells in southern Maine. Several small beaches dot the mid-Maine coast, notably those at Popham, Reid, and Pemaquid state parks. The mid-coast waters are a bit chilly for swimming, but there, as at other beaches, visitors can sunbathe, fish, and enjoy beautiful coastal scenery.

Moosehorn National Wildlife Refuge, near Calais, provides a habitat for many native animals and includes numerous scenic nature trails and observation areas.

Old Gaol Museum, in York Village, is the oldest public building in Maine and one of the oldest in North America. It was built in 1653 as a jail (gaol) and now houses historic artifacts.

Portland Head Light, on Cape Elizabeth near Portland, is one of the country's oldest lighthouses. Built in 1791, it was the first of four lighthouses authorized by George Washington to be put into service.

Seashore Trolley Museum, in Kennebunkport, houses a large collection of vintage electric trolley cars.

Wadsworth-Longfellow House, in Portland, was the home of the poet Henry Wadsworth Longfellow. Part of the three-story brick house was built by Longfellow's grandfather, General Peleg Wadsworth, in 1785. The home contains possessions of the Wadsworth and the Longfellow families.

State Areas. Maine has about 35 state recreational areas. For more information, contact the Maine Bureau of Parks and Recreation, State House, Augusta, Maine, 04333.

Enjoying a dockside lobster dinner is one of the many pleasures of a visit to Maine, which has a long-standing tourist industry. Maine lobsters are renowned for their delectable taste and fine quality.

have all found buyers beyond Maine's boundaries.

The state's fishing industry has experienced major changes. Overfishing and new conservation regulations have hit the industry hard. However, Maine is the nation's foremost harvester of lobsters and ranks second in the number of soft-shell clams caught. Deep-sea fishing brings in valuable amounts of cod, flounder, pollock, haddock, and herring.

Mining and Construction

Granite from Maine has been used in the construction of many of the nation's important buildings and monuments. The major mineral products today are sand and gravel, which are used in road construction, landscaping, and cement.

Maine's construction industry is relatively strong. Building construction, which flourished in the 1980's, has weakened in recent years. But other areas, such as the building of roads, bridges, and treatment plants, have experienced substantial growth.

Energy

Maine is New England's leading producer of hydroelectric power. Hydroelectric plants are located on the Androscoggin, Kennebec, Penobscot, and Saco rivers. A nuclear power plant was set up in 1972 but was shut down temporarily in 1995. The state also has petroleum-powered plants and imports some electric power from Canada.

Transportation

Maine has more than 20,000 miles of roads. The Maine Turnpike runs from Kittery to Augusta, the capital, and a second four-lane coastal highway runs from Portland to Augusta. Another four-lane highway continues north from the capital to Houlton.

Maine's first railroad was built between Bangor and Old Town in 1836 to haul lumber. Today freight service is provided by several railroads, the largest of which are the Maine Central, Bangor and Aroostook, and Canadian Pacific. Ferry service is available from Portland and Bar Harbor to Nova Scotia. The harbor at Portland is one of the largest in the United States.

Maine has about 45 commercial and municipal airports and half that many seaplane bases. Portland International is Maine's busiest airport, with flights connecting south along the Atlantic seaboard and elsewhere. Bangor International Airport is the closest American airport to Europe.

Communication

Maine has some 60 newspapers, including 9 dailies. The *Bangor Daily News* is the largest. Other papers include Augusta's *Kennebec Journal* (the longest-running paper in Maine, founded in 1825), Waterville's *Central Maine Morning Sentinel*, and Portland's *Portland*

The State House, in Augusta, was designed by noted architect Charles Bulfinch and built of native granite. Augusta has been the state capital since 1832.

GOVERNMENT

State Government

Governor: 4-year term
State senators: 35; 2-year terms
State representatives: 151;
2-year terms
Number of counties: 16

Federal Government

U.S. senators: 2
U.S. representatives: 2
Number of electoral votes: 4

For the name of the current governor, see STATE GOVERNMENTS in Volume S. For the names of current U.S. senators and representatives, see UNITED STATES, CONGRESS OF THE in Volume UV.

Press Herald. The periodicals *Downeast* and *The Maine Antiques Digest* have readerships that extend outside the state. Maine has some 58 radio stations and 10 television stations.

CITIES

Small cities are the rule in Maine. Only Portland has more than 60,000 people.

Augusta, the capital, is on the Kennebec River about 45 miles (70 kilometers) from the Atlantic Ocean. In 1628, Pilgrims of the Plymouth Colony had a prosperous fur-trading post on this site. Fort Western was built there first, in 1754, to protect settlers.

Augusta was incorporated as a town in 1797. It replaced Portland as the capital of Maine in 1832. The main activities of the city are related to the work of the state government. Industries include the manufacture of electronic components, fabricated structural steel, glass containers, and precision tools.

INDEX TO MAINE MAP

Portland, Maine's largest city, was built on the site of Falmouth, a settlement dating from the 1630's. Renamed Portland in 1786, it was the state capital from 1820 to 1832.

Portland is called the Forest City because of its thousands of shade trees. It is the chief

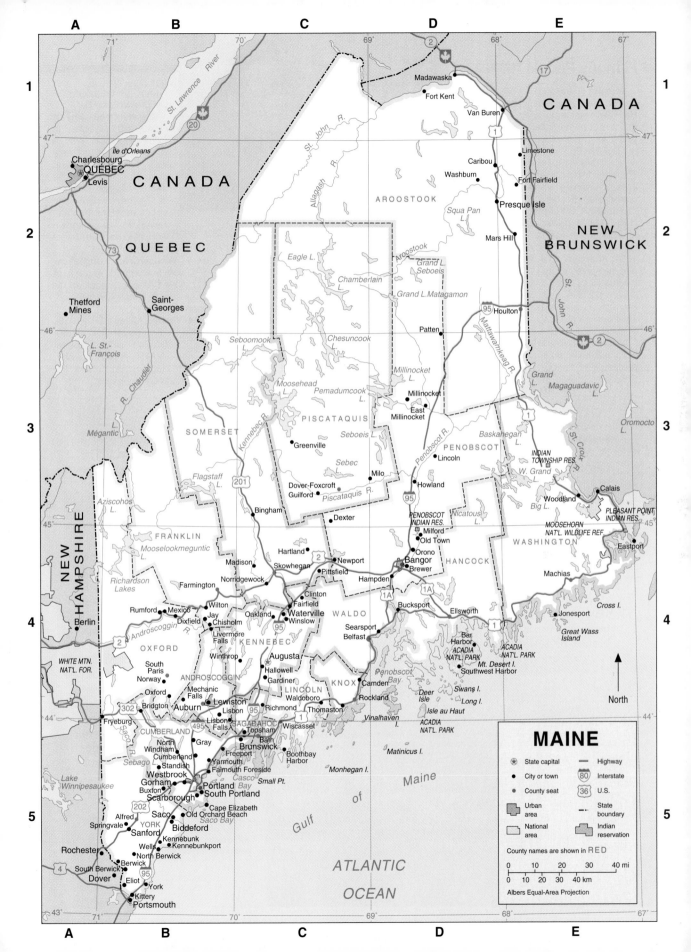

MAINE

State capital	Highway
City or town	Interstate
County seat	U.S.
Urban area	State boundary
National area	Indian reservation

County names are shown in RED

0   10   20   30   40 mi
0 10 20 30 40 km
Albers Equal-Area Projection

North

CANADA

QUEBEC

NEW BRUNSWICK

NEW HAMPSHIRE

ATLANTIC OCEAN

Gulf of Maine

St. Lawrence River

Charlesbourg
QUÉBEC
Levis
Île d'Orleans

Thetford Mines
Saint-Georges

L. St.-François

Mégantic

Aziscohos L.

Berlin

WHITE MTN. NAT'L. FOR.

Madawaska
Fort Kent
Van Buren

Limestone
Caribou
Washburn
Fort Fairfield
Presque Isle
Mars Hill

AROOSTOOK

Squa Pan L.
Aroostook

Eagle L.
Chamberlain L.
Grand L. Seboeis
Grand L. Matagamon

Houlton
Patten

Seboomook L.
Chesuncook
Millinocket L.
Pemadumcook L.
Moosehead L.

Mattawamkeag R.
Grand Magaguadavic L.
Oromocto

Millinocket
East Millinocket

PISCATAQUIS

Greenville
Seboeis L.
Sebec
Milo
Dover-Foxcroft
Guilford
Piscataquis R.

Lincoln
Howland

PENOBSCOT
Penobscot R.
Baskahegan L.
Nicatous L.

INDIAN TOWNSHIP RES.
W. Grand L.
Big L.
Woodland
Calais
PLEASANT POINT INDIAN RES.
Eastport
MOOSEHORN NAT'L. WILDLIFE REF.

St. Croix R.

SOMERSET

Kennebec R.

Flagstaff L.

Bingham
Dexter

PENOBSCOT INDIAN RES.
Milford
Old Town
Orono
Bangor
Brewer
Hampden

WASHINGTON

Machias
Cross I.
Jonesport
Great Wass Island

FRANKLIN

Mooselookmeguntic L.
Richardson Lakes

Madison
Hartland
Skowhagen
Newport
Pittsfield
Norridgewock
Clinton
Fairfield
Waterville
Winslow
Oakland

HANCOCK

Bucksport
Ellsworth
Bar Harbor
ACADIA NAT'L. PARK
ACADIA NAT'L. PARK
Mt. Desert I.
Southwest Harbor
Swans I.
Long I.

Farmington
Rumford
Mexico
Dixfield
Jay
Chisholm
Wilton
Livermore Falls

OXFORD

Androscoggin R.

KENNEBEC

WALDO

Searsport
Belfast
Camden
Rockland
Thomaston

Penobscot Bay
Deer Isle
Isle au Haut
Vinalhaven I.
ACADIA NAT'L. PARK

South Paris
Norway
Oxford
Bridgton

ANDROSCOGGIN

Winthrop
Augusta
Hallowell
Gardiner

KNOX
LINCOLN

Waldoboro

Mechanic Falls
Auburn
Lewiston
Lisbon
Lisbon Falls
Richmond

SAGADAHOC

Wiscasset
Boothbay Harbor

Matinicus I.
Monhegan I.

Fryeburg
Saco R.

CUMBERLAND

North Windham
Cumberland
Standish
Gray
Yarmouth
Falmouth Foreside
Topsham
Freeport
Brunswick
Bath
Small Pt.
Casco Bay

Lake Winnipesaukee
Sebago L.

Westbrook
Gorham
Buxton
Scarborough
Portland
South Portland
Cape Elizabeth
Old Orchard Beach
Saco
Biddeford

YORK

Rochester
Springvale
Sanford
Alfred
Kennebunk
Kennebunkport
Wells
North Berwick

Dover
South Berwick
Berwick
Eliot
York
Kittery
Portsmouth

Famous People

Martha Ballard (1735–1812), born in Massachusetts, settled in Hallowell, Maine, in 1777, where she was a homemaker, midwife, and healer. Her story, related in the Pulitzer Prize-winning *A Midwife's Tale* (1991) by Laurel Thatcher Ulrich, illuminates the lives of ordinary women on the northeastern frontier.

James Gillespie Blaine (1830–93), a newspaper editor and political leader, was born in Pennsylvania and moved to Augusta in 1854. After serving in the Maine legislature, he served in the U.S. House of Representatives (1873–76) and in the Senate (1876–81). He was an unsuccessful Republican candidate for president in 1884 and served twice as U.S. secretary of state (1881; 1889–92).

Joshua Chamberlain (1828–1914), born in Brewer, was a Civil War hero. A professor of rhetoric and languages at Bowdoin College, he joined the Union

Joshua Chamberlain

Sarah Orne Jewett

Army in 1862. He served with distinction in 24 engagements, earning the Congressional Medal of Honor for his leadership at the Battle of Gettysburg and rising to the rank of brigadier general. After the war, Chamberlain served as governor of Maine (1866–70) and president of Bowdoin College (1871–83).

Dorothea Lynde Dix (1802–87), born in Hampden, was a social reformer who helped improve conditions for the mentally ill. She also was an educator and author. A biography of Dix is in Volume D.

Sarah Orne Jewett (1849–1909), born in South Berwick, was a writer whose usual theme was the New England character. Her stories and novels are often set in Maine, where she spent most of her life. Jewett's best-known work is *The Country of the Pointed Firs* (1896).

Henry Wadsworth Longfellow (1807–82), born in Portland, was one of the most beloved American poets of his day. A biography of Longfellow is included in Volume L.

Edna St. Vincent Millay (1892–1950), born in Rockland, began her career with the publication of her poem "Renascence" in 1912. A prolific writer, she won the Pulitzer Prize in 1923 for *The Harp Weaver and Other Poems*.

---

seaport and an industrial and cultural center. A few of its products are processed foods, dairy and meat products, machinery components, cement and concrete, and insulation.

Lewiston, the second largest city in Maine, is located on the Androscoggin River. Its twin town, Auburn, stands on the opposite bank of the river. Both cities have extensive shoe manufacturing operations.

▶ GOVERNMENT

Maine entered the Union in 1820. The state constitution adopted at that time has been in force ever since. The executive branch of government is headed by a governor. The legislative branch is made up of a senate and a house of representatives. The legislature holds yearly sessions. The Supreme Judicial Court is the highest court in the state. Maine also has a superior court and regional courts.

▶ HISTORY

Native peoples inhabited what is now Maine some 11,000 years ago. They hunted game and fished the lakes and coastal waters. One early group is known as the Red Paint people because ocher—an earthy red or yellow mineral often used as a pigment—has been found at their gravesites.

The last major Native American group, the Woodland Indians, appeared about 2700 B.C. and were living in the region when the first Europeans arrived. Makers of pottery, they probably also developed the birch-bark canoe and the bow and arrow.

Portland is Maine's largest city and a center of business and industry. Situated on Casco Bay, it has an excellent deepwater harbor.

Edmund Sixtus Muskie (1914–96), born in Rumford, helped revive Maine's Democratic Party in the 1950's and became a national political figure. He served as governor of Maine (1955–59) and as a U.S. senator (1959–80). He became an authority on pollution and helped pass a national clean water act. In 1972, Muskie ran unsuccessfully for the Democratic presidential nomination. He later served as U.S. secretary of state under President Jimmy Carter.

Sir William Pepperell (1696–1759), born in Kittery, was a wealthy colonial merchant and shipbuilder. In 1745 he led New England's militia in capturing the French fortress on Cape Breton Island, Nova Scotia. Later he was invited to England, where he was made a baronet. He was the first American to receive this honor.

Edmund Sixtus Muskie

Margaret Chase Smith

John Poor (1808–71), born in Andover, was a lawyer and railroad executive. In 1845 he persuaded Canadian entrepreneurs to build a rail line from Montreal to Portland rather than to Boston. The line was completed in 1853, enabling Portland to serve as central Canada's winter port. Poor also consolidated numerous Maine railroads into the Maine Central Railroad and shepherded the creation of a line from Portland to Halifax, Nova Scotia.

Edwin Arlington Robinson (1869–1935), born in Head Tide, was a Pulitzer Prize-winning poet. Educated at Harvard, he began publishing poems in 1896 but first gained widespread notice for the collection *The Man Against the Sky* (1916). His poems were frequently set in small-town Maine.

Margaret Chase Smith (1897–1995), born in Skowhegan, was Maine's first congresswoman and the first woman to win election to both houses of Congress. She was first elected to the House of Representatives in 1940, succeeding her late husband. In 1948 she was elected to the Senate, where she served until 1973. Smith was one of the first senators to denounce Senator Joseph McCarthy's anticommunist activities. In 1964 she was an unsuccessful candidate for the Republican presidential nomination.

Exploration and Settlement

Giovanni da Verrazano, exploring for France, visited the Maine coast in 1524 while searching for a route to the Orient. In 1604, French explorer Samuel de Champlain established a colony on the St. Croix River and named Mount Desert Island. Three years later the English founded the Popham Colony at the mouth of the Kennebec River. Both colonies failed after only one winter, largely because of the severe cold. However, the explorers had discovered the rich fisheries along the Maine coast, and their reports drew English fishermen to the area.

During the 1600's permanent settlements were established—at Pemaquid in about 1628, and later at Kittery, York, Wells, Saco, and Falmouth (now Portland).

Sir Ferdinando Gorges, who had helped finance the Popham colony, received a royal charter in 1639 to the territory called Maine, extending from the Piscataqua River to the Kennebec River. A few years after his death in 1647, some of the Maine settlements agreed to join the Massachusetts Bay Colony. In 1677, Massachusetts purchased the title to Maine from the Gorges heirs. In 1691, a new charter to Massachusetts included Acadia, the eastern third of the region, as well.

Between 1675 and 1763, Maine experienced a series of wars between the English colonists and the French and Native Americans. The conflicts did not end until France gave up its claim to Maine and other regions of North America. Without French support, the Native Americans dared not stand in the way of the settlers streaming into Maine.

By the late 1760's, Maine citizens were already angry with the British over laws such as the one claiming the colony's largest white pines for use as masts on British warships. These grievances escalated into conflict. On June 12, 1775, the settlers of Machias captured a British cutter, *Margaretta*, which had been sent to guard a local loyalist merchant, in what has been claimed to be the first naval action of the American Revolutionary War.

Statehood and Development

Once the war was over, a movement for statehood began to grow. But most people wanted Maine to remain a part of Massachusetts. Feelings changed after the War of 1812. During the war, the British occupied all of eastern Maine; despite requests for help, Massachusetts left Maine to its fate. This, plus a growing sense of regional identity, brought an easy vote for statehood in 1819.

Maine's entry into the Union was delayed because of the struggle in Congress to maintain the balance between free and slaveholding states. Finally, under the Missouri Compromise, Maine entered as a free state in 1820 and Missouri as a slave state in 1821.

The period between 1820 and the start of the Civil War in 1861 saw tremendous economic growth. Numerous new farms and better agricultural techniques meant greatly increased production of farm products. The lumbering, granite, lime, deep-sea fishing, and shipbuilding industries were all booming. At the same time, textile manufacturing and shoemaking were evolving from home or shop to factory industries.

Still, there were problems. The northern border between Maine and New Brunswick had never been settled. In the 1820's and 1830's, hostile encounters occurred over the rights to cut timber in the areas of the Aroostook, Allagash, and northern St. John rivers. In 1839, Maine and New Brunswick soldiers rushed to the region ready to do battle, but the two sides were calmed and a truce was arranged. The boundary was finally decided by the Webster-Ashburton Treaty in 1842.

Civil War to Modern Times

Maine, early on, supported the abolition of slavery and sent some 73,000 men to fight for the Union in the Civil War (1861–65). Many of its soldiers fought in the bloodiest engagements, and a number had decisive roles in the outcome of key battles.

After the war and into the 1900's, Maine's traditional industries experienced numerous changes. Deep-sea fishing declined in favor of inshore fishing, which focused on lobsters, clams, and sardines. Metal shipbuilding replaced the building of wooden ships.

Several new industries were established in the later 1800's. The pulp and paper industry came to the region, setting up great plants on major rivers. Hydroelectric power was also introduced. In the later 1800's, resort centers such as Old Orchard Beach, Bar Harbor, and Sebago Lake became famous. With the advent of car travel in the early 1900's, tourism increased.

During the same period, Maine's inhabitants fought over the prohibition of alcoholic beverages. In 1850 the state passed a bill called the Maine Law, which forbade the sale of liquor. Despite resistance, the law was maintained until the repeal of national prohibition in 1933.

Recent History

Through the early 1900's, Maine was still largely rural, with most people living on farms or in small villages. Many depended on secondary, often seasonal work—lumbering, ice cutting, or factory piecework, for example. During the Great Depression of the 1930's, only the textile and shoe industries remained fairly strong.

The economy revived during World War II. Massive shipbuilding efforts in Bath and Portland and other war-related industrial production had the state's economy booming. Eighty thousand Maine men and women served in the military. Much of the home production was carried on by women, who had long worked in mills and factories but now took over traditionally male jobs. When the war ended, Maine's economy again declined.

The 1950's through the 1970's brought substantial change. Maine's education system was dramatically upgraded, and a strong effort was made to create new jobs and bring in new industries. Tough environmental laws were passed to control water and air pollution, protect wetlands, and regulate waste disposal. Some of the results were dramatic: Many streams and rivers, once polluted, are now clean enough for recreation and fishing.

The economy has not shown the same success. The new environmental regulations caused a number of industries to close down or move elsewhere. It was hoped that new, clean industries would come to Maine, and a few have. But the economy remains highly dependent on the pulp and paper industry, tourism, and shipbuilding and ship repair.

In 1980, the federal government awarded Maine's Penobscot and Passamaquoddy Indians $81.5 million in payment for lands that were taken from them in the late 1800's and early 1900's. Later, monetary agreements were also made with members of the Maliceet and Micmac tribes living in Maine.

Today, Maine's leaders are moving to reinvigorate Maine's economy while preserving the unique quality of life that has drawn so many people Down East.

EDWIN A. CHURCHILL
Maine State Museum

MAJOR, JOHN (1943–   )

John Major served as prime minister of Great Britain from November 1990 to May 1997. Born on March 29, 1943, Major grew up in a working-class neighborhood in Brixton. He left school at 16 and went to work, first as a concrete-mixer, then as an insurance company clerk. He later established himself with the Standard Charter Bank and became an aide to the bank chairman. In 1970 he married Norma Johnson, with whom he had two children.

Major first ran for Parliament as a Conservative in 1974 but did not win the election. He finally won a seat in 1979, representing Huntingdonshire (now Huntingdon).

Soon after Major entered the House of Commons, he won the respect of Prime Minister Thatcher, a Conservative who had come to power in 1979. Thatcher promoted him rapidly, and he eventually made his reputation in the financial field. He served as chief executive to the treasury (1987–89), and after a brief period as foreign secretary (1989), he became chancellor of the exchequer, the nation's chief finance minister (1989–90).

In 1990, Major succeeded Thatcher as the leader of the Conservative Party. He became prime minister when the Conservatives swept the general elections in 1992.

Major was handicapped from the start by Great Britain's long-standing economic and unemployment problems. He also faced opposition within his own party for his support of the European Union (EU). Among his achievements was the coordination of peace talks between Catholics and Protestants in Northern Ireland.

In the 1997 elections, the Conservatives were defeated in a general election for the first time since 1974. Major resigned as party leader and was succeeded as prime minister by Tony Blair, the leader of the Labour Party.

JEREMY BLACK
University of Exeter

MALAGASY REPUBLIC.   See MADAGASCAR.

MALARIA

Malaria is an ancient disease that is carried from person to person by the female mosquito. The mosquito transmits disease during a bite if it injects a parasite into a person's blood. The parasite that most often causes the disease in people is called *Plasmodium falciparum*.

Only mosquitoes infected with the parasite spread disease. In some places, however, infected mosquitoes are common. In these places, a child has a chance of being bitten by an infected mosquito once a day.

After the parasite enters the blood, it passes through several stages of its life cycle, including stages that affect the liver and the red blood cells. At these stages, a person feels sick, with fevers and flu-like symptoms. Symptoms tend to be more severe in young children, pregnant mothers, and travelers who have been infected for the first time. If treatment of malaria is delayed, life-threatening complications can occur. They include brain involvement (coma and seizures), kidney failure, and severe anemia. About 1 million people, mostly children, die each year from malaria.

Uneven Success. Over the past 50 years, malaria was eliminated in the United States and many other areas. Insecticides were used to kill mosquitoes, and effective drugs were available to treat people.

However, malaria still exists in some areas. It is especially bad in sub-Saharan Africa. Mosquitoes have developed resistance to pesticides, and the parasite has developed resistance to the cheapest drugs.

The first anti-malarial drug was quinine, a natural extract of the so-called fever tree. It became ineffective because of resis-

Sleeping under a bednet helps protect against malaria-infected mosquitoes. Some bednets are treated with insecticides.

tance. Its most effective replacement, the synthetic chloroquine, has also lost effectiveness. Resistance to chloroquine exceeds 50 percent in many countries.

Epidemics and deaths have surged. Each year, there are 300 million to 500 million cases of malaria. Most at risk are the very poor, who cannot buy effective drugs, even if they cost only a few dollars.

Poverty worsens malaria, and malaria worsens poverty. Treatment is costly, and productivity is lost whenever people suffer the effects of malaria, which include premature death.

Prevention and Treatment. The use of existing tools to prevent and treat malaria can cut the disease's impact by half. One way to prevent malaria is to target the mosquito: get rid of breeding sites, use insecticide-treated bednets, and spray insecticides on walls. The use of DDT, a controversial pesticide, has been reconsidered. Agricultural use harms the environment, but household use seems safer.

The same drugs that are used to treat the sick can also be used to prevent illness. However, using drugs for prevention over an entire continent is impractical. Instead, the drugs go to high-risk groups, such as pregnant women and travelers.

Newer, more effective drugs already exist, but they need to be used more widely. One new drug, artemisinin, is derived from a Chinese herb. Resistance to the drug has not been detected. However, artemisinin tends to be expensive.

Many organizations are trying to find ways to help pay for artemisinin and other new drugs. These organizations include private institutions, government agencies, and international organizations.

Additional Tools. Future efforts will depend on new tools, such as new drugs and vaccines. Finding new tools is costly, but development projects are already attracting support, including aid from partnerships between public and private institutions.

In 2004, one such partnership helped test a vaccine that prevented the onset of signs and symptoms of malaria in 30 percent of children. Researchers hope to create a vaccine that will prevent more than 50 percent of severe disease.

N. REGINA RABINOVICH, M.D.
Bill & Melinda Gates Foundation

MALAWI

Malawi is a nation in southeast Africa. Its name, which means "broad water," is taken from the huge lake along its eastern border.

▶ PEOPLE

Most Malawians are of Bantu origin. The chief groups are the Chewa, Nyanja, Tumbuka, Yao, and Lomwe. Chichewa is the official language. Nearly 80 percent of the people are Christians, mainly Protestants.

Primary school education in Malawi is free, and nearly all children go to school, although it is not compulsory. Malawi's largest university is the University of Malawi in Zomba.

▶ LAND

About one-fifth of Malawi's area is made up of lakes. The largest, Lake Malawi (also known as Lake Nyasa), is one of Africa's largest lakes. It lies within the Great Rift Valley, which runs through the country from north to south. On either side of the lake are towering plateaus. To the south lies the Shire River valley and the Shire Highlands. Mount Mulanje, Malawi's highest point, rises 9,848 feet (3,002 meters) in the Mulanje Mountains in the southeast.

Because Malawi is mountainous, it does not have an extremely warm climate. Generally, temperatures average from 65 to 85°F (18 to 30°C). Rainfall is heaviest in the mountains, where as much as 100 inches (2,500 millimeters) may fall in a year.

Malawi's chief natural resource is limestone, used as building stone. There are also known deposits of uranium, coal, and bauxite (to make aluminum).

▶ ECONOMY

Malawi's farms produce enough food for the people's own use, with some left over for export. The primary food crops are maize (corn), potatoes, cassava (a starchy root), sorghum, millet, and groundnuts (peanuts). Tobacco, sugarcane, cotton, and tea are the country's leading exports. Tea is grown in the Shire Highlands and the Mulanje Mountains. Tobacco and coffee are grown in the northern highlands. Cotton is grown in the lowlands. Most of Malawi's industry involves the processing of agricultural products for export.

Malawi's wildlife, scenic beauty, and pleasant climate have made tourism increasingly important to the economy.

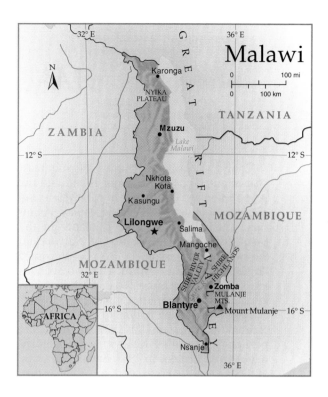

▶ MAJOR CITIES

Lilongwe, the capital of Malawi since 1975, has a population of about 600,000. Ministerial and financial government offices are located there. **Blantyre**, with about 650,000 people, is Malawi's largest city as well as its commercial and manufacturing center. This city is home to the government's executive and judicial offices. **Zomba**, Malawi's former capital, remains the home of the legislature.

▶ HISTORY AND GOVERNMENT

Malawi was settled by Bantu peoples. The Portuguese were the first Europeans to enter

---

FACTS and figures

REPUBLIC OF MALAWI is the official name of the country.

LOCATION: Southeastern Africa.

AREA: 45,745 sq mi (118,480 km²).

POPULATION: 12,100,000 (estimate).

CAPITAL: Lilongwe.

LARGEST CITY: Blantyre.

MAJOR LANGUAGE: English, Chichewa (both official).

MAJOR RELIGIOUS GROUPS: Christian (mainly Protestant), Muslim, traditional African religions.

GOVERNMENT: Republic. **Head of state and government**—president. **Legislature**—National Assembly.

CHIEF PRODUCTS: Agricultural—tobacco, sugarcane, cotton, tea, maize (corn), potatoes, cassava, sorghum, millet, groundnuts (peanuts). **Manufactured**—tobacco products, processed foods and beverages, sawmill products, cement. **Mineral**—limestone.

MONETARY UNIT: Kwacha (1 kwacha = 100 tabala).

---

the area, in the 1600's. In 1859, a Scottish medical missionary named David Livingstone made the first exploration of the region, discovering Lake Malawi, which he called Lake Nyasa. The city of Blantyre is named after his birthplace in Scotland.

Nyasaland, as the region was then called, became a British protectorate in 1891 and became part of the British Federation of Rhodesia and Nyasaland in 1953. Nyasaland became self-governing in 1963 and won complete independence as Malawi in 1964.

Malawi is a republic under a president who serves as head of both state and government. The legislature is the National Assembly. After independence, Malawi's president, Hastings Kamuzu Banda, headed the country's only legal political party. In 1993, however, Malawians voted to introduce a multiparty democracy. The first elections under the new system, held in 1994, resulted in Banda's defeat and the election of Bakili Muluzi as president. Muluzi won a second term in 1999. He was succeeded by Bingu wa Mutharika in 2004.

HUGH C. BROOKS
Director, Center for African Studies
St. John's University (New York)

MALAYSIA

Malaysia is the only country of Southeast Asia situated on both a major island and the Asian mainland. In the west, Malaysia occupies the southern half of the Malay Peninsula, which it shares with Thailand. In the east, it includes the states of Sabah and Sarawak on the island of Borneo, the third largest island in the world. The two sections are separated by more than 400 miles (645 kilometers) of the South China Sea.

The independent nation of Malaysia was created in two steps. In 1957, its mainland portion (then called Malaya) won independence from Britain. In 1963, Sabah, Sarawak, and Singapore were added to Malaya, thus creating the nation of Malaysia. (Singapore later became an independent nation.)

▶ **PEOPLE**

Most of Malaysia's 24 million people live on the Malay Peninsula, chiefly in towns or cities on or near the western coast. Native Malays make up the largest single ethnic group (58 percent), followed by Chinese (24 percent) and Indians (8 percent). There are also a small number of indigenous people, the Orang Asli. Sabah and Sarawak on Borneo are inhabited mainly by Dayaks and peoples of non-Malay origins.

Language. Malay (officially called Bahasa Melayu) is the national language. English is used in

The Petronas Towers in Kuala Lumpur (*below*), Malaysia's capital, are among the world's tallest buildings. Malaysians include tribespeople on Borneo (*right*), ethnic Chinese (*far right*), and native Malays (*below right*).

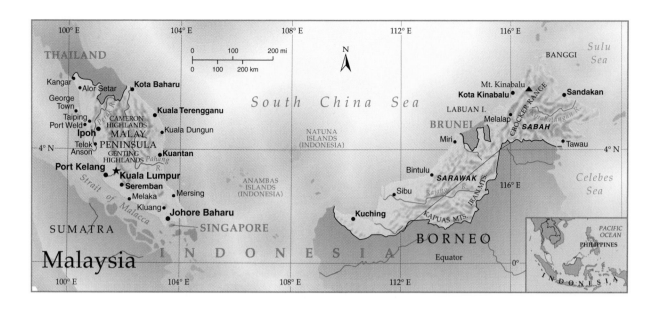

Malaysia

business and government. Chinese is also widely spoken.

Religion. The official religion of Malaysia is Islam (the Muslim religion), but the constitution guarantees freedom of worship to all. Many ethnic Chinese are Buddhists or Taoists. Most Indians are Hindus. Some of the tribal peoples of Sabah and Sarawak are Christians, while others follow the traditional native religions of their ancestors.

Education. Children receive nine years of free public education—six years of primary school and three years of lower secondary school. Students who pass a series of examinations may go to upper secondary school for two years. Institutions of higher learning include teacher-training colleges, technical colleges, and several universities. The largest university is the University of Malaya, in Kuala Lumpur.

Housing. In Malay villages, wooden houses with thatch-palm roofs are often raised above the ground on pilings to protect them from dampness. In towns and cities, many of these traditional houses have been

Many Malaysians have adopted a more modern lifestyle than their traditional clothing might suggest.

replaced by modern architecture. The Dayaks in Sarawak often live in villages made up of longhouses, which may contain an entire village of fifty families or more.

Dress. The traditional national costume of Malay women is a sarong tied around the waist, a *baju* (a loose blouse), and a *selendang* (a scarf draped over one shoulder). Malay men wear loose shirts, trousers, and a *songkok* (a black velvet cap with no brim). Indian women wear saris (long, loose robes). Chinese women wear the pajamalike *sam-foo* or a *cheongsam* (a straight dress with side slits). Most Indian, Chinese, and Malay men in towns and cities wear Western-style clothes.

Food and Drink. Curry and spices flavor Malay dishes of rice, fish, vegetables, and meat. Chinese and Indian people cook their own national dishes. People drink mostly mineral water, tea, and coffee. Islam forbids alcoholic beverages.

Holidays. The country's most important holidays are the Hari Raya Puasa (an Islamic holiday, celebrating the end of the fasting month of Ramadan), Divali (a

The lush green valleys of the Cameron Highlands on the Malay Peninsula provide fertile farmland for a variety of subsistence and commercial crops.

Hindu festival of lights), Christmas (a Christian holiday, celebrating the birth of Christ), the Chinese New Year, and Freedom Day (August 31).

▶ LAND

Land Regions. Malaysia is divided into two distinct regions: West (or Peninsular) Malaysia and East Malaysia (Sabah and Sarawak on the island of Borneo).

A mountain chain—made up of the Cameron Highlands and Genting Highlands—runs down the middle of the Malay Peninsula, rising in places to more than 7,000 feet (2,100 meters). Low plains extend down to both the eastern and western seacoasts. Except for the Pahang River valley, the land east of the mountains is underdeveloped and covered by dense forests. The eastern coast has only two good harbors, Kota Baharu and Kuantan. The western coast has good harbors at George Town, Port Kelang (formerly Port Swettenham), Telok Anson, and Port Weld.

About three-quarters of East Malaysia consists of sparsely populated jungle. The coastline of both Sabah and Sarawak is made up of alluvial and swampy land. Farther inland in Sarawak, the rolling country is intersected by mountain ranges. To the south, the Kapuas Mountains and Iran Mountains separate Malaysian Borneo from Indonesian Borneo. To the north in Sabah, low hills along the coast rise into a central mountain range that contains Mount Kinabalu, which at 13,455 feet (4,101 meters) is the nation's highest peak.

Rivers and Coastal Waters. The Pahang River, the longest on the Malay Peninsula, flows south and east before emptying into the South China Sea. In the west, the Perak River rises on the border with Thailand and flows south into the Strait of Malacca, a narrow waterway separating West Malaysia from the Indonesian island of Sumatra. There are many rivers in Sabah, the longest being the Kinabatangan, which waters Sabah's largest plain. In Sarawak, the Rajang River has the longest navigable stretch.

FACTS and figures

MALAYSIA is the official name of the country.
LOCATION: Southeast Asia.
AREA: 127,317 sq mi (329,750 km²).
POPULATION: 24,000,000 (estimate).
CAPITAL AND LARGEST CITY: Kuala Lumpur.
MAJOR LANGUAGES: Bahasa Melayu (official), English, Chinese, Tamil, others.
MAJOR RELIGIOUS GROUPS: Muslim (official), Buddhist, Daoist, Hindu, Christian.
GOVERNMENT: Constitutional monarchy. **Head of state**—*yang di-pertuan agong* (paramount ruler). **Head of government**—prime minister. **Legislature**—*Dewan Negara* (Senate) and *Dewan Rakyat* (House of Representatives).
CHIEF PRODUCTS: Agricultural—rice, rubber, palm tree kernels, cacao, coconuts, poultry, pigs. **Manufactured**—processed rubber, processed palm oil, electronics, smelted tin, timber and wood products, refined petroleum, processed foods. **Mineral**—tin, petroleum, natural gas, iron ore, bauxite (aluminum ore), gold.
MONETARY UNIT: Ringgit (1 ringgit = 100 sen).

Climate. Malaysia has two main seasons during which most precipitation occurs—the Northeast Monsoon (November to March) and the Southwest Monsoon (May to September). Annual rainfall averages from 80 to 100 inches (2,000 to 2,500 millimeters). During the Southwest Monsoon, lines of thunderstorms called sumatras form along the Strait of Malacca.

Natural Resources. The Malay Peninsula has a vast supply of rubber and palm oil and a large amount of timber. Tin, iron ore, bauxite, and gold are also found. Sarawak has considerable deposits of bauxite (aluminum ore).

Malaysia's forests abound in palm, teak, camphor, sandalwood, and ebony trees. However, in Sarawak these forests are being cut down. Elephants, rhinoceroses, crocodiles, lizards, wild pigs, and tigers once roamed through the country's forests, hills, and swamplands but are now scarce. There is a great variety of butterflies, other insects, birds, and reptiles.

▶ **ECONOMY**

Malaysia's wealth of natural resources and high-technology industries have greatly helped in the development of its economy.

Services. From banking and real estate to government and local commerce, services account for nearly 47 percent of Malaysia's economy. Service industries also employ about half the entire workforce. Industries related to tourism account for part of this total. Favored destinations include the less developed regions of mainland Malaysia, where natural jungle and habitat abound, and Sarawak on Borneo, where the more adventuresome travel up the River Skrang to visit tribespeople still living in longhouses.

Manufacturing. Malaysia's manufacturing sector accounts for about 45 percent of the economy. Chief products include electronics and electrical goods, textiles, clothing and footwear, petroleum, wood and metal products, and processed rubber. Traditional Malaysian handicrafts, such as basketware, jewelry, silverware, and batik cloth, are also important, particularly in Sarawak.

Agriculture. Farming and fishing account for about 8 percent of the country's wealth. Most Malaysian farmers practice subsistence agriculture, growing food mainly for their own use. Rice is the chief food crop. Poultry and pigs are also raised. The major commercial crops are rubber, palm tree kernels, cacao, and coconuts.

Mining. Tin mining has been important in Malaysia since colonial times. A famous by-product of Malaysia's tin is Selangor pewter, which is exported around the world. Significant petroleum and natural gas reserves are mined in the South China Sea off the coast of Sabah.

Trade. International trade is one of Malaysia's fastest-growing economic sectors. Chief exports include electronic equipment, petroleum and liquefied natural gas, wood and wood products, palm oil, rubber, textiles, footwear, and chemicals.

Transportation. The peninsula has a very good interstate highway system, and passenger rail service operates along the Malay Peninsula, between Singapore and Bangkok, Thailand. In Sabah, a railway joins Kota Kinabalu with the inland town of Melalap. The country has several international airports, notably Kuala Lumpur International Airport.

Communication. Malaysians have access to a well-developed and sophisticated communications network. State-operated radio and

Oil rigs mine petroleum from the South China Sea for export. International trade is one of the fastest-growing sectors of Malaysia's economy.

television stations broadcast throughout West Malaysia and some parts of East Malaysia. Internet use is growing rapidly. Bernama, the national news agency, transmits Malaysian government information around the world. Leading newspapers include the *New Straits Times* and the *Star*.

MAJOR CITIES

Malaysia's urban centers have grown rapidly, as many people have moved from the countryside to the cities and towns.

Kuala Lumpur, with a population of more than 1 million, is Malaysia's capital and largest city. Founded in 1857 as a tin-mining camp on the Kelang River, it developed rapidly during the period of British rule. The city is noted for its Moorish Islamic architecture as well as the modern Petronas Towers, which at 1,483 feet (452 meters) are among the world's tallest skyscrapers. **Putrajaya**, a new city, was built nearby to serve as the government's administrative capital.

Other major cities on the peninsula are **Ipoh**, **George Town**, and **Johore Baharu**. On Borneo, **Kota Kinabalu** serves as the capital and major port of Sabah, while **Kuching** is the chief city and capital of Sarawak.

CULTURAL HERITAGE

In Malaysia, art is found mostly in the form of handicrafts, especially batik textiles. Native to Malaysia and Indonesia, batik cloth designs are produced by coating the cloth with wax, cutting designs out of the wax, and then dyeing the unwaxed areas.

Malaysia has many museums. Among the most notable are the National Museum in Kuala Lumpur and the Sarawak State Museum in Kuching, which is noted for its collection of traditional Malay and Chinese furniture.

Wayang (shadow plays), the traditional theater of Malaysia, are performed with puppets casting shadows on a screen. The plays are presented on platforms or in huts lighted by lanterns, colored lights, or torches. The *wayang* tell traditional stories of the struggle between good and evil. Malay operas and the traditional Malay dramas called *menora* are

Malaysia's economy grew rapidly throughout much of the prime ministership of Mahathir bin Mohamad (1981–2003).

also popular. Indian plays and dances and Chinese musical plays, puppet shows, and classical dramas are also performed.

GOVERNMENT

Malaysia is a constitutional monarchy with a parliamentary form of government. The head of state is the *yang di-pertuan agong* (paramount ruler). He is elected by (and from among) the rajas (rulers) of the nine original Malay states to serve a 5-year term. Actual executive power is exercised by the prime minister, who is appointed by the paramount ruler. The legislature is made up of two houses, the *Dewan Negara* (Senate) and the *Dewan Rakyat* (House of Representatives). The prime minister must be a member of the House of Representatives and must have the support of that body to remain in power. The prime minister is assisted by a cabinet of ministers. Since independence, the United National Malay Organization (UNMO) has been the dominant political power. The prime minister is always a Malay and is the head of the UMNO Party.

Malaysia consists of 13 states and three federal territories.

HISTORY

The modern history of Malaysia began about 1400, when a Malay ruler founded a settlement at Malacca (present-day Melaka). Arab missionaries and traders brought the Muslim religion to Malacca, and from there it spread to the rest of the Malay Peninsula (as well as to the islands of Indonesia). As a center of trade, Malacca soon became the most powerful area in Southeast Asia.

In 1511 the Portuguese captured Malacca. In 1641 the Dutch took the city from the Portuguese. The British obtained a foothold on the Malay Peninsula in 1786 by taking control of the island of Penang, and in 1824 the Dutch ceded Malacca to Britain.

Meanwhile, Sir Thomas Stamford Raffles of the British East India Company had founded a British settlement at Singapore in 1819. And in 1841 an Englishman, Sir James Brooke, was installed as rajah of part of Sarawak. Both Sarawak and British North

Borneo came under Britain's protection in 1888.

British Rule. At this time, the Malay Peninsula was politically divided into nine states, which eventually came under British protection. By the time World War II (1939–45) began, the British controlled all of Malaya. During the war, the Japanese occupied Malaya, but the British recaptured the peninsula in 1945. Three years later, Britain brought the nine Malay states together by establishing the Federation of Malaya.

In 1957 the Federation of Malaya achieved independence. At the same time, Britain also gave up Penang and Malacca, which then joined with Malaya.

Creation of Malaysia. In 1959, the British crown colony of Singapore gained self-government within the Commonwealth of Nations. Then in 1961, the Malayan prime minister, Tunku Abdul Rahman, conceived the idea of forming a Malaysian federation by joining the Malayan states with Singapore and the territories of British Borneo (Brunei, Sabah, and Sarawak). Malaysia officially came into existence on September 16, 1963. Brunei chose not to join, and Singapore withdrew from the federation in 1965.

Under Mahathir bin Mohamad, who was first elected prime minister in 1981, Malaysia experienced nearly two decades of rapid economic growth. But in 1997, Malaysia experienced a serious economic downturn with much of the rest of Southeast Asia.

In 2002, the World Court awarded Malaysia title to two islands in the Celebes Sea—Ligitan and Sipadan—ending a long-standing dispute with Indonesia. The following year, Mahathir, Asia's longest-serving elected leader, retired. Abdullah Ahmad Badawi succeeded him as prime minister. Abdullah was elected in his own right in 2004.

THOMAS FRANK BARTON
Indiana University
Reviewed by PATRICK M. MAYERCHAK
Department of International Studies
Virginia Military Institute

See also BORNEO.

MALCOLM X (1925–1965)

Malcolm X was a leader of the Black Muslims, a group whose ideas concerning black nationalism influenced the Black Power movement of the late 1960's.

He was born Malcolm Little on May 19, 1925, in Omaha, Nebraska. While he was serving time in prison (1946–52) for burglary, he embraced the teachings of Elijah Muhammad, the leader of the Nation of Islam (Black Muslims). On his release, Malcolm joined the Nation and adopted the letter X as his surname in the belief that all African-American surnames were slave names.

For attracting many new members to the Nation, Malcolm was named assistant minister of Temple Number One in Detroit. He then established temples in Boston and Philadelphia and was chosen minister of Temple Number Seven in Harlem, in New York City.

The eloquent, charismatic, and outspoken Malcolm X brought great visibility to the Black Muslims. He was eager to spread the Nation's theories of black separatism and hatred of whites, but he angered the more conservative Muhammad by speaking out on political and social issues. After Malcolm declared that the 1963 assassination of President John F. Kennedy was the result of hatred in America, Muhammad suspended Malcolm's ministry.

During a Muslim pilgrimage to Mecca in 1964, Malcolm concluded that America's racial problem was not the fault of whites but of its political and economic systems. On his return, he formed the Organization of Afro-American Unity (OAAU) to work for human rights for African Americans. He was speaking at an OAAU meeting in Harlem when he was assassinated by three Muslims on February 21, 1965. *The Autobiography of Malcolm X* (as dictated to Alex Haley) was published soon after.

JIM HASKINS
Author, *One More River to Cross: The Stories of Twelve Black Americans*

MALDIVES

The Republic of Maldives is a small nation in the Indian Ocean, lying southwest of India and Sri Lanka. It consists of nearly 1,200 small islands, most of which are uninhabited.

People. The Maldivians are believed to be descendants of people from India, Sri Lanka, and from Arab lands. Their language, Dhivehi, is related to Sinhala, a language of Sri Lanka. English is also spoken. Most Maldivians are Sunni Muslims (followers of Islam). Educational standards are high, and the literacy rate is nearly 100 percent.

Land. The Maldives islands form an archipelago (a chain of islands) consisting of some 26 atolls. (The word "atoll," meaning a ring of coral encircling a lagoon, is Maldivian in origin.) Each atoll is made up of many small islets—about 1,190 in all. The only large town is Male, the capital, on Male atoll. The climate is generally hot and humid. Monsoons (seasonal winds) bring considerable rainfall.

Economy. Tourism and fishing are the leading industries. Agriculture is limited, and most food must be imported. The main crop is coconuts, which are used to make copra (dried coconut meat) and other products. The chief exports are fish products and clothing.

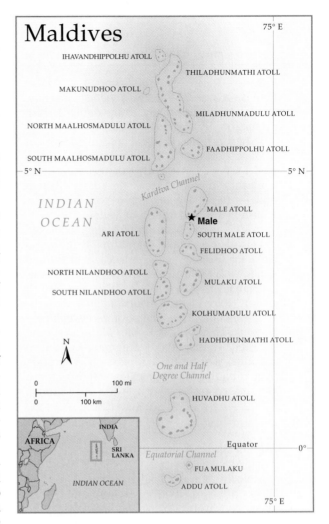

FACTS and figures

REPUBLIC OF MALDIVES (Dhivehi Raajjeyge Jumhooriyyaa) is the official name of the country.

LOCATION: Indian Ocean, South Asia.

AREA: 116 sq mi (300 km²).

POPULATION: 330,000 (estimate).

CAPITAL AND LARGEST CITY: Male.

MAJOR LANGUAGE: Dhivehi.

MAJOR RELIGIOUS GROUP: Sunni Muslim.

GOVERNMENT: Republic. **Head of state and government**—president. **Legislature**—Majlis (People's Council).

CHIEF PRODUCTS: Agricultural—Fish, coconuts. **Manufactured**—boats, clothing, handicrafts, fish products, coconut products (copra, coconut fiber, coconut palm mats). **Mineral**—sand.

MONETARY UNIT: Rufiyaa, or Maldivian rupee (1 rufiyaa = 100 laris).

History and Government. According to legend, the islands' first ruler was a Sinhalese prince whose ship became stranded in Maldivian waters. Arab traders introduced Islam to the islands in the 1100's. Maldives later fell under Portuguese and Dutch control, then became a British dependency in 1887. The islands won independence in 1965 and became a republic in 1968. In 1985, Maldives was a founding member of the South Asian Association of Regional Cooperation (SAARC).

The government is headed by a president, elected for a 5-year term. The legislature is the Majlis. Most of its members are elected by the people. Eight are appointed by the president, who also appoints a cabinet. The current president is Maumoon Abdul Gayoom, who first took office in 1978.

Reviewed by ALEXANDER MELAMID
New York University

MALI

Mali is a large but thinly populated nation in West Africa. It was once one of the richest and most powerful of the ancient West African empires. Today, however, Mali is one of the world's poorest countries.

▶ PEOPLE

Mali's people can be divided into several groups. Those who have traditionally lived in the north and raised livestock are the Tuaregs, Moors, and Fulani. The more fertile and heavily populated southern part of the country is the home of several African peoples, mostly farmers. The most numerous are the Bambara. Others include the Sénoufo, the Soninké, the Dogon, the Songhaï (who also live farther north), and the Malinké.

French is the official language, but African languages are spoken as well. The most common of these is Bambara. Most people are Muslim. Some Malians follow traditional African religions, and a few are Christians.

Malian children must attend school for nine years, but only about 60 percent do. However, the government has made significant efforts to enroll and retain students.

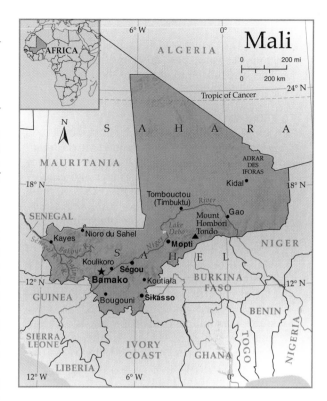

▶ LAND

Africa's vast Sahara desert covers the northern half of Mali. The semi-arid southern fringe of the Sahara, called the Sahel, runs through the center of the country, and grasslands cover the south. In the northeast are rugged hills and Mali's only mountain range, the Adrar des Iforas. Mali's highest point, Mount Hombori Tondo, is in the southeast. It has an elevation of 3,788 feet (1,155 meters).

The Niger River sweeps across the middle of southern Mali in a great arc. The Niger Valley is situated approximately in the center of the country between the cities of Ségou and Tombouctou (also known as Timbuktu). Mali's other chief rivers are the Bakoye, Bafing, and Senegal, which form part of its southwestern border with Senegal.

Mali's climate is tropical, although temperature and rainfall

Visitors to a market in Mopti travel by bullock and cart. Mali, in West Africa, is one of the world's poorest countries.

vary. The south—Mali's chief farming region—is warm and receives the most rain. The arid northern desert is hotter but gets very little rain.

▶ ECONOMY

Mali is one of the world's least developed countries and is heavily dependent on financial aid. Agriculture and fishing account for about half the country's earnings and employ about 80 percent of the workforce. The main food crops are millet, rice, corn, vegetables, and peanuts. Cotton is the most important export crop. Livestock is also exported.

Services account for almost 40 percent of Mali's economy and include tourism, transportation, utilities, and communications.

The country has many natural resources, including gold, phosphates, kaolin, salt, limestone, uranium, and hydropower. It also has undeveloped deposits of bauxite, iron ore, manganese, tin, and copper. Mining is a growing industry, and gold is a primary export. Other important industries are construction and food processing.

▶ MAJOR CITIES

Bamako, Mali's capital and largest city, has a population of approximately 1 million. Located in southwestern Mali, it is an important market city in West Africa. Other large towns include **Sikasso**, **Ségou**, and **Mopti**. **Tombouctou**, once an important trading city, is now a small town.

▶ HISTORY AND GOVERNMENT

Several ancient empires once thrived in what is now Mali, including the Mali Empire, which reached its height between 1200 and 1400. Its greatest emperor was Mansa Musa (ruled 1312–37), who founded Tombouctou and made it a center of learning and culture.

The French explored and conquered the region in the late 1800's. Then known as French Sudan (Soudan), Mali became a part of French West Africa. In 1959 it joined with Senegal to form the Mali Federation. The federation was dissolved in 1960, and the Republic of Mali was created.

Mali's first president, Modibo Keita, established a socialist government. Economic difficulties and discontent with Keita's rule brought about his overthrow in 1968 by army officers led by Colonel Moussa Traoré, who formed a military government.

A new constitution was approved in 1974. It provided for a single political party, called the Democratic Union of the Malian People (UDPM). Traoré was elected president in 1979 and re-elected in 1985. However, continuing economic problems and dissatisfaction with his dictatorial rule led to a rebellion in 1991, and Traoré was overthrown in a military coup led by Lieutenant Colonel Amadou Toumani Touré. Touré was president between 1991–92. In 1992, following the approval of a new multiparty constitution, Alpha Oumar Konaré of the Alliance for Democracy was elected president. He introduced economic and political reforms and ended a rebellion by Tuaregs and other groups in the north. He was re-elected in 1997.

In 2002, Touré again became president. This was considered significant as it was the first time since independence that there had been a peaceful transition in Mali from one democratically elected leader to another.

Mali's government is headed by a president, who is elected to a maximum of two 5-year terms. The president appoints a prime minister, who appoints other members of a Council of Ministers. Mali's legislature is the National Assembly, which has 147 seats. Its members are also elected to 5-year terms.

Reviewed by SUSANNA WING
Haverford College

FACTS and figures

REPUBLIC OF MALI (République du Mali) is the official name of the country.

LOCATION: West Africa.

AREA: 478,764 sq mi (1,240,000 km²).

POPULATION: 11,600,000 (estimate).

CAPITAL AND LARGEST CITY: Bamako.

MAJOR LANGUAGES: French (official), Bambara, other African languages.

MAJOR RELIGIOUS GROUP: Muslim.

GOVERNMENT: Republic. **Head of state**—president. **Head of government**—prime minister. **Legislature**—National Assembly.

CHIEF PRODUCTS: Agricultural—cotton, millet, rice, corn, vegetables, peanuts, cattle, sheep, goats. **Manufactured**—processed foods. **Mineral**—gold, phosphates, kaolin, salt, limestone, uranium, bauxite, iron ore, manganese, tin, copper.

MONETARY UNIT: African Financial Community (CFA) franc (1 CFA franc = 100 centimes).

MALTA

Malta

The nation of Malta is composed of several small, rocky islands in the Mediterranean Sea about 58 miles (93 kilometers) south of the Italian island of Sicily. The country owes its historical importance to its strategic location in the central Mediterranean and its natural deep-sea harbors.

▶ PEOPLE

The Maltese people today reflect their country's rich cultural heritage. Their earliest ancestors included the Phoenicians, an ancient seafaring people from the Middle East, and the Carthaginians, a related people who once ruled a great empire in North Africa and the Mediterranean.

Most Maltese are Roman Catholics. They trace their Christian faith to Saint Paul, who, according to the New Testament, was shipwrecked on Malta in A.D. 60.

Both Maltese and English are official languages. Maltese is a Semitic language, originating from Arabic. The Arabs occupied and settled Malta from 870 to 1091. But the language has also been influenced by Italian.

Education is required for all children between the ages of 5 and 16. Students seeking higher education generally attend the University of Malta in Msida, founded in 1592.

▶ LAND

Three main islands—Malta, Gozo, and Comino—and two tiny uninhabited islets make up the nation-state of Malta. Most of the land is covered with low, rolling hills. There are no rivers or mountains. The highest point, Ta'Dmejrek, is 830 feet (253 meters) and located near Dingli on the island of Malta. The climate is dry and hot in the summer and mild, with periods of rainfall, in the winter.

▶ ECONOMY

Tourism is Malta's most important economic activity. Many vacationers, mostly from northern Europe, are attracted to the country's beautiful beaches, the capital city of Valletta, and prehistoric temples dating from about 4000 B.C.

Factories produce electronic products, processed foods, textiles, footwear, clothing, and

The rocky island of Malta has many deep-sea harbors, and fishing villages like this one are a common site on its coastline.

tobacco products. Important sources of income include the ports of Valletta and Marsaxlokk, which house shipyards and yacht marinas and handle much of Malta's external trade.

Malta has few natural resources, except for limestone and salt. Farming is difficult because of the shortage of land and dry climate. Potatoes, cauliflower, and grapes are grown. Some potatoes and wine are exported, but Malta must import most of its food to meet its needs.

▶ MAJOR CITIES

Valletta is Malta's capital. Founded in 1566, it has a population of about 7,000. Located on the main island of Malta, Valletta is built on a high ridge between two excellent natural harbors. It is the administrative and cultural center of Malta.

Birkirkara, also located on Malta, is the nation's largest city, with a population of about 22,000. The city marks the line between the island's agricultural region in the north and its urban area in the south.

Sliema, with a population of about 12,500, is a major tourist area with many hotels, shops, and restaurants. A waterfront promenade connects this fashionable city to **San Giljan (St. Julian's)**, Malta's chief leisure and entertainment center. Both cities lie across the harbor from Valletta.

▶ HISTORY AND GOVERNMENT

One group after another has conquered this small nation. The Phoenicians, Carthaginians, Romans, Byzantines, and Arabs all held Malta in turn. In 1091 the islands were conquered by the Normans and became part of the Kingdom of Sicily. In 1530, Holy Roman Emperor Charles V gave Malta to the Knights Hospitalers of Saint John (also called the Knights of Malta). Under their rule Malta became a Christian fortress. After they defeated the Turks in 1565, their leader, Jean de la Valette, built the capital Valletta. The Knights built beautiful churches, monasteries, and palaces, many of which still stand. They also developed the islands' harbors and gave Malta a European identity.

Napoleon captured Malta from the Knights in 1798. But the Maltese rose against the French and besieged them, defeating them with the help of the British in 1800. Britain formally annexed Malta in 1814 and made it its chief base in the Mediterranean. During World War II (1939–45), bombings brought devastation and hardship. For its bravery, the whole population was awarded the George Cross.

Malta was granted internal self-rule in 1947, and it became an independent country within the British Commonwealth of Nations in 1964. In 1974, the islands became an independent republic, although Britain retained a military base there until 1979. Malta became a neutral state in 1987.

Malta's government is based on the 1974 constitution. The legislature is the unicameral (one-house) House of Representatives, which elects the president; there are usually 65 seats, and members serve 5-year terms. The president is the head of state, and the prime minister, appointed by the president, is the head of government; both serve 5-year terms.

In 2003, the Maltese voted to join the European Union (EU), and Malta became a member in May 2004. Earlier that year, Lawrence Gonzi was elected leader of the Nationalist Party and appointed prime minister. Former prime minister Edward Fenech-Adami was elected president of Malta.

Reviewed by DOMINIC FENECH
University of Malta

FACTS and figures

REPUBLIC OF MALTA (Repubblika ta' Malta) is the official name of the country.

LOCATION: Mediterranean Sea, south of the island of Sicily.

AREA: 122 sq mi (316 km²).

POPULATION: 400,000 (estimate).

CAPITAL: Valletta.

LARGEST CITY: Birkirkara.

MAJOR LANGUAGE: Maltese, English (both official).

MAJOR RELIGIOUS GROUP: Roman Catholic.

GOVERNMENT: Republic. **Head of state**—president. **Head of government**—prime minister. **Legislature**—House of Representatives.

CHIEF PRODUCTS: Agricultural—Potatoes, cauliflower, grapes, wheat, barley, tomatoes, citrus fruits, cut flowers, livestock products (meat, milk, eggs). **Manufactured**—electronic products, ships, processed foods, textiles, footwear, clothing, tobacco products. **Mineral**—limestone, salt.

MONETARY UNIT: Maltese lira (1 lira = 100 cents).

MAMMALS

The Earth teems with life. In the pitch-black night of a tropical rain forest, a bat hovers in front of a flower, lapping up nectar with its long tongue. Hundreds of feet under the surface of the ocean, a whale patrols the waters. A norway rat scampers through city alleys exploring the contents of trash cans, while high atop a South American plateau, a camel-like vicuna grazes. On the frozen Arctic Ocean, a huge polar bear waits patiently by a hole in the ice, ready to catch the first seal that comes up to breathe. A dog, its tail wagging, runs through the high grasses of a field, barking a friendly greeting to a smiling child.

A polar bear is much different from a child. A whale looks nothing like a bat, and each lives in a vastly different place. But they, and the other animals mentioned, have very much in common. They are all vertebrates (animals with backbones) belonging to the group of animals called mammals.

▶ THE CHARACTERISTICS OF MAMMALS

However small or large, mammals share a combination of characteristics that identify them as a group, although not every species of mammal has each characteristic. Some of the characteristics are found only in mammals, while some are shared with other animal groups.

The most important characteristic of mammals is the one that sets them apart from all other creatures: Mammals nourish their young with milk they produce. In fact, mammals get their name from the mammary glands, which are the chest glands of the female that are used to produce milk.

In addition to being the only animals that nurse their offspring, mammals also are the only animals that have hair. Some mammals have bodies covered with hair, and others have bodies that are partially covered with hair. Still others have hair on their bodies only at particular times in their lives.

Mammals, with their approximately 4,000 different species, are the dominant form of animal life on Earth. Their ability to adapt has allowed them to populate environments around the world, ranging from frozen tundra to tropical forests and from the depths of the oceans to the tops of mountains.

Mammals also have a set of internal characteristics that they share. Some, such as a muscular diaphragm that aids breathing, are unique to them.

A distinguishing feature of a mammal's skeleton is the way its mouthparts are formed. While other vertebrates have jaws made up of several bones, a mammal has

The adaptable creatures known as mammals appeared on Earth more than 190 million years ago. Over time they developed into the life-forms that dominate the Earth. Today there are 20 orders of living mammals. In the following pages, an animal from each of the orders is illustrated.

**Flying lemur
Order: Dermoptera**

only one bone on each side of its lower jaw. The long jaw bones of the mammal form a strong base for the several types of teeth that perform the tasks of chewing, tearing, and grinding food. This arrangement of teeth enables the mammal to feed very efficiently and get the maximum energy from the food it eats.

WONDER QUESTION

How big do mammals grow?

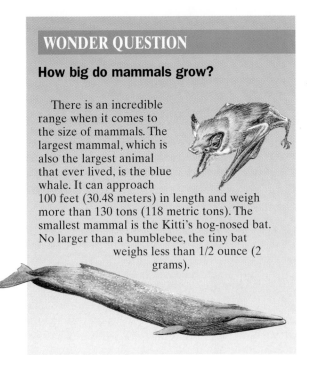

There is an incredible range when it comes to the size of mammals. The largest mammal, which is also the largest animal that ever lived, is the blue whale. It can approach 100 feet (30.48 meters) in length and weigh more than 130 tons (118 metric tons). The smallest mammal is the Kitti's hog-nosed bat. No larger than a bumblebee, the tiny bat weighs less than 1/2 ounce (2 grams).

**Brown Bear
Order: Carnivora**

Another skeletal characteristic of most mammals can be found in the bones of the vertebral column, or spine. The vertebral column provides a protective structure for the spinal cord. The spinal cord is the structure that carries messages from body parts to the brain and relays instructions from the brain to the rest of the body. Although the number of bones in the vertebral column varies with the species of mammal, all mammals—except manatees and sloths—have the same number of neck bones. Whether they are large or small, most mammals have seven neck bones.

Unlike most animals, mammals are **endothermic**, or warm-blooded. This means they are able to maintain a constant body temperature. Through internal regulation, mammals are able to produce heat or lose heat so that their internal temperature stays about the same even though their surroundings may become cooler or warmer. They are able to maintain this process as long as they have enough to eat and outside conditions do not become extreme.

Nourishment is carried through the circulatory system. Blood carries food and oxygen to cells, removes wastes from cells, such as carbon dioxide. The efficient blood circulation is made possible by the mammal's four-chambered heart that pumps blood separately to the lungs and to the rest of the body.

The large, well-developed brain of the mammal is another feature that sets it apart from other animals. The effect of this characteristic is seen in the mammal's ability to learn quickly and adapt its behavior to changes in its environment. Several mammals, most notably humans, chimpanzees, and dolphins, exhibit high levels of intelligence.

A mammal's ability to see, hear, smell, taste, and touch provide it with information about the outside world. Information gathered by the senses is processed in the brain. Some senses are better or less developed in certain mammals than in others. For example, a lion gets much of its information about its surroundings through its excellent vision. Moles, which live in dark underground tunnels, do not see very well. However, the snout and paws of a

and reproduce only at certain times of year. For example, whitetail deer mate in the autumn and polar bears mate in the spring. The age at which a mammal is ready to mate also varies. The female deer mouse is ready to mate when only a month old and in a year can have three or four litters, each with up to nine young. The female African elephant may not be ready to mate until she is more than 20 years of age. After that, she usually produces an offspring, called a calf, about every five years.

Only mammals produce milk to feed their offspring (*right*). They also are the only animals with hair, such as a fur coat or whiskers (*left*). Most mammals, whether their necks are long or short, have just seven neck bones (*above*).

mole are very sensitive to touch. This enables the mole to feel its way about and gather the information it needs to survive in its underground environment.

▶ THE LIFE CYCLE OF MAMMALS

There is great variation in the life cycles of mammals. But no matter how different their lives, all mammals go through similar stages in producing and caring for their offspring.

Mating

The process of producing offspring begins when male and female mammals come together to mate. The females of most mammal species, and the males of some as well, mate

During the mating season, chemical changes occur inside the bodies of mammals. Many female mammals, such as whitetail deer, signal that they are ready to mate by releasing scented chemicals that attract males. Sometimes changes take place on the outside of the body as well, such as the neck swelling that occurs in the male, or bull, elk.

Most species of mammals do not form permanent bonds with a mate. They mate with many different individuals, and after mating, the males and females separate. Plains baboons, sea lions, and tigers are among those

Mole
Order: Insectivora

Beaver
Order: Rodentia

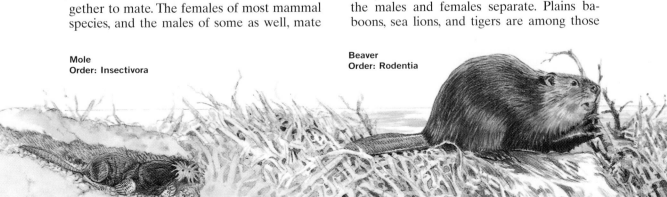

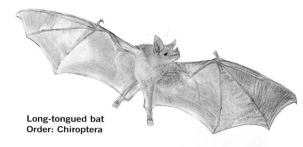

Long-tongued bat
Order: Chiroptera

after the young are born, the females begin to mate with the males. Males battle each other, each one fighting fiercely to gather his own group of females, called a harem, with which to mate. Male tigers patrol large territories and try to keep other males outside of them. More than one female tiger may live within a single male's territory, and he may mate with most or all of them.

A few species of mammals do seek just one mate. Following mating, they remain together to raise their young. Some, such as beavers, stay together for life, raising young that eventually set out on their own. Tiny South American monkeys called tamarins also stay together. The parents and young form a close family group, with the father tamarin and the older offspring helping the mother care for her young.

Rival male walruses (*above*), which may weigh as much as 3,000 pounds (1,360 kilograms), battle to protect their territory and their mates from other males. The platypus (*right*) has all the major features of a mammal, except for one—it lays eggs.

Reproduction

Male and female mammals reproduce by the process of sexual reproduction. In sexual reproduction, an egg (the female sex cell) is fertilized when it is united with sperm (the male sex cell). The egg is fertilized within the female's body. To accomplish this task, the male uses a special organ, called the penis, to release the sperm into the female.

The young develop within the female from the fertilized egg, or embryo. The differences in how an embryo develops have been used to group mammals into three distinct groups: monotremes, marsupials, and placentals.

Monotremes (Egg-Laying Mammals). Unlike most mammals, monotremes do not give birth to live young. Instead, they lay eggs from which the young hatch. The platypus and echidnas are the only egg-laying mammals. ·After a female platypus mates, she builds a nest of leaves in her burrow. She lays her eggs, usually two, in the nest and keeps them warm with her body. The young emerge from the eggs after about ten days. They feed on milk that trickles from pores on the mother's abdomen.

mammals that do not take one mate for life. Baboons live in groups called troops. At mating time, the female plains baboons may mate with several males in their troop. The dominant, or most powerful, male baboons get to mate with the most females. In the late spring and early summer, female California sea lions gather on beaches to have their young. Within a week or so

Impala
Order: Artiodactyla

Chimpanzee
Order: Primates

The female echidna, or spiny anteater, develops a pouchlike fold of skin on the underside of her body. She usually lays a single egg, which rolls into the fold. There, the egg stays warm until the young echidna hatches and begins to feed on milk from the mother's mammary glands, which open into the pouch.

Marsupials (Pouched Mammals). Marsupials, such as kangaroos, koalas, and wombats, give birth to offspring that are not fully formed. After birth, the young marsupials attach themselves to their mother's nipples, which are most often located in a pouch on the female's stomach. There the young continue to develop and grow as they feed on mother's milk.

Placental Mammals. Most mammals are placentals. The young of a placental mammal grows to full development inside a hollow organ, called a uterus, within the mother's abdomen. The placenta is the structure that unites the growing mammal with the mother's uterus. Oxygen and food pass from the mother through the placenta and into the developing mammal's bloodstream.

The time of growth before birth is called the gestation period, and the length of this period depends on the species. Gestation in mammals ranges from about 12 days (in opossums) to about 22 months (in elephants). Generally, mammals that have a long gestation period are born more well developed and more capable of normal activities, such as walking and running, than those with a short gestation period.

Care of the Young

In most species of mammals, it is the female who provides the care for offspring, starting with the nursing of the young. There are rare exceptions, such as the father tamarins, but most males depart after mating. The mother keeps a watch on her young,

While horses (*above*) and other placental mammals give birth to fully formed live young, opossums and other marsupials produce undeveloped offspring (*left*) that are naked, blind, and helpless at birth.

guarding them and protecting them from danger. If she belongs to a species whose young live in a nest or burrow, she keeps it clean. When her young are ready to begin eating foods other than her milk, she helps teach them the skills they need to find and eat the food.

Mammals, such as deer mice, that mate frequently and have many young at one time usually provide care for a short period of time only. Young deer mice stop feeding on milk in about two or three weeks. Shortly

African elephant
Order: Proboscidea

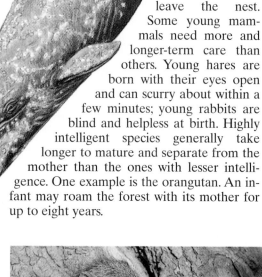

**Gray whale
Order: Cetacea**

afterward they leave the nest. Some young mammals need more and longer-term care than others. Young hares are born with their eyes open and can scurry about within a few minutes; young rabbits are blind and helpless at birth. Highly intelligent species generally take longer to mature and separate from the mother than the ones with lesser intelligence. One example is the orangutan. An infant may roam the forest with its mother for up to eight years.

A polar bear (*left*) spends most of its life roaming the icy Arctic landscape by itself. But most mammals, including these sociable baboons (*above*), form complex groups with multiple members.

▶ HOW MAMMALS LIVE

The way a mammal lives depends on its species, although closely related species may have similar lifestyles. Climate, habitat, diet, and many other factors shape a mammal's life.

Social Life

A male grizzly bear wanders the wilderness alone, unless he is with his mate. He has no family ties and may even kill his own cubs if he happens to find them unprotected by their mother. Solitary mammals such as these live apart from others of their kind. They seek out others only when it is time to mate.

Many mammals are social; that is, they live in groups and interact on a regular basis with members of their own species. Some groups change depending on the season, and others are restricted to members of a certain age or sex. Within many social groups, the members have a certain rank, or status. The dominant members of a group usually achieve their status by fighting and, ultimately, winning. Their position allows them privileges such as the first choice of mates or more food.

The impala, an African antelope, forms groups that are based on both age and sex. Each adult male tries to establish its own territory, or living space. Females, with their young, roam in herds through the territories of several adult males. Each of the males tries to keep the females within his territory so that when the time is right, he can mate with them.

The females always stay with their herd, which includes their male and female offspring. When the young males mature, they leave the females. They do not leave by choice. The male that rules the territory usually chases them away. However, they do not remain alone for long. The young males gather in what scientists call bachelor herds. They stay with the bachelor herd until they can stake out their own territories.

Each way of living has advantages and disadvantages. The lone mammal has an advantage because it only needs to provide food and lodging for itself. If the solitary mammal is hunting prey or avoiding an enemy, it is less likely to be seen than a group. On the other hand, when there is danger, the chances of survival are greater in a group. Members of a group can alert others to an impending attack as well as help bring down an enemy. Living in a group also can make it easier for members to find mates.

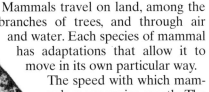

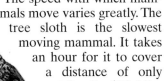

The bodies of mammals are adapted for movement. Most mammals use four legs to leap and bound over the land or move through the trees (*below*). Others use well-developed fins, tails, or limbs to swim through water (*left*). Only one, the bat, uses wings to fly.

Locomotion

Mammals travel on land, among the branches of trees, and through air and water. Each species of mammal has adaptations that allow it to move in its own particular way.

The speed with which mammals move varies greatly. The tree sloth is the slowest moving mammal. It takes an hour for it to cover a distance of only 1/2 mile (0.8 kilometer). The fastest speed a human being can reach is about 20 miles (32 kilometers) an hour, and that can be kept up for only a few minutes. The fastest mammal is the cheetah. It can approach speeds of close to 70 miles (113 kilometers) an hour.

Hooded seal
Order: Pinnipedia

On Land. All of the land dwellers have four limbs. Most use all four limbs to get around. Human beings are the only mammals that stand erect, walking and running on two feet only. Chimpanzees sometimes walk upright, but most often they move about on the ground using all four limbs.

When walking, people walk flat on the soles of their feet. So do other slow-moving mammals, such as bears and raccoons. Dogs and cats are among the many land-dwelling mammals that walk on their toes, with their heels not touching the ground. Horses, deer, and antelopes move about on the very tips of their toes, which are encased in hard, protective hooves. Their limbs are adapted for swift, sustained movement.

Some mammals spend little time walking or running. Kangaroos, for instance, hop most of the time. In hopping, the two hind legs move together. Kangaroos use only their powerful hind legs when they hop, holding their small front legs close to their chests.

In the Trees. Many mammals spend most of their lives in the trees. Most of them have sharp, curved claws that help them hold on as they climb. Sloths, which spend much of their lives hanging upside down from branches, have enormous claws that they use as hooks. Many tree dwellers, such as monkeys and

Manatee
Order: Sirenia

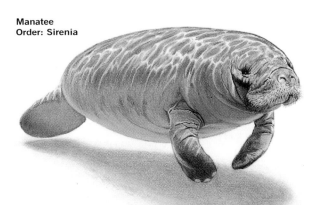

Food provides mammals with the energy and raw materials needed to carry on the functions necessary for life. The majority of mammals, large and small, feed on plant matter (*above*). Others survive by eating other animals (*right*) or both plants and animals (*below*).

broad, flat tails move up and down, propelling them through the water.

In the Air. A few mammals, such as the flying squirrel and the flying lemur, can glide from tree to tree. They have developed thin flaps of skin that stretch between their legs on either side. They spread their legs as they leap, stretching out their flaps. The flaps, which act like sails or parachutes to trap air, hold the animals aloft as they glide for long distances from tree to tree.

The only group of mammals that can truly fly are the bats. Their forelimbs have become adapted for flight. Bats have very long and slender arms and fingers. These provide the framework for thin membranes of skin that stretch between them to form wings.

Food and Feeding

Anything that can be eaten serves as food for mammals. Most mammals are herbivores; that is, they eat only plant matter. Zebras, cattle, and deer are among the herbivores. They graze on grasses, flowers, leaves, sprouts, and similar vegetation. Grazing mammals have spadelike incisors (front teeth) that they use to seize and break off the tough plant matter that makes up their diet. Their molars (cheek teeth) have broad grinding surfaces that mash the vegetation into a pulpy mass before it is swallowed.

opossums, have tails that are adapted for grasping. When wrapped around a branch, the tail serves as another hand.

In the Water. Practically all mammals, except possibly the great apes, can swim to some extent. Some so-called land animals spend much of the time in the water. They have special adaptations that make them expert swimmers. For example, otters and beavers have webbed hind feet. The beaver also has a broad, flat tail that can be used as either a rudder or an oar.

Seals, sea lions, and walruses spend most of their lives in the water and are even more specialized. Speedy, graceful, and streamlined in the water, they are awkward on land. Their four limbs have become shortened and flattened into flippers, which propel and steer them through the water.

The most specialized of all, however, are the sea cows and the whales, which live in the water from birth until death. They use their short, flat forelimbs for steering, while their

Some mammals, such as lions and weasels, feed on other animals. These carnivores, or meat eaters, have long, sharp canines (side teeth) for stabbing their victims. Their canines have sharp edges for cutting flesh into pieces. Insect eaters, such as bats and shrews, have many sharp, cutting teeth—ideal for

Aardvark
Order: Tubulidentata

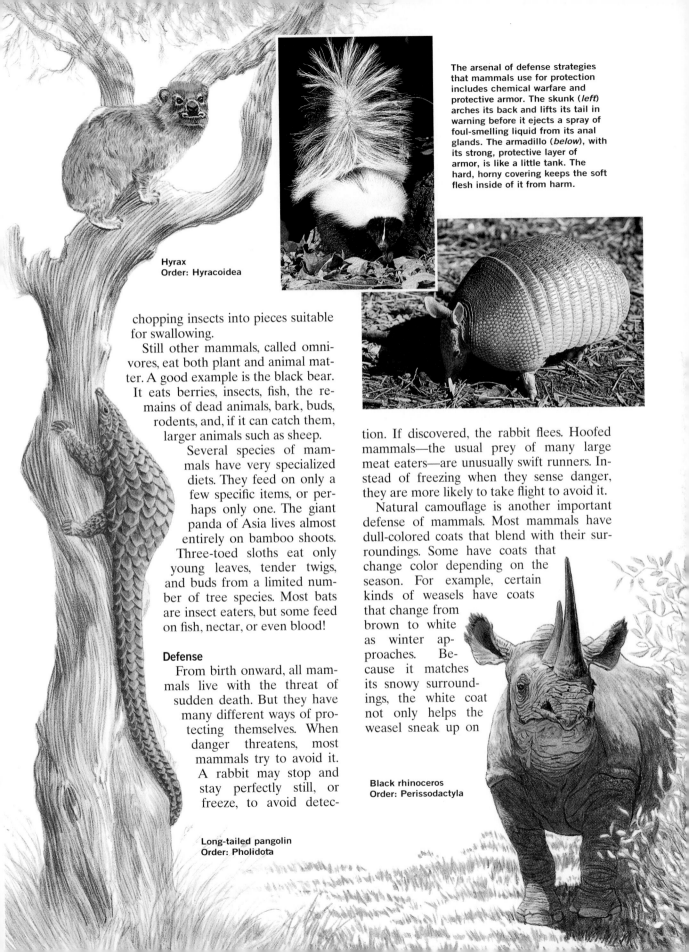

Hyrax
Order: Hyracoidea

The arsenal of defense strategies that mammals use for protection includes chemical warfare and protective armor. The skunk (*left*) arches its back and lifts its tail in warning before it ejects a spray of foul-smelling liquid from its anal glands. The armadillo (*below*), with its strong, protective layer of armor, is like a little tank. The hard, horny covering keeps the soft flesh inside of it from harm.

chopping insects into pieces suitable for swallowing.

Still other mammals, called omnivores, eat both plant and animal matter. A good example is the black bear. It eats berries, insects, fish, the remains of dead animals, bark, buds, rodents, and, if it can catch them, larger animals such as sheep.

Several species of mammals have very specialized diets. They feed on only a few specific items, or perhaps only one. The giant panda of Asia lives almost entirely on bamboo shoots. Three-toed sloths eat only young leaves, tender twigs, and buds from a limited number of tree species. Most bats are insect eaters, but some feed on fish, nectar, or even blood!

Defense

From birth onward, all mammals live with the threat of sudden death. But they have many different ways of protecting themselves. When danger threatens, most mammals try to avoid it. A rabbit may stop and stay perfectly still, or freeze, to avoid detec-

tion. If discovered, the rabbit flees. Hoofed mammals—the usual prey of many large meat eaters—are unusually swift runners. Instead of freezing when they sense danger, they are more likely to take flight to avoid it.

Natural camouflage is another important defense of mammals. Most mammals have dull-colored coats that blend with their surroundings. Some have coats that change color depending on the season. For example, certain kinds of weasels have coats that change from brown to white as winter approaches. Because it matches its snowy surroundings, the white coat not only helps the weasel sneak up on

Black rhinoceros
Order: Perissodactyla

Long-tailed pangolin
Order: Pholidota

prey, but it also conceals the weasel from animals that might attack it.

Patterns such as stripes and spots also create natural camouflage. The stripes of a zebra break up its outline and confuse predators. At dusk, zebras can be difficult to see even if they are out in the open. A spotted fawn curled up at the base of a tree is practically invisible as long as it remains motionless.

A few animals have body armor. The pangolins of Africa and Asia have coats of tough, overlapping scales, except on their bellies. When threatened, pangolins roll up into a tight ball. Even leopards have a difficult time penetrating such a ball of scales. Porcupines are covered with thousands of long, barbed quills. When alarmed, they raise their quills. Few predators can get past this spiny defense.

Pen-tailed shrew
Order: Scandentia

When danger presents itself, most mammals would rather flee than fight. If there is no choice, most will fight, and many have deadly weapons. Cats attack with razor-sharp teeth and claws. Hoofed mammals slash about with their

Koala
Order: Marsupialia

hooves or rely on horns or antlers as weapons of attack. A big kangaroo can rip open an enemy with its clawed hind legs. Even a rabbit will kick out desperately if cornered. The elephant tramples its victim or tosses him with its tusks. The walrus stabs with a pair of downward-pointing tusks.

Skunks rely on a chemical attack, spraying the enemy with a choking, overpowering scent that is squeezed from glands on either side of the tail. Hit in the face, the enemy is blinded for the moment and usually retreats.

Migration

Migration is the seasonal movement of animals over the same routes, year after year, from one place to another. Mammals may migrate to find food, to reach breeding grounds, or to avoid harsh weather. Throughout the dry season, huge herds of wildebeests circle the ranges and hills of Africa's Serengeti Plain in search of green grass and water. Gray whales summer in the cold waters off Alaska. In winter, they can be found in the warm, sheltered lagoons along the coast of Baja California in Mexico. Here

Some mammals travel hundreds of miles during a migration. However, bighorn sheep simply move up and down the mountainside to find more favorable conditions, including better feeding grounds and less severe climate.

their young are born. Caribou spend the summer on the Arctic tundra, then move south for the winter to the shelter of the boreal forests.

Not all migratory journeys cover long distances. Mountain sheep and elk just travel up and down the mountainside. They may travel only a few miles as the seasons change, but the differences in the weather of the high mountains and the lower valleys are significant.

During the winter when there is little food, this hibernating chipmunk is freed from activities, such as long periods of foraging in the cold, that could prove fatal.

Hibernation

Some mammals, including woodchucks, groundhogs, chipmunks, and some species of bats, have a special method of escaping bad weather and food shortages. These animals hibernate. In the late summer and into the fall, a hibernating mammal stuffs itself with food. As cold weather approaches, it enters its home, where it is shielded from the cold, and goes into a sleeplike state. Its body temperature drops, and its heartbeat and breathing slow down. Some hibernating animals survive on stored fat, while others wake up periodically and eat food they have stored away in their homes.

Bears also avoid severe winter conditions by remaining protected in their dens. Although they sleep and their breathing and heartbeat slow down, their body temperature remains relatively unchanged. Scientists think this is because of the bears' large body size, and most consider bears to be hibernators.

▶ THE FIRST MAMMALS

Scientists believe that the ancestors of mammals were reptiles that appeared 250 million years ago. These large reptiles were called therapsids. For 50 million years, they ruled the Earth. Some were as small as rats, others

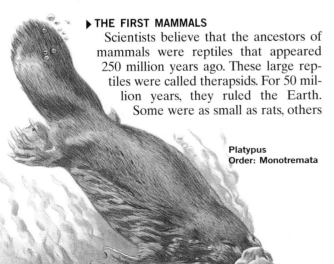

Platypus
Order: Monotremata

as large as moose. Some ate plants, some other animals. Like mammals, therapsids had more than one type of teeth, for different types of feeding. Scientists suspect that some therapsids may have been able to maintain their internal body temperature. They might even have had hair. Certainly, many lived in cool climates.

When the dinosaurs began to dominate the Earth, the therapsids gradually disappeared. By about 200 million years ago, only a few very small therapsids remained. Some of those had evolved traits that combined features of reptiles and mammals. Over time more and more changes took place, until about 190 million years ago when the creatures we call mammals began to roam the Earth.

Rabbit
Order: Lagomorpha

As long as the dinosaurs existed, mammals remained small. They resembled present-day rodents, such as squirrels and rats, and insectivores, such as shrews. After the dinosaurs disappeared about 65 million years ago, the mammal population began to expand. Mammals began to vary in size, shape, and living habits. Gradually they spread to almost all corners of the Earth and occupied all sorts of surroundings. Today mammals are the dominant animals on this planet. Their stable body temperature and high intelligence have enabled them to exploit a vast number of living places and lifestyles.

▶ THE FUTURE OF MAMMALS

Many species of animals, including several mammals, are declining in numbers. Others are threatened with extinction. The most serious threat to these animals comes from the human activities that destroy their habitats.

Forced from the natural wilderness areas they once roamed searching for food and mates, these elk graze on the protected grounds of a park.

Water pollution, for instance, can threaten not only animals that live in the water but land animals that use the water for drinking or as a food source, such as the brown bears that catch fish. Physical destruction of habitat presents the most serious danger. Forests are leveled and grasslands are plowed under as lumber is harvested and room is made for farms, ranches, and other forms of development. Once these habitats are destroyed, the animals that live there have no home left, so they vanish.

At times, governments are pressured to contain animal populations. As human populations increase, especially in developing countries, people crowd out animals as they settle in newly developed areas. Sometimes the animals are viewed as threats to the settlers. This is particularly true of species that are large or fierce, such as the African elephant. Many areas that elephants once roamed are now covered by farms. Without sufficient range, the elephants often raid crops, sometimes killing people in the process. The elephants are placed in further peril as the farmers and other settlers pressure their governments to destroy the elephants.

However, people have helped threatened animals instead of harming them. Conservation organizations all over the world work with governments on plans to save threatened animals, such as elephants, and still allow the people who live with them to make a living. Organizations such as the Wildlife Conservation Society send scientists to study animals' habits and needs and work with governments to establish parks and other places where the animals are safe.

Wildlife agencies also help reintroduce mammal species to habitats. Wildlife biologists captured fishers from northern New England and released them in Connecticut, where they had become extinct. The new fisher population is now growing there. During 1995, wolves captured in Canada were released by U.S. government scientists on remote regions of public land in Idaho, Montana, and Wyoming, including Yellowstone National Park. Wolves had been exterminated in these areas (and in many other areas) during the 1800's and 1900's, because ranchers and farmers complained that the wolves preyed on livestock. The results of the wolf program seem to be successful, as some of the wolves have reproduced. Conservationists hope this is a sign that new wolf populations may once again thrive in the western wilderness.

EDWARD R. RICCIUTI
Coauthor, *The Audubon Society Book of Wild Animals*

See also ANIMALS; EGGS AND EMBRYOS; ENDANGERED SPECIES; EVOLUTION; FOSSILS; HIBERNATION; HOMING AND MIGRATION; KINGDOMS OF LIVING THINGS; LIFE; REPRODUCTION; articles on individual animals.

MANAGEMENT. See BUSINESS; INDUSTRY; LABOR-MANAGEMENT RELATIONS.

Three-toed sloth
Order: Edentata

MANATEES

If you stand on the banks of some of Florida's lush waterways, you might occasionally hear a peculiar rush of air coming out of the water. It is the sound of a manatee as it pops its head above the surface to breathe.

Manatees also live in the warm coastal waters of the Caribbean Islands, central America, northeastern South America, and western Africa. They belong to the sirenians—one of three orders of mammals that spend all or most of their lives in water. (The other two are cetaceans, which include whales, and pinnipeds, which include seals.) Scientists believe they originally evolved from land animals.

Above: A manatee and her two calves swim in a Florida river. *Left:* This dugong lives in the waters of Indonesia. Dugongs are close relatives of manatees.

Sirenians get their name from the sirens, or singing mermaids, of Greek mythology. It is believed that early sailors may have mistaken these creatures for mermaids when looking at them from a distance. Up close, however, the animals look more like seals than humans.

Characteristics of Manatees. Manatees have a large flexible muzzle with strong but sensitive whiskers. Their smooth round bodies get their shape from stores of blubber (fat). Two front flippers each have five "fingers" joined together, but there are no hind limbs. A broad tail serves as a paddle, used for moving through the water. Some manatees may reach up to 13 feet (4 meters) in length and weigh up to 3,300 pounds (1,500 kilograms).

Horny plates at the front of their mouths are well suited to grazing on their vegetarian diet of mainly aquatic plants and some algae. Adults eat about 10 percent of their body weight in vegetation each day. Because of this huge appetite, some manatees have been used to clear canals clogged by vegetation.

Female manatees give birth about a year after becoming pregnant. By the end of its first year, a calf no longer needs to nurse. But it will typically stay with its mother for another year as it learns where to feed.

Threats to Manatees and Their Relatives. Populations of sirenians have decreased dramatically over the years because of hunting and other human activities. All three kinds, or species, of manatees—the Caribbean manatee, the Amazonian manatee, and the West African manatee—are considered to be either threatened or endangered. Florida's roughly 2,500 manatees may be the largest population.

Also at risk is a relative of the manatee called the dugong. It lives along the coasts of eastern Africa, southern India, Southeast Asia, the Philippines, Indonesia, and Australia. Overhunting has nearly wiped out many dugong populations. The only other modern-day sirenian, the huge Steller's sea cow, was hunted into extinction by 1768, just 27 years after its discovery in the Arctic.

Most sirenians are now protected by laws that prohibit poaching (illegal hunting). However, in many places of the world, it is impossible to enforce those laws. In addition, many manatees are seriously injured or killed by motor-boat propellers, which cut their bodies, and also by fishing lines and nets, in which they become tangled and drown. An equally important threat is the destruction of their habitat, brought about by pollution, dredging of waterways, and other human activities.

In recent years, campaigns have been launched to increase people's awareness of these gentle creatures and the dangers they continue to face. Limits have been set for the speed of boats in areas where manatees live. Also, some wildlife sanctuaries have been established to protect their natural habitats.

Reviewed by DANIEL K. ODELL
Research biologist, SeaWorld, Inc.

MANCHESTER. See NEW HAMPSHIRE (Cities).
MANCHURIA. See CHINA.

MANDELA, NELSON (1918–   )

Nelson Mandela personified the struggle for majority rule in South Africa. He was the leader of the resistance to the white minority government's policy of apartheid, or racial separation. Imprisoned for more than 27 years for his actions, he emerged to play a key role in negotiating governmental changes, and in 1994, he was elected the first black president of South Africa.

Nelson Rolihlahla Mandela was born on July 18, 1918, near Umtata, South Africa. His family were hereditary councilors to the chiefs of the Thembu, a group of the Xhosa people. He was educated as a lawyer and it was while practicing law in Johannesburg that he joined the African National Congress (ANC) in 1944. Dissatisfied with its leadership, he helped found, within the ANC, the Youth League, which spearheaded the fight against discrimination in South Africa.

Mandela's first marriage ended in divorce. In 1958 he married Winnie Madikizela, a leader in the anti-apartheid movement in her own right. They were divorced in 1996. In 1998, on his 80th birthday, he married Graca Machel.

Mandela at first adopted a policy of nonviolent resistance to the government. But after the shooting of 70 black Africans by police at Sharpeville in 1960, he turned to violent action instead. Arrested by the police, he was tried and, in 1964, sentenced to life imprisonment.

By the 1980's, however, the South African government had concluded that its racial policies were doomed. In 1990, President F. W. de Klerk released Mandela. The two shared the 1993 Nobel Peace Prize for their efforts to end apartheid. In the 1994 elections, the ANC won a majority of seats in the new South African parliament, and Mandela, as the ANC leader, became president. In December 1997, Thabo Mbeki succeeded Mandela as head of the ANC.

BRUCE FETTER
University of Wisconsin, Milwaukee

See also SOUTH AFRICA (History).

MANET, ÉDOUARD (1832–1883)

Édouard Manet is widely regarded as a forerunner of the modern movement in painting. He was born on January 23, 1832, in Paris, the son of wealthy parents. Rather than study law, as his father wished, Édouard became an apprentice on a ship. When he returned home with his luggage full of drawings, his father allowed him to study art. In 1850 he entered the studio of Thomas Couture, an excellent teacher. After six years he left to work on his own—painting everyday life in Paris.

In 1861, Manet's painting *The Guitar Player* was accepted by the Paris Salon, the official exhibition of the French Academy of Fine Arts. *Déjeuner sur l'herbe* was refused by the Salon in 1863. Its subject—a female nude, accompanied by two clothed gentlemen, seated on the grass of a public park—was considered improper. *Olympia*, a painting of a reclining female nude, was accepted in 1865, but it caused a great scandal. After that, most of Manet's works were rejected by the Academy.

Manet was somewhat like the realist painters of his day in his choice of subjects and his manner of painting them. He was also often called the leader of the impressionists. But he never thought of himself as an impressionist painter. He remained firmly rooted in classical composition. And he longed for recognition by the Academy.

Manet died on April 30, 1883. By then he was beginning to be recognized as a pioneer of modern painting. *Olympia* was exhibited in the Louvre in Paris in 1907.

Reviewed by FRANK GETLEIN
Author, *The French Impressionists*

MANGANESE. See IRON AND STEEL.

Manet's painting *Olympia* caused a scandal when it was first exhibited. Today it is acclaimed as a masterpiece of early modern art.

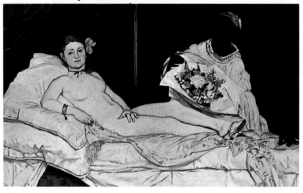

MANILA

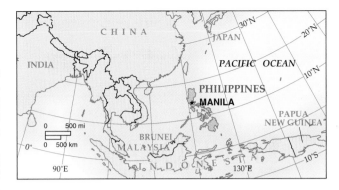

Manila is the capital and largest city of the Republic of the Philippines. Early in its history it was known as Maynila, meaning "place of the nila flower." Now it is often called the Pearl of the Orient because of its natural beauty.

The city lies on a warm and humid coastal plain in the southwest part of the island of Luzon. It is an ideal seaport because of its location on the eastern shore of Manila Bay at the mouth of the Pasig River. The city covers an approximate area of 15 square miles (39 square kilometers) and has a population of more than 1.6 million. Metro-Manila, which includes Manila, Quezon City, and many other nearby cities and towns, has a population of about 6 million.

The City. Near the port is the old Spanish city of Intramuros, which is surrounded by thick walls. Fort Santiago and San Agustin, the oldest church in the Philippines, are located there. Nearby Rizal Park is a popular gathering place. Other attractions include Malacañang Palace, the official home of the president of the Philippines; the modern Cultural Center complex, built on land reclaimed from Manila Bay; and the National Museum of the Philippines, known for its anthropological and geological exhibits. Manila also has more than a dozen colleges and universities. The oldest, the University of Santo Tomás, was founded by Spanish missionaries in 1611.

Economic Activity. Manila is the nation's center of trade, finance, publishing, and manufacturing. Electronics, chemicals, textiles, shoes, coconut oil, and processed foods are among the products manufactured there. Imported and exported goods are shipped to and from the busy docks on Manila Bay. Tourism and shipbuilding are also important to the economy.

History. In 1521 the Portuguese explorer Ferdinand Magellan claimed the Philippines for Spain. Manila became Spain's island headquarters in 1571. British forces occupied Manila from 1762 until 1763, but with this brief exception, Spain controlled Manila for more than 300 years.

In 1898 during the Spanish-American War, U.S. warships under Commodore George Dewey defeated the Spanish fleet in the Battle of Manila Bay. Manila was captured four months later, and at the war's end, the Philippines were ceded to the United States.

In 1942 during World War II, the Japanese bombed Manila, then occupied the city. Manila was liberated by American forces in 1945. After the war, the destroyed city was completely rebuilt.

When the Philippines became independent in 1946, Manila became the nation's capital. Two years later, Quezon City replaced Manila as the seat of government. But Manila again became the official capital in 1976. In recent years, the government has done much to provide housing, hospitals, roads, and schools for Manila's poor. It has also encouraged the building of hotels, a new airport, and a modern convention center to serve the important tourist industry.

CAROLINA S. MOULTON
Philippine Consulate
(New York City)

Manila, the capital of the Philippines, is a busy port city in the South Pacific.

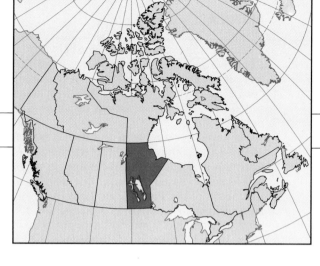

MANITOBA

Manitoba's flag (above) was officially proclaimed in 1966. The coat of arms (opposite page), granted in 1992, includes a unicorn, a symbol of Great Britain, and a beaver, which is Canada's national animal as well as a symbol of economic and historic importance in Manitoba. The provincial bird is the great gray owl (right), and the provincial flower is the prairie crocus (opposite page).

Manitoba, the first western province to join the Canadian Confederation, takes its name from the Cree and Ojibway words meaning "the strait of the Great Spirit," referring to the roar of the waves through the narrow strait in Lake Manitoba.

▶ THE LAND

The geography of Manitoba is mainly the result of the Ice Age. Millions of years ago, glaciers covered much of North America. When they receded, they leveled the land, scraped off much of the soil, and left behind the enormous Lake Agassiz. This later drained into Hudson Bay, leaving three large lakes—Winnipeg, Winnipegosis, and Manitoba—and a fertile plain in the valley of the Red River. The area to the north and east is known as the Canadian Shield and is rich in forests, minerals, and water resources. The areas to the south and west are called the Manitoba Lowland and Saskatchewan Plain. The Saskatchewan Plain has some of the richest agricultural land in Canada.

Manitoba is essentially a low-lying province with the exception of the west, where the Manitoba Escarpment rises abruptly. But even here, the highest point is Baldy Mountain, which stands a mere 2,727 feet (831 meters) above sea level.

Climate

Like the other Prairie Provinces (Alberta and Saskatchewan), Manitoba has a continental climate with long, cold winters and short, hot summers. Average January temper-atures range from –3°F (–19°C) in Winnipeg to –16°F (–28°C) on the northern coast of the province. Average July temperatures range from 68°F (20°C) in the south to 54°F (12°C) in northern Manitoba.

Farmers can usually count on about 100 to 120 frost-free days in the southern areas of the province, but farming is not profitable north of The Pas. Many communities farther to the north are built on permafrost, or land that is permanently frozen.

Annual precipitation in the form of snow or rain varies widely, but an average of about 20 inches (500 millimeters) falls in Winnipeg. The southwestern region is considerably drier.

Natural Resources

Manitoba has a variety of natural resources. The northern regions are rich in minerals, forests, and hydroelectric power. The southern regions are ideally suited for growing crops and raising livestock.

The most important minerals are nickel, copper, zinc, gold, cadmium, and silver. Nickel is mined in the northern part of the province.

Forests cover just over half the entire area of Manitoba. This is more than three times the amount of land that is devoted to agriculture. Common tree species are black spruce, trembling aspen, jack pine, white spruce, balsam poplar, and white birch. Among the forested areas are hundreds of lakes, many of them well stocked with walleye, pike, and trout.

FACTS AND FIGURES

Location: Mid-Canada. **Latitude**—49° N to 60° N. **Longitude**—89° W to 102° W.

Joined Canadian Confederation: July 15, 1870, as the 5th province.

Population: 1,119,583 (2001 census). **Rank among provinces**—5th.

Capital and Largest City: Winnipeg, pop. 619,544 (2001 census).

Physical Features: Area—250,115 sq mi (647,797 km²). **Rank among provinces**—6th. **Rivers**—Assiniboine, Nelson, Churchill, Red, Winnipeg. **Lakes**—Winnipeg, Winnipegosis, Manitoba, Southern Indian, Island, Cedar, Moose. **Highest point**—2,729 ft (832 m), Baldy Mountain.

Industries and Products: Manufacturing; agriculture; mining; lumber.

Government: Self-governing province. **Titular head of government**—lieutenant governor, appointed by the governor-general in council. **Actual head of government**—premier, leader of the majority in the legislature. **Provincial representation in federal parliament**—6 appointed senators; 14 elected member(s) of the House of Commons. **Voting age for provincial elections**—18.

Provincial Bird: Great gray owl.

Provincial Flower: Prairie crocus.

Provincial Motto: *Gloriosus et liber* (Glorious and free).

Manitoba's river system has also provided the province with a continuing source of wealth. The first hydroelectric dams were built on the Winnipeg River, which flows into Lake Winnipeg, but most of the larger dams are on the Nelson River, which flows north from Lake Winnipeg to Hudson Bay.

▶ THE PEOPLE AND THEIR WORK

More than half of Manitoba's people live in metropolitan Winnipeg. But it was not always this way. When Manitoba became a province in 1870, most people lived on farms. Later, many immigrant groups settled on the land. These groups included British, Ukrainians, and Poles. Among the early settlers were Mennonites from Ukraine. Another group were Hutterites, who originated in Russia and went to Canada by way of the United States. Icelanders settled mainly near the lakes; the métis (people of mixed Indian and European ancestry) settled in distinctive communities. Later immigrants have settled mainly in Winnipeg and have come from the West Indies, the Philippines, India, Pakistan, and Hong Kong.

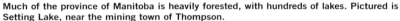

Much of the province of Manitoba is heavily forested, with hundreds of lakes. Pictured is Setting Lake, near the mining town of Thompson.

Below: Wheat is harvested in a Manitoba field. *Left:* A field of canola grows in the Minnedosa Valley in the northwestern part of the province. *Below left:* A friendly young Manitoban.

Manitoba has the most ethnically mixed population of all the provinces. People of British origin are still the most numerous, making up approximately 40 percent of the population. Germans are next in number, followed by Ukrainian, Irish, and French. Manitoba still has the largest concentration of French Canadians in western Canada. Native Indians number approximately 93,000 and live on 61 reservations and also in the cities. Métis number some 57,000.

Industries and Products

Agriculture remained Manitoba's main source of wealth until the early 1900's, when it was overtaken by manufacturing and mining. Agriculture is still very important in Manitoba. Today, however, service industries dominate the economy.

Services. Service industries account for about 75 percent of the provincial economy. Leading services are business, social, and personal services such as health care and services related to tourism. Wholesale and retail trade, finance, and communication are also important.

Manufacturing. The leading manufactured products in Manitoba are food and beverages, machinery, transportation equipment, printed materials, and clothing.

Manufacturing has long been an important part of Manitoba's economy. The first factories were often based on local needs and included dairies, bakeries, and lumber mills. While some factories have remained in smaller towns—steel mills in Selkirk and meat-packing plants in Brandon, for example—many smaller industries moved to Winnipeg, which also became the center for clothing and other manufactures.

Agriculture. Wheat remains the most important crop that is grown in Manitoba. Other major grain crops are barley, canola, flaxseed, oats, and rye. The raising of livestock—especially beef cattle, hogs, and poultry—is a thriving business.

Agriculture in Manitoba is more diversified than in the other two Prairie Provinces. Many specialty crops, such as sunflower seeds, as well as sugar beets, corn, potatoes, and other vegetables are grown in the rich soil of the southern Red River Valley and near Portage la Prairie.

Mines and Mining. Nickel is the most important mineral in Manitoba. It comes chiefly from mines at Thompson. Copper and zinc are mined at Flin Flon. Other minerals are gold, cadmium, and silver. Together, these account for more than 70 percent of mineral production. Industrial minerals, such as silica sand, limestone, granite, bentonite, and dolomite, and oil are also mined.

Transportation and Communication

Centrally located in Canada, Winnipeg is the focal point of road, air, and rail routes. Both the Canadian National and Canadian Pacific railways pass through Winnipeg, and a branch line reaches north to Churchill on the shore of Hudson Bay. Winnipeg International Airport is one of the largest airports in Canada. It is largely concerned with domestic flights.

Manitoba has six English-language daily newspapers. Many other communities have weekly newspapers, and several ethnic groups publish their own newspapers.

Within Manitoba there are radio stations in all the cities and in several of the smaller towns. Broadcasting is also available in French and some native languages. Television stations operate in Brandon, Portage la Prairie, and Thompson, in addition to five stations in Winnipeg. Of these, one is French language. Most households in Manitoba have cable television, which provides access to programs in both Canada and the United States.

▶ EDUCATION AND CULTURE

The first schools in Manitoba were provided by private teachers or by churches. In 1871, a public school system was established. Today there are 47 school districts. Classes are taught in English and French as well as some other languages.

Higher education is provided by the University of Manitoba, St. Boniface College, and the University of Winnipeg, all located in Winnipeg, and Brandon University in Brandon. Three community colleges offer technical and commercial training.

Complementing Manitoba's educational system is a rich cultural and artistic tradition. Best known are the Winnipeg Symphony Orchestra, the Royal Winnipeg Ballet, the Manitoba Theater Center, and the Winnipeg Art Gallery. Libraries are found in most small towns, and the Provincial Archives in Winnipeg contain the invaluable records of the Hudson's Bay Company.

▶ PLACES OF INTEREST

The following are among the many scenic, historical, and recreational areas.

Assiniboine Park, in Winnipeg, contains one of the largest zoos in Canada.

Delta Waterfowl and Wetlands Research Station, on Lake Winnipeg, is an important wildlife research center. It provides many opportunities for observing and learning about nature.

Below: Visitors stroll through the colorful English Garden in Assiniboine Park. *Right:* Located at the junction of the Red and Assiniboine rivers, the Forks site in Winnipeg offers many attractions.

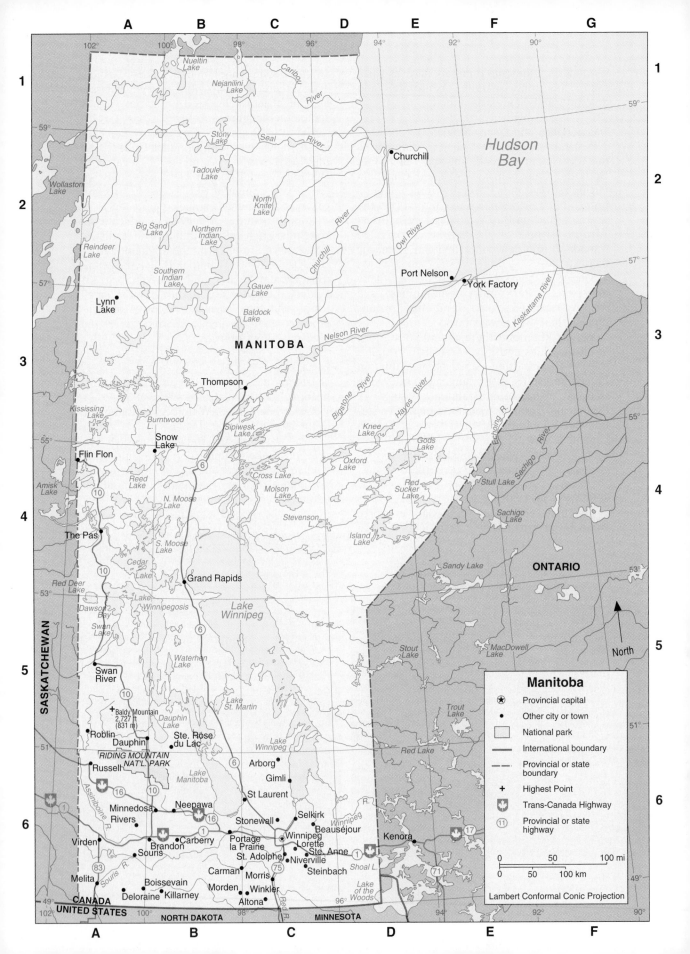

INDEX TO MANITOBA MAP

International Peace Garden, on the boundary between Manitoba and North Dakota, is a monument to peaceful relations between Canada and the United States.

Lower Fort Garry, on the banks of the Red River north of Winnipeg, is a museum and the oldest stone fort in western Canada.

Manitoba Museum of Man and Nature, in Winnipeg, has a replica of the *Nonsuch*, the ship that opened up fur trade in the 1600's.

Mennonite Heritage Village, at Steinbach, recreates a traditional Mennonite village of the late 1800's.

Oak Hammock Marsh Interpretive Center, north of Winnipeg, is home to over 250 species of birds and hundreds of species of mammals, amphibians, and reptiles.

St. Andrew's Church, north of Winnipeg, is the oldest stone church in western Canada.

St. Boniface Museum, in Winnipeg, is the city's oldest building. It was built in 1846.

CITIES AND TOWNS

A diagonal line from the southeast corner of Manitoba northwest to The Pas divides the almost uninhabited North and the well-settled South. Winnipeg, the capital, is the largest city and the chief industrial and transportation center of Manitoba. The city's metropolitan population is about 671,000. An article on Winnipeg appears in Volume WXYZ.

Brandon, with a population of almost 40,000, is Manitoba's second largest city. It is an industrial and marketing center and the home of a provincial university. Smaller communities include Thompson, a northern mining town, and Portage la Prairie, a retail center west of Winnipeg.

GOVERNMENT

The titular head of government is the lieutenant governor, who acts as the representative of the Queen of England but is appointed by the prime minister with the assent of the governor-general. There are 57 members elected to the legislative assembly. The leader of the party with the most members is appointed premier. He or she then chooses a cabinet to take charge of the various government departments. Manitoba is represented in the federal parliament by 14 elected members of the House of Commons and by 6 appointed members of the Senate.

HISTORY

The first inhabitants of North America, ancestors of the people now known as Native Americans, arrived soon after the end of the Ice Age. They came originally from Asia across the Bering Strait to Alaska and gradually spread throughout the continent.

In 1612 a British explorer and trader, Sir Thomas Button, visited the western coast of Hudson Bay and traded with the Indians for furs. Other English traders followed, and in 1670, King Charles II of England granted a charter to the Hudson's Bay Company giving them ownership of all lands draining into Hudson Bay. This area was named Rupert's Land, in honor of the king's cousin Prince Rupert, and included vast areas of western Canada and modern-day Manitoba.

From 1670 to 1870, the Hudson's Bay Company controlled the vast interior of British North America. York Factory on Hudson Bay and, later, Fort Garry served as the principal forts and trading posts in the fur trade. In 1811, Lord Selkirk, a Scottish philanthropist, bought 116,000 square miles (300,400 square kilometers) of land from the Hudson's Bay Company and established a settlement to be called Assiniboia. Its center was at the junction of the Red and Assiniboine rivers (now downtown Winnipeg).

The first settlers arrived in 1812, and despite many hardships they gradually prospered. Ownership of the settlement reverted

The Canadian government was determined to take over the colony. Canada purchased the land of the Hudson's Bay Company in 1869 and sent survey teams even before the deal was complete. The métis resented this, and under the leadership of Louis Riel, they seized control of the settlement. They then sent representatives to Ottawa to negotiate terms for admission to confederation, or union, as the province of Manitoba. The federal government sent in a military force. Riel fled, and a provincial government was established. Manitoba became Canada's fifth province on July 15, 1870.

With peace restored, immigrants flooded into the new province from Ontario and from many countries of Europe. By 1881, when the provincial boundaries were extended, the population had reached 62,000. From the late 1890's to 1912, when the boundaries were extended to their present limits, Manitobans enjoyed prosperous times.

But those years also brought a demand for social changes. In 1916, Manitoba became the first province to give the vote to women, and the first woman member took her seat in the legislature four years later.

The aftermath of World War I brought serious troubles as returning veterans faced rising unemployment and a higher cost of living. Growing anger led to the Winnipeg General Strike in 1919. The workers demanded better wages and the right to bargain as members of a union. Police and armed troops quelled the violence that followed, but in the long term, unionism was strengthened. Winnipeg has had a strong labor movement ever since.

In the 1920's, conditions improved as industries grew and agricultural prices rose, but Manitoba shared fully in the Great Depression of the 1930's. Poor crops and a long drought continued until the outbreak of World War II in 1939.

After the war, prosperity gradually returned until a recession struck the province in the 1980's. In the future, much depends on how effectively Manitoba manages its resources and how successfully the province competes in the global economy and in the world of computer technology.

KEITH WILSON
Professor Emeritus, University of Manitoba

MANKILLER, WILMA. See OKLAHOMA (Famous People).

to the Hudson's Bay Company in 1835. The small colony gradually took on the characteristics of a settled community, with churches, schools, and a government under the control of a governor appointed by the company.

For many years, it was an isolated settlement. By the 1850's, however, trade routes and postal services were opened to St. Paul, Minnesota, and the first newspaper began publication. Many retired fur traders and voyageurs settled in the colony, and the population soon reached 12,000.

MANN, HORACE (1796–1859)

The man who has been called the father of the American free public school was born on a farm in Franklin, Massachusetts, on May 4, 1796. Perhaps it was his own lack of proper schooling that led Horace Mann to struggle for the important reforms in education that he helped bring about.

When Horace Mann was still a boy, his father and brother died. The young Horace had to take over many of their chores. Like most of the children in his town, he was unable to go to school more than eight or ten weeks each year. Then, in 1816, a classics teacher named Samuel Barrett arrived in the town. He began teaching Latin to Horace. In addition, Reverend William Williams, a Baptist minister who lived near the Mann farm, taught him geometry. Both teachers helped Horace, an apt student, enter the sophomore class at Brown University. In 1819, Horace graduated with honors. He went on to study law in Connecticut, and in 1823, he became a member of the Massachusetts bar.

Mann was married twice. In 1830 he married Charlotte Messer, who died two years later. His second wife was Mary Tyler Peabody, whom he married in May 1843. They had three children.

Mann entered politics and served in the Massachusetts legislature from 1827 to 1837. As president of the state senate, he signed a historic education bill that became a law on April 20, 1837. This bill set up a state board of education. Mann was asked to be the board's first secretary. He willingly gave up a successful legal practice and political career because of his great desire to serve the cause of education.

During the twelve years that he was secretary of the board of education, Mann reorganized the public school system. Through his efforts the first state-supported normal school —for the training of elementary-school teachers—was established in 1839 in Lexington, Massachusetts. By 1840 there were three normal schools in Massachusetts.

Under Mann's leadership, a law was passed that increased the school year to a minimum of six months. Through his efforts more public money was made available for building schools, and the teachers received badly needed increases in their salaries. The twelve annual reports he submitted are still read by students of American education.

Mann was elected to the United States House of Representatives in 1848 to fill the vacancy caused by the death of John Quincy Adams. In 1852, Mann was offered the nomination for governor of Massachusetts. He declined in order to accept the presidency of Antioch College in Yellow Springs, Ohio. He continued as president of Antioch until his death there on August 2, 1859. In his last commencement address at Antioch, Mann said, "Be ashamed to die until you have won some victory for humanity."

Reviewed by JONATHAN C. MESSERLI
Author, *Horace Mann, A Biography*

MANNERS. See ETIQUETTE.

MANUFACTURING

The objects you use every day at home and at school were made from raw materials. Someone took these materials and turned them into pencils, books, shirts, or chairs. Making raw materials into useful products is called manufacturing.

Manufacturing is the shaping and changing of materials. This can be done by cutting away unwanted pieces, beating or stretching the material, or changing it by heating or chemical processing. When the materials are prepared and shaped, the final product can be made.

People in small, non-industrialized societies use the simplest manufacturing methods and tools. People in industrialized nations usually have developed more complex methods and tools with which to manufacture products.

The development of modern manufacturing was based on two things—sources of power and machines. For centuries the only sources of power were human and animal strength and waterwheels. Machines could not be used efficiently because there was no good way to power them. The invention of a practical steam engine in the 1700's provided the power that was needed. The rapid growth of industry at that time, known as the Industrial Revolution, was based on the power of the

Computers are now important in many manufacturing processes. In this Canadian assembly plant, one worker at a control station directs many complex operations.

steam engine. Later other sources of power, such as electricity, were developed.

The discovery of a cheap way to produce steel was another important event. For many years, iron was the chief industrial metal. But steel is stronger and easier to work than iron. When Henry Bessemer introduced a cheap steelmaking process in 1856, steel began to replace iron for most uses. Besides being used to make tools and machines for factories, steel became valuable as a raw material for a great number of products.

Organizing Manufacturing for Mass Production

Until the Industrial Revolution, artisans did their work in small shops or in their own homes. In making textiles, for instance, spinners would spin the yarn in their homes. The yarn was then taken to the weavers' cottages, where it was woven into cloth. Most products people used were custom-made—produced by individuals for a specific customer at the customer's request.

The Industrial Revolution introduced many changes. Industries began using machinery to produce goods. The new machines could not be jammed into a worker's cottage, so factories were built to house the machinery. In a system known as mass production, hundreds of workers in a factory could produce great quantities of an item. Mass production was a more efficient way to produce goods—production costs were lower, and products were more affordable to more people.

Three things are needed for a mass production system: machine technology—the tools and skills needed to produce items by machinery rather than by hand; a factory system—a method of organizing and managing workers and machines; and a mass market—a large number of people with the desire and money to buy mass-produced goods. A mass market needs a system of transportation to move the goods from factory to store and a means of letting people know about the goods through advertising.

Among the most important elements in the new system of manufacturing were the standardization of parts, assembly-line production, and automation.

Standardized parts are important to mass production. Instead of making one part at a time, large quantities of a part are made. For example, a clock manufacturer will make all the mainsprings of the same type clock the same, all the minute hands the same, and so on. Since a particular part is identical to all its mates, the parts are interchangeable. A manufacturer wanting to put a clock together can use any one of the mainsprings made.

Speed of production is one of the advantages of this method. The separate parts can be put together rapidly to make many duplicates of a product. Another advantage is that it is cheaper for workers to make parts in large quantities than to make a few at a time.

The idea of standardized parts was developed early in the 1800's by two Americans—Simeon North and Eli Whitney, the inventor of the cotton gin. Both North and Whitney had their own workshops for manufacturing guns for the U.S. Government. Each man had the idea independently of the other to use standardized parts for the guns. After all the separate parts were made, a gun was assembled by passing it from one worker to another, with each worker adding a new part. Other manufacturers soon started using this method. Some of the first products, besides guns, to be made with standardized parts were clocks, watches, sewing machines, and farm machinery.

Rapid production was achieved by using both standardized parts and a moving assembly line. Henry Ford (1863–1947) was one of the first manufacturers to use this method in making automobiles. The bare frame of the famous Model T Ford started at one end of the assembly line. As the frame moved slowly along the conveyor, parts were added. Each worker was responsible for putting on a part —a fan belt or a door handle, for example.

With this method the time needed to assemble a car was eventually reduced from over 12 hours to only 1½ hours. Soon cars were being mass-produced by the thousands.

Automation

Production can be faster and easier if machines run and control themselves. This is called automation. The word is a short way of saying "automatic mechanization."

Advancement in automation has been rapid since World War II. At that time, research was focused on devices that could automatically guide airplanes, missiles, and rockets. Much of this research has been applied to making automatic controls for factory machinery.

In many factories today, at least part of the production is performed by automated machines. Some of these machines are robots, with "arms" and "hands" that perform tasks on the assembly line. There are some fully automated factories that use few workers but turn out large quantities of products. Bottles, cans, lightbulbs, paper, and cigarettes are some of the things made by automated production. Many oil refineries are automated.

New Materials

Chemically made (synthetic) substances are among the most important new materials that are manufactured. One of the first such materials was the artificial textile fiber rayon. It is made of cellulose. Many other synthetic fibers, such as nylon, Dacron, and Orlon, were developed later. These fibers are replacing natural fibers such as wool and cotton for many purposes. To learn more about these new fibers, see the article NYLON AND OTHER SYNTHETIC FIBERS in Volume N.

Plastics, which are also chemically produced, have come into wide use in the past 25 years. Plastics are used for a great variety of products—everything from raincoats to ballpoint pens. Most of the new plastics are made from coal, natural gas, and petroleum. An article on plastics appears in Volume P.

Manufacturing Around the World

Between 1800 and 1900, the United States changed from an agricultural to an industrial country. The greatest changes were made after

Electronic robots work on many automobile assembly lines. They can work almost nonstop, need little care, and, if programmed properly, do not make mistakes.

the U.S. Civil War. In 1820 more than 70 percent of the people were engaged in farming. By 1900 this figure had dropped to about 40 percent, and by 1990 less than 3 percent of all workers were employed in farming. As industry grew, people left the farms and moved to jobs in factories. Automated farm machinery helped food production remain high even with the loss of farmworkers.

The number of production workers in manufacturing has also dropped, mostly because of automation. The number of office jobs has increased, and more people have gone into professional jobs as lawyers, doctors, and teachers.

Most of Europe is highly industrialized. In Asia, Japan is the leading industrial country. But in many nations of the world, industrialization is not yet well established. This is especially true in parts of Africa, Asia, and South America. However, with the growth of international manufacturing companies, many of these countries are becoming industrialized in the hopes of improving their economies.

PHILMORE B. WASS
University of Connecticut

See also AUTOMATION; INDUSTRIAL DESIGN; INDUSTRIAL REVOLUTION; INDUSTRY; IRON AND STEEL; ROBOTS.

MANUSCRIPTS, ILLUMINATED. See ILLUMINATED MANUSCRIPTS.

Mao Zedong's portrait leads a Beijing parade.

MAO ZEDONG (1893–1976)

Mao Zedong (or Tse-tung) was a revolutionary leader, founder of the People's Republic of China, and its ruler for nearly thirty years. He was born on December 26, 1893, in a small village in Hunan province, in South China. His father, a stern man, was a successful rice merchant and farmer.

Early Years. Mao went to a nearby primary school. When he was 13, his father made him give up schooling for farm work. By that time, however, the boy already had a great love for books—especially those filled with adventures and rebellion.

Mao worked on the farm for three years and then returned to school, where he was a brilliant but rebellious student. When the Chinese revolution against the Qing (or Manchu) dynasty broke out in 1911, he joined the revolutionary army. Mao stayed in the army for six months and then resumed his schooling. He was disappointed with the new Chinese Republic and thought the revolution had failed to win needed reforms. At school Mao headed a group of students who debated how to achieve those reforms.

In 1918 Mao went to Beijing (Peking), where he worked in the university library as a fetcher of newspapers. On the side he edited a monthly paper of his own. On May 4, 1919, the university students rebelled against the government. An associate of Mao's was the guiding spirit of this movement, which protested the transfer of former German lands, or "concessions," in China to Japan. Though most of these students were Socialists, a few called themselves Communists.

The Struggle for Power. Mao was one of the founding members of the Chinese Communist Party, which met in Shangahi in 1921. Within six years he had become one of the party's most important members.

The Communists joined forces with the Kuomintang, China's chief party of reform. But suddenly, in 1927, Chiang Kai-shek, leader of the Kuomintang, turned on the Communists and began to massacre them. Mao and his followers set up a base in the mountains of Jiangxi province and fought off five Kuomintang attacks. Then, with Zhou Enlai (Chou En-lai) and other Communist Party chiefs, he led the Communist armies on the Long March. This 6,000-mile (9,700-kilometer) trek took them to the borders of Tibet and then north to the valley of Yenan, in Shaanxi province, where, in 1936, they set up a powerful base.

In the following year the Japanese invaded China. For a time the Kuomintang and the Communists united against the common enemy—but this unity did not last long. Chiang Kai-shek's armies were forced to retreat while the Communist guerrilla armies fought on behind the Japanese lines. By the time the Japanese were defeated in 1945, it was clear that the Communists had more support among the Chinese people than did Chiang Kai-shek's forces. A civil war followed, ending in a Communist victory in 1949.

The People's Republic. In Beijing, on October 1, 1949, Mao proclaimed the People's Republic of China. The landlords were stripped of their holdings, the government took control of industry, and communes (communities where everything is owned in common) were set up. The entire country came under the control of the Communist Party. The control was so rigid that Mao feared the revolutionary spirit would die out. At various times, without much success, he tried to lessen the power of the Communist bureaucrats (government officials). The Great Proletarian Cultural Revolution in the late 1960's, led largely by Mao's wife, Jiang Qing, was just such an effort. It attempted to cleanse the bureaucracy by giving power to young revolutionaries called Red Guards.

Mao's health began to fail in the late 1960's. He died in 1976 at the age of 82.

ROBERT PAYNE
Author, *Mao Tse-tung*

MAPLE SYRUP
AND MAPLE SUGAR

Maple syrup and maple sugar are two products made from the sap of maple trees. Maple syrup is a sweet, tasty liquid; maple sugar is made by boiling maple syrup. Eighty percent of the maple syrup and sugar produced in North America comes from Quebec, Canada. In the United States the leading producers are Vermont and New York.

The Sugar Maple Tree. The sugar maple tree, sometimes called the hard or rock maple, is the best maple for sugar making. The sap from it is sweeter than the sap of black, silver, and other maple trees. The sugar maple lives a long time. It is easy to grow, but it grows slowly. The trees are not ready to be tapped (opened) for production until they are about 40 years old and about 12 inches (30 centimeters) in diameter.

During the winter, the starch that the tree made during the previous summer and stored in its roots has turned to sugar. In early spring, sap begins to rise in the trees, gathering sugar with it.

Many factors, such as the tree's age and size, determine the flow of the sap and the quality of the final product. The tree's health during the previous summer and the tree's overall condition also affect the sap. The weather, both during the previous summer and during the sugaring season, are very important. Freezing nights and thawing days—days of 35 to 50°F (2 to 10°C)—provide ideal weather conditions for sap flowing.

Producing Syrup and Sugar. At the beginning of the sugaring season, a small hole is bored in the tree trunk, about 3 feet (90 centimeters) above the ground. A spout is driven in, and a bucket is hung on it. Modern producers use plastic tubing connected to the spouts. From the tubes the sap flows into a pipeline system that takes it to storage tanks in the sugarhouse, where the syrup and sugar are made. Adding a vacuum pump to the pipeline can increase the flow of sap.

Immediately after the sap is collected, it is filtered. Then it is boiled in huge evaporating pans. When the sap has been boiled to 219°F (104°C), it has become maple syrup. It must be boiled for a longer period of time and a higher temperature for maple sugar.

A Vermont farmer pours maple sap into a bucket. After it is collected, the sap is taken to a sugarhouse and processed to make delicious maple products.

Saps vary in sweetness. Some saps have 1 percent sugar. Others contain up to 4 percent. It takes an average of 35 gallons (130 liters) of sap to make 1 gallon (4 liters) of syrup. On average a single tap may yield about 10 gallons (38 liters) of sap.

History. Long before Europeans appeared in North America, the Native Americans were producing their own maple syrup and sugar. When the settlers arrived, the Native Americans showed them the method of getting sap from trees and heating it to make a dark, thick syrup. Sugar from sugarcane was scarce, and maple sugar was often the only sweetener the settlers could get.

Today, cane sugar is comparatively inexpensive and plentiful. Maple sugar is still used. But because of its high cost, it has become something of a delicacy. It is used to make candies and flavorings. Maple syrup is used on waffles, pancakes, French toast, ice-cream sundaes, and other foods. It can be used in baking, as a substitute for molasses.

MAURICE TESSIER
Agriculture Canada

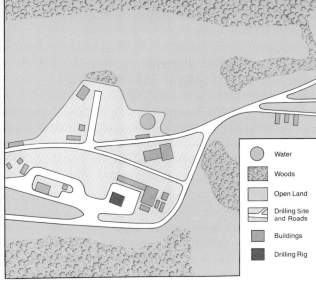

This photograph and map both show the same oil-drilling site. Unlike the photograph, the map uses symbols to represent things. Find the drilling rig in the photograph. Then use the map legend to find the drilling rig on the map.

Legend:
- Water
- Woods
- Open Land
- Drilling Site and Roads
- Buildings
- Drilling Rig

MAPS AND GLOBES

A map is a kind of picture of an area as seen from above. It will usually include symbols and other information to make it easier to understand. A map could show the street on which you live—or the entire world. Maps help people find their way from one place to another and record all kinds of information about people, places, and things.

Because our planet is round, a round globe gives the most accurate picture of the shapes and sizes of the land and water areas of the earth. But flat maps are cheaper and easier to handle, and they can show small areas in greater detail than a globe. For these reasons flat maps are more widely used than globes.

Maps have taken different forms through history. Long ago, Middle Easterners drew maps on clay tablets and directed travelers by arranging stones on the ground. Polynesians once sailed the Pacific using maps made of palm fiber and shells. Later, maps drawn on sheepskin told of trade and treasure routes. Maps once took a long time to make and were very rare and costly. It was not until the printing press and the process of copper engraving had been invented that maps could be produced cheaply and in large quantities. They then became part of everyday life.

The first maps were designed to help people move from place to place. Today maps come in many forms and are used for many purposes. Maps can show how land is used and who owns it. They can depict physical features such as mountains and lakes or record information about population or economic activities. There are even weather, undersea, and star maps. A person who makes maps is called a **cartographer.** The science of map making is known as **cartography.**

▶MAP SKILLS

To be able to use maps, you must know how to read them. The language of maps is simple, and good maps include instructions to help you understand them. Once you become familiar with the language of maps, you can use them to find out about many things.

Finding Location

One basic use of maps is to locate specific places or features. All location is relative. You need a starting point. All else can then be described as being a certain distance and direction from this point. The earth has two natural starting points—the North and South poles. Because people needed a way to describe location between the two poles, the ancient Greeks invented a **geographic grid.** This grid is still in use today. It is made up of two sets of imaginary lines that cross each other at regular intervals. One set of lines is a series of circles running east and west around the earth parallel to the poles. The other set stretches north and south between the poles. The east-west lines are called **parallels of latitude.** The north-south lines are known as **meridians of**

SOME MAP AND GLOBE TERMS

Arctic Circle—a line of latitude around the north polar region at 66° 30′ N. The **Antarctic Circle** is a line of latitude around the south polar region at 66° 30′ S.

Atlas—a bound volume of maps.

Cartography—the science of map making. A **cartographer** is a person who makes maps.

Compass rose—a symbol used to show direction on a map.

Co-ordinates—a set of two numbers (usually latitude and longitude) used in specifying the location of a point.

Degree—a circle can be divided into 360 equal degrees. A degree, represented by the symbol °, is divided into 60 **minutes,** represented by the symbol ′. Latitude and longitude are shown in degrees.

Globe—a round representation of the earth.

Great circle—an imaginary circle on the earth's surface that divides the earth into two equal parts.

Grid—a network of evenly spaced horizontal and perpendicular lines. Lines of latitude and longitude form an imaginary **geographic grid** on the surface of the earth.

Hemisphere—half of a round object. The equator divides the earth into the **Northern and Southern hemispheres.** The prime meridian and the 180th meridian divide it into the **Eastern and Western hemispheres.**

International date line—an imaginary line at roughly 180° longitude, where a calendar day begins and ends.

Latitude—the distance in degrees north or south of the **equator** (° latitude). A **parallel of latitude** is an imaginary line circling the earth and connecting points on the earth's surface having the same latitude. Parallels of latitude never meet. They are numbered from 0° to 90° north and south of the equator.

> **High latitudes** are latitudes between 60° and the pole in the Northern and Southern hemispheres.
> **Low latitudes** are latitudes extending north and south of the equator to 30° latitude.
> **Middle latitudes** are latitudes between the high and low latitudes.

Longitude—the distance in degrees east or west of the **prime meridian** (0° longitude). A **meridian of longitude** is an imaginary line connecting points on the earth's surface having the same longitude. Meridians of longitude meet at the poles. They are numbered from 0° to 180° east and west of the prime meridian.

Map projection—the method by which the curved surface of the earth is represented on a flat map.

North Pole—the point farthest north on the earth's surface (90° N). The **South Pole** is the point farthest south on the earth's surface (90° S).

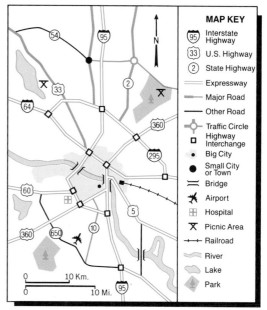

One of the most widely used kinds of maps is the road map. The symbols in the legend make the map easier to understand. On this map, north is at the top. If you were traveling from north to south, you might orient the map by turning it upside down, so that its directions would coincide with directions on the ground.

Orienting a map—making the map's directions coincide with directions on the ground.

Scale—the ratio between distance on a map and distance on the area being mapped.

Sea level—the level that the ocean would reach if it were as still as the water in a pond. Height, or **elevation,** is always measured from sea level, which is the same all over the world. **Contour lines** connect places of equal elevation on a map.

Symbol—something that represents something else. Letters, drawings, lines, and color are used as symbols on maps. The map **legend,** or **key,** is the place on the map where the symbols are explained.

Tropic of Cancer—a line of latitude lying 23° 30′ north of the equator. The **Tropic of Capricorn** is a line of latitude lying 23° 30′ south of the equator.

The globe on the left has been divided at the equator (0° latitude) into two equal halves—the Northern and Southern hemispheres. The globe on the right has been divided in half at the prime meridian (0° longitude) into the Eastern and Western hemispheres.

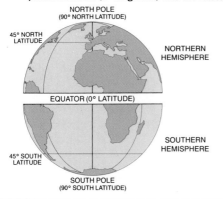

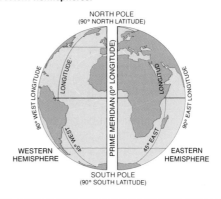

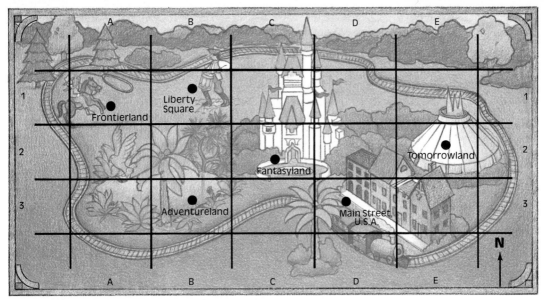

A map grid makes it easier for you to locate places on the map. To find Fantasyland on this map of the Magic Kingdom in Walt Disney World, follow section C to where it crosses section 2. Where on the map would you tell someone to look for Tomorrowland?

longitude. All latitude-longitude grid lines are circles or parts of circles and are shown in degrees (°).

Why do map makers need two sets of lines? Giving location only in latitude would be like telling people that you lived on Main Street instead of telling them that you lived at the corner of Main Street and Second Avenue. A place at 30 degrees north latitude (usually written 30° N) could be in Spain or China, in the middle of the Atlantic or Pacific oceans, or even near New Orleans, Louisiana. But any place on earth can be located exactly if you know both its latitude and its longitude.

There are other kinds of map grids that help you locate places. Many maps have a series of letters beginning with ''A'' running across the top and bottom of the map, and a series of numbers beginning with ''1'' running along the right and left margins. To find a place located at A-3 in the **map index** (the list of place names on the map), you just look in the box formed where sections A and 3 cross each other.

Finding Direction

Another thing maps tell us is direction. On most modern maps, north is at the top of the map. But ''north'' and ''up'' are not the same. ''Up'' is away from the surface of the earth. ''North'' is toward the North Pole. If you face north, east will be to your right, west will be to your left, and south will be behind you.

It is easy to find north on a globe—just look for the North Pole. On a flat map an arrow or

compass rose will tell you which way north is. If you are drawing a map of your town and want to add a compass rose, use a compass—holding it flat—to find north. Many places have features oriented to direction—for example, a city may have a North First Street or an East Meadow Drive.

A map can show direction and distance. If you look at the compass rose, you will be able to tell that the cabin is north of the picnic grounds. Use the map scale and a ruler to find out how far north of the picnic grounds the cabin is. Compare this map's scale to the scale on the map of Chad on the facing page. Which map shows a larger area on the ground?

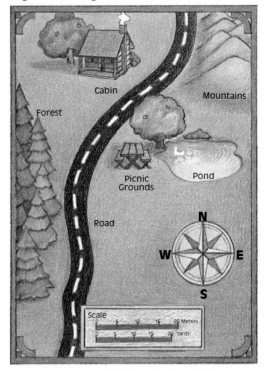

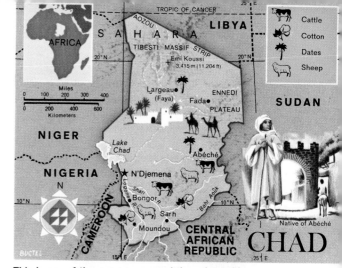

This is one of the many maps used throughout this encyclopedia. Why do you think the tiny map of Africa inserted in the corner is called a locator map? The symbols in the map legend represent the chief products of Chad. Most of these symbols are in southern Chad. Northern Chad, in the Sahara, receives very little rainfall. Where do you think most Chadians live? Why?

Finding Distance

Maps can do more than tell us where and which way. They can also tell us how far. Because areas being mapped are usually hundreds or thousands of times larger than the map itself, cartographers had to find a way to describe the relationship between the map and the area being mapped. So they let a small length on the map represent a large one on the ground. This relationship is called **scale.**

Expressions of scale can be written in several ways. The most common expression of scale on road maps and maps in textbooks or encyclopedias is the **graphic,** or bar, **scale.** This is a line that is subdivided to show distance on the area being mapped. To find the distance between two cities on a map with a graphic scale, mark the distance between the two places on the edge of a piece of paper or on a ruler. Place the paper or ruler along the graphic scale and read the distance. If you want to measure distances along waterways or other curved features, use a piece of string.

A **verbal scale** gives the relationship between the map and the ground in simple English. It might read, ''1 centimeter equals 100 kilometers'' (''1 inch equals 160 miles'').

Cartographers can show elevation on a flat piece of paper by using contour lines to link places of equal elevation. Contour maps are often used to show ocean depths as well as the height of land above sea level. This contour map includes a side view of the mountain being mapped so that you can see the relationship between the contour lines and the area being mapped.

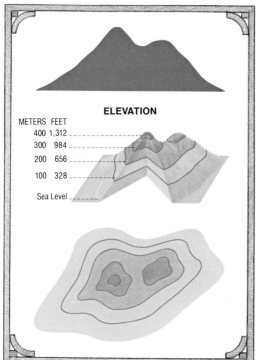

Another scale often used on flat maps is a **representative fraction (RF)** or ratio. This states the relationship between a unit of measurement on the map and the same unit of measurement on the area being mapped. Thus 1/10,000 or 1:10,000 means that 1 centimeter, inch, or other unit on the map represents 10,000 centimeters, inches, or other units on the area being mapped. With an RF scale it does not matter what system of measurement is being used. The larger the second number in the RF, the smaller the scale. The smaller the second number, the larger the scale will be. You can convert a graphic or verbal scale into an RF by multiplying the number of kilometers per centimeter by 100,000 (the number of centimeters in a kilometer) or the number of miles per inch by 63,360 (the number of inches in a mile).

There is another way to find approximate distances between points north and south of each other. Each degree of latitude equals about 111 kilometers (69 miles). If you find the difference in degrees of latitude between two north-south points and multiply it by 111 (or 69), you will get an approximate distance. This method will not work with east-west distances, because meridians of longitude are not the same distance apart along their entire length.

Distances over large areas are measured by **great circles** rather than straight lines. A great circle divides the globe into two equal halves.

The **equator** is a great circle. It divides the earth into the **Northern Hemisphere** and the **Southern Hemisphere.** Any meridian when joined with its opposite is also a great circle. The **prime meridian** (0° longitude) forms a great circle when linked with the 180th meridian. This great circle divides the globe into the **Eastern and Western hemispheres.**

Stretch a string between New York City and Moscow on a flat map and figure the distance between the two cities. Next, take a globe and turn it until both cities lie on the **horizon ring** (the ring going around the globe or from pole to pole). If you position one of the cities at the zero mark on the horizon ring, you can read the distance between the cities. Compare the distance you calculated on the flat map and the distance on the great circle route. Can you see why navigators use great circles to find the shortest distance between two points?

Using Maps to Find Time

Meridians of longitude can be used to tell time at any place in the world. The earth rotates from west to east at the rate of 15 degrees of longitude an hour (360 degrees in 24 hours). The time 15 degrees west of a point is 1 hour earlier; 15 degrees east it is 1 hour later. Thus, when it is 6 P.M. on the East Coast of the United States, it is only 3 P.M. on the West Coast. There has to be some place on the globe for an old calendar day to end and a new one to begin. This place is the international date line, a line roughly following the 180th meridian. If you cross the international date line heading west, "today" becomes "tomorrow." If you cross the line heading east, "today" becomes "yesterday."

Using Map Symbols

Relief or **physical maps** show natural features, such as mountains, oceans, rivers, and islands. **Cultural maps** include people-made features, such as political boundaries, highways, towns, oil wells, and dams. Cartographers often use **symbols** to stand for various features on a map. Map symbols often look like what they represent. The outline of an airplane, for example, may be used to locate airports. Colors, lettering, and lines are also used as symbols. Water, for example, is almost always blue.

Symbols and other information to help you understand the map are usually placed in a box called the **map legend,** or **key.** Since not all maps use the same symbols, it is important to refer to the map legend when using a map.

Physical relief features, such as mountains, hills, and valleys, are among the hardest things to show on a map. This is because they must be shown from above, rather than from ground level. Cartographers deal with this problem by using **contour lines** to show elevation above sea level. The contour lines link points with the same elevation. Color and shading are also used to show elevation.

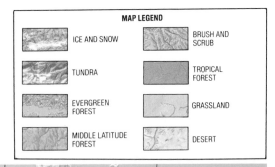

MAP INDEX	
Barranquilla	B-1
Bogotá	B-2
Caracas	C-1
Cartagena	B-1
Maracaibo	B-1
Medellín	B-2
Panama City	B-2
Puerto Rico	C-1

This is part of a physical-cultural map of South America. It shows both natural features of the land and cultural features such as political boundaries and cities. The map legend will help you identify different kinds of vegetation in the region. Use the grid and the map index to find Bogotá and Barranquilla. What direction would you travel to get from Bogotá to Barranquilla? How far would you travel?

MAP LEGEND

ICE AND SNOW

TUNDRA

EVERGREEN FOREST

MIDDLE LATITUDE FOREST

BRUSH AND SCRUB

TROPICAL FOREST

GRASSLAND

DESERT

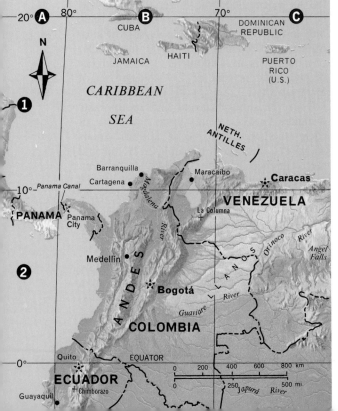

MAP PROJECTIONS

It is impossible to show the surface of the round earth accurately on a flat map. Some parts of the area being mapped will always be distorted (changed in size or shape) or broken apart as they are flattened. The smaller the area being mapped, the less distortion there will be. A city, for example, can be shown on a flat map with no apparent distortion. But distortion is a major problem on flat maps of large areas.

In map making, cartographers project the geographic grid of the round earth onto a flat piece of paper. They generally use mathematical formulas to determine the arrangement and spacing of the lines of latitude and longitude on which the flat map will be drawn. There are many kinds of map projections. Each was invented to keep relatively unchanged some particular property or properties of the round earth, such as distance, area, shape, or direction. The cartographer chooses a projection that will most accurately present the information needed by the people who will be using the map.

Cylindrical Projections. Imagine a cylinder of thin paper enclosing a transparent globe. A light source inside the globe projects the latitude-longitude grid and the continents onto the cylinder. This projection stretches the areas of the land masses toward the top and bottom of the map, although shapes remain true. Compare the sizes and shapes of Greenland and Africa on the Mercator projection below and on a globe. What does this tell you about distortion in a Mercator projection? The Mercator projection was invented by the great Flemish map maker Gerhard Mercator in 1569. It is still useful to navigators because it shows the true direction between any two points.

Conic Projections. Imagine a paper dunce cap (cone) placed over the Northern Hemisphere of a transparent globe. A light in the middle of the globe projects the grid and land features of the hemisphere onto the cone. At the point where the cone touches the globe, distance and direction and shape are true. This kind of projection works well for maps of countries. (A cartographer could make a fairly accurate map of the United States from the conic projection below.) But it is not appropriate for world maps because shapes and sizes away from the point where the cone touches the globe are badly distorted. **Polyconic projections** combine many conic projections, each touching the earth's surface at a different point.

Plane Projections. This time, imagine that a light is projected onto a piece of paper touching the globe at only one point. The point at which the globe and the paper touch is often the North or South pole, but it could be anywhere. Plane projections emphasizing the round shape of the earth are popular for mapping hemispheres. But shapes and sizes are greatly distorted away from the center. The azimuthal equidistant projection below is often used by pilots flying great circle routes over the North Pole. Every point is the correct distance and direction from the center.

Some Other Projections. Interrupted projections like the one below can show the whole world. Land areas are usually accurate, but water areas are broken apart. **Oval projections** like the mollweide projection below can show the whole world without interruption. Area and distance are true, but shape and direction are badly distorted toward the outer edges of the map.

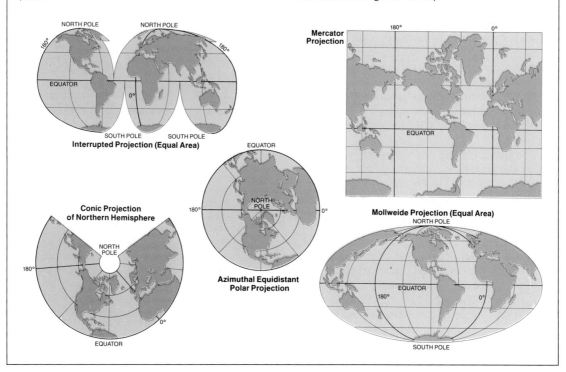

Interrupted Projection (Equal Area)

Conic Projection of Northern Hemisphere

Azimuthal Equidistant Polar Projection

Mercator Projection

Mollweide Projection (Equal Area)

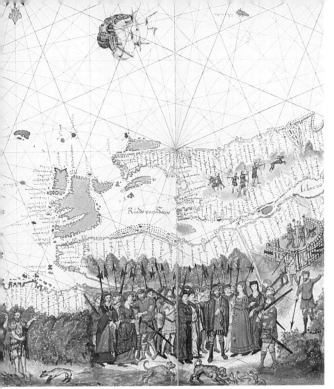

The work of a French map maker of the mid-1500's, this map shows a portion of the northeast coast of Canada as described by explorer Jacques Cartier.

▶A HISTORY OF MAP MAKING

Civilizations throughout history have made and used maps. The oldest surviving maps date back to Babylonian times, more than 4,000 years ago. The ancient Greek geographers, including Herodotus, Pytheas, Eratosthenes, Hipparchus, and Strabo, are recognized as the founders of scientific cartography. Claudius Ptolemy, who lived in the second century A.D., is perhaps the most famous Greek geographer. He explained some of the basic principles of map making in his *Geography*. This work included a number of maps, directions for making a simple projection, and the latitude and longitude for many places in the world.

The Romans used maps to wage war, build roads and aqueducts, and administer their conquered provinces. They were not interested in mathematics, or in how maps were made. After the fall of the Roman Empire, European maps were made mostly in monasteries. Maps usually showed the Holy Land at the center of the world. Scientific cartography during this period was preserved and advanced chiefly by Islamic scholars. The Chinese also made many maps. The oldest printed Chinese map (1155) was made about 300 years before the first map was printed in Europe.

The Age of Exploration and Discovery (1470–1700) increased people's knowledge of the world and led to great advances in cartography. The oldest existing globe (1492) was the work of the German merchant and navigator Martin Behaim. The first map to use the name America was made 15 years later by another German, Martin Waldseemüller. In 1570 the Flemish publisher Abraham Ortelius reproduced many maps of the same size and bound them into the first modern atlas, *Theatrum Orbis Terrarum*. But the term **atlas** did not come to be used for a bound volume of maps until after Gerhard Mercator published his book of maps entitled *Atlas* in 1595.

European explorers and navigators made and used sailing charts. But little attention was given to mapping the inland areas of the continents until the 1700's, when all sorts of commercial and military activities created a great demand for accurate maps. Elaborately decorated atlases were published in Belgium and the Netherlands. France became the leading center of scientific cartography. A new tech-

---

BE YOUR OWN MAP MAKER

Let's explore the nature of contours by making and mapping a mountain. You will need a waterproof container, a large piece of modeling clay, and an old ballpoint pen. Set aside a small piece of the clay. Use the rest to form a make-believe mountain in the shape of an irregular cone. Place the mountain in the container. Put the small piece of clay on the bottom of the container and press the zero end of the ruler into it so that the ruler stands upright. Pour water into the container until it reaches the 2.5 centimeter (1 inch) mark on the ruler. With the pen, draw a line around the mountain where the water touches it. Continue to add water and draw contour lines at 2.5-centimeter (1-inch) intervals until the water covers the mountain. Remove the mountain from the container and look at it from above. The lines you have drawn mark off the contours.

To make a map of your mountain, use a fine wire or a piece of fishing line to cut apart the contour intervals. Cut through each contour line, beginning with the highest one, until all the contour intervals have been removed from the mountain.

Place the lowest contour interval on a heavy piece of paper and trace around its base. Remove the clay interval and set it aside. Place the next higher interval on the paper, positioning it correctly within the first interval's outline. After you have traced around it, place it on top of the clay base. Continue tracing around the clay intervals until you have rebuilt the mountain. When the mountain has been rebuilt, the contour map is complete. Compare the map and the mountain as viewed from above. Can you see why contour lines are a useful way to show relief on a flat map?

nique for measuring latitude and longitude enabled Jean Dominique Cassini (1625–1712) to construct a much more accurate map of the world. Jean's son, Jean Jacques Cassini, began a survey of France in 1733. This was the first of many national surveys undertaken by various European countries during the late 1700's and 1800's. Gradually, surveying and mapping became a government responsibility.

As the United States expanded westward, so many facts needed recording on official documents and verification on official maps that cartographic activity became primarily government sponsored. The U.S. Geological Survey, founded in 1879, began a national mapping program that continues to this day.

Ptolemy and Mercator would be amazed by our maps. Modern cartographers, assisted by computers, remote sensing devices, and satellite photographs, can even make maps of the moon, Mars, and the ocean depths.

MICHAEL L. HAWKINS
University of Georgia

See also CLIMATE; EQUATOR; GEOGRAPHY; INTERNATIONAL DATE LINE; LATITUDE AND LONGITUDE; TIME.

MARAT, JEAN PAUL. See FRENCH REVOLUTION (Profiles).
MARBLE. See ROCKS (Metamorphic Rock).

MARBLES

Marbles is a game that is played all over the world. The history of the game goes back to the ancient civilizations of the Nile Valley and the Tigris and Euphrates valleys. Small balls of clay, flint, and bone have been found in the tombs of pharaohs and in caves in Europe dating to prehistoric times. Statues from the pre-Christian era show children playing at "knucklebones," which may have been an early marbles game. (Children in Iran still use sheep's knucklebones for marbles in a game called *ashog*.) The ancient Indian peoples of North America played marbles.

Marbles are mentioned in the writings of the Roman poet Ovid, and historians believe that Emperor Augustus played marbles. As long ago as the 1500's, marbles, or "Taws," was played in England. The game spread to America, and it is known that George Washington and Thomas Jefferson were marbles players. Abraham Lincoln was expert at a marbles game called "Old Bowler."

A Circle Game. Many marbles games are played in a circle. One of these, "Ringer," is perhaps the most famous. Thirteen marbles are placed in the shape of a cross in the center of a circle 10 feet (3 meters) in diameter. The surface should be hard and level so that shooters can aim accurately. The players try to knock marbles out of the circle by shooting at them—with a special shooting marble—from the edge of the circle. The winner is the first player to knock seven marbles out of the circle. To shoot, a player must "knuckle down," which means that the shooting hand must be turned so that four knuckles rest on the ground. The marble is held in the curved index finger and propelled by the thumb.

Pot, or Hole, Games. "Pot," or "Hole," games are somewhat like miniature golf. The object is to get your shooter into the hole and to knock your opponent's shooter out. If you knock a marble out, you win it. Games can either be played just for fun or for "keepsies." In "keepsies," all marbles won are kept by the winner.

FRED FERRETTI
Author, *The Great American Marble Book*

Marbles are smooth and perfectly round. They may be as small as peas or as large as golf balls. Glassies—glass marbles—may be clear or opaque. A purie is clear (pure) glass, such as the gold marble in the left corner. To the right of the gold purie is a blue aggie. Aggies are made of agate, marble, or limestone.

March

March was originally the first month of the year in the Roman calendar. The Romans named the month after Mars, the god of war. Later March became the third month.

Place in year: 3rd month.
Number of days: 31.
Flowers: Jonquil and daffodil.
Birthstone: Bloodstone or aquamarine.
Zodiac signs: Pisces, the Fishes (February 19–March 20), and Aries, the Ram (March 21–April 19).

1
- **Frédéric Chopin** born 1810
- U.S. Articles of Confederation ratified, 1781
- Ohio became the 17th state, 1803
- Nebraska became the 37th state, 1867

2
- **Samuel Houston** born 1793
- **Pope Leo XIII** born 1810
- **Pope Pius XII** born 1876
- **Dr. Seuss (Theodor Geisel)** born 1904
- **Mikhail Gorbachev** born 1931
- Texas declared its independence from Mexico, 1836
- First round-the-world nonstop airline flight successfully completed, 1949

3
- **Alexander Graham Bell** born 1847
- Missouri Compromise passed, 1820
- Massachusetts became first state to pass child labor laws regulating work hours, 1842
- Florida became the 27th state, 1845
- "The Star Spangled Banner" officially declared the national anthem of the U.S., 1931
- Feast of Dolls (Hina-Matsuri) in Japan
- Independence Day in Morocco

4
- William Penn received the charter to Pennsylvania, 1681
- U. S. Constitution went into effect, 1789
- Vermont became the 14th state, 1791
- Frances Perkins became first woman to be appointed to a U.S. presidential Cabinet, 1933

5
- Redcoats shot at a mob in the Boston Massacre, 1770
- Independence Day in Equatorial Guinea

6
- **Michelangelo** born 1475
- **Elizabeth Barrett Browning** born 1806
- Antonio Santa Anna, Mexican general, captured the Alamo, 1836
- Independence Day in Ghana

7
- **Luther Burbank** born 1849
- **Tomáš Masaryk** born 1850
- **Piet Mondrian** born 1872
- U.S. Congress ratified first treaty with a South American country, Republic of Colombia, 1825
- Alexander Graham Bell patented the telephone, 1876

8
- **Oliver Wendell Holmes, Jr.,** born 1841
- **Kenneth Grahame** born 1859

9
- The *Merrimack* fought the *Monitor* in the U.S. Civil War, 1862

10
- First paper money issued by the U.S., 1862

12
- **William Lyon Mackenzie** born 1795
- Juliette Low founded the organization that became the Girl Scouts of the U.S.A., Savannah, Georgia, 1912
- National holiday in Mauritius

13
- **Joseph Priestley** born 1733

14
- **Albert Einstein** born 1879
- Eli Whitney patented the cotton gin, 1794

15
- **Andrew Jackson** born 1767
- Julius Caesar assassinated, 44 B.C.
- Maine became the 23rd state, 1820

16
- **James Madison** born 1751
- U.S. Military Academy founded at West Point, New York, 1802
- U.S. Marines won major victory at Iwo Jima during World War II, 1945

17
- **Kate Greenaway** born 1846
- **Bobby Jones, Jr.,** born 1902
- *St. Patrick's Day* in Ireland and the U.S.

18
- **John C. Calhoun** born 1782
- **Grover Cleveland** born 1837
- Plans announced for formation of NATO, 1949

19
- **David Livingstone** born 1813
- **William Jennings Bryan** born 1860

20
- **Henrik Ibsen** born 1828
- **Martin Brian Mulroney** born 1939

21
- **Johann Sebastian Bach** born 1685
- **Benito Juárez** born 1806
- Vernal equinox, in which day and night are each just 12 hours long all over the world

22
- **Anthony van Dyck** born 1599
- Massacre of settlers in Jamestown, Virginia, 1622

23
- Patrick Henry delivered famous speech in which he declared "Give me liberty or give me death," 1775
- National holiday in Pakistan

25
- **Arturo Toscanini** born 1867
- **Béla Bartók** born 1881
- British Parliament abolished slave trade, 1807
- Independence Day in Greece

26
- **Benjamin Thompson** born 1753
- **Robert Frost** born 1874

- **Tennessee Williams** born 1911
- First savings bank of the U.S. chartered, in New York City, 1819
- Independence Day in Bangladesh

28
- Most serious accident in nuclear power industry's history, Three Mile Island, Pennsylvania, 1979

29
- **John Tyler** born 1790

30
- **Francisco Goya** born 1746
- **Vincent van Gogh** born 1853
- U.S. agreed to purchase Alaska from Russia for $7,200,000, 1867
- Fifteenth Amendment to U.S. Constitution, stating that a person cannot be denied the right to vote because of race or color, ratified, 1870

31
- **René Descartes** born 1596
- **Joseph Haydn** born 1732
- Commodore Matthew C. Perry signed treaty between the U.S. and Japan, 1854
- U.S. acquired the Virgin Islands from Denmark, 1917
- Daylight Saving Time introduced in the U.S., 1918
- Newfoundland became the 10th province of Canada, 1949
- National holiday in Malta

Holidays that may occur in either March or February: *Shrove Tuesday,* or *Mardi Gras; Ash Wednesday; Purim.* Holidays that may occur in either March or April: *Palm Sunday; Easter; Passover.*

The calendar listing identifies people who were born on the indicated day in boldface type, **like this.** You will find a biography of each of these birthday people in *The New Book of Knowledge.* In addition to citing some historical events and historical firsts, the calendar also lists the holidays and some of the festivals celebrated in the United States. These holidays are printed in italic type, *like this.* See the article HOLIDAYS for more information.

Many holidays and festivals of nations around the world are included in the calendar as well. When the term "national holiday" is used, it means that the nation celebrates an important patriotic event on that day—in most cases the winning of independence. Consult *The New Book of Knowledge* article on the individual nation for further information on its national holiday.

Marconi is shown at age 22 with his wireless receiver, now known as the radio. Several years later, Marconi sent the first radio message across the Atlantic Ocean.

MARCONI, GUGLIELMO (1874–1937)

Guglielmo Marconi, the inventor of wireless telegraphy, was born in Bologna, Italy, on April 25, 1874. He was the son of a successful Italian businessman. His mother was Irish. He was not a strong child and was also very shy, so his parents decided to have him educated at home by private teachers instead of sending him to school.

Guglielmo spent a great deal of his free time reading in the library of the Marconi home. The library had a good collection of science books. Almost as soon as Guglielmo could read, he began to read these books.

By the time he was 12 years old, Guglielmo was working with wires and batteries in an attic workshop he had set up. Then, when he was about 16 years old, he began to study electricity under the guidance of a physics professor. But he never became a regular student at any university.

In the summer of 1894, while on vacation, Marconi read a magazine article about the work of a German scientist, Heinrich Hertz, who had died earlier that year. Hertz had produced certain kinds of electric waves by means of electric sparks. They were called Hertzian waves. (They are now called radio waves.)

Marconi's imagination was fired by what he had read. He thought it might be possible to use these radio waves to send wireless dot-and-dash messages like those used in the telegraph. When he returned from his vacation, Marconi began to experiment in order to work out his ideas. His father encouraged him in this and set aside a part of the garden for these experiments. Within a year, Marconi was successfully sending weak dot-and-dash signals to a receiver across the garden. Before long he was able to send stronger signals that could be received by an assistant 8 miles (13 kilometers) away.

Marconi then recognized that he had a useful invention. He also thought that its greatest use would probably be in communicating with ships at sea. With his father's financial help, he went to England, one of the world's great shipping countries, to perfect his wireless. He felt his invention would be readily received there.

By 1899, Marconi was able to send messages across the English Channel to France, about 28 miles (45 kilometers) away. But his great dream was to set up wireless communication across the Atlantic Ocean. To do this he set sail for America and, on December 6, 1901, landed in Newfoundland. Assistants remained behind to operate a powerful transmitter on the coast of England.

On December 12, 1901, Marconi received a signal in dot-and-dash code sent from the station in England, 3,000 miles (4,800 kilometers) away. Wireless communication across the Atlantic was a success. And within a few years the usefulness of wireless communication from ships at sea was also proved.

Many countries now showered honors on Marconi. He became a wealthy man. In 1909 he won the Nobel Prize in physics for his invention of the wireless.

Marconi continued improving his wireless, which had come to be called radio. During World War I, he became commander of the Italian Army's wireless service. By means of radio, his own invention, the world learned of his death in Rome on July 20, 1937.

DAVID C. KNIGHT
Author, science books for children

MARCO POLO. See POLO, MARCO.

MARCOS, FERDINAND. See PHILIPPINES (History).

MARDI GRAS. See CARNIVALS.

MARGUERITE OF NAVARRE. See RENAISSANCE (Profiles).

MARIA THERESA. See HABSBURGS.

MARIE ANTOINETTE (1755–1793)

Marie Antoinette was the beautiful and willful queen of France who was executed during the French Revolution. Born in Vienna on November 2, 1755, she was the daughter of Maria Theresa and Francis I of Austria. At 15 she married Louis, the dauphin, or crown prince, of France. When his grandfather died in 1774, the prince became King Louis XVI. Marie Antoinette became the queen.

The queen was a lighthearted woman who wastefully spent fortunes, not unusual for royalty of the day. But unemployment and hunger were widespread among the lower classes, and they blamed the queen for their miseries. They could easily believe the legend that when told that the people had no bread, she quipped, "Then let them eat cake."

In 1789 the French Revolution began, and there was widespread rioting. The people stormed the palace. The king and queen were imprisoned in August 1792. On January 21, 1793, the king was beheaded.

The following October at the height of the Reign of Terror, Marie Antoinette was charged with treason and brought before a revolutionary tribunal. She was treated like a commoner. Throughout her trial the queen remained serene and dignified. She calmly heard her sentence pronounced. On October 16, 1793, she went to her death on the guillotine.

OWEN CONNELLY
University of South Carolina

See also FRENCH REVOLUTION.

MARIJUANA. See DRUG ABUSE.

MARINES. See UNITED STATES, ARMED FORCES OF THE.

MARION, FRANCIS (1732–1795)

One of the most successful officers of the Revolutionary War was a South Carolinian named Francis Marion. Although he had no military training, he became an elusive and skillful soldier. He became known for using the protection of rivers, hills, and swamps to evade the enemy. An angry British officer once exclaimed, "But as for this damned old fox, the Devil himself could not catch him!" The nickname stuck—Marion became known as the Swamp Fox.

Francis Marion was born in 1732 in Berkeley County, South Carolina. Before the war began he fought with the state militia against the Indians. He also served one term in the South Carolina Provincial Congress.

When the Revolutionary War began in 1775, Marion was made a captain in the Continental Army. His leadership qualities were quickly recognized. In 1776, after successfully defending Charleston against British attack, he was made a general. In May 1780, Marion and his followers, who were called Marion's Brigade, evacuated Charleston before the British took the city. Thereafter, they used guerrilla tactics of surprise attack and rapid movement to fight the enemy.

As fighting slowed between 1782 and 1783, General Marion worked to heal the wounds of war. After the war he was twice elected to the state legislature. He was also a delegate to the state's Constitutional Convention in 1790.

On April 20, 1786, at the age of 53, Marion married his cousin, Mary Esther Videau. They lived happily at their plantation at Pond Bluff, near Charleston, until his death on February 27, 1795.

JOSEPH T. STUKES
Francis Marion College

MARIONETTES. See PUPPETS AND MARIONETTES.

MARIS, ROGER. See NORTH DAKOTA (Famous People).

MARKETING. See SALES AND MARKETING.

MARKHAM, EDWIN. See OREGON (Famous People).

MARLBOROUGH, DUKE OF (1650–1722)

John Churchill, the 1st duke of Marlborough, was one of the most outstanding generals of his age. He was born in Devon, England, on May 26, 1650, and commissioned as an ensign at the age of 17. In 1678, Churchill married the vivacious Sarah Jennings, the best friend of Princess (later Queen) Anne. In 1685, shortly after Anne's father succeeded the throne as James II, Churchill helped put down a rebellion that sought to overthrow the king and was promoted to major-general. But during the Glorious Revolution of 1688, Churchill deserted King James in favor of William III, whom he later served in the War of the Grand Alliance (1688–97) against France. For his services, Churchill was given the title earl of Marlborough.

When his wife's friend Anne became queen in 1702, Marlborough, as he was then called, was promoted to commander in chief and was made a duke. He reached the peak of his fame during the War of the Spanish Succession (1701–14), winning a brilliant series of battles against the French at Schellenberg and Blenheim (1704), Ramillies (1706), Oudenaarde (1708), and Malplaquet (1709). Blenheim Palace, near Oxford, was built as a tribute to his achievements.

Marlborough's career later suffered when his wife quarreled with the queen, and a new government, headed by the Tory Party, came to power. Accused of embezzlement, Marlborough was dismissed from his offices in 1711. He left the country, returning only when George I came to the throne in 1714. Although Marlborough was made a captain-general, he exercised little influence thereafter. Sir Winston Churchill, prime minister of Great Britain (1940–45 and 1951–55), was a direct descendant of the duke of Marlborough.

JEREMY BLACK
Author, *Eighteenth-Century Europe, 1700–89*

MARLOWE, CHRISTOPHER (1564–1593)

The great English poet and dramatist Christopher Marlowe was born in Canterbury, England, in February 1564, two months before William Shakespeare. Like Shakespeare, he grew up enjoying the advantages of a prosperous middle-class family.

He went on scholarship to the King's School in Canterbury, and from there to Corpus Christi College of Cambridge University. His Cambridge scholarship was for students preparing to enter the ministry. After receiving his M.A. in 1587, Marlowe decided against becoming a clergyman. Instead, he went to London, where he wrote plays and poetry and associated with other writers. Marlowe also became involved with men of questionable character and had several brushes with the law. He was fatally stabbed under mysterious circumstances at an inn in Deptford on May 30, 1593.

Marlowe's literary fame rests on a few plays that became very popular on the London stage. These include *Tamburlaine the Great*, parts I and II (1587), about a shepherd who becomes a ruthless conqueror; *The Jew of Malta* (1588), about a wealthy but wicked person who is finally killed by a device intended to trap his enemies; *Edward II* (1591–92), based on the life of an English king who was horribly assassinated; and *The Tragical History of the Life and Death of Dr. Faustus* (1592), about a learned man who obtains superhuman powers but in the end must surrender both his power and his soul to the devil.

Marlowe is famous for developing "the mighty line," the kind of unrhymed verse that Shakespeare and others adapted for their plays. An example is Faustus' greeting to Helen of Troy: "Was this the face that launched a thousand ships, / And burned the topless towers of Ilium?" His ever-popular plays are still performed today.

JAY L. HALIO
University of Delaware

MARQUETTE, JACQUES. See JOLLIET, LOUIS, AND JACQUES MARQUETTE.

MARRIAGE CUSTOMS. See WEDDING CUSTOMS AROUND THE WORLD.

MARS

If you could visit any object in the solar system, which one would you choose? Would you decide to travel to the Earth's airless moon, to desolate Mercury, or to the baking-hot surface of Venus? Or, would you choose Mars, a planet with orange sandy deserts, great canyons, magnificent volcanoes, and gleaming ice caps?

Mars is the fourth planet from the sun, and the first planet beyond the Earth. Although Mars is smaller than the Earth, it has more land area because it has no oceans, lakes, or streams.

Mars looks distinctly orange or red in color, which has earned it the nickname the Red Planet. The color led the ancient Romans to name the planet Mars, after their god of war. Mars actually gets its color from minerals that contain oxides of iron. Ordinary rust is an oxide of iron, and it is dark orange in color. If you were to go for a walk on Mars, you would see dark orange or brown boulders and drifts of fine orange sand.

Mars has a very thin atmosphere and, on average, the planet is much colder than Antarctica. The temperature at low latitudes during a summer day can occasionally reach 60°F (16°C) but falls to about –100°F (–73°C) at night. Near the Martian poles during the winter, the temperature can fall as low as –150°F (–101°C).

The Orbit of Mars

The orbit of Mars is more elliptical (oval shaped) than that of most of the other planets. Because of this, the distance from Mars to the sun varies throughout the Martian year. At its closest approach, called **perihelion**, Mars is 128.4 million miles (206.7 million kilometers) from the sun. When Mars is at its greatest distance from the sun, called **aphelion**, it is 154.8 million miles (249.2 million kilometers) away. Mars is farther from the sun than the Earth, so it travels more slowly in its orbit. One Martian year—the time Mars takes to orbit once around the sun—is 687 Earth days.

Because the Earth moves faster than Mars in its journey around the sun, the Earth catches up with and passes Mars about every two years. At these times the planets are said to be in **opposition**. When these planets are

This striking image of Mars shows the great rift canyon Valles Marineris; three huge volcanoes, which can be seen in the upper left; and what appear to be ancient riverbeds running north of the canyon.

closest to one another, Mars is 34.6 million miles (55.7 million kilometers) from Earth. However, the distance between Earth and Mars can vary greatly from one opposition to the next due to the elliptical orbit of Mars.

Rotation and Size of Mars

The turning of a planet on its axis is called **rotation**. The Earth rotates on its axis every 23 hours 56 minutes. Mars has a similar period of rotation—24 hours 37 minutes. Another similarity between the Earth and Mars is the tilt of the planet on its axis. The Earth is tilted 23.5 degrees; Mars is tilted 25.2 degrees. So, like the Earth, Mars has seasonal changes in temperature. Because of its longer period of revolution, however, seasons on Mars last longer than those on Earth.

Mars is only a little more than one-ninth the mass of the Earth, and its average density is less. The diameter of Mars is 4,200 miles (6,760 kilometers), a little more than one-half

The Composition of Mars

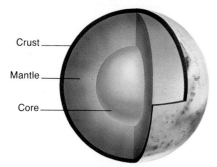

Crust

Mantle

Core

Mars

Position in the solar system	Fourth planet from the sun
Distance from the sun (average)	142,000,000 miles (228,000,000 kilometers)
Revolution around the sun	687 Earth days
Diameter	4,200 miles (6,760 kilometers) About ½ the diameter of Earth
Mass	642 quintillion tons About ⅛ the mass of Earth
Density	3.9 grams per cubic centimeter
Rotation on its axis	24 hours 37 minutes
Tilt of rotational axis	25.2°
Natural satellites known	2
Rings known	None
Surface	Desertlike, with sand and boulders
Atmosphere	Carbon dioxide
Temperature (average in mid-summer)	Ranges from –40°F (–40°C) to –121°F (–95°C)
Symbol	
In mythology	Mars, Roman god of war

that of the Earth. Primarily because of its smaller mass, the pull of gravity on Mars' surface is weaker than the pull of gravity on the Earth's surface. A weak magnetic field was first detected by the *Mars Global Surveyor* spacecraft shortly after it entered orbit around Mars in 1997.

The Martian Surface

The surface of the Earth's moon is covered with impact craters—the cup-shaped scars left when meteors and asteroids strike the surface—and so are the surfaces of Mercury and the moons of the outer planets. Astronomers expected that the surface of Mars would also be covered by craters. Instead,

they discovered that only about two-thirds of Mars is covered with them.

This tells astronomers that something may have removed the craters. On the Earth, wind and water erode craters, and sediments and lava from volcanic activity fill them. Much of the surface of the moon is still covered with craters because there is no wind or water and there is no longer any volcanic activity on the moon as there is on the Earth.

On areas of Mars where there are no craters, astronomers do see signs that once there may have been strong wind and water action on the planet that could have eroded them. There are so many physical features that look like dry streambeds, gullies, and channels that it appears as if streams and rivers once flowed on the surface.

Water on Mars. Under current conditions, Mars is too cold and its surface pressure is too low for liquid water to exist. To learn if liquid water ever existed there, several space probes have been sent to study the planet from orbit and on its surface.

The *Mars Pathfinder* landed on Mars in 1997 and together with its mobile rover *Sojourner* analyzed the chemistry of rocks and soil and studied the planet's atmosphere. The mission found strong indications that water may have flowed on Mars long ago.

In 2000, the *Mars Global Surveyor* in orbit around the planet photographed gullies apparently formed recently by flowing water.

Two years later, the *Mars Odyssey* orbiter analyzed gamma rays and neutrons emitted from the surface and detected the presence of hydrogen, the key component of water. This led to the conclusion that water did exist on Mars, but it lay frozen in several regions beneath the surface of the planet.

When the twin rovers *Spirit* and *Opportunity* landed on opposite sides of Mars in 2004, they found even more compelling evidence that liquid water existed on the planet long ago. This evidence includes the altered composition and distinct patterns of cracks in some rocks that are consistent with the appearance and physical properties of rocks on Earth that have come in contact with liquid water. To learn about the significance of water on Mars, see the Wonder Question "Is there life on Mars?" accompanying this article.

Volcanoes. When the *Mariner 9* spacecraft arrived at Mars in 1971, a big dust storm was in progress. The probe's cameras showed nothing but dust and four mysterious spots. As the storm subsided, scientists were surprised to learn that the spots were the tops of four giant volcanoes. The largest of these, Olympus Mons ("Mons" means "mountain"), is about 373 miles (600 kilometers) across and rises about 17 miles (27 kilometers) above the surrounding plain. In contrast, Mount Everest, the highest mountain on the Earth, is only about 5½ miles (9 kilometers) from base to peak.

Olympus Mons is a **shield volcano**—a volcano built up from successive eruptions of lava or lava flows. Geologists think that Olympus Mons took at least a billion years to grow and that it stopped erupting about a billion years ago.

Olympus Mons is located near the equator of Mars in a volcanic region called Tharsis. Any impact craters there have all been buried under vast flows of lava. Three other large shield volcanoes are in this region: Ascraeus Mons, Pavonis Mons, and Arsia Mons.

The surface of the Tharsis region tells geologists that the crust of Mars does not move, as the Earth's crust does. (The movement of the Earth's crust is called continental drift.) To form Tharsis, molten rock flowed from inside Mars for billions of years, always coming out in the same region. For this reason the Tharsis volcanoes are larger than any volcanoes on Earth. However, there are more volcanoes on Earth than there are on Mars. Mars has probably not been geologically active for a long time.

Gigantic Canyon. East of Tharsis is a canyon so big—it stretches over 2,500 miles (4,000 kilometers)—that the Grand Canyon and the Colorado River would be lost inside of it. From the rim of this vast canyon, called Valles Marineris, there is a drop of up to 6 miles (10 kilometers) to the floor, and the canyon is 100 miles (160 kilometers) wide in

Among the prominent features of Mars are its volcanoes. Olympus Mons (*left*) is one of the largest known volcanoes in the solar system.

Mars has many features on its surface (*right*) that appear to have been formed by the flowing of liquid water sometime in the planet's past.

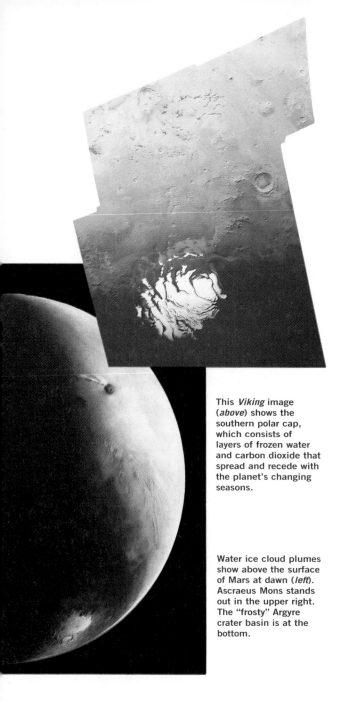

This *Viking* image (*above*) shows the southern polar cap, which consists of layers of frozen water and carbon dioxide that spread and recede with the planet's changing seasons.

Water ice cloud plumes show above the surface of Mars at dawn (*left*). Ascraeus Mons stands out in the upper right. The "frosty" Argyre crater basin is at the bottom.

During the Martian summers, the polar caps shrink. However, the ice does not melt; because of the planet's low surface pressure, the ice changes directly into a vapor and dissipates into the atmosphere. In the winter, water and carbon dioxide freeze and enlarge the polar caps. The ice near the edges of the polar caps is probably quite thin. Ice near the centers never evaporates, so the ice could be quite thick. The reason astronomers think there could be such thick ice is that pictures of the polar caps show dozens of layers of ice. If each layer were 10 to 15 feet (3 to 5 meters) thick, the total thickness would be hundreds of feet.

However, there is not enough water in the polar caps to cause much erosion if it became liquid. If all the carbon dioxide and water in the polar caps melted, Mars would still be drier than the driest desert on Earth.

Atmosphere and Weather

The atmosphere of Mars at its surface is 95.3 percent carbon dioxide, 2.7 percent nitrogen, and 1.6 percent argon. There is only a very small amount of oxygen present.

As the summer season approaches, Mars sometimes has violent dust storms. Sunshine warms the ground, and winds rise, whipping fine yellow dust from the ground. Because sunlight warms dusty air more than clear air, the winds grow stronger and the dust storms spread. In less than a week, the atmosphere can change from clear to dusty. Once a dust storm has started, it takes weeks or months before the air is clear again. Sometimes these dust storms can engulf much of the planet, and when seen from Earth, Mars appears as an almost featureless disk.

There is very little water vapor in the Martian atmosphere—it is drier than the driest of the Earth's deserts. Even though Mars is extremely dry, however, water sometimes plays a role in its weather. On windy days, thin ice clouds form on the downwind side of the big volcanoes in Tharsis. Deep down in the canyons on chilly mornings, the air sometimes becomes foggy.

After the *Viking 1* and *Viking 2* space probes landed on the surface of Mars in 1976, their cameras took pictures of the landscape for two years. Some of the images taken during the Martian winter showed white frost on the ground.

places. Scientists think Valles Marineris is a rift valley, a huge crack that formed where the crust of Mars pulled apart. Along the walls of the canyon are channels apparently cut by flowing water long ago.

Polar Caps. The polar regions of Mars are quite cold. The ice at the poles consists of frozen water and carbon dioxide. Carbon dioxide freezes at a temperature of $-195°F$ ($-126°C$).

Is there life on Mars?

Scientists, storytellers, and many others have pondered this question for centuries. Today we know that the Red Planet is not home to a vast civilization of "Martians." But just because Mars has no exotic cities bustling with aliens or crumbling ruins filled with artifacts from a long-extinct culture, it does not mean some form of life has never existed on the planet.

As we have seen on Earth, life can assume many shapes and sizes. But no matter what form it takes, every known kind of life needs water to survive. This is why space probes to Mars have increasingly focused on searching for evidence of this precious substance on the planet's surface.

Although frozen water has been found on Mars, as well as strong evidence for the past existence of water in liquid form, no sign of life has been discovered. But only a tiny fraction of the planet has been explored.

Evidence of Martian life may have even been found here on Earth. In 1996, a team of scientists

This meteorite from Mars was found in Antarctica and contained formations that appeared to be fossilized bacteria (*inset*).

announced they had detected what appeared to be fossilized bacteria and other signs of life in an ancient Martian meteorite that had crashed in Antarctica. Other researchers were skeptical of this conclusion, arguing that the meteorite contained no signs of life. The debate will no doubt continue until more convincing evidence can be found in samples of Martian soil or rock brought back to Earth by future space probes.

Satellites

Two small satellites, or moons, orbit Mars. They are named for the two horses, Phobos ("fear") and Deimos ("terror"), that pulled the chariot of Ares, the god of war in Greek mythology. Phobos is the closer of the two to Mars. Its orbit is only 2,462 miles (3,964 kilometers) above the surface of Mars. It takes Phobos only 7½ hours to complete one orbit. In its longest dimension, Phobos measures 8½ miles (13.7 kilometers), and it is 6 miles (9.7 kilometers) wide in the middle. The surface of Phobos is

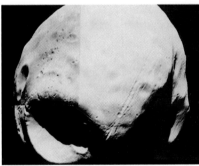

Phobos showing the Stickney crater.

covered with craters, and there are cracks in it. A large meteorite may have caused these cracks. Deimos is smaller than Phobos and orbits above Mars at a distance of 14,700 miles (23,667 kilometers). It is 5 miles (8 kilometers) long and 3½ miles (5.6 kilometers) wide. Deimos has a smoother surface than that of Phobos.

Phobos and Deimos are very dark. Astronomers believe that they are made of car-

bonaceous chondrite, which is a dark-colored mix of rock and tarlike compounds. Asteroids and meteorites sometimes contain carbonaceous material. Some astronomers suspect that Phobos and Deimos were once asteroids that strayed close to Mars and were captured by the planet's gravitational field.

If you were standing on the surface of Phobos, Mars would fill half of the sky above you. As you gazed toward the Red Planet, you would see the mighty volcano Olympus Mons and the vast canyon of Valles Marineris. Imagine what an adventure awaits the astronauts who will someday explore Mars.

RICHARD BERRY
Author, *Discover the Stars*
Reviewed by WILLIAM A. GUTSCH, JR.
President, The Challenger Center for Space
Science Education

See also ASTRONOMY; PLANETS; SATELLITES; SOLAR SYSTEM; SPACE PROBES.

MARSALIS, WYNTON. See JAZZ (Profiles).

MARSHALL, GEORGE C. (1880–1959)

George Catlett Marshall had two brilliant careers. As chief of staff of the U.S. Army during World War II (1941–45), he commanded the largest U.S. military force ever assembled. In peacetime, he served his country as a statesman. He was the only person ever to serve both as secretary of state (1947–49) and as secretary of defense (1950–51).

Marshall was born on December 31, 1880, in Uniontown, Pennsylvania. At the age of 16, he entered the Virginia Military Institute. He was commissioned a second lieutenant in 1902, the same year he married Elizabeth Carter Coles. After tours of duty in the United States and in the Philippines, Marshall studied and later taught at the Army Staff College.

During the United States' participation (1917–18) in World War I (1914–18), Marshall served in France as a staff officer and won recognition for his role in directing the St. Mihiel and Meuse-Argonne offensives. From 1919 to 1924 he was aide to General John J. Pershing in Washington, D.C. In 1930, three years after the death of his first wife, Marshall married Katherine Boyce Brown, a widow with three children.

In 1938, Marshall was promoted, first to assistant chief and later to deputy chief of staff. Then in 1939, the year World War II began in Europe, he was named chief of staff of the Army. Marshall, predicting that the United States would eventually become involved in the war, recommended military preparedness.

When the United States entered the war in December 1941, following the Japanese attack on Pearl Harbor, Marshall supervised all U.S. Army operations both in Europe and in the Pacific. He increased the size of the U.S. Army (which at that time included the Army Air Corps) from 200,000 to more than 8.5 million and helped train and supply the Allied troops. The British prime minister, Winston Churchill, called Marshall the "true organizer of victory." In 1944 he became the first officer to receive the new rank of five-star general of the Army. He retired from the service in 1945, at the end of the war.

In November 1945, President Harry S. Truman sent Marshall to China as his personal representative. There he was unsuccessful in helping to negotiate a settlement of the civil

George C. Marshall won the 1953 Nobel peace prize for the Marshall Plan, which revived Europe's economy after World War II.

war between Chinese Nationalist and Communist forces. Then in 1947, Truman named Marshall secretary of state. He was the first professional soldier to hold that post.

As the Cold War between the United States and the Soviet Union took shape, Marshall adopted a strong anti-Soviet, anti-Communist policy. He helped formulate the Truman Doctrine to aid nations that the Communists sought to influence.

The Marshall Plan

George Marshall was responsible for developing the Marshall Plan, which is also known as the European Recovery Program. The purpose of this plan was to provide economic and technical assistance to the war-torn nations of Europe and to curb the spread of communism there following World War II.

In 1948 the U.S. Congress established the Economic Cooperation Administration (ECA) to administer the Marshall Plan, and 16 nations in Western Europe formed the Organization for European Economic Cooperation (OEEC) to co-ordinate and distribute the funds. (The Soviet Union and other Communist European nations were invited to join the program, but they declined.) From 1948 to 1952 the participating countries received more than $13 billion in U.S. aid, including food, machinery, and other products.

In 1949, Marshall resigned as secretary of state to serve as president of the American Red Cross. The following year, during the Korean War, he was appointed secretary of defense, but he retired in 1951 due to ill health. He received the Nobel peace prize in 1953 for the success of the Marshall Plan. He died in Washington, D.C., on October 16, 1959, and was buried in Arlington National Cemetery.

Reviewed by FORREST C. POGUE
Author, *George C. Marshall*

MARSHALL, JOHN
(1755–1835)

The story of Chief Justice John Marshall is the story of how the Supreme Court truly became the third great branch of the United States Government. It is also the story of the United States Constitution. For in his 34 years as chief justice, Marshall gave a new, broader meaning to the Constitution, strengthening not only the Supreme 'Court but also the federal government itself.

John Marshall was born on September 24, 1755, in a log cabin near Germantown, on the Virginia frontier. He had almost no formal schooling, receiving most of his education from his father, Thomas Marshall, a planter. But the vigorous frontier life did much to develop young Marshall's independent, self-reliant character. During the Revolutionary War both father and son joined the patriot army. John Marshall's service in the Revolution had a great influence on his life and career. Years later, he said of this period: "I was confirmed in the habit of considering America as my country and Congress as my government." At that time most Americans felt greater loyalty to their own states than to the country as a whole.

Marshall studied law at the College of William and Mary in Virginia, and in 1780 he was admitted to the bar. Later he opened a law office in Richmond. In 1783 he married Marie Ambler. They had ten children.

As his law practice grew, Marshall rose to political prominence. He became Federalist Party leader in Virginia, and President Washington twice offered him important posts—as attorney general and as minister to France. Marshall refused both for financial reasons. In 1799 he was elected to Congress, serving until 1800, when President John Adams appointed him secretary of state. In 1801, Adams appointed him chief justice. Two months later, Marshall administered the oath of office to the new president, Thomas Jefferson. Jefferson, as leader of the Democratic-Republican Party, believed in the strict interpretation of the Constitution. Marshall's view was different. He believed that the Con-stitution was "intended to endure for ages to come" and must be "adapted to the various *crises* of human affairs."

Of Marshall's hundreds of decisions, only a few can be cited here. His first important case, and one of the most important in the history of the Court, was *Marbury* v. *Madison* (1803).

William Marbury was one of the Federalist "midnight" justices of the peace appointed by President Adams during the last days of his administration. Secretary of State James Madison, acting under President Jefferson's orders, refused to deliver Marbury's commission of appointment. Marbury then asked the Supreme Court to issue a writ forcing Madison to deliver it. In his decision, Marshall declared that Marbury was entitled to the writ, but he added that the Supreme Court could not issue it because the section of the law authorizing such a writ was unconstitutional.

Marbury did not get his appointment. But Marshall had firmly established the principle of **judicial review**, under which the Court could declare a law of Congress unconstitutional. Later, in *Fletcher* v. *Peck* (1810), Marshall ruled that the Court could also find a state law unconstitutional.

The most important of Marshall's decisions in establishing the supremacy of the federal government over a state's government in the event of a conflict was *McCulloch* v. *Maryland* (1819). James McCulloch, cashier of the Baltimore branch of the Bank of the United States, had refused to pay a tax levied by the state of Maryland. Maryland then sued him. Marshall first declared that the federal law by which Congress had created the bank was constitutional because it was within "the letter and spirit of the Constitution." He then ruled that no state could tax a federal agency.

John Marshall, who has been called the Great Chief Justice, died on July 6, 1835.

Reviewed by RICHARD B. MORRIS
Editor, *Encyclopedia of American History*

See also SUPREME COURT OF THE UNITED STATES.

MARSHALL, THOMAS R. See VICE PRESIDENCY OF THE UNITED STATES.

MARSHALL, THURGOOD. See MARYLAND (Famous People).

MARSHALL ISLANDS

The Republic of the Marshall Islands is a small nation situated in the northwestern Pacific Ocean. It consists of more than 1,200 small islands, most of them uninhabited. The islands are scattered over 750,000 square miles (1,942,500 square kilometers) of ocean. Politically, the Marshall Islands is an independent country in free association with the United States. Its capital is Majuro.

People. The Marshallese are Micronesians, like most of the other peoples of this part of the Pacific. (Micronesia means "small islands.") Their ancestors may have first arrived in the region from Asia about 2,000 years ago. The people speak Marshallese (Kajin Majol) and English. Most of the people are Christian, mainly Protestant. Nearly three-quarters of adults can read and write.

Land. The Marshall Islands consists of some 28 atolls (an atoll is a ring of coral encircling a lagoon) and 5 low coral islands. Each atoll is made up of many small islets—about 1,225 in all. The atolls and islands are divided into two roughly parallel chains—the Ratak (Sunrise) on the east and the Ralik (Sunset) on the west. Kwajalein, in the Ralik chain, is the largest atoll in the world. About half the population lives on Majuro atoll in

A Marshallese woman preparing coconuts.

the Ratak chain. The highest elevation, 34 feet (10 meters), is found on Likiep atoll.

The climate is tropical. Average annual temperature is about 80°F (27°C). Rainfall is heaviest in the south, where it reaches 150 inches (3,800 millimeters) or more a year.

Economy. The islets generally have poor soil, in which only coconut palms, pandanus (fruit-bearing trees), and breadfruit trees will grow well. Copra, or dried coconut meat, is the only important agricultural export. Very little food is grown locally. Income from tourism is low but increasing, and prospects for economic development are limited, except for fishing. As a result, the republic depends on food aid as well as financial assistance from the United States.

History and Government. Spanish navigators first sighted the islands in 1526. They were named for a British sea captain, John Marshall, who explored them in 1788. American whalers followed in the 1820's; missionaries arrived in 1857. The islands became a German protectorate in 1886. They were occupied by the Japanese from 1914, classified as a League of Nations mandate in 1920, and possessed by the Japanese military through the end of World War II (1939–45). During World War II, Kwajalein was the scene of bitter fighting between U.S. and Japanese forces. In 1947 the Marshalls were administered by the

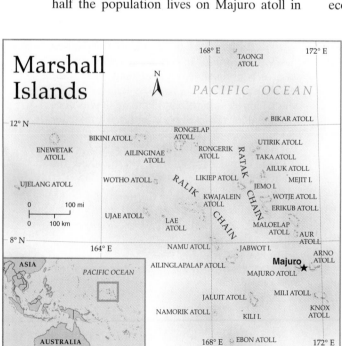

Marshall Islands

PACIFIC OCEAN

168° E
172° E

TAONGI ATOLL

BIKAR ATOLL

12° N

RONGELAP ATOLL

BIKINI ATOLL

UTIRIK ATOLL

ENEWETAK ATOLL

AILINGINAE ATOLL

RONGERIK ATOLL

TAKA ATOLL

AILUK ATOLL

UJELANG ATOLL

WOTHO ATOLL

LIKIEP ATOLL

MEJIT I.

JEMO I.

KWAJALEIN ATOLL

WOTJE ATOLL

ERIKUB ATOLL

UJAE ATOLL

LAE ATOLL

MALOELAP ATOLL

AUR ATOLL

8° N

164° E

NAMU ATOLL

JABWOT I.

ARNO ATOLL

ASIA

PACIFIC OCEAN

AILINGLAPALAP ATOLL

Majuro

MAJURO ATOLL

JALUIT ATOLL

MILI ATOLL

NAMORIK ATOLL

KNOX ATOLL

KILI I.

AUSTRALIA

168° E

EBON ATOLL

172° E

0 100 mi
0 100 km

RALIK CHAIN

RATAK CHAIN

United States as part of the United Nations Trust Territory of the Pacific Islands.

The United States began using Bikini atoll for atomic bomb testing in 1946, and in 1947 it started using Enewetak (or Eniwetok) for the same purpose. Many Marshallese were either permanently relocated from their homes or harmed by fallout from the atomic tests, and some compensation was paid them by the United States. Kwajalein has been leased for long-range missile tests since 1959.

The Trust Territory effectively ended when the Marshall Islands entered into a Compact of Free Association with the United States in 1986. Under its terms, citizens of the Marshall Islands receive visa-free entry into the United States in exchange for U.S. military access to the islands. Under the first compact agreement (1986–2001), the United States provided about $1 billion in payments and programs, including the rental of Kwajalein, nuclear testing compensation, and government funding. A 2003 compact agreement renewed the Kwajalein lease until 2066, and continues economic provisions through 2023.

The government includes a legislature, the Nitijela, made up of 33 members elected for four years. The Nitijela elects the president, who is the head of state and government. A

FACTS and figures

REPUBLIC OF THE MARSHALL ISLANDS is the official name of the country.

LOCATION: Northwestern Pacific Ocean.

AREA: 70 sq mi (180 km^2).

POPULATION: 56,000 (estimate).

CAPITAL AND LARGEST CITY: Majuro.

MAJOR LANGUAGE: Marshallese, English (both official).

MAJOR RELIGIOUS GROUP: Christian (Protestant).

GOVERNMENT: Republic in free association with the United States. **Head of state and government**—president. **Legislature**—Nitijela.

CHIEF PRODUCTS: Agricultural—coconuts, copra, taro, breadfruit, pandanus, pigs, chicken. **Manufactured**—coconut products, handicrafts, fish.

MONETARY UNIT: U.S. dollar (1 dollar = 100 cents).

twelve-member Council of Chiefs (Iroij) is consulted on questions of land and custom. The nation's first two presidents were traditional chiefs; the first non-chief president, Kessai Note, was elected in 1999 and won a second term in 2004.

JULIE WALSH KROEKER
Executive Director, Small Island Networks

MARSHES. See WETLANDS.

MARSUPIALS

A kangaroo hopping across an Australian grassland may seem very different from an opossum climbing a tree in a Canadian forest. But they are related. Both belong to a group of mammals called marsupials.

Scientists have identified more than 270 kinds, or species, of marsupials. Some, such as kangaroos, koalas, and opossums, are well known. Others include bandicoots, numbats, phalangers, wombats, and the doglike Tasmanian devil. The largest marsupial species is the red kangaroo. It can be almost 7 feet (2 meters) tall and may weigh up to 180 pounds (80 kilograms). The smallest is the flat-headed marsupial mouse. It is about 4½ inches (11 centimeters) long, including its tail, and it weighs less than ⅙ ounce (5 grams).

The oldest known marsupials lived about 80 million years ago in North America. At this time many of the continents were connected. The marsupials probably spread from North America to what would become South America, Antarctica, and Australia. When the continents drifted apart, the marsupials became isolated from one another. They evolved in different ways. Many species became extinct as the climate changed and as they faced growing competition from other mammals for food. For example, scientists attribute the extinction of a rhinoceros-sized, wombat-like marsupial to the arrival of humans in Australia and the drier climate at the end of the last Ice Age.

Today most marsupials are found in Australia and nearby islands. Opossums are the only kind found in North and South America.

There is no typical marsupial—each species differs in appearance, size, and way of life from all the others. Some marsupials make their home on the ground, others in trees. Still others burrow into the ground. Most are small animals that range in size from that of a

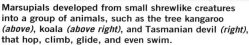
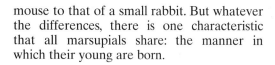

Marsupials developed from small shrewlike creatures into a group of animals, such as the tree kangaroo *(above)*, koala *(above right)*, and Tasmanian devil *(right)*, that hop, climb, glide, and even swim.

mouse to that of a small rabbit. But whatever the differences, there is one characteristic that all marsupials share: the manner in which their young are born.

▶ **BIRTH AND EARLY DEVELOPMENT**

The offspring of most mammals receive nourishment from the mother before birth. Food is passed to the unborn young through a special organ called the placenta. Animals that are nourished through a placenta are often called placental mammals. At birth, the young placental mammals are well developed and look like their adult parents, only much smaller.

The placentas of most female marsupials are different from those of other mammals. Their young are born at a very early stage. The newborn marsupials are less developed and look very different from their parents. They complete their development attached to their mother's nipples, feeding on her milk. They remain attached until they are nearly able to survive on their own.

Immediately after birth, a newborn marsupial instinctively crawls from the birth canal at the base of the mother's tail through the fur to her belly. There it finds a nipple, which it grips with its mouth. In most species, the nipples are located in a pouch, called a **marsupium**. Numbats and a few other kinds of marsupials do not have pouches. The nipples and babies are protected only by the long hairs that cover the mother's belly.

The amount of time spent in the pouch varies. A baby kangaroo—called a joey—begins to take short trips from the pouch in about four months, but it spends most of its time there for up to eleven months. Virginia opossum babies remain in their mother's pouch for about two months. A koala baby stays in the pouch for about seven months.

▶ **EATING HABITS**

When they are no longer nursing, marsupial young must find their own food. Some search for food during the day. However, most species will begin their search after the sun sets. They are nocturnal—that is, active at night.

Some marsupials, including kangaroos, koalas, wombats, and opossums, eat mainly plant matter. However, they may be very choosy about the kind they will eat. For instance, koalas eat only leaves of eucalyptus

The opossum *(left)* uses its tail to hold tightly to the branches of a tree as it searches for food. Even though the young kangaroo *(above)* is too big to fit in the pouch, it returns to its mother for milk.

trees. Other marsupials, such as native cats, are meat eaters that hunt and eat other animals. The numbat and marsupial anteater use the strong claws on their front feet to tear apart ant hills and termite nests. Then they lick up the insects with their long tongues.

▶ LOCOMOTION

Each marsupial species has special adaptations that help it survive in its habitat. The great variety within the species can be observed in the different methods of locomotion they use. Marsupials move by running, jumping, climbing, gliding, and swimming.

Most kangaroos have short front limbs and powerful back legs and tails. They can move fairly quickly as they hop across open land. Exceptions are the tree kangaroos. Their front and back legs are closer to the same length, which is a better arrangement for climbing.

Koalas' fingers are arranged to give them a firm grip on tree trunks. Opossums are also climbers. Most opossums have **prehensile**, or grasping, tails that can be wrapped around branches. The yapok, or water opossum, has webbed rear feet, which help it swim well.

Gliding possums have folds of skin along the sides of the body. When the limbs are stretched out, the folds open like sails and enable the animals to glide from branch to branch, or from a tree to the ground.

Marsupial moles have large claws on their front feet. They use the claws to dig underground in sandy deserts. The moles also have a horny shield on the front of the snout, which allows the animals to use their heads to bore through the sand.

▶ MARSUPIALS AND THEIR ENVIRONMENT

Some marsupials, such as opossums and marsupial mice, are quite common. Other marsupials are less adaptable, and they are threatened with extinction.

European settlers introduced sheep, cattle, dogs, cats, and other placental mammals to Australia. These mammals compete with the marsupials for food. Other placental mammals such as dingoes (a type of wild dog) and foxes hunt marsupials. People have hunted marsupials, too. They slaughtered kangaroos and koalas for their beautiful fur. When Europeans first arrived in Australia, an animal known as the Tasmanian wolf was common. Now the species is assumed to be extinct.

Although some marsupials are protected by law, they are still in danger. Today the major threat to marsupials is the destruction of their habitats. As forests are cleared for housing, and grasslands are plowed for the planting of crops, the homes and food supplies of these once common animals are destroyed.

JENNY TESAR
Author, *Introduction to Animals*
Reviewed by JAMES G. DOHERTY
Curator of Mammals, The Bronx Zoo

See also KANGAROOS; KOALAS.

MARTEL, CHARLES. See MIDDLE AGES (Profiles).

MARTIAL ARTS

The term "martial arts" refers to many different forms of hand-to-hand combat. Most of the well-known martial arts originated in Asia, and many are practiced today as methods of self-defense and as sports.

▶ TECHNIQUES AND WEAPONS

Numerous techniques and weapons are used in martial arts. Unarmed martial artists

Martial arts, such as tae kwon do (*above*), include many ancient forms of hand-to-hand combat.

employ various kinds of strikes (with hands, feet, or knees), throws (with feet, hips, or hands), and grapples (choke-holds, pinnings, and armlocks, or reversing the joints of the body).

Weapons used in martial arts are simple handheld objects that resemble sickles, oars, flails, and walking sticks. A variety of swords are also used. In hojojitsu, a Japanese martial art, the only weapon is a strong, light cord used to tie up an opponent.

▶ MAJOR MARTIAL ARTS

Listed here are some of the more popular martial arts practiced today.

Aikido. Aikido, founded about 1925 in Japan, is a defensive art based on swordsmanship and jujitsu. It uses wristlocks and armlocks to throw and control an attacker.

Judo. Judo was created in Japan in 1882. It utilizes throwing and grappling in the sport form and includes striking in the self-defense form. Judo was the first Asian martial art admitted to the Olympics (1964). For more information, see the article JUDO in Volume JK.

Jujitsu. Jujitsu has been practiced, in various forms, in Japan for more than 600 years. Self-defense forms use throwing, grappling, kicking, and striking techniques. Sport jujitsu has grown very popular in recent years.

Karate. Karate originated on the island of Okinawa and was brought to Japan in 1922. It is basically a striking art, using blows with the fist, open hand, elbow, knee, or foot to subdue an opponent. For more information, see the article KARATE in Volume JK.

Kung Fu. Kung fu is an ancient form of Chinese self-defense that is practiced in many forms. Like many of the martial arts of Southeast Asia, kung fu employs a "soft style" of striking. This means that rather than blocking an attack with brute power, the attack is avoided and a counterstrike is performed.

Tae Kwon Do. Tae kwon do is sometimes known as Korean karate. There is much more emphasis on kicking, as well as on properly executed routines of imagined attacks and defenses.

Other Martial Arts. Other kinds of martial arts include sumo, a stylized form of Japanese wrestling; kickboxing, a combat sport involving kicks to the body and head; and kendo, a Japanese art of fencing with wooden swords. Boxing and wrestling are also considered martial arts, although they are seldom used today in combat or for self-defense.

PHILIP S. PORTER
Founder, United States Martial Arts Association

MARTINEZ, MARIA. See INDIANS, AMERICAN (Profiles).

MARX, KARL
(1818–1883)

Karl Marx, a German thinker and revolutionary, was one of the most influential figures of all time. His theories on society and economics, known as Marxism, provided the framework for the Communist governments that developed in the 1900's.

Karl Heinrich Marx was born to a Jewish family in Trier, Prussia (now Germany), on May 5, 1818. His parents later converted to Christianity, but Marx renounced all religion. In 1843, after completing studies in law and philosophy, Marx married Jenny von Westphalen. By then he had earned a reputation as a radical thinker and turned to journalism to earn a living.

Marx observed the miserable conditions under which workers lived during the early days of industrialization. Their lives were marked by poverty, unemployment, child labor, and other evils. In response, Marx published the *Communist Manifesto* (1848), coauthored with his lifelong friend Friedrich Engels. This radical work urged workers to rise up, overthrow their governments, and start a new economic system. Marx was arrested in Germany. Later he was expelled from France and Belgium. In 1849 he finally found refuge in England, where he and his family lived in acute poverty.

Marx devoted long years to studying capitalism, an economic system that is based on a continuous quest for profit. Profit is made possible when workers sell their labor power to employers who own the "means of production" (factories, farmlands, mills, and the like). As a result of his study, Marx wrote his now famous book *Das Kapital* (*Capital*). In it Marx predicted that capitalist societies would be replaced by socialist societies, where all the people would own the means of production. In democratic societies, he expected that change would come peacefully after capitalism had failed. In countries where democracy did not exist, he called for revolution. The first volume of *Das Kapital* appeared in 1867.

Two additional volumes were edited and published by Engels after Marx's death in London on March 14, 1883.

Marx's Ideas. Four main ideas are found in Marx's writings. The first is his belief that the most important feature of a society is its economic system—that is, the way in which people earn their living. It is the basis of the society's culture—its art, science, philosophy, and religion.

The second idea is that in all societies (except primitive societies of the past and socialist societies) the economic system divides people into classes—masters and slaves, capitalists and workers—and that these classes are always in conflict.

The third idea is that labor is the source of all value. Under capitalism, profits result when workers produce goods that have more value than the workers' wages. Marx believed that this system exploited (took unfair advantage of) the workers and that this exploitation would stop only if society as a whole, instead of individuals, owned the means of production.

Finally, Marx thought of history as a process in which human freedom is always being extended. He thought that people will be free to choose their way of living only when private ownership of the means of production is abolished. Then, when capitalism falls, a classless society will result.

Marx expected socialism to come first to highly industrialized countries, but the opposite happened. Marxism was adopted in underdeveloped societies, notably the Communist nations of China and North Korea (since 1948), Cuba (since 1959), and the former Soviet Union (1922–91). That is why, in spite of great changes, the study of his thought is still important today.

SIDNEY HOOK
Author, *The Ambiguous Legacy: Marx and the Marxists*

See also CAPITALISM; COMMUNISM; SOCIALISM.

MARX BROTHERS. See MOTION PICTURES (Profiles: Movie Stars).

MARY, QUEEN OF SCOTS (1542–1587)

Mary Stuart, queen of Scotland, was one of the most romantic and tragic figures in British history. She inherited the Scottish throne as a child and later reigned briefly as queen of France. A woman of great beauty, charm, and intelligence, she was also passionate and ambitious. Her romantic involvements cost her the Scottish crown. Her ambition to be queen of England led to years of captivity and, finally, to her execution.

Mary was born at Linlithgow Palace near Edinburgh, Scotland, on December 7 or 8, 1542. She was the daughter of King James V of Scotland and his French wife, Mary of Guise. Her father died when she was a week old, and the infant princess became queen of Scotland. Her mother governed as regent for her. At the age of 5, Mary was promised in marriage to the French dauphin (the heir to the throne), Francis, and was sent to France to be educated. She was brought up as a Roman Catholic. Her intelligence impressed her teachers, and her grace and charm captivated the elegant French court. In 1558, at the age of 15, she married the young dauphin. The following year he became King Francis II, and Mary became queen of France. She reigned less than two years. The sickly king died in 1560, and Mary returned to Scotland.

She arrived home a Catholic queen in a country that had become largely Protestant. Mary's own religious views were moderate, but her desire to advance the Catholic faith aroused the hostility of many Protestants. Her position as monarch was weak, for much power rested with the Scottish nobility. In 1565, Mary chose as her second husband a cousin, Henry Stewart, Lord Darnley, who was a Catholic. It was a poor choice. Many Scottish lords disapproved of the match, and some took up arms against her.

Mary's great ambition was to gain the throne of England, which was then occupied by her cousin Elizabeth I. Mary's claims to the English crown were strong. As the great-granddaughter of King Henry VII of England, she was next in line to the throne after the childless Elizabeth.

In 1566, Mary gave birth to a son who was to become King James VI of Scotland and, later, King James I of England. But by then the handsome Darnley had proved to be a

Mary, Queen of Scots, as she appeared in 1560—the year her mother and her first husband died.

weak and vicious man, and Mary had grown to hate him. Darnley was jealous of Mary's attentions to her Italian secretary, David Rizzio. Suspecting that Rizzio's influence was turning Mary against him, Darnley and a group of sympathetic lords murdered him in 1566.

Mary never forgave Darnley and turned for affection and support to James Hepburn, Earl of Bothwell. In 1567, Darnley was found murdered. Bothwell was widely believed to have planned the murder, but he was acquitted. Mary's part in the crime has remained unclear. It is thought that she knew of the plan to kill Darnley and probably agreed to it. Soon after, she married Bothwell. The marriage aroused a storm of protest. She was forced to give up the Scottish throne in favor of her son, James, and was imprisoned. In 1568 she escaped and raised a small band of loyal followers. But they were defeated in battle and Mary fled to England.

For the next 19 years she was held prisoner in England. Her presence incited many plots against the English throne and was a constant threat to Elizabeth. Catholics did not recognize Elizabeth's title to the throne and believed Mary to be the rightful queen of England. She was finally put on trial and convicted of having taken part in a plot to assassinate Elizabeth. Fearing the effect that Mary's execution would have, Elizabeth delayed signing the death warrant for three months. At last, on February 8, 1587, Mary—still proclaiming her innocence—was beheaded.

Reviewed by ELLIOT ROSE
University of Toronto

MARY, VIRGIN

Mary was the mother of Jesus Christ. Tradition has it that she was the daughter of Anne and Joachim and was a member of the house of David, the royal house of Israel. As a young woman, she was promised in marriage to Joseph, also a descendent of David.

The Gospels of the New Testament tell us that the Angel Gabriel visited Mary and told her that she would have a son, whose name was to be Jesus. Mary and Joseph married in Nazareth and then went to Bethlehem, where Jesus was born about 6 B.C. The Gospels state that God, through the Holy Spirit, caused the birth of Jesus and that Mary was a virgin when he was born. Therefore she is often referred to as the Virgin Mary, but she is also known as the Mother of God and Our Lady.

The Gospels place Mary at the wedding feast in Cana, where Jesus performed his first public miracle. The Scripture says that at Mary's request, Jesus turned water into wine.

Mary, the mother of Jesus Christ, was often portrayed in Early Renaissance art. This fresco by Italian artist Pinturicchio makes up the central panel of a church altarpiece in Perugia, Italy.

Mary was also present at the Crucifixion of Jesus. At that time Jesus entrusted his mother to the care of the Apostle John. The last mention of Mary in Scripture is in the Acts of the Apostles. There we read that after the Resurrection and Ascension of Jesus, Mary was with his followers in Jerusalem, praying and waiting for the coming of the Holy Spirit.

Reviewed by MSGR. GEORGE E. TIFFANY
Editor in Chief, *The Contemporary Church*

MARY I (1516–1558)

Mary Tudor was the first English queen to reign in her own right. She was born in 1516 to King Henry VIII and his first wife, Catherine of Aragon, the daughter of Ferdinand and Isabella of Spain. Mary's early childhood was a happy one. Henry eventually became very cruel to her, however, and in 1527 he tried to divorce her mother in order to marry Anne Boleyn. Pope Clement VII refused to recognize the divorce, so Henry broke from the Catholic Church and formed the Protestant Church of England. Not only did Henry reject Mary's Catholic faith, he also prevented Mary from seeing her mother.

In 1547, Mary's Protestant half-brother, Edward VI, succeeded Henry VIII on the throne. When young Edward died in 1553, his Protestant protector, the Duke of Northumberland, tried to prevent the Catholic Mary from taking the throne. He arranged for the succession of his own Protestant candidate, Lady Jane Grey, a cousin of Mary and Edward. However, Mary ably defeated this conspiracy. Lady Jane Grey, the "nine days' queen," was accused of treason and beheaded. Mary took her place on the throne.

Mary I, the eldest daughter of Henry VIII, tried to restore the authority of the Catholic Church in England. Her execution of Protestants earned her the nickname Bloody Mary.

Mary soon became unpopular. In 1554 she married Prince Philip of Spain (later Philip II), whom the English despised. Then, seeking to restore the Roman Catholic Church, she violently executed hundreds of Protestants.

Mary's last years were very unhappy. Because she was unable to bear children, her husband left her in 1557. Then she drew England into Spain's war against France, during which England lost Calais, its last possession in France. Increasingly plagued by melancholy and illness, Mary died in 1558 and was succeeded by her Protestant half-sister, the popular Elizabeth I.

MICHAEL HUGHES
University College of Wales

MARYLAND

Maryland earned one of its nicknames, the Old Line State, because of the heroism of its troops during the Revolutionary War. The soldiers of the Maryland Line were considered among the finest in the Continental Army. They fought with great courage in many battles until independence was won in 1783. Maryland is also called the Free State, in part because it was the first American colony to offer religious toleration to its people.

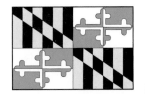

State flag

Maryland is one of the Middle Atlantic states of the United States. Located midway between the North and the South, it is also traditionally midway in its temperament and politics. The state is a cultural crossroads as well, and has sometimes been called the nation in miniature.

Due to its central location, Maryland provided the site for the United States capital: All the land that now makes up the District of Columbia was donated by Maryland.

The first national road was the Cumberland Road, which began in Maryland and through which thousands of settlers made their way west. The nation's first passenger railroad, the Baltimore and Ohio, followed a similar route over the mountains. The fast sailing ship called the Baltimore Clipper connected Maryland to Europe, South America, and Asia. Orville and Wilbur Wright brought their first airplane to Maryland, where they supervised the construction of the world's first airport.

The crossroads sometimes brought war to Maryland. In the French and Indian War, General Edward Braddock led British and American troops from Fort Cumberland into the west. During the Revolutionary War, the Continental Congress fled from Philadelphia to Baltimore and later to Annapolis, where its members ratified the Treaty of Paris, ending the war, in 1783.

In the War of 1812, Baltimore held fast against the British invasion; it was during this attack that Francis Scott Key, straining to see the flag through the dawn light, wrote "The Star-Spangled Banner." In the Civil War, both Union and Confederate armies fought major battles across the state. In the two world wars and in the Korean and Vietnam wars, Baltimore was a major port of embarkation (departure) for troops.

Maryland has been an educational crossroads as well. Each year hundreds of young persons come to Annapolis to study at the United States Naval Academy. Many others come to Baltimore and College Park to study at Johns Hopkins University or the University of Maryland.

Maryland is dominated by two great cities: Washington, D.C., whose suburbs spread over several southern counties, and Baltimore, whose suburbs encompass several northern counties. These two cities have almost grown together. They are part of a supercity, or megalopolis, that stretches from Richmond, Virginia, to Boston, Massachusetts.

In earlier days, Maryland was a land of farms, especially tobacco farms, and fishing, mainly for the oysters and crabs of the Chesapeake Bay. These activities continue, but today most residents are city dwellers or suburbanites who work in government, the service industries, retail trade, or manufacturing.

▶LAND

Maryland is a small state, but geographically it is one of the most divided. In the east, the Chesapeake Bay almost cuts the state in two. The area east of the bay is called the Eastern Shore, and the area to the west is

Opposite page, clockwise from left: Seasoned and steamed, Maryland crabs are a famous delicacy. The Blue Ridge Mountains cross north-central Maryland. The Baltimore skyline seen from the city's Inner Harbor.

State flower:
Black-eyed Susan

State tree:
White oak

FACTS AND FIGURES

Location: Eastern United States; bordered on the north by Pennsylvania, on the east by Delaware and the Atlantic Ocean, and on the south and west by Virginia and West Virginia.

Area: 12,297 sq mi (31,849 km²); rank, 42nd.

Population: 5,296,486 (2000 census); rank, 19th.

Elevation: *Highest*—3,360 ft (1,024 m) at Backbone Mountain, in Garrett County; *lowest*—sea level.

Capital: Annapolis.

Statehood: April 28, 1788; 7th state.

State Motto: *Fatti maschii parole femine* ("Manly deeds, womanly words").

State Song: "Maryland, My Maryland."

Nicknames: Old Line State; Free State.

Abbreviations: MD; Md.

State bird:
Baltimore oriole

Right: The Chesapeake Bay Bridge spans Maryland's Chesapeake Bay near Annapolis, linking the state's Eastern and Western shores. *Below:* A series of rapids in the Potomac River occurs at scenic Great Falls. The Potomac forms much of Maryland's border with Virginia.

called the Western Shore. The counties south of Washington, D.C., are called Southern Maryland, and the mountain area to the west is called Western Maryland. The state is less than 2 miles (3 kilometers) wide at Hancock, in Washington County. Farther west at Cumberland it is about 5 miles (8 kilometers) wide.

Land Regions

Maryland extends inland from the Atlantic Ocean across belts, or regions, of landforms that stretch from New England far into the South.

The Coastal Plain. The lowlands surrounding Chesapeake Bay belong to the natural region called the Coastal Plain, which extends along the Atlantic coast from New Jersey to Florida. This region in Maryland makes up about half the state, including the Eastern Shore, the Western Shore as far inland as

Washington, D.C., and Baltimore. Areas on the Eastern Shore are low and marshy.

The Appalachian Region, which extends from Washington, D.C., and Baltimore to the west, is subdivided into four increasingly hilly sections. The **Piedmont**, or foothills, is the easternmost of these four sections. It extends west to Frederick. The countryside is rolling and fertile. It is made up of the worn-down remains of ancient mountains that are among the oldest in the world.

The **Blue Ridge Mountains**, between Frederick and Hagerstown, are part of a long, narrow chain that stretches from Pennsylvania to Georgia. The Appalachian Trail, a scenic path for hikers, follows the crest of the mountains. Thirty-eight miles (61 kilometers) of the trail pass through Maryland.

The **Appalachian Ridge and Valley** extends from Hagerstown in the east to Cumberland in the west. The fertile valley was the scene of many Civil War battles. The **Allegheny Plateau** extends west from Cumberland and includes the most rugged section of Maryland. Some of its mountain ridges are rich in coal.

Rivers, Lakes, and Coastal Waters

Maryland has two important waterways—Chesapeake Bay and the Potomac River. Chesapeake Bay is the drowned valley of the Susquehanna River. The bay once isolated the Eastern Shore from the rest of the state. Now the William Preston Lane, Jr., Memorial Bridge (better known as the Chesapeake Bay Bridge) connects the two parts. The bay is about 195 miles (315 kilometers) long.

The Potomac River forms most of Maryland's southern border. Maryland owns the entire watercourse to the shores of Virginia.

This unusual arrangement has caused some difficulties with Virginia over fishing and seafood rights. The Potomac and the many other rivers in the state are used for recreation.

Dams in the rivers create large artificial lakes, or reservoirs. Their main purpose is to store water for cities or produce hydroelectric power. Some of them are used for recreation as well. The largest reservoir in the state is Deep Creek Lake, on the Youghiogheny River, of the Ohio River drainage system. It was built to produce hydroelectric power. Another large power development is on the Susquehanna River at Conowingo.

Baltimore is a major port city, and the state has built canals to enhance its trade. The Chesapeake and Delaware Canal cuts across the northern neck of the Eastern Shore and Delaware so that ships from Baltimore can easily reach the ocean. The Susquehanna Canal reaches into central Pennsylvania.

Maryland is an Atlantic coastal state, though it actually has only 31 miles (50 kilometers) of shoreland on the Atlantic.

Climate

Maryland's climate is midway between the climate of the warmer southern part of the United States and that of the colder north. January temperatures average 29°F (−2°C) in the west and 39°F (4°C) along the coast. The average July temperature is 68°F (20°C) in the west and 76°F (24°C) along the coast.

The rainfall throughout the state is usually adequate for growing crops. However, precip-itation varies considerably from year to year. Average annual rainfall is nearly 42 inches (1,067 millimeters); average annual snowfall is 25 inches (63.5 centimeters). Frost-free growing days average 185 days, ranging from 130 days in the west to 230 days in the southern Chesapeake area.

Plant and Animal Life

Forests cover slightly more than 40 percent of Maryland's land. Most are privately owned commercial forests. Three fourths of the saw-timber is hardwood, such as oak and hickory. The rest is softwood, chiefly pine.

Chesapeake Bay is rich in bluefish, rock-fish, sea trout, crabs, oysters, and diamond-back terrapin. There are many wild geese and ducks. Maryland's forests are home to rabbits, mink, opossum, squirrels, foxes, and deer, as well as grouse, partridge, and wild turkeys.

Natural Resources

Maryland's natural resources are as varied as its landforms and its climate. These resources include soils and minerals in addition to water, forests, and wildlife.

Maryland has been a leader among the states in environmental conservation. The legislature has passed strict laws to protect the wetlands of Chesapeake Bay, the quality of the water in rivers and the bay, and the quality of the air.

Soils. The state's great variety of soils is a result of the variety of underlying rocks. Some soils are stony and some are stiff clays, but

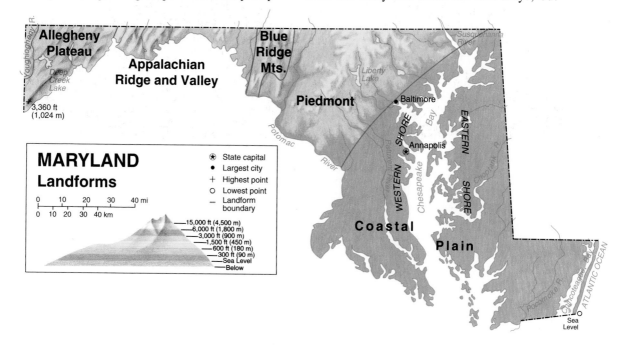

MARYLAND
Landforms

0   10   20   30   40 mi
0   10   20   30   40 km

⊛ State capital
• Largest city
+ Highest point
○ Lowest point
— Landform boundary

15,000 ft (4,500 m)
6,000 ft (1,800 m)
3,000 ft (900 m)
1,500 ft (450 m)
600 ft (180 m)
300 ft (90 m)
Sea Level
Below

Allegheny Plateau
Appalachian Ridge and Valley
Blue Ridge Mts.
Piedmont
3,360 ft (1,024 m)
Deep Creek Lake
Liberty Lake
Baltimore
Annapolis
WESTERN SHORE
EASTERN SHORE
Chesapeake Bay
Coastal Plain
Potomac River
Sea Level
ATLANTIC OCEAN

most are of medium texture and provide good drainage. The sandiest soils are on the south end of the Eastern Shore. Sandy soils warm earliest in the spring. If properly fertilized, they can produce early vegetable crops.

Minerals. The Piedmont section of Maryland has underlying rocks that contain a great variety of minerals. Unfortunately for Maryland, the minerals exist only in small amounts and so are not profitable to mine. The Piedmont and the Great Valley have deposits of various granites, marbles, and sandstones. Sand and gravel come mostly from the Western Shore counties. Coal and natural gas are found in the western part of the state.

▶ **PEOPLE**

In area, Maryland is one of the smallest states, but in density of population it ranks among the highest. Before 1850, most of the people were farmers, and population was spread widely over the state. Then it became a manufacturing state, and by 1920 more than half the people lived within the city of Baltimore. Now about 72 percent of Maryland's people live in what the United States Census Bureau calls suburban areas, mostly outside Baltimore and Washington, D.C.

The first settlers in Maryland came from the British Isles. Among them were wealthy people and farmers and other workers. Black slaves added to the supply of laborers. Most of the native Indians gradually moved away from the area. In the early 1700's, farmers of German and Scotch-Irish stock arrived by way of Pennsylvania.

Baltimore especially has been a melting pot of people from all over the world. There were English, Scotch-Irish, and Africans from the earliest days of the colony. After the Revolutionary War, many Germans and Irish arrived; often they worked on the canals and railroads around Baltimore. After the Civil War, as manufacturing boomed, many Jews, Poles, Italians, and Russians arrived. In recent years many Asians and Hispanics have migrated to the city and its suburbs.

Maryland has always had a large black population. At the time of the Civil War, Baltimore had the second highest population of free blacks in the nation. Today, blacks make up about 28 percent of the state's population.

Education

In 1686, Maryland's General Assembly levied a tax on tobacco to support King William's School in Annapolis, and in 1723 it levied a tax on wild animal skins to support a public school in each county.

The money was too little, however, and the population too scattered for the schools to work very well. Again in 1826 the state tried to establish a free school system for all, but it was not until 1864 that Maryland's modern public school system became a reality. Today, Maryland's school systems have an excellent reputation.

As in the rest of the United States, good colleges developed in Maryland before good public schools. In 1782, William Smith, who had helped found the University of Pennsylvania, came to Maryland and persuaded the state to establish a college at Chestertown. The institution was named Washington College after George Washington, who donated money. Two years later, the state transformed King William's School, in Annapolis, into St. John's College.

The University of Maryland began in 1807 as a medical school and later added a school of law, a school of dentistry (the first in the world), and a college of agriculture (the second in the country). Today the University of Maryland system, with headquarters in Col-

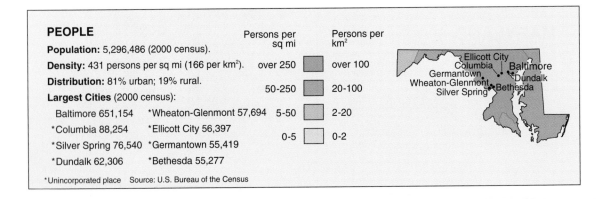

PEOPLE

Population: 5,296,486 (2000 census).

Density: 431 persons per sq mi (166 per km²).

Distribution: 81% urban; 19% rural.

Largest Cities (2000 census):

Baltimore 651,154   *Wheaton-Glenmont 57,694

*Columbia 88,254   *Ellicott City 56,397

*Silver Spring 76,540   *Germantown 55,419

*Dundalk 62,306   *Bethesda 55,277

Persons per sq mi	Persons per km²
over 250	over 100
50-250	20-100
5-50	2-20
0-5	0-2

*Unincorporated place   Source: U.S. Bureau of the Census

Above: Two young spectators enjoy a close-up view of undersea life at the National Aquarium in Baltimore. *Top right:* Marylanders test their speed and skill at an oyster-shucking contest. *Bottom right:* Graduation day is a proud occasion for the men and women of the United States Naval Academy in Annapolis.

lege Park, has eleven campuses throughout the state. In addition, Maryland has 19 community colleges.

The United States Naval Academy opened in 1845 in Annapolis. In 1876, Johns Hopkins University opened in Baltimore. The first research university in the United States, it is internationally known for its research, especially in medicine. Other private colleges in Maryland include Goucher College in Towson, Hood College in Frederick, Loyola College in Baltimore, and Western Maryland College in Westminster.

Libraries, Museums, and the Arts

Maryland's best-known library is the Enoch Pratt Free Library system in Baltimore. It was established in the 1880's. Today every large community in the state has a public library system. Many special libraries are maintained by colleges, universities, and professional organizations. Some of the museums include libraries. The National Library of Medicine and the National Agricultural Library are located in the Maryland suburbs of Washington, D.C.

In Baltimore, the Walters Art Gallery and the Baltimore Museum of Art have large and distinguished collections of European, Asian, and American art. The Peale Museum in Baltimore and the Washington Museum of Fine Arts in Hagerstown are smaller. The Maryland Historical Society in Baltimore, the Chesapeake Maritime Museum in St. Michael's, the Hall of Records in Annapolis, and the U.S. Naval Academy Museum in Annapolis have historical and maritime materials. The Maryland Science Center, the Baltimore and Ohio Railroad Museum, the Baltimore Museum of Industry, and the National Aquarium, all in Baltimore, attract enthusiastic visitors.

Many concert series are given in Maryland, but the chief musical events take place in Baltimore. The Baltimore Symphony is one of the major orchestras in the nation. The Maryland Symphony Orchestra, based in Hagerstown, was founded in 1982. The Baltimore Opera Company presents grand opera.

▶ ECONOMY

Maryland's economic development has mirrored that of the nation: It was dominated by agriculture and rural life until the Civil War, by industry and urban life until World War II, and by services and suburban life since then.

Services

About 75 percent of the Maryland work force is engaged in a service occupation. This is not only the largest but also the most rapidly growing type of employment. A leading service activity is government work, because of the many bureaus and military establishments that spread into the Maryland suburbs from Washington, D.C. These include the National Institutes of Health, the National Bureau of Standards, the National Aeronautics and Space Administration, and the research parks

of Johns Hopkins University and the University of Maryland.

Other service occupations include business, social, and personal services such as data processing, health care, and auto repair; wholesale and retail trade; finance, insurance, and real estate; and transportation, communication, and utilities.

Manufacturing

Manufacturing in Maryland is widely diversified among many different industries. The leading manufacturing activity is food processing, including the preparation of poultry, vegetables, and seafood from the state's farms and fisheries. Next in importance are the manufacture of electrical equipment, printed materials, and chemical products.

Agriculture

Only about 1 percent of the work force is engaged directly in agriculture, but farms still occupy about 40 percent of the land. The leading product is poultry, most of which is raised on the Eastern Shore. Dairy products are next in importance. Many dairy farms are located in the counties just west of Baltimore and Washington. Third in importance are greenhouse and nursery products, including sod for suburban lawns. Tobacco, which once dominated the state economy, is now grown on only a few small fields in southern Maryland.

About 44 percent of the state is forested. The pine forests of the Eastern Shore provide

Left: The harvesting of clams is an important part of the Chesapeake Bay's flourishing fishing industry. *Below:* A cargo ship awaits unloading at the docks of Baltimore, one of the nation's leading port cities.

Goddard Space Flight Center, a branch of NASA, is in Greenbelt. Many government and military establishments have spread into Maryland from Washington, D.C.

raw material for paper products, while hardwood from the forests of the west are used for furniture and fuel.

A flourishing fishing industry is centered around the Chesapeake Bay. It includes the trapping of crabs in summer, dredging for oysters in winter, and fishing for bluefish, rockfish, and flounder all year round. The state is making great efforts to control industrial pollution and urban development around the bay in order to protect this natural resource.

Mining and Construction

Small amounts of stone, sand, and limestone are mined in the state. Coal mining, once a major industry in Maryland, is now small. The construction industry flourishes during times of prosperity, especially to provide housing and office buildings for the booming suburbs.

Transportation

Baltimore is one of the leading port cities in the United States, with modern state-managed loading facilities and warehouses. Interstate highways and railroads radiate out from the port—northeast to New York, north to central Pennsylvania, west into Ohio, and south to Washington, D.C., and Knoxville, Tennessee. Wide tunnels under Baltimore Harbor speed traffic around the city.

Magnificent 8-lane, 8-mile (13-kilometer) bridges cross the Chesapeake Bay. The bay itself is a center of boating and excursion travel. Western Maryland is noted for its scenic country roads and hiking trails.

The Baltimore-Washington International Airport, near Baltimore, is a center of air travel. Many smaller airports are located throughout the state.

Communication

The *Maryland Gazette*, begun in Annapolis in 1745, was one of the earliest newspapers in the American colonies. The *Afro-American* of Baltimore was one of the first black newspapers and remains one of the finest. The Baltimore *Sun* has won many awards as one of the nation's best daily newspapers.

Maryland has about 80 general-circulation newspapers, 100 radio stations, and 18 television stations.

PRODUCTS AND INDUSTRIES

Manufacturing: Electrical equipment, processed foods, printed materials, chemical products.

Agriculture: Poultry and eggs, dairy products, greenhouse and nursery products, vegetables and melons, soybeans, seafood.

Minerals: Stone, sand, coal.

Services: Wholesale and retail trade; finance, insurance, and real estate; business, social, and personal services; transportation, communication, and utilities; government.

*Gross state product is the total value of goods and services produced in a year.

Percentage of Gross State Product* by Industry

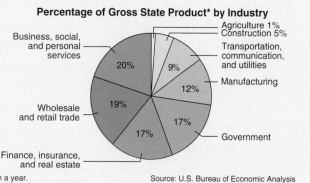

- Agriculture 1%
- Construction 5%
- Transportation, communication, and utilities 9%
- Manufacturing 12%
- Government 17%
- Finance, insurance, and real estate 17%
- Wholesale and retail trade 19%
- Business, social, and personal services 20%

Source: U.S. Bureau of Economic Analysis

Places of Interest

Antietam National Battlefield Site

Colonial plantation reconstruction, St. Mary's City

Chesapeake Bay Maritime Museum Lighthouse, St. Michael's

Chesapeake and Ohio Canal National Historical Park

Antietam National Battlefield Site, near Sharpsburg, commemorates an important battle of the Civil War fought at Antietam Creek on September 17, 1862. It includes a historical museum and a marked tour of the battlefield.

Catoctin Mountain Park, in Frederick County, contains the presidential retreat Camp David.

The Chesapeake and Ohio Canal National Historical Park follows the route of the 184-mile (296-kilometer) C & O Canal that once ran from Washington, D.C., to Cumberland, Maryland. The canal was planned by George Washington and was finished in 1850. The park has facilities for picnicking, boating, and hiking.

Deep Creek Lake State Park is a beautiful mountain park in Western Maryland.

Fort McHenry National Monument and Historic Shrine preserves Fort McHenry in Baltimore harbor. The successful defense of this fort on September 13–14, 1814, inspired Francis Scott Key to write the national anthem of the United States.

Fort Washington Park, on the Potomac River south of Washington, D.C., preserves a fort of the 1800's that guarded the approaches to Washington.

Hampton National Historic Site, near Towson, is a fine example of a Georgian-style mansion, built in the late 1700's.

Harborplace, in Baltimore, is a favorite tourist area, with many shops and restaurants. It is part of one of the most famous examples of urban renewal in the United States. Also in this area are the Maryland Science Center and the National Aquarium. The USS *Constellation*, a national historic landmark, is docked nearby.

Harpers Ferry National Historical Park, a scenic and historic area at the meeting of the Shenandoah and Potomac rivers, is shared by West Virginia and Maryland. It is described in the article WEST VIRGINIA.

Monocacy National Battlefield, near Frederick, is the site of a Civil War battle. The Union troops lost, but they prevented Washington, D.C., from falling to the Confederates.

Ocean City, a resort city on the Atlantic Ocean, attracts more than a half million tourists each summer.

St. Mary's City, near the mouth of the Potomac River, is the site of the first settlement in Maryland; it has many archaeological exhibits and restored buildings, as well as an operating colonial era farm.

State Recreation Areas. Maryland has more than 50 state parks and forests and more than 200 restored or protected historical sites. Famous historical areas on the Eastern Shore include almost the entire towns of Chestertown and St. Michael's; on the Western Shore they include Ellicott City, St. Mary's City, and parts of Annapolis and Baltimore. For additional information, write to the Division of Tourism, 217 East Redwood Street, Baltimore, Maryland 21201.

▶CITIES

Most of Maryland's population is concentrated in the chain of suburbs that extends from Baltimore to Washington, D.C. Almost half the population resides in the rapidly growing suburbs around Washington. These suburbs include Bethesda, Silver Spring, and Rockville in Montgomery County and College Park and Bowie in Prince George's County. Large numbers of people live in the suburbs of Baltimore, which include Dundalk and Towson. Other important cities have a character all their own.

Annapolis, the state capital, was founded in 1648 by Puritans from Virginia, who called it Providence. In 1694, when it became the colonial capital, it was renamed for Princess Anne (later Queen Anne of England). With its narrow streets and colonial-era buildings, the city is almost a living museum. Its main business is state government. Annapolis is also the site of the United States Naval Academy and St. John's College. It is a popular tourist destination.

Baltimore, founded in 1729, is located on the Patapsco River near the Chesapeake Bay. It is a port city and industrial center. Baltimore's population declined after World War II, but in recent years it has undergone major urban renewal. An article on Baltimore appears in Volume B.

Right: With its narrow streets and quaint colonial-era buildings, the historic district of Annapolis, Maryland's capital, is a reminder of life in the 1700's. *Below:* Baltimore's restored Inner Harbor offers many attractions, including Harborplace, a group of shops and restaurants, and—anchored in the harbor—the *Constellation*, the oldest U.S. warship still afloat.

Columbia, located between Baltimore and Washington, was founded in 1965 by a famous city planner, John Rouse. It is composed of nine villages clustered around an urban core. Industries are located on the outer fringes.

Frederick, in central Maryland, was settled in 1745, mainly by German settlers. It was once the largest city in Maryland. According to a legend, made famous in a poem by John Greenleaf Whittier, Barbara Fritchie defiantly waved the Union flag in front of her home when Confederate troops marched through Frederick during the Civil War.

Hagerstown, in the Great Valley of Maryland, was founded in 1791 by Jonathan Hager. It is an agricultural and industrial center.

Cumberland is one of the largest cities of Western Maryland. It is a gateway city through the Appalachian Mountains to the west.

The State House in Annapolis is a historic site as well as the state capitol. The treaty ending the Revolutionary War was ratified there by Congress in 1783.

▶ **GOVERNMENT**

Maryland is governed under its fourth state constitution, which was adopted in 1867.

The governor is at the head of the executive branch of the state government. The other elected executive officials are the lieutenant governor, comptroller, and attorney general. The governor appoints the secretary of state and many other state officials.

The state legislature, called the General Assembly, meets yearly. It has two bodies, the senate and the house of delegates.

The Court of Appeals is the highest court in the judicial branch of the state. The governor appoints the chief judge of this court.

GOVERNMENT

State Government
Governor: 4-year term
State senators: 47; 4-year terms
State representatives: 141; 4-year terms
Number of counties: 23, and one independent city (Baltimore)

Federal Government
U.S. senators: 2
U.S. representatives: 8
Number of electoral votes: 10

For the name of the current governor, see STATE GOVERNMENTS in Volume S. For the names of current U.S. senators and representatives, see UNITED STATES, CONGRESS OF THE in Volume U-V.

INDEX TO MARYLAND MAP

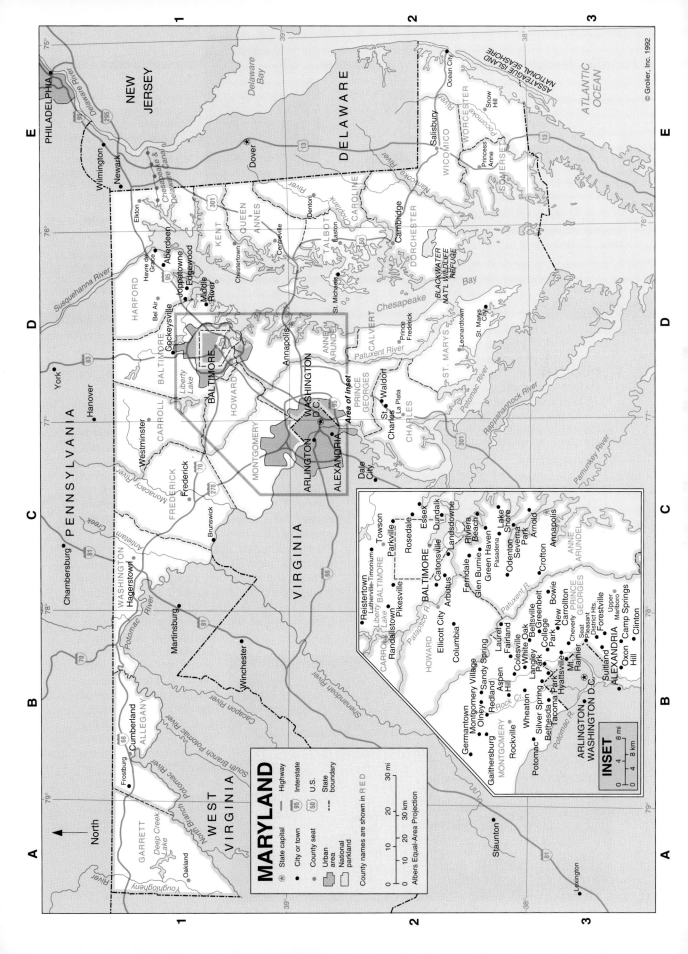

Charles Carroll of Carrollton

Thurgood Marshall

Margaret Brent (1600–1671?) is sometimes called America's first feminist. In the 1630's she became one of the colony's largest landowners and a battlefield leader in Maryland's wars against invaders from Virginia. She claimed not one but two votes in the Maryland General Assembly.

Charles Carroll of Carrollton (1737–1832), born in Annapolis, was said to be the richest man in America in his day. He was a signer of the Declaration of Independence, a United States senator (1789–92), an opponent of slavery, and a founder of the Baltimore and Ohio Railroad.

Daniel Coit Gilman (1831–1906) was the first president of Johns Hopkins University. He helped develop the university's educational program, which emphasized scholarship and research and which served as a model for other American universities. Gilman also helped design Johns Hopkins Hospital and School of Medicine.

Lilly May Carroll Jackson (1889–1975), a black descendant of Charles Carroll of Carrollton, was the head of the Baltimore chapter of the National Association for the Advancement of Colored People (NAACP) for more than twenty years. During that time the chapter became the nation's largest. She helped Maryland become the first segregated state to integrate its schools and public facilities.

Thurgood Marshall (1908–93), born in Baltimore, was the first black to become a justice of the U.S. Supreme

▶ **HISTORY**

Before Europeans came to North America, Maryland was the home of many Indian tribes. Most of them lived around the inlets of Chesapeake Bay in bark houses, usually in stockaded villages. They hunted and fished and raised some crops.

Discovery and Exploration

The first European to see Maryland was probably John Cabot, an Italian captain working for the English. Cabot sailed down the Atlantic coast in 1498.

In 1608, Captain John Smith, with 14 other men from the Virginia colony, started up the Chesapeake, hoping to find a passage to the Indian Sea. He inspected the inlets and islands of the Eastern Shore and was welcomed by the Indians. He returned to Virginia to make a map of the area.

Settlement and Growth

The first Lord Baltimore, George Calvert, was a native of Yorkshire, England. His service to King James I gained for him a grant of land in Newfoundland. This location proved to be too cold. Lord Baltimore persuaded King Charles I, James's successor, to grant him a charter for a new colony, which became the colony of Maryland.

Lord Baltimore died before the charter was signed on June 20, 1632. His son Cecil, the second Lord Baltimore, succeeded him. Cecil organized a colonizing expedition to Maryland in two vessels, the *Ark* and the *Dove*, in 1634. Lord Baltimore did not go with the ships. In charge was his brother, Leonard Calvert, assisted by Father Andrew White, a Jesuit priest. The members of the Calvert family were Catholic, as were many of the colony's leaders, but most of the settlers were Protestant.

The British attack on Fort McHenry during the War of 1812 inspired Francis Scott Key to write "The Star-Spangled Banner."

Court. As special counsel for the NAACP, he won numerous civil rights cases before state and federal courts. Marshall also served on the U.S. Court of Appeals (1962–65) and as solicitor general of the United States (1965–67).

Henry Louis Mencken (1880–1956), a Baltimore journalist, was a leading literary voice of the 1920's. His sharp wit and lively social criticism reflected the intellectual mood of the times. He was a newspaper columnist, co-editor of the magazine *The Smart Set*, and founder and editor of the magazine *The American Mercury*. His books include *The American Language*, a linguistic study.

Charles Willson Peale (1741–1827), born in Queen Annes County, was a leading artist of his day. He painted portraits of many Revolutionary figures, including George Washington. His son Rembrandt Peale founded the Baltimore Museum and Gallery of Fine Arts, now the Peale Museum.

Albert C. Ritchie (1876–1936) was a four-time governor of Maryland (1919–35). He supported such progressive reforms as regulation of public utilities, a merit system for state employees, and public health programs.

George Herman (Babe) Ruth (1895–1948), born in Baltimore, was one of the greatest baseball players in the history of the game. Ruth, who started his career with the Baltimore Orioles, was one of the first five players selected to the Baseball Hall of Fame. A biography of Ruth appears in Volume Q-R.

Babe Ruth

The colonists landed at St. Clements Island (now Blakiston Island) in the Potomac River on March 25, 1634. Later they bought a village from the Indians and moved into what is now St. Mary's City.

For the colony's first fifty years, life in Maryland was extremely hard. People lived in tiny cabins widely scattered along the shores of the Chesapeake, growing tobacco and corn. One difficulty was that Virginians did not want to give up their trade with the Indians of Maryland. In 1631 the Virginians had established a trading post at Kent Island. Led by William Claiborne, they fought with the Maryland settlers for many years until the Virginians were finally driven off.

Catholics and Protestants in Maryland lived together in harmony. In 1649, Lord Baltimore and the people of the colony agreed to the famous "Acts of Religion," which made this religious tolerance official. It was the first such act in America. However, it was repealed a few years later, for in 1692 the people of Maryland made the Church of England the established church, which meant that everyone had to pay taxes for its support. This situation lasted until after the Revolutionary War, when separation of church and state again became an American principle.

Gradually, beginning about 1660, Maryland settlers began to buy black slaves, whose labor brought enormous prosperity to the colony. The population surged, the first towns began to appear, and rich planters began to build fine estates in the English style. Life, at least for the rich, was very grand.

The Revolution and Statehood

Like other colonists, Marylanders opposed the taxes and trade restrictions imposed by the British. In July 1776, Maryland delegates to the Second Continental Congress voted for independence. Four months later Maryland was the first of the former colonies to adopt a state constitution.

During the war, troops from Maryland took part from the first battle at Boston to the final surrender, but little fighting took place in the state. The most famous campaign of the Fifth Regiment, known as the Old Line, was at Brooklyn in the Battle of Long Island. There the Maryland troops delayed the British and covered the retreat of George Washington's army. Maryland's nickname, the Old Line State, comes from this battle. The Third Continental Congress met in Baltimore in 1776 and 1777. The famous Ninth Continental Congress met at the State House in Annapolis in 1783. This Congress ratified the Treaty of Paris, ending the Revolutionary War. On April 28, 1788, Maryland became the seventh state to ratify the Constitution.

The War of 1812 was a kind of civil war in Maryland, for the cities were in favor of it and the countryside opposed it. The British sailed up the Patuxent River to burn the public buildings in Washington, D.C. A few days later, the British moved on to Baltimore but were halted there by city forces; this event inspired Francis Scott Key to write the verses that became the national anthem.

Tension continued between the cities, which enjoyed rapid economic growth, and the slave-owning planters, whose power was diminishing. These tensions looked ahead to the divisions of the Civil War. Baltimore grew enormously, and its famous Clipper ships engaged in worldwide commerce. Banks and factories sprang up, canals and railroads reached into the back country, and immigrants poured in from Europe. In 1830, the Baltimore and Ohio Railroad was the first to use a coal-burning steam locomotive. In 1844, Samuel F. B. Morse built the first telegraph line from Washington, D.C., to Baltimore. Baltimore became the second largest city in the country, after New York.

The Civil War

Slavery was declining in this urban environment, and by the time of the Civil War almost half the blacks in Maryland were free. Nevertheless, many owners continued to profit from slavery, and the state was mostly sympathetic to the South when the war began. In 1861, when the first Northern troops marched southward, a number were attacked and killed by the people of Baltimore. This was the first blood shed in the war.

As the war went on, Maryland became increasingly loyal to the Union. In 1863 the Confederates seized many Maryland towns, but they were defeated when they reached Gettysburg, Pennsylvania. In 1864 a Confederate invasion led by General Jubal A. Early angered the people, and the Confederates were quickly driven off. The state freed its remaining slaves before the war ended.

The cities, with their railroads and industry, surged to new power after the war. Baltimore, in particular, became a major manufacturing center for steel, canned goods, and clothing. The coal mining industry developed in Western Maryland, and Eastern Shore cities boomed with seafood and canning industries. New waves of immigrants arrived. However, labor conditions in the factories were often harsh. As a result, unions were formed, and there was often bitter struggle between factory owners and workers. About a hundred people were killed in the Great Strike of 1877, centering in Baltimore. In 1910, Maryland workers won the first workers' compensation law in the nation, providing insurance against injury and unemployment.

The 1900's

Beginning about 1900, a group of managers and professional people began working for improvements in industry and labor. These reformers attacked the old political system, which gave government jobs to loyal followers of the political parties, and provided instead a system that gave jobs to well-educated people. The reformers also improved schools and developed paved roads, public health programs, and public parks. When the nation outlawed the sale of alcoholic beverages, from 1917 to 1933, Maryland opposed the movement. Speakeasies (establishments that sold alcohol illegally) flourished throughout the state.

During the Great Depression of the 1930's, most people in Maryland, like most people in the rest of the country, looked to the national government for leadership. During World War II many federal agencies moved from Washington, D.C., into the Maryland suburbs. Women and blacks joined the work force in increasing numbers, bringing many families into the growing middle class.

In the postwar years, Maryland took a leading role in the civil rights movement. Black leaders such as Lilly May Jackson and Thurgood Marshall led the struggle against segregation, and in 1954 Baltimore became the first large segregated city to integrate its public schools. Racial tension during the 1960's led to rioting, first in Cambridge and later in Baltimore. People slowly accepted integration, however, and the state moved forward with its own program of affirmative action.

The movement to the suburbs caused cities like Baltimore to decline, but today Maryland is making great efforts to restore them. James Rouse, who built the city of Columbia, Maryland, was chiefly responsible for rebuilding Baltimore. Decaying old warehouses were swept away around the harbor, and Harborplace, also designed by Rouse, brings the city millions of visitors.

GEORGE BEISHLAG
Towson State University
Reviewed by GEORGE H. CALLCOTT
University of Maryland—College Park

MASARYK, TOMÁŠ (1850–1937)

Tomáš Garrigue Masaryk was a founder and the first president of Czechoslovakia (now divided into the Czech Republic and Slovakia). He was born on March 7, 1850, in Hodonín, Moravia, then part of the Austro-Hungarian Empire. His father was a coachman on an estate belonging to the Austrian imperial family. Masaryk studied at the universities of Vienna and Leipzig. At Leipzig he met an American music student, Charlotte Garrigue. They were married in 1878. In 1882 he was appointed a professor of philosophy at the newly formed Czech University in Prague. There he began his career as a scholar and political leader. His writings quickly made him famous.

Prague was the center of Czech nationalism. Masaryk soon became a leader of the Young Czech Party, which sought greater self-government. In 1891 he was elected to the Austrian parliament. But he returned to teaching two years later. In 1900 he formed the Progressive (Realist) Party. He hoped to unite the Slovaks (who were ruled by Hungary) and the Czechs in a self-governing federation within the empire. In 1907 he was again elected to parliament.

When World War I broke out in 1914, Masaryk began to organize a movement for complete independence. He was warned that he might be arrested, and he left Prague for London. There he and other patriots, including Eduard Beneš, formed a Czechoslovak national council. In 1918 Austria was on the brink of defeat, and the council declared itself a provisional government. On October 28 of that year, Masaryk proclaimed the independence of the Czechoslovak nation. He was elected president and returned to Prague. He was re-elected three times and served until his retirement in 1935. His friend Beneš succeeded him as president. Masaryk died near Prague on September 14, 1937. His son, Jan Garrigue Masaryk, held several important posts in the Czechoslovak Government.

Reviewed by R. E. ALLEN
Columbia University

MASERS. See LASERS.

MASON-DIXON LINE

The Mason-Dixon line is the southern border of Pennsylvania, just north of 39° 43′ north latitude. The states north of this line abolished slavery during and soon after the Revolutionary War. And the line came to symbolize the entire border between slave and free states, or between the South and the North.

The colonial charters of Maryland and Pennsylvania left their common border in dispute. In 1732, commissioners from both colonies agreed to a border. But minor differences delayed the survey that would mark the actual line. The commissioners finally hired two English astronomers, Charles Mason and Jeremiah Dixon, who made the survey from 1763 to 1767. Their most difficult task was placing their first marker, southwest of Philadelphia. This marker, called the Stargazer's Stone, was set at the point where the borders of Pennsylvania, Maryland, and Delaware meet. It became the point on which all future surveys of federal land west of Pennsylvania rested. From the Stargazer's Stone, Mason and Dixon

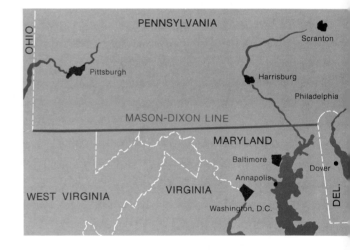

pushed due west to Maryland's western border. Later, Pennsylvania and Virginia extended the line to Pennsylvania's western border.

Mason and Dixon were very accurate. Later surveys resulted in no major changes in their line. Today many people still say the South is located "below the Mason-Dixon line."

ARI HOOGENBOOM
City University of New York, Brooklyn College

MASONRY. See BRICKS AND MASONRY.

MASSACHUSETTS

The name Massachusetts *comes from the Massachuset Indians, an Algonquian tribe that once lived around the Great Blue Hill near present-day Boston. The Massachuset ceased to exist as an independent tribe before their culture could be recorded, but it is believed that in their language,* Massachusetts *meant "near the great hill."*

Massachusetts is nicknamed the Bay State, after the Massachusetts Bay Colony, founded by English Puritans in 1630 on Massachusetts Bay, an inlet of the Atlantic Ocean. Although Plymouth had been settled by the Pilgrims ten years earlier, the Massachusetts Bay Colony was the first to receive an official royal charter from King Charles I of England.

State flag

The Commonwealth of Massachusetts is located in the northeastern United States in the region known as New England. Except for Maine, it is the most easterly of the fifty states. Massachusetts is also one of the most densely populated states, even though it is near the smallest in area.

Boston, its capital and largest city, is an international cultural center, famous for its extraordinary educational institutions and medical facilities. Since colonial times, Boston has been called the Cradle of Liberty, as Bostonians were the primary organizers of the American independence movement that gave rise to the Revolutionary War.

In fact, ever since the Pilgrims founded Plymouth Colony in 1620, the citizens of Massachusetts have played an immeasurable role in shaping the course of American political, economic, and social history. The state has produced exceptional leaders in the fields of politics, industry, education, the arts and sciences, religion, and social welfare.

In the 1800's as the United States transformed itself into an urban, industrialized society, Massachusetts led the way in the production of manufactured goods. Today, with its research activities and advancements in high technology industries, Massachusetts remains in the forefront of modern industry.

▶LAND

Nothing expresses the varied character of Massachusetts quite so much as its surface features. There are some flat areas, but most of the land is broken and hilly. Some parts are quite rugged, even though the elevations are not high. Only a small part of the state is more than 1,000 feet (300 meters) above sea level; much of it is less than 500 feet (150 meters) above sea level.

Land Regions

Massachusetts may be divided into several regions—the Coastal Plain, the Seaboard Lowland, the New England Upland, the Connecticut Valley Lowland, and the Taconic Mountains.

The Coastal Plain is an extensive landform that makes up most of the eastern coast of the United States. In Massachusetts it covers Cape Cod and the islands of Nantucket and Martha's Vineyard. The northern side of Cape Cod is a long ridge that was formed by glaciers during the ice ages. The southern side is low and sandy and is pitted with small lakes and ponds. The hooked northern end of Cape Cod was formed by the action of currents and waves. Sand was deposited in the form of a curved sandbar and was whipped by the wind into huge piles called dunes.

The Seaboard Lowland makes up the rest of Massachusetts' coastal lands. This area, also called the Coastal Lowland, has a rough ter-

Opposite page, clockwise from left: **Faneuil Hall, an old meeting hall in Boston, was the site of many revolutionary activities. Beach enthusiasts dig for clams along the Atlantic shore. The bustling port city of Boston, the state capital, is the cultural center of New England. Admirers dubbed it the Hub of the Universe.**

*State flower:
Mayflower*

*State tree:
American elm*

FACTS AND FIGURES

Location: Northeastern United States; bordered on the north by Vermont and New Hampshire, on the east by the Atlantic Ocean, on the south by Connecticut and Rhode Island, and on the west by New York.

Area: 9,241 sq mi (23,934 km²); rank, 45th.

Population: 6,349,097 (2000 census); rank, 13th.

Elevation: *Highest*—3,491 ft (1,064 m) at Mount Greylock; *lowest*—sea level along the Atlantic Ocean.

Capital: Boston.

Statehood: February 6, 1788; 6th state.

State Motto: *Ense petit placidam sub libertate quietem* ("By the sword we seek peace, but peace only under liberty").

State Song: "All Hail to Massachusetts."

Nickname: Bay State.

Abbreviations: MA; Mass.

*State bird:
Chickadee*

The craggy beauty of Gay Head Cliffs on Martha's Vineyard in the Atlantic Ocean contrasts greatly with the gently sloping lowlands of the Connecticut River Valley in central Massachusetts.

rain, except for a few small basins. The largest of these are the Boston and the Narragansett basins. The Boston Basin contains many oval-shaped hills called **drumlins**. The most famous drumlins are Bunker Hill and Beacon Hill.

The coastline is rough and rocky, with many sheltered harbors and small offshore islands. In some places the waves have formed sandbars, or **tombolos**, that tie the islands to the mainland. Good examples of tombolos are found at Duxbury, Nahant, and Marblehead.

The New England Upland covers most of the rest of the state. It is divided into two sections, the Eastern and the Western uplands, that are separated by the **Connecticut Valley Lowland.** The Eastern Upland rises gradually to elevations as high as 1,000 feet (300 meters), then drops sharply, with broad terraces descending like steps into the Connecticut Valley. This wide river valley, which stretches from northern Massachusetts to southern Connecticut, is mostly flat but is occasionally broken by ridges. Mount Tom and Mount Holyoke are peaks in these ridges. Then, out of the valley, the Western Upland makes a spectacular westward rise.

The Western Upland, an extension of the Green Mountains of Vermont, is known locally as the Berkshire Hills or, simply, the Berkshires. It ends abruptly, dropping sharply to the Berkshire Valley—a narrow trough that runs along the base of the Taconic Mountains.

The Taconic Mountains are old and worn down, but they have steep slopes. Mount Greylock lies in this range. At 3,491 feet (1,064 meters), it is the highest point in the state.

Rivers, Lakes, and Coastal Waters

The Connecticut River is the principal river of Massachusetts. Its most important tributaries are the Westfield, Deerfield, Millers, and Chicopee rivers. This major river system drains the Connecticut Valley Lowland and the Eastern and Western uplands. Northeastern Massachusetts is drained by the Merrimack River and its tributaries, the Concord and the Nashua.

Massachusetts has many natural lakes, most of which are in the eastern part of the state. Often they are called ponds. Among the largest are Assawompset, Watuppa, and Long ponds. Artificial lakes include Quabbin and Wachusett reservoirs. Both of these supply water to the Boston metropolitan area.

The general coastline of Massachusetts is 192 miles (309 kilometers) long. With all the islands, bays, and inlets, the shoreline measures 1,519 miles (2,444 kilometers). Massachusetts' largest bay is Cape Cod Bay.

Climate

The word for the weather in Massachusetts is "variable." A fine day is often followed by two or three stormy or cloudy days. Winters are cold and wet. Summers are pleasantly warm. Temperatures in Boston average about 30°F (−1°C) in January and 73°F (23°C) in July. Coastal areas and the higher elevations in the western part of the state have slightly cooler July temperatures than other areas in the state. Massachusetts does not have a true rainy season. The rainfall is fairly evenly distributed throughout the year. All parts of the state have snow, but snows are heaviest in the west. Annual precipitation from rain and snow is about 44 inches (1,120 millimeters) in the Boston area.

Plant and Animal Life

In colonial days, Massachusetts was covered with forests. Huge oaks, maples, and white pines supplied the settlers with all their needs for building and fuel, but much forest land was lost to overcutting. Today nearly 65 percent of the state is forested.

Dozens of varieties of animals inhabit the land, mostly deer, bats, chipmunks, foxes, raccoons, squirrels, and other small woodland mammals. Cape Cod, the islands, and southeastern Massachusetts are significant stopping points on one of the two most important bird migration corridors in the nation.

Dozens of varieties of fish and shellfish abound in the coastal waters. Whales, once common in the offshore waters, still can be seen.

Natural Resources

Massachusetts is not richly endowed with forests or fertile soils, and the only minerals mined there are building stone, sand and gravel, limestone, and clay. The state's most valuable natural resource by far is the marine life found in its offshore waters. Due to the lack of raw materials and an agricultural base, the people of Massachusetts turned first to fishing, then commerce and industry in order to prosper.

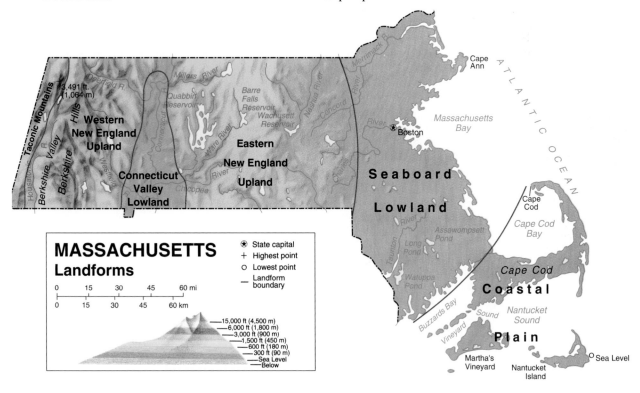

MASSACHUSETTS Landforms

✳	State capital
+	Highest point
O	Lowest point
—	Landform boundary

0 15 30 45 60 mi
0 15 30 45 60 km

15,000 ft (4,500 m)
6,000 ft (1,800 m)
3,000 ft (900 m)
1,500 ft (450 m)
600 ft (180 m)
300 ft (90 m)
Sea Level
Below

Harvard University (*left*) in Cambridge is one of the world's most renowned educational institutions. Boston's outdoor markets (*near right*) bring city residents together. The Boston Celtics (*far right*) play at the FleetCenter.

▶ **PEOPLE**

In 1830 most of the citizens of Massachusetts were native-born of Yankee stock—descendants of the original English settlers. Only 1 percent were foreign-born. Then in the 1840's, due to a potato crop failure and widespread famine in Ireland, thousands of Irish immigrants fled to the United States. By 1846, 1,000 per month were entering the port of Boston. French and English Canadians and Germans followed the Irish, and by the 1870's, 25 percent of Massachusetts' residents were foreign-born.

Another big surge in immigration occurred between 1890 and 1910. Large numbers arrived from Italy and Portugal and from the eastern European countries. The Portuguese were attracted by commercial fishing. But most of the newcomers found jobs in the growing textile and shoe industries. Since 1960 there has been a marked increase in the number of immigrants. The growth in services and high-tech industries has attracted the majority of newcomers from Asia, the West Indies, Latin America, Africa, Puerto Rico, and from the southern United States.

Education

The present-day system of public education had its start when the Massachusetts Board of Education was established in 1837. Horace Mann, the first secretary of the board, supervised the founding of an efficient system of public schools. A biography of this famous educator is included in Volume M.

Massachusetts has many private preparatory schools. Among them are Phillips Academy, in Andover; Deerfield Academy, in Deerfield; Groton School, in Groton; and St. Mark's School, in Southborough.

Harvard University, in Cambridge, founded in 1636, is the oldest institution of higher learning in the United States. Other well-known private institutions that were established originally for men are Amherst College, in Amherst; College of the Holy Cross, in Worcester; and Williams College, in Williamstown. Outstanding women's colleges include Mount Holyoke College, in South Hadley (the first women's college in the United States); Radcliffe College, in Cambridge; Simmons College, in Boston; Smith College, in Northampton; and Wellesley College, in Wellesley. Among the many other private institutions are Boston College, in Chestnut Hill; Boston University, in Boston; Brandeis University, in Waltham; the Massachusetts Institute of Technology (MIT), in Cambridge; Northeastern University, in Boston, and Wheaton College, in Norton.

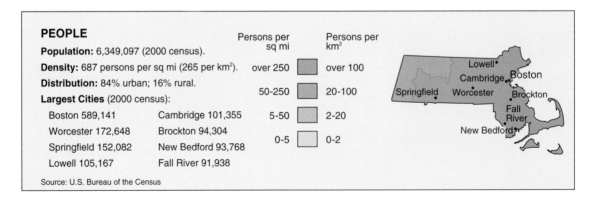

PEOPLE

Population: 6,349,097 (2000 census).

Density: 687 persons per sq mi (265 per km²).

Distribution: 84% urban; 16% rural.

Largest Cities (2000 census):

Boston 589,141	Cambridge 101,355
Worcester 172,648	Brockton 94,304
Springfield 152,082	New Bedford 93,768
Lowell 105,167	Fall River 91,938

Source: U.S. Bureau of the Census

Persons per sq mi	Persons per km²
over 250	over 100
50-250	20-100
5-50	2-20
0-5	0-2

Massachusetts also has many state-supported institutions of higher education. The University of Massachusetts has five campuses—in Amherst, Dartmouth, Lowell, Boston, and a medical school in Worcester. The Massachusetts State College system includes colleges in Bridgewater, Fitchburg, Framingham, North Adams, Salem, Westfield, and Worcester. Other members of the system are the Massachusetts College of Art, in Boston, and the Massachusetts Maritime Academy, in Buzzards Bay. Massachusetts also supports approximately 15 community colleges.

Libraries, Museums, and the Arts

Massachusetts' first library was established in 1638. In that year, a young minister, John Harvard, died. He left his library and half his fortune to the newly founded College of Massachusetts Bay Colony, which was renamed Harvard College in 1639. It is now Harvard University.

The Boston Public Library is among the largest in the nation. The Massachusetts Historical Society in Boston, the oldest historical society in the United States, has the private papers of Thomas Jefferson, the Adams Papers, and other historical documents. Important collections pertaining to American history are also found in the Boston Athenaeum and in libraries of the Essex Institute, in Salem, and the American Antiquarian Society, in Worcester. The John Fitzgerald Kennedy Library, in Boston, houses presidential papers and a museum.

Massachusetts is noted for its many museums. Outstanding art collections are on view at the Museum of Fine Arts and the Isabella Stewart Gardner Museum, both in Boston. Important college museums include the William Hayes Fogg Art Museum of Harvard University, in Cambridge, and Smith College Museum of Art, in Northampton. Outstanding science museums of interest include the Museum of Science, in Boston; the Peabody Museum of Archaeology and Ethnology, in Cambridge; the Whaling Museum, in New Bedford; and Pilgrim Hall, in Plymouth.

The Boston Symphony Orchestra, founded in 1881, is one of the world's great orchestras. In the summer the orchestra performs outdoors at Tanglewood, near Lenox, where the Berkshire Music Festival is held. Also well known are the Boston Pops orchestra and the Opera Company of Boston.

Sports

Boston has professional teams in every major sport. The Boston Red Sox of the American League play baseball at Fenway Park, one of the nation's oldest and most famous ballparks. The Boston Celtics of the National Basketball Association play at the FleetCenter, as do the Boston Bruins of the National Hockey League. The New England Patriots of the National Football League play nearby at Foxboro Stadium.

Since 1897, Boston has hosted the Boston Marathon. This oldest of modern-day marathons is held every year on Patriot's Day, the third Monday in April.

▶ECONOMY

Massachusetts has a diversified economy. Services and commercial activities, such as banking, insurance, real estate, and wholesale and retail trade provide the largest number of jobs and contribute the most to the gross state product (GSP)—the total value of goods and services the state produces in one year. Manufacturing is of secondary importance, followed by government and transportation and public utilities. Agriculture, construction, and mining contribute relatively little to the overall value of the state's economy.

Services

Massachusetts service industries produce about 72 percent of the GSP. Tourism, business, legal, medical, community, social, and personal services combined account for 22 percent. Financial services, including insurance, banking, and real estate, account for 17 percent. Boston is the major wholesale and retail trade center in New England; wholesale and retail trade of personal and industrial goods also account for 17 percent of the GSP. State and municipal government services account for 9 percent of the GSP, and transportation and public utility services account for an additional 7 percent (see below).

Manufacturing

Manufacturing accounts for about 22 percent of the GSP, second only to the service industries. The state's chief manufactured products are nonelectrical machinery and electric and electronic equipment, such as computers. Other leading manufactures include scientific instruments and measuring devices, fabricated metal products, paper, rubber, plastic, and leather products, printing and publishing, and transportation equipment. Textiles and shoes are still produced, but they are not as important as they once were.

Cranberries are a Massachusetts specialty. Every September, harvesters flood the bogs in which they grow and scoop up the berries that rise to the top.

Agriculture

Only a very small number of workers in Massachusetts make a living from agriculture, and it accounts for less than 1 percent of the GSP. The main sources of agricultural income are greenhouse and nursery products, dairy products, beef cattle, hogs, apples, hay, and asparagus. In addition, Massachusetts has long been famous for its cranberries, grown in specially prepared bogs.

Fisheries. It is said that many people went to the Massachusetts colony not for religious freedom or farming but for the good fishing to be found in that part of the world. At present the main commercial fish and shellfish include haddock, scallops, flounder, cod, ocean perch, and lobster.

Mining and Construction

The state's mining industry is not significant. Building stone and sand and gravel are

---

PRODUCTS AND INDUSTRIES

Manufacturing: Nonelectrical machinery, electric and electronic equipment, scientific instruments and measuring devices, fabricated metal products, paper, rubber, plastic, and leather products, printing and publishing, transportation equipment.

Agriculture: Greenhouse and nursery products, dairy products, beef cattle, hogs, apples, hay, asparagus, cranberries, fish and shellfish.

Minerals: Building stone, sand and gravel, limestone, clay.

Services: Wholesale and retail trade; finance, insurance, and real estate; business, social, and personal services; transportation, communication, and utilities; government.

*Gross state product is the total value of goods and services produced in a year.

Percentage of Gross State Product* by Industry

Manufacturing — 22%

Business, social, and personal services — 22%

Finance, insurance, and real estate — 17%

Mining 1%
Agriculture 1%
Construction 4%
Transportation, communication, and utilities — 7%
Government — 9%
Wholesale and retail trade — 17%

Source: U.S. Bureau of Economic Analysis

quarried, and limestone and clay are also mined. But Massachusetts has a very active construction industry. Commercial, public, and residential building projects contribute nearly 5 percent to the GSP.

Transportation

By the end of the Revolutionary War, a good system of roads was badly needed due to the growth of industry in different sections of the state. Massachusetts formed private companies to build and maintain roads. Today the state has a network of excellent highways. One of the most notable is the Massachusetts Turnpike, which crosses the state from east to west. Another is the superhighway Route 128 that circles Boston and its inner suburbs.

Boston has been a leading port since the earliest days. There are numerous other small harbors with port facilities, such as Gloucester and New Bedford. The first railroad track was laid between Quincy and Milton in 1826. By 1836, three important railroads had been completed. Today Massachusetts' railroads provide mainly freight service, but commuter lines serve the Boston area.

There are about 50 commercial and municipal airports and several seaplane bases. The major airport is Boston's Logan International.

Communication

The Boston *News-Letter*, started in 1704, was the first regularly issued paper in the United States. Some of the largest and best-known newspapers today are *The Boston Globe*, *The Boston Herald*, and *The Christian Science Monitor*, all published in Boston.

Fishing was Massachusetts' first successful commercial enterprise, but recent overharvesting has begun to threaten the industry.

There are more than 40 other daily newspapers in Massachusetts and more than 200 weeklies and other papers. Massachusetts has about 100 radio stations and about a dozen commercial television stations.

▶CITIES

Massachusetts is one of the most densely populated of the 50 states, and more than 84 percent of its residents live in urban areas, or cities and towns. Boston is the largest city in the state. Other well-settled areas are around Springfield in the Connecticut Valley Low-

Boston is Massachusetts' largest and capital city. It is one of the nation's major centers of education, culture, finance, insurance, wholesale and retail trade, banking, real estate, scientific research and development, publishing, and tourism.

Places of Interest

Plimoth Plantation, near Plymouth

Rockport Harbor, Cape Ann

Revolutionary War re-enactment, in Sudbury

Adams National Historic Site, in Quincy, was the home of the Adams family for more than 100 years.

Boston has dozens of locations famous in the history of the state and of the nation, including Faneuil Hall, where Revolutionary War patriots met; the Old North Church, where lanterns signaled Paul Revere to begin his famous "midnight ride"; the Old State House, the seat of the colonial government, and Black Heritage Trail. For a detailed description of attractions, see the article BOSTON in Volume B.

Cape Ann, the northern arm of Massachusetts Bay, has several charming coastal towns, including an artists' colony at Rockport and the historic fishing village of Gloucester.

Cape Cod is a peninsula jutting into the Atlantic Ocean. The cape's lovely beaches, quaint villages, summer theaters, gift shops, and artist colonies attract many vacationers.

Concord, near Boston, was settled in 1635. It was the site of the first Provincial Congress in 1774 and of the Battle of Concord on April 19, 1775. By the mid-1800's, Concord had become a literary center. Among the writers who lived and worked there were Ralph Waldo Emerson, Henry David Thoreau, Nathaniel Hawthorne, and Louisa May Alcott.

Historic Deerfield, settled in 1669, preserves twelve museum-houses depicting the culture of colonial New England.

John F. Kennedy Library, in Boston, houses Kennedy's presidential papers.

Lowell National Historical Park, in Lowell, commemorates the nation's first planned industrial community.

Martha's Vineyard, an island south of Woods Hole, was named for the wild grapes that once grew there. Settled in 1642, it soon became a fishing and whaling center. Its many attractions include beaches, small historic towns, and the brightly colored cliffs at Gay Head.

Minute Man National Historical Park, in Lexington, preserves the site where minutemen fired on British troops retreating from the battles of Lexington and Concord on April 19, 1775, the first day of the Revolutionary War.

Nantucket Island, south of Cape Cod, takes its name from an Indian word meaning "the faraway land." Once the most important whaling port in the world, today the island is a summer resort.

Old Sturbridge Village, near Sturbridge, is a "living history" theme park that shows what a New England farming village looked like in the 1830's.

Plimoth Plantation, near Plymouth, is a "living history" park that re-creates life in the Pilgrim's original village in 1627. For more information, see the article PLYMOUTH COLONY in Volume P.

Plymouth, located southeast of Boston, is the site of the first permanent white settlement in New England. The best-known monument is Plymouth

Rock. It is said that the Pilgrims stepped ashore on this rock when they landed in December 1620. The *Mayflower II*, a reproduction of the ship that brought the Pilgrims to Massachusetts, is moored at State Pier. For more information, see the article MAYFLOWER in this volume.

Provincetown, on Cape Cod, was the site of the first landing of the Pilgrims, in November 1620. The Pilgrim Memorial Monument commemorates the event. Today Provincetown is a fishing village and a summer resort.

Salem, located near Boston, was the scene of the famous witchcraft trials of 1692. By 1800, Salem had become a leading port; many fine mansions that once belonged to sea captains are now open to the public, including the one used by Nathaniel Hawthorne as the setting for his novel *The House of the Seven Gables*.

Saugus Iron Works National Historic Site, at Saugus, is a reconstruction of an ironworks that began operating in 1646.

Walden Pond State Reservation is located near Concord. Walden Pond was a favorite retreat for the writer Henry David Thoreau.

State Recreation Areas. Massachusetts has hundreds of national and state parks, scenic trails, national historic sites, and historical parks. To obtain information on these and other places of interest, write to the Massachusetts Office of Travel and Tourism, 100 Cambridge Street, 13th Floor, Boston, Mass. 02202.

land, Worcester in the central part of the state, Lowell and Lawrence in the northeast, and Brockton, Fall River, and New Bedford in the southeast.

The Boston metropolitan area is the major cultural center of New England. It includes many other cities and towns, including Cambridge, Newton, and Quincy, and each of these alone ranks among the largest cities in the state. The total population of the Boston metropolitan area is about 5.8 million.

Boston, the state capital, was founded in 1630 by John Winthrop as the main colony of the Massachusetts Bay Company. Boston contains many of the state's most important historical sites from the days of the Revolutionary War. An article about the city appears in Volume B.

Worcester, the second largest city in the state, is an industrial and educational center. About 20 towns fall within its metropolitan area, whose population is approaching 440,000. The city itself has more than ten colleges and universities, including Worcester Polytechnic Institute. Worcester's American Antiquarian Society claims to have the world's largest collection of early American newspapers, sheet music, and children's books.

Springfield is the state's third largest city, but the population of its greater metropolitan area, which includes Chicopee and Holyoke, is larger than Worcester's. This industrial region is known for the manufacture of clothing, electrical machinery, chemicals, and paper.

Springfield is the financial and industrial center of southwestern Massachusetts. It is also home to the Naismith Memorial Basketball Hall of Fame.

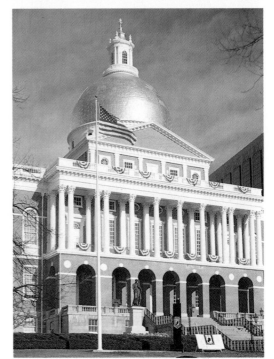

Massachusetts' capitol building, called the State House, is located in the heart of Boston. Designed by Charles Bulfinch, it was completed in 1795.

▶ **GOVERNMENT**

Massachusetts is governed by a constitution that was adopted in 1780. Amendments may be proposed by the legislature or by petition of the voters.

The governor, who is elected for a term of four years, is assisted by a governor's council and several other elected executive officers. The state legislature, known as the General Court of Massachusetts, consists of a senate and a house of representatives.

The court system is headed by the Supreme Judicial Court, the oldest court in the United States in continuous existence. Other courts include superior and district courts and the juvenile court of Boston.

GOVERNMENT

State Government
Governor: 4-year term
State senators: 40; 2-year terms
State representatives: 160;
2-year terms
Number of counties: 14

Federal Government
U.S. senators: 2
U.S. representatives: 10
Number of electoral votes: 12

For the name of the current governor, see STATE GOVERNMENTS in Volume S. For the names of current U.S. senators and representatives, see UNITED STATES, CONGRESS OF THE in Volume U-V.

English pilgrims set their boat, the *Mayflower*, ashore at Plymouth in 1620 and established the first permanent European settlement in Massachusetts.

▶ **HISTORY**

Before the Europeans came to North America, several Algonkian-speaking Indian tribes inhabited Massachusetts. Most of them lived and prospered near the coast or in the Connecticut Valley Lowland.

Settlement and Colonial Days

Europeans sailed along the shores of present-day New England long before the first colonists came to Massachusetts. Giovanni Verrazano was the first to record such a voyage, in 1524.

In 1602, Bartholomew Gosnold, an English navigator, explored Massachusetts Bay and named its curved peninsula Cape Cod, because of the abundance of codfish in the area. When Captain John Smith visited the area in 1614, he called it New England. His descriptions of the fine timber and the abundance of fish and wildlife attracted many Europeans, who came in search of opportunities. But soon the Indians fell prey to the foreigners' diseases, and the resulting epidemics wiped out more than 80 percent of the southeastern coastal tribes.

The first permanent colony in Massachusetts was Plymouth, settled by the Pilgrims in 1620. (For more information, see the article PLYMOUTH COLONY in Volume P.) Gradually other settlements were established along the coast for fishing and trading. The Massachusetts Bay Company, a company of English Puritans, started a colony in 1630. Under the leadership of John Winthrop, they founded Boston, which prospered. Fishing and whaling stimulated shipbuilding and trade.

INDEX TO MASSACHUSETTS MAP

• County Seat   Counties in parentheses   ★ State Capital

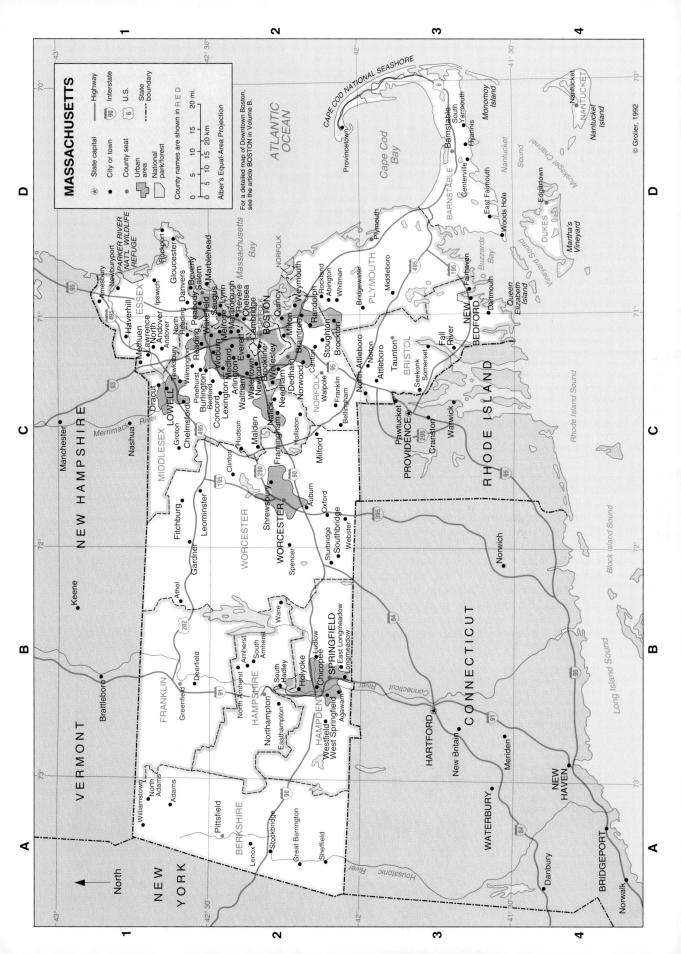

MASSACHUSETTS

✹	State capital
●	City or town
●	County seat
	Urban area
	National park/forest

Highway
Interstate
U.S.
State boundary

90 Interstate
6 U.S.

County names are shown in RED.

For a detailed map of Downtown Boston, see the article BOSTON in Volume B.

0 5 10 15 20 mi.
0 5 10 15 20 km

Alber's Equal-Area Projection

© Grolier, 1992

North

VERMONT

NEW HAMPSHIRE

NEW YORK

CONNECTICUT

RHODE ISLAND

ATLANTIC OCEAN

Massachusetts Bay

Cape Cod Bay

CAPE COD NATIONAL SEASHORE

Buzzards Bay

Nantucket Sound

Vineyard Sound

Muskeget Channel

Rhode Island Sound

Block Island Sound

Long Island Sound

BERKSHIRE
FRANKLIN
HAMPSHIRE
HAMPDEN
WORCESTER
MIDDLESEX
ESSEX
SUFFOLK
NORFOLK
PLYMOUTH
BRISTOL
BARNSTABLE
DUKES
NANTUCKET

Merrimack River
Connecticut River
Housatonic River

Manchester
Nashua
Keene
Brattleboro
Williamstown
North Adams
Adams
Pittsfield
Lenox
Stockbridge
Great Barrington
Sheffield
Greenfield
Deerfield
North Amherst
Amherst
South Amherst
Northampton
Easthampton
South Hadley
Holyoke
Chicopee
Ludlow
SPRINGFIELD
East Longmeadow
Longmeadow
Agawam
West Springfield
Westfield
Ware
Athol
Gardner
Fitchburg
Leominster
Clinton
Spencer
WORCESTER
Shrewsbury
Auburn
Oxford
Sturbridge
Southbridge
Webster
HARTFORD
New Britain
Meriden
NEW HAVEN
WATERBURY
Danbury
BRIDGEPORT
Norwalk
Norwich
Fitchburg
Brattleboro

Lowell
Dracut
Tewksbury
Methuen
Lawrence
North Andover
Andover
Haverhill
Amesbury
Newburyport
PARKER RIVER NATL WILDLIFE REFUGE
Rockport
Gloucester
Ipswich
Danvers
Beverly
Salem
Marblehead
Peabody
Lynn
Saugus
Revere
Chelsea
Wakefield
Melrose
Medford
Everett
Woburn
Reading
North Reading
Wilmington
Pinehurst
Burlington
Bedford
Concord
Lexington
Arlington
Cambridge
Watertown
Newton
Waltham
BOSTON
Brookline
Wellesley
Needham
Dedham
Norwood
Walpole
Franklin
Bellingham
Milford
Holliston
Framingham
Natick
Malden
Hudson
Groton
Chelmsford

Quincy
Milton
Braintree
Randolph
Stoughton
Rockland
Abington
Whitman
Brockton
Bridgewater
Middleboro
Plymouth
Weymouth
Norton
Attleboro
North Attleboro
Taunton
Seekonk
Somerset
Fall River
NEW BEDFORD
Dartmouth
Fairhaven
Queen Elizabeth Island
PROVIDENCE
Pawtucket
Cranston
Warwick

Barnstable
South Yarmouth
Hyannis
Centerville
East Falmouth
Woods Hole
Provincetown

Nantucket
Monomoy Island
Nantucket Island
Edgartown
Martha's Vineyard

Interstate 95, 93, 495, 290, 195, 90, 84, 91, 395, 295, 195
U.S. 202, 97, 6

Famous People

Horatio Alger, Jr. (1834–99), born in Revere, wrote more than 100 enormously popular books for boys. A Unitarian minister, he left the ministry in 1866 to devote himself to helping orphans and runaways and to writing. His "rags to riches" novels, which include *Ragged Dick* (1867) and *Tattered Tom* (1871), support his theory that any honest, hardworking boy with a little pluck can make a success of himself in America. The term "Alger hero" still applies to anyone who becomes successful by this formula.

William Bradford (1590–1657), born in Austerfield, England, was one of the Pilgrim leaders who established Plymouth Colony (1620). He served as its governor for more than 30 years and recorded early Pilgrim life in his historical account, *Of Plymouth Plantation*.

Edward William Brooke (1919–), born in Washington, D.C., was an influential Republican politician in Massachusetts. As state attorney general (1963–66), Brooke exposed corruption and organized crime in the government. In 1966 he became the first black to be elected to the U.S. Senate by popular vote. Reelected in 1972, he served until 1979.

Mary Baker Eddy (1821–1910), founder of the Christian Science religion, was born near Concord, N.H., but performed her life's work in Boston. In 1879 she founded the First Church of Christ, Scientist, to promote healing through prayer. In 1908, Eddy also founded the internationally-renowned newspaper *The Christian Science Monitor*.

William Lloyd Garrison (1805–79), a journalist, radical abolitionist, and advocate for women's rights, was born in Newburyport. As editor of the Boston-based antislavery publication *The Liberator* (1831–65), Garrison lashed out against slavery, declaring it an abomination in God's sight. A founder of the American Anti-Slavery Society, he once called the U.S. Constitution "a covenant with death and an agreement with Hell" because it protected slavery.

Julia Ward Howe (1819–1910), an author and abolitionist, spent her adult life in Boston, although she was born in New York City. Howe and her husband edited the *Commonwealth*, a major antislavery periodical. She published three books of verse and a biography of Margaret Fuller (1883) but is best known for "The Battle Hymn of the Republic," first published in the *Atlantic Monthly* in 1862.

Cotton Mather

Increase Mather (1639–1723), born in Dorchester, was a strict Puritan, who used his position as teacher of Boston's Second Congregational Church (New North Church) to shape the culture of second-generation New Englanders. He attacked those who did not conform to traditional church practices. He cautioned against unfounded accusations at the Salem Witch Trials (1692), and his publication *Cases of Conscience Concerning Evil Spirits* (1693) helped put an end to them. He also served as president of Harvard College from 1685 until 1701. Increase's eldest son, **Cotton Mather** (1663–1728), born in Boston, was also a congregational minister. A noted scholar, Cotton wrote more than 450 books on scientific

---

At first the Indians and the colonists were friendly. A few Indians, such as Samoset and Squanto, welcomed the English. When the colonists' crops failed, the Indians taught the newcomers how to plant corn, beans, pumpkins, and squash and where to find lobsters and clams. But discontent soon grew among the Indians. The settlers believed the Indians were inferior and were intolerant of their way of life. The settlers also aggressively took over the Indians' land.

A few tribes decided to adopt some of the settlers' ways. A mission was established at Natick in 1651. There, John Eliot, known as the Apostle to the Indians, led an effort to educate Indians and to convert them to Christianity. This mission was known as the praying town of Natick. Other praying towns were

The famous Boston Tea Party took place on December 16, 1773. American colonial patriots, dressed as Indians, raided British merchant ships and dumped crates of British tea into Boston Harbor to protest the tea tax. The raid so infuriated the British, Parliament passed the so-called Intolerable Acts, which led directly to the Revolutionary War.

and religious topics. His *Magnalia Christi Americana* (1702), which recorded the Puritans' effort to establish Christianity in the New World, is one of the most important pieces of early American scholarship. His writings and preachings about witchcraft may have stimulated the hysteria that led to the Salem Witch Trials (1692), although he later criticized the executions.

Sylvia Plath (1932–63), born in Boston, was one of the finest "confessional poets" of her generation. Plath's savage imagery produced such brilliant collections as *Ariel* (1965), *Crossing the Water* (1971), and *Winter Trees* (1971), all published after her suicide at the age of 30. Her semi-autobiographical novel, *The Bell Jar* (1963), which described a young woman's mental breakdown, became a cult classic.

John Winthrop (1588–1649), born in Edwardstone, England, was a founder (1630) and four-term governor of the Massachusetts Bay Colony. A strict Puritan leader, Winthrop established the Congregational Church of New England, which shaped the Puritan settlement into a Bible commonwealth. His *Journal* (1630–49) is the most valuable surviving record of the colony's early years.

Robert F. and John F. Kennedy

Consult the Index to find more information in *The New Book of Knowledge* about the following people who were either born in Massachusetts or are otherwise associated with the state:

ADAMS, Charles Francis
ADAMS, Henry
ADAMS, John
ADAMS, John Quincy
ADAMS, Samuel
ALCOTT, Louisa May
ANTHONY, Susan B.
BARTON, Clara
BERNSTEIN, Leonard
BRADSTREET, Anne
BRANDEIS, Louis Dembitz
BRYANT, William Cullen
BUSH, George
COOLIDGE, Calvin
DAVIS, Bette
DE MILLE, Cecil B.
DICKINSON, Emily

DIX, Dorothea
DU BOIS, W.E.B.
EMERSON, Ralph Waldo
FRANKLIN, Benjamin
FULLER, Margaret
HANCOCK, John
HAWTHORNE, Nathaniel
HOLMES, Oliver Wendell
HOLMES, Oliver Wendell, Jr.
HOMER, Winslow
HOWE, Elias
KENNEDY, John F.
KENNEDY, Robert F. and Edward M.
LODGE, Henry Cabot
LOWELL FAMILY

MANN, Horace
MORSE, Samuel F. B.
MOTT, Lucretia Coffin
POE, Edgar Allan
REVERE, Paul
SAMOSET
SEUSS, Dr.
STONE, Lucy
THOREAU, Henry David
WALKER, David
WEBSTER, Daniel
WHEATLEY, Phillis
WHISTLER, James Abbott McNeil
WHITNEY, Eli
WHITTIER, John Greenleaf
WYETH, N. C.

established, and by 1674 more than 1,000 Indians had been converted.

Other groups of Indians refused to give up their way of life. Some moved far into the interior, and some fought the settlers. The largest group, the Wampanoag under the leadership of Chief Massasoit, aided the English for many years. But Massasoit's son, King Philip (Metacomet), believed that Indian life would soon be destroyed. In fact, the colonists' increasing need for land led to King Philip's War (1675–76), in which the colonists attacked the Wampanoag, killed King Philip, and very nearly eliminated the Indians from Massachusetts.

The Revolutionary War

From 1691 up to the time of the Revolutionary War, there was constant quarreling between the colonists and the English government, mostly about taxes. Boston became the center of resistance. Events such as the Boston Massacre in 1770 and the Boston Tea Party in 1773 led finally to the Revolu-

tionary War. The first battles were fought at Lexington and Concord. (For more information about these and other events of the struggle in Massachusetts, see the article REVOLUTIONARY WAR in Volume R.)

Statehood

In 1780 the people of Massachusetts ratified (approved) a state constitution, which later served as a model for the Constitution of the United States. On February 6, 1788, Massachusetts became the sixth state of the Union. (Although Massachusetts, along with Virginia, Kentucky, and Pennsylvania, calls itself a commonwealth, there is no legal difference between a commonwealth and a state.)

Industrial, Cultural, and Social Developments

After the Revolutionary War, trade in and out of Boston Harbor flourished. The Northwest fur trade, new markets for codfish in the West Indies, and the opening up of China to American products brought fabulous wealth to a handful of merchant families. These fortu-

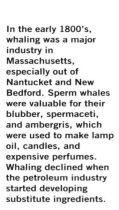

In the early 1800's, whaling was a major industry in Massachusetts, especially out of Nantucket and New Bedford. Sperm whales were valuable for their blubber, spermaceti, and ambergris, which were used to make lamp oil, candles, and expensive perfumes. Whaling declined when the petroleum industry started developing substitute ingredients.

nate few, which included the Cabots and the Lowells, became known as the Boston Brahmins, nicknamed for India's elite class. Also during this period, Massachusetts' whaling industry boomed, as whale products furnished oil for lamps and wax for candles.

In the early years of the 1800's, as a result of Europe's instability due to the Napoleonic Wars, the Brahmins chose to invest their wealth at home rather than abroad. The result was the creation of New England's massive textile industry—centered around Waltham, Lawrence, and Lowell—and the beginning of the industrialization of the nation.

The first industrial workers were Yankee farm women and children, who left poor, rural areas to work in the booming factory towns. Soon large numbers of Irish, Canadians, and other immigrants poured into Massachusetts. The invention of a stitching machine in the 1850's helped to promote factory production of shoes. By 1900 almost half the nation's shoes were made in New England, with Massachusetts the leading state. The production of textiles and shoes led to another industry—the manufacture of machinery for the factories. By the end of the century, the state had become an urban society.

With its newfound prosperity as a commercial and industrial center, Boston also became the literary and publishing hub of the United States. Writers of this period were concerned with ideas on religion, democracy, the frontier, the common person, and science and industry. In addition, Boston became the center of the abolitionist, or antislavery, movement.

Labor Unrest

Industry prospered, but working conditions were often extremely poor, and strikes were frequent. Between 1881 and 1900, there were nearly 2,000 strikes and lockouts. In 1911 a labor law reduced the work week for women to 54 hours, but manufacturers struck back by cutting wages. This action led to a strike of more than 22,000 textile workers in Lawrence in 1912. The city came under siege and the state militia was called in. This strike became a milestone event in the struggle of American laborers for better working conditions.

Massachusetts' industries declined dramatically after World War I. In the 1920's, many businesses moved to the South, where labor was less expensive. By 1931, near the start of the Great Depression, only 44 percent of the state's working population was fully employed. The shipping, shoe, and textile industries bounced back during World War II but declined again after 1945.

In the 1950's, Massachusetts' industry turned toward services and also to science and technology. The state's exceptional educational institutions, including Harvard and MIT, attracted top engineers and physicists, whose research led to the development of the high-tech industries that flourish in Massachusetts today.

RICHARD O. RIESS
Salem State College
Reviewed by JACK TAGER
University of Massachusetts

See also BOSTON.

MASS MEDIA. See ADVERTISING; COMMUNICATION.

MASS PRODUCTION.   See Manufacturing.
MATA HARI.   See Spies (Profiles).
MATCHES.   See Fire.

MATERIALS SCIENCE

A material is the substance out of which something is made. Some materials, such as sand, cotton, gold, and the soil of the earth, are natural. Others, such as glass, polyester fabrics, steel, and concrete, are produced by people from natural materials. As human knowledge of these substances has grown, the materials of civilization have advanced from bricks to advanced ceramics, from bronze to miracle alloys, from glass to optical fibers.

Modern materials have remarkable properties. Some new adhesive materials join objects together so tightly that the objects will break before the joint does; other new materials are so smooth that nearly nothing can stick to them. Superconductors carry electricity without any loss of energy. Tiny silicon chips make it possible for hand-held computers to solve complicated problems.

Because human-made materials are so important, a science has developed to study them and to find ways of making new ones. This science, called materials science, has developed out of metallurgy, chemistry, and physics during the second half of the 1900's. To understand why a material has its particular properties, the materials scientist studies not only what atoms and molecules it is made of, but also the way its atoms are arranged and bonded together. All of these together make up the material's **microstructure**. How changes in these structures will affect the properties of a material is also examined. Thus it is reasonable to say that materials science is the study of microstructure, and that **materials engineering** is using the knowledge of microstructure to make new substances and devices.

▶ PROPERTIES OF MATERIALS

Matter can exist in three distinct states: gas, liquid, and solid. Materials science deals mainly with solid matter and how it behaves. The usefulness of a material is described by its **properties**. The properties of a material tell you whether it is light or heavy, hard or soft, brittle or flexible, strong or weak. They also tell you how well electricity or heat flows through it, whether it is magnetic and how

powerful a magnet it can be, and what happens when light or other electromagnetic waves strike it. Its properties may change dramatically at high temperatures or at low temperatures, in a vacuum or under high pressure, or when it is in contact with other materials.

Materials science deals with understanding why each material has its particular properties. From that understanding, materials scientists are able to invent new materials that have just the properties they need.

Atomic Arrangements

To understand a material, the materials scientist usually begins with the arrangements of its atoms or molecules and how they are held together. In most solids the atoms are arranged in a regular three-dimensional pattern that repeats itself over and over again like a stack of building blocks. This pattern is called a **crystal lattice**, and the material is said to form crystals or to be crystalline.

In a crystal lattice, the atoms are arranged in planes. In each plane, the atoms have a square, rectangular, triangular, or hexagonal (in the shape of a six-sided figure) arrangement. The planes are stacked one beside (or above) another so that the atoms of one plane are either lined up with the atoms on the neighboring planes or lined up with the spaces between those atoms. Only seven basic arrangements of atoms are possible. You can read more about those basic arrangements in the article Crystals in Volume C.

Although there are only seven basic arrangements of atoms in a crystal, there are infinitely many crystalline materials. That is because the atoms that go into that arrangement can be different, and the crystals can be imperfect. With different atoms, the same crystal lattice arrangement can have many different sizes, and the imperfections influence the material's properties in important ways.

Atomic Bonding

Many properties of a material are determined by the bonds that hold its atoms together. In solids, the bonds are of three types: **metallic**, **covalent**, and **ionic**. Atoms are made up of a tiny, positively charged inner core, called a nucleus, surrounded by a cloud of negatively charged electrons. The bonds between the atoms result from the interaction of their electrons.

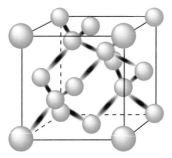

Each carbon atom in a diamond is joined to four other carbon atoms by covalent bonds. The atoms form a crystal in which the arrangement shown here repeats over and over in every direction. A diamond's hardness is due to the strength of its covalent bonds.

Most of the electrons of an atom are strongly attracted to the nucleus because the nucleus and electrons have opposite electrical charges. However, the electrons in the outer part of the cloud are not held by this attraction as tightly as the others, and when two atoms come close together, their outer electrons may be attracted by both atoms almost equally.

In metals, these outer electrons cease to belong to any one atom and move freely through the crystal lattice. As a result, solids held together with metallic bonds are good electrical conductors. Metallic bonding and free electrons are responsible for this high electrical conductivity and other properties characteristic of all metals, such as their ability to conduct heat and their shininess.

Covalent bonds are formed when two atoms share their outer electrons. Electrons spend part of their time with one atom and the remainder with another. The electrons stay close to the two bonding atoms, so covalent solids are poor conductors of electricity. Diamond and silicon are typical covalent solids.

Atoms are more chemically stable when they have certain numbers of outer electrons. When they have the right number for maximum stability, they are said to have a "complete outer shell." If one atom has a complete outer shell plus one more outer electron, it gives up that extra electron easily and becomes a positively charged ion. If another atom has one electron less than a complete outer shell, it attracts another electron to become a negatively charged ion. When those two atoms come together, the first easily gives up an electron to the second, forming an **ionic bond**. Bonding results from attraction between the oppositely charged ions. Like covalent solids, ionic solids are poor conductors of electricity because each electron is bound to a particular ion and is thus not free to move around in the crystal lattice. Sodium chloride —ordinary table salt—is a typical ionic solid.

Grains and Crystal Defects

In some crystals, the pattern of atoms repeats perfectly or almost perfectly for millions or even billions of atoms in every direction. When this happens, even though the spacing of the atoms in the crystal lattice is very small, we can see evidence of its regularity in pieces of material large enough to hold in our hands. Have you ever noticed the sharp rectangular shape of salt crystals, the smooth surfaces and distinct corners of a gemstone, the precise shapes of pieces of certain minerals dug up from the ground? Because of those smooth surfaces and sharp corners, you know that you are looking at a crystal.

But in most crystalline materials, the regularity is not so obvious. These materials are made up of many tiny regions, each as perfect as those large ones but much smaller. The material does not appear to be a perfect crystal because the atomic planes of one of those tiny regions, called **crystallites** or **grains**, are not lined up with the planes of another.

Even when crystals appear to be perfect, they can have a variety of imperfections, which materials scientists call **defects**. Sometimes there is no atom in the crystal lattice at a place where one would be expected. Sometimes an extra atom is squeezed into the crystal lattice at a point where no atom should be found. These two types of **point defects** are called **vacancies** and **interstitials**.

Another type of defect is called a **line defect** or a **dislocation**. It occurs when the atomic planes of one section of the crystal lattice are slightly offset—or slipped, as a materials scientist would say—from another. Line defects

When magnified 250 times, the boundaries of the tiny crystal grains of molybdenum metal are visible.

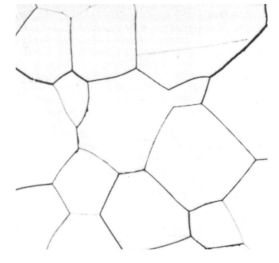

move easily when stress is applied to the solid and when it is heated to a high temperature because the parts of the solid on opposite sides of the line defect can slip past each other.

Two types of defects fall into the category known as **planar defects**. One of these, called a **grain boundary**, occurs where two different grains meet. The other occurs in a crystal that has different arrangements in neighboring planes. Normally, the planes follow one another in a repeating sequence. But in a **stacking fault**, a plane is out of order or missing.

A **volume defect** or **inclusion** is a small region of a crystal that is entirely different from the crystal that surrounds it. For example, diamond and graphite are two different crystalline forms of carbon. If a diamond gemstone has inclusions of graphite, its value is greatly diminished even though it is still pure crystalline carbon.

Finally, a material can contain **impurities**, atoms or molecules that are not the same type as those making up the rest of the crystal. Impurities can occur as single atoms or inclusions. Impurities are not always undesirable. For example, they are responsible for the coloring of certain gems. Sometimes scientists introduce impurities into certain materials on purpose. This is called **doping**. Transistors are made from crystals of semiconducting materials such as silicon, carefully doped with different impurities in different regions.

Microstructure and Properties of Materials

How the properties of materials depend on microstructure is best shown by examples.

Imagine that you have been given the task of hammering a cube-shaped piece of metal into an elongated (lengthened) rectangular block. When you carry out this task, you will notice that as you hammer on the block to reduce its thickness, it becomes longer and wider at the same time. You will also notice that it is relatively easy to change the shape in the beginning, but it becomes increasingly difficult as you go along. What is happening?

Materials scientists explain this behavior in terms of crystal defects. The block was made from molten (melted) metal, and when it solidified, it had a high number of point defects. Because of the high temperature, these point defects moved around, and many of them came together to form dislocations. Hammering the metal cube forces parts of the block to slip past one another. As a result of this, the shape of the block changes. If dislocations were not present, the force required to change the shape would be extremely high because there would be no parts of the material that could move easily.

Hammering increases the number of dislocations. Around each dislocation, the crystal lattice is distorted; for example, there may be a bulge. If two bulges come together, they push against each other and it becomes more difficult to move the material and change the shape of the block. That is why you have to hammer harder at the end than at the beginning.

Thus, having some dislocations is helpful, but having too many works against you. Understanding how to create defects such as dislocations by heating and stressing materials has led to an understanding of such important industrial metalworking techniques as rolling and forging. Those techniques are used to make metals into sheets from which people form car bodies, the shells of home appliances, and many other important products.

Semiconductors. In crystalline materials with ionic and covalent bonds, the electrons that complete the outer shells are able to move from one atomic bond to a neighboring one. In some materials, this movement is easier than others, especially as the temperature of the material increases. As the electrons move more freely, those materials become better conductors of electricity. Such materials are called semiconductors.

Semiconductors are very important in modern technology. Transistors, integrated circuits (microchips), and tiny lasers are made from semiconducting materials. Doping the semiconductors—carefully adding impurity

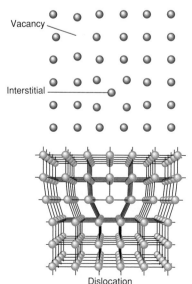

These sketches show common crystal defects. A vacancy occurs when an atom is missing from the crystal lattice. An interstitial is an atom squeezed in where one would not be expected. A dislocation occurs when one plane of atoms is offset by another. The crystal lattice is distorted by defects because the atoms nearby are slightly out of place.

Vacancy

Interstitial

Dislocation

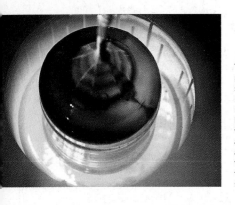

This large, nearly perfect crystal of silicon can be turned into thousands of integrated circuits by slicing it into wafers, carefully adding impurities, and then creating tiny metal pathways to carry electric signals.

atoms in small amounts—causes large changes in their electrical and light-related properties. Silicon is the most frequently used semiconducting material because it is common and relatively easy to work with. But other semiconductors, such as gallium arsenide, are becoming increasingly important because their electrical properties and the way they interact with light may lead to better and faster computers and many other useful devices.

The way integrated circuits and other semiconducting devices are made is an excellent example of the role of materials science, microstructure, and materials engineering in modern technology. For silicon semiconductors, the process starts with silicon dioxide in the form of common sand and ends with thin wafers (slices) of nearly perfect crystalline silicon. Each wafer can be transformed into many integrated circuits in a process that includes many steps, including doping. You can learn more about it in the article TRANSISTORS, DIODES, AND INTEGRATED CIRCUITS.

Superconductors. Under ordinary circumstances, all materials, no matter how well they conduct electricity, have some resistance to the flow of current. It takes energy to keep that current flowing, and the energy becomes heat that can sometimes be a problem. But as the temperature of some materials is lowered to $-240°F$ ($-150°C$) or less, they suddenly lose all their electrical resistance. Thus a current, once started, can flow forever without the need for additional energy and without producing heat. Such materials are called superconductors.

Until 1986, superconductivity had only been seen in materials cooled in expensive liquid helium. But then a breakthrough discovery of new higher-temperature superconductors changed things dramatically. Now there is great scientific and engineering activity that may lead to powerful new computers, trains that ride above rails on a magnetic field produced by superconducting magnets, and transmission of electric power over long distances with very little loss of energy.

Understanding superconductivity involves the activity of many scientists, including materials scientists, who are studying the crystal structure of the new materials in careful detail. They are seeking to discover the arrangement of atoms within crystal planes, the arrangement of the planes themselves, and the role of defects and of small changes in the chemical makeup of these new superconductors. As they gain this understanding, they improve both the properties of these materials and our ability to make them into useful devices.

Glass Fibers. Not all useful materials are crystalline. One of the oldest human-made materials is glass, which is produced by melting sand (silicon dioxide). Although glass can be cut into shapes that appear to be crystals, its molecules have the same disorderly arrangement as do the molecules of a liquid. Materials of this kind are called **amorphous**, which means "without form."

In modern technology, thin glass fibers have become increasingly important for communication. Just as wires can transmit electrical signals, carrying telephone messages, computer data, and information of all sorts, glass fibers can carry signals as pulses of light. Glass fibers are lighter and less expensive than copper wires, and a fiber of the same size can carry much more information for much less cost than copper.

Glass fibers for lightwave communication are not made of ordinary glass. They have been specially made so that light pulses travel through them with a minimum of loss and without changing their shape. (The pulse shape carries the information.) The development of these glass fibers in the 1980's is a remarkable achievement of materials science and engineering.

▶**THE TOOLS OF MATERIALS SCIENCE**

The study of microstructures requires special tools and techniques that enable materials scientists to see things as small as atoms themselves. One major technique is X-ray diffraction. When X rays reflect from a perfect crystal onto a photographic film, they produce a pattern of dots that tell the materials scientist the basic crystal structure and the spacing between the various crystal planes. This **X-ray crystallography** is often a useful starting point in understanding the properties of a material.

Besides crystallography, a very important tool is microscopy. Depending on the level of detail the materials scientist needs to see, there are several different kinds of microscopes to choose from.

Optical microscopy uses ordinary light (optical) microscopes. A materials scientist considers it a low-magnification technique and uses it to develop a large-scale picture of the microstructure.

Electron microscopes can be used to see much smaller features than optical microscopes. Using **scanning electron microscopy**, a materials scientist sees a close-up television picture of line, planar, and volume defects that are present on the etched surface of a sample. Scanning electron microscopy can also be used to perform microscopic chemical analysis. The electrons that create the image also cause the material to give off X rays. Because each chemical element gives off its own characteristic X rays, analysis of the X rays can tell the scientist what elements are present in what concentration at various places in the material.

Materials scientists use **transmission electron microscopy** to study finer details of microstructures of materials. In this technique, to obtain images of line, planar, and volume defects, a beam of electrons is transmitted through a very, very thin sample.

An important development is the **scanning tunneling microscope**. This technique reveals individual atoms near the surface of the material under study.

The only technique available to produce images of single point defects is a **field ion emission microscope**. An extremely sharp tip of the material being studied is imaged by bouncing helium atoms from the tip onto a television-like screen. The image shows the position of atoms as well as of point defects in the tip. Line, planar, and volume defects can also be studied using this technique.

▶ **MATERIALS THROUGHOUT HISTORY**

The importance of materials in the history of civilization can be seen in the names of major historical periods. Civilization began more than 2 million years ago in a time that is

A scanning electron microscope reveals the layered crystal structure and the crystal defects in this superconducting material that contains bismuth, strontium, calcium, copper, and oxygen. The scale line on the photo is about 40 millionths of an inch (1 millionth of a meter) long.

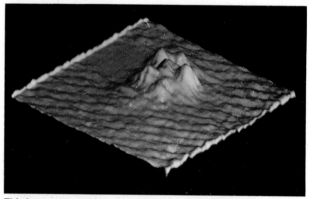

This image, created by a scanning tunneling microscope, shows the shape of a phthalate molecule attached to a smooth graphite surface. The carbon atoms of the graphite can be seen as bumps arranged in straight lines.

now called the Stone Age. The Bronze Age began around 3500 B.C., when people discovered how to make and use the important alloy bronze in tools and weapons. Then from 1900 B.C. to 1200 B.C. human civilization underwent a slow and gradual transition from the Bronze Age to the Iron Age.

By the mid-1700's, people knew how to make large quantities of steel with great strength and quality. This, together with the invention of the steam engine, ushered in the Industrial Revolution. The pace of development of new materials has been increasing ever since then. A means to produce aluminum inexpensively and the discovery of a new fiber called nylon were major breakthroughs. Today new lighter, stronger plastics and new synthetic fabrics are the best-known examples of the amazing new materials that constantly appear on the scene. We have truly entered the Materials Age.

SUBHASH MAHAJAN
Professor of Metallurgical Engineering
and Materials Science
Carnegie Mellon University

See also ALLOYS; ATOMS; CRYSTALS; ELECTRON MICROSCOPE; METALS AND METALLURGY; MICROSCOPES.

MATHEMATICS

What is mathematics? Mathematics is the study of numbers, and counting, and measuring, but that is only the beginning. Mathematics involves the study of number patterns and relationships, too. It is also a way to communicate and analyze ideas, and perhaps more than anything, it is a way of reasoning that is unique to human beings.

Mathematics is divided into pure, or theoretical, mathematics and applied mathematics. Theoretical mathematicians focus mainly on problems and questions within the world of pure mathematics—they develop theorems (unproved ideas), proofs of theorems, and formulas. They also explore new fields that fit into the category of pure mathematics.

Applied mathematicians focus on how to apply mathematical principles to questions people have about the world around them. For example, when mathematics is used to determine the amount of weight that a bridge can hold, or the speed of a falling object, or the distance of a star from the Earth, it is considered applied, because mathematical models and techniques are being applied, or used, to solve practical problems.

Although theoretical mathematicians may not be directly involved in solving practical problems, it often happens that the mathematical tools they develop help engineers, physicists, and other scientists solve such problems.

▶THE BRANCHES OF MATHEMATICS

Over the thousands of years of its history, mathematics has grown to be a very broad field that includes many specialized branches as well as a wide range of topics. In this article we will look at some of the main branches of mathematics.

Number Theory

At a very early age, we all learn how to count using the counting numbers: 1, 2, 3, 4, 5, 6, 7, 8, 9, and so on. The counting numbers are just one category of numbers. There are many other kinds of numbers that can be grouped by their properties, or characteristics. You may be familiar with groups of numbers such as even and odd numbers, positive and negative numbers, prime and composite numbers, or rational and irrational numbers. **Number theory** is the study of numbers and their properties. One of the interesting things a number theorist does is to look at sets of numbers and study their patterns

Varied geometric shapes and patterns in the design of this building contribute to its beauty. The framing patterns in the walls and ceiling also help make the building structurally sound.

and relationships. (For more information about number patterns, see the article NUMBER PATTERNS in Volume N.)

Arithmetic

Arithmetic focuses on computation with numbers using the basic operations of addition, subtraction, multiplication, and division. We use arithmetic almost every day of our lives. Although calculators, computers, and cash registers are used regularly to do computations for us, there are still many situations in which we must do the arithmetic ourselves. Estimating a grocery bill, keeping score at a baseball game, sharing a batch of cookies equally among friends, figuring out how much food your dog or cat eats every week—all are examples of practical ways in which arithmetic is used.

Geometry

Geometry is the study of shape, space, and measurement. Look at the objects around you and you will undoubtedly see examples of lines, circles, rectangles, squares, triangles, and other geometric shapes or figures. Geometry examines the properties of those shapes and investigates how to make complicated shapes from simpler ones. Plane geometry examines figures such as squares, circles, and triangles that sit on a plane surface. Solid geometry examines figures that are three-dimensional such as cubes and spheres.

Euclidean geometry, named after the Greek mathematician Euclid, is an example of an axiomatic system of geometry. An **axiom** is something that is assumed to be true. For example, two axioms that are assumed to be true in Euclidean geometry are that a straight line can be drawn between any two points and that parallel lines never meet. If certain things are accepted as axioms, other things can follow logically from them, and an axiomatic system can be built around them.

Non-Euclidean geometry differs from Euclidean geometry in that its axioms are different from those in Euclidean geometry, and entire new systems of geometric lines and figures were developed for it. Topology is a related field of study that focuses on figures and three-dimensional shapes that are twisted, stretched, and transformed in various ways. Analytic geometry, also called coordinate geometry, and trigonometry are fields of mathematics that combine geometry and another branch of mathematics, algebra. In analytic geometry, algebra is used to plot lines, curves, and shapes. Trigonometry focuses on measuring and determining relationships among angles and sides in triangles. It is often used by astronomers and navigators to determine the measurements of areas too far away to be measured directly.

Algebra

Algebra makes use of symbols, often letters such as x and y, to represent unknown or unspecified quantities in a mathematical problem. Algebra can be more complex than arithmetic, but it operates with many of the same basic rules.

In algebra, just as in arithmetic, there are equations, or mathematical sentences, in which everything on one side of an equal sign must be equivalent to whatever is on the other side of the equal sign. For example, the equation $x + 3 = 7$ means "When I add three to some unknown number, I will end up with seven." The only number that can be substituted for x that will make this mathematical statement true is 4.

It is much easier to write the equation $x + 3 = 7$ in letters and numbers than it is to write the same information in words. Mathematicians and scientists, therefore, use the symbols of algebra as a kind of shorthand for recording and communicating their ideas.

Calculus

The world around us is in constant change and motion. Grass grows, a tennis ball flies through the air, water flows down a river, the moon appears to move across the sky. One of the most important fields of study within mathematics is calculus, the study of change and motion. Calculus, perhaps more than any other field within mathematics, is a mixture of pure and applied mathematics.

The scientific field that makes the greatest use of calculus is physics. Physicists observe the motion and change of objects and create models to describe the patterns in those changes. We might want to know, for example, how fast a ball would be traveling after 10 seconds if we dropped it off a very high cliff. Calculus enables us to determine that, at any instant, the speed of a falling object is 32 times the number of seconds it has been fall-

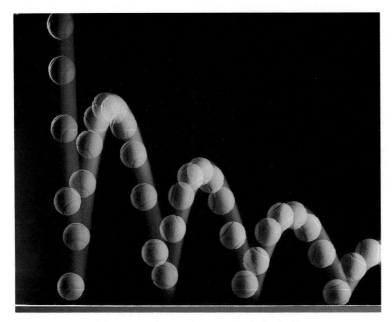

This stop-motion photograph of a bouncing tennis ball illustrates the subject matter of calculus, the branch of mathematics that studies motion and rates of change.

ing. In this case, at 10 seconds the ball would be traveling at a rate of about 320 feet (98 meters) per second.

Probability and Statistics

Probability and statistics are often considered together. Probability theory provides us with a way to know how likely certain events are to occur, and statistics gives us procedures for collecting, organizing, and displaying information about those events.

Probability theory is used in many different situations, from calculating the odds in games of chance, to determining how likely it is that a person may inherit a particular disease, to making predictions about elections based on political polls. For instance, when you roll a single die, there is a one in six chance of rolling a 4. This probability can also be shown as the ratio 1:6, or as the fraction $\frac{1}{6}$. There is also a one in six chance of rolling a 2. We can figure out these probabilities because there are six different sides to each die, and each number on it has the same chance of being rolled. If you roll two dice, there are different probabilities that could add up to any sum from 2 to 12. Probability theory allows us to say exactly how likely each of those occurrences would be.

Statistical theory also has many applications. It may be used to determine how many people watch a particular television show, or to study how air pollution affects plant growth, or to predict the behavior of molecules in a gas. Statistics is important in all of these activities because it contains rules for dealing with large bodies of information and numbers of objects. For example, in most statistical investigations a small number of objects or people, called a sample, are studied to find out the likely behavior of a large number of the same kind of objects or people. Statistical theory also allows us to look at and study patterns over time and to use what is learned to make predictions.

Set Theory

Set theory is a relatively new branch of mathematics. It examines the properties of **sets**, or collections of objects, ideas, or numbers. A set might consist of the members of a team, such as a football team or a debating team; all the maple trees in Vermont; or the numbers 1, 2, 3, 4, 5, 6, 7, 8, and 9.

Set theory also provides rules for performing operations with sets. For instance, the union of two sets is all of the members of the two sets combined. The set of numbers listed above can be seen as the union of all of the even numbers—2, 4, 6, 8—and all of the odd numbers—1, 3, 5, 7, 9—between 0 and 10.

Another important operation with sets is called intersection. Intersection is the combining of sets with particular elements that are common to both of them. For example, in a regular deck of playing cards, you might consider all the red cards in the deck as one set and all the tens in the deck as another set. The ten of hearts and the ten of diamonds are common to both sets and are called the intersection of the two sets. Sets are often used to solve problems in many other branches of mathematics.

Logic

In many ways, logic, or the science of reasoning, is the common link among all the branches of mathematics. Logic unifies them by establishing formal rules of reasoning that apply to all the branches. These rules help mathematicians establish the truth of certain ideas within a system or to draw conclusions from axioms.

In mathematics, many of the logical arguments are stated by using letters and other symbols to represent words, phrases, and even whole sentences. For this reason, mathematical logic is often called symbolic logic.

The Impact of Computer Technology

Computer technology has had a dramatic impact on most branches of pure and applied mathematics. The computer is an ideal tool for creating visual models and simulations of situations and ideas that cannot be created for observation and study in other ways. The computer is also ideal for solving problems with extremely large numbers and for detecting and studying patterns over long periods of time.

These capabilities of the computer have also led to tremendous progress in areas such as probability and topology as well as in the newer fields of chaos theory and fractal geometry. In the field of chaos theory, mathematicians and scientists have found that certain systems called dynamic systems—the weather system or the human circulatory system, for example—are highly sensitive to small changes in the system's conditions. These tiny changes can bring about very large or dramatically different outcomes in such systems. The changes seem to put the system into a state of chaos, or random disorder. For instance, when a stream of air reaches a certain velocity, the air suddenly becomes violently disturbed or turbulent. We say it becomes chaotic. A surprising feature of chaotic systems is that there are patterns to the chaos, and even an underlying orderliness. Chaos theory involves the study of the patterns of behavior of chaotic systems. Computers are useful in studying the patterns and order within chaotic systems.

The study of fractal geometry deals with visual patterns in objects or geometric shapes that repeat at different scales over and over again. For example, if you look at a fern leaf, you may notice that each branch of the leaf looks like a smaller version of the whole leaf. Similarly, each leaflet off a main branch of the leaf also looks like a miniature of the original. Computers have made it possible to create fractal patterns from mathematical models and to study how these patterns may develop and change.

▶EVERYDAY MATHEMATICS

Mathematics is all around us. It is used in many ways, from figuring out how much money we are spending or saving, to remembering phone numbers and addresses. You can

To produce this fractal image of a fern, a computer was instructed to follow a series of complex mathematical steps.

probably think of a number of ways you use mathematics in a typical day, but you may be surprised at some of the ways in which mathematics affects our lives.

Games and Puzzles

Many games and puzzles, even those for young children, incorporate mathematics. For example, hopscotch involves counting. In dominoes, the matching of dots in numerical patterns is important. Many board games use dice or spinners, which means counting and even probability are important parts of playing the game. Logic and spatial reasoning are essential strategies for winning at chess.

Many children and adults also enjoy solving math puzzles, games, and tricks. Here is a trick you can try with your family and friends. Have them follow these instructions:

1. Write down a favorite number.
2. Add 12 to that number, double the result, and subtract 6.
3. Divide that number in half.
4. Subtract the original number.

No matter what number anyone starts with, the final result will always be 9! (If you like working math puzzles and games, try some in NUMBER PUZZLES AND GAMES in Volume N.)

Mathematics in the Kitchen

Mathematics appears frequently in the kitchen. At breakfast you can read the side of a cereal box to find what percentage of each ingredient is in the cereal, how much of each ingredient is in each serving, and the nutritional value of each serving. You may even look for a pattern in the bar code on the box. There is a mathematical procedure used to create the bar code so that it can tell the store's scanner what kind of cereal is in the box and how much it costs.

At dinnertime, you may find that you have a fish that should be cooked 8 minutes per pound (18 minutes per kilogram). If you have a $2\frac{1}{2}$-pound fish, how long should you cook it? You will not know that the fish should be cooked for 20 minutes unless you can do the mathematical calculation.

Statistics in the News

Newspapers and magazines contain many articles that use statistical information as a way to organize data and present it to readers. Statistics may be used to demonstrate the effectiveness of a drug in lowering blood pressure, or to show historical patterns of immigration, or to provide evidence that a program is helpful in keeping students from dropping out of school. Such information is often presented through tables, charts, or graphs.

Statistics are especially abundant in the sports pages. There we find the scores of recent games, major records, rankings of teams, and individual player statistics.

▶ MATHEMATICS IN CAREERS

Think about a career you might want to enter, and you can be assured that mathematics will somehow be a part of it. It is much more difficult to think of occupations that do not require some sound understanding of mathematics than those that do. A few of the many areas that require knowledge of some branch of mathematics are mentioned below.

Business and Industry

No matter what type of business or industry they may work in, people need to know more mathematics than simple arithmetic to be successful at their jobs. For example, businesspeople need to know how to figure out the costs of producing and selling their products in order to determine whether or not their businesses are profitable. Stockbrokers use mathematical formulas to evaluate the stock market and to make investment decisions. Engineers and designers of machine tools need to understand many areas of mathematics in order to create good designs and precise and accurate blueprints that can be used to manufacture tools that will work properly. Bankers need to know about interest rates so they can tell their customers how much they will make on money kept in savings accounts or how much they will be charged for an automobile loan.

The Arts

Although we do not usually think of artists as mathematicians, there are several mathematical concepts, or ideas, that are very important in many of the creative arts. For instance, both painting and sculpture require an understanding of the mathematical principles of proportion, symmetry, and perspective. A knowledge of geometry can help these artists see their work as the putting together and the taking apart of basic shapes and figures in two dimensions, as in painting, or in three dimensions, as in sculpture.

Musicians must be able to count beats in a piece of music, to distinguish between half-notes and eighth-notes, and to be able to change from one rhythmic pattern to another.

The Sciences

Physicists are probably the scientists who most commonly make use of mathematics, but mathematics is used in all branches of science. Geologists may use mathematical analysis to determine the interior structure of the Earth or the age of a rock. Biologists study the probability of changes in genes and the geometry of proteins. Archaeologists might use mathematics to establish the age of a fossil or to make a statistical analysis of the shapes of arrow points. Astronomers need a solid background in mathematics to predict the next solar eclipse or to determine the distance from Earth to a major star.

Health

Knowledge of mathematics is also important in careers in medicine. Physicians use various kinds of mathematical calculations to diagnose symptoms, evaluate tests, and prescribe appropriate medications and procedures for their patients. A dietitian must be familiar with the mathematics of proportions in order to suggest the proper amounts of calories, protein, fat, vitamins, and carbohydrates in a diet, particularly for those people who must limit the kinds of things they can eat.

Mathematics

In addition to the many occupations that use mathematics, there are careers for which a strong background in mathematics is a necessary requirement. Careers such as teaching and research in mathematics, engineering, actuarial work in the insurance industry, computer programming, and accounting as well as careers in statistical analysis in many different fields can be especially interesting and challenging for people who want to go beyond the mathematics they learn in school.

Other Occupations

Mathematics is important to a broad range of other occupations. For example, airplane pilots and navigators must be skilled in reading instruments, graphs, and charts. Meteorol-

Basic mathematics skills are important to many aspects of managing a small business, including setting prices and monitoring sales and costs.

ogists use mathematics to measure things such as wind speed, barometric pressure, snowfall amounts, and the probability that it will rain tomorrow. To the architect, the use of calculus, trigonometry, and geometry is indispensable in designing bridges and buildings that are safe to use and beautiful to look at.

The examples given in this article are but a very few of the ways mathematics enters into our world. As the workplace becomes more complex and the use of technology expands, the list of occupations in which mathematics is important will continue to grow.

Although it is important to recognize how useful mathematics can be in our lives, it is equally important to understand that mathematics is also filled with mysteries to explore, games to play, patterns to discover, and symmetries to admire. The science of mathematics is one of the great achievements of humankind. To become part of that achievement, you need only open your mind to it.

JIM O'KEEFE
Assistant Professor of Mathematics
Lesley College

See also ALGEBRA; ARITHMETIC; GEOMETRY; MATHEMATICS, HISTORY OF; NUMBER PATTERNS; NUMBER PUZZLES AND GAMES; NUMBERS AND NUMBER SYSTEMS; NUMERALS AND NUMERATION SYSTEMS; SETS; STATISTICS; TOPOLOGY; TRIGONOMETRY.

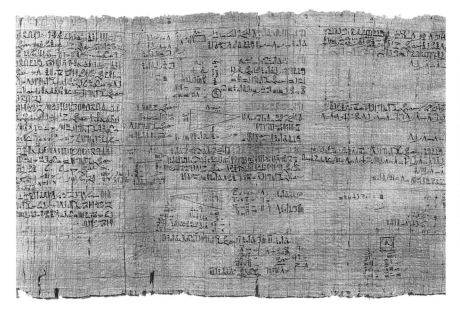

This fragment of the Ahmes, or Rhind papyrus, dates from about 1650 B.C. It demonstrates solutions to two geometry problems—how to calculate the areas of a triangle and a trapezoid. Egyptians used geometry for many projects, including measuring the areas of farms. This was important to the Egyptian pharaoh, who collected taxes based on the size of each farm.

MATHEMATICS, HISTORY OF

We know from the objects and structures that early human beings left behind that they used mathematics to keep track of things in their lives. They had a sense of quantity and number, were able to count, and had methods for measuring time and distance. They were also familiar with geometry, that part of mathematics involved with lines, surfaces, and shapes.

It was not until writing was invented and the first large civilizations developed, however, that enough information could survive to put together a useful history of mathematics.

▶ MATHEMATICS IN THE EARLIEST CIVILIZATIONS

The history of mathematics begins in Sumer, a civilization located in what is now northern Iraq, about 3000 B.C. Sumerian students used reeds to write numbers and words in soft clay tablets that were then baked hard and kept. From such notebooks we know that Sumerian students learned methods for calculating and that they also studied measurement and geometry. Other Sumerian tablets and monuments show how mathematics was used in business, trade, and government.

The first name that appears in the written record of mathematics is found in the Ahmes papyrus, also called the Rhind papyrus. Ahmes was an Egyptian scribe who in about 1650 B.C. made a copy of a document that had been written much earlier. The Ahmes papyrus is a kind of handbook. It contains more than 80 mathematical problems, most dealing with practical matters. One problem, for example, explains how to divide six loaves of bread among ten people.

Around the time of Ahmes, a Chinese scribe wrote one of the earliest books of Chinese mathematics, the *Chou Pei Suan Ching*. This volume, along with later books, shows that the mathematics of China probably developed independently from the mathematics of Sumer and Egypt but that all three were similar in many ways.

Each of these civilizations had a well-developed numeration system and knew how to use simple fractions. They had devised methods for multiplying, for finding square roots, and for figuring out how to measure areas and the volume of geometric figures. The Babylonians (who were the successors of the Sumerians), the Egyptians, and the later Chinese also had some idea of what is known as the Pythagorean theorem, which describes relationships among the sides of a right triangle. This theorem, or idea, is important in the measurement of areas. It may have been used to help lay out foundations for the pyramids of Egypt. The Babylonians also devised a numeration system based on groups of 60. We use such a system today to measure time.

Greek Mathematics

Until about 600 B.C., mathematics was used primarily for counting, calculating, and measuring and for solving problems of a practical nature. Then the people of ancient Greece began to approach mathematics in a different way. They used logical reasoning to explore mathematical ideas and to solve all types of problems. For almost a thousand years, the study of mathematics was centered in Greece and its colonies.

Thales of Miletus, a Greek who was born about 600 B.C., began the new way to study geometry. He was the first to develop proofs for a system of mathematics based on step-by-step reasoning, or logical deduction. He stated, for example, that some things were always true for perfect lines and shapes. One example was his proof that a line through the center of a circle always separates the circle into two identical parts. Instead of experimenting and demonstrating his idea by drawing and measuring many circles of different sizes, Thales used reasoning to show that this idea would be true for all circles.

Pythagoras of Samos, a contemporary of Thales, was interested in number theory, the study of numbers and their properties. He and his followers, who were called Pythagoreans, formed a secret society based on the belief that everything in the universe could be understood in terms of numbers. Many of their ideas were concerned with what they believed to be the mystical or magical properties of numbers. Nevertheless, the Pythagoreans also found important relationships and patterns among numbers that are still studied today. Both Thales and Pythagoras traveled widely and probably learned the mathematics of Egypt and Babylonia. The Pythagorean theorem about right triangles was most likely picked up from the Babylonians but became associated with Pythagoras, whose followers devised the first proof of this theorem.

In the 300 years following the work of Thales and Pythagoras, Greek culture spread throughout the Mediterranean region. By 300 B.C. Alexandria in Egypt and various Mediterranean islands were important centers of Greek learning. Alexandria contained a great library, and scholars gathered at its famous museum, which was more like a university than what we think of today as a museum. Among the scholars who came together at the museum, the most famous is Euclid, who organized all that was then known about geometry into a single logical structure. In his work, *Elements*, Euclid set down definitions, axioms, and the proofs for about 500 geometric theorems. Euclid's *Elements* was considered a model of logical reasoning and argument, and it became the main textbook for geometry for the next 2,000 years. High school students today still study Euclidean geometry.

The greatest mathematician of ancient Greece was Archimedes of Syracuse, who lived in the 200's B.C. Archimedes was also a scientist, and he applied mathematics to problems of physics, including how levers work and how objects float or sink in a liquid. Much of Archimedes' work involved finding areas of plane or flat geometric figures as well as areas and volumes of solid figures. He was also responsible for advances in other branches of mathematics, especially in number theory.

From the 300's B.C. to the A.D. 400's, the political and financial center of Europe, northern Africa, and eastern Asia was the city of Rome, but the center of mathematics continued to be the Greek colonies and especially Alexandria. Geometry steadily advanced, and during the 100's B.C. the astronomer Hipparchus invented trigonometry, the branch of mathematics that makes it possible to calculate distances that cannot be measured directly. Many geometric models were also devised during this period by Greek mathematicians and scientists such as Ptolemy and Aristarchus to describe the motions of the planets.

As time went on, interest in new areas of mathematics other than geometry grew, and in about A.D. 250, Diophantus developed methods for finding exact solutions to equations in algebra, a branch of mathematics that uses numbers and symbols to solve problems involving unknown quantities. Diophantus was the first to use a letter notation for unknown quantities. For this, he is called the "father of algebra."

Near the end of this period, Hypatia, the first known woman mathematician, taught mathematics at the museum in Alexandria. She also wrote several books about the work of earlier Greek mathematicians. Her death in A.D. 415 marks the end of the period of Greek dominance in mathematics.

THE EARLY MIDDLE AGES

A few years after the death of Hypatia, the Roman Empire collapsed. For the next thousand years, significant progress in mathematics was made, not in western Europe and the Mediterranean centers of Greek tradition but in India, China, and the Arab empire.

India

In India mathematicians made many original contributions to mathematics. They introduced a method of writing numbers based on nine different digits, and later included zero as the tenth digit. The Indians were the first to recognize and use zero as a number and not just as a placeholder in their system of numbers and numerals, or number symbols. Indian mathematicians used negative numbers as well and developed rules for computing with certain numbers called irrational numbers, such as $\sqrt{2}$, the square root of 2. They also changed the trigonometry of Hipparchus into a form more like that used today.

Some of the most important contributions to mathematics in India were made by Aryabhata in the 500's, Brahmagupta in the 600's, Mahavira in the 800's, and Bhaskara in the 1100's.

Arab Mathematicians

The expansion of Arab rule in the 700's and 800's B.C. led to some of the ways in which they influenced the development of mathematics. The Arabs tended to take the best ideas of the people they conquered, including those of the people of India and the people of many Greek colonies along the southern Mediterranean, and to use and spread those ideas. The Arabs, for example, learned to write numbers using the Indian, or Hindu, system and then introduced this Hindu-Arabic numeration system to the rest of the world. They also translated important Greek works, such as Euclid's *Elements*, into Arabic. Arab scholars also encountered and spread mathematical discoveries made in another part of the world, China. But Arab mathematicians made their own important contributions as well. Two stand out in very different ways.

An extraordinary mathematician and astronomer, al-Khwarizmi, lived and worked in Baghdad during the A.D. 800's in the House of Wisdom, an institution similar to the museum in Alexandria. There he wrote *Al jabr wa'l mhqabalah*, known to the West as *Algebra*. Al-Khwarizmi's *Algebra* was a considerable advance over the work of Diophantus. In it general rules are given for solving equations, while geometric demonstrations explain why the rules work. The book greatly advanced the study of mathematics at that time. The topics covered compare to those in a modern algebra textbook for high school.

Omar Khayyam, who lived during the 1100's and worked in what is now Iran, is best known today as a poet. Omar, however, was a skilled mathematician as well. He wrote an *Algebra*, even more advanced than that of al-Khwarizmi, in which he proposed and solved higher-level equations. In his *Algebra*, Omar solved equations that included cubes, squares, roots, and numbers. His method used the geometric curves we call circles, parabolas, ellipses, and hyperbolas.

During the Crusades (about A.D. 1100–1300), Europeans came into close contact with Arab learning, and they began to translate the Arabic versions of Greek and Indian works as well as original Arabic writings into Latin, the scholarly language of Europe. As these translations spread, European engineers applied their mathematical principles to the construction of buildings, and artists gained additional insights into the idea of perspective to apply to their work.

MATHEMATICS RETURNS TO THE WEST

About a century after the time of Omar Khayyam, the Italian mathematician Leonardo of Pisa—better known by his nickname of Fibonacci—introduced the main achievements of Arab mathematics into Europe. Fibonacci had been educated among the Arabs in North Africa, and he strongly promoted the use of the Hindu-Arabic numeration system, which was made up of the digits 1 through 9 and 0. He also demonstrated how to use this system in arithmetic. Eventually, Europeans were convinced to use the new numerals and methods of calculation, which are still used today. Fibonacci is best known now as the author of a problem that gives rise to a sequence known as the Fibonacci numbers: 1, 1, 2, 3, 5, 8, 13, and so forth. Can you figure out the rule and predict the next number in the sequence?

Fibonacci's main work was published in 1202. Then, books were still copied by hand, and changes such as the use of Hindu-Arabic numerals were slow to spread. However,

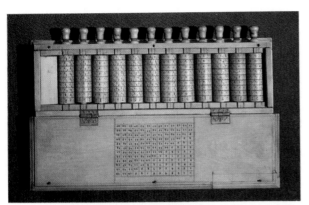

In 1617, John Napier invented a mechanical calculator consisting of columns representing the numbers 0 to 9 and their multiples. Multiplication was done on "Napier's bones" by rotating the columns.

printing with movable type was invented in the 1400's, and mathematics entered a time of rapid growth about a hundred years later.

(*Did you figure out the next number in the Fibonacci sequence of numbers? It is 21, the sum of the previous two numbers.*)

Advances in Algebra

The publication of a mathematics book called *Ars Magna* ("The Great Art") in 1545 is considered to be the beginning of modern mathematics. The author was an Italian scholar and physician, Geronimo Cardano, known as Cardan in English. In his book, Cardan introduced two methods for solving higher-level algebraic equations without using geometry. The book caused a scandal because Cardan did not invent these methods but borrowed the first from Niccolo Tartaglia and bought the second from Luigi Ferrari. He did, however, acknowledge both men in his book.

About the end of the 1500's, François Viète, a French lawyer who made a hobby of mathematics, achieved another breakthrough in algebra. In a book published in 1591, Viète advanced the use of symbols in mathematical equations. He wrote general equations using symbols such as plus and minus signs to indicate operations, a set of letter symbols to indicate known quantities, and another for variables, or unknown quantities. We use the same method today. For example, we write $ax + bx + c = 0$ to mean any equation where a, b, and c are known quantities but x is a variable. Viète showed how to make statements about whole classes of equations.

About the time that Viète was working on general algebra, John Napier and Henry Briggs in Great Britain were developing logarithms, numerical tools based on the idea that every number can be expressed as the power of another number. Logarithms make computation with large numbers much easier.

Descartes, Fermat, and Pascal

Extraordinary scientific advances were made by Nicolaus Copernicus in Italy during the early 1500's and by Johannes Kepler in Germany and Galileo in Italy during the late 1500's and early 1600's. Each of them used their extensive knowledge of mathematics to demonstrate their work in physics and astronomy, which helped bring about important new discoveries in mathematics throughout the 1600's.

One of the most important advances in mathematics occurred in the late 1630's. It was the discovery of how to solve geometric problems with algebra. Two Frenchmen, René Descartes, a soldier, mathematician, and scientist, and Pierre de Fermat, a lawyer and a

WONDER QUESTION

Who invented mathematical signs?

If you look at any mathematics book written before the 1500's, it will be very hard to understand. Although the Hindu-Arabic numerals familiar to us may have been used, everything else was different. The signs and symbols that make up the rest of the language of mathematics as we study it today had not yet been invented.

The familiar + sign for addition and the − sign for subtraction first appeared in 1489 in a German arithmetic handbook. They may have been borrowed from signs used by merchants to mark certain packages. A + was marked on packages with too much of whatever the package contained, while a − meant too little.

The = sign for "equals" was invented in 1557 by the English mathematician Robert Recorde. Another Englishman, William Oughtred, invented the × sign for multiplication in 1631. The ÷ sign for division was actually invented earlier by the German mathematician Johann Heinrich Rahn, but his book was not published until 1659.

politician who avidly pursued the study of mathematics as well, worked independently of one another but share the credit for this discovery.

Although Fermat's work was more advanced, Descartes, who championed mathematics as the highest form of reasoning, published his findings first, in 1637, and is thus credited with starting this revolution in mathematical thinking. Fermat's manuscript had circulated among mathematicians even earlier, but it was not published until 1679, after the author's death.

Today the combination of algebra and geometry is called coordinate or analytic geometry. In it, lines and curves can be drawn by turning algebraic equations into graphs, and it is frequently used to solve problems in physics.

Descartes's work was closer to the algebra of Viète, but Fermat's work was much closer to what is called coordinate or analytic geometry today. Fermat also used his new method to find high and low points of curves, to find tangents to curves, and to find areas between a curve and a straight line. The logic of his methods was the same as that which Isaac Newton and Gottfried Leibniz were to use a few years later as the foundation of calculus. Fermat also greatly extended the theory of numbers well beyond the work of the Greeks.

Probability Theory

Fermat was also one of the early contributors to a whole new branch of mathematics that today is known as probability theory. Probability theory, the mathematical study of chance, had its beginnings in the correspondence between Fermat and a remarkable young Frenchman, Blaise Pascal.

A well-known gambler had asked Pascal for help in resolving some problems having to do with games of chance. The gambler wanted advice about the odds of getting a certain combination of dice in 24 rolls, and he also wanted to know how to divide the stakes fairly when a game was suddenly interrupted. Between them, Pascal and Fermat were able to provide the gambler with answers, and in doing so, they worked out and established the founda-

---

Georg Cantor (1845–1918) was born in Denmark but spent most of his life in Germany. Cantor explored the idea of mathematical infinity and was the first to treat infinity seriously as a number. In 1874 he published a paper on the infinite set, defined as a set that can be put into one-to-one correspondence with a subset of itself. Cantor also developed a system of arithmetic for working with infinite sets. His work was at first attacked by other mathematicians, but it was finally accepted and honored for its originality in the early 1900's.

Leonhard Euler

Georg Cantor

Leonhard Euler (1707--83) of Switzerland made important contributions to most branches of mathematics. Euler spent most of his professional life in Russia and Germany. There he taught and wrote more than 900 books. Blind for the last 17 years of his life, Euler was capable of doing lengthy and complex calculations in his head and was thus able to continue his research. He is known particularly for his work in analysis, a branch of mathematics largely concerned with calculus and infinite series. He also introduced or brought into general use many mathematical symbols, including π (pi).

Pierre de Fermat (1601–65), a French lawyer and civil servant, was one of the greatest amateur mathematicians. Fermat, who spent his days doing exacting, detailed work, loved to spend his leisure time with mathematics. Although most of his work was not published during his lifetime, his ideas were shared with other mathematicians through the many letters

Pierre de Fermat

tions of probability theory. Pascal, in addition to his work in other branches of mathematics, invented one of the first calculating machines.

▶ CALCULUS

During the second half of the 1600's, the character of mathematics changed dramatically. Two great mathematicians invented, independently but almost simultaneously, a new mathematical tool called calculus. Calculus was introduced in England by Isaac Newton, one of the giants in the history of mathematics, and in Germany by Gottfried Leibniz. Calculus deals with problems involving motion, change, and the rate of change. Today calculus is used to solve difficult problems in many branches of mathematics, such as number theory, geometry, the theory of equations, and probability, and it is the basis of almost all work in physics and engineering.

Newton was the first to develop calculus, which he did during 1665 and 1666 while he was living in the country to avoid an epidemic of plague in London. He did not publish his findings, however, until 1687.

Leibniz discovered calculus independently about ten years after Newton, but he published his work first, in 1684. Although Newton and Leibniz had a friendly relationship for years, an unfortunate feud developed over the question of who was the first inventor of calculus. Spurred on by their followers, the men continued their feud for the rest of their lives.

Newton and Leibniz each did much more than invent calculus. Newton, who was also a scientist, applied calculus to solving problems of gravitation and motion. He developed new general forms of analytic geometry and contributed to the theory of equations. Leibniz investigated ways of combining logic with mathematics and developed a method for solving sets of equations.

Applications and Extensions of Calculus

Throughout the late 1600's and the 1700's, a number of European mathematicians applied and extended the ideas of calculus, creating the basis for modern mathematics. They included the Swiss mathematicians Jakob and Johann Bernoulli, Johann's son Daniel Ber-

---

he wrote. A highly original thinker, Fermat is recognized as a founder of modern number theory and of probability theory. He was also a cofounder, along with René Descartes, of coordinate or analytic geometry.

Sofia Kovalevskaia (1850–91) was born in Russia at a time when women were not encouraged to study mathematics. Her tutor convinced her father to allow her to pursue her natural aptitude for the subject. Kovalevskaia had to get special permission to attend lectures at Heidelberg University in Germany, and she later studied privately with the famous mathematician Karl Weierstrass. She was the first woman to be granted a doctorate in mathematics and one of the first women to achieve full professorship at a European university. Kovalevskaia is best known for her work with partial differential equations, which involve several functions and have important applications in physics and engineering.

Omar Khayyám (1050–1123?) was an important Arab mathematician and poet. Acclaimed in his native Persia as a scientist, Omar came to the attention of the West in 1859 when his *Rubáiyát*, a collection of poetry, was published in an English translation. His most important mathematical work was *Algebra*, which was used as a textbook in Persia for hun-

Sofia Kovalevskaia

dreds of years. In it Omar set forth rules for solving high-level algebraic equations, including cubic equations. He also used astronomical observations to reform the Persian calendar, making it one of the most accurate of the time.

Alan Turing (1912–54) was an English mathematician and a pioneer in computer theory. His special field of study was mathematical logic. In 1936 Turing proposed his idea for a machine that could solve any problem capable of being solved, as long as the problem could be stated in mathematical terms. This theory eventually led to the design

and construction of one of the first electronic computers. During World War II (1939–45), Turing served in the Government Code and Cypher unit. He led the way in breaking the German "Enigma" code, saving many lives. Turing also posed questions about whether machines capable of thinking could be built, and he devised a test for artificial intelligence, called the Turing test.

John von Neumann (1903–57) was one of the most versatile and influential mathematicians of the 1900's. As a child in Hungary, Von Neumann exhibited an early brilliance in mathematics, mastering calculus by age 8. As a young man, he taught in Germany and made important contributions in set theory, logic, abstract algebra, and quantum theory. Von Neumann came to the United States in 1930, and during World War II (1939–45), he worked on the Manhattan Project, which developed the first atomic bomb. Best known as a primary creator of the modern computer, he was also a founder of game theory. Game theory was developed to design economic strategies, but it has also been applied to problems in transportation, communication, and military strategy.

noulli, Leonhard Euler, also of Switzerland, and three Frenchmen, Adrien Marie Legendre, Joseph Louis de Lagrange, and Pierre Simon de Laplace.

Jakob and Johann Bernoulli played important roles in the development of calculus, showing how it could be applied to many fields. Jakob also advanced the study of probability, and the Bernoulli theorem—the law of large numbers in probability—is named for him. Johann Bernoulli is considered one of the founders of a different form of calculus, known as the calculus of variations, for his work on finding the curve down which an object would slide the fastest. The methods of the calculus of variations are generally applied to problems in physics and engineering. The Bernoulli principle (which explains the force that allows airplanes to fly) is the work of Johann's son Daniel, whose most important work was in applying mathematical principles to the field of hydrodynamics.

Leonhard Euler was a student of Jean Bernoulli. Euler became one of the great mathematicians of the 1700's and one of the greatest in history. His name is associated with elements of almost all branches of pure mathematics as well as research in many areas of applied mathematics. He is credited with establishing many mathematical notations, or symbols, including the use of e as a number, often called the base of the natural logarithms, and the use of π (pi) to indicate the ratio of the circumference of a circle to its diameter.

Legendre, Lagrange, and Laplace were leading French mathematicians, and they all served on the committee that developed the first version of the metric system. Legendre is noted for advances in differential equations, calculus, the theory of numbers, and applied mathematics. Lagrange, one of the most respected mathematicians and scientists of the late 1800's, reshaped the calculus of variations into a form similar to the one in use today. In addition to his important work in astronomy, Laplace's work in probability theory was so complete that no other mathematician added to his ideas on the subject for more than a hundred years.

▶THE 1800'S

The period of the 1800's has been called the Golden Age of Mathematics. Many advances were made during this time, including a calculus that used imaginary numbers and several non-Euclidean geometries—all became hallmarks of a century during which mathematicians began a new search for a way to establish a logical basis for calculus and other branches of mathematics.

During much of the century, mathematicians also continued to apply calculus and related ideas to solving new problems. New mathematical tools were developed in response to the inventions and discoveries of the 1800's, but many of the most striking developments were in mathematics itself.

Non-Euclidean Geometry

The greatest mathematician of the 1800's is generally acknowledged to be Germany's Carl Friedrich Gauss. For his doctoral thesis, Gauss proved his famous theorem, now called the fundamental theorem of algebra, that all ordinary equations have solutions. Throughout his life, Gauss was responsible for new ideas and advances in most branches of mathematics, although he did not always publish his results. When his private mathematical notes were published after his death, it became apparent that Gauss had been the first person to write about almost every topic in mathematics developed during the century.

Gauss was the first to recognize that the geometry of the Greeks was only one of several that were logically consistent. He thought, however, that people would not be ready to accept such a radical view and did not let his ideas become widely known.

Three other mathematicians, all from different countries—a Russian, Nikolai Lobachevsky, a Hungarian, János Bolyai, and a German, Bernhard Riemann—all came to the same conclusion. Each of them independently investigated what is now known as non-Euclidean geometry, a geometry different from that of Euclid.

One of the basic ideas in Euclid's geometry is that only one straight line can be drawn parallel to a given line through a given point not on the line. Another basic idea is that the three angles of a triangle always add up to 180 degrees. Gauss, Lobachevsky, and Bolyai all worked with a geometry in which more than a single line can be parallel to a given line through a point not on the line. In this geometry there are fewer than 180 degrees in a

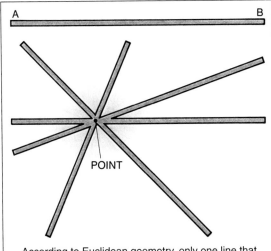

According to Euclidean geometry, only one line that is parallel to line AB can be drawn through any given point.

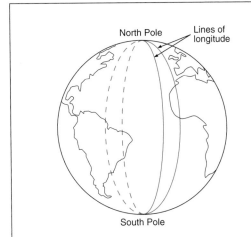

In Riemann's non-Euclidean geometry, lines on the surface of a sphere, like the lines of longitude on a globe, cannot be parallel because they cross each other at two points.

triangle. Bernhard Riemann's geometry has no parallel lines and has triangles with more than 180 degrees.

Mathematicians did not begin to accept any of these ideas until Gauss's papers were published after his death in 1855. Today non-Euclidean geometry is thought to describe the universe better than Euclid's geometry does.

New Branches Begin

Several new branches of mathematics had their beginnings during the 1800's. French-men Augustin Louis Cauchy and Évariste Galois, Irishman William Rowan Hamilton, and American Josiah Willard Gibbs each helped lay the foundations for a new, more complex system of algebra called abstract algebra. This system deals with special structures called groups, rings, and fields.

In the middle of the 1800's, the ideas of abstract algebra, especially the concept of a group, were beginning to be applied to geometry. Methods had been developed to change one geometric figure into another. For example, suitable algebraic operations could change the location of the center of a circle, its size, or even its shape into an ellipse or a line, and such transformations could be organized into groups. In the 1870's, the German mathematician Felix Klein developed the study of such groups of transformations further, and he became a founder of a new kind of geometry called transformational geometry. It includes the study of properties that do not change when an object is rotated, flipped, or stretched. This concept, along with the ideas and non-Euclidean geometry of Bernhard Riemann, later led to the development of topology in the 1900's.

Both Descartes and Leibniz had been interested in the concept of an algebra of ideas, but it was not advanced until the rise of abstract algebra in the 1800's. The first successes came in England, where in 1847 George Boole published the first of several methods for making an algebra of logic. It used various symbols to stand for ideas and the relationships of ideas, and it is called symbolic logic. A German mathematician, Gottlob Frege, also used symbolic logic, but to examine the foundations of mathematics itself. His work became the starting point for the development of foundations as a mathematical discipline. The structure of symbolic logic also became the basis for electronic computers.

In the second half of the 1800's, the work of a number of mathematicians, including Riemann, German mathematician Karl Theodore Weierstrass, and Russian mathematician Sofia Kovalevskaia, focused on the re-examination of the foundations of calculus. Then attempts to develop a better understanding of these issues led German mathematician Georg Cantor to develop the theory of infinite sets, those sets whose elements cannot be counted because they are infinite. Cantor later developed set theory, which has applications in algebra, geometry, probability, calculus, and other branches of mathematics.

MATHEMATICS IN THE 1900'S

A major force in mathematics during the 1900's was the person often called the leading mathematician of the century, David Hilbert of Germany. In a famous speech in 1900, Hilbert listed 23 unsolved problems or questions he thought could be resolved. Although many were solved during Hilbert's lifetime, some were ultimately proved unsolvable, and some are still being worked on today.

Hilbert himself devoted considerable attention to trying to put mathematics on a logical basis, and in 1928 he had called for a proof that all mathematical statements could be proved either true or false. But in 1936 English mathematician Alan Turing and others demonstrated that such a proof is impossible, for there are always some mathematical statements beyond proof.

Chaos Theory and Fractals

Among the notable mathematical fields of the 1900's are chaos theory and a branch of geometry known as fractal geometry.

Chaos theory describes the significant but unpredictable results of small changes in systems. It started with a weather-forecasting problem explored by the American meteorologist Edward Lorenz in 1962. Lorenz discov-

When equations describing thermal convection, such as heat moving through the atmosphere, are graphed, repeating butterfly-like curves are formed. These curves, representing chaotic motions, create an image called a strange attractor. Originally demonstrated by Edward Lorenz, an early developer of chaos theory, it is also known as the Lorenz butterfly.

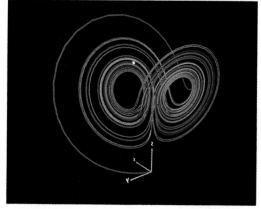

ered that even the tiniest miscalculation in weather information would lead to large mistakes in weather predictions. Thus Lorenz concluded that perfect long-range weather predictions were impossible. Similar effects in other systems were investigated by Mitchell Feigenbaum, an American physicist, and others. They found that chaos theory could be applied to all kinds of systems and situations, from air turbulence to heart rhythms.

Fractals are geometric objects or shapes that exhibit self-similarity, which means that any part of the object is similar in detail to the whole object. For example, if you view the large-scale features of a coastline from an airplane, they are similar to the small-scale details of any part of the coastline seen close up. Many fractal images are generated on computers. The word "fractal" was coined in 1975 by Benoit Mandelbrot, who is one of the leading researchers of fractal images.

Computers and the Future of Mathematics

Computers have become an indispensable tool for today's mathematicians. The basic concepts on which nearly all modern computers are built were developed by one of the leading mathematicians of the 1900's, John von Neumann, a Hungarian who came to the United States in 1930.

Computers are used to find proofs for old and new mathematical conjectures and theorems. They have been very useful in some of the newer fields, such as chaos theory, fractals, and game theory, and in the use of probability theory to find approximate solutions to otherwise unsolvable problems. Game theory also uses probability theory to devise strategies for everything from card games to military tactics. As mathematicians continue to pursue answers to unsolved problems and open up new fields of study, computers will continue to ease their way.

BRYAN BUNCH
Coauthor, *The Timetables of Science*

See also ALGEBRA; ARITHMETIC; COMPUTERS; GEOMETRY; MATHEMATICS; NUMBER PATTERNS; NUMBERS AND NUMBER SYSTEMS; NUMERALS AND NUMERATION SYSTEMS; SETS; STATISTICS; TOPOLOGY; TRIGONOMETRY; articles on individual mathematicians.

MATHER, COTTON. See MASSACHUSETTS (Famous People).

MATHER, INCREASE. See MASSACHUSETTS (Famous People).

MATHIAS, BOB. See OLYMPIC GAMES (Profiles).

MATISSE, HENRI (1869–1954)

The French artist Henri Matisse was born in Le Cateau in northern France on December 31, 1869. He grew up in a nearby town where his father was a grain merchant. When Matisse finished school, his father sent him to Paris to study law. At the end of two years he returned home. Matisse worked as a law clerk, but early every morning he took drawing lessons. Then in 1890, while he was recovering from an illness, his mother gave him a box of paints. From that time forward Matisse devoted his life to painting. In 1891, much against his father's wishes, Matisse left for Paris to become an artist.

For five years Matisse studied with the painter Gustave Moreau. To earn money, he made copies of famous paintings in the Louvre. By 1897 he had begun to paint in the style of the impressionists, experimenting with the effects of pure (unmixed) colors.

In 1899, Matisse married Amélie Parayre. They had two sons and a daughter—Jean, Pierre, and Marguerite. To help support the family, Madame Matisse set up a hat shop.

Matisse became the leader of a group of painters who used color in a very untraditional way. They used it to express their emotions rather than to represent nature. In 1905, paintings by these artists were accepted for an important exhibition of the French Academy of Art. The public was scandalized by the painters' daring use of color. One outraged art critic labeled the artists *les fauves* ("the wild beasts"). Despite this criticism, Matisse's reputation grew. He set up an art school, and collectors were eager to buy his paintings. Soon he became one of the most famous living painters.

Around 1910, Matisse's style changed. Using calmer colors, he painted simple figures with dark outlines. These paintings have powerful rhythms. During World War I, Matisse's paintings were somber in color and spirit, but after the war they became gay and decorative. About 1925, Matisse again began experimenting. After many lifelike studies he created simple compositions in flat colors.

Matisse was an accomplished sculptor as well as a painter. His sculpture follows the same development as his painting. He also illustrated many books and made designs for tapestries, carpets, and glass.

French artist Henri Matisse exhibited *Woman with the Hat,* a portrait of his wife, in Paris in 1905. Its unconventional colors made the painting controversial.

During World War II, Matisse refused to leave France. Shortly after the war, he began to design a chapel in the town of Vence. Because of illness, Matisse often worked in bed, sketching large designs with a piece of charcoal attached to a long pole. To create the designs for the stained-glass windows, he cut up pieces of colored paper and experimented with their arrangement. The chapel was completed in 1951, when Matisse was 82. The inside walls are covered with simple designs painted in black on white ceramic tiles. Brilliantly colored light floods into the chapel through stained-glass windows.

By his constant searching and experimenting, Matisse opened up new paths of art. His works were the result of much planning. Before beginning a painting he made many studies and sketches, but the final work he did quickly. Matisse continued drawing and painting until his death on November 3, 1954.

Reviewed by PIERRE MATISSE

MATTER

Matter is the name given to anything that possesses two qualities, or properties—it must take up space, and it must have mass.

The first property is easy to understand. Everything solid around you—people, books, tables, pens, and so on—takes up space. The amount of space that an object takes up has a special name—it is called **volume**.

The volume of an object is measured in cubic inches (or cubic centimeters).The cubic measurement expresses the volume that the object would have if it were shaped into a cube —that is, a box with sides all of the same length. You can squeeze a piece of modeling clay into a ball, a cube, or any other shape you wish. But whatever shape you give it, the clay always takes up the same amount of space. Its volume stays the same.

Once you have pushed clay into a particular shape, it will keep that shape if left alone. Anything that keeps its shape when left alone is a **solid**.

What about water? You cannot shape water into a ball, a cube, or any other definite shape —it simply flattens out. But if you place water in an empty container, the water will press against the bottom and sides. No matter what the shape of the container may be, the water will take that shape.

Substances that behave in this way are **liquids**. Liquids change their shape easily, but they take up space, as solids do. And no mat-

ter what shape a particular amount of liquid may take, its volume remains the same.

Now let us look at the empty container. Was it really empty before the water was poured in? No, the container had air in it. Air is a mixture of several kinds of **gases**, and gases also take up space. When we pour water into the container, we push out the gases.

Solids, liquids, and gases are the three general forms of matter. They are the three **states of matter**. Try the experiments on pages 172–173, and you will see that all matter, whatever state it is in, takes up space.

▶MASS

What is mass? To understand what it is, let's begin with something everyone knows. It is harder to throw a large, heavy ball than a small, light one. A very large rock is hard to get moving at all. In the same way, a quickly moving Ping-Pong ball is easy to stop. A quickly moving baseball is harder to stop and calls for a padded glove. A large, heavy rock moving as fast as the baseball is so hard to stop that you had better just get out of its way.

Any piece of matter, if it is at rest (not moving), tends to remain at rest. If it is moving, it tends to keep on moving. That is what people mean when they say that matter possesses **inertia**. It takes an effort to put matter into motion or bring it to rest. The more effort it takes for any piece of matter, the more inertia that matter has. The amount of inertia a particular piece of matter has represents its **mass**.

STUDY THE FORMS OF MATTER

Matter may be in the form of a solid, a liquid, or a gas. These experiments will help you see that all matter, whatever its form, takes up space. You will need a toy block, a dishpan or bucket, two or more drinking glasses of different shapes, and a piece of newspaper. Work at a sink or a place where spilled water will not damage anything.

SOLIDS. Fill the pan with water to the very top. Hold the block with two fingers and push it down into the water so that it is just covered. You will see some of the water running out of the pan. This happens because the solid block takes up space — the space that was taken up by the overflowing water.

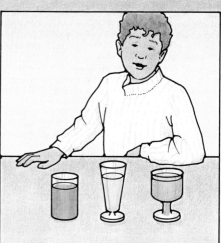

LIQUIDS. Pour water into each of the glasses. You can see that the water takes up space inside the glass. Notice also that the water, like any liquid, takes the shape of the container it is in.

All matter has inertia. Inertia is the tendency for an object at rest to remain at rest and for a moving object to continue moving. It takes great effort to push a car from a resting position, but once in motion, the car is fairly easy to push.

Much effort is needed to start the car moving.

Less effort is needed to keep the car moving.

Mass and Weight

Any piece of matter attracts all other pieces of matter. For ordinary pieces of matter, this attraction is tiny. For a huge piece of matter, such as the earth, the force of attraction is very strong. We call it the force of **gravity**. The more mass a piece of matter has, the more it is attracted by the earth's gravity.

We feel the attraction of the earth as weight. An object with a large mass (a truck, for example) is strongly attracted, so it has a large weight. It is heavy and hard to lift. On the other hand, an object of little mass (an insect, let us say) is light and easy to lift.

Since mass and weight go together on the earth's surface, people sometimes talk as though the two were the same thing. They are not. For one thing, weight changes from place to place, but mass does not. An object on a high mountain weighs a little less than it would in the valley below. Up on the mountaintop the object is farther from the center of the earth. It is less strongly attracted toward the center of the earth, so it weighs less.

The moon is a smaller body than the earth. It has less mass. The moon, therefore, produces a weaker force of attraction. An astronaut weighing 154 pounds (70 kilograms) on the earth weighs only about one sixth that much on the moon.

Yet any object would have the same mass —the same amount of inertia—whether it was in a valley, on a mountaintop, or on the moon. An object might feel very light on the moon, but it would be just as hard to set in motion as on the earth. Once in motion, it would be just as hard to stop it as on the earth.

Because mass doesn't change from place to place but weight does, mass is considered the more important property of matter.

Density

It is sometimes useful to speak of mass and volume together. Iron is often said to be "heavier" than aluminum. This means that a certain volume of iron is heavier than the same volume of aluminum. The quantity of mass in a particular volume is called its density. For example, the density of aluminum is 168.7 pounds per cubic foot (2.7 grams per cubic centimeter), while iron has a density of 491 pounds per cubic foot (7.8 grams per cubic centimeter). Iron is about three times denser than aluminum.

GASES. Crumple a piece of newspaper into a ball. Force the ball down into the bottom of a glass. It should fit tightly enough to stay in place when you turn the glass upside down. Push the upside-down glass straight down into the water so that it is completely covered. Then lift the glass straight up out of the water. You will find that the paper ball and the inside wall of the glass are dry. No water can enter because something else is already taking up space in the glass — the mixture of gases we call air.

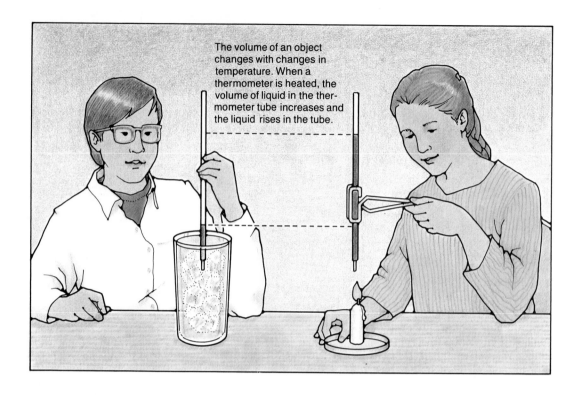

The volume of an object changes with changes in temperature. When a thermometer is heated, the volume of liquid in the thermometer tube increases and the liquid rises in the tube.

▶TEMPERATURE AND VOLUME

When a solid or a liquid changes shape, it does not change volume. Yet the volume of an object almost always changes with changes in temperature. If a solid or liquid is heated, the volume generally increases and the substance takes up more room. If the solid or liquid is cooled, however, the volume generally decreases and the substance takes up less room.

You can see this very easily with the colored liquid in a thermometer. Whenever the temperature goes up, the liquid expands (takes up more space) and it rises higher in its tube. When the temperature goes down, the liquid contracts (takes up less space) and its level drops. We tell the temperature by the height of the liquid.

Gases change volume even more easily. In fact, you can make a gas change volume just by compressing it (squeezing it together). As you know, a tire flattens somewhat under the weight of a car. Its air is compressed by the weight. If the little valve in the tire were opened, the air would escape and expand. If you could trap the air in a container, you would find that it took up much more room outside than it did inside. As the air escaped, it expanded.

▶THE CONSERVATION LAWS

Although the volume of a piece of matter can be changed easily, its mass cannot. In the 1800's scientists became certain that it was impossible to change the mass of a particular piece of matter. They felt sure that mass could not be destroyed and could not be created. They stated this as the **law of conservation of mass**. (It could also be called the law of conservation of matter, for matter and mass go hand in hand. You can't have one without the other.)

Scientists also concluded that the same was true of energy. Energy might change from one form to another, but it could be neither created nor destroyed. This was the **law of conservation of energy**.

In 1905 a scientist named Albert Einstein worked out a theory that matter and energy were not entirely different things. Matter, he said, could be converted (changed) into energy, and energy into matter. Matter is a very rich form of energy, and a little matter could be converted into a great deal of energy. On the other hand, a great deal of energy could be converted into only a small quantity of matter.

However, the sum total of matter and energy could be neither created nor destroyed.

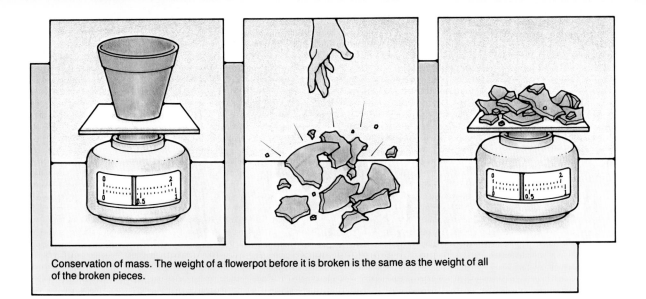

Conservation of mass. The weight of a flowerpot before it is broken is the same as the weight of all of the broken pieces.

For that reason scientists now speak of the **law of conservation of mass-energy**.

▶WHAT MATTER IS MADE OF

What is matter made of? There is an important clue in some of the ways that gases differ from liquids and solids.

If water is cooled, it eventually freezes and becomes ice. Ice is the solid form of water. Equal volumes of water and ice differ by less than 10 percent in mass—that is, liquids and solids do not differ very much in density.

If water is heated, it eventually boils and forms steam. Steam is the gaseous form of water, and there is a tremendous difference between the density of steam and the density of water. As steam forms during boiling, it is only about $\frac{1}{1700}$ as dense as water or ice.

That is true of gases generally. Gases are always much less dense than liquids and solids. It is as though matter had been thinned out in forming gases.

Then, too, it is very hard to compress liquids and solids. Even when they are squeezed together under great pressure, they are compressed only very slightly. Gases, on the other hand, are easy to compress. A quantity of a gas that fits into a given amount of space can easily be compressed to fit into $\frac{1}{10}$ of that amount of space.

It would seem then that a gas can be easily compressed because its matter does not really fill up its volume. And that is the case. Gas is made up of tiny particles of matter separated by empty space. That explains why a gas has such a low density. The matter in it is spread

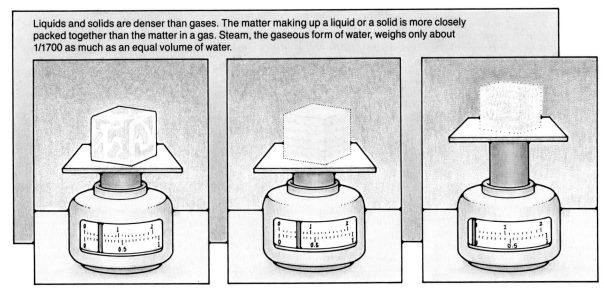

Liquids and solids are denser than gases. The matter making up a liquid or a solid is more closely packed together than the matter in a gas. Steam, the gaseous form of water, weighs only about 1/1700 as much as an equal volume of water.

As you blow up a balloon, you compress air—that is, you push together the particles of the gases that make up air.

out. It would also explain gas compression. The little particles making up gas are just pushed closer together.

In liquids and solids, the little particles are already almost touching. That is why liquids and solids are much denser than gases and hard to compress. The particles cannot be pushed together more closely.

These little particles are called **atoms**. A substance that is made up of only one kind of atom is called an **element**. Iron is an element because it is built up only of iron atoms. Aluminum is another element; it is built up only of aluminum atoms. Other metals such as mercury, gold, and copper are elements. Nonmetals such as sulfur and phosphorus are elements, so are gases such as oxygen, hydrogen, and nitrogen.

There are as many different elements as there are different varieties of atoms. Some elements do not exist on the earth but have been formed in tiny amounts in laboratories. Other elements exist in nature but are very rare. Only about a dozen elements are really common on the earth. Stars like our sun are made up almost entirely of two elements, hydrogen and helium, though many other elements are present in small quantities.

Atoms usually form tight bonds with other atoms of the same type or with one or more different atoms. A group of tightly bonded atoms is called a **molecule**. Some molecules are small and are made up of only two or three atoms. Other molecules are much larger and can contain thousands of atoms.

Substances made up of two or more different atoms are called **compounds**. Water is an example of a compound. Each molecule of water is made up of three atoms: two hydrogen atoms and one oxygen atom.

A model of a water molecule. A water molecule contains two hydrogen atoms (H) and one oxygen atom (O).

A model of a simple organic compound, methane. A methane molecule contains one carbon atom (C) and four hydrogen atoms (H).

Atoms can combine in many thousands of different ways. Every different molecule represents a different substance. That is why matter appears in so many different forms.

For example, atoms of the element carbon can combine in long chains and complicated rings. Other kinds of atoms can add to these chains and rings, making hundreds of thousands of different molecules. Some of these are very large and complicated. Living organisms contain many such large molecules that are based on carbon. These carbon-containing substances have come to be called **organic compounds**.

▶**PHYSICAL AND CHEMICAL CHANGES**

Matter can be made to change its properties in a number of different ways.

For example, a metal like copper can be beaten into different shapes. It can be drawn out into wires. It can be broken up into fragments. It is still copper. An electric current can be passed through it. It can be heated until it glows red-hot. It is still copper. Copper powder can be mixed with iron filings and still be copper. Copper can be heated until it melts. It can then be heated further until it boils and forms gaseous copper. It is still copper.

Such changes alter the properties of matter but not its atomic makeup. They are called **physical changes**. The science of physics is particularly concerned with energy and with the physical changes of matter.

Often, however, changes in properties also involve changes in atomic makeup. For instance, suppose iron is allowed to stand in damp air. Atoms of oxygen from the air and atoms of hydrogen from the moisture join the iron atoms. The resulting molecules have properties that are entirely different from those of the original iron. In place of a hard gray metal there is crumbly, reddish brown rust.

Or suppose copper is dropped into a compound called nitric acid. Nitrogen and oxygen atoms join the copper atoms. In place of the reddish metal, there is a blue, brittle nonmetal, called copper nitrate.

Such changes alter the atomic makeup of the molecules of a substance. They are called **chemical changes**. The science of chemistry is chiefly concerned with such chemical changes.

When wood is heated, a chemical change takes place. The wood does not melt. Instead,

Changes in Matter

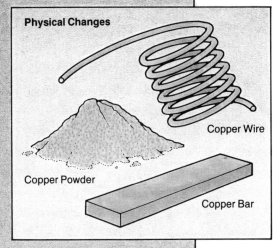

Physical Changes

Copper Wire

Copper Powder

Copper Bar

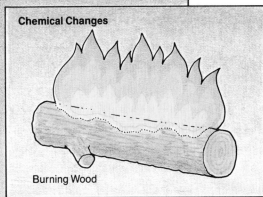

Chemical Changes

Burning Wood

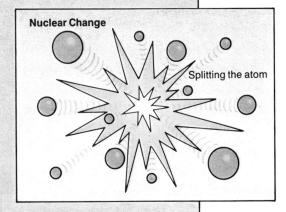

Nuclear Change

Splitting the atom

Matter can be made to change its properties in three main ways. In a physical change a substance has the same atomic makeup, but its form is altered. In a chemical change the atomic makeup of a substance is changed as well as its properties. In a nuclear change the central core, or nucleus, of an atom is altered. In this process great amounts of energy are released.

its rather complicated molecules break up into smaller ones. The gases, consisting of these simpler molecules, combine very rapidly with the oxygen of the air. As they do so, energy is given off in the form of light and heat. We say the wood is burning.

Many chemical changes produce energy. We use the energy of burning wood, coal, or oil to produce electricity (another form of energy). Chemical changes can produce energy so quickly as to give rise to an explosion. An automobile runs because of the energy of small explosions of gasoline in its cylinders.

Human beings—and all other living organisms—make use of the energy produced by chemical changes within the body.

Chemical changes proceed most rapidly and easily when different substances make a great deal of contact. Molecules can interchange atoms only where such contact takes place. Powdered iron, for instance, will rust much more quickly than a solid piece of iron.

▶NUCLEAR CHANGES

Atoms are made up of still smaller parts, called subatomic particles. The more massive of these particles are called protons and neutrons. They form a tiny but extremely dense **atomic nucleus** at the very center of the atom. Around this nucleus are the less massive electrons. The protons and electrons carry electric charges, but the neutrons do not.

Ordinary chemical changes affect the electrons at the surface of the atom. However, there are also changes that can take place in the atomic nucleus. These are **nuclear changes**.

Nuclear changes involve much larger quantities of energy than ordinary chemical changes do. The first nuclear change to be discovered was radioactivity. The atomic nuclei of radioactive elements give off subatomic particles or little groups of subatomic particles. As this happens, energy is released in the process.

Sometimes a nucleus can be made to break apart. More energy is produced in this process of **nuclear fission** than in ordinary radioactivity. Energy can be produced very quickly as a result of fission. This is the kind of energy that powers an atomic bomb.

Still greater energy can be produced with the nuclei of hydrogen atoms. Several of these very tiny nuclei can be made to join together, thus forming the more complicated nucleus of the element helium. This joining together of nuclei is called **nuclear fusion**. Energy released by nuclear fusion is the kind that powers the sun and other stars. A little bit of nuclear fusion on earth powers the hydrogen bomb.

Nuclear scientists have learned to create fission reactions that proceed in a slow and orderly fashion. Taking place within nuclear reactors, these can produce power for ships and submarines. They can produce electricity for peaceful uses. Scientists are trying to tame the more powerful fusion reactions, too.

To bring about controlled fusion reactions, hydrogen must be heated to extremely high temperatures of millions of degrees. At such temperatures the atoms themselves break up into clouds of electrically charged subatomic particles. Matter composed of such broken-up atoms is called **plasma**. Plasma is sometimes called a **fourth state of matter**.

The sun and all other stars are made up of plasma. On earth the gases inside fluorescent bulbs are examples of a low temperature plasma.

The broken atoms in plasma can be packed together much more tightly than ordinary atoms can be. In some stars the plasma is packed together very tightly indeed. The result is that the brightly glowing star shrinks down into a volume no larger, perhaps, than that of our earth. Such a star is a white dwarf. The matter in a white dwarf can be thousands of times as dense as the densest material on earth. Yet it can be packed even more tightly. Eventually, the particles are converted into neutrons, and these are squeezed so tightly that they touch. Such neutron stars may be only a few kilometers across and yet contain as much matter as our sun.

In contrast, the space between the planets and between our sun and other stars has practically no matter in it. On the earth, scientists can take most of the air out of a container, leaving a volume of space with almost no matter in it. Such space is called a **vacuum**. This means that most of the universe is a vacuum.

ISAAC ASIMOV
Boston University School of Medicine

See also CHEMISTRY; ELEMENTS, CHEMICAL; GASES; GRAVITY AND GRAVITATION; HEAT; LIQUIDS; NUCLEAR ENERGY; SOLIDS.

MAURITANIA

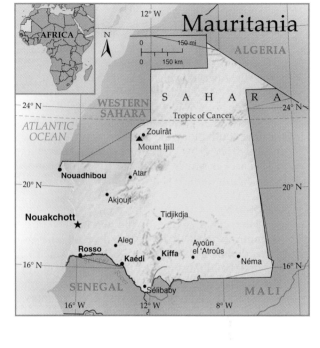

Mauritania is a large nation in northwestern Africa, bordering the Atlantic Ocean. Although nearly as large as France and Spain combined, it is mostly desert and can support only a relatively small population. A former French colony, it gained complete independence in 1960. Mauritania takes its name from its dominant ethnic group, the Moors (or *Maures* in French).

▶ **PEOPLE**

About 30 percent of Mauritania's people are Moors, an ethnic group of mixed Arab and Berber ancestry. Traditionally, they have been nomads of the north, moving from place to place with their herds of camels and flocks of sheep and goats. These animals have provided the Moors with food, transportation, and other necessities of life. Today many Moors live in settled areas.

Blacks living mainly in the south make up another 30 percent of the population. They include the Fulani, cattle herders who travel with their animals to find grazing land, as well as the Tukulor, Sarakolé, and Wolof, who are farmers. Fishing is a traditional occupation of the people living along the Atlantic coast. The remaining 40 percent of the population is a mixture of Moor and black.

Almost all Mauritanians are Muslim (followers of Islam). Islam is the state religion, but freedom of worship is guaranteed by law. Arabic and Wolof are the official languages, but many educated Mauritanians also speak French and English. In the south, people speak a variety of African languages.

Education is mandatory for six years. Classes are taught in Arabic, French, and African languages. This is because blacks objected to using only Arabic (the language of the Moors) in the schools.

▶ **LAND**

Mauritania has about 435 miles (700 kilometers) of coastline along the Atlantic Ocean. The country's northern, central, and eastern regions, which make up more than half the land, are part of the great Sahara desert. Here, vast stretches of sand are broken only by occasional rocky peaks and plateaus. Part of Mauritania lies in a region called the Sahel, the semi-desert fringe of the Sahara. It is grazing land, where cattle, sheep, and goats can be raised. But drought and overuse of the scant vegetation have led

Rural women learning to read. Although primary education is now mandatory, many Mauritanians cannot read or write.

to its deterioration and the steady encroachment of the Sahara farther south each year. The country's highest point is Mount Ijill in the northwest, which has an elevation of 3,001 feet (915 meters).

Aside from a few desert oases, only about 10 percent of Mauritania's land, in the extreme south along the Senegal River, is fertile enough to grow crops throughout the year. This area is wetter and cooler than the rest of the country, which is hot and dry.

▶ ECONOMY

Mauritania is one of the world's poorest countries; most of its people live on one or two dollars a day. It depends heavily on foreign aid and must import much of its food. Its economy has traditionally been based on livestock and a few food crops, such as dates, millet, sorghum, rice, and corn. Fish and fish products are also important and are a source of export income. A long drought in the 1970's wiped out many of the cattle herds, an economic disaster from which Mauritania has not yet recovered. In the south, a more recent concern has been the devastation of crops by floods and locusts.

Mauritania has several important minerals, including iron ore, which accounts for about 40 percent of all exports. It also has gypsum, copper, phosphates, diamonds, gold, and oil.

Services, including government, account for about 45 percent of the country's economy.

FACTS and figures

ISLAMIC REPUBLIC OF MAURITANIA is the official name of the country. It is called République Islamique de Mauritanie in French.

LOCATION: Northwestern Africa.

AREA: 397,954 sq mi (1,030,700 km²).

POPULATION: 3,100,000 (estimate).

CAPITAL AND LARGEST CITY: Nouakchott.

MAJOR LANGUAGES: Arabic and Wolof (both official), Fulani, Soninké, French, English.

MAJOR RELIGIOUS GROUP: Muslim.

GOVERNMENT: Republic. **Head of state**—president. **Head of government**—prime minister. **Legislature**—National Assembly and Senate.

CHIEF PRODUCTS: Agricultural—dates, millet, sorghum, rice, corn, livestock. **Manufactured**—processed fish, livestock products. **Mineral**—iron ore, gypsum, copper, phosphates, diamonds, gold, oil.

MONETARY UNIT: Ouguiya (1 ouguiya = 5 khoums).

▶ MAJOR CITIES

Nouakchott, the capital, is the largest city, with a population of about 558,000. It has grown in recent years due to drought in the surrounding countryside.

Nouadhibou, the second largest city, is Mauritania's major port on the Atlantic. It has a population of about 72,000.

▶ HISTORY AND GOVERNMENT

The original inhabitants of what is now Mauritania were peoples called Bafours. They were farmers, fishermen, and nomads. They were displaced by Berber tribes from North Africa between the 200's and the 600's.

The first Europeans to arrive were the Portuguese in the 1400's. Portuguese, Dutch, French, and British all competed for control of the region. In the late 1800's, French explorers penetrated the interior and signed agreements with the Moorish chieftains. The region became a French protectorate in 1903 and part of French West Africa in 1920.

Mauritania won self-government in 1958 and complete independence in 1960. It acquired part of the territory of Spanish Sahara (now Western Sahara) in 1976 but relinquished its rights to the territory in 1979.

Mauritania's first president, Moktar Ould Daddah, governed until 1978, when he was overthrown by the army, which established a military government. Muhammad Ould Haidalla became chief of state in 1980.

A second military coup, in 1984, ousted Haidalla and brought Colonel Maawiya Ould Sid Ahmed Taya to power as military ruler and president. Demands for political reform led to the adoption of a new constitution in 1991, which provided for a multiparty political system with an elected president and legislature. The president, who serves as head of state, appoints a prime minister who heads the government.

Taya was elected president in 1992 and reelected in 1997 and 2003. However, some opposition political parties disputed these results, charging that the elections had been rigged in Taya's favor. In 2005, Taya was overthrown by a group identified as the Military Council for Justice and Democracy. The coup was condemned by other African leaders and by the United Nations.

Reviewed by SUSANNA WING
Haverford College

MAURITIUS

Mauritius is a small, densely populated island nation in the Indian Ocean. It lies about 500 miles (800 kilometers) east of Madagascar, which is situated off the southeastern coast of Africa. The country is made up of one main island, also called Mauritius, and several smaller ones. Port Louis, located on the main island, is the capital and largest city.

People. Most Mauritians are of Indian ancestry. Most are Hindus in religion, with smaller numbers of Muslims. The next largest group, the Creoles, are of African, Malagasy (people from Madagascar), Indian, and European descent. Most Creoles are Christians.

The official language is English. But most Mauritians speak French and Creole, a language derived from French. Primary and secondary education is free and required of all children between the ages of 6 and 11.

Land. The main island is volcanic in origin and almost completely surrounded by coral reefs. Black mountain peaks rise steeply above lush vegetation. The highest point is Piton de la Rivière Noire, which rises to 2,711 feet (826 meters).

Economy. Agriculture is a vital part of the country's economy but is no longer its mainstay. Main agricultural products include sugarcane, tea, and corn. Tourism is an equally important industry. Clothing, textiles, and processed sugar are the leading exports.

History and Government. The Portuguese were the first to know of Mauritius, in the early 1500's. It was claimed in 1598 by the Dutch, who named it after Prince Maurice of Nassau, then ruled by France from 1715 to 1810, when it came under British control.

Africans, Malagasy, and people from Southeast Asia had been brought to the islands as slaves by the Dutch, the French, and the British. Slavery was abolished in 1835, and Indian laborers were later hired to work on the sugarcane plantations.

Mauritius gained independence from Britain in 1968 and adopted a government based on the British model. The present constitution was amended in 1992. It provides for a president, who is elected to a 5-year term by the legislative body, the National Assembly. Most legislators are elected by popular vote to serve 5-year terms. The government is headed by a prime minister, who leads the majority or largest political party in the National Assembly. Anerood Jugnauth, the current president, was elected in 2003. Navin Ramgoolam, leader of the Social Alliance Party, became prime minister in 2005.

Reviewed by MARIE JOYCE S. FORTUNÉ
University of California, Los Angeles

MAXWELL, JAMES CLERK. See PHYSICS, HISTORY OF (Profiles).

FACTS and figures

REPUBLIC OF MAURITIUS is the official name of the country.

LOCATION: Indian Ocean, southeast of Africa.

AREA: 784 sq mi (2,030 km²).

POPULATION: 1,200,000 (estimate).

CAPITAL AND LARGEST CITY: Port Louis.

MAJOR LANGUAGES: English (official), French, Creole, Bhojpuri.

MAJOR RELIGIOUS GROUPS: Hindu, Christian.

GOVERNMENT: Republic. **Head of state**—president. **Head of government**—prime minister. **Legislature**—National Assembly.

CHIEF PRODUCTS: Agricultural—sugarcane, tea, corn, potatoes, bananas. **Manufactured**—processed foods (including refined sugar), textiles, clothing.

MONETARY UNIT: Mauritian rupee (1 rupee = 100 cents).

May

The month of May was probably named for Maia Majesta, the Roman goddess of spring. In the Southern Hemisphere, May is one of the chilly months of autumn, but in the Northern Hemisphere, May is a warm and merry month. The earth blooms and people rejoice.

Place in year: 5th month.
Number of days: 31.
Flowers: Hawthorne and lily of the valley.
Birthstone: Emerald.
Zodiac signs: Taurus, the Bull (April 20–May 20), and Gemini, the Twins (May 21–June 20).

1
- England, Scotland, and Wales became Great Britain, 1707
- Admiral Dewey won the Battle of Manila Bay, 1898
- Empire State Building dedicated, 1931
- *May Day*

2
- Hudson's Bay Company chartered, 1670
- Prokofiev's *Peter and the Wolf* premiered at a children's concert in Moscow, U.S.S.R., 1936

3
- Constitution Day in Japan; Poland

4
- **Horace Mann** born 1796
- **Thomas Henry Huxley** born 1825
- Rhode Island declared its independence from England, 1776
- Haymarket Riot took place in Chicago, 1886

5
- **Karl Marx** born 1818
- Napoleon died at St. Helena, 1821
- First U.S. suborbital space flight made by Alan B. Shepard, Jr., 1961
- Children's Day in Japan

6
- **Sigmund Freud** born 1856
- **Robert E. Peary** born 1856
- The dirigible *Hindenburg* blew up and burned killing 36 persons, 1937
- Dr. Roger Bannister of England became the first person to run a mile in less than 4 minutes, 1954

7
- **Robert Browning** born 1812
- **Johannes Brahms** born 1833
- **Peter Ilyich Tchaikovsky** born 1840
- The *Lusitania* torpedoed and sunk by a German submarine, 1915

8
- **Harry S Truman** born 1884
- The German High Command surrender to the Allies, ending World War II in Europe, became effective, 1945

9
- **John Brown** born 1800
- **Sir James Matthew Barrie** born 1860

10
- Second Continental Congress met, 1775
- Ethan Allen and his "Green Mountain Boys" captured Fort Ticonderoga in New York during the Revolutionary War, 1775
- First transcontinental railroad in the U.S. competed at Promontory, Utah, 1869
- *Confederate Memorial Day* in North Carolina; South Carolina

11
- **Salvador Dali** born 1904
- Minnesota became the 32nd state, 1858

12
- **Florence Nightingale** born 1820
- **Dante Gabriel Rossetti** born 1828

13
- **Georges Braque** born 1882
- U.S. declared war on Mexico, 1846
- Pope John Paul II wounded in an assassination attempt in Rome, 1981

14
- Lewis and Clark started trip up Missouri River, 1804
- State of Israel established, 1948
- Skylab, first orbiting U.S. space laboratory, launched, 1973
- *National Flag Day* in Paraguay

15
- **Pierre Curie** born 1859
- Edith Cresson became France's first woman premier, 1991

16
- U.S. Senate voted for acquittal in the impeachment trial of Andrew Johnson, 1868

17
- **Edward Jenner** born 1749
- U.S. Supreme Court issued *Brown* v. *Board of Education* decision, ruling segregation of schools unconstitutional, 1954
- *Constitution Day* in Nauru; Norway

18
- **Bertrand Russell** born 1872
- **Pope John Paul II** born 1920

19
- Mount St. Helens in state of Washington erupted, killing more than 60 people, 1980
- Jacques Cartier sailed from France on his second voyage to Canada, 1535

20
- **Honoré de Balzac** born 1799
- Charles Lindbergh took off on first nonstop transatlantic solo flight, 1927
- *National Day* in Cameroon

21
- **Albrecht Dürer** born 1471
- **Alexander Pope** born 1688
- Clara Barton founded American Red Cross, 1881
- Amelia Earhart completed first solo flight by a woman across the Atlantic, 1932

22
- **Richard Wagner** born 1813
- **Mary Cassatt** born 1844
- **Sir Arthur Conan Doyle** born 1859
- The American ship *Savannah* became first steamship to cross the Atlantic, 1819

23
- **Carolus Linnaeus** born 1707
- South Carolina ratified the Constitution, 1788
- New York Public Library incorporated, 1895

24
- **Queen Victoria** born 1819
- First permanent English settlement in the U.S. founded at Jamestown, Virginia, 1607
- First public telegraph message ("What hath God wrought!") sent by Samuel F. B. Morse from Washington, D.C., to Baltimore, Maryland, 1844

25
- **Ralph Waldo Emerson** born 1803
- **Tito (Josip Broz)** born 1892
- Constitutional Convention opened in Philadelphia, 1787

26
- Organization of African Unity (OAU) charter adopted by heads of most independent African states, 1963
- *Independence Day* in Jordan

27
- San Francisco's Golden Gate Bridge opened, 1937

28
- **William Pitt the Younger** born 1759
- **John Louis Rodolphe Agassiz** born 1807
- **James Francis (Jim) Thorpe** born 1888

29
- **Patrick Henry** born 1736
- **John F. Kennedy** born 1917
- Rhode Island ratified the Constitution, 1790
- Wisconsin became the 30th state, 1848
- Sir Edmund Hillary of New Zealand and Tenzing Norkay of Nepal became first to reach summit of Mount Everest, 1953

30
- **Peter the Great** born 1672
- Joan of Arc burned at the stake, 1431
- Kansas-Nebraska Act passed, 1854
- *Memorial Day* first celebrated in the U.S., 1868
- First Indianapolis 500 Automobile Race held, 1911

31
- **Walt Whitman** born 1819
- Seventeenth Amendment to U.S. Constitution, providing for direct election of senators, went into effect, 1913
- *Republic Day* in South Africa

Second Sunday in May: *Mother's Day.* **Third Saturday in May:** *Armed Forces Day.* **Last Monday in May:** *Memorial Day.* **Monday before May 25:** *Victoria Day* in Canada.

The calendar listing identifies people who were born on the indicated day in boldface type, **like this.** You will find a biography of each of these birthday people in *The New Book of Knowledge.* In addition to citing some historical events and historical firsts, the calendar also lists the holidays and some of the festivals celebrated in the United States. These holidays are printed in italic type, *like this.* See the article HOLIDAYS for more information.

Many holidays and festivals of nations around the world are included in the calendar as well. When the term "national holiday" is used, it means that the nation celebrates an important patriotic event on that day—in most cases the winning of independence. Consult *The New Book of Knowledge* article on the individual nation for further information on its national holiday.

MAYA

The Maya are an American Indian people who have lived in western Central America for at least 3,000 years. Today, with a population of nearly 5 million, they continue to speak Maya languages and to carry on traditions that go back to the time of their famous ancestors.

During their Classic period, A.D. 200–900, the ancient Maya made advances in painting, sculpture, astronomy, and writing. They built magnificent cities, then abandoned them. In the mid-20th century, many of the palaces and pyramids were cleared of jungle growth and could again be appreciated for their beauty. More recently, scholars have begun to decipher Maya writing and to read the inscriptions on the ancient walls. As a result, the Maya of the Classic period are better known now than they were just a few years ago.

▶SOCIAL ORDER

Maya cities were built with the co-operation of thousands of people. At the top of the social order stood the king, whose power was granted by the gods. From him, authority flowed downward through the many layers of society.

The King

No pains were spared to establish the dignity of the ruler. His official title was "Great Sun," and his royal ancestry could be traced back to legendary kings or even to the gods.

Ordinarily, rulership was passed from father to son. In rare cases the ruler was a woman.

The Stele. To impress his subjects, the king had a stone pillar, called a **stele**, carved with his portrait. Sometimes he was shown wearing the costume of a god. Surrounding the portrait were inscriptions telling of his deeds, along with the dates of important events in his life. These free-standing steles are one of the most typical features of ancient Maya culture. When the king died, a pyramid might be erected over his tomb, with a small temple at the very top. Evidently there was a close connection between the respect paid to kings and the worship of gods.

The City State

There was never a single Maya empire. Rather there were dozens of cities, each with its own government. Among the largest were Tikal in Guatemala, Copán in Honduras, and Palenque (pah-LAYNG-kay) in southern Mexico. In the hope of increasing his power, the king of one of these cities might marry off his sister or daughter to the king of another city. More often, however, a city's influence was extended by conquest.

Warfare. The king himself was the leader of his warriors. His greatest achievement was to capture a rival king and bring him home to be sacrificed. In close combat the warriors wore armor of quilted cotton and used axes, clubs, and long spears. The Maya of the Classic period did not use the bow and arrow.

A conquered city was ruled in the king's name by a group of nobles called governors.

A drawing of how the city of Copán—one of the most important Maya cities—would have looked in late Classic times.

Social Classes. The governors formed one of several classes that were close to the king. Those who served him at home as personal servants, including musicians, formed another class. Still another was the priestly class in charge of religious ceremonies.

An aerial view of one of the larger cities shows a central plaza, surrounded by palaces, pyramids, and temple structures. Behind these are smaller plazas. Farther removed are yet smaller courtyards and smaller buildings. Such arrangements suggest that the ruling classes were ranked so that the most important lived nearest the king.

Beyond the stone buildings are the remains of outlying settlements. These were occupied by the common people whose main business was farming. The entire population, including the residents of these suburbs, might have reached as many as 50,000 for a great city like Tikal.

Temple I at Tikal, Guatemala. This is a good example of Maya architecture.

▶WAY OF LIFE

The vast region stretching from central Mexico to northwest Costa Rica is known to archaeologists as Mesoamerica. Within this area, ancient Indian cultures built cities, traded with each other, and shared customs. It is not surprising, therefore, to find that the Maya have much in common with the Aztecs and other Mesoamerican peoples, even though they developed their own particular way of life.

Work

The main work of the ancient Maya was farming. Without large food supplies their cities could not have been built. In the swampy lowlands, raised fields were made by scooping up the rich, wet soil. In hilly country, the slopes were terraced to hold moisture and prevent erosion.

Maize (corn) was the most important crop. Beans, squash, tomatoes, chili peppers, cacao (chocolate), and avocados were also grown.

Weaving. Another important crop was cotton. Women wove cloth from the fiber, using a long loom strapped around the middle of the body and attached at the far end to a post or tree.

For themselves they made long wrap-around cotton skirts and loose-fitting blouses; for the men, loincloths and capes. Among the nobles, fancy dress might include a turban wound around the head or necklaces and ear ornaments of jade and feathers, as well as other precious materials.

House Construction. The simpler houses were made of wooden poles set closely together and roofed with thatch. Wooden beds were covered with kapok-filled mattresses. In the stone palaces of the nobles, sleeping platforms were built into the walls.

Transportation. Most men, if they were commoners, were farmers. But many men worked as porters, carrying goods from town to town. There were no beasts of burden and no wheeled vehicles. Yet the Maya were great merchants, bringing goods from as far away as central Mexico and setting up markets in all the cities.

Religion

The Sun God, the Maize God, the planet Venus, and numerous Death gods were among the deities that watched over the Maya world. The Moon Goddess was the most important of the female deities. Often she is shown spinning or weaving.

Blood Offerings. The gods were worshiped, or "nourished," with gifts of blood. Men and women pierced their earlobes or their tongues and ran strips of bark paper through the wound. The blood-soaked paper would then be burned as an offering. Prisoners of war were bled for the same purpose, and some were sacrificed.

Death Gods. The gods of the underworld were among the most feared. When a king died, his tomb was furnished with painted vases showing mythical heroes who had outwitted the lords of death. Following the example of the heroes, the king himself, it was believed, might survive the trials of the underworld and achieve everlasting life.

Arts and Learning

The ancient Maya are celebrated for their artistic and intellectual accomplishments. Few Maya books survive, but Maya artworks are prized possessions in museums around the world.

Books and Writing. Books that open like a folding screen were made of bark paper and painted in red and black. The symbols, found also in stone carvings and on painted vases, can be read more or less like letters in the modern alphabet. They make up the only true writing system developed in ancient America.

Astronomy. A folding-screen book now called the Dresden Codex is the finest of the surviving Maya books. Written after the Classic period, parts of it are thought to have been adapted from a Classic source. In this codex is a table for predicting the phases of the planet Venus: when it appears as evening star and when as morning star. The Maya were keen observers of the planets, especially Venus, which they held to be a god that guided them to victory in war.

The Long Count. Many of the peoples in Mesoamerica had accurate calendars, but the calendars ran out after 52 years and had to be started all over again. The Maya had this kind of calendar, too. But they also had a Long Count, which started from a fixed point in the distant past—like the modern calendar, which counts years from the birth of Christ.

Pottery and Painting. Figurines and vases made of fired clay are among the most admired of Maya artworks. Some vases have a carved surface. Others are painted with lifelike scenes. The painters, using a fine brush, achieved a delicacy of line that was well suited to depicting human figures and facial expressions.

Architecture and Sculpture. Sometimes painters working in a bold style filled interior spaces with scenes of battles and ceremonies. Stone buildings, however, were roofed by means of the corbel arch, not a true arch but a steep peak made by laying stones closer and closer together. Thus the interiors were dark and narrow and had to be lit by torches.

Inside walls were usually left bare and were probably darkened by smoke. But the exteriors of important buildings were sometimes completely covered with sculpture. Today the exteriors are the color of natural stone. To visualize them as the Maya saw them, one must imagine them as they originally were, vividly tinted with reds, blues, yellows, and greens.

▶HISTORY

Unlike the Aztecs, the Maya have a long history, spanning thousands of years. Although their time of greatest fame may have passed, they remain a vital people with prospects for the future.

Pre-Columbian Era

It is not known where or when Maya civilization began. The Maya kings themselves traced their origin to the Olmecs, who had built cities along the Gulf of Mexico between 1200 and 100 B.C. The Olmecs are known to have had the Long Count and evidently invented the bar-and-dot method of writing numbers.

Classic Period. During the last years of the Olmecs, the Maya were already building cities of their own. Their writing system and art style matured about A.D. 200, which marks the beginning of the Classic period.

Suddenly, about the year 900, many of the cities were abandoned. No one knows the reason for this Maya "collapse." Disease, food

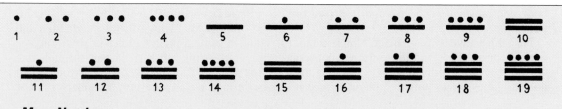

Maya Numbers   Higher numbers are written by placing these symbols for the first 19 numbers in different positions.

A special photograph of a Maya painted vase showing a palace scene. All sides of the vase can be seen in one picture.

shortages, rebellions, severe drought, and a foreign invasion have all been suggested as the cause.

Postclassic Period. The collapse was not the end of the Maya. Cities continued to thrive in the Guatemala highlands and in Yucatán. The important city of Chichén Itzá belongs to this period. Typical of the Postclassic, the architecture of Chichén Itzá shows strong influences from central Mexico.

Colonial Era

By the time the Spaniards arrived, in the 1520's, the Maya were living in smaller, more hastily built cities than those their ancestors had known. As in the past, they were divided into rival factions. In 1523 the Guatemalan Maya were conquered by Pedro de Alvarado with the help of Indian allies. The conquest of Yucatán was accomplished in the 1540's by Francisco de Montejo and his son.

As a conquered people, the Maya were brought into the Spanish *encomienda* system. This meant that the land was now owned by Spaniards, for whom the Indian people were forced to work.

Burning of the Books. Hoping to end the worship of Maya gods, Christian missionaries collected the ancient books and burned them. But the Maya promptly learned to use the European's alphabetic script and prepared new books to preserve their traditions. Among these are the *Popol Vuh*, written in Guatemala in the 1550's, and the *Books of Chilam Balam*, written in Yucatán.

The Modern Maya

The Maya of today speak about 30 closely related languages. Among the best-known groups are the Tzotzil and Yucatec of southern Mexico and the Ixil, Quiché, and Kekchi of Guatemala. Christianity has been accepted, but prayers are still made to Maya gods. Maize is grown in small family plots, but many Maya still work on large plantations owned by non-Indians.

Sacred stories, or myths, that go back to the Classic period are still told in many communities. In Guatemala, Maya scholars have prepared new Spanish translations of the *Popol Vuh*. Meanwhile, in Yucatán, *Books of Chilam Balam* are still kept in a few villages, where they are read publicly in annual ceremonies. A thousand years after the abandonment of Tikal and Palenque, the Maya have not lost their respect for the written word.

Crisis in Guatemala. Fearing revolution, the military government of Guatemala began to attack Indian villages in the early 1980's. Entire communities were massacred and hundreds of thousands of people were driven from their homes. Many fled to neighboring Mexico until the civil war ended in 1996.

JOHN BIERHORST
Author, *The Mythology of
Mexico and Central America*

See also INDIANS, AMERICAN.

MAYER, LOUIS B. See LOS ANGELES (Famous People).

MAYER, MARIA GOEPPERT. See PHYSICS, HISTORY OF (Profiles).

MAYFLOWER

The *Mayflower* was the little three-masted sailing ship that brought the Pilgrims from England to the New World in 1620. About 90 feet (27 meters) long, it was roughly the size of a harbor tugboat. The *Mayflower* was not really a passenger ship at all. It was just a sea "tramp" that usually carried any cargo it could find. Before the Pilgrims hired it, the ship had been carrying wine from France to England.

On September 20, 1620, the *Mayflower* sailed from Plymouth, England. Aboard were just over 100 men, women, and children, including a crew of about 28 men under Captain Christopher Jones.

The *Mayflower* crossed the Atlantic Ocean at its stormiest season. Sometimes the decks were full of water, and the wind and rain blew through the passengers' quarters. The Atlantic seas almost rolled the little ship over. One young man was washed overboard but managed to hang onto a trailing rope and was rescued. At mealtimes the passengers ate the same food day after day—sea biscuits, salted meat, dried fish, and cheese—and washed it down with beer. Some of them were seasick for weeks on end. The *Mayflower* was so old that once, during a storm, one of the main supporting timbers inside the tiny ship broke. To support the broken beam a printing press was

placed underneath it. The press was part of the equipment that the Pilgrims were taking to the New World.

Shortly before the *Mayflower* reached land, William Butten, the 22-year-old servant of Deacon Samuel Fuller, died and was buried at sea. But the number of passengers remained unchanged. A son, Peregrine, was born on shipboard to William and Susanna White a month after the vessel arrived safely.

After ten weeks the Pilgrims made the first landfall where Provincetown, Massachusetts, is today, then proceeded to the site of Plymouth, across Cape Cod Bay. The *Mayflower* sailed for England the following April.

Today anchored near a reconstruction of the early colony at Plymouth is the *Mayflower II*, a replica of the wonderful old ship that brought the Pilgrims. More than 250,000 visitors go aboard the ship each year. They gain a new admiration for the courage and fortitude of the people who sailed in such a vessel to America more than 350 years earlier.

ALAN VILLIERS
Master, *Mayflower II*

See also THIRTEEN AMERICAN COLONIES; PLYMOUTH COLONY.

MAYFLOWER COMPACT. See PLYMOUTH COLONY.

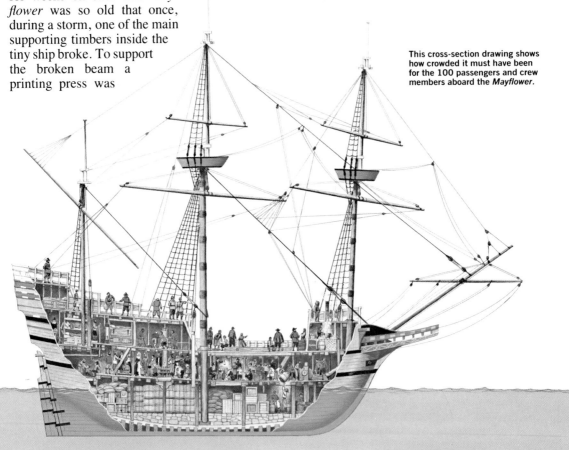

This cross-section drawing shows how crowded it must have been for the 100 passengers and crew members aboard the *Mayflower*.

MAZZINI, GIUSEPPE (1805–1872)

Giuseppe Mazzini was an Italian patriot who helped unite the numerous states of Italy into one nation. He was born in Genoa on June 22, 1805. While a student at the University of Genoa, he joined the Carbonari, a secret revolutionary society dedicated to overthrowing ruling monarchies in order to establish republican governments.

In 1830, Mazzini was imprisoned for conspiracy. After his release in 1831, he left Italy for France and founded a society called Young Italy, which plotted against the governments of the Italian states. Mazzini also formed a group called Young Europe to unite revolutionaries from all European countries. In 1837, he moved to England, which he considered a second home.

In 1848, revolutions broke out in the Italian states, and Mazzini returned to Italy. A revolutionary republic was established in Rome, with Mazzini as a governor. But French troops defeated the republican army, and once again, Mazzini fled.

For the next ten years, he continued his revolutionary activities. Then in 1860, after wars and revolts against Austria and the Italian states, most of Italy was united under King Victor Emmanuel II of Sardinia. In 1861 a united Italian kingdom was officially proclaimed. But Mazzini remained opposed to the monarchy.

In 1870 his attempt to stir up a new republican uprising failed. He was sentenced to prison but was pardoned because of ill health. He died in Pisa on March 10, 1872. Although Mazzini's hopes for a united Italian republic were not realized in his lifetime, his ideas strongly influenced Italy's future.

EMILIANA P. NOETHER
University of Connecticut

McAULIFFE, CHRISTA. See NEW HAMPSHIRE (Famous People).

McCARRAN, PATRICK ANTHONY. See NEVADA (Famous People).

McCARTHY, JOSEPH R. See UNITED STATES, CONGRESS OF THE (Profiles: Senators).

McCARTHY, MARY. See WASHINGTON (Famous People).

McCLELLAN, GEORGE B. See CIVIL WAR, UNITED STATES (Profiles: Union).

McCLINTOCK, BARBARA (1902–1992)

Barbara McClintock was one of America's foremost scientists in the field of genetics, which is the study of how traits are passed on from one generation to the next. Her work led to a new genetic theory and the 1983 Nobel Prize in physiology or medicine.

McClintock was born on June 16, 1902, in Hartford, Connecticut. She first became interested in science in high school and took great pleasure in solving scientific problems. "It was a tremendous joy, the whole process of finding that answer, just pure joy," she recalled. After earning her Ph.D. in botany from Cornell University (1927), she taught and conducted research at several universities.

In 1941, she joined the Carnegie Institution's Department of Genetics in Cold Spring Harbor on Long Island, New York. There, McClintock studied the way that certain traits, such as the color of corn kernels, are passed on from one generation of corn to the next. For a long time, scientists had believed that genes (the units of heredity) were fixed in place on the chromosomes of cells. McClintock discov-

ered that some genes can change their positions on the chromosomes. She went on to show that such a "jumping gene" can change the inherited traits of future generations as it changes position and affects neighboring genes.

When McClintock first presented the results of her experiments in 1951, few scientists were willing to accept her findings. However, as new discoveries were made during the years that followed, McClintock's ideas were accepted. She received the Nobel Prize in 1983 —in part for her work done in the 1940's. She continued to work out of her laboratory in Cold Spring Harbor until her death on September 2, 1992.

KARYN L. BERTSCHI
Science Writer

See also GENETICS.

Cyrus McCormick demonstrated his first reaping machine in a Virginia wheat field in 1831. Later improved models made possible the extensive farming of wheat in the Midwest.

McCORMICK, CYRUS (1809–1884)

Cyrus McCormick is known as the inventor of the reaper, a machine for harvesting grain. The invention of this machine was one of the most important developments of the 1800's.

Cyrus McCormick was born on February 15, 1809, on a farm in Rockbridge County, Virginia. He had little schooling. As a boy he spent a lot of time helping his father.

Cyrus' father, Robert McCormick, was also an inventor of farm machines. Like many others, he tried to invent a reaper. And like the others, he was not successful. In 1831, Cyrus McCormick, benefiting from his father's mistakes, built a reaper that worked. He was not entirely satisfied with it, however, and worked to improve his invention. He did not patent the reaper until 1834. Even then he did not try to manufacture or sell it because he had become involved in iron manufacturing.

In 1837, McCormick's iron business failed, and he lost a great deal of money. He decided to return to his work on the reaper, and began manufacturing and marketing his machine.

At first, many farmers chose not to use the reaper. The early models exhausted the horses that pulled them; and the machines often clogged and were generally unreliable.

McCormick realized that the reaper was better suited to the flat fields of the Midwest than to the small, hilly farms of the East. In 1847 he left Virginia to open a factory in Chicago, the center of the wheat country. By 1855 he had completely redesigned his reaper. Even though other people began making reapers, McCormick's business did extremely well. It prospered because he used advanced equipment to make very reliable reapers. McCormick also provided services to his customers that others did not, such as written guarantees and mail-order parts. He advertised heavily and was among the first to offer credit. In addition he established a large network of agencies to sell and service his products. McCormick became a millionaire.

In 1858, McCormick married Nancy Fowler. They had seven children. McCormick died on May 13, 1884.

TERRY S. REYNOLDS
Michigan Technological University

See also FARMS AND FARMING.

McGOVERN, GEORGE. See SOUTH DAKOTA (Famous People).

WILLIAM MCKINLEY (1843-1901)
25th President of the United States

FACTS ABOUT MC KINLEY

Birthplace: Niles, Ohio
Religion: Methodist
College Attended: Allegheny College, Meadville, Pennsylvania
Occupation: Lawyer
Married: Ida Saxton
Children: Katherine, Ida (both died in infancy)
Political Party: Republican
Office Held Before Becoming President: Governor of Ohio
President Who Preceded Him: Grover Cleveland
Age on Becoming President: 54
Years in the Presidency: 1897–1901 (died in office after being shot)
Vice President: Garret A. Hobart (first term, died 1899); Theodore Roosevelt (second term)
President Who Succeeded Him: Theodore Roosevelt
Age at Death: 58
Burial Place: Canton, Ohio

DURING MC KINLEY'S PRESIDENCY

Below: The Spanish-American War broke out (1898) after the battleship USS *Maine* was blown up in the harbor of Havana, Cuba. Puerto Rico, Guam, and the Philippines became territories of the United States as a result of the U.S. victory in the war. U.S. Marines took part in an international expedition (1900) to relieve the foreign legations in Peking, China, during the Boxer Rebellion. *Above:* Dr. Walter Reed, working in Cuba, discovered (1900) that yellow fever is transmitted by a type of mosquito. *Center:* The U.S. Navy's first submarine, the *Holland,* was commissioned (1900).

MC KINLEY, WILLIAM. William McKinley was one of the kindliest and most peace-loving of U.S. presidents. Yet he led the United States at a time when most Americans were determined to go to war. And the life of this gentle and sympathetic man was brought tragically to an end by bullets from an assassin's gun.

▶ EARLY YEARS

McKinley was born in Niles, Ohio, on January 29, 1843, the seventh child of William and Nancy Allison McKinley. Young McKinley grew up a serious boy, possessed of a quiet determination to succeed. He attended school in Poland, Ohio, and then went to Allegheny College in Meadville, Pennsylvania. He left college before graduating and became a teacher in a rural school. When the Civil War broke out in 1861, the 17-year-old McKinley enlisted as a private in the 23rd Ohio Volunteer Infantry Regiment. Though short and slight, he impressed his superiors with his initiative, and he rose to become a brevet major.

At the war's end, McKinley left the Army and returned to Ohio to study law. In 1867 he opened a law office in Canton, Ohio. There he remained, except when public duty interfered, for the rest of his life. Within two years he was elected prosecuting attorney, and a career in politics began to open up for him.

In 1871, McKinley married Ida Saxton, daughter of Canton's most prominent banker. They were devoted to each other. However, after the death of their two young children, both girls, Ida became ill and remained an invalid for the rest of her life.

▶ CONGRESSMAN AND GOVERNOR

In 1876, McKinley was elected, as a Republican, to the U.S. House of Representatives. He was re-elected almost continuously until 1890. In that year the Republicans lost the election because of a tariff—the McKinley Tariff.

In 1890 the business interests of the country were determined to pass a high tariff, or tax on foreign goods, in order to protect

American industry from competition. McKinley firmly believed in such a policy, and overcoming all opposition, he got his tariff bill passed. However, resentment over the tariff, especially in the West and South, cost the Republicans heavily in the election, and McKinley lost his seat in Congress.

Undiscouraged by his defeat, McKinley won the governorship of Ohio in 1891. Earlier he had impressed a wealthy Cleveland businessman, who offered to help McKinley further his political career. This businessman was Marcus Alonzo Hanna (1837–1904), one of the most influential men in the Republican Party. A close relationship developed between the two men and grew into a lifelong friendship. Under Mark Hanna's steady direction McKinley would attain the presidency.

In 1892 McKinley was appointed chairman of the Republican National Convention. Some members of his party were so enthusiastic about McKinley that they wanted him to become the Republican presidential candidate. But McKinley felt that he was not yet ready for so important an office. Instead he gave his support to the renomination of President Benjamin Harrison. McKinley's decision not to seek the nomination was a fortunate one. While Harrison was defeated by Grover Cleveland in the election of 1892, McKinley went on to be elected governor of Ohio for a second term.

By 1896, McKinley felt ready to accept his party's nomination for the presidency. At the Republican National Convention in St. Louis, Missouri, he was nominated on the first ballot. The Republicans were confident of victory, for the Democratic administration of President Grover Cleveland had been plagued by an economic depression.

▶ THE CAMPAIGN OF 1896

The Democrats, with William Jennings Bryan as their candidate, campaigned on the issue of "free silver." Many people, especially farmers in the West, felt their economic hardships would end if the government restored unlimited coinage of silver money. Bryan toured the country urging such a policy. He was a forceful orator, and McKinley was hard pressed to compete with him.

Taking his friend Mark Hanna's advice, McKinley did not try to out-talk Bryan. Instead, he stayed at his home in Canton and conducted a "front-porch" campaign, speaking to groups of people who flocked to his home to listen to him. Businessmen and workers in the East gave him their support, and a good farm crop in the West helped restore prosperity. McKinley received 7,102,246 popular votes to Bryan's 6,492,559 and 271 electoral votes to Bryan's 176.

▶ PRESIDENT

McKinley's first term of office was an eventful one for the United States. The nation was seething with new growth, and many different interests sought dominance. McKinley seemed ideally suited to the task of harmonizing such clashing interests.

Cuba and the Spanish-American War

The most important event in McKinley's administration resulted from a crisis in Cuba. Revolts by Cubans against Spanish rule had

During the campaign of 1896 Republicans praised the McKinley tariff bill, as shown in this cartoon.

THE TWO BILLS.
A combination that is hard to beat.

broken out, and the Cubans appealed to the United States for help. Stories of Spanish cruelty toward the Cubans began to arouse American public opinion against Spain. Soon an avalanche of sympathy for *Cuba Libre* ("Free Cuba") began to descend on McKinley. The President, above all a man of peace, had already pledged his opposition to any armed interference in another country's affairs. In his annual message to Congress he urged that Spain "be given a reasonable chance" to right the situation. Yet his concern over the plight of the Cuban people was real. He issued a Christmas Eve appeal for public contributions to a Cuban relief fund. And at his initiative over $250,000 of aid was sent to Cuba by the Red Cross.

Early in 1898 two events occurred that left McKinley helpless to avoid war with Spain. The first was a private letter written by the Spanish minister in Washington, D.C. Intercepted by a Cuban, who turned it over to a reporter, the letter was published in American newspapers. In it the minister, De Lôme, called McKinley "a would-be politician . . . weak and a bidder for the admiration of the crowd. . . ." Though the minister promptly resigned and the Spanish Government apologized, the De Lôme letter turned popular opinion even more strongly against Spain.

Then, a few days later, the United States battleship *Maine* was blown up in Havana harbor, with a loss of 260 American lives. Newspapers across the country blazed the headline that Spain was responsible and that war was now certain. Actually, no one knows to this day what caused the disaster. But without waiting further, Congress rushed through a bill appropriating $50,000,000 for national defense.

Though McKinley continued to press for peace, Congress and the vast majority of the American public were convinced that war was the only honorable road left open to the United States. A popular newspaper cartoon of the day showed an angry Uncle Sam straining to fight Spain while the President held him back by the coattails. The caption read, "Let go of him, McKinley!"

Soon the President feared that unless he gave way, Congress would declare war over his head. Finally he decided to yield to popular demand, and in April, 1898, war with

IMPORTANT DATES IN THE LIFE OF WILLIAM MC KINLEY	
1843	Born at Niles, Ohio, January 29.
1861–1865	Served in the 23rd Ohio Volunteer Infantry Regiment, Union Army.
1867	Opened a law office in Canton, Ohio.
1869	Elected prosecuting attorney of Stark County, Ohio.
1871	Married Ida Saxton.
1877–84; 1885–91	Served in the United States House of Representatives.
1892–1896	Governor of Ohio.
1897–1901	25th president of the United States.
1901	Shot by Leon F. Czolgosz at Buffalo, New York, September 6; died September 14.

Spain was declared. Yet McKinley always felt that, left to himself, "I could have concluded an arrangement with the Spanish government under which the Spanish troops would have been withdrawn from Cuba without a war."

The Spanish-American War lasted less than four months and resulted in a victory for the United States. The United States won control over the former Spanish possessions of Puerto Rico, Guam, and the Philippines, while Cuba gained its independence.

The Issue of Imperialism

After the war some Americans were undecided as to whether the United States should keep the territory won from Spain. They argued that the United States should not hold on to such possessions as the Philippine Islands, which were far from the country's shores. As the islands of Hawaii had also been acquired during this time, there was a growing fear that the United States was becoming an imperialist power.

McKinley was tormented by his conscience as to what course he should take. Though he felt that the United States had had to interfere in Cuba for "humanity's sake," he found it hard to justify holding the Philippines. However, others in his party urged him to keep them as legitimate possessions. Finally, after walking "the floor of the White House night after night until midnight," McKinley decided to accept the islands for the United States.

China and the Open-Door Policy

With major possessions in the Far East, American interest in China and in world politics in general increased. At the time, Great Britain, France, Germany, and Japan were acquiring large "spheres of influence" in China. In 1899, McKinley's secretary of state, John Hay (1838–1905), called on the other powers to allow equality of trade in China. After the unsuccessful Boxer Rebellion in 1900, in which the Chinese revolted against foreign domination, Hay declared that it was American policy to respect the independence of China. He called on the other countries to do the same. This policy of equality of trade with China and respect for its territorial integrity was the basis of the famous Open-Door policy.

The American share of the indemnity, or the payment for losses, exacted from China after the revolt was later turned into a scholarship fund to enable Chinese students to study in the United States.

The Election of 1900

The election of 1900 found McKinley more popular than ever. Bryan, who was again the Democratic candidate, tried to raise the issue of imperialism. But its effect was limited by the fact that the United States was prospering more than ever. The "full dinner pail" became a McKinley slogan. The result was an

Although Ida Saxton McKinley was an invalid when William McKinley became President, she entertained frequently at the White House. She died in 1907 and is buried beside her husband in Canton, Ohio.

easy victory for McKinley and his vice president, Theodore Roosevelt.

▶ASSASSINATION

On the afternoon of September 6, 1901, at a public reception in Buffalo, New York, a man suddenly walked up to the President with a handkerchief-covered revolver in his outstretched hand. Two shots rang out, striking McKinley at point-blank range. While being carried to an ambulance, he pleaded with police not to beat the assassin. Eight days later McKinley died, and Vice President Theodore Roosevelt was sworn in as 26th president. The assassin, Leon F. Czolgosz, was an anarchist —one who rebels against governmental authority. He was speedily brought to trial and sentenced to death on September 26. Czolgosz was executed in the prison at Auburn, New York, on October 29.

Amid great mourning, McKinley was buried in Canton, Ohio. Ida McKinley died in 1907 and was buried beside her husband in a great memorial tomb. Another memorial to McKinley was erected at Niles.

With the passing of McKinley, the United States, too, passed from one era to another—from an era of internal growth and expansion to one of growing participation and leadership in world affairs.

ANDREW BRYCE
Author, *Narrative History of the United States*

See also BRYAN, WILLIAM JENNINGS; SPANISH-AMERICAN WAR.

MCLOUGHLIN, JOHN. See OREGON (Famous People).

McKinley was shot on September 6, 1901, in Buffalo, New York, by Leon F. Czolgosz, an anarchist. McKinley died eight days later.

MEAD, MARGARET (1901–1978)

By the time Margaret Mead was 10 years old, she was studying her two younger sisters the way her mother, a sociologist, had studied her. She made notes on how they developed and took their places in the family. Those notes were her first attempt at cultural anthropology—the study of the culture, or ways of life, of the different peoples who make up the family of humankind.

Margaret Mead was born in Philadelphia, Pennsylvania, on December 16, 1901. She thought she might become a writer, lawyer, or psychologist. But as a senior at Barnard College, she was inspired by the anthropologist Franz Boas to study age-old ways of life that were rapidly dying out. Her first field trip, in 1925, took her to the Samoan Islands in the Pacific Ocean. The book she later wrote, *Coming of Age in Samoa* (1928), helped change people's thinking all over the world. It showed that what people had thought was unchangeable "human nature" was really learned behavior formed by a particular culture. This helped people understand their own culture and other human beings.

Margaret Mead was associated with the American Museum of Natural History throughout her career. As a curator of ethnology (the study of races and cultures), she studied other Pacific island cultures. She wrote

The anthropologist Margaret Mead helped people understand their own culture and that of other human beings.

Growing Up in New Guinea (1930) about one of them. She studied American Indians, too.

When she began to explore relationships between modern men and women, she drew on her work among primitive societies. This is reflected in her book *Male and Female* (1949). As one of the best-known and most respected anthropologists, Margaret Mead was a sought-after writer, lecturer, and teacher. She died on November 15, 1978, in New York City.

SAM AND BERYL EPSTEIN
Authors, *She Never Looked Back:
Margaret Mead in Samoa*

MEADE, GEORGE GORDON.   See CIVIL WAR, UNITED STATES (Profiles: Union).
MEAN, MEDIAN, MODE.   See STATISTICS.
MEANY, GEORGE.   See LABOR MOVEMENT (Profiles).
MEASLES.   See DISEASES (Descriptions of Some Diseases).
MEASUREMENT.   See WEIGHTS AND MEASURES.

MEAT AND MEAT PACKING

Meat is any part of an animal that people use for food. In ages past, people had fresh meat only after a successful hunt. Later, animals were raised for meat, but usually they were slaughtered only in autumn. To keep the meat from spoiling, people learned to salt it. The modern meat industry supplies fresh meat year-round. The development of railroads and refrigeration made this possible.

▶RAISING ANIMALS FOR MARKET

Methods of raising animals are constantly being changed and improved through scientific research. Farmers depend on this research to be sure that the feed their animals eat keeps the animals healthy and makes them grow as rapidly as possible.

Hogs

The outdoor pigsty, where pigs wallowed in mud and ate garbage, is no longer used to raise pigs that go to market. Today many pigs are raised in temperature-controlled "pig parlors," with automatic feeding, watering, and cleaning systems. These systems allow one person to care for several hundred animals.

Hot dogs, or frankfurters, are the most popular kind of sausage in the world. They are made from cooked or smoked beef, pork, or veal mixed with spices and cereals.

Hogs are usually ready for market at the age of 6 months. Lean hogs weighing about 200 pounds (90 kilograms) are considered best for market. There are several methods of marketing hogs. Some farmers sell their hogs directly to meat packers; others sell through auction or to local dealers.

Hog's meat is called **pork**. It is the primary meat in many countries, such as Austria, Belgium, the People's Republic of China, Japan, Poland, Spain, and Sweden. Great quantities of pork also are produced in the United States and Canada.

Cattle

It takes more time and money to raise beef cattle than hogs. The best beef comes from 18- to 24-month-old **steers** (males that were desexed as calves) or young **heifers** (females that have not borne calves). **Veal** is the meat of very young, usually male, calves.

In Argentina, Australia, Brazil, Chile, Great Britain, Mexico, the United States, and Russia, more beef is produced than any other type of meat. Canada, France, and Italy produce approximately the same amounts of beef and pork each year.

Sheep

The meat of mature sheep is called **mutton**. When the sheep is less than one year old, its meat is called **lamb**. In many countries, including Algeria, New Zealand, and Turkey, mutton and lamb are the most popular meats. In the United States and Canada, they are eaten much less frequently than beef and pork.

Variety Meats

Variety meats are the edible, non-fleshy parts of butchered animals. They include sweetbreads (the thymus glands of young animals); tripe (the stomach tissue of even-toed hoofed animals); chitterlings (hog intestines); heads, hearts, tongues, tails, and feet (except lamb); and organ meats, such as brains, livers, and kidneys. Variety meats are not as widely popular in the United States as they are in Europe, where many people consider them a delicacy.

Meat Consumption

In the United States, meat is considered an important source of protein. The consumption of red meat has declined in recent years as chicken and other poultry have become more popular.

In 1997 the U.S. Department of Agriculture recorded that each year the average person in the United States eats 67 pounds (30 kilograms) of beef; 49 pounds (22 kilograms) of pork; 1 pound (0.5 kilogram) of veal; and 1 pound (0.5 kilogram) of lamb (as compared with 90 pounds, or 41 kilograms, of poultry).

▶ MEAT PROCESSING

At meat-packing plants, livestock are butchered and processed into different cuts of meat. The first step is to make the animal unable to feel pain. The animal may be anesthetized by gas or stunned by a hard blow or electric shock. When the animal can no longer feel pain, it is lifted up and attached to a conveyor rail. The main artery above its heart is opened, and the blood drains out.

The next step is not taken until the bleeding has stopped. Some hog carcasses are then placed in hot water to loosen the hair. A dehairing machine scrapes the hair off. The heads and hides are removed from some pork and all beef carcasses. Next, the carcasses are opened and the internal organs removed.

After an animal has been slaughtered, its head, hide, and internal organs are removed. Inspectors check all meats, such as the split carcasses of beef above, to ensure they are disease-free and meet government standards.

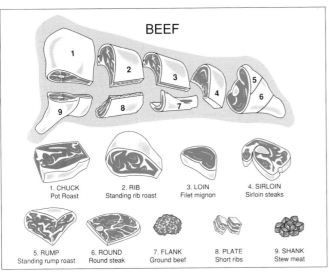

BEEF

1. CHUCK
Pot Roast

2. RIB
Standing rib roast

3. LOIN
Filet mignon

4. SIRLOIN
Sirloin steaks

5. RUMP
Standing rump roast

6. ROUND
Round steak

7. FLANK
Ground beef

8. PLATE
Short ribs

9. SHANK
Stew meat

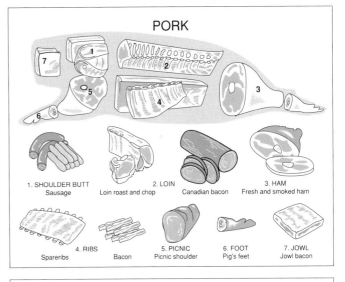

PORK

1. SHOULDER BUTT
Sausage

2. LOIN
Loin roast and chop

Canadian bacon

3. HAM
Fresh and smoked ham

4. RIBS
Spareribs

Bacon

5. PICNIC
Picnic shoulder

6. FOOT
Pig's feet

7. JOWL
Jowl bacon

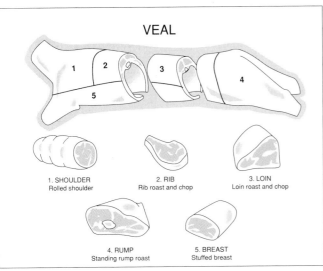

VEAL

1. SHOULDER
Rolled shoulder

2. RIB
Rib roast and chop

3. LOIN
Loin roast and chop

4. RUMP
Standing rump roast

5. BREAST
Stuffed breast

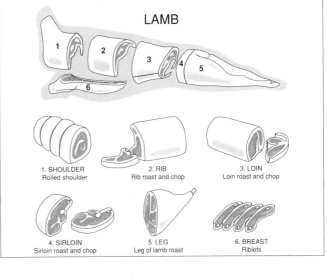

LAMB

1. SHOULDER
Rolled shoulder

2. RIB
Rib roast and chop

3. LOIN
Loin roast and chop

4. SIRLOIN
Sirloin roast and chop

5. LEG
Leg of lamb roast

6. BREAST
Riblets

The carcass is split by sawing along the backbone. The two sides each go along the overhead rail to be trimmed, washed, and carefully inspected. Then the sides are sent to a cooler to be chilled for 24 to 36 hours. After this, they may be cut into different parts, such as steaks, chops, or roasts. Or the sides may not be cut until they are sent to retail outlets.

▶PRESERVING MEAT

Before refrigerators came into widespread use, meat was eaten fresh or preserved by curing and smoking processes. Cured meats were heavily salted to keep them from spoiling. Today the curing process, which involves injecting a solution of salt, water, and sometimes sugar into the meat, is used mostly to enhance flavor. Smoking, a curing process that exposes meat to the smoke of burning hardwood, also gives meat a distinctive flavor and aroma. Smoked meats include most ham, bacon, and sausages.

Two other common methods of preserving meat are canning and freezing. Canned goods containing meats, such as sandwich spreads, chile con carne, beef stew, and corned-beef hash, may be stored unopened for several years. Meat can also be frozen, but for a more limited period of time. Uncooked beef and lamb may be kept up to 6 months in the freezer (3 months if cooked); uncooked pork and veal can be kept frozen for 4 months (2 months if cooked).

▶MEAT INSPECTION AND GRADING

Meat is inspected and graded in most countries. Inspection assures that meat is wholesome and safe to eat. **Quality** grades tell how tender, juicy, and flavorful meat is supposed to be. **Yield** grades indicate how much of the carcass can be sold as cuts of meat.

Animals are inspected before entering the slaughterhouse because diseased or injured animals cannot be slaughtered for food. The animals are also inspected during the slaughter process to be sure there are no diseased tissues. Inspectors make sure that the plant and equipment are kept clean, that the workers are clean and healthy, and that ingredients added to meat products are clean and wholesome.

All meat that is offered for sale in the United States must pass inspection by either the U.S. Department of Agriculture or an in-dividual state inspection agency that has regulations equal to or better than the federal regulations. Meat that has been inspected is stamped, using a purple dye that is fully edible. A round stamp indicates federal inspection, and a stamp in the shape of the borders of a state indicates state inspection. Both stamps assure the consumer that the product has been inspected and found to be free from disease, clean, and truthfully labeled.

Beef and lamb carcasses may carry a grade stamp in addition to the inspection stamp. There are eight official U.S. grades for beef. The most tender cuts are said to be well marbled, meaning they have a high fat content. These cuts are graded prime and choice. Good and standard grades are leaner. They may be fairly tender but not juicy. Commercial grade will be juicy but tough. It can be made tender by cooking slowly with moist heat. Utility grade is very lean and can be used for ground beef and the like. Canner and cutter grades are extra lean and are used mostly in luncheon meats and frankfurters.

▶ANIMAL NUTRIENTS AND BY-PRODUCTS

Meat has many nutrients. It contains fats, proteins, and some carbohydrates and is a good source of minerals, such as iron, copper, potassium, and phosphorus. Meat also contains vitamins B_1 (thiamine), B_2 (riboflavin), niacin, B_6 (pyridoxine), pantothenic acid, and B_{12}.

Much of an animal slaughtered for meat is not edible. Not more than half the weight of a typical steer, for example, is actually beef. But the rest of the animal does not go to waste. Almost every part of it can be used for some purpose.

The glands of meat animals are used to make medicines, such as pepsin, cortisone, and insulin. Steer hides and pigskins are made into leather products, including wearing apparel and athletic equipment. Hog hair is used to make brushes and upholstery. Animal fats make soaps, cosmetics, and animal feed. Bones, horns, and hooves are made into buttons, bone china, gelatin, and glue. Lamb's wool is turned into yarn and clothing. Other inedible parts are used as fertilizers.

JOHN C. FORREST
Purdue University

See also CATTLE; FOOD PRESERVATION; FOOD REGULATIONS AND LAWS; POULTRY.

MECCA

Mecca, the birthplace of the prophet Mohammed (570–632), is the holiest city of Islam, the religion of the Muslims. It is also the site of an ancient shrine called the Kaaba. Muslims all over the world face toward Mecca when they pray.

Mecca lies in a hot, sandy valley in west central Saudi Arabia. The valley is unfit for cultivation. But it was on a major ancient caravan route from the southern part of the Arabian Peninsula to Syria, and it has a good water supply. This, together with the presence of the Kaaba, explains why a great and wealthy city grew up on this unfavorable spot.

Mecca was a holy city long before Mohammed was born. Pilgrims from all over Arabia once came to worship the various gods of the Arab tribes at the Kaaba. About 610, a Meccan named Mohammed began to preach the way of life that became known as Islam.

The leaders of Mecca did not accept Mohammed's teachings, and he was forced to move from Mecca to Medina in 622. In 630, Mohammed and his followers conquered Mecca. The city later became part of several great Muslim empires, including those of the Egyptians and the Turks. After World War II, it became part of Saudi Arabia.

All Muslims who are able to do so must make a pilgrimage (*hajj*) to Mecca at least once in their lifetimes. While in Mecca, the pilgrims wear special clothes. They cannot shave, cut their hair or nails, or uproot plants. They pray within the walls of the Great Mosque, a huge temple that encloses the Kaaba. They walk around the windowless Kaaba seven times and kiss the sacred Black Stone embedded in one corner. According to Muslim tradition, this stone was sent down from heaven when the shrine was built by Abraham and his son Ishmael.

Only Muslims can enter the holy city, which has a permanent population of about 370,000. Taking care of pilgrims has been the chief business of the city for centuries. More than 1,000,000 people visit Mecca each year.

JOHN A. WILLIAMS
American University in Cairo

See also ISLAM; MOHAMMED.

Pilgrims from all over the world pray at the Kaaba, Islam's most sacred shrine.

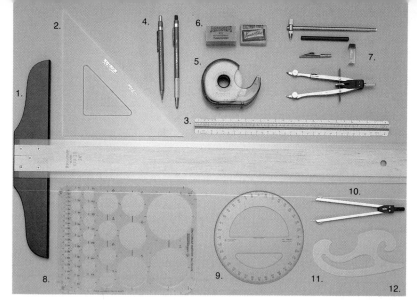

Drafting instruments and tools include:

1. T-square
2. triangle
3. architect's scale
4. pencils
5. drafting tape
6. eraser
7. compass
8. template
9. protractor
10. dividers
11. French curve
12. drafting board

MECHANICAL DRAWING

Before a building is built, a bridge is constructed, or any product manufactured, a plan must be made. Architects, engineers, and designers must sketch the objects they wish to create. A drawing using special lines and symbols is then made that shows the exact size and shape of the object. These drawings are called mechanical drawings because they are done by hand with drafting instruments and tools. **Drafters** are the people who specialize in making mechanical drawings. Using these drawings as plans, builders and artisans can visualize and make the finished objects.

Drafters use special drawing sheets made of vellum (a type of paper), cloth, or film. They attach the drawing sheet to a **drafting board**, and draw, or draft, with special pencils and pens. Horizontal lines are drawn along the edge of a **T-square**; vertical and diagonal lines are drawn with **triangles** placed on the top edge of the T-square; and circles and arcs are drawn with a **compass**. Various shapes may also be drawn with **templates**.

Other instruments include the **architect's scale**, for measuring distances; **dividers**, for transferring measurements from one place to another on the drawing; **French curves**, for drawing irregular curves; the **protractor**, for measuring angles; the **eraser**; and **drafting tape**, for attaching the paper to the board.

A mechanical drawing may be **multiview**, usually showing two or three sides of an object. Each side (front, top, right side) is shown separately. The drafter adds dimensions so that a machinist, carpenter, or other builder can make or construct the product. A mechanical drawing may also be **pictorial**, showing the overall appearance of an object.

Today many designs are created through Computer Aided Drafting (CAD). When done on a computer, a mechanical drawing is made with the same standards and techniques used by an expert drafter.

MARSHALL A. BUTLER
Montclair State College (New Jersey)

A multiview mechanical drawing of a portable radio shows three sides separately; a pictorial mechanical drawing shows the radio as it would actually appear.

MULTIVIEW   PICTORIAL

TOP

3

5

FRONT   RIGHT SIDE   FRONT   RIGHT SIDE

TOP

MECHANICS. See WORK, POWER, AND MACHINES.

MEDAL OF HONOR. See DECORATIONS AND MEDALS.

MEDICAID. See HEALTH AND HUMAN SERVICES, UNITED STATES DEPARTMENT OF.

MEDICARE. See HEALTH AND HUMAN SERVICES, UNITED STATES DEPARTMENT OF.

MEDICI

The Medici were one of the great Italian ruling families during the late Middle Ages and the early modern era. This was a time when Italy was divided into many states, one of which was the city-state of Florence. Beginning as merchants and bankers, the Medici became the unofficial rulers of Florence, their native city, in the mid-1400's. From 1532 to 1743, when the family line came to an end, the Medici reigned first as dukes and then grand dukes in Florence and the surrounding region of Tuscany.

In addition to their roles as bankers and rulers, the Medici were generous patrons of the arts. Florence under the Medici was one of the leading cities of the Italian Renaissance, the period during which great art and learning flourished. The family also included among its members several popes and two queens of France.

Beginnings. The origins of the Medici are clouded in obscurity. By the late 1200's and early 1300's, however, the family had prospered, thanks to its investments in the wool industry and in banking. Giovanni di Bicci (1360–1429) was the real founder of the family's fortunes. A shrewd, careful, and immensely talented businessman, he established the Medici bank in 1397. With its numerous branches, it soon became the largest bank in Europe. After 1410 the Medici became bankers to the popes. The company founded by Giovanni also dealt in luxury goods, such as carpets, jewels, spices, and works of art.

Giovanni de' Medici's policy had always been to remain aloof from politics. But eventually, his great wealth drew him into the political arena, in order to protect the large investments the family had made in the government of Florence.

Bankers to Rulers: Cosimo. Giovanni's oldest son, Cosimo (1389–1464), continued his father's shrewd management of the Medici bank. By the mid-1400's he was considered one of Europe's richest men, on a par with the wealthiest kings and princes. By then, the source of Medici distinction and power came not only from their bank, but from their position as one of Florence's principal ruling families as well.

In 1433, following a sharp clash with their chief rivals, the Albizzi, Cosimo and his fam-

Under Lorenzo (1449–92), called the Magnificent, the Medici reached the height of their power and influence. A great patron of the arts, he was also the unofficial ruler of what was then the city-state of Florence.

ily were exiled to the city of Venice. But less than one year later, they were triumphantly recalled. For the next sixty years, the Medici dominated the city's affairs. Although Cosimo never made himself Florence's official ruler, he established a political organization that governed the city harshly but efficiently.

Cosimo's son Piero (1416–69) and his grandson Lorenzo (1449–92) were more drawn to politics and to the pleasures of the arts than to commerce and banking. As a result, the Medici bank went into a period of decline, finally going bankrupt in 1494.

Lorenzo the Magnificent. When Piero died in 1469, he was succeeded as ruler of Florence by his eldest son, the 20-year-old Lorenzo. Known as Lorenzo the Magnificent, he created about him a court that was a gathering point for politicians, intellectuals, and artists. Lorenzo himself was not only a brilliant politician but a talented amateur poet, who also dabbled in philosophy. A careful judge of character, ferocious in punishing his opponents, he personified the Renaissance ruler. Under Lorenzo, Medici power and prestige reached its height in the 1400's. So great was

Far left: Cosimo I (1519–74) expanded the Medici realm, becoming grand duke of Tuscany, which was ruled by the family until the 1700's. *Left:* Marie de Médicis (1573–1642), seen here as a child, became queen of France when she married Henry IV in 1600.

his influence that he was able to have his second son, Giovanni (1475–1521), made a cardinal of the church when the boy was barely a teenager. Giovanni later became pope as Leo X.

Period of Change. In 1494 the French king Charles VIII invaded Italy, provoking a political crisis. With the death of Lorenzo and the French invasion, the fortunes of the Medici entered a period of change. Expelled from Florence once again, they allied themselves with Spain, the Holy Roman Empire (the federation of the German states), and the pope, who then had considerable military strength.

With the help of these powers, the Medici returned to Florence in 1512. The coronation of Giovanni as Pope Leo X in 1513 helped solidify Medici control in the city. The family was to suffer another brief period of exile, however, from 1527 to 1531, before they were restored as overlords of Florence.

Dukes and Grand Dukes. In 1532, Alessandro de' Medici (1510–37) was formally made hereditary duke of Florence. This was done at the insistence of Pope Clement VII (1478–1534), born Giulio de' Medici, a nephew of Lorenzo the Magnificent. For the first time since the 1400's, the Medici were recognized by law as rulers of Florence. Alessandro was succeeded in 1537 by a distant cousin, Cosimo I (1519–74). Cosimo expanded his realm by

annexing the neighboring and once powerful city of Siena. He became grand duke of Tuscany, which was governed by his descendants until the 1700's.

Later Medici. During these centuries, some members of the family continued to serve in the church, while others gained fame in war. Several Medici women married into distinguished foreign families. Caterina (1519–89), a great-granddaughter of Lorenzo the Magnificent, was the wife of King Henry II of France and the mother of three French kings. She is better known by the French form of her name, Catherine de Médicis. Her distant relative Marie de Médicis (1573–1642) married Henry IV of France.

The last reigning Medici was Anna Maria (1667–1743). After her death, Tuscany passed to the Austrian emperor. By the terms of Anna Maria's will, however, none of the great works of art collected over the generations by the Medici could be removed from Florence. There, as they have for centuries, they continue to be admired by the countless visitors to the city.

ANTHONY MOLHO
Brown University
Editor, *Economic and Social Foundations of the Italian Renaissance*

See also FLORENCE; ITALY, ART AND ARCHITECTURE OF; RENAISSANCE; RENAISSANCE ART AND ARCHITECTURE.

MEDICINE

The practice of medicine is one of the most ancient professions. It is devoted to the detection and cure of illness, the prevention of disease, and the maintenance of good health for all people in a society.

▶ ELEMENTS OF MEDICAL CARE

At one time the practice of medicine focused almost entirely on diagnosing and treating illnesses. Today we are aware of the importance of preventing diseases as well. Therefore, people no longer visit the doctor only when they are ill. Regular trips to the doctor help ensure that medical problems are found before they become serious and that people are educated in the role they can take in maintaining their own good health.

Prevention

Disease prevention includes living a healthy lifestyle as well as taking steps to prevent specific diseases. For good health, an individual should eat a balanced diet, get regular exercise, and maintain a clean living environment. Avoiding tobacco products and addictive drugs is also important.

Another step in disease prevention is immunization. An immunization prepares the body to encounter a specific pathogen (germ), so that the body can more easily fight it off and prevent disease. Effective vaccines against diphtheria, tetanus, poliomyelitis, measles, mumps, rubella, hepatitis B, chicken pox, and influenza are available. Newer vaccines developed in the 1990's prevent ear in-

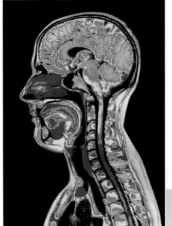

The practice of medicine involves preventing, diagnosing, and treating illness. Vaccination (*above*) helps prevent disease, techniques such as magnetic resonance imaging (*left*) are used to diagnose conditions, and surgery (*below*) is sometimes necessary to treat an illness.

fections, meningococcal meningitis (infection of the brain), and pneumonia. Vaccines for smallpox and tuberculosis were routinely used until the 1960's but are rarely used today because these diseases have been largely eliminated. Special vaccines for smallpox, anthrax, cholera, typhoid, and plague are available for use during emergencies or epidemics.

In the United States, state and regional governments have passed laws requiring routine immunization of all children. Doctors and other health care workers must maintain immunization records and provide these records to the children's schools before the children can attend. Such vaccination programs protect groups of children from serious diseases and also help prevent epidemics that could affect thousands of people.

Diagnosis

The term **diagnosis** describes a process by which the exact nature of a disease is discovered. A doctor takes several steps to arrive at a diagnosis. First the doctor asks the patient questions to gather information about the signs and symptoms of the illness. This is called taking a clinical history. The clinical history is followed by a detailed physical examination. Clinical instruments such as a stethoscope, otoscope, and ophthalmoscope may be used during the checkup to examine the heart and lungs, the ears, and the eyes. A **sphygmomanometer** is used to obtain blood pressure, and a thermometer is used to determine body temperature. Most often, these simple steps give the doctor enough information to make an accurate diagnosis.

Occasionally, further tests may be needed. For example, diagnostic tests such as X rays or magnetic resonance imaging (MRI) might be used to view tissues or organs inside the body. Or laboratory tests might be conducted; for example, a throat culture might be done to determine if a sore throat is strep throat.

Treatment

An accurate diagnosis enables a physician to prescribe the appropriate treatment. The doctor may prescribe antibiotics for bacterial infections, anti-inflammatory agents for fevers and pains, and lotions or creams for skin conditions. Surgery may be necessary for conditions that require the removal of a diseased organ, such as an inflamed appendix, or the repair and reconstruction of body parts. Treatment may be short term for acute conditions such as sore throats, ear infections, or upset stomachs, while it may be long term—

The New Book of Knowledge contains biographies of many people who contributed to medical progress. Consult the appropriate volumes to find entries on the following physicians and scientists.

BARNARD, CHRISTIAAN
EHRLICH, PAUL
FLEMING, SIR ALEXANDER
HARVEY, WILLIAM
JENNER, EDWARD
KOCH, ROBERT
LEEUWENHOEK, ANTON VAN
LISTER, JOSEPH
PASTEUR, LOUIS

Medical Milestone

ERADICATION OF SMALLPOX

On October 26, 1977, a Somali youth, Ali Maow Maalin, recovered from smallpox and was proclaimed the last known victim of a disease that had terrorized mankind for thousands of years. Smallpox evolved in Africa about 3,000 years ago and had spread around the globe. In the 1900's more than 300 million people died from smallpox.

Ancient doctors had tried inducing immunity to smallpox in healthy people by injecting them with smallpox pus. This was known as **variolation**. Variolation could be effective but it was also dangerous, as it often caused smallpox in the recipient.

During an epidemic of smallpox in 1778, a Scottish country doctor named Edward Jenner noted that cowboys and milkmaids who had previously had cowpox did not get smallpox, and he wondered if cowpox was protective. Jenner decided to test his theory in the summer of 1796. When a local milkmaid came to him for treatment of cowpox, Jenner obtained pus from her skin sores. Then, after getting permission from

lasting months or years—for chronic conditions such as diabetes, high blood pressure, asthma, arthritis, and most cancers. After the primary treatment, a period of recovery or rehabilitation may be required. Additional therapy may be prescribed during this period.

▶ HEALTH CARE PROVIDERS

Experts involved in the delivery of health care are known as health care professionals. Physicians, surgeons, nurses, and dentists are the most visible health care workers, but large groups of specialists working in hospitals, clinics, pharmacies, nursing homes, health care-related research institutions, and private industries are also crucial for providing effective health care.

Until the early 1900's, doctors known as general practitioners were responsible for the health of all people in a community. The general practitioner made diagnoses, prescribed medicines, performed minor surgeries, and helped pregnant women during labor and delivery. When more serious surgery was needed, a general surgeon carried out the procedure.

the parents of James Phipps, a boy with no known history of smallpox or cowpox, he deposited the cowpox pus over scratches he made on the boy's arms. The boy developed cowpox and recovered, as expected. Six weeks later Jenner did one of the most daring experiments in medical history: He inoculated James with the pus from a smallpox victim. James did not develop smallpox. With this experiment Jenner demonstrated that cowpox pus inoculation could prevent smallpox.

Although initially met with criticism and ridicule, cowpox inoculation for smallpox spread widely. In 1881, Louis Pasteur named the technique **vaccination** for the vaccinia virus that causes cowpox.

The last steps in the eradication of smallpox took place in the 1970's. With funding from the World Health Organization, some 200,000 workers began a massive vaccination program in Africa and Asia. With Maalin's recovery in 1977, the eradication of smallpox was complete.

Although smallpox has been eliminated as a naturally occurring public health

Edward Jenner vaccinated a young boy with the cowpox virus and then exposed him to smallpox. The vaccine was a success.

threat, a few laboratories have maintained the smallpox virus for research and vaccine production. New fears that the virus could be used as a biological weapon have prompted government and health authorities in the United States to re-examine the need for vaccination against smallpox.

Advances in medical science in the 1900's were so rapid that it became impossible for a single person to master all aspects of health care. Doctors began to concentrate on narrow but complex fields of medicine, such as diseases of children, surgery of the brain or heart, or the science of cancer. These fields became known as medical subspecialties.

Many other people are involved in the health care process. Nurses are registered and licensed by the state. They care for the sick and also educate healthy people to help them stay well. Some nurses concentrate on a specific area of care, such as surgery or pediatric care. Physician assistants are certified to provide basic health care under the supervision of a physician. Physical therapists are trained to treat disorders or injuries using exercise, massage, or

A single snake wrapped around a staff is the official symbol of the American Medical Association and a symbol of the medical profession in general.

other physical methods. Pharmacists are scientists trained in the preparation and dispensing of drugs. They are knowledgeable about drug interactions and side effects. And a number of medical technicians are trained to perform specific roles in the hospital or other health care settings. For example, respiratory therapists evaluate, treat, and care for patients with breathing disorders under the direction of a physician. In an emergency, EMT's (emergency medical technicians) arrive with the ambulance to provide care until a hospital can be reached.

▶ HISTORY OF MEDICINE

The history of medicine is a story of the human struggle against disease and death. It is also an account of the growth of knowledge related to the human body, health and hygiene, and causes and cures of illness. This growth in medical knowledge began with the earliest people but did not proceed in an orderly manner. Long periods of little progress were separated by bursts of spectacular achievement.

Prehistoric Medicine

Medicine of some sort has been practiced since prehistoric times. In early tribal societies, people did not distinguish between medicine and magic. They believed diseases were caused by demons. Sorcerers performed rituals or gave out herbal remedies in order to confuse or calm the evil spirits. The tribal doctors also offered surgical treatments. A common operation was **trepanation**, or drilling a hole in the skull. Archaeological evidence suggests that this procedure was done while the patients were alive, and the patients lived for some time after the surgery. Trepanation may have been performed to drive away the demons believed to cause the symptoms of brain disorders we now know to be epilepsy or coma.

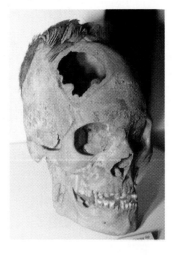

Fossilized skulls showing evidence of trepanation indicate that healers performed surgical procedures in prehistoric times.

Ancient Medicine

About 7,000 to 10,000 years ago in the ancient cultures of Babylonia, Egypt, India, China, Greece, and Rome, a more scientific outlook toward diseases and their treatment began to evolve. Doctors started to think of diseases as dysfunctions of the body as well as demonic spells. Treatment with magic, sorcery, and rituals did not cease completely, but new treatments involved a more fact-based approach toward health and illness.

Babylonia. Science and learning flourished under the Babylonian king Hammurabi about 1695 B.C. In 1901, at an excavation site

---

Medical Milestone

THE BATTLE AGAINST TUBERCULOSIS

Tuberculosis (TB) is caused by the bacterium *Mycobacterium tuberculosis*. This disease has been called the captain of men of death.

In medieval Europe a popular remedy for TB was the ceremonial "touching by the king." In very elaborate ceremonies, kings would stroke and bless hundreds of TB victims and give them gold coins as souvenirs. Despite its popularity, this cure did not work.

On March 24, 1882, in Berlin, Robert Koch announced that a tiny blue rod-shaped bacterium was the cause of TB. He found the bacteria in the lungs and saliva of TB patients by using a microscope and new staining methods. He also infected animals with TB by injecting them with the bacteria. Knowledge of the cause of TB was crucial for finding a cure for the disease; Koch was awarded the 1905 Nobel Prize in physiology or medicine for his

The blue rod-shaped bacterium *Mycobacterium tuberculosis* was identified as the cause of tuberculosis, an infection of the lungs, in 1882.

discovery, and the World Health Organization proclaimed March 24 as World TB Day.

TB remains a problem in certain parts of the world, but it is much less of a menace than it was 100 years ago because of the development of antibiotics. Selman Waksman developed the first effective remedy for TB. From soil samples, Waksman and his associates at the Agriculture College of Rutgers University extracted a chemical agent that killed the TB bacterium. Waksman named it streptomycin. He also coined the term "antibiotic" to describe compounds derived from living organisms that killed other living organisms. Waksman was honored with the 1952 Nobel Prize in physiology or medicine.

in Iran, archaeologists discovered slabs of rock that list more than 300 laws and regulations of Hammurabi. Some of these laws relate to medicine. They indicate that doctors were well paid, but they were punished harshly for mistakes, especially those made during surgical procedures. Historians believe that these laws were not strictly enforced, as medicine remained a popular profession.

Egypt. The Egyptians recorded in papyrus books descriptions of infections, specific diseases of women and children, treatments of war wounds, methods of public health, and the science of mummification. The medical practices outlined in these books resemble those of modern medicine in their definition of diseases, descriptions of signs and symptoms, and suggestions concerning therapy and prognosis (prediction of disease outcome).

Egyptian healers used opium for pain relief, castor oil for constipation, and turpentine as an antiseptic to kill germs. Personal hygiene and daily cleansing were emphasized. Public health was also important—there was a strict royal decree against polluting the Nile. Magic and prayer were part of all treatments, but the Egyptian doctors also used a variety of drugs prepared from herbs, spices, minerals, and metallic substances.

Eastern Medicine. *Ayurveda*, the ancient form of medicine practiced by Hindus of India, began between 200 B.C. and A.D. 200 and remains in practice today. Unlike other forms of ancient medicine, *Ayurveda*, meaning "knowledge of life," focused on healing both the body and the mind. Hindu doctors treated disease with both prayer and medicines. They used medicinal herbs and developed surgical instruments. And they performed complex operations such as plastic surgery.

Ancient Chinese medicine was based on the principle of yin and yang. Yin is passive, cold, and female. Yang is active, warm, and male. All things were believed to be made up of both yin and yang. The Chinese thought illness was caused by an imbalance between the yin and yang in a patient. They used acupuncture and herbal remedies to restore the balance. Chinese doctors also recognized the importance of good hygiene. Today many Chinese herbal remedies, such as ginseng, are used in Western cultures as "alternative" medicine.

Medical Milestone

PASTEUR AND THE GERM THEORY OF DISEASE

The son of a humble village tanner, Louis Pasteur studied science and earned a doctorate from the prestigious École Normale in Paris. While working as a chemist in the heart of French wine country, he was sought out by the owners of a winery. They were facing financial disaster because their wines were turning sour. After a series of brilliant experiments, Pasteur discovered that solutions of beet sugar

Louis Pasteur became famous for the theory that diseases were caused by micro-organisms. He also developed the first vaccine against rabies.

fermented naturally in the presence of yeast but became sour if contaminated by bacteria. Pasteur suggested heating the fermenting solution to 131°F (55°C) prior to brewing to kill off any bacteria. This process became known as **pasteurization**. It saved the wineries and also helped other food processing industries.

From this and other similar studies, Pasteur concluded that bacteria caused the decay of organic materials. Over time, he understood the implications of his discoveries and formed the theory that diseases can be caused by micro-organisms invisible to the naked eye. This became known as the germ theory of disease. In 1888 the Pasteur Institute was built in Paris and dedicated to the research and treatment of infectious diseases.

Greece and Rome. The Greek physician Hippocrates is considered the father of modern medicine because he was one of the first to insist that diseases were caused by natural forces. He believed that cures should be based on scientific principles. His ideas triggered a revolution in medicine.

Not all of Hippocrates' ideas were correct. For example, he developed a theory that the body was made up of four **humours**—black bile, yellow bile, blood, and phlegm—and that disease occurred when the humours were out of balance. But Hippocrates also taught the value of listening to a patient's complaints and examining a patient systematically. He emphasized treatment with herbs, fresh air, exercise, and a healthy diet.

Hippocrates formulated a set of codes describing proper conduct for doctors. The codes have survived through history and today are known as the Hippocratic Oath. A modified version of the oath is still used in most medical schools as part of the graduation ceremonies.

Ancient Roman medicine emphasized public health. Sanitation, sewage disposal, and the water system were more advanced than anything that followed in the Western world prior to the 1800's. Medical students were educated at public expense, and physicians were provided for the poor and incorporated into the armed forces.

The Medieval Period

During the Middle Ages (500–1500), medicine was influenced by Christian theology. The Christian emphasis on charity and concern for the sick led to the establishment of hospitals that were maintained by monastic orders.

The first European medical school was founded at Salerno, near Naples, Italy, in the 700's. Because the area was still part of the Byzantine Empire, many Greek texts were available for study. By the 1000's the school had become a world center of medical knowledge.

Medicine also flourished in the Islamic empire during this period. Islamic medicine combined elements of a number of other systems. It was strongly influenced by Greek medicine, the medical writings of the Talmud (studies of the Hebrew scriptures), and the teachings from Egypt and Asia. Islamic physicians discovered the use of many medicinal herbs, and the basic chemical processes of distillation and crystallization. The words "alkali" (basic), "alcohol," and "syrup" originated with Islamic medicine.

The Renaissance

The period known as the Renaissance was marked by a revolution in scientific, artistic, and other intellectual thought. The invention of the printing press aided the growth of knowledge because it allowed the works of many scientists to be more widely distributed.

It was during this period that Ambroise Paré, a French army surgeon, transformed the art of surgery. For centuries, it had been standard practice to pour boiling oil on surgical wounds, such as those of amputations. Then one day Paré ran out of oil, so he simply bandaged the wounds on his patients. The next morning his patients were doing well, and the wounds were healing better than if he had used oil. Paré and others used this new method of treatment with great success.

At about the same time, an anatomy professor named Andreas Vesalius began performing dissections of human cadavers. Before this, most information about human anatomy had come from animal dissections, particularly the work of Claudius Galen (130–200), a Greek physician. Vesalius discovered numerous errors that had been passed on for centuries. With the help of a local artist, Vesalius

Two of many famous figures in the history of medicine were Hippocrates (*top*), known as the father of medicine, and Ambroise Paré (*above*), who is regarded as the father of modern surgery.

wrote and published an illustrated book of anatomy, *The Structure of the Human Body*, which clarified many issues relating to anatomy of the body organs.

Quackery became common during this period as many people who were untrained in medicine pretended to be able to cure disease. In 1511, a group of English doctors petitioned Henry VIII and requested that a guild be formed to develop formal medical education and licensing processes. They felt this was the only way to protect the public from quacks. The king agreed and founded the first organized medical group, the Royal College of Physicians of London.

The 1600's and 1700's

In the 1600's and 1700's, discoveries in chemistry and physics had a significant impact on medical progress. English chemist Robert Boyle, his pupil Robert Hooke, and John Mayow studied the effects of lack of air

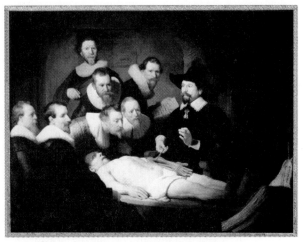

A famous painting by Dutch artist Rembrandt depicts an anatomy lesson in 1632. In the painting, a surgeon demonstrates the function of a muscle in the arm.

on animals and began to understand the requirement for oxygen, although they did not discover this gas. The invention of the microscope enabled scientists such as Anton van

Medical Milestone

CONQUEST OF PAIN

Before anesthesia was developed, surgery was very painful. Whether pulling teeth or amputating legs, surgeons worked swiftly while strong assistants held down the squirming patients. In 1799, English scientist Humphry Davy discovered that nitrous oxide caused uncontrollable laughter when inhaled. Thus he called it the laughing gas. Soon there were laughing gas parties in England and the United States. There were also ether parties, using a gas developed by Michael Faraday. Yet no one paid attention to the anesthetic properties of these agents.

In 1844, Horace Wells, a New England dentist, witnessed a live demonstration of the effects of laughing gas. Wells noticed that a volunteer who fell off the podium did not feel any pain, despite sustaining a large wound. He wondered if the gas could be

William Morton is recognized for his contribution to the field of anesthesia. He demonstrated the usefulness of ether as a painkiller during surgery.

used to ease the pain in his dental patients and decided to experiment.

With the help of a fellow dentist, Wells had a tooth painlessly extracted while inhaling the gas. Early the next year, he attempted a public demonstration of his anesthetic gas, but it did not go well. Wells did not administer sufficient gas, and the patient groaned during the tooth extraction.

William Morton, a former student of Wells, developed an inhaler to administer ether. In 1846, in a well-orchestrated demonstration, Morton administered ether during a minor surgery. The ether was effective and the demonstration was a success.

As ether was gaining popularity, another anesthetic agent was also being used. James Young Simpson began using chloroform to reduce pain in women during childbirth. After Queen Victoria used chloroform during childbirth, it became a commonly used method and remained so for 100 years.

THE RISE OF MODERN SURGERY

During the decades following the introduction of anesthetics, more and more surgeons began using these painkillers during operations. They attempted longer and more complex operations as there was no need to finish the operation quickly. Despite the improvements, surgery remained dangerous. Wound infections were a frequent and serious complication of surgical operations, but for many years their cause was not understood.

In Vienna, Hungarian physician Ignaz Semmelweis insisted that the fatal infections some women suffered after delivery of their infants were due to poisonous particles transmitted through the unclean hands of doctors and hospital attendants. This theory was ridiculed, because at the time no scientific reason was known that supported it.

Then Louis Pasteur proposed that microorganisms in the air and on hands could produce disease. This led British surgeon Joseph Lister to begin work on infection. In 1867, he published studies that showed surgery was made safer by using antiseptics to sterilize surgical equipment and the surrounding environment. The antiseptic

Joseph Lister (*left*) demonstrated that creating a clean surgical environment made operations more safe. Today sterile techniques are standard procedure in operating rooms (*below*). Medical personnel wear masks and gloves, and all surgical equipment is sterilized before use.

process was implemented gradually, and today operating rooms are made germfree by sterilizing all equipment and supplies, covering surgeons and attendants with sterile gowns, and draping the patient so that only the site of actual operation is exposed.

Leeuwenhoek to see things they had never seen before. And Stephen Hale, an English clergyman, measured blood pressure in horses.

English physician William Harvey studied the circulatory system and the lungs of experimental animals. Harvey published his findings and concluded that blood circulated in the body with the heart acting as a pump. Before this, it was believed that the heart contained holes that allowed blood to pass from the left half to the right and that the heart was a source of heat for the body.

The first vaccination was carried out in 1796, when a Scottish doctor named Edward Jenner recalled that people previously infected with cowpox did not get smallpox. He inoculated a boy with pus from cowpox sores and later exposed him to smallpox. The boy did not get smallpox and the concept of vaccination was proven.

The 1800's

The 1800's brought about increased understanding of the causes of disease. During a cholera outbreak in 1854, London physician John Snow noticed that the closer people lived to a well on Broad Street, the higher the level of cholera incidence. He concluded that the well water was the source of the cholera. At his insistence, the well was closed—and the epidemic ended. Further investigation revealed that the well was contaminated by a ruptured sewer line. Before Snow's observations, cholera was believed to be spread through the air.

The development of anesthetics allowed dramatic progress in surgery. The anesthetic properties of nitrous oxide (laughing gas), ether, and chloroform were discovered in the mid-1800's. In the decades that followed, surgeons began using these painkillers during operations. More complex surgical procedures were attempted and perfected, but wound infections, or **sepsis**, following surgery remained a problem.

The ideas of Ignaz Semmelweis, Louis Pasteur, and Joseph Lister led to the sterile operating rooms we know today. Semmelweis suggested that it was doctors' hands that were spreading diseases among patients. At first he was ridiculed, but Semmelweis' idea was later supported by Pasteur's germ theory of disease, which hypothesized that infectious diseases were caused by invisible microorganisms. Lister then showed that cleaning surgical instruments and the surgical environment with antiseptics killed disease-causing germs and led to safer surgeries with less risk of sepsis.

The 1900's

Medical science advanced more in the 1900's than at any other time in human history. The discovery of vitamins and antibiotics provided new tools for curing disease.

The ability of specific foods to prevent and treat certain diseases had been known for centuries. The ancient Egyptians used cooked liver to treat night blindness, and from the 1700's, sailors recognized the ability of citrus fruits to prevent scurvy during long periods at sea. But the specific curative factors in

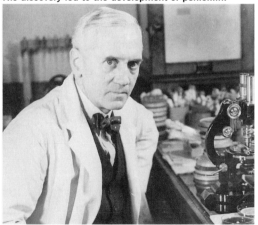

Sir Alexander Fleming made the accidental discovery that a certain mold could inhibit the growth of bacteria. His discovery led to the development of penicillin.

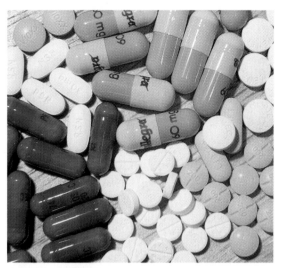

Scientists in the pharmaceutical and biotechnology industry are continually developing new drugs that are essential for treating a variety of illnesses.

these foods (vitamin A and vitamin C) were not discovered until the 1900's.

The first vitamin to be identified was vitamin A, which was termed "fat soluble A" and recognized as a necessary factor for growth in rats in 1914. The term "vitamin" was introduced by Casimir Funk, who isolated thiamine (vitamin B_1). He called it a "vital amine" because of its chemical structure. As more vitamins with different chemical structures were discovered, the term was changed to vitamin.

The discovery that foods contained necessary factors beyond calories led to nutritional cures for other diseases, such as the bone disease rickets, caused by vitamin D deficiency, and pellegra—a disease marked by diarrhea, skin disorders, and dementia—caused by niacin (vitamin B_3) deficiency.

The first antibiotic was synthesized by Paul Ehrlich in 1909. He created arsphenamine, a drug that could kill the bacteria that caused syphilis. The accidental discovery of penicillin by Alexander Fleming in 1928 was another important step. New antibiotics continue to be created today.

In addition to improved treatment of diseases with vitamins and antibiotics, a number of diseases were conquered through immunization. Smallpox has disappeared worldwide. In technologically advanced countries a number of childhood diseases such as poliomyelitis, measles, rubella (German measles), diphtheria, and mumps now occur

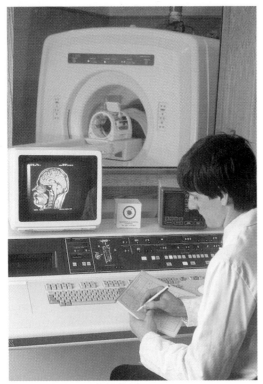

MRI uses powerful magnets and radio waves to generate an image of the body. MRI allows the diagnosis of certain conditions without invasive surgery.

infrequently. New vaccines for preventing other diseases continue to be developed.

Advances in surgery in the 1900's saved the lives of many people. The first successful human organ transplantation—a kidney— was performed by Joseph Murray in 1954. The first heart transplant was performed in 1967 by Christiaan Barnard.

Technological advancements since the 1950's have changed the way physicians diagnose and treat disease. The discovery of X rays led rapidly to their use in medical practice. X rays are also used in medical research to determine the structures of molecules such as DNA, proteins, and vitamins. Techniques such as computed tomography (CT), magnetic resonance imaging (MRI), sonography, and endoscopy allow doctors to see inside the body without invasive surgery.

Basic medical science has become dependent on the use of radioactive forms of elements, which are used to follow specific processes within the body. For example, positron emission tomography (PET) is a form of radioisotopic imaging that allows a physician to observe the flow of blood into an organ.

Radioisotopes have also made possible the detection and quantification of molecules that are present in body tissues in such small concentrations that they could not otherwise be measured.

▶ MEDICAL RESEARCH

An important component of modern medicine is the ongoing research in various fields of science and technology to find and develop new diagnostic methods, clinical procedures, treatments, and cures. Much of this research is done in universities, medical schools, government institutions, and the pharmaceutical and biotechnology industry.

Recent Advancements

The completion of the human genome sequence, which occurred in 2000, is expected to have a significant impact on the practice of medicine. With access to the entire human genetic sequence, scientists and physicians hope to learn more about the nature of human disease and the interrelationship between genes and the environment in causing disease. This should enable the discovery of new treatments and cures.

But even before the human genome sequence was completed, genetic research was changing medicine. For example, scientists have identified at least 1,000 genes that cause

An important part of medicine does not involve patients. Laboratory research is critical for developing new diagnostic techniques, treatments, and cures.

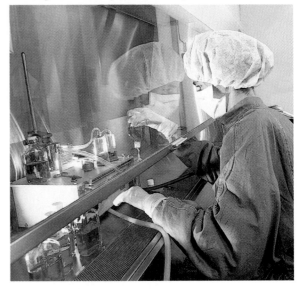

Medical Milestone

THE DISCOVERY OF X RAYS

Wilhelm Roentgen was born in Germany and raised in Holland. After studying in the Netherlands and Switzerland, he returned to Germany where he taught and experimented in physics. Roentgen's colleague, Phillip Lenard, was a pioneer of cathode rays. It was while

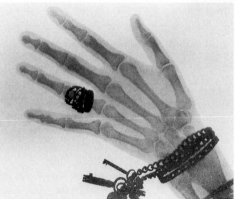

Wilhelm Roentgen's accidental discovery of X rays allowed doctors to diagnose broken bones and other ailments. An image of Roentgen's wife's hand (*above*) was one of the first X rays.

pursuing experiments on cathode rays that Roentgen stumbled onto his discovery of a new kind of ray.

In 1895, Roentgen was testing whether black cardboard sheets could block the passage of cathode rays. He switched on the electricity to test the setup of his experiment and noticed a faint green glow on a screen set 3 feet (1 meter) away. The glow appeared to be coming from the cathode ray tube and passing through the black cardboard, but he knew that cathode rays could not travel that far. He repeated the experiment 17 times, and each time he produced the same light shimmering through almost anything placed in front of it. He named the new rays X rays, because their nature was unknown.

Over the next months, Roentgen showed that his X rays could pass through wooden blocks, heavy books, tin boxes, and even human flesh. He asked his wife, Anna Bertha, to keep her hand in front of the rays for 15 minutes, and obtained the first radiograph of a human body. Within days of publishing his discovery, Roentgen became an international celebrity. Doctors realized the value of X rays in clinical medicine. Within a year, commercial X-ray machines were being used for diagnostic purposes. Roentgen won the first Nobel Prize in physics in 1901 for his discovery.

---

specific diseases when the genes are defective. Gene therapy techniques, in which a functional gene is incorporated into the cells of a patient with a defective gene, are being used experimentally to treat cystic fibrosis, hemophilia, and other illnesses.

An understanding of genetics has also led to improved treatments for certain cancers. Researchers have found that different kinds of cancers occur in specific areas of the body, such as the breast and colon. These cancers have specific genetic fingerprints, and some cancers respond better to certain therapies than others. By identifying the genetic fingerprint of the cancer, oncologists can determine which treatment strategy is most likely to be effective.

Similarly, genes that are linked to increased risk of developing cancer have been identified. People with a family history of cancer may be screened for these genes and choose to begin preventative treatments if they have a high-risk gene.

Immunology research focuses on understanding the immune system and finding new cures. Problems within the immune system can lead to noninfectious and autoimmune diseases such as rheumatoid arthritis, lupus erythematosus, and cancer and infectious diseases such as acquired immunodeficiency syndrome (AIDS). Many cancer cells have been shown to be capable of combining with unique antibodies—the components of the immune system that target cells for destruc-

Medical Milestone

GROWTH OF PSYCHIATRY

In the 1700's, the field of psychiatry did not exist, and patients suffering from mental disorders were treated badly. They were branded as insane, chained, and thrown into jails. Sometimes they were burned as witches or warlocks.

Phillipe Pinel was a shy and studious doctor who helped change psychiatric care. Born in St. André d'Alayrac in southern France, he studied theology and medicine and moved to Paris in 1778. In August of 1793, Pinel was placed in charge of Bicêtre—a dungeon serving as an insane asylum. Pinel did not believe the mentally ill patients were being treated as they should be, and he appealed to the authorities for reform. He wanted all the patients to be released from their chains. When questioned whether such a step would be safe for the general public, Pinel is reported to have said " … these mentally ill are intractable [incurable] only because they are deprived of fresh air and their liberty." The authorities permitted the inmates to be unchained under Pinel's supervision. This act ranks as one of the

The circulating swing was one of many methods used by early psychiatrists in their attempts to treat patients with mental illness.

greatest milestones in medicine and was the moment modern psychiatry was born.

Pinel believed that kindness and freedom of the body were the first steps for curing a sick mind. He trained assistants, guards, and nurses to follow this method. Pinel maintained notes and data on his works, and published two books: *On the Classification of Diseases* and *Treaties on Madness*.

---

tion—so cancers may one day be treated using vaccines that will cause the body to produce anti-tumor antibodies.

In 1981, the first cases of AIDS were reported by the U.S. Centers for Disease Control and Prevention. A French team, in collaboration with American scientists, isolated the human immunodeficiency virus (HIV)—the virus that causes AIDS—in 1984. It was a triumph for science that within only three years, a previously unknown disease was described and the cause found. Since then, numerous treatments for AIDS have been developed, and HIV-positive individuals receiving antiviral drug therapy remain symptom-free for longer periods than ever. However, the fight against AIDS is ongoing, and at present there is an intense effort to develop an AIDS vaccine.

Progress in technology is changing the way surgeries are performed. In robot-assisted surgery, the surgeon sits at a video console that displays a magnified image of the surgical site. The surgeon maneuvers robotic arms that carry out the surgery in real time. The mechanical arms are steadier than the human hand. The precision of robot-assisted surgery also allows smaller incisions to be made, which helps the patient heal more quickly. Robotic arms have been used experimentally for several types of surgery and are now approved for routine use in certain heart and gallbladder surgeries.

The human immunodeficiency virus (HIV), the virus that causes AIDS, was identified in 1984, but scientists still have much to learn about this virus.

Organ transplant surgery has also become very sophisticated, but finding enough donor organs remains a problem. Therefore, medical researchers have begun experimenting with artificial organs to use in serious cases when a donor organ cannot be found. In 2001, the first totally implantable artificial heart was placed in a human being. The AbioCor heart is battery operated and has no wires or tubes that pass through the skin. This makes it quite different from previous artificial hearts, such as the Jarvik-7. Because the Jarvik-7 required tubes that led from the patient to large machines, the patient could not move around easily and infections were a problem. By mid-2002 the AbioCor had been implanted in seven people.

Biomedical engineering has led to new options for those in need of prosthetic (artificial) limbs. A prosthetic leg equipped with

The titanium AbioCor artificial heart may one day be an important life-saving tool. It could be implanted in patients when a donor heart cannot be found.

 ## Medical Milestone

A COMMON DRUG WITH UNCOMMON POWERS

Among the medical advances that have made the greatest impact on human health is the inexpensive, tiny white aspirin tablet. In 1758, an English Reverend, Edmund Stone, accidentally chewed a twig of the willow tree and discovered that the bitter twig reduced his fever and body aches. Then he prepared a dry powder extract from the bark of the willow tree and used it to treat many patients.

Unknown to the Reverend, willow tree bark had a long history. Hippocrates and the Egyptians used extracts from willow tree bark and other plants to control fevers, eye disease, and pain. The British dismissed the effects of the Reverend's extracts, but the Europeans did not. The French, Swiss, and Germans raced to find the fever-reducing ingredient in Stone's bark. Eventually the active ingredient, salicylic acid, was isolated from the bark. This compound proved effective for reducing pain and fever, but it irritated the stomach.

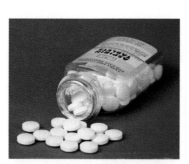

Aspirin, a painkiller derived from the bark of a willow tree, is also used as a blood thinner.

In the 1890's, a young chemist named Felix Hoffmann was working for the Bayer division of a German chemical company. He was interested in finding a safer alternative for salicylic acid for his father, who suffered from severe arthritis. Felix prepared a modified form of the compound called acetylsalicylic acid that reduced his father's pain. Four years later, Hoffmann and a colleague at Bayer coined the term "aspirin" from the "a" for acetyl and "spirin" from the German *Spiraure*, for the meadowsweet tree of the Spirea family that yielded the salicylic acid.

The full power of aspirin was yet to be learned. In the 1960's, a new group of hormones called prostaglandins was discovered. It was found that aspirin's painkilling properties were due to its ability to interfere with the prostaglandins. Later other uses of aspirin, including preventive treatment against coronary heart disease and stroke, were discovered.

biosensors and linked to a computer allows the person who wears it to move more naturally than with a standard prosthetic leg.

Potential Future Developments

Several medical advances are on the horizon. **Nanotechnology research** is producing miniature cameras that will be swallowed or injected into the bloodstream to take pictures of the inside of the body. These pictures will be relayed to external monitors, which will display the images, allowing accurate diagnosis without invasive surgery.

Some people feel that pain management needs to be more aggressive. Researchers hope to better understand different types of pain so that they can improve treatments.

Stem cell research may lead to new treatments for many injuries or diseases. Stem cells have the potential to become any cell type within the body. Unlike liver cells, for example, which only behave as liver cells, stem cells could become liver cells, brain cells, or other cells. Stem cells injected into an injured or diseased region could replace the

damaged cells and restore function. Stem cells harvested during cloning procedures could be used to create donor tissue that would be a perfect genetic match.

Genetic engineering research aims to provide cures for many inherited diseases. Functional genes may be incorporated into the genetic information of cells to replace defective genes. It may be possible to select the traits that are desirable in offspring by inserting particular genes into human embryos. But not everyone approves of such manipulations.

▶ MEDICAL ETHICS

Medical ethics weighs the moral and social issues that arise in medicine. With the recent medical advances in stem cell research, genetics, and cloning, many new issues of medical ethics have arisen.

Human stem cells come from two sources, adults and embryos. Many people are concerned about the use and destruction of human embryos, which some consider potential human lives. In 2001, President George W. Bush banned the use of federal funds for research conducted using embryonic stem

 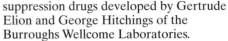

Medical Milestone

ORGAN TRANSPLANTATION

Research in organ transplant surgery began during the early 1900's, when Alexis Carrel, a daring French surgeon and philosopher, perfected a method for connecting large blood vessels end-to-end. He also practiced organ transplantation in experimental dogs. Although Carrel's work made organ transplantation technically possible, rejection of the transplanted organ by the body remained a problem.

Following advances in immunology, methods were developed to suppress the body's immune system so that organs could be successfully transplanted from one person to another. Among these methods were the immune

South African surgeon Christiaan Barnard performed the first successful human-to-human heart transplant in 1967.

suppression drugs developed by Gertrude Elion and George Hitchings of the Burroughs Wellcome Laboratories.

The first successful human organ transplant operation took place on December 23, 1954. Joseph Murray removed a kidney from a healthy man and transplanted it into the donor's identical twin, whose kidneys had failed. The operation was a technical marvel. The transplanted kidney began working almost instantly, and both the donor and the recipient remained healthy.

Soon doctors began perfecting the techniques for transplanting skin, hearts, pancreases, livers and intestines. In 2000, more than 22,000 organ transplants were performed in the United States.

ANTIBIOTICS

The development of antibiotics in the 1900's revolutionized the fight against disease. A pioneer in this field was German bacteriologist Paul Ehrlich. In 1909, Ehrlich synthesized arsphenamine, a drug that could destroy the bacterium that caused syphilis. The German physician Gerhard Domagk, working 25 years after Ehrlich, developed the first effective sulfa drug, or sulfonamide, which was used to treat streptococcal disease.

In 1928, Sir Alexander Fleming accidentally contaminated his experimental petri dishes with a mold called *Penicillium notatum*, which was often used in making cheese. He noted that no bacteria grew in the area around the mold. Fleming proposed that the mold contained antibacterial properties.

It took 13 more years to show that an extract from this mold actually killed bacteria in the body. Howard Florey and

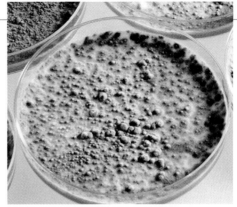

The mold *Penicillium notatum* (*above*) grew accidentally on petri dishes of Sir Alexander Fleming, allowing him to see the mold's ability to inhibit the growth of bacteria.

Ernst Chain headed the team that isolated the extract, which was called penicillin. During World War II, penicillin was manufactured on a huge scale and shown to be safe and effective in treating many diseases, including gonorrhea, syphilis, and meningitis. Many antibiotics are now in use.

---

research conducted using embryonic stem cells, other than the approximately 70 stem cell lines already created. Some scientists believe that adult stem cells have the same potential as embryonic stem cells, without the ethical issues, but other scientists do not think adult stem cells will be as useful. In 2004, voters in California approved a proposition that promised funding for embryonic stem cell research. Other states may follow suit. Many countries are creating their own policies on stem cell research.

The rise of animal cloning has led to concern that humans will be cloned. Most people do not think cloning should be used to reproduce new humans, but medical ethicists ask if there are times when human cloning would be acceptable. Even as cloning sparks new debate, older debates remain open. For example, we still ask how death should be defined for purposes of organ transplantation or for stopping care of the terminally ill.

In the United States these ethical problems are difficult to solve legally. Most cases fall under state law, so that similar cases must be tried in several jurisdictions before legal precedents are firmly established.

Yet another question of medical ethics is that of access to health care. Medical care can be very expensive, and not all people can afford to pay for it. Some nations, such as Canada and the United Kingdom, have government policies of universal health care, in which the government pays for medical expenses of all citizens using tax dollars. The United States does not have such a policy.

Cloned pigs may one day be used as a source of organs for implantation into humans, a controversial technique known as xenotransplantation.

SOLVING THE HUMAN GENOME

On June 26, 2000, President Bill Clinton proclaimed that the first survey of the entire human genome had been completed, a milestone widely regarded as one of the greatest in biological sciences.

The success of the Human Genome Project could not have happened without a biochemical revolution that began in the late 1800's and technological advances in molecular biology and computer sciences during the second half of the 1900's. These milestones in genetics research are described in more detail in the article GENETICS.

Today at least 1,000 gene defects that cause disease have been identified. Genetic markers are available for assessing the risk of developing diseases such as cancers of the breast and cervix, Alzheimer's disease, diabetes, high blood pressure, and heart

J. Craig Venter and Francis Collins led the two teams that successfully unraveled the sequence of the human genome, an achievement that was announced in 2000.

disease. Gene therapies for cystic fibrosis and muscular dystrophy are on the horizon. And the availability of the complete human genome sequence is sure to lead to a greater understanding of the causes and cures of disease.

▶ **HEALTH CARE COVERAGE**

The 1900's were a time of change regarding the social aspects of medical care. About 1900, health care was the concern of family physicians. Doctors treated patients in neighborhood clinics or made house calls when requested. As hospitals became more modern, doctors began providing care in hospital-based clinics or inpatient wards. Federal, state, and city governments developed extensive health care-related policies and monitored the quality of care provided. Medical costs increased greatly in the second half of the 1900's. In 2002, 10 to 12 percent of the U.S. gross national product was devoted to health care needs.

In the 1980's and 1990's, health coverage in the United States began to switch from private insurance to managed care. Doctors became associated with insurance groups called health management organizations (HMO's), and individuals prepaid for medical services on a schedule, rather than paying larger fees when medical care was given.

Changes in the United States health care system are likely to continue. Some would like to see the U.S. government provide health care coverage for all citizens. But the establishment of a national health plan is

considered less probable than the expansion of insurance coverage to selected groups. Numerous proposals to reform health care are under discussion by lawmakers.

▶ **TRENDS IN MEDICINE**

New ideas lead to changes in medicine, and old ideas are sometimes revived. In the United States and other Western nations, the use of alternative or complementary treatments based on Eastern medicine has grown since the 1960's. This includes the use of herbal remedies, massage, and acupuncture. In recognition of this trend, the National Institutes of Health established an office of alternative medicine in 1992. It grew to become the National Center for Complementary and Alternative Medicine in 1998. The center aims to test the scientific principles behind these alternative healing techniques. Some insurance companies and HMO's now cover expenses for certain alternative therapies, such as therapeutic massage. But many doctors will continue to recommend traditional therapy until the scientific basis for alternative treatments is better understood.

TONSE N. K. RAJU, M.D.
National Institutes of Health

MEDIEVAL PERIOD. See MIDDLE AGES.

MEDITERRANEAN SEA

The Mediterranean is the world's largest inland sea. Its name comes from Latin words meaning "in the midst of lands," for it is bounded by three continents—Europe on the north, Africa on the south, and Asia on the east. The Mediterranean has been one of the world's most important waterways since ancient times and was the birthplace of Western civilization.

The Mediterranean Sea extends from the Strait of Gibraltar, where it joins the Atlantic Ocean, to the shores of western Asia. It includes a number of smaller seas, among them the Ligurian, Tyrrhenian, Adriatic, Ionian, and Aegean seas. The Black Sea is often considered a part of the Mediterranean as well and is connected to it by the Bosporus and Dardanelles straits and the Sea of Marmara. An underwater ridge running from Sicily to Tunisia divides the Mediterranean into western and eastern basins. The Suez Canal gives it an outlet to the Red Sea.

Including the Black Sea, the Mediterranean has an area of about 969,100 square miles (2,510,000 square kilometers). From east to west it covers a span of about 2,300 miles (3,700 kilometers) and has an average width of about 500 miles (800 kilometers). It reaches its deepest point, 16,896 feet (5,150 meters), in the Matapan Trench in the Ionian Sea.

Numerous islands and island groups are scattered like stepping stones across the

The Greek island of Mykonos is one of dozens of picturesque islands in the Aegean Sea, an arm of the Mediterranean Sea that lies between Greece and Turkey.

Mediterranean. The largest are Sicily and Sardinia (both belonging to Italy), Corsica (part of France), Crete (part of Greece), the Balearic Islands (part of Spain), the Dodecanese (belonging to Greece), and the island nation of Cyprus.

Much of the Mediterranean is bordered by narrow coastal plains. On the more mountainous north, where the peninsulas of Italy and Greece extend deeply into the sea, the coastline is indented by many bays and gulfs. The southern coast is less deeply indented

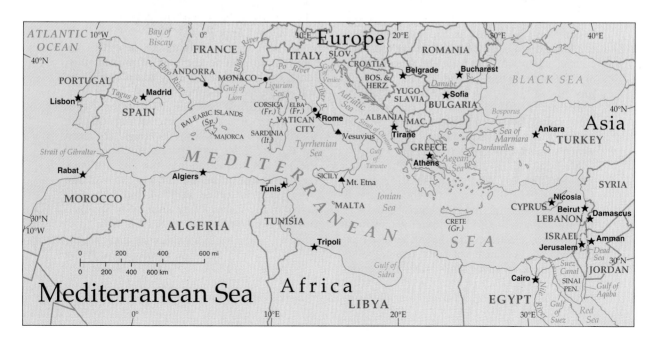

and has fewer good harbors. The major rivers emptying into the Mediterranean are the Ebro, Rhône, Po, Tiber, and Nile.

The Mediterranean climate is marked by long, hot, and dry summers and mild, rainy winters. Rainfall generally decreases and temperatures rise as one travels from north to south. A variety of winds blow across the region, including the blustery mistral of the lower Rhône, the cold, northerly bora of the Adriatic, and the hot, dry sirocco from the Sahara, the great desert of northern Africa.

Agriculture has traditionally been the chief occupation of Mediterranean peoples. Grains, wine grapes, olives, and citrus fruits are leading crops. While fishing is a major economic activity, most of the catch is for local markets. The generally mild, sunny climate and numerous historic sites have long made tourism an important industry.

History. The ancient Egyptians and the Minoans of Crete were among the earliest peoples to trade in the eastern Mediterranean.

The Phoenicians first navigated the entire length of the sea, establishing colonies along its coasts and sailing beyond the Strait of Gibraltar into the Atlantic Ocean. They were followed by the ancient Greeks, whose civilization spread rapidly across the western Mediterranean.

The Romans, who built an empire that eventually encompassed nearly all of the Mediterranean, called it *mare nostrum* ("our sea"). During the Middle Ages, the Italian city-states of Venice and Genoa grew wealthy from the Mediterranean trade.

The Mediterranean declined in importance in the late 1400's and early 1500's, with the discovery of the Americas and of a sea route to Asia around the southern tip of Africa. It again became economically important as a highway of commerce after the Suez Canal opened in 1869, providing a shorter route to Asia.

ANTHONY SAS
University of South Carolina

MEERKATS. See MONGOOSES, MEERKATS, AND THEIR RELATIVES.
MEIGHEN, ARTHUR. See CANADA, GOVERNMENT OF (Profiles).

MEIR, GOLDA (1898–1978)

Golda Meir, prime minister of Israel from 1969 to 1974, led her country during one of its most critical times. Clear-headed and determined but with a warm and sincere personality, she was one of the most respected of Israeli political figures.

She was born Golda (or Goldie) Mabovitch in Kiev, Ukraine, on May 3, 1898. When she was 8, the family immigrated to the United States, settling in Milwaukee, Wisconsin, where she later taught school. Meir also became active in the Zionist national movement to establish a Jewish state in Palestine. In 1917 she married Morris Myerson. (She later simplified the name to "Meir.") In 1921 they moved to Palestine, which was then governed by Britain.

Meir served as a delegate to the World Zionist Congress. And when Israel became a nation in 1948, she was one of the signers of its declaration of independence. She was briefly ambassador to the Soviet Union and in 1949 was elected to the Israeli Knesset, or parliament. As minister of labor, from 1949 to 1956, she dealt successfully with the enormous problems of employment and housing for Israel's large numbers of new immigrants. Appointed foreign minister in 1956, she forcefully championed Israel before the United Nations and established friendly relations with newly independent African countries. Age and poor health led her to resign in 1966, although she continued in politics as head of the Labor Party.

In 1969, Meir reluctantly came out of retirement to assume the post of prime minister. Expected to serve only temporarily, she was to remain in office for five years. Her most severe test came in 1973, when Egypt and Syria attacked Israel, setting off the fourth Arab-Israeli war. Although criticized for the military's unpreparedness, she rallied the nation to repel the invasion and win back territories lost in the first days of the war. She resigned from office in 1974, but remained active in the Labor Party until 1976. She died in Jerusalem on December 8, 1978.

ARTHUR CAMPBELL TURNER
Coauthor, *Ideology and Power in the Middle East*

MELBOURNE

Melbourne is Australia's second largest city. It is the capital, largest city, and chief port of the state of Victoria. With a population of nearly 3,000,000, it is an important world metropolis.

Though a large part of Melbourne is a bustling business and industrial area, the city also contains many quiet tree-lined streets with homes fronted by lovely gardens. Broad, attractive avenues are lined with fine, stately buildings. The city's climate is temperate and comfortable, with an average annual temperature of 58°F (14°C).

▶ TRADE, FINANCE, AND INDUSTRY

With its broad, modern harbor Melbourne is one of Australia's major ports. Docks are situated in Melbourne itself and also in Port Melbourne and Williamstown, both of which lie nearby on Hobson's Bay. Because of its location Melbourne is an important agricultural depot.

Melbourne is highly industrialized. Its modern factories produce railway rolling stock (locomotives, passenger and freight cars), power-station equipment, structural steel, and other heavy engineering equipment. Because many leading banks and insurance companies have made Melbourne their headquarters, the city is recognized as the financial center of Australia. The Melbourne Stock Exchange is the largest stock exchange on the continent.

▶ TRANSPORTATION

Melbourne is a vital transportation center. Highways and railway lines connect the city with Sydney, Brisbane, and Adelaide. The new international airport at Tullamarine, on the outskirts of the city, is one of the most modern in the world.

▶ CULTURE AND RECREATION

Melbourne has many excellent theaters and art galleries. The National Gallery of Victoria has one of the finest collections of paintings in the Commonwealth of Nations. The city also maintains an excellent library system and several fine museums, such as the Museum of Applied Science and the National Museum. Centers of learning include the University of Melbourne, the Royal Australian College of Surgeons, the Australian Institute of International Affairs, the Conservatorium of Music, and the Walter and Eliza Hall Institute of Medical Research.

Australians are a sports-minded people. The Melbourne Cup is one of the world's greatest horse races. It is run at Flemington Race Course at Melbourne each year on the first Tuesday in November, a day of national celebration. Melbourne is also the home of the "Australian Rules," an Australian brand of football. In 1956 the city was the site of the Olympic Games.

▶ PLACES OF INTEREST

One attractive sight in Melbourne is the natural beauty of the Botanic Gardens. In Fitzroy Gardens stands a cottage that once belonged to the family of Captain James Cook, the first European to visit eastern Australia. The cottage was brought to Australia from Yorkshire, England, in 1934. Other places of interest are the Victoria Parliament House; the Royal Mint; the Shrine of Remembrance, a World War I memorial; and the recently completed Victorian Arts Center.

▶ HISTORY

Melbourne was first settled in 1835, by two groups of settlers from Tasmania, an island that lies south of Victoria. The city was named in 1837 in honor of Lord Melbourne, prime minister of Great Britain at the time. The discovery of gold at Ballarat and other places in 1851 changed Melbourne into a boom city. From 1901 to 1927, Melbourne was the seat of the federal government pending the development of Canberra. When Parliament House opened in Canberra, the seat of the national government was transferred there. Sydney has surpassed Melbourne as Australia's largest city. But Melbourne is still a major center of commerce, transportation, and culture.

Reviewed by SHARYN KALNINS
Australian Capital Territory Schools Authority

MELONS

Melons belong to the Cucurbitaceae, or gourd, family, which also includes cucumbers, pumpkins, squash, and watermelons. Tremendous diversity exists in the shape, size, texture, sweetness, and taste of melons. The two most common types are summer melons and winter melons.

Summer melons include muskmelons, cantaloupes, Ogen melons, and Persian melons. Muskmelons are spherical or elongated with heavy netting on the outer rind and orange flesh. The two types of muskmelons grown in the United States are referred to as western shippers and eastern types. Western shippers—commonly called cantaloupes—lack vein tracts, have firm flesh, and are shipped from California, Arizona, and Texas to destinations across North America. Eastern muskmelon types are generally not shipped because they have softer flesh and deteriorate much more quickly than western types. True cantaloupes are grown in Europe and are seldom seen in the United States.

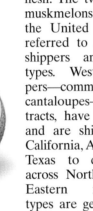

Cantaloupe

The Ogen melon gets its name from the Kibbutz Ha'Ogen in Israel, where the melon was originally grown. An Ogen melon is round and very aromatic, and its rind typically turns from green to golden when ripe. The flesh is soft, light green, and sweet.

Muskmelon

Persian melons are usually larger than cantaloupes or muskmelons. Their surface is completely covered with a fine netting and they have no vein tracts.

The winter melons include honeydew, canary, casaba, Christmas, and Crenshaw melons. They are also called inodorus melons because they do not give off a fragrant aroma. They require more time to mature than summer melons, and most will keep for two to three months after harvest.

Honeydew melon

The honeydew is the most common winter melon available in the United States. Honeydews are generally larger than cantaloupes. They have a smooth rind and firm green or orange flesh.

Canary melons are oval or round in shape. They have a smooth rind, which turns from green to bright golden yellow when ripe, and a sweet, firm, light green flesh. Casaba melons also turn

Christmas melon

from green to yellow when ripe. However, casaba are often teardrop shaped, with a wrinkled rind and white, firm, sweet flesh. A variation of the casaba melon is the Christmas melon. The Christmas melon has a spotted green and yellow rind and green or white flesh.

Although classified as a winter melon, the Crenshaw melon does not ship or store well, and it has a very soft skin that bruises easily when handled. The Crenshaw melon has juicy, soft, flavorful orange flesh.

Melons require a long, warm growing season to produce high-yielding, sweet fruit. Dry, warm climates are best for growing melons. Humid growing conditions increase the likelihood that crops will be infected by disease or plant pests. Also, long periods of wet weather result in melons that are less sweet than those grown in drier conditions.

Melons originated in Africa. In the 1400's, the melon was brought from Turkish Armenia to the papal estate of Cantaluppe, near Rome, Italy. Cantaloupe gets its name from this source. Melons were originally brought to the New World by Columbus.

JONATHAN SCHULTHEIS
North Carolina State University

MELVILLE, HERMAN (1819–1891)

Herman Melville is best known for his novels of the sea. The greatest of these, *Moby Dick,* is not only an exciting adventure story but a complex novel of ideas.

Herman Melville was born in New York City on August 1, 1819. His father was a well-to-do merchant whose business collapsed in 1830. The family then moved to Albany, New York, the home of Mrs. Melville's parents. After his father died in 1832, Herman tried to earn money for his family by working in his uncle's bank and later as a teacher. In 1839 he went to seek his fortune at sea as a member of the crew of a merchant ship.

In 1841, Melville sailed on the whaler *Acushnet* and started on the greatest adventure of his life. When the ship docked at Nuku-Hiva, one of the Marquesas Islands, in 1842, Melville jumped ship and fled into the jungle. He stayed briefly with a native tribe before sailing on an Australian whaler to Tahiti and on another whaler to Hawaii. He reached home in 1844 after spending 14 months on a U.S. Navy frigate.

Melville immediately began to write of his experiences. *Typee* (1846), *Omoo* (1847), *Mardi* (1849), *Redburn* (1849), and *White-Jacket* (1850) followed each other quickly. In 1847, Melville married Elizabeth Shaw, and in 1850 he moved his family to Pittsfield, Massachusetts. There he became a friend of the writer Nathaniel Hawthorne.

When *Moby Dick* was published in 1851, it disappointed readers who preferred Melville's simpler early novels. Its commercial failure was a severe disappointment to Melville, *Pierre,* a novel published in 1852, was even less successful. But Melville continued to write poetry and short stories. *Benito Cereno* and *Bartleby the Scrivener* are among his finest stories.

After attempting unsuccessfully to earn a living by giving public lectures, Melville took a position as a customs inspector in New York City, where he worked until his retirement in 1885. He died on September 28, 1891. The manuscript for *Billy Budd,* a short novel, was discovered among Melville's papers after his death and was published in 1924.

Reviewed by ERWIN HESTER
East Carolina University

Herman Melville drew on his own experiences as a sailor for his novels. *Moby Dick* was a failure when it was first published but is now regarded as a masterpiece.

▶MOBY DICK

Melville's story of Moby Dick, the great white whale, is told by Ishmael, a schoolmaster who signs on a whaling ship, the *Pequod.* Its captain is Ahab, who is obsessed with finding and killing Moby Dick, the great white whale that bit off Ahab's leg on an earlier voyage. When Ishmael arrives at the port of New Bedford, he finds he must share a room in the Spouter Inn with a man who appears to be a savage cannibal. But Queequeg turns out to be the son of a king. In the following passage, Ishmael tells Queequeg's story.

A Sag Harbour ship visited his father's bay, and Queequeg sought a passage to Christian lands. But the ship, having her full complement of seamen, spurned his suit; and not all the King his father's influence could prevail. But Queequeg vowed a vow. Alone in his canoe, he paddled off to a distant strait, which he knew the ship must pass through when she quitted the island. On one side was a coral reef; on the other a low tongue of land, covered with mangrove thickets that grew out into the water. Hiding his canoe, still afloat, among these thick-

Moby Dick is a novel of ideas, but it is also filled with adventure. This illustration by Rockwell Kent shows the crew of the *Pequod* battling a whale.

ets, with its prow seaward, he sat down in the stern, paddle low in hand; and when the ship was gliding by, like a flash he darted out; gained her side; with one backward dash of his foot capsized and sank his canoe; climbed up the chains; and throwing himself at full length upon the deck, grappled a ring-bolt there, and swore not to let it go, though hacked in pieces.

In vain the captain threatened to throw him overboard; suspended a cutlass over his naked wrists; Queequeg was the son of a King, and Queequeg budged not. Struck by his desperate dauntlessness, and his wild desire to visit Christendom, the captain at last relented, and told him he might make himself at home. But this fine young savage—this sea Prince of Wales, never saw the captain's cabin. They put him down among the sailors, and made a whaleman of him. But like the Czar Peter content to toil in the shipyards of foreign cities, Queequeg disdained no seeming ignominy, if thereby he might happily gain the power of enlightening his untutored countrymen. For at bottom—so he told me—he was actuated by a profound desire to learn among the Christians the arts whereby to make his people still happier than they were; and more than that still better than they were. But, alas! the practices of whalemen soon convinced him that even Christians could be both miserable and wicked; infinitely more so than all his father's heathens. Arrived at last in old Sag Harbour; and seeing what the sailors did there; and then going on to Nantucket, and seeing how they spent their wages in *that* place also, poor Queequeg gave it up for lost. Thought he, it's a wicked world in all meridians; I'll die a pagan.

And thus an old idolater at heart, he yet lived among these Christians, wore their clothes, and tried to talk their gibberish. Hence the queer ways about him, though now some time from home.

By hints, I asked him whether he did not propose going back, and having a coronation; since he might now consider his father dead and gone, he being very old and feeble at the last accounts. He answered no, not yet; and added that he was fearful Christianity, or rather Christians, had unfitted him for ascending the pure and undefiled throne of thirty pagan Kings before him. But by and by, he said, he would return,—as soon as he felt himself baptized again. For the nonce, however, he proposed to sail about, and sow his wild oats in all four oceans. They had made a harpooneer of him, and that barbed iron was in lieu of a sceptre now.

I asked him what might be his immediate purpose, touching his future movements. He answered, to go to sea again, in his old vocation. Upon this, I told him that whaling was my own design, and informed him of my intention to sail out of Nantucket, as being the most promising port for an adventurous whaleman to embark from. He at once resolved to accompany me to that island, ship aboard the same vessel, get into the same watch, the same boat, the same mess with me, in short to share my every hap; with both my hands in his, boldly dip into the potluck of both worlds. To all this I joyously assented; for besides the affection I now felt for Queequeg, he was an experienced harpooneer, and as such, could not fail to be of great usefulness to one, who, like me, was wholly ignorant of the mysteries of whaling, though well acquainted with the sea, as known to merchant seamen.

MEMORY. See LEARNING; BRAIN.

MEMPHIS

Memphis, Tennessee's largest city, is situated in the southwestern corner of the state. It stands atop a high bluff overlooking the Mississippi River. The "Bluff City" has a rich history and heritage. More than 650,000 people live in Memphis, and the metropolitan area has a population of more than 1.1 million.

Memphis is an important world cotton and lumber market and a major distributing center for livestock, soybeans, and other agricultural products. Memphis processes or manufactures food products, machinery, and a variety of other goods. Each year, 11 million tons of cargo pass through the city's port, the second largest port in the United States. A number of large corporations have their headquarters in Memphis.

The city is a leading medical and educational center. The University of Tennessee's Center for the Health Sciences, the state's chief medical school, is located there. Memphis University is one of several institutions of higher education in the city. Others include LeMoyne-Owen College, Christian Brothers College, and Memphis Academy of the Arts.

Among the museums of Memphis are the Brooks Memorial Art Gallery and the National Civil Rights Museum, which opened in 1991. But the cultural heritage of the city is perhaps best expressed through its music. One of the best-known places in Memphis is Beale Street, where in the early 1900's W. C. Handy, the "Father of the Blues," wrote and

Memphis, Tennessee's largest city, is situated on the Mississippi River. Rich in history, it is a commercial and cultural center for much of the mid-South.

played the music for which he was to become famous. Elvis Presley, who popularized rock and roll in the 1950's, began his recording career in Memphis. Presley's home, Graceland, remains the city's most popular tourist attraction. Other styles of popular music are also associated with Memphis, and the city is a major recording center.

Memphis has a number of sizable parks. Other attractions include the 22,000-seat Pyramid sports arena, the remodeled Beale Street, the historic Peabody Hotel, and Mud Island Park, a theme park on the banks of the Mississippi. Among the city's annual events are the Memphis in May International Festival, and the Mid-South Fair.

The site of the city of Memphis was originally inhabited by Chickasaw Indians. A succession of Spanish, French, and English frontiersmen competed for possession of the strategic bluff overlooking the river. The area was ceded to the U.S. government by the Chickasaws in 1818. The next year, the city was founded and named for Memphis, the ancient Egyptian capital. By the 1860's, the rough river town had become one of the nation's busiest ports.

During the Civil War, Union forces defeated Confederate defenders of the city in a river battle in 1862. Union forces occupied Memphis for the remainder of the war.

A series of devastating yellow fever epidemics struck Memphis in the 1870's. By the 1890's, however, the city was growing again. Memphis entered the 1900's as a leader in the cotton and lumber businesses. It has since grown to become one of the important cities of the modern South.

Reviewed by WAYNE C. MOORE
Tennessee State Library and Archives

MENCKEN, HENRY LOUIS. See MARYLAND (Famous People).

MENDEL, GREGOR JOHANN (1822–1884)

Gregor Johann Mendel, an Austrian priest, first discovered the scientific laws of plant and animal heredity. These laws describe how traits such as eye color in human beings and tallness in plants are passed on from generation to generation.

Mendel, the son of a farmer, was born on July 22, 1822, in a small village in what was then Austria but is now the Czech Republic. He was named Johann but took the name Gregor when he became a priest. He was an excellent student, and his parents enrolled him in a high school in a nearby city. When his father became ill and had to sell the farm, Mendel turned to tutoring to pay his way through high school. He was helped later by his younger sister who paid his university expenses from her wedding dowry. At the university, Mendel completed a two-year course of philosophy, physics, and higher mathematics. In 1843 he entered the Augustinian monastery in Brünn (now Brno) as a novice. He was ordained into the priesthood at the age of 25.

Mendel's first assignment was in the town hospital. But because he could not bear to witness the suffering of the sick, he was transferred to a position as a teacher in an elementary school. Father Gregor, as he was then known, was well liked by his pupils and fellow teachers. In 1851 he was sent to the University of Vienna to study science. There Mendel studied mathematical statistics and experimental botany, the two subjects that were later to be of great value to him.

After two years at the university, Mendel returned to Brünn as a substitute teacher of physics and natural history at the technical school there. He was a good teacher. But his extreme nervousness when taking examinations kept him from completing the university test to become a fully licensed science teacher. For 14 years he remained a substitute teacher, but he did much more than teach. His university courses had given him a sound knowledge of the theory of plant and animal breeding as it was then understood. To satisfy his curiosity about the ways in which such plant traits as color, height, and seed shape were inherited, he used his spare time to carry out a series of

Gregor Mendel, a monk, carried out his experiments in genetics on pea plants in the monastery garden.

experiments with pea plants. Between 1856 and 1863, he grew more than 28,000 plants on which he kept careful records.

From his records, Mendel saw clearly that there was a predictable pattern by which plant traits were passed from generation to generation—a pattern that had never been reported before. He explained this pattern in principles, or rules, that are now known as the Mendelian Laws of Heredity.

In 1868, Mendel became abbot of the monastery. His new duties made it difficult for him to continue with his experiments. He published detailed reports on his findings, but his ideas were ignored, perhaps because he was not a professional scientist. When Mendel died on January 6, 1884, the world of science was still unaware of his genius. But in 1900, three scientists wrote separate articles describing his work and brought it to the attention of biologists everywhere.

Some questions about Mendel's experimental methods cannot be answered because all the facts are not known. Nevertheless, it was Mendel who created a new kind of experiment combining biology and statistics. And it is Mendel alone who is still honored as the founder of the modern science of genetics.

LOUIS I. KUSLAN
Southern Connecticut State University

See also GENETICS.

MENDELEEV, DMITRI I. See CHEMISTRY, HISTORY OF (The Periodic Table).

MENDELSSOHN, FELIX (1809–1847)

The composer Jakob Ludwig Felix Mendelssohn-Bartholdy was born on February 3, 1809, in Hamburg, Germany. In 1812 the family moved to Berlin, where Felix began his musical studies. Felix was a true child prodigy. At an early age he developed into an outstanding pianist and organist, as well as composer. His compositions were often played by a group of musicians that gathered at the house of his music-loving parents on Sunday afternoons. Felix received his first training in conducting on these occasions. At 17 he wrote one of his masterpieces, an orchestral overture to Shakespeare's *A Midsummer Night's Dream*. Years later he composed his famous Wedding March for the same play.

In 1829 the young Mendelssohn directed the first performance in almost 100 years of Johann Sebastian Bach's *St. Matthew Passion*. The performance led to a widespread revival of interest in all of the music of this almost forgotten German composer. Today Bach is considered one of the greatest composers in history.

Mendelssohn traveled widely and became famous as both a pianist and a conductor. From 1829 to 1832 he made a tour that included England, Scotland, Germany, Austria, Italy, Switzerland, and France. Both his *Italian Symphony* (1833) and *Scottish Symphony* (1842) were inspired by these travels.

In 1835 he became conductor of the celebrated Gewandhaus Orchestra in Leipzig, Germany. He founded a conservatory of music in this city that became one of the best schools of its kind. Mendelssohn was also a talented painter and poet. He was a friend of the writer Johann Wolfgang von Goethe and set some of Goethe's poems to music. In 1837, Mendelssohn married Cécile Jeanrenaud, whom he had met while serving as director of a choral society in Frankfurt am Main. The marriage was a very happy one.

Despite his full schedule, Mendelssohn continued to compose. In 1836 he completed his oratorio *St. Paul*. He also continued traveling, particularly to England, where the elegance of his music was as much admired as in Mendelssohn's own country. In 1846 he conducted the first performance of his second oratorio, *Elijah*, in Birmingham, England.

The strain of this busy life proved too great for Mendelssohn's health, which had always been delicate. He died of a stroke on November 4, 1847, at his home in Leipzig. Though only 38 at his death, he left rich musical heritage. His best-known works include two piano concertos, the Violin Concerto in E minor, several symphonies, a wealth of chamber music, and many solo piano pieces, including the famous *Songs Without Words*.

KARL GEIRINGER
Professor of Music
University of California—Santa Barbara

MENSTRUATION

Sometime between the ages of 10 and 15, most girls begin to menstruate. Menstruation is a flow of bloody fluid from the uterus, the body organ where babies can develop. Women and girls who are old enough to have children have a menstrual period every month. In fact, the word "menstruation" comes from *mensis,* the Latin word for month.

▶ROLE IN REPRODUCTION

Menstruation plays an important role in human reproduction. The uterus, an organ in the pelvis that looks like a small upside-down pear, gets ready for pregnancy every month by thickening its lining, called the endometrium.

Once a month, a tiny egg cell is released from one of two ovaries, small organs on either side of the uterus. The egg cell, or ovum, travels down the Fallopian tube to the uterus. If it is fertilized by a male sperm cell, it settles down on the lining of the uterus. There it will develop into a baby.

If the egg cell is not fertilized, the lining of the uterus breaks down and is washed away. The blood and cells of the lining leave through the vagina, a canal that opens just behind the place where urine leaves the body. The flow normally lasts three to seven days, a time called the menstrual period. The total amount of blood lost is usually less than 30 milliliters

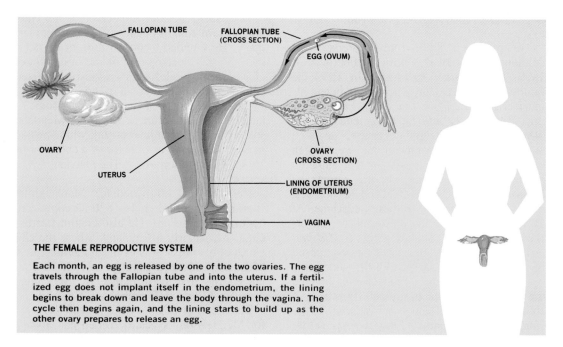

THE FEMALE REPRODUCTIVE SYSTEM

Each month, an egg is released by one of the two ovaries. The egg travels through the Fallopian tube and into the uterus. If a fertilized egg does not implant itself in the endometrium, the lining begins to break down and leave the body through the vagina. The cycle then begins again, and the lining starts to build up as the other ovary prepares to release an egg.

(1 ounce). Then the lining of the uterus begins to thicken again.

This cycle is controlled by hormones, or chemical messengers, that are produced by the ovaries and the pituitary gland. It usually repeats itself about every 28 days, but anywhere from 21 to 40 days is normal. In the first year or so of menstruation, it is common to have irregular periods.

Menstruation starts about two years after the appearance of some other signs that a girl is growing up, such as the first growth of breasts and body hair. Girls who are very thin often begin to menstruate later than others. Menstruation stops when a woman is about 50. This is called menopause. Periods also stop temporarily during pregnancy.

▶**MANAGING MENSTRUATION**

The flow of blood can be absorbed with a pad (called a sanitary napkin) worn outside the opening of the vagina or with a tampon, a roll of absorbent material that is worn inside. (A tampon cannot get lost inside.) A girl who has her period can continue all her usual activities, including sports and (with tampons) swimming. She need not take unusual care of her health. For example, she will not catch cold if she washes her hair, as was once thought.

Regular periods are a sign of good health, but even healthy women occasionally miss a period. Missed periods can be a sign of pregnancy. They can also result from emotional strain, sudden or extreme weight loss, or a medical problem. A woman who misses several periods or skips periods often should consult a doctor.

Some women have crampy pains in the lower abdomen on the first day or two of their periods. These cramps are caused by contractions of the uterus, which is made of strong muscle. They are not imaginary and are not caused by emotions. The best mild pain relievers for them are ones that contain aspirin. If the pain is severe, a doctor can prescribe other medication and look for less common causes of painful periods.

For a few days before each period, some women have various unpleasant symptoms. These include fatigue, irritability, breast soreness, and bloating of the abdomen. These symptoms together are called premenstrual tension. They are more common in older women than in teenagers. Doctors do not agree on what causes them. Some women find they feel better if they eat less salt for a few days before their periods. If the symptoms are severe, there are a number of treatments that can be tried.

JEAN PASCOE, M.D.
Miriam Hospital/Brown University

See also REPRODUCTION.

MENTAL ILLNESS

An illness is an unhealthy condition that interferes with normal body activities. Illnesses can be caused by damage to some part of the body or by an abnormally functioning bodily organ. According to the Surgeon General of the United States, mental illnesses are "disorders of the brain that disrupt a person's thinking, feeling, moods, and ability to relate to others."

Just as with other medical illnesses, mental illnesses have special names (diagnoses) and cause particular symptoms for the people who have them. These illnesses need to be treated by a psychiatrist, psychologist, social worker, psychiatric nurse, or other mental health expert. Although not all mental illnesses are curable, the symptoms will get better with proper treatment. Mental illnesses are, therefore, similar to physical illnesses.

Diabetes, for example, is a physical illness caused when the pancreas cannot produce enough insulin to allow the body to use sugar from the blood for energy. In some people, the pancreas does not make enough insulin from early in life, while other people have diabetes because of injuries to the pancreas or from being overweight. Just as problems with the pancreas can cause diabetes, problems in the brain can also cause illnesses. These problems can be caused by many different factors, including genetics and the environment.

▶ TYPES OF MENTAL ILLNESS

In the United States, the different mental illnesses are classified in a book written by the American Psychiatric Association. The book is titled *Diagnostic and Statistical Manual of Mental Disorders, Fourth Edition*, or DSM-IV. The DSM-IV lists over 400 separate disorders. The most common diagnoses are discussed in this article.

Mood Disorders

Most people experience a wide range of different feelings and emotions every day. Typical feelings include joy, excitement, fear, sadness, anger, jealousy, pride, and shame. The term "mood" refers to a feeling that lasts for hours, days, weeks, or longer. When a particular mood is so strong and long lasting that it interferes with normal activities, it is referred to as a **mood disorder**.

One kind of mood disorder is **depression**, which is extreme sadness that causes loss of pleasure in almost all activities. Children with depression may feel more irritability than sadness. **Major depressive disorder** is diagnosed when depression lasts for two weeks or more and is accompanied by sleep problems (either too much or too little), weight change, hopelessness, and trouble concentrating. A less severe but more lasting form of depression is **dysthymic disorder**.

Depression is one of the most common psychiatric disorders. Approximately 20% of women will have a major depressive episode during their lives, almost twice the number seen in men.

People with **bipolar disorder** (also called manic depression) have repeated episodes of depression that alternate with periods of mania. Or, depression and mania can be separated by periods of normal mood. **Mania** is a mood that is excessively happy or irritable combined with symptoms such as decreased need for sleep, excessive talking, and racing thoughts. People with mania may have thoughts that are **grandiose**, for example, believing they have special powers. Bipolar disorder is less frequent than major depressive disorder and occurs equally in men and women.

Although depression and bipolar disorder most commonly begin in adulthood, children and adolescents can also have these illnesses. Mood disorders of all types tend to run in families. This is particularly true for mood problems in children. Mood disorders that start in childhood tend to be more serious and to continue longer. All types of mood disorders can be severe and chronic illnesses, but they can usually be well controlled with medicine and other therapy. If left untreated, however, they sometimes result in suicide.

Anxiety Disorders

Everyone feels fear and anxiety sometimes. A normal fear is associated with a specific danger in the immediate future. For example, you might be afraid of being struck by lightning if you are standing outside during a thunderstorm. Anxiety refers to a more general feeling of worry about the future even when there is no immediate danger. Some anxiety can be good—it motivates people to work or study in order to keep a job or do well in school. But too much anxiety can interfere with normal activities to the point that a person cannot concentrate, make decisions, or even go outside.

A panic attack is a sudden feeling of intense anxiety that usually includes a fear of dying or going crazy. The anxiety is combined with physical symptoms such as sweating, increased heart rate, shortness of breath, dizziness, numbness, or choking. When people who have had panic attacks begin to constantly fear having them again, they have what is called **panic disorder**.

People with panic disorder may begin to avoid places or situations where they would feel trapped if they had a panic attack. This is called **agoraphobia**. In some cases, agoraphobia prevents people from traveling or leaving home. Individuals with **social phobia** have intense and unreasonable fears of social situations where they might feel overwhelming embarrassment if they had to speak or perform in public.

People with **obsessive-compulsive disorder (OCD)** have unwanted thoughts, or **obsessions**, about a particular danger, such as being contaminated by germs if they touch a doorknob. These obsessions cause them to feel intense anxiety and distress. To reduce the

stress, they repeatedly perform a certain act (**compulsion**) that is related to the obsession. For example, they might wash their hands again and again to remove the germs. Some people with OCD spend many hours each day doing compulsive acts and are unable to stop the behavior, even though they realize their fears are exaggerated.

Post-traumatic stress disorder (PTSD) is seen only after someone has experienced a very frightening or life-threatening situation, such as a serious accident, an earthquake, or physical or sexual abuse. After such an event, some people have problems with intense memories and nightmares of the event. They may also have flashbacks (feeling as though the event is happening again) when they encounter reminders of the situation. People with PTSD also have symptoms of numbing, which is an absence of normal feelings, as well as hyperarousal, which is the presence of abnormally intense feelings such as anger and fear.

Generalized anxiety disorder is a continued state of worry about many upcoming events, such as work or school, along with physical symptoms including restlessness, fatigue, muscle tension, and sleep problems. Anxiety disorders are very common in children, adolescents, and adults and are frequently seen along with mood disorders and other psychiatric problems.

Problems Primarily Affecting Memory

The two types of illnesses that affect memory are delirium and dementia. **Delirium** is a condition in which people lose awareness of who they are, where they are, or what day it is. People who are delirious may be confused and have trouble communicating. They may also **hallucinate** (see and hear things that are not really there). Delirium comes on quickly and is usually caused by some physical effect on the brain from a medical condition, poison, or drug.

Unlike delirium, which occurs quickly, **dementia** is a gradual loss of memory and judgment. People with dementia lose the ability to make decisions, perform routine activities, and recognize familiar objects, places, and

Alzheimer's disease results from the destruction of brain tissue. People with Alzheimer's disease eventually need help with routine activities, such as eating meals.

people. Dementia is caused by physical damage or deterioration of the brain because of injury, illness, or inherited genetic problems. One type of dementia, **Alzheimer's disease**, affects approximately 2 to 4 percent of people over age 65.

Schizophrenia and Other Psychotic Disorders

Psychosis is a term that usually refers to a group of symptoms including hallucinations, delusions, and disorganized thoughts and speech. These symptoms can be seen with a number of medical conditions and in people who are intoxicated with certain substances.

The most serious illness with psychotic symptoms is **schizophrenia**. People with schizophrenia may have hallucinations. They may also believe falsely that people are following them or trying to hurt them. These false beliefs are called **delusions**. Hallucinations and delusions can cause a great deal of distress and fear. People with schizophrenia may also have disorganized thoughts and speech, making it difficult for them to study, work, and interact normally with others.

Schizophrenia occurs in people throughout the world. It usually starts when individuals are in their 20's, and tends to run in families. People with schizophrenia may need lifelong care, but with new treatments and medications, many people have been able to live independent, productive lives.

Problems with Alcohol and Other Drugs

A person who repeatedly uses alcohol or other drugs—such as cocaine, heroin, and opiate painkillers—may find that using the substance leads to serious consequences in his or her life. The consequences may include missing school or work, having conflicts at home, or participating in dangerous behavior, such as driving while intoxicated. If someone continues to use a substance despite having these types of problems repeatedly, the condition is called substance abuse.

Use of alcohol, nicotine, and other drugs can also result in addiction. This means a person develops physical symptoms if he or she stops using the drug (withdrawal) or has to use increasing amounts of the drug to get the same effect (tolerance). People taking addictive substances may be unable to stop their drug use even when they know that it is causing them harm.

Eating Disorders

Two major mental illnesses involve abnormal eating behaviors. People with **anorexia nervosa** are intensely afraid of gaining weight and believe themselves to be fat even when they are thin or underweight. To avoid gaining weight, people with anorexia nervosa starve themselves and may exercise excessively. Anorexia can cause lifelong problems of weak bones and hormone imbalance and can be fatal if a person's weight falls too low.

The second major type of eating disorder is **bulimia nervosa**. People with bulimia feel uncontrollable urges to eat excessively large amounts of food (this is called **bingeing**). The binges are followed by attempts to remove the food from the body by vomiting, using laxatives, or exercising. Some people have a combination of anorexia and bulimia.

Anorexia nervosa and bulimia nervosa are seen mostly in young women, typically starting in adolescence. But eating disorders can also affect men. In some people the symptoms gradually lessen with age, but many people continue to have problems with eating behavior as adults.

Disorders of Infants, Children, and Adolescents

Some mental illnesses typically start early in life, although they may not be diagnosed until later or may continue into adulthood. The most frequently occurring of these disorders include mental retardation, learning and communication problems, developmental disorders, and attention and disruptive behavior disorders.

Mental retardation affects approximately 1 percent of the population. It is characterized by a general, below-average ability to learn (low IQ) and trouble participating in daily activities. The severity of mental retardation can range from mild (the largest percentage of cases) to profound (the most serious type, which happens in the smallest percentage of cases). People who have mild mental retardation can often live and work independently. Those with profound mental retardation usually need close supervision throughout life. For more information about mental retardation, see the article RETARDATION, MENTAL in Volume QR.

Individuals with **learning and communication disorders** have normal intelligence but have difficulty in a particular learning area, such as reading, mathematics, or writing. Others may have trouble expressing themselves or understanding language.

Children with **pervasive developmental disorders (PDD)** have severe problems in several areas of development. These problems cause difficulty relating to others. Many children with PDD also have trouble with language and are unable to communicate normally. Often they show unusual interests or body movements. Two of the more frequently seen types of PDD are **autistic disorder** and **Asperger's disorder**. For more information about autistic disorder and Asperger's disorder, see the article AUTISM in Volume A.

Attention-deficit/hyperactivity disorder (ADHD) is seen in approximately 3 to 5 percent of school-age children, mostly in boys. The two major types of symptoms are inattention and hyperactivity or impulsiveness. Children with ADHD may lose things, be easily distracted, and have trouble paying attention. They may also seem to be constantly talking and unable to sit still. All of these behaviors are normal in children to some degree. ADHD is diagnosed only when the behaviors are persistent and interfere with normal daily activities at school and at home. See the article ADHD in Volume A to learn more.

Personality Disorders

The term "personality" refers to the typical ways that someone thinks, feels, acts, and reacts to situations in his or her life. For example, some people may be shy in new situations, prefer a regular routine, plan ahead, make decisions slowly, and become worried easily. Other people enjoy meeting others, get bored with routine, do not plan very far ahead, make decisions quickly, and seldom become worried or anxious. Both of these personality types are normal, as are many other possible patterns.

People with personality disorders are those who have developed patterns of thinking, feeling, and behavior that are much different from those usu-

ally seen. For example, people with **paranoid personality disorder** are highly suspicious of other people's intentions. **Schizoid personality disorder** is characterized by a strong lack of interest in having relationships with other people. Those with **histrionic personality disorder** are highly emotional and seek excessive attention from others. Individuals with **antisocial personality disorder** disregard other people's rights, and people with **obsessive-compulsive personality disorder** are excessively preoccupied with things being perfect and in order. People with personality disorders are unable to change their behavior even though it causes problems with personal relationships or an inability to cope with daily activities.

Since personality is formed over a long period of time during childhood and adolescence, personality disorders do not appear until late adolescence or young adulthood. Without treatment, symptoms tend to last for many years, although some will gradually get better as a person grows older.

▶ CAUSES OF MENTAL ILLNESS

The exact causes of mental illness are still being discovered, but it is clear that many result from a combination of biological, psychological, and social problems. For some types of mental illness, such as depression, people inherit genes that make them more likely than other people to develop the illness, but only if certain things happen to them during their lives. This is known as genetic vulnerability. Mental illnesses that seem to have a high level of genetic vulnerability include ADHD, mood disorders, schizophrenia, and some anxiety disorders.

On the other hand, some mental illnesses show less evidence of being controlled by heredity and seem to be the result of life experiences. For example, post-

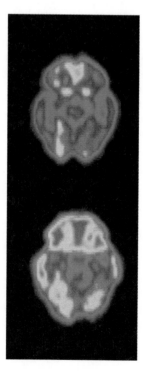

A PET scan shows increased activity in the frontal lobe of the brain of a person with obsessive-compulsive disorder (bottom) compared with the brain of a person without the disorder (top).

traumatic stress disorder occurs only if some-one has been through a life-threatening event or traumatic situation. Other mental illnesses, such as substance-abuse disorders, seem to be caused in almost equal parts by genetics and experience, including cultural values.

▶ TREATMENT OF MENTAL ILLNESS

Just as with physical illnesses, the best treatment for a mental illness is different for different people. Treatment depends upon the diagnosis, whether there is more than one diagnosis, and what psychological and social factors are making the illness worse. Since many mental illnesses are caused by a combination of brain biology and experiences, the best treatments often combine biological and non-biological therapies.

The most important biological treatments are medications and electroconvulsive therapy (ECT). Although there are still no medicines that cure most mental illnesses, many new drugs help relieve specific symptoms such as depression, anxiety, obsessions, inattention, and sleep problems. Specialized studies have begun to show how these medicines affect the parts of the brain that are working abnormally in different illnesses.

ECT is a treatment during which the patient is put under anesthesia and given a medicine to prevent muscle contractions. A pulse of electricity is then given to the brain through electrodes placed on either one or both sides of the head. The way that ECT works is not yet known; however, it has become a safe and effective way of treating severe cases of depression and mania that do not respond to other treatments.

Non-biological treatments are often grouped under the term **psychotherapy**. A patient undergoing psychotherapy usually has a series of meetings with a mental health professional. The different types of psychotherapy emphasize different approaches for dealing with mental illness. **Cognitive-behavioral** therapy uses training methods that help people have more self-control over their symptoms. **Family therapy** can help change the way people behave toward each other at home in order to lower stress, provide more support, or change habits that may contribute to symptoms. **Individual psychotherapy** helps people understand how experiences in the past affect their behavior in

Mental health professionals use many different techniques to help people with mental disorders. Here, a social worker uses puppets to interact with a child.

the present. **Group therapy** involves several people with the same type of problem working together with a therapist. It is often helpful in teaching people new ways to cope with their illness because they learn from each other and share their experiences with others dealing with the same problems.

An exciting discovery has been that certain methods of psychotherapy cause physical changes in the brain similar to those seen with drug treatment. For example, cognitive-behavioral therapy and medicine each increase blood flow to the part of the brain affected in obsessive-compulsive disorder.

▶ MENTAL HEALTH PROFESSIONS

In the United States, there are four main professions devoted to treating mental illness. **Psychiatrists** are doctors who specialize in evaluating, diagnosing, and treating people with psychiatric disorders. They can prescribe medication and use all of the other treatments that help people with mental illness. There are also sub-specialists in psychiatry who concentrate on certain age groups, such as children, or types of problems, such as substance abuse.

Psychologists are behavioral scientists who study both normal and abnormal functioning, and also treat patients with mental and emotional problems using non-biological treatments. **Social workers** are professionals devoted to helping people function the best they can in their environment. This can mean

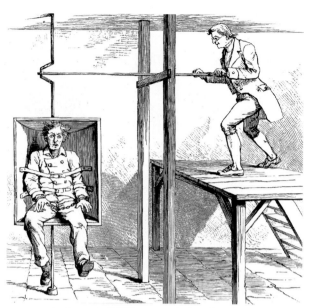

In the early 1800's, some doctors thought certain mental illnesses could be treated by increasing blood flow to the brain by spinning patients in a circulating swing.

providing services or therapy directly to people or working for change to improve social conditions. **Nurses** are medical professionals who are trained both to provide direct medical care and to help patients and families learn to provide self-care. Nurses with advanced training in psychiatric nursing often work with mentally ill patients either in the hospital or in the community. Some are able to prescribe medication.

The best care for patients usually involves having an assessment by a psychiatrist, psychologist, social worker, or psychiatric nurse who will either provide treatment or refer the patient to another specialist if necessary. For patients with complicated, long-lasting, and serious mental illnesses, a group of mental health professionals working together (a treatment team) can provide the combination of treatments that will be most successful.

▶ WHERE TO GET HELP

People who need mental health treatment will often go first to their regular physician. Many physicians can help with uncomplicated problems but will usually need to refer someone to a specialist for a problem that is complicated or severe. Similarly, most schools have counselors available to meet with students to help with less serious problems or to refer students and their parents to a mental health specialist in the community. Most communities have public clinics or mental health centers where people can go directly if they are in need of help. Some communities have hotlines, which are telephone numbers available 24 hours a day with volunteers or staff who can help with an emergency or suggest how to find professional help.

▶ HISTORY OF ATTITUDES TOWARD MENTAL ILLNESS

Until the 1600's, most cultures did not distinguish mental illness from physical illness. During the 1600's, French philosopher René Descartes developed the idea that the mind and the body were separate. With time, particularly in European cultures, brain illnesses whose symptoms were mostly problems with feelings, thinking, and behavior were considered problems of the mind and not the body. As a result, people began to think differently about mental as opposed to physical disease.

One of the most important results of this separation of illness into two categories was that diseases of the mind (mental illness) came to be seen as caused by some personal failure or weakness. While many caring physicians and religious leaders did their best to help the mentally ill, those with mental diseases were often looked at as inferior, or bad, by society. These negative attitudes have only slowly begun to change.

During the past twenty years, scientists have started to discover the brain abnormalities that cause the symptoms of mental disorders. These discoveries have led to new treatments as well as new information to contradict the ideas that have been used to stigmatize the mentally ill. Future progress will depend upon more new discoveries about the brain as well as a change in the attitudes of society, which have prevented people who suffer from these illnesses from receiving the care they need.

Robert Racusin, M.D.
Associate Professor of Psychiatry
Dartmouth Medical School

MENTAL RETARDATION. See Retardation, Mental.

MERCHANT MARINE. See United States, Armed Forces of the.

MERCURY (ELEMENT). See Elements, Chemical.

MERCURY

To the ancient Romans, Mercury was the swift messenger of the gods. This was certainly a good name to give to the small planet closest to the sun. Of the nine planets in the solar system, the planet Mercury travels around the sun the fastest. It completes one full orbit in only 88 Earth days—less than one fourth the time the Earth takes to make its trip around the sun.

Mercury is not easy to see from the Earth. Because it lies so close to the sun, it can only be observed as a faint starlike object appearing near the horizon during the twilight hours just after sunset or just before sunrise. Even astronomers with telescopes can see little of the planet. Mercury is just too small and too far away for telescopes on Earth to observe much of it. Information about Mercury increased greatly in 1974 and 1975 when the U.S. spacecraft *Mariner 10* made three separate flights past the planet. During its mission, *Mariner 10* transmitted more than 2,700 images and other information back to scientists on Earth. This information taught astronomers a great deal about the planet.

A mosaic of Mercury made from *Mariner 10* photographs shows bright ray craters (*above*) and a detail of the fractured and ridged surface of the Caloris Basin (*left*).

Mercury's Surface

The images transmitted by *Mariner 10* revealed that Mercury looks a lot like the Earth's moon. The surface of this small planet has thousands and thousands of craters and large dark areas of flat plains covering its surface. Another interesting feature is a series of cliffs that is hundreds of miles long.

Craters. Most of Mercury's craters were caused by large meteorites that crashed into the planet's surface between 3.7 and 4.5 billion years ago during a period known as the Great Bombardment. This period of heavy bombardment by meteorites, which occurred early in the history of the solar system, also left craters on the Earth's moon and on many other objects in the solar system.

There are some differences between the craters on Mercury and those on the Earth's moon. Most of Mercury's craters are flatter and have thinner rims or walls. This may be because the force of gravity is greater on Mercury than it is on the moon, and a stronger gravitational force may have caused the crater rims on the planet to crumble somewhat. By observing how some of Mercury's craters lie inside or on top of others, scientists can determine which craters formed first. This can help them understand something about how the planet and its surface features evolved.

The largest craterlike feature on Mercury, which is known as the Caloris Basin, is more than 800 miles (1,280 kilometers) in diameter. It was formed billions of years ago when a huge object, perhaps as much as 100 miles (160 kilometers) in diameter, crashed into the planet. Around the Caloris Basin are the Caloris Mountains. These mountains are actually huge piles of material that were thrown out of the Caloris Basin by the colossal impact of the meteor that formed it. The impact may also

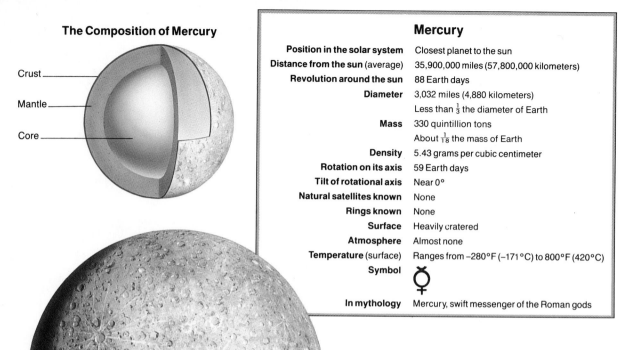

The Composition of Mercury

Crust

Mantle

Core

Mercury	
Position in the solar system	Closest planet to the sun
Distance from the sun (average)	35,900,000 miles (57,800,000 kilometers)
Revolution around the sun	88 Earth days
Diameter	3,032 miles (4,880 kilometers)
	Less than $\frac{1}{3}$ the diameter of Earth
Mass	330 quintillion tons
	About $\frac{1}{18}$ the mass of Earth
Density	5.43 grams per cubic centimeter
Rotation on its axis	59 Earth days
Tilt of rotational axis	Near 0°
Natural satellites known	None
Rings known	None
Surface	Heavily cratered
Atmosphere	Almost none
Temperature (surface)	Ranges from –280°F (–171°C) to 800°F (420°C)
Symbol	☿
In mythology	Mercury, swift messenger of the Roman gods

have formed an area on Mercury that scientists call the "weird terrain," which is almost opposite the Caloris Basin. It consists of hills, ridges, and grooves that cut across craters. This "weird terrain" may have been formed by shock waves that raced through the center of the planet and outward from the Caloris Basin at the time of the impact.

Although most of the craters on Mercury's surface are billions of years old, some have probably been formed within the last hundred million years, while other craters could still form today. Some of the younger craters are called ray craters because bright rays appear to run outward from their centers in all directions. The rays are probably lighter colored material that sprayed outward at the time of impact.

Other Surface Features. Each of the dark, flat plains on Mercury's surface is called a *mare* (the Latin word for "sea"), just as they are on the moon. The word *mare* was chosen in earlier times by observers of the moon who thought that the dark areas on its surface might be seas or oceans. Astronomers now know, however, that there is no surface water on either the moon or on Mercury. These dark areas are actually places where lava has flowed upward from the interior of the moon and the planet and has filled low-lying areas.

The lava of Mercury's plains became solid millions of years ago. Because there are few craters within these plains, astronomers know that they date from a time after the Great Bombardment. The few craters found within the plains were caused by meteorites that struck the planet after the plains had formed.

Another interesting surface feature of Mercury is a series of cliffs hundreds of miles long. These cliffs, called scarps, were probably formed early in Mercury's history. After the planet first formed out of a cloud of gas and dust, internal heat may have caused its interior to become molten. Heavy elements sank to the center of the planet, while lighter elements flowed upward through cracks in its surface to form the plains. Later, as the interior of Mercury cooled, its core solidified and expanded just as water expands when it freezes. This expansion may have pushed sections of the planet's surface upward to form the scarps.

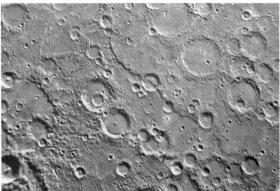

Close-ups of Mercury show a newer crater in the center of a much older crater (*left*) as well as ridges and grooves cutting across craters in an area affected by the impact that created the Caloris Basin (*above*).

Mercury's surface is probably covered in most places by a thin layer of very fine dust. Some of this dust has come from meteorites striking the planet and throwing fine particles of rock and other material up from its surface. The dust also comes from the constant heating and cooling of Mercury's surface during its days and nights. This causes surface rocks to expand and contract again and again until they finally crack and break down into very fine particles.

Mercury's Interior and Its Magnetic Field

Astronomers think that the interior of Mercury consists of a core of iron, nickel, and perhaps other heavy elements. The core of Mercury may be larger than the Earth's moon. Surrounding the core may be a rocky zone about 360 miles (580 kilometers) thick and

over that a light crust no more than 40 miles (65 kilometers) thick.

The existence of a magnetic field around Mercury suggests that the planet's core may consist partly of molten iron. As the molten iron core circulates, as it does within the Earth, it creates an electrical current that then generates a magnetic field. Although the magnetic field of Mercury is much weaker than that of the Earth, it is stronger than the magnetic fields of the moon and of the planets Venus and Mars.

Mercury's Revolution and Rotation

Mercury completes its revolution, or orbit, around the sun in only 88 Earth days, the fastest of any planet. Compared to its fast revolution, Mercury rotates quite slowly. The planet rotates once on its axis (relative to the stars) in about 59 Earth days—the slowest rotation of any planet except Venus. It rotates once on its axis (relative to the sun) in about 176 Earth days. Therefore, a day on Mercury (as

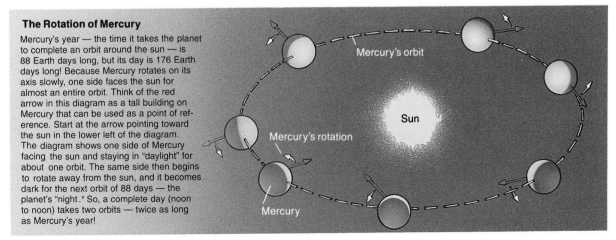

The Rotation of Mercury

Mercury's year — the time it takes the planet to complete an orbit around the sun — is 88 Earth days long, but its day is 176 Earth days long! Because Mercury rotates on its axis slowly, one side faces the sun for almost an entire orbit. Think of the red arrow in this diagram as a tall building on Mercury that can be used as a point of reference. Start at the arrow pointing toward the sun in the lower left of the diagram. The diagram shows one side of Mercury facing the sun and staying in "daylight" for about one orbit. The same side then begins to rotate away from the sun, and it becomes dark for the next orbit of 88 days — the planet's "night." So, a complete day (noon to noon) takes two orbits — twice as long as Mercury's year!

Mercury's orbit

Sun

Mercury's rotation

Mercury

During a transit of Mercury, the planet passes between Earth and the sun. From Earth, Mercury then appears as a tiny black dot against the huge face of the sun.

measured from noon to noon) is twice as long as the planet's year!

Mercury travels around the sun in an elliptical, or oval-shaped, orbit. Combined with its speed of revolution and rotation, this results in an odd movement of the sun as seen from the planet's surface. At some places on Mercury's surface, the sun rises above the horizon very slowly at dawn, then stops and goes back down, and finally rises again and moves across the sky. At other places on the planet's surface, this slight back-and-forth motion of the sun happens around midday.

Mercury's Atmosphere

On Mercury the sun appears more than twice as large as it does on the Earth because of the planet's closeness to the sun. But even with such a large, brilliant sun, it is possible to see bright stars in the planet's sky during the daytime. The reason for this is that Mercury has an extremely thin atmosphere. The planet's weak gravitational force, combined with the heat from the sun, allowed most of the planet's gases to boil away into space long ago. However, an extremely thin veil of helium gas surrounds Mercury. In addition, a very thin atmosphere of sodium, potassium, and oxygen gases has been detected.

The lack of a substantial atmosphere affects the surface of Mercury in a variety of ways. There are no natural forces to erode the surface of the planet, which is why craters and other features on the planet's surface have remained relatively unchanged for millions or perhaps even billions of years. The surface of the planet also experiences enormous temperature differences from day to night because there is no atmosphere to trap the sun's heat energy. For example, at the planet's equator the midday temperature may reach 800°F (420°C), while the nighttime temperature may plunge to –280°F (–170°C).

Recent studies have convinced some scientists that ice may exist on the floors of deep craters near Mercury's polar regions. They believe that the sun's rays may never reach the bottoms of these deep craters, so it may be cold enough for ice to exist there. Since Mercury has no surface water (or water vapor in an atmosphere), they argue that such ice could have been deposited on the planet by comets that crashed into its surface over a period of billions of years.

Scientists hope many questions about Mercury will be answered by the *MESSENGER* (MErcury Surface, Space ENvironment, GEochemistry, and Ranging) space probe, launched in 2004. *MESSENGER* is scheduled to do two flybys of the planet before entering its orbit in 2011.

Mercury's Phases

From the Earth, Mercury appears to change in shape and size. These changes, or phases, happen because different parts of Mercury's sunlit surface are visible from the Earth at different times. When Mercury lies almost opposite the sun as seen from Earth, we see almost all of its sunlit surface, and the planet appears as a bright round spot. However, when Mercury is closer to Earth, less and less of its sunlit surface can be seen, and the planet appears as a half circle or a larger thin crescent. Since its orbit is tilted a little to the Earth's orbit, Mercury does not appear to pass directly between the Earth and the sun every time it swings between them. Once in a while, however, Mercury, the sun, and Earth lie almost in a straight line, and Mercury can be seen as a tiny black spot moving across the face of the sun. This rare event, called a transit of Mercury, occurs only about 13 times every 100 years. A telescope and protective equipment are needed to view it safely.

WILLIAM A. GUTSCH, JR.
President, The Challenger Center for Space
Science Education

See also ASTRONOMY; PLANETS; SOLAR SYSTEM; SPACE PROBES.

MERRIAM, EVE. See CHILDREN'S LITERATURE (Profiles).

MESOPOTAMIA

Mesopotamia was an ancient region located around the Tigris and Euphrates rivers, in present-day Iraq, eastern Syria, and southeastern Turkey. In southern Mesopotamia, about 3500 B.C., the world's first civilization arose.

The northern region of Mesopotamia was called Assyria, and the southern region was called Babylonia. Babylonia was divided into Akkad in the north and Sumer in the south.

Early Communities. People lived in Mesopotamia before 100,000 B.C., hunting animals and harvesting wild plants for food. Between 7500 and 5000 B.C., these people began living in villages; domesticating animals such as cows, sheep, and goats; and cultivating various grains. They also engaged in trade with neighboring regions.

Sumer and Akkad. Between 3500 and 3000 B.C., the world's first civilization arose in Sumer. People developed efficient irrigation systems, invented writing, and built large cities with monumental (large-scale) architecture. Each city-state ruled its surrounding countryside.

For more than 1,500 years, Mesopotamia was characterized by these city-states. They often fought one another but remained independent except for three main periods, during which one city established an empire over the others. These cities were Akkad (2320–2220 B.C.), Ur (2100–2020 B.C.), and Babylon (1760–1740 B.C.).

One notable ruler, Sargon of Akkad, used his large army to establish the first empire to control all of southern Mesopotamia. He spoke a Semitic language (one belonging to a family of languages that also includes Arabic, Hebrew, and others) and appointed Akkadians as governors over each city. For more on the history and culture of southern Mesopotamia between 3500 and 2000 B.C., see the articles BABYLONIA in Volume B and SUMER in Volume S.

Old Babylonian Empire. After Ur fell in 2004 B.C., Babylon rose to power under Hammurabi (reigned about 1792–50 B.C.), who is best known from inscriptions on several stone monuments discovered in the early A.D. 1900's. The inscriptions are called the Code of Hammurabi, and they provide rules for proper conduct in Babylonian society. Hammurabi gradually conquered the other city-states in Mesopotamia and the surrounding regions. His empire lasted until 1740 B.C., when southern Mesopotamia was divided among various lesser rulers.

The Kassites, whose homeland is unknown, invaded Mesopotamia in the early 1700's B.C. They brought an end to independent city-states in the region, created the unified state of Babylonia, and established a dynasty that survived from about 1475 to 1155 B.C. Babylonia became a major power in western Asia, rivaling Egypt for many years. After 1155, Babylonia became politically

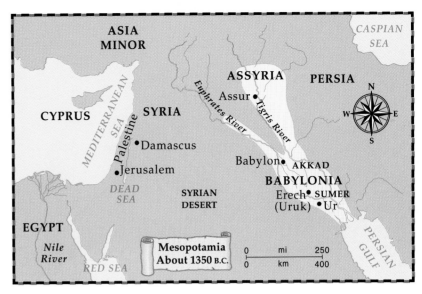

Above: This bronze sculpture dates from the 2200's B.C. and may represent the ruler Sargon of Akkad, whose empire was the first to control all of southern Mesopotamia.

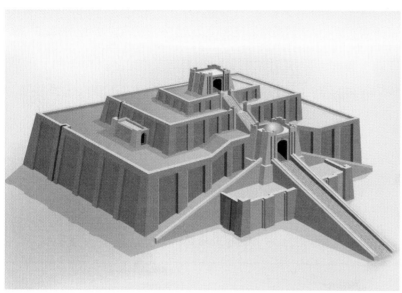

Mesopotamia's ziggurats were pyramid-shaped towers made of baked clay bricks. Ziggurats had as many as eight levels and were topped with a temple or shrine used for religious rituals.

weaker and was governed by a series of minor dynasties until it fell to the Assyrians in the 600's B.C.

Assyrian Empire. Before 2000 B.C., northern Mesopotamia was relatively undeveloped; only small settlements existed, and few people knew how to write. About 1950 B.C., Assur, a town on the Tigris River, became the center of a wealthy trading network that expanded far into the region of modern-day Turkey. About 1350 B.C., Assur conquered the rest of northern Mesopotamia and became the capital of the unified state of Assyria. The Middle Assyrian Empire ruled from about 1300 to 1200 B.C., and the Neo-Assyrian Empire ruled from about 875 to 612 B.C. Assyrians spoke a Semitic language closely related to Babylonian, but they copied Babylonian literature and used the Babylonian language for their official royal inscriptions.

Neo-Babylonian Empire. In 612 B.C., the Neo-Assyrian Empire collapsed under attacks from Babylonia and Media, a state in western Iran. It was succeeded by the Neo-Babylonian Empire, which inherited much of Assyria's territory in western Asia. Nebuchadnezzar II, who reigned from 604 to 562 B.C., made Babylon the most magnificent city on Earth. For his queen he built the Hanging Gardens, one of the seven wonders of the ancient world. The Neo-Babylonian Empire was the last independent state in Mesopotamia. It fell to the Persians, another Iranian people, in 539 B.C.

Persian Empire and Decline of Mesopotamia. Babylonia became the wealthiest province of the Persian Empire and by itself financially supported the royal court for four months of each year. After controlling Mesopotamia for little more than 200 years, however, the Persians were conquered in 331 B.C. by Alexander the Great of Macedonia, a kingdom north of Greece. For more information on the Persian Empire, see the article PERSIA, ANCIENT in Volume P.

Beginning with Alexander's introduction of Greek culture, Mesopotamia was increasingly influenced by foreign cultures. Parthians and Sassanians, Iranian peoples, controlled the region in later years, and Mesopotamia's unique culture eventually disappeared.

Art, Architecture, and Literature. The Mesopotamians were a creative people. Figurines and statues of clay, gypsum, or bronze have been found by archaeologists. Palaces were decorated with relief sculptures or with molded bricks colored by glazes. Pottery was often painted in geometric designs.

The most distinctive kind of Mesopotamian architecture was the ziggurat. Ziggurats were pyramid-shaped towers built of baked clay bricks. These structures had as many as eight levels and were topped with a temple or shrine where rites were performed.

One of the world's first writing systems was developed in Sumer. Called cuneiform, its characters were formed with wedge-shaped lines, and the many examples found on clay and stone have revealed a rich literary tradition. Royal inscriptions on buildings include hymns, prayers, and blessings, as well as accounts of battles. Other examples contain myths about gods and the creation of the world and epics about heroic figures. See the article CUNEIFORM in Volume C.

JOHN BRINKMAN
The Oriental Institute

METABOLISM. See BODY CHEMISTRY.

METALS AND METALLURGY

Automobiles, airplanes, bicycles, and thousands of other items are made of metals in some form or another. The science of metals is called **metallurgy**. It is concerned with the characteristics of metals, the extraction, or removal, of metals from metal-bearing ores, the purification of metals, and the different ways metals can be used or shaped into products.

Basic Properties of Metals

Metals are chemical elements that cannot be broken down into other substances. All metals have physical characteristics, or properties, that make them different from other elements. Polished metals reflect light with a characteristic shine called metallic luster. Two of the physical properties of metals are **ductility** and **malleability**. Ductility is the ability of metals to be pulled or stretched into different shapes. Malleability is their ability to be hammered or squeezed. Another property of metals is the ability to conduct heat and electricity.

While all metals have certain physical properties, the amount of each property differs depending upon the type of metal. Gold, for example, is the most ductile and malleable metal. It can be hammered, squeezed, stretched, or pulled into sheets and wire that are thinner and finer than any other metal. Mercury is a metal with a very low melting point and it becomes liquid at room temperature. Tungsten has the highest melting point of any metal—over 6000°F (about 3300°C). The lightest metal, lithium, weighs about half as much as water. Osmium, the heaviest metal, is 22½ times heavier than water and 3 times heavier than iron.

In addition to their physical properties, metals also have certain chemical properties. Two of the most important are **oxidation** and **reduction**. **Oxidation** refers to the ability of metals to combine with oxygen or other nonmetals. **Reduction** is the ability of oxidized metals to be separated from nonmetals and be made pure again. A few metals, such as gold, platinum, silver, and sometimes copper, are found in the earth in a pure form. Most metals, however, are chemically combined with other elements. Chemical compounds found in nature are called **minerals**. Minerals that are valuable for the metals they contain are called **ores**. The properties of oxidation and reduction play an important role in removing metals from their ores and purifying them.

▶### EXTRACTING METAL FROM ORES

Various processes are used to extract pure metal from a metal-bearing ore. The most important ones are concentration, leaching, pyrometallurgy, and electrolysis.

Concentration. When first mined, metal-bearing ores usually contain large amounts of unwanted material, such as clay and stone. This material, called **gangue**, can be removed through a process called concentration. The first step in concentration is to crush the ore so that the gangue is no longer attached to the metal. The gangue and metal are then separated through one of several methods.

One method, known as **flotation**, is based on the fact that certain minerals can become attached to bubbles. The crushed ore is put into a tank of special liquid through which air is bubbled. Each bubble carries a small particle of the metallic part of the ore to the top of the tank. The gangue settles to the bottom.

Another method, **gravity concentration**, is based on the fact that the metallic part of some ores is heavier than the gangue. A current of air or water carries away the gangue, while the metallic part of the ore sinks. When prospectors panned for gold, they were using gravity concentration. By shaking a pan of ore in running water, they washed away the gangue, leaving the heavier particles of gold at the bottom of the pan. Today, large gravity concentration machines use the same principle.

Leaching. This method is often used with poorer quality ores. Ore is treated with a liquid that dissolves the mineral containing the metal, leaving the gangue behind. The metal is then removed chemically from the liquid and mineral mixture. **Amalgamation** is a method that uses mercury in the leaching process.

Pyrometallurgy. This process uses heat to extract metal from ores. There are several methods of pyrometallurgy. In **sintering**, heat is used to cause small particles of metal powder to stick together, forming large chunks that are easy to handle. In **roasting**, ore is heated in air, causing it to oxidize and change to a form that makes the metal easier to extract. In **smelting**, ore is heated in a furnace along with a reducing agent and a flux. The reducing agent is a substance that combines chemically with the nonmetal in the ore and separates it from the metal. The heat of the furnace melts the metal, which then runs off and is collected. The flux is a substance that combines with gangue and other unwanted material to form a waste known as slag, which is easily removed from the surface.

Electrolysis. Some metals, such as magnesium and aluminum, are very active chemically, and powerful methods are needed to separate them from their ores. The method commonly used is electrolysis, a process that uses electricity to separate chemical elements. In electrolysis, the ore must first be purified chemically and then melted. The pure metal is then obtained by running an electric current through the purified, melted ore.

▶ **REFINING METALS**

After a metal is removed from its ore, it must be refined, or purified. Even very small amounts of impurities in a metal can cause it to lose its strength or other properties. Three methods of refining metal are electrorefining, distillation, and pyrometallurgy.

Electrorefining. In this process, thin sheets of pure metal and large slabs of impure metal are submerged in a liquid chemical solution. An electric current is passed through the solution, causing pure metal to be removed from the slabs and deposited onto the thin metal sheets. Impurities fall to the bottom of the tank or are dissolved in the solution.

Distillation. Metals with fairly low boiling points, such as zinc, mercury, and magnesium, may be refined by distillation. In this process, the metal is heated and boiled off, leaving the impurities behind. The vapor is collected and cooled, forming the solid pure metal.

Pyrometallurgy. This process uses heat to burn away impurities. When metal is melted in the presence of air, impurities combine with oxygen and either boil off or combine with other substances to form slag, which is then easily removed.

▶ **SHAPING METALS**

A variety of ways have been developed to shape metals into finished products. Among these methods are forging, casting, extrusion, rolling, drawing, and powder metallurgy.

Forging. Forging—the beating or squeezing of metal into a desired shape—is one of the oldest forms of metalworking. In early

forging, a metal such as iron was first softened by heating it in a fire, then placed on a steel block called an anvil and slowly beaten into shape with a hammer. Modern **drop forging** uses the same principles, but the anvil is much larger and the hammer is replaced by a steel block called a ram, which may weigh several tons. A machine called a drop hammer lifts and drops the ram onto a heated piece of metal in order to shape it. By attaching dies—blocks of steel with shapes cut into them—to the ram and anvil, complicated shapes can be made. **Press forging** uses a hydraulic press. The ram in this press is attached to water-driven cylinders that exert tremendous pressure to squeeze the metal into shape.

Casting. When molten metal is poured into a mold and left to cool, it becomes solid and takes the shape of the mold. This process is called casting. In **sand casting**, the mold is made of special sand that holds together when liquid metal is poured into it. The first step in sand casting is to make a model of the object to be cast. The model is then put into a box and sand is packed around half of it, forming half of the mold. This process is repeated in another box to make the other half of the mold. The two halves of the mold are then clamped together and the liquid metal is poured in through holes in the mold. When the metal has solidified, the mold is opened and the cast object is removed. The surface of the object is then smoothed by machine to remove rough edges. **Die casting** uses metal molds called dies. In gravity die casting, the molten metal is simply poured into the mold as in sand casting. In pressure die casting, the molten metal is put into the mold under great pressure, filling it very quickly. This method can produce hundreds of copies of an object in a short time. In **centrifugal casting**, the mold is spun at high speed as the metal is poured into it. Centrifugal force throws the metal against the walls of the mold, leaving the center hollow. This method is often used for casting pipes and other hollow, tube-shaped objects.

Extrusion. Extrusion is a method of shaping metal that uses pressure to squeeze objects into a particular shape. In extrusion, a metal block is heated to make it softer. Then a ram forces the metal through an opening in a steel plate. The strip of metal that is extruded (forced out) can be made into many different shapes by changing the shape of the opening.

Rolling. Metal sheets are made by rolling molten metal blocks between heavy rollers. These rollers are slowly brought closer and closer together as the hot metal passes between them. This process is repeated until the metal reaches the desired thickness, which can range from thick plates of metal to very thin sheets called foil. Rollers with grooves cut into them are used to form shapes other than flat sheets, such as rails for railroad tracks.

Drawing. Drawing, or pulling, is a process used to make metal wire. In this process, molten metal rods are pulled through special dies that have small holes in them. One end of a metal rod is put into the die and is then gripped by a powerful tool and pulled through the

SOME IMPORTANT METALS

METAL	METAL-BEARING ORES	SPECIAL PROPERTIES	IMPORTANT USES
Aluminum	Bauxite	Lightweight	Cans, airplanes, cooking utensils, foil
Antimony	Stibnite	Hardens lead	Storage-battery plates, pewter
Chromium	Chromite	Resists oxidation and corrosion at high temperatures	Chrome plating, stainless steel
Cobalt	Nickel and copper ores	Resists corrosion at high temperatures	Jet aircraft, turbines, cutting-tool steel
Copper	Chalcocite, chalcopyrite	Second best conductor of heat and electricity; corrosion-resistant	Electrical wire, water pipes, brass, bronze
Gold	Native	Most malleable and ductile metal; corrosion-resistant	Jewelry, dental alloys
Iridium	Nickel and copper ores	Most corrosion-resistant metal	High-temperature equipment
Iron	Hematite, limonite, magnetite	Most useful metal; magnetic	Steel, iron castings
Lead	Galena	Low melting point; high density	Storage batteries, solder, ammunition
Magnesium	Seawater, magnesite	Lightest structural metal	Aircraft, tools
Manganese	Pyrolusite, cryptomelane	Neutralizes sulfur in steel; strengthens steel	Steel, aluminum alloys
Mercury	Cinnabar	Liquid at room temperature	Thermometers, vacuum pumps, electric switches
Molybdenum	Molybdenite, powellite	Toughens and strengthens steel; high melting point	Steel, X-ray tubes, solid lubricants
Nickel	Pentlandite, pyrrhotite	Corrosion-resistant; magnetic	Coins, stainless steel, noncorrosive equipment, electrical resistance wire
Platinum	Native, nickel and copper ores	Corrosion-resistant; catalyst	Jewelry, industrial chemical reactions
Silver	Argentite, lead ores	Best conductor of heat and electricity; malleable; light-sensitive	Coins, tableware, jewelry, photography
Tin	Cassiterite	Low melting point; corrosion-resistant	Solder, bronze, pewter
Titanium	Ilmenite, rutile	Lightweight and strong	Aircraft, gas-turbine engines
Tungsten	Wolframite, scheelite	Highest melting point of any metal; catalyst	Electric lamp filaments, tungsten carbide tools, industrial chemical reactions
Uranium	Pitchblende, carnotite	Radioactive	Nuclear fuel
Vanadium	Carnotite	Makes steel tougher and more elastic	Steel, titanium alloys
Zinc	Sphalerite, smithsonite	Corrosion-resistant	Galvanizing, brass, dry-cell batteries

hole. This process is repeated several times using smaller and smaller dies. Each time, the wire comes out longer and thinner.

Powder Metallurgy. In this process, the metal to be shaped is first ground to a fine powder. This powder is then poured into a die or a mold where it is compressed under high pressure and heated until the powders weld together into the desired shape. Powder metallurgy can also be used to mix certain nonmetals with metals. For example, graphite, which is an excellent lubricant, can be mixed with bronze to make self-lubricating bronze bearings. Diamond powder can be mixed with different metals to make grinding wheels.

▶ USES OF METALS

The special properties of some metals make them very important for certain uses. The high melting point of tungsten, for example, makes it very useful for electric lamp filaments or other items that must conduct or withstand high temperatures. Platinum is very resistant to chemicals, so it is very useful for making laboratory equipment.

There is usually more than one reason to use a particular metal. For example, silver is the best conductor of electricity, but it is expensive. Copper and aluminum are cheaper and are also good conductors of electricity, so they are usually used for electrical wiring.

A metal seldom has all the properties needed for a specific use. For this reason, metallurgists develop **alloys**—mixtures of metals —that are better suited to special purposes. In addition to creating alloys, metallurgists can change the properties of metals by treating them in special ways. For example, if a metal becomes hard and brittle after it has been worked, it can be softened and made malleable again by heating it until it is red-hot and then allowing it to cool. This is called **annealing**. Steel, an iron alloy, can be made harder and stronger by **quenching**—heating it red-hot and cooling it quickly by plunging it into water or oil. Quenched steel can be made softer and more ductile by **tempering**—heating it again, but not red-hot, and then allowing it to cool slowly.

▶ HISTORY OF METALLURGY

Copper and gold were probably the first metals people learned how to use. Scientists have determined that copper was used as long

ago as 5000 B.C. and gold was first used about 4000 B.C. Within another thousand years, silver and lead were also discovered, but copper was still used most often because it was the strongest and most plentiful metal known.

By about 3000 B.C., people had learned how to pound metal into useful shapes, such as tools and weapons, and they had discovered the processes of annealing, melting, casting, and smelting. They also had learned how to extract copper from copper ores. Actually, the metal they extracted was a kind of bronze, an alloy of copper and tin. After the discovery of tin, people learned how to mix copper and tin to produce better bronze alloys. During a period called the **Bronze Age**, from about 3500 B.C. to 1200 B.C., bronze was the most important metal in use.

Around 1900 B.C. some people learned how to work with iron. By about 1200 B.C., this knowledge had spread throughout the civilized world, and iron replaced bronze for most uses. This was the beginning of the **Iron Age**. Iron, in the form of steel, is still one of our most important metals.

By the time of the ancient Romans, seven metals—gold, copper, silver, lead, tin, iron, and mercury—were known, and ways of extracting and working these metals had been discovered. During the Middle Ages, the metals antimony and bismuth were discovered, as were other methods of metalworking.

During the 1700's at the time of the Industrial Revolution, great advances were made in metallurgy. One was the discovery of improved methods for making and working steel. Another was the invention of steam power, which led to the invention of machines that could work metal better and more efficiently. Many new metals were also discovered.

In recent years, advances in metallurgy have led to an increased use of metals and metal alloys. However, the work of metallurgists is by no means finished. There will be new uses for metals and a need for new and better alloys and metalworking processes to meet the challenges of the future.

JOHN MOORE
Department of Metallurgical and
Materials Engineering
Colorado School of Mines

See also ALLOYS; DIES AND MOLDS; MINERALS; MINES AND MINING; ORES; ROCKS; WIRE; articles on individual metals, such as ALUMINUM.

METAMORPHOSIS

The crawling caterpillar becomes a moth or a butterfly. The tadpole swimming in shallow water changes into a frog or a toad. Many other animals also undergo a change in form and appearance during the development from egg to adult. This change is called metamorphosis.

The word "metamorphosis" comes from a Greek word meaning "change of form." During the distinctive stages of metamorphosis, more than just the shape and appearance of an animal changes. So does its way of life. For example, the young creature that emerges from a starfish egg is much too small to live and feed in the same way as the adult starfish. The young starfish, or **larva**, swims near the surface of the sea, feeding on microscopic plants until it has grown to many times its original size. Then it sinks to the seafloor and remains there while it changes into a little crawling starfish. On the seafloor, it feeds on mussels, clams, and other shelled animals.

A monarch butterfly begins its metamorphosis as a small, tough-shelled egg (a). A hungry wormlike larva, called a caterpillar, hatches from the egg (b). When the caterpillar reaches full size, it becomes a pupa and forms a hard shell (c). Within the shell, pupal structures develop into those of an adult. The newly emerged adult (d) is ready for flight once its outer structures harden and its wings expand (e).

Most frogs start life in water as a fertilized egg covered by a protective jellylike substance (a). A tiny fishlike larva, called a tadpole, emerges from the egg (b). As its growth continues, the tadpole becomes more froglike—legs and lungs form, and internal systems develop to accommodate the habits of an adult frog, such as eating live animals (c). When the tadpole has become an adult frog, its metamorphosis is complete (d).

▶ COMPLETE METAMORPHOSIS

Metamorphosis is said to be complete when there is a clear distinction between the stages of development. Animals such as frogs and butterflies exhibit complete metamorphosis.

The Life Cycle of a Frog. A frog lives most of its life out of water as a four-legged hopping creature, but it lays its eggs in water. The larva that hatches from each egg must therefore be able to breathe in the water, as a fish does. It must also be able to take its food from the water. The frog larva, called a **tadpole**, has gills like a fish and swims by means of its long, thick tail. It feeds on water plants and grows to many times its original size. Small legs begin to grow. The tadpole's body thickens and begins to look more like that of a little frog.

When the tadpole reaches a certain size, metamorphosis takes place. Quite suddenly, during the course of a day or so, the legs grow larger and the tail starts to shrink. The gills stop working, and lungs, which have been developing inside the tadpole's body, begin to work.

At this time, unless the frog crawls out of the water, it will drown. It has changed from a fishlike animal that breathes underwater to an air-breathing land animal. It no longer eats plants. It feeds on worms and insects.

The Life Cycle of a Butterfly. Most insects undergo metamorphosis. Insects that fly are able to do so only when they are fully grown. Until then they must live and feed in a way different from that of the adult.

The greatest change in insects is seen in butterflies and moths. The small moth or butterfly egg usually hatches into a crawling larva, or caterpillar. The caterpillar feeds until it grows

From an egg deposited in a sticky mass beneath the water's surface (a), the young dragonfly nymph emerges (b). Although it has no wings, the thick-bodied nymph resembles the adult dragonfly. Through a series of molts (c), a process in which the skin is shed, the nymph gradually changes its form to that of an adult dragonfly. Still wingless, the nymph crawls out of the water. During its final molt, a winged adult emerges and pulls itself away from the nymphal skin (d). With crumpled wings expanded, the fully developed adult can now fly (e).

to a certain size. Then it spins a covering around itself called a cocoon, or it may burrow into the ground or hide behind loose bark. The caterpillar goes into a resting stage and is now called a **pupa**. Inside the skin of the pupa, a big change takes place. The larva gradually changes into an adult.

The butterfly or moth that emerges from the pupa is practically a new creature. The metamorphosis of butterflies and moths, with its four distinct forms, is more complete than that of any other animal group.

▶ INCOMPLETE METAMORPHOSIS

Primitive insects, such as dragonflies, undergo incomplete metamorphosis. While complete metamorphosis is a relatively quick transformation with distinct stages, incomplete metamorphosis involves a gradual transformation. When the young hatch from the eggs, they closely resemble the adult form. They go through a series of stages, looking progressively more like adults with each stage.

The Life Cycle of a Dragonfly. Dragonflies may take two to three years to develop from an egg to an adult. The young that emerges from the egg is called a **nymph**. The nymph lives underwater. It breathes in the same way that a fish does—by using gills. It also uses gills to help it move about in the water. Jets of water, ejected from the gills, propel the nymph about.

As the nymph grows, it gets too big for its tough external covering, or skin. In order for it to continue growing, it must shed its skin, a process called molting. Through a series of molts, the dragonfly nymph approaches adult size and structure.

Because the adult dragonfly lives out of the water, the final molt must take place above the water's surface. The mature nymph crawls up a stem and clings tightly. When the skin splits, the winged adult emerges. It crawls free of its nymphal skin and remains on the stem until its soft wings are stiff and fully expanded. Usually within two hours, it is ready to fly.

N. J. BERRILL
McGill University

METEOROLOGY. See WEATHER.

METEORS AND METEORITES. See COMETS, METEORITES, AND ASTEROIDS.

METRIC SYSTEM. See WEIGHTS AND MEASURES.

METROPOLITAN MUSEUM OF ART

The Metropolitan Museum of Art houses the largest collection of art in the United States. It was incorporated in 1870 by the state of New York. The incentive to establish the museum came from members of the Union League Club, who aroused interest in and support for a public art museum.

In 1880 the City of New York built a permanent home for the Metropolitan Museum on the Fifth Avenue side of Central Park. Though the city still contributes to the maintenance of the building, most of the museum's funds come from private contributions.

▶THE COLLECTIONS

Every year more than 4,000,000 people visit the Metropolitan Museum to see its widely varied collections. The exhibitions include works from every age—from prehistoric pottery to modern paintings—and of every type—from heavy armor to delicate lace. Among the masterpieces are paintings by Raphael, Rembrandt, Vermeer, and El Greco.

One of the outstanding attractions of the museum is its collection of Egyptian art. The exhibit includes the tomb of Perneb and a series of life-size statues of Queen Hapshetsut, dating from about 1500 B.C. The tomb of Perneb, built about 4,400 years ago, has been reconstructed so visitors may enter it. In 1968 the museum added the ancient Temple of Dendur to its collection. This was a gift of the Egyptian Government to the people of the United States for their role in moving ancient monuments away from the danger of flooding when the Aswan High Dam was being built.

Greek and Roman statues have been placed so that you may walk around them and see each one from every possible angle. A bedroom from Boscoreale is decorated with wall paintings that were perfectly preserved under ashes when Vesuvius erupted in A.D. 79. Vases from Greece, China, and Japan, displayed in glass cases, show an endless variety of design and color.

The large and exciting Equestrian Court on the first floor contains life-size figures of armored riders beneath a display of bright heraldic banners. Most of the armor is from the Middle Ages and the Renaissance.

Decorative art objects—including silver, porcelain, and textiles in all styles—are dis-

The Metropolitan Museum of Art's vast collection of Egyptian art is one of the largest in the world outside of Cairo. It is displayed in thirty-two galleries.

played in glass cases. Whole rooms from palaces and great houses have been reconstructed and furnished, to show changes in styles and tastes over a period of 500 years.

In addition to a fine collection of American painting and sculpture, the museum has an entire wing devoted to American decorative arts. Rooms from 17th-, 18th-, and 19th-century houses have been reconstructed with their original woodwork and filled with furniture, silver, glass, and paintings.

Another great attraction of the museum is the Costume Institute, a center for fashion designers. Its collections include clothing from all over the world, representing many styles and periods.

The museum's collection of Islamic art is one of the most comprehensive in the world. In new galleries opened in 1975, the visitor can view a complete survey of Islamic art, from architectural elements to paintings and manuscripts, carpets, ceramics, metalwork, glass, jewelry, and textiles.

The Crosby Brown Collection of Musical Instruments, which came as a gift in 1889, is one of the world's richest and most systematic collections of musical instruments. It forms the nucleus of the museum's musical holdings, which include some 800 instruments from Europe, Asia, the Middle East, Oceania, Africa, and the Americas.

The Michael C. Rockefeller Wing of the Metropolitan is designed to exhibit an unusually extensive collection of primitive art. The museum's holdings include the Michael C. Rockefeller collection, which was transferred to the Metropolitan in 1969, and the museum's collection of pre-Columbian art. These two collections consist of more than 7,500 objects from three separate cultural areas—Africa, Central and South America, and Oceania.

To complement the museum's collection of East Asian art, a reconstruction of a Ming dynasty courtyard was installed in 1981. Twenty-seven engineers and artisans from the People's Republic of China worked for many months to construct the peaceful garden setting.

▶**THE CLOISTERS**

Overlooking the Hudson River in Fort Tryon Park is the Cloisters—a branch of the Metropolitan Museum devoted to European art of the Middle Ages. The Cloisters looks like a medieval monastery. It is made up of sections from medieval buildings, consisting mainly of five cloisters and a Romanesque chapel. A cloister is a covered walk running around an open court and opening onto it. An entire 12th-century Spanish apse (a large projecting semicircular portion of a building, generally found at the eastern end of a church) was added to the building in 1961. In this authentic medieval setting, many fine examples of sculpture, frescoed walls, painted altarpieces, stained-glass windows, tapestries, and chalices from the 11th to the 15th century are exhibited. The site of the Cloisters, the building, and most of the collections were a gift to the people of New York from John D. Rockefeller, Jr. (1874–1960).

Reviewed by PHILIPPE DE MONTEBELLO
Director, Metropolitan Museum of Art

MEXICAN WAR

In 1846 the United States and Mexico went to war. One of the causes of the war was the annexation by the United States of the former Mexican province of Texas. Americans who had settled in Texas had revolted against Mexico, formed an independent republic, and asked that Texas become part of the United States.

Many Americans wanted to obtain more than just Texas. They sought to acquire, by purchase or conquest, other Mexican territories, including California. These Americans felt that it was necessary for the United States to expand westward. They believed that it was the "manifest destiny" of the United States to span the continent from the Atlantic to the Pacific and from the Canadian border south to the Rio Grande, the river that is now the boundary between the United States and Mexico. This desire for expansion also played a part in bringing about the war.

▶**EVENTS LEADING UP TO THE WAR**

The years before the war were difficult times for Mexico. Revolutions and changes of government kept the nation in turmoil. Unable to develop the territories of Texas and California, Mexico at first welcomed American settlers there. Later the Mexican Government began to fear the growing power and independence of the settlers, especially in Texas, and passed strict laws to control them. The Texans rebelled and in 1836 declared their independence. Texas then applied to the United States for annexation and statehood.

There was much opposition in the United States to Texas' request. Mexico had threatened war if the United States took over Texas. In addition, Texas would enter the Union as a slave-owning state, and this was unacceptable to the free states, who opposed the expansion of slavery. It was not until 1845 that the United States agreed to annex Texas. Mexico then broke diplomatic relations. Mexico did not declare war, but other disputes arose. The United States claimed the Rio Grande as part of Texas' border. Mexico insisted that the boundary was the Nueces River. There was also a disputed claim by U.S. citizens against Mexico for $3,000,000 for loss of property.

United States President James K. Polk sent a minister, John Slidell, to Mexico. Slidell was to offer to cancel the American money claims and to pay Mexico from $25,000,000 to $40,000,000 if it would accept the Rio Grande boundary and sell California and the New Mexico territory to the United States. However, the Mexican Government refused to receive Slidell.

▶ **OUTBREAK OF WAR**

President Polk then ordered U.S. forces in Texas to advance to the Rio Grande. On April 25, 1846, Mexican troops crossed the Rio Grande and attacked U.S. troops in the disputed area. On May 11, 1846, Polk asked Congress for a declaration of war. On May 13, Congress declared that "by the act of …Mexico" a state of war existed.

The commander of the U.S. forces in Texas was General Zachary Taylor, who was nicknamed Old Rough and Ready. His victories in the Mexican War later helped him win election as president of the United States. Even before war was formally declared, Taylor had defeated Mexican armies at Palo Alto and Resaca de la Palma. Now, Taylor's men advanced well into Mexico. On September 24, 1846, after a long, hard-fought battle, they captured the fortified city of Monterrey.

California and New Mexico. Meanwhile the war had spread westward. In June 1846, American settlers in California rebelled against Mexican rule. An expedition under General Stephen W. Kearny occupied Santa Fe, taking control of New Mexico, and then marched on to California. United States naval forces played an important part in the war in California by lending support to Kearny's troops. The conquest of California was completed in early 1847 with the defeat of Mexican forces near Los Angeles.

In February 1847, U.S. troops under Colonel Alexander W. Doniphan, marching from Santa Fe, occupied the Mexican city of Chihuahua after heavy fighting.

Buena Vista. At about the same time, General Taylor was advancing on the city of Buena Vista. The Americans and Mexicans clashed in a desperate, hard-fought battle. The advantage swung first to one side, then to the other. As Captain Braxton B. Bragg (a future Confederate general in the U.S. Civil War) brought his artillery into action, Taylor ordered him to "Double-shot your guns and give 'em hell!" When the sounds of battle died away, the Mexicans were in retreat.

Veracruz. Rather than continue the long advance from the north, the United States decided to strike at the heart of Mexico. On March 9, 1847, a seaborne expedition under General Winfield Scott landed near Veracruz on the coast of the Gulf of Mexico. Scott, the highest-ranking general in the U.S. Army, was known for his strict discipline and handsome uniforms. Artillery commanded by Captain Robert E. Lee (who as a general would command Confederate forces in the Civil War) opened the battle. The shelling forced the surrender of Veracruz. The Americans swept on, winning the battles of Cerro Gordo, Contreras, and Churubusco.

Mexico City. Finally, Mexico City, the capital, loomed before the Americans. Above the city stood the Castle of Chapultepec. The battle for Mexico City brought heavy losses on both sides. Second Lieutenant Ulysses S. Grant (later commander of all Union forces in the Civil War) had a cannon hoisted into a church tower, where his gun raked Mexican soldiers in the streets below.

On September 13, 1847, the Americans stormed the Castle of Chapultepec, all that stood between them and victory. It was defended by a small group of soldiers and about 100 young cadets of the Mexican military academy. The cadets, some as young as 14, were known as *los niños* ("the boys"). They fought bravely but were unable to prevent the capture of the castle.

The Peace Treaty. With the fall of Mexico City, the war was practically over. But a treaty of peace remained to be signed. The treaty was signed on February 2, 1848, at the town of Guadalupe Hidalgo. The Treaty of Guadalupe Hidalgo went into effect on July 4, 1848. It established the Rio Grande as the boundary of Texas. Mexico ceded to the United States all of present-day California, Utah, and Nevada, and most of what is now Arizona and New Mexico. In return, the United States paid Mexico $15,000,000, and Mexican debts to American citizens were cancelled.

FAIRFAX DOWNEY
Author, *Texas and the War with Mexico*

See also MEXICO; POLK, JAMES K.; TAYLOR, ZACHARY; TERRITORIAL EXPANSION OF THE UNITED STATES.

MEXICO

Mexico is the northernmost country of Latin America, which includes the mainly Spanish- and Portuguese-speaking countries of the Western Hemisphere. It is located in North America, between the United States on the north and Guatemala and Belize on the south. To its West is the Pacific Ocean and to its east, the Gulf of Mexico and the Caribbean Sea.

A land of sharp contrasts, Mexico has snowcapped mountains, broad plateaus, lush tropical rain forests, and parched deserts. It is almost three times larger than the U.S. state of Texas and, with over 100 million people, is the third most populous country in the hemisphere, after the United States and Brazil.

Mexico is rich in natural resources, such as oil, and in attractions that lure some 20 million visitors each year. But its real wealth lies in its people, whose achievements span thousands of years—from building monumental cities before the birth of Christ, to creating a trillion-dollar economy in the 21st century.

Home to some of the most advanced ancient civilizations in Latin America, Mexico became a colony of Spain in the early 1500's and remained so until achieving independence in 1810.

Violent political struggles dominated the country in the 1800's but subsided not long after the Mexican Revolution (1910–17). For most of the 1900's, from 1929 until 2000, one political party, the Institutional Revolutionary Party (PRI), ruled Mexico. In 2000, demanding a greater say in their government and other reforms, Mexicans ended 71 years of PRI presidential rule by choosing a president from the opposition National Action Party (PAN).

▶ PEOPLE

Most Mexicans (60 percent) are mestizos—that is, of mixed Indian and European (mainly Spanish) ancestry. Thirty percent are of Indian ancestry. People of largely European ancestry make up the remainder.

Language. Spanish is the official language. In fact, Mexico is home to the largest number of Spanish-speaking people in the world. Some 8 percent of Mexicans also speak native Indian languages—chiefly Nahuatl, Mayan, Mixteco, and Zapoteco.

Religion. Freedom of worship is guaranteed under Mexico's constitution. Some 89 percent of Mexicans are Roman Catholics; another 6 percent are Protestant.

Education. The federal government determines what is taught in schools. The law requires six years of primary education for all children, followed by three years of secondary school. Qualified students may attend upper secondary schools to prepare to enter a university or to be trained for technical or commercial jobs.

Education at state-run schools is free from primary grades through the university level. There are also private and parochial schools in large cities. Over 92 percent of Mexicans age 15 and older can read and write.

Mexico has hundreds of institutions of higher learning. The largest is the National Autonomous University of Mexico, or UNAM as it is popularly known. It is located in Mexico City and has about 270,000 students. Founded in 1551, UNAM is the oldest university in North America.

Museums. Mexico's museums testify to the country's rich cultural and artistic heritage. Mexico City is home to some of Mexico's best-known museums, including the Papalote Museo del Niño, a museum designed for children, and the world-class National Anthropology Museum, which displays thousands of archaeological pieces from Mexico's past. In the city of Monterrey, artifacts ranging from ancient to modern times are housed in the beautifully designed Museum of Mexican History.

Food and Drink. Mexico's cuisine is very diverse, with different regions serving their own specialties. *Mole poblano de pollo*, chicken with a chocolate and almond sauce, is popular in the state of Puebla. In the Yucatán, chicken wrapped in banana leaves, or *pollo pibil*, is a favorite. Also popular are roast goat, sun-dried beef, fish stews, shrimp, and mussels. Staples include tortillas, which are flat, thin corn or wheat cakes; rice; beans; chili peppers; and tomatoes.

Cactus and maguey plants provide both food and drink. One variety of cacti produces tender shoots for salads. Another type provides the prickly pear used in desserts and preserves. The maguey is a source of two kinds of alcoholic drink—the fiery tequila and the milder, milk-colored pulque.

National Holidays. Each year, on the Day of the Dead, November 2, Mexicans remember and pay respect to their dead. They visit cemeteries and pray, sing, and eat foods favored by loved ones who have died. On December 12, pilgrims make their way to Mexico City's shrine of the Virgin of Guadalupe, the country's patron saint.

The Christmas season extends from December 16 through January 6. Each day through December 24, Christmas Eve,

There are many faces of Mexico, reflecting its rich and diverse heritage. Most Mexicans are of mixed Indian and European (mostly Spanish) ancestry. About a third of the people are of Indian ancestry.

FACTS and figures

UNITED MEXICAN STATES (Estados Unidos Mexicanos) is the official name of the country.

LOCATION: North America.

AREA: 761,600 sq mi (1,972,550 km²).

POPULATION: 106 million (estimate).

CAPITAL AND LARGEST CITY: Mexico City.

MAJOR LANGUAGES: Spanish (official); Maya, Nahuatl, and other Indian languages.

MAJOR RELIGIOUS GROUPS: Roman Catholic, Protestant.

GOVERNMENT: Federal Republic. **Head of state and government**—president. **Legislature**—National Congress (made up of the Senate and the Federal Chamber of Deputies).

CHIEF PRODUCTS: Agricultural—corn, wheat, soybeans, rice, beans, cotton, coffee, fruit, tomatoes; beef, poultry, dairy products; lumber. **Manufactured**—food and beverages, tobacco, chemicals, iron and steel, textiles, clothing, motor vehicles. **Mineral**—petroleum and natural gas, silver, copper, manganese, zinc, lead, iron ore, sulfur, gold.

MONETARY UNIT: Peso (1 peso = 100 centavos).

families re-enact Mary and Joseph's journey to Bethlehem with special prayers and songs. Children play a game to receive their holiday treats. A *piñata*, a brightly colored toy, is suspended over the head of a blindfolded child, who tries to break it with a stick. Once the *piñata* breaks, the children share the candies, fruits, and coins that pour out of it. December 25, Christ-

mas Day, is a national holiday. On January 6, children receive their Christmas presents from the Three Kings, referring to the legend of the Three Wise Men who gave gifts to the baby Jesus.

Mexico also has a number of civic holidays. The most important is September 16, on which Mexicans celebrate their country's independence from Spain. On the night of the 15th, the Mexican president comes out on the balcony of the National Palace in Mexico City, rings a bell that is symbolic of Mexico's independence, and shouts "*¡Mexicanos, que Viva México!*" ("Mexicans, long live Mexico!"). Thousands of Mexicans gathered in the Zócalo, or Main Square, answer "¡Viva!" The ceremony is followed by fireworks and music and is re-enacted in cities all over Mexico.

Another holiday, Cinco de Mayo (the fifth of May), honors the Mexican victory over the French army in the city of Puebla de los Angeles in 1862. Once a regional holiday, Cinco de Mayo is now a popular celebration along the U.S.-Mexican border and in areas of the United States where Mexicans live. On Revolution Day, November 20, Mexicans observe the anniversary of their 1910 Revolution.

Sports and recreation. Soccer is very popular in Mexico, as is baseball. Fans also go to see bullfighting, which is considered more of a spectacle and art than a sport. Mexicans also enjoy jai alai, a kind of fast handball that originated in Spain.

▶ LAND

The north of Mexico consists mainly of flatlands and hills. In the south are sierras, canyons, and ravines. The east has mountains and volcanoes, and the west, plains, hills and sierras. In the central area, hills surround plains and valleys.

The Mexican Plateau. The Mexican Plateau (also known as the Central Plateau) is Mexico's most extensive geographical feature. It contains most of Mexico's population and many of its important cities. It also accounts for the

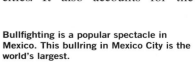

Bullfighting is a popular spectacle in Mexico. This bullring in Mexico City is the world's largest.

largest share of the country's agricultural output, industry, and mineral wealth.

The northern part of the plateau is dry, requiring irrigation for farming, and much of it is sparsely populated. The plateau rises as one moves southward, toward central Mexico. This is the heartland of the country. It is well watered, has fertile soil, and is densely populated.

Mountain Ranges. High, rugged mountain ranges border the Mexican Plateau. On the west is the Sierra Madre Occidental, which has a number of spectacular volcanoes. A second range, the Sierra Madre Oriental, lies along the eastern edge of the plateau and joins with the Sierra Madre Occidental near Mexico City. At their juncture stands the country's highest peak—the snowcapped volcano of Orizaba (or Citlaltépetl), which rises 18,700 feet (5,700 meters).

South of Mexico City is the Sierra Madre del Sur, whose mountains lie along the Pacific Ocean. Other Pacific highland regions are the Southern Uplands and the Chiapas Highlands, which extend to Guatemala.

Coastal Plains and Lowlands. The Pacific Coastal Plain extends from the U.S. border to Cape Corrientes, about halfway down the western coast of Mexico, and includes the long, narrow peninsula of Baja California (Lower California). The Gulf Coastal Plain, bordering the Gulf of Mexico, and the Yucatán Peninsula in the southeast are the most extensive lowland areas. The Yucatán is especially notable for its ancient Maya temples.

Rivers, Lakes, and Coastal Waters. On its north, Mexico shares a 1,900-mile (3,100-kilometer) border with the United States. Along part of this border runs Mexico's most famous river, the Río Bravo del Norte (called the Río Grande in the United States). Other major rivers include the Río Balsas, which flows into the Pacific; the Río Grijalva and Río Usumacinta, which flow into the Bay of Campeche; and the Río Pánuco, which flows into the Gulf of Mexico. Lake Chapala in Jalisco and Michoacán states is the largest lake in Mexico. Mexico is known for its beaches, with major tourist resorts located on its east and west coasts.

Climate. Mexico's climate generally varies from tropical and wet to temperate and dry, depending on region and elevation. The coastal plains are hot and humid, with heavy rainfall. The north is dry, with extremes of temperature, while the region around Mexico City has a pleasant, temperate climate. Temperatures usually fall as elevation increases. Most of Mexico receives inadequate rainfall, except for the coastal areas and parts of the central region.

Natural Resources. Because of its generally dry climate, Mexico has only limited land suitable for farming. It has a wealth of mineral resources, however. It ranks fifth in the world in oil production and is the world's leading exporter of silver. It also has large deposits of copper, manganese, zinc, and lead.

Forests cover nearly one-quarter of the land. The government has established reserves but Mexico's forests remain threatened by overlogging and the clearing of land for farming.

There is a wide variety of animal life. Wolves, bears, coyotes, foxes, and deer are found in the cooler north and mountainous areas, while tropical Mexico is home to jaguars, ocelots, tapirs, monkeys, and colorful parrots, macaws, and other birds. The burro (a

Mexico's landscape ranges from parched deserts to tropical rain forests. At left, dotted with cactus, is the Central Desert of Baja California in the north; below, the rain forests lying along the Agua Azul River in Chiapas, in the south.

small donkey) is sometimes used as a pack animal in rural areas. The waters of the Pacific coast and the Gulf of Mexico abound in fish and shellfish.

▶ **ECONOMY**

Before 1940, Mexico was much as it had been for generations. There were few roads that could be used year-round, and most of its people worked in agriculture. They no longer do so. Today, most Mexicans work in service industries, such as tourism, or in manufacturing. The land is now farmed largely by big agricultural companies. Modern transportation and communication systems make the country an attractive place for investors from other countries.

The oil and gas industry is an important source of income. Although the industry is owned by the government, some foreign investment is allowed and more may be permitted in the future to raise the production and export of oil. The added income could provide Mexico with the funds it needs to pay for education, health, and other services for its people.

Mexico is relatively wealthy and industrialized compared with many other developing countries. However, its wealth is very unevenly distributed among its people. The richest 10 percent of Mexicans receive 60 percent of the country's income, while the poorest 30 percent receive a little over 4 percent of it. At present, over 40 percent of Mexico's people are poor, meaning they do not have enough money to pay for the food, health services, education, and other goods and services they need. Poverty is worse in the countryside, where some 30 percent of Mexican families do not have enough to eat, compared to close to 10 percent in the cities.

Many Mexicans leave their country, at least temporarily, to work—often illegally—in the United States. The money these workers send to their families in Mexico is an important source of income for the country. Negotiations to make these migrations legal are a major element of Mexican-U.S. relations.

Services. Tourism and other service industries dominate Mexico's economy, employing nearly 60 percent of Mexico's workers and contributing nearly 70 percent to the domestic economy. Tourism is Mexico's largest source of income from other countries. Over 20 million tourists visited Mexico in 2004.

Manufacturing and Mining. Manufacturing and mining employ just over one-quarter of Mexico's workers and contribute about one-quarter to the domestic economy. Major industries include those producing food and beverages, tobacco, chemicals, iron and steel, petroleum, textiles, clothing, and motor vehicles. Mexico's mines produce silver, copper, manganese, zinc, lead, and other minerals.

Agriculture, Fishing, and Forestry. Although 18 percent of Mexico's workers are employed

The lavish tourist hotels in Acapulco (*left*) contrast with a shantytown (*below*) in Mexico City, often home to recent arrivals from rural areas.

in agriculture, the sector contributes less than 4 percent to the domestic economy. In central and southern Mexico, farmers grow food crops of corn and beans on small plots of land. In contrast, in the north, large, modern irrigated farms produce specialty fruits and vegetables (especially strawberries, melons, cucumbers, and tomatoes). Cotton and coffee are also major commercial crops.

Mexico's fishing industry centers on shrimp and other shellfish, sardines, tuna, and pompano. The forestry industry produces lumber cut from mahogany and other tropical hardwoods, pine, and oak.

Energy. Hydroelectric power accounts for nearly one-quarter of Mexico's energy capacity and steam plants burning fuel oil and natural gas make up the remainder. Mexico is a major producer and exporter of oil. The state-owned oil company, Petróleos Mexicanos, known as PEMEX, provides the government with billions of dollars in tax revenue and export income each year.

Trade. Mexico's main trading partner is the United States, which buys about 90 percent of its exports each year. Mexico's main exports to the United States are oil (over 1.5 million barrels a day), manufactured goods, and fruits and vegetables. Mexico has trade agreements with many countries. The most important is the North American Free Trade Agreement, or NAFTA, which encourages trade among Canada, Mexico, and the United States. Since NAFTA went into force in 1994, Mexico has increased its trade with the United States and Canada. Mexico has been a member of the World Trade Organization

(WTO) since the group was created in 1995. (The WTO is an international organization used by countries to facilitate and regulate their trade.)

Transportation. For transporting people and goods, Mexico offers extensive bus, rail, and highway systems; deepwater ports; and over 200 airports with paved runways.

Communication. Telephone service is adequate for business and government; however, most Mexicans tend to use mobile telephones rather than landlines. There are also an estimated 10 million Internet users.

▶ **MAJOR CITIES**

Most Mexicans lived in rural areas until the 1950's, when many moved to the cities. By 2003, about 75 percent lived in cities. Nine Mexican cities have more than 1 million people. In descending order by population, they are Mexico City, Guadalajara, Ecatepec de Morelos, Puebla, Nezahualcóyotl, Ciudad Juárez, Tijuana, Monterrey, and León.

Mexico City is Mexico's capital and largest city. Over 8 million people live in Mexico City proper and more than 17 million in its metropolitan area. See the article on Mexico City following this article. To the northwest of Mexico City is **Guadalajara**, Mexico's second largest city and the capital of Jalisco state. It is a major industrial and commercial city and a popular tourist center.

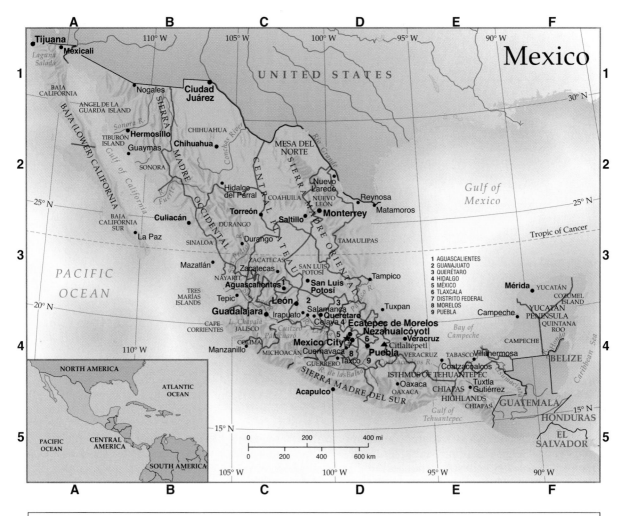

Mexico

A B C D E F

UNITED STATES

Tijuana
Mexicali
Laguna Salada
BAJA CALIFORNIA
Nogales
Ciudad Juárez
ANGEL DE LA GUARDA ISLAND
Sonora R.
SIERRA MADRE OCCIDENTAL
TIBURON ISLAND
Hermosillo
Chihuahua
CHIHUAHUA
MESA DEL NORTE
SONORA
Guaymas
Gulf of California
Fuerte R.
Hidalgo del Parral
Conchas River
Rio Grande
Nuevo Laredo
NUEVO LEÓN
Reynosa
Matamoros
BAJA (LOWER) CALIFORNIA
Culiacán
Torreón
COAHUILA
Saltillo
Monterrey
BAJA CALIFORNIA SUR
La Paz
DURANGO
Durango
SINALOA
TAMAULIPAS
Verde R.
ZACATECAS
SAN LUIS POTOSÍ
SIERRA MADRE ORIENTAL
CENTRAL PLATEAU
Mazatlán
Zacatecas
NAYARIT
Aguascalientes
Tampico
TRES MARÍAS ISLANDS
Tepic
León
San Luis Potosí
Pánuco R.
Tuxpan
Guadalajara
Irapuato
Salamanca
Querétaro
Celaya
Ecatepec de Morelos
Nezahualcóyotl
Veracruz
JALISCO
L. Chapala
Cuitzeo
Pátzcuaro
Mexico City
Citlaltépetl
CAPE CORRIENTES
COLIMA
Manzanillo
MICHOACÁN
Cuernavaca
Puebla
VERACRUZ
TABASCO
Villahermosa
GUERRERO
Taxco
Balsas R.
Coatzacoalcos
SIERRA MADRE DEL SUR
R. de las Balsas
ISTHMUS OF TEHUANTEPEC
Oaxaca
Tuxtla Gutiérrez
CHIAPAS
Acapulco
OAXACA
CHIAPAS HIGHLANDS
GUATEMALA
HONDURAS
EL SALVADOR
Gulf of Tehuantepec
PACIFIC OCEAN
Bay of Campeche
Mérida
YUCATÁN
COZUMEL ISLAND
YUCATÁN PENINSULA
Campeche
QUINTANA ROO
CAMPECHE
Hondo R.
BELIZE
Caribbean Sea
Gulf of Mexico

1 AGUASCALIENTES
2 GUANAJUATO
3 QUERÉTARO
4 HIDALGO
5 MÉXICO
6 TLAXCALA
7 DISTRITO FEDERAL
8 MORELOS
9 PUEBLA

110° W 105° W 100° W 95° W 90° W
30° N
25° N
Tropic of Cancer
20° N
15° N

0   200   400 mi
0   200   400   600 km
105° W   100° W   95° W   90° W

A B C D E F

Inset

NORTH AMERICA
ATLANTIC OCEAN
PACIFIC OCEAN
CENTRAL AMERICA
SOUTH AMERICA

INDEX TO MEXICO POLITICAL MAP

★ State Capital   States in parentheses   ⊛ National Capital

PEMEX, the state oil company, is a major source of revenue for the government. This PEMEX worker (left) is adjusting a pipeline at a refinery in the state of Chiapas.

A large portion of Mexico's manufacturing is concentrated in the central region of the country in the state of Mexico. Many industrial workers in the state of Mexico live in **Nezahualcóyotl**. The state is also home to the commercial city of **Ecatepec de Morelos**. To the north of Mexico City is the industrial city of **León**, the center of the country's shoe production. To Mexico City's south is **Puebla**, the capital of Puebla state. Once known primarily for its textiles and pottery, Puebla now also produces automobiles.

In the northern state of Nuevo León lies the city of **Monterrey**, the state's capital and another important center of industry. Also in the north is **Ciudad Juárez**, which lies on the Río Grande, and **Tijuana**, in northern Baja California. Both are commercial cities with large tourist industries. **Acapulco**, a famous resort city, lies on the Pacific coast of southern Mexico. **Veracruz** is Mexico's chief port on the Gulf of Mexico.

▶ CULTURAL HERITAGE

Art and Music. Mexico is internationally recognized for its contribution to the arts. Many of its famous painters and architects have been inspired by the country's past. Among them are painters Diego Rivera and José Clemente Orozco, who painted murals in public places so that all Mexicans could see them. Other artists include painters David Alfaro Siqueiros, Rufino Tamayo, and Frida Kahlo, as well as architects Juan O'Gorman and Luís Barragán. The composer Carlos Chávez frequently utilized Mexican folk elements in his work.

Literature. Mexican writers include the critic, poet, and scholar Alfonso Reyes, the writer and scholar Carlos Fuentes, and the poet Octavio Paz, winner of the Nobel Prize for literature in 1990.

For more information on the arts in Mexico see LATIN AMERICA, ART AND ARCHITECTURE OF; LATIN AMERICA, LITERATURE OF; and LATIN AMERICA, MUSIC OF in Volume L.

Film. Mexico has a large motion-picture industry. Its most famous directors include the Spanish-born Luis Buñuel, Emilio Fernández, and Alfonso Arau Incháustegui, whose film *Like Water for Chocolate* (1992) was popular in Mexico as well as outside the country.

▶ GOVERNMENT

Mexico is a federal republic composed of 31 states and the Federal District of Mexico City. The government is based on the Constitution of 1917. The head of state and government is the president, who is elected for a single 6-year term. The legislative body is the Congress, made up of the Senate, whose members are elected for six years, and the Chamber of Deputies, which is elected for three years. The third branch of government is the judiciary, or court system. The federal judiciary is headed by the Supreme Court. Each Supreme Court justice is appointed by the Senate from among three names presented by the president.

Each state government has its own elected governor and legislature. The state governments have authority over local matters.

▶ HISTORY

Mexico is an ancient land that had seen the rise and fall of great Indian empires long before the arrival of the Europeans. The Olmec were the first, followed by the Maya, Toltec, Zapotec, and Mixtec. The Indian civilizations made important breakthroughs in agriculture and science. They built great cities and created remarkable works of art. At the time of the Spanish conquest, the most powerful Indian empire was that of the Aztecs.

See the article on the Aztecs in Volume A and the one on the Maya in this volume. Also see the appropriate sections in the article INDIANS, AMERICAN in Volume I.

The Spanish Conquest. The first Spaniards to reach Mexico landed on the coast of Yucatán in 1517 but were soon expelled. In 1518 a second expedition explored part of the coast of the Gulf of Mexico. This time Indians and Spaniards exchanged gifts. A third expedition, led by Hernando Cortés, landed on the Gulf coast in 1519 and founded the city of Veracruz. From this point, within less than three years, Cortés conquered the country.

Several factors helped Cortés. His army, which had fewer than 600 men, was disciplined and equipped with some horses and a few cannons. The Indians had never seen either horses or cannons. Cortés also had military support from Indians who opposed the Aztecs. In addition, many Aztecs were killed by an epidemic of smallpox, a disease new to them, brought by the Spaniards. There is also a legend that the Aztec emperor Montezuma II welcomed Cortés because he believed he was the Indian god Quetzalcóatl. In 1521, the Aztec capital Tenochtitlán (the site of present-day Mexico City) fell to the Spaniards, and the rest of Mexico followed soon after. See the article on Hernando Cortés in Volume C. An article on Montezuma appears in this volume.

The Colonial Period. For 300 years, Mexico, then known as New Spain, was ruled as a Spanish colony. The colony's wealth lay in its silver mines and agriculture. The Indians taught the Spanish how to cultivate corn, tomatoes, and cacao (from which chocolate is made), crops that were unknown in Europe. In turn, the Spanish introduced sugarcane, wheat and rice, and large-scale cattle and sheep raising.

But only a relative few enjoyed the colony's prosperity. The ruling minority consisted of colonists born in Spain. They owned the large estates, controlled all important government posts, and dominated business. The *criollos*, or Spaniards born in the colony, were next in importance. Although often wealthy, they were allowed only minor government offices. Next came the mestizos, who often worked as supervisors or storekeepers or served as soldiers or priests. Indians were at the bottom of the social scale. They labored in the mines or on the large estates under conditions of virtual slavery.

Wars of Independence. In 1808, the French emperor Napoleon I invaded Spain and placed his brother Joseph on the throne. The resulting conflict sparked the Mexican independence movement, whose first leader was a priest, Miguel Hidalgo y Costilla.

On September 16, 1810, Hidalgo summoned his parishioners to revolt. His army, composed mainly of mestizos and Indians, grew rapidly and won several victories, but it was defeated by troops loyal to Spain in 1811. Hidalgo was captured and executed.

Another priest, José María Morelos y Pavón, Hidalgo's former student, kept the struggle alive. After two years of fighting and several victories, in 1813, Morelos called together a congress, which declared Mexico's independence and drafted a constitution.

But Morelos was defeated in battle soon after. In 1815 he, too, was executed, and leadership of the movement passed to Vicente Guerrero. The final victory was achieved after an officer loyal to Spain, Colonel Agustín de Iturbide, switched sides. Eventually, Spain was forced to sign the Treaty of Córdoba in 1821, acknowledging Mexico's independence.

The Struggle to Build a Nation. Although independent, Mexico as yet had no real government. Iturbide seized power in 1822, declaring himself emperor. Once again Guerrero rose to fight him, along with Antonio López de Santa Anna, an army offi-

A Maya-Toltec temple and sculpture at Chichén Itzá reflect the past glories of Mexico's great Indian civilizations.

cer. Their successful revolt overthrew Iturbide, and in 1824 Mexico became a republic. For a short period, the country enjoyed constitutional rule under Guadalupe Victoria, its first president, and Guerrero, its second.

Mexico's progress to nationhood, however, was slow and difficult. Conflicts between conservatives and liberals weakened and divided the country. The conservatives supported a strong national government and sought to maintain their traditional privileges. The liberals wanted decentralized rule, much less church influence, and broad social reforms.

The Era of Santa Anna. Elected president in 1832, Santa Anna dominated Mexico for more than 20 years. It was a time of political turmoil, with a succession of governments. Foreign wars also sapped the country's strength. A dispute with France over Mexican debts brought French troops to Veracruz in 1838. The French were repulsed, but in a war with the United States (1846–48), Mexico lost nearly half its territory. See the article on the Mexican War in this volume.

War of the Reform: Juárez. The liberals forced Santa Anna to flee Mexico in 1855 and then began the work of leading the country out of chaos. Among their leaders was Benito Juárez, a Zapotec Indian, who became one of Mexico's greatest statesmen. Juárez played a leading role in framing the Constitution of 1857, which limited the power of the

army and the church, recognized civil marriage, and called for freedom of religion, press, and assembly.

Conservatives violently opposed the constitution, and Mexico was plunged into a civil war known as the War of the Reform (1857–61). With a liberal victory in 1861, Juárez became provisional president. But the conflict had bankrupted the country. When Juárez suspended payment on debts owed to France, Spain, and Britain, troops of the three countries occupied Veracruz.

The French Monarchy. The British and Spanish soon departed, but France's emperor Napoleon III, urged on by the conservatives, seized the opportunity to establish a monarchy in Mexico. French troops invaded in 1862 and captured Mexico City the following year. Juárez' government, forced to flee the capital, began a campaign of guerrilla warfare. Meanwhile, Napoleon III and the conservatives had chosen Ferdinand Maximilian, archduke of Austria, as emperor of Mexico. Maximilian arrived in 1864 with his wife, the empress Carlota, to assume the throne.

Maximilian was a weak ruler. Because he accepted liberal reforms that cost the church

Hernando Cortés (*left*), here being received by the Aztec emperor Montezuma II, conquered Mexico in 1521, beginning 300 years of rule by Spain. The first, unsuccessful, revolt against Spanish rule was led by a priest, Father Hidalgo y Costilla (*above*), who called on his parishioners to rise in 1810. Mexico achieved independence in 1821.

much of its land, he lost the support of church and conservative political leaders. Napoleon III, under pressure from the United States, withdrew the French troops in 1866, leaving Maximilian isolated in the nation he supposedly ruled. In 1867, he was captured by Benito Juárez' troops and executed.

The Republic Restored. Once again free to govern as president, Juárez laid the foundation for Mexico's industry as well as its transportation and communications systems. Most important, he introduced free public education that reached out to the great mass of Indians and mestizos who could neither read nor write. He died in office in 1872. See the article on Benito Juárez in Volume JK.

The Long Rule of Porfirio Díaz. General Porfirio Díaz seized power in 1876 and served several terms as president. Known as Don Porfirio, he ruled Mexico with an iron hand for nearly 35 years. He brought stability to the country, built railroads, improved harbors, and promoted agriculture. He also established the country's oil industry, promoted good relations with other countries, and encouraged foreign investment in Mexico.

At the same time, under Díaz, conservative groups—the church, the aristocracy, and the army—regained many of their old privileges. The Indians had less land than ever, city and rural workers were impoverished, and political opposition was suppressed.

The Revolution of 1910. Díaz' dictatorial rule brought about a revolution in 1910. Pancho Villa, a former bandit and guerrilla fighter, led the uprising in the north. In the south, Emiliano Zapata, a tough peasant leader, took up the cause of the landless Indians. Díaz was forced to resign, and Francisco I. Madero, the liberal son of a wealthy landowner and a champion of political reform, was elected president in 1911.

In the years that followed, Mexico was torn by almost continuous violence in the struggle among rival revolutionary leaders. Victoriano Huerta, a general supported by the conservatives, had Madero assassinated in 1913 and seized power. Villa and Zapata rebelled against Huerta, as did Venustiano Carranza, the governor of Coahuila state. Huerta was deposed and Carranza became president in 1914.

By 1915, however, Carranza was at war with both Villa and Zapata, who opposed the slow pace of land reform. U.S. president Woodrow Wilson twice intervened on behalf of Carranza. He had ordered U.S. troops to invade Veracruz in 1914. In 1915 he dispatched a cavalry force against Villa, who had raided a U.S. border town. In 1916 the victorious Carranza called for a convention to draft a new constitution.

The Constitution of 1917. The 1917 Constitution revived Juárez' ideal of free public education and government control of church property and wealth. It regulated hours and wages for workers and upheld their right to unionize and strike. It also affirmed the government's right to reclaim ownership of all land, as well as the resources beneath the surface, in the name of the nation. Although socially progressive, many provisions of the new constitution were not carried out because of a lack of funds and political will.

The Post-Constitutional Era. Carranza was himself deposed in 1920 (and later killed), when he tried to prevent Alvaro Obregón from becoming president. Obregón was a cautious man who was elected in 1920 and achieved some results in land distribution, education, and labor reform. His successor, in 1924, was Plutarco Elías Calles, who expanded the distribution of land. He also enforced the constitutional provisions against the church, which led to the bloody but unsuccessful Cristero revolt (1926–27) by militant Catholics.

Under Calles' successors, however, reform slowed. He was succeeded in the presidency by Emilio Portes Gil (1928–30), Pascual Ortiz Rubio (1930–32), and Abelardo Rodríguez (1932–34).

A New Political Party. Although he retired as president in 1928, Calles remained for some six years thereafter the most powerful figure in Mexican political life. In 1929, to stabilize the country's fragmented political system, he created a new party, the National Revolutionary Party, to include the various revolutionary factions. It was the predecessor of the PRI, which remained Mexico's dominant party until losing the presidency to the opposition PAN party in 2000.

Lázaro Cárdenas, elected president in 1934, restored the revolutionary fervor of an earlier time. He recast the party, making it national and bringing it under presidential control, and he undertook bold economic and social changes. He nationalized the oil industry (much of which was foreign owned) and the railroads; distributed more land to the poor than any previous president; and greatly increased the number of schools.

A New Direction. The presidents after Cárdenas stressed Mexico's industrial development, placing less emphasis on social and economic reforms. This policy began during the administration of Manuel Ávila Camacho (1940–46), who also made peace with the church and took Mexico into World War II on the side of the Allies. It continued under his successors—Miguel Alemán Valdés (1946–52), Adolfo Ruiz Cortines (1952–58), and Adolfo López Mateos (1958–64). In 1953, women won the right to vote in national elections and to run for office.

Pancho Villa (center), a revolutionary leader and bandit, was a dramatic figure in the early 1900's, when Mexico was torn by political turmoil. Stability was achieved after the adoption of a new constitution in 1917.

Mexico's industrialization emphasized producing for the Mexican market and was accompanied by migration both within Mexico to its cities and to the United States under the joint U.S./Mexico Bracero program. High population growth, urbanization, and unemployment became major concerns. Criticism of the government intensified during the presidencies of Gustavo Díaz Ordaz (1964–70) and Luis Echeverría Álvarez (1970–76). It was under Echeverría that a national family-planning program was launched to slow high population growth.

From Prosperity to Crisis. The discovery of new oil resources ushered in a period of prosperity during the presidency of José López Portillo (1976–82). But his free-spending poli-

Vicente Fox Quesada, elected president of Mexico in 2000, has worked to improve Mexico's economy, expand trade, and provide education and jobs for the poor.

cies and falling oil prices led to an economic crisis in 1982. His successor, Miguel de la Madrid Hurtado (1982–88), sought to bring the country's enormous foreign debt under control. He also linked Mexico economically to the international community through the General Agreement on Tariffs and Trade (GATT). For more information, see the article GENERAL AGREEMENT ON TARIFFS AND TRADE (GATT) in Volume G.

Efforts to improve the economy continued under Carlos Salinas de Gortari (1988–94), who returned the government-controlled banking system to private ownership and sold off state-owned steel mills, copper mines, and airlines. Even more important was his negotiation of NAFTA with the United States and Canada. But the Salinas years also saw an increase in drug trafficking, official corruption (particularly within the country's police forces), and a revolt in poverty-stricken Chiapas state by the Zapatista National Liberation Army, a guerrilla group.

The 1994 presidential election was marred by the assassination of the PRI candidate, Luis Donaldo Colosio. He was replaced by PRI candidate Ernesto Zedillo Ponce de León, who, soon after winning the election, had to steer Mexico through a severe economic crisis. To prevent a default on Mexican government bonds, the United States loaned Mexico $12.5 billion in 1995.

To restore the reputation of the PRI, which had come under increasing attack because of its single-party rule and entrenched corruption, Zedillo introduced political reforms intended to make Mexico a true multiparty democracy. He promised fair and honest elections, consultations with the opposition on key issues, a strengthened judiciary, and political democratization. Zedillo's reforms contributed in 1997 to the PRI's loss of control of the lower house of the legislature for the first time in the party's history.

Recent Events. In early 1998, opposition candidates won six gubernatorial races, but by the end of the year the PRI appeared to be regaining strength. Nevertheless, in 2000 PAN opposition candidate, Vicente Fox Quesada, was elected president. He received over 42 percent of the vote versus 36 percent for the PRI and 17 percent for the Democratic Revolution Party (PRD). Fox was the first president in 71 years who was not a member of the governing political party.

Fox's platform emphasized economic policies and programs to benefit the poor, both by transferring income to them and by investing in their education and health. He also promised to reduce corruption and make the country more democratic. But Fox's PAN party did not have a majority in Congress and this limited his ability to get his programs adopted.

Relations between Mexico and the United States made little progress after the September 11, 2001 attacks, which focused U.S. attention on terrorism. Relations revived after the November 2004 re-election of U.S. President George W. Bush. Several issues are up for negotiation, the most important of which is a program to regulate emigration from Mexico to the United States.

GEORGE W. GRAYSON
Author, *The United States and Mexico: Patterns of Influence*

LAURA RANDALL
Professor Emerita
Hunter College of the City University of New York
Author, *The Changing Structure of Mexico*

MEXICO CITY

Mexico City is Mexico's capital and largest city. One of the world's biggest cities, it is home to more than 8.6 million people in the city proper and more than 17 million in its metropolitan area, including the Federal District, of which it is a part.

Located in the Mexican Plateau, Mexico City is built on the site of Tenochtitlán, the capital of Mexico's ancient Aztec empire. The city lies at the feet of snowcapped mountains and the Popocatépetl and Iztaccíhuatl volcanoes. Its climate is temperate.

The City. At the heart of the city is the Plaza of the Constitution, better known as the Zócalo, which features some of the finest Spanish colonial architecture in the Americas. On its eastern side is the National Palace, which houses the offices of the president of Mexico. The Metropolitan Cathedral, the largest in Latin America, stands on its northern side, and the Municipal Palace, or city hall, on its southern side.

A short distance away, down Avenida Juárez, is the Palace of Fine Arts, home to Mexico's national ballet company. It features the work of Mexico's most famous mural painters, Diego Rivera, José Clemente Orozco, and David Alfaro Siquieros.

Where Avenida Juárez ends, the Paseo de la Reforma, a broad, tree-lined boulevard, begins. It leads to a park called Chapultepec,

The Independence Monument is one of Mexico City's landmarks. It stands in the heart of the Paseo de la Reforma, the city's main boulevard.

which means "hill of grasshoppers" in Nahuatl, the Aztec language. Within it are a zoo and the National Museum of Anthropology.

Outside the downtown area is the National Autonomous University of Mexico, one of the oldest in the hemisphere. On the city's outskirts are the ruins of Teotihuacán (200 B.C.–A.D. 750), an ancient city famous for its towering pyramids.

Mexico City's most famous church is the Basilica of Our Lady of Guadalupe. It stands on the spot where Juan Diego, a poor man, saw Mexico's patron saint, Our Lady of Guadalupe, in a vision in 1531. Diego became a saint of the Catholic Church in 2002. Thousands of pilgrims visit the shrine daily.

Many tourists begin their visit to Mexico at Mexico City's Benito Juárez airport, then travel about using the city's buses, taxis, and an underground subway, or metro.

Economic Activity. More than a third of Mexico's economic activity takes place in Mexico City. Services dominate the city's economy, including government administration, tourism, and trade. The balance consists largely of manufacturing and construction.

History. The Aztecs built their capital, Tenochtitlán, in the 1300's. The city was destroyed by the Spanish in 1521, and a new city was erected on the site. It remained the capital of the colony of New Spain until Mexico achieved independence in 1821.

The city's population grew steadily in the first half of the 1900's and then dramatically, beginning in 1950, as people flowed in from rural areas. As the city grew, so did pollution, the result of the city's geographic location and its many cars and factories. Despite more than a decade of pollution-control measures, air pollution remains a serious problem.

Reviewed by LAURA RANDALL
Professor Emerita, Hunter College, CUNY

See also MEXICO.

MIAMI

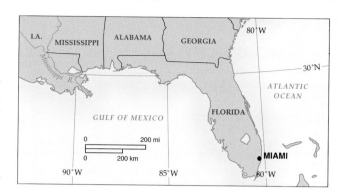

Miami is a resort city situated on Biscayne Bay, an arm of the Atlantic Ocean, near the southern tip of Florida. It is noted for its subtropical climate, winter sunshine, sports, and large hotels along palm-fringed beaches. Miami is also a gateway to Everglades National Park and the Florida Keys.

Miami was founded soon after the frost of 1894–95 spoiled central Florida's orange crop. Farmers near the southern trading post of Fort Dallas, where the Miami River empties into Biscayne Bay, escaped the frost. At a settler's suggestion, Henry Flagler (1830–1913), a businessman and promoter, built a railroad line to this settlement and drained the swamps. He installed waterworks, developed the land, and built a resort hotel. The town was incorporated as Miami in 1896 with about 1,500 people. The climate soon drew settlers, vacationers, and real estate dealers. John S. Collins, a New Jersey horticulturist, started the Miami Beach Improvement Company, which drained a mangrove swamp across the bay from Miami and built it into a long, thin island—Miami Beach. It was incorporated in 1915. The company advertised delightful, springlike winter

Miami's subtropical climate and its location on the Atlantic Ocean make it one of the most popular vacation resorts in the United States.

temperatures and balmy summers with gentle trade winds. A land rush began during the 1920's.

Miami's population today is about 362,000. About half the people are Hispanic, largely of Cuban origin. The metropolitan area, which includes Miami Beach, Coral Gables, Hialeah, and Fort Lauderdale, is the largest in Florida, with nearly 4 million people.

Miami's main business is tourism. Each year more than 10 million vacationers come to the area to enjoy swimming, sunbathing, sailing, golfing, and other recreational activities. Miami's industries turn out furniture, food products, plastics, electrical equipment, clothing, and other products.

Horse racing is enjoyed at Gulfstream Park, Hialeah Park, and Calder Race Course. Greyhound races, jai alai games, golf tournaments, and boat races attract crowds. On New Year's Day, college football teams compete in the Orange Bowl, the home stadium of the University of Miami Hurricanes. The Miami Dolphins of the National Football League and the Florida Marlins of baseball's National League play at Pro Player Stadium. The Miami Heat of the National Basketball Association plays at AmericanAirlines Arena.

Miami's cultural institutions include the Miami Symphony Orchestra, the Historical Museum of Southern Florida, and the Center for the Fine Arts. Educational institutions in the area include the University of Miami, in Coral Gables; Florida International University in Miami; and Miami-Dade Community College, in Miami.

Reviewed by ROBERT S. CHAUVIN
Stetson University

MICE. See RODENTS.

MICHEAUX, OSCAR DEVERAUX. See SOUTH DAKOTA (Famous People).

The Creation of Adam is one of nine scenes painted by Michelangelo on the ceiling of the Sistine Chapel.

MICHELANGELO (1475–1564)

Michelangelo devoted his whole life to the creation of magnificent works of art. His work was all that interested him, and he had no use for the easy ways of doing things. He lived a long and productive life, creating art that influenced almost all countries in all ages.

Michelangelo Buonarroti was born in Caprese near Florence, Italy, on March 6, 1475. On that day his father, Judge Buonarroti, thought he saw lucky signs in the sky. He was sure the boy would have heavenly powers. For this reason he named his son Michelangelo—*angelo* in Italian means "angel." Michelangelo was a sickly child, but though he remained small and thin throughout his life, he had amazing strength and energy.

Remembering the heavenly signs, Judge Buonarroti sent Michelangelo to school with the hope that the boy would become a great scholar. But Michelangelo was interested in art and sketched or painted day and night. His father and uncles were horrified that he wanted to be an artist. They thought art was a low occupation fit only for peasants. They beat Michelangelo cruelly to make him forget his dream, but the beatings made him more determined. Finally, in 1488, they agreed to let him study with Domenico Ghirlandaio (1449–94), a popular Florentine painter.

In Ghirlandaio's workshop Michelangelo studied the art of the old masters and learned to paint **frescoes**—paintings done on wet plaster. Although he was only 13, Michelangelo was highly skilled. Ghirlandaio paid him a small salary, which the boy gave to his father. The other students did not like Michelangelo because of his hot-tempered, critical ways. And they were jealous of his talent. From the very beginning of his career, he scorned anyone whose goals were less than his—and Michelangelo's goal was perfection in art. He was very outspoken and did not hesitate to attack the ideas of others.

Florence at that time was ruled by the powerful Medici family, who were great lovers of art. When Michelangelo was 16, Ghirlandaio sent him to study sculpture with Bertoldo de Giovanni (1420?–91). Bertoldo supervised the garden of Lorenzo de' Medici, a meeting place for Florentine scholars and artists. Lorenzo, the ruling prince, was so impressed with the ability of the young genius that he gave Michelangelo the privileges of a son. This was a wonderful opportunity for the boy, but his father was sadder than ever. He thought that Michelangelo would be nothing more than a lowly stonecutter and mason.

In the 2 years that Michelangelo lived with Lorenzo he met the most outstanding men of the day. Although he learned a great deal from them, he never copied their courteous ways. These men often talked about the philosophy

The *Last Judgment* (1536–41) was painted on the western wall of the Sistine Chapel.

and art of ancient Greece. Michelangelo came to love the great size and power of Greek sculpture. He admired the Greeks' attempt to capture ideal beauty in their statues. At night he studied anatomy (the structure of the human body). Secretly he cut up dead bodies to see how they were put together. To create overpowering, perfect human forms in marble became his one mission in life.

While living with Lorenzo, Michelangelo once criticized the work of Pietro Torrigiano (1472–1528), a fellow student. Torrigiano became so enraged at Michelangelo's straightforward remarks that he smashed Michelangelo's nose and scarred his face for life. All Florentines came to hate Torrigiano for this black deed.

In 1492 Lorenzo de' Medici died. Within 2

years Michelangelo left Florence and traveled through Italy. He went to Rome in 1496. There he created his first major work. The *Pietà,* completed in 1499, is a sad and graceful statue of Jesus in Mary's lap. Michelangelo's work was well received, and he returned to Florence in 1501 as a famous sculptor.

When Michelangelo was 26, he began a statue that amazed all the critics of his day. The piece of marble that he used was thin and scarred and more than 16 feet long; in fact, other sculptors had refused to use it. But Michelangelo never turned away from a difficult problem. From this poor piece of marble he carved his glorious *David.* The statue of the Bible hero became the most popular work of art in Florence. The citizens felt that the youthful warrior was a symbol of the strength and vigor of their city.

After the *David* was unveiled in 1504, Michelangelo was commissioned to do more work than he could finish. He was asked to design tombs, libraries, and statues. The Medicis ordered a great deal of work. Although the popes also ordered quantities of work from him, they did not give Michelangelo much money or help. When he was 30, the sculptor was chosen by Pope Julius II to design his tomb—the largest in the Christian world. It was so large that a new chapel in St. Peter's Basilica had to be constructed to hold it. For 8 months Michelangelo supervised the quarrying of the marble for the tomb. But when he came to Rome to discuss the project, the Pope refused to see him. Furious, Michelangelo left Rome and went back to Florence. When the Pope threatened war if the sculptor did not return, Michelangelo finally agreed to continue his work.

It took Michelangelo 40 years to finish the tomb. In the meantime he had many more quarrels with Julius and later popes. Julius wanted Michelangelo to paint the ceiling of the Sistine Chapel in St. Peter's. Michelangelo protested at first, saying that he was a sculptor, not a painter. He finally began the project and worked on it feverishly. He locked out his assistants and painted the entire area—over 3,000 square feet—by himself. To paint the ceiling, he had to lie on his back on a scaffold. He slept in his clothes to save time. But Julius was so impatient that he once threatened to throw Michelangelo off the scaffold if he did

The *Pietà* (1498–99) is in St. Peter's Basilica, Rome.

not hurry. Despite the Pope's threats, it took Michelangelo 4 years to finish the fresco.

The overpowering figures on the Sistine ceiling tell the story of man's creation and earliest history according to the Bible. The ceiling is considered by many to be the greatest single work of art ever created by one man. Twenty-four years later, in 1536, Michelangelo began The *Last Judgment,* a fresco on the altar wall of the Sistine Chapel. It is a perfect companion piece to the ceiling painting.

St. Peter's Basilica was constantly being enlarged and changed. Michelangelo was appointed chief architect of St. Peter's in 1547. The dome that he designed for the building has often been called the crowning glory of the Renaissance period. It has been copied in many lands for churches and public buildings.

It is said that when Michelangelo was 60, he could still carve faster than three ordinary sculptors. He lived to be 89, working steadily until his death in Rome on February 18, 1564. Unlike the unhappy Judge Buonarroti, the rest of the world thinks that Michelangelo fulfilled the prophecy of the stars.

Reviewed by AARON H. JACOBSEN
Author, *The Renaissance Sketchbook*

MICHIGAN

When the Revolutionary War ended in 1783, one of the tasks of the new American government was to determine what to do with the lands west of the original 13 states. Thomas Jefferson, always with an idea or solution to a problem, suggested in 1784 that the area be divided into ten additional states. The area around the Great Lakes he designated Michigania, a name that originated from a Native American term michigama, *meaning "large lake" or "big water." Although Jefferson's plan was not adopted, the name endured, and in 1805 the area around the Great Lakes became known as the Michigan Territory. Statehood followed in 1837.*

Michigan is called the Wolverine State, after a fierce, bearlike animal belonging to the weasel family. Wolverines, noted for their strength and cunning, were prized by fur trappers long ago for their thick, glossy pelts.

State flag

Michigan is a midwestern state, located in the east north central region of the country. It is made up of two separate peninsulas that are almost entirely surrounded by four of the five Great Lakes—Superior, Michigan, Huron, and Erie. The Lower Peninsula, which is shaped like a giant mitten, contains all of Michigan's large cities and 97 percent of its population. The Upper Peninsula, once an important center for the mining of copper and iron, is heavily forested and sparsely settled. Together these two peninsulas have the longest freshwater shoreline of any state or even any country in the world.

Michigan shares a 720-mile (1,160-kilometer) international border with Canada. Three great steel bridges and two underwater tunnels connect the state with the province of Ontario. Oceangoing ships on the St. Lawrence Seaway call at Michigan's many ports, notably Detroit, Michigan's most populous city and largest industrial center.

A variety of nicknames describe Michigan, in addition to the Wolverine State. License plates advertise it as the Great Lakes State. It is also known as a Water Wonderland. The Great Lakes, along with thousands of inland lakes, endless miles of beaches and sand dunes, and thousands of acres of hills and forestlands, attract millions of vacationers. Boating in the summer, hunting in the fall, and skiing in the winter have made tourism a profitable statewide industry.

Perhaps the name that defines Michigan most accurately is the Automobile State. The manufacture of motor vehicles, which developed in the Detroit area early in the 1900's, transformed Michigan from an agricultural state into an industrial giant. For nearly one hundred years, the production of cars, trucks, and industrial machinery has defined Michigan's economy. The nation's largest motor vehicle manufacturers—General Motors, Ford, and DaimlerChrysler—are all headquartered in southeastern Michigan. These companies, known as the Big Three, form the heart of the nation's automobile industry, one of the most profitable industrial enterprises the world has ever known.

▶ LAND

Michigan's shoreline, including its islands, measures 3,288 miles (5,292 kilometers), a distance longer than the Atlantic coastline from Maine to Florida. The state's two peninsulas are separated by the Straits of Mackinac, a narrow passageway between Lake Michigan and Lake Huron. The Lower Peninsula contains about 70 percent of the state's total land area.

Opposite page, clockwise from left: The Renaissance Center is one of Detroit's most modern landmarks. Michigan harvests more cherries than any other state. Lakeside cottages are a favorite summer retreat for Michiganders as well as out-of-state visitors.

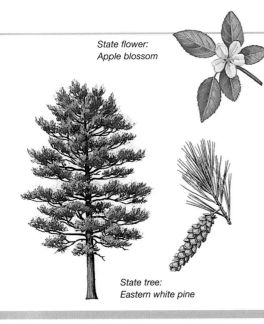

FACTS AND FIGURES

Location: East north central United States; bordered on the north by Lake Superior, on the east by Lake Huron and Lake Erie, on the south by Indiana and Ohio, and on the west by Wisconsin and Lake Michigan.

Area: 96,705 sq mi (250,465 km^2); rank, 11th.

Population: 9,938,444 (2000 census); rank, 8th.

Elevation: *Highest*—1,979 ft (603 m) at Mount Arvon in Baraga County; *lowest*—572 ft (174 m) at Lake Erie.

Capital: Lansing.

Statehood: January 26, 1837; 26th state.

State Motto: *Si quaeris peninsulam amoenam, circumspice* ("If you seek a pleasant peninsula, look about you").

State Song: "Michigan, My Michigan."

Nicknames: Wolverine State; Great Lakes State; Water Wonderland; Automobile State.

Abbreviations: MI; Mich.

State bird: Robin

Water is a consistent and prominent feature of Michigan's beautiful landscape. *Left:* Lake of the Clouds, on the Upper Peninsula (popularly known as the U. P.), lies within the heavily forested Porcupine Mountains. *Opposite page:* Mountains of sand accumulate in various places along the eastern shores of Lake Michigan. Warren Dunes, in the southwestern part of the state, is a popular state park.

Land Regions

The present surface features of Michigan are largely the result of glaciation. During the Ice Age, the great weight of the glaciers pressed down on the land, gouging out numerous basins and grinding down entire ranges of hills. As the climate gradually grew warmer and the great masses of ice began to melt, a blanket of rich soil called till was deposited on the land, and basins filled with water, forming many of today's lakes.

The entire Lower Peninsula and the eastern half of the Upper Peninsula are part of a large region of the United States known as the Central Lowland. The western section of the Upper Peninsula is part of the Superior Upland, also known as the Laurentian Upland or the Canadian Shield.

The Central Lowland, in Michigan, is known as the Michigan Basin. It is made up of layer upon layer of rocks formed from sediment that was deposited in an ancient sea long before the Ice Age.

The northern and southern halves of the Lower Peninsula are divided by a moraine, a ridge that was formed by a glacier. It separates the rivers that flow west into Lake Michigan from those that flow east into Lake Huron. The southern half of the Lower Peninsula is level to gently rolling. High bluffs and dunes line the shores of Lake Michigan. The eastern section of the Upper Peninsula is mostly low swampland, although hills rise as high as 1,000 feet (305 meters) along the shores of Lake Superior.

The Superior Upland, covering the western half of the Upper Peninsula, contains crystallized rocks and many metallic minerals. The main surface features are rugged, forested hills, including the Copper, Gogebic, and Menominee ranges and the Porcupine Mountains. The highest point in the state is found at Mount Arvon in Baraga County.

Rivers and Lakes

Michigan has two major types of rivers. The first type flow into the Great Lakes from the interior of the two peninsulas. Examples are the Escanaba, Menominee, and Tahquamenon rivers in the Upper Peninsula and the Grand, Muskegon, Kalamazoo, Raisin, and St. Joseph rivers in the Lower Peninsula. (The St. Joseph River is one of the few rivers in the world that flows alternately in north and south directions.) The second type drain one great lake into another. The St. Marys, St. Clair, and Detroit rivers are of this type. These three rivers also serve as international boundaries between the United States and Canada. Rapids and waterfalls are major scenic attractions on the state's nearly 36,000 miles (58,000 kilometers) of rivers. Numerous small dams and reservoirs are located along rivers throughout the state.

Lake St. Clair is a link in the waterway that joins Lake Huron to Lake Erie. Houghton Lake, in the northern part of the Lower Peninsula, is the largest lake in the state. More than 11,000 smaller lakes lie within the borders of the state.

Climate

Michigan has a humid continental climate with cold winters and warm summers. Spring in Michigan is usually short, and often winter seems to change suddenly to summer. Autumn is a time of great beauty, when warm, sunny days and frosty nights change the leaves to brilliant shades of yellow and red. Winters are snowy and cold, especially in the north.

The Lower Peninsula is generally warmer than the Upper Peninsula. Average temperatures in July range from 65°F (18°C) in the north to 73°F (23°C) in the south. Average temperatures in January range from 15°F (-9°C) in the north to 26°F (-3°C) in the south.

Precipitation, or the amount of rain and snow, varies widely in different locations but is fairly evenly distributed throughout the year. Amounts range from about 25 to 35 inches (630 to 890 millimeters). Michigan's many winter resorts make good use of the state's often heavy snowfall.

The growing season is shortest in the interior areas of the Upper Peninsula and longest near lakes in the southern part of the Lower Peninsula.

Plant and Animal Life

Michigan has a great variety of wildlife. Animals found in the state's forests include moose, black bears, and deer, as well as many smaller animals such as squirrels, beavers, porcupines, foxes, and rabbits. Canadian geese stop by on their way south in the winter and north in the summer. Game birds include pheasant, partridge, ducks, and wild geese. The lakes and streams are well stocked with trout, pike, bass, perch, and salmon.

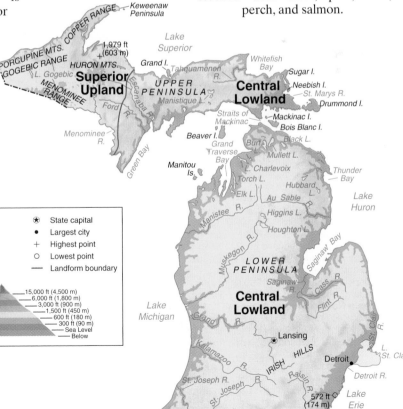

MICHIGAN Landforms

```
0   20   40   60   80   100 mi
0  20 40 60 80 100 km
```

⊛ State capital
• Largest city
+ Highest point
○ Lowest point
— Landform boundary

15,000 ft (4,500 m)
6,000 ft (1,800 m)
3,000 ft (900 m)
1,500 ft (450 m)
600 ft (180 m)
300 ft (90 m)
Sea Level
Below

Isle Royale

Keweenaw Peninsula

COPPER RANGE

PORCUPINE MTS.

GOGEBIC RANGE

HURON MTS.

1,979 ft (603 m)

L. Gogebic

Superior Upland

MENOMINEE RANGE

Ford

Menominee R.

Escanaba R.

Green Bay

Lake Superior

Grand I.

Tahquamenon R.

UPPER PENINSULA

Manistique L.

Whitefish Bay

Sugar I.

Neebish I.

St. Marys R.

Drummond I.

Central Lowland

Straits of Mackinac

Mackinac I.

Bois Blanc I.

Beaver I.

Grand Traverse Bay

Burt L.

Black L.

Mullett L.

L. Charlevoix

Torch L.

Hubbard L.

Thunder Bay

Elk L.

Au Sable R.

Higgins L.

Houghton L.

Manitou Is.

Manistee R.

Muskegon R.

Lake Huron

Saginaw Bay

Saginaw R.

Cass R.

Flint R.

LOWER PENINSULA

Central Lowland

Lake Michigan

Grand R.

Kalamazoo R.

St. Joseph R.

Joseph R.

✶ Lansing

IRISH HILLS

Raisin R.

Detroit

St. Clair R.

Detroit R.

L. St. Clair

572 ft (174 m)

Lake Erie

Places of Interest

Henry Ford Museum, Dearborn

Tulip Festival, Holland

Fort Mackinac, Mackinac Island

Fort Michilimackinac, in Mackinaw City, is a reproduction of the colonial fort and trading post used by the French and later the British in the earliest days of European settlement. Nearby, visitors can also go aboard the *Welcome*, a reconstructed ship that sailed the Great Lakes in the Revolutionary War days.

Hartwick Pines State Park, near Grayling, contains thousands of acres of pine and hemlock, practically the only remnants of Michigan's once-great virgin forests. The park includes a historical museum and reproductions of parts of a logging camp.

Henry Ford Museum and Greenfield Village, in Dearborn, were built with funds provided by Henry Ford. One million artifacts, celebrating American history and popular culture, are housed in 12 acres (4.9 hectares) of exhibit space. Furniture, cars, and entire buildings, from Thomas Edison's laboratory to a 1950's hamburger stand, are featured.

Isle Royale National Park encompasses a wilderness area on Isle Royale and about 200 surrounding islets in the western part of Lake Superior. Much of the area is covered with dense forests, where wolves and moose still roam. Visitors may hike to an ancient pit copper mine or paddle the streams and coves.

Ludington State Park, near Ludington, has a long stretch of beach on Lake Michigan, sand dunes, and forested areas. The park is adjacent to Big Point Sable Lighthouse.

Mackinac Island (pronounced MACK-in-aw) is a popular summer resort, located in the straits of Mackinac between Lake Huron and Lake Michigan. The Indians originally called it *michilimackinac*, meaning "Great Turtle." No automobiles are allowed on the island, but visitors may ride bicycles or in horse-drawn carriages. Today most of the island is a state park, featuring geological formations, such as Arch Rock, and nature trails. Points of interest include Fort Mackinac, established by the British in 1780, and the John Jacob Astor House, built about 1817.

National Ski Hall of Fame and Ski Museum, in Ishpeming, contains a collection of national trophies and historic ski equipment and publications.

Sleeping Bear Dunes National Lakeshore, along the coast in Leelanau County, encompasses many islands, beaches, dunes, and inland lakes. The largest dune rises 500 feet (152 meters).

Sojourner Truth's Grave, located at Oak Hill Cemetery in Battle Creek, marks the burial place of one of the antislavery movement's most famous spokeswomen. Born a slave in New York, Truth settled in Battle Creek, where she died in 1883.

Tahquamenon Falls State Park, near Newberry, features one of the largest falls in the eastern United States. The Tahquamenon River plays an important part in Henry Wadsworth Longfellow's poem "The Song of Hiawatha."

Tulip Festival, in Holland, takes place every May, when thousands of tulips are in bloom. Costumed in Dutch clothing and wearing wooden shoes, the townspeople celebrate Holland's Dutch heritage with parades and dances.

State Parks. Most of Michigan's 99 state parks include camping facilities. For more information, contact the Michigan Travel Bureau, 333 South Capitol Avenue, Lansing, Michigan 48909.

Woods cover half the state's area. Pine trees and varieties of evergreens are common in Michigan, particularly up north. During the spring, the state is full of blossoms from the many varieties of fruit trees. Because there is still much uncultivated land in the state, wildflowers and wild mushrooms (morels) can be found in significant numbers.

Natural Resources

Water is one of Michigan's most valuable resources, together with minerals and forests. The state practices timber management and fire control, and great efforts are made to keep pollutants from entering rivers and lakes. The state has a strict program for the preservation of wetlands as well.

The quality of Michigan's soils varies widely from one part of the state to another. The richest soils are in the southern part of the Lower Peninsula, where vegetables and grain crops are grown. Soils in other areas produce grasses that make good grazing lands. Some soils are suited only to forests.

▶ PEOPLE

Michigan is one of the most populous and ethnically diverse states in the nation. The earliest European settlers to the area were French and British fur traders. When the Erie Canal opened in 1825, settlers began to pour in from the eastern states and from Germany to settle and farm the land. In 1847 a large group arrived from the Netherlands and established the city of Holland. A logging boom, which started about 1850, attracted loggers from Finland, Norway, Sweden, and Canada. At about the same time, the development of iron and copper mining in the Upper Peninsula attracted miners from England, Finland, and Wales.

Industrialization again transformed the population. Auto manufacturing required a large labor force, and between 1910 and 1930, Detroit's population nearly quadrupled. Thousands of Germans, Austrians, Swiss, Belgians, Canadians, Greeks, Irish, Italians, Romanians, and Russians came. A particularly large group came from Poland and settled in Hamtramck, a community now entirely surrounded by Detroit. Great numbers of African Americans also migrated to Michigan from the South. Today they make up

Above: The growth of Detroit's automobile industry in the early 1900's attracted immigrants from all over Europe. Greeks are among those who have maintained strong cultural ties with their native land. *Left:* The pier at East Tawas Harbor, near the entrance of Saginaw Bay on Lake Huron, is a popular fishing spot.

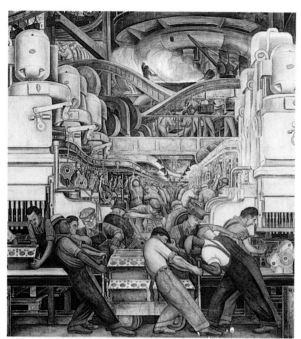

The *Detroit Industry* frescoes (1933) featured at the Detroit Institute of Art are considered among the finest works by the Mexican artist Diego Rivera.

about 14 percent of the population. More recently, Arab, Hispanic, and Asian groups have settled in the largest cities. More than 50,000 Michiganders are descended from the region's original Native American population.

Education

Michigan has been a pioneer in the development of public education. It was the first state to appoint a superintendent of public instruction, the Reverend John Davis Pierce, who drew up a plan for the nation's first public school system, made up of three divisions—the elementary school, the high school, and the university.

About half a million students attend the state's 13 public universities and 29 community colleges. Three universities in the state are specifically authorized by the state constitution. The oldest of these, the University of Michigan, was founded in Detroit in 1817 but was moved to Ann Arbor in 1841. Today it has two branch campuses in Dearborn and Flint. Michigan State University, located in East Lansing, was chartered in 1855 as the nation's first agricultural college. It has seven branch campuses statewide. Wayne State University, founded in 1868, is located in the center of Detroit.

Other state-supported universities include Central Michigan in Mount Pleasant, Eastern Michigan in Ypsilanti, Ferris State in Big Rapids, Northern Michigan in Marquette, Michigan Technological in Houghton, Western Michigan in Kalamazoo, Lake Superior State in Sault Sainte Marie, and Saginaw Valley State College in University Center. Private schools include Albion College in Albion, Hillsdale College in Hillsdale, and Hope College in Holland.

Libraries, Museums, and the Arts

The public library in Detroit is the largest of the state's 350 public libraries. Its main branch contains the Burton Collection, housing some of the area's earliest documents. The Bentley Historical Library, at the University of Michigan in Ann Arbor, contains important manuscripts relating to the history of the state after 1837. The William L. Clements Library, also at the university, holds an important collection of rare books on American history. The Walter Reuther Library, at Wayne State University in Detroit, houses important historical sources on the history of labor. The Gerald R. Ford Library, in Ann Arbor, houses the official documents and papers of the nation's 38th president.

Michigan has many fine museums. Detroit, in particular, features a wide range of art, history, and science museums. For more information, see the article DETROIT in Volume D.

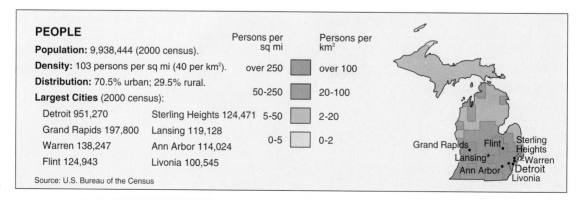

PEOPLE

Population: 9,938,444 (2000 census).

Density: 103 persons per sq mi (40 per km²).

Distribution: 70.5% urban; 29.5% rural.

Largest Cities (2000 census):

Detroit 951,270	Sterling Heights 124,471
Grand Rapids 197,800	Lansing 119,128
Warren 138,247	Ann Arbor 114,024
Flint 124,943	Livonia 100,545

Persons per sq mi	Persons per km²
over 250	over 100
50-250	20-100
5-50	2-20
0-5	0-2

Source: U.S. Bureau of the Census

Collections outside Detroit also are impressive. The Henry Ford Museum and Greenfield Village in Dearborn hold a vast array of historic artifacts. The State Museum and Archives in Lansing contain important resources on state history and government. The Michigan Historical Museum, also in Lansing, has a collection of Native American and pioneer objects. The Holland Museum in Holland displays Dutch decorative arts, while the Public Museum of Grand Rapids features a collection of locally made furniture. Also in Grand Rapids is the Gerald R. Ford Museum, containing objects and artifacts from Ford's brief presidency.

The Detroit Symphony Orchestra, established in 1914, performs at Orchestra Hall and is one of the nation's leading orchestras. Michigan is also noted for the National Music Camp at Interlochen, attended each summer by students from all over the United

Association, the Detroit Shock of the Women's National Basketball Association, and the Detroit Tigers of baseball's American League. Michiganders also root for such college teams as the University of Michigan Wolverines and the Michigan State Spartans.

▶ **ECONOMY**

Since the early 1900's, Michigan has been one of the world's leading manufacturing centers. The health of the state's economy has generally been determined by the strength of the automobile industry.

Services

More than 73 percent of all Michiganders are employed in the service industries. Business and personal services, from office supplies to medical care, make up the largest segment, followed by financial services; wholesale and retail trade; government ser-

The University of Michigan pep squad cheers on the Wolverines football team, which is regularly ranked among the top teams in the Big Ten college conference. Michigan Stadium in Ann Arbor can seat more than 100,000 fans.

States. Cranbrook, an educational and cultural center in Bloomfield Hills, includes the Cranbrook Institute of Science and the Cranbrook Academy of Art Museum.

Sports

Detroit hosts several major league sports teams, including the Detroit Lions of the National Football League, the Detroit Red Wings of the National Hockey League, the Detroit Pistons of the National Basketball

vices, including the administration of the public schools; gas and electric utilities; transportation services, such as trucking; and communication, including television services. Tourism, which draws on most of these services, provides a significant source of income.

Manufacturing

The design and manufacture of motor vehicles of all kinds is Michigan's leading industry. More cars, buses, and trucks are produced

Above: The manufacture of automobiles and other transport vehicles has been Michigan's leading industry for nearly a century. Robots now perform many of the tasks that once required skilled human labor. *Right:* A wide variety of fruits are grown in Michigan, particularly in the counties bordering Lake Michigan.

there than in any other state. Industrial machinery and equipment, metals and metal products, and chemicals and pharmaceuticals rank next in importance. Processed foods, especially breakfast cereals, also bring a large income. Other manufactured goods include printed materials, rubber and plastic products, furniture, and paper.

Agriculture

Michigan is a leading dairy state, and milk is its most important farm product. Cattle, pigs, and hogs are raised for livestock. Major field crops include corn, hay, soybeans, and wheat. A fruit belt extends through the western counties along Lake Michigan, producing large quantities of tart cherries, apples, blueberries, and pears. Grapes grown in Berrien County are used in the production of wine.

Each year Michigan's commercial fishing industry nets nearly 16 million pounds (7.2

million kilograms) of fish from the Great Lakes. Whitefish accounts for more than 75 percent of the value of the annual haul.

Mining and Construction

Michigan ranks second to Minnesota in the mining of iron ore, but production on the Upper Peninsula has declined because most of the high-grade ores have been used up. Copper mining on the Keweenaw Peninsula, once an important industry, ended many years ago.

Oil and natural gas are found in the northern part of the Lower Peninsula. Salt is mined throughout the central regions and the Detroit area. Iodine, bromine, and magnesium contribute to Michigan's pharmaceutical industry.

Michigan is a leading producer of portland cement, which is made from limestone and sandstone quarried in the state. It also ranks

---

PRODUCTS AND INDUSTRIES

Manufacturing: Motor vehicles, industrial machinery, metals and metal products, chemicals.

Agriculture: Dairy products, corn, hay, cattle.

Minerals: Natural gas, iron ore, petroleum, limestone, sand and gravel, salt.

Services: Wholesale and retail trade; finance, insurance, and real estate; business, social, and personal services; transportation, communication, and utilities; government.

*Gross state product is the total value of goods and services produced in a year.

Percentage of Gross State Product* by Industry

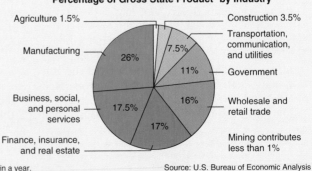

Agriculture 1.5%
Construction 3.5%
Transportation, communication, and utilities 7.5%
Government 11%
Manufacturing 26%
Wholesale and retail trade 16%
Business, social, and personal services 17.5%
Finance, insurance, and real estate 17%
Mining contributes less than 1%

Source: U.S. Bureau of Economic Analysis

high in the production of gypsum, used in making plaster and other building materials.

A steady construction industry is dedicated to the building and repair of roads, bridges, residences, office buildings, shopping centers, and tourist facilities and accommodations.

Transportation

Due to the concentration of the automobile industry, Michigan has been a pioneer in highway development and has an extensive road system.

The first railroads in Michigan were built during the 1830's. Ferry service across the Straits of Mackinac connected the Upper and Lower peninsulas from 1881 until the Mackinac Bridge was completed in 1957. It is one of the longest suspension bridges in the world. Three other bridges—the International, the Ambassador, and the Blue Water—connect Michigan to the Canadian province of Ontario. An underwater tunnel built in 1913 connects Detroit and Windsor, Ontario; a second tunnel, completed in 1995, connects Port Huron and Sarnia, Ontario.

The Great Lakes have been important to transportation since the pioneer days. Ships on the Great Lakes now include oceangoing vessels from the St. Lawrence Seaway. These large freighters haul ores mined in the upper areas of the Great Lakes and transport them back to ports on the Atlantic Ocean.

Located on the St. Marys River, linking Lake Superior to Lake Huron, are the famous Soo Canals, named after their location between the twin cities of Sault (pronounced SOO) Sainte Marie, Michigan, and Sault Sainte Marie, Ontario. These two parallel systems, toll-free and government-operated, are among the busiest in the world.

Michigan has more than 400 public air strips. Daily jet connections to all parts of the world are made from the Detroit Metropolitan Airport, the state's principal airport.

Communication

Michigan has about 50 daily newspapers. The leading dailies are the Detroit *Free Press*, the *Detroit News*, the *Grand Rapids Press*, and the Flint *Journal*.

One of the nation's first commercial radio broadcasting stations, WWJ, opened in Detroit in 1920. The state now has more than 280 radio stations and about 30 television stations, many accessed through several cable systems. Ann Arbor serves as one of several hubs in the international computer information system known as the Internet.

▶ CITIES

All of Michigan's largest cities are situated in the Lower Peninsula. Nearly half the people of the entire state live in the Detroit metropolitan area.

Lansing, the state capital, is located in south central Michigan in a shallow valley formed by three rivers—the Grand, the Red Cedar, and the Sycamore. Originally named Michigan, the city was settled in 1837. It has been the seat of government since 1847, when members of the legislature decided to move the capital from Detroit. Today it is an impor-

The United States operates four locks on the Soo Canals on the St. Marys River, making it possible for ships to travel between Lakes Huron and Superior.

Above: Detroit, which rises along the north bank of the Detroit River, is actually built up over one of the nation's largest salt mines. *Right:* Monroe Center is a pleasant shopping area in Grand Rapids.

tant industrial center, producing automobiles, school buses, trucks, and tools. It is also a trading center for the surrounding farmlands. East Lansing, a separate community, is the home of Michigan State University.

Detroit, long known as Motor City and the Automobile Capital of the World, is Michigan's largest and most populous city. Large cities in the Detroit metropolitan area include Warren, Sterling Heights, Livonia, Dearborn, and Southfield. For more information, see the article DETROIT in Volume D.

Grand Rapids, Michigan's second largest and fastest growing city, is situated at the rapids of the Grand River. Established as a fur trading post in 1827, Grand Rapids developed a strong lumber industry. During the first half of the 1900's, the city was the most important furniture-manufacturing center in the nation. Today it has a diverse economy and several local colleges.

Flint is second only to Detroit in the manufacture of motor vehicles and automotive parts. Founded in 1819 as a fur-trading post on the Flint River northwest of Detroit, Flint later became a center for the carriage-making industry. The Flint Institute of Arts, the Robert L. Longway Planetarium, and a branch campus of the University of Michigan are located there.

Saginaw is situated on the Saginaw River, about 16 miles (25 kilometers) from Saginaw Bay, an inlet of Lake Huron. Originally a fur-trading post, the land was ceded to the U.S. government in 1819 by the Ojibwa (Chippewa) Indians. It later became an important lumbering center. Saginaw's economy is now dominated by automobile manufacturing and metallurgy.

Kalamazoo, in southwestern Michigan, takes its name from an Indian word meaning "where the water boils in the pot." The name first applied to the local river, which had many bubbling springs. Paper manufacturing and pharmaceuticals are two of Kalamazoo's main industries. It is home to Western Michigan University and Kalamazoo College.

Battle Creek, in south central Michigan, is known as the Cereal Bowl of America. First settled in 1831, the city rose to prominence after both W. K. Kellogg and C. W. Post set up breakfast cereal factories there in the early 1900's.

Marquette is the principal city of the Upper Peninsula. It now has a small but diverse economy including service industries and some shipping and manufacturing.

▶ GOVERNMENT

Michigan has had four state constitutions. The first one was drawn up in 1835. The most recent one was adopted in 1963.

The executive branch of the state government is headed by the governor, who is elected every four years. Other executive officers include a lieutenant governor, a secretary of state, and an attorney general.

The state legislature is made up of a senate and house of representatives. These two bodies are reapportioned after the national census is taken every ten years.

The highest court of the state's judicial branch is the supreme court, made up of seven justices. The state also has one court of appeals and 56 circuit courts. Each county has a probate and a district court, and some cities have municipal courts.

▶ HISTORY

Before European settlers came, an estimated 15,000 Indians belonging to three major tribes lived in the forests of Michigan. The Ottawa and the Potawatomi lived along the shores of Lake Michigan. The Ojibwa (Chippewa) lived in the northern part of the Lower Peninsula and in the Upper Peninsula.

Exploration and Settlement

The French explorer Étienne Brulé may have been the first European to see Michigan. It is known that he visited Lake Superior, probably in 1622. Others soon followed to explore and trade for furs.

In 1641, French Jesuit missionaries came to the site of Sault Sainte Marie on the St. Marys River to work among the Indians. Fa-

Lansing replaced Detroit as Michigan's capital city in 1847. The state capitol building is located in the center of the downtown area.

ther Jacques Marquette established a mission there in 1668. It became the first permanent settlement in Michigan.

The Lower Peninsula was explored and settled later. The most important settlement was at Fort Michilimackinac, in present-day Mackinaw City, located at the straits that divide the two peninsulas. First established in 1671 as a Jesuit mission, it later served as a fur-trading post. By 1690 it had become a military outpost with a fort to protect the French fur trade from English competitors. Other settlements followed, including Fort St. Joseph (1691) at the site of present-day Niles and Fort Pontchartrain (1701) at the site of present-day Detroit.

GOVERNMENT

State Government
　Governor: 4-year term
　State senators: 38; 4-year terms
　State representatives: 110;
　 2-year terms
　Number of counties: 83

Federal Government
　U.S. senators: 2
　U.S. representatives: 15
　Number of electoral votes: 17

For the name of the current governor, see STATE GOVERNMENTS in Volume S. For the names of current U.S. senators and representatives, see UNITED STATES, CONGRESS OF THE in Volume U-V.

Michigan was held by the French until the end of the French and Indian War in 1763, when it, along with most of the North American continent, came under British control. Later, during the Revolutionary War, British posts in Michigan served as bases for attacks against American settlements in Ohio and western Pennsylvania. The United States took control of the Michigan region at the end of the war in 1783.

Territorial Days and the War of 1812

In 1787, Michigan was included in the newly formed Northwest Territory. In 1805, Michigan was reorganized as a separate territory, even though it had few settlements.

During the War of 1812, Michigan once again fell into British hands. After war was declared, Governor William Hull surrendered Detroit, and with it Michigan, to the British. In 1813, an American lieutenant, Oliver Hazard Perry, won an important naval victory on Lake Erie. Soon afterward American troops reoccupied Detroit, and Michigan was restored to American control.

Statehood and Early Development

Westward immigration surged with the opening of the Erie Canal in 1825. People from the eastern states and from Europe went to Michigan to farm the southern part of the Lower Peninsula. At this time the towns of Ann Arbor, Marshall, Monroe, Adrian, Grand Rapids, and Niles were established. Bolstered by its growing population, Michigan applied for statehood in 1834, but Congress delayed its decision until a border dispute with Ohio could be resolved. In 1836, Congress awarded the land in question to Ohio but granted Michigan the Upper Peninsula when it was admitted to the Union as the 26th state in 1837.

Mining and Lumbering

In the latter part of the 1800's, investors found that money could be made from the state's vast natural resources. Copper- and iron-mining companies were formed in the Upper Peninsula, attracting a new wave of immigrants. Similar companies were formed in the Lower Peninsula to log the tremen-

INDEX TO MICHIGAN MAP

● County Seat   Counties in parentheses   ★ State Capital

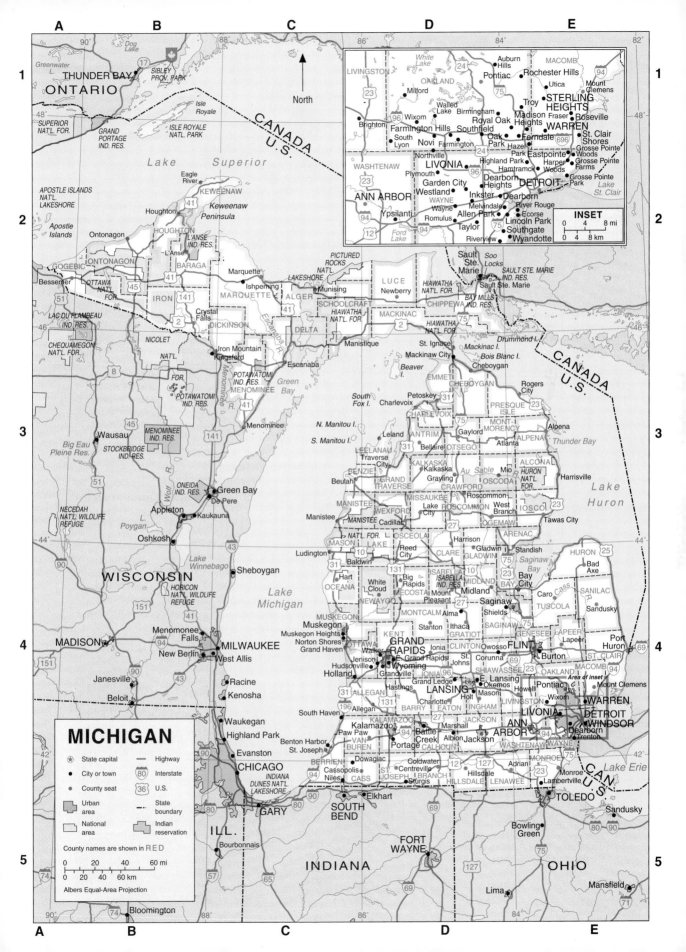

Famous People

Consult the Index to find more information in *The New Book of Knowledge* about the following people who were born in Michigan or are otherwise associated with the state: automobile tycoon HENRY FORD (1863–1947), U.S. senator VANDENBERG, ARTHUR HENDRICK (1884–1951), aviator CHARLES LINDBERGH (1902–74), Nobel Peace Prize winner RALPH BUNCHE (1904–71), labor leader WALTER P. REUTHER (1907–70), President GERALD R. FORD (1913–), and boxing champions Joe Louis (1914–81) and Sugar Ray Robinson (1921–89).

Henry Ford

Aretha Franklin

(Charles) Bruce Catton (1899–1978), born in Petoskey, was a popular author of historical works on the Civil War. *A Stillness at Appomattox* (1953), the last book in his trilogy on the Army of the Potomac (as the Union Army was called), won a Pulitzer Prize and the National Book Award. Other works include the *Centennial History of the Civil War* (3 volumes, 1961–65) and two biographical works on General Ulysses S. Grant, *Grant Moves South* (1960) and *Grant Takes Command* (1969).

Thomas E. (Edmund) Dewey (1902–71), born in Owosso, was a prominent Republican politician. As a special prosecutor for New York City, he convicted many members of organized crime. Dewey later served three terms as governor of New York State (1943–54). He ran for president of the United States twice but was defeated first by Franklin D. Roosevelt (1944) and then by Harry S. Truman (1948).

Edna Ferber (1887–1968), born in Kalamazoo, was a novelist and playwright. *So Big* (1924), about a midwestern farm community, won a Pulitzer Prize in 1925. *Show Boat* (1926), adapted by Jerome Kern and Oscar Hammerstein II, became a successful Broadway musical. She also wrote several popular stage comedies with George S. Kaufman, notably *Dinner at Eight* (1932) and *Stage Door* (1936).

Aretha Franklin (1942–), known as the Queen of Soul, was born in Memphis, Tennessee, but was raised in Detroit. The daughter of the Baptist reverend Charles L. Franklin, Aretha began singing gospel at her father's church and made her first recording at the age of 12. At 18 she signed with Columbia records but moved to the Atlantic label in 1966. The following year, *Billboard* magazine named her top

---

dous stocks of native white pine. As a result, the towns of Bay City, Saginaw, and Traverse City sprang up. For many decades logging teams moved northwest across the state, chopping down trees but not replanting them, leading to the industry's decline.

The Civil War Years

Before and during the Civil War (1861–65), Michigan was a center of a strong antislavery movement. The state became a major stop on the Underground Railroad that helped runaway slaves escape to Canada.

Michigan contributed greatly to the Union cause. More than 90,000 of its citizens—about 23 percent of the men in the state—fought for the Union. Nearly 14,000 died from wounds or disease.

Henry Ford's assembly-line production methods had each worker dedicated to a specific task. This efficient method made the manufacturing of automobiles more cost-effective. The workers shown here in 1928 assembled Ford Model A's at the Rouge plant in Dearborn.

The Industrial Period

In the early 1900's, Michigan began to transform itself from an agricultural to an industrial state. Several innovators, including Ransom E. Olds, Henry Ford, William C. Durant, and David D. Buick, began developing motorized transport vehicles.

Ford's particular achievement was to build simple cars that the average person could afford. To keep costs down, he pioneered the moving assembly-line process in 1913 that

female vocalist. From 1967 to 1975, she won an unprecedented string of Grammy Awards, most of them for best female rhythm and blues vocals. Franklin has recorded more than 50 albums. Her most enduring single is "Respect" (1967).

Berry Gordy, Jr. (1929–), born in Detroit, founded the Motown Recording Corporation, one of the largest, most successful businesses ever owned by an African American. In the 1950's, while working on the Ford automobile assembly line, Gordy began writing songs with his sister, Gwen, and Billy Davis. In 1959, he formed the Motown Recording Corporation, housed in a two-story building with a sign out front reading "Hitsville U.S.A." Motown's first hit came in 1961 with Smokey Robinson's "Shop Around." Gordy developed several of the most popular recording artists of all time, among them the Four Tops, the Tempta-

Gerald R. Ford

W. K. Kellogg

tions, Stevie Wonder, Marvin Gaye, Diana Ross and the Supremes, and the Jackson Five—all known for their distinctive Motown Sound. The original Motown studios are now preserved as a museum in Detroit.

W. K. (Will Keith) Kellogg (1860–1951), born in Battle Creek, founded a breakfast cereal empire. As a young man, he worked with his brother, Dr. John H. Kellogg, at the Battle Creek Sanitarium, where they developed toasted corn and wheat flakes and other vegetarian foods. In 1906, W. K. founded the Battle Creek

Toasted Corn Flake Company and sold his product through intensive advertising. He later added other breakfast foods to the company's line, making it the largest manufacturer of prepared cereal. In 1930, with $45 million, he established the W. K. Kellogg Foundation to fund charitable programs.

Ringgold Wilmer (Ring) Lardner (1885–1933), born in Niles, began writing as a reporter for the *South Bend Times*. He became known in 1916 when the *Saturday Evening Post* published his satirical collection of short stories, *You Know Me, Al*. Lardner's comical stories, often about sports figures and ordinary people, were narrated by characters who were prone to misusing or mispronouncing words. Other popular works included *Gullible's Travels* (1917); *Treat 'Em Rough* (1918); and *How to Write Short Stories (with Samples)* (1924).

made production extremely efficient. More than any other innovation, this one idea was critical to the state's emergence as a world leader in the production of automobiles.

Michigan's economy prospered throughout the 1920's, but it fell into sharp decline with the Great Depression of the 1930's. The auto industry was particularly hard hit, leading to massive unemployment. Hardship sparked the creation of the United Automobile Workers (UAW) union, which was formally recognized in 1937, following the resolution of a bitter confrontation between the owners of General Motors and their workers, known as the Flint "sit-down" strike.

World War II

When World War II broke out in Europe in 1939, Michigan industry began to recover. Automobile factories were immediately reorganized to speed up the manufacture of planes and tanks to supply to the armed forces overseas. Between 1939 and 1945, the industry was operating at full capacity, delivering nearly $50 billion in war materials, earning the state the nickname the Arsenal of Democracy.

Modern Times

After the war, Michigan continued to prosper, although its principal industries faced aggressive competition, both at home and from abroad. Furniture production, once dominated by firms in Grand Rapids, could not compete with new factories operating in the southern states. The automobile industry prospered until the 1970's, when fuel shortages and increased imports—particularly from Japan—forced Michigan manufacturers to develop new technologies to enhance quality and keep costs down. At the same time, economic opportunities and populations started shifting to suburban areas, causing Michigan's inner cities to fall into poverty and decay. Rebuilding the cities, maintaining the health of the automobile industry, and finding ways to strengthen and diversify the economy remain the state's most pressing challenges.

HERBERT L. ZOBEL
Eastern Michigan University

Reviewed by FRANCIS X. BLOUIN, JR.
The University of Michigan, Ann Arbor

See also DETROIT.

MICHIGAN, LAKE. See GREAT LAKES.

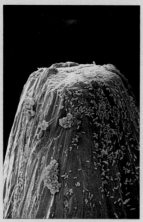
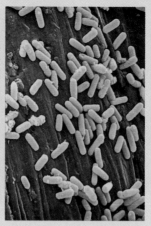
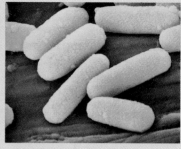

The point of a household pin is magnified over 4,000 times to show bacteria swarming over it—a dramatic demonstration of the minute size and vast number of microbes in our environment.

MICROBIOLOGY

A world of living creatures too small to see with our eyes is all around us—and in us, too. They cannot be seen, yet these minute life forms make their presence known by the things they do. They cause bread dough to rise and green scum to form on ponds. They even are responsible for the sore throat that occurs when you have a cold. These creatures are called microbes, or micro-organisms. When they cause disease they are called germs. Microbiology is the study of these microbes.

Microbes are billions of years old. Fossil records show that they were the first forms of life on earth. However, humans have only known about microbes for about 300 years. Their existence could not be proven until the invention of the microscope in the 1600's.

Since the time of discovery, scientists have been able to demonstrate how important these tiny organisms are to the balance of nature. Without them, plants and animals—including human beings—would stop living.

▶ THE WORLD OF MICROBES

The first microbiologists (scientists who study microbes) found that microbes were curious creatures. They did not fit readily into either the plant or animal kingdom. Microbes do some of the same things that both plants and animals do. Some get their energy from sunlight, as plants do. Other microbes move and find their food, as animals do. Microbes also have unique properties of their own. Most are simple creatures made of a single cell, while plants and animals are complex organisms made of many cells and a variety of different kinds of cells.

Most microbes measure less than $\frac{4}{1,000}$ inch (0.1 millimeter) across. Many of them must be studied with microscopes that magnify objects at least 1,000 times. Some are so tiny that they can be seen only with electron microscopes that magnify objects many thousands of times.

Upon examination, a microbe, like every other living cell, is seen to have a skin that covers it. This outer covering is called a **membrane**. The molecules and fluid needed for cell life are enclosed by the membrane. Some microbes also have an inner membrane that covers parts within the cell, such as genes. Genes, which are made of a substance called DNA (*d*eoxyribo*n*ucleic *a*cid), are the basic units of heredity. They carry the characteristics that are inherited by the next generation of cells from the parent cell. The membrane around genes forms a body inside the cell called a nucleus. Depending on the type of microbe, a cell may have other bodies that contain substances such as fat or protein. A cell may also have parts, such as whiplike structures called **flagella**, that are used for movement.

Most microbes are small, one-celled organisms with an outer covering that encloses molecules, fluid, genes, and other substances necessary for cell life. Some microbes, such as this rod-shaped soil bacteria called *Pseudomonas fluorescens*, also have whiplike structures, or flagella, that help them move about.

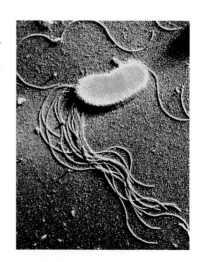

Types of Microbes

Microbiologists have identified many different types of microbes. Bacteria, algae, fungi, protozoa, and viruses are the major types. Some microbes, such as bacteria, are simple, one-celled organisms that do not have a membrane around their genetic material. Other types of microbes, including algae, fungi, and protozoa, consist of larger and more complex cells. These complex cells have a membrane around their genes forming a true nucleus.

Bacteria. Bacteria (plural of bacterium) are small, single-celled organisms without a nucleus. Nearly all bacteria are so small that they can only be seen under the highest magnification of a **light microscope**. Most have a thick wall around their cell.

Under the microscope, bacteria appear in three common shapes: rod-shaped, spherical, or spiral. These patterns help identify the type of bacteria. A rod-shaped bacterium is called a bacillus. A round or spherical bacterium is called a coccus. A wavy or corkscrew- or comma-shaped bacterium is called a spiral.

Some bacteria are stationary, while others can move or "swim." Many bacteria move with the help of flagella, the whiplike structures found on the outside of cells. Flagella spin like motorboat propellers and move the microbe to the food, air, or light they need to survive.

Bacteria need food and energy to live, just as all living creatures do. Some bacteria can make their own food from basic materials such as water and carbon. These organisms get the energy necessary to make the food from sunlight or from simple chemicals found in the soil, water, or air.

Bacteria are great at recycling. Most kinds of bacteria feed on nutrients produced by other living organisms. Bacteria that grow on dead plants and animals break them down to simple

Rod-shaped bacteria (colored red) coat the surface of a human tooth.

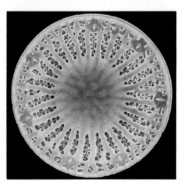
The pores of this diatom form a delicate radiating pattern.

chemicals. These simple chemicals can then be used as food by other microbes as well as by plants and animals. Other living organisms would not be able to survive if microbes, such as bacteria, did not process nutrients. However, bacteria can also be harmful and cause life-threatening disease.

Algae. Some algae (plural of alga) are small, single-celled organisms that are hard to see. Their presence becomes known when green scum forms in the quiet waters of ponds and lakes or when green stains appear on soil or rocks. Other algae, such as seaweed, are many-celled organisms made up of chains of several cells. The long, tangled chains can be seen growing along rocky beaches or in shallow coastal waters.

Within their cells, algae have a nucleus. Algae cells also contain pigments—the chemical substances that give algae its color and help in the manufacture of food. In the same manner as plants, algae use a process called photosynthesis to manufacture food. During photosynthesis, algae absorb energy from the sun and use it to power the formation of food from the raw materials (carbon dioxide and water) around them. It is with cell pigments, such as chlorophyll, that algae are able to capture the energy of sunlight.

Algae live in fresh waters and salty oceans. They are very important sources of food for other water creatures. Some small water algae, called diatoms, have very hard shell-like cell walls that can have unique, interesting shapes. Algae also live in soil and on trees.

Fungi. If you have seen fuzzy molds on stale bread, used yeast to bake, or eaten mushrooms, you may have seen the effects of fungi or even used fungi without knowing it. Molds, yeasts, and mushrooms are all types of fungi. Fungi (plural of fungus) are complex cells with a nucleus inside their cell fluid, or **cyto-**

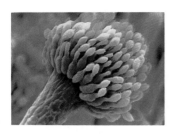

Aspergillus fumigatus is one of the more than 100,000 kinds of fungi. Its branching cells end in swollen, budlike reproductive structures called spores.

plasm. All fungi get their food and energy from other organisms. Some feed on living plants and animals, others live on dead and decaying plant and animal matter.

Some fungi are small and made of one cell, such as yeast. Some are large organisms with many cells, like mushrooms. Moldlike fungi form masses of long branching cells, or **filaments**, as they grow. Under the microscope, the mass looks like a collection of tangled hairs. These filaments can make millions of reproductive bodies, called **spores**. Each spore can form or reproduce into a new mold. The spores, which can be different colors, give the fungi their characteristic colors.

Fungi live in water, soil, and decaying leaves. They can cause the death of plants and the rotting of grains and food. Humans can sometimes be infected by fungi. Athlete's foot is a skin infection that is caused by one kind of fungus.

Protozoa. Protozoa (plural of protozoan) are single-celled microbes with at least one nucleus. Although most of the about 40,000 kinds of protozoa live in water, they also are found in moist earth, air, plants, and animals —including human beings. If you look at a drop of water under the microscope, you will see several types of protozoa. They are exciting to watch because they can move. Many get their food by eating other small microbes.

One type of protozoan is the **amoeba**. It moves by sending out fingerlike extensions of its cell membrane called **pseudopods**, or "false feet." The amoeba also uses pseudopods to find and eat food. As the amoeba moves slowly toward food, its pseudopods reach out and surround the food. Then the pseudopods draw the food into the cell body. Once the food is inside the cell, the amoeba digests it.

Another common protozoan you may see in pond water is the **paramecium**. This creature looks like a slipper with thin hairs covering it. These hairs are called **cilia**; they are used in locomotion and as the cell feeds. The cilia beat together rapidly to move the paramecium. Cilia also are used to sweep food and water into a funnel-like groove on the paramecium's side and into the

The paramecium is a tiny, one-celled organism.

cell body. A membrane bubble, or **vacuole**, forms around the food. The food vacuole floats in the cell until the food is digested. Waste material exits a small opening at the end of the cell. The paramecium also has a way to remove extra water from its cell so it does not burst.

Other protozoa move using flagella that stick outside one end of the cell. These protozoa are called flagellates. Protozoan flagella are like flexible whips that can bend in any direction. Some flagellates have several flagella, but most have one or two.

The Humongous Fungus

Except for mushrooms dotting the forest floor, there is little evidence of the massive organism that thrives within a forest near Crystal Falls, Michigan. However, scientists claim the giant has been a forest resident for more than 1,500 years!

The organism, which occupies more than 37 acres (15 hectares), is a fungus called *Armillaria bulbosa*. The mushrooms are just a small part of the fungus. The larger portion is an expansive network of rootlike tentacles that spread beneath the surface. All together, the fungus weighs more than 100 tons — close to the weight of an adult blue whale!

Scientists studying the gigantic fungus have found that it is a single organism. That is, the fungus is one individual living thing. Its size, along with its age, makes the humongous fungus one of the oldest and largest of all living organisms.

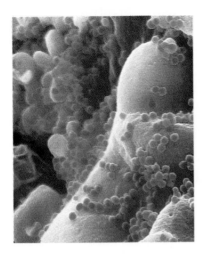

Because a virus cannot grow or reproduce on its own, it must take over living cells to survive. The deadly AIDS virus seeks out the cells of the immune system. Eventually it destroys the cells and renders the immune system helpless against infection. Here AIDS viruses (tinted blue) emerge from an infected white blood cell called a T helper cell.

Viruses. Viruses (plural of virus) are very different from other types of microbes. They are so small that most can only be seen with a powerful electron microscope. Viruses are not cells; they are very simple creatures. A virus has genetic material surrounded by a protective protein coat. Its genes can be made of either DNA or a related substance called RNA (ribonucleic acid). Some viruses have an additional layer called an envelope.

Viruses cannot reproduce unless they are inside the cell of another organism. All viruses are **parasites**, or creatures that live on and are harmful to other creatures. They get all their food and energy from the cell they infect. Often they change or damage the host cell. Viruses cause many different diseases, among them the common cold, flu, chickenpox, mumps, and AIDS.

▶THE STUDY OF MICROBES

The existence of microbes could not be proved until the discovery of the microscope. It was in the 1660's, after Anton van Leeuwenhoek constructed powerful microscope lenses, that it finally became possible to study and illustrate various microbes.

Leeuwenhoek, a Dutch store keeper and amateur scientist, was probably the very first to see microbes. He had a hobby of grinding lenses and building small, but powerful, single-lens microscopes. The lenses were no larger than the head of a pin and could magnify an object more than 200 times. He used these lenses to discover the world of "small animacules" in rainwater, teeth scrapings, and other living and nonliving materials. The creatures astonished and delighted him. Leeuwenhoek carefully drew what he saw and sent letters about his discoveries to other scientists.

Interest in microbes faded after Leeuwenhoek's death, for several reasons. Leeuwenhoek never showed his children or an apprentice how to grind the lenses used in his microscopes. Also, scientists during this time saw microbes as "interesting creatures," but not worth studying. They did not realize how many different ways microbes affect other living things.

In the centuries that followed, scientists began to think about microbes in a different way. It was proven that microbes came from living things rather than arising from nonliving matter. Interest continued to increase with the further development of the light microscope. With improved instruments, scientists could examine all but the smallest microbes.

The 1800's brought an explosion of discoveries. It was then that Robert Koch, a country doctor in Germany, and Louis Pasteur, a French professor of chemistry, made their

---

Did you know that . . .

pizza is a tasty meal because of microbes? Yeast, a type of fungus, is used to make the dough for the crust. The cheese that melts atop the crust would not be as flavorful if bacteria were not added to the cheese as it is made.

While some microbes, such as yeast and bacteria, are valued for what they add to food, other microbes are themselves eaten as a food. One example is a fungus that is used as a pizza topping—the mushroom.

Events in the Development of Microbiology

Ancient Life
Fossil remains of microbes resembling blue-green algae are captured in rock that is more than 2 billion years old.

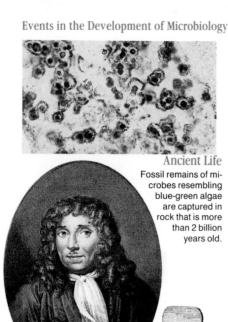

1673 Anton van Leeuwenhoek (1632–1723) becomes the first to view the mysterious and exciting world of microbes through a small, single-lens microscope that he has built (*right*).

1796 Edward Jenner (1749–1823) conducts the first vaccination by injecting the fluid from a dairymaid's cowpox lesion into a young boy's arm. The vaccination successfully protects the child from smallpox.

1884 Louis Pasteur (1822–85) works in his laboratory on a vaccine to combat the dread disease called rabies. A year later, the vaccine is ready and is used successfully.

1865 Joseph Lister (1827–1912) concludes that microbes cause wound infections. He begins to use carbolic acid on wounds to kill microbes and reduce infection after surgery.

contributions to the study of microbes. Both made many discoveries that advanced the science of microbiology.

Koch was able to show that bacteria caused disease. He also developed the methods of studying microbes that are still used today. Koch was able to grow, or culture, one kind of microbe from a mixture of different kinds of microbes. He was able to obtain what is called a **pure culture**. This process allowed him to tell what each microbe did. Koch originally spread samples containing bacteria on potato slices or solidified gelatin. Later, it was suggested that he add agar, a thickener used in cooking, to his nutrients. Today, his solid nutrient agar is still used to isolate microbes.

Pasteur expanded on Koch's disease theories and demonstrated the importance of microbes in agricultural and industrial processes. One such instance occurred when the French government asked Pasteur to solve the problem of the sour taste in wine. He showed that certain yeasts, which are types of fungi, made good wine. In addition, he showed that wine became sour when other microbes were also in the wine. Pasteur solved the problem by heating the wine and killing the unwanted microbes. This process of heating wine, milk, and food to make it safe is called **pasteurization**. Today, we are able to preserve food and prevent food poisoning by using Pasteur's method.

Tremendous strides were made in microbiology during the late 1800's. But it was not until the 1900's that the field of microbiology was opened up to its fullest extent. It was then that it became possible to observe the smallest of microbes, the viruses. With the development of the electron microscope in the 1930's, scientists were given the opportunity to study viruses and microscopic particles such as prions, viroids, and plasmids.

1910 Paul Ehrlich (1854–1915) introduces chemotherapy — a way to control and treat disease by using substances that will attack disease-causing microbes but will not damage the rest of the body.

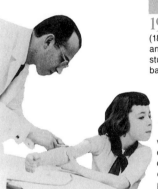

1905 Robert Koch (1843–1910) receives the Nobel Prize for his trailblazing work, which includes identifying the organism responsible for tuberculosis (rod-shaped microbes in drawing *above*) and discovering a tuberculosis skin-testing material.

1928 Sir Alexander Fleming (1881–1955) discovers the first antibiotic, penicillin, as he studies the relationship between bacteria and the mold *Penicillium*.

1953 Jonas Salk (1914–95) vaccinates a young girl during the test trials of the vaccine he has developed to prevent poliomyelitis. It proves to be the first effective polio vaccine.

▶MICROBIOLOGY IN THE 1900'S

The early scientists laid the foundation for many developments in the 1900's. It was in the early 1900's that the concept of the gene as the basic unit of heredity was fully appreciated. Scientists learned that DNA controls the shape, behavior, and growth of microbes. Further studies led researchers to the discovery that in nature, microbes can exchange, or recombine, pieces of DNA. The exchange of DNA gives the next generation of microbes new traits. This information set the stage for significant new applications of microbiology within medicine, agriculture, and industry.

Modern-day scientists have developed a new set of methods called recombinant-DNA technology. These methods artificially give microbes new genes and new traits. A revolution in research has resulted. With careful experimenting, helpful genes can be put into bacteria. For example, the gene for the human hormone insulin can be put into bacteria. These bacteria can act like factories and make large amounts of insulin. This insulin can then be used to treat people with diabetes.

In the same way that developments such as the discovery of the microscope and antibiotics brought exciting changes to the world, so will recombinant-DNA technology. Solutions for worldwide problems of disease, food production, and waste disposal are possible using these methods. The wide-ranging possibilities ensure that microbes will continue to be very important creatures in our world.

Cynthia V. Sommer
Department of Biological Sciences
University of Wisconsin at Milwaukee

See also Algae; Antibiotics; Bacteria; Cells; Diseases; Fermentation; Fungi; Koch, Robert; Leeuwenhoek, Anton Van; Microscopes; Pasteur, Louis; Viruses.

MICROCHIPS. See Computers.

MICRONESIA, Federated States of

The Federated States of Micronesia (FSM) is an island nation in the northwestern Pacific Ocean. It is made up of more than 600 small islands and islets scattered over a vast area of the Pacific. The name Micronesia means "small islands."

The FSM is made up of four states—Chuuk (formerly Truk), Pohnpei (formerly Ponape), Yap, and Kosrae. Each state is composed of one or more islands, plus atolls (rings of coral surrounding a lagoon). The capital, Palikir, is situated on the island of Pohnpei, the country's largest island.

People. The population of the Federated States is about 136,000. Most of the people are Micronesians, but this term includes peoples of varied cultures and languages. Two islands are inhabited by Polynesians, a distinct ethnic group. About half the population lives on the islands of Chuuk. Nearly one-third lives on the islands of Pohnpei.

Nine languages are spoken in the FSM, including English. The people are Christians, with almost equal numbers of Protestants and Roman Catholics.

Land. The FSM covers 271 square miles (702 square kilometers). It includes most of the islands of the Caroline chain, except for the most westerly, which are part of the Republic of Palau. The islands are of two basic kinds: high volcanic islands and smaller atolls that are only several feet above sea level. The highest point, Dolohmwar, is 2,595 feet (791 meters) high.

The climate is tropical. Annual temperatures average about 80°F (27°C), and rainfall in the higher elevations exceeds 200 inches (5,000 millimeters) a year. The islands are subject to typhoons—severe storms that can cause great damage.

Economy. Tropical fruits and vegetables, copra (dried coconut meat), and cassava (an edible root) are the islands' basic food crops. The country's chief exports are fish, clothing, bananas, and black pepper. However, the FSM depends on economic assistance from the United States.

History and Government. Spanish navigators sighted the islands in the 1500's and claimed them for Spain. Spain sold them to Germany in 1899. Japan occupied the islands from the beginning of World War I (1914–18) until the end of World War II (1939–45). In 1947 the United Nations placed the islands under the administration of the United States, as part of the Trust Territory of the Pacific Islands.

In 1982 the FSM entered into a Compact of Free Association with the United States. The Compact went into full effect in 1986. Under its terms, the FSM became an independent nation, although still dependent on the United States for defense and financial aid. The FSM was admitted to the United Nations in 1991.

The government consists of a president and vice president. Both are elected by the one-house legislature to serve 4-year terms. Joseph J. Urusemal was elected president in 2003.

WARD BARRETT
Author, *Mission in the Marianas*

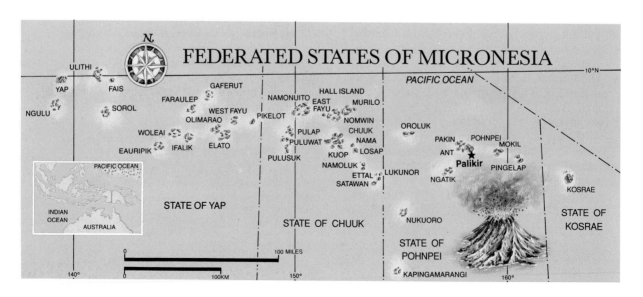

FEDERATED STATES OF MICRONESIA

MICROPHONES. See RADIO.

MICROPROCESSORS. See COMPUTERS.

MICROSCOPES

A microscope is a device that magnifies small objects. The first microscope was developed about 1595 and was only as strong as a magnifying glass. Today, there are dozens of microscopes capable of letting us see and analyze objects as small as atoms!

▶ USE OF MICROSCOPES

When most people think of microscopes, biology and medicine probably come to mind. And the desire to learn about living things was most likely the main reason for the invention of the microscope. Today, however, microscopes are used in many other fields.

For example, geologists use microscopes to examine rocks and minerals and materials scientists use them to study plastics and polymers. Engineers use microscopes to study surface properties and structures of metals.

Forensic science is the study of crime scenes for the purpose of presenting evidence in courts of law. Evidence such as dust, glass, body fluids, hair, inks, and micro-organisms can be analyzed using microscopy.

Microscopes are also used in the service, manufacturing, and pharmaceutical industries to ensure the safety and quality of products. Scientists in these industries examine their products microscopically to identify any flaws or contaminants.

▶ COMMON LIGHT MICROSCOPES

Light microscopes, also called optical microscopes, use light and lenses to magnify images. If light waves reflected off an object are passed through a lens in a certain way, they will refract, or bend. The refracted light waves are spread out and appear to be coming from a bigger object. The simplest light microscope is the magnifying glass. It is a single lens that can magnify an image up to 25 times.

The **compound light microscope** (also called a **brightfield microscope**) is the type found in most classrooms. All compound mi-

croscopes contain two magnifying lenses and work similarly. Visible light from the base passes through a condenser, through the specimen, and then into the objective lens, forming a magnified primary image. The primary image is further magnified as it passes through the ocular lens. The final image is projected onto the retina of the eye. The total magnification is calculated by multiplying the magnifying power of the objective lens by that of the ocular lens. Most microscopes give

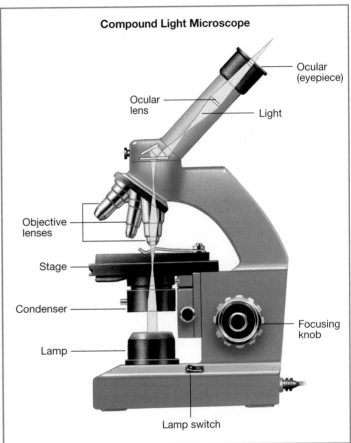

Compound Light Microscope

Ocular (eyepiece)

Ocular lens

Light

Objective lenses

Stage

Condenser

Lamp

Focusing knob

Lamp switch

How to Care for Your Microscope

For information on the care and use of your microscope, read the instruction manual. Store your microscope in its box when you are not using it. Clean its lenses by blotting them with lens paper. Rubbing a speck of dust across a lens could scratch it. Do not touch the lenses with your fingers. The natural oil from your skin is hard to clean off a lens.

a choice of several objective lenses mounted on a rotating disc, each providing a different magnification.

A simple microscope, the **stereoscopic (dissecting) microscope**, is useful for viewing objects too small to be studied with the eye alone, but too large to be seen with a compound light microscope. A specimen is placed on a stage, or platform, and illuminated from above, producing an image similar to that seen with a magnifying glass. Magnifications rarely exceed 50 times.

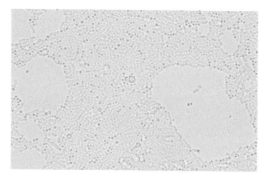

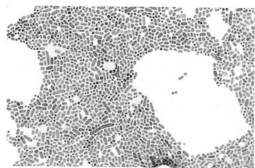

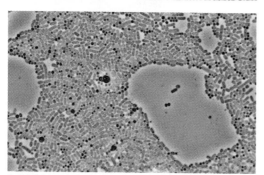

Scientists use stains or special lenses to help them view colorless biological specimens through a microscope. *Top:* Unstained bacterial cells magnified 400 times are still difficult to see. *Middle:* Bacterial cells stained with iodine and magnified 400 times are more visible. *Bottom:* Bacterial cells viewed with a phase contrast microscope are visible without the use of stain.

▶ **VIEWING SPECIMENS**

To be viewed by a compound light microscope, a specimen must be translucent (thin enough to permit the passage of light). Microorganisms in a drop of water are thin enough to view, but what about a piece of liver? The liver must first be preserved and hardened using chemical procedures. It is then sliced very thin on a machine called a **microtome**, which is similar to a meat-slicing machine, and a thin slice is mounted on a glass slide. Sometimes a thin piece of glass, called a coverslip, is placed over a specimen to protect it and make it lie flat. A liver slice prepared this way is nearly colorless; therefore, the image will not be very detailed. A specimen must also have contrast to make structural details more visible.

Color must be added to provide contrast to many biological specimens. A common way to chemically add color is by using a stain, or dye. Different stains can be used to label distinct structures of the liver. Stains can be used to add color to living microorganisms as well. Some stains are toxic to living organisms, but there are a few special stains called **vital dyes** that add color without killing living cells.

▶ **RESOLUTION AND MAGNIFICATION**

Some particles, such as viruses, are too small to be seen with a compound microscope. Even if one built a light microscope capable of magnifying 1 million times, viruses would still be invisible. Why? Because viruses are smaller than the average wavelength of visible light.

Every optical instrument has a **resolving power**, defined as the ability to distinguish closely spaced objects and create a clear image. The resolving power depends on the wavelength of whatever produces the image (white light in the case of a light microscope) and the ability of the objective lens to capture the image-forming rays as they leave the specimen.

Resolving power limits the magnification of a microscope. If an object is too small to be seen by a particular microscope, increasing the magnification will be of no use. An object that is smaller than the wavelength of light cannot be seen with an ordinary light microscope. The maximum usable magnification for an average compound microscope is about

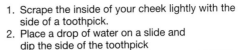

Some Things to See with Your Microscope

See For Yourself

Here are suggestions of things you can see with your microscope.

Basic Materials:

Flat microscope slides
Depression slides (these have a little hollow in the center)
Coverslips (small, thin pieces of glass or plastic used to cover specimens)
A pair of sharp-pointed tweezers
A medicine dropper (pipette)
Single-edge razor blades (handle carefully)
Two saucers or cups (use paper cups or saucers for easy cleanup)
A spoon (use plastic spoons for easy cleanup)
Toothpicks
Iodine

The Cells of an Onion Skin

Plant cells have a hard, outer cell wall made of cellulose. This rigid wall is responsible for the square or rectangular shape of many plant cells. A small circular spot in the cell is the nucleus.

1. Cut a few slices from an onion and separate the rings.
2. Gently break one area of a ring without completely separating the pieces.
3. Pull one piece across the other to separate a thin layer of onion skin or use tweezers to pull off a piece of skin from the underside of a ring.

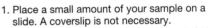

Onion cells

4. Spread the skin on a microscope slide. If you wish to stain the cells, place a drop of iodine on the onion skin. Allow the preparation to sit for two minutes.
5. Pick up a coverslip with the tweezers and cover the onion skin on the slide to keep it from drying out.
6. Using the microscope's focusing controls, place the objective lens as close as possible to the coverslip.
7. While looking through the eyepiece, slowly raise the lens until the specimen is in focus.

A Type of Body Cell

There are many types of cells in the human body. Some cells, like those found in your muscles, are very long and designed to cause movement. Others, like those covering the internal and external surfaces of the body, can be small and thin. These cells are called epithelial cells, and some can be found lining the inside of your cheek.

1. Scrape the inside of your cheek lightly with the side of a toothpick.
2. Place a drop of water on a slide and dip the side of the toothpick into the water.
3. Using tweezers, place a coverslip on the drop of water.
4. Prepare for observation using the procedures described under (6) and (7) above.

Kitchen Microscopy

There are many interesting things to look at right in your own kitchen. The spice and seasoning cabinet has herbs and spices made from plant leaves, flowers, seeds, roots, and bark. Some, like common salt, are mineral compounds.

Potato starch granules

1. Place a small amount of your sample on a slide. A coverslip is not necessary.
2. Using the microscope's focusing controls, place the objective lens as close as possible to the specimen without actually touching it.
3. Bring the specimen into focus as you did above.

Thin slices of green, yellow, and red peppers and potatoes can easily be studied. Pepper cells contain pigmented granules that give the peppers their color. Potato cells also have granules, but these contain starch. When stained with iodine, potato granules become dark blue.

1. Using a razor blade, shave off a very thin slice of vegetable and place it on a slide.
2. Potato slices must first be stained with a solution of iodine and water. (Combine $1/4$ teaspoon iodine and 1 teaspoon water in a saucer). Place one or two drops of the solution on the potato slice. Pepper slices should not be stained.
3. Focus as you did in previous observations.

Micro-organisms in pond water

Life in Pond or Aquarium Water

Pond and aquarium water provide homes for a large variety of organisms.

1. Obtain a water sample in a jar from a dirty region of a pond or from the filter of an aquarium.
2. Put a drop of water on a depression slide and cover it with a cover slip. Make sure your drop contains some visible debris.
3. Focus as you did in previous observations.

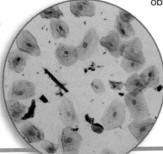

Human cheek cells

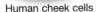

Range of Vision Using Microscopes Compared with Human Eye Alone

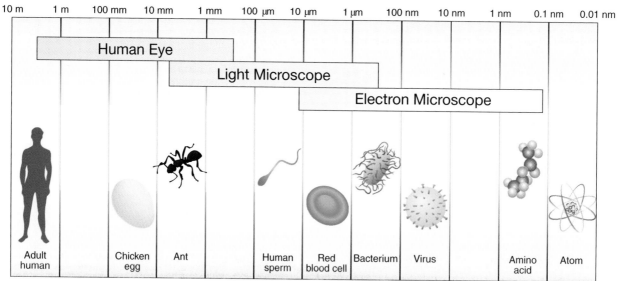

Scientists measure sizes using the metric system. A millimeter (abbreviated mm) is one-thousandth of a meter. A micrometer (μm) is one-millionth of a meter. And a nanometer (nm) is one-billionth of a meter. With the unaided eye, we cannot see things that are less than a millimeter in size. But with an electron microscope, scientists can see molecules, such as amino acids, that are less than a billionth of a meter in size. And the newest microscopes allow scientists to see objects as small as atoms.

1,500 times. If an ocular lens with a magnification of 10 times (10X) is used in combination with a 10X, 20X, or 40X objective lens, the final magnification for each view would be 100X, 200X, and 400X, respectively. As the magnification increases, the objective lens captures fewer image-forming rays, and the magnified image becomes less distinct.

Magnifications above 400X require a different kind of objective lens to capture more of the image-forming rays. This is an **oil immersion** lens. A drop of oil is placed on the coverslip over the specimen, and a 100X oil immersion lens is carefully lowered into the oil. The oil acts as another lens, directing more image-forming rays into the 100X objective lens and producing a clear image (and better resolution) at 1000X.

Some light microscopes obtain higher resolutions by changing the wavelength of the light used to create the image or the ability of the objective lens to capture the image-forming rays (see the section Other Light Microscopes below). To see very small objects like viruses, drastic changes in the way the image is created are required (see the section Electron Microscopes below).

▶ OTHER LIGHT MICROSCOPES

Some microscopes are designed to compensate for the problems of contrast and resolution that limit the function of the compound microscope. For example, the **phase contrast microscope** makes it easier to see living cells without staining them. This microscope processes light rays differently so that uncolored specimens appear colored. A compound microscope can be converted into a phase contrast microscope by changing the lenses and a few other parts. Phase contrast lenses are expensive and are not used in most school laboratories.

A **dark field microscope** can be constructed by placing an opaque disc underneath the condenser of a compound microscope to block the passage of light through the specimen. A powerful light directed at the specimen from above is reflected back from the specimen into the objective lens, producing an illuminated object on a dark background. Dark field microscopy is ideal for looking at small organisms suspended in a liquid.

The **laser scanning confocal microscope** was created for specialized use in research, hospital, and industrial laboratories. It uses a laser beam to increase the amount of light entering the objective lens and to scan different layers of the specimen. This produces two-dimensional, layered images that can be fed into a computer to produce a three-dimensional reconstruction of the specimen.

The **fluorescence microscope** uses ultraviolet light to create contrast. Specimens treated with special dyes emit visible light when exposed to ultraviolet radiation. The fluorescence microscope produces high-contrast images that are used to diagnose infections caused by many types of microorganisms.

Another light microscope is the **stimulated emission depletion microscope**. Through the use of lasers, this microscope allows the viewer to see cellular features one-eighteenth the size that can be observed using standard light microscopes. Although its resolving power is much less than an electron microscope, the stimulated emission depletion microscope is very useful because it can be used to view living tissue. The electron microscope is mainly limited to observing dead tissue.

▶ ELECTRON MICROSCOPES

German physicist Ernst Ruska knew that electrons traveled at much shorter wavelengths than light. In 1931, he built a microscope that produced an image by passing electrons through a very thin specimen. The shorter wavelength of electrons gave this **transmission electron microscope (TEM)** more resolving power, thereby increasing its usable magnification. Today, TEM's are capable of magnifications as high as 1 million times. Such magnification has permitted the internal structures of viruses and cells to be routinely studied in laboratories.

Just as the compound microscope passes light through a specimen to create an image, the TEM does the same with electrons. But neither microscope can observe details on the surface of an object. To view surface details, it is necessary to use a **scanning electron microscope (SEM)**, which can show tiny surface features on biological and non-biological specimens by passing a beam of electrons across the surface of a specimen rather than through it.

The TEM and SEM are by far the most commonly used electron microscopes. However, there are other types. For example, the **scanning transmission electron microscope** can simultaneously provide highly detailed images and molecular information about the specimen.

In 1986, the Nobel Prize was awarded to Ernst Ruska for his design of the first electron microscope, and to Gerd Binnig and Heinrich Rohrer for the design of the **scanning tunneling microscope (STM)**. The STM uses a very fine, pen-like electrode to scan a small area of a specimen's surface at a close distance to produce three-dimensional images of individual atoms. The **atomic force microscope** measures atomic-level forces between a sharp probe and electrons on the

A transmission electron microscope (TEM) uses electrons to produce a magnified image of a specimen, which is shown on a monitor. TEM's can magnify objects up to 1 million times.

surface of a specimen. These measurements can be used to construct a highly detailed image of the surface of an object.

An **atom-probe field ion microscope** can simultaneously create images and provide chemical data of atoms on metal surfaces. When a sharp needle made of the metal specimen is electrically heated in a helium-filled chamber, helium atoms bouncing off the needle tip form a pattern on a television screen that can be quantified by an atom probe.

How to Build Van Leeuwenhoek's Microscope

Van Leeuwenhoek's original microscope was a very simple piece of equipment. A small spherical lens was supported on the end of a nail-like structure that was mounted to a metal plate. The specimen, which was attached to the end of a screw, sat behind the lens. The entire contraption was held up to the light, and the user looked through the lens at the magnified image of the specimen.

A model similar to Van Leeuwenhoek's microscope can be made with a paper clip or a small piece of solid wire.

Materials Needed:
  A small paper clip or 3-inch (7.6-centimeter) piece of solid wire
  A small pair of needle nose pliers
  Water in a cup
  Motor oil, grease, or petroleum jelly
  Distilled (preferred) or tap water
  Alligator clip (optional)

1. Straighten a small paper clip, or use a 3-inch (7.6-centimeter) piece of solid wire.
2. Using a small pair of pliers, bend a small loop—about $1/16$ inch (0.2 centimeter) in diameter—at the end of the straightened paper clip or length of wire. Do not scratch the loop.
3. Rub a small amount of motor oil or grease (petroleum jelly will also work) on the loop, making a very thin coating.
4. Dip the loop into distilled water (or tap water), then slowly remove it from the water. A small drop of water should stick to the loop, forming a "lens."
5. Hold the water lens up to your eye and place the object you wish to study in front of the lens. If the object cannot be held with your fingers, pierce it with the end of another extended paper clip or a piece of wire. An alligator clip (available at electronics stores) also works well for holding a specimen.
6. Look toward a light source.
7. Focus by moving the specimen away from or closer to the lens.

▶ HISTORY OF LIGHT MICROSCOPES

The invention of the microscope was preceded by the use of lenses. In the first century A.D., the Roman philospher Seneca described the magnification produced by "a globe of glass filled with water." Between A.D. 23 and 79, Pliny the Elder, a famous Roman scholar, described the use of an emerald by Emperor Nero to better view the combat of the gladiators. However, it was the widespread use of lenses for eyeglasses in the 1400's that paved the way for the invention of the microscope.

About 1595, a young Dutchman named Zacharias Jansen and his father Hans invented the first microscope. This microscope was a long brass tube with two lenses and a maximum magnification of 9X. Within a few dozen years, there were several microscope manufacturers, including Galileo, who is more famous for his work with telescopes.

The early microscopes were good for observing insect parts, but they were too crude to view smaller objects. Then in the 1660's, Robert Hooke of England viewed smaller objects with an instrument built by Christopher Cock. While looking at thin slices of cork, Hooke used the term "cell" to describe the small air spaces he observed. In 1665, Hooke published *Micrographia*, one of the first books demonstrating the importance of microscopy.

Anton van Leeuwenhoek, an amateur scientist from Holland, became fascinated with Hooke's pictures of magnified textiles. He began making incredible discoveries using a tiny single-lens microscope of his own design. In 1673, van Leeuwenhoek began writing letters about his discoveries to the Royal Society of London. Throughout his life, he wrote letters describing the specimens he viewed with his microscope, which included bee mouthparts and stingers, human lice, algae, protozoa, blood cells, microscopic nematodes, bacteria, and spermatozoa.

Gradually, improvements continued to be made to the design of the microscope. Microscopes became increasingly stable and easy to use, but the images were still blurry (spherical aberration) with colorful halos around objects (chromatic aberration). An achromatic lens for the microscope was designed in 1800, and spherical aberration was fixed in 1830. Through trial and error, improvements were made to objective lenses. The relationship between resolution, wavelength, and how much of the image is collected by the objective lens was not completely understood until German physicist Ernst Abbe published his resolution formula in 1877.

MARTIN A. LEVIN
Eastern Connecticut State University

See also ELECTRON MICROSCOPE; LENSES; LIGHT; RADIATION.

Microwaves are used to carry telephone and other communications signals. At this transmitting station, signals are sent in two ways. Large dish antennae beam microwaves to satellites, which can relay the signals a third of the way around the world. Small antennae atop the tower send signals to the next station in a ground radio relay. Microwaves travel in a straight path, so one tower must be in the line of sight of the next tower.

MICROWAVES

You are probably familiar with the microwave oven. Many families and restaurants use this appliance to cook foods in a fraction of the time that conventional ovens take. In a microwave oven, invisible microwaves, cousins to the radio waves that are picked up by your transistor radio, actually cook the food. But food preparation is only one of many uses that people have found for microwaves.

▶WHAT MICROWAVES ARE

Microwaves form part of the spectrum (range) of electromagnetic waves, which also includes light and radio waves. Like all electromagnetic waves, microwaves travel at a speed of 186,000 miles (300,000 kilometers) a second. They differ from other electromagnetic waves in length and in certain other ways.

The waves of the electromagnetic spectrum vary greatly in length. Hundreds of thousands of light waves could fit in a space the length of your thumbnail. But the waves that carry radio programs may be longer than a football field. Microwaves lie midway between light waves and radio waves. They range in length from less than four hundredths of an inch (1 millimeter) to about a foot (30 centimeters).

Microwaves are actually very short radio waves. Like other radio waves, they can be used to carry messages, such as telephone conversations and television signals. They can pass easily through fog and clouds and many solid materials, including concrete. They are reflected by metal, however.

Microwaves can also be focused into a tight beam that travels in a straight path. In this way they are more like light waves than radio waves. And microwaves are strongly absorbed by certain materials. The microwaves used in a microwave oven, for example, are strongly absorbed by the moisture in food.

▶HOW MICROWAVES ARE USED

Microwaves are used in radar, in communications, and in a variety of other ways in science and industry.

Radar and Navigation. "Radar" stands for *ra*dio *d*etection *a*nd *r*anging. Radar was developed during World War II and was one of the first uses of microwaves. Today it is used aboard aircraft and ships and at airports and harbors, to detect objects at night and in heavy fog. At an airport, for example, a beam of microwaves from a transmitter constantly scans the sky. When the beam hits an incoming aircraft, a signal is bounced back. By processing this echo electronically, it is possible to work out the size, speed, and distance of the aircraft.

Because it can penetrate clouds and work in the dark, radar is used by observation satellites to map the surface of the Earth. Sensitive microwave radars are used by the military to identify targets. An automatic landing system using microwaves is under development for civilian aircraft.

Communications. Microwaves are used to carry the signals of telephone conversations, television programs, and other forms of communication over long distances. Because they are shorter than radio waves, they can carry more signals. And because they can be focused like light waves, the signals can be directed to specific destinations.

You may have seen tall towers with microwave antenna dishes in your community. These microwave towers are used to transmit communications signals in a system called **microwave radio relay.** The signals are focused by the dishes and beamed from one tower to the next. Communications satellites are also used to relay microwave signals.

Heating. Some other uses of microwaves stem from their ability to heat certain materials. The microwaves in a microwave oven are tuned to be absorbed by the moisture in food. As they are absorbed, the microwaves cause the water molecules to jiggle, or vibrate. This heats the food. But containers made of polystyrene, ceramics, and many other materials remain cool because they contain no moisture and thus do not absorb the microwaves. (Containers may become warm from contact with the food, however.)

Besides cooking, microwaves are used in special heating processes. A medical treatment called diathermy uses the heating effects of microwaves to help heal muscle and tendon strains. Exposure to the microwaves is carefully controlled in diathermy treatments.

Other Uses. Detecting microwaves from outer space is an important part of radio astronomy. By analyzing this microwave radiation, astronomers learn about distant stars and even the possible origins of the universe.

Microwave weapons have been proposed as a way of destroying enemy missiles. In these weapons, the microwaves would be produced by an explosion high over the Earth. They would damage the electronic controls needed to launch the missiles.

Some scientists believe that microwaves could be used to transmit electrical power. If this is so, microwaves may one day help solve Earth's energy problems. One idea is to place

Why do foods cook faster in a microwave oven?

Food placed in a microwave oven cooks far more quickly than food placed in a conventional oven. For example, a potato will bake in about four minutes in a microwave oven, but it will need at least ten times that long in a conventional oven. In the conventional oven, the heat is created by infrared radiation, which is given off by the hot element and walls of the oven. The infrared waves cannot penetrate the potato, so the potato cooks slowly—the outside is heated first, and then the heat is slowly transferred to the inside. But microwaves can penetrate deep into the potato, where they are absorbed by the moisture it contains. Thus the food is heated through much more quickly.

satellites with giant solar panels in orbit around the Earth. The solar panels would convert sunlight into electricity, which would be beamed to Earth using microwaves.

Researchers have used microwaves to power small aircraft. However, as distance increases, microwave beams spread out. Less power reaches the aircraft. Beaming power to aircraft may be easier with lasers.

▶ SAFETY CONCERNS

A very strong dose of microwave radiation would be dangerous. If a person accidentally stood directly in front of a working radar dish, for example, the microwaves would heat up parts of the body and could damage internal organs. But the effects of long-term exposure to lower levels of microwave radiation are less clear, and scientists do not all agree about the risks. Some scientists and doctors think that over very long periods, such exposure could have harmful effects.

Governments have therefore set safety standards for exposure to microwaves. These standards vary from country to country. Microwave ovens must meet a number of safety standards before they are sold to the public. They should be safe if they are used according to manufacturers' instructions.

F. DAVID PEAT
Coauthor, *The Looking Glass Universe*

See also RADAR AND SONAR; RADIATION; RADIO; RADIO ASTRONOMY; TELECOMMUNICATIONS.

MIDAS. See GREEK MYTHOLOGY (Profiles).

MIDDLE AGES

The medieval period, known as the Middle Ages, covers nearly 1,000 years of European history. According to some historians, the era began in A.D. 476 when a German chieftain overthrew the last emperor of the Western Roman Empire. It lasted until about 1500, when the Renaissance, a period of tremendous innovation, became firmly established throughout western Europe.

The Middle Ages were once viewed as a time of ignorance—a "dark age" between the glories of the ancient world and the flowering of learning and culture that occurred during the Renaissance. But a great many things happened in Europe during these years.

Sir Lancelot, a legendary knight, does battle in this medieval scene. During the Middle Ages, knights went into battle in the service of feudal lords. In exchange, the knights received grants of land.

▶ THE EARLY MIDDLE AGES

At its height, the Roman Empire controlled most of western Europe. Roman rule provided a sort of glue that unified the region. Roman armies kept the peace. Roman roads linked various parts of Europe, and Roman aqueducts brought water to towns and cities. But by A.D. 400, the Roman Empire had been split into eastern and western halves. Germanic tribes had begun to move into the Western Empire, and Roman armies could no longer control them. In 410, the Visigoths (or West Goths) invaded Italy and plundered the city of Rome itself. It was hard for people of those times to believe that Roman power had grown so weak. "Who would believe," Saint Jerome, a Christian writer, asked, "that Rome, which had spread over the whole earth by means of its victories, could now fall so low?" The Eastern Empire (or Byzantine Empire), with its capital at Constantinople (now Istanbul, Turkey), continued to flourish. But the Western Empire fell apart.

Various Germanic tribes settled in what are today the countries of western Europe—the Visigoths in Spain, the Lombards in Italy, the Anglo-Saxons in England, and the Franks in France and western Germany. They lived alongside the inhabitants of the old empire. They did not wish to destroy all signs of Roman civilization. They adopted many of their neighbors' ways, including the Christian religion. But they lived under their own laws and under the rule of their own chiefs or kings.

Without a central government, life changed greatly. Roads and water-supply systems fell into disrepair. There was little trade, with the result that cities and towns became less important. The people in each region produced almost everything they used, which was often little more than the bare necessities. Learning also declined. Few Germanic people could read Latin, so they learned little about the civilization they had conquered.

During most of the early Middle Ages, Europe was carved up into small regions ruled by local lords. Each lord made his own laws, and this often led to conflict and disorder. Lords fought among themselves, and they tried to defend their lands from outside threats. One of the most serious threats came from Muslims from North Africa, who invaded Europe through Spain in 711.

Historians used to call the early Middle Ages the Dark Ages because this time was marked by confusion, disorder, and the breakdown of civilization in western Europe. But scholars today see this period as a time of change, rather than darkness, in Europe. As Rome's power crumbled, religion became the one thing shared by people throughout the former Roman realm. Today Christianity has many branches, but in western Europe during the Middle Ages there was only one. The Catholic Church, headed by the pope, played a central role in medieval life.

Charlemagne's Empire

During the early Middle Ages, several rulers tried to establish larger kingdoms. The most successful was the great Frankish king Charlemagne (742?–814), whose empire included much of western and central Europe. Charlemagne wanted to rule as the emperors of Rome had in ancient times. He was even crowned emperor of the Romans by Pope Leo III in 800. Charlemagne maintained order throughout his realm and kept close check on the great nobles and landlords, who were in the habit of doing as they wished. Into every district he sent special agents who saw that the nobles obeyed his commands.

Charlemagne also rewarded nobles for their military support. In exchange for providing knights, who were mounted warriors, he gave nobles grants of land called **fiefs**, or fiefdoms. This practice laid the foundation of **feudalism**, a system of government in which land was exchanged for military service by knights.

Charlemagne also encouraged interest in the Christian religion and ancient Latin learning. He established a palace school for the sons of nobles, gave support to scholars, and set scribes to work copying various ancient books to preserve their contents for future generations.

Charlemagne accomplished much, but his empire did not last long after his death. Later Frankish rulers could neither govern nor protect a large empire. Vikings from the Scandinavian lands found that there was no one to keep them from raiding the coast and sailing up the rivers to plunder the countryside. Muslim Arabs threatened in the south, as they had before Charlemagne became king.

With the breakup of Charlemagne's empire, local lords and their knights offered people the best protection. Europe became a patchwork of feudal realms. Feudal lords did give people some protection, but they also disturbed the peace with their private wars.

▶ THE HIGH MIDDLE AGES

After the year 1000, feudal realms began to grow into stable states. European kingdoms expanded their territory and their influence. Beginning in 1096, they united to fight in the **Crusades**, or "wars for the cross." This series of wars was aimed at gaining control of Christian holy places in Palestine, which was ruled by Muslims.

Kings and Nobles

Strong kings in several states succeeded in bringing their feudal lords under control and reducing the number of private wars.

France. In 987, the feudal lords of what is today France elected a king, Hugh Capet, the count of Paris (938?–96). Hugh had little power, but he founded a dynasty that eventually controlled all of France. Among the Capetian kings was Louis VI (1081–1137), who personally led campaigns to bring feudal lords under his control. His grandson, Philip II (1165–1223), or

Musicians and scribes surround the Spanish ruler Alfonso the Wise (1221–84). Medieval kings and nobles enjoyed comforts, but everyday life was hard for most people.

Philip Augustus, appointed special officials, called bailiffs, who traveled within their districts to keep watch on the nobles, somewhat as Charlemagne's agents had done.

Louis IX (1214–70), famous for his piety and sense of justice, did his best to see that no man was treated unfairly in his realm. He would sit under a tree and invite anyone who had been unable to get justice from his lord or the regular courts to come and state his case. After his death, the Roman Catholic Church declared him a saint. His grandson Philip IV (1268–1314) did even more to enhance the power and prestige of the king. By the end of his reign, France was the leading state of Europe.

England. William the Conqueror (1028?–87), duke of Normandy, invaded England in 1066 and won its crown by conquest. As William I of England, he withheld power and independence from his nobles so none could rise against him. The kings of England thus had greater power over their feudal lords than did the French monarchs.

William's son Henry I (1068–1135) and his great-grandson Henry II (1133–89) further strengthened the king's powers. Henry II encouraged people to look to the royal courts for justice rather than to their local courts or those of the lords. He did so partly by having the royal courts offer better service and fairer judgments.

By limiting the powers of feudal lords, English kings built a well-governed state. But the English discovered that royal powers needed limits as well. King John (1167?–1216), a reckless and unjust ruler, was reviled by both nobles and common people. In 1215 he faced a revolt of the lords. To keep his throne, John agreed to issue a charter called **Magna Carta**. In it he stated certain limits on his power. Among other things John promised that he would have no freeman arrested or punished except "by the law of the land." This was the first known document to decree that the head of the government was not

The wife of the lord of the manor oversaw many tasks. Among them were spinning and weaving.

above the law. Constitutional governments today are based on this idea.

In time the power of English kings became increasingly limited by Parliament, an assembly made up of the chief nobles, bishops of the church, and representatives of knights and townspeople. A king would assemble his Parliament before attempting to collect special taxes. Parliament could often obtain privileges and concessions from the king in exchange for voting to give him the money he wanted. Thus Parliament gradually increased its power over the king. The Parliament of the Middle Ages was very different from the modern British Parliament, but the modern representative body grew out of the older one.

Germany, Italy, and Spain. The German kings, like those of France and England, tried to reduce the independence of their feudal lords. In the 900's, the Saxon king Otto I (the Great) (912–73) extended his control over much of Germany and even revived the name Holy Roman Empire. But Otto and his successors never matched Charlemagne's empire, which had extended south almost to Rome.

Through the mid-1200's, various German kings tried to rule northern Italy, but they all failed. Germany remained a collection of small principalities until the 1800's. So did much of Italy. Among the strongest Italian city-states was Venice, which built a trading empire. In 1130 southern Italy and Sicily united as the Kingdom of Sicily.

The history of Spain in the Middle Ages is largely a story of struggle between Muslims and Christians. Christians gradually gained the upper hand, and as they did, several strong feudal states appeared, including Aragon, Castile, Navarre, and Portugal. When they were not fighting the Muslims, these states fought each other. But in the late 1400's, Aragon and Castile united to form the kingdom of Spain.

MEDIEVAL LIFE

Although Europe was politically divided in the Middle Ages, daily life did not vary greatly from one realm to the next. Medieval society was tightly structured. Many people lived their entire lives in one village or manor. They were born to a certain social position and stayed in that position. Those who wanted something more had few choices. For all but the wealthiest, life was extremely hard.

The Manorial System

Medieval land holdings ranged from small estates called manors to huge fiefs as big as small countries. The lord of a large fief, such as a baron, might give individual manors to his knights, in exchange for their service. Those knights thus became lords of their own small manors. But they still owed allegiance to the baron.

A lord's word was law on his manor. But knights and barons were often away, fighting battles. Much of the daily management of the manor fell to the lord's wife. She oversaw planting, spinning, weaving, and other activities. She made sure servants did their jobs and ran the household smoothly. Often she also handled the household financial accounts. But despite these responsibilities, women in medieval times had few rights. They were expected to obey their husbands and fathers in all things. Upper-class girls were married off early, as a way for powerful families to form alliances and build their wealth.

Most of the people on a feudal manor were peasants who spent their lives working in the fields. A great many of the peasants were **serfs**—that is, they were not free. Serfs could not leave their manor to try and find a better place. They belonged to the manor at which they were born and could move or change jobs only if their lord gave permission. The lords did not freely give away their serfs any more than they gave away their land or livestock. When a lord agreed to let one of his serfs marry a serf from another manor, he usually demanded a payment to make up for the loss.

Serfs led difficult lives. They had to till the land of the lord, as well as the strips in the manor fields in which they grew their own food. They knew little about the world and rarely met anyone from outside their village. They did not travel, nor could they read.

Town Life

There were few towns, particularly in northwestern Europe, during the early Middle Ages. The rule of the feudal lords discouraged trade, and towns lived by trade. Each lord collected a toll, for "protection," from all merchants who came into his neighborhood. A merchant paid many such tolls in traveling from one land to another. For example, a merchant taking a boatload of goods down

Towns became increasingly important as centers of trade during the late Middle Ages. Here, merchants in Paris, France, display their wares.

the Loire River from Orléans had to pay 74 different tolls. Needless to say, the many tolls made goods expensive and trade difficult even in times of peace. During the frequent private wars trade became still more risky.

As private wars became less frequent, trade became easier. Towns grew in both number and size. Townspeople were better off than the serfs, for they were free. But their position was beneath that of the lords. Thus the townspeople became known as the middle class.

Most townspeople were merchants and artisans. Some merchants were little more than peddlers carrying their packs from village to village. Others brought goods by ship, riverboat, or pack train from distant lands to sell in town markets and fairs.

As towns grew larger, some people opened shops stocked with goods bought from the traveling merchants. One shopkeeper might sell drugs and spices brought from distant lands. Another shop might have furs or fine cloth and carpets from the East. Towns also had butchers, bakers, and barbers. Artisans manufactured shoes, hats, cloth, ironware, and other goods in their workshops.

The right to do business in a town was a guarded privilege. The merchants and artisans banded together in special organizations for each trade or craft, called **guilds**. Only

The church played an important role in medieval life. Priests conducted services in Latin, and beautiful cathedrals were built in major towns.

members of the guilds could sell goods or practice a trade within the town walls. Guild members all charged the same prices for the same quality work, and they limited the number of people permitted to follow a particular occupation. The shoemakers' guild, for example, wanted to make sure that there were

Consult the Index to find more information in *The New Book of Knowledge* about the following selected notable figures of the Middle Ages: popes Gregory VII and Leo III; saints Thomas Aquinas, Joan of Arc, Francis of Assisi, and Thomas à Becket; writers Geoffrey Chaucer and Dante Alighieri; scientist and philosopher Roger Bacon; inventor and printer Johann Gutenberg; and explorers Marco Polo, Christopher Columbus, and Vasco da Gama. Also refer to the biographies of individual emperors and other monarchs, such as Charlemagne, Eleanor of Aquitaine, Ferdinand and Isabella, and William I (the Conqueror).

Peter Abelard (1079–1142), born near Nantes, France, was a scholar and poet. The son of a knight, he gave up his inheritance to study philosophy. His brilliant writings explored the relation of language to truth, among other things. Abelard taught and studied in several cities, but primarily in Paris. There he became involved in a romance with one of his private students, Héloïse, the niece of a leading clergyman. They married secretly, but scandal and the wrath of Héloïse's uncle forced them apart. He became a monk, and she became a nun.

Bede, Saint (673–735), a priest, scholar, and historian, was born in Northumbria, England. Known as the Venerable Bede (a title of respect), he is best remembered for his *Historia ecclesiastica gentis Anglorum* (*Ecclesiastical History of the English People*), completed in 731. The *Historia* is primarily an account of the conversion of the Anglo-Saxons to Christianity and a history of the church, but it also contains much political history. To this day it remains a primary source for the early history of the Anglo-Saxons. Bede was canonized (made a saint) in 1899.

Charles Martel ("the Hammer") (688?–741), grandfather of Charlemagne, was a Frank-

Eleanor of Aquitaine

ish leader who stopped a Muslim invasion of Europe. He reunited Charlemagne's Frankish kingdom by 719, and then extended his rule over neighboring regions. In 732 a Muslim force advanced from Spain as far as Poitiers, in central France. Charles defeated the invaders at the Battle of Tours. Afterward, there were no major Muslim invasions north of Spain.

Geoffrey of Monmouth (1100?–54), bishop of Saint Asaph in Wales, was an English chronicler whose works are one of the main sources of legends about King Arthur. His most famous work, *Historia Regum Britanniae* (*History of the Kings of Britain*), was completed about 1136. A fictional history, it begins with the conquest of giants and ends with the prophecies of a sorcerer named Merlin. It inspired future authors of Arthurian legends, including Chrétien de Troyes and Sir Thomas Malory.

---

never more shoemakers in a particular town than could make a good living there.

Towns became increasingly important during the later Middle Ages. The middle class grew richer, and the kings began to choose middle-class lawyers to advise them on matters of government. Many merchants and craftsmen had their sons study law because it provided an opportunity for a young man to get ahead in the world.

The Role of the Church

Every town and almost every village in the Middle Ages had a church, where a priest conducted worship services, baptized babies, married young people, and buried the dead in the churchyard. In addition, the priests taught the children at least the most important Christian prayers and beliefs.

The church grew great and powerful during the Middle Ages. It had its own laws and courts in which to try any person who broke church law. Church leaders also claimed that accused priests could only be tried by a church court. The church also collected tax payments for its support.

The church was governed by bishops and archbishops under the authority of the pope at Rome. Church leaders were involved in politics as well as spiritual matters. Some popes were very powerful. They rallied kings and lords to fight in the Crusades and to oppose heretics, those whose beliefs did not agree with the teachings of the church. But sometimes kings opposed the popes in bitter struggles.

The church was also served by monks and nuns. Monks were men who lived together in a house called a monastery. They were under the rule of an abbot, and they devoted their lives mainly to prayer and religious service. The nuns were women who followed a similar life in houses usually called convents. Monks and nuns gave all of their property to the monastery or convent. They vowed never to marry and agreed to live under strict rules.

Some monks worked in the monastery's fields, fed the poor who came to the monastery gate, or took care of travelers who asked for shelter. Others copied books in the monastery scriptorium, or writing room. Since there were no printing presses, all

Godfrey of Bouillon (1060?–1100), born in Baisy, Brabant, was a French crusader and the first Christian ruler of Jerusalem after that city's capture in 1099. The duke of Lower Lorraine, Godfrey signed on for the First Crusade in 1096. He sold most of his possessions to raise an army, and his men were the first to storm the walls of Jerusalem. Elected to rule the city, Godfrey declined the title of king and called himself Defender of the Holy Sepulchre. He proved to be a weak ruler but was later portrayed in stories as "the perfect Christian knight."

Godfrey of Bouillon

Saladin

John Wycliffe

Innocent III (Lothar of Segni) (1161?–1216) was born in Anagni, Italy. He became pope in 1198, and his reign is thought to mark the height of the medieval church's power. Pope Innocent III increased the prestige of his office and required kings to accept the authority of the church. He launched the Fourth Crusade (1202–04), which set out for Palestine but changed course and attacked Constantinople. He also launched the brutal Albigensian Crusade to repress French heretics.

Saladin (1138?–93), born in Tikrit, Mesopotamia, was a Muslim ruler who battled the Crusaders. He began his career as a military commander and rose to power quickly, becoming ruler of Egypt in 1171. By 1186 he had extended his rule over Syria and northern Mesopotamia. Next he turned to Palestine, much of which had been captured by Christians in the First Crusade. In 1187, Saladin regained control of Jerusalem. He then blocked the Third Crusade, which was launched to retake the city.

John Wycliffe (1330?–84), born in Yorkshire, England, was a philosopher and church reformer. He studied and taught at Oxford University for most of his life. Wycliffe began the first English-language translation of the Bible. He urged the clergy to give up property and serve the poor, and he said that the church should be subject to the law of the land in all nonreligious matters. He also criticized many traditional church doctrines. His views foreshadowed the Protestant Reformation of the 1500's.

books had to be copied by hand. A few monks conducted schools where they taught boys to read and write Latin. It was necessary to learn Latin because both the Bible and the church services were in that language. Poetry and history were also written in Latin.

Bishops, too, established schools, called cathedral schools. Some cathedral schools became great centers of learning called universities. A number of the greatest thinkers of the Middle Ages, including Peter Abelard (1079–1142), Saint Albertus Magnus (1193?–80), and Saint Thomas Aquinas (1225?–74), studied and taught at Paris. University students began their studies with the seven liberal arts. These were Latin grammar, rhetoric (how to write and speak), logic (how to reason), arithmetic, geometry, astronomy, and music. Students could also go on to study law, medicine, arts (philosophy), or theology. The church also encouraged artists to erect magnificent cathedrals in stone and glass.

▶ **THE LATE MIDDLE AGES**

The years between 1300 and 1500 brought many changes to Europe. France and England fought the costly Hundred Years' War (1337–1453). This was really a series of wars, in which English rulers tried to win back lands they had once held in France.

From about 1347 to 1350, a terrible plague called the Black Death killed as many as one-third of Europe's total population. Farmland stood idle, with few laborers to work it. Discontented peasants rebelled, and many serfs were able to gain their freedom. At the same time, the church's power began to decline. But in the cities, the influence of the middle class increased, and there was a growing spirit of freedom. This change came first in the cities of Italy, in the 1300's. Historians consider this to be the beginning of a new age called the Renaissance, meaning "rebirth."

KENNETH S. COOPER
George Peabody College

See also CHARLEMAGNE; CHRISTIANITY, HISTORY OF; CRUSADES; FEUDALISM; GUILDS; HOLY ROMAN EMPIRE; HUNDRED YEARS' WAR; KNIGHTS, KNIGHTHOOD, AND CHIVALRY; MIDDLE AGES, MUSIC OF THE.

MIDDLE AGES, ART OF THE. See BYZANTINE ART AND ARCHITECTURE; GOTHIC ART AND ARCHITECTURE; ILLUMINATED MANUSCRIPTS; ROMANESQUE ART AND ARCHITECTURE; STAINED-GLASS WINDOWS.

MIDDLE AGES, MUSIC OF THE

Music from the Middle Ages, referred to as medieval music, represents nearly 1,000 years of European musical development and is the ancestor of all later Western music. In the history of music, the medieval period extends from about A.D. 500 to about 1450. Since much of the music has been lost, our knowledge of medieval music is incomplete. Though writings of the period tell of many other kinds of music, church music is almost all that remains of music composed before the year 1000.

Various forms of chant, especially the Gregorian, were sung in the Christian churches of medieval Europe.

▶ CHURCH MUSIC

The music of the early Christian Church was chant, or plainsong. A chant is a single line of melody sung to Latin texts without harmony or instrumental accompaniment. In the Middle Ages, various forms of chant were used throughout Europe. These included Gallican chant in France, Mozarabic chant in Spain, and Ambrosian chant in the Italian city of Milan. The type of chant used in Rome, Italy, came to be known as Gregorian chant. This was because the first standard collection of chants was thought to have been ordered by Pope Gregory I (reigned 590–604). It is widely believed now, however, that the standardization took place about 200 years later.

Gregorian chant eventually became the dominant form of chant in all Christian churches. It is the only music that has been used continuously from the beginning of the Middle Ages to the present day.

The names of the people who shaped the chants are unknown. They were not composers in the modern sense, for they mostly improved, decorated, and added to existing melodies to make new ones. The chant as it exists today is the work of generations of musicians, covering a period of several centuries. It was preserved and developed mainly by monks in monasteries.

▶ THE RISE OF POLYPHONIC MUSIC

Polyphony, music in which two or more melodies are sung or played at the same time, emerged around the year 800 and made a significant contribution to medieval music. One form of polyphonic music was **organum** (the Latin word for *organ*), which combined a chant sung at one pitch with parallel melodies sung at different pitches. The leading composers of organum, Léonin and Pérotin, flourished in the late 1100's and early 1200's in Paris.

The **motet**, developed in the 1200's and 1300's, was an important form of polyphony. Motets (from the French word *mot*, meaning "word") added new music and words to an existing line of melody. In some motets two or more different texts, often in different languages, were sung together.

The leading composer of this period was Guillaume de Machaut (1300?–77) of France. He and his French contemporaries used elaborate rhythmic schemes in which rhythms were repeated but the melodies changed. The Italian composer Francesco Landini

The organetto was often used in secular, or nonreligious, music in the Middle Ages.

(1325?–97) was famous not only for his music but also for his organ playing.

At first, church polyphony was performed only in cathedrals, monasteries, royal chapels, and a few large city churches. Outside of these places polyphony was confined, in most of Europe, to the upper classes. Ordinary people heard polyphonic music if they worshiped in a cathedral or monastic church. Otherwise they would hear it only if there was some unusual public ceremony, such as a royal wedding procession. For an event like this, the king's musicians would perform a piece specially composed for the occasion. In the 1300's, polyphony began influencing secular (nonreligious) music.

▶ SECULAR MUSIC

During the Middle Ages most secular music was learned by ear. This was because the composers and performers of this music, called **minstrels**, were usually unable to read or write. The music therefore was usually not written down. Minstrels made their living by chanting long poems about heroic deeds, such as the *Song of Roland*, and playing dance music on various instruments. They also entertained with acrobatic stunts, juggling, and magic tricks. From the 1000's onward some minstrels became members of feudal households and learned to write music. Thus, a few dances from the 1200's and 1300's have survived.

Related to the minstrels were the poet-musician **troubadours** of southern France and their northern counterparts, the **trouvères**, who flourished from about 1100 to 1300. Most troubadours and some trouvères belonged to the nobility, or the upper class, and all their music was designed for those audiences. Troubadours and trouvères often wrote both the words

Among the wind instruments used during the Middle Ages were an early form of bagpipe (on left) and the shawm (on right).

Psalteries, made in several shapes, were played either with a bow or by plucking the strings.

and music of their songs, which were generally performed with instrumental accompaniment. These were often love songs that told of knights and their ladies. Other songs dealt with the religious Crusades.

The counterparts to troubadours and trouvères in Germany at this time were called **minnesingers**. Similar entertainers were called **skalds** in Scandinavia (Denmark, Sweden, and Norway) and **bards** in Ireland.

▶ MEDIEVAL MUSICAL INSTRUMENTS

Some of the musical instruments used during the Middle Ages bear strong resemblances to those used today, although they often had very different names. The shawm (or shalmei) resembled an oboe or clarinet. The rebec was a small stringed instrument played with a bow, similar to the violin and its family of instruments. The psaltery resembled a small, hand-held harp.

Other musical instruments of this time were quite different from modern instruments. The organetto, for instance, was a kind of small, portable organ. It consisted of a keyboard, vertical pipes, and bellows, which were worked by the player's left hand. The hurdy-gurdy used a crank to turn a circular bow against four strings, and piano-like keys were pressed to change the tone. The gemshorn was a type of flute made from the horn of an animal, such as oxen.

Some kinds of medieval instruments have remained in use up to the present day, often with little change in their design. These instruments include the harp, harpsichord, drum, and recorder.

Reviewed by GUSTAVE REESE
Author, *Music in the Middle Ages*

The Middle East has been the home of varied peoples since ancient times. The many faces of the region include (*top from far left*) these Egyptian schoolchildren, a Syrian Bedouin chief, young Turkish shepherd women, (*bottom from far left*) a Saudi computer operator, and an Iranian *mullah*, or interpreter of Islamic religious law. Arabs, Turks, and Iranians are the three main Middle Eastern ethnic groups.

MIDDLE EAST

The Middle East is a geographical region that has been of great importance in history since ancient times. Strategically located, it is a natural land bridge connecting the continents of Asia, Africa, and Europe. It was the site of some of the world's earliest civilizations and the birthplace of three great religions—Judaism, Christianity, and Islam. In recent times its enormous deposits of oil have made the Middle East more important than ever.

Defining the Middle East. There has never been agreement on a definition of the Middle East. Historically, the region includes the lands that were formerly part of the Ottoman (Turkish) Empire plus Persia (modern Iran), an ancient empire in its own right. Thus, the area occupied by the modern-day nations that emerged from the breakup of the Ottoman Empire, together with Iran, would come close to what we generally mean by the Middle East. An earlier term, the Near East, was at one time in common use. It usually referred to lands in the Balkan Peninsula of southeastern Europe that were also once under Ottoman rule, in addition to territory now considered part of the Middle East.

The core of the Middle East today consists of the numerous countries of Southwest Asia and the African nations of Egypt and Libya. Tunisia, Algeria, and Morocco are sometimes included in the region. Afghanistan and Sudan are occasionally included.

▶THE PEOPLE

Population Comparisons. The Middle East has a population of about 246 million, or nearly as many people as the United States. The distribution of the population varies widely. The fertile regions are very densely settled; many others are only lightly populated; while others, particularly in the deserts, are completely empty of human life. The most populous Middle Eastern countries are Turkey, Egypt, and Iran, each with more than 50 million people. The Persian Gulf states of Bahrain and Qatar have the smallest populations, about 400,000 each. Saudi Arabia, although greatest in area, has a relatively small population for its size, a little more than 10 million, because much of its land is desert.

Ethnic Groups. Since ancient times, the Middle East has attracted migrating peoples. Mixing with the earlier inhabitants of the region, they produced the peoples that make up the Middle East today. They can be classified into three main ethnic groups—Arabs, Turks, and Iranians. There are, in addition, smaller numbers of Kurds, who are scattered across Turkey, Iran, and Iraq; Jews (of varied ethnic origin), who live chiefly in Israel; Pakistanis; Armenians; and Greeks, who live mainly on the island nation of Cyprus.

Language and Religion. Language and religion are basic elements of cultural identity in the Middle East. The major languages of the region, which correspond to the three main ethnic groups, are Arabic, the most widely used language; Turkish; and Persian (or Farsi), the language of the Iranians. Kurdish is related to Persian. The Hebrew spoken in Israel is, like Arabic, a Semitic tongue. Educated people throughout the Middle East frequently speak English or French as well.

Islam, the religion of the Muslims, is the predominant faith of the Middle East. There are two main branches: Sunni Islam, the larger branch; and Shi'i Islam, found mainly in Iran,

Iraq, and Lebanon. Christianity is practiced by some Arabs, particularly in Lebanon; by the Greeks of Cyprus; and the Copts in Egypt. Judaism was the faith of ancient Israel and is the religion of the modern state of Israel.

Way of Life. No more than 10 percent of the people of the region ever followed the nomadic way of life, represented by the desert Bedouin, and even fewer do so today. Early civilization in the Middle East was centered in agriculture and the majority of the people still earn their livelihood as settled farmers.

At one time most of the region's people inhabited villages or small towns, living and working much as their ancestors had done for centuries. This has changed dramatically as increasing numbers of people have been drawn to the cities, where about half the population of the region now resides.

Three of the world's great religions—Judaism, Christianity, and Islam—were born in the Middle East. An elderly celebrant (*right*) blows the *shofar*, or ram's horn, which ushers in the Jewish New Year. A dignitary of the Greek Orthodox Church (*below right*) represents one of the region's many Christian denominations. Muslims, followers of Islam, kneel in prayer (*below*). Although Islam is the youngest of the three religions, it is the dominant faith of the Middle East today.

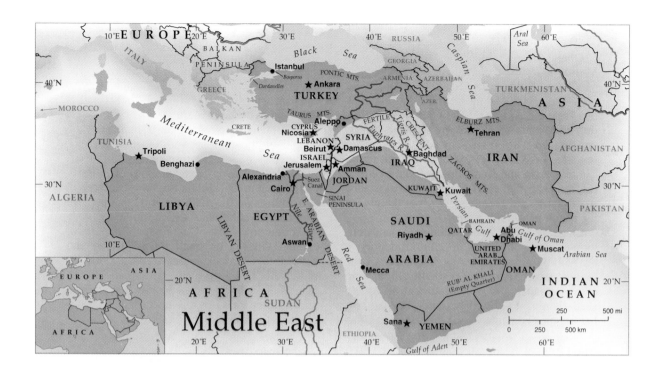

CORE COUNTRIES OF THE MIDDLE EAST

COUNTRY	CAPITAL	AREA	
		(sq mi)	(km²)
Bahrain	Manama	240	622
Cyprus	Nicosia	3,572	9,251
Egypt	Cairo	386,662	1,001,499
Iran	Tehran	636,294	1,648,000
Iraq	Baghdad	169,235	438,317
Israel	Jerusalem	8,019	20,770
Jordan	Amman	35,475	91,880
Kuwait	Kuwait	6,880	17,818
Lebanon	Beirut	4,015	10,400
Libya	Tripoli	679,362	1,759,540
Oman	Muscat	82,030	212,457
Qatar	Doha	4,247	11,000
Saudi Arabia	Riyadh	830,000	2,149,690
Syria	Damascus	71,498	185,180
Turkey	Ankara	301,381	780,576
United Arab Emirates	Abu Dhabi	32,278	83,600
Yemen	Sana	203,849	527,969

▶THE LAND

The Middle East is a vast region. With a total area of nearly 3,500,000 square miles (9,000,000 square kilometers), it is only slightly smaller than the United States. Saudi Arabia is the largest of the core countries of the Middle East in area. Bahrain, an island nation in the Persian Gulf, is the smallest of the Middle Eastern states.

Mountains, Plateaus, Deserts. On the north the region is almost completely ringed by mountain ranges. Lesser chains of hills and mountains extend along the coastal areas of the eastern Mediterranean. The Arabian Peninsula, which makes up more than one quarter of the region's area, is bounded by mountainous heights in the west and south. Most of the region's interior is flat and contains some of the world's most forbidding deserts—among them the Libyan (or Western), the Arabian (or Eastern), and the aptly named Rub' al Khali, or Empty Quarter, of Saudi Arabia.

Fertile River Valleys. The region's two major river systems are the Nile and the Tigris and Euphrates. The Nile, the world's longest river, is the lifeblood of Egypt, most of which is otherwise desert. The Tigris and Euphrates rise in Turkey, flow through Syria, and join in Iraq, there forming the region long known as Mesopotamia (meaning land between rivers). These river valleys contain much of the region's limited fertile land and are the most densely populated areas, and it was here that the first known civilizations arose thousands of years ago.

Climate: A Hot, Dry Land. Hot, dry weather is common to the Middle East for much of the year except in the highest mountains, where snow is frequent. The rainy season in most places lasts from about October to April. In

Life in the Middle East depends on the availability of water. A pipeline (*above*) will carry scarce water to Saudi Arabia's desolate *Rub' al Khali*, or Empty Quarter. The Nile River valley of Egypt (*right*) is one of the region's few fertile areas.

the southern part of the Arabian Peninsula, rain comes mainly between May and September. But there is only light, brief rainfall in most of the region and in some areas it never rains at all. In the deserts, which are baked by the blazing sun, the daytime temperature often rises to more than 125°F (52°C). Yet at night the deserts are cool or even cold.

Life itself in the Middle East has long been dependent upon the amount and location of

WONDER QUESTION

What is the Fertile Crescent?

The name Fertile Crescent refers to an area of the Middle East, where the earliest known civilizations are believed to have developed. The name itself comes from the crescent (as in a quarter moon) or arclike shape of the region, which extends northward along the coast of the Mediterranean Sea, eastward across the valley of the Tigris and Euphrates rivers, and then southward to the head of the Persian Gulf. The region includes land in what is now Israel, Lebanon, Syria, Iraq, and Iran. (The region can be seen on the map accompanying this article, where it appears in a lighter yellow shade.) A relatively well watered region, agriculture first originated here some 8,000 or more years ago. It was also the site of the first towns and cities. The early Babylonian and Assyrian empires were located in this region.

water. Rain-bearing winds are often unable to penetrate into the interior of the region because they are blocked by the surrounding mountains. The best-watered areas are usually the strips of land lying between the mountains and the sea, but the Middle East generally suffers from a severe shortage of water due to the limited rainfall.

Water and History. Long ago the availability of water determined where people could live in the Middle East and how they would earn their livelihood. The amount of available water limited the farmer's choice of crops. It compelled the nomads, who traveled from place to place seeking grazing land for their herds, to rely on goats, sheep, and camels, since cattle could not easily survive in the harsh, dry environment. The location of sources of water also determined the routes of travel and trade.

From earliest times the power of Middle Eastern empires depended on ready supplies of water. It is no accident that the valleys of the Nile and the Tigris and Euphrates rivers were—and remain—main centers of life in the region. Some of the oldest irrigation systems in the world were developed in the Middle East. Many are still in use, along with newer systems.

Dams and Distilling Seawater. Modern methods of providing regular supplies of water in the region include the Aswan High Dam, which irrigates large areas of Egypt and provides hydroelectric power as well. In Israel a pipeline system has been built to divert water from the Jordan River to the desert areas of the Negev. Turkey in 1990 completed the great Ataturk Dam to harness the waters of the Euphrates River. Saudi Arabia, Kuwait, and other countries of the Arabian Peninsula are converting seawater into drinking water by various distilling processes. The success of programs to raise the standard of living throughout the Middle East will depend to a large extent on the outcome of the various water projects.

Chief Cities. Early Middle Eastern civilization developed great cities, and cities continue to play an important role in the life of the region. The largest city of the Middle East is Cairo, the capital of Egypt. Founded by Arab conquerors in the A.D. 900's, it has a population of about 6 million in the city proper and some 14 million in its metropolitan area. The older Egyptian port city of Alexandria, rebuilt by Alexander the Great in the 300's B.C., was famed for its great library, the largest in the ancient world. Istanbul, the major city of Turkey, lies on one of the world's most historic sites, spanning Europe and Asia. As Constantinople, it was once the capital of the Roman and Byzantine empires.

The Galata Bridge crosses the Golden Horn, which separates the old and new parts of Istanbul, Turkey's largest city. Formerly known as Constantinople, the city was at one time the capital of the Roman and Byzantine empires.

A Saudi Arabian oil refinery (*right*) symbolizes the economic importance of the Middle East, which has half of the world's known oil reserves. The oil deposits are unequally distributed, however, and for much of the region, agriculture, as in this Israeli farmer's banana crop, remains the chief economic activity.

Baghdad, capital of Iraq, lies on the Euphrates River. Founded in the A.D. 700's, it was the seat of the Abbasid dynasty of Muslim rulers, whose most renowned figure was Harun al-Rashid, famed in the West as the caliph in *The Arabian Nights.* Damascus, Syria's capital, is one of the world's oldest cities, dating back to at least 732 B.C. It was the site of St. Paul's conversion to Christianity, and from A.D. 66 to 750 served as the capital of the Muslim Ummayyad dynasty.

The importance of Jerusalem, Israel's capital, is far greater than its size, containing as it does, places holy to Jews, Christians, and Muslims. Tehran, capital of Iran, is a relatively new city by Middle Eastern standards, first gaining prominence in the 1500's.

▶ECONOMIC ACTIVITY

Agriculture. Although only about 15 percent of the land is suitable for farming, agriculture remains the region's most important economic activity. Wheat, barley, and rice are chief food crops. Figs and dates are grown in desert oases and citrus fruits in the Mediterranean coastal region. The major commercial crops are cotton, coffee, and tobacco. Livestock raising is especially important to the agricultural economy.

Oil and Industry. The discovery of vast oil deposits revolutionized the Middle East's economy. More than half of the world's

known oil reserves are found in the region, although they are not equally distributed. Saudi Arabia has the largest deposits and is the world's leading oil producer and exporter. Iran, Iraq, and the small Persian Gulf state of Kuwait are the other major producers. Aside from oil, chrome, coal, sulphur, and magnesium mined in Turkey, and phosphates from Jordan, the region is generally poor in mineral resources.

Turkey, Egypt, and Israel are the most industrially developed countries of the region. The processing of agricultural products, petroleum refining and the production of petrochemicals, textiles, and such traditional crafts as rug weaving are the chief areas of industrial activity. Heavy industry, including machinery and steel production and motor vehicle assembly, is being encouraged.

Perhaps the most important underlying problem of the Middle East today is that of modernization. How are the traditional societies of the region to cope with the modern world? How are they to use the new oil wealth wisely, in order to change but not destroy existing structures of society? There is also serious political tension between the countries that have oil and those that do not and between the rich and poor within countries.

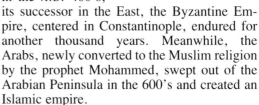

Alexander the Great carved out a Middle Eastern empire in the 300's B.C., based on Greek civilization.

▶HISTORY

Early History. The Middle East has been called the cradle of civilization. More than 8,000 years ago, people in this part of the world discovered the methods of agriculture that freed them from the need to wander about in search of food as hunters and gatherers. The development of settled communities and the earliest forms of government followed. Between 4000 and 3000 B.C., city-states, most notably Sumer, began to emerge in the southern part of the fertile region between the Tigris and Euphrates rivers.

Before the beginning of the Christian era, the Middle East had already seen the rise and eventual fall of numerous kingdoms and empires—those of the Egyptians, Hittites, Babylonians, Assyrians, and Persians among them. Their great contributions to civilization included codes of law, writing systems, mechanical inventions such as the wheel, and the development of sciences, such as astronomy, and mathematics. Judaism, the first great monotheistic religion (the faith in but one God), evolved among a relatively small group of people, the ancient Hebrews.

Greeks, Romans, Arabs. Alexander the Great invaded the region with an army of Macedonians and Greeks in the 300's B.C. and carved out a vast empire based on Greek culture. The Romans began their own conquest of the region some three centuries later. When the Roman Empire in the West collapsed in the A.D. 400's, its successor in the East, the Byzantine Empire, centered in Constantinople, endured for another thousand years. Meanwhile, the Arabs, newly converted to the Muslim religion by the prophet Mohammed, swept out of the Arabian Peninsula in the 600's and created an Islamic empire.

The Ottoman Empire. Other conquerors—Seljuk Turks, European crusaders, and Mongols—followed in their turn. The last great empire of the region was that of the Ottoman Turks, who reached the height of their power in the 1500's, when all of the Middle East, except for Persia, came under their sway. From this high point, Ottoman power slowly declined, although the crumbling empire was to last, at least in name, until the early 1900's.

Period of Nationalism. The final breakup of what remained of the Ottoman Empire came about as a result of World War I (1914–18), in which the Turks sided with the Central Powers, led by Germany and Austria-Hungary. Their defeat by the Allies, headed

Calah (or Nimrud), situated on the Tigris River, was one of the capitals of the Assyrian Empire, which reached the height of its power in the 600's B.C.

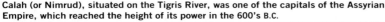

The Middle East has continued to be torn by conflicts and disputes in modern times. Here U.S. Army tank crews pause for a moment during the 1991 Persian Gulf War, in which an alliance led by the United States defeated Iraqi forces that had invaded and occupied the small Persian Gulf nation of Kuwait.

by Britain and France, split the empire apart, reducing Turkey to its present territory. During the war many Arabs fought with the Allies against the Turks, hoping to gain their independence. But after the war, much of the region came under British and French control through the League of Nations.

Two Arab nations, Saudi Arabia and Iraq, were created in 1932. Most of the rest won their independence during or shortly after World War II (1939–45). These years also saw the large-scale development of the region's oil resources.

Recent Conflicts. Since World War II, the Middle East has been torn by conflicts, including five wars between Israel and its Arab neighbors. Israel signed a peace treaty with Egypt in 1979. However, its relations with the rest of the Arab world remained hostile until 1993. That year, Israel and the Palestine Liberation Organization (PLO) signed the first in a series of accords granting limited self-rule to Palestinian Arabs in Israeli-occupied territories. Israel and Jordan also signed a

peace treaty, in 1994. Israel withdrew its forces from southern Lebanon in 2000. But at the same time violence again erupted between the Israelis and Palestinians. Relations improved with the death in 2004 of the long-time Palestinian leader Yasir Arafat. In 2005, prospects for peace improved further when Israel turned over all its settlements in the Gaza Strip (including its border crossings into Egypt and Israel) and some in the West Bank to the Palestinians.

Lebanon fought a civil war from the mid-1970's until 1990 and was long occupied by Israel and Syria. Iran and Iraq fought a bitter war from 1980 to 1988. Iraq invaded Kuwait in 1990, which led to the Persian Gulf War (1991). Iraq was quickly defeated by a U.S.-led multinational coalition. The United States led a second war against Iraq in 2003 and overthrew its dictator, Saddam Hussein. Iraq held democratic elections in 2005, despite a deadly anti-Western insurgency.

Syrian forces remained in Lebanon until 2005. They were forced out after the Lebanese staged an anti-Syrian revolution, in which they blamed Syrian officials for the assassination of former Lebanese prime minister Rafiq Hariri.

HYMAN KUBLIN
Author, *The Rim of Asia*

Reviewed by ARTHUR CAMPBELL TURNER
Coauthor, *Power and Ideology
in the Middle East*

See also articles on individual countries and cities of the Middle East.

MIDSUMMER NIGHT'S DREAM, A. See SHAKE-SPEARE, WILLIAM.

MIES VAN DER ROHE, LUDWIG (1886–1969)

Ludwig Mies van der Rohe was one of the most influential architects of the 1900's. He is known simply as Mies, and the type of building he designed—a simple and elegant "glass box"—is called Miesian. Today, Miesian skyscrapers dominate the skylines of cities everywhere. In his designs for skyscrapers and other structures, Mies eliminated surface decoration to expose a building's main elements: a skeleton of steel beams filled in with rectangles of glass. This concept, which he expressed in the phrase "less is more," is a key part of the style of modern architecture known as the **international style**.

Mies was born on March 27, 1886, in Aachen, Germany. He studied under well-known architects and produced interesting designs. By the end of World War I (1914–18), he had already turned his attention to designing glass skyscrapers.

Mies was dedicated to the philosophy of simple, functional design as taught by the Bauhaus, a German design school. He served as director of the Bauhaus from 1930 to 1933. Several years later, he immigrated to the United States and became director of architecture at the Illinois Institute of Technology (IIT) in Chicago. While at IIT, he designed a master plan for the campus featuring spacious

The Lake Shore Drive Apartments, Chicago, were built by architect Mies van der Rohe. Their simple glass-and-steel design typifies the international style.

buildings with interiors that could be rearranged easily to accommodate changing functions. Mies spoke of this concept of design as "universal space." His Crown Hall (1955) on the IIT campus is a good example of this approach.

Other examples of Mies's later work are the Lake Shore Drive Apartments (1951) in Chicago; the Seagram Building (1958) in New York City, designed with Philip Johnson; and the New National Gallery (1968) in Berlin. Mies died on August 17, 1969.

HOWARD E. WOODEN
Director Emeritus
The Wichita Art Museum

MIGRATION OF ANIMALS. See HOMING AND MIGRATION.
MIGRATION OF PEOPLE. See IMMIGRATION.

MILK

Early records often mention people's use of milk and milk products. In 1922 a British-American expedition discovered a temple near Babylon. The temple is thought to be 5,000 years old, and on one of the walls is a milking scene. In the Bible, milk stands for riches and plenty. Palestine is described as a good land because it is "flowing with milk and honey."

What is milk, and why has it been of great importance in human history? Milk is the white liquid produced by the female of the warm-blooded animals for the feeding of her young. Animals that produce milk are called **mammals**. Blood is pumped from the heart to the udder (mammary gland). The mammary gland is able to separate different substances from the blood and combine them to make milk. Milk has been called nature's most perfect food. It provides all the nutrients (nourishing substances) that human babies and other young mammals need for growth until they are able to eat other food. But from ancient times people have continued to drink milk beyond babyhood. They enjoy it, and they know that it provides most of the nutrients needed for good health.

Today the cow and the goat are the major animals that supply milk for human use. But people also use milk from several other animals native to their homelands. In Asia the camel, the horse, and the yak are sources of milk. The Inuit and the people of Lapland use the milk of caribou and reindeer.

▶ **WHAT MILK CONTAINS**

Milk contains several hundred different substances. It is best known as a source of calcium, phosphorus, and protein. Milk contains large amounts of vitamin B_2 (riboflavin) and some vitamin A. Milk fat, milk sugar (lactose), and the major milk protein, **casein,** are found only in milk and nowhere else in nature.

Milk Fat. The fat in milk is shaped into tiny droplets. They can be seen easily under a microscope. When milk stands for a while, the fat will rise to the surface and form a layer of cream. Farmers used to skim off the cream by repeatedly dipping a dish with tiny holes into the cream layer. In 1877 the Swedish engineer Carl Gustav de Laval invented the centrifugal cream separator, which rapidly removed the cream by spinning the milk in a bowl. The cream was sent out through one

spout, and the skim milk flowed out through another.

Cream contains five to ten times more fat than the original milk. By adding skim milk, which has almost no fat, the cream can be made less rich. In the United States, whipping cream has at least 30 percent fat. Light cream has at least 18 percent fat, and half-and-half, 10 percent fat or more. The golden color and rich look of cream come from **carotene.** Fresh, green fodder—such as spring pasture grass—provides the carotene pigment in milk fat. In the body, carotene is changed into an important nutrient, vitamin A.

Protein. There are two kinds of proteins in milk—the casein and the whey proteins. Milk proteins are noted for their high food value. Casein makes up about 80 percent of the total protein and is the basis of all cheese. When milk sours, the casein forms into a jellylike structure. This lumpy mass is called the curd, or clabber. Cottage cheese, which is made from skim milk, is mostly casein.

Whey is the pale, greenish-colored liquid that separates from the casein, or curd. Whey has all of the milk sugar, almost all of the minerals, vitamin B_2 (riboflavin), and other water-soluble vitamins. The whey proteins add up to 20 percent of the total milk protein. The whey gets its greenish color from the vitamin B_2. When milk is heated to boiling and allowed to stand for a few minutes, a "skin," or "scum," forms on the surface. This happens because the whey proteins are sensitive to heat. The change in the flavor of milk when it is boiled is caused by changes in the whey proteins as they are heated.

Lactose. Lactose (milk sugar) is a special kind of sugar found in milk. It is not as sweet or as easy to dissolve as table sugar. When milk becomes sour, it does so because the lactose has been fermented by bacteria and has turned into lactic acid. The lactic acid gives the milk a sour flavor.

Some people cannot drink milk—or can drink only small amounts—because they have trouble digesting lactose. This digestive disorder is called **lactose intolerance.**

Lactose may be made in a pure form as a finely ground white powder for use in medicines and the production of penicillin.

Reviewed by ROBERT L. BRADLEY, JR.
University of Wisconsin

See also CHEESE; DAIRYING AND DAIRY PRODUCTS.

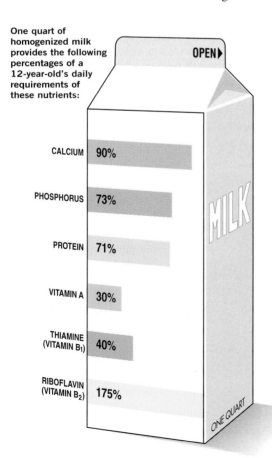

One quart of homogenized milk provides the following percentages of a 12-year-old's daily requirements of these nutrients:

CALCIUM	90%
PHOSPHORUS	73%
PROTEIN	71%
VITAMIN A	30%
THIAMINE (VITAMIN B_1)	40%
RIBOFLAVIN (VITAMIN B_2)	175%

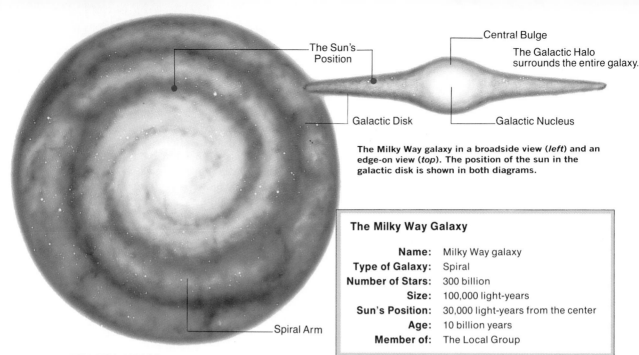

The Sun's Position

Central Bulge

The Galactic Halo surrounds the entire galaxy.

Galactic Disk

Galactic Nucleus

The Milky Way galaxy in a broadside view (*left*) and an edge-on view (*top*). The position of the sun in the galactic disk is shown in both diagrams.

Spiral Arm

The Milky Way Galaxy

Name:	Milky Way galaxy
Type of Galaxy:	Spiral
Number of Stars:	300 billion
Size:	100,000 light-years
Sun's Position:	30,000 light-years from the center
Age:	10 billion years
Member of:	The Local Group

MILKY WAY

Did you know that you live in a galaxy? You do, and so does every other person you know. Astronomers call our galaxy the Milky Way. It is only one of billions of galaxies in the universe, but it is the galaxy human beings call home.

Galaxies are enormous groups of stars. Astronomers estimate that the Milky Way galaxy contains more than 300 billion stars, as well as huge clouds of dust particles and gases.

If you could travel far beyond the Milky Way galaxy and look back at it, what would it look like? Astronomers think it would look like a gigantic pinwheel with a bright center and a thin disk of stars spiraling outward. Our entire solar system would be a tiny, almost invisible speck about two-thirds of the way out from the galaxy's center. Astronomers have calculated that its distance from the center is about 30,000 light-years. (A light-year is the distance light travels in one year: about 6 trillion miles, or 10 trillion kilometers.)

From our position within the Milky Way galaxy, it is possible to see only a tiny part of it. If you look up at the sky on a clear, dark night you will see a faint, shimmering band of starlight crossing overhead, which is also called the Milky Way. People in ancient times thought this band of starlight was a road or a river in the sky. Some believed it was milk that a goddess had spilled across the heavens. This is how the galaxy got its name.

▶THE GALAXY'S SIZE AND SHAPE

Galaxies come in a variety of sizes and shapes. The Milky Way galaxy has a diameter of about 100,000 light-years, and it is one of the most common galactic shapes—a spiral. Galaxies may also have elliptical or irregular shapes. The distinguishing feature of a spiral galaxy is a series of long curving arms that spiral outward from a bright center.

Astronomers know that the Milky Way galaxy is located among a larger group of galaxies that are clustered together in one section of the universe. Similar galactic clusters exist in other sections of the universe as well. The

Many galaxies have a spiral shape similar to the shape of the Milky Way galaxy. This spiral galaxy, M83, is about 10 million light-years away.

galactic cluster the Milky Way belongs to is called the Local Group. Galaxies like the Milky Way have four major parts: the nucleus, central bulge, disk, and halo.

The Nucleus. Astronomers do not know for sure what lies at the nucleus, or center, of the Milky Way galaxy. Huge clouds of dust and gas block our view of the nucleus, so astronomers use radio waves and infrared light to determine what is there. The nucleus gives off huge amounts of energy and exerts a powerful gravitational pull on the rest of the galaxy. Astronomers conclude that matter must be concentrated and very dense there. In the universe, a region only 4 light-years across may contain as much matter as 10 million stars the size of the sun. Astronomers are not sure what causes the energy and gravitational forces in the nucleus of the Milky Way. It may be that the region contains millions of stars concentrated in a very small area. Some astronomers think the nucleus may contain a massive **black hole**, an extremely dense object with such a strong gravitational pull that nothing, not even light, can escape from it.

The Central Bulge. Surrounding the galactic nucleus is a dense cloud of stars about 3,000 light-years across. This is the central bulge, and it contains vast numbers of old stars that may date back to the beginning of the galaxy.

The Disk. Extending out from the central bulge is an area called the galactic disk. This area contains many young stars and also most of the galaxy's dust and gases. The disk is enormous—more than 80,000 light-years across. But it is also very thin—only about 1,000 light-years in thickness. Within the galactic disk are the Milky Way galaxy's spiral arms. These arms contain millions of stars, some of which are grouped together in masses called galactic clusters. Most of the stars in the disk are yellowish stars like the sun, but many of those in the spiral arms are young bright blue and white stars. Our solar system is located along the inner edge of one of the spiral arms—the Cygnus Arm. It orbits the center of the Milky Way galaxy once every 250 million years. Since its formation several billion years ago, the solar system has probably circled the galaxy fewer than twenty times.

The Halo. Surrounding the Milky Way galaxy is a vast spherical halo of stars. The halo is very faint because the stars in it are far apart, and many are older, dimmer stars.

WONDER QUESTION

How far away is the nearest galaxy?

The nearest large galaxy to the Milky Way galaxy is about 2.2 million light-years away. Known as the Andromeda galaxy, it is approximately one and a half times larger than the Milky Way galaxy. But more than a dozen small galaxies are closer. Two of the closest ones are the Large Magellanic Cloud and the Small Magellanic Cloud. These small galaxies are ten times closer than the Andromeda galaxy, and they are ten times smaller. Astronomers think that the Magellanic Clouds orbit our own galaxy much like the moon orbits Earth.

About a dozen very faint, very small galaxies lie mainly between the Magellanic Clouds and the Andromeda galaxy. They have names such as "Leo" and "Sagittarius," after the constellations in which they are seen. One of these so-called dwarf galaxies is so close that it is invading our own galaxy. The dwarf galaxy orbits around the center of the Milky Way and may be left over from its birth.

▶**THE MILKY WAY'S AGE**

Astronomers estimate that the Milky Way galaxy is about 10 billion years old. It was probably formed from clouds of gas floating in the early universe. Astronomers think that the universe itself may be 14 to 15 billion years old.

RICHARD BERRY
Author, *Discover the Stars*

See also ASTRONOMY; STARS; UNIVERSE.

MILLIKAN, ROBERT ANDREWS (1868–1953)

Robert Andrews Millikan was the first scientist to isolate the electron (one of the particles that make up the atom), to show that it carried a constant charge, and to measure this charge. This discovery was enormously important to our understanding of how the atom is constructed.

Millikan was born on March 22, 1868, in Morrison, Illinois. He studied physics at the universities of Berlin and Göttingen in Germany, which were the leading scientific centers of the world at the time. From 1896 to 1921, he taught physics at the University of Chicago.

Robert Millikan displays his cosmic ray machine, 1931.

It was at the University of Chicago that Millikan devised an experiment to measure the electric charge of a single electron. This experiment became known as the "oil-drop experiment" because it measured the electricity in the tiny droplets of an oil mist. The experiment was later used by others involved in electron research. For his work on the electron and its charge, Millikan won the Nobel prize for physics in 1923.

Robert Millikan was a pioneer in the study of cosmic rays. In 1921, he had become director of the Norman Bridge Laboratory of Physics at the California Institute of Technology, in Pasadena. There he studied X rays and high-energy rays from outer space, which he named cosmic rays. Millikan continued to chair the institute's executive council until he retired in 1945.

Millikan's books include *The Electron*; *Science and the New Civilization*; *Time, Matter, and Value*; and *Protons, Photons, Neutrons, and Cosmic Rays*.

During his lifetime, Millikan was the recipient of many awards. He died on December 19, 1953, in San Marino, California.

RACHEL KRANZ
Editor, Biographies
The Young Adult Reader's Adviser

See also ATOMS.

MILLIPEDES. See CENTIPEDES AND MILLIPEDES.

MILNE, A. A. (1882–1956)

Winnie-the-Pooh, Piglet, Eeyore, Tigger, and Kanga with little Roo in her pocket—these are some of the best-loved characters in children's literature. They began as stuffed toy animals that belonged to a boy named Christopher Robin. They came to life in the imagination of the boy's father, the writer A. A. Milne.

Alan Alexander Milne was born in London on January 18, 1882. His father, who was headmaster of a small private school, often read aloud to his three sons, Barry, Ken, and Alan.

Milne was very good at mathematics when he was a boy. Later, he attended Trinity College, Cambridge, to study that subject. But he soon became more interested in writing. In 1903, he returned to London to try to make a living as a free-lance writer. He wrote humorous articles and light verse. After two years, publishers were "getting used" to him, as Milne described it. He became an assistant editor for the humor magazine *Punch* in 1906. In 1913 he married Dorothy (Daphne) de Sélincourt.

Milne served in the army in World War I. After the war, he began to write plays, many of which are still performed. The best known is *Mr. Pim Passes By* (1919). He wrote other works for adults—novels, essays, and his autobiography, *It's Too Late Now* (1939). *The Red House Mystery* (1921), a detective

A. A. Milne's stories about young Christopher Robin, his bear Winnie-the-Pooh, and their friends are known to children all over the world.

novel, is still popular. So is *Toad of Toad Hall* (1929), his play based on Kenneth Grahame's *Wind in the Willows*. But it was poems and stories for children that made him famous.

Christopher Robin—or Billy Moon, as he called himself—was born in 1920. One day Milne wrote a poem about him called "Vespers" and gave it to his wife as a present. She sent the poem to a magazine, and it was published. Milne wrote more poems, which were published in two books, *When We Were Very Young* (1924) and *Now We are Six* (1927).

In 1925, the Milnes bought a farmhouse in Sussex. This "enchanted place on the top of the Forest" was the setting for Milne's stories about Christopher Robin and Pooh. Other toy animals, as well as creatures of the forest, joined in the adventures described in *Winnie-the-Pooh* (1926) and *The House at Pooh Corner* (1928).

A. A. Milne had a special talent for presenting small children as they are. He takes us into their private world of make-believe and funny words—of "wheezles and sneezles," "haycorns," "expotitions," and "biffalo-buffalo-bisons." All the pictures in the Christopher Robin books were drawn by the well-known artist Ernest H. Shepard. His tiny pen-and-ink figures exactly capture the mood of the books.

A. A. Milne died on January 31, 1956. Pooh, Piglet, and the others now live at the New York Public Library.

Reviewed by CHRISTOPHER MILNE
Author, *The Enchanted Places*

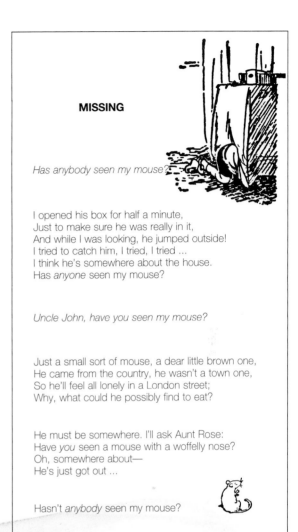

MISSING

Has anybody seen my mouse?

I opened his box for half a minute,
Just to make sure he was really in it,
And while I was looking, he jumped outside!
I tried to catch him, I tried, I tried ...
I think he's somewhere about the house.
Has *anyone* seen my mouse?

Uncle John, have you seen my mouse?

Just a small sort of mouse, a dear little brown one,
He came from the country, he wasn't a town one,
So he'll feel all lonely in a London street;
Why, what could he possibly find to eat?

He must be somewhere. I'll ask Aunt Rose:
Have *you* seen a mouse with a woffelly nose?
Oh, somewhere about—
He's just got out ...

Hasn't *anybody* seen my mouse?

So they all went off on an Expotition to the North Pole: Rabbit, Christopher Robin, Pooh, Piglet, Owl, and Kanga and Roo.

Two of Milton's best-known early poems are *L'Allegro* and *Il Penseroso*. They contrast the outlook of a merry person (L'Allegro) with that of a more thoughtful one (Il Penseroso). In this selection from *L'Allegro,* the poet, in a carefree mood, calls on the spirit of mirth to keep him company.

Haste thee nymph, and bring with thee
Jest and youthful Jollity,
Quips and Cranks, and wanton Wiles,
Nods, and Becks, and Wreathed Smiles,
Such as hang on Hebe's cheek,
And love to live in dimple sleek;
Sport that wrinkled Care derides,
And Laughter holding both his sides.
Come, and trip it as ye go
On the light fantastic toe,
And in thy right hand lead with thee,
The Mountain Nymph, sweet Liberty;
And if I give thee honor due,
Mirth, admit me of thy crew
To live with her, and live with thee,
In unreproved pleasures free.

John Milton, from a 1667 miniature by W. Faithorne.

MILTON, JOHN (1608–1674)

John Milton, one of England's greatest writers, was born into a prosperous London family on December 9, 1608. His father encouraged his early interest in music and languages. John attended St. Paul's School in London before entering Christ's College, Cambridge, at the age of 16. There he began writing poetry in English and Latin.

Milton was graduated in 1632. But he was not satisfied with his formal schooling. In his sonnet "How Soon Hath Time" (1632), he expressed his anxiety about having little to show for his education. While other people of his age were beginning their careers in law or business or the church, Milton lived alone at his father's country house. For nearly six years he read widely in many subjects. Then he rounded out his education with a lengthy stay in Italy. His first important publications were *Comus*, a masque (short play) first performed at Ludlow Castle in 1634, and *Lycidas* (1637), a magnificent elegy on the death of a former classmate.

On the eve of the English Civil War (1642–49), Milton began writing pamphlets supporting the cause of the Puritans, who favored religious liberty and a parliamentary form of government without a king. One of these, *Areopagitica* (1644), is among the earliest and most eloquent pleas for freedom of the press. Milton's writings brought him to the attention of Oliver Cromwell, who became Lord Protector after the execution of Charles I in 1649. He appointed Milton secretary for foreign languages in the new government.

By 1652, Milton had gone blind. He responded to this affliction with renewed creativity. With the help of secretaries, he continued in his government post until the restoration of the monarchy in 1660. He then lived in retirement with his family while he completed his masterpiece, *Paradise Lost* (1667). This work is the greatest epic poem in the English language. It expands the story of the fall of Satan and of Adam and Eve in the Garden of Eden.

In 1671, Milton published *Paradise Regained*, a shorter epic, and *Samson Agonistes*, the story of Samson written in the form of a Greek tragedy. When he died on November 8, 1674, Milton had won a place in English literature next to Shakespeare.

DAYTON HASKIN
Boston College

MILWAUKEE

Milwaukee is the largest city in Wisconsin. It is located on the western shore of Lake Michigan, where three rivers—the Menominee, the Kinnickinnic, and the Milwaukee—flow together. It is an important port on the Great Lakes, with a route to the Atlantic Ocean by way of the St. Lawrence Seaway.

Milwaukee is noted for its excellent government, low crime rate, and beautiful harbor. The city covers 106 square miles (275 square kilometers) and has a population of about 600,000. More than 1.6 million live in the greater metropolitan area.

Known as the Machine Shop of the World, Milwaukee is among the leading industrial cities of the United States. It is known especially for the manufacture of motorcycles, tractors, outboard motors, diesel and gasoline engines, mining machinery, and equipment for electric power plants. Beer and processed foods are also important products.

Milwaukee is a regional center of culture, education, and recreation. There are numerous art museums and a performing arts center, where people enjoy symphony concerts, opera, ballet, theater, and other cultural activities. The Milwaukee County Public Museum is one of the largest science and history museums in the country. The Milwaukee County Zoo, which includes the Children's Zoo, ranks among the country's best. Milwaukee County is famed for its park system. The city's best-known colleges and universities are Marquette University and a branch of the University of Wisconsin. Sports fans in the city root for the Milwaukee Bucks basketball team and the Milwaukee Brewers baseball team.

The name "Milwaukee" comes from the Indian word *Millioke*, which probably meant "good land." French fur trappers camped there as early as the mid-1600's.

The first permanent settler, Solomon Juneau (1793–1856), built a trading post between the Milwaukee River and Lake Michigan in 1818. Villages grew up around Juneau's post and around the cabins of other nearby pioneers. During the 1830's, many settlers came, including a number of Irish, English, German, and Scandinavian immigrants. The villages joined in a town, which was incorporated in 1846. Juneau served as the first mayor.

Milwaukee's population greatly increased, due mainly to a flood of German refugees escaping revolutions in Europe in 1848. Many of these immigrants were important intellectual and political leaders, who set a high cultural tone for the frontier city. The Germans also established the art of making fine beer and set up beer gardens and music societies. Other sizable groups in Milwaukee's population today include African Americans and people of Polish and Hispanic descent.

JAMES JOHN FLANNERY
University of Wisconsin, Milwaukee

Milwaukee, Wisconsin's largest city, is located on the western shore of Lake Michigan. It is a leading center of industry in the Midwest.

Gold

Hematite

Siderite

Chalcopyrite

Beryl

Halite

Barite

MINERALS

Minerals are everywhere around us. In fact, they are the most common solid substances found on earth. More than 2,000 different kinds of minerals have been identified. Rock, sand, soil, particles in the air, and even the human body contain the substances that people call minerals.

▶ WHAT ARE MINERALS?

Minerals are naturally occurring substances. They are inorganic; that is, they are not alive and never have been alive. Some people describe any material taken from the earth as a mineral. However, **mineralogists**, scientists who study minerals, use four characteristics to distinguish minerals from all other materials: A mineral is found in nature—it is not made by people or produced artificially; it is made up of inorganic (nonliving) substances; it has the same chemical makeup wherever it is found on earth, so long as it comes from the same rock type; and it has atoms that come together in a regular pattern to form a solid unit called a crystal.

▶ IDENTIFYING MINERALS

All minerals have distinctive physical properties that are used to identify them. Minerals also have distinctive chemical compositions. Both the physical properties and the chemical composition can be used to learn a mineral's identity.

Scientists are able to put all minerals into one of seven groups based on their chemical composition. Each of the minerals pictured here represents one of the main mineral groups. The chart (*next page*) lists each mineral shown along with the group it belongs to and its chemical composition.

Characteristics of Minerals

Often a mineral can be recognized by its physical characteristics alone. Color, luster, cleavage, and hardness are the main properties that are used to identify a mineral.

Color. The color of a mineral helps identify it. Color is not always a good clue to a mineral's identity, because many minerals are found in several colors. But most minerals are usually not found in certain colors. For example, quartz is typically clear, milky white, smoky gray, or pink, but not black. Hornblende is generally very dark green or black rather than light colored.

Luster. One of the easiest things to notice about a mineral is its luster. Minerals that shine like metal have a metallic luster. All

The Main Mineral Groups		
Group Name	Examples	Chemical Composition
Sulfates	**Barite**, gypsum, anhydrite	Metals, sulfur, oxygen
Silicates	**Beryl**, quartz, feldspar, talc	Metals, silicon, oxygen
Sulfides	**Chalcopyrite**, galena, pyrite	Sulfur, metals
Elements	**Gold**, copper, sulfur, silver	Uncombined elements
Halides	**Halite**, fluorite	Metals, chlorine, fluorine, iodine, bromine
Oxides	**Hematite**, bauxite	Metals, oxygen
Carbonates	**Siderate**, calcite, dolomite	Metals, carbon, oxygen

other minerals have a nonmetallic luster. There are several ways of describing nonmetallic luster. The terms used are pearly, glassy, silky, or dull.

Some minerals have such a distinct luster and color that these two characteristics are all you need to identify them. Other minerals are difficult, if not impossible, to identify using only color and luster. For example, pyrite, gold, and chalcopyrite are three minerals that are very similar in color and luster.

Cleavage. Certain minerals break in a very definite way. This is called a mineral's cleavage. Galena, the mineral from which lead is extracted, cleaves into little cubes. Mica cleaves easily into very thin sheets, almost like paper. Calcite cleaves into pieces that look like little slanting bricks. Feldspar cleaves in two directions: It splits into pieces with surfaces that join each other almost at right angles. A broken piece of feldspar looks as if it had little steps on its surface.

Many minerals have no definite cleavage. They break into irregular chunks. Quartz is one of these minerals.

Hardness. Some minerals are harder than others. Some, such as gypsum, are so soft that they can be scratched easily. A diamond is so hard that it cannot be scratched by any other known substance.

Geologists use a standard scale of hardness, called **Mohs' scale**, to describe a mineral's hardness. The scale was developed about one hundred years ago by a German scientist, Friedrich Mohs. In Mohs' scale, ten standard minerals are given a number from 1 to 10. Talc is number 1, quartz is number 7, and diamond is number 10. Talc is the softest mineral on the scale, and diamond is the hardest.

A mineral on Mohs' scale can scratch any other listed below it. For example, topaz can scratch quartz, and quartz can scratch feldspar and every other mineral below it on the scale. In turn, a mineral can be scratched by every

How to Identify Minerals

Amateur geologists have long collected minerals and rocks. When an interesting specimen is found, rock hunters can use resources such as reference books with pictures to help identify minerals. There are also simple tests that can be used to help in the identification. The hardness of a mineral, from the softest (talc) to the hardest (diamond), can be found using the scratch tests and the corresponding hardness scale on the chart below. For example, a mineral that can be scratched by a fingernail would have a hardness of approximately 1 to 2, and a mineral that can scratch window glass would have a hardness of approximately 6 to 9.

Talc

Diamond

Scratch Tests	Hardness Scale
Can be scratched by a fingernail	1–2
Can be scratched by a penny	3
Can be scratched by a knife blade	4–5
It can scratch window glass	6–9
It can scratch all common materials	10

mineral above it on the scale. Talc can be scratched by every other mineral, while corundum can be scratched only by diamond.

Thus an unknown mineral that cannot be scratched by fluorite (which has a hardness of 4) but can be scratched by feldspar (which has a hardness of 6) has a hardness that falls between them. The mineral may be apatite (which has a hardness of 5). Its color, luster, and cleavage will further help to identify it.

Tests That Identify Minerals

Along with examining a mineral's physical properties, indirect methods such as laboratory tests also can be used to identify a mineral.

Because of their chemical compositions, minerals have characteristic reactions to specific physical and chemical tests. These reactions are then used in determining a mineral's identity.

Streak. Sometimes the powder of a mineral has a color different from that of a large piece of the mineral. You can best see the powder by scratching the mineral across a hard dull-white surface, such as a white porcelain plate or even the back of a bathroom tile. The trail of powdered mineral that is made on the surface is called the streak of the mineral.

Habit. The typical form or appearance of a mineral is called its habit. Crystals, fibers,

The Shapes of Mineral Crystals

Most minerals have a characteristic crystal shape that can be used to help identify one mineral from another. The shape is formed by the regular pattern of a mineral's atoms. Below are the six basic crystal shapes with a mineral example of each.

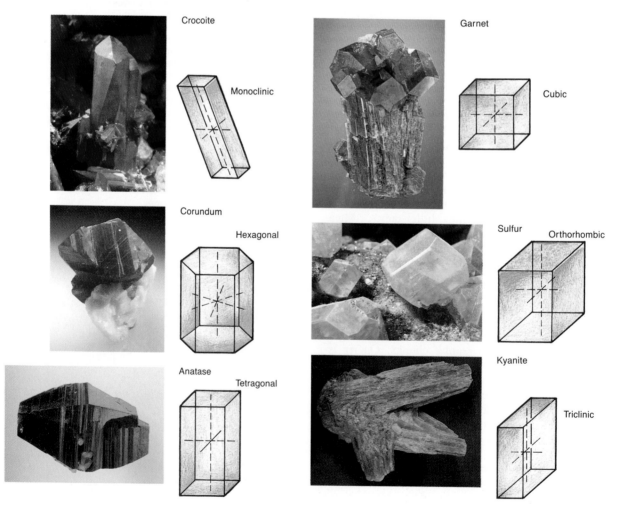

Crocoite — Monoclinic

Garnet — Cubic

Corundum — Hexagonal

Sulfur — Orthorhombic

Anatase — Tetragonal

Kyanite — Triclinic

Minerals are retrieved from deposits close to the earth's surface as well as from deposits buried deep beneath the surface. The open-pit, or surface, method is used to mine copper from this North American mine (*right*). Underground mining methods are used to mine garnet deposits in this South African mine (*above*).

nuggets, and grains are all typical mineral forms. Some minerals are generally in crystal form, such as diamonds. Others, including serpentine asbestos, are found in a fibrous form. Gold is found in the form of nuggets. Still other minerals are found in more than one form. Halite may be found as crystals, grains, or large chunks.

Special Properties. Some minerals have special identifying properties. Halite, which has several forms, can best be identified by its taste. If you were to touch a clean piece of it with your tongue, you would get a salty taste. The mineral kaolin (sometimes called kaolinite) is identified by its earthy smell. It has the distinct smell of dry, freshly plowed earth. Talc has a greasy, slippery feel that no other mineral has. Weight helps in identifying some minerals. Those with iron or lead in them are much heavier than most other minerals.

Pure clear calcite, called Iceland spar, has double refraction. For example, if you look at a pin through a piece of Iceland spar, you will see two pins on the other side. Print seen through clear calcite appears double. Calcite has one other property that no other mineral has: It effervesces, or bubbles, strongly in hydrochloric acid. Because limestone and marble are almost entirely calcite, they are tested with acid. Other minerals do effervesce, but only weakly.

▶**PROCESSING AND USING MINERALS**

Since ancient times, people have searched for rocks rich in minerals. Prospectors have studied rock formations and changes on the earth's surface to locate possible mineral-rich sites. Today's mineral prospectors have elaborate methods of searching for minerals. Modern techniques of exploration include detailed geologic maps and photographs taken high above the earth's surface.

Once a rock deposit containing minerals is located, it is tested to see if it is possible to profitably extract the minerals. When the mineral is close to the surface, an open-pit, or surface, mine is developed. Underground deposits are mined using deep excavations called shafts.

The rock that is mined may contain a variety of minerals. It must be processed to retrieve the minerals that are useful. Water, chemicals, heat, and filtering are all used to separate the rock and impurities from the minerals. Then the extracted minerals are refined and made into finished products.

The goods that can be produced from minerals are an important part of everyday life. Industry, such as agriculture, transportation, construction, and communications, could not exist without minerals and the products made from them. Computers, glass, plaster, fertilizers, cement, and cosmetics are just a few of the many products containing minerals that we depend on.

Reviewed by JEFF STEINER
Earth Sciences
City University of New York

See also CRYSTALS; EARTH; EARTH, HISTORY OF; GEOLOGY; MINES AND MINING; ORES; ROCKS; VOLCANOES.

Open-pit mines, such as this copper mine in Utah, are the chief sources of ore. Ore can be taken more easily from a surface mine than from an underground mine.

MINES AND MINING

Mining is a fascinating—and difficult—task. The earth does not give up its mineral riches easily. People must tear them from the earth with picks and shovels, drills, and explosives. But the work is well worth the trouble. Our modern civilization could not exist without the materials provided by mining.

Most of our food and clothing come from materials on the surface of the earth. But many other important things—including metals, fuels, chemicals, and plastics—are made from materials that are dug out of the earth. Even food and clothing could not be provided in abundance without mineral fertilizers to grow food and without metal machinery to weave cloth.

The materials that miners dig from the earth are minerals. A **mineral** is a chemical element or compound that occurs naturally in the earth. A **rock** is a combination of two or more minerals. An **ore** is a deposit in the earth that is rich enough in some mineral to make mining it worthwhile.

Some of the most important metals that are mined are aluminum, copper, gold, iron, lead, nickel, silver, tin, and zinc. These metals are used every day for hundreds of purposes. Other metals, such as beryllium, are less well known. Beryllium is used to make lightweight alloys (combinations of metals) needed in space vehicles and nuclear equipment.

Not all minerals are metals. Useful nonmetallic minerals include salt and sand and gravel. Precious stones such as diamonds, emeralds, rubies, and sapphires are nonmetallic minerals. Other nonmetals have uses in a variety of industries. Fluorspar is needed for refining aluminum. Gypsum is used for making plaster of paris. Phosphate rock is a main ingredient of fertilizers. Sulfur is used in hundreds of chemical products.

▶ **WHERE DEPOSITS ARE FOUND**

Nonmetallic minerals are found in deposits scattered all over the earth. But the large deposits of metallic ores tend to be grouped in certain areas. The chief centers for gold mining, for instance, are in South Africa, Russia, northern Canada, Japan, and the southwestern United States. Important areas that produce copper are in the southwestern and northern United States, Russia, Japan, Chile, and Zambia. Many areas that are rich in deposits of one metallic ore also have other metals. The technical name for such an area is **metallogenetic province**.

Finding and extracting ore is the work of geologists, mining engineers, and metallurgical engineers. Geologists are scientists who study the earth's crust. With their special

Geologists take ore samples for testing. If the samples contain enough high-grade ore, a mine will be opened.

A satellite photograph shows the area around Salt Lake City, Utah. Such pictures help locate ore deposits.

knowledge and instruments, they can find ore deposits that untrained people might never discover. Mining engineers work out ways to get the minerals out of the earth efficiently and safely. Metallurgical engineers figure out how to process the ore to extract valuable metals.

Searching for Ore

The first step in mining is to find a rich mineral deposit, or ore body. Some ore bodies lie exposed on the surface of the earth. This happens when wind, rain, creeks, or rivers have worn away the soil and rock covering them. Because such ore bodies are not hidden from view, most of them have been located by now.

In the past, prospectors—with burros, picks and shovels, and gold pans—searched for rich deposits of gold. Their place has been taken by trained geologists who use scientific instruments and methods to locate deposits of all the important minerals.

One method used to find ore is **geologic analysis.** Geologists carefully study the earth around a known ore deposit. They note such things as the shape of the folded rock layers, the location of faults (breaks in the rock layers), the kinds of rocks and minerals present, and the way the rocks have been changed by forces in the earth's crust. Then the geologists look for another area that has the same char-

acteristics. There is a good chance that there will be ore deposits in that area, too.

To aid in the search for ore, geologists use aerial and satellite photographs and maps that are made from photographs. The formations of land, rocks, and vegetation as seen from the air can reveal much to a trained eye about what lies under the surface of the earth.

Geologists sometimes create small artificial earthquakes to get a better idea of the underlying rock formations. They place sticks of dynamite in shallow holes and set off the blast. This sends vibrations through the earth, which are picked up by devices called **geophones.** Another way of creating vibrations is to "hammer" on the ground with a mechanical device mounted on a truck. Patterns of the vibrations are recorded on graphs by electrically operated pens. A study of the patterns shows what the rock layers and faults, or cracks, are like under the surface.

Measuring differences in the force of gravity with sensitive instruments helps locate mineral-bearing rocks. It is known that rocks containing certain minerals exert more gravity pull than other rocks. When the instruments register very strong gravity forces, samples of the underlying rock may be drilled out for further testing.

Some minerals are magnetic. They can be detected by instruments that measure differences in the strength of the earth's magnetic fields. One magnetic detector, called an **airborne magnetometer,** is trailed behind a low-flying airplane. In this way, a great deal of ground can be checked in a very short time. Magnetic methods led to discoveries of large iron ore deposits in Brazil and Labrador.

Electricity is sometimes used to help locate ore deposits. Ores that contain metals usually conduct more electric current than other minerals and rocks. Metal rods called **electrodes** are stuck into the earth's surface. Electric current is passed through the electrodes, and the amount of current flow is measured. Where the current flow is greatest, metal ore may be present.

Some ores betray their presence by giving off radioactivity—a stream of charged particles. If the ores are not too deep underground, the radioactivity can be detected by a device called a **Geiger counter.** Uranium, thorium, and radium are three important radioactive minerals.

Workers drill holes to attach wire mesh to the ceiling of a nickel mine. The mesh will keep debris from falling.

Geochemical analysis is a newer method for locating ores. Scientists have found that the water in streams, springs, and wells usually contains traces of any metals that are in the area. Many plants also contain traces of the metals. Samples of water and plants are tested with chemicals to find out what metals they contain. When an area shows a concentration of some valuable metal, geologists take a closer look to see whether the deposits are large enough to be mined.

Today, space technology provides valuable new tools to geologists. High-altitude aircraft and earth-orbiting satellites take photographs, radar images, and other measurements that help locate ore deposits.

Drilling and Sampling

When geologists have located a possible ore deposit, they use drilling and sampling to decide whether the deposit is worth mining. Drills with hollow, diamond-tipped cutting bits are used to bore into the rock to get the samples. The drills can cut out a core of rock about 5 centimeters (2 inches) in diameter to a depth of more than 100 meters (330 feet).

The rock samples are tested for the amount of a certain mineral they contain. If the rock has a high percentage of the mineral, the deposit is a **high-grade ore.** Lower percentages of mineral content mean that the deposit is a **low-grade ore** or a **marginal ore.** Low-grade ores usually are considered worth mining if they are not too difficult to dig up. It must also be possible to separate the valuable minerals from the worthless materials cheaply and easily. Marginal ores contain so little of the mineral being sought that they usually are not considered worth mining unless the mineral is extremely valuable. But sometimes marginal ores become worth mining—for example, when a new use is found for a mineral, making it more in demand, or when supplies of higher-grade ores containing the mineral are exhausted.

▶PLANNING A MINE

When it is known how rich and how large the mineral deposit is, a decision must be made about whether to open a mine. A mine, like a highway or a building, is a carefully engineered structure. A team of experts studies the question. The team includes geologists, mining engineers, business managers, and other specialists. They decide what kind of mine should be dug, how much ore could be mined each day, and what the equipment, supplies, labor, and transportation would cost. The mining company will open the mine only if the costs do not seem too high for the amount of ore that could be obtained. The company must make more money from selling the minerals than it spends in mining them.

The method to be used in mining the ore has a great deal to do with how expensive it might be to open a mine. There are two chief methods of mining ore—underground mining and surface mining. Underground mining is usually the more costly method because it requires more labor. In many cases, the large power equipment used in surface mining cannot be put to work underground.

▶ UNDERGROUND MINING

Underground mining is used to extract ores that are deep beneath the earth's surface. To reach the ore, deep shafts and horizontal passageways called **drifts** must be dug. This is very expensive. A large amount of money must be invested before any ore is extracted or any metal produced.

The shaft that is dug down to the ore is usually vertical. An elevator called a **cage** is installed to carry workers and materials up and down. If the ore is not too deeply buried, a sloping shaft may be built, and inclined-rail transportation may be used.

At the bottom of the shaft, a larger opening is dug to make room for workers and equipment. From this spot, working drifts, or roadways, are dug. The ore can now be extracted. How it is removed depends on the kind of ore being mined and how the ore bed, or vein, is placed. Coal, for instance, is usually found in veins that are nearly horizontal. Metallic ores are often found in veins that run almost vertically in the earth. Coal is fairly soft and can be dug out by machines. Most ores must be drilled and blasted out.

Excavating ore from an underground mine is usually called **stoping.** This involves drilling and blasting the ore with explosives so that it is broken into pieces for easy removal.

Open stoping is a system of digging "rooms" out of the ore while leaving pillars of ore to hold up the roof. This is also called

Coils of slow-burning fuse attached to dynamite in the rock are lit to set off the blast.

Timbers are often used to support the mine tunnels.

the room-and-pillar method of mining. Often supports of timber, steel, or concrete are used to help hold the overlying rock in place. Sometimes the pillars of ore are cut away after all the other ore has been extracted. The roof of each room is allowed to collapse as the miners work back toward the main shaft.

If the ore pillars are not strong enough to allow open stoping, **filled stoping** may be used. As ore is cut out, the walls that are left are buttressed with timbers, and the holes are filled with sand. Without support, the weight of rock and earth from above would cause the working areas to cave in. One important type of filled stoping is called the timbered cut-and-fill method.

Many coal deposits and a few ore deposits lie nearly horizontal in the earth. If the overlying ground is not too strong, they can be mined by **longwall stoping.** An excavation (or stope) is dug into the ore vein. The miners drill and blast the ore off the face of one wall of the stope. As the ore is dug out, the rock and ore above will cave in. The stope's walls must be held up by timber or steel supports. When all the ore is taken from one wall of the stope, the supports are removed and that wall caves in. Then the miners start digging ore from the wall on the other side.

Caving is another method that can be used to remove ore. Openings are cut under large blocks of ore. Small pillars are left to hold the ore in place. When everyone is safely out of the openings, the pillars are blasted. The weight of the ore and rock above it causes the ore to cave in. The broken pieces of ore are scooped up, usually by automatic loading machines, and carried away.

Ore is transported to the main shaft by underground railway trains. At the shaft it is loaded onto elevators called **skips** and hoisted to the surface.

Safety in Underground Mines

Huge fans circulate fresh air through the mine tunnels. A fresh air supply is important for several reasons. Drilling and blasting in the passageways and stopes stir up dust. Miners

Ore cars, which run on train tracks, are used to carry mineral-laden rock from an underground mine.

could not work long if they had to breathe this dust-filled air all the time. The dust from quartz, a form of silica, is especially harmful. Inhaling this dust for long periods of time can cause a lung disease called **silicosis.** Gases from explosives are also released into the air when blasting is going on. These gases are harmful to breathe. Besides fouling the air, the dust and gases may cause fires or explosions. Thus, good ventilation of a mine is a necessary safety precaution. Some mines also are very hot from the earth's heat. They must be air-conditioned so that the miners are comfortable while they work.

Another problem is groundwater, which constantly seeps into mines. The water must be pumped out all the time, even when the miners are not working. If pumping stopped even for a few weeks or months, the drifts and stopes might be flooded.

Miners have to be careful of such dangers as falling rock, cave-ins, large digging and loading machinery, and the explosives used for blasting. In spite of all these hazards, the number of mine accidents and deaths has steadily decreased. Mining companies, miners' unions, and the government are continually looking for ways to make mining safer. Miners must take special training courses and safety-education programs.

▶ SURFACE MINING

Surface mines extract ore that lies near the surface of the earth. The work is faster and easier than underground mining. No shafts, drifts, or stopes have to be dug. All the heavy digging and loading can be done by large power equipment, which cannot be taken into most underground mines.

Surface mines are of two types—open-pit bench mines and strip mines. An open-pit bench mine looks like a bowl lined with a series of benches or terraces. Strip mines are used to mine coal. They follow the coal bed across the countryside.

The ease and speed of surface mining make it less expensive than underground mining. Even very low-grade ores can sometimes be mined with profit in open-pit mines. Huge quantities of ore are taken from open-pit mines. More minerals are obtained from these mines than are obtained from underground mines.

Before the ore can be mined, the soil and rock covering it, called the **overburden,** must be removed. Giant diesel-powered scrapers gouge out tons of the material at a time. The total weight of waste material is usually several times as great as the weight of the ore.

When enough ore is uncovered and blasted loose, large power shovels go into action. They scoop up the ore and dump it into trucks. The largest hauling trucks can carry as much as 350 tons of ore in one load. Because of their great size and weight, these trucks travel on specially built roads from the mines to the processing plants.

▶ PLACER MINING

Valuable minerals are sometimes found in the sand and soil deposited by rivers and streams. Gold, platinum, and zircon, for example, are often found in these **placer deposits.** The minerals are recovered by a specialized type of mining, called **placer mining.**

Large dredges and power shovels dig up the soil and dump it into long troughs. The material is washed over with water. The minerals, which are heavier than the soil, sink to the bottom and are recovered. Placer mining is not used as widely as underground and surface mining. There are not as many placer deposits as there are deposits of minerals buried in the earth.

▶ MILLING AND PROCESSING

Some minerals, such as sulfur and salt, are sometimes found in an almost pure state in the earth. They are not mixed with other materials. They can be sold directly to customers without much processing. But in most cases, minerals must go through several processing treatments before they can be used. Metallic ores, for instance, go through many processing operations before the useful metals are obtained. Sometimes the processing is done in plants at the mine site, and sometimes the ore is shipped to processing plants elsewhere. The ways in which metallic ores are processed are described in the article METALS AND METALLURGY in this volume (Volume M).

▶ HISTORY OF MINING

Mining is such an ancient occupation that no one can say exactly when it began. The

This massive strip-mining machine scoops up 200 tons of earth with each bite. It is used to mine coal.

Greek myth of the Golden Fleece grew out of tales about a primitive kind of mining. The Golden Fleece was a sheepskin used to catch particles of gold washed down a stream.

One of the earliest mining ventures recorded in history was the Egyptian expedition into the Sinai peninsula sometime around 2600 B.C. The Egyptians went to Sinai to mine turquoise. While there, they also found and mined a more useful mineral—copper.

The ancient Greeks mined silver in the mines of Laurion, south of Athens. The mines may have been opened as early as 1400 B.C. by an earlier Greek people, the Mycenaeans. The Greeks worked the mines from about 600 to 350 B.C. Several of the shafts went to a depth of 120 meters (400 feet). Other metals, such as lead, zinc, and iron, were later mined from these old diggings.

By 1940, machines such as this conveyor belt were being used to help miners load coal into cars.

The Romans had mines everywhere, from Africa to Britain. Among their most valuable mines were the Río Tinto mines in Spain, which yielded large quantities of gold, silver, copper, tin, lead, and iron.

Mining became a really large-scale operation in the 1700's and 1800's, when the Industrial Revolution was under way. Large amounts of coal were needed for smelting iron and stoking factory furnaces, and coal mining expanded rapidly. The development of modern mining techniques started at this time.

Most of the exciting stories about mining are connected with the search for precious metals and stones, usually gold and diamonds. Gold fever reached its height in the 1800's. The California gold rush started in 1848, after the discovery of rich gold deposits at John Sutter's sawmill on the American River.

One of the California prospectors was an Australian, Edward H. Hargraves. He noticed that the rocks and terrain of the California goldfields resembled those in his native land. Hargraves went back to Australia and found rich gold deposits there in 1851. This started the Australian gold rush.

Two other large gold deposits were found later in the century. In 1896, a gold strike in the Klondike region of Canada's Yukon Territory started a gold rush in Canada and Alaska. Ten years earlier, in 1886, mining had begun in the richest goldfield ever discovered, the Witwatersrand area in South Africa.

The world's largest diamond deposits were found in South Africa about 1870. These became the famous Kimberley diamond mines.

Some of the money made from these mines led to other mineral discoveries. An Englishman, Cecil Rhodes, used money from his interest in the Kimberley mines to finance exploration into the interior of Africa, where more gold and diamonds were found. Even more valuable were the copper deposits that were discovered.

The widespread prospecting for gold and diamonds often led to the uncovering of other minerals. Prospectors may have been disappointed when they found lead, copper, iron, or other minerals instead of gold, but the discoveries were important. As modern industry grew, these minerals were more in demand.

The radium used in early radioactivity experiments came from ores that eventually also provided the first uranium. Uranium was used to develop the atomic bomb during World War II. Later, atomic, or nuclear, technology developed to include nonmilitary uses.

▶MINING IN THE FUTURE

In the future, mining will probably be more important than ever before. As developing countries build industries to support better living standards for their people, there will be greater demand for minerals. This could result in temporary shortages and higher prices for many minerals.

All over the world geologists are hunting for new mineral deposits. New ways to search for hidden deposits are being developed, as are better mining machines and methods. Gigantic drill bits, able to bore large mine shafts in a single operation, are being tested. Miners are using super-hot torches that can burn through rock too hard for drills.

The demand for minerals is increasing, but it is not likely that the world will run out of minerals. There are still supplies available, especially of low-grade ores and common rocks. As high-grade ores are used up, less rich ores will have to be used. Already modern technology enables us to process ores that were once thought to be too low in grade to be of any value. Scientists and engineers are continually experimenting with ways to extract valuable minerals from these ores.

Reviewed by WILLIAM H. DRESHER
International Copper Research Association, Inc.

See also COAL AND COAL MINING; ENGINEERING; METALS AND METALLURGY.

MINNEAPOLIS–SAINT PAUL

Minneapolis and Saint Paul are Minnesota's Twin Cities. Saint Paul is the state capital, Minneapolis the state's biggest city. Both are industrial cities noted for their parks, lakes, and beautiful homes.

The cities grew up near Fort Snelling, an army post at the junction of the Minnesota and Mississippi rivers. Saint Paul began in 1840 as Pig's Eye—the nickname of its first settler, Pierre "Pig's Eye" Parrant. The name was later changed to Saint Paul, after a log-cabin church built within the settlement. In 1847 a pioneer built a sawmill upriver at St. Anthony Falls. A village grew up there and became known as Minneapolis (*minne*, Indian for "water," and *polis*, Greek for "city").

When Minnesota became a territory in 1849 and a state in 1858, Saint Paul, then the larger city, was the natural choice for the capital. Yet by 1880, Minneapolis had become the larger of the Twin Cities—a lead it has held ever since. Its population is more than 382,000, while Saint Paul's is 287,000. The metropolitan area of both cities is nearly 3 million.

The Twin Cities have a diversified economy. Some of the biggest flour companies in the world are headquartered there, as well as the largest cash grain market in the United States. The South Saint Paul stockyards are among the largest in the country. Local factories produce processed foods, automobiles, building materials, computers, electronic equipment, television sets, and plastics.

The St. Anthony Falls prevent large-scale shipping north of Minneapolis. Saint Paul is the largest port on the upper Mississippi and is also a busy motor freight terminal. The Twin Cities are a major railroad hub.

Minneapolis is a lake town, a college town, and a trade, industrial, and financial center. Scenic drives link its 22 lakes and more than 150 parks. Enclosed walkways connect many downtown buildings to keep out the winter cold. The University of Minnesota, in Minneapolis, is one of the largest in the country. The city is also the home of the Minnesota Symphony Orchestra and the Tyrone Guthrie Repertory Theatre. Its museums include the Walker Art Center and Minneapolis Institute of Arts. One of the tallest buildings west of the Mississippi River is the 57-story IDS Center, designed by the architect Philip Johnson.

Included among Saint Paul's attractions are the State Historical Society's museum, the Science Museum of Minnesota, and the world-famous Como Park Zoo and Conservatory. The Agricultural College of the University of Minnesota is one of Saint Paul's many colleges and universities. The cities also host Minnesota's professional sports teams—the Twins (baseball) and the Vikings (football) play in the Metrodome; the Lynx and Timberwolves (basketball) play in the Target Center; and the Wild (hockey) play in the Xcel Energy Center.

Reviewed by LEWIS WIXON
St. Cloud State University

Minneapolis (*below*) is the largest city in Minnesota. St. Paul, its "twin city" and the state capital, is situated directly across the Mississippi River.

MINNESOTA

Minnesota earned the popular nickname the Land of 10,000 Lakes due to the extraordinary number of lakes, rivers, and ponds that decorate its landscape. The state may actually have more than twice this number of crystal-blue lakes, carved out by giant glaciers in ancient times.

The name Minnesota *can be translated from a variety of native Sioux dialects. The most widely accepted interpretation is "sky-tinted water." Others claim that it means "clouded water" and was first used to describe the Minnesota River and the light-colored particles of clay it carried in its flow.*

The state's popular nickname, the Gopher State, has a far less gracious origin. It has been traced to an 1850's political cartoon, in which a group of railroad promoters were equated with gophers, the pesky animals that once plagued Minnesota's prairie homesteaders.

The largest of all the midwestern states, Minnesota is located along the U.S.-Canadian border, about halfway between the Atlantic and Pacific oceans. Minnesota is considered one of the Great Lakes states. Duluth, the state's fourth largest city, lies on Lake Superior and is home to one of the world's largest inland ports. Plains cover much of the landscape, but more rugged country, containing fantastic deposits of iron ore, lies to the north.

With more than 4.9 million residents, Minnesota is the 21st most populous state. More than half of the population is concentrated in the southeast, in the single metropolitan area of the Twin Cities of Minneapolis and St. Paul. Rochester, another populous southeastern city, is home to the Mayo Clinic, a world-renowned medical facility.

About three quarters of all working Minnesotans are employed in the service industries. Manufacturing also contributes significantly to the economy, particularly the production of computers and other electric machinery. Food-processing industries use Minnesota cream to churn out much of the nation's butter and cheese. Because of its dairy and also its wheat production, Minnesota has also been called the Bread and Butter State. But its official nickname is the North Star State because of its northerly location.

State flag

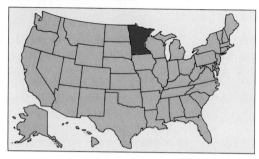

▶ LAND

Minnesota lies approximately in the center of the North American continent. An unusual part of the state is the Northwest Angle. This piece of land, which is about 150 square miles (390 square kilometers) in area, juts farther north than any other part of the continental United States except Alaska.

Land Regions

Minnesota is made up of two major landforms—the Superior Upland and the Central Lowland. The Superior Upland is in the upper northeast; the Central Lowland covers most of the state. All of Minnesota's surface features were created or affected in some way by the glaciers that once covered most of the region. As these glaciers melted, they slowly moved across the state, leaving behind tons of drift—sand, gravel, and rocks of all sizes. Like giant bulldozers, they scooped out thousands of depressions that filled with water and became lakes and ponds.

The Superior Upland, in the northeast, belongs to a large upland region that extends into Canada. It is often called Arrowhead Country because its shape resembles an arrowhead. The region's low ranges of hills include the Mesabi and the Vermilion ranges, known for their deposits of iron ore. Eagle Mountain, the highest point in the state,

Most of Minnesota's water-speckled landscape is so sparsely populated, timber wolves and other wild animals may roam free in the far north. Most Minnesotans live in or near the Twin Cities of Minneapolis (*pictured*) and St. Paul in the southeast.

State flower:
Showy (pink and white)
lady's slipper

State tree:
Red (Norway) pine

FACTS AND FIGURES

Location: North central United States; bordered on the north by Canada (Manitoba and Ontario), on the east by Lake Superior and Wisconsin, on the south by Iowa, and on the west by North Dakota and South Dakota.

Area: 86,943 sq mi (225,182 km²); rank, 12th.

Population: 4,919,479 (2000 census); rank, 21st.

Elevation: *Highest*—2,301 ft (701 m) at Eagle Mountain; *lowest*—602 ft (183 m) along Lake Superior.

Capital: St. Paul.

Statehood: May 11, 1858; 32nd state.

State Motto: *L'Etoile du Nord* ("The Star of the North").

State Song: "Hail! Minnesota."

Nickname: North Star State (official); Gopher State; Land of 10,000 Lakes; Land of Sky-Blue Waters; Bread and Butter State.

Abbreviations: MN; Minn.

State bird:
Loon

Clockwise from top: White birch trees grace Superior National Forest along the north shore of Lake Superior. The entire state is dotted with thousands of small ponds and lakes that provide a recreational haven for vacationers. Prairie grasses cover the gently rolling central lowlands in the southern half of the state.

is located in this region. Surprisingly, it is not far from the state's lowest point, located nearby on the shore of Lake Superior.

The Central Lowland covers the rest of Minnesota and is subdivided into four regions.

The **northwestern lake plain** is a very flat area that was once the bottom of an ancient glacial lake called Lake Agassiz. Wide sandy ridges extend through this plain in a north–south direction. To the east of these ridges lies an area of marshes and peat bogs known as the Big Bog.

The **central hill and lake area** stretches from northern Minnesota all the way south to the Iowa border. The Minnesota River cuts through this region at an angle. North of the river there are many low glacial hills, small valleys, and cold, clear lakes. The land south of the river is gently rolling.

The **southwestern ridges** are hills that rise more than 1,800 feet (540 meters). These are the second highest elevations in the state. The hills in this area were probably created by the plowlike action of glaciers. Sometimes the hills are called the *Coteau des Prairies*, which is French for "little hills of the prairies."

The **driftless area** covers a small corner of southeastern Minnesota, the only part that was not affected by glaciers. It is called driftless because it contains no drift, or glacial deposits. But streams created by melting ice masses flowed into and across the area, cutting many deep valleys between flat ridges.

Rivers and Lakes

Three major river systems run through Minnesota. The Red River of the North and the Rainy River flow north toward Hudson Bay; the St. Louis and other rivers in the east drain eastward into the Great Lakes and the St. Lawrence system; and the Mississippi and its main tributaries, the Minnesota and the St. Croix, flow south toward the Gulf of Mexico.

Among the largest of the state's thousands of freshwater lakes are Red Lake, Leech Lake, Mille Lacs Lake, and Lake Winnibigoshish. Minnesota shares with Canada many small lakes and two large ones—Lake of the Woods and Rainy Lake.

Climate

Minnesota is subject to extremes in weather. Summers can be very hot and winters are long and cold.

During the winters, the northwest wind often brings cold air from the Canadian Arctic. Many of the lakes and rivers freeze, and snowfall is heavy in most areas. Temperatures as low as −59°F (−51°C) have been recorded at International Falls, a city on Rainy River at the Canadian border. To the south, around Minneapolis-St. Paul, January temperatures average about 11°F (−12°C).

The southern half of the state is generally warmer and more humid in summer than the northern half, and yet the average July temperature in Minneapolis-St. Paul is a mild 74°F (23°C). Occasionally there are hot, cloudless days, and these are often accompanied by thunderstorms that may bring heavy downfalls and an occasional tornado.

A moderate amount of precipitation falls in Minnesota. The annual amount from rain and snow averages about 28 inches (710 millimeters), although an occasional blizzard may leave as much as 2 feet (61 centimeters) of snow. Severe dry spells are uncommon.

Plant and Animal Life

Forests cover almost 35 percent of Minnesota. Three million acres (1.2 million hectares) of the state's most spectacular woodlands can be found in the northeast in Superior National Forest. It is here, and in the state's other 65 state forests, that balsam fir, pine, spruce, aspen, and white birch grow. In the south, ash, black walnut, elm, maple, and oak trees are more common. Tall prairie grasses also extend throughout the state, and wildflowers abound in the spring.

In the far north, timber wolves roam free, sharing the land with large populations of white tailed deer and smaller numbers of moose and black bears. Gophers still inhabit the grasslands, while beavers and muskrats live in the many rivers and ponds that are filled with bass, northern pike, trout, muskie, walleye, and other game fish. Lake Superior contains lake herring, lake trout, coho salmon, whitefish, and sturgeon.

Natural Resources

Minnesota has developed its many natural resources but at the same time has attempted to preserve its natural beauty. Air pollution and water pollution, especially of Lake Supe-

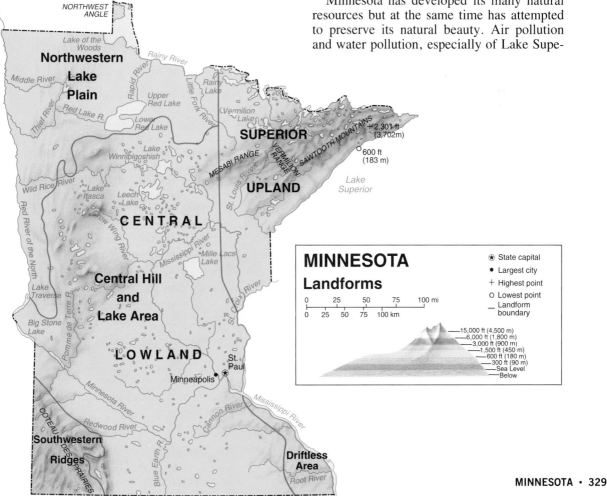

MINNESOTA
Landforms

The Twin Cities of Minneapolis-St. Paul are renowned for their seasonal festivities. In the winter, St. Paul hosts the Winter Carnival, where fantastic palaces are sculpted from gigantic blocks of ice (*left*). In the summer, Minneapolis, nicknamed the City of Lakes, hosts the Aquatennial festival, featuring water sports (*below*) and sand-castle-building contests (*opposite page*).

rior, by mineral-processing and paper-milling plants has been a major concern, but new methods of waste disposal have largely overcome the problem.

Most of the state's woodlands are located in the northeastern third of the state. They provide wood for the paper industry. So much of the state's original timber was used up after more than a century of lumbering that today deliberate attempts are made to plant more trees than are chopped down.

Seventy percent of the country's iron ore is mined in Minnesota, most of it in the form of taconite. Minnesota's soil also contains deposits of granite, limestone, clay, sand and gravel, and smaller amounts of nickel, copper, gold, vanadium, and feldspar. The state's rich soil is responsible for its bountiful farms.

▶ PEOPLE

Seven out of every ten Minnesotans live in cities or towns. Most inhabit the southeastern quarter of the state, although there are a few concentrated areas along the Mesabi Range and in and around Duluth in the northeast.

The first residents of Minnesota were Dakota Sioux and Ojibwa (Chippewa) Indians. Beginning in the 1600's, French traders came to

barter with the Native Americans and were soon followed by British traders. As American pioneers began to settle the land between 1830 and 1850, workers were needed for farming, lumbering, and building towns and railroads. Minnesotans began advertising their rich land to lure more settlers. Pamphlets distributed throughout northern Europe described the state as the land of opportunity. As a result, German and Irish immigrants poured in, followed by Swedes, Norwegians, and Danes. Most of Minnesota's present population is descended from these original pioneers.

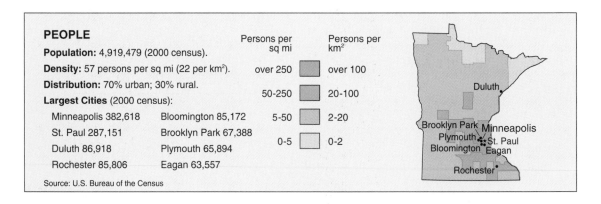

PEOPLE

Population: 4,919,479 (2000 census).

Density: 57 persons per sq mi (22 per km²).

Distribution: 70% urban; 30% rural.

Largest Cities (2000 census):

Minneapolis 382,618	Bloomington 85,172
St. Paul 287,151	Brooklyn Park 67,388
Duluth 86,918	Plymouth 65,894
Rochester 85,806	Eagan 63,557

Persons per sq mi	Persons per km²
over 250	over 100
50-250	20-100
5-50	2-20
0-5	0-2

Source: U.S. Bureau of the Census

Employment of migrant farm laborers, beginning in the 1920's, brought a growing number of Hispanic Americans to the state, and today they make up about 3 percent of the population. The African American community has always been concentrated in the Twin Cities. In addition, since 1980, refugees from Southeast Asia have created a large Hmong community centered in St. Paul. Together these groups make up about 9 percent of the state's total population.

The Native American population reached its lowest point about 1900, and although it has since been increasing, Native Americans still make up only 1 percent of the entire state population. Many live in the Minneapolis–St. Paul and Duluth metropolitan areas. Others live on the dozen Ojibwa and Sioux reservations scattered throughout the state. Among the largest are the Ojibwa's White Earth, Red Lake, and Leech Lake Indian reservations.

Education

Minnesota is proud of the high quality of education offered in its schools and its 28 public and private colleges and universities. The state's leading institution of higher learning is the state-supported University of Min-

nesota, founded in 1851. Its main campus is located in Minneapolis–St. Paul, but branches also include the Mayo Graduate School of Medicine at Rochester, a university campus and a medical school at Duluth, a campus at Morris, and a technical school at Crookston.

Minnesota State University campuses are located in Bemidji, Mankato, Marshall, Moorhead, St. Cloud, St. Paul, and Winona. The state also supports a community college system. Private institutions include Carleton College and St. Olaf College, both in Northfield; Gustavus Adolphus College in St. Peter; St. John's University in Collegeville; and Concordia College at Moorhead. Hamline University, Macalester College, the University of St. Thomas, and the College of St. Catherine all are located in St. Paul.

Libraries, Museums, and the Arts

Minnesota has approximately 330 public libraries. The largest of these is the Minneapolis Public Library, which also contains the Minneapolis Planetarium. The Mayo Clinic and Foundation Library in Rochester houses a large collection of medical works. The James J. Hill Reference Library in St. Paul specializes in business, economics, technology, and science texts. The Minnesota Historical Society Library, also in St. Paul, includes collections on state history and heritage.

Most of the more widely known museums are in the Minneapolis–St. Paul area. The Minneapolis Institute of Arts, with a collection of major works of art, is the largest in the state. It is located in the Minneapolis Society of Fine Arts Park, along with the Minneapolis College of Art and Design and the Children's Theatre Company and school. The Minnesota History Center and the Minnesota Science Museum are in St. Paul. Suburban Apple Valley is home to the impressive 485-acre (196-hectare) Minnesota Zoo. Its Sky Train monorail allows visitors a bird's-eye view of the outdoor animal habitats.

The state's cultural institutions include the Minnesota Opera Company and the internationally acclaimed Saint Paul Chamber Orchestra, which perform in St. Paul's Ordway Theatre, and the Minnesota Symphony Orchestra, which is housed in Orchestra Hall in Minneapolis. The equally famed Tyrone Guthrie Theater in Minneapolis is considered one of the nation's finest repertory theaters.

▶ ECONOMY

Minnesota's economy is supported by a healthy balance of diverse industries. Services make up the largest segment, followed by manufacturing, government, transportation, agriculture, and mining and construction. The state's location on the Great Lakes and its access to the St. Lawrence Seaway and the Mississippi River make it a major marketing and distribution center of the Midwest.

Services

Minnesota's service industries produce about 70 percent of the state's gross state product (GSP), the total value of goods and services the state produces in one year. Services employ more than three quarters of the state's work force.

Wholesale and retail trade, or the buying and selling of industrial and personal goods, accounts for 18 percent of the total GSP. Financial services, which include banking, insurance, and real estate, make up another 18 percent, while government services, including the maintenance of hospitals, schools, and military bases, account for 10 percent. Tourism, business, legal, medical, recreational, community, social, and personal services combined add up to 15 percent of the GSP. Transportation and communication are also service industries and account for an additional 9 percent.

Manufacturing

After 1950 manufacturing surpassed agriculture in economic value. Today it employs almost one fifth of the state's work force and accounts for 21 percent of the GSP.

Machinery, mainly office machines and computers, heads the list in value. It is followed closely by food processing, such as butter and cheese manufacturing, meat packaging, sugar refining, and vegetable canning. Minneapolis was once a leading flour-milling center in the United States, and cereals continue to be processed there.

The Minneapolis-St. Paul area is also a large printing and publishing center. Fabricated metal products are produced in St. Paul. Wood pulp and paper products are produced throughout the state. Crude oil is refined near Minneapolis and Duluth. Among the other products manufactured in Minnesota are scientific instruments, such as temperature regulators and rocket guidance systems. The manufacture of refrigerators, cellophane tape, and snowmobiles is also notable.

Agriculture

In the late 1800's and early 1900's, Minnesota milled more flour than any other state, and it was widely known as the nation's breadbasket. Farmers later earned a reputation in producing livestock. Today's farmers in western and central Minnesota raise beef cattle,

Food processing is one of Minnesota's most profitable manufacturing industries. Dairy-processing plants churn milk into butter and cheese.

hogs, and turkeys. Dairy farmers in the east-central and southeastern regions produce butter, cheese (especially blue cheese), and eggs. All together, livestock and dairy products bring in about half the state's farm income. Other important crops are corn, soybeans, hay, wheat, sugar beets, potatoes, wild rice, green peas, honey, apples, barley, and oats. Indeed, Minnesota is one of the nation's leading producers of corn and soybeans. Although agriculture has been surpassed in importance by manufacturing, it still accounts for a full 5 percent of the GSP.

Mining and Construction

Iron ore, Minnesota's leading mineral, is taken from the Mesabi, Vermilion, and Cuyuna ranges. Most of the best pockets of ore have been exhausted, but the iron-bearing taconite rock of the Mesabi Range is still one of the nation's leading sources of iron.

Sand and gravel are quarried throughout the state for use in the construction of roads and buildings. Central Minnesota has large deposits of granite, which is used as building stone and for monuments. Limestone and clay are also mined.

Together mining and construction account for about 4 percent of the GSP and employ the same percent of the state's work force.

Transportation and Communication

Minnesota has a highly varied transportation network. The first railroad connected St. Paul and St. Anthony in 1862, and by 1900, almost every town was served by railroad. The state's modern highway system had its beginning in 1920 when the people voted to approve a network of roads. The Minneapolis-St. Paul International Airport is the largest of more than 140 airports in the state. And Duluth is one of the world's leading freight ports.

Minnesota has 30 daily newspapers and 290 weeklies. The *Star Tribune*, published in Minneapolis, and the *St. Paul Pioneer Press* have the largest circulations. There are 18 television stations and 190 radio stations in the state.

Above: Dairy products and livestock from eastern Minnesota farms account for about half of the state's total agricultural income.
Right: The harbor at Duluth, one of the nation's busiest inland ports, lies at the western end of Lake Superior and the St. Lawrence Seaway. Enormous freight cargoes of iron ore and agricultural products, particularly grain, are shipped from Duluth. The city is also an important commercial and manufacturing center.

Places of Interest

Charles A. Lindbergh House and Interpretive Center in Little Falls, maintains the boyhood home of Charles A. Lindbergh, the famous aviator, and tells the story of three generations of the Lindbergh family.

Grand Portage National Monument, in northeastern Minnesota, includes the 9-mile (14-kilometer) portage that was a vital link between Lake Superior and a navigable point on the Pigeon River. Visitors can see this trail, which was used by Indians, traders, explorers, and missionaries, and a partially reconstructed fur depot of the North West Company.

Itasca State Park, Minnesota's oldest state park, is near Park Rapids and contains Lake Itasca, the source of the Mississippi River. The importance of the lake was realized in 1832 by Henry Rowe Schoolcraft, an explorer and specialist in the life and culture of the Indian people of the Lake Superior region. It is said that he coined the word Itasca from two Latin words meaning "truth" and "head." He believed that Lake Itasca was the "true head" of the Mississippi.

James J. Hill Mansion, in St. Paul, was a home of Minnesota's richest and most powerful financier. Hill, who was nicknamed the Empire Builder, built railroads that connected the Twin Cities with Canada and the Pacific Northwest.

Kensington Rune Stone, on display in Alexandria, was discovered in 1898. It contains a message many believed was carved by Vikings in 1328, although scholars now generally agree that the artifact is a forgery.

Mayo Clinic, in Rochester, was founded in 1889 by William and Charles Mayo. The Mayo brothers had worked with their father, William Worrall Mayo, on the surgical staff of St. Mary's Hospital, the establishment from which the Mayo Clinic developed. Today the family clinic is a world-renowned medical research and treatment center.

Minnehaha Falls, in Minneapolis, is the "laughing water" Henry Wadsworth Longfellow referred to in his epic poem, "The Song of Hiawatha."

Old Fort Snelling stands on a high bluff overlooking the junction of the Minnesota and Mississippi rivers. It has been restored to the way it looked in the 1820's, when it was the main outpost of the Upper Mississippi Valley.

Paul Bunyan and Babe statues, in Bemidji, celebrate the folklore of the legendary lumberjack and his blue ox. The statues are among the country's oldest examples of roadside art.

Pipestone National Monument, near Pipestone, contains the famous red stone quarries, mined by the Indians to make their calumets, or ceremonial pipes. Today the stone is called catlinite after George Catlin, a noted artist and traveler who visited the quarries in 1836. Points of interest within the monument are the quarries, Winnewissa Falls, Lake Hiawatha, and a museum.

Split Rock Lighthouse State Park, near Beaver Bay, overlooks Lake Superior and contains the Split Rock Lighthouse, perched high on a cliff.

Voyageurs National Park, near International Falls, preserves a vast and beautiful area of woods and lakes. The lakes were once the route of French voyageurs, or travelers, who were employed by early fur-trading companies to transport goods and traders by canoe. It is Minnesota's only national park.

State Parks. For more information on state parks and other places of interest, contact the Minnesota Office of Tourism, 375 Jackson Street, 250 Skyway Level, St. Paul, Minn. 55101

Split Rock Lighthouse State Park, overlooking Lake Superior

Old Fort Snelling, near Minneapolis

Paul Bunyan and Babe statues, in Bemidji

Minneapolis is Minnesota's largest city. Founded as a U.S. military outpost on the Mississippi River, by the end of the 1800's it was known as the flour-milling capital of the world. Today it is a major financial, commercial, industrial, and transportation center.

▶ **CITIES**

Most of Minnesota's large cities, except Duluth, are located in the southeastern part of the state. The two largest cities, Minneapolis and St. Paul, are so close together that they are commonly referred to as the Twin Cities.

Minneapolis–St. Paul spans the Mississippi River. Minneapolis is the state's largest city; St. Paul is the state capital. Together they lead the state in trade and industry while also serving as a major midwestern educational and cultural center.

The population of the Twin Cities' metropolitan area is about 3 million. Other cities within this area include Bloomington, St. Louis Park, Richfield, Edina, Minnetonka, Brooklyn Park, Roseville, and Coon Rapids. For more information, refer to the article MINNEAPOLIS–SAINT PAUL in this volume.

Bloomington is located south of Minneapolis on the north bank of the Minnesota River. Once a scenic suburb of Minneapolis, it grew into a full-blown city after World War II. For many years, Bloomington Stadium was home to the Minnesota Twins, making the city the state's baseball capital. In 1992 the Mall of America, one of the world's largest shopping centers, replaced the stadium.

Duluth is situated at the mouth of the St. Louis River, opposite the city of Superior, Wisconsin. Its location on the western end of the St. Lawrence Seaway and its fine harbor make it one of the world's leading inland ports. It handles large freight shipments of iron ore, grain, flour, and dairy products.

Rochester lies about 75 miles (120 kilometers) southeast of the Twin Cities. It was once an agricultural town in rolling farm country but is now more industrial. Early in the 1900's Rochester became famous as a medical center when the Mayo Clinic began to draw patients from throughout the Midwest.

▶ **GOVERNMENT**

Minnesota's government is similar to that of most other states. Its constitution, adopted in 1857, provides for a government of three branches.

The state's executive branch is headed by the governor. The legislative branch consists of two houses, a senate and a house of representatives. In 1972, voters approved a constitutional amendment permitting the legislature to hold a session every year instead of just in odd-numbered years. The judicial branch is headed by the Minnesota Supreme Court, consisting of a chief justice and eight associate justices. The state's major trial courts are called district courts.

GOVERNMENT

State Government
Governor: 4-year term
State senators: 67; 4-year terms
State representatives: 134;
 2-year terms
Number of counties: 87

Federal Government
U.S. senators: 2
U.S. representatives: 8
Number of electoral votes: 10

For the name of the current governor, see STATE GOVERNMENTS in Volume S. For the names of current U.S. senators and representatives, see UNITED STATES, CONGRESS OF THE in Volume U-V.

St. Paul has been Minnesota's capital since 1849. The marble-domed state capitol building, completed in 1904, was modeled after St. Peter's Basilica in Rome.

INDEX TO MINNESOTA MAP

▶HISTORY

About 10,000 years ago, as the glaciers of the last Ice Age were disappearing, small bands of Indian hunters entered Minnesota. They were probably following herds of large animals, such as elk or giant bison. Over the centuries, their descendants made the land their home and slowly adopted new ways. They fashioned tools and ornaments from native copper, made baskets and pottery, and built thousands of sacred mounds for religious and burial purposes. When they learned to plant gardens of corn and squash and harvest the wild rice growing in lakes and swamps, life became easier, and the population grew.

European Influences

French traders came west to Minnesota with migrating Ojibwa Indians. Soon the region was part of a great trading network that reached from the St. Lawrence River through the Great Lakes and on to the Mississippi River and the Great Plains.

In the 1760's, France lost its North American territories to England, and British traders took control over trade. In the early 1800's they were followed by Americans, who claimed the country and all of its valuable natural resources for themselves.

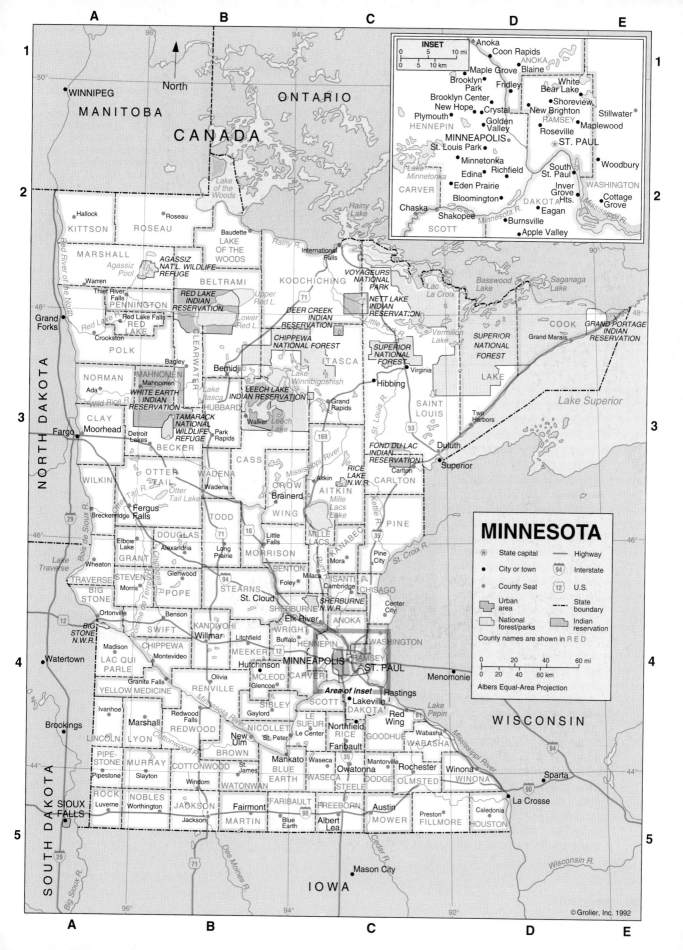

MINNESOTA

INSET

Anoka
Coon Rapids
Maple Grove
Brooklyn Park
Fridley
Blaine
White Bear Lake
Brooklyn Center
New Hope
Crystal
Shoreview
New Brighton
Stillwater
Plymouth
Golden Valley
MINNEAPOLIS
St. Louis Park
Roseville
ST. PAUL
Maplewood
Minnetonka
Richfield
Woodbury
Lake Minnetonka
Edina
South St. Paul
CARVER
Eden Prairie
Inver Grove Hts.
Eagan
Cottage Grove
Chaska
Bloomington
WASHINGTON
DAKOTA
Shakopee
Burnsville
SCOTT
Apple Valley

HENNEPIN
RAMSEY
ANOKA

Legend

- State capital
- City or town
- County Seat
- Highway
- **94** Interstate
- **12** U.S.
- Urban area
- National forest/parks
- Indian reservation
- State boundary

County names are shown in RED

Albers Equal-Area Projection

MANITOBA
ONTARIO
CANADA

WINNIPEG

KITTSON
ROSEAU
Hallock
Roseau
Lake of the Woods
LAKE OF THE WOODS
Baudette
MARSHALL
AGASSIZ NAT'L. WILDLIFE REFUGE
Agassiz Pool
BELTRAMI
KOOCHICHING
International Falls
VOYAGEURS NATIONAL PARK
Rainy Lake
Warren
Thief River Falls
PENNINGTON
RED LAKE INDIAN RESERVATION
Upper Red L.
DEER CREEK INDIAN RESERVATION
NETT LAKE INDIAN RESERVATION
Lac La Croix
Basswood Lake
Saganaga Lake
Grand Forks
Red Lake Falls
RED LAKE
Lower Red L.
CHIPPEWA NATIONAL FOREST
SUPERIOR NATIONAL FOREST
Crookston
CLEARWATER
POLK
Bagley
Bemidji
Lake Winnibigoshish
ITASCA
Virginia
Vermilion Lake
SUPERIOR NATIONAL FOREST
COOK
Grand Marais
GRAND PORTAGE INDIAN RESERVATION
NORMAN
MAHNOMEN
Mahnomen
Lake Itasca
LEECH LAKE INDIAN RESERVATION
Hibbing
SAINT LOUIS
LAKE
Lake Superior
Ada
WHITE EARTH INDIAN RESERVATION
Grand Rapids
HUBBARD
Leech Lake
Two Harbors
CLAY
TAMARACK NATIONAL WILDLIFE REFUGE
Walker
Moorhead
Detroit Lakes
BECKER
Park Rapids
CASS
FOND DU LAC INDIAN RESERVATION
Carlton
Duluth
Superior
Fargo
WILKIN
OTTER TAIL
WADENA
Wadena
Aitkin
RICE LAKE N.W.R.
CARLTON
Otter Tail Lake
CROW WING
AITKIN
Fergus Falls
Breckenridge
TODD
Brainerd
Mille Lacs Lake
PINE
DOUGLAS
Little Falls
MILLE LACS
Elbow Lake
Alexandria
Long Prairie
MORRISON
KANABEC
Wheaton
GRANT
Glenwood
BENTON
Mora
Pine City
STEVENS
POPE
Foley
Milaca
ISANTI
St. Cloud
Cambridge
CHISAGO
Ortonville
Morris
STEARNS
SHERBURNE N.W.R.
Center City
BIG STONE N.W.R.
Benson
SHERBURNE
ANOKA
Lake Traverse
TRAVERSE
BIG STONE
SWIFT
KANDIYOHI
Elk River
WASHINGTON
Madison
CHIPPEWA
Willmar
Litchfield
MEEKER
WRIGHT
Buffalo
HENNEPIN
RAMSEY
Menomonie
Watertown
LAC QUI PARLE
Montevideo
Hutchinson
MINNEAPOLIS
ST. PAUL
YELLOW MEDICINE
Olivia
McLEOD
CARVER
Granite Falls
Glencoe
Hastings
Ivanhoe
RENVILLE
SCOTT
DAKOTA
Area of inset
Lakeville
Redwood Falls
SIBLEY
Red Wing
Brookings
LINCOLN
LYON
Marshall
Gaylord
NICOLLET
Le Center
RICE
GOODHUE
Lake Pepin
REDWOOD
New Ulm
St. Peter
Northfield
Faribault
Wabasha
WISCONSIN
PIPESTONE
MURRAY
COTTONWOOD
BROWN
St. James
BLUE EARTH
Waseca
Mantorville
Rochester
WABASHA
Pipestone
Slayton
Windom
WASECA
DODGE
OLMSTED
Winona
WINONA
Mankato
Owatonna
Sparta
ROCK
NOBLES
JACKSON
Fairmont
FARIBAULT
STEELE
MOWER
La Crosse
Luverne
Worthington
MARTIN
Blue Earth
Albert Lea
Austin
Preston
FILLMORE
HOUSTON
Caledonia
SIOUX FALLS
Jackson
FREEBORN
WATONWAN

NORTH DAKOTA
SOUTH DAKOTA
IOWA
Mason City

North

© Grolier, Inc. 1992

Famous People

Consult the Index to find more information in *The New Book of Knowledge* about the following people who were born in Minnesota or are otherwise associated with the state: authors Sinclair Lewis (1885–1951) and F. Scott Fitzgerald (1896–1940); U.S. Supreme Court Justice William O. Douglas (1898–1980); aviation pioneer Charles A. Lindbergh (1902–74); Vice President Hubert H. Humphrey (1911–78) and Walter F. Mondale (1928–); actress and singer Judy Garland (1922–69); and folk rock musician Bob Dylan (1941–).

Judy Garland

Sinclair Lewis

Warren Earl Burger (1907–95), born in St. Paul, was chief justice of the U.S. Supreme Court from 1969 to 1986. A former judge of the U.S. Court of Appeals for the District of Columbia, Burger was appointed to the high court by President Richard M. Nixon. Burger's court was more conservative than that of his predecessor, Earl Warren. It upheld the use of capital punishment and limited the rights of defendants in criminal cases. Yet it also assured a woman's right to have an abortion and upheld busing as a means to desegregate schools.

J. (Jean) Paul Getty (1892–1976), born in Minneapolis, was one of the world's wealthiest businessmen. An oilman, Getty amassed a fortune of more than $1 billion. In 1953, Getty founded the J. Paul Getty Trust, headquartered in Los Angeles, to promote the visual arts. An avid collector, he founded the J. Paul Getty Museum in Malibu, California.

Louis Hennepin (1640?–1701), born in Flanders (in present-day Belgium), was a missionary, explorer, and author. As chaplain to Robert Cavalier, Sieur de La Salle, Hennepin explored the Great Lakes (1679) and accompanied the first expedition to the upper valley of the Mis-

Settlement and Statehood

The first United States official to visit Minnesota was a young army officer named Zebulon Pike (1779–1813). In 1805 he was sent up the Mississippi River to find a site on which to build a fort to guard against trespassing British fur traders. Pike selected a site at the junction of the Minnesota and Mississippi rivers. Fort Snelling was erected there and completed in 1820. For thirty years the fort's limestone walls and towers symbolized American power and served as the primary outpost for settlers.

Out on the prairie where lumber was scarce, the pioneers built sod houses with blocks of turf taken straight from the ground.

Through a long series of treaties, few of which were honored, the United States took the land from the Dakota and Ojibwa tribes. Settlements at Stillwater, St. Paul, and St. Anthony were established soon after the first treaty was signed in 1837. The Indians later tried to take back their land, but after their defeat in the Dakota War (1862), the tribe was banished to the western plains.

In 1849, Minnesota became a territory, and great waves of immigrants began pouring in from northern Europe. Nine years later, the territory was admitted to the Union as the 32nd state.

The Growth of Industry

During the next forty years, pioneers transformed the Minnesota wilderness. They turned the prairies into farms, built railroads, and cut down the pine forests to build new towns and cities. Minneapolis grew so large it absorbed the village of St. Anthony, and by the 1880's Minneapolis had become known as Mill City, the country's most important flour-milling center.

In the 1890's iron mines began to transform the face of northeastern Minnesota. The rich ore that poured from the great open pit mines of the Mesabi Range made possible America's Age of Steel.

By 1900 lumber and wheat were the leading products of Minnesota. But dairy products and livestock soon became more important. As manufacturing developed, more and more people left their farms to settle in the cities and towns.

sissippi River (1680), where he named the Falls of St. Anthony at the site of present-day Minneapolis. Captured but later released by the Sioux, Hennepin sailed for France in 1691. He wrote several accounts of his travels, including *A New Discovery* (1697).

Garrison Keillor (1942–), born Gary Edward Keillor in Anoka, earned fame as the author and host of *A Prairie Home Companion*, a humorous radio show featuring a fictitious Minnesota town called Lake Wobegon. Keillor's publications include *Lake Wobegon Days* (1982), *WLT: A Radio Romance* (1991), and *The Book of Guys* (1993).

Elizabeth Kenny (1886–1952), born in Warialda, New South Wales, Australia, was a nurse who became known for her method of treating victims of polio. Known as Sister Kenny, she favored stimulating paralyzed muscles rather than the accepted treatment of immobilizing

Charles M. Schulz

afflicted limbs. In 1940, Kenny demonstrated her methods in the United States. In 1942 she opened the Elizabeth Kenny Institute in Minneapolis.

William Worrall Mayo (1819–1911), an immigrant from Manchester, England, became a leading physician in Minnesota

and in 1889 the chief of staff of St. Mary's Hospital in Rochester. His sons, **William James** (1861–1939), born in Le Sueur, and **Charles Horace** (1865–1939), born in Rochester, also worked as staff physicians at St. Mary's. As the family's reputation grew, they established the Mayo Clinic in Rochester, where many different physicians, all with different specialty areas, could assess and treat patients at one facility. In 1915, the brothers also founded the Mayo Foundation for Medical Education and Research and the Mayo Graduate School of Medicine.

Charles M(onroe) Schulz (1922–2000), born in Minneapolis, created the popular comic strip "Peanuts." First appearing in 1950 as "Li'l Folks," Schulz's cartoon characters, featuring the hapless Charlie Brown and his beagle, Snoopy, reflected Schulz's own childhood dilemmas. The strip has been adapted for films and television specials.

Labor and Politics

In the 1900's, Minnesota began the transition from an agricultural heartland to an urban industrial state. But not everyone benefited equally from the growth and profits. In 1890 industrial workers organized the Minnesota Federation of Labor to protect themselves from greedy industrialists. And in 1915, farmers formed the **Nonpartisan League**, a socialist group that offered protection against the powerful bankers, railroad tycoons, and mill owners, who took advantage of the farmers and made huge profits by controlling the sale and distribution of the farmers' products.

Also at this time, many frustrated miners joined a radical union called the Industrial Workers of the World (IWW), and a strong Communist movement developed in northern Minnesota. In the 1920's, supporters of the Nonpartisan League united with industrial workers to form the Farmer-Labor Party.

Minnesota thus became known for turbulent politics and its unconventional political parties. For six years during the Great Depression of the 1930's, the Farmer-Labor Party controlled the state. Defeated in 1938, it united with the Democratic Party in 1944.

Minnesota also developed a reputation as an isolationist state; except for World War II, Minnesotans generally opposed U.S. participation in foreign wars. Anti-war feelings were

particularly strong in Minnesota during the Vietnam War years. In 1967, one of Minnesota's U.S. senators, Eugene J. McCarthy (1916–2005), provoked national controversy when he became the first national politician to openly challenge the country's commitment to the war in Southeast Asia.

Toward the end of the 1960's, Minnesota also had developed a strong women's movement. By the 1990's, approximately 21 percent of the state legislature and more than 50 percent of the judges on the state supreme court were women.

Modern Times

By the 1980's, service industries had taken the lead in the state's economy and employed two thirds of Minnesota's labor force. In that decade, Minnesota faced economic problems, due largely to a nationwide recession, and the number of farms declined even more sharply. But the state's diverse economy has helped it through tough economic times, and Minnesotans continue to maintain the high quality of life associated with the state.

LEWIS DIXON
THOMAS P. DOCKENDORFF
St. Cloud State University

Reviewed by RHODA GILMAN
Minnesota Historical Society

See also MINNEAPOLIS–SAINT PAUL.

An Inspector at the Royal Canadian Mint checks blanks that will be stamped to make pennies.

MINT

A mint is a place where coins are made. Today mints are nearly always under government authority and supervision.

Coins were made in the ancient kingdom of Lydia, in Asia Minor, in the 700's B.C. From there the art of coining spread throughout the Mediterranean world and into Persia and India. Somewhat later, coining began independently in China. It spread from there to Japan and Korea.

The foundations of modern minting, or coin making, were laid by the Romans. They minted silver coins in the Temple of Juno Moneta as far back as 269 B.C. In Latin, *moneta* came to mean mint or coin. The English words "money" and "mint" developed from this Latin word.

Gold and silver coins existed in Britain before Roman rule. During the Middle Ages, the chief mint in Britain was located in the Tower of London. The British Royal Mint was founded in 1810. It continues to make coins today.

The first coins minted in Britain's North American colonies were made by John Hull in Massachusetts Bay Colony. In 1652, the Boston mint began to make coins that showed a pine tree. Pine-tree shillings and similar six-penny and three-penny coins were widely circulated in New England.

▶ THE UNITED STATES MINT

The states were permitted to coin money immediately after the Revolutionary War, but they do not have that right today. Under the Constitution, only Congress has the right to coin money and to regulate its value.

The first United States mint was established at Philadelphia, Pennsylvania, in 1792. At first the secretary of state supervised the mint. In 1799 it became an independent agency, under the president. Then, in 1873, Congress created the Bureau of the Mint, as part of the Department of the Treasury at Washington, D.C. In 1984 the bureau's name was changed to United States Mint. The director of the mint is appointed by the president.

The bureau mints 1-cent, 5-cent, 10-cent, 25-cent, 50-cent, and 1-dollar coins. It also makes the dies (engraving stamps) and tools used in minting. The bureau mints coins for some foreign governments, and it sells coin sets and commemorative medals to the general public.

The United States Mint is in charge of the mint at Philadelphia and another mint at Denver, Colorado. Coins made at Denver bear a mintmark—the letter D. The bureau also keeps the government's holdings in silver and gold bullion (bars). Gold is kept at Fort Knox, Kentucky, and silver is kept at West Point, New York. The assay office, which judges the value of ores and bullion, is located at San Francisco, California.

The nation's paper money is designed and printed by the Bureau of Engraving and Printing. This bureau is also a part of the Department of the Treasury.

▶ THE ROYAL CANADIAN MINT

Canada's mint began operation in 1908, as a branch of the British Royal Mint. It was called the Ottawa Mint until 1931, when it became the Royal Canadian Mint. It is headed by a seven-member board of directors, who report to Parliament. Coins are produced at a plant in Winnipeg, Manitoba. The mint also buys and sells precious metals and produces medals, plaques, and the like.

STELLA HACKEL SIMS
Former Director, United States Mint

See also COINS AND COIN COLLECTING; MONEY.

MIRACLE PLAYS. See ENGLISH LITERATURE (Middle English Literature).

A mirage of a lake appears on the hot sands of Death Valley in the California desert. The water in the lake is actually an image of the sky.

MIRAGE

Suppose you are riding along a country road on a hot day in summer. If you look ahead about a quarter of a mile, you may suddenly see a silvery lake covering the road. You may even see another car reflected in this lake, as in a mirror. When you come up to the place where you saw the lake, you find that the pavement is perfectly dry. What you saw was not really water. It was only an appearance that is called a **mirage**.

The lake seemed to be there because of something that happens to light rays passing through the air. Usually the light by which you see things travels through the air in straight lines. This is true as long as the air is all at the same temperature. But air, like most other materials, expands and becomes less dense (thinner) when it is warmed. As a result, light is bent aside when it goes from a layer of air at one temperature to a layer at a different temperature.

On a sunny day the road pavement becomes quite hot. This warms the air just above the road, while the air higher up stays cooler. Light coming down from the sky through these layers is bent upward again to your eyes. The bright patch of light looks like water.

Now suppose there is a car on the road ahead of you. You may see both the car and an upside-down mirage of it.

Some of the light rays from the car travel through air that is all at the same temperature, and so these rays are straight. They show you the car where it really is.

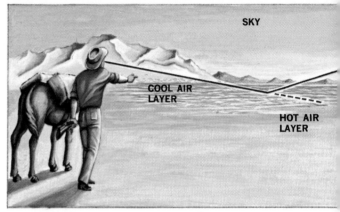

The shallow lower layer of air close to the desert sand is made very hot by the sand. The air above the lower layer is cooler. Light rays passing from the cooler layer to the hot layer of air are refracted (bent) up. They form an image of the sky that looks like a lake.

There are also some rays that reach your eyes by a different path. Rays starting downward from the car will gradually bend upward again when they enter the warmer air near the pavement. These rays come into your eyes from below, and you think you are looking at an upside-down car beneath the real one.

Mirages of this kind are often seen in hot, desert countries. There are stories of thirsty travelers in the desert who imagine they see ahead of them a refreshing pool of water, only to find that it is not really there. What they actually saw was light from the sky, bent upward by hot air just above the sand.

An opposite kind of mirage is sometimes seen over the ocean or in the polar regions. A distant ship or mountain may appear to be

The center iceberg in the distance is a looming mirage. The iceberg is actually out of sight beyond the horizon. Light rays from the iceberg are bent, forming the mirage.

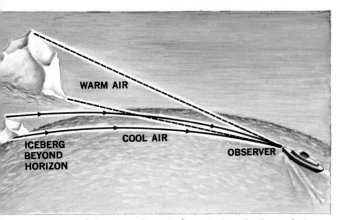

A looming mirage is formed when the layer of air near the cold ocean is cooler than the air above it. Light that usually would pass overhead is bent down, and an observer sees an image of something that may actually be over the horizon.

raised up in the sky. This kind of mirage is called **looming**. The object itself may really be out of the line of sight, below the horizon.

In a looming mirage, air near the ground or near the surface of the ocean is cooler than it is higher up. When this happens, light that would otherwise pass overhead is bent down to the eye. As a result, a person thinks he sees the distant object much nearer and taller than it really is. Travelers have told of seeing whole towns—with their trees, towers, and houses —raised high in the sky as a result of a looming mirage. This is probably where the expression "castles in the air" comes from.

There are other ways in which the air bends light and fools your eyes. These, too, are sometimes called mirages. Look across the top of a car that has been standing in the sun. Things you see in the distance appear to shimmer. The air warmed by the car roof rises and changes the direction of the light that passes through it.

The twinkling of the stars is caused by warm and cool patches of air drifting through the earth's atmosphere. That is why large observatories are usually located on mountaintops or in other places where the temperature of the air is steady, which makes the seeing good.

Astronomers are now using balloons and rockets to send telescopic cameras to great heights. With most of the atmosphere out of the way below them, these instruments are able to get much sharper and clearer pictures of the sun, planets, and stars than have ever been seen before.

The bending of light by the air makes the sun look flattened or oval when it is very low in the sky. This bending also makes the sun seem to rise about 2 minutes before it actually comes up over the horizon and keeps it in view about 2 minutes after it really has sunk below the horizon.

IRA M. FREEMAN
Rutgers—The State University

See also LENSES; LIGHT.

MIRÓ, JOAN (1893–1983)

The Spanish painter Joan Miró is recognized worldwide as one of the most distinguished artists of the surrealist movement. He was born on April 20, 1893, in the Catalonian town of Montroig, near Barcelona. At the age of 14, he studied at the Barcelona School of Fine Arts.

Miró's earliest works were clearly realistic. But in his 20's he visited Paris and became acquainted with such innovative artists as Pablo Picasso and Max Ernst. By 1924, Miró had developed a distinctly unrealistic style reminiscent of primitive cave drawings or the humorous drawings of young children. Indeed, he generally painted bold, abstract shapes and loved bright colors and strong color contrasts. His works consist of playful fantasy forms that seem to originate in the unconscious imagination or in dreams.

In 1925, Miró participated in the first surrealist exhibition in Paris, and in 1928 held his first exhibition in New York City. During the 1930's, he designed ballet settings and costumes. After the close of World War II, he spent considerable time in Paris and undertook major projects in sculpture, ceramics, weaving, and mural painting. He also produced several handsome sets of original color prints.

Works by Joan Miró, such as *Woman Before the Eclipse*, have bold, playful shapes.

One of Miró's most impressive works consists of two ceramic walls located outside the UNESCO building in Paris. One of the walls is titled *Wall of the Sun,* and the other *Wall of the Moon.* These were completed in 1958 in collaboration with José Artigas, a noted ceramist whom Miró had met many years earlier. In 1978, Miró designed a large-scale tapestry for the court garden of the East Wing of the National Gallery of Art in Washington, D.C. Miró died on December 25, 1983, at the age of 90, at his home in Palma, Spain.

HOWARD E. WOODEN
Director Emeritus
The Wichita Art Museum

MIRRORS. See LIGHT.

MISSILES

Have you ever thrown a ball or shot an arrow? If so, you have launched a missile. A ball or arrow or any other object that is sent toward a target with force may be called a missile.

For modern missiles, that force is provided by the action of a rocket. **Ballistic missiles** are fitted with rockets that give them an initial push into their flight. ("Ballistic" comes from the Greek word *ballein,* meaning "to throw.") Then the rocket turns off, and the missile coasts downward toward its target, pulled by the force of gravity. Another kind of missile is powered to its target by a rocket engine. This is called a **continually powered missile**.

▶ **THE STORY OF MISSILES**

Rocket missiles date back to the 1200's in China. The Chinese invented both gunpowder and the rocket. Their rockets were tubes made of bamboo or heavy paper. The tubes were closed at one end and packed with gunpowder. The Chinese lashed the tubes to arrows. When the gunpowder was set afire, the arrows sped toward the enemy. These "arrows of flying fire," as the Chinese called them, were the first rocket missiles.

The Chinese invention spread to other countries. The rockets were made larger, and explosives were placed in their tips. In the 1790's, troops of the Prince of Mysore, in India, used rocket missiles against British soldiers, killing many of them. These rockets interested an English army officer, William Congreve, who designed rockets of his own. During the War of 1812, between England and the United States, Congreve rocket missiles bombarded Fort McHenry in Baltimore, Maryland. Francis Scott Key mentioned these rockets in his poem "The Star-Spangled Banner," which became the national anthem of the United States.

These early missiles were not very safe or accurate, and big guns were used much more commonly in warfare. But after World War I, work began in many nations to improve the safety, accuracy, range, and payloads (carrying capacity) of missiles. Many people thought it was a waste of time, and in most countries the work went very slowly. There was great interest in Germany, though, and the first modern missiles were developed and used by Germany in World War II. Several countries used rocket missiles before the war ended, but the first ballistic missile was the German V-2. Each missile carried more than half a ton of explosives. During the war, more than 1,000 V-2's were fired across the English Channel against Britain.

Since the end of World War II, there has been rapid development of both ballistic and continually powered missiles. They are used for many military purposes. Missiles of both types play a major role today in the military forces of most nations. Ballistic missiles also carry spacecraft into space.

▶MISSILE DESIGN

Modern missiles contain many thousands of parts—from tiny electronic components to large structures weighing many pounds. Most missiles have three major systems. They are propulsion, which includes the fuel, fuel tank, and motor; the guidance and control system, which steers the missile; and the payload, which is usually the explosive warhead that blows up when the missile reaches its target. Other systems, such as the electrical system and the hydraulic system, help the major systems operate correctly.

Propulsion System

The purpose of the propulsion system is to provide the missile with forward motion. The needed energy is stored in the fuel carried by the missile. The energy of the fuel is released during **combustion**, or burning. Combustion is a chemical reaction between the fuel and oxygen. For this reason, both fuel and oxygen are needed to power a rocket. Missiles that fly in the atmosphere at low altitudes can use the oxygen in the air for burning. They are called **air-breathing missiles**. But missiles that fly higher than about 12 miles (20 kilometers) cannot get enough oxygen from the thin air. Such missiles must carry a chemical sub-

The Patriot missile, designed to protect airfields, was used by the United States against Iraqi ballistic missiles during the 1991 Persian Gulf war.

stance, called an oxidizer, that supplies the necessary oxygen.

Missile Motor. There are two main parts to the missile motor: the combustion chamber and the nozzle. The fuel is burned in the combustion chamber. As the fuel burns, very hot, rapidly moving gases are produced. These gases rush out through the nozzle at the rear of the missile, pushing it forward. Air coming out of an inflated balloon moves the balloon forward in just the same way.

Missile Fuels. Missiles can use **liquid fuels**, like gasoline or kerosene, or **solid fuels**, which can be a mixture of plastic, powdered metal, flammable chemicals, and other dry substances. Fuels and oxidizers are sometimes grouped together and called **propellants**. Solid fuels are easier to store in a missile and are safer. Many liquid fuels contain more energy than a solid fuel of the same volume. Solid fuels were used in all practical missiles until World War II. These early missiles were small and did not need to be very powerful.

Liquid fuels are very complicated to use. Engines that burn liquids must have many more parts than those that burn solids. It also takes much more time to prepare a liquid-fuel missile for launching than it does to prepare a solid-fuel missile. To overcome these difficulties, scientists and engineers have developed efficient solid propellants. Today most large missiles, such as the U.S. Minuteman and Poseidon, use solid propellants. Solid propellants are mixed with a compound similar to rubber and poured into a metal or plastic container, where they are allowed to harden. An open space is left in the center, where the burning takes place.

Guidance and Control System

Some missiles are unguided. They have fins, like feathers on an arrow. They are pointed in the direction they are meant to go and then are fired. The pressure of the air on the fins keeps these missiles on a steady course. Once such a missile is on its way, nothing controls or steers it.

But most modern missiles have some kind of guidance system. In ballistic missiles, the guidance operates during the early part of the

SOME IMPORTANT MISSILES*

ROCKET	COUNTRY	RANGE	WARHEAD
SSM (surface-to-surface missiles)			
Titan II (B)†	U.S.A.	9,300 mi (15,000 km)	Nuclear
Minuteman III (B)	U.S.A.	8,100 mi (13,000 km)	Nuclear
Pershing (B)	U.S.A.	460 mi (740 km)	Nuclear
Vigilant	Britain	4,510 ft (1,375 m)	High explosive
Harpoon	U.S.A.	55 mi (90 km)	High explosive
Scud	Russia	280 mi (450 km)	High explosive
SS-18	Russia	6,500 mi (10,500 km)	Nuclear
SAM (surface-to-air missiles)			
Hawk	U.S.A.	22 mi (35 km)	High explosive
Patriot	U.S.A.	30 mi (48 km)	High explosive
Seacat	Britain	3 mi (4.8 km)	High explosive
Guideline/SAN-2	Russia	27 mi (43 km)	High explosive
Gammon/SA-5	Russia	155 mi (250 km)	High explosive
AAM (air-to-air missiles)			
Sparrow III	U.S.A.	15.5 mi (25 km)	High explosive
Red Top	Britain	7.4 mi (12 km)	High explosive
Matra R 530	France	11 mi (18 km)	High explosive
Sidewinder	U.S.A.	11 mi (18 km)	High explosive
Phoenix	U.S.A.	102 mi (165 km)	High explosive
Atoll/AA-2	Russia	4 mi (6.4 km)	High explosive
Acrid/AA-6	Russia	31 mi (50 km)	High explosive
ASM (air-to-surface missiles)			
Blue Steel	Britain	500 mi (810 km)	High explosive
Robot RB-04	Sweden	6 mi (9.7 km)	High explosive
Bullpup/AGM-12C	U.S.A.	10.5 mi (17 km)	High explosive
Kennel/AS-1	Russia	56 mi (90 km)	Not known
Kangaroo/AS-3	Russia	350 mi (565 km)	Not known
SLM (submarine-launched missiles)			
Polaris A-3 (B)	U.S.A.	2,870 mi (4,620 km)	Nuclear
Subroc (B)	U.S.A.	35 mi (56 km)	Nuclear
Asroc (B)	U.S.A.	1.2–6.2 mi (2–10 km)	Nuclear or High explosive
Poseidon C-3 (B)	U.S.A.	2,870 mi (4,620 km)	Nuclear
SS-N-8 (B)	Russia	4,840 mi (7,800 km)	Nuclear
Serb/SS-N-5 (B)	Russia	745 mi (1,200 km)	Nuclear

* The People's Republic of China has some important missiles, but details about them are not available.

† (B) = Ballistic missile.

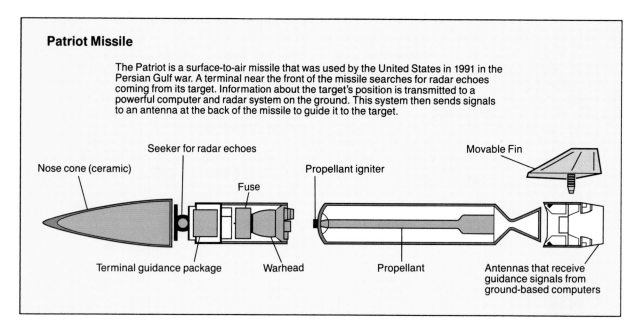

Patriot Missile

The Patriot is a surface-to-air missile that was used by the United States in 1991 in the Persian Gulf war. A terminal near the front of the missile searches for radar echoes coming from its target. Information about the target's position is transmitted to a powerful computer and radar system on the ground. This system then sends signals to an antenna at the back of the missile to guide it to the target.

Nose cone (ceramic)

Seeker for radar echoes

Fuse

Propellant igniter

Movable Fin

Terminal guidance package

Warhead

Propellant

Antennas that receive guidance signals from ground-based computers

missile's flight. In continually guided rocket missiles, the guidance system controls the motion of the missile all the way from launch to target.

Inertial Guidance. Many missiles are kept on a straight course by a guidance system called inertial guidance. This system is made up of devices that can keep track of the distance the missile has traveled and the changes of direction it has made. By comparing the actual path the missile has traveled with the path it must follow to reach the target, the missile "brain," or computer, guides the missile to its target.

Landmark Sensors. Another missile guidance system guides the missile to a target by providing it with a way to "recognize" landmarks in the way the human eye recognizes the corner drugstore and the supermarket signs. In the case of a missile, such landmarks could be mountaintops, rivers, lakes, roads, and railroad tracks. Your brain knows about the familiar landmarks of the neighborhood because it has stored them in a kind of visual map. The missile brain, or computer, knows about the landmarks the missile must recognize because a computer operator has put the coded map information or coded distance information into the computer.

The information stored in the computer may say, for example, "Go past three mountains, each a little higher than the last, then turn east," or "The target is 250 miles (400 kilometers) away."

But of course, knowing about these guidance clues is not enough. There must be a way to detect them and recognize them. As you travel toward the supermarket, your eyes see, or sense, the drugstore and the red sign. A signal then moves from your eyes to your brain. And the brain sends out a signal that orders certain muscles in your body to move, or steer, you in a certain direction.

The missile's sensor is like your eyes. It may be radar, a small television camera, or another device that helps it locate landmarks. When the sensor tells the missile's computer that the missile is over a landmark, the computer may decide to change course. If so, it sends electric signals to the steering devices in the missile that then change its direction.

Steering Systems. There are two basic types of missile steering systems. One system is used in missiles that travel in the atmosphere. It involves moving fins at the end of the missile. Air rushing against the fins changes the direction of the missile. But where the air is very thin or does not exist at all, a rocket steering system is used. The nozzle of the main rocket is moved, so that it points in a direction exactly opposite to the new direction the missile must follow. This makes the gases produced by the burning fuel also move in exactly the opposite direction. Then the force of the rushing gases makes the missile move in the new direction. Another rocket steering system involves firing small rockets built into the sides of the missile.

Missiles may use many combinations of the different guidance devices. Ballistic missiles are guided during the first part of their flight by an inertial guidance system. When the computer on the missile decides that the guidance system has put the missile in the right direction at the right speed, the engines shut off, and the guidance system stops working. From then on, the missile is pulled toward the earth by the force of gravity. If the guidance system has worked properly, the missile is nearing the target area, and it dives directly toward the target.

The biggest missiles are usually ballistic missiles. They may have to travel to targets as far away as 6,500 miles (10,500 kilometers). The Minuteman and the Poseidon are ballistic missiles.

Smaller missiles are usually guided all the way to their target. One such missile, the **cruise missile**, has an inertial guidance system as well as a sensor and a computer with map information. This system allows the missile to follow the contours of the terrain it flies over. For example, the cruise missile can fly just over the tops of mountains and then drop down low over valley floors. Because it can fly so low, the cruise missile is difficult to detect on the radar screens of an enemy. This missile can be launched from a plane, submarine, ship, or from the ground and still find its target thousands of miles away.

Homing Devices. Another kind of missile guidance system is the homing device. Homing devices enable a missile to follow a trail in much the same way that a bloodhound follows a smell. For the missile, the trail may be light, heat, or some other kind of energy given off by the target. If, for example, the target is much brighter or warmer than the surrounding area, the missile could home in on it. Homing may be the only guidance system for a short-range missile—one that must travel a short distance. Long-range missiles may be guided by homing devices during the last part of the flight.

Payloads or Warheads

The type of warhead carried by a missile depends on the purpose of the missile. Very early missiles did not carry an explosive. They depended on the weight of the missile to do damage when the missile itself hit the target. During World War II, missiles had warheads consisting of explosives similar to dynamite. Most small missiles today have this type of warhead. They explode when they hit the target or sense that they are close to it.

A missile guides itself to a target by sensing the target's heat radiation.

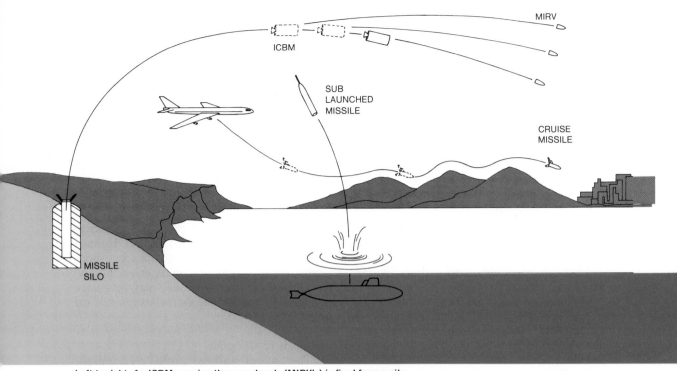

Left to right: An ICBM carrying three warheads (MIRV's) is fired from a silo.
A cruise missile is fired from a plane. A submarine-launched missile takes flight.

Large missiles today carry nuclear warheads. Sometimes one missile can carry more than one warhead, each of which can hit a separate target. The targets may be many kilometers apart. This warhead system is called a MIRV (*m*ultiple *i*ndependently targeted *re*-entry *v*ehicle) system. For example, each **submarine-launched** Poseidon missile can carry as many as 14 MIRV warheads. This means that one Poseidon missile could strike 14 different targets.

Smaller missiles can carry less powerful nuclear warheads, but even these can do a great deal of damage. None of these missiles has ever been used against an enemy. But they are the most powerful weapons that any nation has, and many people consider them an important measure of military strength.

▶ TYPES OF MISSILES

Missiles are classified in several different ways. A missile can be either a defensive weapon or an offensive weapon. Missiles are also classified according to their launch and target locations.

Launch and Target Classifications

In the United States, it is common to classify missiles by a series of letters. The first letter stands for the launch site of the missile. The second letter stands for the location of the missile's target. The first and second letters are either S or A. An S means the surface of the earth or of the ocean. A stands for air. The third letter in this system is simply M, for missile. So SSM, for example, is a surface-to-surface missile. It may be launched from the ground toward a target on the ground, or it may be launched from a ship or a submarine toward a target on the ground. Submarine-launched missiles (SLM) are listed separately in the table on page 345.

SSM—Surface-to-Surface Missiles. These include the very largest rockets, such as the **intercontinental ballistic missiles** (ICBM's). This group of missiles can travel from continent to continent. They are guided only while gaining speed. An ICBM can carry nuclear warheads. The Russian SS-18, for example, can carry a nuclear charge with destructive power equal to that of 25,000,000 tons of TNT. It can deliver this incredible destructive force to a target as far as 6,500 miles (10,500 kilometers) away. ICBM's are stored underground in structures called silos to protect them from enemy attack. Many small surface-to-surface missiles, such as the ballistic Scud used in the Persian Gulf War, are designed for use against tanks, fortifications, and troops. These are mostly continually guided rockets that carry a high-explosive warhead.

The Polaris is a long-range ballistic missile that can be fired from a submerged submarine. Each Polaris nuclear submarine carries 16 such missiles and can launch them all within five minutes or so. Polaris missiles, equipped with MIRV warheads, can reach surface targets as far as 2,870 miles (4,620 kilometers) away.

The Poseidon is an improved submarine-launched missile of the United States. The Poseidon has a greater accuracy than the Polaris, and it can be fitted with a 14-MIRV warhead.

SAM—Surface-to-Air Missiles. Surface-to-air, or anti-aircraft, missiles are meant as defensive weapons against enemy planes. Some SAM's, such as the French missile Roland, are placed on mobile launching platforms that can be moved to stay with the tanks they protect.

The United States has a SAM missile, called Red-eye, that can be carried by soldiers very much like a rifle. It is fired from a tube held on the shoulder. The missile homes to the engine heat of low-flying planes. The Patriot is designed to protect airfields from attacking bombers.

AAM—Air-to-Air Missiles. Air-to-air missiles are launched by planes toward other planes. Most AAM's have guidance systems that use radar or heat homing sensors to steer the missiles to the other airplane. These missiles usually carry high explosives. The Phoenix of the United States is the most capable air-to-air missile in the world today.

ASM—Air-to-Surface Missiles. ASM's are used by aircraft to attack targets on the ground or on water. Some are used only on targets the pilot can see. The Shrike, which delivers a high-explosive warhead, is such a missile. It was used by the United States in Vietnam and by the Israelis during the 1973 Israeli-Arab War. Other ASM's, such as the nuclear-armed SRAM, a United States Air Force missile, might be called flying bombs. A bomber pilot could launch one or two of them at a point 40 to 100 miles (60 to 160 kilometers) from the target. The missile, using inertial guidance, could then go on to deliver the nuclear warhead by itself while the plane returned to its base. The new cruise missile that has been developed by the United States can do the same, traveling to a target as far as 1,550 miles (2,500 kilometers) away from where its launch point is located.

Cruise Missiles

The United States has developed a new long-range, continually guided cruise missile. The new missile can carry a nuclear warhead almost as far as a ballistic missile. There are three basic types of cruise missiles—ALCM, an air-launched cruise missile; GLCM, a ground-launched cruise missile; and SLCM, a sea-launched cruise missile. All these cruise missiles are different variations of a basic cruise missile developed by the U.S. Navy and originally meant to be launched by submarine.

▶ AN EQUAL THREAT

Any one missile is used for only a relatively short period of time. Improvements in propulsion, guidance and control, structure, and warheads are made so fast that one type of missile is replaced by a better one in a very few years.

Improvements in missiles have brought us the frightening vision of death and destruction. It is now possible to send thousands of powerful nuclear warheads from one continent to another. Many people have begun to realize that most of the life on earth could be killed just by pushing the launching buttons of the U.S. and Russian ballistic missiles. With this in mind, leaders of the nations possessing the most dangerous weapons have signed agreements that limit the number of nuclear-armed missiles each can have. The goal has been to make certain that no nation has more nuclear weapons than any other. So far, this equalization of nuclear weapons has kept nations from using them.

Without quite realizing what has been happening, people now find themselves trapped and their way of life threatened by the nuclear weapons they have made. The weapons remain only a threat—so far. But as missiles are improved, it will be necessary to conclude new agreements, keeping the threat so nearly equal for all that the deadly buttons capable of igniting nuclear destruction will never be pushed.

KOSTA M. TSIPIS
Massachusetts Institute of Technology

See also ROCKETS.

MISSISSIPPI

Mississippi takes its unusual name from the Mississippi River, which forms the state's western boundary. Native Americans called the river Miss-Sipi, *meaning "Big River" or "Father of Waters." In 1798, American settlers adopted the name for the territory they founded. When the territory became a state, political leaders voted, by a narrow margin, to keep the name Mississippi. Their second choice was Washington.*

Mississippi's official nickname, the Magnolia State, honors the beautiful magnolia tree that blooms throughout the state. Residents also take pride in the fact that Mississippi is also known as the Hospitality State.

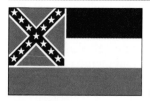

State flag

Mississippi is located in the south central United States in a region called the Deep South. From the earliest days of settlement, the quality of Mississippi's soils encouraged agricultural production. Before the Civil War ended in 1865, vast numbers of black slaves cleared the land to cultivate cotton and other valuable crops. The use of forced labor created great tensions between blacks and whites that still have not been fully resolved.

As the introduction of farm machinery and synthetic fibers for clothing eliminated many jobs in the cotton business, many Mississippi farm families were forced to seek work in cities and towns, especially in the southern half of the state, where most of Mississippi's metropolitan areas are found, including Jackson, the state's largest city.

Today more and more Mississippians find jobs in manufacturing and the service industries. Although fields white with cotton can still be seen every autumn, Mississippi today is better known for its forest products, seafood, and farm-raised catfish.

▶ LAND

Low hills are the primary land feature of Mississippi. Three narrow lowland regions angle across the state: the Jackson Prairie, the Flatwoods, and the Black Prairie. These lands are called prairies because much of their area was once covered with grass.

The highest point in the state, Woodall Mountain, rises in northeastern Mississippi a modest 806 feet (246 meters) above sea level. From there the land slopes to the south and southwest toward the Mississippi River and the Gulf Coast.

Land Regions

Mississippi has two distinct land regions: The Mississippi Alluvial Plain and the East Gulf Coastal Plain.

The Mississippi Alluvial Plain, commonly called the Delta, is a large lowland area that covers the entire western border of the state, along the Mississippi River. Flattened by glaciers thousands of years ago, the Delta is covered with a rich, thick layer of topsoil that has been deposited by receding Mississippi floodwaters. In places, the topsoil measures 30 feet (9 meters) deep.

The East Gulf Coastal Plain, which covers most of the state, can be divided into several subregions. The Tennessee River Hills in the northeast form the highest region of Mississippi. Tributary streams of the Tennessee River have cut narrow ravines in the land and flow in short, swift courses to the east. The Loess, or Bluff, Hills, running the length of the state from north to south, parallel the Mississippi River east of the Delta. The Coastal Pine Meadows is a narrow stretch of lowland plain along the Gulf of Mexico. The land is composed mostly of sand and silt. The

Opposite page, clockwise from left: An old-fashioned riverboat ferries tourists along the Mississippi River. The Medgar Evers Memorial in Jackson pays tribute to the slain civil rights leader. The lovely magnolia is Mississippi's state flower.

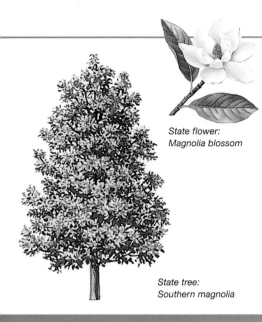

State tree:
Southern magnolia

State flower:
Magnolia blossom

FACTS AND FIGURES

Location: South central United States; bordered on the north by Tennessee, on the east by Alabama, on the south by Louisiana and the Gulf of Mexico, and on the west by Arkansas and Louisiana.

Area: 48,286 sq mi (125,060 km^2); rank, 32nd.

Population: 2,844,658 (2000 census); rank, 31st.

Elevation: *Highest*—806 ft (246 m) at Woodall Mountain; *lowest*—sea level, along the Gulf of Mexico.

Capital: Jackson.

Statehood: December 10, 1817; 20th state.

State Motto: *Virtute et armis* ("By valor and arms").

State Song: "Go, Mississippi."

Nicknames: Magnolia State; Hospitality State.

Abbreviations: MS; Miss.

State bird:
Mockingbird

Below: Pine forests, known as the Piney Woods, cover Mississippi's southeastern regions. The state is a leader in tree planting and farming.
Right: Ship Island, part of the Gulf Islands National Seashore, was cut in two by Hurricane Camille in 1969.

gently rolling Pine Hills, also known as the Piney Woods, cover much of the southern part of the state. The North Central Hills are composed of moist, clay-based soils and are higher than the Pine Hills. Shortleaf pines and hardwood trees grow in this area. Finally, reaching up into northeastern Mississippi, is a region called the Black Belt or the Black Prairie, named for its fertile black soil.

Rivers, Lakes, and Coastal Waters

The Mississippi River, one of the nation's most important rivers, serves as Mississippi's western boundary. Its tributaries in the state include the Homochitto, the Big Black, and the Yazoo, formed by the joining of the Tallahatchie and the Yalobusha rivers. The Pearl and Pascagoula rivers both flow directly into the Gulf of Mexico. The Tombigbee River flows from northeastern Mississippi into Alabama. Small, slow-moving streams called bayous are found along the Mississippi River and the Gulf coast.

Water on the eastern side of the Pontotoc Ridge, which lies in the northeastern corner of Mississippi, flows into the Tennessee and Tombigbee rivers. Water on the western side drains into the Mississippi River.

Mississippi has no large natural lakes. But along the Mississippi River, especially north of Vicksburg, there are many oxbow lakes. An oxbow lake is created when a river changes its course and leaves water behind in the original channel.

Reservoirs, dams, and levees (artificial banks) have been built along Mississippi's many rivers. These structures help contain water during heavy rains and floods. The reservoirs also function as recreation centers for swimming, fishing, and boating.

In the northeastern part of the state is the Tennessee-Tombigbee Waterway, a project that was completed in 1985 to stimulate the area's economy by increasing shipping. This waterway links the Tennessee River to the Gulf of Mexico through a 234-mile (377-kilometer) system of locks and canals.

Mississippi's coastline is only 44 miles (71 kilometers) long, but numerous bays, rivers, and creeks make the tidal shoreline much longer. A number of islands parallel the coast, separated from the mainland by Mississippi Sound. The largest islands are named Petit Bois, Horn, Ship, and Cat.

Climate

Mississippi is located in the humid subtropics and has a warm, moist climate. Annual rainfall ranges between 48 inches (1,220 millimeters) in the north and 66 inches (1,680 millimeters) in the south. The greatest amount of rainfall occurs during the winter months. Autumn is the driest season.

Temperatures in Mississippi are mild in the winter and hot in the summer. Temperatures average 46°F (8°C) in January and 82°F (28°C) in July and tend to be warmer along the coast.

In the spring, Mississippi is prone to tornadoes, and hurricanes may occur during the summer and fall. Thunderstorms strike throughout the year. Snow and ice storms sometimes occur.

Plant and Animal Life

At one time, great forests covered almost all of Mississippi. Tall deciduous and evergreen trees formed a canopy that kept sunlight from reaching the floor of the forests, preventing the growth of shrubs and bushes. Cypress forests could be found throughout the Delta and along the coast. Swampy areas were covered by patches of thickly grown reeds and briers called canebrakes.

Today forestlands cover only about one-half of Mississippi. Water, red, and black jack oaks, hickory, and walnut trees are abundant in the north. Pine trees cover the south. Moss-covered live oaks are familiar sights along the coast.

Mississippi has one of the highest concentrations of white-tail deer in the nation. Squirrels, opossums, and rabbits also are found in great numbers. Coyotes, bobcats, and foxes are common, and black bears are occasionally sighted. Migrating ducks and geese rest for short periods on the state's waterways. Wild turkeys, quail, and mourning doves are permanent residents. Freshwater rivers and lakes are home to significant numbers of largemouth bass, perch, bream, and catfish. Flounder, marlin, redfish, and mullet are popular saltwater game fish along the Gulf Coast.

Natural Resources

Mississippi's most productive soils are found in the Delta and Loess Hills areas of the state. These are made up mainly of alluvial and eolian deposits, which are materials deposited by rivers and the wind. The soils in the hills and the prairies are less fertile due to overplanting and erosion.

The major forests harvested for timber are located in the southern part of the state and include the famed Piney Woods area. Pine trees provide resin, turpentine, pulp, and other products, including lumber.

Flocks of migrating geese and ducks, such as these mallards, stop to refresh themselves on Mississippi's abundant rivers, lakes, and reservoirs.

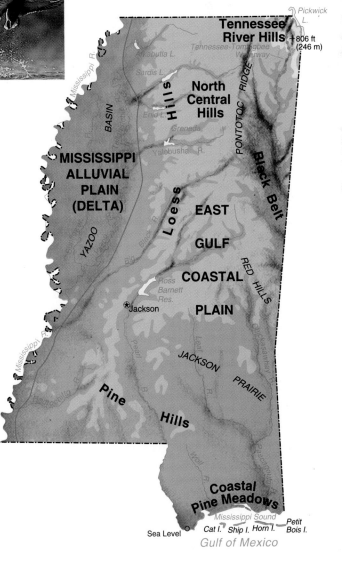

MISSISSIPPI Landforms

| 0 | 25 | 50 | 75 mi |
| 0 | 25 50 | 75 | 100 km |

⊛ State capital
+ Highest point
○ Lowest point
— Landform boundary

15,000 ft (4,500 m)
6,000 ft (1,800 m)
3,000 ft (900 m)
1,500 ft (450 m)
600 ft (180 m)
300 ft (90 m)
Sea Level
Below

Mississippi does not possess a large supply of any single mineral. Petroleum and natural gas are the most important. Along the Gulf Coast and in the Piney Woods, salt deposits run deep into the earth. Other minerals found in the state include lignite, sand and gravel, bauxite, limestone, and clays.

The Mississippi Sound and coastal bays provide excellent breeding and feeding grounds for many forms of aquatic life. Biloxi is the center of the fishing industry, which is especially famous for shrimp.

▶ **PEOPLE**

The original residents of Mississippi were Native Americans, but contact with white settlers caused their numbers to decline, and eventually they were forced to move west of the Mississippi River. Today, few Native Americans remain in Mississippi aside from a band of Choctaws in Neshoba, Leake, and Winston counties.

The influence of early Spanish and French settlers in Mississippi is still apparent in certain surnames and landmarks. Later many Anglo-Americans came, mostly from other Southern states. They brought with them a great number of African American slaves, many of whose descendants now make up more than 36 percent of the state's population. Later immigrants to Mississippi included Chinese and Italians, who went to the Delta to work as farm laborers. The most recent immigrants have been Vietnamese, many of whom fish the state's coastal waters.

Education

Mississippi had no organized system of public education until 1870, five years after the Civil War ended. White citizens opposed the use of state money to educate former slaves and their children, so school laws were not enforced. In 1890 the public education

A young girl awaits her baptism in Lake Ferguson, an old bend in the Mississippi River. About three-quarters of all churchgoing Mississippians are Baptists.

system was re-created, and segregated (separate) schools for black and white students were maintained until the early 1960's.

State-supported schools are Mississippi State University near Starkville; the University of Southern Mississippi in Hattiesburg; the University of Mississippi, with its main campus in Oxford and medical center in Jackson; and Jackson State University, also in Jackson. Others include the Mississippi University for Women in Columbus, Delta State University in Cleveland, Mississippi Valley State University in Itta Bena, and Alcorn State University in Lorman.

Private colleges include Belhaven and Millsaps colleges in Jackson, Mississippi College in Clinton, Tougaloo College in Tougaloo, and Rust College in Holly Springs.

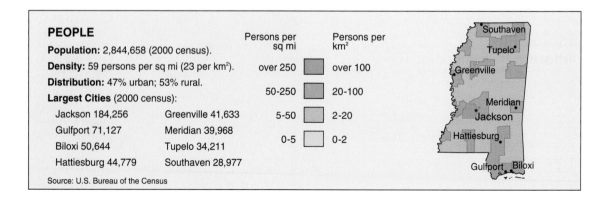

PEOPLE

Population: 2,844,658 (2000 census).

Density: 59 persons per sq mi (23 per km²).

Distribution: 47% urban; 53% rural.

Largest Cities (2000 census):

Jackson 184,256	Greenville 41,633
Gulfport 71,127	Meridian 39,968
Biloxi 50,644	Tupelo 34,211
Hattiesburg 44,779	Southaven 28,977

Persons per sq mi	Persons per km²
over 250	over 100
50-250	20-100
5-50	2-20
0-5	0-2

Southaven
Tupelo
Greenville
Meridian
Jackson
Hattiesburg
Gulfport Biloxi

Source: U.S. Bureau of the Census

Libraries, Museums, and the Arts

All of Mississippi's cities and most of its larger towns have public libraries. Rural areas are served by county or regional libraries. In all, they number more than 250. The library of the Mississippi Department of Archives and History in Jackson and libraries at the state universities contain important historical collections. The Old Capitol building in Jackson, which housed the state government from 1839 until 1903, has the Lauren Rogers Library and Museum of Art in Laurel. The Mary Buie Museum in Oxford contains ancient Greek and Roman art as well as literary prizes awarded to the celebrated Mississippi author William Faulkner. Jackson has its own symphonic orchestra and opera company.

▶ ECONOMY

Until the 1960's most Mississippians worked on farms. Since that time the majority of workers have been employed in service and manufacturing positions. Despite this

Top: Cotton is Mississippi's most important crop. *Above:* Cotton gins separate the seeds and hulls from cotton fibers, which are used to produce clothing, Mississippi's leading manufactured product. *Right:* Channel catfish are raised commercially for food. *Above right:* Catfish farming in the Delta is one of Mississippi's fastest-growing industries.

been restored as the State Historical Museum. The Old Courthouse in Vicksburg is now a museum containing relics from Civil War days.

The fine arts are represented in Mississippi's museums and concert halls. European and American paintings are housed at

Services

Approximately 70 percent of Mississippians work in service-related jobs and generate about two-thirds of all wages and salaries

shift, the state continues to rank last among states in average personal income.

Manufacturing: Clothing, wood products, ships, tile, brick, chemicals, fertilizers, paper, oil, electric and electronic equipment, fabricated metal products.

Agriculture: Cotton, broilers, soybeans, cattle.

Minerals: Petroleum, natural gas, sand and gravel.

Services: Wholesale and retail trade; finance, insurance, and real estate; business, social, and personal services; transportation, communication, and utilities; government.

*Gross state product is the total value of goods and services produced in a year.

Percentage of Gross State Product* by Industry

- Mining 1.5%
- Manufacturing 24.5%
- Construction 3%
- Agriculture 3.5%
- Transportation, communication, and utilities 12%
- Business, social, and personal services 12.5%
- Government 13.5%
- Finance, insurance, and real estate 14.5%
- Wholesale and retail trade 15%

Source: U.S. Bureau of Economic Analysis

Wood products are important to the state's economy. Logs are gathered and transported to sawmills, where they are processed for lumber.

earned each year. A few examples of service-related businesses are wholesale and retail stores; government (local, state, and federal); education; banking, insurance, and real estate; medical facilities; hotels and restaurants; and automobile repair.

Manufacturing

Of all the people employed in Mississippi, one in four works in manufacturing. Important manufactured products include clothing, ships, processed foods, chemicals, and fertilizers. Mississippians manufacture furniture from native lumber, while sawdust is formed into paper and plywood. Other manufacturing enterprises make use of Mississippi's sand, gravel, and clay to produce tiles, bricks, and pottery.

Agriculture

Cotton provides the largest agricultural income in Mississippi, and the state is the nation's third largest grower of cotton. However, synthetic fabrics and international competition have diminished its overall importance to the state's economy.

Mississippi farms also produce poultry, eggs, and milk. Southwestern Mississippi in particular is known for its dairy farms. Beef cattle are raised throughout the state.

Soybeans are the third most important source of agricultural income. Grown in every part of the state, soybeans are used in animal foods, margarine, and mayonnaise. Mississippi ranks fifth among the states in rice production. Soybeans and rice are exported to Europe and Asia.

Over the past 20 years, the production of farm-raised catfish has skyrocketed. In 1975, Mississippi farmers processed less than 20 million pounds (9 million kilograms) of catfish. In 1990, the total annual production reached 290 million pounds (132 million kilograms). There are approximately 90,000 acres (36,000 hectares) of catfish ponds in the state. Other major commercial seafoods from Mississippi are shrimp, menhaden, red snapper, crabs, oysters, and spotted sea trout. Most is frozen or canned; some is ground into fish meal for pet and livestock food.

Mining and Construction

The most important mineral in the state is petroleum, first produced there in 1939. Natural gas was first produced from fields at Amory in 1926. The area along the Gulf Coast contains many salt domes that have pushed through the sedimentary rock. The salt is used to make table salt and various chemicals. Other minerals of economic importance found in the state include lignite, sand and gravel, bauxite, limestone, and clays.

Mississippi's construction industry involves the building and repair of roads, bridges, ports, homes, offices, and the like. Together, mining and construction provide a steady source of income and employ more than 7 percent of the working population.

Transportation

The Mississippi River has long been a significant transportation route for the state. It continues to provide a means for delivering goods and services. Freight traffic also travels on the Tennessee-Tombigbee Waterway. This 234-mile (377-kilometer) system of locks and canals links the Tennessee River to the Gulf of Mexico.

Several railroad companies operate more than 3,600 miles (5,790 kilometers) of mainline track in Mississippi. By far the largest freight carrier is the Illinois Central Gulf Railroad. Amtrak provides passenger trains across the state. Freight also travels over Mississippi's more than 75,000 miles (120,700 kilometers) of highways, which includes three interstate highways. The most famous road in Mississippi is probably Highway 61, which parallels the Mississippi River. It once served as the chief connection between New Orleans and Chicago. Major airline carriers offer passenger service from airports near Jackson, Meridian, Columbus, Hattiesburg, and Gulfport.

Communication

The first newspaper in the state was the *Mississippi Gazette*, which began publication in Natchez in 1799. The oldest paper still in publication is the weekly *Woodville Republican*, founded in 1823. Jackson's *Clarion-Ledger* has the largest circulation of any newspaper in the state. About 22 daily newspapers and 94 weeklies are published. Mississippi has about 20 television stations and 200 radio stations.

▶ CITIES

Mississippi, with its population of more than 2.8 million, is one of the few states in which more people live in rural areas than in cities. Five metropolitan areas have populations greater than 40,000. Jackson is the only city with a population greater than 100,000.

Jackson, the state's capital and largest city, is located on the west bank of the Pearl River. Founded in 1821 on the site of a former French trading post, the city was named in honor of Andrew Jackson, a hero of the War of 1812 who later became president of the United States. Today Jackson is an important regional manufacturing, transportation, and distribution center and the home of several colleges and universities.

Biloxi, the state's third largest city, takes its name from the Biloxi Indians and means "first people." Founded on

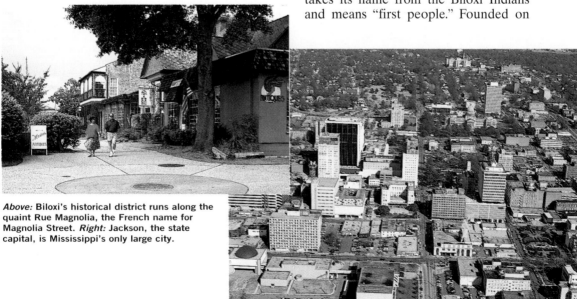

Above: Biloxi's historical district runs along the quaint Rue Magnolia, the French name for Magnolia Street. *Right:* Jackson, the state capital, is Mississippi's only large city.

Places of Interest

Elvis Presley's Birthplace, Tupelo

Vicksburg National Military Park, Vicksburg

Longwood Mansion, Natchez

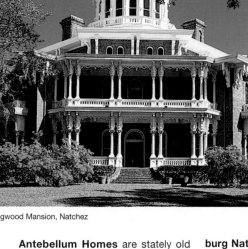
The Natchez Trace, near Jackson

Antebellum Homes are stately old homes that were built before the Civil War. They are located mainly in Vicksburg, Natchez, Holly Springs, Columbus, Port Gibson, and Biloxi.

Civil War Sites are numerous in Mississippi. **Beauvoir**, near Biloxi, was the last home of Jefferson Davis, the president of the Confederate States of America (1861–65). The estate, which has been completely restored, features a museum containing Confederate artifacts and a Confederate cemetery. **Brices Cross Roads National Battlefield Site**, north of Tupelo, commemorates a Confederate victory on June 10, 1864. **Fort Massachusetts**, on Ship Island, was built in 1858 to protect the entrance of the waterway to New Orleans, Louisiana. Located 12 miles (19 kilometers) off-shore, the fort was captured by Union forces in 1861 at the start of the Civil War and was used to hold Confederate prisoners. **Tupelo National Battlefield** in Tupelo commemorates the battle of Tupelo, July 13–14, 1864. **Vicksburg National Military Park** preserves the scene of the city's 47-day siege in 1863. Hundreds of monuments and tablets mark the positions of the armies. The park also preserves trenches, rifle pits, and many cannons in their original positions. **Vicksburg National Cemetery**, containing the graves of thousands of soldiers, adjoins the park.

Elvis Presley's Birthplace, in Tupelo, commemorates the site where rock-and-roll great Elvis Presley was born and spent his early childhood.

Gulf Islands National Seashore includes a number of islands off Mississippi's Gulf Coast, featuring wildlife sanctuaries, historic forts, and white sand beaches.

Natchez Trace Parkway, a scenic roadway from Natchez to Nashville, Tennessee, parallels the old Natchez Trace, a trade route forged by Native Americans more than 1,000 years ago and used by boatmen, before the age of steamships on the Mississippi River, to return north. Along the way are picnic sites, nature trails, museums, and historic sites, such as Indian mounds, Confederate gravesites, and the Ackia Battleground Monument near Tupelo, marking the location of a Chickasaw Indian village.

Old Spanish Fort, in Pascagoula, is considered the oldest building still standing in Mississippi. Built as a fort in 1718, it now operates as a museum.

Petrified Forest, in Flora, contains the fossilized remains of giant trees dating back 36 million years. The site includes nature trails and a geological museum.

State Recreation Areas. Mississippi has six national forests—Holly Springs, Tombigbee, Delta, Bienville, Homochitto, and De Soto. Of these, De Soto is by far the largest. Mississippi's 14 state parks include a variety of woodlands, lakes and bayous, wildlife refuges, and sand beaches. For more information, contact the Department of Wildlife, Fisheries, and Parks, P. O. Box 451, Jackson, Mississippi 39205.

the Gulf Coast by the French in 1717, Biloxi briefly served as the capital of the French colony of Louisiana. Today this port city's chief industry is commercial fishing, particularly of shrimp and oysters. It is also a resort center noted for its gambling casinos, beautiful old buildings, and oak trees hung with Spanish moss.

Hattiesburg, located in south central Mississippi, was founded in 1884 as a railroad hub for the shipment of lumber. Today its economy depends on the city's two colleges and many small industries.

Greenville, located on the Mississippi River, was settled in 1828. It became a major center for the buying and selling of cotton and continues to provide services to farmers. Greenville is Mississippi's largest city in the Delta region.

Meridian, located in central Mississippi, was founded in 1854 as a railroad depot town on the Mobile and Ohio Railroad line. Today the city is a center for manufacturing.

▶ GOVERNMENT

Mississippi has been governed under four constitutions. The present one, written in 1890, provides for three branches of government—executive, legislative, and judicial.

A governor heads the executive branch of state government and serves a 4-year term. A recent amendment allows a governor to be re-elected to office for one additional term. Other elected executive officers include the lieutenant governor, secretary of state, attorney general, treasurer, and superintendent of public education.

The legislative branch makes laws for the state. It is composed of a senate and a house of representatives. All legislators serve 4-year terms and meet annually.

Mississippi's supreme court is the highest court in the judicial branch of state government. It is an appeals court, presided over by nine justices. Chancery courts hear cases involving wills, divorces, and domestic problems. Circuit courts try serious crimes and cases involving large sums of money. County courts and justice courts handle less serious matters. All judges in Mississippi are elected to their offices.

▶ HISTORY

Many Indian tribes once lived in the area that is now Mississippi. The largest tribes were the Chickasaw in the north, the Choctaw in the central and southern parts of the state, and the Natchez in the southwest. Several cities and rivers now bear the names of some of the smaller tribes, such as the Biloxi, the Pascagoula, and the Yazoo.

Exploration and Settlement

A Spanish explorer, Hernando de Soto, was the first European known to travel into the Mississippi region. He arrived in eastern Mississippi in December 1540, searching for gold. He claimed the area for Spain, who ruled the region for 150 years, though they built no settlements.

The state capitol building in Jackson was designed to look like the national capitol in Washington, D.C. Completed in 1903, the building was restored in 1979.

GOVERNMENT

State Government
Governor: 4-year term
State senators: 52; 4-year terms
State representatives: 122;
 4-year terms
Number of counties: 82

Federal Government
U.S. senators: 2
U.S. representatives: 4
Number of electoral votes: 6

For the name of the current governor, see STATE GOVERNMENTS in Volume S. For the names of current U.S. senators and representatives, see UNITED STATES, CONGRESS OF THE in Volume U-V.

In 1682, the French explorer Robert Cavelier, Sieur de La Salle, claimed a vast region for France that included Mississippi. In 1699 his countryman, Pierre Le Moyne, Sieur d'Iberville, established Mississippi's first European settlement, Fort Maurepas, at what is now Ocean Springs. Later the French also built Fort Rosalie on the site of present-day Natchez. After the French and Indian War (1754–63), England took over French territory east of the Mississippi and named it West Florida.

At the time of the Revolutionary War (1775–83), the Spanish saw an opportunity to re-establish power in Mississippi. While the English were busy fighting the American colonists, Spanish troops moved into the Gulf area and in 1799 established a government. After the American colonists won the war in 1783, England recognized the United States' claim to all land north of 31 degrees latitude. Spain, however, did not do so until 1795, when it signed a treaty ceding the southern portions of Mississippi and Alabama to the United States.

Territorial Days

In 1798, the Territory of Mississippi was organized with Natchez as its capital. The territory included most of modern-day Mississippi and Alabama. The area south of 31 degrees latitude was added to the territory in the early 1800's. Under the terms of the Louisiana Purchase of 1803, the Mississippi River became part of the United States. Then in 1811 the first steamboat travelled on the river. Both of these events had a great influence on the development of Mississippi. American control of the river and of steamboat travel meant that Mississippians could transport their goods to many new markets.

During the 19 years of territorial government, the region developed dramatically. In 1798, about 5,000 people lived there, but by 1810, the population had increased to 42,000. Many residents were immigrants from Atlantic Coast states, including slaves brought by their owners to work in tobacco, cotton, and indigo fields.

Statehood and Antebellum Days

On December 10, 1817, the U.S. Congress divided Mississippi into the territory of Alabama and the state of Mississippi, the 20th

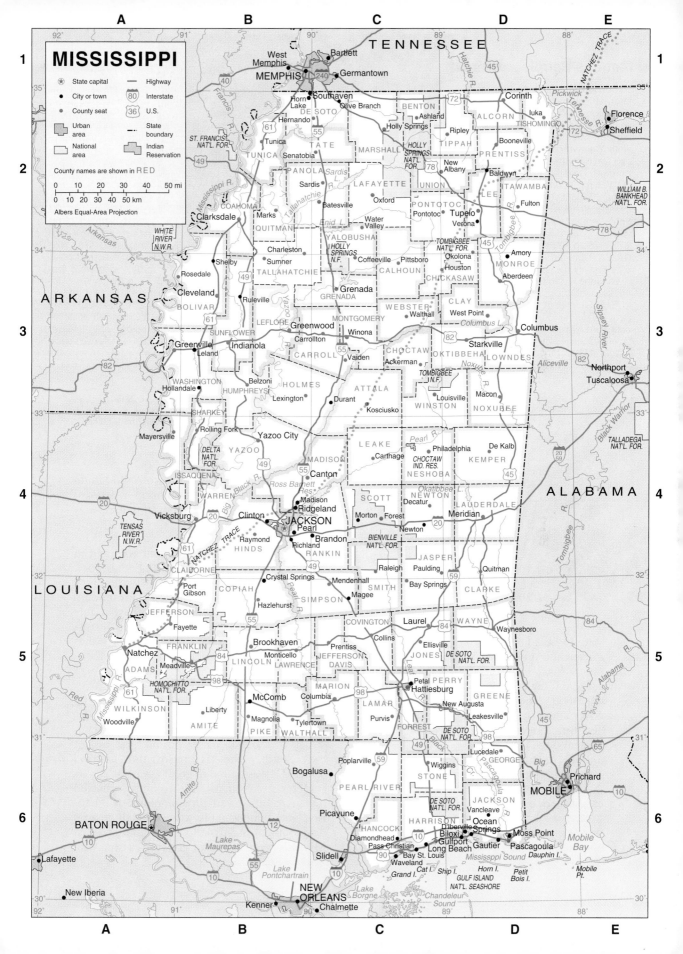

Famous People

Consult the Index to find more information in *The New Book of Knowledge* about the following people who were born in Mississippi or are otherwise associated with the state: Confederate president Jefferson Davis (1808–89); U.S. senator Hiram R. Revels (1822–1901); writers William Faulkner (1897–1962), Richard Wright (1908–60), and Tennessee Williams (1911–83); civil rights activists Fannie Lou Hamer (1917–77) and Medgar W. Evers (1926–63); opera singer Leontyne Price (1927-   ) and the "king of rock and roll," Elvis Presley (1935–77).

Blanche Kelso Bruce (1841–98) was the second African American to serve in the U.S. Senate but the first to serve a full term (1875–81). Born to a slave mother near Farmville, Virginia, Kelso attended Oberlin College after the Civil War broke out in 1861. Later he founded two

Tennessee Williams

Ida Wells-Barnett

schools for African Americans in Missouri before moving to Mississippi to become a planter. In 1874 he was elected to the Senate on the Republican ticket. Kelso worked to promote civil rights, improve navigation on the Mississippi River, and fight election fraud.

James Maury (Jim) Henson (1936–90), born in Greenville, was a gifted puppeteer and the creator of the Mup-

pets, first seen on the award-winning public television program *Sesame Street*. Henson went on to produce *The Muppet Show* (1976–81), which was watched by children and adults all over the world. Among the most beloved of his creations are Kermit the Frog, Bert, Ernie, Big Bird, Miss Piggy, Oscar the Grouch, and the Cookie Monster. The Muppets also were featured in several films, including *The Muppet Movie* (1979).

Belle Kearney (1863–1939), born near Vernon, was a writer and politician known for her autobiography *A Slaveholder's Daughter*. In 1924 she was elected to the Mississippi state senate, the

Until the Civil War ended in 1865, slaves were used to harvest Mississippi's profitable cotton crop. Afterward, the work was performed by sharecroppers, both black and white, for shares of a farm's profits.

state to be admitted into the Union. In 1830, President Andrew Jackson signed the Removal Act, which forced the Choctaw, Chickasaw, and other southeastern tribes to surrender their land in Mississippi to the U.S. government in exchange for lands in "Indian Territory," beyond the Mississippi River in present-day Oklahoma.

With Indian lands vacated, white settlers from the southeast flooded into Mississippi. A cotton empire, based on slave labor, was established on the cheap, fertile lands. By 1861, white Mississippians believed their prosperity and way of life depended on slavery and cotton. To preserve the institution of

slavery, Mississippi withdrew from the Union in January 1861. Other Southern states also seceded, and the Civil War began that April.

The Civil War

Of the several Civil War battles fought in Mississippi, the most important one took place at Vicksburg. After almost two months of siege, Union general Ulysses S. Grant conquered this important river port city in July 1863, giving the Union control of the Mississippi River. Smaller battles and skirmishes occurred in the state, leaving much of Mississippi a wasteland by the war's end in 1865.

Reconstruction and the Slow Growth of Industry

After the Confederate States were defeated, the U.S. government sought to reconstruct, or rebuild, Mississippi and the rest of the South. The Reconstruction Period (1865–77) was a time of great adjustment.

Reconstruction of the economy achieved mixed results. Even though railroads, factories, and lumber mills were built, industrial development in Mississippi was limited. Most Mississippians were still growing cotton, with first woman in the South to rise to such a high political office.

Riley (B. B.) King (1925–), born in Itta Bena, is acknowledged as a major influence on the development of rock music and one of the great blues guitarists. As a teenager, King found work as a disc jockey and singing in clubs in Memphis, Tenn. His stage name, Blues Boy, was soon shortened to B. B. He had his first hit record in 1949. He became known for his energetic stage performances. His many recordings include *B. B. King: The World's Greatest Living Blues Artist* (1973) and *King of the Blues* (1989). He has won several Grammy awards, including the Lifetime Achievement Award in 1987.

Jim Henson

Eudora Welty

Ida Bell Wells-Barnett (1862–1931), born to slave parents in Holly Springs, was a journalist and lecturer who became known for her crusade to stop the lynchings (murders) of African Americans. Educated at Rusk University, she became a schoolteacher in Memphis and began writing articles for the African American newspaper *Free Speech*. After three friends were lynched by whites, she dedicated herself to exposing mob violence, campaigned for protection laws, and published a pamphlet on the subject, *A Red Record* (1895). In 1909 she helped found the National Association for the Advancement of Colored People (NAACP).

Eudora Welty (1909–2001), a distinguished author, was born in Jackson. Most of her works, widely admired for their graceful prose and descriptive detail, are set in Mississippi. Her novels include *Delta Wedding* (1946) and *The Optimist's Daughter* (1972), which won a Pulitzer Prize in 1973. Her volumes of short stories, which won six O. Henry Awards, include *A Sweet Devouring* (1969) and *Collected Stories* (1980). An autobiographical sketch, *One Writer's Beginnings*, was published in 1984.

black farmers typically working as sharecroppers, or tenants, on land owned by whites. In the 1880's and 1890's, overproduction of cotton and declining cotton prices caused many white farmers to fall into debt and lose their land. By the 1920's, the majority of Mississippi farmers—both black and white—were sharecroppers on cotton farms.

In the 1930's, the Great Depression encouraged many sharecroppers, especially blacks seeking social and political equality, to move to other states in search of employment. A vast migration of Mississippians moving northward continued into the 1940's.

World War II

During the years America was engaged in World War II (1941–45), Mississippi experienced dynamic growth. Military bases, manufacturing facilities, and even prisoner-of-war camps provided the economy with a much-needed boost. Industrialization continued after the war, and by 1960, for the first time ever, more Mississippians worked in non-agricultural jobs than worked on farms.

The Civil Rights Movement

In the 1960's, a nationwide movement to secure equality for African Americans made its way into Mississippi, but the struggle for equality was not a peaceful one. Many advocates of social reform, both black and white, were killed, including Medgar Evers, a leader of the National Association for the Advancement of Colored People (NAACP), and three young voting-rights volunteers—James Chaney, Andrew Goodman, and Michael Schwerner. It took the intervention of federal law enforcement officers in 1964 to force the integration of Mississippi's public schools.

In 1969, Charles Evers, the brother of the slain civil rights leader, was elected mayor of Fayette, signaling a major advancement toward racial healing in the state. Many black Mississippians now hold positions in federal, state, and local government.

Modern Times

Mississippi's economy has become more diversified, attracting manufacturing industries and becoming less dependent on agriculture. However, wages tend to be lower than those earned in other states.

The task of strengthening the economy became more difficult in the aftermath of Hurricane Katrina, which hit the Gulf Coast on August 29, 2005. Nearly 20,000 Mississippians had to evacuate their homes, and 221 were killed. In Mississippi, the hardest-hit cities were Gulfport and Biloxi.

BRADLEY G. BOND
University of Southern Mississippi

MISSISSIPPI RIVER

The Mississippi River is the chief river of the United States and one of the major rivers of the world. Native Americans, awed by its vastness, called it *Miss-Sipi*, meaning "the great (or big) river." Of all the rivers in the United States, only the Missouri is longer.

The Mississippi forms the heart of a great inland water system formed by the Ohio, Mississippi, and Missouri rivers and their 2,500 tributaries. This system drains an area of more than 1.2 million square miles (3.1 million square kilometers), stretching from the western slopes of the Appalachians to the Rocky Mountains.

Course of the River

From its source near Lake Itasca in northern Minnesota, the Mississippi River flows through a broad, shallow valley until it reaches the Falls of St. Anthony in Minneapolis. From this point to Cairo, Illinois, it varies in width from about 3 1/2 miles to 1/2 mile (5.6 kilometers to 0.8 kilometer). Below Cairo, where the Mississippi is joined by its principal tributary, the Ohio River, the river widens from 1/2 mile to 1 1/2 miles (0.8 kilometer to 2.4 kilometers) and ranges from 50 to 100 feet (15.2 to 30.5 meters) in depth.

The author Mark Twain, who piloted a steamboat on the Mississippi in the 1800's, described the Mississippi as "the crookedest river in the world." South of Illinois, it flows through a broad plain marked by widely spaced bluffs, slowly winding its way past Memphis, Vicksburg, Natchez, Baton Rouge, and New Orleans. Finally it fans out through the Mississippi Delta into the Gulf of Mexico.

History

Archaeologists believe that the valley through which the Mississippi river flows was inhabited as early as 10,000 B.C. A succession of Native American cultures lived along the river and used it to trade goods with peoples as far away as Montana and Florida. By the time Europeans arrived in the 1500's, the Sioux, Chippewa, Sauk (Sac), Mesquakie (Fox), Creek, and Choctaw were living in the Mississippi Valley region.

The first known European to discover the Mississippi was the Spanish explorer Hernando de Soto. His small expedition crossed the river near present-day Memphis in 1541. In 1673, French explorers in Canada, ambitious to expand the fur trade and spread Christianity beyond the Great Lakes region, sent Father Jacques Marquette, a Jesuit missionary, and Louis Jolliet, a fur trader, to explore the Mississippi. They traveled as far south as the Arkansas River.

In 1682, the French empire-builder, Robert Cavelier, Sieur de La Salle, entered the Mississippi by way of the Illinois River and navigated downstream to the Gulf of Mexico. He claimed all of the land east of the river to the Appalachian Mountains and west of the river to the Rocky Mountains for King Louis XIV and named it Louisiana. When the United States gained its independence from England in 1783, the Mississippi became the western boundary of the new nation. Then in 1803, when the Louisiana Territory was purchased

The Mississippi River originates in Minnesota and flows a distance of 2,340 miles (3,766 kilometers) before emptying into the Gulf of Mexico, just south of New Orleans. Most of the commerce on the river is moved by barges pushed by tugboats. Special carriers have been designed to handle such cargo as petroleum and industrial chemicals.

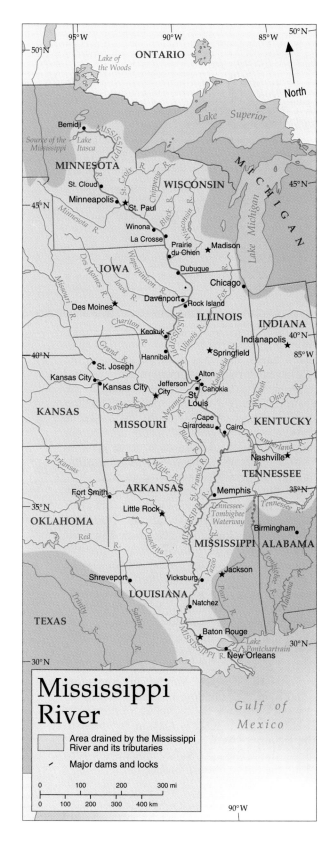

Mississippi River

☐ Area drained by the Mississippi
River and its tributaries

⌐ Major dams and locks

| 0 | 100 | 200 | 300 mi |

| 0 | 100 | 200 | 300 | 400 km |

from France, the Mississippi became the center of a vast American territory that stretched from the Atlantic Ocean all the way to the Rocky Mountains.

Before steamboats were invented, trade and travel on the Mississippi was largely restricted to downriver travel in rafts and barges. Steamboats made it possible for trade and commerce to travel upriver against the strong currents. Steamboats could also transport more goods and deliver them in less time to markets in the North. Steamboat traffic encouraged agricultural development along the river, leading to the growth of cities and industries in the midwestern states.

In the years of slavery before the Civil War (1861–65), the expression "sold downriver" meant the harshest of conditions to the African American slaves, as the most backbreaking work took place on the sugar and cotton plantations in the Deep South. On the other hand, "going upriver" meant escape.

During the Civil War, the Union attempted to control the Mississippi as part of their strategy to win. On May 17, 1863, they began a siege on the city of Vicksburg, the Confederates' stronghold on the river. The city surrendered on July 4, marking one of the turning points in the war that led to the collapse of the Confederacy.

Improving the River

In recent history federal and state funds have been used to improve the river and to control flooding. However, environmentalists have raised concerns, warning of the dangers of tampering with the river and misusing its resources. Costly projects have been undertaken to improve harbors, raise and reinforce levees, build dams and locks to improve navigation, dredge channel depths, and remove obstructions. Despite many efforts, devastating floods have occurred, notably the Great Flood of '93, which cost billions of dollars in property damage and even loss of life.

GUY-HAROLD SMITH
Editor, *Conservation of Natural Resources*
Reviewed by CHARLES T. JONES, JR.
Emeritus Professor of American History
William Woods University

See also FLOODS (The Great Flood of '93); JOLLIET, LOUIS, AND JACQUES MARQUETTE; LA SALLE, ROBERT CAVELIER, SIEUR DE; LOUISIANA PURCHASE.

MISSOULA. See MONTANA (Cities).

MISSOURI

Of all the nicknames of the fifty states, Missouri's—the Show Me State—may be the most spirited. In the early 1890's, many Missourians went to work in the mines of Colorado and found the techniques used there unfamiliar. A saying began, "He is from Missouri, so you have to show him." Later in the decade, a Missouri congressman delivered a speech in which he gave the phrase a whole new meaning. He said, "Frothy eloquence neither convinces or satisfies me. I am from Missouri. You have got to show me." Thereafter, the slogan suggested that Missourians have a questioning attitude and need proof of an argument.

People who live in parts of the state settled by southerners pronounce its name Missourah, *while most others pronounce it* Missouree. *The name comes from a Native American language and means "place (or town) of the big canoes." This referred to the large dugout logs the Indians used for traveling along the region's great Mississippi and Missouri rivers.*

State flag

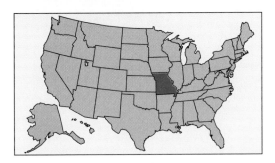

Missouri is a midwestern state, located near the center of the continental United States. More than half of its 5.6 million residents live in two major metropolitan areas—Kansas City, on the Missouri River, and St. Louis, on the Mississippi River. Both cities are centers of manufacturing and finance, and each has a Federal Reserve bank, making Missouri the only state with two.

Missouri farms grow corn and soybeans, while cotton and melons are produced in the southeastern region known as the Boot Heel. Cattle, hog, and poultry farms also make an important contribution to the state's economy. Missourians mine coal and zinc in great quantities and produce about 90 percent of the nation's supply of lead. Yet the service industries, which include tourism, provide even greater income.

Among Missouri's many attractions are the famous Gateway Arch in St. Louis, a monument to America's territorial expansion; recreational sports in Missouri's beautiful lakes and rivers; and the homesteads of two of Missouri's favorite sons—Harry S. Truman, the 33rd president of the United States, and Mark Twain, creator of the fictional characters Tom Sawyer and Huckleberry Finn. An-

other popular attraction is Branson, a town in the Ozarks that has become one of the world's most popular country music capitals.

Much of Missouri's history mirrors the drama of early American politics. The first major political debate over the expansion of slavery occurred when Missouri applied for admission to the Union as a slave state in 1820. Then in 1857, the state was again spotlighted when a Missouri slave named Dred Scott unsuccessfully sued for his freedom, taking his case all the way to the U.S. Supreme Court. Throughout the Civil War (1861–65), Missourians were divided in their loyalties. The state officially sided with the Union but also sent representatives to the Confederate Congress. In addition, during the principal years of western migration, Missouri served as the starting point for the pioneers beginning their long journeys west along the famed Santa Fe and Oregon trails.

▶ LAND

The rich Missouri Valley cuts the state roughly in two, dividing the plains of northern Missouri from the highlands of the south. It extends from Kansas City in the west to the vicinity of St. Charles in the east. Here it meets the Mississippi Valley, which itself runs along the entire eastern border.

Opposite page, clockwise from right: **The Gateway Arch in St. Louis is a monument to all the pioneers who journeyed west of the Mississippi River. Alley Spring Mill is just one of the many picturesque sites on the Ozark National Scenic Riverways. Frog jumping contests are featured during Tom Sawyer Days in Hannibal.**

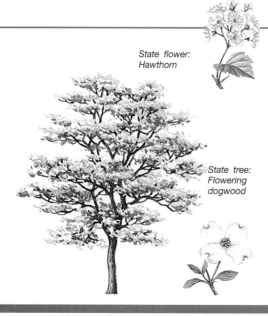

State flower: Hawthorn

State tree: Flowering dogwood

FACTS AND FIGURES

Location: Central United States; bordered on the north by Iowa, on the east by Illinois, Kentucky, and Tennessee, on the south by Arkansas, and on the west by Oklahoma, Kansas, and Nebraska.

Area: 69,709 sq mi (180,546 km²); rank, 21st.

Population: 5,595,211 (2000 census); rank, 17th.

Elevation: *Highest*—1,772 ft (540 m), at Taum Sauk Mountain; *lowest*—230 ft (70 m), near Cardwell.

Capital: Jefferson City.

Statehood: August 10, 1821; 24th state.

State Motto: *Salus populi suprema lex esto* ("The welfare of the people shall be the supreme law").

State Song: "Missouri Waltz."

Nickname: Show Me State.

Abbreviations: MO; Mo.

State bird: Eastern bluebird

Left: The Missouri River is the longest river in the United States. It flows eastward through the state of Missouri before emptying into the Mississippi River, just north of St. Louis. *Below:* Tobacco and other crops thrive on the fertile till plains in the northern part of the state.

Land Regions

Missouri is divided into four major landforms: the Dissected Till Plains of the north, the Osage Plains of the west, the Ozark Plateau highlands of the south, and the Mississippi Alluvial Plain of the southeast.

The Dissected Till Plains, or glaciated plains, that form the northern part of the state make up one of the richest agricultural regions in the world. Thousands of years ago, immense glaciers melted, leaving behind rich deposits of soil, called till. Wind currents created rich deposits of topsoil, called loess, in the northwest part of the state.

The Osage Plains, an extension of the Great Plains of the West, is a triangular-shaped landform in western Missouri that was unaffected by glacial action. Alternately flat and rolling prairie, the section reveals more hills and steeper grades as it approaches the Ozark Plateau.

The Ozark Plateau, covering most of south central Missouri, is the state's largest region. The Ozarks get their picturesque beauty from the high ridges and steep gullies that resulted from the gradual water erosion of elevated lands. The St. Francois Mountains in the eastern Ozarks contain Taum Sauk Mountain, Missouri's highest point, as well as some of the state's most unusual rock formations. A broad upland of tree-covered hills, fast-flowing streams, and deep narrow valleys makes up the rest of the Ozark Plateau.

The Mississippi Alluvial Plain, a lowland region also known as the Mississippi Delta, covers the Boot Heel of southeastern Missouri, from Cape Girardeau well into Arkansas. The Delta's rich topsoil, a product

of the frequent flooding of the Mississippi Valley, has made this a highly productive agricultural region. The soil and the weather in the Delta region provides crops with a two-hundred-day growing season, which allows Missouri to grow a wide variety of agricultural produce.

Rivers and Lakes

Missouri benefits from the nation's two greatest rivers, the Mississippi and the Missouri. Both are major transportation avenues for heavy and bulky cargoes best carried by barges. Many cities, including St. Louis, depend on the rivers for their supply of water. Northern rivers include the Grand, Chariton, and Salt. South central Missouri is drained by the lovely Gasconade, Osage, and Meramec rivers. Farther south the White, Current, and

St. Francis rivers flow. Articles on the Mississippi River and the Missouri River appear in this volume.

All of Missouri's major lakes have been formed by dams on its rivers. The largest of these, the Harry S. Truman Reservoir and Lake of the Ozarks, were created by damming the Osage River. Dams on the White River created Table Rock, Taneycomo, Bull Shoals, and Norfolk lakes on the Missouri-Arkansas border.

Missouri also has 11 of the nation's 75 largest springs. Big Spring, with an average daily flow of 277 million gallons (1,048 million liters) is its largest. Others of importance include Alley, Maramec, and Round.

Climate

Missouri has four distinct seasons. Summers tend to be hot and sultry. In July, the hottest month, the average temperature is 77°F (25°C), but daytime high temperatures of 100°F (38°C) are not uncommon. Winters can be intensely cold for short periods. Temperatures in January, the coldest month, average 30°F (1°C). Missouri's springs and autumns are usually mild and sunny.

Northern Missouri receives an average of 35 inches (889 millimeters) of precipitation (rain and snow) per year, while southern Missouri receives about 46 inches (1,150 millimeters). The most precipitation generally falls in the Boot Heel region.

Plant and Animal Life

Missouri's large size and different climatic zones produce a great variety of plant and animal life. Botanists have classified 2,400 species of wild ferns and flowering plants. Most of Missouri's heavily wooded areas lie in the Ozarks. Among the types of trees found there are oak, linden, maple, papaw, hickory, sweet gum, walnut, pecan, cottonwood, hornbeam, ash, pine, redbud, dogwood, catalpa, red cedar, hazelnut, crab apple, sycamore, hackberry, and sumac.

Deer, red foxes, coyotes, otters, raccoons, opossums, squirrels, rabbits, and skunks abound, while a few black bears can still be found in the Ozarks. Birds native to the state include cardinals, eastern bluebirds, blue jays, crows, hawks, bobwhite quail, turkeys, wrens, red-winged blackbirds, brown thrushes, and woodpeckers. Rivers and lakes hold crappie, bluegill, carp, buffalo sucker, four species of bass, three species of catfish, the misnamed-but-famous spoonbill cat, and many other kinds of fish.

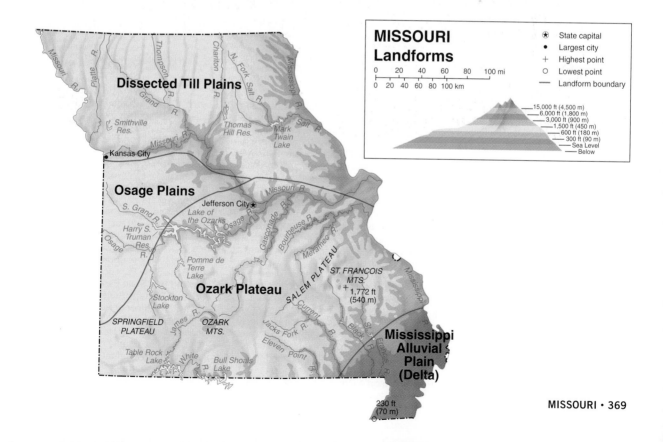

Places of Interest

Harry S. Truman Home, Independence

Country music entertainment, Branson

Elephant Rocks, Johnson's Shut-Ins State Park

Missouri Botanical Garden, St. Louis

Missouri's two great cities, St. Louis and Kansas City, have many attractions, as does its countryside. The Ozarks provide unspoiled scenery, large springs, fast-flowing rivers, lakes, and caves. Branson is located in some of the most picturesque surroundings in the state.

Battle of Lexington State Historic Site, in Lexington, preserves the site of the Civil War's Battle of Lexington, which occurred in September 1861. One can still see the trenches employed by the soldiers. The Anderson House, which was used as a field hospital, also is preserved as a state historic site.

The George Washington Carver National Monument, near Diamond, preserves the birthplace of this great American scientist. The site includes a museum that houses many of his papers and a statue of him as a boy.

Harry S. Truman Library-Museum, in Independence, contains the papers of the late president and also houses a museum. President and Mrs. Truman are

buried in the courtyard on the library grounds. The Truman Home is also located in Independence.

The Jefferson National Expansion Memorial, in St. Louis, commemorates Missouri's role as a gateway to the West. The memorial includes the Old Courthouse as well as the stainless steel Gateway Arch created by architect Eero Saarinen. Visitors may go to the top of the arch on trains located in the structure's legs. In the bottom of the arch is a historical museum featuring artifacts of the American West.

Ozark National Scenic Riverways, a popular national area for camping and canoeing, encompasses 134 miles (216 kilometers) of the beautiful Current and Jack's Fork rivers, two of the best recreational streams in the Midwest. This area, which attracts up to 1.5 million visitors a year, also features Alley Spring Mill and Big Spring.

Wilson's Creek National Battlefield is located just west of Springfield. On

August 10, 1861, Confederate and Union soldiers met in one of the earliest important battles of the Civil War. Union General Nathaniel Lyon lost his life in this battle.

State Parks. Missouri has more than fifty state parks and historic sites. Lake of the Ozarks State Park is the largest of Missouri's state parks. Boating, nature trails, fishing, horseback riding, and campgrounds attract many visitors. Other parks with lakes include Big Lake State Park in Holt County, Lake Wappapello State Park in southeast Missouri, Table Rock State Park near Branson, and Thousand Hills State Park near Kirksville. Johnson's Shut-Ins State Park lies in the northeastern corner of Reynolds County. Nearby are Taum Sauk Mountain, the highest point in Missouri, and Elephant Rocks, a fine example of wind-eroded rocks. For more information, contact the Missouri Department of Natural Resources, Division of State Parks, P.O. Box 176, Jefferson City, Missouri 65102.

Natural Resources

Both the Mississippi and Missouri river valleys provide farmers with excellent soil, varying from the rich loess of the Missouri River bluffs to the productive topsoil of the Boot Heel.

Missourians produce 90 percent of the nation's lead supply and considerable quantities of coal, fire clay, iron ore, zinc, shale, stone, copper, sand and gravel, and silver. At one point Missouri was called the Mineral State.

Missouri's important rivers, many lakes, and abundant rainfall ensure a steady supply of water. In addition to providing plenty of opportunities for recreation and transportation, plentiful water is the key to a variety of manufacturing and agricultural enterprises.

When Europeans first explored Missouri, forests covered about two-thirds of the region. Today little more than one-third is forestland, and much of this lies in the Ozarks. Timber harvesting occurs on private lands and in the national forests, supplying building materials, wood pulp, and numerous other products.

▶ PEOPLE

Originally inhabited by Native Americans, Missouri attracted its first white settlers in the 1700's, but it was not until the Louisiana Purchase in 1803 that the population swelled. During the next several decades, the bulk of settlers came from Kentucky, Tennessee, and Virginia. Many brought slaves, which greatly increased Missouri's African American population. The French had introduced slaves into the region as early as 1720 to work in the lead mines. One hundred years later, African Americans made up about one-sixth of Missouri's population.

Missouri attracted settlers from the northern states as well as immigrants from Ireland, Poland, England, and most of all Germany. By 1860, more than one-third of the population of St. Louis had been born in Germany. After the Civil War, large numbers of Italians, Russians, and European Jews settled in Kansas City and St. Louis.

About 11 percent of Missouri's current residents are African Americans, most of whom live in metropolitan areas. Kansas City has a significant Hispanic population. In recent years, immigrants from Latin America, Southeast Asia, India, and other countries

Sportfishing is extremely popular in Missouri, particularly in the Ozark region. White bass are among the many types of fish found in the state's numerous lakes and rivers.

have increased Missouri's cultural diversity. Few Native Americans remain in the state.

Education

Missouri claims several firsts in education. St. Louis University, which began as an academy in 1818, is the nation's oldest university west of the Mississippi River. The University of Missouri, which received its charter in 1839, was the first state university founded west of the Mississippi River. The first public kindergarten was opened in St. Louis in 1873, and the first school of journalism was founded as a part of the University of Missouri in 1908.

Missouri established a public school system in 1839, although private schools had functioned as early as 1774. The state organized districts in 1874 and in fact ran two separate school systems for black and white children until the 1954 U.S. Supreme Court case *Brown* v. *Board of Education of Topeka* (Kansas) struck down racial segregation. Private institutions include many church-sup-

Right: Among the many interesting sights at the Harry S. Truman Library is the mural *Independence and the Opening of the West*, painted by the famous Missouri artist Thomas Hart Benton. *Below:* Parks and other recreation areas make city life more enjoyable for the seven out of ten Missourians who live in urban areas.

ported schools and three private military academies.

In the fifty years after the Civil War, the state created five regional campuses that became universities: Northeast Missouri State in Kirksville, Northwest Missouri State in Maryville, Southwest Missouri State in Springfield, Southeast Missouri State in Cape Girardeau, and Central Missouri State in Warrensburg. Lincoln University in Jefferson City was established in 1866 for African American students. The University of Missouri added a campus in Rolla to teach mining and engineering in 1871, and additional campuses opened in Kansas City and St. Louis in 1963. In the late 1960's, the legislature established four-year schools in Joplin and in St. Joseph. Students may also attend any of 15 community colleges.

Among Missouri's 25 private colleges and universities are St. Louis University and Washington University in St. Louis, Rockhurst College in Kansas City, Stephens College in Columbia, and Westminster College in Fulton. It was at Westminster that, in 1946, British prime minister Winston Churchill de-

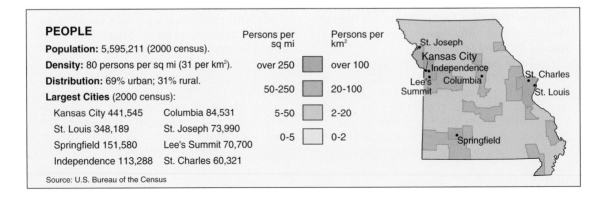

PEOPLE

Population: 5,595,211 (2000 census).

Density: 80 persons per sq mi (31 per km²).

Distribution: 69% urban; 31% rural.

Largest Cities (2000 census):

Kansas City 441,545	Columbia 84,531
St. Louis 348,189	St. Joseph 73,990
Springfield 151,580	Lee's Summit 70,700
Independence 113,288	St. Charles 60,321

Source: U.S. Bureau of the Census

Persons per sq mi	Persons per km²
over 250	over 100
50-250	20-100
5-50	2-20
0-5	0-2

St. Joseph
Kansas City
Independence
Lee's Summit
Columbia
St. Charles
St. Louis
Springfield

livered a famous speech in which he first referred to the political isolation of the Soviet Union and Eastern Europe as an "iron curtain." Today a Winston Churchill Memorial Library is housed on the campus.

Libraries, Museums, and the Arts

Missouri provides state and local tax support for more than one hundred public libraries. The largest of these is the St. Louis Public Library. The Pope Pius XII Memorial Library at St. Louis University contains important special collections, including a complete microfilm edition of the Vatican Library in Rome. The Linda Hall Library in Kansas City houses one of the best collections of science and technology material in the Midwest. The Kansas City Public Library and the Mercantile Library in St. Louis contain significant collections of regional and Western history materials. Two other important history libraries are the State Historical Society in Columbia and the Missouri Historical Society in St. Louis. Missouri's most famous library however, is the Harry S. Truman Library in Independence, containing the papers of the

The Kansas City Chiefs (in red) play in the Western Division of the American Conference of the National Football League. Home games are played in Kansas City's Arrowhead Stadium.

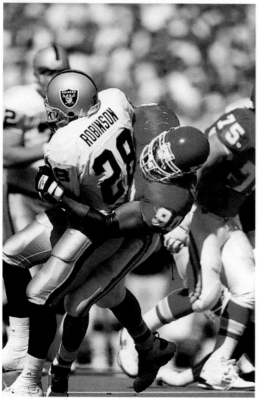

nation's 33rd president. For more information on Missouri's most notable art museums, performing arts centers, and historic sites, refer to the articles on St. Louis and Kansas City in volumes S and J-K, respectively.

Sports

Missouri's major league sports teams include the Kansas City Royals of baseball's American League and St. Louis Cardinals of the National League; the Kansas City Chiefs and St. Louis Rams of the National Football League; and the St. Louis Blues of the National Hockey League.

▶ ECONOMY

As in so many other states, Missouri's service industries employ the most people. Nearly 70 percent of all Missourians work in service industries. Agriculture, fishing, and forest industries employ 3 percent. Manufacturing and all other occupations employ the remaining 27 percent.

Services

Services account for more than 70 percent of the gross state product (GSP). Professional and personal services make up the largest segment, followed by wholesale and retail trade (the buying and selling of personal and industrial goods), financial services (such as banking, insurance, and real estate), transportation and utilities, and government. The people employed in these professions include teachers, lawyers, physicians, architects, custodians, salesclerks, waiters, maids, chefs, entertainers, police and firefighters, and the like. Many of these jobs are supported by Missouri's extensive tourist industry.

Manufacturing

Traditional industries associated with the processing of agricultural products, such as grain milling, meat packing, beer brewing, and wine making, employ many Missourians. Major chemical, electrical, and pharmaceutical companies are headquartered in St. Louis and Kansas City. Missouri is also a top producer of automobiles, with assembly plants for Chrysler, Ford, and General Motors located in Kansas City and St. Louis. In addition, St. Louis is headquarters to McDonnell-Douglas Corporation, one of the nation's largest aircraft defense contractors.

Left: Much of the jet fighter aircraft used by the U.S. military is manufactured in Missouri. *Below:* Hogs, raised in northern Missouri, are one of the state's most valuable farm products.

Agriculture

Cattle and hogs, raised primarily north of the Missouri River, account for more than 50 percent of Missouri's total farm income. They also consume much of the state's corn and hay. Dairy and poultry industries flourish in the Ozarks. Missourians also raise sheep, goats, and riding horses.

Soybeans and corn account for more than 65 percent of the state's total market value of crop sales. They are followed in importance by hay and cotton. Rice, tobacco, wheat, oats, grain sorghum, apples, peaches, grapes, melons, strawberries, walnuts, vegetables, seeds, and other products are also grown. The areas of highest productivity include the Missouri River valley and the Boot Heel counties.

Mining and Construction

Coal underlies about one-third of the state and is mined extensively. The mining of lead has been associated with the state since the

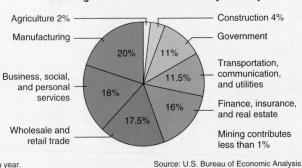

PRODUCTS AND INDUSTRIES

Manufacturing: Transportation equipment, processed foods, chemicals and chemical products, electric and electronic equipment, fabricated metal products, printed materials.

Agriculture: Cattle and calves, soybeans, hogs, corn, wheat, milk and cheese, grain sorghum, turkeys, eggs, cotton, broilers, rice.

Minerals: Lead, cement, iron, stone, coal, lime, marble, zinc, sand and gravel, copper, clays, silver, barite.

Services: Wholesale and retail trade; finance, insurance, and real estate; business, social, and personal services; transportation, communication, and utilities; government.

*Gross state product is the total value of goods and services produced in a year.

Percentage of Gross State Product* by Industry

Agriculture 2%
Manufacturing 20%
Business, social, and personal services 18%
Wholesale and retail trade 17.5%
Construction 4%
Government 11%
Transportation, communication, and utilities 11.5%
Finance, insurance, and real estate 16%
Mining contributes less than 1%

Source: U.S. Bureau of Economic Analysis

early 1700's. Missourians also produce zinc, shale, stone, fire clay for brick making, copper, iron ore, lime, sand and gravel, marble, barite, and silver. Missouri limestone is turned into cement in St. Louis and Kansas City. Silica sand is the basis for glass manufacturing in Crystal City. Marble from Carthage is used for construction in Missouri and in various parts of the world.

Transportation

The Missouri River carries barge traffic throughout much of the year. The Mississippi River, with its extensive system of locks and dams, provides cheap transportation to heavy cargoes in all except the coldest weather.

At one time, practically every town in Missouri had rail transportation with passenger service readily available. Freight hauling now creates most of the income for railroads, and the miles of track have been greatly reduced. Truck and automobile travel, enabled by an extensive and excellent road system, has either replaced or eroded the importance of the railroads. State efforts and the completion of the Interstate Highway System by the federal government created the comprehensive road system that Missouri enjoys. Major airports include Lambert Airport in St. Louis and Mid-Continent International Airport in Kansas City. Regional airports serve Springfield, St. Joseph, Joplin, and Columbia.

Communication

More than two hundred radio stations and more than twenty television stations operate in Missouri. Cable television is available throughout most of the state. Of the many newspapers published in Missouri, two command the most readership. The *St. Louis Post-Dispatch*, founded by Joseph Pulitzer in 1878, has a national reputation for excellence in reporting. *The Kansas City Star*, founded by William Rockhill Nelson in 1880, has a loyal readership throughout western Missouri. Daily papers are also published in St. Joseph, Springfield, Joplin, Independence, and Rolla, and more than three hundred communities publish weeklies.

▶ CITIES

More than 60 percent of Missourians live in the metropolitan areas of the state's two largest cities, Kansas City and St. Louis. The

Kansas City is the largest city in Missouri. Because of its central location in the United States, it has been called the Heart of America. It is also known as the City of Fountains.

people who live in these cities commonly refer to the rest of Missouri as "Outstate."

Jefferson City, the state capital since 1826, was named for Thomas Jefferson, the U.S. president who purchased the Louisiana Territory in 1803. Government is its chief industry, although the city also serves as a trade center for surrounding farmers. Jefferson City is the home of Lincoln University. It is also the location of the state penitentiary.

Kansas City, Missouri's largest city, is a significant commercial, educational, and transportation center. An article on Kansas City appears in Volume J-K.

St. Louis, the state's second largest city but largest metropolitan area, is one of the major cities of the Midwest. An article on St. Louis appears in Volume S.

Springfield, known as the Queen City of the Ozarks, is Missouri's third largest city and one of its fastest growing regions. It was first settled in 1829. The local economy is based on light manufacturing, food processing, livestock, and dairy products. Springfield is the home of Southwest Missouri State University,

Missouri's state capitol building in Jefferson City houses the executive and legislative branches of the state's government. Beautiful murals decorate its walls, and a museum occupies much of the first floor.

Drury College, and Evangel College. It is also the headquarters for Assemblies of God churches.

Independence, the state's fourth largest city, was settled in 1827. It later served as the starting point for western travelers following the Oregon and Santa Fe trails. Independence has oil refineries and manufactures chemicals and farm machinery. It is the world headquarters for the Reorganized Church of Jesus Christ of Latter Day Saints and is also the site of the Harry S. Truman library, museum, and home.

▶ **GOVERNMENT**

Missouri's original constitution of 1820 has been rewritten three times, in 1865, 1875, and

---

INDEX TO MISSOURI MAP

● County Seat   Counties in parentheses   ★ State Capital

GOVERNMENT

State Government
Governor: 4-year term
State senators: 34; 4-year terms
State representatives: 163;
2-year terms
Number of counties: 114 plus
1 independent city (St. Louis)

Federal Government
U.S. senators: 2
U.S. representatives: 9
Number of electoral votes: 11

For the name of the current governor, see STATE GOVERNMENTS in Volume S. For the names of current U.S. senators and representatives, see UNITED STATES, CONGRESS OF THE in Volume U-V.

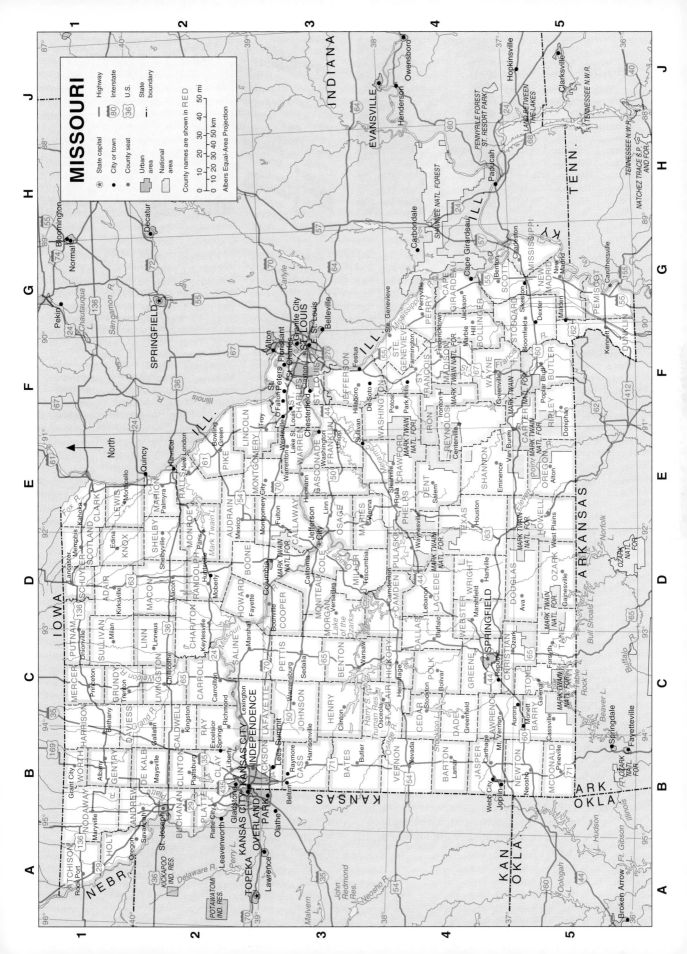

MISSOURI

Legend	
⊛	State capital
●	City or town
⊛	County seat
	Urban area
	National area

Highway	
80	Interstate
36	U.S.
	State boundary

County names are shown in RED

Albers Equal-Area Projection

0 10 20 30 40 50 km
0 10 20 30 40 50 mi

North

Famous People

Consult the Index to find more information in *The New Book of Knowledge* about the following native Missourians: the slave Dred Scott (1795?–1858); poets and writers Mark Twain (1835–1910), Eugene Field (1850–95), T. S. Eliot (1888–1965), Langston Hughes (1902–67), and Maya Angelou (1928–); outlaw Jesse James (1847–82); frontierswoman Calamity Jane (1852–1903); World War I commander John J. Pershing (1860–1948); scientist George Washington Carver (1864– 1943); President Harry S. Truman (1884–1972); artists Charles Marion Russell (1864–1926) and Thomas Hart Benton (1889–1975); civil rights leader Roy Wilkins (1901–81); film director John Huston (1906–87); and journalist Walter Cronkite (1916–).

Josephine Baker (1906–75) , born in St. Louis, rose from poverty to become an international star. In 1924 she was featured on Broadway in *The Chocolate Dandies*, and the following year she caused a sensation starring in

Harry S. Truman

Mark Twain

Jesse James

La Revue Nègre at the Folies-Bergère musical revue in Paris wearing only a string of bananas. She later starred in a number of European films. In the late 1930's, she became a spy for the French government in Fascist-controlled Italy. When France fell to the Nazis during World War II, Baker moved to North Africa and fought in the Free French Army. After the war, she devoted herself to raising her "rainbow tribe," a group of children of all races that she adopted. In 1951, she returned to the United States, where she protested racism by appearing only before integrated audiences.

Lawrence Peter (Yogi) Berra (1925–), born in St. Louis, was a baseball star. He played catcher for the New York Yankees (1946–63) and was chosen to play in the All-Star game 14 times. He was the American League's Most Valuable Player in 1951, 1954, and 1955. Berra managed the Yankees in 1964, then was coach (1965–72) and manager (1972–75) of the New York Mets. He later rejoined the Yankees as coach (1976–83) and manager (1984 and part of 1985), finishing his career as coach of the Houston Astros (1986). Berra was inducted into the Baseball Hall of Fame in 1972.

1945. All provided for a government composed of three branches—executive, legislative, and judicial.

The governor heads the executive branch and is elected to a 4-year term along with a lieutenant governor, auditor, secretary of state, treasurer, and attorney general. The governor may be re-elected to no more than one additional term.

The legislative branch, called the General Assembly, is composed of a house of representatives and a senate. All members of the house must stand for election every two years. State senators serve 4-year terms. Members of both bodies represent districts whose boundaries are based on population. The General Assembly meets annually.

The judicial branch is headed by a seven-member supreme court. Three courts of appeal are located in St. Louis, Kansas City, and Springfield. Forty-five circuit courts and municipal courts for cities of more than 40,000 residents complete the state system. Smaller communities may have municipal and probate courts as well, but they are administered at the local level.

▶ HISTORY

Missouri's rich history dates back many thousands of years. As early as 100 B.C., prosperous Native Americans, known as the Hopewell, inhabited major river sites in the Midwest and traded goods with other native cultures from Canada to Florida. Often today the Hopewell and their successors, the Mississippians, are referred to as the Mound Builders for the huge earthen burial mounds they left behind. For more information, see the article INDIANS, AMERICAN (Empires and Other Extended Groups) and (The Late Prehistoric Period) in Volume I.

If the state had been named after the Native Americans who most influenced the region's early history, it would be called Osage instead of Missouri. The Osage were the largest Indian group living in what is now Missouri when European explorers first discovered the region. Smaller groups included the Sauk, Mesquakie (Fox), and Shawnee. By the end of the 1830's, none of these groups remained. They had been compelled to give up their lands to the white settlers and were pushed west into Kansas and Oklahoma.

Omar Nelson Bradley (1893–1981), born in Clark, was one of the greatest military commanders of World War II. In 1915 he graduated from the U.S. Military Academy at West Point, in the same class as Dwight D. Eisenhower. During the war, as battlefield commander of the Second Army Corps, he participated in the invasion of North Africa and played an important role in the victory in Tunisia in May 1943 as well as in the capture of Sicily the following August. He helped plan the D-Day invasion of Normandy (June 6, 1944), and on August 25 his forces liberated Paris from Nazi occupation. He then took command of the Twelfth Army Group, leading 1 million ground forces until Germany was defeated in May 1945. After the war, he served as head of the Veterans Administration (1945–47), as Army Chief of Staff (1948–49), and as the first chairman of the Joint Chiefs of Staff (1949–53). A five-star general, Bradley supported President Truman's decision to remove General Douglas MacArthur as supreme Allied commander during the Korean War.

Dale Carnegie (1888–1955), born in Maryville, was an author, lecturer, and pioneer in the field of teaching public speaking. He later broadened his courses to instruct people how to be more successful in all aspects of their lives. One of his books, *How to Win Friends and Influence People* (1936), became one of the most popular books of all time. It sold more than 10 million copies and was translated into more than 30 languages. Carnegie also wrote *How to Stop Worrying and Start Living* (1948).

Helen Stephens (1918–94), born in Fulton, became known as the Fulton Flash. A track-and-field star, Stephens won two gold medals in the 1936 Olympics for the 100-meter dash and 400-meter relay. Between

Josephine Baker

1935 and 1937, she ran in 70 matches and never lost one. She also set records throwing the javelin.

Sara Teasdale (1884–1933), born in St. Louis, was one of the most acclaimed American poets of her generation. Her work is generally marked by great simplicity, clarity, and a recurring sense of loss. Her *Love Songs* (1917) won the 1918 Columbia University Poetry Society Prize, the forerunner of the Pulitzer Prize. Although ill throughout most of the 1920's, she still produced excellent poetry, including *Flame and Shadow* (1920), *Dark of the Moon* (1926), and *Strange Victory* (1933) until her death by suicide.

Exploration and Settlement

French explorers, fur traders, and settlers made the first European impact on Missouri. In 1673, explorers Father Jacques Marquette and Louis Jolliet sailed down the Mississippi River and became the first known Europeans to reach the mouth of the Missouri River. In 1682, another French explorer, the nobleman Robert Cavelier, Sieur de La Salle, claimed the entire region for France. For many years the French hunted fur-bearing animals and mined lead in Missouri, but it was not until 1750 that they established the first permanent settlement at Ste. Genevieve.

Then in 1756, the Seven Years' War erupted between England and France and other European powers. In 1762, when the French realized they would lose the war, they ceded to Spain French lands west of the Mississippi River in order to deny the prize to England. Spain officially controlled the area until 1800, when international matters caused it to cede the region back to France.

In 1803, the United States purchased the Louisiana Territory from France, and Missouri became part of the United States. In 1804, President Thomas Jefferson dispatched Meriwether Lewis and William Clark to investigate the enormous new territory. Upon their return in 1806, Lewis and Clark brought news of abundant furs on the upper Missouri River. The trade in furs provided income to many Missourians well into the 1820's.

Territorial Period and Statehood

During the territorial period (1805–21), settlers flocked into Missouri from many parts of the United States, despite a series of earthquakes that hit the New Madrid region in southeastern Missouri in 1811, which scientists now rank among the strongest ever to hit the United States.

By 1819 the fur trade, lead mining, agriculture, and commerce had attracted about 50,000 settlers to Missouri, and in that year, the first bill for statehood was introduced into the U.S. House of Representatives. But statehood was delayed by Congress due to a major debate that was raging over the practice of slavery in Missouri. To keep an equal balance of slave and free states, Congress finally approved what was called the Missouri

Raftsmen Playing Cards, by Missouri artist George Caleb Bingham, shows boatmen passing the time on the Mississippi River in the mid-1800's.

Compromise, allowing Maine to come into the Union as a free state and Missouri to enter as a slave state. Missouri became the 24th state on August 10, 1821. (For more information, see the article on the Missouri Compromise that follows this article.) In autumn of that year, the Santa Fe Trail was established, opening up an important overland trade route between Missouri and the southwestern regions.

Early Politics

Missouri Democrats, led by U.S. senator Thomas Hart Benton, controlled state politics during most of the period before the Civil War. But in the 1850's, the party was split in opinion concerning whether or not slavery should be allowed in new U.S. territories. This political division ended Senator Benton's career and reflected the nation's crisis in its failure to resolve the conflict over slavery. Bloodshed in Kansas between Missouri proslavery forces and Northern "freesoilers" from 1856 to 1858 foreshadowed the civil war that was soon to come. Antislavery forces were further inflamed when in 1857 the U.S. Supreme Court ruled against Dred Scott, a Missouri slave who tried to claim his freedom, and declared that blacks had no rights as citizens in their own homeland.

Civil War (1861–65)

Missourians remained divided during the Civil War. The state officially remained in the Union, but it also sent representatives to the congress of the new government of the Confederate States of America. About 110,000 Missourians fought for the Union, while about 40,000 joined the Confederate forces. Some of the fiercest fighting of the war took place in Missouri. Only Virginia and Tennessee had more battles and skirmishes.

The Outlaw State

During the war, a band of Confederate guerrilla fighters known as Quantrill's Raiders terrorized Union supporters in Kansas and Missouri. Although the rebel leader William Quantrill was killed before the war ended, his comrades, including Frank and Jesse James, continued their terrorist ways after the war, robbing banks and trains and killing people. Missouri became so associated with renegade violence that it became known as the Outlaw State.

Growth and Development

In the fifty years after the Civil War, railroads replaced steamboats as the most important means of transporting goods. In the 1900's, Missouri developed its highway system, diversified its farming, and encouraged the growth of industry. Manufacturing began to rival agriculture in economic importance. By 1900, the population of Kansas City had grown to more than 150,000, while St. Louis exceeded 500,000. By 1910 more than 40 percent of Missouri's population lived in cities.

Missouri's advantages—a central location, abundant water supplies, low energy costs, productive agricultural land, a growing service economy, and a low rate of taxation—continue to make it a pleasant place to live.

LAWRENCE O. CHRISTENSEN
University of Missouri, Rolla

See also KANSAS CITY; SAINT LOUIS.

MISSOURI COMPROMISE

Before the issue of slavery finally brought the United States to civil war, there were many attempts at compromise between the North and the South. One of the most important of these attempts was the Missouri Compromise of 1820.

In 1819 Missouri applied for admission to the Union. The question of whether it should be admitted as a slave state stirred up the conflict between those who were for slavery and those who were against it. Many Northerners were against slavery because they thought it morally wrong or economically unfair. Southern planters had already taken their slaves into the Missouri Territory and naturally wanted slavery to be permitted there.

Slave and free states were evenly balanced at the time—eleven of each. Therefore each side had the same number of senators. A new slave state would upset the balance and give people who favored slavery control of the United States Senate.

In February of 1819 Representative James Tallmadge (1778–1853) of New York introduced a resolution in Congress proposing that no more slaves be brought into Missouri after it became a state and that children of slaves born after the admission of the state be freed at the age of 25.

Southerners were outraged. Northerners greeted the proposal with enthusiasm, holding mass meetings and signing petitions of support. On February 16 and 17, 1819, the resolution passed in the House of Representatives. But the Senate rejected it. Soon afterward Congress adjourned. The debate raged furiously all over the land.

When Congress met in December, Missouri again asked for statehood. Meanwhile Maine, at that time part of Massachusetts, also asked admission as a separate state. The Senate voted to combine the resolutions, admitting Maine as a free state and Missouri as a slave state. The number of slave and free states would then still be even—twelve each.

Then in February 1820, Senator Jesse Burgess Thomas (1777–1853) of Illinois proposed an amendment to the combined resolutions: Admit Missouri as a slave state, but ban slavery in the future from all territory north of 36° 30′ north latitude, Missouri's southern border.

Slave states were already separated from free states by the Mason-Dixon line (the southern boundary of Pennsylvania) and the Ohio River. The new requirement would extend the dividing line westward. If Missouri were admitted as a slave state, it would be the only slave area north of the line.

This proposal angered Southerners. They claimed that all states had equal rights and that Congress had no power to limit the right of a state to decide whether to be slave or free. For months the question of states' rights was debated bitterly in Congress. Thomas Jefferson called the debate "a fire bell in the night" because it appeared to be a warning of great trouble.

The Thomas Amendment passed in the Senate but was rejected in the House. On March 1, 1820, the House voted to admit Missouri as a free state. But in the compromise that both houses of Congress finally accepted, Maine was admitted as a free state (March 1820), and Missouri was authorized to form a state constitution without restrictions on slavery. The Compromise also banned slavery north of 36° 30′. The South won Missouri, but it lost more than it gained. The area north of the dividing line, where slavery was banned "forever," was larger than the area where slavery would be allowed.

The state constitution Missouri presented to Congress was not approved. According to this constitution freed slaves could not enter Missouri. The "Great Compromiser," Henry Clay, then helped work out a second compromise, which stated that Missouri could not deny free black citizens their constitutional rights. Missouri accepted this and became a state in August 1821.

In 1854 the Missouri Compromise was repealed by the Kansas-Nebraska Act. By the terms of this law slavery would not be banned in new states north of 36° 30′. Each entering state had the right of popular sovereignty. This meant that these states could decide for themselves whether to be slave or free. The change further divided North and South and led to fighting in Kansas. The repeal of the Missouri Compromise is one of the events that led to the Civil War.

Reviewed by RICHARD B. MORRIS
Columbia University

See also KANSAS-NEBRASKA ACT.

MISSOURI RIVER

The Missouri River is the longest river in the United States and one of the nation's greatest natural resources. From its headwaters in southwestern Montana, the Missouri flows about 2,466 miles (3,968 kilometers) through a basin of 529,000 square miles (1,370 square kilometers). Including its longest tributaries, it flows 2,683 miles (4,317 kilometers). As it cuts through mountains and prairies, the Missouri gathers huge quantities of sand and silt, earning its nickname the Big Muddy.

The Missouri River drains parts of ten states and two Canadian provinces before discharging 69,000 cubic feet (1,954 cubic meters) of water per second into the Mississippi River, just north of St. Louis. The Missouri's major tributaries include the Yellowstone, Milk, White, Cheyenne, and Platte rivers.

Many Native American tribes inhabited the regions surrounding the Missouri River before the French explorers Father Jacques Marquette and Louis Jolliet discovered the mouth of the river while exploring the Mississippi River in 1673. American explorers Meriwether Lewis and William Clark used the Missouri as a highway to the West while exploring (1804–06) the Louisiana Purchase. After 1814, Army forts and Indian trading posts appeared as far as northern Montana.

Before the Civil War (1861–65), steamboats fostered economic development along the river. Several prosperous cities grew up along its banks, including Kansas City, Council Bluffs, Omaha, Pierre, and Bismarck. Railroads later reduced river traffic but the river remained an important artery of trade and transportation.

In the 1900's, many projects were sponsored by the federal and state governments to control flooding, provide reservoirs, and improve navigation on the river. Yet in spite of all that has been done, disastrous floods occur periodically. One of the worst floods in American history happened in the spring and summer of 1993. Persistent rainfall caused the Missouri and Mississippi rivers to overflow their banks, bursting dams and levees. This disaster affected nine states, drove some 70,000 people from their homes, and caused billions of dollars in damage.

Reviewed by CHARLES T. JONES, JR.
William Woods University

MITCHELL, JOHN N. See WATERGATE (Profiles).
MITCHELL, MARIA. See ASTRONOMY (Profiles).
MITES. See ARACHNIDS

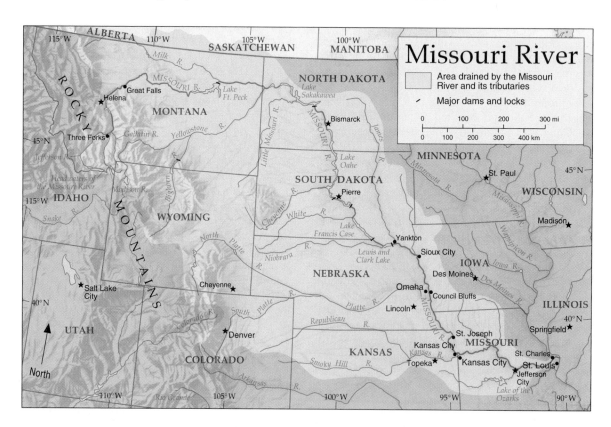

MITTERRAND, FRANÇOIS (1916–1996)

François Maurice Marie Mitterrand was president of France from 1981 to 1995. Born on October 26, 1916, in Jarnac in western France, he studied law and political science at the University of Paris, graduating in 1938. He served in the army in World War II, was wounded and captured by the Germans, and spent some 18 months as a prisoner of war. In 1944 he married Danielle Gouze.

Mitterrand's postwar political career began with his election to the National Assembly in 1946, and over the next twelve years, he held numerous cabinet posts. A critic of Charles de Gaulle, he ran unsuccessfully for president against him in 1965. Named head of the Socialist Party in 1971, Mitterrand made a second attempt at the presidency in 1974 but was defeated by Valéry Giscard d'Estaing. In a second contest against Giscard, however, in 1981, he won election.

Mitterrand's extensive program included the nationalization of large banks and corporations, increased taxation and spending on social services, and decentralization of the government administration. Eventually, however, he was forced to curtail all but the last of these. Mitterrand won re-election in 1988, defeating Jacques Chirac, a Gaullist. But losses by the Socialists in 1993 parliamentary elections compelled him to appoint a conservative, Edouard Balladur, as premier (prime minister). During this period, Mitterrand was limited in his influence over domestic policy, but he nevertheless maintained a strong presence in foreign affairs.

Mitterrand had earlier been diagnosed with incurable cancer. He cooperated with the author of a book on his early life, *A French Youth*, which answered questions about his activities during the war. But he remained aloof from the 1995 presidential election, won by Jacques Chirac. Mitterrand died on January 8, 1996. His most lasting contribution to France will probably be his monument building. These include the renovation of the Louvre, the great art museum; the glittering new opera house at the Bastille; and the new National Library on the banks of the Seine.

DONALD J. HARVEY
City University of New York, Hunter College
Author, *France Since the Revolution*

MOBILE. See ALABAMA (Cities).

MOBUTU SESE SEKO (1930–1997)

Mobutu Sese Seko was president of Zaïre (now the Democratic Republic of Congo) from 1965 to 1997. Originally viewed as a leader who would bring unity to a rich but divided land, Mobuto's dictatorial policies fueled his nation's virtual collapse.

He was born Joseph Désiré Mobutu (he later Africanized his name) on October 14, 1930, in Lisala, in what was then the Belgian Congo. He attended Catholic mission schools and then joined the colonial army, where he quickly rose to sergeant major, the highest rank open to Africans. When the Congo won independence in 1960, Mobutu became one of the highest-ranking officers in the army. During the disorder that accompanied independence, he was implicated in the murder of Prime Minister Patrice Lumumba and seized power, which he relinquished in 1961.

The new government was extremely unstable. In 1965, Mobutu seized power again and reorganized the government to provide for a strong central authority. In 1971 he changed the country's name to Zaïre. In 1973, Mobutu nationalized all foreign companies, turning them over to his friends. His regime became increasingly unpopular, but he skillfully eliminated his enemies. On May 16, 1997, the ailing Mobutu fled as rebel forces advanced on the capital. Rebel leader Laurent Kabila was sworn in as president on May 29. Mobutu died in exile on September 7.

BRUCE FETTER
University of Wisconsin, Milwaukee

MODELING, FASHION

Fashion modeling is big business wherever fashion and advertising exist. Although there are many men and children who are successful models, the vast majority of fashion models are young women who range in age from the teens to the mid-thirties.

A fashion model usually lives and works in a great fashion center, such as Paris, Milan, New York, Tokyo, or Munich. There she may show collections of clothes by famous designers. Or she may be a photographic model whose face smiles at you from the pages of a magazine. She may even lend charm and grace to commercials on national television. Models are usually chosen for their elegance, beauty, and grace. Models are also expressive, animated, and project an image of energy. They set styles of beauty for many women, who copy their makeup, hairdos, and clothes.

Modeling sounds glamorous, but it is really very hard work. To make a picture for a magazine cover, the model may have to stand for hours, holding a difficult pose under strobe lights. The showroom model may be on her feet all day, making hurried changes of clothing in a cramped dressing room. The television model may have to go through many hours of tedious ''takes.''

A model needs a great deal of patience and stamina. But models who reach the top of their profession make a great deal of money and wear some of the world's most beautiful clothes. They work with great photographers and dress designers. Their assignments can take them all over the world.

Not everyone can be a model. There are stringent physical requirements. Most models are tall and slim and have broad shoulders, long legs, and slender waists. Photographers' models must also have beautiful faces that photograph well. Recently, however, there has been a trend toward using models who look like ''real people.''

Generally, models must look fresh and young, so their careers are often over by the time they reach their early- to mid-thirties. However, the advertising media have begun to use more mature models in recent years. Many models go on to acting, dress designing, or editorial work on fashion magazines when their active modeling days are over.

Photographic Modeling. Photographers' models pose for department-store catalogs, newspaper advertisements, and the great fashion magazines, such as *Vogue* and *Harper's Bazaar*. A cover on one of these magazines is a prize assignment and means that the model has reached the top of her profession. Many models also appear in the prestige designer fashion shows, which have become showcases for their introduction to editors and advertising directors who ultimately may hire them.

The requirements for photographic modeling are the hardest to meet. Because the camera makes people seem heavier than they are, the models must be trim. Female models must be a minimum of 5 feet 7 inches tall, although heights of 5 feet 8 inches to 5 feet 11 inches are more desirable. Male models are usually over 6 feet tall and may range up to 6 feet 3 inches. In the late 1970's the earnings of male models began to equal that of women, and there are now many more men's fashions and products than ever before.

Photographers' models must also have faces that photograph well. Women often have angular faces with large eyes, hollowed cheeks, and prominent cheek bones.

A photographers' model must learn to stand for hours in a difficult pose. Since magazines plan their issues many months in advance, she may have to pose in a bathing suit in December or wrap up in furs on a sweltering day in July. She must be an expert with makeup and hair styles—and a bit of an actress too. She may be asked to pose as a college girl in one picture and as a society matron in the next. She must know how to change her hair and makeup so that she will feel, act, and look the part.

Top-level models customarily work exclusively through one representative office, or agency, that guides their careers and establishes and negotiates their fees. Such representatives collect from 15 to 20 percent of a model's income as commission.

Showroom Modeling. In fashion houses and some exclusive shops, clothes are shown to customers by showroom models instead of being displayed on racks. In wholesale houses, too, where large quantities of clothing are sold, models wear sample garments from which buyers make their selections.

Some showroom models are hired by a fashion house and work only for that house.

The designers make their clothes on the models, called "fitting models," and often plan clothing with a favorite model in mind. Other models free-lance, through agencies. These models are hired for special showings and are paid by the hour or the day.

The job of the showroom model is to show off the garments at their best. The model must learn to walk gracefully. Graceful movement is more important than classic beauty or a lovely face. Showroom models are usually tall and slender and wear a size 7 to 12 dress.

Television Modeling. Many fashion and photographers' models take classes that will help make them competent for television modeling. There are several different types of television models. Many models appear as background models for TV commercials or, possibly, TV game shows. Some have learned to combine beauty and acting talent for scenes in TV commercials. Others exhibit cosmetics or other products while describing them and urging consumers to use them. Sometimes one model becomes the major spokesperson for a particular product or product line.

Trade Show Modeling. Also referred to as industrial shows, trade shows exhibit merchandise, such as computers, automobiles, or boats, to dealers and the general public. Since the products are exhibited with great fanfare, models are often used to enhance the look of the product and explain its uses. For this type of modeling, height and perfection of features are secondary to personality, general appeal, and a clear speaking voice. A trade show model is usually provided with a brief familiarization of the exhibitor's product or service and is then expected to distribute literature about the product and answer simple questions.

Child Models. Photogenic children are sometimes hired for magazine and television advertisements. Child models range in age from 3 months to 14 years (when they usually become junior models). They are hired through agencies in the same way adult models are hired. Some child models continue their careers into adulthood. Many make the transition from photographic models to TV commercials, TV series, and films.

Model Agencies

Model agencies conduct business transactions for models. They perform such duties as

Posing for photographs may look glamorous, but it is hard work. Models must be able to hold difficult poses for hours under hot studio lights.

arranging test photos, assisting with makeup and grooming, arranging portfolios (groups of pictures of the model), and introducing models to photographers, designers, and other clients. Agencies will also negotiate fees, bill for payment, and advance payment to models before receiving the fees from clients. Agencies collect a percentage of a model's earnings as commission.

Becoming a Model

A person who wishes to become a model must have the required height and photogenic qualities. If such qualities are present, gracefulness of movement, grooming and makeup techniques, and good speaking characteristics can be acquired.

Most reputable agencies will provide a free evaluation of one's potential for modeling, if given a few snapshots, hair and eye color, weight and height measurements, some garment sizes, and age. A model hopeful should not pay for such an evaluation, nor should money be spent on professional photographs, unless a commitment to represent has been made by an agent.

Every field of modeling is highly competitive. Only one person in a hundred can be a successful model. But the lucky few win high pay, independence, and the chance to work in almost every great city in the world.

G. W. FORD
Ford Model Agency

Reviewed and updated by WILLIAM P. WEINBERG
President, Wilhelmina International Ltd.

MODELMAKING. See AIRPLANE MODELS; AUTOMOBILE MODELS; RAILROADS, MODEL; SHIP MODELS.

Impression: Sunrise (1872), by Claude Monet. Musée Marmottan, Paris.

MODERN ART

It is impossible to say exactly when and where modern art began. The history of art is like a chain to which new links are always being added. Every link is attached to the link before it. For example, the many different styles of the 20th century are outgrowths of the styles used during the 19th century. In turn, 19th-century art developed from the styles of the previous century. If we were to trace the origins of modern art as far back as possible, we would find that it really began with the very first link in the chain—the rock scratchings of cavemen.

▶ REALISM

During the first half of the 19th century the artists of France—then the world's center of artistic activity—began to look for new ways to paint. The French Revolution was over, and the Industrial Revolution was under way. Many artists felt that the formal, classical pictures of such artists as Jacques Louis David (1748–1825) no longer expressed the spirit of the times. These young artists preferred the work of Théodore Géricault (1791–1824) and Eugène Delacroix (1798–1863), who were known as **romantics**. The romantics painted dramatic pictures filled with bright, sometimes raw colors. The painters who admired romanticism thought that this informality and passion better expressed an age in which freedom and individuality had become very important.

Gustave Courbet (1819–77), a Frenchman, said that the aim of painting was to set down without change what was seen by the human eye. He called himself a **realist**. Other artists who claimed to be searching for realism were puzzled by Courbet's statement, for the newly invented camera reproduced exactly what was seen by the eye. Was there no difference between a photograph and a painting? For an answer to that question, some French artists looked to the work of an Englishman, J. M. W. Turner (1775–1851). Turner sacrificed details in order to capture atmosphere. He felt that mist, fog, and light were as real in a scene as trees and water. Nature is ever changing, and Turner tried to suggest the changes that occur from hour to hour and season to season.

Around the middle of the century there were several groups and individual artists who were attempting to develop a realistic style. The painters of the French Barbizon school —so called because they worked in the town of Barbizon, south of Paris—went outdoors to paint. They hoped to capture the qualities of nature that were momentary, fleeting, and very real. In this they differed from Courbet, who painted pictures of peasants at work or relaxing. Courbet thought that paintings of day-to-day activities represented a peak of realism. Édouard Manet (1832–83) combined the ideas of Courbet and the Barbizon painters. He liked to depict the quality of a single moment, and his subject matter was often commonplace.

▶ IMPRESSIONISM

On April 15, 1874, a group of Paris artists opened an exhibition of 165 paintings. During the month-long show visitors crowded the gallery, but their opinion of the work was low. The most common reaction was laughter. One critic wrote a humorous article called "Exhibition of the Impressionists." This name, taken from Claude Monet's painting *Impression: Sunrise,* was meant to be sarcastic. Apparently the artists had no objection to it and began calling themselves impressionists.

Most of the impressionists were mature artists. Their exhibition had not been meant to startle or shock. Instead, its purpose was to display the kind of work that had been rejected from official exhibitions for years. The impressionists, after all, had been developing their approach for a long time. Painters like Camille Pissarro (1830–1903) and Claude Monet (1840–1926) had been experimenting with many techniques since before 1860.

Objects themselves were of little importance to the impressionists. The play of light over a surface, the discovery of hidden colors in shadows—these became the subject matter of impressionist paintings. The impressionists studied scientific color theory and tried to apply what they learned to their painting. If an object was supposed to be purple, they did not mix blue and red paint on their palette and then apply the paint to the canvas. Instead they painted the object with many small dabs of blue and red. The eye of the viewer mixed the color, making it appear purple.

Impressionism was not so "scientific" as the impressionists said it was. A painter named Georges Seurat (1859–91) invented a technique called **pointillism**. Seurat's canvases were painted entirely with tiny dots of colors, premixed according to formula. But most of the impressionists did not wish to paint according to formula. Thus, the works of the impressionists bear individual differences.

Rodin

Impressionism is a kind of painting, but the sculptor Auguste Rodin (1840–1917) is sometimes called an impressionist. Like the painters, he wanted to create surfaces that seemed alive. He accomplished this by modeling his surfaces with many distinct little planes. The planes catch and reflect light and make the surface almost appear to breathe.

Monument to Balzac (1897), by Rodin. Museum of Modern Art, New York.

Rodin was also interested in the space that his sculpture occupied. If a figure had its hands placed on its hips, the triangle of space between the arms and the body was, to him, as important a shape as the arms themselves.

Compared to painting, sculpture had been of little importance after the 17th century. It almost always had represented the human form in a classical manner. Soldiers and statesmen were shown in statues to look like Greek gods. Rodin gave new life to the nearly dead art. Trained in the academic tradition, he modeled naturalistic and dramatic figures. His talent was great and his influence strong. Though his work hardly looks revolutionary today, he revived the art of sculpture.

▶ **POSTIMPRESSIONISM**

Although he was not an impressionist, Edgar Degas (1834–1917) was close to the group and took much from its style. Degas was a collector of Japanese prints. From these prints he learned a great deal about spacious compositions and sharp contrasts of simple shapes. Unlike the impressionists, he used black paint and drew hard edges. But his dancing colors were similar to those used by the impressionists.

Paul Gauguin (1848–1903) was influenced by impressionism and by the work of Degas. But he was not interested in a scientific formula of light. Gauguin liked the flat pattern effects suggested in the work of Degas. He simplified the human figure, treating it as part of an over-all pattern.

Vincent van Gogh (1853–90) loved the effects of shimmering light achieved by the impressionists. He concentrated on this effect, applying paint thickly, in large dabs, making his colors appear to swirl around or explode. The subject matter of his paintings seems to be light alone—its movement and its power.

Gauguin and Van Gogh, along with Seurat and sometimes Degas, are often included in a group called postimpressionists. This term has little meaning because the styles of these painters vary greatly. It does, however, indicate that their styles developed after the impressionists'.

▶ **PAUL CÉZANNE**

Paul Cézanne (1839–1906) was about the same age as most of the impressionists. But in a discussion of art history Cézanne is always mentioned after the impressionists and after Gauguin, Van Gogh, and Seurat. Although he lived only until 1906, he is regarded as the first 20th-century artist.

Cézanne was impatient with impressionism. He thought that the impressionists had created a veil of pleasing color across the canvas without describing the solid forms of nature. In his paintings he tried to show that natural objects had structure and weight—that they were made of more than atmosphere. A landscape, a human body, and a basket of fruit were solid and real to Cézanne, and he was interested in their every surface, or plane.

In most of Cézanne's pictures there is little suggestion of depth. A tree in the foreground and a mountain in the background appear to be the same distance from the viewer's eye. He divided his objects into planes. A face, for example, would be painted according to its separate surfaces, with a different plane for the forehead, the cheeks, the nose, the chin, and so forth. Cézanne would make the face look solid by varying the amount of light that struck each plane and by varying his shading or brushstroke on each plane.

Cézanne was never fully appreciated when he was alive. He was not an impressionist (though many of his friends were). He desired public recognition, but he died feeling that he had failed. In 1907, a year after his death, a memorial exhibition of his work was held in Paris. Its effect was startling, as we shall see.

▶ **FAUVISM**

For the Autumn Salon of 1905—the official exhibition of the French Academy of Art—the Academy jury accepted the works of five painters whose styles had certain things in common. Henri Matisse (1869–1954), André Derain (1880–1954), Albert Marquet (1875–1947), Georges Rouault (1871–1958), and Maurice de Vlaminck (1876–1958) painted with bright, rich colors. Their pictures contained only the barest suggestion that they depicted natural scenes. Colors were pure and flat. Very little shading was employed.

The Academy decided to display the pictures of the five artists in one room, apart from the rest of the Salon. One critic, after

Above left: *Rocky Landscape* (1898?), by Cézanne. Right: *Sunflowers* (1888), by Van Gogh. Both pictures are in the National Gallery, London. Below: *The Red Studio* (1911), by Matisse. Museum of Modern Art, New York.

visiting the exhibition, called the five painters *fauves* ("wild beasts").

The fauves learned about color theories from the impressionists. From Van Gogh and Gauguin they learned to use color boldly. From Cézanne they learned how to make separate forms appear solid. They placed complementary colors next to one another, making the canvas seem to vibrate.

Matisse was the greatest painter of the fauve group. Strongly influenced by Cézanne, he continued working with flat, pure colors in patterns. Throughout his long career he produced a tremendous number of pictures and much fine sculpture.

▶ CUBISM

The early years of the 20th century were exciting ones. Modern science was exploring everything, replacing superstitions with facts. In all areas of life there were reactions against illusions of any kind. Moreover, the new science of anthropology revealed much about the relationship between art and civilization. By studying so-called primitive societies, the anthropologists realized that art was more than just decoration: it was an important part of life.

Two young painters in Paris were very much aware of the scientific discoveries of their day. The Frenchman Georges Braque (1882–1963) and his Spanish-born friend Pablo Picasso (1881–1973) were interested in African sculpture. They found the simple shapes and sharp contrasts beautiful, and they began to develop a new style influenced by African work. Then, they attended the Cézanne exhibition of 1907. Greatly impressed, they returned to the studio they shared to experiment. Within the year, they developed cubism, a style of painting that dominated art until World War II.

The cubists saw no reason why they should paint a subject from just one view. After all, there are countless ways to look at something. Just as Cézanne had done, they divided their subjects according to planes. But instead of showing only the visible side, they tried to suggest all the sides at once. It was almost as though they had smashed their subjects to bits, put all the pieces on a flat board, and then painted what they saw.

In their early cubist paintings Braque and Picasso used only pale, grayish colors applied in small, even dabs. These neutral colors prevented any part of the picture from appearing to come forward or go backward. Later the cubists began using larger areas of brighter colors. Braque remained within the framework of cubism, experimenting and perfecting, until his death in 1963. Picasso has moved on to other things, working in countless styles.

Cubism, by nature, was very influential in the development of the sculpture of the period. The idea of simplifying a shape into its basic planes and forms was, in fact, a sculptural idea. Picasso did a great deal of three-dimensional work within the cubist framework of ideas.

The cubist idea of **collage** (the gluing of paper, cloth, or other materials to a surface)

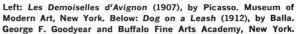

Left: *Les Demoiselles d'Avignon* (1907), by Picasso. Museum of Modern Art, New York. Below: *Dog on a Leash* (1912), by Balla. George F. Goodyear and Buffalo Fine Arts Academy, New York.

was soon developed into the school of **constructivism**—the building of sculpture out of ready-made pieces of shaped materials. Picasso did quite a lot of sculpture using construction as his method.

Sculpture that is constructed, rather than modeled or cut from a block, makes wider use of space shapes than the more traditional type of work. This consciousness of space developed into a new form of sculpture. In the work of sculptors like Jacques Lipchitz (1891–1973) the whole piece is actually a network of empty spaces and solid forms.

▶ **FUTURISM IN ITALY**

Until World War II, Paris remained the art capital of the world. But experiments in art had spread throughout Europe. In Italy, around 1910, a short-lived but important modern movement developed. It was called futurism, and the artists who developed it wanted to express the speed, progress, and even the violence of modern life.

The futurists, led by the poet Filippo Tommaso Marinetti (1876–1944) and the painter Giacomo Balla (1871–1958), were enthusiastic about such modern developments as motion pictures, the airplane, and mechanical weapons. They were actually looking forward to the mechanized war that seemed to be coming. They wanted their art to capture the speed and violence of the new century. They drew objects on their canvases with flowing, overlapping lines, trying to show how things move in ever shifting light.

Futurism lasted until the outbreak of World War I in 1914. Then the war upset the whole scheme of life and the natural development of modern art in Europe.

The futurist artist Umberto Boccioni (1882–1916) was one of the first artists to use space shapes in sculpture. He did this by imitating a natural object in reverse. That is, he would often include a hollowed-out space where one would expect a full, rounded form. A nose, for example, might cut back into the head rather than project from it.

Another method used by futurist sculptors was to exaggerate space in order to give the illusion of movement. For example, the stride of a walking figure would be extended beyond the natural to make it seem as if the figure were really walking.

Composition III (1914), by Kandinsky. Museum of Modern Art, New York.

▶ **GERMAN EXPRESSIONISM**

The fauves in France had counterparts in Germany. In 1905 several young painters in Dresden rented a studio together and formed a group called *Die Brücke* ("The Bridge"). The most famous of the group are Ernst Ludwig Kirchner (1880–1938) and Emil Nolde (1867–1956). In their paintings they wanted to express their passion for life. They felt that the brightness and darkness of their colors and their generous brushwork could express their innermost feelings.

By 1911 the Bridge group had moved to Berlin. They held exhibitions at the gallery of a magazine, *Der Sturm* ("The Attack"). A year later another group of painters began to exhibit at *Der Sturm* gallery. Calling itself *Der Blaue Reiter* ("The Blue Rider"), this group had begun in Munich in southern Germany. The founders were Wassily Kandinsky

Above: *Twittering Machine* (watercolor and ink; 1922), by Klee. Museum of Modern Art, New York. Below: *Opposition of Lines: Red and Yellow* (1937), by Mondrian. Philadelphia Museum of Art.

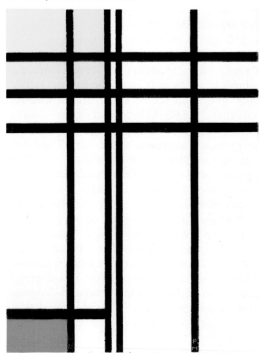

(1866–1944) and Franz Marc (1880–1916).

Kandinsky was a Russian who was strongly influenced by the folk art of his homeland. He came to believe that the strength of all art lay in colors and shapes. He abstracted objects to their simplest forms, and soon no one could identify any natural objects in his paintings. Thus, from 1910 to 1914 he painted the first really abstract works of the 20th century.

Another important Blue Rider artist was Paul Klee (1879–1940). Usually small watercolors, the pictures of this Swiss-born painter are not totally abstract. But his simple figures resemble those that children draw. Although Klee's subject matter is frequently frivolous or fantastic, his pictures are carefully constructed, beautifully painted, and highly sophisticated. Klee is one of the few modern masters whose work is admired universally. His paintings appeal to artists of all modern schools.

▶CONSTRUCTIVISM

In 1912 the Russian painter Kazimir Malevich (1878–1935) met Picasso in Paris and discovered cubism. He was enthusiastic and returned to Russia to start a similar movement. The cubists had broken down objects and simplified them to geometric shapes. Malevich's work emphasized only the geometry itself. With the circle, rectangle, triangle, or square he felt that he could suggest any form in the world. One of Malevich's most famous pictures, *White on White*, is simply a white square placed on an angle within the square of the canvas.

Malevich called his style **suprematism** because geometric forms were regarded as the simplest and therefore the most pure, or supreme, shapes. His followers, however, changed the name to constructivism.

Sculpture

The brothers Naum Gabo (1890–1977) and Antoine Pevsner (1886–1962) are the best known of the constructivist sculptors. The work of these Russian artists was an outgrowth of the cubist construction, but it relied more on the laws of mathematics and geometry. Whereas cubist work was often expressionistic or emotional in character, the constructivists tried to keep their sculpture as impersonal and scientific as possible.

▶NEOPLASTICISM

During the war years (1914–18) a movement was developing in the Netherlands. Its ideas were similar to those of Malevich. Piet Mondrian (1872–1944) and Theo van Doesburg (1883–1931) started a magazine called *De Stijl* ("The Style"). For more than 11 years they published their ideas about art. They influenced industrial designers and architects as well as painters.

Mondrian's neoplasticism was an attempt to remove art from the world of natural forms. He said that geometric forms were the only pure ones—the only fully manageable, or plastic, forms in painting. He divided his rectangular white canvas with black lines, drawn up and down or straight across; there were no diagonals. The lines crossed and formed squares and rectangles, which Mondrian sometimes painted with primary colors —red, yellow, and blue. Thus he produced pictures that were perfectly orderly, with the simplest possible shapes and colors. His idea was the opposite of the futurists'. Instead of capturing the speed and violence of life, Mondrian wanted to describe orderliness.

▶DADAISM

The outbreak of World War I had different effects on the artists of the period. Some artists fought in the war; others continued working in the styles they had developed in the decade before the war. A group of artists from all over Europe protested against the social ills of the time. Meeting in Switzerland—a neutral country—they created work that was anti-war, anti-modern life, and indeed, anti-art. This group called their art dada because the word had nothing to do with anything—it was pure nonsense.

The dadaists wrote nonsense poetry in which the words were gobbledygook, and they created nonsense objects. For example, Man Ray (1890–1976) attached carpet tacks to the bottom of an iron and exhibited it. Marcel Duchamp (1887–1968) exhibited a printed reproduction of the *Mona Lisa* on which he had painted a moustache. When they held exhibitions, the dadaists sometimes encouraged the public to destroy some of their displays. This was their reaction to the new civilization of the 20th century. They thought that governments had become insane and art too serious.

Developable Column (1942), by Pevsner. Museum of Modern Art, New York.

The dadaists set out to make fun of—or even destroy—art, but they failed. They failed because while trying to destroy art they created it. They used the cubist collage to put all kinds of objects together. They pasted together drawings, photographs, buttons, advertisements, rubbish—anything at all.

Many people found the antics of the dadaists foolish, insane, vulgar, and destructive. Nevertheless, new territories of modern art were being opened. Dada forced people to re-examine their opinions of what is ugly and what is beautiful. It forced them to look carefully at everything—even objects that were not supposed to be art. For example, the dada artist Kurt Schwitters (1887–1948) made some of the most admired collages of the period out of ticket stubs, candy wrappers, matchbooks, and similar materials.

One of the most important ideas to develop out of the dada movement was **automatism** —the automatic production of art. This meant that whatever came into the artist's mind was used as part of the work of art. Dada poets, for example, would write down any words that formed in their minds, regardless of how nonsensical these words seemed. Dada painters would draw the first shapes or objects that appeared to them.

Le Cadeau ("The Gift") (1919), by Man Ray. Collection of Mr. and Mrs. Morton G. Neumann, Chicago.

▶SURREALISM

The only style of any importance to develop in the years following World War I was surrealism. This style, an outgrowth of dada, became the most important art movement in Europe during the late 1920's and 1930's. Many artists who were not members of the movement were strongly influenced by it during this period—even Pablo Picasso, the cubist painter.

Many of those who were very important in the dada movement—such as the French writer André Breton (1896–1966) and the German-born painter Max Ernst (1891–1976) —were also the founders of surrealism. This new school combined the dada idea of automatism (free and automatic painting) with the psychology of Sigmund Freud. Freud believed that people's real thoughts were hidden in their unconscious minds and in their dreams. He felt that to understand people you must search their dreams. Only dreams are clear. Daytime life is too full of outside events to be understood.

The surrealists believed that the artist should try to understand this world of dreams. They felt that the job of the artist was to show this unconscious world through his work. Obviously they could not paint while asleep. They believed the next best thing was to let the imagination wander and to paint whatever happened to come to mind.

Probably the most important of the surrealist artists was Max Ernst. Not only was he one of the founders of the movement, but he was also a great innovator, developing new ideas in collage. He invented the technique called frottage (texture rubbings). Ernst worked mostly with the idea of automatism, allowing his imagination complete freedom. He often painted or pasted objects next to one another that had no apparent reason for being together. They were placed in this position as an automatic action.

Max Ernst also worked quite often in sculpture, using the same theory of automatism in this medium. Some of the work he did was modeled from clay, using strange and imaginative forms, while other pieces were constructed of ready-made objects in a collagelike technique.

Another very important artist of this period was Joan Miró (1893–1983), who was born in Spain. Although Miró developed no new techniques, his paintings are good examples of surrealism. Completely forgetting the real world, his mind invented humorous abstract paintings made of colorful and unusual forms.

Working a great deal in sculpture, mostly as construction, Jean (Hans) Arp (1887–1966) also was influential as a surrealist artist. Like Miró, Arp created abstract works, using automatism as a means of freeing his imagination and allowing his unconscious mind full reign. Arp's work was based on simple shapes, often symbolic or suggestive of living forms.

A very important surrealist sculptor is Alberto Giacometti (1901–66), who was born in Switzerland. Some of Giacometti's work seems to use space as its only subject matter. His sculpture often consists of a group of sticklike figures standing on a flat surface. Because the figures are so simple, it becomes obvious to the viewer that the space between them is important. The effect of these strange pieces of sculpture is often eerie and dreamlike.

There were some artists who took an entirely different approach to surrealism; among this group were the Spanish painter Salvador Dali (1904–89), French-born Yves Tanguy (1900–55), and an Italian, Giorgio di Chirico (1888–1978). These artists believed in a more literary approach to surrealism. They tried to illustrate dreams the way one would illustrate a story, using symbolic images. Tanguy and di Chirico were very popular during their own period but did not have a great influence on later artists.

Reviewed by RICHARD W. IRELAND
Maryland Institute College of Art

▶ **MODERN ART IN THE UNITED STATES**

In 1913 an international exhibition of modern art was held in a large armory (military building) in New York City. The Armory Show, as it came to be called, gave the public its first glimpse of some of the important European art movements. And it had a strong influence on American art. During World War I, New York became an active center for modern art. Young artists there came into daily contact with the latest art movements.

In the 1920's, United States artists became convinced that modern art could make a better world. They modeled their art on the highly refined style of the constructivists, and they called for art that associated itself with technology and progress.

During the Depression of the 1930's, when artists found it difficult to support themselves, the U.S. Government provided projects for thousands of artists. As a result, the public became much more aware of modern art.

At the start of this period, in 1929, one of the country's major museums—the Museum of Modern Art in New York City—was founded. During the 1930's and 1940's, the Museum of Modern Art expanded its collection and did much to help people understand the importance of modern art and design. Today the museum has the most important collection of modern art in the world.

Many artists escaped the beginnings of war in Europe during this time. They fled to New York City to live and work. As a result of their activities and the activities of the Museum of Modern Art, New York City became the center of modern art.

Left: *The Little Tear Gland That Says Tic-Tac* (1920), by Max Ernst. Museum of Modern Art, New York.

Chariot (1950), by Alberto Giacometti. Museum of Modern Art, New York.

A Tree Grows in Naples (1960), by Willem de Kooning. Janis Gallery, N.Y.

Above: *Numbers in Color* (1958–59), by Jasper Johns. Albright Art Gallery, Buffalo, N.Y.
Below: *Number I* (1948), by Jackson Pollock. Museum of Modern Art, New York.

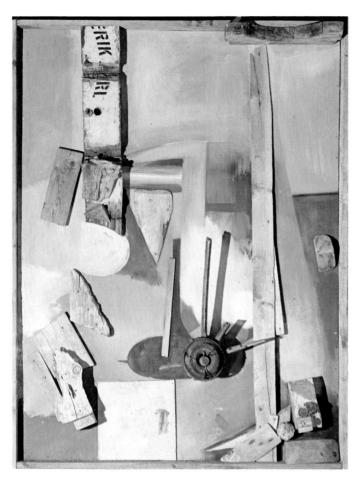

Black Reflections, by Franz Kline. Collection of Ellison Manufacturing Company.

Merzbild mit Regenbogen (Assemblage with Rainbow), by Kurt Schwitters. Collection of Mr. and Mrs. Charles B. Benenson.

Ctesiphon II (1968), by Frank Stella. Collection of Myron Orlovsky.

Abstract Expressionism

During World War II, a significant new style of modern art developed. It became known as the New York school. Arshile Gorky (1904–48), Willem de Kooning (1904–97), Mark Rothko (1903–70), Jackson Pollock (1912–56), and Franz Kline (1919–62) were among the most important painters of this school. They combined abstraction with emphasis on the expressive quality of paint as it is applied to canvas. Pollock became famous for paintings on which he dripped, swirled, spattered, and pushed the paint in many directions. To do this, he spread the canvas on the floor. His paintings had the look of being unplanned, even though they were carefully planned and controlled. Because Pollock and others valued the action of painting so highly, their work was called **action painting**. The style was known as abstract expressionism because it consisted of expressively created abstract forms.

Significant new forms of sculpture also were being developed in the United States. Alexander Calder (1898–1976) and David Smith (1906–65) were the two most important sculptors during this time.

Calder developed the **mobile**—a construction or sculpture with parts that are delicately balanced and move freely in space. Later came his **stabiles**. These are abstract sculptures somewhat like mobiles but stationary. They influenced the form of all outdoor sculpture.

David Smith was a highly productive artist who tried to move modern sculpture in the direction of painting. His early works were welded abstractions that were clearly influenced by cubism and surrealism. His later works were simpler and larger pieces, but they were just as complex in their meaning.

Pop Art and Minimal Art

In the 1960's, many artists felt that abstract expressionism was too specialized to appeal to the general public. As a result, pop art ("popular art") came into being. It went back to everyday subject matter and methods. The artists felt that this was a better way for modern art to mirror U.S. society. Jasper Johns (1930–   ) made careful easel paintings of the United States flag, and Robert Rauschenberg (1925–   ) created "combine" paintings. In these, he combined pieces of junk that he found on New York City streets. Andy Warhol (1930?–87) turned out multiple copies of paintings based on subjects featured in newspapers and advertisements, such as motion picture stars and cans of Campbell's tomato soup. Marisol (Marisol Escobar) (1930–   ) and Louise Nevelson (1900–88) used everyday things or "found objects" to create their sculpture. The observer had to view the subjects, as well as the process of art itself, in a new way.

Some artists objected to the direction that pop art was taking. They felt that the relation between art and the modern world would be better expressed if abstraction was refined and simplified. These feelings were expressed in a kind of art called minimal art ("minimal" means "the least possible"). It made use mainly of simple geometric forms executed in an impersonal style. The paintings of Frank Stella (1936–   ) and the sculpture of Donald Judd (1928–   ) looked simple. Yet they were highly complicated in their meanings. Viewers had to bring their own meanings to these works and wonder what the artist intended. One of minimal art's most important influences on contemporary art was the artists' willingness to join art more closely with an appreciation of beauty. They were concerned with how a simple geometric shape looked in different lights and colors. They wanted to create a more satisfactory means of communication through the use of abstraction.

Conceptual Art

One of the more recent developments in modern art was the concept that the idea of a work of art is more important than the finished product. Sol Lewitt (1928–   ) illustrated this development in his many-lined wall drawings and his modular structures.

Artists went on to include the process of thinking out, or acting upon, the idea. They called it conceptual art, or "idea art." The result was a breaking down of boundaries among all the arts. Artists now convey ideas through performance, theater, music, dance, video, and photography as well as painting, drawing, and sculpture. All of this has revealed a richer field of artistic expression and a new emphasis on variety and complexity. Modern art, as ever, is fully in step with modern life.

PATRICK STEWART
Williams College

See also PAINTING; SCULPTURE; UNITED STATES, ART AND ARCHITECTURE OF THE.

MODERN MUSIC

Music written according to techniques developed from the early 1900's to the present day is called modern music. Like the music composed before 1900, modern music includes a wide variety of styles. In general, however, the term "modern music" refers to compositions that use the basic elements of music—melody, harmony, rhythm, and tone color (the quality of a musical sound)—in untraditional ways. Modern music often has complicated melodies and rhythms, dissonant, or clashing, harmonies, and unusual tone colors. Many listeners find modern music more difficult than earlier music to follow and understand. (To learn more about earlier music, consult the articles BAROQUE MUSIC and CLASSICAL AGE IN MUSIC. A glossary of musical terms appears in the article MUSIC.)

▶ **EARLY DEVELOPMENTS**

Modern music differs from earlier music in several ways. The most important difference is in the way tones, or the musical notes of the scale, are organized. Most music written before 1900 is **tonal**; that is, it is organized around one note, which serves as a **tonal center**, or home tone. This home tone is combined with six other tones to form a scale. (Five additional tones, called chromatic tones, are used to enrich these seven tones.)

From about 1700 until 1900, composers based the structure of their music on keys. If a piece of music was written in the key of D, for example, the melodies and harmonies of the piece would center on D as the tonal center.

The music might move through other chords and even change keys, but it would begin and end in the key of D.

By the end of the 1800's, composers had explored nearly every key relationship and sound effect possible within the system of tonal harmony. Some composers began to search for new ways of organizing sounds. Their search led to a dramatic change in the way music was written.

Atonality. Arnold Schoenberg, an Austrian composer born in 1874, was among the first to break with the tonal system. At first Schoenberg wrote music in a style similar to that of composers of the late 1800's. By the early 1900's, Schoenberg had developed a new musical language, called atonality. The new music had no tonal center. Instead, all the tones were used in a way that gave them equal importance. Schoenberg's atonal music was very original and intensely emotional. However, the lack of a tonal center left the composer with no rules on which to base the structure of a composition. Schoenberg realized that new methods of organizing tones were needed.

Twelve-Tone Music. After seven years of work, Schoenberg developed a new method of composing, known as the twelve-tone technique. The twelve tones were the same as those used by composers of the past: the seven tones of the scale, together with the five chromatic tones. (If you play all the black and white keys from one C to the next C on a piano, you will hear these twelve tones.)

In Schoenberg's system, these tones are arranged in a particular order, or sequence, of

Far left: The Austrian composer Arnold Schoenberg created the twelve-tone method of composing. An important break with earlier composing techniques, the method offered modern composers a rich new field for experimentation. *Near left:* The French composer and conductor Nadia Boulanger taught composition in Paris during the 1900's, influencing a generation of young composers.

the composer's choosing. This sequence of notes, called a **tone row**, becomes the basis for the entire composition. Both melodies and harmonies are taken from the tone row. Its notes must be used in such a way that no one note receives more emphasis than another.

Twelve-tone music sounds very different from music based on tonal harmony. The melodies may seem incomplete and hard to follow, and the harmonies may sound dissonant. But Schoenberg's method offered composers a rich new field for experimentation.

Other Experiments. In the early 1900's, while Schoenberg was still writing atonal music, other composers were also at work developing new musical sounds.

In 1913, a ballet was performed in Paris that was so shocking to the audience that a riot broke out. The ballet was *The Rite of Spring* and its composer was a young Russian named Igor Stravinsky. The ballet music had stark, primitive-sounding melodies and clashing harmonies. Most startling of all were its rhythms. In most earlier music, the rhythm was based on groups of two, three, four, or six beats. Once a grouping, or **meter**, was established for a piece of music, it seldom changed. In *The Rite of Spring*, the meter changes often, sometimes at almost every measure.

Stravinsky proved to be one of the most important composers of the 1900's. He did not turn to atonality, as Schoenberg had. Instead, he used other techniques, such as combining two or more keys at the same time, to produce new harmonic sounds. This technique is called **bitonality** or **polytonality**. Many other composers studied Stravinsky's music and drew ideas from it.

Claude Debussy, a French composer born in the late 1800's, developed a musical style known as **impressionism**. Debussy created a soft, delicate world of sound with rapidly changing, fluid melodies. Debussy often used scales borrowed from Eastern music and from ancient church music.

Béla Bartók borrowed scales and rhythms from the folk songs of his native Hungary for his musical compositions. Bartók spent many years collecting folk music from the Hungarian countryside. He also became an expert in music from the neighboring Balkan states and in the Arabic music of North Africa. Bartók combined these folk sounds with such musical forms as the string quartet and concerto.

The music of Charles Ives, an American composer, was understood by few people of his own day. Ives drew from familiar American melodies—folk tunes, band music, and hymns. Often, several melodies, harmonies, and rhythms are played at the same time, resulting in dissonant sounds. Today Ives is recognized as a prophet of modern music.

Neoclassicism. After the vigorous experiments that took place in the early decades of the 1900's, many composers turned to a more restrained type of music. They began to look to composers of the past for inspiration, especially to Johann Sebastian Bach, Wolfgang Amadeus Mozart, and other composers of the 1700's. This new trend was called neoclassicism, or new classicism. The neoclassic music of the 1900's did not sound like the music of Bach or Mozart, however. Composers used all the newly developed ways of working with rhythm and harmony. Stravinsky changed his style to neoclassicism in the early 1920's, and many other composers joined him. The composers Paul Hindemith, Sergei Prokofiev, and Francis Poulenc were all influenced by neoclassic trends.

During the 1920's, American jazz found its way into concert music in the works of American composers such as Aaron Copland and George Gershwin. European composers also incorporated jazz sounds into their music.

▶MID-1900'S

By the 1930's, the twelve-tone technique had been further developed by Alban Berg and Anton Webern, two composers who were students of Arnold Schoenberg. Webern's music was especially admired by other composers because of its highly organized technique.

After World War II (1939–45), the twelve-tone technique was adopted by many other composers. Soon a number of Webern's followers began to extend the principles of twelve-tone writing to other musical elements —rhythm, tone color, and dynamics (loudness)—as well as melody. The result was a complex type of composition known as total organization, or **serialism**. Major serialist composers included Oliver Messian, Pierre Boulez, and Milton Babbitt.

Electronic Music. As serialism developed, interest in electronic music also grew. Earlier in the 1900's, a few composers, including Edgar Varèse, had begun to explore the use of everyday sounds in their music. Traffic noise, thunder, and other sounds could be recorded on tape and then changed in different ways. Later, computers were developed that could produce musical sounds.

Many composers who were working with serialism turned to electronic music because it offered them total control. By electronic means they could create sounds that would be impossible to produce with voices or with traditional musical instruments. In purely electronic music, the role of the performer is completely eliminated. Often, however, composers combine taped or electronically produced sounds with live performances by singers or instrumentalists.

Chance Music. At the opposite extreme from serialism is a movement known as chance music. Unlike the composer of serial music, who is interested in total organization of a composition, the composer of chance music may select rhythms, melodies, and other elements by throwing dice or flipping a coin. In some cases the performer may compose part or all of the piece on the spot. In this case, the music will sound very different at each performance.

The American composer John Cage was a leading composer of chance music. In one of his most famous pieces, *4'33"*, a pianist sits at a keyboard for four minutes and 33 seconds but plays nothing. The "music" is made up of whatever other sounds can be heard in the auditorium during that time.

Despite their differing philosophies, some serialist composers were attracted to the ideas of Cage and other composers of chance music.

The American composer John Cage is best known for using an element of chance in creating his compositions. He also incorporated nonmusical noises, such as banging doors, into his work and produced unique sounds on the piano by placing objects between the instrument's strings.

They introduced chance elements into their own music. This way of working is typical of modern composers. They often draw from widely varying ideas and techniques in their search for new forms of expression.

▶**LATER TRENDS**

Throughout the 1900's, some composers, including Benjamin Britten, Samuel Barber, and Gian-Carlo Menotti, continued to compose in a tonal style. Several younger composers also turned back to tonality.

After 1965, a new trend known as **minimalism** became popular with both composers and listeners. Minimalist composers such as Steve Reich and Philip Glass rejected the complex style of much modern music in favor of simpler sounds. Their music is marked by short, repeated melody patterns and a steady beat. Many minimalist composers were influenced by Eastern music, particularly the music of India.

In the late 1900's, for the first time, women composers began to gain recognition. Ellen Taaffe Zwilich, Pauline Oliveros, and Vivian Fine are among the women who have made notable contributions to concert music. The woman who may have had the most influence on modern music was Nadia Boulanger, a teacher of composition in Paris. Throughout much of the 1900's she taught and deeply influenced countless young composers from both Europe and the United States.

While the works of early modern masters such as Bartók and Stravinsky have become well established on concert programs, a new composer may have difficulty getting his or her work performed. One reason is that much modern music is very difficult to play or sing. A new work is likely to require many more hours of rehearsal time than a work from the past. Another reason is that concert audiences often seem to prefer earlier music. To overcome these problems, small performing groups have formed that specialize in playing modern music. In addition, recordings have made almost all the important modern works available to everyone.

ALICE TRIMMER
Editor and Consultant

See also BARTÓK, BÉLA; COPLAND, AARON; DEBUSSY, CLAUDE; ELECTRONIC MUSIC; IVES, CHARLES; MUSIC; PROKOFIEV, SERGEI; SCHOENBERG, ARNOLD; STRAVINSKY, IGOR.

MODIGLIANI, AMEDEO (1884–1920)

The artist Amedeo Modigliani was born in Leghorn, Italy, on July 12, 1884. At the moment of his birth, moving men were taking away most of the furniture in his house, for the family business had just failed. The Jewish family had been prosperous, but as Dedo—this was Modigliani's childhood nickname—grew up there was little money. In spite of this, his mother encouraged his early interest in art, and he was given painting lessons at 14.

When he was 16, Modigliani was stricken with tuberculosis, and he was sent south to Naples for the winter. He also visited Rome, Florence, and Venice, and was thrilled by the activity of the big cities. For the first time he saw great Italian painting and sculpture. While he was in Venice he decided that his life's ambition was to be a sculptor—to work directly in stone.

Modigliani went to Paris in 1906. He entered an art school, the Colarossi Academy, and rented a studio in Montmartre, a section of Paris where artists lived, worked, and met. While there, he became friendly with the artists Pablo Picasso and Marc Chagall.

Materials for sculpture were expensive, and he begged stone from workers constructing a nearby building. The stone dust irritated his weakened lungs, but he persisted, happy to be pursuing his ambition. When his money ran out, Modigliani moved from place to place, looking for food and lodging. For a few pennies or a drink, he would draw portraits of people sitting in cafés. It is said that he and the painter Maurice Utrillo peeled vegetables together for room and board.

Occasionally he stole ties from subway tracks to make sculptures in wood. His family helped him as much as they could, but he was always in need of money. He started drinking too much and taking drugs. Yet he drew and painted constantly. When he was in moods in which he felt unappreciated, he would destroy some of his paintings. He worked in stone as often as he could, but in 1916 his poor health forced him to stop.

Modi (as he was then called) made friends with many young artists, writers, and poets. He was often seen around the cafés in his corduroy jacket, red scarf, and broad-rimmed hat. In 1914 he sold a few of his paintings for low prices and began to gain recognition. In 1917 he met a young art student named Jeanne Hebuterne; they fell in love. Even her loving care could not restore Modigliani's ruined health, for he died on January 25, 1920. The final tragedy was her suicide the day of the artist's funeral. Their daughter, Jeanne, was adopted by Modigliani's sister.

Portrait painters usually portray their models with noble and serene expressions. But the faces in Modigliani's paintings appear sad. He did not try to portray his subjects realistically. Instead, his human forms are simple and decorative. Modigliani used few colors, and he used them forcefully. He did not soften them with shading.

The figures Modigliani painted have oval faces, long cylindrical necks, and almond-shaped eyes. His painting and sculpture reveal his interest in black African art, which is also created with simplified shapes.

Reviewed by JEANNE MODIGLIANI

In his portraits, such as *Woman with Red Hair*, Modigliani used simple shapes and muted colors.

MOHAMMED (570?–632)

Mohammed (or Muhammad) is one of history's most important and influential figures. He is considered the prophet of Islam, the world's second largest and fastest-growing religion. Born about A.D. 570 in Mecca, a city in Arabia, Mohammed believed he was chosen by God to clarify the teachings of earlier Christian and Hebrew prophets and to establish a universal faith.

Mohammed was orphaned at age 6 and raised by a grandfather, Abd-al-Muttalib. Later, after his grandfather died, he lived with an uncle, Abu-Talib.

He belonged to a tribe that was prominent in Mecca—the Quraish—but his own family was poor. He received no formal education and probably never learned to read or write. As a boy, Mohammed worked as a trader and may have traveled with caravans to Syria and Iraq. As a young man he worked for a wealthy widow named Khadijah, whom he later married. They had two sons, who both died young, and four daughters.

After his marriage, Mohammed led a comfortable life and often thought about the problems of his people, who were constantly fighting and practicing cruel and selfish acts. He concluded that their religion, with its greed, evil practices, and many gods, was responsible for many of their problems. Like the Christians and Jews, who also lived in Mecca, he came to believe in a single God who was all-powerful and compassionate.

Mohammed often went to a cave outside Mecca to be alone and think. While meditating there one night, when he was about 40, he suddenly felt called to be God's prophet. According to Mohammed, the archangel Gabriel came and commanded him to recite the word of God to the Arabs in their own language, Arabic. The angel told Mohammed what words to recite. These were the beginning of the Koran (or Qur'an), the book that became the foundation of Islam. Other parts of the Koran were revealed to Mohammed during the remaining years of his life.

The Koran, one of the world's most widely studied books, speaks of a single God, the importance of submitting to his will, and a final Day of Judgment. It also features many stories found in the Hebrew and Christian Bible and discusses such matters as ethics, social justice, politics, law, individual and group relationships, and the natural world.

At first Mohammed was unsure of his revelations and did not discuss them openly. In time, however, he began to preach in public and attracted followers. Although influential people initially paid little attention to this, they began to oppose him as he attracted more interest. They did not like his preaching against idols in the name of one God (called Allah), and they did not like his warnings of a Day of Judgment. Although Mohammed tried to reason with his critics, he and his followers were often persecuted.

By the year 621, prospects for the survival of Mohammed and his followers seemed dim. Fearing further persecution, some Muslims (followers of Islam) left the city. Then a fortunate opportunity arose. Two important tribes in Medina (a city north of Mecca that was then called Yathrib) had been feuding for years. Some tribe members had heard Mohammed preach and asked him to mediate their disputes. Secret arrangements were made, and Mohammed and many of his Muslim followers fled to Medina.

Mohammed's flight to Medina (called the **Hegira**) in 622 was the true beginning of the Islamic era. In Medina, Mohammed transformed his religion into one that formed the basis for a world religion, a powerful state, and, eventually, a powerful world empire.

At Medina, Mohammed became a lawgiver, a political leader, and a diplomat, as well as an inspiring religious leader. He established an Islamic community with its own system of government, laws, and institutions. He persuaded many people to accept the teachings of Islam and made alliances with neighboring tribes that brought stability to the area. Mohammed's greatest hope was to make Mecca the sacred capital of all Islam, but the people of Mecca resisted Islam and Mohammed's teachings. Finally, in 630, they agreed to accept Islam, and Mecca became the center of Muslim worship. Shortly after, in A.D. 632, Mohammed died.

Today, when his name is spoken by devout Muslims, it is often followed by the blessing, "Peace be upon him."

SHAHZAD BASHIR
Department of Religion
Carleton College

See also ISLAM; KORAN.

MOLDOVA

Moldova is a new nation of Eastern Europe. It is bordered by Ukraine on the north, east, and southeast, and by Romania on the west. Formerly known as the Moldavian Soviet Socialist Republic, it was for some 67 years a part of the Soviet Union. During the breakup of the Soviet Union in 1991, Moldavia declared its independence, taking the name Republic of Moldova.

The People. In language and culture, the Moldovans are Romanians, and ethnic Romanians make up nearly two-thirds of the country's population. Ukrainians and Russians are the largest ethnic minorities, with more than one-quarter of the population. There are, in addition, smaller numbers of Gagauzi (a Turkish people), Bulgarians, and Belarusians. For most of the period of Soviet rule, Russian was the official language. Moldovan (Romanian) is now the public language and will become the official language over a ten-year transitional period.

Most of the people traditionally have been Eastern Orthodox Christians, although under Soviet rule, the Communist government strongly discouraged religious observance. There is also a significant Jewish community.

The Land. Moldova is the second smallest in area of the former Soviet republics, after Armenia. It lies between two rivers, the Prut, which it shares with Romania, and the Dniester. The central portion of the country is a plateau, the Bessarabian-Moldavian Upland, which rises to about 1,400 feet (427 meters) and extends westward beyond the Prut River. The treeless Beltsy Steppe lies to the north of the plateau and the dry Budzhak Steppe to the south. Both are covered with rich black-earth soil. In the south the only areas of forest are found in the flood plains of the lower Dniester and Prut rivers. Although Moldova has fertile cropland, it has only limited mineral resources. The most important are gypsum and building stone.

Moldovan vineyard workers, wearing traditional dress, bring in some of the grape harvest that will be used to make the country's popular wines.

The climate is mild, with an average annual temperature of about 50°F (10°C). Rainfall ranges from 12 to 20 inches (300 to 500 millimeters) a year.

Chisinau, the capital and largest city, has a population of about 800,000. Situated on the Byk River, a branch of the Dniester, it is a manufacturing city, the site of a university, and a cultural center.

The Economy. Agriculture, including the raising of cattle and other livestock, is the chief economic activity. Grain crops, particularly corn, but also wheat, barley, and rye, take up most of the country's cultivated land. Moldova is famed for its wines. Its other major commercial crops include tobacco, sugar beets, soybeans, and flax (from which linen is made).

Industry is based largely on the processing of foods and other agricultural products. Machinery, textiles, and construction materials are also manufactured. Moldova produces thermal electric and hydroelectric power, some of which is exported.

Early History. The earliest people in what is now Moldova were the Thracians. Between the 300's and 100's B.C., it was inhabited by tribes of Dacians, Scythians, Slavs, and Goths. All of these tribes were strongly influenced by the culture of the Romans, who colonized the region. Latin, the language of the Romans, became the basis for Romanian, as well as other Romance languages. By 1340, Moldavia had achieved independence under its prince, Bogdan. In the mid-1500's, it became a self-governing vassal state of the Ottoman Turkish Empire, which dominated it for the next 300 years.

Russian and Romanian Rule. In 1774 the region was placed under the protection of Russia, which continued to accept the Turks as overlords. In 1812, Bukovina, the northwestern part of the region, was lost to Austria, while Bessarabia fell to Russia. The remaining territories were united with the province of Walachia in 1859 to form Romania.

In 1918, as a result of World War I, Bessarabia passed to Romania, although the new revolutionary Soviet Russian government refused to recognize it. In 1924 the Communist Soviet Union established its own small Moldavian republic, in an area populated mostly by Ukrainians but also containing some Moldavians.

Soviet Rule to Independence. In 1940, during World War II, the Soviet Union forced Romania to cede it Bessarabia and northern Bukovina, from which most of the Moldavian Soviet Socialist Republic was established. It was one of the most artificial of the Soviet republics, because most of its people were Romanians, separated from the Romanian inhabitants of historic Moldavia.

Like other Soviet republics, Moldavia had a state-controlled economic system and a government run by the Communist Party. It declared its sovereignty, or right of self-rule, in June 1990, and on August 27, 1991, it proclaimed complete independence, amid the collapse of the Soviet Union. The new country has been beset by internal disputes, particularly among the Russian and Ukrainian nationalities and over the question of ties with Romania.

Moldova's constitution was adopted in 1994. The government consists of an elected parliament, which appoints a president as head of state and a prime minister as head of the government.

DONALD L. LAYTON
Indiana State University

See also ROMANIA.

MOLDS. See DIES AND MOLDS.

MOLDS (FUNGI). See FUNGI.

MOLECULES. See ATOMS; MATTER.

FACTS and figures

REPUBLIC OF MOLDOVA is the official name of the country.

LOCATION: Eastern Europe.

AREA: 13,000 sq mi (33,700 km²).

POPULATION: 4,400,000 (estimate).

CAPITAL AND LARGEST CITY: Chisinau.

MAJOR LANGUAGES: Romanian (to be official), Russian, Ukrainian.

MAJOR RELIGIOUS GROUP: Eastern Orthodox Christian.

GOVERNMENT: Republic. **Head of state**—president. **Head of government**—prime minister. **Legislature**—parliament.

CHIEF PRODUCTS: Agricultural—corn and other grains, wines, tobacco, sugar beets, soybeans, flax, meat and dairy products. **Manufactured**—processed foods, machinery, textiles, construction materials. **Mineral**—gypsum, building stone.

With its strong claws, the eastern mole scrapes out underground tunnels, leaving scattered mounds of dirt (or molehills) on the surface to mark its path.

MOLES

If there were a contest for the hardest working animal, the first prize would surely go to this small mammal that spends most of its life digging underground tunnels. Using its powerful front limbs and spade-shaped front feet, the mole digs through the dirt pushing a mass of earth, sometimes 20 times its own weight, upward to form a heap on the surface. The mole can dig at the rate of over 18 feet (5.5 meters) an hour. In less than a day, this champion builder can dig a tunnel over 300 feet (91 meters) long!

The mole has very poor eyesight; it relies on keen senses of touch and hearing to find its way underground. Even the thick, soft fur of the mole is well suited to its digging existence. The fur can lie flat in any direction, which is very helpful as the mole moves back and forth in the narrow tunnels.

All moles are part of a group of mammals known as insectivores, or "insect-eaters." The more than 20 different kinds are found in mild climates throughout North America, Europe, and Asia. Moles are small animals, about the size of mice. They range in length from 2½ to 8½ inches (6 to 22 centimeters), plus a tail of ⅗ inch to 8½ inches (1.5 to 22 centimeters). The average weight of a mole is between ³⁄₁₀ ounce and 6 ounces (9 and 170 grams).

Moles and Their Young. During the spring, moles court and mate. Males will search on the surface and travel through tunnels looking for females. Sometimes a male will wander into the burrow of another male by mistake, then a fight occurs.

After the male and female find each other and mate, the female prepares a nest. Six weeks later two to five baby moles are born. The babies are pink and hairless at birth. Their eyes are closed. Hair soon grows, and in three weeks the eyes open. In a very short time, at about 5 weeks, the young moles are ready to leave the nest and begin independent lives.

The Life of a Mole. Moles generally live alone, working tirelessly digging tunnels and searching for food. They stay active all year long and do not hibernate. As winter approaches, however, moles do collect more food and store it in special underground chambers. Their diet consists of large amounts of food—mainly insect larvae and earthworms. They also eat adult insects, snails, baby birds, and small vertebrates.

One North American mole spends part of its time burrowing beneath the ground and part swimming in water. It is the starnose mole. It gets its name from the fleshy starlike ring of feelers around the end of its nose. The starnose mole is an able hunter on land or in water. As the mole hunts, the feelers wave back and forth, helping the animal find its way.

The Mole and its Environment. Moles have few natural enemies. Birds such as owls, ravens, and eagles hunt the mole, but they must wait for the mole to come to the surface. Even though other animals may kill it, the mole has a built-in protection against becoming some mammal's dinner—it tastes bad.

The main danger to moles is from people. At one time moles were hunted for their fur, which was used to make clothing. Today, moles are mainly hunted and killed because they destroy the appearance of lawns and gardens and can cause damage to machinery used to tend yards and farm fields. People use a variety of methods to try and get rid of moles —from flooding the tunnels with water to putting mothballs in their burrows. When left to roam under gardens and fields, moles are very helpful. They eat vast quantities of the insects that feed on crops and garden plants.

JENNY TESAR
Author, *Introduction to Animals*

Reviewed by DOUGLAS FALK
Assistant Curator
New York Zoological Society

MOLIÈRE (1622–1673)

Molière is the stage name of Jean Baptiste Poquelin, a French dramatist and actor who was his country's leading comic playwright and a major influence on world theater. He was born in Paris on January 15, 1622, the son of an upholsterer for King Louis XIII. The family was well off, and Jean, an intelligent boy, received an excellent education at the Collège de Clermont, a Jesuit school.

When Jean was 21, his life took a new turn. He joined a troupe of actors who were opening a theater in Paris. At that time he took the name Molière. When this theater failed, the actors decided to try their luck in the provinces. Molière soon became the leader of the troupe. He acted, danced, wrote plays, and directed. After twelve years of touring the towns of southern France, the company returned to Paris. This time they were a success, especially in performances of Molière's own comedies. King Louis XIV enjoyed them so much that he commanded the actors to stay and become the royal troupe.

Molière wrote his greatest comedies in this period. Among them are *Tartuffe* (1664), *The Misanthrope* (1666), *The Miser* (1668), *The Learned Ladies* (1672), and *The Imaginary Invalid* (1673). The plays typically portray a character with a common human failing, which Molière ridicules by exaggerating. Because misers, hypocrites, and people who worry about their health are always with us, Molière's plays still amuse audiences. They continue to be staged at France's national theater, the Comédie-Française in Paris, and in translation all over the world.

The plays offended certain important people who thought they were being laughed at. But Louis XIV always stood by Molière and often summoned him to perform or to compose a play for some royal occasion. Molière worked very hard and suffered from ill health. He collapsed on February 17, 1673, during a performance of *The Imaginary Invalid* and died later that evening.

Reviewed by WILLIAM D. HOWARTH
Author, *Molière: A Playwright and His Audience*

MOLLUSKS

It is hard to imagine that the slug chewing on a garden plant, the giant squid patrolling the cold, dark waters of the ocean, and the clam burying itself in the sand along the seashore have much in common. But they do. They all belong to the group of animals with soft, fleshy bodies called mollusks. There are at least 100,000 species, or kinds, of living mollusks in this diverse group. In addition, more than 30,000 species of fossil mollusks have been found and described. These abundant creatures make their homes throughout most of the world in a variety of habitats. They can be found in the deepest ocean waters, in humid tropical forests, in dry, hot deserts, or on wooded mountain slopes— wherever there is enough water to keep their bodies moist.

▶ CHARACTERISTICS OF MOLLUSKS

Mollusks are one of the largest groups of animals, consisting of such seemingly different members as snails, octopuses, scallops, and nudibranchs. Although they live on land

and in freshwater, the majority of mollusks make their home in the ocean. In fact, there are more species of mollusks in the ocean than of any other kind of animal, including fish. They are also some of the oldest animals, appearing on Earth more than 500 million years ago.

No matter how greatly the various species of mollusks appear to differ from one another, all mollusks have a similar body plan with distinct organ systems that digest food and excrete waste, circulate oxygen throughout the body, and control the senses. In all species, the fleshy body of the mollusk, called the **visceral mass**, is boneless. Structures that make up the digestive, excretory, and circulatory systems are contained in the visceral mass. The delicate tissues of these organs are covered by the **mantle**, a skinlike organ that also secretes the material that forms the shell. In many mollusks, including snails, oysters, and scallops, the shell is external. Some, such as squid and cuttlefish, have an internal shell-like skeleton. Others, such as slugs and octo-

KINDS OF MOLLUSKS

The vast array of mollusks can be separated by certain distinct characteristics of structure and behavior into seven classes, or large groups. They are Gastropoda (gastropods), Bivalvia (bivalves), Cephalopoda (cephalopods), Scaphopoda (scaphopods), Polyplacophora (polyplacophorans), Monoplacophora (monoplacophorans), and Aplacophora (aplacophorans). Some primitive mollusks, such as the small wormlike aplacophorans that occupy deep ocean waters and the flat-shelled monoplacophorans that were long thought to be extinct, are seldom seen. The most familiar kinds of mollusks are described below.

Gastropods make up the largest class of mollusks. They include snails, whelks, slugs, abalones, and conch. Many of these animals have a single external shell that is coiled. In some gastropods, the shell is very small or internalized.

Bivalves form the second largest class of mollusks. Members of this group include clams, scallops, oysters, mussels, and shipworms. Their flattened bodies dwell inside two hinged shells.

puses, have no shell at all. They only have the mantle to protect their internal organs.

All mollusks have some type of muscular foot. Clams, mussels, snails, and whelks are among the mollusks that have an easily recognizable foot. But the foot of other mol-

lusks, such as squid, octopuses, and cuttlefish, has been modified into arms or tentacles. Depending on the species, the foot is used in locomotion, digging, or feeding. For example, snails use their foot to walk or crawl, while clams dig with their foot and octopuses capture prey with their arms.

In most kinds of mollusks, the sexes are separate; that is, each individual mollusk has either male or female reproductive organs. However, some kinds of mollusks, such as sea hares, nudibranchs, and some snails and slugs, are hermaphrodites. In these, the individual mollusks possess both male and female reproductive organs.

▶ THE LIFE OF MOLLUSKS

Most species of mollusks live independently; that is, they are able to perform the tasks, such as finding food and reproducing, that are necessary for them to survive. However, some mollusks live in a symbiotic relationship with other animals or plants. This means that the mollusk and the organism benefit from their association with each other. Still other mollusks are hosts to parasites. In this relationship, another organism depends on a mollusk to exist but does not provide any help to the mollusk in return. One example of a parasite is the pea crab, which makes its home in the shells of living bivalves such as clams and mussels.

Mollusks demonstrate a wide range of feeding habits. Most bivalves are filter feeders. They draw in water through a tubelike structure, called a siphon, to obtain the microscopic organisms on which they feed. Chitons and many gastropods, including limpets and most snails, graze on algae and plant cells, using a toothed tonguelike organ called a radula. A few snails prey on other animals. They capture their prey by injecting them with poison. Octopuses and other cephalopods are aggressive predators, capturing fish, shellfish, and other mollusks with their strong tentacles. They use their sharp beaklike jaws to tear apart their prey.

The methods of reproduction also vary among mollusks. In most mollusks, fertilization takes place externally. Eggs (the female sex cells) and sperm (the male sex cells) are released into the water at the same time, and fertilization occurs when they unite. While female octopuses stay close to the fertilized eggs to keep them well supplied with oxygen and safe from predators until they hatch, most mollusk parents do not tend the eggs.

In some mollusks, fertilization takes place internally with the male depositing sperm within the female. Depending on the species of mollusk, the fertilized eggs are deposited into the water and, in a short time, either larvae or fully formed mollusks emerge. Or the fertilized eggs remain within the female where they hatch. The larvae grow and develop inside the female and are born fully formed.

When larvae emerge from their eggs, they are tiny creatures with fine hairlike projections, called cilia, sprouting from their bodies. These free-swimming animals drift along in the water, feeding on floating plankton. The protective shell of the mollusk begins to form early in the larval stage. As the larvae mature, their shells become well defined. The cilia grow longer and are used to help the larvae propel themselves through the water. Some larvae settle to the sea bottom or anchor themselves to reefs, stones, or other objects to complete their development into adults.

Many marine animals feed on the defenseless eggs and larvae of mollusks. But as mollusks grow, it becomes increasingly difficult for predators to catch and eat them. When threatened, many mollusks simply pull into their hard shells. To avoid predators, octopuses, squids, and other cephalopods of all ages change their color to match their surroundings. Octopuses and squids have an additional defense: They shoot out a dense cloud of black ink toward an enemy. Other mollusks without shells, including nudibranchs, emit bad-tasting chemicals. Once an enemy attacks and tastes its prey, it quickly releases the mollusk and retreats.

▶ **MOLLUSKS AND THEIR ENVIRONMENT**

Some mollusks are considered pests because of the damage they cause. For instance, shipworms attack wood pier pilings and wooden ships, and land slugs and snails feed on garden plants. There are even mollusks that carry diseases. But the harmful effects of mollusks are outweighed by the benefits they provide. Mollusk shells were used as money by some Native Americans. Food, tools, decorative objects, cameos, pearls, and dyes are all products that have come from mollusks.

Cephalopods, such as octopuses, squids, chambered nautiluses, and cuttlefish, are some of the oldest animals in the world. Except for the chambered nautilus, cephalopods do not have external shells. All members of this group have a prominent head and a muscular foot that has been modified into arms or tentacles.

Scaphopods, which are also called tooth or tusk shells, are a class of mollusks with long, tubelike shells. Their delicate shells are open at both ends. A powerful, muscular foot, which extends out of an opening at one end, is used to burrow into the mud of the seafloor.

Polyplacophorans make their home in shallow ocean waters. Members of this group, which is made up of the various species of chitons, have flat oval bodies covered by eight overlapping shell plates.

Although mollusks are preyed on by many different creatures, including whales, fish, and walruses, human beings are the most serious threat to mollusk populations. The continued harvesting of great numbers of mollusks, such as oysters, from the same areas year after

the largest of all inverte-
brates (animals without a
backbone) is a mollusk?
Mollusks come in an enor-
mous range of sizes. An
adult mollusk can be as
small as a single grain of
sand. Huge clams known
as tridacnid clams grow to
more than 3 feet (1 meter)
in width. But the record
holder is the giant squid.
Giant squids measuring
57 feet (17 meters) in
length, including the tentacles, and weighing more
than 2 tons have been
found. There may be even
larger ones, but
specimens are rare
because squids live in extremely deep waters.

opment of coastal land. Natural events also occur that change mollusk habitats. For example, silt is carried down rivers by fast-moving currents. In places where the currents move more slowly, silt settles to the bottom and sometimes covers oyster beds.

Concern for the preservation of the world's water life and water has prompted many governments to regulate activities that could harm or destroy natural habitats. Regulations that establish when certain mollusks can be harvested and limits to how large a catch can be help preserve mollusk populations. Scientists are also studying their life cycles to find out more about what mollusks need to survive in the ever-changing environments of our world.

CLYDE MACKENZIE
James J. Howard Marine Sciences Laboratory
U.S. Department of Commerce

See also AQUACULTURE; FISHING INDUSTRY; OCTOPUSES, SQUIDS, AND OTHER CEPHALOPODS; OYSTERS, CLAMS, AND OTHER BIVALVES; PEARLS; SHELLS; SNAILS AND SLUGS.

year has led to a decline in mollusk populations as well as in the populations of fish and other water creatures that feed on mollusks. Other human activities also lead to changes in mollusk populations. Mollusk habitats have been altered by pollution and the devel-

MOLTKE, HELMUTH VON (1800–1891)

Count Helmuth von Moltke was the most famous German general of his generation. His brilliant military strategies won victories for the German state of Prussia in several critical wars—against Denmark (1864), Austria (1866), and France (1870–71)—and paved the way for the unification of all the German states in 1871.

Prussia's famous general was born Helmuth Karl Bernhard, Graf (Count) von Moltke, on October 26, 1800, in Parchim, Mecklenburg. He attended the Royal Military Academy in Denmark and became a Prussian officer in 1822. From the outset it was clear that he was more of a military scholar than a fighting soldier. He spoke several languages fluently and throughout his life wrote many volumes of military and historical texts. In 1832, Moltke joined the Prussian General Staff—the planning and organizational branch of the army—and in 1857 was appointed chief of staff.

As head of the Prussian Army, Moltke dedicated himself to making it the best in the world. He was the first to recognize the military value of the railways. The speed with which trains moved the large German armies and their supplies was a significant factor in the German victory over the French in the Franco-Prussian War (1870–71). In recognition of Moltke's achievements, King William I of Prussia promoted him to the rank of field marshal. He remained chief of staff until 1888. He died in Berlin on April 24, 1891.

Moltke's nephew, Helmuth Johannes Ludwig, Graf von Moltke, also held the post of chief of staff in later years (1906–14), but he lacked his uncle's intelligence and ability. In 1914, at the start of World War I, the younger Moltke made disastrous last-minute changes to the Schlieffen Plan (a long-standing, carefully thought-out plan of attack on France), for which he was later relieved of command. As it turned out, his modifications made it impossible for German troops to achieve their supreme goal—to sweep through France and capture Paris quickly. Four years of trench warfare resulted, costing millions of lives.

MICHAEL HUGHES
Author, *Nationalism and Society:
Germany 1800–1945*

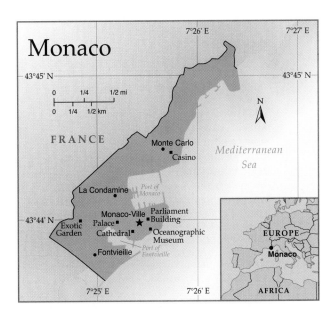

MONACO

Monaco is the second smallest independent state in the world, after Vatican City. Situated on the Mediterranean Sea, it occupies a tiny corner of southwestern Europe, surrounded on three sides by France. Monaco has been ruled for centuries by princes. Its official name is Principality of Monaco.

The most famous building in Monte Carlo is the Casino, which is always crowded with tourists who have come to gamble. The Casino, combined with the region's mild climate, has helped make Monaco a world-famous resort.

People. Monaco has a year-round population of about 32,000. Citizens of Monaco, who are known as Monégasques, make up only about 16 percent of the population. About half of Monaco's residents are French. Most of the remainder include Italians and other Europeans. French is the official language, although Monégasque (a mixture of French and Italian), Italian, English, and other languages also are spoken. Most of the people are Roman Catholics.

Land. Measuring about less than 1 square mile (2 square kilometers) in area, Monaco is smaller than New York City's Central Park. The principality is divided into four districts:

Monte Carlo (the resort and residential area); La Condamine and Fontvieille (the business and industrial districts); and Monaco-Ville (the capital). Monaco-Ville, the oldest part of the country, has cobblestone streets lined with old houses. Built in 1234, its major landmarks are the Prince's Palace, Monaco Cathedral, and the Oceanographic Museum.

Economy. Monaco's economy is based mainly on tourism. Main attractions include the Monte Carlo Casino and the Monaco Formula 1 Grand Prix car race, held every year in May.

Manufacturing accounts for about 30 percent of Monaco's income. Additional revenue comes from taxes on liquor, business registration fees, a small tax on business profits, and tobacco. Monaco has no unemployment, and legal residents pay no direct taxes on income and property.

History and Government. The modern history of Monaco began in the late 1200's when the Grimaldi family (the present ruling house) won control of Monaco. Its independence was recognized by France in 1512. But between 1793 and 1860, Monaco was ruled first by France and then by the Kingdom of Sardinia.

Monaco regained its independence in 1861. Its ruler at that time, Prince Charles III, de-

Monaco, on the Mediterranean Sea, is the world's second smallest nation, after Vatican City. Monaco-Ville (background left) is Monaco's capital and oldest district.

PRINCIPALITY OF MONACO (Principauté de Monaco) is the official name of the country.

LOCATION: Southwestern Europe.

AREA: ¾ sq mi (1.95 km²).

POPULATION: 32,000 (estimate).

CAPITAL AND LARGEST CITY: Monaco-Ville.

MAJOR LANGUAGE: French (official).

MAJOR RELIGIOUS GROUP: Roman Catholic.

GOVERNMENT: Constitutional monarchy. **Head of state**—prince. **Head of government**—minister of state. **Legislature**—National Council.

CHIEF PRODUCTS: Tourism is the mainstay of the economy. The chief manufactured products include small-scale industrial and consumer products.

MONETARY UNIT: Euro (1 euro = 100 cents).

cided to make an industry of tourism. He built a new town, Monte Carlo (Mount Charles), the Casino, and many fine hotels. Under Charles's son, Albert I, Monaco received its first constitution in 1912. In 1918 a treaty with France guaranteed the independence of Monaco as long as there is a male heir to the throne. France maintains limited protection over the principality.

Albert's son, Louis II, ruled until 1949. He was succeeded by his grandson, Rainier III. In 1956, Prince Rainier married Grace Kelly, an American film star, who brought glamour to the small principality. They had three children—Princesses Caroline and Stephanie and Prince Albert. Princess Grace died following a car accident in 1982. Prince Rainier died in 2005 and was succeeded by Prince Albert.

The government of Monaco is based on the Constitution of 1962. The prince, who is the head of state, appoints a minister of state (a French civil servant) to head the government. The members of the legislature, the National Council, are elected directly by the people. Monaco joined the United Nations in 1993. Although not a member of the European Union (EU), Monaco adopted the euro as its official currency in 2002.

Reviewed by TANITH FOWLER CORSI
Center for Global Education
George Mason University

MONDALE, WALTER F. See VICE PRESIDENCY OF THE UNITED STATES.

MONDRIAN, PIET (1872–1944)

Modern artist Piet Mondrian is recognized as a founding master of abstract art. His theory of art influenced the clean lines of modern architecture and commercial design.

Mondrian was born in Amersfoort, the Netherlands, on March 7, 1872. He received his first art lessons from his father. Mondrian enrolled in the Amsterdam Academy of Fine Arts in 1892.

In 1911, Mondrian went to Paris. There he saw the work of the cubists, a group of painters who represented objects from all sides, using combinations of flat shapes. He, too, began to produce some paintings using horizontal and vertical lines and no curves. On white backgrounds, he painted rectangles and squares of red, yellow, and blue. Mondrian's paintings represent

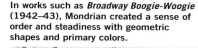

In works such as *Broadway Boogie-Woogie* (1942–43), Mondrian created a sense of order and steadiness with geometric shapes and primary colors.

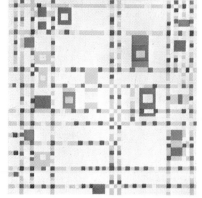

ideas. He believed that there is a logical reason for everything. He expressed his ideas through form and color, which give a sense of order and steadiness.

Mondrian returned to the Netherlands in 1914 and later formed a group of artists that came to be called De Stijl (The Style), after a magazine he helped start. Mondrian coined the term **neoplasticism** to describe the group's work, in which forms are restricted to simple geometric shapes and primary colors.

Mondrian lived in Paris from 1919 until 1938. At the beginning of World War II (1939–45), he moved to London and then to New York City. He continued to create important works, such as *Broadway Boogie-Woogie* (1942–43), until his death in New York on February 1, 1944.

Reviewed by ARIANE RUSKIN
BATTERBERRY
Author, *The Pantheon Story of Art for Young People*

Monet and other impressionists used hundreds of small brushstrokes side by side, often in contrasting colors, to give an impression of solid forms. *Boats at Argenteuil* (1875).

MONET, CLAUDE (1840–1926)

Claude Monet, a French landscape painter, was one of the founders of the style of art known as impressionism. He was born in Paris on November 14, 1840, but spent his childhood in Le Havre. When Monet was 15, he held an exhibit that interested the painter Eugène Boudin. Boudin persuaded him to take his materials outdoors to paint. Monet continued this practice throughout his life.

In 1860, after studying in Paris for a year, Monet joined the army and went to Algeria. He returned to Paris two years later. There he married and had two sons. In the Paris studio of Charles Gleyre, Monet met many other promising young artists, with whom he exhibited in 1874. The critics did not like their works and made fun of these "impressionists." The term was taken from the title of Monet's landscape *Impression: Sunrise*. This painting is reproduced in the article MODERN ART in Volume M.

Impressionism began at the time (the early 1870's) and in the setting of Monet's painting *Boats at Argenteuil*. Argenteuil is a suburb of Paris, on the Seine River. There the artists Monet, Manet, and Renoir painted together and learned from one another. By watching Monet, Manet became convinced for the first time that it was indeed possible to paint outdoors. Monet and Renoir painted so much alike that it was sometimes difficult for them to tell who had painted certain views.

Monet and the other impressionists placed unmixed colors side by side on their canvases to show how light splits into the colors of the prism—like a rainbow. To show how light could completely change the appearance of an object, Monet painted the same scene at different times of the day and year. For example, he painted the Rouen Cathedral 20 times, in conditions varying from a misty summer dawn to a brilliant winter sunset.

Monet's first wife died in 1879, and he later married a woman with several children of her own. In 1883 the couple moved to Giverny, where the artist created the gardens that inspired his paintings of water lilies.

Monet did not become famous or earn much money until he was over 50 years old. Then his paintings began to sell for higher prices. In 1916 the French government bought eight of Monet's paintings of water lilies. Although his eyesight began to fail, Monet painted until his death in Giverny on December 5, 1926.

FRANK GETLEIN
Author, *The French Impressionists*

MONEY

More than 2,000 years ago the Romans were using metal coins similar to those we use today. Many of these early coins were made in the temple of the goddess Juno, or Moneta. It is from the name "Moneta" that we get our word "money."

In most places throughout the world people are familiar with some form of what we call money. Yet, in spite of the fact that it is so widely known, money is very difficult to define. A London banker and the chief of an African tribe have widely different ideas of what money is.

Many people think of money as **currency**—metal coins and paper bills. But money is not simply currency—a United States nickel or dollar bill, a Mexican peso, a Canadian dollar, a French franc, an Italian lira, or a Russian ruble. Money is whatever people agree to use in exchange for goods and services.

Money serves people's purposes in several ways. Bakers, for example, cannot live on just the bread they bake. In today's society, they have to sell their bread to other people so that they can get the money they need to buy life's necessities. In this way, money is serving as a **medium of exchange**.

Because the baker knows how much money a loaf of bread will bring, money can do something else. It tells the baker how much work it takes to buy a new oven. Both the bread and the oven have their own price. So, money helps the baker decide whether he or she can afford a new oven by using it to bake and sell more bread. In this way, money is serving as a **standard of value**.

Finally, money can be saved. The baker can hardly set aside a couple of loaves of bread every day until they can be taken down the street to trade for a television set. Even if the television store were willing to take bread as payment, the loaves would be moldy by the time the baker had enough saved up. But the baker can set aside a little money every day. In this way, money serves as a **store of value**.

▶ **HISTORY OF MONEY**

Down through its long and fascinating history, money has undergone many changes. Long before people thought of making metal coins or paper bills, they needed some way to acquire the things they wanted.

Money is whatever people agree to accept in payment for goods and services. Some American Indians, for example, used beads called wampum during colonial days.

Barter

In early societies, money was unknown, and people relied on a simple system of exchange. Perhaps a good hunter had more animal skins than he could use. His neighbor, a good fisherman, might have too many fish but needed furs to protect his children from the cold. Both soon realized that their problems could be easily solved by exchanging what they did not need, their surplus, for what they did need.

This method of exchanging something not needed for something that is needed is called barter. The word comes from the Italian *barattare* and the French *barater*, which mean "to trade."

On the American frontier, a merchant might let a settler have an ax in return for a sack of wheat. The merchant might then trade the wheat to a miller who would make it into flour. The flour might then be traded to a trapper for animal skins.

Barter is still used today—not only by individuals, but also by corporations. An airline might let people from a fuel company fly on its planes in return for jet fuel. Since the airline probably has a few empty seats on its flights anyway, such a deal could be a significant saving for the airline.

But barter has disadvantages. If the settler on the American frontier had carried his sack of wheat to the merchant just after 40 other settlers had been there, the merchant might have decided that he no longer needed any wheat. That would mean that the settler would not have gotten his ax.

When labor and services became more specialized in growing societies, barter no longer satisfied the demands of payment. A new system of exchange had to be found.

Early Forms of Money

As societies developed, people turned to many different things in the search for a convenient medium of exchange, or money. One of the earliest forms of money was cattle. The richest person was the one who owned the most livestock. Cattle were called *capitale*, and from that Latin word we get our word "capital," meaning "wealth."

But this new method, too, had many drawbacks. A cow or a sheep must be fed and cared for. Some animals are fat and some are lean. A person who wanted to sell something might believe that it was worth much more than one cow. The buyer might not be willing to part with two. A cow and a half was certainly not a practical solution. Difficulties arose over exact values.

The use of cattle as a standard means of exchange decreased when people began to trade with people who lived far away. Again a new medium had to be found. Soon such things as grain and salt came into use. Both of these commodities had certain advantages. They could be weighed exactly. They could be stored in the holds of ships and transported easily. Salt, especially, was fairly scarce, an important quality for something used as a means of exchange. So widespread did the use of salt become that Roman soldiers were sometimes paid in salt. And it is from *salarium,* the Latin word for "salt money," that our own word "salary" comes. We still speak of people as not being worth their salt if they do not do their jobs well.

In early societies around the world, many different objects and products were used as money. The use of colored beads and ornaments was common. After Europeans came to North America, some Indian people began using shell beads, called wampum, as money. (The name "wampum" was taken from the word *wampumpeag,* meaning "string of white beads.") Cowrie shells were used in many areas, including China, India, and Africa.

People on the American frontier used various articles as money. Among these articles were gunpowder, tobacco, and nails, which were in short supply on the frontier. Today, smaller nails are still classified as two-penny nails, for example, and larger nails may be called ten-penny nails. These names are a remnant of the days when nails were used as money.

Coins

The more complex societies became, the less satisfactory livestock and other early media of exchange became. In the search for a better way of trading, people turned to metal. At first they used crude lumps of copper, iron, gold, or silver as money. Decorative metal ornaments became highly valued.

It is difficult to say just when the first metal coins were used. Some historians believe that the Chinese were using miniature metal knives and spades as money as early as 1000 B.C. A few examples of coins made of electrum, a natural alloy of gold and silver, have been found. They were made by the Lydians of Asia Minor about 700 B.C. The Greeks had a silver coin called a drachma; the Roman denarius was a common silver coin during the period of the Empire.

It took many hundreds of years for coins to replace barter and primitive forms of money. As the use of coins increased, their output came to be controlled by the ruler of a country. Governments began to regulate the production of all coins, and it became a crime for individuals to make counterfeits, or imitations, of those issued by authority.

A great step forward in the development of money came with the widespread use of coins in the late Middle Ages. Metals were stamped by the issuing authority and fashioned in uniform weights. People could determine how many coins were required to pay for a particular object or service.

The advantages of coins were many. Coins made it possible for people to trade in a standardized way. They had a set value. They came in various denominations, and prices could be set with some precision. Early coins were made from precious metals, such as gold and silver, which were valuable in their own right and gave people a feeling of wealth.

Paper Money

Paper money came into general use only about three centuries ago. However, some forms of it were known hundreds of years earlier. Many historians believe that the Chinese were printing paper money as early as the 900's A.D. The Italian explorer Marco Polo saw paper money in China in the 1200's. But it was not commonly used until the 1600's, when international trade was expanding at a rapid rate.

In many nations paper money was strongly distrusted when it was first introduced. It was often difficult to accept the idea that the new form of money stood for something real. Eventually, however, people's confidence increased. Paper currency is now standard in every civilized country in the world.

One advantage of paper money is that it is cheaper to make. Another is that it is easier to carry around in large quantities. But advantages can also create problems. The production of coins was dependent on limited supplies of gold and silver. Paper currency can be produced in virtually unlimited quantities. The danger is that creation of too much money will push prices up because if people have more money to spend, they will be willing to spend more of it on a particular object.

At first, governments tried to limit the creation of paper money by requiring that the paper money be backed by gold or silver. In the United States, for example, a dollar once entitled the holder to exchange the dollar bill for a set amount of gold. This **gold standard** assured that new dollars could be created no faster than the government was able to increase the amount of gold in its vaults. But governments decided that letting the production of gold and silver mines determine the amount of money in circulation was too artificial. At times, the amount of money increased too fast. At other times the amount of money grew too slowly. Most countries stopped using the gold standard in the 1930's. By 1972 the nations of the world abandoned the final remnants of the gold standard.

CURRENCY AROUND THE WORLD

When people travel from one country to another, they must change their money into the currency of the country they are visiting. Here are the currencies of some of the countries of the world:

Country	Currency
Argentina	1 **peso** = 100 centavos
Armenia	1 **dram** = 100 luma
Bolivia	1 **boliviano** = 100 centavos
Brazil	1 **real** = 100 centavos
Canada	1 **dollar** = 100 cents
Chile	1 **peso** = 100 centavos
China, People's Republic of	1 **yuan** = 100 fen
China, Republic of (Taiwan)	1 **new dollar** = 100 cents
Denmark	1 **krone** = 100 øre
Estonia	1 **kroon** = 100 senti
France	1 **euro** = 100 cents
Ghana	1 **cedi** = 100 pesewas
Greece	1 **euro** = 100 cents
India	1 **rupee** = 100 paisa
Indonesia	1 **rupiah** = 100 sen
Iran	1 **rial** = 100 dinars
Ireland	1 **euro** = 100 cents
Israel	1 **new shekel** = 100 agorot
Italy	1 **euro** = 100 cents
Japan	Basic currency is the **yen**
Kenya	1 **shilling** = 100 cents
Malaysia	1 **ringgit** = 100 sen
Mexico	1 **peso** = 100 centavos
Nigeria	1 **naira** = 100 kobo
Philippines	1 **peso** = 100 centavos
Poland	1 **zloty** = 100 groszy
Russia	1 **ruble** = 100 kopecks
Singapore	1 **dollar** = 100 cents
South Africa	1 **rand** = 100 cents
Sweden	1 **krona** = 100 öre
Syrian Arab Republic	1 **Syrian pound** = 100 piastres
Thailand	1 **baht** = 100 satangs
United Kingdom	1 **pound sterling** = 100 pence
United States	1 **dollar** = 100 cents

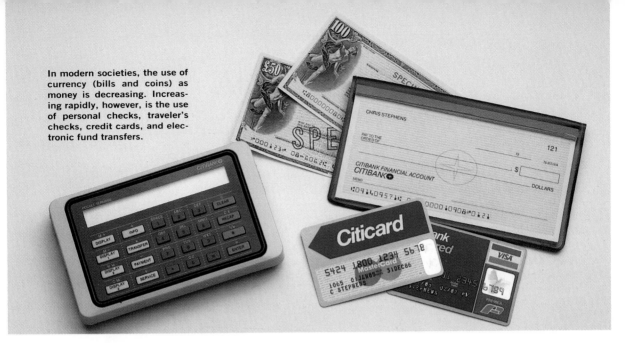

In modern societies, the use of currency (bills and coins) as money is decreasing. Increasing rapidly, however, is the use of personal checks, traveler's checks, credit cards, and electronic fund transfers.

▶MONEY TODAY

In the United States today, the amount of money in circulation is controlled by the **Federal Reserve System**. The Federal Reserve was set up by Congress in 1913. Its purpose is to assure that business gets enough money to expand and to create new jobs. But the Federal Reserve must be careful that new money is not put in circulation so fast that it only pushes prices up. The Federal Reserve controls the amount of money in circulation through its control over banks. In fact, the Federal Reserve is called a **central bank**.

The Federal Reserve controls the amount of money in circulation in two ways. First, it sets the amount of reserves a bank must hold. Lowering the amount required to be held in reserve, for example, increases the amount of money banks can lend. Second, the Federal Reserve buys and sells government securities (bonds). When the Federal Reserve buys government securities, the money goes into the bank accounts of the companies that sold the securities. There, the banks can use the money to make new loans. When the Federal Reserve sells government securities, the money flows out of the banks and into the Federal Reserve. When it is in the Federal Reserve, people cannot use the money for spending.

In a modern society, actual currency—coins and bills—represents a small part of the money in existence. Most money is simply a bookkeeping entry in a bank, representing the value of the goods a merchant has sold or the value of a job a worker has done to earn a paycheck. The money can be moved from one account to another by a **check**, which is a written order from an account holder telling his or her bank to transfer the money to the person or business named in the check. Transfers of money can also be ordered electronically. By passing a plastic card through a special machine that "reads" a coded magnetic tape on the card, a shopper can pay for purchases in a store. The signals picked up from the card are transferred to the banks electronically, where the money is moved from the shopper's account to the merchant's account.

The electronic system is a variation on the **credit card** system. With a credit card, the bank is actually lending its customer money to make purchases. The merchant sends the slip signed by the customer to the bank, the bank pays the merchant, and the customer eventually pays the bank.

Today's system of handling money is far removed from barter, nails, or salt. In the United States, the government decrees that people must accept dollars as payment for debts. In technical terms, the dollar is **legal tender**. It is up to individuals to determine how many dollars—how much money—they will demand as payment for goods or work. Ultimately, the value of money depends on the goods people produce and the work that they do.

Reviewed and revised by G. DAVID WALLACE
Author, *Money Basics*

See also BANKS AND BANKING; COINS AND COIN COLLECTING; CREDIT CARDS; DOLLAR; MINT.

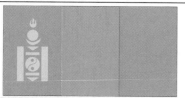

MONGOLIA

In the 1200's, mounted Mongol warriors led by Genghis Khan swept across Asia and parts of Europe. They conquered vast territories and created a great empire. The original home of these warriors was the Mongolian plateau of east central Asia. Today the country of Mongolia occupies the northern half of the plateau. It is occasionally referred to as Outer Mongolia to distinguish it from Inner Mongolia, a region of China.

Outer Mongolia was ruled as a Chinese province until 1911, when it declared its independence. But it soon fell under the influence of its powerful Communist neighbor to the north, the Soviet Union. Mongolia became a Communist country in 1924 and remained so until the breakup of the Soviet Union in 1991.

▶ PEOPLE

Various Mongol tribes include the Halh (Khalkha), who make up approximately 75 percent of the population; the Dörvöd; and the Bayad. The Kazakhs, a Turkic people, are the largest non-Mongol group, followed by Russians and Chinese.

Language. The official language of the country is Khalkha Mongol, which is written in the Cyrillic, or Russian, alphabet. Many Mongols also speak Russian or Chinese.

Religion. For centuries, most Mongols have followed Lamaism, a form of Buddhism introduced from Tibet. The Turkic people are chiefly Muslims. There are also some Mongolian Christians.

Education. Ten years of schooling are required in Mongolia, beginning at age 6. About 83 percent of the adult population is literate (able to read and write).

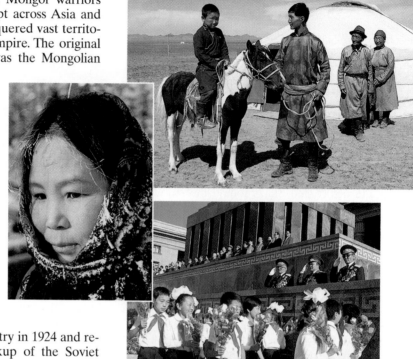

Left and top: Mongols are an ancient people. Traditionally they lived as nomads in open grasslands. *Above:* In Ulaanbaatar, the nation's capital, children celebrate National Day to commemorate Mongolia's declaration of independence from China in 1921.

Way of Life. At one time most of the people were nomads who lived on the open steppes (level, treeless grasslands). Their homes, called yurts, were made of light wooden frames covered by felt cloth. When the nomads traveled, they took their homes with them. The nomads lived off their herds of sheep, goats, cattle, horses, and camels. The animals provided them with transportation and their staple foods—milk, butter, cheese, and meat. The favorite drinks of the nomads were *airag* (fermented mare's milk) and tea. Today the nomad population is declining as more Mongols are moving into towns and cities.

▶ LAND

Mongolia is one of the largest countries in Asia. It occupies a large inland plateau that is shaped like a saucer. Broad rolling plains cover most of the country. At some points mountainous regions break through the plains. Long belts of mountains in the north, principally the Tannu-Ola and Hentiyn ranges, separate Mongolia from Siberia, a region of Russia. Much of northern Mongolia is made up of forests and is fairly rich in wildlife. Reindeer are especially common.

The southern region of Mongolia is called the Gobi, the Mongol word for "desert." Parched and barren, it has long been uninhabited. It is the northernmost desert area in the world.

Mongolia's principal river, the Selenga, begins near the Hangayn Mountains and flows northward, emptying into Lake Baikal in Siberia. Other important rivers are the Kerulen and the Onon in the northeast.

The Mongolian climate is marked by sharp extremes. In much of the region, the summers are short and hot. The winters are long and quite cold, with winter temperatures as low as –52°F (–47°C). Although summer temperatures may rise to over 90°F (32°C), they average about 64°F (18°C). Mongolia has only light annual rainfall, averaging between 2 inches (50 millimeters) in the south and 12 inches (300 millimeters) in the north.

▶ ECONOMY

The raising of livestock is Mongolia's most important economic activity. Sheep and goats are the most numerous, but millions of cattle, horses, and camels are also raised. The Mongols get most of their food, wool, horsehair, and leather from their herds. The animals also furnish such other necessities as clothing, shelter, and transportation.

In recent years the government has encouraged the growth of farming and industry. Large grassland areas on the steppes have been broken by plows and planted with crops for the first time. Many Mongols are now using modern farm machines, such as tractors and harvesters. Grains and potatoes are the leading crops.

An increasing number of people are now employed in industry. Major products include processed foods (particularly meat), textiles, leather goods, and wood products. Mining is also of growing importance. The chief minerals are coal, copper, molybdenum, and fluorspar.

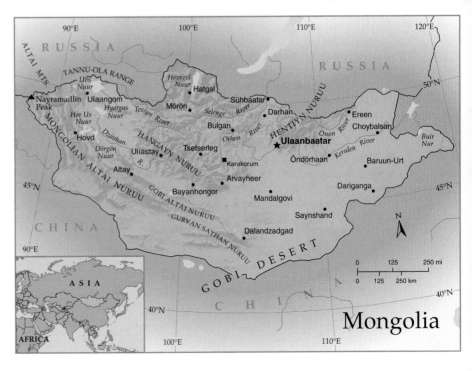

Mongolia

حصاوكريشه وناملك زانى سينه ده وان شنياد هاآتراطه خوار كها يند

وارآ يكاشيدرشه كذاام آن كلكك ايحى ست وتهنى ده آرا يمونهست ونعارد ار دا وبعى دكرا

The fearsome Mongol emperor Genghis Khan, pictured here with his sons, ruled the largest land empire in the history of the world.

MAJOR CITIES

Ulaanbaatar, the capital and largest city of Mongolia, is the country's industrial, cultural, and political center. Its population is approximately 650,000. Ulaanbaatar is home to the National Choibalsan University and the Academy of Sciences. Ulaanbaatar (formerly called Urga) was first settled in 1639 by Lamaist monks and was situated on the caravan route between Russia and China. When Mongolia became a Communist republic in 1924, the city was renamed Ulaanbaatar, which means "Red Hero."

Darhan, with a population of just 87,000, is Mongolia's second most populous city. Built in the late 1960's with financial help from the Soviet Union, Darhan is a regional center of heavy industry and manufacturing.

GOVERNMENT

Mongolia's government is based on a constitution adopted in 1992. It provides for a one-house legislature called the State Great Hural (Assembly), whose members are elected by the people to 4-year terms. The Hural chooses a prime minister to head the government. A president, who serves as head of state and commander in chief of the armed forces, is also elected for four years. Supreme court judges are approved by the Hural.

Mongolia is divided into 18 provinces and three municipalities. The provinces have appointed governors and locally elected assemblies.

HISTORY

Early History. The Mongolian plateau has been inhabited since ancient times. For centuries the people were organized into small local tribes that fought among themselves to protect and conquer new pasturelands. The great era for the Mongols arrived in the 1200's, when the many tribes of Mongolia were united and brought under the leadership of Genghis Khan (1167?–1227). For more information, see the article on Genghis Khan in Volume G.

The victories of Genghis Khan were repeated by his descendants. The greatest of them was his grandson Kublai Khan (1216–94) who ruled Mongolia and China (the Yüan dynasty of China) as chief khan of the Mongols. His empire reached from the Pacific Ocean to eastern Europe.

After the death of Kublai Khan, the Mongol Empire fell apart. In the 1600's, the Manchus, a people from Manchuria in northeastern China, conquered all of China. Mongolia soon became part of their empire, and it remained so for more than two centuries.

Modern Period. In 1911, the Mongols overthrew the Manchus. They then ruled themselves until Chinese troops occupied part of the country in 1919. In 1921, Mongol revolutionaries, led by Sukhe Bator and aided by the Soviet Union, entered what is now Ulaanbaatar and seized control of the government. In 1924 they proclaimed Mongolia a Communist state, although China did not formally recognize its independence until 1946.

Mongolia was long an ally of the Soviet Union and relied heavily on Soviet economic aid. But the revolutionary political changes that eventually broke the Soviet Union apart also affected Mongolia. Massive demonstrations in favor of democracy in 1990 brought some political reforms, including multiparty elections. But the Communist Party, known as the Mongolian People's Revolutionary Party (MPRP), maintained its hold on power.

In 1992 a new constitution abolished Communism and introduced a democratic government and economic reforms. Nevertheless, Mongolia's former economic dependence on the Soviet Union has made its transition from a state-controlled economy to a free-market economy a difficult one.

HYMAN KUBLIN
City University of New York, Brooklyn College

MONGOOSES, MEERKATS, AND THEIR RELATIVES

In an Indian jungle, a small, weasel-like mammal advances toward a cobra. Its hood spread wide, the snake rears and prepares to strike. It faces one of its most dangerous enemies—a mongoose.

This fierce predator is from a family of more than 100 species, or kinds, of meat-eating mammals called the viverrids, which inhabit various parts of the Eastern Hemisphere. Sometimes called weasel cats, viverrids are about the same size as domestic cats, with long bodies and tails.

Mongooses. Many kinds of mongooses live in Africa and Asia; one species lives in southern Europe. Unlike most viverrids, they may be most active during the day, when they hunt snakes, rodents, and other small animals.

Mongooses are famous for killing poisonous snakes. A quick-footed mongoose can dodge a striking cobra and avoid its bite. Before the cobra can strike again, the mongoose leaps and bites it at the back of the head. When the snake has been killed, the mongoose eats it, poison sacs and all. But the mongoose usually dies if the cobra bites it.

About a century ago, mongooses were brought to the Caribbean islands to kill rats. The adaptable rats soon took refuge in trees, where mongooses seldom ventured. The mongooses, in their turn, took to eating eggs, birds, and other small native animals. The same damage has happened in other areas where mongooses have been introduced. As a result, the United States has long forbidden anyone to bring mongooses into the country.

Meerkats. A relative of the mongoose is the meerkat, or suricate, of Africa. It is especially

An Asian mongoose (*above*) prepares to attack a cobra, whose deadly bite the quick-footed mammal is adept at avoiding. Its African relatives, the meerkats (*below*), are more social animals that can stand on their hind legs to watch for predators.

known for standing on its hind legs, using its tail as a support. This posture helps the little animal look out for predators while fellow meerkats forage for food nearby.

Like the prairie dogs of North America, meerkats are social animals. Sometimes they form colonies with squirrels, whose tunnels they occupy. Meerkats will often abandon their homes and build new underground passages when their food supply runs low. Their varied diet includes insects, mice, lizards, birds' eggs, and fruit.

Civets and Genets. Another group of viverrids are the civets, or civet cats, of Africa and Asia. Civets produce a substance with a strong odor called civet musk, which they use to mark their territory. Civet musk has been an important perfume ingredient, although it can now be made artificially. Palm civets often make their homes in palm trees. They are often called toddy cats because they drink the palm sap, or "toddy," that people collect.

Genets are catlike viverrids that live mostly in Africa. Their curved claws can be drawn back into sheaths, and their coats are spotted. The ancient Greeks are said to have tamed genets and kept them as pets and expert mousers.

Other Relatives. Other kinds of viverrids live in Indonesia, home to the binturong, and Madagascar, where the fossa roams. Also called the bear cat, the binturong has black, shaggy fur and a long, bushy tail, which it uses to hold on to branches. It is slow and awkward on the ground, moving like a bear. The fossa resembles a long cat with short, smooth fur. Scientists think the fossa may be a link between the civets and the true cats.

ROBERT M. McCLUNG
Author, science books for children

Clockwise from far left: The tiny pygmy marmoset, the sleepy white-faced capuchin, the watchful De Brazza's monkey, and the hulking mandrill display the great contrasts that can be found among monkeys.

MONKEYS

Monkeys are long-limbed, hairy animals with tails. They are part of a group of mammals, along with human beings, apes, and some primitive animals such as lemurs and lorises, called **primates**. Primitive lemur-like primates were the common ancestors of all monkeys. These tree-dwelling relatives lived more than 55 million years ago.

As the Earth changed over time, old landmasses separated, forming new ones. Some of the early ancestors of monkeys moved from the connected landmasses that formed North America and Europe toward the landmass that formed Central and South America, while others moved toward the landmass that formed Africa. The changes in land also meant changes in the development of monkeys. Two distinct groups of monkeys arose: **New World** monkeys and **Old World** monkeys. New World monkeys, including marmosets, tamarins, douroucoulis, as well as woolly, howler, spider, and squirrel monkeys, populate Central and South America, while Old World monkeys, including macaques, langurs, baboons, guenons, and colobus monkeys, inhabit Africa, Asia, and Europe (Rock of Gibraltar).

▶ CHARACTERISTICS OF MONKEYS

There is a wide range in the size of the 133 different species, or kinds, of monkeys. The smallest monkey, the pygmy marmoset, weighs as little as 4 ounces (113 grams), while the imposing male mandrill can weigh as much as 100 pounds (45 kilograms). Although sizes may differ widely, New World monkeys and Old World monkeys share many of the same general characteristics due to their common ancestors. Monkeys are intelligent animals with large, well-developed brains. They are able to adapt to a wide range of environments, from tropical forests to snowcapped mountains. Some monkeys live their entire lives in the trees, while others make their home on the ground and only seek the shelter of trees when it is time to rest. However, all monkeys have bodies that are well suited to living in the trees, and all are capable of climbing in the trees.

Except for baboons, most monkeys have short, flattened snouts. Like apes and humans, monkeys have keen vision. Their eyes, which are set in the front of the head, look straight forward. They have full-color vision and are able to see in three dimensions. Their long limbs end in hands and feet with flexible fingers and toes that, except for marmosets and tamarins, are tipped with nails instead of claws. Monkeys use their well-developed hands to pick up and hold both large and small objects in much the same manner as people do. The tail of a monkey helps provide balance as it moves about on land and in the trees.

Did you know that...

the only monkeys in Europe are called apes? The so-called Barbary apes live on the Rock of Gibraltar, at the tip of Spain. The "apes" really belong to a group of monkeys called macaques. Barbary apes also live in North Africa, across the Mediterranean Sea from Gibraltar. Scientists are not sure whether the Barbary apes traveled to Gibraltar by themselves or whether people, possibly the Romans, brought them from Africa and released them. They do know that Barbary apes have lived on Gibraltar for more than 1,000 years!

The feature that most readily identifies a monkey as Old World or New World is the nose. Old World monkeys have noses with nostrils that are close together and that open to the front, while the noses of New World monkeys have nostrils that are far apart and that open to the sides.

Other features also identify to which group a monkey belongs. Old World monkeys have special pads on their rumps. The pads are

thick, tough calluses that probably allow them to sit for long periods of time. Except for the colobus monkeys, all of them also have **opposable thumbs**, which means that their thumbs can be turned and placed against other fingers. Although Old World monkeys are well suited to climbing and moving about among the tree branches, many of them live most of their lives on the ground. An additional feature that identifies some Old World monkeys are cheek pouches that they use to temporarily store food when they are feeding.

The differences in their noses reveal that the douc monkey (*left*) is an Old World species and the douroucouli, or night monkey (*below*), is a New World species.

The New World monkeys have typically slender bodies and limbs and long tails. These quick, skillful climbers seldom come down from the tree branches of their forest homes. They move gracefully through the trees, leaping considerable distances between branches. Some of these tree dwellers have a special kind of tail called a **prehensile**, or grasping, tail that serves as another hand, which is a great advantage when moving about in the trees. The thumbs of New World monkeys are not truly opposable, but they are able to move their thumbs and hands to grip objects.

▶ THE LIFE OF MONKEYS

Monkeys are social animals; that is, they live in groups. The kinds of members that make up a group depend on the species. Some, such as marmosets and tamarins, live in family groups that are each headed by a

Not all monkeys are acrobatic tree dwellers like the New World squirrel monkey (*top*) or woolly spider monkey (*middle*). Most Old World monkeys, such as the baboon (*bottom*), seldom leave the ground.

Monkeys exhibit many distinctive behaviors. A Philippine macaque (*top left*) searches for the crabs it feeds on. A langur community (*above*) can include one male, several males, or only males. A chorus of howler monkeys (*bottom left*) unleashes a loud, penetrating song.

on the species. Most male monkeys do not take a very active part in rearing their offspring; however, marmosets, douroucoulis, and tamarins are exceptions.

Group membership can change over time, with members leaving the group and new members joining. Relations within the group are kept agreeable through behaviors such as grooming each other, or cleaning each other's fur. However, not all activities are positive. Some members, especially young males, may be driven from the group by the head male.

▶ MONKEYS AND THEIR ENVIRONMENT

While there are some wild animals that prey on monkeys, it is human beings that pose the most significant threat to monkeys. In some parts of the world, people kill monkeys in large numbers for use as food. Because they share certain primate characteristics with people, monkeys are often captured for use in medical research. But the greatest danger occurs as people destroy the monkey's habitat. Tropical forests are being rapidly cut for timber and to make room for agriculture and ranches.

Conservationists and other concerned people are trying to preserve monkey populations in several ways. Efforts are directed at preventing the destruction of forest habitat and protecting the animals from being killed or taken from their natural homes. Increasingly, monkeys are being bred in captivity so they do not have to be taken from the wild for research. Meanwhile, rare monkeys, such as the lion tamarins, are being bred in zoos to make certain they will not vanish forever.

EDWARD R. RICCIUTI
Coauthor, *The Audubon Society Book of Wild Animals*
Reviewed by JAMES G. DOHERTY
Curator of Mammals
The Bronx Zoo

See also APES; PRIMATES.

mother and father. A family usually contains more than one generation of young. Other species, including plains baboons, live in large groups, or **troops**, with several males and many females. A troop may number 300 animals, although it usually is less than 100. Still others, the langurs (leaf monkeys) and guenons for example, live in groups with only one male but several females and their young.

Living in a group has several advantages. It means that help is readily available to find food. Monkeys spend most of their waking hours feeding or searching for food. Most are not fussy eaters—they will eat many different things, including leaves, fruits, grasses, and other plant matter, as well as animals such as insects, eggs, bats, birds, and small reptiles.

Group living also means that when it is time to breed, there are possible mates close at hand. Some monkeys have regular breeding seasons, but others may breed at any time of the year. Although twin births do occur, especially in marmosets and tamarins, usually a single offspring is born to a female. The baby monkey is cared for and protected by its mother for as long as two years, depending

MONONUCLEOSIS, INFECTIOUS. See DISEASES (Descriptions of Some Diseases).

JAMES MONROE (1758-1831)
5th President of the United States

FACTS ABOUT MONROE

Birthplace: Westmoreland County, Virginia
Religion: Episcopalian
College Attended: College of William and Mary, Williamsburg, Virginia (did not graduate)
Occupation: Lawyer
Married: Elizabeth Kortright
Children: Eliza, James Spence (died in infancy), Maria Hester
Political Party: Democratic-Republican
Offices Held Before Becoming President: Secretary of State, Secretary of War
President Who Preceded Him: James Madison
Age on Becoming President: 58
Years in the Presidency: 1817–1825
Vice President: Daniel D. Tompkins
President Who Succeeded Him: John Quincy Adams
Age at Death: 73
Burial Place: Richmond, Virginia (moved from New York City in 1858)

James Monroe (signature)

DURING MONROE'S PRESIDENCY

Below: Construction was begun on the Erie Canal (1817). Mississippi (1817) and Illinois (1818) were admitted to the Union. Florida was purchased from Spain (1819).
Above: The U.S. ship *Savannah* became the first steam-powered vessel to cross the Atlantic Ocean (1819). Alabama was admitted to the Union (1819). The first public high school opened in Boston, Massachusetts (1820). Under the Missouri Compromise, Maine (1820) and Missouri (1821) were admitted to the Union. The Monroe Doctrine was proclaimed (1823).
Left: The African nation of Liberia adopted its present name and renamed its capital Monrovia in Monroe's honor (1824).

MONROE, JAMES. James Monroe was the last of the Virginia Dynasty of U.S. presidents, which also included Thomas Jefferson and James Madison. A modest man, Monroe was overshadowed by the brilliance of his great contemporaries, but his honesty and integrity won him wide esteem and the unwavering loyalty of his friends. He spent nearly all of his adult life in the public service, steadily rising to ever higher office. As president, he is best known for his proclamation of the Monroe Doctrine, opposing European intervention in the affairs of the countries of the Western Hemisphere. His two terms in office, sometimes called the Era of Good Feelings, were generally a period of national optimism, growth, and expansion for the United States.

▶ EARLY YEARS

Monroe was born on April 28, 1758, in Westmoreland County, Virginia, the son of Spence and Elizabeth Jones Monroe. He was educated by a tutor at home and at a private school, and in 1774 he entered the College of William and Mary in Williamsburg. In 1776, at the age of 18, he left college to join the American forces in the Revolutionary War. Commissioned a lieutenant in the Third Virginia Regiment, he took part, over the next two years, in some of the momentous battles and campaigns of the American Revolution.

Returning to Virginia, Monroe studied law with the man who would help shape his career and affect his whole life—Thomas Jefferson, who was then governor. The friendship between them lasted until Jefferson's death in 1826. Jefferson, who was Monroe's senior by 15 years, unfailingly helped the younger man advance his political career, all the way to the presidency. His confidence in Monroe never wavered. Jefferson said of him, "He is a man whose soul might be turned wrong side outwards, without discovering a blemish. . . ."

ENTRY INTO POLITICS AND MARRIAGE

In 1782, Monroe won election to the Virginia House of Delegates and a year later to the Congress of the Confederation, under which the United States was governed until the adoption of the Constitution. He served in the Confederation Congress until 1786, when he returned to Virginia. In 1788, Monroe was elected to the state convention called to ratify the U.S. Constitution. Along with fellow Virginians Patrick Henry and George Mason, he opposed its adoption, feeling that it centered too much power in the federal, or central, government.

Nevertheless, he accepted the Constitution's ratification and ran for a seat in the House of Representatives in the First Congress of the United States. He was unsuccessful, losing out to James Madison, but in 1790

The beautiful daughter of a wealthy New York merchant, Elizabeth Kortright married James Monroe in 1786.

he won election to the U.S. Senate. Together with Madison and Jefferson, who was then serving as secretary of state, Monroe led the fight against the policies of the Federalist Party. The three helped organize a new political party, the Republicans (also known as the Democratic-Republicans), in opposition to the Federalists.

In 1786, Monroe had married Elizabeth Kortright, the beautiful 17-year-old daughter of a wealthy New York merchant. Of the three children born to them, two daughters, Eliza and Maria Hester, survived. The third child, a son named James Spence, died in infancy.

MINISTER TO FRANCE AND GOVERNOR

In 1794, President George Washington appointed Monroe minister to France. The French had overthrown their king a few years earlier, and Washington hoped to improve relations with the country's revolutionary leaders as well as with their sympathizers in the United States. The French government gave Monroe an enthusiastic reception. Monroe returned the enthusiasm. But his open support for the French and his criticism of a U.S. treaty with Britain (the Jay Treaty) antagonized Washington's pro-British cabinet, and Monroe was recalled in 1796. In 1799 he was elected governor of Virginia, serving until 1802.

DIPLOMAT FOR JEFFERSON

In 1803, Monroe was again sent on a diplomatic mission to France, this time by Jefferson, who had succeeded to the presidency. He was appointed special envoy to assist the regular U.S. minister, Robert R. Livingston. Monroe carried with him to Paris the president's confidence and his special instructions. These were, primarily, to buy the city of New Orleans from the French and to acquire the right of free navigation on the Mississippi River. The French surprised the two diplomats by offering to sell them the whole Louisiana Territory. After some haggling, a treaty was signed in 1803, by which the United States acquired the territory for $15

IMPORTANT DATES IN THE LIFE OF JAMES MONROE

1758	Born in Westmoreland County, Virginia, April 28.
1776	Left the College of William and Mary to join the American forces in the Revolutionary War.
1782	Elected to the Virginia House of Delegates.
1783–86	Served in the Congress of the Confederation.
1786	Married Elizabeth Kortright.
1788	Elected a delegate to the Virginia Ratification Convention.
1790–94	Served in the U.S. Senate.
1794–96	Served as U.S. minister to France.
1799–1802	Served as governor of Virginia.
1803	Helped negotiate the purchase of the Louisiana Territory from France.
1803–07	Served on diplomatic missions to Britain and Spain.
1811	Elected again as governor of Virginia.
1811–17	Served as secretary of state; also held the post of secretary of war (1814–15).
1817–25	Served as fifth president of the United States.
1831	Died in New York City, July 4.

As president, Monroe is probably best remembered for the proclamation, in 1823, of the doctrine that bears his name. Here, Monroe and his cabinet discuss the doctrine, which warned against European interference in the affairs of the nations of the Western Hemisphere.

million. The acquisition doubled the size of the United States and greatly enhanced Monroe's reputation. See the article on the Louisiana Purchase in Volume L.

Pleased with Monroe's diplomatic efforts in France, Jefferson appointed him minister to Britain. He was then dispatched to Spain to help the American minister, Charles Pinckney, negotiate U.S. claims to West Florida, but they were unsuccessful. Returning to Britain, Monroe concluded a commercial treaty with the British in 1806. But the treaty did not resolve the main dispute with Britain—the impressment, or forcing into service, of American seamen in the British navy. Jefferson therefore decided not to submit it to the U.S. Senate for ratification.

▶ **TWO CABINET POSTS**

A disappointed Monroe returned home in 1807. His friends sought to promote him as a candidate for the presidency to succeed Jefferson, but the nomination and the election went to James Madison. Monroe resumed political life in Virginia, serving in the state legislature and, in 1811, as governor again.

He resigned the governorship that same year when Madison appointed him secretary of state. He held this post throughout the War of 1812 with Britain and until the end of Madison's presidency. In 1814, Monroe was named to the additional cabinet post of secretary of war. His energetic policies as war secretary were given some of the credit for U.S. victories at the battles of Plattsburg in 1814 and New Orleans in 1815. They also helped him win his party's nomination for the presidency in 1816. See the article on the War of 1812 in Volume W-X-Y-Z.

In the election of 1816, Monroe easily defeated his Federalist opponent, Rufus King of New York, winning 183 electoral votes to 34 for King. The election result emphasized the loss of political power by the Federalists, who had opposed the War of 1812.

▶ **PRESIDENT**

The Era of Good Feelings. As president, Monroe adopted a policy of tolerance toward his opponents, seeking an end to sectional and political rivalries. Soon after his inauguration, he undertook a goodwill tour of New

England, a Federalist stronghold, and was so well received that a Boston newspaper acclaimed his visit as the beginning of an "era of good feelings." The phrase stuck and became a byword for the period of Monroe's presidency.

Foreign Affairs. Monroe's administration was especially notable for its achievements in foreign affairs. Much of this was due to the able diplomacy of Secretary of State John Quincy Adams. Three important treaties were concluded during Monroe's first term in office. The Rush-Bagot Agreement of 1817 with Britain limited the number of naval vessels permitted on American inland waters, and the Convention of 1818 fixed the northwestern boundary between the United States and British Canada. Under the Adams-Onís (or Transcontinental) Treaty of 1819, the United States acquired East Florida from Spain, which also gave up its claims to West Florida.

Missouri Compromise. A potentially explosive sectional dispute arose in 1819, following Missouri's application for admission to the Union as a slave state. The United States then consisted of an equal number of free states (where slavery was prohibited) and slave states. The Missouri Compromise of 1820 provided for the admission of Missouri as a slave state and Maine as a free state, maintaining the balance. Slavery was also banned from territory north of the 36° 30' line of latitude. See the article on the Missouri Compromise in this volume.

Second Term. Monroe ran unopposed for re-election in 1820 and received all but one of the electoral votes cast. He would have received all if not for one elector, who decided that no one should share that historic honor with George Washington and cast his ballot for John Quincy Adams.

Monroe's attitude toward domestic issues reflected his concept of limited government. He had maintained a cautious stance during the Missouri crisis, allowing it to be resolved by Congress. In 1822 he vetoed the Cumberland Road Bill as being beyond the power of Congress, but recommended a constitutional amendment that would give the federal government the authority to undertake such "great national works."

The Monroe Doctrine. The most memorable event connected with Monroe's presidency was the proclamation of the doctrine that bears his name. It began as a public declaration of U.S. policy, expressed in a message to Congress in 1823. The Monroe Doctrine became a foundation of the country's foreign policy, particularly in regard to Latin America. See the article on the Monroe Doctrine following this article.

▶ **LATER YEARS**

Upon his retirement from the presidency in 1825, Monroe returned to Oak Hill, his home in Virginia. In 1826 he became a regent of the University of Virginia, and in 1829 he presided over the Virginia State Constitutional Convention. After the death of his wife in 1830, Monroe, lonely and ill, went to live with his daughter Maria Hester and her husband, Samuel L. Gouverneur, in New York City. There he died on July 4, 1831, at the age of 73. In 1858, on the 100th anniversary of his birth, his remains were moved to Richmond, Virginia.

SAUL K. PADOVER
Author, *The Genius of America*

MONROE, MARILYN. See MOTION PICTURES (Profiles: Movie Stars).

This striking memorial marks James Monroe's grave in Richmond, Virginia. His remains were moved there in 1858 from New York City, where he had died in 1831.

MONROE DOCTRINE

The Monroe Doctrine, as it later came to be called, was first proclaimed by President James Monroe on December 2, 1823, as part of his annual address to Congress. It was a statement of U.S. policy opposing any European interference in the affairs of the newly independent nations of the Western Hemisphere.

The Doctrine. The doctrine had four main points: (1) The countries of the Western Hemisphere were no longer to be regarded "as subjects for future colonization by any European powers"; (2) the political system of these countries was different from those of Europe; (3) the United States would regard any attempt by European countries "to extend their system" to the Western Hemisphere as a threat to its "peace and safety"; and (4) the United States had no intention of interfering in the affairs of the European powers "in matters relating to themselves."

Historical Background. Monroe had issued this declaration because of reports that Austria, Russia, and Prussia were considering lending their support to France in an attempt to restore, by armed intervention, Spanish power in the Americas. The former Spanish colonies had only recently won their independence. The same reports had reached the British foreign minister, George Canning. The British, for their own reasons, were also reluctant to see these continental powers intrude into the Western Hemisphere.

Canning proposed a joint declaration by the United States and Britain. After consulting his cabinet and previous presidents Thomas Jefferson and James Madison, Monroe was inclined to accept the offer. But he was persuaded by Secretary of State John Quincy Adams to take the step independently, to avoid relying on the British.

Later Influences. Several examples of the doctrine's later influence on U.S. foreign policy can be given.

In 1845, President James K. Polk referred to Monroe's proclamation in the dispute with Britain over the Oregon Territory.

During the early 1860's, when the United States was distracted by a civil war, the French emperor Napoleon III sought to es-

A political cartoon of the early 1900's depicts the U.S. fleet as a powerful symbol of the Monroe Doctrine.

tablish a monarchy in Mexico. In calling for a withdrawal of French troops, Secretary of State William H. Seward evoked the spirit, although not the name, of the Monroe Doctrine. Napoleon III, beset by troubles in Europe, eventually did withdraw them, and the short-lived Mexican empire collapsed.

In 1895, President Grover Cleveland specifically mentioned the doctrine in demanding that Britain arbitrate the boundary dispute between its colony of British Guiana (now Guyana) and Venezuela.

In the early 1900's, President Theodore Roosevelt added what is known as the Roosevelt Corollary to the doctrine. It stated that, although European intervention in the Americas might sometimes be justified, it could not be permitted under the Monroe Doctrine; instead, the United States itself would take action in the country involved. The corollary was used to justify U.S. intervention in several Latin American countries, before it was revoked.

Modern Interpretation. During the 1930's, President Franklin Roosevelt's Good Neighbor Policy resulted in a series of nonintervention treaties with Latin American countries. These meant that the doctrine could not be evoked—short of an armed attack—without the agreement of the American republics. No U.S. president since then has actually pronounced the Monroe Doctrine dead, but it has been left largely unused.

SAMUEL FLAGG BEMIS
Yale University
Author, *A Diplomatic History
of the United States*

MONTANA

In 1864, the U.S. government carved a brand new territory out of what was then the enormous Idaho Territory, crossing the Rocky Mountains on the western frontier. Congressman James M. Ashley of Ohio, the chairman of the House Committee on Territories, attached to the new land the name Montana, from the Spanish word montaña, *meaning "mountainous."*

Long ago the Native Americans called Montana the Land of the Shining Mountains, but later settlers dubbed it the Treasure State due to its vast resources of minerals, timber, and coal. Today it is also known as Big Sky Country. This name, adapted from the title of a popular western novel by A. B. Guthrie, Jr., evokes the vast and open beauty of Montana's unspoiled horizons.

State flag

Located in the northwestern United States, Montana is one of the six Rocky Mountain states. Graced by the astonishing beauty of Glacier and Yellowstone national parks, Montana's western mountain region stands in marked contrast to the gently rolling grasslands of the High Plains country of eastern Montana, described by the early American explorer Meriwether Lewis as "level as a bowling green."

Montana is the nation's fourth largest state, yet it has no major cities. Most of today's people live in the western mountains, where they find employment in mining, logging, and the booming retail trades and service industries.

Active promotion since 1987 has dramatically increased the number of tourists who visit Montana's numerous national parks, forests, and wilderness areas, old mining towns, historical museums, and two world-class ski resorts—Big Mountain, in Whitefish, and Big Sky, south of Bozeman.

For centuries, Native Americans inhabited Montana, living off the bounty of the wildlife in the woodlands and the buffalo on the plains. Pioneers first came to western Montana to trap beaver and other fur-bearing animals and later to exploit its rich mineral deposits. The development of the nation's richest copper lodes, owned by "copper kings" Marcus Daly and William A. Clark in the 1880's, set the pattern for Montana's first hundred years as a state.

Wars with the Native Americans led to two memorable battles in Montana—Custer's Last Stand (1876) and the defeat of Chief Joseph and the Nez Percé (1877). After the final defeat of the Native Americans on the plains and the slaughter of the great buffalo herds in the 1880's, cattle ranching and wheat farming began to flourish in the east. By then, Montana's legend as a land of cowboys and rodeos had begun.

▶ LAND

In eastern Montana, grassy plains roll endlessly toward the horizon. In western Montana, the peaks of 53 mountain chains tower over broad valleys and rushing rivers. The Continental Divide crosses western Montana from north to south, following the crest of the Lewis, Anaconda, Beaverhead, and Centennial mountains.

Land Regions

Montana has two distinct land regions, the Great Plains and the Rocky Mountains.

The Great Plains cover the eastern three-fifths of Montana. Several isolated mountain ranges—such as the Sweetgrass, Judith, Big Snowy, Bears Paw, Little Rocky, Highwood, and Crazy mountains—occasionally interrupt the landscape, rising as high as 5,000 feet (1,500 meters) above the plain.

Clockwise from top: **Butte, a historic mining empire, was built on top of what was called "the richest hill on earth." Bull riders test their mettle at the Yellowstone Rodeo in Gardiner. Cross-country skiers admire the scenery in Glacier National Park.**

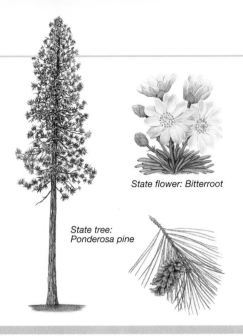

State tree:
Ponderosa pine

State flower: Bitterroot

FACTS AND FIGURES

Location: Northwestern United States; bordered on the north by Canada (British Columbia, Alberta, and Saskatchewan), on the east by North Dakota and South Dakota, on the south by Idaho and Wyoming, and on the west by Idaho.

Area: 147,046 sq mi (380,849 km²); rank, 4th.

Population: 902,195 (2000 census); rank, 44th.

Elevation: *Highest*—12,799 ft (3,901 m) at Granite Peak; *lowest*—1,800 ft (549 m) along the Kootenai River.

Capital: Helena.

Statehood: November 8, 1889; 41st state.

State Motto: *Oro y plata* ("Gold and silver").

State Song: "Montana."

Nicknames: Treasure State; Big Sky Country.

Abbreviations: MT; Mont.

State bird:
Western meadowlark

In the southeast along the Yellowstone River lies a small area of badlands, known for its unusual rock formations carved out by wind and water. Fossils and skeletal remains of several ancient life-forms, including dinosaurs, have been unearthed there.

The Rocky Mountains in Montana include many ranges that generally run in a north-south direction. In the northwest are the Cabinet Mountains, which Montana shares with Idaho, and the Purcell Mountains, which extend southward from Canada. To the east are a series of ranges, including the Whitefish, Mission, Swan, Flathead, and Lewis.

The boundary between Idaho and Montana follows the crests of the Bitterroot Range and the Beaverhead and Centennial mountains. Glaciers have carved out jagged peaks in these wild, almost impassable mountains. Nearby in the southwest are the Spanish Peaks and the Madison and Gallatin ranges. Few ranges in the United States are as rugged or as beautiful as the Absaroka Range, which extends southward into Wyoming. The Bighorn Basin separates the Absaroka Range from the Bighorn Mountains, which Montana shares with Wyoming.

Rivers and Lakes

The major rivers east of the Continental Divide are the Missouri and the Yellowstone. The Missouri River is formed by the joining of the Madison, Gallatin, and Jefferson rivers near Three Forks. The Yellowstone River is the longest free-flowing river in the United States. It rises in northwestern Wyoming, but most of its course is in Montana. It joins the Missouri in North Dakota near the Montana line. Its major tributaries are the Bighorn, Tongue, and Powder rivers.

The major river in northwestern Montana is the Clark Fork of the Columbia River. One of its most important tributaries is the Flathead River, which drains the Kalispell, Mission, and Flathead valleys.

Flathead Lake in Mission Valley is Montana's largest natural lake and one of the largest natural bodies of freshwater west of the Great Lakes. Quake Lake, near Yellowstone National Park, was formed by an earthquake in 1959.

The Bighorn River cuts through Devils Canyon in the Bighorn National Recreation Area, adjoining the lands of the Crow Indian Reservation.

Numerous dams and reservoirs have been built to provide flood control, water for irrigation, and hydroelectric power. They include Fort Peck and Canyon Ferry dams on the Missouri River, Hungry Horse Dam on the South Fork of the Flathead River, and Yellowtail Dam on the Bighorn.

Climate

Statewide television stations and newspapers in Montana publish two weather reports, one for each side of the Continental Divide. West of the Divide, winters are somewhat milder and summers are cooler. The mountains of western Montana lie in the path of relatively warm Pacific winds. The mountains also protect western Montana against cold air masses from the Canadian Arctic that sweep down into the Great Plains several times each winter. Warm winter winds in Montana are called chinooks.

In Great Falls, which lies east of the Divide, the daytime temperature in January usually reaches about 28°F (–2°C). In July it reaches about 84°F (29°C).

Montana, classified as a semiarid region, receives a limited amount of rainfall, usually less than 20 inches (510 millimeters) a year.

Mountain goats roam the rocky terrain of western Montana. *Inset:* Beautiful wildflowers, such as the striking Indian paintbrush, bloom throughout the state.

Most of its moisture comes from the Pacific Ocean and falls in late spring and early summer. Much of the state has a growing season longer than 130 days.

Plant and Animal Life

Montana's trees include aspens, birches, cedars, spruces, firs, and several varieties of pine. Native wildflowers, such as asters, bitterroots, daisies, lupines, poppies, and primroses, add color. The gray-green sagebrush is a common sight on the plains.

Grizzly and black bears can be seen in Montana's national parks. Big-game animals regularly hunted in the state include moose, mountain goat, elk, deer, bighorn sheep, and pronghorn (American antelope). Bison, or buffalo, are limited to herds in the National Bison Range at Moiese and in a few other areas. Among the game birds are pheasant, duck, and grouse. Freshwater fish include trout, whitefish, and grayling.

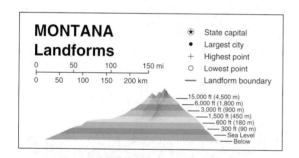

MONTANA
Landforms

⊛	State capital
•	Largest city
+	Highest point
○	Lowest point
—	Landform boundary

0   50   100   150 mi
0   50   100   150   200 km

15,000 ft (4,500 m)
6,000 ft (1,800 m)
3,000 ft (900 m)
1,500 ft (450 m)
600 ft (180 m)
300 ft (90 m)
Sea Level
Below

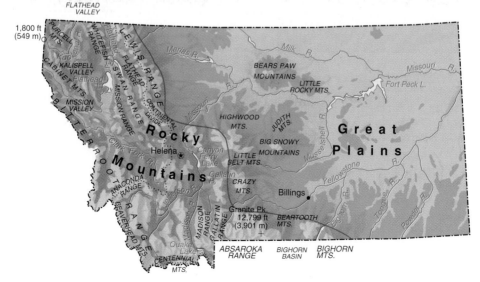

Natural Resources

The poor soils of Montana's forested mountain slopes contrast sharply with the rich, dark soils of the grass-covered plains. In general the mountain soils are thin and not good for cultivation. In the Great Plains and the lowest parts of many western valleys, the soils are usually fertile and productive if enough moisture falls or where irrigation is possible. Fertile alluvial soils lie along the major rivers and their tributaries. The grasslands of eastern Montana, which can withstand droughts and wide extremes of temperature, are most suitable for grazing.

About one-fourth of Montana is covered with forestland, mostly in the mountainous areas. The most commercially important softwood trees are lodgepole and ponderosa pine, Douglas fir, and larch. Hardwood forests east of the Continental Divide make up a very small part of the commercial acreage.

Montana was nicknamed the Treasure State because of its mineral wealth. The Butte district is famous for copper, lead, and zinc. Gold is mined in the mountains. Montana also has enormous supplies of low-sulfur coal and valuable deposits of petroleum and natural gas.

▶ PEOPLE

Montana is sparsely settled, and its small population is unevenly distributed. People cluster in the valleys of the Rocky Mountains in the west and along the rivers and the railroad lines in the eastern plains. A little more than half the people live in cities with a population of 2,500 or more.

Rich gold strikes in western Montana in the early 1860's brought the first rush of settlers. Ranchers were later attracted to Montana's fertile western valleys. The arrival of the railroads in the 1880's brought the greatest gain in population. Railroad companies advertised in European newspapers, telling of opportunities for settlers in the western part of the United States. Soon people began to

Left: Many of today's Montanans are descended from the early miners and cattle ranchers. *Above:* The Crow are one of a dozen Native American tribes in Montana.

PEOPLE

Population: 902,195 (2000 census).

Density: 6 persons per sq mi (2 per km²).

Distribution: 52.5% urban; 47.5% rural.

Largest Cities (2000 census):

Billings 89,847	Bozeman 27,509
Missoula 57,053	Helena 25,780
Great Falls 56,690	Kalispell 14,223
Butte/Silver Bow 34,606	

Source: U.S. Bureau of the Census

Persons per sq mi	Persons per km²
over 250	over 100
50-250	20-100
5-50	2-20
0-5	0-2

Kalispell · Great Falls · Missoula · Helena · Butte/Silver Bow · Billings · Bozeman

Left: The University of Montana in Missoula, shown here hosting a Kutenai Indian powwow, is one of the state's oldest universities. It has a liberal arts college and a school of forestry.

Right: The C. M. Russell Museum in Great Falls features works by this popular artist, known for his paintings of wildlife, cowboys, and Native Americans posed in western landscapes.

arrive from Scotland, England, Wales, Germany, Russia, Canada, and Scandinavia.

Many of today's Montanans are descended from these early miners and ranchers. More recently, small communities of African and Hispanic Americans as well as Laotian and Vietnamese immigrants have developed in the largest cities. Native Americans, who have inhabited Montana for about 12,000 years, make up about 6 percent of the population. They include members of the Blackfoot, Cheyenne, Arapaho, Assiniboin, Atsina, Gros Ventres, and Crow tribes on the plains and the Flathead, Kutenai, Bannock, Shoshoni, and Kalispel tribes in the mountains. Many live on Montana's seven reservations.

Education

In 1864 a boarding school for Native Americans was opened in the mission at St. Ignatius. This was the first school of its kind in the Northwest. Numerous private schools were also established. In 1865, the first territorial legislature approved the establishment of a school system for the Montana Territory. Virginia City was the first place to organize a school district. A state board of education was created in 1893, and by 1897, free county high schools had been established.

Montana State University, in Bozeman, opened in 1893. The University of Montana, in Missoula, was chartered in the same year, but it did not open until 1895. In 1994 these two units took over the administration of the state's four other colleges. Montana Tech in Butte and Western Montana College in Dillon became part of the University of Mon-

tana; Eastern Montana College in Billings and Northern Montana College in Havre are administered by Montana State. Private schools include the College of Great Falls, Carroll College in Helena, and Rocky Mountain College in Billings. The state also supports several community colleges.

Libraries, Museums, and the Arts

The library in Helena, established in 1886, was the first free public library in Montana. Today most counties have some form of library service, and all the major cities have excellent public libraries. The state colleges and universities maintain excellent libraries, notably the Maureen and Mike Mansfield Library at the University of Montana and the Roland R. Renne Library at Montana State.

The Montana Historical Society in Helena maintains state archives and a research library noted for its collection of frontier newspapers. It also exhibits frontier photography and a collection of paintings, sketches, and bronze sculptures by the noted Western artist Charles M. Russell. Other works are displayed in the C. M. Russell Museum in Great Falls.

The Museum of the Plains Indian on the Blackfeet Reservation in Browning explains the history and culture of the Plains Indian. The Museum of the Rockies in Bozeman has historical and paleontological exhibits. The Montana College of Mineral Science and Technology in Butte houses a magnificent collection of minerals. The Butte Historical Society preserves objects relating to the history of southwestern Montana.

For many years, Montana's economy was based on cattle, wheat, lumbering, and the mining of the Treasure State's abundant natural resources, such as coal (shown). By the end of the 1900's, the service industries, especially tourism, had grown in importance.

PRODUCTS AND INDUSTRIES

Manufacturing: Lumber and wood products, petroleum and coal products, food products, printing and publishing.

Agriculture: Cattle, wheat, barley, hay.

Minerals: Coal, petroleum, natural gas, molybdenum, gold, silver, nickel, copper, palladium, talc.

Services: Wholesale and retail trade; finance, insurance, and real estate; business, social, and personal services; transportation, communication, and utilities; government.

*Gross state product is the total value of goods and services produced in a year.

Percentage of Gross State Product* by Industry

- Construction 4%
- Business, social, and personal services — 16.5%
- Finance, insurance, and real estate — 16.5%
- Wholesale and retail trade — 16%
- Mining 5.5%
- Agriculture — 6%
- Manufacturing — 8%
- Transportation, communication, and utilities — 12.5%
- Government — 15%

Source: U.S. Bureau of Economic Analysis

▶ ECONOMY

Traditionally mining, cattle ranching, and wheat farming were Montana's chief sources of income. These continue to be important, but in the last half of the 1900's, services began to produce more income. The travel and recreation industry is the fastest-growing sector of the state's economy.

Services

Montana boasts a growing service economy. Retail trade outlets serve every major city. Health care centers have expanded in Billings and Missoula. Better roads have improved transportation, especially for trucking.

Manufacturing

The production of lumber and wood products, such as paper, is Montana's leading manufacturing industry. Oil refineries are located in the Billings and Cut Bank areas. Other enterprises include food processing, such as flour milling and sugar refining, and the production of concrete, gypsum, and plaster products.

Agriculture

About two-thirds of Montana's total area is agricultural land, more than half of which is classified as pasture for livestock. Beef cattle and spring and winter wheat account for about 75 percent of Montana's total agricultural output. Sheep and hogs are also raised, and barley and oats are grown, mostly in the eastern and central sections. Irrigated land is found in every county. Some is used for pasture, but most is used for growing grains, fruits, vegetables, and sugar beets.

Mining and Construction

Because Montana's coal is near the surface, it can be readily strip-mined. Much of the coal is low in sulfur, which causes less pollution than other types of coal.

Oil production began near Red Lodge in Carbon County in 1915. Production in the Williston Basin began in the 1950's. This vast, oil-rich area stretches across several counties of eastern Montana and parts of the Dakotas and Canada. The Cut Bank field in Glacier County is the leading producer of natural gas.

Silver Bow County was the center of copper production in Montana for more than a century, but falling prices in the 1980's caused the closing of the copper smelters in Anaconda, Great Falls, and Butte, although some Butte mines reopened in 1986. Other metals mined in Montana include gold, silver, nickel, molybdenum, palladium, and platinum. Nonmetallic materials mined include clays, talc, gypsum, phosphate, and sand and gravel.

Transportation

Good transportation is vital in Montana because distances between places are great. Early travelers came by boat on the Missouri River. In 1861 a wagon road, known as the Mullan Trail, was completed from Fort Benton across the mountains to Walla Walla, Washington. Overland trails also connected with the Oregon Trail to the south.

The Northern Pacific Railroad, completed in 1883, was the first of three transcontinental railroads built across Montana. It follows a central route through Miles City, Billings, Bozeman, Butte, Helena, and Missoula. The Great Northern Railroad, completed in 1893, follows a northern route. The Chicago, Milwaukee, Saint Paul, and Pacific Railroad was completed in 1909.

Several interstate highways cross Montana, both from east to west and from north to south. The Going-to-the-Sun Road is a spectacular highway running east and west through Glacier National Park. Another scenic highway leads to the northeast entrance of Yellowstone National Park. This highway dips into Wyoming, where it crosses the Beartooth Pass at almost 11,000 feet (3,353 meters). Airports in Billings, Great Falls, and Bozeman have regularly scheduled commercial flights.

Communication

Montana's first regular newspaper, the *Montana Post*, was printed in Virginia City in 1864. It moved to Helena in 1866. Today the leading newspapers are the Billings *Gazette* and the Great Falls *Tribune*. Eleven daily newspapers and about 70 other papers are published in the state. Montana has more than 15 television and 60 radio stations.

▶ CITIES

Montana's cities are not large. Only Billings, Missoula, and Great Falls have populations of more than 50,000 people. The most populous counties are Yellowstone, Missoula, Cascade, Flathead, and Gallatin.

Helena, the capital of Montana, is situated near the Missouri River in Prickly Pear Valley, a rich agricultural area irrigated by water from Canyon Ferry Reservoir. It owes its existence to the discovery of gold. In 1864 four prospectors, weary of poor diggings, decided to take one last chance in a gulch they had stumbled upon. They found gold, and the place was dubbed Last Chance Gulch. A community grew rapidly around the site. In 1875, Helena became Montana's third territorial capital. When Montana became a state in 1889, Helena was the temporary capital. It became the permanent capital in 1894. Today the city is a center for trade, transportation, and finance as well as government. Its main street is still called Last Chance Gulch.

Billings, Montana's largest city, is located on the Yellowstone River in the south central part of the state. It is in the heart of a highly productive area called the Midland Empire. Industries in the city include

Billings is Montana's most populous city. Founded in 1882 by the Northern Pacific Railroad, it was named for Frederick Billings, the company's president.

Places of Interest

Bannack State Monument, west of Dillon, is a reminder of gold-rush days. The first important gold strike in Montana was made at Grasshopper Creek in 1862, and the town of Bannack grew up there almost overnight. The city later became Montana's first territorial capital. Weathered remains of the first capital building, a jail, a hotel, and many log cabins are preserved.

Gates of the Mountains, 25 miles (40 kilometers) north of Helena, is a deep gorge cut by the Missouri River. The river has eroded the banks into fantastic shapes. The names of the formations tell what they resemble—Indian Head, Beartooth, Bride and Groom, and the like. During the summer, boats carry tourists on regular trips through the gorge.

Glacier National Park, located in the Rocky Mountains of northwestern Montana, was established in 1910. Considered one of the most beautiful places in the United States, the park features spectacular glaciers, lofty peaks, waterfalls, lakes, and forests. It is part of the Waterton-Glacier International Peace Park, shared by the United States and Canada. An article on Glacier National Park is included in Volume G.

Grasshopper Glacier, one of Montana's most remarkable glaciers, is in Custer National Forest southwest of Billings. The glacier gets its name from millions of grasshoppers that were trapped in a severe storm and embedded in the ice as the glacier was being formed.

Little Bighorn Battlefield National Monument, southeast of Hardin, commemorates "Custer's Last Stand" at the Battle of the Little Bighorn on June 25,

Little Bighorn Battlefield National Monument

1876. A granite memorial marks the battlefield, and headstones mark where Lieutenant Colonel George A. Custer and his soldiers fell.

Missouri River Headwaters State Monument, near Three Forks, is one of the most important geographical sites in the West. The Missouri River begins there at the joining of the Jefferson, Madison, and Gallatin rivers. The Lewis and Clark expedition explored the site in July 1805. Lewis and Clark named the rivers in honor of President Thomas Jefferson, Secretary of State James Madison, and Secretary of the Treasury Albert Gallatin.

The National Bison Range, near Moiese on the Flathead Indian Reservation, protects one of the few remaining herds of American bison, or buffalo, in the United States. The range is also a home for other big-game animals, such

as deer, elk, and bighorn sheep. Tours are conducted throughout the range.

Nez Perce National Historic Park includes three separate sites along the 1,000-mile (1,600-kilometer) route that Chief Joseph and the Nez Percé retreated through Idaho and Montana. The **Big Hole Battlefield**, near Wisdom, marks the place where Col. John Gibbon and his forces attacked the Nez Percé encampment on August 9, 1877. On September 13, at **Canyon Creek Battlefield**, near Laurel, the Nez Percé held off Col. Samuel D. Sturgis and the Seventh Cavalry. On October 5, at the **Bear Paw Battlefield**, south of Chinook, Chief Joseph finally surrendered to Col. Nelson A. Miles. A profile of Chief Joseph is included in INDIANS, AMERICAN in Volume I.

Virginia City and Nevada City, two former boomtowns, were founded near the site of a famous gold strike in Alder Gulch. Now ghost towns, they preserve many historic buildings and artifacts of Montana's early mining days.

Yellowstone National Park lies mainly in the northwestern corner of Wyoming, but it extends into both Montana and Idaho. Three of the park's entrances are in Montana. An article on Yellowstone National Park appears in Volume W-X-Y-Z.

State Recreation Areas. Montana has eleven national forests, three national parks, eleven state parks, and dozens of other recreation areas, providing plenty of opportunities for camping, fishing, hunting, hiking, mountain climbing, and winter sports. For more information, contact Travel Montana, 1424 9th Avenue, Helena, Montana 59620.

Nevada City

The National Bison Range

oil refineries and meat-packing plants. Rocky Mountain College and a branch of Montana State University are both located there.

Missoula, Montana's second largest city, was founded in 1860. It lies on the Clark Fork River in western Montana. The Flathead Indians called the place *Im-i-sul-a*, meaning "by the chilling water." The city's main manufactures are paper and plywood. It is the home of the University of Montana.

Great Falls is located on the Missouri River at the mouth of the Sun River. It was incorporated as a city in 1888, after the arrival of the Great Northern Railroad. Great Falls is the financial, industrial, and supply center of an agricultural and mining area called the Golden Triangle. Waterfalls near the city are used to supply hydroelectric power. Downstream are the Great Falls of the Missouri River, for which the city is named.

Butte, the center of Montana's mining empire, sits on top of what has been called "the richest hill on earth." Located in southwestern Montana, it was once home to as much as 20 percent of the state's population. The discovery of gold in 1864 brought the first boom to the area. Since the 1880's, Butte has been most famous for its copper, although production declined in the 1980's. In 1976, Butte and the rest of Silver Bow County were consolidated into a single governmental unit known as Butte/Silver Bow.

▶ **GOVERNMENT**

In 1972, Montana adopted a new constitution that became effective in 1973. It provides for three branches of government and is noteworthy for its open political processes and the protection it gives the environment.

The executive branch of the government is headed by a governor. Other executive officers include a lieutenant governor, secretary of state, attorney general, superintendent of public instruction, state auditor, and several public service commissioners. There is no limit on the number of terms a governor may serve.

The legislative branch, called the Legislative Assembly, is made up of a senate and a house of representatives. Regular sessions of the legislature begin on the first Monday in January in odd-numbered years and continue for about 90 days. Special sessions also may be called.

The copper-domed state capitol building in Helena houses the state legislature. Helena became the permanent state capital in 1894.

GOVERNMENT

State Government
Governor: 4-year term
State senators: 50; 4-year terms
State representatives: 100; 2-year terms
Number of counties: 56

Federal Government
U.S. senators: 2
U.S. representatives: 1
Number of electoral votes: 3

For the name of the current governor, see STATE GOVERNMENTS in Volume S. For the names of current U.S. senators and representative, see UNITED STATES, CONGRESS OF THE in Volume U-V.

The judicial branch is headed by the state supreme court. Voters elect a chief justice and six associate justices to 8-year terms. Each county elects at least one justice of the peace, and many locations also have district, municipal, and police courts.

Most counties elect a county commissioner to administer county affairs. Cities and towns are governed by a mayor (or a city manager) and a city council.

▶ **HISTORY**

Tools, weapons, and other clues studied by scientists indicate that Montana has been inhabited for perhaps 12,000 years. Little is known about these ancient peoples because they developed no written language and built no permanent structures. All of the Native Americans living east of the Continental

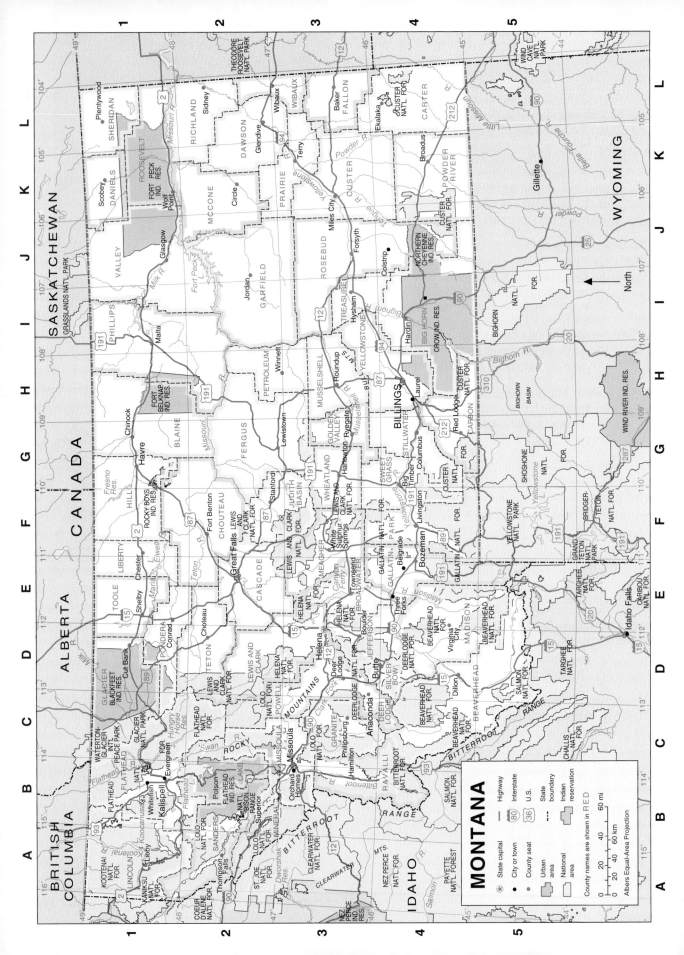

INDEX TO MONTANA MAP

Divide at the time the pioneers first ventured into Montana had moved there after 1600. Most had been displaced as Europeans settled eastern North America.

Exploration and Settlement

Montana's recorded history begins with the expedition of Meriwether Lewis and William Clark, who were sent by President Thomas Jefferson to explore the new American lands acquired by the Louisiana Purchase of 1803. Lewis and Clark crossed the 104th degree of longitude, Montana's eastern border, on April 28, 1805. They traveled the Missouri River to its source, crossed the Continental Divide at Lemhi Pass, and descended the Salmon and Bitterroot rivers before exiting Montana at Lolo Pass. The following year they took separate routes on their return through Montana.

In the following decades, fur traders thoroughly explored Montana. They sought mainly beaver pelts, then in demand for fashionable hats. Numerous outfits eventually consolidated into the American Fur Company with its major trading post at Fort Union, built in 1828 near the junction of the Missouri and Yellowstone rivers.

Pioneer Days

In the 1850's, traces of gold were found in western Montana, but the first important discovery was made at Grasshopper Creek in 1862, making Bannack Montana's first boomtown. Rich finds at Alder Gulch in 1863 and Last Chance Gulch in 1864 established the towns of Virginia City and Helena. Other metals, especially silver and copper, were later discovered and mined.

On May 26, 1864, President Abraham Lincoln signed a bill creating the new territory of Montana out of the larger Idaho Territory. Bannack served as the capital. By 1870, Montana had produced more than $100 million in gold, which helped the U.S. government pay its debts from the Civil War.

Relations with the Native Americans

While western Montana was being settled by miners and prospectors, along with the farmers and businessmen who came to serve their needs, most of the land east of the Rockies was still held by Native Americans. The opening of the West to white settlement caused great conflict. Foreign diseases introduced among the natives devastated the tribes, but more important, the wholesale slaughter of buffalo by the new settlers threatened to destroy the food supply on the plains. Tensions reached a climax when the U.S. Army resolved to displace the natives from their homelands and restrict them to reservations.

Two milestone events of the Indian Wars took place in Montana. On a hot June day in 1876, Lieutenant Colonel George A. Custer and five companies of the U.S. Seventh Cavalry were massacred by the Sioux and Northern Cheyenne Indians on the banks of the Little Bighorn River. The following year, while attempting to escape confinement on a

Famous People

Gary Cooper

Calamity Jane

Calamity Jane (Martha Jane Canary) (1852–1903), born in Princeton, Missouri, became a folk legend of the Wild West. Orphaned by the age of 15, Calamity spent many years in Virginia City, Montana, and drifted in and out of several other mining towns. Known for her manly dress and skill with a rifle and pistol, she became a popular attraction in Buffalo Bill's Wild West shows. She claimed to have been a Pony Express rider and a scout for General George A. Custer. Her diary and other artifacts are preserved at the Western Heritage Center in Billings.

Gary Cooper (1901–61), born in Helena, was one of Hollywood's most popular and enduring film stars, known for his portrayals of strong, soft-spoken heroes. He won two Academy Awards, for *Sergeant York* (1941) and *High Noon* (1952). Other notable films include *The Virginian* (1929), *A Farewell to Arms* (1932), *Mr. Deeds Goes to Town* (1936), *Beau Geste* (1939), *Meet John Doe* (1941), and *For Whom the Bell Tolls* (1943).

George Armstrong Custer (1839–76), born in New Rumley, Ohio, was a dashing cavalry officer of the Civil War who gained greater fame as an "Indian fighter." In 1868, after a year's suspension for disobeying orders, he was given command of the U.S. Seventh Cavalry and sent to Indian Territory (present-day Oklahoma) to fight the Southern Cheyenne. Custer's surprise attack killed most of the villagers, including Chief Black Kettle. Transferred north to protect the crews building the Northern Pacific Railroad, Custer was later placed in command of an expedition to the Black Hills, where gold was rumored to exist. When the Sioux refused to sell this land, which they considered sacred, Custer was ordered to force them onto reservations. On June 25, 1876, Custer and his band of about 260 men were ambushed and killed by the Sioux and Northern Cheyenne at the Little Bighorn River in Montana, a massacre known as Custer's Last Stand.

Marcus Daly (1841–1900) was the first of Montana's powerful "copper kings." An immigrant from Ireland at the age of 15, Daly migrated to Butte in 1876 and acquired an interest in a silver mine. The silver did not last very long, but beneath

---

reservation, a band of Nez Percé, led by the great Chief Joseph, was captured in the mountains of northern Montana.

In the 1880's, most of Montana's Native Americans had been confined to reservations, and some of their tribal lands were sold or leased to settlers under the Dawes Act of 1887. Restricted movement, coupled with the harsh adjustment to farming, brought poverty to Montana's Native American population.

During the 1860's, eastern Montana began to be stocked with cattle. The first large herds were driven up from Texas in 1866. Ranching became very profitable, although transportation to markets remained a problem. The completion of the transcontinental railroads, expansion of the cattle range, and the development of copper mining brought many more people to Montana. After 25 years as a territory, Montana became the nation's 41st state on November 8, 1889.

Economic and Political Progress

Statehood created an arena for significant economic change. Montana's copper interests were brought together under the mighty Anaconda Company, founded by Marcus Daly. Coal deposits, natural gas, and oil were discovered. Railroads allowed for the growth of the lumber industry, and the homestead boom brought thousands of farm families onto the plains. Between 1900 and 1920 the population more than doubled, as progressive reformers restructured the political system, enacting both women's suffrage and prohibition.

In the 1920's, copper mining in Butte was so profitable, Marcus Daly's Anaconda Company was considered the fifth richest corporation in the world.

the mine was a rich deposit of copper. Daly made millions from his copper mines as well as from coal, timber, banking, power plants, irrigation systems, and railroads. He organized the Anaconda Company and built the town of Anaconda as a smelting center.

Pierre-Jean de Smet (1801–73), a Jesuit missionary born in Dendermonde, Belgium, is often called the founder of Montana. He immigrated to the United States in 1821 and was ordained in Missouri in 1827. After founding a mission in 1838 to Christianize the Potowatomi Indians at Council Bluffs, Iowa, he moved west to Montana's Bitterroot Valley, where he established St. Mary's Mission, near present-day

George Armstrong Custer

Stevensville, in 1841. Native Americans called him Black Robe.

Michael Joseph Mansfield (1903–2001), a U.S. congressman and senator, was born in New York City but raised in Montana. A Democrat, Mansfield represented Montana in the U.S. House of Representatives (1943– 53) and in the U.S. Senate (1953–77), where he served as majority leader (1961–77) longer than any other senator. Before entering politics, Mansfield was a copper miner and taught history at the University of Montana. After retiring from Congress, he served as ambassador to Japan (1977–89).

Plenty Coups (1848– 1932) (Indian name: Aleekchea-akoosh), born near Billings, was a chief of the Crow Indians. As a young

man he helped organize scouts for the U.S. Army. He worked for understanding between settlers and Native Americans. Today his ranch is a state park.

Jeannette Rankin (1880–1973), born in Missoula, was the first woman elected to the U.S. House of Representatives, where she served two terms (1917–18 and 1941–42). As a young woman, Rankin campaigned vigorously for woman suffrage (the right to vote), which passed in the state in 1914. A staunch opponent of war, she was the only member of Congress to vote against United States participation in both world wars. In 1971 she became the first person elected to the Susan B. Anthony Hall of Fame.

Charles Marion Russell (1864–1926) was one of the greatest artists devoted to the painting and sculpting of scenes of the American West. Born in St. Louis, Missouri, he went to Montana at the age of 16 to work as a hunter, trapper, and cowboy, all the while developing his skills as an artist. His vivid, dramatic, and often humorous illustrations of cowboys, Native Americans, and animals provide a spirited record of life in the Wild West.

Rising wheat prices during World War I (1914–18) brought unprecedented prosperity to Montana. But over the next twenty years, severe drought crippled agriculture, and Montana became the only state in the nation to lose population.

The Great Depression of the 1930's also hit Montana hard. The federal government's New Deal programs helped with relief, conservation, and public works projects, such as the building of Fort Peck Dam for irrigation, power, flood control, and other purposes. A New Deal program to help the Native Americans was sponsored by Senator Burton K. Wheeler. Prosperity, however, did not return to Montana until the United States entered World War II in 1941.

Modern Montana

After the war, Montana lost thousands of jobs in its dominant industries of mining, logging, agriculture, and energy. The energy crisis of the 1970's produced a brief boom by increasing the value of the state's oil and coal resources, but in the 1980's, a steep recession struck all sectors of the economy. Falling

copper prices led to the closing of most of the state's mines, while farmers also suffered from low prices and poor weather conditions.

Despite unemployment concerns, Montana's Native Americans now actively encourage economic growth and development on the state's seven reservations. In addition, each reservation has a tribal community college with growing numbers of students.

Montana is rapidly changing. The old economic mainstays of mining, timber, agriculture, and energy are still important, even though they employ fewer workers and average personal incomes remain low. As the rural population declines, increasing numbers are moving to the mountains, seeking environmental beauty, residential privacy and safety, and educational and recreational opportunities. Many use new computer technologies to earn a living at home or in small businesses. As always, Montana still beckons the adventurous.

Vincent K. Shaudys
Montana State University

Reviewed by Harry W. Fritz
Author, *Montana: Land of Contrast*

MONTENEGRO. See SERBIA AND MONTENEGRO.

MONTESQUIEU, BARON DE LA BRÈDE ET DE. See ENLIGHTENMENT, AGE OF (Profiles).

MONTESSORI, MARIA. See KINDERGARTEN AND NURSERY SCHOOLS.

MONTEVIDEO

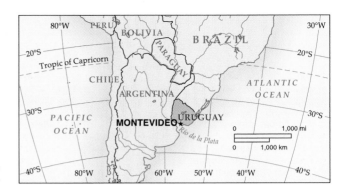

Montevideo is the capital, largest city, and chief port of Uruguay, as well as its most important financial, industrial, and cultural center. Its name most likely came from a Portuguese sailor who, upon seeing a hill near the city, cried out "*Monte vide eu!,*" meaning "I see a hill." About 1.5 million people, nearly one-half of all Uruguayans, live there.

Situated on Uruguay's South Atlantic coast, Montevideo is bordered by the Río de la Plata ("river of silver") estuary and the states of Canelones and San José. The climate is temperate; the average annual temperature is 62°F (16°C). There are four distinct seasons, and rainfall remains constant throughout the year.

The City. One of Montevideo's main attractions is the Old City. This picturesque area has several squares and colonial buildings, including the cathedral and the first city hall, Cabildo. In the port area is the Mercado del Puerto, a lively food and crafts market.

In the modern city, the main boulevard is the Avenida 18 de Julio; it begins at the Plaza Independencia and ends at Batlle Park. Nearby is Centenario Stadium, site of the first

Montevideo, the capital and largest city of Uruguay, is situated on the country's South Atlantic coast. The city is home to about half the country's population.

World Cup soccer game. Another landmark is the Rambla—a road stretching along almost 10 miles (16 kilometers) of sandy beaches and rocky ledges.

A huge Carnival festival is held in Montevideo in February. Traditional music is performed in national competitions, and people dance the candombe, a style that evolved from rhythms brought to Uruguay by African slaves more than 200 years ago. The tango, a famous music style and dance that originated in Montevideo and Buenos Aires during the early 1900's, is also popular.

The University of the Republic (founded 1849), Uruguay's national university, is located in Montevideo. The city is also home to the National Library, the Museum of National History, and the Fine Arts Museum.

Economic Activity. Most of Uruguay's factories, banks, and services are located in Montevideo. Key industries include meat packing, fishing, and textile manufacturing. Montevideo is the administrative capital of the regional trading bloc, the Southern Common Market (Mercosur), which includes Uruguay, Argentina, Brazil, and Paraguay.

History. Montevideo was founded in 1726 by Bruno Mauricio de Zabala, a governor of Buenos Aires, Argentina. The city served as a military outpost used by the Spanish to block Portuguese expansion. A natural deepwater port gave the city added regional importance. In the late 1800's and early 1900's, Montevideo grew as large numbers of immigrants arrived, mainly from Italy and Spain. Since the mid-1990's, there has been a renewed interest in restoring the city's colonial buildings. Despite substantial improvements, several restoration programs were halted during an economic recession in 2002.

ROSSANA CASTIGLIONI
University of Notre Dame

MONTEZUMA II (1470?–1520)

Montezuma (also known as Motecuhzoma or Moctezuma) II was the ruler of the Aztec Empire at the time the Spanish arrived to conquer the land that is now Mexico. Born in Tenochtitlán, the Aztec capital (and the site of present-day Mexico City), Montezuma succeeded his uncle Ahuizotl as ruler of the Aztecs in 1502. A great warrior, he added new regions to the empire but made many enemies in the process.

In 1519, a Spanish army of about 500 men, led by Hernando Cortés, arrived on the Gulf Coast of Mexico, seeking to conquer the land that they had heard was rich in gold and other valuables. With the aid of about 6,000 Tlaxcalans and other enemies of the Aztecs, Cortés advanced toward the city of Tenochtitlán that November. Legend has it that Montezuma mistook the foreigner for the Aztec god Quetzalcóatl, whom he wished to please. More likely, Montezuma recognized Cortés as a powerful leader and diplomatically welcomed him with gifts, hoping the Spanish would leave Mexico and not wage war. Nevertheless, Cortés took

In 1519, the Aztec emperor Montezuma II welcomed the Spanish explorer Hernando Cortés in the capital city of Tenochtitlán.

control over Montezuma and the city.

Cortés left Tenochtitlán in 1520 and put his lieutenant, Pedro de Alvarado, in charge in the city. But Alvarado and his men brutalized the Aztecs to the point of revolution. In the ensuing battles, Montezuma was killed, either by his own angry people or by the Spanish. The following year, Cortés and his Indian allies destroyed Tenochtitlán, bringing the end to the Aztec Empire.

Reviewed by SUSAN D. GILLESPIE
University of Illinois, Urbana

See also CORTÉS, HERNANDO.

MONTGOMERY. See ALABAMA (Cities).

MONTGOMERY, BERNARD LAW (1887–1976)

British field marshal Bernard Law Montgomery was one of the most important commanders of the Allied forces during World War II. Known as "Monty," he became a national hero after routing the Germans at El Alamein in northern Egypt in 1942. He is also remembered for his legendary disagreements with his superior officer, the supreme Allied commander Dwight D. Eisenhower.

Born in London on November 17, 1887, Montgomery was educated at St. Paul's School and the Royal Military College at Sandhurst, from which he graduated in 1908, commissioned as a lieutenant in the infantry. During World War I he saw action in several of the war's most terrible battles.

When World War II broke out in September 1939, Montgomery was a major general, commanding the Eighth Division in Palestine. He returned to Europe to command a division in France but in 1940 was forced to evacuate his troops back to Britain through Dunkirk when France fell to the

Germans. On August 18, 1942, Montgomery took command of the Eighth Army in Egypt. His victory over the German general Erwin Rommel at El Alamein on October 23 earned him a promotion to full general. The following year he led the Eighth Army in the invasions of Sicily and Italy. In 1944, Montgomery was recalled to Britain to command the ground forces in the successful June invasion of Normandy. On September 1, he was promoted to field marshal, Britain's highest military rank.

After the war, Montgomery was given the title Viscount Montgomery of Alamein. He headed the British occupation forces in Germany (1945–46); served as chief of the Imperial General Staff (1946–48); and as deputy supreme commander of the North Atlantic Treaty Organization (NATO) (1951–58). He died on March 25, 1976.

Reviewed by JOHN KEEGAN
Author, *Who's Who in the Second World War*

MONTPELIER. See VERMONT (Cities).

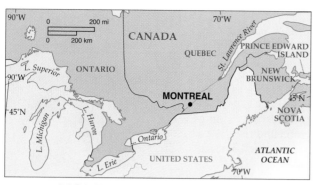

MONTREAL

Montreal, the largest city of Quebec, is also one of the largest cities of Canada and a busy inland port. It stands on an island in the middle of the St. Lawrence River. In the center of the island rises Mount Royal. Montreal is a distinctive and colorful city, with a large French-speaking population and an "old town" with buildings and houses from the 1600's.

▶ **HISTORY**

Montreal Island was first discovered by the French explorer Jacques Cartier in 1535, but it was not permanently settled until 1642. The settlement was made that year under the leadership of Sieur de Maisonneuve. It was named Ville-Marie de Montreal.

The settlement's growth was slow at first. In fact, one hundred years later Montreal still lay inside confining and protective walls in a small area along the St. Lawrence River. Almost from its beginning the colony lived in great danger of attacks by Indians, who feared to lose their lands. Finally, in 1701, a peace treaty was signed with the Indians.

Montreal served as a base for many famous explorers, traders, and missionaries—Marquette, La Salle, Jolliet, and others—who reached points as far north as Hudson Bay and as far south as the Gulf of Mexico.

During the American Revolution an army under the command of General Montgomery occupied Montreal. The Americans hoped that the people of the city would join forces with them in their struggle with the British. But the Montrealers decided to stay loyal to Britain.

Montreal grew rapidly in the first half of the 1800's. Steamboats replaced sailboats. Canals and railways were built. Trade and commerce grew. In 1843 Montreal was important enough to be made the capital of Canada. But this distinction lasted only six years. In 1849 the

Montreal, on the St. Lawrence River in the province of Quebec, is one of Canada's largest cities and the second largest French-language city in the world.

government buildings were severely damaged during a riot. The capital was moved to Quebec and later to Ottawa.

▶ **THE CITY TODAY**

The modern city of Montreal covers most of Montreal Island and has spread eastward onto the mainland. The population of the metropolitan area is more than 3.5 million. Two-thirds of Montreal's residents are French-speaking, making it the second largest French-language city in the world (after Paris). The next largest population group is made up of people of British ancestry. There are also many Italians, Chinese, Germans, Greeks, Portuguese, Spanish, and Central Europeans.

Montreal's center was extensively remodeled during the 1960's and 1970's. Many skyscrapers were built, as well as a network of underground shopping centers that provide climate-controlled environments for winter living. The historic Old Montreal section was also restored. In 1967, Montreal was the site of a world's fair, called Expo '67, and a permanent exhibition continues to occupy the fairgrounds. The Summer Olympic Games were held in Montreal in 1976, spurring further construction, including the massive Olympic Stadium.

Montreal holds a great attraction for tourists from all over North America. The charm of the city comes from the blending of its French and English cultures. Many tourists visit the Church of Notre Dame, which was completed in 1829. Other places of interest include St. Joseph's Oratory and Basilica, the Bonsecours Market, and lovely Dominion Square.

Transportation. Because of its location on the St. Lawrence River, Montreal is one of Canada's leading ports. For many years all goods shipped to and from the Great Lakes had to pass through the port of Montreal. Even after the completion in 1959 of the St. Lawrence Seaway, which allows oceangoing ships to enter the Great Lakes, Montreal kept its importance as a port. The St. Lawrence River is sometimes closed during the winter because of ice, but the Port of Montreal remains open year-round.

Montreal is the hub of a dense road network and the headquarters of Canada's two great railway systems, the Canadian National and the Canadian Pacific. The city is connected by rail to all major cities in North America. A subway system provides transportation within the city.

Two major airports serve the city: Mirabel and Trudeau. Air Canada, the largest commercial airline in Canada, is headquartered in Montreal.

Industry and Commerce. Trade, industry, and services are Montreal's leading economic activities. The main manufactures are metal products, transportation equipment, clothing and other textile products, chemical products, and food and beverages. The city's economic development is due in part to the importance of the port. It is also due to the abundance of hydroelectric power from projects in the Canadian Shield area and from power plants on the St. Lawrence Seaway.

Montreal is also a financial center. Many of the great insurance and banking firms in Canada have their headquarters in the city.

Education and Culture. Montreal has several noted universities. McGill and Concordia are English-language institutions. McGill is well known for its medical school. The Université de Montréal conducts its classes in French, as does the Université de Québec.

There are many excellent museums in the city. The Museum of Fine Arts has a superb collection of French paintings of the 1800's as well as works of the Canadian school. The Museum of Contemporary Art exhibits the work of modern artists. The Château de Ramezay, one of the oldest buildings in Montreal, houses an impressive display of historical documents, furniture, and Indian craft.

Montreal has many fine theaters, libraries, art galleries, and concert halls. The Place des Arts, a performing-arts complex containing three concert halls, is the home of the Montreal Symphony Orchestra.

Sports and Recreation. Sports are a popular activity in Montreal. Winter hockey games, horse racing, and soccer in summer, and autumn football matches attract both spectators and participants. Many people spend summer weekends and holidays in the lake region of

Historic buildings and charming flower-planted plazas lend a European flavor to Old Montreal, site of the early French settlement established in the 1600's.

the Laurentian Mountains. It is also to the Laurentians that skiers swarm in winter.

The Montreal Canadiens, well known to hockey fans throughout North America, are the city's most famous professional team. Each year, Montreal hosts the Canadian Grand Prix Formula One automobile race. The Canadian Football League is represented in the city by the Montreal Alouettes. In 1976 Montreal played host to the Summer Olympic Games.

THEODORE L. HILLS
McGill University

MOODY, HELEN WILLS. See TENNIS (Great Players).

Earth's natural satellite, the moon, affects many vital events on our planet, such as the rising and ebbing of tides. It also plays an eventful role in our art, our music, our literature, and as a mood-setting backdrop to our emotions.

MOON

The moon is Earth's only natural **satellite**—an object that travels in an **orbit**, or curved path, around a larger object. The moon's orbit is elliptical, or oval shaped, which means that its distance from the Earth changes as it travels in its orbit. At its closest point to the Earth, known as **perigee**, the moon is 221,500 miles (356,600 kilometers) away. At its greatest distance, or **apogee**, it is 252,700 miles (406,800 kilometers) away.

The moon travels in its orbit at an average speed of 2,237 miles (3,600 kilometers) per hour. As it gets closer to the Earth, it speeds up because of the Earth's strong gravitational pull. As it gets farther away, it slows down. The Earth's gravitational pull also affects the moon's shape. Although the moon appears perfectly round, it is not. There is a slight bulge on the side of the moon facing the Earth that scientists think is caused by the Earth's gravitational pull.

The moon is quite large in relation to Earth. With a diameter of 2,160 miles (3,478 kilometers), it is about one fourth the diameter of the Earth. The only planet that has a larger satellite in relation to its size is Pluto—Pluto's moon is more than half the size of Pluto.

Rotation and Libration

Like all planets and natural satellites, the moon rotates, or spins, on its own axis. One rotation of the moon takes 27 days, 7 hours, and 43 minutes—just about the same amount of time it takes the moon to orbit the Earth. The fact that these two periods of time are about the same means that the same side of the moon is always facing the Earth (see Figure 1). Because of this, you might think that it is impossible to see the far side of the moon from Earth. To a large extent this is true. However, we do see small sections of the moon's far side at different times as a result of motions called **librations**.

One type of libration involves the moon's axis. The moon's axis, like the Earth's, is slightly tilted. This tilt makes it possible to see other areas of the moon's surface during its orbit around the Earth.

Another kind of libration occurs because of changes in the moon's speed. As the moon circles the Earth, its speed changes slightly. Its rate of rotation on its axis does not change, however. As a result, it is possible to see even a little more of the far side of the moon.

Because of these librations, we are able to see about 59 percent of the moon's surface at one time or another. The rest of the moon's

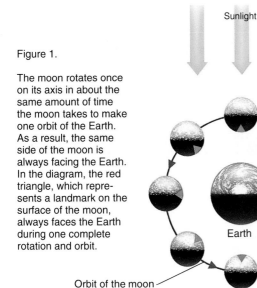

Figure 1.

The moon rotates once on its axis in about the same amount of time the moon takes to make one orbit of the Earth. As a result, the same side of the moon is always facing the Earth. In the diagram, the red triangle, which represents a landmark on the surface of the moon, always faces the Earth during one complete rotation and orbit.

Sunlight

Direction of the moon's rotation

Earth

Orbit of the moon

surface was a mystery, however, until 1959. In that year a Russian space probe, *Lunik III,* circled the moon and took the first pictures of the surface of the moon's far side. Later, other Russian and American space probes took additional pictures of the far side.

Phases of the Moon

The moon has no light of its own. Moonlight is really sunlight that is reflected off the moon's surface. Here on Earth, the amount of moonlight we see varies. Sometimes we can see the entire lighted side of the moon. At other times, we see only a portion of it lit. Because of this, the moon appears to change its shape from night to night. We call these changes the phases of the moon.

These phases occur as a result of the moon's orbit around the Earth. This can be understood best by looking at a diagram (see Figure 2). During its orbit, when the moon is between the sun and the Earth (A), the side facing the Earth receives no sunlight, and the moon is not visible on Earth. This phase is called the **new moon**. Two or

three days after the new moon, as the moon moves farther in its orbit, a small portion of the side of the moon that is lit becomes visible. This is called the **crescent moon**. As the moon travels farther in its orbit, the crescent **waxes**, or grows (B). When half the side that is lit is visible, this phase, which occurs a week after the new moon, is called the **first quarter** (C) because the moon has traveled through one quarter of its orbit. Next comes the moon's **gibbous phase** (D), in which more than half the side that is lit is visible. This is followed by the **full moon** (E). At this point, about two weeks after new moon, the whole side that is lit is visible. A day or two after full moon, the moon begins to **wane**, or shrink. Another gibbous phase (F) appears next, but with the right side of the moon in darkness instead of the left. About three weeks after new moon, the moon is in its **last quarter** (G). At this point, the moon has completed three quarters of one trip around the Earth. At the last quarter, the moon's left half appears lighted and right half appears dark—the opposite of the first quarter moon. The moon appears next as a **waning crescent** (H), and a few days after that, there is another new moon (A).

Shifts of the Moon's Position in the Sky

Because the moon is traveling in an orbit around the Earth as it goes through its phases, we see the moon in a slightly different place in the sky from night to night. When the moon is a waxing crescent, for example, it becomes visi-

The heavily cratered far side of the moon is shown in the top three quarters of this photograph, which was taken by astronauts on *Apollo 16.*

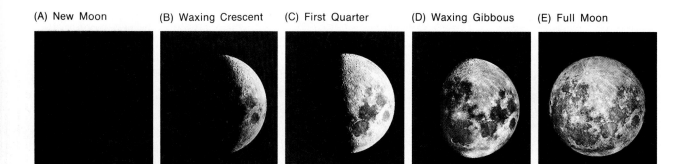

(A) New Moon **(B) Waxing Crescent** **(C) First Quarter** **(D) Waxing Gibbous** **(E) Full Moon**

The Phases of the Moon

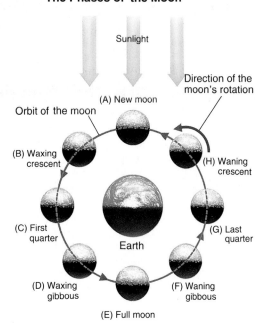

Sunlight

Direction of the moon's rotation

Orbit of the moon

(A) New moon

(B) Waxing crescent

(H) Waning crescent

(C) First quarter

Earth

(G) Last quarter

(D) Waxing gibbous

(F) Waning gibbous

(E) Full moon

Figure 2.

Moonlight is really sunlight reflected off the surface of the moon. The half of the moon facing the sun is always lighted while the other half remains in darkness. Because of the way the moon orbits the Earth as they both orbit the sun, we see different portions of the moon's lighted side while it orbits the Earth. Sometimes we see the entire lighted side of the moon, while at other times we see only a portion of it lit. We call these changing views the phases of the moon.

the day. The first quarter moon, for example, is sometimes visible an hour or two before sunset on a clear day. The waning gibbous moon is sometimes visible for a few hours after sunrise. And the last quarter moon is sometimes visible shortly after sunrise.

Eclipses

Since the moon circles the Earth, you might think that it would pass directly between the Earth and the sun on each orbit. The moon's orbit, however, is slightly tilted, and it passes directly between the Earth and sun only at certain times. When the sun's light is blocked by the moon, and the moon's shadow falls at certain places on Earth, a **solar eclipse**, or eclipse of the sun, occurs.

During a solar eclipse, the diameter of the moon's shadow on the Earth varies from almost nothing up to about 160 miles (258 kilometers). The narrow path that this shadow makes on the surface of the Earth is called the **path of totality**. People who are directly in this path see a total eclipse. People who are outside the path see only a partial eclipse, in which only a portion of the sun is blocked by the moon. During a solar eclipse, the moon's shadow crosses the Earth at speeds of more than 1,000 miles (1,600 kilometers) an hour. The period of time during which the moon completely blocks the sun can last from a little more than seven minutes down to a fraction of a second.

A **lunar eclipse**, or eclipse of the moon, occurs when the Earth passes directly between

ble in the western sky just after sunset and it sets a few hours later. Thereafter, from night to night, the moon appears slightly to the left of where it was at the same time the night before. By first quarter, the moon appears in the southern sky as soon as the sky gets dark. When the moon is full, it appears opposite the sun, rising in the east as the sun sets in the west. By the time the moon is waning, it rises after the sun has set. The last quarter moon typically rises around midnight. The waning crescent moon rises even later, and it is usually visible in the eastern sky within a few hours of sunrise.

Depending on its phases, the moon can sometimes be seen both at night and during

(F) Waning Gibbous

(G) Last Quarter

(H) Waning Crescent

Gravitational Pull of the Moon

If you have ever seen movies or a video of astronauts on the moon, you must have noticed that they did not move in the same way people move on the Earth. They almost seemed to float, despite the cumbersome and heavy space suits and backpacks they wore. This is because the pull of gravity on the surface of the moon is only about one sixth as strong as the pull of gravity on the surface of the Earth, so the weight of an astronaut wearing such equipment is only about 60 pounds (27 kilograms) on the moon while about 350 pounds (158 kilograms) on the Earth.

the sun and the moon and the Earth's shadow blots out the moon. The shadow of the Earth has two sections—a dark inner part called the **umbra** and a fainter outer part surrounding it. If the moon passes entirely through the umbra, there is a total lunar eclipse. If it passes through only a portion of the umbra, there is a partial eclipse.

At the distance of the moon from the Earth, the umbra is considerably larger than the moon, so in passing through it, the moon can stay totally eclipsed for up to about one hour and forty minutes.

An eclipse of the sun can only take place when the moon is new, and an eclipse of the moon can only take place when the moon is full. But we do not see an eclipse every time the moon is new or full. This is because the moon's orbit is slightly tilted relative to the orbit of the Earth around the sun. So the new moon usually passes a little above or below the sun in our sky and the full moon passes a little above or below the shadow cast by the Earth into space. The moon's orbit slowly wobbles, however, so once in a while—at the new or full moon—the Earth, moon, and sun lie along a perfectly straight line and an eclipse occurs.

Sunlight filtered through the Earth's atmosphere during a total eclipse of the moon often casts a reddish or coppery glow over the moon's eclipsed surface.

A solar eclipse can occur when the moon passes between the Earth and the sun. A lunar eclipse can occur when the Earth passes between the sun and the moon and casts a shadow over the moon. When the moon passes entirely through the shadowed area called the umbra, a total eclipse occurs. When it passes through only the penumbra, or through only a portion of the umbra, a partial eclipse occurs.

Penumbra

Umbra

Moon

Earth

Earth

Moon

Sun

Solar eclipse

Lunar eclipse

high tides and two low tides each 25 hours or so. The moon's gravitational pull also causes weak tides in the Earth's atmosphere and in the Earth itself.

The Moon's Surface

If you look up at the moon at night, you can see dark and light areas on its surface even with the naked eye. The pattern formed by these dark and light areas creates the familiar sight commonly called "the man in the moon." The light areas are actually heavily cratered and mountainous terrain known as the lunar highlands. The dark areas are known as **maria** (singular: **mare**), from the Latin word meaning "seas." Early astronomers used this

A section of the spectacular Apennines Mountains, with the Hadley rille snaking along its left side, stretches across the lower right area of this photograph of the moon (*far left*), which was taken from *Apollo 15*. A photo of the crater Clavius (*left*) shows the high walls or rims that surround it and the younger craters that break its surface. This photograph was taken from Earth by telescopes at the Hale Observatories.

The gravitational pull between the Earth, moon, and sun causes the Earth's ocean **tides**. The sun is more massive than the moon but the moon is much closer to the Earth, so the moon has a greater effect on the Earth's tides than the sun does. The tides are caused by the fact that the moon pulls with greater force on the side of the Earth that is closer to the moon than on the side of the Earth that is opposite the moon. This difference in force causes two bulges of water (the high tides) to form on opposite sides of the Earth (the side facing the moon and the side facing away from the moon). As the Earth rotates under these bulges, the oceans are seen to go through two

term because they originally thought the dark areas might be bodies of water.

Mountains. Looking through a telescope, it is possible to see more clearly the light regions known as lunar highlands. These high, mountainous areas contain some peaks as high as Mount Everest on the Earth. Some mountains in these regions form ranges, but most of them form the rims of craters.

Craters. Craters are depressions in the lunar surface that are roughly circular in shape. Millions of craters cover the moon's surface. Many are surrounded by high walls, or rims. Others are ringed by hills, and the smallest are mere pits in the moon's surface.

The walls of craters frequently have different slopes inside and out. The outside crater rim usually slopes gently down toward the surrounding surface. Interior walls, however, usually have steeper slopes. In most craters, the interior floor is lower than the surface outside the crater, sometimes by as much as 10,000 feet (3,048 meters).

Almost all the craters on the moon have been formed by the impact of objects from space. The Earth is bombarded by such objects as well. Many people have seen the light of shooting stars, or meteors, streaking through the night sky. These are actually small pieces of rock or other material moving through the Earth's atmosphere. As they enter the Earth's atmosphere, however, friction causes most of the objects to burn up before reaching the ground. Those that reach the surface are called **meteorites**. The moon has no atmosphere. As a result, there is nothing to stop meteorites from striking the lunar surface, creating craters and grinding lunar rocks into a thin layer of fine dust.

The moon has hundreds of very large craters. Some, such as Clavius, can be seen without a telescope. Clavius is about 145 miles (233 kilometers) in diameter and is surrounded by crater walls up to 17,000 feet (5,182 meters) high. Yet millions of the smallest craters on the moon are less than 1/2500 inch (1/100 millimeter) in diameter.

Most larger craters are **primary craters**, which means that they were formed when an object from space struck the moon's surface. Many smaller craters are **secondary craters**, which means that they were not formed directly by the impact of an object from space. When an object from space strikes the lunar surface, it sends material flying out from the point of impact (the primary crater). As this material crashes onto the lunar surface, it creates secondary craters. Sometimes these impacts send more material flying outward, creating even smaller craters in turn.

By closely examining the moon's craters, it is often possible to tell which ones are older than others. For example, a crater that lies inside another crater or cuts through its walls must be younger than the other one. In this way, astronomers are able to determine relative dating of craters and other lunar features.

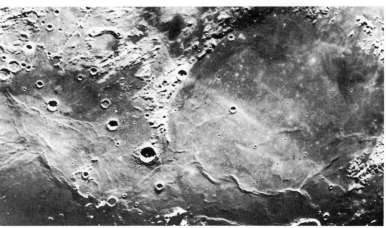

A composite photo of the moon (*above*) made up of 15 images taken by the *Galileo* space probe helps scientists study the composition of the moon's surface soil. Red areas show lunar highlands. Purple areas were formed by explosive volcanic eruptions while blue and orange regions represent different types of lava flows. In a photo taken by the Yerkes Observatory (*right*), moon rilles, valleys, and craters are shown in the area of the Mare Tranquilitatis (left) and the Mare Serenitatis (right).

Rays and Rilles. Some of the moon's craters have light-colored streaks called **rays**, which look like the spokes of a wheel stretching away from the crater. The most noticeable rays are those stretching outward from the crater Tycho. Some of these rays are more than 1,500 miles (2,415 kilometers) long. Giant craters, such as Tycho, were gouged out of the lunar surface by gigantic meteorites. The rays are the broken and ground-up rocks that were blasted outward by the impact of the meteorites. Rayed craters are among the youngest craters on the moon. Astronomers know this because the rays tend to darken with time, and after awhile they are no longer visible.

Powerful telescopes on Earth, lunar probes, and the Apollo astronauts who explored the moon have photographed another feature of the moon's surface called **rilles**. Rilles are cracks and valleys in the lunar surface. They may be straight or they may twist and turn.

Maria and Mascons. The scientist Galileo thought that some areas of the moon were seas, or maria, because they appeared flat, dark, and smooth through his telescope. As telescopes improved, astronomers discovered that the maria are not smooth. They contain many craters—a few large ones and millions of small ones. Astronomers now know that the maria are large plains of solidified lava and that there is no water on the moon.

Astronomers have noted a strange characteristic of those lunar maria that have a roughly circular shape. These areas exert a stronger gravitational pull than do other areas of the moon. Since the gravitational pull exerted by an object depends on the amount of its matter, or mass, scientists reason that the stronger pull of the circular maria is caused by a greater concentration of mass in them. Astronomers

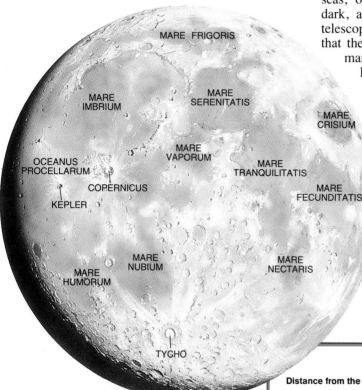

MARE FRIGORIS
MARE IMBRIUM
MARE SERENITATIS
MARE CRISIUM
MARE VAPORUM
OCEANUS PROCELLARUM
MARE TRANQUILITATIS
COPERNICUS
MARE FECUNDITATIS
KEPLER
MARE NUBIUM
MARE NECTARIS
MARE HUMORUM
TYCHO

The Composition of the Moon

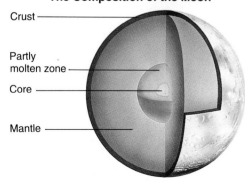

Crust

Partly molten zone

Core

Mantle

Moon

Distance from the Earth (average)	240,000 miles (386,400 kilometers)
Revolution around Earth	27 Earth days 7 hours 43 minutes
Diameter	2,160 miles (3,478 kilometers)
	$\frac{1}{4}$ the diameter of Earth
Mass	74 quintillion tons
	About $\frac{1}{81}$ the mass of Earth
Density	3.36 grams per cubic centimeter
Rotation on its axis	27 Earth days 7 hours 43 minutes
Speed in orbit (average)	2,237 miles (3,600 kilometers) per hour
Tilt of rotational axis	6.68°
Surface	Mountains, craters, and plains
Atmosphere	None
Gravity (compared to Earth's)	About $\frac{1}{6}$, or 0.16 times, the Earth's gravity
Temperature (on sunlit side, at surface)	250°F (120°C)
Symbol	🌙
In mythology	Diana, or Luna, Roman moon goddess

have shortened the term "mass concentration" to **mascons**. The mascons were a problem to the Apollo astronauts who landed on the moon. Because of their stronger gravitational force, mascons can pull a spacecraft slightly off course. Therefore, such changes in course had to be predicted and allowed for when the Apollo spacecraft attempted to land on the lunar surface.

Moon Rocks. Between 1969 and 1972, six teams of Apollo astronauts landed on the moon. Each team consisted of two astronauts. While on the moon, these astronauts collected more than 840 pounds (378 kilograms) of moon soil and rocks to bring back to the Earth for study. A small amount of lunar material also was brought back to the Earth by two Russian space probes.

The rocks collected on the moon are types that are familiar to geologists. Almost all are formed from the cooling of lava. The rocks collected from the maria are mainly basalt—a dark, dense rock. Those collected from the lunar highlands are mainly anorthosite—a type of lava rock that cools more slowly than basalt. Some of the rocks collected in the lunar highlands and the maria were breccia—a type of rock that is compacted and welded together by intense heat and pressure.

Moon rocks have helped scientists learn more about the moon. We now know that the Earth and the moon are generally similar in composition, although some elements that are rare on Earth are somewhat more abundant on the moon (at least among the samples brought back). The age of the oldest lunar rock that has been tested is 4.42 billion years.

The Moon's Interior

While the Apollo astronauts were on the moon, they placed a number of seismometers on its surface. These instruments, which detect movement, measured the strength of the 3,000 or so weak moonquakes that occur on the moon every year. Information about these moonquakes, which was transmitted back to Earth, has enabled scientists to get a partial picture of the moon's interior.

The moon's outer layer, or **crust**, appears to be about 40 miles (64 kilometers) thick on the side of the moon facing the Earth. On the far side of the moon, the crust is nearly twice that thick. Beneath the crust is a thick layer of dense rock, the **mantle**, which extends down

Apollo 11 astronaut Buzz Aldrin deploys an experimental seismometer on the moon. Later versions helped scientists study moonquakes and the structure and movements of the lunar surface. Unless they are covered by dust raised by meteor impacts, Aldrin's footprints will remain on the moon's surface where there is no weather to wear them away.

perhaps 435 miles (700 kilometers). It is not known what lies beneath the mantle.

The Moon's Environment

Scientists have found no evidence to suggest that life has ever existed on the moon. That is not surprising, for the moon's environment is very hostile to life as we know it. Living things need an atmosphere of gases to survive, and the moon has virtually none. On the Earth, every living thing contains carbon and water. On the moon there is almost no carbon. And although scientists have found evidence of ice on the moon, there are no signs of liquid water. Life on Earth also depends on the sun's heat and light, which are forms of **radiation**. Other forms of radiation—some from the sun and some from farther out in space—can be deadly. The Earth's atmosphere helps to filter out most of this deadly radiation. But the moon, without an atmosphere, is continually bombarded by such radiation.

The lack of an atmosphere poses another obstacle to life. The moon's sunlit, or daytime, side is heated to a temperature of about 250°F (120°C) on the surface. The two-week lunar day is followed by two weeks of night, when the temperature falls to –255°F (–160°C). Such extreme temperatures would kill the kinds of living things we know.

Because the moon has no atmosphere, a person on the moon would see a very different sky from the one we see on Earth. On Earth, the daytime sky appears blue because the atmosphere scatters portions of the sun's light. On the moon, there is no air to affect light. As a result, the sky above the moon's surface is always black, even in the daytime. In these black skies, the sun and the stars can be seen at the same time.

Origin of the Moon

Scientists have offered a variety of theories to explain how the moon came into being. One theory, known as the "capture" theory, was based on the idea that the moon once traveled in an orbit around the sun near the Earth. The Earth's strong gravitational force "captured" its neighbor and pulled it into the orbit it now follows around the planet.

A second theory, known as the "fission" theory, suggests that the Earth and the moon were once a single mass of material. As the mass grew, it spun so fast that a part of it formed a bulge. In time, this bulge pulled away and was thrown out into space, forming the moon. The larger part of the mass became the Earth.

Another theory, the "condensation" theory, states that the whole solar system was formed at the same time from a great cloud of dust and gas that whirled in space. More than 99 percent of this cloud collected, or condensed, into a large mass that became the sun. The rest of the cloud condensed into a number of smaller masses, which eventually became the planets and their satellites.

Information about the moon's composition obtained from the *Apollo* missions put all three theories in doubt. Instead, a new hypothesis emerged as the leading theory in the mid-1980's. The "giant impact" theory suggests that the moon was formed when a large object—perhaps as large as Mars—collided with the Earth. The collision blasted large amounts of debris into space, where it formed a ring around the planet. Over time, the orbiting debris collected together to form the moon.

The giant impact theory is not perfect and modifications are still being made. Scientists are not sure at what point in the Earth's formation the collision occurred. Evidence obtained from a computer model suggested it may have occurred when the Earth was almost fully formed.

Early History of the Moon

The moon's early history was unimaginably violent. Millions of rocks, ranging in size from small pebbles to large boulders many miles in diameter, crashed onto the moon's surface. These collisions generated energy that heated up the lunar surface and melted its rock. The moon's surface became a sea of glowing liquid lava hundreds of miles deep.

After millions of years, fewer rocks remained in space, and so fewer crashed into the

WONDER QUESTION

Is there water on the moon?

In 1998, a space probe named *Lunar Prospector* made a surprising discovery while orbiting the moon. The spacecraft detected large amounts of hydrogen—a sign of water—at the moon's poles. At the end of the mission in 1999, scientists directed the probe to crash near the moon's south pole. However, they detected no sign of water in the debris from the impact. Still, some scientists estimate there could be several billion tons of ice deep inside craters. If that is true, future lunar colonists might some day use the water to live on the moon. The water could be converted into hydrogen and oxygen for fuel and oxygen for people to breathe.

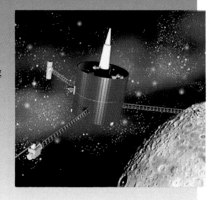

moon. The lighter or less dense materials floated to the surface and eventually formed the moon's crust. The denser materials sank below the surface and formed the mantle and the core of the moon. Because the chemical composition of these materials was different, the rocks of the moon's crust and mantle are also different.

After the moon's crust cooled, some rocks continued crashing onto the moon, blasting huge craters on its surface. During this time, the upper part of the moon's crust was broken, remelted, and mixed almost completely. Then about 4 billion years ago, after the crust was cool and solid, the mantle began heating up as a result of **radioactive decay**. Radioactive decay occurs when unstable radioactive elements such as uranium break down and form other elements. The process generates great amounts of heat, and this is what happened with some elements in the moon's mantle.

The process of radioactive decay generated enough heat to melt portions of the moon's interior, forming lava. Over millions of years, more and more rock was melted, and increasing amounts of lava collected within the mantle. In time, some of this lava worked its way up through the crust and spilled out across huge basins on the lunar surface. As it flowed, the fiery lava cooled and solidified, forming great plains, the lunar maria. Gigantic eruptions of lava took place again and again, over a period of nearly 1 billion years. Then, about 3 billion years ago, the flow of lava came to an end, and the molten rock on the surface cooled. The rock that crystallized in the basins was mainly basalt, a dark rock that led early astronomers to believe that the basins were vast seas. Except for the continuing impact of meteorites, the moon's surface has changed little since the last flows of lava cooled.

Changes on the Earth and the Moon

Most scientists now believe that the Earth was formed in the same general way and at the same time as the moon. After their formation, however, they developed differently.

On both the Earth and the moon, millions of tons of nitrogen, carbon dioxide, water vapor, and other gases were released during the period of lava eruption. On Earth, these substances were held in place by the Earth's gravity, and they formed a protective layer of atmosphere around the planet. Over millions

This striking photograph of the Earth rising over the near side of the moon in the region of the Mare Smythii was taken by the *Apollo 11* astronauts.

of years, as the Earth's crust cooled, the water vapor in the atmosphere condensed into drops of water and fell as rain. Torrents of water poured across the Earth's surface, forming mighty rivers and vast oceans. This rushing water, together with violent winds and changes in the Earth's crust itself, wore away large craters and other evidence of the planet's early history. The planet's atmosphere and its oceans of water also made life possible.

The moon, however, had a weaker gravitational pull because of its smaller size. As a result, it was unable to hold onto the gases produced by lava eruptions, and all the gases escaped into space. Without an atmosphere or water, the moon had no forces of erosion to change its surface. The changes that have occurred in the last 3 billion years have been caused primarily by meteorites crashing onto its surface. For these billions of years, the moon has looked much as we see it today. Its cratered and mountainous surface is like a partial portrait of Earth when it was young.

William A. Gutsch, Jr.
Chairman, American Museum-
Hayden Planetarium

See also Eclipses; Gravity and Gravitation; Satellites; Solar System; Space Exploration and Travel; Space Probes; Tides.

MOORISH ART AND ARCHITECTURE. See Islamic Art and Architecture.

MORE, SIR THOMAS (1478–1535)

Thomas More was a brilliant English scholar, lawyer, and statesman. He was born in London, England, on February 7, 1478. In 1494, More interrupted his language studies at Oxford University to return to London and study law. About this time he considered entering the religious life, and for four years he lived and studied under the direction of a

group of Carthusian monks. Eventually he decided against becoming a monk and resumed his law career. In 1504 he entered Parliament. The next year he married, and his wife bore him four children. When his wife died in 1511, More married again.

Thomas More's deep sense of justice and outstanding legal ability earned him increasingly important positions. He became a royal counselor to King Henry VIII in 1518, was knighted in 1521, and was made lord chancellor, the king's highest legal adviser, following the dismissal of Cardinal Wolsey in 1529. His friendship with the king became strained when he refused to support Henry's plan to disobey the pope's orders and divorce his wife, Queen Catherine of Aragon. More resigned the chancellorship, citing ill health, in 1532.

The dispute reached its climax in 1534 when More refused to take an oath recognizing Henry as head of the church in England. After a year in prison, More was brought to trial on charges of treason, and on the false testimony of a witness, he was found guilty and sentenced to death. Just before his execution on July 6, 1535, More declared, "I am the king's good servant, but God's first."

In addition to his brilliance as a lawyer and statesman, More was a scholar. He wrote many works in Latin and in English, notably *Utopia,* which describes an imaginary country with an ideal society. The Catholic Church declared him a saint in 1935.

KATHLEEN McGOWAN
Catholic Youth Encyclopedia

MORÈS, MARQUIS DE, ANTOINE DE VALLOMBROSA.   See NORTH DAKOTA (Famous People).

MORGAN, JOHN PIERPONT (1837–1913)

J. Pierpont Morgan was one of the most influential bankers and financial leaders in American history. He also was one of the nation's greatest patrons of the arts.

Pierpont Morgan was born in Hartford, Connecticut, on April 17, 1837. While his father, Junius Spencer Morgan, headed a banking firm in London, young Pierpont attended schools in Switzerland and Germany.

After 1857, Pierpont Morgan worked in New York City as an American representative of his father's bank, J. S. Morgan and Company. These were years of huge growth in American industry and commerce. The Morgan Bank, with its reputation for honesty, was largely responsible for acquiring large-scale European investments to finance developing American businesses.

After his father's death in 1890, Pierpont Morgan headed his own New York firm, J. P. Morgan and Company, which became one of the most powerful banking houses in the world. He became famous for reorganizing the railroad companies and for financing huge industries, including United States Steel, the nation's first billion-dollar corporation. He was powerful enough to assist the United States government in periods of financial panic.

Morgan's interests were not limited to financial dealings. He loved books, art, and sailing. His steam yacht, the *Corsair,* was one of the world's most impressive private vessels. When asked how much such an extravagance cost, he reportedly replied, "If you have to ask, you can't afford it!" For many years he served as president of the Metropolitan Museum of Art in New York City, to which he gave thousands of important works of art.

Pierpont Morgan died in Rome, Italy, on March 31, 1913. His extraordinary private library in New York City is open to the public as a museum and research library.

D. W. WRIGHT
Archivist, The Pierpont Morgan Library

MORMONS

The Church of Jesus Christ of Latter-day Saints was founded on April 6, 1830, in Fayette, New York, as a result of the religious experiences of a young farmer named Joseph Smith. According to Smith, on a late September night in 1827 he unearthed from a hill the writings of Christian prophets he claimed had lived in the Western Hemisphere many centuries earlier. Smith translated and published these writings as *The Book of Mormon*. This volume of scripture, now subtitled *Another Testament of Jesus Christ*, was named for Mormon, one of the prophets of old. It is the basis for the nickname by which its church members are known.

Although Smith's organization started with only six members, the new church grew rapidly. But the Latter-day Saints, as they were known, soon faced persecution, not only because Joseph Smith claimed he had seen God but because he added new scripture to the Bible. Smith and his followers were driven out of every place they settled—first New York, then Ohio, and later Missouri. In 1839 they founded the village of Nauvoo in Illinois. But after Joseph Smith was murdered by a hostile mob in 1844, most of the Latter-day Saints followed their new leader, Brigham Young, west to the Rocky Mountains. From Canada to Mexico, they established hundreds of settlements, including Salt Lake City, Utah, which today remains the church's world headquarters. Those followers of Joseph Smith who chose not to go west remained in the Midwest and ultimately founded a separate organization called the Reorganized Church of Jesus Christ of Latter Day Saints.

Beliefs. Although Mormons are Christian, they are neither Catholic nor Protestant; rather, they believe their church is the "restored" church of Jesus Christ. Mormons look upon the president of the church as a prophet, much like Moses and Abraham, and believe that God guides and directs the church by divine revelation through this prophet. Baptism in the church follows the biblical example of immersing, or dipping, a person in water, a symbolic act of washing away one's sins. Because Mormons believe that young children are incapable of sin, children are not baptized until the age of 8, which is considered the age of accountability.

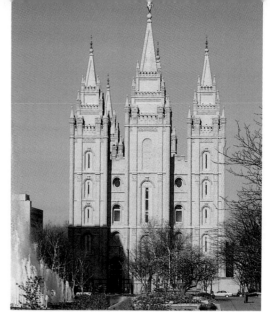

The Mormon Temple in Salt Lake City, Utah, is one of 43 Mormon temples located worldwide. It is reserved for worship and is not open to the public.

Mormons believe that there is life before birth as well as life after death and that all people will be resurrected; however, status after death depends on how accepting and obedient one is to the teachings of Jesus Christ.

Considerable emphasis is placed on the worth of the individual and on the solidarity of the family unit. Strict morality is taught and encouraged; abortion, pornography, and gambling are emphatically opposed. The church has a health code that forbids the use of tobacco, alcoholic beverages, tea, and coffee, and it emphasizes the positive benefits of wise eating habits and physical and spiritual fitness.

Faithful members of the church embrace the principle of tithing, which means that they donate one tenth of their income to the church. This money is used to finance construction, education, and welfare programs as well as missionary and humanitarian services to benefit its members and others.

The church believes in a lay ministry, meaning there is no professional clergy. Only men may serve as ministers, and they are not paid for their services. More than 20,000 congregations are led and staffed by lay members. World membership in the Church of Jesus Christ of Latter-day Saints is approaching 10 million in some 150 nations and territories.

L. DON LeFEVRE
The Church of Jesus Christ of Latter-day Saints

See also SALT LAKE CITY; SMITH, JOSEPH; UTAH; YOUNG, BRIGHAM.

MOROCCO

The Kingdom of Morocco is located on the northwestern coast of Africa, bordering both the Atlantic Ocean and the Mediterranean Sea. Its northern tip lies just a short distance from Spain, across the Strait of Gibraltar. Roughly rectangular in shape, Morocco is a land of fertile plains, high mountains, and barren desert.

▶ THE PEOPLE

Ethnic Groups, Religion, Language. The Moroccans are descended from the early Berber inhabitants of the region and the Arabs who arrived during a series of invasions beginning in the A.D. 600's. From the Arabs, the Berbers acquired the Muslim religion and the Arabic language while, at the same time, keeping their distinctive languages and cultures. Although Arabic is the official and principal language, French is also widely used. In the north, Spanish is spoken.

At one time there were about 200,000 Moroccan Jews. Most were descendants of Jews who had been expelled from Spain in the late 1400's, or fled from other European coun-tries, and settled in the coastal cities. The present Jewish community numbers only about 7,000, largely due to emigration. Morocco has, in addition, about 100,000 foreign residents, most of whom are French or Spanish and live mainly in Casablanca, the country's largest city.

Way of Life. While there has been a continuous movement of people from the countryside to the cities, a slight majority of Moroccans still live in rural areas. Most country people are farmers who grow crops and raise livestock for their own needs, generally on small plots of land. The most densely populated areas are in the north, particularly along the fertile coastal plains. In the southern desert, a few tribes follow the traditional nomadic way of life, stopping at the oases, or watered areas, that dot the otherwise barren landscape. Some nomads pitch their tents on the high, dry plateaus, where their flocks of sheep and goats can graze.

In the past, women in the cities rarely left home. Today, the majority of them readily do so, to go to work, to the mosque (the Muslim

An encampment in the Sahara is the temporary home of a party of nomadic Berbers (*above*), Morocco's earliest inhabitants. A woman of Arab ancestry (*right*) watches her child at play. The Berbers and Arabs are the country's two main ethnic groups.

house of worship), the public baths, and the movies. Women in the rural areas have always had greater freedom than those in the cities, because they must help out in the fields. Children usually take care of the livestock and fetch water from public wells or fountains. Boys usually follow their fathers' occupations.

Dress and Food. The Moroccan national dress is the *jellaba*, a long, hooded robe-like garment. The women's version no longer has the hood, but some women continue the tradition of covering their face with a veil. Most city men and women wear European-style clothing when they go out.

Couscous, or semolina, made from wheat, is the basic food. It is usually served with meat and vegetables. Roast lamb dishes are also popular. Mint tea is the traditional drink. Dates and camel's milk are staple foods of the desert nomad.

Education. Since 1962, when primary education was made compulsory, the number of children enrolled in school has increased greatly. Currently, children are required to attend classes from age 7 to 15, although not all are able to do so. Morocco has more than a dozen universities, the largest of which is Mohammed V University in Rabat, the capital. Al-Qarawiyin University, in Fez, is a center of Islamic studies. Founded in 859, it may be the oldest university in the world.

FACTS and figures

KINGDOM OF MOROCCO is the official name of the country.

LOCATION: Northwestern Africa.

AREA: 172,413 sq mi (446,550 km²), not including Western Sahara.

POPULATION: 29,000,000 (estimate).

CAPITAL: Rabat.

LARGEST CITY: Casablanca.

MAJOR LANGUAGES: Arabic (official), Berber, French, Spanish.

MAJOR RELIGIOUS GROUP: Muslim.

GOVERNMENT: Constitutional monarchy. **Head of state**—king. **Head of government**—prime minister. **Legislature**—Chamber of Representatives and Chamber of Counselors.

CHIEF PRODUCTS: Agricultural—wheat, barley, sugar beets, tomatoes, cotton, wine grapes, livestock. **Manufactured**—fertilizers, textiles, processed foods, refined petroleum products, leather goods, plastics, glassware, machine tools, electrical equipment. **Mineral**—phosphate rock.

MONETARY UNIT: Dirham (1 dirham = 100 centimes).

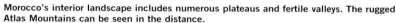

▶ THE LAND

Features. Morocco has three major geographical regions: the fertile coastal plains in the north and northwest; the rugged Atlas

Morocco's interior landscape includes numerous plateaus and fertile valleys. The rugged Atlas Mountains can be seen in the distance.

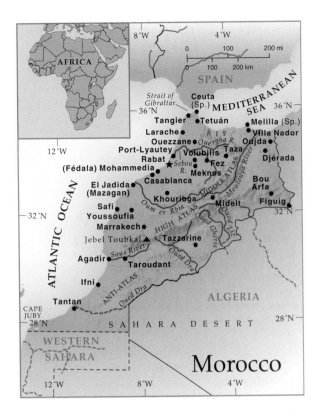

Morocco

Mountains, consisting of several parallel ranges running diagonally through the country; and the Sahara Desert in the south. Another mountain range, the Rif (Er Rif), lies along the Mediterranean coast. The country's highest peak, Jebel Toubkal, rises to 13,665 feet (4,165 meters) in the High Atlas range.

Climate. Temperatures are generally moderate along the Atlantic coastal strip, but they become more extreme inland. The Atlas Mountains act as a barrier to the moisture-laden winds of the Atlantic, helping to create the desert conditions in the south. Rainfall is heaviest in the north and in the mountains, where there is considerable snowfall as well. The Sahara receives slight rainfall.

Natural Resources. Morocco is rich in mineral resources. It has the world's largest reserves of phosphate rock (used to make fertilizers) and deposits of manganese, lead, copper, zinc, iron ore, and other minerals. Forests cover about 12 percent of the land, with the cork oak the most valuable tree. The surrounding waters are an abundant source of fish.

Major Cities. Casablanca, located on Morocco's Atlantic coast, is not only the country's largest city but also its chief port and the center of its commerce and industry. With a population of more than 3 million, it is one of the largest cities in Africa. Rabat, the capital and second largest city, also lies on the coast. The main inland cities are Fez, Marrakech (or Marrakesh) and Meknes. Tangier, the second most important port, is situated near the northern tip of Morocco.

▶ **THE ECONOMY**

Agriculture and Fishing. Agriculture and fishing (along with forestry) employ about 35 percent of the Moroccan workforce. The chief crops include wheat, barley, sugar beets, tomatoes, and cotton. Citrus fruits and wine grapes are leading export crops. Large, mechanized farms account for most of the agricultural production. Fish and fish products make up nearly 15 percent of the country's exports. The fish catch is varied, but sardines are the most important. Cork is the chief forestry product.

Industry. Nearly 25 percent of the labor force is engaged in industry (including manufacturing and mining). The most important manufactures, by value of output, are fertilizers, textiles, processed foods, and refined petroleum products. Leather goods, plastics, glassware, machine tools, and electrical equipment are also produced. Phosphate mining is vital to the economy, with phosphate rock accounting for a significant part of the country's export earnings. With the country's many his-

Casablanca is Morocco's largest city, chief port, and the center of its commerce and industry. This is the Place des Nations Unies (United Nations Square).

torical sites, tourism is a major service industry and an important source of revenue.

▶ HISTORY AND GOVERNMENT

Early History. What is now Morocco was inhabited in the Stone Age by cave dwellers, who left many traces of their presence. In about 2000 B.C. it was settled by Berber tribes, who have formed the basis of the population ever since, despite repeated invasions. The Arabs brought the Islamic religion and culture to the region and, in the early A.D. 700's, joined forces with the Berbers to conquer most of Spain and Portugal. The first Moroccan state was established in about 788 by Idris I, whose descendants ruled for nearly two centuries.

Empires and Foreign Rule. The first great Moroccan empire was founded in the early 1000's by the Almoravids, whose domain eventually extended from Spain to present-day Mali and Algeria. They were overthrown in 1147 by the Almohads, who held sway until 1271. Although by the late 1400's all of Spain and Portugal had been lost to them, later Moroccan dynasties maintained themselves in power until modern times.

Morocco remained relatively free from foreign domination until the middle and late 1800's, when the European countries began to compete for territory in Africa. In 1912, under the Treaty of Fez, most of Morocco was made a protectorate of France, with Spain occupying additional territory, mainly in the north. Rebellions against foreign rule erupted in 1917 and in the 1920's, but all were crushed by military force.

Toward Independence. In 1942, during World War II, Allied forces landed in French Morocco, which had been under the control of France's Vichy government. At the Casablanca Conference in 1943, U.S. president Franklin D. Roosevelt and British prime minister Winston Churchill met to discuss the Allied war aims. Near the end of the war, a movement for independence began, led by the oldest Moroccan political party, the Istiqlal (Independence) Party. Opposition to the French reached its peak in 1953, when they forced the Moroccan ruler, Mohammed V, who had become a symbol of the independence movement, into exile. In 1955 he was allowed to return, and independence was granted in 1956.

King Hassan II came to the Moroccan throne in 1961, succeeding his father, Mohammed V. He ruled until his death on July 23, 1999.

King Mohammed V died in 1961 and was succeeded by his son, Hassan II. Spain gave up most of its Moroccan territory at the same time as France, but it still maintains two small ports on the Mediterranean coast, Ceuta (Sebta) and Melilla.

Recent History. Spain also retained control of the Western Sahara (formerly called Spanish Sahara), a vast but thinly populated region, rich in phosphate rock. Morocco recovered most of the region in 1976 and the rest in 1979. But the territory continues to be contested by the Polisario Front, which seeks independence. The ongoing dispute led Morocco to withdraw from the Organization of African Unity (OAU) in 1984, after several African countries officially recognized the region as the Saharan Arab Democratic Republic. Hassan II died in 1999. He was succeeded by his eldest son, Mohammed VI.

Morocco is a constitutional monarchy. Its government is based on a constitution adopted in 1992. The king, who is both head of state and the country's spiritual leader, appoints a prime minister to head the government. Members of the Chamber of Representatives are elected by the people to 5-year terms. Members of the upper chamber are elected by community councils, trade unions, and professional bodies to 9-year terms.

NAJAT SEBTI
Mohammed V University (Rabat)

MORRIS, ESTHER HOBART. See WYOMING (Famous People).

MORRIS, GOUVERNEUR (1752–1816)

Gouverneur Morris, an American statesman and diplomat, was one of the most active delegates at the Constitutional Convention of 1787. He made his greatest historical contribution as head of the committee that drafted the original Constitution of the United States.

Gouverneur (pronounced gov-er-NEER or GOOV-er-ner) was born on January 31, 1752, at Morrisania, the family manor in New York State. He entered King's College (now Columbia) at the age of 12. He later studied law and passed the bar exam in 1771.

Despite a promising legal career, Morris was drawn into politics by the growing movement toward American independence. While some members of his family were loyal to England, Morris championed self-government for the American colonies. He served in the colonial militia (1775–76) and was a delegate at New York State's constitutional convention (1776). He later served in the Continental Congress (1778–79).

In 1779, Morris moved to Philadelphia to practice law but was soon drawn back to government work. As assistant superintendent of finance (1781–85) under the Congress of Confederation, he was the first to suggest a decimal monetary system for the country and the use of the term "cent."

Morris was one of eight delegates elected to represent Pennsylvania at the Constitutional Convention of 1787, held in Philadelphia. Morris, who made the greatest number of speeches, found himself at odds with many of the delegates and their philosophy for a new, democratic republic. He himself favored a strong central government that would be controlled by the upper classes. He also favored the election of a president for life.

In his later years, Morris served as U.S. minister (1792–94) to France, as a U.S. senator (1800–03) from New York, and as director of the Erie Canal Commission (1810–12). He died on November 6, 1816.

LARRY R. GERLACH
The University of Utah

MORRISON, TONI (1931–   )

The Nobel Prize-winning American novelist Toni Morrison is one of the outstanding writers of her generation. Her novels combine historical detail with vivid, poetic language to portray African American family life, female experience, and culture.

Toni Morrison was born Chloe Anthony Wofford in Lorain, Ohio, on February 18, 1931. She graduated from Howard University in 1953, receiving a master's degree in writing

from Cornell University two years later. In addition to writing fiction and nonfiction, she had a long career as a book editor. She also taught at several universities, including Howard and Princeton.

Through the voices of her characters, Morrison often reveals the effects of racism in the United States. In her first novel, *The Bluest Eye* (1969), a young black girl longs for the white American ideal of beauty. *Beloved* (1987), for which Morrison won the Pulitzer Prize, tells the story of an escaping slave who kills her own child rather than see her grow up in slavery. All Morrison's novels explore the complex stories of our human condition.

Morrison's other novels include *Song of Solomon* (1977), *Tar Baby* (1981), and *Jazz* (1992). Each examines the relationship between racism and self-discovery in American life. Morrison also wrote a number of essays. She received the Nobel Prize for literature in 1993.

Reviewed by PRISCILLA R. RAMSEY
Department of Afro-American Studies
Howard University

MORSE, SAMUEL F. B. (1791–1872)

Until the middle of the 1800's, it was not possible to send a message quickly to someone who was far away. Samuel F. B. Morse, an artist and inventor, developed a way to send long-distance messages, using an electrical machine called a telegraph and an alphabet system called the Morse code.

Samuel Finley Breese Morse was born in Charlestown, Massachusetts, on April 27, 1791. At the age of 14 he entered Yale University, where he attended lectures on chemistry and electricity. Although he was fascinated with these subjects, his main ambition was to become an artist.

Shortly after graduating from Yale, Morse went to England to study art. During the several years he remained abroad, he became well known as an artist. Morse returned to the United States, and in 1815 he became a portrait painter. Three years later he married Lucretia Pickering Walker, with whom he had four children.

In 1823, Morse settled in New York City to lecture and write about art. He was appointed professor of art at the University of the City of New York, which is now called New York University. The position did not pay him a salary, but it allowed him to give private art lessons to students and the opportunity to attend a series of science lectures, which he enjoyed. The subject of several of these lectures was a new device called the electromagnet.

In 1825, Morse's wife died while he was away from the city. Because communication was so slow at that time, he did not learn of Lucretia's death until days after the funeral had taken place.

Several years later, while returning from a second trip to Europe, Morse passed some of the time aboard ship discussing electromagnets with one of the other passengers. The idea suddenly came to him how messages might be sent over great distances with the proper use of an electromagnet, wire, and batteries. As soon as he got back to New York, he began working out his idea. At the same time he also invented a message code system, in which dots and dashes are arranged in different sequences to represent each letter of the alphabet, a system now known as the Morse code.

By this time, Morse had begun to realize that he would never be a great artist. He was

The American inventor Samuel F. B. Morse developed the electric telegraph system and the Morse code to send long-distance messages.

having difficulty making a living as a painter. Fortunately several of his friends were willing to invest money in his new invention. Morse gave up his career as an artist and devoted all of his time to perfecting the telegraph. In 1837 he applied for a patent on his invention.

Soon, Morse felt his instrument was good enough for a long-range test, which he wished to conduct between Washington, D.C., and Baltimore, a distance of 38 miles (61 kilometers). Morse went to the U.S. Congress for help, but Congress refused to grant him any money to finance the test. Disappointed, he went to Europe to try to engage the interest of representatives of foreign governments in his invention, but he was unsuccessful there, too.

Finally, in March 1843, Congress voted to give Morse $30,000 for the test line. By 1844 the line was finished. The first message, "What hath God wrought!" was sent from the Capitol in Washington, D.C., on May 24, 1844. The message was received in Baltimore almost as soon as it was sent. "Writing at a distance" had become a reality.

From that moment on, Morse began receiving honors from all over the world. He also became a wealthy man. After having remained a widower for 23 years, in 1848 Morse married Sarah Elizabeth Griswold. She, too, bore him four children.

On June 10, 1871, the telegraph operators of America unveiled a statue of Morse in Central Park in New York City. Morse died in New York City on April 2, 1872.

DAVID C. KNIGHT
Author, *Let's Find Out About Magnets*

MORSE CODE. See RADIO, AMATEUR.
MORTGAGES. See REAL ESTATE.
MORTON, JELLY ROLL. See JAZZ (Profiles).
MORTON, LEVI P. See VICE PRESIDENCY OF THE UNITED STATES.

MOSAIC

Mosaic is an art in which small pieces of colored materials are placed in cement or plaster to form a picture or pattern. The pieces, called **tesserae**, can be made of practically anything—marble, glass, tile, minerals, shells, seeds, or pebbles. They can be any shape—round or square, octagonal (eight-sided), hexagonal (six-sided), or irregular. Mosaic is most often used to decorate floors, walls, ceilings, jewelry, and furniture. Tesserae for floors are usually flat, while those used on walls are often cone-shaped so that they can be pushed into cement.

As early as 3000 B.C., the Sumerians, Egyptians, and other ancient peoples decorated walls with colored tiles arranged in simple geometric patterns. In the Americas, Aztec and Maya artisans covered such objects as masks, shields, and religious statues with closely fitted pieces of turquoise, shell, and other materials.

The first true mosaics were floors made from colored pebbles. Floor mosaics dating from the 700's to the 300's B.C. have been found in Turkey, northern Greece, and on the island of Crete.

Pebble mosaic spread throughout the Mediterranean world. In time the Greeks and, later, the Romans began to use small cubes of cut stone or glass for floor mosaics. At first these mosaics had simple abstract patterns in just a few colors. Later, artisans imitated painting techniques, creating detailed and realistic images in many colors. In addition to covering floors, panels of mosaic were used like paintings to decorate walls.

A mosaic (*left*) from the church of San Vitale in Ravenna, Italy, depicts St. John the Evangelist. It is one of many outstanding examples of Byzantine mosaic in the church, which was built in the A.D. 500's. A detail of the mosaic (*right*) shows the tiny pieces of colored glass that combine to form the image.

Mosaic technique was an important element of early Christian art. Beginning in the A.D. 300's, mosaic was used to decorate church interiors. The use of mosaic in church decoration reached its height during the Byzantine Empire (330–1453). Elaborate mosaics depicting Christ, saints and prophets, and other biblical subjects cover the walls and ceiling vaults of many Byzantine churches.

The use of mosaic declined greatly after 1400, although it continued in Italy during the Renaissance (1400–1600) and through the 1800's. The art of mosaic was revived in the 1900's, most notably by Mexican artists. Mosaic technique continues to be used today as a form of decoration in both religious and public buildings.

Reviewed by CHARLES McCLENDON
Yale University

See also BYZANTINE ART AND ARCHITECTURE.

MOSCOW

Moscow (Moskva in Russian) is the capital and largest city of Russia, or the Russian Federation, and is the center of the country's political, economic, and cultural life. It was formerly the national capital of the Union of Soviet Socialist Republics, or Soviet Union, before its collapse in 1991. Historically, Moscow was the core around which the Russian Empire grew. With a present-day population of about 9 million, it ranks among the world's major cities.

Moscow has played an important role in Russian history for more than six centuries. Reminders of the time when the czars ruled Russia can be found throughout the historic inner heart of the city. Other parts of Moscow reflect the changes it underwent after the revolutions of 1917, which led to the overthrow of the last czar and to the creation of the Soviet Union.

Location and Climate. Moscow is situated on both banks of the Moskva River, a tributary of the Oka. It is located in the center of the Great Russian Plain, in the European part of Russia. A northern city, Moscow lies in the same latitude as the southern tip of Alaska. Its

winters are long and cold, with frequent snowfall; summers are relatively short but can be quite warm.

▶ **PLACES OF INTEREST**

Moscow has a circular pattern, which developed as the city grew over the centuries from its central core.

The Kremlin. Located in the heart of the inner core of the city, the Kremlin is a fortress that was once the seat of power of the czars and later became the center of the former Soviet government. Its walls, which are 40 to 50 feet (12 to 15 meters) high, extend for almost 1½ miles (2.4 kilometers) and enclose a large triangular-shaped area. Towers are located at intervals along the walls. Five gates permit entrance to the Kremlin.

The Kremlin (the word means a fortress or citadel) lies in the heart of Moscow. It contains palaces dating from czarist times, some of which are now government buildings.

Left: St. Basil's Cathedral was built by Czar Ivan IV in the 1500's. *Above:* Muscovites crowd a street in the city's Arbat section dating from the 1800's.

The main entrance is through the Gate of the Savior, whose tower is more than 200 feet (61 meters) high. Inside the walls are the palaces formerly used by the czars and the buildings that once housed the Soviet government. There are also three cathedrals, two bell towers, two monasteries, and many churches. Many of the religious buildings were closed under the Soviets but were reopened after the breakup of the Soviet Union in 1991.

Several palaces, including the Great Palace, built in the 1800's, are kept just as they were in czarist times and are now museums. These museums contain the beautiful costumes, jewelry, thrones, crowns, carriages, and personal possessions of the former czars, as well as the treasures of the church. The ornate reception halls of the Great Palace are now used for official state ceremonies.

Cathedral Square adjoins the Great Palace and is the site of the Supreme Soviet, or Russian legislature. Dormition Cathedral, Annun-ciation Cathedral, and the bell tower of Czar Ivan the Great dating from the 1500's are grouped together around the square. The slender 300-foot (93-meter) tower is the tallest structure in the Kremlin.

Red Square. The Gate of the Savior opens out from the Kremlin onto Red Square. This large open area, measuring 2,300 by 430 feet (700 by 130 meters), was a marketplace in the Middle Ages. It is now used for important ceremonial occasions, parades, and for strolling by Muscovites (as the people of Moscow are called). In Russian, the square is known as *Krasnaya Ploshchadd*. "Krasnaya" means "beautiful" as well as "red."

At one end of the square stands the many-colored St. Basil's Cathedral, with its distinctively Russian, onion-shaped domes. On one side of the Kremlin wall is the Lenin Mausoleum (tomb). Built of red and black stone, it contains the embalmed body of the leader of the 1917 Bolshevik Revolution and founder of the Soviet Communist government. Behind the mausoleum are the burial places of other Soviet leaders.

Kitai Gorod. The earliest development of the city beyond the immediate area of the Kremlin was *Kitai Gorod* ("Middle City"). It was long the main commercial section of Moscow but has now lost some of its importance. On its western edge is the GUM, or state department store, the largest store of its kind in Russia.

Other Landmarks of the Inner City. There are many other places of interest within the inner part of the city. The Aleksandrovsky Garden lies west of the Kremlin. Nearby is the old Moscow University building, the first university in the country, founded in the mid-1700's. Farther north is the Bolshoi Theater, home of the world-famous ballet company.

Other cultural attractions of special interest include the Pushkin Museum of Fine Arts; the Russian State Library, the nation's largest; the Tretyakov Art Gallery, which contains paintings from earliest Russian times to the present; the Moscow Conservatory, where many Russian composers studied and taught; and the Moscow Art Theater, which first gained renown in the early 1900's for its naturalistic staging of the great Russian dramatists.

The Metro. The Moscow subway, known as the Metro, first opened in 1935. It has more than 100 stations and approximately 100 miles (160 kilometers) of track and is used by millions of Muscovites daily. The Metro is a Russian showplace, with many of its stations elaborately decorated and lighted. The station at Revolution Square is decorated with sculptures; the one at Makakovsky Square is hung with paintings.

Outer Parts of the City. The Sadovoye Ring marks the boundary of the inner city. At one time it enclosed the old city within walls, but it now consists of boulevards. Just beyond the ring are Gorky Park and the Ostankino television tower, which stands more than 1,750 feet (533 meters) high.

More than half of Moscow's total land area now lies within its outermost region, which was formerly countryside. It has the highest concentration of new buildings, mainly large apartment blocks, built to try to relieve the city's chronic housing shortage. The new campus of Moscow State University is situated in this area, as is Dynamo Stadium, which is the home of the Moscow soccer team, Dynamo. Several airports are located on the outskirts of the city.

▶**ECONOMY**

Moscow's economic importance is partly due to its location at the center of the country's transportation system of railroads, airlines, highways, rivers, and canals. It is also a leading Russian manufacturing city. Its chief products are textiles, a wide range of machinery and transportation equipment (including machine tools and electric motors, automobiles, trucks, and aircraft), processed foods, chemicals, and various consumer goods (including radios and television sets).

The outer area of Moscow has the largest concentration of new buildings, including apartment complexes. The tall structure is the Ostankino television tower.

The 70th anniversary of the Bolshevik Revolution, which led to the creation of the Soviet Union, was marked by a jubilant parade in Red Square on November 7, 1987, just a little more than four years before the Soviet breakup in 1991.

▶ HISTORY

Early Period. Although a settlement probably existed earlier on the site, the first written mention of the city dates from 1147, when Prince Yuri Dolgoruki had a protective stockade constructed around the hill where the Kremlin now stands. The stockade, a few log buildings, and a wooden church were Moscow's first structures.

The city grew into importance under Ivan I, who became prince of Moscow in 1325, under the rule of the Tatars. The Tatars, a Mongol people, had conquered the Russian lands in the 1200's. Ivan I became their chief vassal, or subject prince. He collected the heavy taxes demanded by the Tatars and extended his control over surrounding areas.

Capital. Moscow became the capital of a unified Russian state under Ivan III, called the Great, who expelled the Tatars in 1480 and first used the title of czar. He beautified the city, calling in Italian architects to build the Kremlin wall, two of the cathedrals, and many other buildings. The city prospered under succeeding rulers.

Moscow Loses its Place. In 1712, Czar Peter I, known as the Great, transferred the capital to his newly built city of St. Petersburg near the country's western border. Seeking to Westernize Russia, Peter had decided that his country also needed a capital that was, geographically, farther west. However, the czars continued to be crowned in Dormition Cathedral in the Kremlin, for Moscow remained a holy city.

Napoleon's Invasion. In 1812 a French army under Napoleon I invaded Russia and occupied Moscow, which had been abandoned. Fires broke out, possibly set by accident or by the Russians themselves. Much of the city was destroyed (the Kremlin was saved by its strong walls), forcing Napoleon to begin the disastrous retreat from Russia that cost him most of his army. Moscow was quickly rebuilt.

Capital Again. Moscow was restored as the capital in 1918 by the new Communist government, following the overthrow of the monarchy. In 1941, during World War II, Moscow barely escaped capture by invading German armies, which were stopped at its outskirts.

After the war ended in 1945, the number of inhabitants of Moscow increased enormously. The city's limits were extended and massive new housing projects were built. The city was chosen as the site of the 1980 Summer Olympic Games.

Moscow was at the center of the events leading to the breakup of the Soviet Union at the end of 1991. As the capital, it was also the critical site in the armed revolt against Russian president Boris Yeltsin by his opponents in parliament that took place in 1993.

ELIZABETH SEEGER
Author, *The Pageant of Russian History*

MOSES

Moses' story is told in the Bible in the books of Exodus, Leviticus, Numbers, and Deuteronomy. These books, along with Genesis, are sometimes called the Books of Moses. They are known as the Pentateuch.

According to the Bible, Moses was born in Egypt of Hebrew parents in the 1200's B.C., when the Hebrews were slaves of the Egyptians. Pharaoh, the king of Egypt, was afraid that the Hebrews would grow in numbers and become strong. Just before the time of Moses' birth, he ordered that every son born to a Hebrew woman must be cast into the river. Moses' mother put her baby son in a basket among the reeds along the banks of the river. Pharaoh's daughter found him when she came to wash, and she took pity on him. She took him home and raised him as a son.

Moses was treated like a prince at the Egyptian court. He learned to read and write. One day, when he had grown up, he went among his own people, the Hebrews. When he saw a Hebrew slave being beaten by an Egyptian, he killed the Egyptian. Pharaoh heard about Moses' deed and threatened to kill him. Moses fled for his life.

Moses hid in the land of Midian. He lived with Jethro, the priest of Midian, and married Zipporah, one of Jethro's daughters. One day while Moses was tending Jethro's sheep, he saw a flame in the midst of a bush. He stared at it in wonder, for the fire did not burn up the bush. Then God called to Moses from out of the bush. He commanded Moses to return to Egypt and free the Hebrews. God promised to guide Moses and the Hebrews into Canaan, "a land flowing with milk and honey."

Moses obeyed God and returned to Egypt. When Moses asked Pharaoh to free the Hebrews, Pharaoh refused. But each time that he refused, God brought a terrible plague on the land. He turned the waters into blood. He covered the land with frogs and locusts. He made all the cattle of the Egyptians die, but He saved the cattle of the Hebrews. When the tenth plague killed all the firstborn children of the Egyptians, including Pharaoh's own son, Pharaoh finally freed the Hebrews.

Moses took his people out of Egypt and into the wilderness. A pillar of cloud led them by day and a pillar of fire by night. Pharaoh later changed his mind and sent horsemen and chariots after them. His army overtook the Hebrews when they were camped by the Sea of Reeds. The Bible says that God parted the waters, and Moses led his people across on dry land. When the Egyptians tried to follow, the waters closed over them.

The journey through the wilderness was hard, and the people grew tired and hungry. But God provided for them. When they had nothing left to eat, He covered the land with food called manna, and the people ate.

Moses worked to unite his people. At first he settled their quarrels himself. Then he set up courts and judges. In the third month the Hebrews reached Mount Sinai. God called Moses up to the top of the mountain and gave him the Ten Commandments and other laws. This code of laws is called the Law of Moses.

When the people lost faith, they began worshiping other gods. They made a golden calf out of their jewelry and built an altar in front of it. To punish them, God told Moses they would have to wander in the wilderness for 40 years before they enter the promised land.

Moses never lost faith. When he was 120 years old, he led his people to the borders of Canaan. He went to the top of a mountain, and God showed him the promised land. Then Moses died, his work accomplished.

Reviewed by MORTIMER J. COHEN
Author, *Pathways Through the Bible*

See also PASSOVER.

Moses stayed on Mount Sinai for forty days and nights while God instructed him in the law. French painter Marc Chagall shows Moses receiving the Ten Commandments.

Sugaring Off, painted when Grandma Moses was 83 years old, shows people collecting sap from sugar maple trees and boiling it down to make maple syrup and maple candy.

MOSES, GRANDMA (1860–1961)

The artist Grandma Moses became famous for her simple, bright, cheerful paintings of American farm life. Her full name was Anna Mary Robertson Moses. But she was known to everyone as Grandma Moses because she did not begin to paint seriously until she was in her seventies.

Anna Mary Robertson was born on September 7, 1860, on a farm in Greenwich, New York. She was one of ten children. Life on the farm was hard, and Anna had little schooling. Her days were filled with farm chores—feeding the animals, gathering eggs, and making soap. But she often found time to make pictures. Because she had no proper paints, she used house paint, scraps of colored paper, the juice of wild berries, and even laundry bluing for her colors.

Soon, however, she became too busy to draw or paint. At the age of 12, she went to work as a servant for a family nearby. She worked for other people for many years. Then, when she was 27, she married Thomas Moses, a farmer. And they began raising a family of their own. They moved to a farm near Staunton, Virginia, and later to another at Eagle Bridge, New York. Thomas Moses died there in 1927.

As she grew older, Anna Moses could no longer do heavy farmwork. She took up needlework, but her hands became too stiff to continue. Then, in her seventies, she began to paint in oils. Her pictures showed things she recalled from childhood—farm scenes, small villages, picnics, ice-skating, bringing home the Christmas tree. The forms were simple, and the colors bright and cheerful.

Grandma Moses had a fine memory for detail, and her pictures recorded a way of life that was quickly passing away. People everywhere loved these happy scenes, and soon her paintings were shown in art galleries. She continued to paint almost until her death, on December 13, 1961, at the age of 101.

Reviewed by JANE KALLIR
Author, *Grandma Moses: The Artist Behind the Myth*

MOSES, ROBERT. See NEW YORK CITY (Famous People).

MOSLEM. See ISLAM.

MOSQUITOES

Mosquitoes are among the most widespread of flying insects. There are more than 2,000 species, or kinds. They are found on every continent and in every nation, in temperate and tropical climates, and near both fresh water and salt water.

The Mosquito's Body

Mosquitoes range in length from $1/12$ inch to $2^2/5$ inches (0.2 to 6 centimeters). Its thin, scale-covered body is divided into three main parts, or segments: head, thorax, and abdomen. The **head** is small and round. On it are the large compound eyes (many lenses clustered together), the branching antennae, and the mouthparts, which include a long sucking tube, the **proboscis**.

The **thorax** is a rigid, boxlike segment just behind the head. The mosquito's six legs are attached to the thorax, and underneath them are two pairs of **spiracles**, the vents through which the insect breathes. Two large wings are attached to the upper side of the thorax. The wings move in a figure-eight pattern between 250 and 600 times a second—the rate varies with the species. It is the rapid movement of the wings through the air that causes the mosquito's familiar high-pitched buzzing sound. The mosquito can fly forward or backward and can hover in one spot.

The abdomen is the last body segment. It is a slender tubelike structure that has a rounded or pointed end, depending on the kind of mosquito. Along the sides of the abdomen are eight pairs of spiracles.

Life Cycle

Mosquitoes need only a short season of warmth and moisture to carry out their life cycle. A mosquito goes through four life stages—**egg**, **larva**, **pupa**, and **imago** (adult).

In cold climates, where temperatures drop below freezing in winter, fertile females survive in a dormant (resting) state in crevices and holes in barns, houses, and other buildings. When the first warm days of spring arrive, they lay their eggs in a body of still water. This can be a swamp, a puddle, or even water in an old can. The entire development from egg to adult takes three to ten days. The length of time varies according to the species and the climate. As adults, both male and fe-

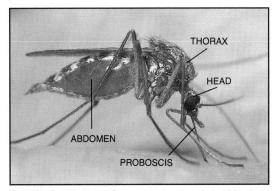

Only the female mosquito uses her proboscis to "bite." Females are led to their victims by special organs in their antennae that are sensitive to heat and chemicals. These organs detect the trail of warm, moist carbon dioxide exhaled by animals, including people.

male mosquitoes feed on the nectar of flowers and fruits. Females also feed on blood. In fact, the females of some species must have a blood meal before they can lay eggs.

Carriers of Disease

Some species of mosquitoes act as vectors, or carriers, of serious diseases. They may transmit disease from animals to humans or from one person to another. Females spread disease by biting, but some parasites are carried on the outside of the mosquito's body and can be spread by touch. The illnesses that are spread by mosquitoes include yellow fever, malaria, and various forms of encephalitis.

For this reason, people have long tried to control populations of mosquitoes and stop their spread. Among the methods tried has been the use of chemical sprays. Since some chemical sprays can have harmful effects on other forms of life, other methods of control are now favored. These methods include encouraging the spread of natural enemies, such as certain flies, and the spread of diseases that attack mosquitoes. One of the simplest and most effective methods is to remove water where the insects develop by draining swamps and puddles.

People who live and work in an area of the world where mosquitoes are plentiful should use repellent sprays and should dress to cover most of their bodies. They should avoid wearing dark clothes and should sleep protected by screens or netting.

WILLIAM WHITE, JR.
Author, *The Mosquito: Its Life Cycle*

MOSSES

Mosses are small green plants that can be found growing throughout the world. Very few people consider mosses to be important plants—they are not used to make foods or beverages or as raw materials to produce clothing or shelter. But, these delicate, nonflowering plants played an important role in wartime. If you were injured during World War I or World War II, when medicines and bandages were often in short supply, a special kind of moss known as sphagnum moss might have been used to dress the wound. For centuries, many different peoples used sphagnum moss to treat injuries because it absorbed a lot of blood and helped prevent infection. Although modern medicines have replaced it, sphagnum moss was a lifesaver in the past.

Characteristics of Mosses

The more than 9,000 different species, or kinds, of mosses are found in a variety of places. Some mosses are aquatic, or live in water, and a few hardy mosses even live in deserts. Those that live in dry places only grow after it rains. Much of the time these mosses are dormant, that is, in a resting condition. But most mosses grow in damp, shady forests.

All mosses are part of an ancient group of plants called **bryophytes**. They are simple nonvascular plants. A nonvas-

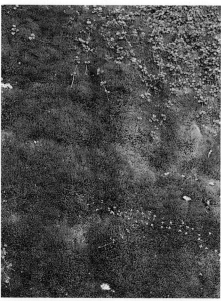

cular plant is one that does not have specialized tissues to transport water and other materials through the plant. Although the small multicellular mosses do not have true roots, stems, or leaves, they do have structures that are rootlike, stemlike, and leaflike. Each moss plant usually consists of a leafy stalk that is 1 to 6 inches (2.5 to 15 centimeters) tall. Tiny threadlike structures called **rhizoids** anchor the leafy stalk in the soil or on the tree trunk or damp rock.

Types of Mosses

The different species of mosses are separated into three groups: true mosses, peat mosses, and granite mosses. Most mosses are true mosses. Peat mosses are those that grow in wet habitats, including bogs. Granite mosses are found in mountainous regions

Mosses are some of the most primitive members of the plant kingdom. They can be found in moist places or in areas that are damp part of the year. The three groups of mosses include peat mosses (*below*), which are the most commercially important mosses; true mosses (*below left*), which are the most common kind of mosses; and granite mosses (*left*), which grow directly on rock.

growing directly on rock. Some granite mosses grow high up on mountains where no other plants can exist.

Life Cycle of a Moss

Mosses have a life cycle that consists of two phases. In one phase, the leafy green moss plant is known as a **gametophyte**. In the other phase, the moss plant is known as a **sporophyte**. During their life cycles, mosses go back and forth between the gametophyte and the sporophyte phases in a process called **alternation of generations**.

During the gametophyte phase, the moss plant forms male and female **gametes**, or reproductive cells. The male gametes, or sperm, are formed in structures called **antheridia**, and the female gametes, or eggs, are produced in **archegonia**. Sometimes the antheridia and archegonia are produced on one plant; other times, they are on separate plants. When it rains or when there is a heavy dew, the antheridia takes in the moisture, swells, and then bursts. Hundreds of sperm are released into the wet surroundings. The sperm swim to the archegonia. Once a sperm enters an archegonium (singular of archegonia), it can unite with an egg to form a **zygote**.

With the formation of a zygote, the sporophyte phase of the life cycle begins. The zygote grows and develops into a mature sporophyte with a podlike structure called a **spore case** at the top. The spore case contains hundreds of tiny reproductive cells, or **spores**. When the spores ripen, they are released from the spore case and carried by wind or rain to a new location. If conditions are favorable, the spore grows into a new gametophyte plant, completing the life cycle.

The two phases of the life cycle of a moss, each with its own distinct plant form, exist within a cluster of hair cap moss. The plant of the sporophyte phase consists of a long thin stalk topped with a podlike spore case. The sporophyte grows attached to the leafy green plant of the gametophyte phase, depending on it for all of its nourishment.

The Importance of Mosses

Sphagnum mosses, which are also known as peat mosses, are the mosses most important to humans. Peat mosses often grow in bogs in cooler areas of the United States, Canada, and Europe. After many years, dead peat mosses accumulate in the bog, forming a fuel known as peat. When peat is cut into blocks and dried, it can be burned for energy. People in Ireland, Scotland, and other places in Europe have used peat for centuries.

Mosses are important contributors to the quality of the environment. They usually grow in dense clusters, forming a carpetlike covering over large areas. The moss "carpet" acts like a huge sponge when it rains. The plants absorb much of the rainwater, helping prevent flooding and soil erosion.

Mosses also help form and enrich soil. Over time, mosses growing on rocks break the rocks into smaller and smaller pieces. The pieces of rock and the dust and debris held in place by the mosses are added to the layer of soil. As the soil accumulates, other plants, such as grasses and ferns, become established. When mosses die and decompose, their nutrients are added to the soil. These nutrients enrich the soil and provide food for other plants.

LINDA R. BERG
Coauthor, *The World of Biology*

See also PLANTS; WETLANDS.

MOTELS. See HOTELS AND MOTELS.

MOTHERWELL, ROBERT. See WASHINGTON (Famous People).

MOTHS. See BUTTERFLIES AND MOTHS.

MOTION

Things are in motion everywhere. Cars move along roads. Water flows in rivers. Airplanes move across the skies. The planets move through space around the sun.

The place from which you watch a particular motion is called your frame of reference. For example, if you are standing on the ground watching a car pass by, your frame of reference is the Earth's surface. To you, it appears that the car is moving. But a given motion can look different to people in different frames of reference. To someone whose frame of reference is the car, the car does not appear to be moving.

There are two basic kinds of motion. If an object moves at a constant speed, covering the same distance each second without changing direction, we say that it is in **uniform motion**. A car moving down the street at 30 miles (48 kilometers) per hour is in uniform motion. If the speed or direction of the object changes, then it is in **accelerated motion**. A car speeding up from a stop sign or after slowing down to go around a curve is in accelerated motion.

In general, the motion we encounter every day consists of a mixture of uniform and accelerated motions. If someone throws a baseball, for example, the ball moves at a steady rate in the horizontal direction. If it leaves the thrower's hand traveling at 50 miles (80 kilometers) per hour parallel to the ground, it will move at about that same speed throughout its course. In this direction, its motion is uniform. At the same time, however, the ball moves up and down under the influence of gravity. This is accelerated motion because the vertical speed of the ball is changing throughout its course. Thus the motion of the ball is a combination of uniform motion in the horizontal direction and accelerated motion in the vertical direction.

Except for situations in which a frame of reference is moving near the speed of light, all motion takes place according to three scientific laws. These laws, discovered about 300 years ago by Isaac Newton, explain how things move and how motions change.

▶NEWTON'S FIRST LAW OF MOTION

When you throw a ball into the air, you say that the ball is in motion. When the ball lands, it rolls until it comes to a stop. Then it is no longer in motion. An object that is not in motion is said to be at rest. Newton's first law of motion states that an object in motion tends to stay in motion. This law also states that an object at rest tends to stay at rest.

You can demonstrate the first law of motion using a toy cart with a smooth, flat top. Put a heavy object on the cart. If you suddenly jerk the cart into motion, you can pull it out from under the object. Now put the item back on the cart and give the cart a good push. Let it run into a wall while it is moving quickly. The wall stops the cart and the object slides along the top of the cart until it also hits the wall.

You have observed two facts about motion. First, when the heavy object was at rest, it tended to stay at rest. It just fell straight down when the cart was suddenly jerked out from under it. Second, when the object was in motion along with the cart, it tended to stay in motion until it was stopped by the wall. You have probably noticed these effects on your body. If you are in a car that suddenly starts to move, your body presses back against the seat of the car. Your body is at rest before the car begins to move, and it tends to stay at rest. If you are in a moving car that comes to a sudden stop, however, your body pitches forward. Your body is in motion with the car, and it tends to stay in motion. This tendency to continue at rest or continue in motion is called **inertia**.

Newton's first law explains why people should always wear seat belts when riding in a car. In a moving car, you are carried along at the same speed as the car. If the car stops suddenly, you will keep moving unless a force such as a seatbelt acts on you. If you are not wearing a seat belt, that force will not be exerted until you hit the dashboard or windshield of the car.

Forces

A force—a push or a pull—is needed to overcome the inertia of an object. That is, a force must be used to put an object at rest into motion or to stop a moving object or change its motion while it is moving.

To put a cart in motion, you must push or pull it. If you want to change the direction in which the cart moves, you must pull or push it from another direction. You can speed the cart up or slow it down, but in each case you have to use force.

Demonstrating Laws of Motion

A toy cart, some small rocks, and a spring scale can be used to demonstrate some laws of motion: (1) an object in motion tends to stay in motion; (2) a force such as a push or a pull is needed to change the motion of an object; and (3) the speed of an object in motion depends on the strength of the force that put it in motion and the mass of the object.

If no forces act on a moving object, it will stay in motion forever, moving along at the same speed and in the same direction. But you have noticed that objects in motion come to a rest even when no force seems to be pushing against them. For example, if you roll a ball on the ground, the ball soon comes to a stop. When a cart is moving along the floor, it eventually stops moving even if it does not run into anything.

Why do things in motion come to a stop? The answer is an unseen force called **friction**. Friction is a force between two surfaces that works against movement. One surface tends to work against, or resist, any motion of the other surface. For example, there is friction between the floor and the surface of the ball or the wheels of the cart. The floor resists the motion of these surfaces and makes them come to a stop. Friction exists between any two surfaces that touch, slide, or roll on one another.

▶ **NEWTON'S SECOND LAW OF MOTION**

An object moves because a force is applied to make the object move. The speed of the object depends on how strong the force is.

You can demonstrate this with a rubber band, a cart, and either a spring balance or a spring scale.

Acceleration and Force

Attach a rubber band to the front of the cart and hook the spring scale to the rubber band. Pull the scale lightly with one hand while holding the cart in place with the other. Read the scale to see how hard you are pulling. Then release the cart and notice its speed.

Next, hold the cart in place again and pull twice as hard on the spring scale. When you release the cart this time, it moves forward much more quickly. If the speed of the cart was measured both times, you would find that the cart moved forward about twice as quickly the second time.

The cart speeds up when it starts to move. Any change in an object's speed is called **acceleration**. An increase in speed is called positive acceleration, while a decrease in speed is called negative acceleration, or **deceleration**.

Newton's second law of motion states that there is a relationship between force and acceleration. It says that the amount of acceleration depends on the strength of the applied force. Pulling twice as hard on the cart will make the cart move about twice as fast. If you pulled three times as hard on the cart, you would make it move three times as fast.

Acceleration can mean a change in direction as well as in speed. A force is needed to change the direction of an object, so a change in force can also mean a change in direction as well as a change in speed. According to Newton's second law of motion, the change in direction of a moving object depends on the applied force.

Acceleration and Mass

There is yet another part to Newton's second law of motion. You can observe it as follows. First weigh the cart. Then attach a rubber band and spring scale to it again. Pull on the scale while holding the cart in place. Notice the reading on the scale. Let go of the cart and see how much it accelerates.

Next, add some heavy objects to the cart until it weighs twice as much as it did before. Hold the cart in place again and pull on the scale. Be sure you are pulling just as hard as you did the first time. When you release the cart, note that there is less acceleration. A certain amount of force will accelerate a light object more than it will a heavy one. The amount of acceleration depends on the object's weight.

In this experiment the cart with heavy objects on it weighs twice as much as the cart weighs by itself. A scientist would say that the cart and its load have twice as much mass as the cart alone. Mass is the amount of matter in an object. The cart accelerates twice as much without the load as it does with it.

Suppose you try to start your bicycle when carrying a passenger. You will find that it is harder to accelerate with a passenger on board than it is when you are riding alone. This is because you are trying to accelerate a greater mass.

If you could measure the force, mass, and acceleration involved in any motion, you would find that they are always related. Newton's second law of motion says that a given force accelerates a small mass more than it does a larger mass.

Acceleration and Direction

One of the hardest things to understand about acceleration and force is that it requires a force to keep something moving around a curve at a constant speed. For instance, think about what happens when you swing a ball on a string above your head. As long as you continue to pull on the string, the ball keeps moving in a circle at a constant speed. But if you let the string go, the ball flies off in a straight line. As long as a force acts—in this case, the force you exert by pulling on the string—the object can move in a circle. As soon as you stop exerting the force—when you let go of the string—the object moves in a straight line. The Earth moving in its orbit around the sun obeys the same laws. As long as the sun exerts a gravitational force on the Earth, it continues moving in a circular orbit. If the force of gravity were turned off, the Earth would fly off into space, just as the ball does when you let go of the string.

▶NEWTON'S THIRD LAW OF MOTION

In science, the word "action" is often used for the word "force." Newton found that every **action** is accompanied by a response, or a **reaction**. Both the action and the reaction are forces, but the reaction acts in a direction opposite to the action. In addition, the strength of the reaction is always equal to the strength of the action. Newton's third law says that for every action there is an equal and opposite reaction.

Action and reaction are involved in every motion. You can observe both with a balloon. If you blow up the balloon and release it, it flutters around until most of the air has escaped. The air escapes with a certain amount of force. This is the action. The movement of the balloon around the room is the reaction to the force of the escaping air.

A giant rocket works on the same principle. As gases explode from a rocket's engine, the action is very strong because the gases escape at high speeds and in large amounts. This means that the reaction is equally strong and the rocket rises from the ground and travels into space.

The motions of people traveling in cars, of rockets lifting off the surface of the Earth, and of the planets orbiting the sun take place in accord with Newton's three laws of motion. All objects at rest tend to remain at rest and all objects in motion tend to remain in motion. The force, mass, and acceleration involved in any motion are always related to one another in the same ways. Whenever there is an action, there is always an equal and an opposite reaction.

JAMES TREFIL
Clarence J. Robinson Professor of Physics,
George Mason University

See also ENERGY; NEWTON, ISAAC; RELATIVITY.

MOTION PICTURES

Motion pictures—also called movies or films—are one of the most popular forms of entertainment today. Millions of people, in all the countries of the world, go to movie theaters to enjoy an entertaining story and to see their favorite movie stars. Film is truly an international medium for entertainment.

Film entertainment is both art and business. It is art because it is made by creative people with visions and passions. Films make us laugh and cry; they motivate us to imagine and they require us to think. The film art form is in many ways a composite of all the others, including writing, performance, visual ele-

Motion pictures are one of the most popular forms of entertainment. Although nearly every country has its own film industry, the big-budget products of Hollywood are internationally successful. Most films are made for theatrical release, and audiences eagerly line up to see their favorite stars on the big screen. Today, many films, both classics and newer releases, are available on videotape for home viewing.

ments, sound, music, and design. Some of the most important artists of our time have chosen film as their means of communication.

Film is also a business because most films are made for profit. Films cost a great deal of money to make, and people and companies who make them often do so in the hopes of attaining great fame and fortune.

Filmmaking is the first form of creative communication to be completely dependent on industrial technology. In filmmaking, technology, business, and art combine to produce a dynamic and powerful form of communication. For filmmakers to be effective they must understand and work with elements and processes belonging to each of these aspects of filmmaking.

This article investigates the technical, creative, and financial aspects of the filmmaking process, focusing on the mainstream, mass-produced filmmaking style of the United States. This discussion is followed by a history of motion pictures.

▶FILM TECHNOLOGY

When watching a film, viewers experience a life-like image in which characters and objects appear to move as they do in the real world. This is actually an illusion of movement produced by the rapid projection of a series of still images onto a movie screen.

The illusion of motion effect can be explained by looking at the way the human eye

and brain function. In a naturally occurring phenomenon called **persistence of vision**, the retina of the eye retains an image for a fraction of a second longer than an object is actually in front of it. When a rapid succession of images is presented before the eye, each image will superimpose, or overlap, onto the next.

While persistence of vision explains the physical basis for the illusion of motion, many theorists feel that there is a psychological element involved as well. Some psychologists believe that the human brain struggles to find meaning in everything it perceives. When a series of superimposing images showing consecutive movements are presented to the eye, the brain fills in the gaps and helps create the illusion of continuous movement.

Equipment

A motion picture **camera** is capable of taking many individual pictures, called **frames**, every second. It functions as a kind of photographic machine gun, which many of the earliest motion picture cameras resembled. For every photograph to be properly shot, the film must remain still behind the lens for a small fraction of time. In other words, the machine has to stop, take a picture, move, stop, take a picture, move, and so forth. This stopping and starting action, called **intermittent motion**, is the basis of all modern motion picture cameras.

Motion picture **film** is made of thin, flexible plastic layered with light-sensitive chemicals. Long strips of this flexible film can be rolled

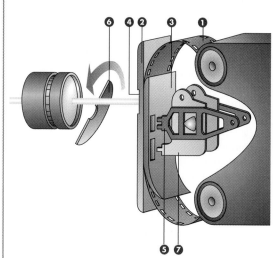

THE MOTION PICTURE CAMERA: INTERMITTENT MOTION

Motion picture film does not move continuously through the camera. Instead, the film stops briefly behind the lens while a picture is taken, then moves on, one frame at a time. The mechanism that controls this stop-and-start, or intermittent, motion must be precisely coordinated.

The unexposed film ❶ is fed off a supply reel and positioned behind the lens at the camera gate ❷. A pressure plate ❸ presses lightly against the film to keep it in the proper position. Light reaches the film through an opening in the gate called the aperture ❹. The rectangular shape of the aperture determines the shape, or aspect ratio, of the film image. A registration pin ❺ holds the film steady as a shutter ❻ opens, allowing light to expose the frame. Once the frame has been exposed, the shutter closes, blocking light from the film as a claw ❼ engages the sprocket holes at the edge of the film and pulls the next frame into position.

This process is repeated 24 times every second.

and then run intermittently through the camera. The most commonly used motion picture film is 35 millimeters wide, but a number of other film sizes, or formats, exist. Motion picture film has perforations (holes) running along both sides, which the camera uses to advance the film, then keep it still while a frame is exposed. The picture in each frame is located in the center of the film between the perforations. The shape of the picture, called the **aspect ratio**, is determined by the size of the film strip and the type of camera used.

The motion picture camera has changed very little since its invention in the late 1800's, and today's units continue to employ the same basic mechanisms. All of the parts must move intermittently in precise coordination for the camera to produce a working motion picture. In modern motion pictures, this process of intermittent motion is repeated 24 times every second.

The **lens** is an optical device that bends light rays to form an image on the film. Depending on its characteristics, a lens can give an image distinct creative qualities. The choice of lens for a particular shot is an important creative decision.

Motion picture **projectors** function in the same manner as motion picture cameras and have similar parts. The main difference between them is the location of the light source. During shooting the light source is outside the camera (light reflecting from objects) and is captured on the film. During projection the light source is located inside the projector and travels through the film, acquiring its qualities of color and intensity and transferring them onto the screen.

▶MAKING A MOTION PICTURE

A film is very rarely made by one person; usually dozens of people contribute different skills toward the making of a film. In large-scale film productions, technical crews are organized into various departments, dividing the tremendous amount of detail-oriented work among many people with specialized skills.

The people who assume much of the control of all these workers and the jobs they perform are the producers and the director. The **executive producer** and **producer** are involved with raising funds to finance the project. Because they are ultimately responsible for the commercial success of the film, they also carefully choose the material for the film, hire the director and actors and other members of the creative team, and exercise final decision-making power over the finished product.

Making a motion picture is usually a team effort. A variety of technical crews work behind the scenes to create the final product seen on the screen.

The **director** provides the film with an overall creative vision by interpreting the screenplay and translating it into visual terms. The director works with the actors and other creative and technical personnel to bring this vision to the screen.

What the audience feels and thinks about what they see is not only determined by what happens in the film but also by how the images are constructed. Like paintings, film images have the power to evoke emotions and thoughts by the way they look. The director interprets the screenplay to determine color, texture, lighting, composition, movement, and many other subtle elements of each shot and each scene.

The making of a film can be broken into the following stages: conception, development, pre-production, production, post-production, and distribution. Each of these stages is equally important in making a film successful.

Conception

The making of a film typically begins with an idea for a story. A **screenwriter** conceives the pictures, people, dialogue, and actions of the film, writing them into a standard story format called a **screenplay**. A screenwriter creates a screenplay with the hope of selling

Development

In recent years this stage of filmmaking has grown in importance. With the ever-increasing budgets required to make films, production companies want to make sure their investments will turn into successful commercial products.

Development executives are experts at analyzing the structure, plot, and characters of a screenplay and making suggestions to improve its potential for success. In many cases they also recommend a director, actors to play major roles, and other creative collaborators.

Set design is an important part of the pre-production stage of filmmaking. *Left:* An elaborate set for a science fiction space film is constructed on a sound stage. *Above:* The completed set, enhanced by props and special lighting, is ready for filming.

it to a production company. Because of this commercial intent, most screenplays adhere to accepted ways of telling a story that have proven successful in the past.

Sometimes the idea for a screenplay is born in the mind of the writer. At other times a screenwriter is hired to turn someone else's idea into a screenplay. Such is the case with films based on novels or historical events. The process of writing a screenplay is a very laborious one. The writer must not only plot the story but also create characters who speak and behave in a believable manner. Screenwriters work through a process of writing and rewriting that can take many months and result in numerous revisions.

In other words, their job is to put together a package that includes all the creative elements for a successful film. The development stage ends when the production company approves the project and finds financing for it.

Pre-Production

During the pre-production stage, key creative and technical personnel are chosen, and a complete plan is developed for the making of the film.

The **unit production manager** (UPM) is in charge of the day-to-day supervision of the film project throughout the production process. The UPM ensures that all necessary production elements are present during filming, from the cameras and lights to the actors and director.

The **director of photography** (DP) is responsible for realizing the visual style of the film as designed by the director. The DP chooses the film, lenses, camera placement, and lighting techniques that will achieve the director's creative goals. The DP is also in charge of running the camera technical crews on the set and ensuring that work flows smoothly.

Actors learn the words and mannerisms of the characters in the screenplay in order to portray them in the film. They must understand how to move and speak in a way that looks natural but is well suited to the camera. Unlike the other participants in a film project, who work behind the scenes, actors connect with the film's audience. Popular actors can contribute greatly to the success of a film; producers usually try to choose actors who are not only talented but have box-office appeal.

The **production designer** collaborates with the director and the director of photography to discover the colors, textures, and shapes that best support the visual look and emotional theme of the film. The **set designer**, supervised by the production designer, draws detailed plans and builds models of the film sets.

The **costume designer** creates clothing for the actors appropriate to the characters, locations, and time periods of the film. **Hair and make-up artists** are hired to create hairstyles and apply make-up to perfect the appearance of the actors and help them create convincing portrayals of their characters.

Below left: The proper makeup can help an actor create a convincing character. Makeup artists for fantasy and science fiction films must be especially creative. *Above:* Costume designers create clothing appropriate to the characters and time period of the film.

All these creative and technical people are involved in the planning of the film. The screenplay is transformed into a series of visual images called a **shot list**, and pictures of the images, called **storyboards**, are drawn. Costumes are designed, locations are scouted and prepared, and sets are built on sound stages. Actors rehearse, and the director finalizes the visual, narrative, and performance styles of the film, making final revisions in the screenplay with the screenwriter. Efficiency and economy are the basic driving forces.

Production

This stage is composed of the shooting of all the photographic components, called **shots**, that will later be assembled to create the final film. A grouping of shots in which time and space seem to be continuous is called a **scene**. In other words, a scene is a sequence of shots that together show one occurrence in the film, such as a person waking up, somebody walking a dog, or a rocket reaching the moon. When the action of the film jumps to another space or time, a new scene begins.

Each day of shooting is organized around photographing specific parts of the film. Scenes that use the same locations, actors, or other elements are shot together even if they will ultimately belong to different sections of the film.

While the producers continue to be in charge of making the whole process run

Just as verbal communication is made of words and sentences, film communication is made of shots and scenes. A shot is a single, uninterrupted photographic sequence that can last from a fraction of a second to many minutes. The shot starts with the director calling "Action!" and ends with the call to "Cut!"

Shots vary according to where the camera is positioned and how much of the subject matter is seen.

TYPES OF SHOTS

The examples below show various ways that a human subject can be framed in a shot. Through different combinations of shots, any action in a film can be shown. The director chooses the combination that is best for the mood and content of the film.

Extreme Close-up
A shot showing only a part of the face.

Medium Shot
The subject is seen from approximately the knees up.

Close-up
A full face shot that may also include the neck and the top edge of the shoulders.

Long Shot
The full body is seen within the frame.

Medium Close-up
The subject is seen from approximately the waist up.

Establishing Shot
The subject and its surroundings are seen within the frame.

smoothly, the director and the other creative contributors focus on the creative aspects of the picture: visual style, story development, and performance. For each scene, multiple camera angles are shot and often repeated to provide many alternatives for the editing of the film in post-production. The director also coaches the actors' performances and makes final decisions regarding lighting and camera placement.

The director receives organizational support from the **assistant director** (AD) and **script supervisor** at the production stage. The AD is in charge of meeting the production schedule so that work gets done on time. This involves getting actors onto the set when necessary and coordinating action, stunts, and extras. The script supervisor keeps track of important details within scenes being filmed, making sure props, costumes, and other elements remain consistent from shot to shot. This continuity is essential to maintaining realism in a film.

The director of photography guides the work of the **camera operator**, who is responsible for cleaning, loading, and setting up the camera. This includes adjusting the lens aperture and focus as well as framing and shooting the images. The camera operator must constantly adjust the camera to maintain a shot's composition as characters change position or action moves across the frame.

Below: Before filming a scene, actors and director go over the dialogue and action as written in the script. *Above:* A film crew goes on location to film a beach scene. Technical personnel include the boom operator (holding the microphone), the gaffer (aiming the light), and the camera operator.

The field of special effects is one of the most complex and interesting areas of filmmaking. Large teams of special effects artists and technicians employ a variety of techniques to create the illusions central to many science fiction, fantasy, and action films.

SPECIAL EFFECTS

Models can be constructed in miniature and filmed to appear much larger than they are. What looks like a giant spacecraft on screen may really be a tiny model less than a foot long! **Puppets** are often used to create imaginary creatures for science fiction films. They can be made to move through animation. Or they can be manipulated by puppeteers working out of camera range or, in the case of larger puppets, hidden inside the figures.

Miniature models and puppets can be animated using **stop-motion photography**. The specially designed, jointed figures are photographed one frame at a time. After each frame is photographed, the camera stops and the figures are repositioned slightly, bringing them through a series of movements. When the film is run at normal speed, the figures appear to move. In a related technique, called **go-motion**, the figure is moved by means of rods attached to its body and connected to a motor controlled by a computer. The figure is moved as it is filmed one frame at a time. Later, when the sequence is combined with the rest of the film, the rods are concealed through optical techniques or erased by computer.

Miniature stop-motion puppets may double for actors in certain scenes. The puppets can be made to perform feats that would be too dangerous for actors or even for stunt people.

Camera speeds can be altered to create certain effects; sequences are sometimes filmed at speeds that are faster or slower than normal. For example, to obtain the effect of a high-speed chase, the camera may be slowly walked down a road, filming at a very slow speed of less than a frame per second. When this film is run at the usual speed of 24 frames per second, the effect is that of speeding along at 100 miles per hour. Conversely, filming at a higher rate will slow down the action when the sequence is projected at 24 frames per second. This technique is often used when filming a miniature action, such as the explosion of a model building, to create the illusion of greater mass and size.

Matte paintings are created when a set or location is required that is difficult or impossible to build or find. If well done, a painting can fool viewers into thinking they are looking at a real-life scene. The painting is integrated with the live-action film footage in a variety of ways—by projecting a live-action scene onto a painting done on glass, or by filming a painting directly onto an area of unexposed film that was blocked out during live-action filming.

Animation is used to create special effects such as lightning bolts or flying ghosts. Animation is also used to block out things that filmmakers do not want seen, such as the rods that move a model in go-motion. Today, much special-effects animation is done with computers.

Optical compositing is the process of combining several separately filmed images such as a model of a dinosaur or a spaceship, a matte painting of background scenery, and footage of actors moving and speaking. Increasingly, this process is being replaced by **digital compositing**, in which computers are used to combine separate images into a single composite image. Film images can be converted into digital form and manipulated or combined. Some images are generated entirely by computer; that is, they exist only in digitized memory. For example, computer-generated images of dinosaurs were combined with live-action puppets and actors to create the dinosaurs in *Jurassic Park*.

Special effects helped create an exciting movie scene that appears to take place on a military jet in mid flight. Computer graphics produced the jet's smoke trail ❶. The actor hanging from the jet's missile was filmed on a set ❷, as was the jet itself, actually a fiberglass model ❹. These images were combined on a computer, together with a photograph of a city skyline ❸, to create the final composite shot ❺

The **key grip** assists the camera operator by setting up the camera tripod and dolly. The dolly is a wheeled platform that allows the camera to move freely around the set. The grip is an expert at smoothly pushing the dolly during a shot. The **gaffer** specializes in setting up and aiming the dozens of lighting instruments required to illuminate a scene.

The **production sound mixer** operates the sound-recording equipment. The mixer decides on the type and number of microphones to use and where they should be placed to obtain the best possible sound recording. Working with the mixer is the **boom operator**, who uses a long pole called a boom to constantly adjust the microphone's distance and angle from the sound sources in a given scene.

Post-Production

During post-production, all the visual and sound components of the film are combined.

Editing. Which shots will be used in the final film and in which order is determined during the editing process. To preserve the quality of the original film footage, a working copy is made for editing. The **editor** uses this copy, called a work print, to create a finished film. The work print gives the editor the creative freedom to make many cuts without fear of damaging the original footage.

The editor makes thousands of complex decisions about when and why to change from one shot to another. Then the appropriate pieces of film are spliced—glued together with a special clear adhesive tape. This rough version is called the assembly edit, or first cut. After viewing this first version of the film, the editor makes adjustments, taking some parts out and rearranging the order of shots to make scenes work better.

After the initial editing, the producers and director view the film and give their opinions. At this point they may decide to reshoot some shots and scenes or add new scenes to the film. Ultimately, the editor answers to the film's producers, who bear final responsibility for the film's success.

Most special effects sequences are also composed during post-production. This area of filmmaking is discussed in the feature on the opposite page.

The **negative cutter** takes the editor's work print and returns to the camera negative—the actual film stock shot during production—to

The camera operator shoots the film, framing the shots and adjusting the camera lens and position. The camera is set up on a movable platform called a dolly.

assemble the final film. This is more a technical than a creative process, requiring a clean environment, precise cutting, and steady hands to make liquid-cement splices in the delicate original footage.

Sound. Once the images and basic dialogue are edited to the producer's satisfaction, the sound work begins. Sound editing and mixing is a complex, subtle process that plays an important role in the viewer's perception of the film. The final version of the film may have dozens of layers of sound, all recorded at different volumes and needing to be heard at varying levels throughout the film. Each layer of sound is called a **track**. There are

The editor views all the film footage, deciding which shots to use and in what order. The editor's work print is used as a guide in assembling the final film.

The post-production sound mixer combines all the sound tracks for dialogue, sound effects, and music into a single track.

separate tracks for music, for dialogue, for sound effects such as slamming doors, and for background sounds such as city traffic. The **sound designer/editor** is charged with finding and inserting sound effects and background sounds.

Many sound effects are not properly recorded during production or simply do not match the type of sound desired. The **foley artist** specializes in matching tricky sounds that are difficult to synchronize during editing. For example, to record footsteps, the foley artist walks in place in a gravel-filled pit rigged with microphones while watching the filmed action on a screen.

All the sound tracks are ultimately mixed, or combined into a single track, to create the final sound of the film with the correct volume for each sound. The **post-production sound mixer** accomplishes this using a mixing console—a vast sound-recording device with a volume control for each sound track.

At the film-processing laboratory, picture and sound are brought together, and multiple copies are printed for distribution of the film to movie theaters across the country.

Distribution

Once the film is completed, a final and very important process begins. Based on the projected commercial appeal of the film, a distribution company creates a strategy to promote awareness and anticipation among potential viewers and to deliver the film to them. A marketing plan is designed to create an image for the film based on what the company believes people want to see.

The distribution company places advertisements in major newspapers and magazines, on billboards, over radio, and on television. The distributors hope that the image presented of the film will attract enough viewers to ensure the film's financial success.

Once movie theater owners have committed to show the film, the distributor makes as many prints of the film as are needed for screening. A mass-appeal film might be shown in 1,200 to 2,000 theaters at the same time, while a more specialized film may show in only 10 to 200 theaters at one time.

FABIAN WAGMISTER
JOHN BELANGER
Department of Film and Television
University of California, Los Angeles

Profiles MOVIE STARS

Fred Astaire (Frederick Austerlitz) (1899–1987) was a dancer, singer, and actor whose graceful, sophisticated style dominated Hollywood musicals from the 1930's through the 1950's. Born in Omaha, Neb., he began his career in vaudeville with his older sister Adele as a dancing partner. Paired with Ginger Rogers and other dancers, he starred in more than 30 musicals, including *Top Hat* (1935), *Easter Parade (1948)*, and *Silk Stockings* (1957).

Ingrid Bergman (1915–82), born in Stockholm, Sweden, was best known for her roles in Hollywood films. A star in Sweden, she gained international fame with her first American film, *Intermezzo* (1939). She exuded a radiant, wholesome beauty in such Hollywood classics as *Casablanca* (1943), *For Whom the Bell Tolls* (1943), and *Notorious* (1946). Bergman won Academy

Humphrey Bogart

Awards for best actress in *Gaslight* (1944) and *Anastasia* (1956) and for best supporting actress in *Murder on the Orient Express* (1974).

Humphrey Bogart (1899–1957), born in New York City, was famous for his portrayals of hardened, cynical characters, starting with the role of a gangster in stage and screen versions of *The Petrified Forest* (1935 and 1936). He appeared in more than 50 motion pictures, notably *The Maltese Falcon* (1941), *Casablanca* (1943), *The Big Sleep* (1946), and *The Treasure of the Sierra Madre* (1948). He won an Academy Award for best actor for his performance in *The African Queen* (1951).

Marlon Brando (1924–2004), born in Omaha, Neb., practiced the naturalistic acting style known as the Method. After gaining fame on Broadway for his performance in *A Streetcar Named Desire* (1947), he made his motion picture debut in *The Men* (1950). He then did the film version of *A Streetcar Named Desire* (1952) and followed it with *On the Waterfront* (1953), for which he won an Academy Award. His other films include *The Young Lions* (1958); *Mutiny on the Bounty* (1962); *The Godfather* (1972), for which he won a second Academy Award; and *Apocalypse Now* (1979).

James Cagney (1899–1986) was born in New York City. Cagney was famous for his "tough guy" roles in such films as *Public Enemy* (1931), *Lady Killer* (1933), *White Heat* (1949), and *Mr. Roberts* (1955). He started his career in musical comedy in the 1920's and later sang and danced in the film *Yankee Doodle Dandy* (1942), winning an Academy Award for his portrayal of the composer George M. Cohan.

▶ HISTORY OF MOTION PICTURES

In the early 1890's, inventors were working on ways to photograph and then project images to create the illusion of motion—to create motion pictures.

In order to capture and project moving images, inventors had to develop three types of technologies. First, they needed a way to capture images on a strip of film: they needed a motion picture camera. Second, they required film that was flexible enough to move easily through the camera: they needed to develop the proper film **stock**, or material. Finally, inventors needed to develop a way to project the still images they photographed onto a flat screen at a rate that would maintain the illusion of motion: they needed a projector.

The Silent Era (1896–1927)

By the turn of the century, the three technologies necessary for motion pictures—camera, film stock, and projector—had been invented. In the United States, Thomas Edison and William Dickson invented the kinetoscope, a machine that allowed one viewer at a time to peep into a small viewfinder to see about 20 seconds of full motion. In France, the Lumière brothers invented a small portable camera, which made the job of shooting a film easier. This camera, which they called the *cinematographe*, was able to run film at 16 frames per second, a speed that made movement seem natural. (Later, sound filmmakers would standardize film speed at 24 frames per second).

It was the novelty of the film medium itself that drew crowds to kinetoscope parlors and cafés featuring Edison and Lumière films. The films consisted of single shots of simple actions or scenic views. The image remained static, or still, and distant. The films had no recorded synchronous sound (sound occurring at the same time as the action). Instead, they were presented with live musical accompaniment, such as a pianist, or with a lecturer.

The First Story Films. After 1897, filmmakers realized that people were more likely to go see a film if it presented interesting characters in interesting situations—elements that make up a story. Two pioneers of early film storytelling were Georges Méliès, a French magician, and Edwin S. Porter, an American camera technician. In Méliès' *A Trip to the Moon* (1902), a humorous science fiction tale, he used special effects to tell a simple story. In a technique called stop-motion photography, Méliès would stop the camera on a scene showing one or two characters. He would then add another character to the scene and turn the camera back on. When he projected the film, the third character seemed to magically appear.

Porter was one of the first filmmakers to adapt stories from novels and plays, and his story films were very popular. He used various

Bette Davis (Ruth Elizabeth Davis) (1908–89) was born in Lowell, Mass. She was one of Hollywood's most popular actresses, known for her distinctive clipped speech and outspoken personality. Davis twice won Academy Awards, as best actress in *Dangerous* (1935) and *Jezebel* (1938). Her other films include *The Little Foxes* (1941), *All About Eve* (1950), *Whatever Happened to Baby Jane?* (1962), and *The Whales of August* (1987).

Robert De Niro (1943–), born in New York City, studied at the Actors Studio. He was known for his realistic performances, especially in the films of director Martin Scorsese. These include *Mean Streets* (1973), *Taxi Driver* (1976), *Raging Bull* (1980), for which he won an Academy Award, and *Cape Fear* (1991). De Niro also won an Academy Award for *The Godfather, Part II* (1974).

Marlene Dietrich

Henry Fonda

Marlene Dietrich (Maria Magdalena von Losch) (1904–92), born in Berlin, Germany, projected an air of mystery and sensuality in her many films. After winning international fame in the German film *The Blue Angel* (1930), she went to the United States. Her Hollywood films include *Morocco* (1930), *Destry Rides Again* (1939), and *Witness for the Prosecution* (1957).

Clint Eastwood (1930–), born in San Francisco, Calif., is known for his portrayals of strong, silent loners in Westerns and action films. He became an international star in a series of Italian Westerns, beginning with *A Fistful of Dollars* (1964). His other films include *Dirty Harry* (1971), *High Plains Drifter* (1973), and *Pale Rider* (1985), which he also directed. Eastwood received Academy Awards as best director for *Unforgiven* (1992) and *Million Dollar Baby* (2004).

Henry Fonda (1905–82) was born in Grand Island, Neb. He was known for his portrayal of popular heroes of great honesty, as in the films *Young Mr. Lincoln* (1939), *The Grapes of Wrath* (1940), and *Mr. Roberts* (1955). Fonda received the Academy Award for best actor in 1982 for *On Golden Pond*.

The Great Train Robbery (1903), an 11-minute film by Edwin S. Porter, was one of the first American films to tell a story. Its exciting plot thrilled audiences.

story films. Many of the patrons were recent immigrants, for whom going to the nickelodeon was an inexpensive way to learn about their new country.

As fiction films became more popular, filmmakers kept experimenting with different ways to tell a story. One of the most famous of these filmmakers was D. W. Griffith, who made more than 450 fictional films between 1908 and 1915. Griffith was one of the first filmmakers to use all the techniques of making a film, from framing to editing, to emphasize the psychology of characters and the drama of stories.

techniques, such as the close-up, to enhance suspense. In *The Great Train Robbery* (1903), his best-known film, a robber shown in a close-up shoots a gun directly into the camera (the gun was loaded with blanks).

The first films were shown in **nickelodeons**, small theaters that usually seated less than 200 people. Admission to nickelodeons was usually a nickel (hence the name), and their numbers increased with the rise in popularity of

Griffith's films are controversial, however. His films often presented stereotyped portrayals of African Americans and other groups. His most famous film, *The Birth of a Nation* (1915), has been criticized for glorifying the Ku Klux Klan, a racist organization that terrorized and murdered thousands of African Americans. The film was boycotted by the NAACP and other organizations.

Hollywood and the Studio System. By the time Griffith began to perfect the craft of film

Profiles

Clark Gable (1901–60), born in Cadiz, Ohio, was known as the king of Hollywood. His popularity as an actor remained strong throughout his career. In most of his films he played likable, adventurous heroes. He won an Academy Award for his performance in the comedy *It Happened One Night* (1934) but is best remembered for his role as Rhett Butler in *Gone with the Wind* (1939). His other films include *Mutiny on the Bounty* (1935), *Boom Town* (1940), and *The Misfits* (1961).

Greta Garbo (Greta Gustafsson) (1905–90) was born in Stockholm, Sweden. Her acting talent and classic beauty, enhanced by an air of mystery, made her a Hollywood star. Her films include *Mata Hari* (1931), *Grand Hotel* (1932), *Anna Karenina* (1935), *Camille* (1937), and *Ninotchka* (1939). Known

Greta Garbo

Lillian Gish

for her shyness, she retired from public life in 1941 but remained a legendary figure.

Judy Garland (Frances Ethel Gumm) (1922–69) was born in Grand Rapids, Minn. Her distinctive, emotion-filled singing style made her a star of Hollywood musicals of the 1940's. She began her career at age 5 as one of the singing Gumm Sisters. At 17, she

won fame as Dorothy in *The Wizard of Oz* (1939), a performance highlighted by her rendition of the Academy Award-winning song "Over The Rainbow." Her later films include *Meet Me in St. Louis* (1944), *Easter Parade* (1948), and *A Star Is Born* (1954). Her daughter **Liza Minnelli** (1946–) is a well-known singer and actress.

Lillian Gish (1893–1993), born in Springfield, Ohio, was called the First Lady of the Silent Screen. She is best known for the silent films she made with director D. W. Griffith, including *The Birth of a Nation* (1915) and *Orphans of the Storm* (1922). But she also had a distinguished stage career and appeared in character roles in many sound films, including *Duel in the Sun* (1947) and *The Night of the Hunter* (1955). Her sister **Dorothy Gish** (1898–1968) was adept at comedy and appeared on stage as well as in films.

storytelling, silent film was fast becoming a major industry. The little nickelodeons were expanded into large theaters. During and after World War I (1914–18), Hollywood, an area within Los Angeles, California, became the center of U.S. film production. This period is marked by the emergence of the **studio system**, in which a few companies controlled all aspects of filmmaking. These companies cooperated to keep independent and foreign companies out of the American market.

It soon became apparent to film studios that filmgoers came to movies to see their favorite actors. Rudolph Valentino's romantic exploits in *The Sheik* (1921) and other films drew millions of adoring women to theaters. Audiences also flocked to see Mary Pickford, known as America's Sweetheart, in such films as *Pollyanna* (1920) and *Little Annie Rooney* (1925).

Charlie Chaplin, Buster Keaton, Harold Lloyd, and other popular stars of **slapstick** comedies were known for their elaborate physical dexterity and imaginative sight gags.

Studios took advantage of

Harold Lloyd dangles precariously from a New York skyscraper in *Safety Last* (1923). Slapstick comedies were among the most popular films of the silent era.

the emerging popularity of these performers and began advertising their films as starring a particular actor. Thus emerged the **star system**. In order to control their stars, studios signed actors to multi-year contracts so that they could work for only one studio at a time.

The monopoly created by the studio and star systems left little room for diversity in films. Minorities, if shown at all, were presented in stereotyped ways. In response, African Americans began

Cary Grant (Alexander Archibald Leach) (1904–86) was born in Bristol, England. He went to the United States in 1920 and appeared in plays and musicals before making his first film, *This Is the Night* (1932). Grant soon became known for sophisticated comedies such as *The Awful Truth* (1937), *Bringing Up Baby* (1938), and *The Philadelphia Story* (1940). He made more than 70 films, including the Alfred Hitchcock thrillers *Notorious* (1946), *To Catch a Thief* (1955), and *North by Northwest* (1959). In 1969, he received a special Academy Award for his contributions to the film industry.

Katharine Hepburn (1909–2003), born in Hartford, Conn., is best known for her portrayals of strong-minded, outspoken women. Hepburn made a series of popular film comedies in the 1930's and co-starred in nine films with Spencer Tracy, beginning with *Woman of the Year* (1942). Among her

Cary Grant

Katharine Hepburn

best-known films are *A Bill of Divorcement* (1932), *Bringing Up Baby* (1938), *The Philadelphia Story* (1940), *The African Queen* (1951), *The Lion in Winter* (1968), and *On Golden Pond* (1981). She received four Academy Awards for best actress.

Dustin Hoffman (1937–   ) was born in Los Angeles, Calif. Originally a stage and television actor, he first achieved fame

with his performance in *The Graduate* (1967). His other films include *Midnight Cowboy* (1969), *Little Big Man* (1970), and *All the President's Men* (1976). He won Academy Awards for best actor for *Kramer vs. Kramer* (1979) and *Rain Man* (1988).

Laurel and Hardy were an American film comedy team. **Stan Laurel** (Arthur Stanley Jefferson) (1890–1965), born in Ulverson, England, and **Oliver Norvell Hardy** (1892–1957), born in Atlanta, Ga., were both vaudeville performers before they met in 1926. In more than 100 feature films, among them *Pardon Us* (1931), *Pack Up Your Troubles* (1932), *Babes in Toyland* (1934), and *Block-Heads* (1938), timid Laurel suffered the insults of Hardy, the blustering bully.

German directors of silent films often used unrealistic sets and distorted camera angles to reflect a character's state of mind. A famous example is *The Cabinet of Dr. Caligari* (1920).

making their own films. The most famous of the early African American directors, Oscar Micheaux, made more than 30 films on topics of interest to African Americans.

European Silent Films. Though Hollywood came to dominate the world's film market after World War I, many European film directors earned international reputations. German filmmakers such as F. W. Murnau and Robert Wiene used expressionistic techniques, including stylized sets and distorted camera angles, to create imaginative and intriguing works of art. Wiene's masterpiece, *The Cabinet of Dr. Caligari* (1920), influenced filmmakers in Europe and the United States.

Another influential and internationally recognized filmmaker was the Soviet director Sergei Eisenstein. Eisenstein introduced the editing technique known as **montage**, in which separate images are combined in a sequence to create a particular effect. Eisenstein's films, including *The Battleship Potemkin* (1925) and *October* (1927), supported the socialist ideals of the 1917 Bolshevik Revolution.

Many talented Europeans worked in Hollywood during this period. Among them was the German director Ernst Lubitsch, who became one of the most respected American filmmakers of the late silent period.

Classical Cinema (1927–60)

The introduction of sound ushered in a golden age of motion pictures in the 1930's. During this period, as well as in the 1940's and 1950's, the popularity of motion pictures rose considerably, both in the United States and around the world. The films that were produced during these years are sometimes referred to as classical.

The Arrival of Sound. In order for the sounds of spoken dialogue to be synchronized with the movement of the actors' lips, sound had to

Marx Brothers

Marx Brothers, Chico (Leonard) (1887–1961), **Harpo** (Adolph or Arthur) (1888–1964), **Groucho** (Julius Henry) (1890–1977), American comedians, were born in New York City. Given to zany frolicking, they developed their stage characters in a vaudeville team, appearing at various times with their two other brothers, **Gummo** (Milton) (1894–1977) and **Zeppo** (Herbert) (1901–79). They starred on Broadway in *The Cocoanuts* (1925) and *Animal Crackers* (1928), both of which were later made into popular films (1929

and 1930). Their other films include *Duck Soup* (1933), *A Night at the Opera* (1935), and *A Day at the Races* (1937).

Marilyn Monroe (Norma Jean Baker) (1926–62) was born in Los Angeles, Calif. Her great beauty caused her to be cast as a sex symbol, and she became internationally famous in a succession of hit comedies. These included *Gentlemen Prefer Blondes* (1953), *The Seven-Year Itch* (1955), and *Some Like It Hot* (1959). She also performed well in dramatic roles in *Bus Stop* (1956) and *The Misfits* (1961). But personal problems and the pressures of stardom proved too great, and she died of an overdose of sleeping pills at 36. Her tragic story became a Hollywood legend.

Marilyn Monroe

Paul Newman (1925–   ) was born in Shaker Heights, Ohio. His portrayals of independent but charming characters have made him one of the most popular film stars of all time. His screen successes include *Somebody Up There Likes Me* (1956), *The Hustler* (1961), *Butch Cassidy and the Sundance Kid* (1969), *The Sting* (1973), and *The Color of Money* (1986), for which he won an Academy Award. Newman is well known as a professional racing car driver and is active in drug education programs and other charitable activities.

be recorded at the same time that scenes were actually being filmed. In a process known as sound-on-film, this soundtrack was added to the film. The era of sound pictures began with *The Jazz Singer* (1927), a silent film that incorporated musical sequences and a few lines of spoken dialogue. The popular success of this film revealed the possibilities of sound.

Studios initially resisted the transition to sound. They needed to develop effective sound equipment as well as projectors that could run sound films. This was costly, especially since America during this period was in the midst of the Great Depression. Many filmmakers also resisted the transition to sound because they felt it would distract from the images—for example, the sight gags used by slapstick comedians. Eventually, however, studios and filmmakers adapted to using sound-on-film, and movies with synchronous sound soon came to dominate the motion picture world.

As motion pictures grew more popular, local governments and religious organizations became concerned with their impact on social standards. Censorship of films increased. To avoid censorship and maintain control over their products, the major Hollywood studios created the Motion Picture Producers and Distributors of America (MPPDA). In 1934 the MPPDA adopted the Production Code, a set of rules restricting filmmakers from depicting controversial subjects. For example, the code prohibited filmmakers from showing violence or using profanity.

Classical Hollywood Films. Despite the Production Code, the Hollywood film industry continued to prosper. One of the factors for this success is the division of films into **genres**, or categories marked by similar styles and themes. Film genres include the gangster film, the screwball comedy, the musical, melodrama, film noir, the Western, and the science fiction film.

The **gangster film** was particularly popular during the early 1930's, a time when alcohol was illegal and real gangsters such as Al Ca-

James Cagney played a ruthless gangster in *The Public Enemy* (1931). Gangster films of the 1930's dramatized the real-life violence of America's prohibition era.

pone dominated newspaper headlines. Gangster films capitalized on the notoriety of real-life villains, often romanticizing them. *Little Caesar* (1930), which starred Edward G. Robinson, and *The Public Enemy* (1931), which starred James Cagney, are two famous gangster films that featured two popular stars of the period.

Jack Nicholson (1937–), born in Neptune, N.J., first gained recognition in *Easy Rider* (1969). He made a specialty of playing witty, cynical outsiders, as in *Chinatown* (1974) and *One Flew Over the Cuckoo's Nest* (1975), for which he won an Academy Award for best actor. He won an Academy Award for best supporting actor in *Terms of Endearment* (1983) and another for best actor in *As Good As It Gets* (1997). Other films include *Prizzi's Honor* (1985), *Batman* (1989), and *About Schmidt* (2002).

Mary Pickford (Gladys Marie Smith) (1894–1979), born in Toronto, Canada, was known as America's Sweetheart. She was a highly popular star of silent films, including *Rebecca of Sunnybrook Farm* (1917), *The Poor Little Rich Girl* (1917), and *Pollyanna* (1920). A shrewd businesswoman, Pickford founded the film studio United Artists Corporation in 1919 with Charlie Chaplin, D. W. Griffith, and Douglas Fairbanks.

Jack Nicholson

Sidney Poitier (1927–), born in Miami, Fla., was one of the first African American actors to play leading roles in major films. His best-known films include *The Defiant Ones* (1958), *Lilies of the Field* (1963), for which he received an Academy Award, *In the Heat of the Night* (1967), and *Guess Who's Coming to Dinner* (1967). Poitier also produced and directed films.

James Stewart (1908–97), born in Indiana, Pa., is best known for the soft-spoken, small-town characters he played in such films as *You Can't Take It With You* (1938), *It's a Wonderful Life* (1946), and *Harvey* (1951). He acted on Broadway before signing a film contract with MGM in 1935. His films for director Alfred Hitchcock, including *Rear Window* (1954) and *Vertigo* (1958), are considered among his best. Stewart received an Academy Award for *The Philadelphia Story* (1940) and the American Film Institute's Life Achievement Award (1980).

Screwball comedies, such as *Bringing Up Baby* (1938) with Katharine Hepburn and Cary Grant, often placed wisecracking characters in hilarious predicaments.

The **screwball comedy**, which was most popular in the 1930's, relied on the frantic actions and wisecracks of its leading characters. Films from this genre were usually about the middle and upper classes and usually featured elaborate sets and costumes. Classical screwball comedies include *It Happened One Night* (1934) and *Bringing Up Baby* (1938).

The heyday of the **musical** ran from the mid-1920's to the mid-1950's. The studio most famous for musicals is Metro-Goldwyn-Mayer (MGM). Its musicals included *The Wizard of Oz* (1939), *Cabin in the Sky* (1943), which featured an all-black cast, and *Singin' in the Rain* (1952), which starred dancer Gene Kelly.

Though present in early films, **melodrama** took a different turn in the 1940's, when many men in the country were off to war and women made up the majority of the film audience. Also known as "women's films," melodrama during this period revolved around women working or handling difficulties in their relationships and families. Notable among these are the works of Douglas Sirk, including *All I Desire* (1953) and *Written on the Wind* (1956).

Film noir, a French term meaning "black film," features gritty urban settings and dark, mysterious subjects. At the heart of a film noir story is a crime, a guilty person, and a world in which right and wrong are not that easy to tell apart. Classic films from this genre include *Double Indemnity* (1944) and *Gun Crazy* (1949).

The **Western** is a long-standing genre, seen as early as 1903 with Porter's *The Great Train Robbery*. The popularity of this genre is probably due to its timeless themes of good versus evil, human against nature, and the individual in and out of society. Among the many classical Westerns are *Red River* (1948) and *The Searchers* (1956).

Science fiction films of the early 1950's share themes that reflect America's anxiety

Profiles

Meryl Streep
(Mary Louise Streep) (1949–), born in Summit, N.J., earned a master of fine arts at Yale University before embarking on a stage and film career. She won an Academy Award as best supporting actress for her performance in *Kramer vs. Kramer* (1979). Three years later she won the Academy's best actress award for *Sophie's Choice* (1982). She also starred in *Silkwood* (1983), *Out of Africa* (1985), *Heartburn* (1986), and *The River Wild* (1994).

Meryl Streep

Shirley Temple (1928–),
born in Santa Monica, Calif., was one of the most popular child stars of all time. She captivated movie audiences in such films as *Bright Eyes* (1934), for which she received a special Academy Award, *The Little Colonel* (1935), and *Heidi* (1937). She ended her acting career at age 21 and later became active in politics. As Shirley Temple Black (her married name), she served as a delegate to the United Nations (1969–70), as U.S. ambassador to Ghana (1974–76), and as U.S. chief of protocol (1976–77).

Rudolph Valentino (Rodolpho d'Antonguolla (1895–1926) was born in Castellaneta, Italy. His portrayals of dashing, passionate lovers made him a popular star of American silent movies. His first major film was *The Four Horsemen of the Apocalypse* (1921); others include *The Sheik* (1921) and *Blood and Sand* (1922).

Ethel Waters (1896–1977),
born in Chester, Pa., was one of the most admired African American actresses of her time. She began her career as a nightclub singer and made her Broadway debut in 1927. She acted and sang in the Broadway hit *Cabin in the Sky*, repeating her role in the 1943 film version. Her greatest success was her portrayal of the wise and patient cook in Carson McCullers' *The Member of the Wedding* (1950), a role she performed both on Broadway (1950) and on film (1953). Her autobiography, *His Eye Is on the Sparrow* (1951), was a best-seller.

John Wayne (Marion Michael Morrison) (1907–79), born in Winterset, Iowa, began his career as a prop boy at Fox studios. In his films, he came to personify a strong and rugged leader of men, often playing a cowboy or a soldier. His films include *Stagecoach* (1939), *Red River* (1948), *Sands of Iwo Jima* (1950), and *The Quiet Man* (1952). He won an Academy Award as best actor for his performance in *True Grit* (1969).

John Wayne starred in many great Westerns directed by John Ford. Scenic locations in Monument Valley, on the Arizona-Utah border, were a Ford trademark.

While genres dominated the kind of films Hollywood produced from the 1930's to the 1960's, a few directors emerged as individual artists. While there are many directors of this caliber, four stand out: Frank Capra, John Ford, Orson Welles, and Alfred Hitchcock. These filmmakers expanded Hollywood filmmaking to create original and imaginative works of art.

Another famed and creative filmmaker was Walt Disney, who is probably best known for his animated work. Three of the most notable Disney animated films are *Snow White* (1938), *Pinocchio* (1940), and *Cinderella* (1950). These films helped create an animation industry and made "Disney" a household name.

International Film. During the 1930's, France emerged as a center of European filmmaking. Outstanding among French directors was Jean Renoir, whose *Grand Illusion* (1937) and *Rules of the Game* (1939) are considered masterpieces.

Several European film movements arose after World War II (1939–45), receiving international acclaim. One of the most influential was Italian **neorealism**, a style of filmmaking that used nonprofessional actors, location shooting, and simple shots to convey a sense of reality. Among the most prominent neorealist filmmakers were Vittorio De Sica and Roberto Rossellini. Federico Fellini used neorealistic elements in his early films.

over the Cold War and the potential hazards of modern science. Typical themes are alien invasions, monster attacks, and sinister scientists bent on taking over society. Among the best-known science fiction films are *War of the Worlds* (1953) and *Forbidden Planet* (1956).

D I R E C T O R S *Profiles*

Woody Allen (Allen Stewart Konigsberg) (1935–), born in Brooklyn, N.Y., is an actor and writer as well as a director. His highly personal work, set mainly in New York City, focuses on the fears and insecurities of modern life. Allen's first film project as director-screenwriter-star was *Take the Money and Run* (1969). Among his other films are *Bananas* (1971), *Sleeper* (1975), *Annie Hall* (1977), which won an Academy Award for best picture, *Manhattan* (1979), *Hannah and Her Sisters* (1986), which also won a best picture Academy Award, *Crimes and Misdemeanors* (1989), and *Bullets Over Broadway* (1994).

Woody Allen

Ingmar Bergman (1918–), a Swedish film director born in Uppsala, won international recognition for his thought-provoking films. He began his career as a stage director, then turned to writing and directing films. *The Seventh Seal* (1957), a stark and brooding work about the individual's search for meaning in life, is considered a masterpiece. Other Bergman films include *Wild Strawberries* (1957), *Persona* (1966), *Cries and Whispers* (1972), and *Fanny and Alexander* (1983).

Frank Capra (1897–1991), an American director born in Palermo, Sicily, was best known for his sentimental films about the triumphs of ordinary people. These include *It Happened One Night* (1934), *Mr. Deeds Goes to Town* (1936), and *You Can't Take It with You* (1938), all of which won Academy Awards for best picture. Capra began his film career directing and writing jokes for silent slapstick comedies. Most of his own films were comedies, but he also directed some dramas, such as *Lost Horizon* (1937), that became film classics. His autobiography, *The Name Above the Title*, was published in 1971.

Cecil B. De Mille (1881–1959), born in Ashfield, Mass., was known for his spectacular movies featuring elaborate sets, beautiful costumes, and very large casts. Some of his movies, like *The Ten Commandments* (1923; remade 1956) and *The King of Kings* (1927), were based on Bible stories. Others, such as *Union Pacific* (1939), dramatized events from American history. *The Greatest Show on Earth*, a colorful De Mille movie about the circus, won an Academy Award as best film of 1952.

Another important international film movement was the French **New Wave**. It was begun by film critics who became filmmakers with the goal of restoring the artistic role of the director and loosening the conservative style of earlier French films. Typified by the work of François Truffaut, especially *Jules and Jim* (1961), and by the early work of Jean Luc Godard, especially *Breathless* (1959), the French New Wave influenced international moviemaking throughout the 1960's.

Swedish director Ingmar Bergman developed an impressive command of film techniques with which he explored complex human relationships. Luis Buñuel, a Spaniard who worked mainly in France and Mexico, made some of his best films during this period.

Partly due to the rise of international film festivals such as Cannes, non-European filmmakers became better known in the postwar period. Filmmakers such as Satyajit Ray of India, Akira Kurosawa of Japan, and Emilio Fernandez of Mexico received wide recognition for their artistry.

Technical Innovations. By the end of the classical period, Hollywood found itself in competition with more than just the international film scene. By the 1950's, more and more Americans were opting to stay home and watch television rather than go to see a movie.

At first, Hollywood responded with an array of gimmicks designed to bring audiences back into the theaters. An innovation called **3-D**, in which viewers wore special glasses that made the movie image appear three-dimensional, met with only temporary success. Eventually, however, Hollywood was successful in winning back movie audiences with the use of wide-screen projection techniques (Cinerama and Cinemascope) and stereo sound, and by the almost total transition to color film.

The Bicycle Thief (1948), directed by Vittorio De Sica, is an outstanding example of Italian neorealism, a film movement that arose after World War II.

Profiles

Federico Fellini (1920–94), Italian film director, was born in Rimini. Fellini's films often blend reality with sequences of dreamlike fantasy. Many characters in his films confuse reality with what they would like to believe is real. Three of Fellini's films, *La Strada* (1954), *La Dolce Vita* (1960), and *Amarcord* (1974), received Academy Awards as best foreign film. His other works include *8½* (1963), *Satyricon* (1969), and *City of Women* (1981).

John Ford (Sean O'Feeney) (1895–1973) was born in Cape Elizabeth, Me. Many of his films focus on themes from America's past. Ford went to Hollywood in 1913 and began to write and direct silent films. His first great success was *The Iron Horse* (1924). He won Academy Awards for best director for *The Informer* (1935), *The Grapes of Wrath* (1940), *How Green Was My Valley* (1941), and *The Quiet Man* (1952). Among his many other films are the Western masterpieces *Stagecoach*

(1939), *She Wore a Yellow Ribbon* (1949), and *The Searchers* (1956).

D. W. Griffith (David Lewelyn Wark Griffith) (1875–1948) was born in LaGrange, Ky. His first important film was *The Birth of a Nation* (1915), the first American spectacular. He pioneered the use of techniques such as the fade-out, flashback, close-up, and crowd scene. Among his major works are *Intolerance* (1916), *Broken Blossoms* (1919), and *Way Down East* (1920).

Alfred Hitchcock (1899–1980), British-American master of the thriller genre, was born in London, England. After directing several British films, including *The 39 Steps* (1935), he went to Hollywood in 1939. His

Alfred Hitchcock

first American film, *Rebecca* (1940), won an Academy Award for best picture. Later Hitchcock films, such as *Rear Window* (1954), *Vertigo* (1958), *North by Northwest* (1959), and *Psycho* (1960), often mix suspense with sex, humor, and horror. Hitchcock received the American Film Institute's Life Achievement Award in 1979.

John Huston (1906–87) was born in Nevada, Mo., the son of noted actor Walter Huston. He made his directing debut with a classic detective story, *The Maltese Falcon* (1941), and went on to direct more than 40 other films. They include *The African Queen* (1951), *Moby Dick* (1956), and *The Man Who Would Be King* (1975). He directed the Academy Award-winning performances of his father in *The Treasure of the Sierra Madre* (1948)

Contemporary Film (After 1960)

In the contemporary period, the film industry adapted to many changes, including rapidly changing social values, a younger film audience, and an increasingly international film market.

Changing Themes. Later Hollywood filmmakers adapted the established genres of the classical period; often their work addressed the political and social changes that were sweeping the country. Two significant films that reflected the ideals of the civil rights movement are *Guess Who's Coming to Dinner?* (1967) and *In the Heat of the Night* (1967). Both starred the African American actor Sidney Poitier. Films of social criticism included *The Graduate* (1967), *M*A*S*H* (1970), and *One Flew Over the Cuckoo's Nest* (1975).

At the same time that these new themes were being explored, the power of the Production Code was diminishing. In 1968 it was replaced by a new rating system that indicated the level of audience maturity a film demanded. Because it rated the finished film rather than restricting what filmmakers could depict, the new system allowed for more creative freedom.

The Godfather (1972), the story of a powerful crime family, was directed by Francis Ford Coppola. Marlon Brando (second from left) starred in the title role.

Films are presently classified as G (general), PG (parental guidance suggested), PG-13 (some material may be inappropriate for children under 13), R (persons under 17 must be accompanied by an adult), or NC-17 (persons under 17 not admitted).

It is also during this period that young people became the largest group of Americans to attend the movies. Studios responded by providing a number of films targeted directly at this emerging audience. Known as teen pics in the 1960's, these films range from *Beach Blanket Bingo* (1965) to such later films as *The Breakfast Club* (1985) and *Wayne's World* (1992). Even younger audiences were targeted

and his daughter Anjelica in *Prizzi's Honor* (1985). Huston was also a screenwriter and character actor.

Akira Kurosawa (1910–98), a noted Japanese film director, was born in Tokyo. Kurosawa became internationally known following the success of his film *Rashomon* in 1950. His films are often complex psychological studies of the central characters. They are set in modern Japan, as well as in Japan's historical past. His other films include *The Lower Depths* (1957), *High and Low* (1963), *Dersu Uzala* (1975), and *Ran* (1985).

Spike Lee (Shelton Jackson Lee) (1957–), a leading African American filmmaker, was born in Atlanta, Ga., and studied filmmaking at New York University. His debut film, the independently produced *She's Gotta Have It* (1986), attracted international attention, winning a prize at the Cannes Film Festival. Lee's films, which also include *Do the Right Thing* (1989) and *Malcolm X* (1992), focus on the black experience in the United

States and often comment on tensions between blacks and whites. Also an actor, Lee frequently appeared in his own films.

Satyajit Ray (1921–92), one of India's greatest filmmakers, was born in Calcutta. His best-known films, particularly the series known as the Apu Trilogy, depict Indian village and family life with great beauty and simplicity. The trilogy—*Pather*

Spike Lee

Panchali (1955), *Aparajito* (1956), and *The World of Apu* (1959)—explores the coming of age of a young boy, Apu, in his rural Bengali village. Ray's later films include *Charulata* (1964), *Distant Thunder* (1973), and *The Visitor* (1992).

Leni Riefenstahl (1902–2003), a German director born in Berlin, is known primarily as the favorite filmmaker of Adolf Hitler. Her best-known, though controversial, work is *Triumph of the Will* (1935), a masterful propaganda film documenting a Nazi political rally of 1934. Another impressive documentary, *Olympia* (1938), covers the 1936 Olympic Games in Berlin. Because of her role in glorifying the Nazi regime, she was imprisoned for several years after World War II. For the rest of her life, she worked primarily as a magazine photographer. Her last film was *Underwater Impressions* (2002).

Videos and cable television have expanded the American market for such foreign films as *Fanny and Alexander* (1983), by acclaimed Swedish director Ingmar Bergman.

Blockbuster Hollywood films such as *E.T.: The Extra-Terrestrial* (1982) earned millions of dollars from theater receipts and merchandising spin-offs.

with films that revolve around child characters, such as *Home Alone* (1990), and numerous feature-length animated films.

Viewing Alternatives. The 1970's saw the rise of independent filmmakers, individuals who finance and control their own pictures and often receive financial backing from private sources. Independent films competed with the major studios for audiences. Further competition came from the international film scene. In addition to films from Europe, the films of Australia, China, Cuba, Argentina, and many other nations now reached a world audience, exposing audiences to the perspectives of other cultures.

Beginning in the 1980's, the growing popularity of home viewing of movies, on video and on cable television, created a major market for independent and foreign films as well as for the products of Hollywood studios.

Recent Trends. Despite a smaller movie audience and competition from independent and foreign films, Hollywood earned more money during the contemporary period than ever be-

Profiles

Martin Scorsese (1942–   ), born in Flushing, N.Y., became known for films featuring gritty urban settings and realistic, sometimes violent, plots. Outstanding examples are *Mean Streets* (1973), *Taxi Driver* (1976), *Raging Bull* (1980), and *Good Fellas* (1990), all of which star the actor Robert De Niro. Scorsese sometimes departed from this trademark style, exploring the life of Jesus Christ in *The Last Temptation of Christ* (1988) and examining New York society at the end of the 1800's in The *Age of Innocence* (1993).

Steven Spielberg (1947–   ) was born in Cincinnati, Ohio, and studied film at Long Beach State College in California. He made his first feature film, *The Sugarland Express*, in 1974. He then directed a series of immensely popular action and fantasy films—including *Jaws* (1975), *Close Encounters of the Third Kind* (1977), *Raiders of the Lost Ark* (1981), and *E.T.: The Extra-Terrestrial* (1982)—that set records in box-office earnings. In 1993, Spielberg surpassed his previous box-office successes with the science fiction spectacular *Jurassic Park*. In the same year he also directed *Schindler's List*, a drama about the Holocaust that won an Academy Award for best picture.

Orson Welles (George Orson Welles) (1915–85), an innovative American director, producer, and actor, was born in Kenosha, Wis. He began his acting career in Ireland and in 1937 established the Mercury Theatre in New York. In 1938 he broadcast the radio drama *The War of the Worlds* (so realistic that it created panic among listeners). His first film, *Citizen Kane* (1941), is regarded as one of the most impressive achievements in the history of film. Its artistic style had a great impact on later films. Among Welles' other films are *The Magnificent Ambersons* (1942), *Macbeth* (1948), and *A Touch of Evil* (1958).

Martin Scorsese

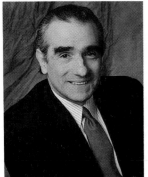

Steven Spielberg

Orson Welles

The work of innovative directors continues to shape the American film industry. *Left:* Spike Lee explored racial tensions in a Brooklyn community in *Do the Right Thing* (1989). *Below:* In *Schindler's List* (1993), Steven Spielberg told the story of a German industrialist who saved Jewish lives during World War II.

fore. Studios increased their profits by linking their films with toys, computer games, and posters. Films such as *Star Wars* (1977), *E.T.: The Extra-Terrestrial* (1982), *Jurassic Park* (1993), and *The Lion King* (1994) earned hundreds of millions of dollars from both theater receipts and the sale of dolls, games, posters, and other merchandising spin-offs.

Star power also increased in this period of American filmmaking. Salaries rose to fantastic numbers, with many of the larger stars—the superstars—earning well over $5 million per picture. Sylvester Stallone, Arnold Schwarzenegger, and other actors became heroes of American popular culture. Their action films, usually depicting heavy violence, emphasize thrilling special effects and the actors' imposing physical strength over story and character development.

While the contemporary American film industry has frequently stressed commercial success, it has also produced many innovative directors who, like their predecessors, influenced the Hollywood style. Many of these directors learned their craft in film schools such as New York University, the University of Southern California, and the University of California at Los Angeles.

Steven Spielberg and George Lucas specialized in epic fantasy and science fiction films that broke new ground in visual technology and special effects. Woody Allen, Francis Ford Coppola, and Martin Scorsese each brought a distinctive style and highly personal vision to filmmaking. Spike Lee expressed his views of the African American experience in such films as *Do the Right Thing* (1989) and *Malcolm X* (1992). A trend toward cultural diversity in American movies was reflected in the growing popularity of films by Chicano filmmakers such as Luis Valdez and Asian Americans such as Wayne Wang.

DANIEL L. BERNARDI
Department of Film and Television
University of California, Los Angeles

MOTORBOATS. See BOATS AND BOATING.

MOTORCYCLES

Some people say the motorcycle is a modern version of the horse, and in many ways this is true. A rider sits on a motorcycle much as if it were a horse. Like a horse, a motorcycle goes farther and faster than the rider could go on foot. And a motorcycle can be ridden along a trail in the backwoods where a car could not go. But a motorcycle can also be used on streets and highways.

A motorcycle is a two-wheeled vehicle powered by a gasoline engine. On the handlebars are controls for the throttle, the clutch, and the brake. The throttle regulates the speed of the motorcycle by controlling the amount of gasoline flowing into the engine. The clutch puts the motorcycle into gear, and the brake stops the motorcycle.

▶ USES FOR MOTORCYCLES

The first practical motorcycle was built by Gottlieb Daimler, a German inventor, in 1885. Since that time, the motorcycle's special characteristics have made it useful in many ways.

Transportation. Motorcycles generally use much less gasoline than cars. Their engines are simpler and less expensive to tune up and repair than car engines. This makes motorcycles an economical way to drive to school or work.

Recreation. Because motorcycles are fun to ride, many people use them for pleasure.

Some people like to carry light luggage on their motorcycles and take long cross-country tours. Other people enjoy riding their motorcycles along dirt trails in the desert, forest, or mountains. Motorcycle racing is a popular sport. Some races over rough country test the rider's skill as well as the speed of the motorcycle.

Professional Work. Many police departments find that motorcycles are just right for their work. Their motorcycles are fast, and because a motorcycle is narrow, it can get through a traffic jam more easily than a car. Forest rangers use motorcycles to patrol rugged country. Motorcycles are used by the armed forces for transportation in remote areas.

▶ TYPES OF MOTORCYCLES

Motorcycles differ in their design and construction, depending on their intended use. They are all similar in that they have two wheels, an engine, a seat for the rider, and other common features. But because riding on a paved road is very different from riding on soft dirt, the motorcycles designed for these conditions are also different.

Dirt Motorcycles. Motorcycles designed for use on dirt roads and trails tend to be small and light because it is difficult to steer a heavy motorcycle over a rough or rocky surface. To keep their weight low, these motorcycles usually do not have headlights and tail-

Motorcycle competitions are spectacular and exciting. Left: A racer takes his motorcycle into the air to hurdle a barrier. Below: Motorcyclists are bunched together at the start of a cross-country race.

lights, license plates, horns, turn signals, or other equipment required on public roads. Often dirt motorcycles have very large wheels, especially in the front, to help them ride up and over rocks and logs. The tires have deep grooves to give traction in soft dirt and mud.

Dual-Purpose Motorcycles. These motorcycles can be used on public roads and on dirt trails. They are designed and built very much like dirt motorcycles. But they are also fitted with the equipment necessary for legal operation on paved roads—lights, a horn, and turn signals. Often this equipment is designed to be easily removed, to protect it from damage, and to reduce weight on dirt trails.

Street Motorcycles. Motorcycles intended for use on paved roads are available in a wide range of sizes. There are small, light models that provide inexpensive around-town transportation. But street motorcycles can be quite large and heavy. The biggest ones are designed to carry two people on long trips.

Mopeds. The word "moped" comes from a combination of "motor" and "pedal." In many ways a moped is just a bicycle with a motor. It is pedaled like a bicycle, but once the moped is under way, the motor can be engaged to keep it going. Mopeds are designed to travel at low speeds. They use very little gasoline and are popular for low-cost transportation.

▶ **MOTORCYCLE SAFETY**

Although motorcycles can be useful and enjoyable, they can also be dangerous. Riders must be completely alert for dangerous traffic situations and road conditions. Because riders are not enclosed as they would be in a car, even a small mishap can cause serious injury. That is why it is important for riders to wear safety helmets. Boots, gloves, and heavy clothing that covers the arms and legs also provide valuable protection.

GEORGE ELLIOTT
Editorial Director, *Popular Cycling*

MOTORS, ELECTRIC. See ELECTRIC MOTORS.

MOTT, LUCRETIA COFFIN. See WOMEN'S RIGHTS MOVEMENT (Profiles).

MOUNTAIN CLIMBING

Mountain climbing is part of a wider activity called mountaineering. Mountaineers are people who know how to move safely through and over mountains, and mountain climbers are people who use mountaineering knowledge and skill to climb a particular mountain peak.

For many years, mountaineering and mountain climbing were practiced not for fun, but because they were useful. Mountaineers rescued people, hunted in rough terrain, and guided travelers over difficult paths and mountain passes. People once thought demons and monsters lived on the highest peaks, and they stayed away from them if they could.

In the 1300's, people in Europe began to climb mountains for pleasure or sport. By the 1700's, the number of climbers had increased greatly and many people were eager to scale Europe's unclimbed peaks. By the mid-1800's, vacationers were climbing peaks in the Alps on a regular basis. Soon every important peak in Europe had been climbed.

As the Alps were conquered, climbers began to go to other mountain areas in Africa, North and South America, and Asia. Most of the highest mountains in the world had been climbed by the mid-1900's. Perhaps the most famous climb was the successful ascent to the summit of Mount Everest by Edmund Hillary, a New Zealander, and Tenzing Norgay, a Sherpa of Nepal, on May 29, 1953.

▶ **MOUNTAIN CLIMBING TODAY**

After the ascent of Mount Everest, mountain climbing became popular. Increasing numbers of people around the world now engage in the sport. In many places, climbing clubs provide climbers with information on routes, terrain, and other matters. The oldest and most famous climbing club is the Alpine Club of London.

A Typical Climb

The approach to some mountains may take climbers through pastures, forests, or open meadows. These climbers do not need special equipment—just good lungs and strong legs. In some cases, climbers may be able to stay on trails all the way to the summit. Usually, however, mountain climbing involves moving up and over steep rock cliffs and ridges.

In dangerous situations, climbers may need to use a piton, carabiner, and rope to make their ascent of a mountain safer.

When descending areas covered with snow and ice, climbers may use a method called rappelling, in which they let themselves down steep slopes or rocks walls on a double rope.

FIRST ASCENTS OF THE HIGHEST PEAKS

MOUNTAIN	HEIGHT	LOCATION	DATE CLIMBED
Mont Blanc	15,771 ft (4,807 m)	Alps (Europe)	1786
Mount Elbrus	18,510 ft (5,642 m)	Caucasus (Eurasia)	1868
Kilimanjaro	19,341 ft (5,895 m)	Tanzania (Africa)	1889
Aconcagua	22,834 ft (6,960 m)	Andes (S. America)	1897
Mount McKinley	20,320 ft (6,194 m)	Alaska (N. America)	1913
Mount Everest	29,035 ft (8,850 m)	Himalayas (Asia)	1953

Mountain routes are graded according to difficulty. Grade I rock can be climbed quite easily with only an occasional use of the hands. On Grade II and III rock, climbers rope themselves together so that if a person slips, the others can keep him or her from falling. Grade IV and V rock becomes increasingly steeper and more dangerous. At this point, all climbers stop at the safest possible spot. The second climber in line lets out rope to the leader, who continues to climb. Once at the next safe spot, the leader helps the others up one by one. If there are no safe spots, one can be made by pounding an iron spike, or **piton**, into a crack in the rock, attaching a steel snap link, or **carabiner**, and running a rope through it to help catch a climber who slips or falls. If there is no crack, one may be drilled for a special bolt that acts as a piton.

Grade VI rock and higher is vertical or overhanging sections of rock that cannot be ascended using just the feet and hands. Instead, special climbing methods are required. In one method, the lead climber makes a ladder of pitons and rope. The other climbers pull on the rope to hold the leader against the top piton while he or she pounds in the next piton above. The climber can stand in a stirrup hooked to the piton and may use a short portable ladder to climb farther up.

When climbers encounter snow and ice, they can cut steps with ice axes and then climb using special steel frames with sharp spikes, or **crampons**, strapped to their boots.

Climbing can be dangerous. Carelessness or faulty equipment may lead to a slip or a fall. Loose rock, bad weather, and sickness are other factors that can make climbing dangerous. To ensure safe ascents, climbers must keep their equipment in good working order, avoid situations that are beyond their level of ability, and use good judgment.

WOODROW WILSON SAYRE
Author, *Four Against Everest*

See also EVEREST, MOUNT.

Majestic Mount Everest —the highest mountain in the world—rises in the eastern Himalayas between Nepal and Tibet. At its highest point, it towers a lofty 29,035 feet (8,850 meters) above sea level.

MOUNTAINS

When you hear the word "mountain," what do you think of? Rocky peaks rising above the clouds? High pine-covered ridges stretching across the horizon? The perfect cone of a snow-covered volcano sloping down to a flat plain? As different as they are, these all are mountains. A mountain is a landform that stands high above the land around it. Mountains generally have steep slopes and defined peaks or ridges. They rise at least 1,000 feet (300 meters) above the surrounding land.

▶ THE DISTRIBUTION OF MOUNTAINS

Some mountains, such as single volcanoes, stand alone. They are isolated mountain peaks. Others are part of a local group of mountains called a **range**. The San Juan Mountains in Colorado and the Wind River Mountains in Wyoming are mountain ranges. They are part of one hundred or so neighboring mountain ranges that are linked together to form the Rocky Mountain **system**. The mountain ranges in a system, or **chain**, are roughly aligned and extend over a large area. They are similar in structure and age. Where systems are made up of ranges and groups of mountains that differ in origin and age, they may form **cordilleras**.

▶ HOW MOUNTAINS ARE FORMED

Mountains are formed as geologic forces, such as heat and pressure, produce changes on and beneath the Earth's surface. Some of the changes, such as molten rock bursting through the Earth's crust, can take place suddenly. But most of the changes that create mountains occur over thousands, even millions, of years.

A theory called **plate tectonics** helps explain how mountain building occurs. According to this theory, the Earth's surface is composed of huge slabs, or plates, of solid rock. Tremendous forces within the Earth keep the plates constantly moving—a few inches a year—carrying continents and ocean basins across the surface of the Earth. Sometimes plates collide. The immense forces of these slow collisions last for millions of years. Towering mountain ranges are thrust up along the plate boundaries as the long-lasting pressures cause layers of rock to crumple and fold.

Based on the composition and arrangement of the rocks that form them, mountains can be divided into four general types: folded mountains, fault-block mountains, volcanoes, and erosional mountains. Most mountain systems include a combination of the different types of mountains.

Folded Mountains

With the high impact of a head-on collision, the body of a car may crumple and become folded like the pleats of an accordion. A similar thing happens where two plates collide. The rock crumples into folds like accordion pleats, forming peaks and valleys. The Alps in Europe and the Appalachians in the eastern United States are examples of folded mountains. Erosion by wind, water, or glaciers further shapes the mountains. Even after folded mountains have been almost completely worn away, the curved layers of underlying rock show where folded mountains once towered.

Fault-Block Mountains

When rock suddenly comes under great pressure, it may not fold. Instead, it may crack. The rocks on either side of a crack may move, forming a **fault**. The upward or downward movement of rock layers along a fault creates fault-block mountains. As with folded mountains, erosion also shapes fault-block mountains, forming jagged peaks and carving deep valleys. The Sierra Nevada, in California, include fault-block mountains. The steep ridges of the mountains along the eastern edge were formed as huge blocks of the Earth's crust tilted upward. With other fault-block mountains, the blocks do not tilt. They remain level as one block is lifted high above the other. The Ruwenzori range in Africa is an example of this type of fault-block range.

Volcanoes

Folded mountains and fault-block mountains arise gradually over the course of hundreds of thousands or millions of years. Volcanic mountains, on the other hand, can sprout from a level plain in a matter of days or weeks. A volcano is a mountain formed when hot, molten rock from deep within the Earth rises to the surface. The ash and molten rock, or lava, from a volcano can shoot out violently, forming a steep-sided mountain, such as Mount St. Helens in Washington or Mount Fuji in Japan. The lava also can seep slowly, forming a mountain with a gentle slope. One such volcano is Mauna Loa; although most of this mountain is submerged beneath the Pacific Ocean, the top part forms part of the island of Hawaii.

Erosional Mountains

The erosion of thick regions of soft sedimentary rock can also form mountains. For example, a mountainous part of southeastern

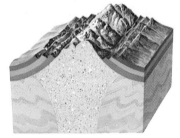

Erosional Mountains
Wind, water, and ice erode the softer top layers of rock, carving out mountainous forms.

Fault-Block Mountains
Movements of rock layers along a fault may thrust large blocks of crust upward, creating fault-block mountains.

Volcanic Mountains

Hot, molten rock from deep inside the Earth rises to the surface and erupts through openings in the crust to form the mountainous peaks of volcanoes.

Folded Mountains

Plates smash together in collisions lasting millions of years. As the layers of rock are relentlessly squeezed together, folded mountains form.

Small independent towns have been established in the valleys of the folded mountains known as the Alps (*right*). Volcanic eruptions are often viewed as violent, harmful events, but volcanoes (*top right*) yield valuable rocks and minerals. They are also sources of geothermal energy. The rounded summits and deep valleys of the Catskill Mountains (*opposite page*), located in New York, were formed as the processes of erosion carved through a once-level plateau.

New York was once a high plateau. Streams and rivers draining the plateau cut down through the flat layers of rock, carving out deep valleys. The remaining hills, formed by erosion of the once-level plateau, are known as the Catskill Mountains.

▶ **MOUNTAINS OF THE WORLD**

Mountain systems are found on all of the world's seven continents. The systems on each continent are unique in size, age, appearance, and geological history.

North America

The Rocky Mountains, part of the North American Cordillera, form the major mountain system of North America. They stretch for 3,000 miles (4,800 kilometers) from the Canadian provinces of Alberta and British Columbia in the north to the United States–Mexico border in the south. In parts of the United States, the system is more than 300 miles (480 kilometers) wide. The highest peak in the Rockies is Mount Elbert in Colorado, which stands 14,433 feet (4,399 meters) tall.

The formation of the Rockies began about 100 million years ago. They formed as a result of collisions between the North American plate and two other plates. Volcanoes frequently erupted in the region from 250 to 80 million years ago, causing further changes in the landscape. Regional uplift, which occurred several times, and erosion also contributed to the present landscape. This complex geological history has resulted in a mixture of different mountain types throughout the Rocky Mountain system: folded mountains, fault-block mountains, and volcanic mountains.

South America

The towering Andes form the main mountain system of South America. They stretch more than 4,500 miles (7,240 kilometers) down the west coast of the continent from western Venezuela to the southern tip of Chile and Argentina. The highest peak in the Andes is Aconcagua, at 22,834 feet (6,960 meters). It lies on the border of Argentina and Chile.

Mountain building started as the South American plate collided with the ocean plate off the west coast of the continent. The collision, which occurred about 100 million years ago, was followed by an intense period of volcanic eruptions. Volcanic activity has continued off and on until very recently. So the Andes contain a combination of folded and volcanic mountains.

Europe

The Alps are the most prominent mountain chain of Europe, forming a 660-mile (1,060-kilometer) crescent from the Mediterranean coast of Italy and France across Switzerland and into central Austria. The name "alp" actually means "high mountain valley." The highest peak in the Alps is France's Mont Blanc, which stands 15,771 feet (4,807 meters) tall.

These magnificent mountains formed over a period of 200 million years, as the plates bearing the continents of Europe and Africa began to move toward each other. As Europe and Africa got closer together, the large sea that separated the two continents began to shrink. Around 65 million years ago, islands at the edges of the sea rammed into Europe, forming folded mountains. Then, about 30 million

WONDER QUESTION

What is the longest mountain chain in the world?

It has only lately been mapped. It has never been climbed. Until the late 1940's, no one even knew it was there. Known as the Mid-Atlantic Ridge, the world's longest mountain chain runs down the middle of the Atlantic Ocean. The Mid-Atlantic Ridge is more than 10,000 miles (16,000 kilometers) long, and in places, 1,000 miles (1,600 kilometers) wide. The mountains that form it rise more than 6,000 feet (1,800 meters) above the ocean floor. The Mid-Atlantic Ridge begins in the Arctic Ocean north of Russia, snakes under the Arctic ice, and breaks through the surface of the water at Iceland. Extending south almost to Antarctica, the Mid-Atlantic Ridge joins other chains that curve around the southern tip of Africa and run into the Indian Ocean. All together, submerged chains of this oceanic mountain system extend for more than 50,000 miles (80,000 kilometers) and cover an area larger than that covered by all of the continents combined.

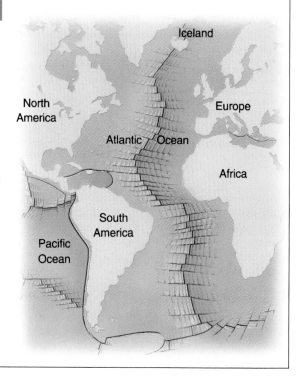

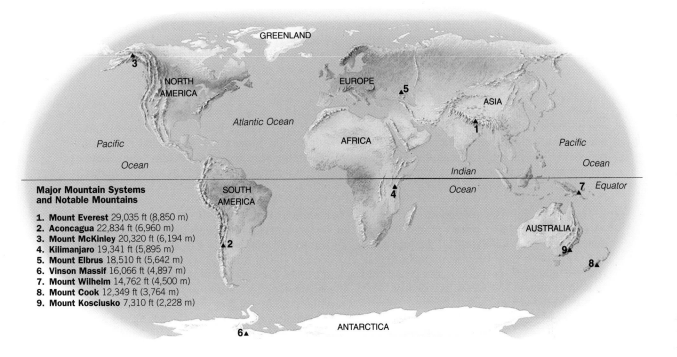

Major Mountain Systems and Notable Mountains

1. **Mount Everest** 29,035 ft (8,850 m)
2. **Aconcagua** 22,834 ft (6,960 m)
3. **Mount McKinley** 20,320 ft (6,194 m)
4. **Kilimanjaro** 19,341 ft (5,895 m)
5. **Mount Elbrus** 18,510 ft (5,642 m)
6. **Vinson Massif** 16,066 ft (4,897 m)
7. **Mount Wilhelm** 14,762 ft (4,500 m)
8. **Mount Cook** 12,349 ft (3,764 m)
9. **Mount Kosciusko** 7,310 ft (2,228 m)

years ago, Europe and Africa collided. One result of this collision was the Alps. Erosion wore the Alps flat within the next 25 million years. Less than 5 million years ago, geologic activity once again uplifted the land. Glaciers helped carve out the deep valleys and, thus, the dramatic peaks of today's Alps.

Asia

The highest mountain chain in the world is the Himalayas, in Asia. Forming a nearly impassable barrier, the Himalayas stretch for about 1,500 miles (2,414 kilometers), dividing China from Pakistan, India, Nepal, and Bhutan. With more than 30 peaks rising above 24,000 feet (7,300 meters), the Himalayas are often called the roof of the world. Mount Everest, at 29,035 feet (8,850 meters), is the tallest mountain in the world. Tibet, a part of China, lies north of the Himalayan range. The average altitude of this region is more than 16,000 feet (4,900 meters)—higher than the highest mountain in the continental United States.

More than 100 million years ago, India was a large island off the east coast of the African landmass. Over the past 140 million years, the plate carrying India has moved northwestward. About 50 million years ago, India crashed into the southern coast of Asia. The collision formed the mighty folded mountains of the Himalayas. But the mountain building did not end with that initial collision. India has continued to plow into Asia, moving an additional 1,250 miles (2,000 kilometers) northward and thrusting the Himalayas even higher.

Africa

Compared with Europe and Asia, Africa has very few mountain ranges. The Atlas Mountains, which stretch across Morocco and Algeria at the northern edge of the continent, are an extension of the high mountains of southern Europe. Ancient mountains also ring the southern tip of the continent at the Cape of Good Hope. These mountains have been worn down to low hills.

A fault system near the eastern edge of Africa creates a prominent valley known as the East African Rift Valley. Volcanic mountains—including Kilimanjaro, the highest peak in Africa at 19,341 feet (5,895 meters)—lie near the Rift Valley. Another set of mountains, the Ruwenzori range, also formed as a result of geological activity along the Rift Valley. This range of fault-block mountains lies along the border of Uganda and the Democratic Republic of Congo. Formed in only the past few million years, the Ruwenzori range has two peaks more than 16,000 feet (4,900 meters) high. These and the other range peaks taller than 14,500 feet (4,400 meters) are permanently covered with snow.

Australia

Australia has a single system of mountains and plateaus called the Great Dividing Range, which curves down the eastern coast of the continent. The highest range in this system is known as the Australian Alps; Mount Kosciusko is its highest peak, standing 7,310 feet (2,228 meters) tall.

The Australian Alps formed more than 300 million years ago and were uplifted by geologic forces as recently as 30 million years ago. They have since been worn down to massive but gentle slopes. Some peaks are high enough to remain snow covered for five to six months of the year.

Antarctica

Almost the entire continent of Antarctica is covered with an ice sheet more than 5,000 feet (1,525 meters) thick. Underneath this ice, however, are mountains, valleys, and plains, as on other continents. The highest mountain

range in Antarctica is the Sentinel Range. The Vinson Massif, at 16,066 feet (4,897 meters), is the highest peak in that range. These mountains are quite similar in age and composition to the Andes of South America.

▶ THE IMPORTANCE OF MOUNTAINS

Mountains have had a great effect on many things that influence civilization. Mountains affect the migration of peoples, the climate and vegetation, and the way people make a living.

Mountain Travel

To American pioneers traveling westward across the plains, the Rocky Mountains first looked like a smudge of gray smoke on the horizon. As they got closer, they could make out the looming barrier of the mountains. The only way to get past this barrier was to find the passes, where valleys from both sides met and the terrain remained lower and more level. Even today, with roads constructed, mountain travel is not easy. Steep slopes continue to challenge travelers, while hazards such as snow, ice, mud slides, and avalanches can make roads completely impassable.

Mountain ranges create complex climate regions and, subsequently, a variety of biomes. The Sierra Nevada, for instance, has, among other environments, lush forests with plentiful animal and plant life as well as barren, forbidding areas.

Climate

Mountain climate is another factor that makes traveling or living in the mountains very difficult. High altitude makes the weather colder than it would be at sea level at the same latitude. It might be summer and unbearably hot in the foothills of the mountains, but the passes might still be blocked with snow. High altitude also makes for frequent storms. As the air begins to rise over the mountains, it cools. Cool air cannot hold as much moisture as warm air can, so the moisture condenses and falls as rain or snow. Storms can be frequent, often daily, occurrences in the mountains. They can whip up quickly and without much warning, causing discomfort and hazards for mountain travelers and residents alike.

The rainfall pattern in the mountains causes the windward side of mountains to have a very different climate from the leeward side. Air rising up mountain slopes generally drops all its moisture on the windward side. Thus, the leeward side of the mountains generally gets little rain.

Resources

Mountains provide important resources. Because of the way mountains catch and cause precipitation, they play an important role in supplying water for large regions. Many rivers have their sources in mountains. The steep inclines of mountain rivers make them good sources for hydroelectric power.

The forests on the sides of mountains supply lumber for building and for making paper and other products. Many important minerals also are found in mountainous regions. The intense heat and pressures involved in the formation of mountains help concentrate elements and bring them close to the Earth's surface. That is why mountains often have mines of minerals such as silver and copper.

Human Activities

In some parts of the world, mountainous regions have been settled for many centuries. In these regions, people tend to rely mainly on herd animals for their livelihood. Farming may also provide food and cash crops.

But mountains have never been prime land for agriculture. Recently, however, mountainous regions in many parts of the world have experienced an economic boom. Visitors

Human activity, such as heavy logging, can strip a mountain of its natural resources, leaving the slopes scarred and vulnerable to erosion.

flock to the mountains for recreational activities such as camping, fishing, and skiing.

As better roads bring more people into remote mountain areas, the environment is likely to suffer. Erosion occurs when mountainous areas are heavily logged, because the trees are not there to keep soil from washing down the slopes. Mining may increase the occurrence of landslides and mudslides. And careless campers can cause forest fires.

Misuse of our mountain resources can do more than simply spoil a beautiful landscape. Mountains are islands of life. Damage to a particular mountain environment can cause species of plants or animals unique to that mountain to become extinct.

ELIZABETH KAPLAN
Series Coauthor, *Ask Isaac Asimov*
Reviewed by KEVIN BURKE
University of Houston

See also ALPS; ANDES; BIOMES; EARTH; EARTH, HISTORY OF; EARTHQUAKES; EVEREST, MOUNT; HIMALAYAS; MINERALS; ORES; ROCKS; ROCKY MOUNTAINS; VOLCANOES.

MOUNTBATTEN, LOUIS. See WORLD WAR II (Profiles: Allied Powers).

MOUSE. See RODENTS.

MOZAMBIQUE

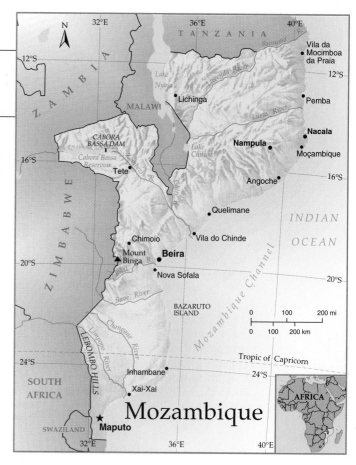

Mozambique

The nation of Mozambique is located in southeastern Africa, along the coast of the Indian Ocean. Parts of Mozambique—a large country nearly twice the size of California—were occupied for many centuries by the Portuguese. The country won its independence in 1975 after a long and bitter struggle.

▶ PEOPLE

Most of the people of Mozambique belong to indigenous (native) ethnic groups such as the Shangaan, the Chokwe, the Manyika, and several others. At one time there was a large Portuguese population, but most left the country after it declared independence.

Language. Portuguese is the official language, but most of the population speaks various Bantu languages, such as Makua, Tsonga, Tonga, and Yao.

Religion. Half the people practice traditional African religions. Of the remaining population, 30 percent is Christian and 20 percent is Muslim.

Education. Primary school is compulsory for children ages 6 to 13, although secondary school is not. None of this schooling is paid for by the state. Only institutions of higher education are financed by the state.

▶ LAND

Mozambique's landscape consists of low coastal plains that rise to inland plateaus. The climate is tropical to subtropical, with two distinct seasons—hot and rainy, and cool and dry. The country's rivers are significant hydroelectric sources, providing 75 percent of the country's energy. The Cabora Bassa Dam on the Zambezi River also supplies electricity to neighboring countries in southern Africa.

Merchants sell vegetables, spices, and other agricultural products at a marketplace in Maputo, the capital and largest city of Mozambique.

▶ ECONOMY

Prior to 1992, Mozambique's economy was badly hurt by civil war and poor governmental management. After economic reforms, the country had one of the world's highest growth rates in the late 1990's. But its gains were wiped out by devastating floods in 2000 that killed thousands of people and left another million homeless. The economy rebounded significantly in 2001.

Mozambique's economy is based primarily on agriculture, which employs over 80 percent of the people. The chief food crops are cassava (a starchy root), corn, and rice. Cash crops (crops grown for export) include cotton, cashew nuts, sugarcane, and tea. The processing of these and other crops is the main form of industry. Prawns, a kind of shellfish, are the country's most important export. Although the land holds valuable mineral deposits, only coal is mined in any quantity.

▶ MAJOR CITIES

Maputo (formerly Lourenço Marques) is the capital and largest city. Founded in 1544, today it has a population of about 1 million and is the chief port and the center of the railroad system. Beaches, hotels, restaurants, and yacht clubs make the city a popular tourist attraction. **Matolo**, a suburb of Maputo, is Mozambique's second largest city. It has a population of about 440,000 and is a major port for the export of coal. **Beira**, with a population of about 413,000, is the third largest city. Like Maputo, its beachfronts attract many tourists.

▶ HISTORY AND GOVERNMENT

Before the arrival of the Portuguese, the area of Mozambique was occupied by the Karanga, Tonga, Zimba, and other cultural groups. Karanga chiefs presided over strong dynasties. Among the Tonga, clusters of small villages were ruled by chiefs who held little power. Chiefs also ruled the Zimba.

The arrival of the Portuguese explorer Vasco da Gama in 1498 marked the first European contact with the region. In 1505, a settlement was founded at present-day Nova Sofala, where the Portuguese began trading gold. After gaining control of the coast, the Portuguese moved inland. From the 1600's to the mid-1800's, the slave trade was the colony's chief source of income.

FACTS and figures

REPUBLIC OF MOZAMBIQUE (República de Moçambique) is the official name of the country.

LOCATION: Southeastern Africa.

AREA: 309,496 sq mi (801,590 km²).

POPULATION: 19,400,000 (estimate).

CAPITAL AND LARGEST CITY: Maputo.

MAJOR LANGUAGES: Portuguese (official), various African languages.

MAJOR RELIGIOUS GROUPS: Traditional African, Christian, Muslim.

GOVERNMENT: Republic. **Head of state**—president. **Head of government**—prime minister. **Legislature**—Assembly of the Republic.

CHIEF PRODUCTS: Agricultural—cotton, cashew nuts, sugarcane, tea, cassava, corn, rice, fruits, livestock. **Manufactured**—processed foods, chemicals, textiles, cement, glass. **Mineral**—petroleum products, asbestos.

MONETARY UNIT: Metical (1 metical = 100 centavos).

By the 1950's, Mozambique's people wanted to govern themselves. In 1964 the Mozambique Liberation Front (FRELIMO) was formed and began a guerrilla war that lasted ten years. In 1974 Portugal acknowledged Mozambique's right to independence, which was officially proclaimed in 1975.

Recent History. Samora Machel, a leader in the independence struggle, became the country's first president. After his death in 1986, he was succeeded as president and head of FRELIMO by Joaquím Alberto Chissano. A long civil war, which pitted FRELIMO against the Mozambique National Resistance (RENAMO), ended in a cease-fire in 1992.

A new constitution established in 1990 provided for a president, elected to a 5-year term, as head of state and a prime minister, appointed by the president, as head of government. Members of the legislature, the Assembly of the Republic, are elected to 5-year terms. Chissano and FRELIMO were reelected in 1994 and again in 1999. Chissano's protegé, Armando Guebuza, was elected president in 2004.

ROBERT O. COLLINS
University of California, Santa Barbara
Reviewed by CASSANDRA R. VENEY
Illinois State University

MOZART, WOLFGANG AMADEUS (1756–1791)

Wolfgang Amadeus Mozart was born on January 27, 1756, in Salzburg, Austria. His father, Leopold, a musician at the Archbishop's court there, was a well-known composer. By the age of 5 Wolfgang was writing little minuets and playing the harpsichord. His father taught him composition, counterpoint, and harmony. His sister, Maria Anna, was an excellent musician too. In 1762 Leopold decided to take his two child prodigies on tour. The children played at the Imperial Court in Vienna. The Emperor was delighted and called Wolfgang "a little magician."

A year later the Mozart family toured Germany, France, and England. Everybody admired Wolfgang. In London, at the age of 8, he wrote his first symphony. Four years later, in Vienna, he composed his first two operas. In 1769 the Archbishop of Salzburg made Wolfgang concertmaster at his court.

In the same year father and son took the first of three trips to Italy, where Wolfgang composed several operas. In Italy the boy studied opera in the country of its origin. He also wrote many symphonies, serenades, sonatas, concertos, and much church music and chamber music.

Wolfgang's salary at the Archbishop's court in Salzburg was rather small. In 1773 his father took him to Vienna to find him a more suitable position but was not successful. In Vienna they heard the latest symphonies and quartets of Joseph Haydn, whose music deeply influenced Wolfgang.

Wolfgang was not happy in Salzburg. In 1777 he took his mother and set off again for Germany and France to seek his fortune. He found no job, and to complete his misery, his mother died in Paris. So once more he returned to his position in Salzburg. In 1781 he quarreled with the Archbishop and was dismissed from his service. Mozart then decided to settle in Vienna.

▶MOZART'S VIENNA YEARS

In 1782 Mozart married Constanze Weber, whom he loved very much. Although he was plagued by troubles, including the deaths of four of his children and his wife's ill health, his greatest works were written during his years in Vienna. There he composed the operas *The Abduction from the Seraglio* (1782), *The Marriage of Figaro* (1786), and *Così fan tutte* (1790). There, too, he wrote his famous last three symphonies, his finest piano concertos, and many other masterpieces. He became a friend of Haydn's and dedicated six string quartets to him. The Viennese flocked to Mozart's concerts to hear him play his concertos. He made several trips to Prague, where his opera *Don Giovanni* (1787) had its premiere performance.

About 1788 Mozart began falling seriously into debt. People found his latest music difficult and stayed away from his concerts. Yet during this period he composed his last three symphonies—E flat, G minor, and the *Jupiter* in C—in less than seven weeks.

In the summer of 1791 Mozart began suffering from fever and severe headaches. However, he completed his opera *The Magic Flute*, which was first performed in September 1791. His last work, the *Requiem* (mass for the dead), he left unfinished. On December 4 Mozart fell into a coma; he died the following day at the age of 35. The cause of his death is uncertain. Because he was so poor, Mozart's coffin was dumped into an unmarked pauper's grave. To this day no one knows where this great and unique composer lies buried.

H. C. ROBBINS LANDON
Coeditor, *The Mozart Companion*

The Mozarts: Leopold playing the violin, Wolfgang at the keyboard, and Maria singing.

MUIR, JOHN (1838–1914)

Few Americans are better known for their conservation efforts than John Muir. Naturalist, explorer, and writer, Muir rallied public support for national conservation laws at a time when few people saw the importance of protecting wilderness areas.

John Muir was born in Dunbar, Scotland, on June 21, 1838. His family went to the United States when he was 10 years old, starting a farm in Kingston, Wisconsin. Muir studied at the University of Wisconsin for several years but never received a degree. He worked at various odd jobs until he was in an industrial accident and was temporarily blinded. After he recovered, Muir made a walking trip that lasted 2½ years, recording his observations of plants and animals along the way.

In 1868, Muir went to San Francisco and then east into the California wilderness. He saw the grandeur of the Sierra Nevada and the beauty of Yosemite Valley. He stayed in Yosemite for six years, studying the forests and rock formations and developing a theory on how glaciers shaped the region. His vivid writings about the area helped the U.S. Congress decide to establish the Yosemite wilderness area as a national park in 1890.

In 1879, Muir made the first of several trips to Alaska. After returning to California, he married and settled down for several years to manage a fruit farm. But the urge to travel and explore never left Muir. He continued his journeys, roaming through Europe, South America, Africa, and Australia.

Muir also had a strong urge to write, keeping more than sixty volumes of journals during his lifetime. His magazine articles and books, including *The Mountains of California* (1894) and *The Yosemite* (1912), describe the beauty of the landscape. In 1892 he founded the Sierra Club, a conservation organization dedicated to protecting wilderness areas.

Muir died in Los Angeles on December 24, 1914. Muir Woods National Monument in California and Muir Glacier in Alaska are named in his honor.

BARBARA WIESE
Nature Writer

See also NATURE, STUDY OF; YOSEMITE NATIONAL PARK.

MUKDEN. See SHENYANG.

MULRONEY, MARTIN BRIAN (1939–)

Brian Mulroney, a leader of Canada's Progressive Conservative Party (1983–93), served as Canada's 18th prime minister from 1984 to 1993.

He was born on March 20, 1939, in Baie Comeau, Quebec, the third of six children in a middle-class, English-speaking family. He received a B.A. degree from St. Francis Xavier University in Nova Scotia and a law degree from Laval University in Quebec.

A successful businessman, Mulroney became president of the Iron Ore Company of Canada. He lost his first bid for the party leadership in 1976, but he ran again in 1983 and was elected party leader. He won his seat in Parliament in a by-election in Nova Scotia.

Two of Mulroney's goals as prime minister were to increase harmony between the federal and provincial governments and to lower trade barriers. In 1987 he signed a free-trade pact with the United States. Opposition from the Liberals led Mulroney to call an election in 1988, which his party won handily.

In 1987, Mulroney proposed a constitutional amendment, known as the Meech Lake Accord, to recognize French-speaking Quebec as a "distinct society" within the Canadian federation. It was signed by all ten provincial premiers but failed to win approval in 1990. Mulroney then sponsored another reform plan, by which Quebecers would be awarded "special status." This plan, too, was rejected in a 1992 national referendum.

Economic recession, unemployment, and uneven support for the proposed North American Free Trade Agreement (NAFTA) further eroded Mulroney's popularity. When he resigned in 1993, he had the lowest approval rating of any prime minister in the century. He was succeeded in office by Kim Campbell.

Reviewed by DESMOND MORTON
University of Toronto

MULTIPLE SCLEROSIS. See DISEASES (Descriptions of Some Diseases).

MULTIPLICATION. See ARITHMETIC.

The unwrapped mummy of King Ramses II shows the results of the sophisticated mummification techniques used by ancient Egyptians.

MUMMIES

A mummy is the body of a human or animal that has been preserved after death. What makes a mummy different from a skeleton or a fossil is that its soft tissue—such as skin, muscle, and internal organs—has also been preserved.

When conditions are just right, a body can be preserved naturally—for example, by rapid drying after burial in the desert or by being frozen in a glacier. In other cases, people have deliberately created mummies by treating, or embalming, bodies in order to preserve them.

The word "mummy" comes from the Persian word *mumiai*, meaning "tar." When the first European travelers visited Egypt and saw the preserved corpses of the ancient Egyptians, they mistook the dark resins coating the bodies for tar.

▶ EGYPTIAN MUMMIES

Egyptian mummies are the most famous examples of human-made mummies. The ancient Egyptians used a sophisticated process to preserve the bodies of their dead, particularly their royalty, because they believed in resurrection—that the body as well as the spirit would rise again in the afterlife.

The most important step in Egyptian mummification was dehydration—the removal of all moisture from the body. Without moisture, bacteria cannot thrive in the tissue and cause

it to decay. Dehydration required two steps. First the internal organs were removed from the body. A long hooked wire was used to extract the brain through the nostrils, and the other internal organs were then removed through a small incision in the abdomen. The only organ not removed was the heart. The ancient Egyptians believed the heart was the source of thought and would be needed immediately in the afterlife.

Next the body was covered for 35 days with a saltlike substance called natron, which drew any remaining moisture from the body. After dehydration, the body was coated with resin and wrapped tightly in long strips of linen. The internal organs were also dehydrated and placed in four containers called canopic jars. The body was then placed in a coffin. For the body of a pharaoh, several magnificently decorated coffins were used, placed one inside the other.

▶ OTHER MUMMIES

Although the mummies of ancient Egypt are the best known, the Egyptians were not the first people to deliberately preserve their dead. The oldest mummies yet discovered

Did you know that...

the ancient Egyptians also mummified animals? Pets were mummified and placed in their owners' tombs so they could accompany them to the next world. Other animals were raised to be sacrificed and mummified as offerings to the gods.

Among the animals sacrificed were cats, ibises, and falcons, and they each had their own cemeteries. The most famous cat cemetery was at Bubastis, the city of the cat goddess Bastet. Millions of ibis and falcon mummies were buried in miles of underground tunnels beneath the ancient city of Memphis.

were made by the Chinchorro of Chile, who practiced mummification about 2,000 years earlier than the ancient Egyptians. The Chinchorro removed all the soft tissue from the body; packed mud, sticks, and straw around the bones; and then put the skin back on the body. The body was then covered with an ash paste and finally painted with manganese, which provided a hard, black coating when dried.

Only occasionally did the ancient Chinese mummify their dead. A famous example is the noblewoman who was mummified more than 2,000 years ago by being immersed in a solution of mercury, which kills bacteria. When scientists discovered her tomb in 1972, her limbs were still flexible, and her stomach contained perfectly preserved melon seeds from her last meal.

▶ **NATURAL MUMMIES**

Various environmental factors can contribute to the natural mummification of a body. Sometimes extreme cold will preserve a body, as was the case with a Stone Age man discovered in 1991 high in the Alps along the border between Austria and Italy. Soon after his death, about 3300 B.C., the Iceman, as he came to be known, was covered with snow and preserved in ice. Often when a body freezes, the tissues' moisture leaves in the form of a gas, a process called sublimation. Because of this process, the Iceman's mummy weighed only about 28 pounds (13 kilograms) when it was discovered.

Cold temperature was also responsible for the many Inca mummies discovered high in the Andes mountains of South America, where the Inca regularly made human sacrifices to their gods. In 1999, thousands of Inca mummies were found in a Peruvian cemetery dating back to the late 1400's. The area's dry

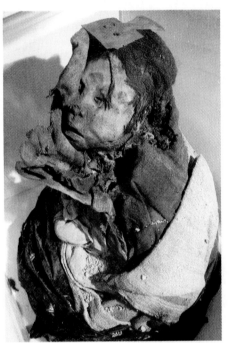

Bodies can be naturally mummified under the right environmental conditions. Cold mountain temperatures preserved this Inca child after she was sacrificed in the 1500's.

environment even preserved the colorful feathered headdresses adorning some of the bodies.

Naturally preserved bodies have also been found in the bogs of Denmark and other northern European countries. The highly acidic and oxygen-poor environment of the bog prevented decay, leaving skin and even clothing intact. When these bodies were discovered, they were so well preserved that at first they were thought to be recent murder victims (many had been deliberately killed, possibly as sacrifices). However, most of the bodies actually date back to between 500 B.C. and A.D. 1.

▶ **STUDYING MUMMIES**

The study of mummies has provided scientists with important information about ancient cultures. Many tools of modern medicine, such as X rays, computed tomography (CT) scans, and DNA analysis, have been used to examine mummies. Analysis of Egyptian mummies has revealed that most were infected with parasites and that those who had lived near swamps suffered from malaria and were anemic because of it. Evidence of tooth problems pointed to an unexpected source: Egyptians used stone to grind wheat into flour, and bits of sand and grit were baked into their bread. Over years of eating the gritty bread, their teeth were worn down, leading to infection.

X rays of the Iceman from the Alps revealed that he had arthritis in several joints. Tattoos on the skin covering those joints may have been an attempt to relieve the pain, perhaps an early form of acupuncture.

BOB BRIER
Author, *Encyclopedia of Mummies*

MUMPS. See DISEASES (Descriptions of Some Diseases).

Municipal, or local, governments provide essential services to the residents of their communities. Local tax dollars and other fees are collected to pay the operating costs and salaries of municipal employees, which may include firefighters (*left*), police officers (*below left*), and emergency medical teams (*bottom left*).

MUNICIPAL GOVERNMENT

A municipality is a specific area that usually has authority over its own government. Municipal government, therefore, refers to government in municipalities, such as cities, towns, and counties. It is sometimes called local government because it serves a limited range of people.

Units of local government in the United States include counties, towns, villages, cities, school districts, and special districts. Some units are more characteristic of certain regions of the United States—for example, towns in New England and counties in the South. The various states have different rules under which a unit of local government may be established.

Citizens of all ages support their local government through the payment of various taxes and fees. In return, local government provides road maintenance, schools, sewers, water, fire and police protection, and other services as required by its citizens.

▶THE ORIGINS OF AMERICAN MUNICIPAL GOVERNMENT

American local government received its heritage from English political institutions. Before the Revolutionary War, charters were given to the American colonies by the king of England. The charter is the basic law of a local government, defining its powers, duties, and organization. As small settlements grew into flourishing towns and cities, they were granted their own charters.

A central system of justice, based on the English court system, was established. Each territory was given a county seat where circuit court was held. The court sessions were held in taverns, the central meeting place for the community, until a courthouse could be constructed. In order to pay the costs of the court system, including the courthouses and jails, representatives of the towns were elected to set tax rates. They formed a legislative body, which was called the county board of supervisors or commissioners.

After the Revolutionary War, the power to grant charters was placed in the state legislatures. In most states, charters are granted to municipal corporations and, in some cases, to counties and townships. When a city has its own charter (and therefore its own separate government), it is **incorporated**. Some states have "home rule" laws, which grant local governments some freedom to draft their own charters and manage their own affairs.

▶ TYPES OF MODERN LOCAL GOVERNMENT

There are six basic types of municipal government in the United States. Counties, towns, villages, and cities are composed of the executive (or chief officer's) branch, the legislative (lawmaking) body, and the judicial (court-related) branch. School districts and special districts are formed to provide specific services.

Counties

A county acts as an arm of the state government. It carries out programs such as social services for the poor and health and mental-health programs. It also provides services and facilities that are too costly for a town government, such as airports, jails, and major road repair.

The county also supervises elections through its board of elections; maintains law enforcement through the sheriff's department; prosecutes crimes through the district attorney; and selects juries and presides over trials in the county court. The county may also provide parks and playgrounds, libraries, and community colleges.

The chief officer of the county may be a county executive, county manager, or the traditional board of supervisors or commission-

ers. The county treasurer or finance director assists in preparing the budget. County services benefit the people of all the towns and cities within the county.

Towns

Towns developed as colonial taxing units to meet expenses for items such as roads, public education, relief of the poor, and to share the county court costs. The town or township may still provide these services in addition to fire and police protection, streetlights, public libraries, recreational facilities, hospitals and emergency medical services, water supply, trash disposal, tax assessments (estimates of property value), and building regulations.

All municipal governments have zoning boards, or planning committees, made up of individuals who determine how the land in their districts will be used. Some areas are zoned to permit residential housing only. Other zones may permit the operation of commercial businesses or heavy industry.

The chief officer may be the town supervisor, town manager, town or township board, or, in the case of the New England states, the town meeting. Town meetings are an example of direct democracy in action. In a direct democracy, the people themselves decide on questions by voting. When the town meeting is not in session, the governing body is the board of selectmen, usually consisting of three to nine members. The power to levy taxes rests with the town meeting, not with the board of selectmen. In many New England

Most small towns across the United States have a Town Hall, which handle the administrative functions of the municipal government. Many of these offices have a sign similar to this one displayed outside their building. The signs describe the types of offices and services provided.

towns, a town manager is hired for more efficient local government.

The chief officer plans the budget and supervises the various departments. The town justice or justice of the peace presides over the town court for traffic violations and other misdemeanors (lesser crimes).

Villages

Although it may be located within the boundaries of a town, a village has its own government, with an elected mayor and a board of trustees. Villages developed when clusters of people within the sprawling towns began to need specific services of their own. A village may also have its own court and village justice system. Villages and towns often contract with each other to share services and facilities.

Cities

Cities are municipalities chartered by the state. Cities provide large-scale services such as police and fire protection, streetlighting, health care and hospitals, education, libraries, recreational facilities, traffic control, refuse disposal, water supply, and mass transportation systems.

City governments often face the additional problem of large populations crowded into limited space in deteriorating older buildings. Urban-renewal boards help to halt housing decay and to obtain federal government funds for new housing construction.

Forms of City Government. There are four major forms of city government in the United States. One is the **strong mayor-council** form, in which the elected mayor has full power to appoint or remove city officials, administer the departments, prepare the budget, and veto the city council's ordinances or laws. In the **weak mayor-council** form, the mayor is a ceremonial figure, but the council has strong administrative powers. In the **council-manager** form, the city council hires a professionally trained executive or manager to administer the budget and departments. A **commission** is composed of an elected board whose members administer the various departments and also act as the legislative body or council.

Canadian cities, like cities in the United States, are usually headed by an elected mayor and council. Governmental responsibilities are spread among a series of boards and commissions. The government of Toronto, Canada's largest city, is organized like the Canadian federal government, but on a smaller scale.

Cities may have several courts—police court for crimes, city court for civil disputes, and traffic court

YEARLY BUDGET OF A TYPICAL NEW ENGLAND TOWN

INCOME

- LOCAL REVENUES (from fees, licenses, permits) 3%
- STATE REVENUES (money from the state for social services and other programs) 23%
- TAXES 74%

EXPENSES

- GENERAL GOVERNMENT 7%
- CAPITAL EXPENDITURES 9%
- SERVICES (highway, public health and safety, culture, recreation) 12%
- EDUCATION 72%

The town represented in this chart receives most of its income from property (and other) taxes. Most of the money is spent on education, which includes buying textbooks and paying teachers. Some money goes for general government expenses, such as the salaries of town officials. Examples of capital expenditures are a new police car or a computer for the town clerk.

for traffic violations. Cities may also have their own jails.

New York City, the largest city in the United States, has a unique regional government, consisting of five boroughs (Manhattan, the Bronx, Queens, Brooklyn, and Staten Island), with five elected district attorneys.

The chief executive of the city of New York is an elected mayor who administers the budget and supervises the many vast departments. These include social services to the poor, health and mental-health facilities, and city colleges.

New York City has a city council headed by the council president; a city comptroller (treasurer); and five borough presidents. The city funds the majority of its services through income taxes, corporation taxes, property taxes, sales taxes, and large amounts of state and federal aid.

School Districts

The independent school district is found throughout most of the United States and in parts of Canada. It is organized and financed separately from other units of local government. These districts maintain schools from kindergarten through junior college, depending on the size of the population, the area, and the wealth of the district. A typical school district is governed by an elected board of education, which chooses a superintendent of schools.

Special Districts

Special districts are units that operate separately from the regular governmental machinery. They are established by state law to provide a single service, such as fire protection, water supply, or public housing. These districts may be called authorities, boards, or commissions.

▶**INTERGOVERNMENTAL RELATIONS**

Although local units of government are created by the state, they are independent of one another. The county does not control the city, and the school district has no power over the town. State laws have priority over all forms of local government within the state's boundaries, just as the laws of the federal government have priority over the state's. All these units may agree to share services and frequently do.

In recent years, contact between local governments and the federal government has been growing. Federal financial aid, which is given mainly to state governments, is now also given directly to local governments. State authority is gradually giving way to the demands of local units for the right to run their own affairs without too much interference from the state. As these developments take place, local, state, and federal governments learn to live with and co-operate with one another.

▶**CANADIAN MUNICIPALITIES**

Federal and provincial governments in Canada are modeled on those of England, but Canada's local government units, which are generally called municipalities, are run much like those of the United States. In some parts of Canada the population is so small that there is no local government at all. These areas are under direct provincial control.

▶**PROBLEMS OF MUNICIPAL GOVERNMENT**

In the United States and most of the major Western nations, many people choose to live in or near cities. But as the populations of these cities grow, municipal and local governments need more money with which to operate and provide services.

In many Western countries, even democratic representation in national parliaments and legislatures has become a problem. Populations have shifted, and areas that have many representatives in national government now have small populations. On the other hand, some areas with large populations now have relatively small representation.

It is especially important that these and other problems be solved, for municipal government is the form of government that affects the everyday lives of most people.

EUGENE J. BOCKMAN
Commissioner, Department of Records and
Information Services, City of New York
Reviewed by MARILYN E. ROTHSTEIN
Author, *What Every Citizen Should Know:
A Guide to Local Government*

MURRAY, PHILIP. See LABOR MOVEMENT (Profiles).

MURROW, EDWARD R. See JOURNALISM (Profiles); NORTH CAROLINA (Famous People).

MUSCAT AND OMAN. See OMAN.

MUSCLES. See BODY, HUMAN; MUSCULAR SYSTEM.

MUSCULAR DYSTROPHY. See DISEASES (Descriptions of Some Diseases).

MUSCULAR SYSTEM

Every moment of your life, even when you are asleep, some of the muscles of your body are working. As you read this book, tiny muscles move your eyeballs back and forth and help to give you a clear view of the words. Muscles in your arm and hand work when you turn a page. Even if you try to sit very still, muscles in your back are working to keep you from slumping over. At the same time, other kinds of muscles in your inner organs are helping you to breathe and to digest your most recent meal.

More than 650 muscles make up the muscular system of the human body. These tough, elastic tissues, which account for nearly half the weight of the whole adult body, are responsible for all body movements. Movements such as walking, running, or jumping are easily observed. However, muscles are also responsible for other movements such as those that open and close the pupil of the eye, force food through the intestines, and keep blood flowing through the body.

▶ KINDS OF MUSCLES

There are three main types of muscles: skeletal, cardiac, and smooth. Each has its own characteristic appearance and function. But no matter what the task, each kind of muscle performs its work in the same manner—by contracting and relaxing.

Skeletal Muscles

Skeletal muscles are the ones whose work can be seen and felt when you move. Their contractions move arms, legs, and other body parts. Sometimes they are called **voluntary** muscles because you can control their work by thinking of what you want to do.

The smallest structural unit of a skeletal muscle, or any muscle, is the **muscle cell**. The muscle cell is also called a **muscle fiber** because it is long and threadlike. Groups of skeletal muscle fibers are wrapped in a sheath of connective tissue. These bundles in turn are

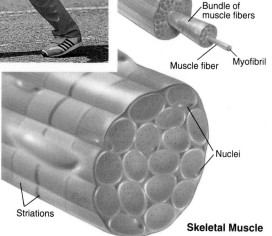

Skeletal muscles cover the body's frame, holding the bones of the skeleton together, creating the body's shape, and coordinating its every motion. Skeletal, or striated, muscle is formed from many fibers, or cells, bundled together and enclosed in connective tissue. Each fiber has many nuclei — centers that control growth processes — as well as light and dark bands called striations.

Skeletal muscle

Bundle of muscle fibers

Muscle fiber   Myofibril

Nuclei

Striations

Skeletal Muscle

grouped into larger bundles and wrapped in a connective tissue sheath, to form the muscle. Tough ropes of connective tissue called **tendons** or flat sheets called **aponeuroses** tie the ends of skeletal muscles firmly to the bones that they move.

Because skeletal muscles can pull but cannot push, they usually work in pairs to produce movement. As one muscle contracts, becoming short and thick, it pulls on the tendons that are attached to the bone, and the bone moves. At the same time, the partner muscle relaxes, becoming long and thin, allowing the bone to move freely. A muscle pair works in the opposite manner to perform the opposite task. For example, when the biceps muscle on the inner part of the upper arm contracts, the triceps muscle on the other side of the upper arm relaxes. The action of contracting and relaxing pulls the lower part of the arm up. When the triceps muscle contracts, the biceps muscle relaxes. This time the con-

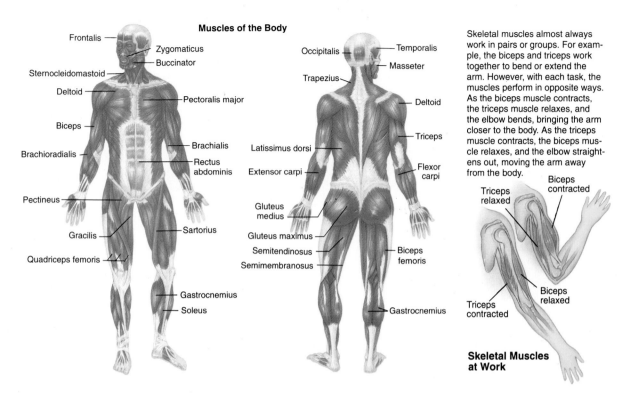

Muscles of the Body

Frontalis
Zygomaticus
Buccinator
Sternocleidomastoid
Deltoid
Biceps
Brachioradialis
Pectoralis major
Brachialis
Rectus abdominis
Pectineus
Gracilis
Sartorius
Quadriceps femoris
Gastrocnemius
Soleus

Occipitalis
Temporalis
Masseter
Trapezius
Deltoid
Triceps
Latissimus dorsi
Extensor carpi
Flexor carpi
Gluteus medius
Gluteus maximus
Semitendinosus
Semimembranosus
Biceps femoris
Gastrocnemius

Skeletal muscles almost always work in pairs or groups. For example, the biceps and triceps work together to bend or extend the arm. However, with each task, the muscles perform in opposite ways. As the biceps muscle contracts, the triceps muscle relaxes, and the elbow bends, bringing the arm closer to the body. As the triceps muscle contracts, the biceps muscle relaxes, and the elbow straightens out, moving the arm away from the body.

Triceps relaxed
Biceps contracted
Biceps relaxed
Triceps contracted

Skeletal Muscles at Work

tracting and relaxing pulls the lower part of the arm down and the arm straightens out.

Cardiac Muscle

Cardiac muscle forms the walls of the heart —the powerful pump that sends blood flowing through blood vessels to all parts of the body. The heartbeat is actually the contraction of the cardiac muscle, and it goes on continually, about once a second, all through your life. This kind of muscle works without your thinking about it. Because you cannot control its work consciously, the cardiac muscle is also known as an **involuntary** muscle.

Cardiac muscle cells are not grouped into bundles. Instead, the muscle fibers are connected to each other and form thin layers that are wrapped in connective tissue. The cardiac muscle layers are arranged in a spiral that winds around the heart. The individual muscle cells are linked together so that all cells in each chamber of the heart are joined into a network of cells, called a **syncytium**, that all contract and relax at the same time.

Smooth Muscles

Smooth muscles are found in the walls of the blood vessels, the stomach and other digestive organs, the urinary tract, and various other body organs. Smooth muscles can work along steadily without getting tired. Like the cardiac muscle, smooth muscles work without your thinking or even knowing about them.

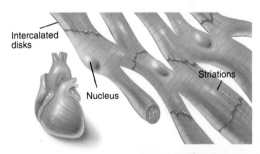

Intercalated disks
Nucleus
Striations

Cardiac Muscle

Thin layers of cardiac muscle form the heart, making this fist-sized organ strong enough to beat more than 2.5 billion times in a 75-year lifetime. Cardiac muscle shares characteristics with both skeletal and smooth muscle. It is striated like skeletal muscle, and like smooth muscle, it acts without our conscious control and has only one nucleus in each of its fibers.

WONDER QUESTION

What is the levator labii superioris alaeque nasi?

In addition to being the muscle with the longest name, the levator labii superioris alaeque nasi is the face muscle that curls the upper lip. When translated, its Latin name means "elevator of the upper lip and the side of the nose." The muscle runs down the sides of the nose and branches to the nostril and upper lip. Elvis Presley (*right*) was well known for using this muscle for dramatic effect during his singing and acting performances.

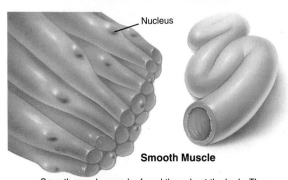

Smooth Muscle

Smooth muscles can be found throughout the body. The smooth-appearing fibers, each with a single nucleus, are grouped in a variety of forms, such as sheets or bundles. The wide range of tasks performed by smooth muscles include changing the diameter of the pupil to monitor the amount of light that enters, propelling food through the intestines, and even helping push a baby from a woman's uterus.

Smooth muscle cells may be grouped into cords, bundles, or sheets. In tubular organs such as the intestines, smooth muscle fibers called **circular fibers** run around the central opening and others called **longitudinal fibers** run along the length of the tube. Contractions of the circular fibers make the tube get narrower and longer. Circular fibers around the opening of an organ form a muscle called a **sphincter**, which can pinch the opening shut.

There is a sphincter at the bottom of the stomach, for example, which opens to squirt partly digested food into the small intestine. Contractions of longitudinal fibers make a tubular organ get shorter and thicker. In the intestines the circular and longitudinal smooth muscles take turns contracting, to mix the food and send it moving along.

▶ **HOW A MUSCLE WORKS**

The contractions of some muscle tissue may start with a message carried by a nerve cell. Other muscle tissue may be stimulated to contract by chemical messengers called **hormones** and by chemical changes in the tissues that are around them. Still other muscle tissue may be set off by either nerve messages or chemical messengers.

Whatever the stimulation, the contraction of muscle cells is an "all-or-nothing" process. If the message to contract is strong enough, the muscle fiber contracts completely. But if the message is not strong enough, a muscle does not contract at all. The strength of contraction of the whole muscle and how long it stays contracted depend on how many of its muscle fibers are working at once. Muscles can be used with widely different amounts of force because they are made up of many muscle cells. With the same muscles a person can deliver a karate chop that splits a board or gently pick up an egg without cracking its shell.

Within muscle cells, threadlike filaments of proteins called **actin** and **myosin** can be found. These proteins are what make the cells contract. When a muscle cell contracts, actin filaments slide into the spaces between the thicker myosin filaments, causing the muscle to shorten. When the muscle cell relaxes, the two kinds of filaments slide apart, causing the muscle to lengthen. The ebb and flow of calcium ions within the muscle fiber aids the process of contraction. When calcium ions are set free deep inside the muscle cell, their action helps the actin and myosin slide together. When the calcium ions are removed and stored away, the contraction stops until a new message to contract comes along.

The work of muscle contraction is powered by the energy from food materials, which is stored in a chemical called **ATP** (*a*denosine *tri*phosphate). The muscles have a supply of this quick energy source. They also have a back-up supply of chemical energy stored in a kind of starch called **glycogen**. The stored energy sources are good for quick surges of power that last only a few seconds. But for longer work, muscles need new sources of fuel that require oxygen to help release their stored energy. These supplies are delivered by the blood, which also carries away the muscle cells' waste products.

Muscles can change in size and shape, depending on how and how much they are used. Exercise causes the individual muscle fibers to gradually **hypertrophy**, or grow larger and stronger, increasing the size and strength of the whole muscle. But when muscles are not used—when a person is sick in bed for a long time, for example—muscle fibers begin to **atrophy**, or waste away, becoming small and weak.

▶**DISORDERS OF THE MUSCULAR SYSTEM**

Pain, cold, or overexercise can provoke a muscle **spasm**, which is a sudden, involuntary, painful muscle contraction. When a muscle spasm lasts for a long time, it is called a **cramp**. Spasms can occur either in skeletal muscles or in smooth muscles. In a tubular organ such as the intestines, a smooth-muscle spasm may temporarily close off the tube or its opening.

Overuse of skeletal muscles may cause tiny tears in some of the muscle fibers. That is why you may feel sore the day after exercising hard. The body can repair this damage, but a severe **muscle strain** may take weeks or even months to heal fully. Warm-up exercises before heavy exertion can help to prevent sports injuries.

A variety of diseases can affect the muscles and cause them to atrophy. Some muscle diseases attack the nervous system and prevent messages from getting to the muscles. Without instructions from the nervous system, muscles are **paralyzed**, or unable to move. In a disease called **myasthenia gravis**, muscle weakness and paralysis occur because signals from the nerves cannot be transmitted to the muscles.

In other muscle diseases, the muscle itself does not work properly. **Muscular dystrophy** is a hereditary disease in which an individual gradually loses the use of skeletal muscles. The muscles grow weaker but become larger because as the muscle fibers atrophy, they are replaced by fat deposits.

ALVIN SILVERSTEIN
VIRGINIA SILVERSTEIN
Coauthors, *The Muscular System*

See also BODY, HUMAN; SKELETAL SYSTEM.

How a Muscle Works

Relaxation

Actin filament

Myosin filament

Myofibril

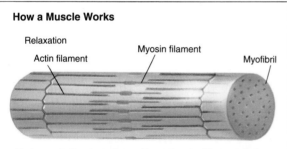

Each muscle fiber is made up of long strands of tissue called myofibrils. Within a myofibril are parallel filaments of two proteins — actin and myosin. It is the action of these proteins, powered by ATP, that produces muscle contraction.

Contraction

The signal to contract travels from the brain and spinal cord along nerve fibers to the body's muscles. During contraction, the thick myosin filaments and the thinner actin filaments slide past each other. The muscle shortens, or contracts, as the sliding movements are repeated throughout the muscle's myofibrils.

Museums are popular destinations for field trips. Teachers or tour guides use the museums' exhibits to teach students about many different branches of knowledge.

MUSEUMS

Museums are places where collections of objects are preserved, studied, and displayed. The objects may be anything found in nature or made by people. There are museums devoted to just about every conceivable branch of knowledge, such as art, science, history, industry, and technology.

Museum exhibits teach us about our world—the materials Earth is made of, the trees and plants that cover it, and the animals that have lived on it since its beginning. Exhibits also teach us about the activities of people—their history and development and their accomplishments in arts, crafts, science, and technology. We can see wonderful examples of what people have been able to create out of clay, stone, wood, and metal or with a paintbrush and paints.

Museums also conduct educational programs, such as tours, lectures, films, music recitals, hands-on workshops, and field trips. They also publish pamphlets, guides, and catalogs. All of these are designed to help visitors gain a better understanding of the collections. Many museums also conduct research programs, the results of which are published so that many people can benefit from them.

Museums acquire their collections in many ways. They may buy items from dealers, private collectors, or at auction sales, and they also accept gifts and bequests (items donated to museums according to someone's will). Large museums accept only objects or collections that meet their standards. Museums also arrange loan exhibitions of important objects from dealers, private owners, and other museums. Often museums collect more objects than they have room to display. Objects not on display are kept in storage or in study collections that can be used by students, researchers, and scholars. Some museums, such as children's museums and halls of fame, do not collect. They produce exhibitions without artifacts, specimens, or works of art.

Museums are supported in various ways. Most museums in the United States are operated as charitable (not-for-profit) organizations, seeking financial support from individual donors, foundations and corporations, and grants by local, state, and federal government. Additional money is raised through private gifts, membership dues, and admission fees. Outside the United States, many museums are supported mostly or totally by national, regional, or city governments.

▶ KINDS OF MUSEUMS

Most museums focus on science, history, or art. General museums may cover more than one of these subjects. Other museums specialize in only one subject, such as modern art or science in industry. Sometimes a museum features a single product, such as glass at the Corning Museum of Glass in Corning, New York, or the work of a single artist, such as that of Auguste Rodin at the Rodin museums in Paris, France, and Philadelphia, Pennsylvania.

Science Museums

Besides the general science museum, there are museums that specialize in a particular field of science. Among the most common are museums of natural history, museums of industry and technology, and planetariums.

Museums of Natural History. Natural history museums are concerned with all the objects found in nature and all living things, from plants to humans. Many natural history museums have anthropology departments that focus on the evolution and development of human beings and their environment. Some museums are devoted entirely to the field of anthropology. **Botanical gardens** and **arboretums** are museums of living plants, **zoos** are museums of living animals, and **aquariums** are museums of fish and other marine life.

Large natural history museums will often include displays of entire habitats, sometimes filling whole exhibition halls. Models of animals are arranged in settings exactly like the ones the animals inhabited in the wild. The American Museum of Natural History in New York City, founded in 1869, has many famous displays of habitats.

Nature centers are similar to natural history museums but also offer outdoor exhibits and trails to help visitors learn about the natural environment.

Museums of Industry and Technology. Museums of industry and technology are museums of applied science. They illustrate the ways in which science is put to practical use and made to work for us. They often feature hands-on or interactive exhibits that help visitors better understand scientific principles and concepts.

The Deutsches Museum in Munich, Germany, which opened in 1903, was the first museum of this kind. It exhibited the first diesel engine, the first dynamo (power generator), and early automobiles. For the first time, visitors to a museum were allowed to operate machines or push buttons that set machines in motion.

Planetariums. A planetarium is a museum of astronomy that houses a theater with a special projector that displays images of the stars and planets on the inner surface of a domed ceiling.

Dinosaur skeletons are a favorite attraction at museums of natural history. They are often displayed in settings that suggest the environment in which the animals may have lived.

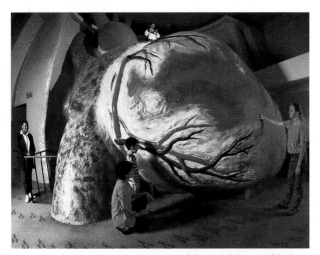

Some museums encourage visitors to interact with the exhibits. At Philadelphia's Franklin Institute, people can walk through a giant model of a human heart.

Planetariums were first developed during the 1800's in Munich, Germany. The Adler Planetarium and Astronomy Museum in Chicago, Illinois, was founded in 1930. It was the first of many planetariums to appear in the United States.

History Museums

A history museum may tell the story of a nation, a community, an event, or an industry. The homes of many famous individuals, such as George Washington's estate at Mount Vernon, Virginia, and William Shakespeare's home at Stratford-on-Avon, England, are now historic house museums.

Other museums are devoted to the history, arts, and contributions of particular cultures. Native Americans have created many museums to tell the story of their tribes and to foster a sense of pride in their heritage. Similar museums have been established for Japanese Americans and African Americans.

The first museum dedicated to peasant life, folk art, and folklore was established in Sweden in 1891. Located in Skansen, near Stockholm on the island of Djurgarden, it was the first outdoor folk art museum in the world. It is a collection of peasant cottages, barns, windmills, and other structures from all parts of Sweden that illustrate the life of the country's people throughout the centuries.

The Skansen museum led to interest in the reconstruction of whole villages that would show the life and customs of earlier times. Old Sturbridge Village in Massachusetts is a reconstructed New England village with authentic houses and shops. Another noted reconstruction project in the United States is Colonial Williamsburg. This capital of Virginia in the 1700's has been rebuilt to look as it did in colonial times. These kinds of museums often include costumed actors who help demonstrate how people of the particular time lived and worked. This is why these museums are sometimes called **living history museums**.

There are also history museums that commemorate a historic event, such as the Holocaust, D-Day, or the civil rights movement. Other history museums are housed in buildings in which historic events have taken place. For instance, the sixth floor of the book depository building in Dallas, Texas, from which point Lee Harvey Oswald shot and killed President Kennedy in 1963, is now a museum.

Living history museums reconstruct entire villages, using costumed staff to show how people lived and worked during a particular time period.

Art Museums

Art museums display paintings and sculptures from many periods. They may also have collections of furniture, ceramics, tapestries, medals, and other examples of decorative art. Some museums of art are called galleries, such as the National Gallery of Art in Washington, D.C. Other art museums are called institutes, such as the Art Institute of Chicago, Illinois.

Almost every country in the world has at least one art museum that is a source of national pride. In the Netherlands the outstanding museum is the Rijksmuseum Amsterdam. It contains a noted collection of paintings, sculpture, and historical objects. The Gold Museum of the Bank of the Republic in Bogotá, the capital of Colombia, has a collection of more than 36,000 objects made of gold, many representing the gods, myths, and customs of native Indian cultures. The Picasso Museum in Barcelona, Spain, contains the largest collection of Picasso's work in the world.

The greatest collections of art from the Renaissance (1300–1600) are found in Florence, Italy. The Uffizi Gallery is noted for its fine collection of paintings showing the development of Italian art from the 1300's to the 1700's. The Pitti Gallery is housed in the palace of the Pitti family, a leading Florentine family from the 1400's. It contains important works by Raphael, Titian, and Rubens. The Vatican Museum in Rome is a complex of several museums. Perhaps the most famous part of the complex is the Sistine Chapel, in which Michelangelo painted his famous frescoes of scenes from the Bible.

The Louvre in Paris is the greatest art museum in France. The building dates back to 1190, when King Philip Augustus ordered that a fortress be built to house "his jewels, his dogs, and his prisoners of war." It later became a royal palace. After the French Revolution it was opened to the public as one of the first national museums.

The British Museum in London is especially rich in its collection of ancient sculpture. Most famous are the Elgin Marbles, which are sculptures from the Parthenon in Greece. The British Museum also owns the historic Rosetta Stone, a tablet on which the same text was written in three different languages and thus provided the key to deciphering ancient Egyptian hieroglyphic writing.

Russia is home to two of the world's most prominent art museums. In Moscow, parts of the Kremlin, the former palace of the czars, are now public museums. The State Hermitage Museum in St. Petersburg is one of the largest museums in the world. Its collection of Western art was begun by Czar Peter

The Solomon R. Guggenheim Museum in New York City was designed by Frank Lloyd Wright to showcase the museum's collection of abstract art.

the Great in 1703 and built upon by his successors. Today the Hermitage houses art from all over the world.

The first museum in the United States was established by the Charleston Library Society in Charleston, South Carolina, in 1773. The older art museums in the United States—the Corcoran Gallery of Art in Washington, D.C. (founded in 1869); the Metropolitan Museum of Art in New York City (1870); the Museum of Fine Arts in Boston, Massachusetts (1870); the Art Institute of Chicago (1879); and the M. H. de Young Memorial Museum in San Francisco, California (1895)—used the great museums of Europe as models for their buildings and collections.

CHILDREN'S MUSEUMS

Children's museums encourage young people to participate in a wide variety of activities that teach them about the world they live in. Some museum programs teach children to make their own models and crafts. Others have hands-on exhibits, allowing children to touch dinosaur bones, work levers, and experiment with weights and measures.

The world's first museum dedicated to children was the Brooklyn Children's Museum, founded in New York in 1899. The idea of having special museums or departments and exhibition space in museums set aside especially for young people caught on, and today museums for children can be found throughout the world. Visitors to Sweden's Xperiment Huset can make some of the largest soap bubbles in the world. At Great Britain's Eureka! The Museum for Children, visitors to the Global Garden exhibit learn all about Earth's many different environments. At Austria's ZOOM Kindermuseum,

Children's museums provide young people with many kinds of hands-on exhibits and activities, such as cleaning dinosaur bones (*above*).

children of all ages learn about life above and below the waves in the ZOOM Ocean exhibit. And the Chicago Children's Museum includes Treehouse Trails, an exhibit that allows children to learn all about nature by exploring waterfalls and the homes of various animals.

A unique art museum building is the Solomon R. Guggenheim Museum in New York City, which opened in 1959. The museum specializes in modern abstract paintings and sculpture. The building was designed by the noted American architect Frank Lloyd Wright. Visitors take the elevator to the top floor and view displays while walking down the gently sloping ramp that circles the inside walls of the building in a continuous spiral.

The fine objects in museums are often used as sources of design. The Victoria and Albert Museum in London was established in 1852 to help businesses and industries improve the design of their products by showing the best examples of old crafts. The museum grouped its collections according to the materials from which objects were made, such as glass, wood, metal, and textile.

▶ MUSEUM EMPLOYEES

The visitor to a large museum is likely to see guards in the exhibition galleries and sales clerks in the gift shops, but there are many more people busy behind the scenes.

The museum **director** is in charge of all museum activities and often has major responsibility for raising funds to support the museum. Large museums are divided into departments, each under the care of a **curator**. A curator is an expert in a particular field, such as ancient art, modern painting, reptiles, or fossils. Curators perform research and develop exhibitions about their field of study. Larger museums may also employ **collection managers** and **collection technicians** who are responsible for the day-to-day care and storage of objects in particular departments. **Educators** organize programs in the exhibition halls to help visitors learn more about the objects on display. Educators also organize tours, often led by volunteer **docents**, and work with teachers to develop programs that complement classroom instruction.

Museums often maintain their own workshops, staffed by designers, carpenters, painters, photographers, and other experts. The artists and taxidermists (people who mount animal skins on life-size animal forms) who work on habitat displays for museums of natural history are known as **preparators**. Large art, history, and anthropology museums employ specialists called **conservators** who take care of the old paintings, sculptures, and other objects that have been damaged by time or accident. These people clean the artworks and artifacts and preserve them. Although some restoration may be necessary, they do as little repainting on old canvases as possible. Some conservators are responsible for controlling the climate (such as the temperature and the humidity) in the museum to ensure the preservation of the objects. They may also oversee the proper storage and exhibition of the objects.

In smaller museums there may be just one or two staff members who must perform all the duties of curator, educator, and other jobs. And museums of all sizes use volunteers who work for free helping wherever they are needed.

If you wish to work in a leading position in a museum, you must have a college degree, and often a graduate degree in a discipline related to the type of museum collections with which you would like to work, such as art history, biology, or history. Graduate degrees in museum studies are also offered at universities throughout the United States and elsewhere. These programs provide the training needed to work in many museum positions.

▶ HISTORY OF MUSEUMS

The word "museum" comes from the Greek word *mouseion*, meaning "temple of the Muses." The Muses were goddesses of the arts, whose lives were removed from the cares of everyday life.

One of the first institutions to be called a *mouseion* was founded in Alexandria, Egypt, about 290 B.C. and adjoined the great Library of Alexandria. The museum col-

lected every kind of information that could be of interest to scholars. It displayed art and curiosities that included statues, astronomical and surgical instruments, elephant tusks, and hides of unusual animals. Temples of the ancient Greeks and Romans sometimes included collections of art and natural history specimens, but they were not displayed in any form resembling today's exhibitions.

In the Middle Ages (500–1500), great cathedrals and monasteries became storehouses for richly ornamented objects such as chalices (cups or goblets, generally used during the celebration of Mass), book covers, and reliquaries (containers for relics of saints and martyrs). These treasuries were opened to the public only for special holy days or for the feast day of the patron saint of the church.

During the Renaissance, princes and noble families in Europe took a renewed interest in art, history, and the natural world. They collected works of art; objects of gold, silver, and other precious metals; and curiosities and rare things found in nature or brought from faraway places. Wealthy families, such as the Medici of Italy, took pride in surrounding themselves with their beautiful possessions. These private collections, found throughout Europe, were known by many names—cabinets of rarities, closets of curios, and others—and they were visited by scholars, artists, and other important persons.

The works of art in the Louvre, in Paris, originally belonged to the kings of France. The museum was one of the first in the world to allow the public to view its collections.

New museums continue to open. Many, such as the United States Holocaust Memorial Museum in Washington, D.C., reflect contemporary social issues.

The objects gathered by wealthy Renaissance collectors became the core collections of some of today's great museums. The Uffizi Gallery in Florence, Italy, is located in a palace built in the 1500's and contains some of the paintings and sculptures once owned by Lorenzo de' Medici (1449–92), a leading citizen of Florence. The Ashmolean Museum at Oxford University, England, opened in 1683, was based on the collections of Elias Ashmole (1617–92), an English collector. The Ashmolean is the oldest science museum in the United Kingdom. Later in the same century, Sir Hans Sloane (1660–1753), a noted British doctor and naturalist, began an important collection of plants and objects related to his scientific work. This collection and others provided the basis of the British Museum, which was founded in 1753.

In 1793, during the French Revolution, the Republican government made the Louvre a national museum. It contained the collections of the kings of France. Later, other royal collections were opened to the public. In 1809, Joseph Bonaparte, then king of Spain, decided that there should be an art museum in Madrid. The Prado, one of Madrid's large civic buildings, was chosen to house the great collections of the kings of Spain.

In the mid-1800's, scholars as well as the public were allowed to visit part of the Hermitage collection in Russia. The collection was housed in the Winter Palace and other buildings dating from the time of Catherine the Great.

The idea of public service and the wish to spread knowledge did not become an important part of museum work until the 1800's, when museums became places where knowledge could be gained by anyone. They ceased to be showcases to be seen only by a chosen few. Art treasures were moved from old curio cabinets and placed with other precious objects already on display. Objects of scientific interest were collected, and museums of natural history were opened.

In the 1800's, buildings were specially designed as museums. Before that, churches, monasteries, palaces, or state buildings that no longer served their original purposes were used as museums. One of the first buildings in Europe planned as a museum was the Altes (Old) Museum in Berlin, Germany. It was constructed in 1830. By the early 1900's, every major city in the United States, Europe, and Central and South America had museums displaying the natural wonders of the world as well as the history, art, and cultural heritage of people around the world.

New museums and collections are constantly being developed. Museums worldwide are renewing their commitment to public service and have become increasingly sensitive to current issues and tastes. Some, such as the Experience Music Project in Seattle, Washington, and the International Spy Museum in Washington, D.C., go beyond traditional exhibitions to create experiences that both entertain and educate the public. Today's museums are important members of their communities, and their exhibitions and educational programs have made them dynamic centers of learning for everyone.

Reviewed by BRUCE CRAIG
Director for Research and Planning
Smithsonian Center for Education and
Museum Studies

See also HERMITAGE MUSEUM; LOUVRE; METROPOLITAN MUSEUM OF ART; NATIONAL GALLERY (LONDON); NATIONAL GALLERY OF ART (WASHINGTON, D.C.); NATIONAL GALLERY OF CANADA; PRADO; SMITHSONIAN INSTITUTION; TAXIDERMY; UFFIZI GALLERY.

MUSHROOMS

Mushrooms are fleshy organisms that belong to the Kingdom Fungi. They grow from decaying materials and have no chlorophyll. They usually grow in the temperate regions of the Earth during the time of year when the weather is warm and moist. They are most likely to be found in pastures, meadows, and woodlands.

Mushrooms are of many different colors: white, orange, red, brown, and beautiful glimmering pastels. Mushrooms also have many different shapes and sizes. The most common varieties have short, thick stems and umbrella-like fleshy caps.

Inside each cap are many thin sheets of flesh, which grow between the stem and the cap edge. These are the gills, on which tiny spores grow as the mushroom ages. The spores are scattered about by wind, water, and living things. They settle on the ground and new fungi form from them.

Some mushrooms are delicious as food. A few kinds of mushrooms, which many people call **toadstools**, are poisonous. Others are too tough or not tasty enough to serve as food, even though they are not poisonous.

Common Edible Mushrooms. Edible mushrooms are prepared and enjoyed in a number of ways. They are eaten raw, cooked and eaten by themselves, eaten with meat, combined with other vegetables, or used in soups and sauces. Mushrooms do not stay fresh long, so many of the mushrooms grown are canned, frozen, or dried before being sold. There is no completely safe way for anyone but an expert to distinguish wild edible mushrooms from very similar poisonous varieties. So it is much wiser to buy the mushrooms you eat than to collect wild ones.

The **common mushroom**, or field mushroom, is the main kind of mushroom raised. Since the air where mushrooms are grown should always be cool and moist, mushrooms are raised in caves or indoors on shelves filled with partly decayed animal and plant materials. Mushroom **spawn**, or root growth, that is planted in this material grows rapidly and soon fills the bed with a mass of tiny

Mushrooms, like other types of fungi, are unable to produce their own food. They survive by feeding on plants or substances produced from plants.

threadlike rootlets. The mushrooms do not show above the ground until the rootlets are well grown.

The availability and popularity of wild mushrooms have increased over time. Varieties that were once found only in European countries are now harvested and sold in markets around the world. They include **morels**, which have unusual pitted, spongelike heads, and the **horse mushroom**, which looks very much like the common mushroom with an added collar around its neck. Another popular, and delicious, wild mushroom is the **puffball**. This is a perfectly round mushroom with no stem at all and no gills.

Poisonous Mushrooms. The **false morels** are among the varieties of poisonous mushrooms. They are easily confused with edible morels. The most deadly poison is contained in the loveliest of all mushrooms—the purewhite, deadly *Amanita verna*, or, as it is sometimes called, the **Destroying Angel**. It has a tall, stately stem and a wide, graceful cap.

Fairy Rings. Sometimes in grassy areas, mushrooms are found growing in circles called fairy rings. There was once a superstition that fairies whirled in circles as they danced, thus wearing down the grass so that the mushrooms might grow. Actually, fairy rings are a grass disease that grows steadily and evenly in the soil, spreading out in a larger circle every year.

Reviewed by LEON R. KNEEBONE
Mushroom Research Center
Pennsylvania State University

See also FUNGI; MICROBIOLOGY.

Music is a vital part of our lives. Traditional Japanese music and the modern sounds of American jazz are each expressions of a particular culture. Playing in a string quartet or a marching band is a social activity as well as a musical one. Live performances by music stars are exciting listening experiences. Recorded music can be enjoyed almost anywhere.

MUSIC

Music may be defined as sound organized into meaningful patterns that express human emotion and meaning. Music can include a wide variety of forms—from a long and complex classical symphony performed by a large orchestra to a simple, traditional folk song.

The word music comes from "Muse," the name for the goddesses of ancient Greek mythology who presided over the arts and sciences. Unlike other fine arts, such as painting, sculpture, and literature, music is a performance art and thus exists only in time. Because of this, music can be difficult to explain and analyze. What is known is that music is a universal language that enables every culture to present its own distinctive voice.

The beginnings of music predate recorded history. Music was no doubt performed by early people in religious rites, at public gatherings, as accompaniment to dancing and storytelling, and simply for pleasure. Archaeologists have discovered musical instruments dating back almost 30,000 years. Early people made rattles from dried gourds and drums from hollow logs. They blew into bones or reeds to make whistling sounds. These instruments accompanied singing and marked the rhythm of dances.

Music remains an important part of modern life. Religious music continues to uplift worshipers. What would a wedding be like without special music to celebrate the occasion? Music has long been useful to the military, signaling the troops and providing a steady beat for marching. Parades show off local marching bands, young people unwind at weekend dances, and the car stereo provides easy listening for long vacation trips.

Music is a social activity. Friends get together to sing songs or play the piano and guitar. School music activities give students opportunities to participate in bands, choirs, and orchestras. Music classes are available for the study of music appreciation, conducting, and music theory. Community bands and choral societies provide the public with further opportunities for making music. Listening to live music is also a popular activity. Concerts by famous singers and rock bands are held throughout the world, while productions of opera and musical theater entertain thousands of people each year.

Music has a large impact on the economy. Each year the recording industry makes billions of dollars from the sale of tapes, compact discs, and records. Music publishers sell songbooks and sheet music to those who perform their own music. Radio broadcasts bring music into our daily lives, and television airs opera productions, symphony concerts, and music videos.

Each of us is most familiar with the musical traditions of our own culture. In North America, the most commonly heard music is part of a tradition known as Western music. It is based on sounds developed in Western Europe over a period of thousands of years. However, other cultures have established their own means of expression. Their music may be structured in an entirely different manner from that of Western music. An appreciation of the music of other cultures is a key to understanding other peoples; it also can provide insights into the music of our own culture.

▶ELEMENTS OF MUSIC

A single musical sound is called a tone. The music of nearly every culture is based on sets of tones arranged according to ascending or descending pitch. These sets of tones are called **scales**. The characteristic sound of a scale is determined by the distance, or **inter-**

SCALES

The way a scale sounds is determined by the intervals between its tones. The patterns of half and whole steps that make up most Western scales are best seen on the keys of a piano. The half step, the smallest interval, is the distance between two adjacent piano keys.

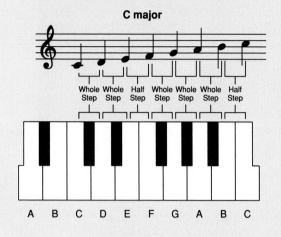

C major

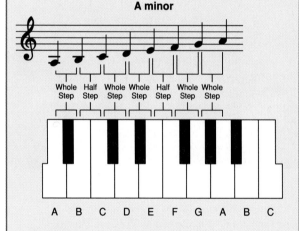

A minor

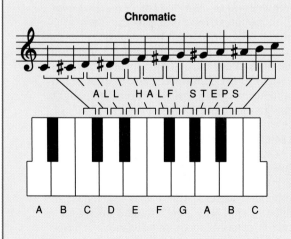

Chromatic

val, between one tone and the next. In Western music, the smallest possible distance between two tones is a **half step**. A **whole step** is equal to two half steps.

A scale consists of a never-changing series of half and whole steps. Most Western scales are made up of seven consecutive tones. These scales and the tones particular to them are called **diatonic**. The most common Western scale, the major scale, is made up of the following interval pattern: whole step, whole step, half step, whole step, whole step, whole step, half step. Another important scale, the natural minor scale, has a different interval pattern: whole step, half step, whole step, whole step, half step, whole step, whole step. A third type of scale, called the chromatic scale, has twelve consecutive tones and consists completely of half steps.

Scales are rooted on a central tone, called the **tonic**, which is the first and main tone of a scale. All the other tones of the scale are related to this home tone.

The scale is the basic organizing system of music. But music is made up of several other important elements. These are melody, rhythm, harmony, timbre (sometimes called tone color), and form.

Melody is a series of tones arranged in a particular pattern. Often the pattern is so distinctive that the melody can be remembered long after the sounds have faded away. Melodies can be arranged in short segments, or **phrases**, similar to the way that words are arranged into sentences.

Rhythm is the way that music is organized in time. The duration, or length, of musical tones can vary, thus creating longer and shorter

This article discusses the importance of music in human life. It describes the basic elements of music and explains music notation, the system by which music is written down. The article also gives an overview of music around the world and includes a feature tracking the development of Western musical forms.

More information on the historical development of music can be found in articles on the music of individual countries and regions, such as ITALY, MUSIC OF and AFRICA, MUSIC OF, and in articles on periods of music such as BAROQUE MUSIC and CLASSICAL AGE IN MUSIC. There are also articles on specific kinds of music, such as COUNTRY MUSIC, ELECTRONIC MUSIC, and ROCK MUSIC, and on musical forms, such as BALLADS and OPERA. Information on musical instruments appears in the article MUSICAL INSTRUMENTS and in articles on individual instruments, such as GUITAR and PIANO. Articles on the ensemble playing of music include BANDS AND BAND MUSIC and ORCHESTRA.

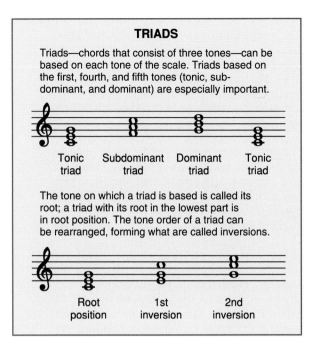

tones. The pattern formed by this variation of tone length is called rhythm. One aspect of rhythm is a regular pulse, or beat. When we march or dance to music we are feeling the underlying beat of the music, or its **meter**. This basic beat can be broken into subdivisions of two or three beats.

Harmony is produced when tones are sounded together at the same time. When three or more tones are played at the same time, a **chord** is formed. The sound quality of a chord is determined by the intervals between its tones. A common type of chord is called a **triad**. It consists of three tones, each of which are two diatonic scale steps apart—for example, the first, third, and fifth tones of a major or minor scale. The tone on which a triad is based is called its **root**. The order of the tones of a triad can be rearranged—the root need not always be the lowest tone. For example, the third tone can be the lowest tone, followed by the fifth and first tones. The rearranged triads are called **inversions**.

Triads can be based on each tone of the scale. Three important triads are the tonic triad, based on the first tone of the scale, the subdominant triad, based on the fourth tone, and the dominant triad, based on the fifth tone. Much Western music is based on these three important triads and their relationship to each other.

Timbre. Every source of musical sound—voice or instrument—has a distinctive tone quality known as its timbre. Timbre is influenced by the size and shape of the instrument or the nature of the voice. An oboe, for example, produces a very different sound than a flute, even when both play the same notes. And we can easily distinguish between a deep bass voice and a high soprano voice singing the same tune.

Form is the structure of a musical work. It refers to the manner in which the sections or parts of a work are put together to create a unified whole. The most basic form is called binary form, or A-B. It occurs when one section (A) is followed by a second, contrasting section (B). If that second section is followed by the return of the original music (A), this expanded form is known as ternary form, or A-B-A.

Another common form, called theme and variations, occurs when the original melody returns in many new ways. A single melody may have a different accompaniment, develop new harmonies, have new rhythms, or even change mode. Yet another form, called rondo, has a recurring melody that alternates with contrasting sections. A written representation of this form is A-B-A-C-A.

Many more complex forms of both vocal and instrumental music have been developed over time. The development of musical forms in Western music is outlined in the feature that begins on page 542.

▶ **MUSICAL NOTATION**

For a very long time music was not written down but was sung or played from memory. This meant that a piece of music might change over time. Gradually, composers developed a way to write down their music so that it would be sung or played exactly as they had composed it. The method that they developed for writing music is called notation. Notation gives musicians information about the pitch of the music; about duration, or length of the tones; and about expression, or the feeling with which the music should be performed.

Pitch indicates how high or low a musical tone may be. In musical notation, tones are represented by symbols called **notes**. In Western music, the letters A, B, C, D, E, F, and G are used to name the notes. These letters are repeated every eight notes. The interval be-

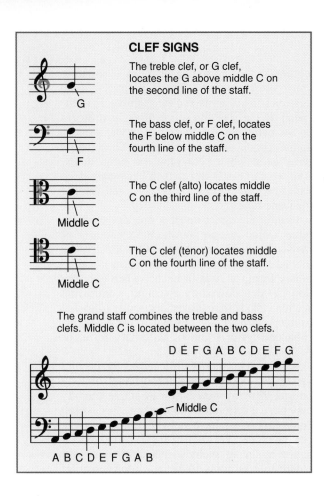

CLEF SIGNS

The treble clef, or G clef, locates the G above middle C on the second line of the staff.

The bass clef, or F clef, locates the F below middle C on the fourth line of the staff.

The C clef (alto) locates middle C on the third line of the staff.

The C clef (tenor) locates middle C on the fourth line of the staff.

The grand staff combines the treble and bass clefs. Middle C is located between the two clefs.

staff lines that extend the staff higher or lower than the five original lines. Vertical lines called **bar lines** appear at regular intervals along the staff. They divide the music into smaller units called **measures**.

At the beginning of the staff is a **clef sign**, which indicates the pitch of each line and space on the staff. The **treble clef**, or **G clef**, is used for high notes, such as those sung by the soprano voice or played by the violin and flute. In music for the piano, the right-hand part is written in the treble clef. The treble clef sign curls around the second line of the staff, marking the location of the note G above middle C.

The **bass clef**, or **F clef**, is used for lower notes, such as those played by the cello and bassoon. The left-hand part in piano music is written in the bass clef. The two dots of the bass clef enclose the fourth line of the staff, marking the location of the note F below middle C. A third clef, the **C clef**, is used in music for the viola and for the higher notes of such instruments as the cello and bassoon. The C clef is a movable clef. That is, it can be placed on different lines of the staff, but it always indicates where middle C is located—on the line where the two curved arms of the C clef meet.

Another sign that tells about pitch is the **key signature**, which indicates the **key**, or tonal center, of the work. It uses sharp signs or flat signs to show which notes should be played sharp or flat throughout the musical work. The same key signature can represent either a major key or a minor key. For example, the key of F major and the key of D minor are both represented by a key signature with one flat.

tween two notes with the same letter name is called an **octave**. A **sharp** sign (♯) placed in front of a note raises the pitch of the note a half tone; a **flat** sign (♭) placed in front of a note lowers the pitch of the note a half tone.

Notes are placed on a **staff**—five parallel horizontal lines and the spaces between them. Each line and space of the staff stands for a particular pitch. **Ledger lines** are temporary

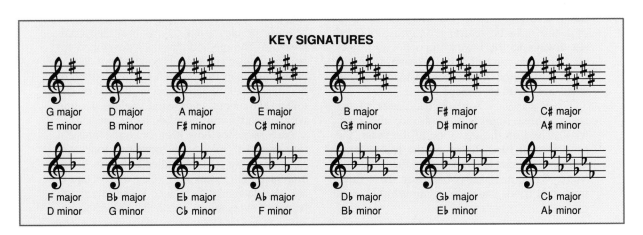

KEY SIGNATURES

| G major / E minor | D major / B minor | A major / F♯ minor | E major / C♯ minor | B major / G♯ minor | F♯ major / D♯ minor | C♯ major / A♯ minor |
| F major / D minor | B♭ major / G minor | E♭ major / C♭ minor | A♭ major / F minor | D♭ major / B♭ minor | G♭ major / E♭ minor | C♭ major / A♭ minor |

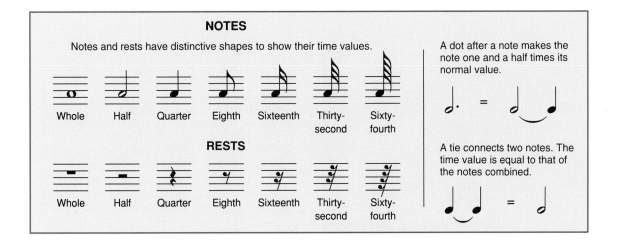

NOTES

Notes and rests have distinctive shapes to show their time values.

Whole Half Quarter Eighth Sixteenth Thirty-second Sixty-fourth

A dot after a note makes the note one and a half times its normal value.

RESTS

Whole Half Quarter Eighth Sixteenth Thirty-second Sixty-fourth

A tie connects two notes. The time value is equal to that of the notes combined.

Sharp signs and flat signs may also be placed next to a note on the staff to raise or lower the note a half tone. These **accidentals** can be reversed by using the natural sign (♮), which returns the affected note to its original form. Unlike the sharps and flats in key signatures, accidentals apply only to the notes in a single measure. They are canceled automatically after each bar line.

Duration. Whereas pitch indicates how high or low a musical note should be, duration indicates how long a note should be held. Each note is given a distinctive shape that indicates its duration. The whole note has the longest time value. Next is the half note, followed by the quarter note, the eighth note, the sixteenth note, and so on. Note values are based on divisions of two. Two half notes equal one whole note, two quarter notes equal one half note, and two eighth notes equal one quarter note. The chart on page 540 shows the values of notes in relation to each other.

A **dot** after a note makes that note one and a half times its normal value. For example, a dotted half note equals a half note plus a quarter note. A **tie** connects two notes of the same pitch and makes the total duration equal to the original notes combined. The second of the two notes is not sounded but simply held. For example, two tied quarter notes sound exactly like a half note.

Music does not consist only of sounds. **Rests**, or periods of silence in the music, are also important. For every note value there is a corresponding rest—there are whole rests, half rests, quarter rests, and so on. The symbols used for the rests have unique shapes that signify their time values.

As mentioned earlier, all the notes and rests in a piece of music are divided into measures, which are marked off by bar lines. The measures represent units of time, and each measure contains a certain number of beats. The basic, recurring pattern of stressed and unstressed beats in a piece of music is called the **meter**. The meter is indicated at the beginning of each piece of music by a **time signature**. The time signature appears in the form of a fraction, such as $\frac{3}{4}$, $\frac{4}{4}$, or $\frac{6}{8}$. The top number tells the number of beats per measure. The bottom number indicates what kind of note gets one beat. For example, in music with $\frac{3}{4}$ time, there are three beats to a measure, and a quarter note gets one beat. Therefore, three quarter notes, or their equivalent, will appear in every measure.

WONDER QUESTION

What is the origin of the clef signs?

The clef signs originated during the Middle Ages, when plainsong, or chant, was sung in the services of the Roman Catholic Church. The scribes who wrote out the music placed the letters C, F, and G on certain lines of the staff to show the pitch of that line and, thus, the pitch of the remaining lines and spaces. In this way singers could locate the proper pitch of the music. The letters were written in the Gothic script used at the time and gradually evolved into the symbols used today.

Clef is a French word meaning "key." The signs were called keys because they unlocked the secrets of the staff.

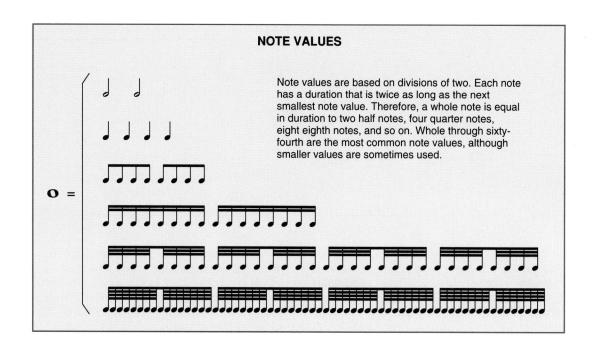

NOTE VALUES

Note values are based on divisions of two. Each note has a duration that is twice as long as the next smallest note value. Therefore, a whole note is equal in duration to two half notes, four quarter notes, eight eighth notes, and so on. Whole through sixty-fourth are the most common note values, although smaller values are sometimes used.

Musical Terms

A cappella—music sung without instrumental accompaniment.
Accelerando—gradually faster tempo.
Accent—stress on a beat.
Accidental—a symbol that raises or lowers the pitch of a note; see **sharp**, **flat**, and **natural**.
Adagio—slow tempo.
Agitato—agitated.
Al fine—to the end.
Allegretto—moderately fast tempo.
Allegro—fast tempo.
Andante—slow tempo.
Animato—animated or lively.
Arpeggio—the tones of a chord played one note at a time, in ascending or descending succession.
A tempo—return to the original speed.
Atonality—absence of a tonal center, or key.
Augmented—an interval made larger.
Bar line—a vertical line on a staff that separates measures.
Beat—a steady pulse in music.
Cadence—a progression of chords that brings a piece of music to a temporary or final conclusion.
Caesura—a pause in the flow of the music.
Cantabile—in a singing style.
Chord—three or more tones sounded at the same time.
Chromatic scale—a scale consisting of a series of half steps.
Clef—a sign used to indicate the pitches of the lines and spaces on a staff; common clef signs are the **bass clef**, **treble clef**, and **C clef**.
Coda—a closing section of a movement.
Common time—a term for $\frac{4}{4}$ time: four beats to a measure, with a quarter note getting one beat.
Con brio—with fire.
Counterpoint—music with two melodic lines.
Crescendo—gradual increase in loudness.
Da capo (D.C.)—direction to go back to the beginning of a piece of music.
Decrescendo—gradual decrease in loudness.
Diatonic—the seven tones that make up a major or minor scale.

Diminished—an interval made smaller.
Diminuendo—gradually growing softer.
Dissonance—clashing musical tones.
Dolce—sweetly.
Dominant—the fifth tone of a diatonic scale; the chord built on that tone.
Double bar—sign indicating the end of a musical work.
Downbeat—the first beat of a measure.
Dynamics—degrees of loudness and softness in music.
Ensemble—a group of musicians playing together.
Fermata—sign to sustain a note roughly twice its normal value; also known as a hold or pause.
Finale—closing section of a musical work.
Fine—the end.
Flat—sign that lowers the pitch of a note one half step.
Form—the musical structure of a composition.
Forte (f)—loud.
Fortissimo (ff)—very loud.
Glissando—sliding from one pitch to another and including all the notes in between.
Grace note—a very short note occurring before a main note.
Grand staff—the treble and bass clefs combined.
Half step—the smallest interval between two notes in Western music.
Harmony—two or more tones sounded together.
Improvisation—spontaneously creating new musical ideas while playing, often used in jazz.
Interval—the distance between two notes.
Inversion—a change in relative position of the tones of an interval, a chord, or a melody.
Key—the tonal center of a composition.
Key signature—set of sharps or flats at the beginning of a piece of music that indicates the key.
Largo—very slow tempo.
Leading tone—the seventh tone of a diatonic scale.
Ledger line—a short line for a note that lies above or below the five lines of the staff.
Legato—smoothly.
Leitmotiv—recurring musical theme, used especially in the operas of Wagner.
Maestoso—majestic.

Expression in music can be achieved in numerous ways. Major and minor keys can create differing moods. In addition, words and symbols are written on the music that tell how loudly or softly to play and about the feeling with which to perform the music.

Contrasts of loud and soft sounds, called **dynamics**, can add musical variety. The most common indication of dynamics are the Italian terms *piano* ("soft"), abbreviated *p*, and *forte* ("loud"), abbreviated *f*. Music does not always stay at one steady volume, however. The

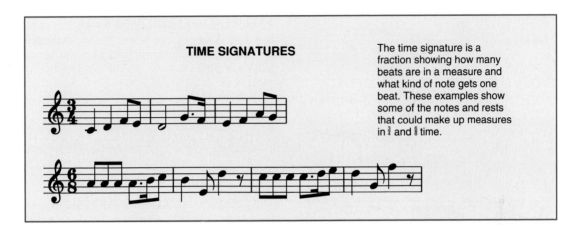

TIME SIGNATURES

The time signature is a fraction showing how many beats are in a measure and what kind of note gets one beat. These examples show some of the notes and rests that could make up measures in ¾ and ⁶⁄₈ time.

Major scale—a scale having a pattern of two whole steps, one half step, three whole steps, and one half step.

Measure—a unit of musical time, containing a specified number of beats; also called a **bar**.

Melody—a series of tones arranged in a particular pattern.

Meter—recurring pattern of beats in a piece of music.

Metronome—a device that gives an exact tempo for music.

Mezzo forte (mf)—moderately loud.

Mezzo piano (mp)—moderately soft.

Microtone—a musical interval smaller than a half step.

Minor scale—a scale having the basic pattern of one whole step, one half step, two whole steps, one half step, and two whole steps.

Moderato—moderate tempo.

Modulation—a change of key, or tonal center.

Monophonic—music that has a single melodic line.

Motif or **motive**—a short melodic idea.

Musique concrète—electronic music made from natural sounds that are recorded and modified.

Natural—sign that cancels a flat, sharp, or other accidental.

Note—the written sign for a tone.

Octave—an interval of an eighth.

Opus (op.)—"work" in Latin; used with a number to indicate the published order of a composer's works.

Phrase—a short segment of music, ending with a cadence.

Pianissimo (pp)—very soft.

Piano (p)—soft.

Pitch—relative highness or lowness of a musical tone.

Polyphonic—music that has two or more melodic lines sounding at the same time.

Presto—very fast tempo.

Refrain—a section of a composition that is repeated.

Relative—the relationship between a major and minor key that have the same key signature; for example, B minor is the **relative minor** of D major.

Repeat signs—symbols showing a section of a composition that is to be played again.

Resolution—the point at which a dissonant note changes to match the prevailing harmony.

Rest—a sign indicating a specified period of silence.

Rhythm—the organization of music in time, involving patterns of long and short note values superimposed on the prevailing meter.

Ritardando—gradually slower tempo.

Scale—a series of related tones arranged in ascending or descending order.

Score—the notation of a musical composition.

Sequence—a musical idea repeated at a higher or lower pitch.

Sforzando (sfz)—sudden accent on a single note or chord.

Sharp—sign that raises the pitch of a note one half step.

Slur—sign indicating legato performance.

Solo—one performer.

Sostenuto—sustained.

Staccato—a short sounding of a note or chord.

Staff—five parallel horizontal lines and the spaces between them, on which notes are written.

Subdominant—the fourth tone of a diatonic scale; the chord built on that tone.

Suspension—dissonance produced by holding over a tone from one chord to a new chord.

Syncopation—a rhythmic pattern stressing beats that normally are unaccented.

Tempo—the speed of the music.

Timbre—quality of tone; also called **tone color**.

Time signature—a fraction that tells how many beats are in a measure of music and what kind of note gets one beat.

Tone—a musical sound.

Tonic—the first and main tone of a diatonic scale; the chord built on that tone.

Transposition—changing the tonality of a musical work to a lower key.

Tremolo—rapid repetition of one tone.

Triad—a three-note chord, with each note a third apart.

Trill—rapid alternation of two adjacent notes.

Tutti—all performers.

Twelve-tone technique—a method of composing in which a single arrangement of the twelve tones of the chromatic scale forms the basis for an entire musical work.

Vibrato—a slight wavering of the pitch.

Vivace—very fast tempo.

EXPRESSION

Words and symbols indicate the expression with which notes should be played. A dot under or over a note means *staccato* (short and clear-cut), and a curving line means *legato* (smooth and connected).

Staccato

Legato

term *crescendo*, or its symbol ◁, shows a gradual increase in loudness, while *decrescendo*, or its symbol ▷, indicates a steady fade in the sound. **Accents** are strong stresses on beats that create sudden pulses in dynamic levels. Common notations for accents are ∧, >, and sfz., which stands for the Italian word *sforzando* ("forced").

Notes can be played somewhat shorter than their full value. A dot above a note indicates that the note should be played in a shortened manner, called *staccato*. In another manner of

An early example of written music

Middle Ages (500–1400)

Plainsong, or chant, the earliest known Western musical form, was used in services of the Roman Catholic Church. It consisted of a single line of vocal melody sung without instrumental accompaniment. This kind of music is called monophonic music.

History of Western Musical Forms

Gradually, composers began to write polyphonic music, in which two or more melodies are sung or played at the same time. **Organum**, developed in the 800's, combined plainsong sung at one pitch with parallel melodies sung at a higher or lower pitch. Another polyphonic form, the **motet**, created in the 1200's, added new music and texts to the original melody line.

Secular (nonreligious) songs were also composed during the Middle Ages. The **rondeau**, the **virelai**, and the **ballade** were all song forms that made use of a recurring section called the refrain.

Renaissance (1400–1600)

The **mass**, the musical setting of the Roman Catholic liturgy, was the most important form of sacred music during the Renaissance. French composer Josquin des Prez and Italian composer Giovanni da Palestrina were two noted composers of masses.

The motet became an important form of sacred vocal music in the Renaissance. It had a Latin text and was usually written for unaccompanied chorus. Another sacred vocal form was the **chorale**, devel-

Josquin des Prez

performing, called *legato*, notes are held their full value and are played as smoothly as possible. *Legato* is indicated by a curving line, called a slur, drawn over or under two or more notes of different pitch.

The rate of speed, or **tempo**, at which a piece of music is performed, is an important factor in expression. Tempo indications are used to show how fast or slowly a piece of music should be performed. Most of these terms are Italian words, and they originally indicated a feeling rather than a strict speed. For example, *andante*, which today indicates a slow tempo, originally meant a walking pace; *allegro*, which composers now use to show a fast tempo, originally denoted a lively mood.

▶ MUSIC AROUND THE WORLD

Western music refers to the musical traditions developed by the peoples of Europe. As Europeans migrated to the New World, their music took root in North and South America, as well as Australia and New Zealand. Western music has its origins in musical theories developed in ancient Greece. Although few

A medieval church choir

oped in Germany in the 1500's following the Protestant Reformation. A four-part setting of a hymn tune, the chorale is used in the Lutheran service. The **anthem** was used in services of the Church of England and had an English text. Some anthems are composed for choir alone, while others add soloists and organ accompaniment. (Today, patriotic songs are often called anthems.)

New secular forms for voice also arose. The **canon** is a form in which an initial theme is imitated by a second voice at regular intervals. The **catch** is a canon for three or more voices. The **madrigal**, a song for several voices, flourished in Italy and England. Its music often closely reflects the meaning of its words. The **chanson** is the French counterpart of the madrigal. Many chansons were light and simple. In those by composer Clement Janequin, singers imitate natural sounds such as birdcalls and the sounds of battle.

Baroque Period (1600–1750)

Opera was developed in Italy during the 1600's and quickly spread throughout Europe. Opera uses several vocal forms. **Recitative**, or speech-song, has a rhythmic flow that imitates the inflections of human speech. It serves to advance the action of the story.

The **aria** is the main lyrical form for solo voice in opera. It shows the emotional state of a character. Arias of the 1700's were often in A-B-A form.

The **cantata** is a sacred or secular work for voices and instruments. Cantatas of the early 1600's were solo works. By the 1700's, German composer Johann Sebastian Bach had perfected the sacred cantata, which usually had a chorus as well as solo arias and recitatives.

Oratorio is a musical setting of a dramatic, often religious, text. It is similar to opera but has no cos-

Musicians at a royal court

Why are so many musical terms written in Italian?

Italy played a major role in the development of the forms, instruments, and performing styles of Western music. As a result, Italian became the international language of music. Today the Italian words for many terms indicating tempo and expression are still used worldwide. However, a composer may choose to use his or her own native language for these directions.

examples of music remain from this culture, the writings of its music theorists had a great influence on music, especially that of the Renaissance. Those musical traditions can be traced in a direct line from the medieval period to the present day.

The highly structured type of music that arose out of these traditions is called art music or, sometimes, classical music. Art music has had a long and complex history. The accompanying feature on Western musical forms traces this history through the development of the forms by which the music is structured.

Score of *Euridice*, an early opera

Stradivari violin

tumes or staging. The oratorio uses aria and recitative, but the chorus rather than the solo voice is emphasized. Oratorio reached a peak with the work of Germany's George Frederick Handel, whose *Messiah* is perhaps the best-known example of the form ever composed. The **Passion** is a particular type of oratorio that tells the story of the suffering and death of Christ.

The **concerto grosso** of the 1600's was an instrumental form in which a small group of instruments alternated back and forth with a full ensemble. Arcangelo Corelli and Antonio Vivaldi, as well as Bach and Handel, were masters of this form.

The **suite**, an important baroque instrumental form, is a group of stylized dances in related keys. The dances, usually arranged in alternating tempos, included the allemande, courante, saraband, and the final fast-paced gigue. A suite sometimes began with a prelude, and optional dances such as the minuet were often added after the saraband. Another name for suite is **partita**.

The **fugue** is a complex keyboard form in which a main theme and other imitating voices combine to form a whole in a technique known as counterpoint. Well-known examples are found in Bach's *Well-Tempered Clavier*, a collection of 48 preludes and fugues, and *Art of the Fugue*. Other baroque keyboard forms include the **chaconne**, a slow composition

J. S. Bach conducting a chamber orchestra

with variations over a repeating bass line; the **minuet**, a courtly dance of French origin set in triple time; and the **toccata** ("touch piece"), a piece designed to display the skill of the player.

Classical Period (1750–1825)

The **sonata**, an instrumental solo form first developed in the baroque era, dominated music from 1750

Art music is generally seen as the artistic expression of an individual composer, who uses music notation to show how his or her music should be performed. Another important type of Western music, folk music, may not have a known author. Rather than being written down, it is often passed along orally from one generation to the next. No formal knowledge of music is required. An article on folk music appears in Volume F.

Western music also includes a third type of music, known as popular music. This term refers to music written as a commercial product that appeals to a wide audience. Popular songs tend to express universal emotions such as love, anger, and despair, and they often reflect the social climate of the time and place in which they are written.

The elements of popular music are generally much simpler and easier to understand than those of art music. However, art music and popular music often overlap, and it is impossible to completely separate the two. Varieties of popular music in the United States include rock music, country music, and jazz. Articles on all three subjects can be found by

to 1900. It consists of three or four movements. The first movement is usually fast and has three main parts. The first, called the exposition, contains at least two main musical themes, which usually contrast in style and mood. The second, called the development, modifies these themes and presents them in new combinations. The final section, called the recapitulation, restates the original themes. This three-part structure of the first movement is called the **sonata-allegro** form. Of the remaining movements of the sonata, the second is slow and songlike; the third is either a minuet or scherzo in triple meter; and the last movement (finale), often the fastest, may be in the sonata-allegro or the rondo form. Austria's Franz Joseph Haydn and Wolfgang Amadeus Mozart and Germany's Ludwig van Beethoven all wrote sonatas for keyboard instruments.

The **string quartet**, an instrumental work for two violins, viola, and cello, became a favorite form of chamber music in the mid-1700's and has retained its popularity

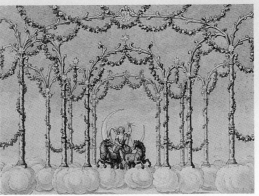
Stage design for Mozart's opera *The Magic Flute*

Franz Joseph Haydn

Handel's score of *Messiah*

over the years. Haydn is considered to be the father of the string quartet.

The **symphony**, a long work for orchestra, reached its modern form in the late 1700's with the Viennese classical symphony. The four movements of the classical symphony follow the same scheme as the sonata: a fast first movement in sonata-allegro form; a slow, songlike second movement; a quick scherzo or minuet for the third movement; and a fast rondo as the finale. The great masters of the classical symphony were Haydn, Mozart, and Beethoven.

The **concerto**, a work for a single instrument with orchestra, was firmly established in the late 1700's with the piano concertos of Mozart. Concertos generally have three movements (fast-slow-fast) and most often feature the piano or violin.

Small instrumental forms were also popular in the classical period. The **divertimento** and the **serenade** are light works of five or more movements each. The **interlude**, a short musical composition, was often played or sung between parts of a larger work.

consulting the appropriate volumes of this encyclopedia.

African music refers to the music of the peoples of Africa living south of the Sahara. Much musical variety occurs among the hundreds of different groups living in this vast region, but some common characteristics can be seen. For most Africans, music is a vital part of everyday life, and there are special songs for many different occasions.

African music is often based on a leader-response format, in which a soloist sings a phrase that is answered by a group of singers.

Many African languages use slight variations in voice inflection to convey meaning. A word may mean different things depending on whether the voice rises in pitch or trails off at the end of a syllable. In African music this subtle modulation of vocal sounds is more important than changes in loudness and softness.

However, it is rhythm that is most important in African music. Interacting layers of rhythm are sounded by a variety of instruments, including drums, gongs, xylophones, rattles, and bells. One of the most distinctive African instruments is the *mbira*, or thumb piano (also

Beethoven's studio

Ludwig van Beethoven

The **overture** is an orchestral piece that serves as an introduction to a concert or an opera. Some, such as Mozart's overture to his opera *The Marriage of Figaro*, are performed today as independent works. Other overtures, called concert overtures, were originally written as independent compositions for orchestra.

Romantic Period (1825–1900)

Instrumental forms multiplied in the romantic age, especially those intended for a single instrument. Much of this more intimate music was written for piano and reached a high level in the works of Polish composer Frédéric Chopin. The **etude** ("study") is a keyboard

work that is intended to strengthen a technical aspect of playing. The **fantasia** or **fantasy** is a form that allows the composer great freedom. The **impromptu** is a single-movement piano composition that appears to be created spontaneously.

The **rhapsody** is another form with considerable freedom, which was popularized by Hungarian Franz Liszt. The **prelude** is a short keyboard work of an introductory nature. Chopin wrote 24 preludes, one for each major and minor key. The **nocturne**—literally, "night song"—sets a peaceful evening mood. The **barcarole** ("boat song") evokes the water with a gentle, rocking rhythm. The **berceuse** is a musical lullaby that has quiet dynamics and simple harmonies.

The **song** also flourished, with composers setting works by famous poets to music. A **song cycle** is a group of songs that have a common story line. **Lied** (the German word for "song") is an art song in which voice and piano are equal partners in expressing the

Franz Schubert playing in an intimate setting

Frédéric Chopin

called *kalimba*), which consists of metal tongues attached to a solid or hollow piece of wood. The tongues are stroked with the thumbs to produce soft tones.

African music has had a strong influence on the music of other regions of the world. Elements of African music can be found in much American music, particularly jazz, and in the music of Latin America and the Caribbean. For more information, see the article AFRICA, MUSIC OF in Volume A.

Asian music encompasses the music of the peoples of the continent of Asia. While there are many regional differences in the music of Asia, one common thread is the dominance of melody.

Chinese music is classified according to northern and southern styles. The pentatonic, or five-tone, scale is an important ingredient in both, but various forms of seven-tone scales exist as well. Southern Chinese folk songs have smooth, flowing melodies, while the northern style favors angular melodies with large leaps between tones. Instruments commonly used in Chinese music include stringed instruments such as the *pipa*, a lute, and the

Franz Liszt conducting a large orchestra

text. The lied reached its peak in the romantic period with the works of Austrian and German composers such as Franz Schubert, Robert Schumann, and Johannes Brahms and later Hugo Wolf, Richard Strauss, and Gustav Mahler. **Mélodie** is the French term for a solo song with piano accompaniment. French composers Hector Berlioz, Charles Gounod, and Camille Saint-Saëns wrote songs that reflected the subtleties of the French language.

Symphonies changed greatly in the 1800's, becoming longer and much more complex. Composers added newly invented or improved instruments to the orchestra. Famous symphonies of the romantic period include Berlioz' *Symphonie fantastique*,

Brahms' score of *German Requiem*

Schubert's *Unfinished Symphony*, and Mahler's *Symphony of a Thousand*. Important symphony composers of the late 1800's include Brahms, Russia's Peter Ilyich Tchaikovsky, and Austria's Anton Bruckner.

For many romantic composers, the restrictions of the old symphonic form were too limiting. They wrote orchestral music that expressed ideas from history, literature, or art. Often the story behind the music was described in a printed program, and the music came to be called **program music**. Two masters of this form were Franz Liszt, who called his works **symphonic poems**, and Richard Strauss, who called his **tone poems**.

Modern Period (after 1900)

The 1900's marked a shift in the development of Western musical forms. Some composers continued to work within the old forms, while others looked for

Poster for Wagner's opera *Lohengrin*

ch'in, a type of zither. Flutes and percussion instruments are also used.

The traditional music of Japan is based primarily on pentatonic scales, sometimes supplemented with two additional tones. The most common style of Japanese music is heterophony, in which a single melody is played with slight variations on several different instruments at the same time. Typical instruments include various flutes, the *koto* (a type of zither), and the *shamisen* (lute). Japanese music is closely linked with other forms of expression, such as dance, drama, and song.

The music of India is based on melodic formulas called *ragas*. Drone harmonies that sustain (hold) certain notes accompany these melodies. Performing style is improvised; that is, the performer makes up some of the music as it is played. The *sitar*, an Indian stringed instrument, is capable of playing in microtones, intervals smaller than the half steps of Western major and minor scales. For more information, see INDIA, MUSIC OF in Volume I.

Other regions of Asia with distinctive musical traditions include the Middle East, where the melodic formulas on which the music is

new ways to structure their music. A wide variety of highly individual musical styles has been the result.

Impressionism is used to describe music that uses a wide range of instrumental colors and unusual rhythm patterns to express subtle feelings and perceptions. French composers Claude Debussy and Maurice Ravel were leading impressionists. Another movement, called **expressionism**, was started by Austria's Arnold Schoenberg and Alban Berg. Expressionist music, such as Berg's opera *Wozzeck*, reflects intense emotions and extremes of behavior through techniques such as dissonance.

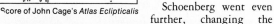
Score of John Cage's *Atlas Eclipticalis*

Schoenberg went even further, changing the basic building blocks with which his music was made. He developed a system, called **twelve-tone music**, or **serialism**, in which all twelve tones of the chromatic scale are used equally. The twelve tones are arranged in a particular sequence, called a tone row, which forms the basis for the entire composition.

Unlike serial music, which involves total organization by the composer, **chance music** leaves some choices to the performer. The music may change each time it is performed. For example, the composer may let the performer choose the order in which to perform various sections of the work. American composer John Cage was a leader in chance music.

After World War II, composers began to experiment with new technology. **Electronic music** is a medium in which sounds of instruments and from

Arnold Schoenberg

nature could be altered, and completely new sounds could be produced. In the 1960's, composers produced pure electronic music by using synthesizers to generate sound waves. The composer could control the pitch, duration, and timbre of the electronically produced tones. Some composers combined taped or electronically produced sounds with live performances by singers or instrumentalists.

Minimalism is a movement that began in the United States during the 1960's, pioneered by composers Philip Glass and Steve Reich. This music relies heavily on repetition. Simple melodies and harmonies are played over and over again, with some freedom given to the performers to improvise.

The late 1900's saw a return to traditional instruments, tonality, and melodic expression in a trend known as the **new romanticism**. The Polish composer Krzysztof Penderecki was one of the leaders in this movement.

Composer using electronic equipment

Above left: Music is a key element in the ceremonial dances of native American Indians. *Below left:* Traditional instruments of India include the *tabla*, a pair of drums, and the *sarod*, a stringed instrument. *Above:* Percussion instruments are especially important in expressing the rhythms of African music.

based are called *maqams*, and Indonesia, where large orchestras called gamelans are famous for their rhythmic combinations.

Native American music is the music of the native peoples of North and South America. The music of the Indians of North America is primarily vocal, with intricate melodies but no harmony. Traditionally, the men performed ceremonial music, while the women sang in domestic rituals. In the culture of the Plains Indians, musical phrases usually started on high pitches and descended to lower tones. Ceremonial dances often were accompanied by instruments such as wooden rattles and flutes made from reeds or bones.

In South America before European conquest, the Aztecs, Incas, and Mayas sang songs composed of two, three, and sometimes five tones. There were songs for different aspects of daily life, including hunting, entertaining, and religious rituals. Music was produced mainly by the human voice, but a variety of percussion and wind instruments were also used.

MICHAEL E. YACHANIN
Hartt School of Music
University of Hartford

Biographies of the following composers can be found in the appropriate volumes:

BACH, Johann Sebastian
BARTÓK, Béla
BEETHOVEN, Ludwig van
BERLIOZ, Hector
BRAHMS, Johannes
CHOPIN, Frédéric
COPLAND, Aaron
DEBUSSY, Claude
DONIZETTI, Gaetano
DVOŘÁK, Antonin
ELGAR, Sir Edward
FRANCK, César
GLUCK, Christoph
GRIEG, Edvard
HANDEL, George Frederick
HAYDN, Joseph
IVES, Charles
LISZT, Franz

MACDOWELL, Edward
MAHLER, Gustav
MENDELSSOHN, Felix
MOZART, Wolfgang Amadeus
PROKOFIEV, Sergei
PUCCINI, Giacomo
SCHOENBERG, Arnold
SCHUBERT, Franz
SCHUMANN, Robert
SIBELIUS, Jean
STRAUSS, Johann, Jr.
STRAUSS, Richard
STRAVINSKY, Igor
TCHAIKOVSKY, Peter Ilyich
VERDI, Giuseppe
WAGNER, Richard

MUSICAL INSTRUMENTS

Musical instruments are devices used to make musical sounds. How are these sounds produced? When an instrument is played, it gives off vibrations, called **sound waves**. These vibrations spread out through the air until they break against our ears, just as a stone dropped into water makes waves that spread out to the sides of a pond. All musical instruments emit sound waves when they are played. But each instrument emits them in its own individual pattern. It is through the different patterns in the sound waves that we hear different kinds of sounds.

A choppy sea combines many wave patterns, large and small. Sound waves can also combine into complex patterns. The more complex the sound waves, the more complicated the sound. Some instruments make more complicated sounds than others. Many instruments playing together sound more complicated than one playing alone. The science of sound is called **acoustics**, and the study of the sounds made by musical instruments is called musical acoustics.

Most musical instruments fall into three major categories: **stringed instruments**, **wind instruments**, and **percussion instruments**.

You can observe the working principle of a stringed instrument by stretching a rubber band across the top of

an empty, open box and plucking it in the middle. You can see the vibrations and hear the "twang" of the sound waves they produce. Similarly, blowing across the top of an empty bottle demonstrates the working principle of a wind instrument. The soft, cooing sound it makes comes from the air in the bottle, which your breath has set quivering with invisible vibrations. And tapping a very thin wooden board with your knuckles demonstrates the working principle of a percussion instrument. You can feel the vibrations in the hand that is holding the wood. These vibrations produce the sound waves that carry the tapping sound to your ears.

Besides the three traditional categories of instruments, an additional category, **electronic instruments**, has arisen since the early 1900's. In these instruments, sound waves are altered or generated electronically, amplified (made louder), and played through loudspeakers. Electronic instruments can produce all the sounds that ordinary musical instruments can make—and many more. (See ELECTRONIC MUSIC in Volume E.)

Most of the instruments described in this article are those in the modern symphony orchestra, with a few of their ancestors included. For more information, see the article ORCHESTRA in Volume O. Other musical instruments, ancient and modern, are described in articles throughout this encyclopedia.

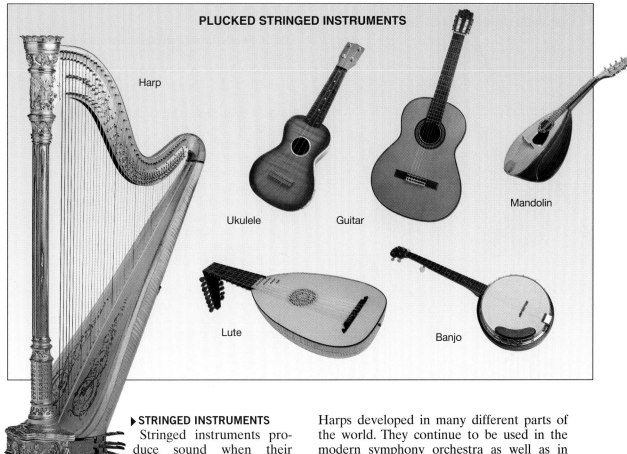

PLUCKED STRINGED INSTRUMENTS

Harp

Ukulele

Guitar

Mandolin

Lute

Banjo

▶ **STRINGED INSTRUMENTS**

Stringed instruments produce sound when their strings are made to vibrate. This is done by plucking, bowing, or striking. The vibrations pass into the wooden body of the instrument. This sends them out into the air more loudly than the thin string could by itself.

Plucked Stringed Instruments. A hunting bow makes a twang when the arrow leaves the string. Prehistoric people attached a gourd or other hollow object to the bow, so that it sounded louder and more musical. This is the **musical bow**. It inspired the **harp** and other stringed instruments. The harp dates back to ancient times: Early harps were first found in the Middle East dating from 3300 B.C.

This article discusses the major categories of musical instruments and gives an overview of many instruments played in a modern symphony orchestra. It also describes the ways in which different musical instruments produce various sounds. More information can be found in the articles KEYBOARD INSTRUMENTS, PERCUSSION INSTRUMENTS, STRINGED INSTRUMENTS, and WIND INSTRUMENTS, and also in articles on individual instruments, including CLARINET, DRUM, GUITAR, HARMONICA, HARP, ORGAN, PIANO, RECORDER, and VIOLIN.

Harps developed in many different parts of the world. They continue to be used in the modern symphony orchestra as well as in many other types of music and ensembles. The strings of the modern harp are stretched across a triangular frame and are plucked or strummed by the harpist.

The **guitar** is another stringed instrument that is played by plucking or strumming the strings. The guitar is shaped like other well-known string instruments, the violin, viola, cello, and double bass, with a curvy body and a fingerboard that extends out of the instrument. Along its neck are **frets**, small pieces of metal under the strings. One can change the note that is played by pressing a finger behind one of the frets and plucking that string. This shortens the length of the string that is vibrating, and changes the pitch. The **banjo** is played in a similar way, but it has a round body and a longer neck.

Bowed Stringed Instruments. Bowed stringed instruments are played with a wooden bow that has horsehair (or sometimes plastic) stretched from one end to the other. Drawing the bow across the strings creates the sound. These instruments do not date to ancient times, as plucked instruments

BOWED STRINGED INSTRUMENTS

Violin

Viola

Cello

Double
bass

do, but **viols**, bowed stringed instruments with frets, existed by the late Middle Ages. By the 1500's and 1600's, they were a complete family—from the highest (treble) to the lowest (bass). But viols went out of use, gradually replaced by the more brilliant and versatile **violin** family.

Viols were valued especially in chamber music. Some of the best of this music was composed in England during the 1600's. It is now sometimes played again on the family of viols, for which it was originally intended. The sound is warmer, and much softer than the sound of the violin family.

Violins were first made early in the 1500's, and they also came to be a complete family: violin, **viola**, **cello**, and **double bass**. The sound of the violin family is not only unusually beautiful; it is also unusually varied. There are many different colorings of tone and styles of bowing, making it a very adaptable family. The violin family rapidly became the foundation of the orchestra.

The string quartet, made up of first and second violins, viola, and cello, is equally successful. The composers Joseph Haydn, Wolfgang Amadeus Mozart, and Ludwig van Beethoven wrote some of their finest music for just this combination of instruments. The string quartet remains a favorite of many modern composers. Moreover, the violin and cello are extraordinary solo instruments.

Stringed Instruments That Are Struck. Stringed instruments whose strings are struck to produce sound are the keyboard instruments. Of this family, the **piano** is by far the best known. It has a hammer action— the hammers are attached to the keys by levers.

Grand piano

When a key is pressed down, a felt-covered hammer jumps up and strikes the string, immediately falling back again when the key is let go. The sound can be made soft and muted or loud and powerful, exactly as required. Like the violin, this, too, is a most versatile instrument. It is wonderful as a solo instrument, and also when it accompanies other instruments or the human voice.

The piano came to prominence after the violin. Mozart made it very popular; Beethoven made it essential. Before that, the **harpsichord** had been the main stringed instrument with a keyboard. Johann Sebastian Bach, for example, composed no music for the piano but much for the harpsichord. Harpsichord music sounds good on the piano, but it sounds even better on its own instrument. For this reason the harpsichord has once more come back into use.

The strings of the harpsichord are plucked by a small piece of leather or quill when the keys are pressed. This gives a clear and ringing sound, not as powerful as the piano at its loudest, but more brilliant. The **clavichord**, the earliest type of stringed keyboard instrument, is much less powerful. It is so quiet that it can be heard only in a small room. But some consider it more expressive, in its quiet way, than any other keyboard instrument. The strings of the clavichord are struck by short metal blades called tangents.

There is a story that Handel, as a child, practiced the piano secretly at night in an attic. This cannot be true; the whole household would have been awakened. It was probably a clavichord, which no one would have heard.

▶ **WIND INSTRUMENTS**

There are two ways to produce sounds on wind instruments. First, sound can be produced by blowing air across a fixed edge. This is what happens, as we have seen, when you blow across the top of a bottle. It is the way all flute instruments produce sound. Sound can also be produced by blowing air across a piece of flexible, springy material (or between two such pieces). You may have done this with a piece of grass held between your thumbs, making a "squeaker," which can emit a very piercing sound. This is the way all reed instruments work. The piece of grass vibrates, and so do the reeds of reed instruments (reeds are made out of cane, a plant related to bamboo). In brass instruments the principle is the same, but the player's own lips vibrate instead. In singing, the vocal cords vibrate.

Woodwind Instruments. Woodwinds are one kind of wind instrument. They are called woodwinds because they are, or were at one time, made of wood, and one uses wind, or air, to play them. Some wind instruments are now made of other materials. The flute is made of metal—either silver, gold, or platinum. The oboe, clarinet, and bassoon are still made of wood, but they now have metal keys. **Flutes** have a pure tone. The player blows air across a mouth hole in the side. The **piccolo** is a small flute, and it makes a higher sound (it has the highest range in the orchestra).

The **oboe** is a reed instrument. Two nearly flat pieces of reed are bound together so that the player's breath flows between them and makes them vibrate. This is called a double reed. The tone is deep, round, and beautiful.

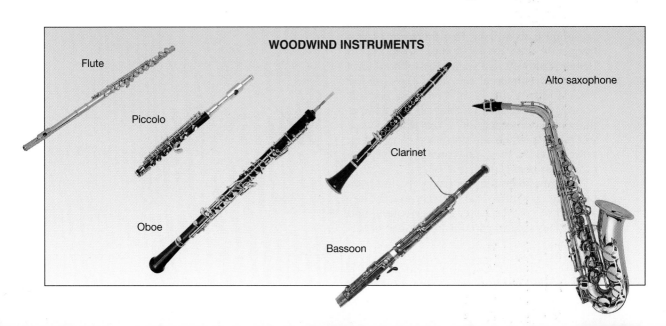

WOODWIND INSTRUMENTS

Flute

Piccolo

Oboe

Clarinet

Bassoon

Alto saxophone

The oboe is used as a solo instrument and in chamber music, but it is most often heard in the orchestra. It often plays melancholy or wistful sounding solos, and it is the instrument that is used to tune the orchestra at the beginning of each rehearsal or performance. The **English horn** is closely related to the oboe, but it has a lower and darker sound. The **bassoon** is another near relative of the oboe, often playing bass to it in the orchestra. It can be used by composers for tragic or comical effect, but it is most often for eloquent and serious passages. It produces a tone somewhat like that of the oboe and English horn but deeper and heavier.

The **clarinet** possesses a tone all its own. The reed is single, and the player's breath flows between the reed and a mouthpiece to make it vibrate. The bodies of oboes and bassoons are tapering tubes, in the shape of a long, narrow cone. But the clarinet is a straight tube, in the shape of a long, narrow cylinder. This in itself gives it a different tone. On high notes the clarinet sounds clear and silky. It is ideally suited for solos and chamber music. And in the orchestra, the clarinet creates a striking contrast to the tone of the flutes and oboes.

The **saxophone**, too, has a single reed. But its tapering tube is very much wider than that of the oboe. This is what gives it its rich tone. The saxophone is well adapted to dance music and jazz of all kinds. Its tone flows along easily. It was not invented until about 1840. Very few composers have used it in the orchestra.

Brass Instruments. Brass instruments are another type of wind instrument. The **trumpet** is the smallest, the highest sounding, and the most brilliant of all the brass instruments. Its sound is so brilliant that the trumpet was frequently used to stir soldiers to battle. In Britain, trumpets are used at royal weddings and other ceremonial occasions. They are the loudest instruments in the orchestra. For this reason, they could never play all the time, as the violins sometimes do. Even when played softly, the trumpets are sharp and clear. When played loudly, they ring out above all the other instruments.

The **trombones** are like trumpets that have been tamed a little—but not very much. They are larger, so they have a lower sound, and their tubes slide in and out to produce differ-ent notes. Their tone is not quite as dazzling, especially when played softly. They can sound beautifully mellow or extremely powerful.

The **French horns** are prized mainly for their warm, mellow tone. Some of the most tender melodies are given French horns to play.

The **tuba** is a bass instrument that is seldom used to play a tune. It makes a solid and sonorous (full, rich) sound that acts as a firm

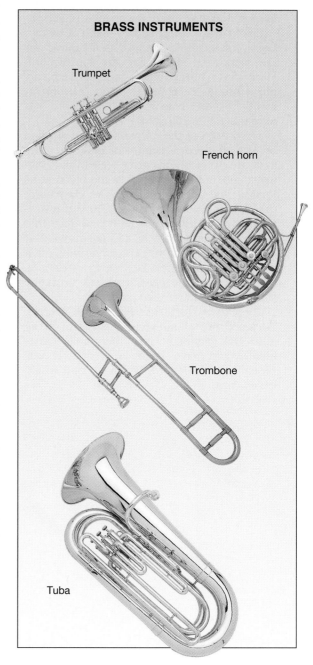

BRASS INSTRUMENTS

Trumpet

French horn

Trombone

Tuba

foundation for the other instruments to stand upon.

Other Wind Instruments Other wind instruments include the pipe organ, accordion, harmonica, and bagpipe.

The **pipe organ** is like a collection of many different wind instruments, linked up by machinery so that one performer can play them all. There may be several keyboards, including one that is played with the feet (the pedal board). The pipes are arranged in groups, called **stops**, each of which has a certain sound color. The wind is supplied by machinery. This powerful instrument can produce an enormous variety of sounds.

The accordion and harmonica have sets of reeds that vibrate when blown by a stream of air. The bagpipe has a windbag that supplies air to several reed pipes. The player fills the windbag with air by either blowing into a tube or by putting pressure on a bellows with his or her arm.

▶ PERCUSSION INSTRUMENTS

Percussion instruments are instruments that are played by striking, shaking, or scraping them. There is an incredible variety of percussion instruments from all over the world.

Bells and gongs, bars of wood or metal, and even bowls and thin stones make fine percussion instruments. The orchestras of Asian peoples, such as the Javanese gamelan orchestras, have a vast array of these and other kinds of percussion instruments, including drums of every size and shape. In symphony orchestras, percussion sections have become much more varied over time, as music from other cultures has influenced symphonic music. The bowl-shaped **kettledrums**, or **timpani**, are almost always present in the orchestra. They give a clear, definite note and a sonorous tone that can be as soft or as loud as the player wishes. Other types of drums are also used: the **snare**, for example, that is also often heard in band music, and the deep **bass drum**.

PERCUSSION INSTRUMENTS

Timpani

Snare drum

Triangle

Cymbals are metal discs that are struck, either against each other or with a mallet of some sort. They can be incredibly loud and ringing, or soft, adding a sheen to the sound of the orchestra. Other percussion instruments include the tambourine, which is shaken or struck and makes a loud rattling sound. The **triangle** is a metal rod left open at one corner. The **xylophone** is a row of wooden bars, and it has a dry and eerie sound. The **glockenspiel** has metal bars that produce a bright ringing sound.

ROBERT DONINGTON
Author, *The Instruments of Music*

Reviewed by SARAH JOHNSON
Director of Education and
Community Partnerships
The Philadelphia Orchestra

Did you know that...

many nontraditional instruments have found their way into the percussion section in the last century? These instruments include car horns, cowbells, water glasses, a musical whistle, and even a musical saw, which is played with a bow, like a violin.

Porgy and Bess, with music by George Gershwin, is a landmark of American musical theater. The term "musical theater" is used to describe works for the stage that tell a story with speech, song, and dance. Such works are typically referred to as musicals.

MUSICAL THEATER

The term "musical theater" is used to describe a work for the stage that tells a story with speech, song, and dance. Such works are often simply called musicals.

Opera is a form of musical theater. This term is mainly used to refer to a drama set to music, in which all of the dialogue is sung. It is typically performed by specially trained singers on a huge stage filled with splendid scenery. When we speak today of musical theater, however, we usually mean less elaborate and more popular combinations of songs, dances, story, and spectacle, in which dialogue as well as song is used to tell the story.

The main components of a musical are the libretto (the book, or story of the musical), the music, and the lyrics (the words to the music). Sometimes two or even all three of these elements are written by the same person. But in many cases a librettist, a composer, and a lyricist collaborate (work together closely) on a production.

Other key people involved in a musical theater production are the choreographer, who arranges the dancing, and the performers, who bring the words, music, and dances to life on stage.

▶ HISTORY

Music and theater have gone together from the beginning. In ancient Greek dramas, many passages, especially those assigned to the chorus, were intoned, or chanted. Theater died out with the collapse of the Roman Empire and was not revived until well into the Middle Ages. Even then, its new beginnings involved a combination of music and drama. The origins of both modern drama and modern musical theater can be traced to scenes that were acted out and sung as part of some medieval church services.

The earliest examples of musical theater on the English-speaking stage occurred in the 1700's and were called **ballad operas**. The most famous ballad opera is *The Beggar's Opera* (1728), the masterpiece of English composer John Gay. Ballad operas were not real operas but comic or romantic plays into which songs were inserted. The songs were not written specifically for the plays. Instead, the authors took popular songs of the day and gave them new lyrics that related to the story being told. For example, one of the earliest-known uses of the melody of "Yankee Doodle" is in the American ballad opera *The Disappointment* (1767).

Modern popular musical theater took its present shape mainly in the last half of the 1800's. Three principal types quickly stood out: operetta, musical comedy, and revue.

Operetta

Operetta was the first to emerge. As its name suggests, it can be seen as an offshoot of opera, although from early on much of its dialogue was spoken rather than sung. The first great writers of operetta appeared in

The Gaiety shows of the 1890's were England's first musical comedies. As this poster indicates, they often featured fashionably dressed ladies.

France, where the new form was called **opéra bouffe** (comic opera). The most important of these writers was Jacques Offenbach, many of whose delightful works are still enjoyed today. Whether set in the present or in the distant past, most opéra bouffe wittily spoofed contemporary society and its often absurd behavior.

The operettas of Austrian composer Johann Strauss, notably *Die Fledermaus* (*The Bat*; 1874), were influential. In England, the foremost composers of operettas were William Schwenk Gilbert and Arthur Sullivan. Their *H.M.S. Pinafore* (1878) introduced musical theater to stages around the world; such later works as *The Pirates of Penzance* (1880) and *The Mikado* (1885) were equally popular. Like opéra bouffe, the Gilbert and Sullivan operettas spoofed modern manners.

Franz Lehar, an Austrian composer, earned lasting fame with *Die Lustige Witwe* (*The Merry Widow*; 1905), considered by many to have been the most successful popular musical of all time. With its dance-based melodies, it introduced a slightly softer, less artificial form of operetta that became a model for a generation of composers.

In the United States, the earliest successful operettas blended comedy and romance. The first to have longstanding popularity was *Robin Hood* (1891), which had music by Reginald DeKoven and a libretto by Harry B. Smith.

The first important American composer for the theater was Victor Herbert. His music combined traditional melodies of his native Ireland, influences of his continental European musical training, and American musical styles. Among his still-admired works are *Babes in Toyland* (1903) and *Naughty Marietta* (1910). Two other European-born composers, Rudolf Friml and Sigmund Romberg, were Herbert's major successors as composers of American operetta. See the article OPERETTA in Volume O.

Musical Comedy and Revue

The other two types of popular musical theater, musical comedy and revue, share similar backgrounds. Both developed from two earlier forms of popular entertainment, **farce-comedy** and **vaudeville**. (The ballad opera was an additional source of musical comedy.) In farce-comedy, an American entertainment of the 1800's, a series of songs, dances, and other acts were performed, loosely unified by a very simple story. In time these simple plots developed complications, and the songs came to be written especially for the situations on stage. In vaudeville, a succession of performers came on stage, did their acts, and exited. There was no plot.

The revue was by far the shortest lived of the main types of musical theater. It consisted of an evening of songs, dances, and skits performed by a group of players. Except for a few very early revues, there was no hint of a plot, and the songs and skits often flitted from one subject to another. Perhaps the most elaborate revues were those produced by Florenz Ziegfeld, whose opulent *Ziegfeld Follies* were staged from 1907 through 1931.

In musical comedy there is usually as much spoken dialogue as song. The story is often lighter than in operetta. The songs are simpler, with smaller ranges, and are much easier to sing. In England, the first true musical comedies were the Gaiety shows, produced in the 1890's by George Edwardes at his theaters. They featured contemporary stories, with songs in the latest musical styles, such as ragtime. Fashionably dressed leading ladies and chorus girls sometimes stepped to the latest dances.

In the United States, the musical plays of George M. Cohan, such as *Little Johnny Jones* (1904), were influential. But the first truly modern American musical comedies began in 1915 with the Princess Theater shows of composer Jerome Kern. Among the Princess hits were *Very Good, Eddie!* (1915) and *Oh, Boy!* (1917). At about the same time, other talented composers, notably Irving Berlin and Cole Porter, also were beginning to write uniquely American works. For many decades thereafter, American musicals, particularly those produced in New York City's Broadway theater district, set the standard for musicals worldwide.

Kern and others introduced jazz into their show music, but it was George Gershwin who became the most famous composer of jazz-based musicals, among them *Lady, Be Good!* (1924) and *Oh, Kay!* (1926). Other leading composers included Vincent Youmans, whose *No, No, Nanette* (1925) was the most successful of all musical comedies of the era, and Ray Henderson, who wrote the music for the tremendously popular *Good News* (1927).

From the mid-1920's to the start of World War II, Richard Rodgers, his lyricist Lorenz Hart, and their librettists provided Broadway with such shows as *A Connecticut Yankee* (1927) and *On Your Toes* (1937). Among the early hits of the prolific Cole Porter were *Fifty Million Frenchmen* (1929), *Gay Divorce* (1932), and *Anything Goes* (1934).

The Modern American Musical

In 1927, Jerome Kern and Oscar Hammerstein wrote what was the first genuine American operetta, *Show Boat*. It took an American story and set it to distinctly American music, but with all the lush beauty of operetta. However, with the onset of the Great Depression and a demand for lighter entertainment, *Show Boat* remained unequaled for many years. In the 1930's, George Gershwin and his lyricist brother Ira experimented with reworking traditional forms. Harking back to opéra bouffe, they satirized American politics in *Of Thee I Sing* (1931), the first musical to win a Pulitzer Prize. They also experimented with opera in *Porgy and Bess* (1935).

Yet it was not until 1943 that musicals and attitudes toward musicals altered dramatically with composer Richard Rodgers and librettist-lyricist Oscar Hammerstein's *Oklahoma!* Although not, as claimed, the first musical to truly integrate song, dance, and story, it did raise the standards for American musicals. Other outstanding Rodgers and Hammerstein works include *Carousel* (1945), *South Pacific* (1949), *The King and I* (1951), and *The Sound of Music* (1959).

A scene from *Cats*, a musical by English composer Andrew Lloyd Webber. This and other long-running hits by Lloyd Webber drew large audiences and did much to enliven contemporary musical theater.

This great era of the Broadway musical produced many memorable shows, among them Irving Berlin's *Annie Get Your Gun* (1946), Cole Porter's *Kiss Me, Kate* (1948), Frank Loesser's *Guys and Dolls* (1950), Frederick Loewe and Alan Jay Lerner's *My Fair Lady* (1956), Leonard Bernstein's *West Side Story* (1957), and Jerry Bock's *Fiddler on the Roof* (1964).

By the mid-1960's, Broadway creativity had begun to fade. Many of the long-running hits, such as *A Chorus Line* (1975), were inspired more by brilliant directors than by creative writers. Many saw the imaginative, free-spirited works of Stephen Sondheim as exceptions. Yet these musicals, which included *A Little Night Music* (1973), *Sweeney Todd*

Oklahoma!, by Richard Rodgers and Oscar Hammerstein, was first staged in 1943. Its skillful blending of song, dance, and story raised the standards for American musicals and ushered in a golden age of the Broadway musical.

(1979), and *Sunday in the Park with George* (1984), were rarely commercial successes.

At the same time that Broadway faded, English composers, led by Andrew Lloyd Webber, began creating rock-inspired musicals. Lloyd Webber enjoyed huge hits, such as *Jesus Christ Superstar* (1971), *Cats* (1982), *The Phantom of the Opera* (1988), and *Sunset Boulevard* (1994). *Les Misérables* (1987), with music by French composer Claude-Michel Schönberg, was another outstanding musical of European origin.

In addition to these imports, the Broadway shows that continued to draw large audiences were revivals of hits of the past and "new" musicals—such as *Ain't Misbehavin'* (1978) and *Jelly's Last Jam* (1992)—constructed around the music of popular composers.

GERALD BORDMAN
Author, *American Musical Theatre: A Chronicle*

MUSIC FESTIVALS

A music festival is a series of musical performances held at regular intervals, often during the summer months. Many music festivals are organized around a central theme, such as the music of a particular composer or a certain type of music.

European Festivals. The Bayreuth Festival, held every July and August in Bayreuth, Germany, is dedicated to the performance of Richard Wagner's operas. It was first held in 1876, when Wagner himself conducted the first complete performance of his monumental *Ring of the Nibelung*. Salzburg, Austria, the birthplace of Wolfgang Amadeus Mozart, is the location of a summer festival dedicated mainly to Mozart's music. The first Mozart festival was held there in 1877, but the Salzburg Festival as we know it today came into being in 1920. The Vienna Philharmonic Orchestra performs at the festival.

The Glyndebourne Festival, held every May and June since 1934 in Sussex, England, is famous for its opera productions. Mozart's operas are given prominence, but other composers are also represented. The Edinburgh Festival, in Edinburgh, Scotland, presents operas, dramas, ballets, concerts, and films. Organized in 1947, it is held each year from late August into September.

Opera is the main feature of the Florence May Festival (the Maggio Musicale Fiorentino), begun in 1933. But there are also symphony concerts, recitals by famous soloists, and chamber music performances. Another major Italian festival is the Festival of Two Worlds, founded by the American composer Gian-Carlo Menotti in 1958 and held every summer in Spoleto, Italy. Its presentations include operas, ballets, chamber music, dramas, and solo recitals.

Two other noted European summer music festivals are the Lucerne Festival, held in Lucerne, Switzerland, and the Holland Music Festival, held in Amsterdam, The Hague, and Scheveningen. Both present concerts of orchestral, choral, and chamber music.

Montreux, Switzerland, is famous for its annual jazz festival. Other important jazz festivals are held each year in Nice, France, and Berlin, Germany.

North American Festivals. The Berkshire Music Festival, or Tanglewood, is perhaps the most famous American music festival. It is held annually in July and August at the Tanglewood estate, near Lenox, Massachusetts. Tanglewood has been the summer home of the Boston Symphony Orchestra since 1937, and performances by the symphony remain the festival's main attraction.

An annual music festival is held at Wolf Trap Farm in Virginia near Washington, D.C.

Tanglewood, a summer music festival in Massachusetts, provides a relaxed atmosphere for enjoying concerts by the Boston Symphony Orchestra and other performers.

This festival, established in 1971, is sponsored by the federal government under the National Park Service. The Spoleto Festival, U.S.A., a counterpart to the Festival of Two Worlds in Spoleto, Italy, was begun by Gian-Carlo Menotti in Charleston, South Carolina, in 1977. It is held annually in late spring.

Aspen, Colorado, is the site of both a summer music school and a festival. Concerts, recitals, and chamber music performances are given. Ann Arbor, Michigan, has been the location of a significant music festival since 1893. Each May, a schedule of symphonic and choral works is performed.

In 1950 the pianist Rudolf Serkin became a founder and director of a festival of chamber music in Marlboro, Vermont. This festival has been held annually in July and August ever since. May is the month of an annual Bach festival in Bethlehem, Pennsylvania. Annual music festivals are held at Saratoga Springs, New York, summer home of the Philadelphia Orchestra, and Ravinia, Illinois, where the Chicago Symphony plays in summer.

Jazz festivals are held annually in many cities throughout the United States, notably New Orleans, Louisiana; Monterey, California; and New York City.

In Canada, summer music festivals are held in Stratford, Ontario, between June and October; in Banff, Alberta, in August; and in Guelph, Ontario, from late April to mid-May. Montreal hosts one of the world's largest jazz festivals for ten days in June and July.

DAVID EWEN
Author, *Encyclopedia of Concert Music*

MUSKIE, EDMUND SIXTUS.   See MAINE (Famous People).

MUSLIM.   See ISLAM.

MUSSOLINI, BENITO (1883–1945)

From the early 1920's through World War II (1939–45), Italy was ruled by one man—Benito Mussolini. Called *Il Duce* ("The Leader"), he was the founder of fascism.

Mussolini was born in Dovia, Italy, on July 29, 1883. His father, a blacksmith, taught him socialist ideas. His mother kept a one-room school in their home. As a child, Benito was aggressive, temperamental, and undisciplined. These traits remained with him all his life.

When he was 18, Mussolini qualified to teach school. But his interests and disposition soon led him into politics. His speaking ability quickly made him a leader of Italy's Socialist Party. During this period he met Rachele Guidi, who later became his wife; they had five children. In 1912, Mussolini became editor of the Socialist newspaper *Avanti!* ("Forward!"). He unexpectedly broke with the Socialists in 1914 and started his own newspaper, *Il Popolo d'Italia* ("The Italian People").

Italy's role in World War I (1914–18) nearly ruined its economy. Waves of strikes and political demonstrations swept the country. In 1919, Mussolini organized the Fascist Party. His promise to make Italy great gained him the support of Italian nationalists. Conservative business leaders supported him as a defense against a working-class uprising. His small but merciless army of fascists (known as blackshirts because of their uniform) soon became an important political force.

In 1922, Mussolini organized a fascist march on Rome to gain control of the country. Fearing a revolution, King Victor Emmanuel III asked him to form a new government. In 1923, Mussolini set up what he called the Corporate State, headed by the Grand Council of Fascism. Using both propaganda and force, he put down individual freedom and turned Italy into a police state.

Mussolini then began to dream of building an Italian empire. In 1936 he conquered Ethiopia. Unable to find support for his aggressive actions elsewhere, he formed an alliance with the German dictator Adolf Hitler. Soon after World War II began, Italy became Germany's military ally. Losses in the war made Mussolini unpopular at home. In 1943 he was driven from power and imprisoned. Hitler arranged his rescue and made him head of a German-controlled government in northern Italy. On April 28, 1945, he was captured by Italian partisans and executed.

Reviewed by JULES ARCHER
Author, *Twentieth-Century Caesar:
Benito Mussolini*

See also FASCISM.

MUSTELIDS.   See OTTERS AND OTHER MUSTELIDS.

MYANMAR

Myanmar, formerly known as Burma, is a nation of Southeast Asia. About the size of the U.S. state of Texas, it is the largest of the mainland Southeast Asian countries. Myanmar has sometimes been called the Land of Pagodas because of the many pagodas, or Buddhist shrines, that dot the landscape.

Although it is surrounded by several other nations, Myanmar has been isolated for much of its long history both by the mountains that enclose it on three sides and by its rulers who chose to separate the country from its neighbors. In 1989, Burma's leaders changed its name to "Myanmar," which is "Burma" in the Burmese language.

▶ PEOPLE

The Burmese are Myanmar's largest ethnic group, making up about two-thirds of the population. The main non-Burmese peoples include the Shan, the Karen, and the Rakhine. Other groups include the Kachin, the Chin, and the Mon. There are also ethnic Indians, Bangladeshis, and Chinese.

Language. More than 120 different languages and dialects are spoken, but Burmese, the language of the Burmese, is the most widely used. Burmese is related to Tibetan, which in turn is related to Chinese.

Religion. The first Burmese kings adopted Buddhism (which originated in India) from the Mon people, whom they conquered in the A.D. 1000's. Today almost all Burmese are Buddhists, as are the Shan and Mon.

Some of the smaller ethnic groups still follow ancient tribal religions, while others were converted to Christianity by British and American missionaries. Myanmar also has

Clockwise from left: The Shwe Dagon pagoda in Yangon is perhaps the most magnificent of the country's many Buddhist shrines. Buddhist monks serve as teachers as well as spiritual leaders in Myanmar's society. A Burmese woman sells produce at a local marketplace.

Myanmar

substantial Hindu and Muslim minorities, chiefly the Indians and Bangladeshis.

Education. Basic education consists of one year of kindergarten, followed by four years of primary school, four years of middle school, and two years of high school. However, there are shortages of schools and teachers in the smaller and remote areas. The country's major universities are located in the cities of Yangon, the capital, and Mandalay.

All formal education is government sponsored. But because schools are crowded and standards have fallen, many families in the cities and towns send their children to private tutoring schools in addition to public schools.

Rural Life. Most Burmese live in villages and are farmers. Farmhouses are often built on poles and have walls of matting and roofs made of palm-leaf thatch. The typical house has a porch, which serves as both a living and dining area. The houses are grouped together along dirt paths, with each house having a small garden where vegetables and fruits are grown and where domestic animals may be kept. Most farmers plow their land with water buffalo.

City Life. Although most Burmese still live in rural areas, the cities have grown rapidly. People take buses from their homes to work. There are many businesses, including factories that produce clothing and food, and many people are employed by the government. Automobile use has increased recently and resulted in traffic problems.

Food. Rice is the staple food and is eaten at every meal. Vegetables, fish, and dishes flavored with curry powder (a mixture of ground spices) are also popular. A sauce or paste made from fish or shrimp is commonly used as a seasoning. Coconut and coconut milk are also important ingredients, as are fruits such as mangoes, papaya, and bananas. Meat is rarely eaten.

Dress. Most Burmese wear a sarong-like skirt called a *longyi* (or *lungyi*), with men's and women's garments differing in patterns

Left: A typical rural house stands on stilts and is roofed with palm-leaf thatch. *Above:* Workers harvest rice from a paddy. Rice is the staple food in this primarily agricultural nation.

Left: Mountains and forests cover much of Myanmar's land. The mountains form a natural boundary between the country and its neighbors. *Below:* Workers use an elephant to haul a huge teak log from a forest. Myanmar exports more of this valuable hardwood than any other country.

and the way they are tied. On formal occasions men wear a colorful cloth headdress called a *gaungbaung.* Women go bareheaded but often wear flowers in their hair. Young, unmarried women frequently tie their hair in a ponytail. Married women traditionally wear their hair in a bun.

▶ LAND

Myanmar is a generally mountainous land just north of the equator. It is bordered by China on the north and northeast, Thailand and Laos on the east, and India and Bangladesh on the west.

Land Regions. Myanmar is made up of two land regions: the central lowlands and a surrounding arc of mountains. The lowlands consist of valleys surrounding the Irrawaddy and Sittang rivers and their tributaries. Mountains form a natural boundary between Myanmar and its neighboring countries. Major ranges include the Patkai and the Kumon in the north, the Dawna and the Bilauktaung in the south, and the Manipur Hills in the northwest. Mount Hkakabo is the highest peak, rising to 19,290 feet (5,880 meters).

Rivers and Coastal Waters. The Irrawaddy is Myanmar's major river. It is the chief communications link between central and southern Myanmar, and it was the "road to Mandalay" in Rudyard Kipling's famous poem "Mandalay." The Salween River to the east is not navigable (usable by ships) for most of its length. The Sittang River drains the eastern part of central Myanmar.

In the south, Myanmar has a long coastline on the Bay of Bengal and the Andaman Sea, arms of the Indian Ocean.

Climate. Myanmar has three seasons, based on the monsoon winds. From October through February the winds bring dry weather with warm days and cool nights. In March the hot dry season begins. The rainy season begins in June, as humid winds sweep in from the Bay of Bengal, bringing up to 200 inches (5,000 millimeters) of rainfall along the coast. The rains are scattered by the mountains, however, and central Myanmar remains relatively dry. It is after the first rains that the hard, dry, compacted ground is moistened and farmers can plow and plant their rice and other crops.

Natural Resources. Forests, which cover nearly half the land, are one of Myanmar's most valuable natural resources. Myanmar has about 75 percent of the world's reserves of teak and is the leading supplier of this valuable hardwood, which is used chiefly in making furniture.

Myanmar has extensive mineral deposits, including tin, antimony, zinc, copper, tungsten, lead, coal, and limestone. It is also famed for gemstones such as jade, rubies, and sapphires. Petroleum production was once significant, but the country's output has diminished recently. There are, however, large reserves of natural gas onshore and offshore.

UNION OF MYANMAR is the official name of the country. Historically, however, it has been known as Burma.

LOCATION: Southeast Asia.

AREA: 261,218 sq mi (676,555 km²).

POPULATION: 49,340,000 (estimate).

CAPITAL AND LARGEST CITY: Yangon.

MAJOR LANGUAGES: Burmese, numerous other languages.

MAJOR RELIGIOUS GROUP: Buddhist.

GOVERNMENT: Military regime. **Head of state and government**—prime minister.

CHIEF PRODUCTS: Agricultural—rice, corn, oilseed, sugarcane, pulses. **Manufactured**—processed foods, textiles, footwear, wood and wood products, construction materials, pharmaceuticals, fertilizer. **Mineral**—copper, tin, tungsten, iron, natural gas.

MONETARY UNIT: Kyat (1 kyat = 100 pyas).

▶ **ECONOMY**

Since 1988, Myanmar's government has built many roads, bridges, and small irrigation systems throughout the country. The government has also encouraged tourism, but with limited success. Trade with China and Thailand has grown, but the country imports more goods than it exports.

Agriculture. The country's most important crop is rice, which is grown in wet, irrigated fields on the plains and in dry fields in the highlands. At one time, Myanmar was the world's leading exporter of rice. Corn, oilseed, sugarcane, and pulses (edible seeds of various legumes) are also grown.

Manufacturing. Chief manufactured products include processed foods, textiles, footwear, lumber, various metals, and fertilizers. In the past, consumer goods were often brought into the country illegally because Myanmar's industry could not produce them efficiently and they could not be legally imported. The government has since legalized this trade.

▶ **MAJOR CITIES**

Yangon (formerly Rangoon), in the south, is the country's capital, largest city, and chief seaport. It has a population of more than 4 million. One of the city's most impressive sites is the thousand-year-old Shwe Dagon pagoda, the most revered Buddhist shrine in Southeast Asia. Most of Myanmar's industry is located in and around the city.

Mandalay, the second largest city, lies on the Irrawaddy River in central Myanmar and has a population of more than 530,000. The capital of the kingdom of Burma from 1860 to 1885, it is the country's cultural center. Other important cities are **Moulmein,** a port on the Salween River in the southeast; **Bassein** in the delta region in the south; and **Pegu,** a city near Yangon that was once a Mon capital.

▶ **CULTURAL HERITAGE**

Myanmar's most notable works of art are its pagodas. Thousands of these beautiful and historic shrines are located throughout the country, particularly in the ancient city of Pagan. Wood carving, another popular art form, is often used to decorate monasteries. Traditional dance and music are practiced in state schools and in private groups. Literature is closely censored by the government.

Yangon (formerly Rangoon) is Myanmar's capital and largest city. It is the country's chief seaport as well as a center of industry.

GOVERNMENT

Myanmar is governed by a military regime. The head of state is the chairman of the State Peace and Development Council (SPDC). General Than Shwe ruled as both head of state and government from 1992 until he appointed a prime minister to assist him in 2003.

HISTORY

After migrating south from China in the A.D. 700's, the Burmese unified the country. The classical age of Burma collapsed when Pagan fell to the troops of China's Mongol emperor Kublai Khan in 1287.

Following a period of Shan rule, two powerful Burmese kingdoms arose. The Toungoo dynasty (1484–1752) controlled Burma and northern Thailand. The Konbaung dynasty (1752–1885) pushed into eastern India, bringing Burma into conflict with Britain, who then ruled India as a colony.

British Rule. Beginning in 1824, three wars were fought between the British and Burmese. These Anglo-Burmese wars gradually eliminated Burma as an independent kingdom, and in 1886, all of Burma was incorporated into British India. In 1937, Britain gave Burma limited self-government.

During World War II (1939–45), the Japanese invaded Burma and established a Burmese state under Japanese rule. Burma was reoccupied by the British in 1945, but General Aung San (considered the father of independent Burma) negotiated his country's eventual independence. Aung San was assassinated in 1947.

Independence. In 1948, Burma became an independent nation, with U Nu as its first prime minister. Until 1958, the Union of Burma was a parliamentary democracy. But some ethnic groups, along with Communists and other dissidents, were in revolt against the central government.

In 1958 the military, led by General U Ne Win, overthrew U Nu and took control of the country. Ne Win relinquished power to U Nu after elections in 1960 but seized control of the government again in 1962. In 1974 a new constitution established a highly centralized government under a single political party, the Burma Socialist Program Party (BSPP), which was dominated by the military. Military rule created social and economic inequality as well as political repression.

The opposition leader Aung San Suu Kyi won the Nobel Peace Prize in 1991 for her nonviolent struggle for democracy and human rights in Myanmar.

Recent Events. In 1988, massive student and urban demonstrations caused Ne Win to resign. But a new military group, the State Law and Order Restoration Council (SLORC), quickly seized power. The main opposition party, the National League for Democracy (NLD), was led by Aung San's daughter, Aung San Suu Kyi. She was placed under house arrest for her pro-democracy views in 1989. Suu Kyi remained under protective custody until 1995, despite being awarded the Nobel Peace Prize in 1991.

SLORC was replaced in November 1997 by the SPDC, with the military remaining firmly in control. Earlier that year, the country was admitted to the Association of Southeast Asian Nations (ASEAN).

In 2000, Suu Kyi was again placed under house arrest. She was released in 2002, but the United Nations remained outspoken about Myanmar's human rights abuses. In 2003, Suu Kyi was again imprisoned and held despite international pressure to release her, including the threat of economic sanctions by the United States and European Union.

On December 26, 2004, a massive earthquake in the Indian Ocean caused a sea surge (tsunami) that killed dozens of Burmese and destroyed many villages, mostly in the Irrawaddy Delta.

THOMAS F. BARTON
Indiana University
Reviewed by DAVID I. STEINBERG
Georgetown University
Author, *Burma: The State of Myanmar*

MYCENAEAN CULTURE

The Mycenaean culture flourished on the mainland of Greece during the Late Bronze Age, from about 1425 to 1100 B.C. Named after Mycenae, its major city, this culture was the direct ancestor of the great civilization of ancient Greece that later developed in the region.

The Mycenaeans were skilled metalworkers. This gold mask was found in an ancient tomb and is known as the Mask of Agamemnon, after Mycenae's legendary king.

What is known about the Mycenaeans comes from two major sources: archaeological evidence, especially clay tablets that have been found at several sites throughout the region; and the myths and legends of the ancient Greeks, which contain references to the Mycenaeans.

Society. Mycenaean society consisted of several probably independent kingdoms centered on large and heavily fortified cities. Each city contained a palace with a major hall, or *megaron*. Inside the hall was a central hearth and a throne. The head of a kingdom's government was known as a *wanax* and was similar to a king. The government of each kingdom was responsible for distributing goods and taxing the people.

Several distinct classes of people lived in a Mycenaean kingdom. The upper class helped the *wanax* govern the kingdom. The middle class consisted mostly of farmers, and the lower class consisted of free and slave laborers. In at least one kingdom, centered on the city of Pylos, slaves were able to own land and animals and give offerings to the gods. The Mycenaeans worshiped a number of gods, some of which—such as Athena, Poseidon, and Zeus—were also worshiped by the ancient Greeks.

The Mycenaean economy was based on agriculture. Wheat and barley were the main crops, and horses, sheep, and other farm animals were domesticated. Pottery and textiles were among the items exported, while ivory and various metals were imported.

The Mycenaeans spoke an early form of the Greek language. Clay tablets were inscribed in a script now known as Linear B, and most examples known today consist of administrative and economic records.

Mycenaean wall paintings typically showed human and animal figures in styles and poses that varied little from work to work. Common themes included war and hunting. Metalwork was a Mycenaean specialty, particularly the combining of different metals to decorate objects such as dagger blades. Terracotta (clay) and ivory figurines, painted pottery, engraved gems, and jewelry were also produced in abundance. For more information on the art of the Mycenaeans and the later ancient Greeks, see the article GREECE, ART AND ARCHITECTURE OF in Volume G.

Decline. Beginning in the mid-1200's B.C. the Mycenaean culture began to decline. The ultimate cause is debated; economic collapse, foreign invasion, internal conflicts, and climatic changes may all have played a part. By about 1100 B.C. everything that defined the Mycenaean culture had disappeared.

WILLIAM R. BIERS
Professor Emeritus
University of Missouri, Columbia

Mycenaean Culture
About 1250 B.C.

MYSTERY AND DETECTIVE STORIES

The term "mystery story" is a very broad and loose way of describing a wide variety of fiction written during many different historical periods. It is used to describe one of the earliest forms of narrative, the adventure story. Later fictional forms—the Gothic story, the crime story, the spy story, and the detective story—also are considered types of mystery stories. Of all the forms, the detective story is the most complicated and the most popular.

▶ ADVENTURE STORIES

The basic plot of an adventure story involves a determined and virtuous hero who must overcome many obstacles to achieve an important goal. These obstacles may include getting from one place to another or finishing a task before an appointed time, or they may be connected to human nature. The human obstacles are the most complicated: They include the hero's own limitations, such as fear, exhaustion, and injury, as well as the complexities of the people—both good and bad—encountered in the course of the story. Adventure stories are considered mystery stories because usually the hero must untangle a seemingly unsolvable problem.

Many of the world's best-known myths, epics, and fables are adventure stories. In modern times, works such as *Treasure Island* (1883), by Robert Louis Stevenson, *King Solomon's Mines* (1885), by H. Rider Haggard, and *The Prisoner of Zenda* (1894), by Anthony Hope, all contain the main elements of the adventure story. At the beginning of the 1900's, writers such as John Buchan, Edgar Wallace, and Sax Rohmer gained large readerships writing **thrillers**, a new term applied to the adventure story. By then, the adventure story borrowed elements from other kinds of mystery fiction.

▶ GOTHIC STORIES

The Gothic story began as a reaction to the emphasis placed on reason and order by writers and thinkers in the early 1700's. Gothic stories are tales of horror and the supernatural. The setting—an ancient castle, for example, filled with eerie sights and sounds—helps create an atmosphere of mystery and

An illustration for *The Woman in White*, by Wilkie Collins, an English writer who contributed greatly to the development of mystery and detective novels.

suspense. Some danger threatens the innocent victim of the story, who is often a young woman.

The first Gothic novel is generally considered to be *The Castle of Otranto* (1764), by Horace Walpole, followed by *The Mysteries of Udolpho* (1794), by Ann Radcliffe. *Frankenstein* (1817), by Mary Shelley, includes many elements of the Gothic novel. In the United States, the tales of Edgar Allan Poe are the most important examples of Gothic fiction.

In the mid-1800's a group of English writers combined the main features of the Gothic novel with some of the features of the crime story and detective story to create what is called the **sensation novel**. The most famous writer of sensation novels was Wilkie Collins, author of *The Woman in White* (1860) and *The Moonstone* (1868).

Biographies of two of the most famous writers of detective fiction, Arthur Conan Doyle and Edgar Allan Poe, can be found in volumes D and P.

Raymond Chandler

Agatha Christie

Raymond Chandler (1888–1959), born in Chicago, Ill., helped create the form known as hard-boiled detective fiction. After losing his job during the Great Depression, he turned to writing, publishing his first story in 1933. His seven novels, featuring the tough-minded private detective Philip Marlowe, were highly successful. Several, including *The Big Sleep* (1939), *Farewell, My Lovely* (1940), and *The Long Goodbye* (1953), were made into films. Chandler also wrote a number of screenplays.

Agatha Christie (1890–1976), born in Torquay, England, is famous for her detective stories, many of which feature the Belgian detective Hercule Poirot or the English amateur sleuth Jane Marple. A prolific writer, she published some 100 novels, stories, and plays. *The Murder of Roger Ackroyd* (1926), *Murder on the Orient Express* (1934), and *Ten Little Indians* (1939) are among her best-known novels. Her plays include *The Mousetrap* (1952), which became one of the longest-running plays in London theater history, and *Witness for the Prosecution* (1953).

Wilkie Collins (1824–89), born in London, England, has been called the father of the detective novel. Trained in the law, he eventually turned full time to writing. His early novels appeared in *Household Words*, a magazine published by his friend Charles Dickens. In the 1860's he became famous as the author of sensation novels, notably *The Woman in White* (1860) and *The Moonstone* (1868). In these he established many of the conventions of the modern detective novel.

Ian Fleming (1908–64), born in London, England, is best known as the creator of James Bond, Agent 007 of Her Majesty's Secret Service. An officer in British Naval Intelligence during World War II, Fleming began to write the spy thrillers that made him famous in 1953. Featuring Bond's fantastic exploits in the world of international intrigue, they include *From Russia With Love* (1957), *Dr. No* (1958), *Goldfinger* (1959), and *You Only Live Twice* (1964). Many were made into popular films.

Dashiell Hammett (1894–1961), born in St. Mary's County, Md., pioneered the style of American detective fiction known as hard-boiled. Many of his novels are based on his own experiences as a detective with the Pinkerton agency. His

---

In the 1900's, some elements of Gothic fiction were retained in works by a number of writers, mainly women, who wrote suspenseful stories featuring innocent heroines. Among the best known of these writers are American novelist Mary Roberts Rinehart (*The Circular Staircase*; 1908) and English novelist Daphne du Maurier (*Rebecca*; 1938).

▶ CRIME STORIES

The origins of the crime story can be traced to the early 1700's, when a number of noted English writers, including John Gay, Henry Fielding, and Daniel Defoe, wrote accounts of the lives of well-known criminals. In the mid-1700's, the chaplains at Newgate Prison in London began to publish biographies of the prison's inmates to warn readers about crime and to supplement their own meager incomes. From this time onward, stories about sensational crimes and notorious criminals became a common form of journalism. It became common, too, for these true accounts to provide the basis for different kinds of mystery fiction.

Some detective stories look back in history and present investigations and solutions to actual crimes. Criminals' lives form the basis for other novels, such as *Little Caesar* (1929), by American writer William Riley Burnett, that examine the psychology of underworld figures. Still other crime novels, such as *Thieves Like Us* (1937), by American author Edward Anderson, examine crime and criminals from a sociological point of view.

▶ SPY STORIES

Spy stories did not arrive on the literary scene until the end of the 1800's. Before this time, the spy was viewed as a vile and dishonorable traitor and was the subject of very few literary works. Later, with the rise of nation-first successful novel, *The Maltese Falcon* (1930), became a classic of detective fiction and its lead character, Sam Spade, a model of the tough private eye. Hammett's other books, several of which were made into films, include *The Glass Key* (1931) and *The Thin Man* (1932).

Tony Hillerman (1925–), born in Sacred Heart, Okla., is best known for his mysteries set among the Navajo people of the American Southwest. His novels, which often feature Navajo tribal police officers Joe Leaphorn and Jim Chee, are admired for their insight into Native American culture as well as for their intricate plots. They include *The Blessing Way* (1970), *Skinwalkers* (1986), and *Coyote Waits* (1990).

John Le Carré (David Cornwell) (1931–), born in Poole, England, became famous for his realistic spy novels. Le Carré, who worked in the British Foreign Service (1960–64), won international acclaim with *The Spy Who Came in From the Cold* (1963). His best-known character is George Smiley, a British agent who appears in several novels. His other

Ian Fleming

Sara Paretsky

novels include *Tinker, Tailor, Soldier, Spy* (1974), *The Little Drummer Girl* (1983), and *The Night Manager* (1993).

Sara Paretsky (1947–), born in Ames, Iowa, is the creator of V. I. Warshawski, a gutsy female private investigator. The character, whose cases often involve such contemporary issues as corporate fraud and medical ethics, was introduced in *Indemnity Only* (1982). Other Warshawski mysteries include *Killing Orders* (1985), *Bitter Medicine* (1987), and *Guardian Angel* (1991).

Ellery Queen is the pen name of two cousins, **Frederic Dannay** (1905–82) and **Manfred B. Lee** (1905–71), both born in Brooklyn, N. Y. They began their mystery-writing collaboration with *The*

Roman Hat Mystery (1929), their winning entry in a writing contest. "Ellery Queen" was also the name of their detective hero, who became famous through novels, films, and radio and television series.

Dorothy L. Sayers (1893–1957), born in Oxford, England, is known for her mystery stories featuring the aristocratic amateur detective Lord Peter Wimsey. Sayers, a graduate of Oxford University, worked for a time in an advertising agency. Wimsey was introduced in *Whose Body?* (1923) and later appeared in *Clouds of Witness* (1927), *Murder Must Advertise* (1932), *The Nine Tailors* (1934), and other stories.

Georges Simenon (1903–89), born in Liège, Belgium, is one of the world's most widely read writers. More than 100 of his novels are detective stories featuring Paris police inspector Jules Maigret. The first of these, *The Strange Case of Peter the Lett*, appeared in 1930. The Maigret stories are known for their accurate portrayal of police procedure.

---

alism and modern methods of warfare, spying, or espionage, came to be seen by many as a necessary government activity. The spy novel rose in popularity during World War II (1939–45) and the "cold war" that followed. English writers, in particular, contributed greatly to this form.

Spy novels can be divided into two separate categories: the realistic spy story and the spy-adventure story. The realistic school presents the difficult and dangerous work of espionage without glamorizing it. It began with Joseph Conrad's *The Secret Agent* (1907), which was based on an actual incident, and continued with the works of Eric Ambler and, later, John LeCarré and Len Deighton.

The spy-adventure story follows the basic plot of the adventure story, in which the hero must overcome a series of obstacles. In these stories, the spy hero is often presented as an exciting, romantic figure. Ian Fleming, with

his books about the fantastic exploits of British secret agent James Bond, and Tom Clancy are among the best known of the adventure school of spy writers.

▶ **DETECTIVE STORIES**

The detective story became popular during the 1900's. Unlike other kinds of fictional heroes, the detective is a relatively recent creation: The first modern police force, the London Metropolitan Police, was organized in 1829, and not until nearly twenty years later were plainclothes detectives (officers who do not wear uniforms on duty) made a part of organized law enforcement.

The most important difference between detective stories and other kinds of mystery fiction is the way the writer tells the story. First, the narrative does not begin at the beginning of the story but picks up the action after the most important event (usually, but not always, some kind of crime) has occurred. Second, the identity of the villain is usually revealed before readers learn the complete details about the beginning. Finally, in addition to changing the normal order of the story, detective story writers intend to surprise their readers when they reveal the "real" facts at the end.

Edgar Allan Poe invented the detective story in the 1840's. In "The Murders in the Rue Morgue" (1841), "The Purloined Letter" (1844), and other short stories, he introduced many of the techniques on which detective stories would come to depend. These include the locked room murder, in which a seemingly impossible crime has been committed; the armchair detective, who solves the crime through pure intellectual reasoning; the red herring, or false clue; and many more. Another of Poe's inventions is the depiction of the detective hero as a misunderstood genius. Almost every important detective story writer owes something to Poe.

Poe's genius detective, however, is not a very sympathetic hero. The creation of a sympathetic detective-hero is one of the key contributions of Charles Dickens to the detective story. Dickens included a murder mystery among the plots of his novel *Bleak House* (1853). In the character of Inspector Bucket, who solves the mystery, Dickens combined genius with humane qualities.

The first writer to really take advantage of Poe's inventions, however, was the French novelist Émile Gaboriau. In a series of novels, beginning with *The Widow Lerouge* (1866), he introduced detectives who use scientific method to solve crimes. His novels describe innovations in police work, such as taking casts of footprints with plaster of Paris, and portray the detective as a master of disguise. But Gaboriau had a difficult time making the detective story long enough to fill up a novel, and so he usually simply split it apart and put a long romantic story in the middle.

Expanding the detective story into a full-length novel was one of the accomplishments of Wilkie Collins. In *The Moonstone* (1868), a tale of the disappearance of a fabulous gem, the story is presented from several characters' points of view. The facts of the case emerge as readers begin to see the events from more than one perspective.

It was Arthur Conan Doyle who combined several of these ideas to create one of the best-known fictional detectives of all time, Sherlock Holmes. Holmes was introduced in the novel *A Study in Scarlet* (1887), but Doyle's real success began when he wrote short stories about his detective for a new magazine called the *Strand*. With the publication of the Sherlock Holmes stories in the *Strand*, the detective story became a very popular form. By the beginning of the 1900's, many writers in England and the United States were producing detective stories for popular magazines. Most of these stories featured eccentric, genius detectives patterned after Sherlock Holmes.

The Modern Detective Story

The modern detective novel began about the time of World War I (1914–18). It began with a revolt against Sherlock Holmes and the other detectives who appeared in popular magazines. Writers began to feel that the portrayals of these detectives and their methods were not very realistic. The reaction against this kind of detective story took two very different forms.

In Britain and the United States, a number of writers, including E. C. Bentley, Dorothy

Sherlock Holmes (right) discusses a case with Dr. Watson. The famous fictional detective was the creation of English writer Arthur Conan Doyle.

Sayers, Agatha Christie, Margery Allingham, Michael Innes, Ellery Queen, and John Dickson Carr, began to write detective stories that were aimed at more sophisticated readers. These writers came from different kinds of backgrounds than the earlier detective writers. Among them were scholars, professors, and, especially, women. They contributed to what is now considered a golden age of detective fiction, in the 1920's and 1930's.

Their stories were full of references to classical literature and culture. They took special care in describing how detectives solved problems, and they wrote in a sophisticated and witty style. These writers abandoned the idea of the genius detective, focusing instead on the human aspects of their detectives and other characters. And they approached writing as a game played by the writer, who hides clues in the novel, and the reader, who tries to find them before the end of the book. They also transformed the detective story into a novel that concentrated on solving one very complicated problem and that introduced a cast of characters who all had some connection with the case. The form they perfected is known as the **classic** detective story.

In the United States, the revolt against Sherlock Holmes led to the creation of the form known as **hard-boiled** detective fiction. The hard-boiled story first appeared in inexpensive magazines written primarily for male readers. In these magazines (called pulp magazines after the cheap pulpwood paper they were printed on), writers such as Dashiell Hammett, Raymond Chandler, Horace McCoy, Frederick Nebel, and Carroll John Daly wrote stories featuring tough private detectives. The detective heroes are loners who are both cynical and romantic. Although they have learned to distrust others, they never give up their ideals. The stories include a great deal of violence because they take place in a world of real criminals, where government is either incompetent or corrupt. They are written in a style that is appropriate to their characters

American hard-boiled detective fiction first appeared in pulp magazines such as *Black Mask*.

and their setting: the language of the streets, full of action, vulgarity, slang, and wisecracks.

These two kinds of modern detective stories, the classic and the hard-boiled, continue to provide patterns for contemporary detective story writers. Writers such as Robert B. Parker, Sue Grafton, Loren Estleman, and Sara Paretsky write novels in the tradition of Hammett and Chandler. They add new social problems, such as drugs and homelessness, and they explore a wider variety of urban centers, from Detroit and Boston to New Orleans and Miami, but their characters and style remain consistent with the hard-boiled tradition.

Other writers, including Emma Lathen, Tony Hillerman, Amanda Cross, John Mortimer, and Charlotte MacLeod, write novels in the classic tradition. They explore new backgrounds—for example, Hillerman's books are set in the American Southwest and feature Native American detectives—but their characters, plots, and style are very similar to those of Agatha Christie or Dorothy Sayers.

The **police procedural** novel is the most recent kind of detective story. While earlier detective fiction had included police officers, the modern police procedural novel owes more to police dramas made for radio and, later, television. Like these shows, the police procedural novel focuses on the day-to-day routines of police departments and officers. Lawrence Treat, Joseph Wambaugh, Hillary Waugh, Elizabeth Linington, and other writers realistically examine crime and police crime-solving methods, as well as the pressures of police work on the ordinary people who perform it.

Detective stories, with their intriguing plots and fascinating characters and settings, remain one of the most popular kinds of mystery fiction. They continue to reflect society's changing attitudes toward crime, criminals, and those who solve crimes and bring criminals to justice.

LEROY L. PANEK
Author, *An Introduction to the Detective Story*

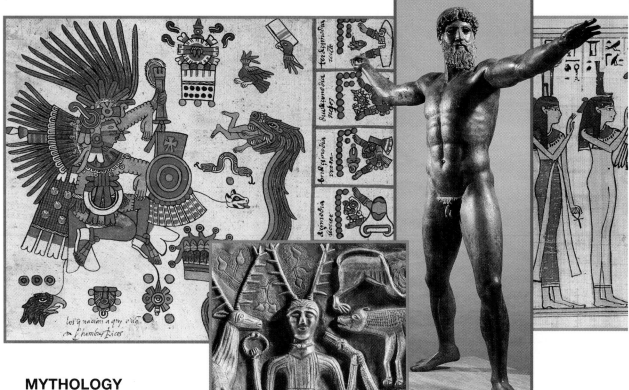

MYTHOLOGY

What is a myth? A myth is a kind of story, usually having one or more of the following four characteristics. First, myths tend to be stories about gods or supernatural beings, who have powers and abilities greater than those of humans. Second, myths usually tell about events set in the very distant past, often in the period before, or just after, humans first appeared on earth. Third, myths are frequently origin stories, explaining how the world or particular things within the world first came to be or how human customs and ways of life were first established. Fourth, myths are stories that were probably regarded as true and perhaps sacred by their original tellers (although this can sometimes be difficult to establish).

The term "mythology" is used in two ways. It sometimes is used to refer to a group of related myths: The entire set of myths told within a society is called that society's mythology, and myths about the sea and sea creatures might be described collectively as marine mythology. "Mythology" may also refer to the study of myth. A scholar who specializes in this field of study is called a mythologist.

Today many people first become acquainted with myths by reading some of the hundreds of such stories that have been collected in books. While this is a good introduction to mythology, it is important to realize that most myths were not originally written and read but rather were remembered and passed along orally (by word of mouth) by skilled storytellers. In addition, while only one version of any particular myth may be published, most myths developed many different versions as they were passed along. Particular storytellers added their own distinctive twists or combined myths or parts of myths in unique ways. They did not always remember stories word for word and may have unintentionally changed a story in repeating it. The many published collections of myths have done much to educate us about myth, but they sometimes convey the false impression that there is one and only one version of any particular myth.

Myths often concern the activities of gods and other supernatural beings. The study of mythology can provide a valuable key to understanding the various cultures of the world. *Left to right:* Quetzalcoatl, an important Aztec creator god; the horned Celtic god Cernunnos; Poseidon, Greek god of the sea; the Egyptian sun god Re, falcon-headed and crowned with a solar disk; Athena, Greek goddess of war, wisdom, and crafts; a female fertility spirit of the Baga people of Guinea.

▶ OTHER KINDS OF ORAL LITERATURE

Myths are not the only stories that were originally passed along orally. **Legends**, like myths, are stories about the past that are believed to be true. But while myths deal with gods and supernatural beings and with deeds set in the very distant past, legends tell of interesting or remarkable events that have occurred to human characters within human history, often in the very recent past. **Epics** are in some respects like legends, but they have some additional specific qualities. Epics are long narrative poems, frequently sung or recited, that recount

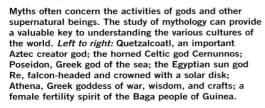

Thor, Norse god of thunder and lightning, clutches the magical hammer that is his main weapon and the symbol of his power.

and praise the great deeds and adventures of human heroes. Almost everyone has heard or read **folktales** or **fairytales**; these are stories, such as "Little Red Riding Hood" and "Snow White," that are set in no particular time ("once upon a time"), are told for entertainment, and are generally thought of by those who tell them as fiction.

These terms, each designating a type of oral story, are useful general categories. Yet it is not always possible to precisely classify a particular story, and myths frequently overlap with other types of stories. For example, perhaps the best-known epics in the Western world are the *Iliad* and the *Odyssey*, two works composed by the Greek poet Homer in the 700's B.C. but believed to have existed as oral stories long before then. For the most part the *Iliad* and the *Odyssey* concentrate on the adventures of great human heroes: their wars, travels, adventures, speeches, and romances. But both works continually refer to the actions and strategies of the Greek gods, picturing them as exerting great influence on human affairs.

MYTH AND SOCIETY

Myths serve a number of functions in a society. In addition to explaining how things came to be, they teach people the values and beliefs of the community in which they live. Myths usually have religious significance to those who tell and believe them, and they are often closely related to certain

aspects of religion, especially ritual. Rituals are repeated, formal actions, often performed on specific dates, that express and dramatize important ideas, especially religious ideas. Many rituals involve acting out a story that is told in a particular myth. The people of a community hear the same myths and participate in the same rituals many times over, thus thoroughly learning the teachings on which their way of life is based.

By studying the myths of various cultures, we can learn about their customs and ways of viewing the world. For many years, the most frequently studied myths were those of the ancient Greeks and Romans. Today scholars study myths of nearly all peoples of the world, including ancient Egyptians, African and Pacific island peoples, pre-Christian societies of Western Europe (Celtic and Norse, for example), and Native Americans.

KINDS OF MYTHS

Some myths are unique to one society. Others are found in more than one region, and still others are found almost everywhere. Mythologists have found many similar themes occurring in cultures throughout the world.

Most myths deal in some way with origins. Among the most fascinating origin stories are those that tell of the beginnings of the earth and the cosmos (universe). Many stories liken this process to mating and birth, while others tell of a creator god who makes the world. A very widespread myth is one explaining the origins of fire. Other myths explain crucial events in human life, notably death.

The Birth of the Cosmos

The version most familiar to many Western readers is the Greek myth handed down

to us in the *Theogony* ("origin of the gods") by Hesiod, a Greek poet from the same era as Homer. The poem describes the origin of the main features of the physical cosmos—Earth, Sky, Ocean, Rivers, Night—but gives even greater attention to the origin of elements depicting human fortune and misfortune, such as Desire, Love, Blame, Grief, and Deceit.

Of the many matings and births that are recounted in the *Theogony*, one is singled out for particular attention: the mating of Earth and Sky, which produces the gods and, later, humans. This is only one of many myths in the world that gives special emphasis to Sky and Earth as the parents of the cosmos; different versions of this story are found through much of the world, including Asia, the Middle East, and the Pacific.

Why has this way of portraying the origin and nature of the cosmos been adopted by so many cultures? Obviously, birth is one of the most natural and readily understandable images for explaining how something new appears in the world; we use the image of birth even in many common figures of speech to express origin ("the birth of a nation," "the birth of an idea").

The image of a family also provides a way of classifying the many different aspects and elements of the cosmos. For example, the *Theogony* tells of the Muses, a group of nine goddesses who inspire artistic creation. The Muses are said to be sisters, whose mother is Memory (Mnemosyne). By portraying the Muses as sisters, Hesiod was implying that the different arts are related to one another. By making Memory their common parent, Hesiod was suggesting that the different arts share a common dependence on this skill. At another point, the poem says that Law (Themis) gives birth to Good Order, Justice, and Peace. Once again the image of a family serves to express a relationship between different but related qualities. The entire cosmos, when pictured as a family, has an order and a structure.

On the other hand, not all aspects of family life are harmonious, and the *Theogony* also tells of strife among family members. One of the most memorable instances involves a great battle between different generations of the children of Sky and Earth, which results in the elder generation, the Titans, being overthrown and driven underground by Zeus and the other gods who inhabit Mount Olympus. Even the stories of the relationships among the Olympian gods—Zeus and his children and other relatives—are full of quarreling and scheming. The complexity and variety of relationships found in family life were used by Hesiod and other myth tellers to portray the complexity and variety of the cosmos in general. Since most people have had some experience of family life, portraying the cosmos as a family makes it more easily understandable.

Creator Gods

Another way in which many myths account for the origin of the universe is through the idea of a powerful god who creates the cosmos through either deliberate or accidental actions. In most such creation stories, the actions of the creator god or gods in some way resemble those of human

artisans. In some accounts, the creators must try several times before getting the world to turn out as they would like it. Such an account appears in the *Popol Vuh*, a saga of the Maya, a people of Central America. It tells of an attempt by the gods to create beings who will praise them. Dissatisfied with the results of their first several attempts, the gods discard them before finally creating humans. Some of the discarded beings become monkeys, thus suggesting why the world has species that in some ways resemble humans.

Many societies portray the creator as an uninhibited, prank-loving being who possesses many opposite qualities: selfishness and generosity, silliness and seriousness, destructiveness and creativity. Mythologists refer to such figures as **tricksters**. Unlike the Maya gods, who methodically craft the world, tricksters are often portrayed as creating or modifying the world out of whim and accident, and often in a carefree spirit. Coyote, for example, is a particularly well known trickster among many Native American tribes. Coyote is jealous of the abilities of other animals and attempts to

Maya gods create the first human being from corn and other plant material.

Coyote, a Native American trickster figure, has a carefree, whimsical nature.

imitate them or obtain their powers or possessions—often with comical results. His antics are often reminiscent of those of a spoiled child. Yet Coyote, even when acting on childish whim, also does many beneficial things for humans; he rids the world of monsters, modifies the natural world in ways that are helpful to humans, and invents useful objects, such as fish traps.

The Origins of Fire

Among the most widespread myths are those that tell about the origin and nature of fire and about how humans first acquired fire and learned how to use it. Many of these stories picture the first humans as originally living in a crude and unhappy state, in which human life is little different from the life of animals. In some myths, it is a god who first gives fire to humans. In others, humans acquire fire by stealing it from its original owners, who are often pictured as either gods or as animals who have been designated as the original keepers of fire. Often it is not fire alone that is acquired; rather, the fire is accompanied by many other things that will be useful for human life. These things include customs—rules about proper behavior for humans—and technology, such as implements for farming, fishing, and hunting, or techniques for making clothing. Fire and the goods that accompany it allow humans to leave their initial sorry state and begin to live in a desirable way.

Sometimes fire and other goods are brought by a **culture hero**; this is a term that mythologists use to designate a character in a myth who enables people to take the first step toward a truly human way of life. Such characters allow, and indeed require, tellers and hearers of such stories to think about what things are really essential to human life and what it is to be human. Culture heroes are common in myths throughout the world. Coyote, the Native American trickster, is a culture hero. The best-known culture hero in Greek mythology is Prometheus, a Titan who gives fire to humans.

The human fascination with the acquisition of fire extends to other stories about the nature of fire. The most common and widespread method for starting fires has always been to rub together sticks or stones. There is a charming myth, found through much of the world, that explains how fire came to be located in sticks and stones. Details vary from society to society, but the general plot remains constant. Fire is being pursued by an enemy, such as water, which threatens to extinguish it. As a last resort, fire hides itself from its pursuer by jumping into wood and stones, where to this day it can be found by those who need it.

Prometheus, a figure in Greek mythology, gives humans the gift of fire.

The Origins of Death

Of the many cosmic questions that are posed in myths, few have given rise to as much mythical speculation as the question of why humans cannot live forever but instead must die. Some myths account for this fact in terms of some great human failing, while others attribute it to a rather minor error in the distant past. In some African myths, for example, the moon sends an animal or insect to inform humans that just as the moon always returns to life after it has died, so will humans also be immortal. The animal, usually as a result of mere forgetfulness, delivers the wrong message, telling humans that they will not be immortal. Because of this foolish mistake, humans die. We have all had the experience of making a small mistake that causes major trouble for ourselves and others. Myth tellers seem especially intrigued by the fact that small mistakes and minor events can have very large consequences. In fact, many origin myths are not about big events that occurred in the past but about small events that turn out to have big consequences.

▶ **MYTH AND SCIENCE**

As we have seen, myths attempt to explain the origin and nature of the world and the nature of life and death. But science also attempts to explain such things. What, then, is the relationship between these two approaches to explaining the world? What do myth and science have in common, and how do they differ? We can attempt to answer these questions by considering some examples of myths from the Pacific islands.

Many Pacific island societies have origin stories that, like Hesiod's *Theogony*, portray the cosmos as a large family. Sky and Earth are the first parents, and their children are the many kinds of plant and animal species, and even rocks and stones. How the children of Sky and Earth develop the characteristics of different species forms the plot of many stories.

In an African myth about the origins of death, a hare brings the people a message from the moon.

For example, the Maori, the original Polynesian people of what is now New Zealand, have a number of stories that explain the existence of different kinds of animals as resulting from arguments about the best ways to live. One story tells about an argument between insects about the best way to attack humans. One group of Sky and Earth's children wants to attack humans in broad daylight in great swarms, while another group wants to attack more secretly, under cover of darkness. Unable to resolve their dispute, the two groups agree to part. The first group becomes the sandflies, and the second becomes the mosquitos.

Another story tells of arguments about whether life on land or in the sea offers greater security. The arguing parties are unable to agree, so some go off to the sea to become fish, while others head inland to become land animals. One group, although having sea parents, decides to head inland: These are the lizards. This story thus provides an explanation not only of why there are both fish and animals on earth but of why lizards, although land animals, resemble fish.

If we compare these mythical explanations of the origin of species with scientific explanations, we can see that both myth and science are based on careful observation of nature. Like scientists, the tellers of these and similar myths have paid careful attention to the details of appearance and behavior of different species. Scientists have generally concluded that reptiles share some characteristics with fish. The myth tellers have come to a similar conclusion. Scientists who study evolution are concerned with the ways in which different strategies of behavior contribute to the survival of different species. The Maori accounts also emphasize this issue,

in the form of arguments between species about the merits of their different ways of life.

But now let us look instead at the differences between myth and science, of which two are particularly important. First, technical instruments of science, such as microscopes, allow scientists to see levels of organization in matter—cells and molecules, for example—that are not visible to the naked eye. Most myth tellers, on the other hand, comment on the world of nature as it is visible in ordinary experience. Second, the explanations offered by many myths seem to treat all the species of the world as though they are humans. The Maori stories treat mosquitos, sandflies, fish, lizards, and even, in some cases, rocks and stones as if they are capable of having discussions the way humans can. The division of the children of Sky and Earth into different species is accounted for as though they were human tribes deciding to live by different rules. As we have seen, most myths draw on familiar human experiences to explain all of nature. Attributing human qualities to things that are (at least according to science) non-human is called **anthropomorphization** ("to

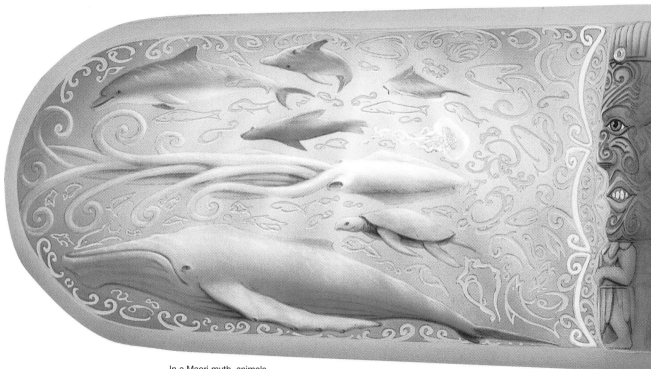

In a Maori myth, animals choose between life on land and life in the sea.

make human"). Many scientists would point to the tendency of myth to treat everything in the world as if it were human or humanlike as the main difference between myth and science.

Why do humans anthropomorphize? It would seem that we feel we can understand the other entities and species in the world if we think of them as being like ourselves. And we like stories in which animals, fish, and lizards act like humans, partly because we like hearing and learning about ourselves.

Some mythologists and scientists have referred to myth as "proto-science," or early science, because they feel that while myth at one time provided the best way to explain the universe, science now is the best way. Thus, they believe, there is no longer any need for myth. Others point out that myths serve many other functions besides explaining the world. Myths give us clever and memorable stories; they stimulate our imaginations and our appreciation of the complexity and beauty of nature; they give us insights into our own behavior; and they teach us values and lessons about good and evil. In fact, some mythologists argue that myths should not be compared with science but rather with the fine arts, such as music, painting, sculpture, and poetry. Because of these additional functions of myth, it is probably incorrect to think that it will ever be completely replaced by science.

▶ MYTH AND TRUTH

We sometimes hear someone say, "That's not true—it's just a myth!" The speaker seems to be suggesting that myths are false. Earlier we noted that scholars apply the term "myth" to stories that are believed to be true. But in its popular usage, the term "myth" sometimes implies two different attitudes regarding truth and falsity: the attitude of those who originally tell a particular myth, and the attitude of those who regard themselves as outside the community that created and believes it. In other words, for the speaker above, "myth" means "stories or ideas that some people think are true but that I think are false."

Because of this difference in the scholarly and popular uses of the term, conflicts sometimes arise. For example, scholars frequently refer to Bible stories as myths because they

have the four defining characteristics: They are set in the distant past, are about supernatural beings, are about origins, and are believed by those who tell them to be true. Members of many religious faiths have expressed misgivings about this term being applied to their particular religious stories; however, it is important to realize that the use of the term in its scholarly sense does not imply falsity.

erly, and by failing to honor corn and to consider it valuable. Feeling mistreated, the Corn Maidens leave the village, with the corn from the storerooms following them. The people, unable to get any corn to grow, begin to starve. Realizing their desperate situation, they initiate a series of rituals and prayers and send out search parties to find the Corn Maidens and bring them back. The searchers finally locate the Corn Maidens and convince

In a Zuni myth, the Corn Maidens return to the village after the people promise to treat them properly.

▶ MYTH AND VALUES

In the southwestern part of North America, Native Americans have survived for centuries by farming in an extremely arid environment. Their success is due in part to their extreme care not to waste food, water, or other products of the earth. Some of the tribes of this area tell a story about a group of sisters, called Corn Maidens, who represent the different varieties of corn. In the version told by the Zuni tribe, things go well for the people until they mistreat the Corn Maidens—by wasting corn, by storing it improp-

them that from now on they will be properly honored and cared for. The Corn Maidens promise to return each year and fill all the corn bins, as long as they are well treated.

The myth of the Corn Maidens is also expressed as a ritual; that is, a yearly pageant portrays the scene of the Corn Maidens returning to the village. The reenactment dramatizes the yearly cycle of corn harvesting and each year reminds the people of their promise to treat the corn properly. The importance of corn is dramatized in many other rituals as well, including the use of corn in ceremonies for the naming of children. Myths and rituals about the importance of this staple together remind participants of basic values on which their survival rests.

There are similarities between the Corn Maidens myths and certain other myths told by other Native American tribes. The myth of the Corn Maidens is found in an area in which corn is a staple. In the Great Plains region, by contrast, buffalo was the central source of food,

WONDER QUESTION

Why are similar myths found throughout the world?

Of particular interest to mythologists are myths that are found almost everywhere in the world. How did they come to be so widely distributed? One theory is that stories created in early times spread as the societies in which they originated broke into separate groups that migrated to different parts of the world.

A second theory is that myths were passed back and forth between neighboring societies and carried along trade routes, just as goods and ideas have long been exchanged among different peoples.

Other mythologists present a third theory. They argue that all people, no matter where they live, share some common experiences and react to these experiences in similar ways. It is only natural that people in different parts of the world would have similar stories to explain the origin of the world and the nature of the various things in it.

There is some truth to all three of these theories. Although the exact history is difficult to reconstruct, the distribution of similar stories throughout the world clearly has resulted from a combination of all three processes.

clothing, and other necessities of life. The Plains Indians tell a story about White Buffalo Woman, who, like the Corn Maidens, is said to have been mistreated and to have departed until the people learned to treat her properly. On the northwest coast of North America, salmon from the Columbia and other rivers formed the most important food source. In this area occurs a similar story about a salmon woman, who represents the flesh of salmon.

Although the details of each story differ, the message remains the same: It is necessary to treat nature, the source of nourishment and life, with care and respect if it is to continue to provide for humans. It is a message of particular importance today.

▶ **MYTH IN THE MODERN WORLD**

In the 1800's, many thinkers predicted that myth, and our fascination with it, would disappear in the new world of science and technology. That has not happened; indeed, the growth of science and technology has been paralleled by an equally large growth of interest in mythology. Many new books, and even radio and television series, have dealt with mythology; and, as in previous times, painters, playwrights, poets, and composers of music have continued to base many works of art on traditional myths.

In addition, some mythologists believe that modern forms of popular culture, such as comic books, cartoons, movies, and television series, have given rise to a new kind of mythology. For example, cartoon characters such as Mickey Mouse and Bugs Bunny, while not portrayed as gods, are able to do things that ordinary animals and even humans cannot. They seem eternal, or at least not to age. Like the characters in traditional myths, they are highly anthropomorphized—we see ourselves in them. Movie stars are powerful and idealized figures, whose activities are eagerly followed by their fans. Although not gods, they seem to live and work in a world that is very remote from everyday human experience. And popular television shows often reflect and reinforce the values of the culture in which they appear. Like myths, they form a body of stories with which many people in the culture are familiar.

Some mythologists think that these modern media creations teach, inspire, and influence people today as fully as traditional myths did in the past and that this makes it appropriate to refer to them as mythology. Not all mythologists accept this new use of the term, and whether it will last remains to be seen. Certainly there is much to think about regarding the place of myth in the modern world.

GREGORY SCHREMPP
Folklore Institute, Indiana University
See also GREEK MYTHOLOGY; NORSE MYTHOLOGY.

Index

HOW TO USE THE DICTIONARY INDEX

See the beginning of the blue pages in Volume 1.

occupational safety **O:**13
office machines **O:**55–60
paper-making machines **P:**53, 55–56
pneumatic systems **H:**314
pumps **P:**540–41
robots **R:**252–56
sewing machines **C:**380
simple machines **W:**247–51
wheels, machinery depends on **W:**160
picture(s)
    paper-making machines **P:**54–55, 56
Machine screws **N:**3
Machine tools **T:**230–32
Machmeters (to measure speed of airplanes) **S:**500
Mach numbers (measures of supersonic flight speed)
    A:40–41, 567; **S:**500, 501, 502
Machu Picchu (ancient Inca city, Peru) **A:**367; **P:**162
    picture(s) **A:**234, 367; **I:**107; **L:**60; **P:**165; **W:**217
Macías Nguema, Francisco (Equatorial Guinean president)
    E:310
Macías Nguema Biyogo (island, Equatorial Guinea) *see* Bioko
Macintosh, Charles (Scottish inventor and chemist) **R:**348
Macintosh, William (Creek Indian chief) **I:**178 *profile*
Macintosh computer **C:**493
Mack, Connie (American baseball manager) **B:**91
Mackay, John William (American miner and financier)
    N:134–35 *profile*
Mackenzie, Alexander (Canadian prime minister) **C:**76
    profile; **O:**135, 137
    picture(s) **C:**76
Mackenzie, Sir Alexander (Scottish explorer) **E:**407; **M:**5
    Alberta **A:**171
    Arctic region **A:**380
    British Columbia **B:**407
    Canada's early fur trade **C:**82
    North West Company (fur traders) **F:**521
    Northwest Territories **N:**343
Mackenzie, William Lyon (Canadian leader) **M:**5; **T:**243
Mackenzie Mountains (Canada) **N:**340; **Y:**370
Mackenzie River (Canada) **N:**340, 341, 342; **R:**243
    Arctic Basin of Canada **C:**57
    Great Slave Lake **L:**31
    Mackenzie's explorations **F:**521; **M:**5
    picture(s) **R:**243
Mackerel (fish) **F:**196, 218
Mackerel sky (of cirrocumulus clouds) **C:**385
Mackinac, Straits of (Great Lakes) **G:**328; **M:**258, 267
Mackinac Bridge (Michigan) **M:**267
Mackinac Island (Michigan) **M:**262
    picture(s)
        Fort Mackinac **M:**262
MacKinnon, Catharine Alice (American attorney) **W:**214
    profile
MacLachlan, Patricia (American author) **C:**234 *profile*
MacLeod, Colin (American biologist) **B:**187
Macleod, John James Rickard (Scottish physiologist) **B:**59
Macmillan, Harold (British prime minister) **M:**6
Macmillan, Kirkpatrick (Scottish inventor) **B:**177; **I:**281
Macmillan, Terry (American writer) **A:**219
MacNelly, Jeff (American editorial cartoonist) **C:**129
Macon (Georgia) **G:**141
Macphail, Agnes Campbell (Canadian politician) **O:**137
Macramé (art of decorative knotting) **M:**6–7b; **T:**142
Macro lenses (for cameras) **P:**207
    picture(s) **P:**206
Macromolecules (giant molecules) **B:**295–96
Macronutrients (elements essential to plant growth) **F:**96
Macrophages (immune system cells) **B:**261; **I:**96; **L:**350
    picture(s) **B:**285; **L:**350
Macula (of the eye) **E:**430, 432
Macumba (Brazilian dance music) **L:**72
Macy's (department store)
    picture(s) **D:**118; **N:**218
MAD (magazine) **C:**454

Madagascar **A:**47; **M:**8–9
    chameleons **L:**277
    language **A:**57
    New Year customs **N:**209
    map(s) **M:**9
    picture(s)
        bricks drying in the sun **B:**390
        flag **F:**235
Madama Butterfly (opera by Giacomo Puccini) **O:**156; **P:**525
Madame Bovary (novel by Gustave Flaubert) **F:**441; **N:**360;
    R:114
Madame Julie Récamier (painting by David) **P:**29
    picture(s) **P:**26
Mad cow disease **C:**154; **D:**5, 208; **U:**56
MADD *see* Mothers Against Drunk Driving
Madder root (plant used for dyeing) **D:**376, 377, 378, 379
    picture(s) **D:**377
Maddox, USS (destroyer) **V:**336
Madeira (group of islands off northwestern coast of Africa)
    I:366; **P:**393
Madeline Island (Wisconsin) **W:**200
    picture(s) **W:**200
Mademoiselle Pogany (sculpture by Constantin Brancusi)
    picture(s) **B:**370
Maderno, Carlo (Italian architect) **I:**400
Madero, Francisco (Mexican president) **M:**250
Madison (capital of Wisconsin) **W:**192, 194, 198, 201, 205
    Monona Terrace **W:**200
    picture(s) **W:**204
Madison, Dolley (Dorothea Payne Todd Madison) (wife of James
    Madison) **F:**166; **M:**12; **N:**320–21 *profile*
    first to serve ice cream at White House **I:**22
    White House, history of **W:**165
    picture(s) **F:**166; **M:**12
Madison, James (4th president of the United States) **M:**10–13
    Bill of Rights **B:**182
    Constitutional Convention **U:**146
    The Federalist **F:**78
    Montpelier **V:**354
    political parties, views on **P:**370
    picture(s) **M:**10, 11; **P:**445
Madison Cave isopod (crustacean) **E:**208
Madison Square Garden (sports arena, New York City) **N:**231
Mádl, Ferenc (president of Hungary) **H:**299
Madonna (American rock singer) **R:**262d–263 *profile,* 264
    picture(s) **R:**262d
Madonna and Angels (sculpture by Luca della Robbia)
    picture(s) **S:**98
Madonna and Child (sculpture by Michelangelo)
    picture(s) **R:**168
Madonna and Child with Angels (painting by Piero della
    Francesca)
    picture(s) **F:**449
Madonna del Granduca, The (painting by Raphael) **P:**21
Madonna della Costa (painting by Giotto) **U:**3
Madonna Enthroned (painting by Giotto di Bondone)
    picture(s) **G:**211
Madonna of the Chair (*Madonna della Sedia*) (painting by
    Raphael)
    picture(s) **R:**106
Madonna of the Rocks (painting by da Vinci) **P:**21
    picture(s) **P:**21
Madonna of the Trees (painting by Giovanni Bellini)
    picture(s) **B:**140
Madonna of Vladimir (Byzantine painting) **B:**493
Madonna with a Rabbit (painting by Titian)
    picture(s)
        detail **T:**213
Madonna with Saints and Members of the Pesaro Family (painting
    by Titian) **P:**23
    picture(s) **P:**22
Madonna with the Chancellor Rolin (painting by Jan van Eyck)
    picture(s) **D:**358
Madonna with the Long Neck, The (painting by Parmigianino)
    picture(s) **I:**399

Madras (Chennai) (capital of Tamil Nadu, India)   **I:**130; **M:**14
 picture(s)   **M:**14
Madrasahs (Islamic schools)   **I:**356
 picture(s)   **U:**257
Madrid (capital of Spain)   **M:**15; **S:**372, 374
 bombings (2004)   **Q:**2; **S:**379
 Prado   **P:**423–24
 picture(s)
  Avenida de José Antonio   **S:**374
  bullfighting   **B:**450
  pedestrians resting under trees   **E:**362
  Prado   **P:**423
Madrid, University of (Spain)   **M:**15
Madrid Hurtado, Miguel de la *see* De la Madrid Hurtado, Miguel
Madrigal (in music)   **M:**539
 English madrigals   **E:**291
 Renaissance music   **I:**410; **R:**161, 173
 vocal chamber music   **C:**184
Maduro, Ricardo (president of Honduras)   **H:**209
Maelstrom (Norwegian strait famous for its whirlpool)   **I:**366
Maestoso (musical term)   **M:**536
Maeterlinck, Count Maurice (Belgian poet, dramatist, and
  essayist)   **B:**134; **D:**304
Mafia (organized crime group)   **O:**223, 224–25
Magars (a people of Nepal)   **N:**107
Magazine Mountain (Arkansas)   **A:**408
Magazine repeating firearms   **G:**422
Magazines   **M:**16–20
 advertising   **A:**30, 33
 bibliographic form   **R:**183
 cartoons, history of   **C:**127, 129
 comics   **C:**453–54
 commercial art   **C:**457
 illustration and illustrators   **I:**81, 82
 indexes   **I:**115
 journalism   **J:**135–36, 140
 libraries, professional publications for   **L:**181
 mass communication media   **C:**471
 publishing   **P:**523
 Reader's Guide to Periodical Literature   **R:**129
 short stories   **S:**162
 writing as a career   **W:**331
Magdalena River (Colombia)   **C:**404, 406; **R:**243; **S:**280
Magdalen Islands (Canada)   **I:**366
Magdeburg (Germany)
 picture(s)
  Thirty Years' War   **T:**179
  World War II   **W:**293
Magdeburg hemispheres (used to illustrate pressure of air)
  V:265
Magellan (space probe)   **S:**358, 359; **V:**303a
 picture(s)   **S:**359
Magellan, Ferdinand (Portuguese explorer)   **E:**406; **M:**21; **P:**2,
  5
 picture(s)   **E:**398–99
Magellan, Strait of (South America)   **E:**406; **M:**21
Magellanic Clouds (galaxies)   **M:**309; **S:**431; **U:**214
 picture(s)   **U:**215
Magen David *see* Star of David
Magen David Adom (Israeli equivalent of the Red Cross)
  R:126
Magenta (color)   **C:**425
Maggie: A Girl of the Streets (novel by Stephen Crane)   **A:**213;
  C:582
Maggiore, Lake (Italy)   **L:**31
Maghrib (region in northern Africa)   **A:**185
Magi (priests of the ancient Medes and Persians)   **J:**86
Magic   **M:**22–25
 African traditional religions   **A:**60
 fire to drive away evil spirits   **F:**142
 Houdini, Harry   **W:**206
 Japanese origami   **O:**229
 prehistoric art   **P:**437
 prehistoric medicine   **M:**206

 prehistoric sculpture   **S:**92–93
 superstition   **S:**503–4
 witchcraft   **W:**208–9
Magical Mystery Tour (motion picture, 1967)   **B:**108
Magical realism (in literature)   **L:**70; **N:**363
Magic Flute, The (opera by Mozart)   **G:**185; **O:**156
 picture(s)   **O:**157
  stage design   **M:**541
Magie, Elizabeth (American game inventor)   **G:**14
Maginot Line (of fortifications)   **F:**379; **W:**296, 298
Magistrate (judge)   **J:**163
Maglevs (magnetic levitation vehicles)   **M:**33; **S:**141;
  T:291–92
 picture(s)   **M:**33; **T:**291
Magma (liquid underground rock)   **G:**113, 114; **R:**265–66
 volcanoes, products of   **V:**379–80, 382, 385, 386
Magna Carta (charter to limit the power of the English king)
  E:239; **M:**26
 basis for English Bill of Rights   **B:**184
 checks on power of kings in Middle Ages   **M:**291
 civil rights, historical origins of   **C:**326
 John   **J:**112
 taxation principle set forth   **T:**25
 what feudal lords owed vassals   **F:**101
Magnes (mythical discoverer of lodestone)   **M:**28
Magnesia (region, Greece)   **M:**27, 28
Magnesite (component of heat-resistant materials)   **A:**520
Magnesium   **E:**174; **M:**27
 alloys   **A:**192
 minerals in the ocean   **O:**28; **T:**129
 minerals needed by the body   **V:**371–72
 table(s)
  food sources and DRI's   **V:**372
  ores, properties, and uses   **M:**235
Magnesium sulfate *see* Kieserite
Magnetic compass *see* Compass, magnetic
Magnetic confinement (in nuclear fusion)   **N:**368
Magnetic deviation (difference between true poles and
  magnetic poles)   **M:**29
Magnetic dip (amount that the magnetic field of a place points
  up or down)   **M:**29
Magnetic domains (clusters of atoms)   **M:**31–32, 33
 picture(s)   **M:**32
Magnetic energy   **E:**213
Magnetic field   **M:**28–29, 30, 31–32
 animal compasses   **H:**202
 Earth   **A:**471; **E:**11; **M:**29; **R:**48–49
 electromagnetic waves   **L:**219–20
 experiments and other science activities   **E:**394
 Jupiter   **J:**159–60; **P:**279
 Mars   **M:**106; **P:**279
 Mercury   **M:**229; **P:**276
 Neptune   **N:**111; **P:**282
 radiation belts   **C:**563
 Saturn   **S:**57
 sun   **S:**493, 494, 496
 Uranus   **P:**281
 Venus has none   **P:**276
 picture(s)   **M:**29
Magnetic Hill (New Brunswick)   **N:**138e–138f
Magnetic induction   **E:**141; **T:**272
Magnetic levitation vehicles *see* Maglevs
Magnetic monopole (theoretical isolated north or south
  magnetic pole)   **M:**30
Magnetic poles *see* Poles, magnetic
Magnetic resonance imaging (MRI) (medical technique)
  D:204–5; **I:**86; **M:**204
 brain disorders   **B:**369
 electromagnets   **E:**139
 electronics   **E:**161
 modern magnetic devices   **M:**33
 photography, special uses of   **P:**208
 picture(s)   **D:**205; **M:**203, 208d
  brain   **B:**362, 369

Magnetic tape
  communication, history of   **C:**467
  computers   **C:**482
  electronic music   **E:**155, 156
  high-fidelity systems   **H:**132
  motion picture soundtracks   **S:**267a
  recording industry   **R:**123
  sound recording   **S:**267–67a
  videotapes   **V:**332d, 332e
  picture(s)
    sound recording   **S:**267
Magnetite (iron ore)   **I:**330; **M:**32
Magnetocaloric refrigerators   **R:**135
Magnetohydrodynamic (MHD) generators   **P:**423
Magnetometers (instruments that measure Earth's magnetism)
  M:320; **P:**169; **S:**520; **U:**18
Magnetopause (outer boundary of the magnetosphere)   **R:**49
Magnetophone (early tape recorder)   **S:**267b
Magnetos (electric generators with permanent magnets)
  E:134
Magnetosphere (planet's magnetic field)
  Earth   **E:**11; **R:**49
  Jupiter   **J:**161
  picture(s)
    Earth   **R:**49
Magnets and magnetism   **M:**28–33 *see also* Electromagnetism
  alternative medicine   **A:**194e
  Earth's magnetism   **E:**11; **G:**111
  electric generators   **E:**133–34
  electricity and magnetism   **E:**140–41; **P:**230, 235
  electric motors   **E:**152–54
  Faraday's experiments in electromagnetism   **F:**47
  magnetic resonance imaging   **I:**86
  mineral detection   **M:**319–20
  radiation, effect on   **R:**47
  radiation belts   **R:**48–49
  telegraph, uses in   **T:**51
  telephone   **T:**53
  picture(s)
    horseshoe magnet   **M:**28
Magnet schools   **E:**87; **S:**61
Magnet therapy (type of alternative therapy)   **A:**194e
Magnifiers   **M:**281–86
  concave mirrors   **L:**214
  lenses of magnifiers and microscopes   **L:**146–47
  optical instruments   **O:**178, 179
Magnifying glasses   **L:**144–45; **M:**281; **O:**179
Magnitude (of earthquakes)   **E:**38, 39–40
Magnitude (brightness) (of stars)   **S:**428
Magnolia (flowering tree)
  picture(s)   **L:**315; **M:**351; **P:**300
Magnolia State (nickname for Mississippi)   **M:**350, 351
Magog (in Old Testament)   **G:**201
Magog, Lake (British Columbia)
  picture(s)   **B:**403
Magritte, René (Belgian painter)
  picture(s)
    painting of men in bowler hats   **B:**133
Magsaysay, Ramón (Philippine statesman)   **P:**188
Maguey (plant)   **M:**241; **R:**336
Magyar (language)   **H:**295
Magyars (European people)   **B:**422b; **H:**294, 298
Mahabharata (epic poem)   **H:**139, 140, 141; **I:**140; **T:**162
Mahaka (Hawaii)   **H:**52
Mahathir bin Mohamad (Malaysian prime minister)   **M:**59
  picture(s)   **M:**58
Mahatma ("Great Soul") (name given to Gandhi)   **G:**23
Mahavira (founder of Jainism)   **R:**150
Mahavira (Indian mathematician)   **M:**164
Mahayana Buddhism   **B:**424–25
Mahé (island, Seychelles)   **S:**131
Mahendra (king of Nepal)   **N:**110
Mahfouz, Naguib (Egyptian writer)   **A:**342
Mahican (Indians of North America)   **I:**177

Mah-jongg (game)   **G:**15–16
  picture(s)   **G:**21
Mahler, Gustav (Austrian composer and conductor)   **G:**188;
  M:34; **O:**197
Mahogany (wood)   **F:**512:
  picture(s)   **W:**224
Mahout (elephant trainer)   **E:**184
Mahuad Witt, Jamil (Ecuadorian president)   **E:**69
Maia Majesta (Roman goddess)   **M:**182
Maiasaur (dinosaur)   **D:**173
Maid Marian (in the Robin Hood legends)   **R:**251
Maid of Orléans (name for Joan of Arc)   **J:**110
Maids of Honor, The (painting by Velázquez) *see* Meninas, Las
Maidu (Indians of North America)   **I:**187
Maigret, Jules (fictional character)   **M:**565
Mail *see* Postal service
Mail, electronic *see* E-mail
Mailer, Norman (American author)   **A:**217; **N:**363
Mailgram (combination letter-telegram)   **P:**400
Mail handling cars (of railroads)   **R:**82
Mailing lists (for direct-mail advertising)   **M:**35
Mailing machines   **O:**60
Maillol, Aristide (French sculptor)   **S:**103
Mail order   **D:**118; **I:**76; **M:**34–35
Maiman, Theodore H. (American scientist)   **I:**283; **L:**46d
Mainassara, Ibrahim Bare (president of Niger)   **N:**252
Main battle tanks (MBT's)   **T:**14
Maine   **M:**36–50
  boundary settlements   **T:**104–5
  lumber industry, history of   **L:**338
  Missouri Compromise   **M:**381
  thirteen American colonies   **T:**170, 174
  map(s)   **M:**47
  picture(s)
    Acadia National Park   **M:**44; **U:**77
    Aroostook County farm   **M:**40
    Augusta   **M:**46
    Bath Iron Works   **M:**42
    Bowdoin College   **M:**41
    coastal town   **M:**37
    fly-fishing   **M:**41
    Friendship's tide water levels   **T:**193
    Katahdin, Mount   **M:**37
    lobstering   **M:**43
    lobsters   **M:**45
    Moosehead Lake   **M:**39
    Mount Desert Island   **M:**38
    painter on Monhegan Island   **M:**40
    Portland   **M:**44, 48
    Portland Head Light   **L:**228; **M:**44
    potato growing   **M:**43
    York   **M:**44
Maine, University of   **M:**42
Maine, **USS** (battleship)   **M:**193; **S:**392c; **T:**110
  mast is a national memorial   **N:**27
  picture(s)   **T:**111
    newspaper coverage of sinking   **N:**204
Maine coon cat   **C:**138
Mainframe computers   **O:**55
Mainmast (of a sailing ship)   **S:**157
Mainsail (of a sailboat)   **S:**8
Main sequence stars   **S:**429
  picture(s)
    section of Hertzsprung-Russell diagram   **A:**473
Mainsprings (in watches and clocks)   **C:**370, 371, 372;
  W:45, 46
Mainstreaming (of handicapped children into regular
  classrooms)   **E:**85 *see also* Inclusion
  picture(s)   **E:**86
Main Street (novel by Sinclair Lewis)   **A:**214b; **L:**162
Maintenance (support payments to a former spouse)   **D:**230
Maintenance of membership (in labor contracts)   **L:**8
Maintenon, Marquise de (French noblewoman)   **L:**313
Maison Carrée (Roman temple, Nîmes, France)   **A:**373

Maisonneuve, Paul de Chomedey, Sieur de (French colonist)
M:444
Maisons-Laffitte, Château de (France)
picture(s) F:425
Maize *see* Corn
Majapahit (former Indonesian kingdom) I:211
Majolica (pottery) D:77–78; P:412
picture(s) D:77; P:412
Ma Jolie (Woman with a Zither or Guitar) (painting by Picasso)
C:612
Major (field of concentration in higher education) U:220–21
Major, John (British prime minister) E:255; M:51
Major, John C. (Canadian Supreme Court justice)
picture(s) S:505
Majorca (island, Spain) I:362; S:373
Major depressive disorder (mental illness) M:221
Major Indoor Soccer League (MISL) S:218b–219
Majority (method of deciding an election) E:126
Majority leaders (in Congress) U:168, 169
Major leagues (in baseball) B:84, 85
selected major league records B:85
Major League Soccer S:218b
Major medical insurance I:252
Major minerals (in nutrition) V:371
Major scale (in music) M:532, 537
Majuro (capital of the Marshall Islands) M:112
Makah (Indians of North America) I:188
Makalu, Mount (Nepal–Tibet)
picture(s) E:12
Makarios III, Archbishop (Greek Orthodox prelate and Cypriot
statesman) C:617
Makarov, Sergei (Russian hockey player) I:31
Makarova, Natalia (Russian dancer)
picture(s) B:33
Makeup
clowns C:386–87
cosmetics C:560–61
motion picture makeup artists M:481
plays P:337, 338; T:158
picture(s)
plays T:158
Maki, Oili (Finnish artist)
picture(s)
Purple Sea (tapestry) T:22
Makin Island (Pacific Ocean) W:308
Makira (island) *see* San Christobel
Makiritare (Indians of South America) I:197
Maksutov-Cassegrain telescope T:59
diagram(s) T:59
Malabo (capital of Equatorial Guinea) E:309
picture(s) E:310
Malacca (now Melaka) (Malaysia) M:58, 59
Malacca, Strait of P:2
Malachi (book of the Old Testament) B:160, 162
Malacology (study of mollusks) S:151
Málaga (Spain) S:375
Malagasy (language) A:57; M:8, 9
Malagasy Republic *see* Madagascar
Malaita (Pacific island) S:252
Malakal (Sudan) S:479
Malamud, Bernard (American writer) A:219
Malamutes (dogs) *see* Alaskan malamutes
Malapropisms (twisting of words) H:290
Malaria (protozoan disease) D:189; M:51–52
Anopheles mosquitoes H:260
caused by plasmodium protozoan P:497
pioneer life P:255
Tanzania T:17
vaccine needed V:261
vectors of disease V:283–84, 285
Malaspina Glacier (Alaska) A:148; G:223
Malawi M:52–53
map(s) M:53
picture(s)
flag F:235

Malawi (Nyasa), Lake (Africa) F:182; L:26, 32; M:52, 53
Malay (language) M:54; S:180, 329
Malaya, Federation of M:59
Malaya, University of (Kuala Lumpur, Malaysia) M:55
Malayan tapirs (mammals) H:217
Malayo-Polynesian languages A:445; L:40
Malays (a people of Asia) A:444–45
Indonesian population I:206
Malaysia M:54, 55, 58
Singapore S:179–80
picture(s) I:206
Malaysia M:54–59
Borneo B:336, 337
economy S:332, 333
ethnic Chinese population S:328
folk dance F:300
food F:332
Kuala Lumpur S:334
Singapore was formerly a part of S:179, 181
tin production A:442
World War II in Malaya W:303, 304
map(s) M:55
picture(s)
Cameron Highlands M:56
flag F:235
Kuala Lumpur M:54; S:334
oil rig M:57
people M:54, 55
Malcolm III (king of Scotland) S:88
Malcolm X (American civil rights leader) A:79o; M:59
picture(s) M:59
Malcolm X (motion picture, 1992) M:497
Maldives D:183; M:60
map(s) M:60
picture(s)
flag F:235
Male (capital of Maldives) M:60
Maletsunyane Falls (Lesotho) W:59
Malevich, Kazimir (Russian painter) C:612; M:392; R:379
Malherbe, François de (French poet) F:435, 438
Malheur National Wildlife Refuge (Oregon) O:210
Mali M:61–62
dance D:25
early western African empire A:66, 79d
mosques of mud A:76
poetry A:76b, 76c
pottery sculpture P:411
map(s) M:61
picture(s)
flag F:235
headdress A:74
sculpture A:72
travel by bullock and cart M:61
Maliceets (Indians of North America) M:41, 50
Mali Federation (former union of Senegal and French Sudan)
M:62; S:118
Malignant melanoma (type of skin cancer) D:123, 124
Malignant tumors (in cancer) C:92
Maligne Lake (Jasper National Park)
picture(s) J:54
Malindi (Kenya) K:233
Malinké (Mandingo; Mandinka) (a people of Africa) G:8, 406,
407; M:61; S:117
African epic poetry A:76c
music A:78
Malinowski, Bronislaw (Polish-born anthropologist) A:304
Maliseet (Indians of North America) N:138b, 138f
Mall, The (Washington, D.C.) W:32
Mallaig (Scotland) S:87
Mallard ducks (birds)
picture(s) B:219; D:345; M:353
Malleability (property of metals) M:233
Mallet, Anatole (Swiss engineer and inventor) L:288
Mallet, Pierre and Paul (French explorers) N:91

Mallets (large hammers)　**T:**227
　in croquet　**C:**595
　picture(s)　**T:**227
Mall of America (shopping center, Minnesota)　**M:**335
Mallorca (island) *see* Majorca
Malls, shopping *see* Shopping centers
Malmö (Sweden)　**S:**527
Malnutrition (poor nutrition)　**N:**429 *see also* Nutrition
　blindness, causes of　**B:**257
　famine　**F:**44
　food supply　**F:**350
　nutritional diseases　**D:**196
　picture(s)　**N:**258
Malocclusion (Bad bite) (in dentistry)　**O:**232, 233
Malone, Karl (American basketball player)
　picture(s)　**O:**113; **U:**248
Malory, Sir Thomas (English author)　**A:**438a–438b; **E:**269;
　H:175
Malpeque (Prince Edward Island)　**P:**466
Malpighi, Marcello (Italian anatomy professor)　**B:**201; **F:**133
Malplaquet, Battle of (1709)　**S:**377
Malpractice (negligent practice by a professional)　**D:**237–38
Malraux, André (French writer and political figure)　**F:**443
Malt (sprouted grain used in brewing and distilling)　**B:**60b,
　114; **G:**284–85; **W:**161
Malta (island nation in the Mediterranean)　**M:63–64**
　map(s)　**M:**63
　picture(s)　**M:**63
　　flag　**F:**235
Maltese (language)　**M:**63
Maltese Falcon, The (novel by Dashiell Hammett)　**M:**565
Malthus, Thomas R. (English economist)　**B:**250b; **P:**387–88
Malthusian theory of overpopulation　**P:**387–88
Maltose (malt sugar)　**H:**211; **S:**482
Maluku *see* Moluccas
Mama, Papa Is Wounded! (painting by Tanguy)
　picture(s)　**S:**518
Mamaia (Romania)　**R:**298
Mamas and the Papas, The (American rock group)　**R:**262c
Mambas (snakes)　**S:**211, 216, 217
　picture(s)　**B:**197
Mambo (dance)　**D:**29
Mameli, Goffredo (Italian poet)　**N:**21
Mamet, David Alan (American playwright)　**A:**218; **D:**307
Mamluk rugs
　picture(s)　**R:**354
Mammals (animals)　**A:**266; **M:65–76** *see also* Hoofed
　　mammals; the names of mammals
　bats are winged mammals　**B:**100
　cetaceans (marine mammals)　**W:**149–53
　cloning　**L:**210
　color vision　**C:**428
　dolphins and porpoises　**D:**273–78
　Earth, history of　**E:**28, 29
　egg-laying monotremes　**P:**331–32
　eggs and embryos　**E:**96, 97
　elephants　**E:**179–84
　even-toed　**F:**81–82
　evolution　**E:**374
　feet　**F:**81–82
　fossils　**F:**387
　fur　**F:**501–5
　hands　**F:**83–84
　hibernation　**H:**127–28
　hoofed *see* Hoofed mammals
　How big do mammals grow?　**M:**66
　human beings　**H:**281–83
　largest animals　**A:**271
　life spans　**A:**82–83
　marsupials　**M:**113–15
　milk producers　**M:**306
　mongooses, meerkats, and their relatives　**M:**419
　monkeys　**M:**420–22
　ocean life　**O:**25

odd-toed　**F:**81–82
　pets　**P:**177–78
　prehistoric animals, development of　**P:**433–34
　primates　**P:**455–57
　rodents are gnawing mammals　**R:**274–78
　sexual reproduction　**R:**178–79
　smallest on land　**A:**271
　wetlands　**W:**145–46, 148
　whales　**W:**149–53
　without feet　**F:**82–83
　picture(s)
　　prehistoric animals　**P:**434
Mammary gland (milk-producing gland)　**G:**227; **M:**65, 306
Mammogram (X-ray of the breast)　**C:**93
Mammoth Cave (Kentucky)　**K:**214, 220
Mammoth Hot Springs (Wyoming)
　picture(s)　**N:**47
Mammoths (extinct mammals)　**E:**183
　fossilized tusks a source of ivory　**I:**415–16
　fossils　**F:**382
　Ice Age　**I:**415–16
　picture(s)　**P:**434
　　geologists removing remains from Earth's crust
　　　G:119
　　Mammoth Site (South Dakota)　**S:**317
Mamprusi (a people of Africa)　**G:**194
Man *see* Human beings
Man, Isle of (in the Irish Sea)　**F:**10; **I:**366; **U:**51, 62
Management (owners and managers in industry)　**I:**224; **L:**4;
　W:346
Management and Budget, Office of (United States)　**P:**451
Managua (capital of Nicaragua)　**N:**244, 246
Manama (capital of Bahrain)　**B:**19
Manapouri, Lake (New Zealand)　**N:**238
Manassa Mauler (nickname) *see* Dempsey, Jack
Manassas (Virginia, site of Civil War battles of Bull Run)
　C:337, 339; **J:**9
Manasseh, Prayer of (apocryphal book of the Bible)　**B:**164
Manatees (aquatic mammals)　**F:**265; **I:**420; **M:77**
　picture(s)　**A:**278; **M:**71, 77
Manaus (Brazil)　**B:**375, 379, 381
　picture(s)　**B:**382
Mancala (Wari) (ancient game)　**G:**10–11
Manchester (England)　**U:**57, 59
Manchester (New Hampshire)　**N:**157, 159, 162
Manchester Ship Canal (England)　**U:**59
Manchester terriers (dogs)　**D:**248
Manchu dynasty *see* Qing dynasty
Manchuria (northeast area of China)　**C:**270
　Japanese occupation　**C:**271; **W:**294–95, 318
　Shenyang　**S:**152
Manchurian Plain (China)　**C:**262
Manchurian tigers
　picture(s)　**T:**198
Manchus (Asian people)　**C:**270; **K:**298, 303; **T:**9 *see also*
　Qing dynasty
Manco Capac (Inca legendary emperor)　**I:**110
Mandalay (Myanmar)　**M:**558, 560
Mandan (Indians of North America)　**I:**180; **N:**333
Mandarin (citrus fruit)　**O:**189
　picture(s)　**O:**186
Mandarin Chinese (language)　**A:**445; **C:**258
Mandarin duck (bird)　**D:**346
Mandated territory
　Iraq, history of　**I:**315
　Palestine　**I:**375; **P:**41
　Transjordan　**J:**132
Mande (language)　**A:**56
Mandeans (religious sect of Iraq)　**I:**314–15
Mandela, Nelson (South African president)　**A:**69; **M:78;**
　S:273
　picture(s)　**A:**69; **S:**273; **W:**275
Mandela, Nomzamo Winifred (Winnie) (South African political
　activist)　**M:**78
Mandelbaum Gate (in Jerusalem)　**J:**84

Mandelbrot, Benoit (American mathematician)   M:170
Mandeville (Jamaica)   J:16, 18
Mandeville, Bernard (Dutch-English satirist)   E:298
Mandibles (jaws of ants)   A:318–19
Mandingo (Mandinka) (a people of Africa) see Malinké
Mandolin
    picture(s)   M:547; S:469
Mandrills (Drills) (monkeys)   A:270; M:420
    picture(s)   A:270; M:420; P:455
Mandyako (a people of Africa)   G:407
Mane, Ansumane (political leader of Guinea-Bissau)   G:408
Manes (of horses)   H:237
Manes (of lions)   L:252
Manet, Édouard (French painter)   F:430; M:78
    impressionism   I:103, 105; P:29
    modern art   M:387
    watercolor painting   W:56
    picture(s)
        The Balcony (painting)   I:104
        Olympia (painting)   M:78
        portrait of Berthe Morisot   W:55
Manganese (element)   E:174
    alloys   A:192
    minerals in the ocean   O:28
    paints used by prehistoric people   P:15
    steel   I:329
    table(s)   M:235
Mangas Coloradas (Apache Indian leader)   I:184
Mangbetu-Azande (a people of Africa)   C:499
Manger, Itzik (Yiddish poet)   Y:361
Mango (tropical fruit)   T:317
    picture(s)   T:317
Mangroves (shrubs and trees)   J:157; W:146
    picture(s)   P:293
Manhattan (borough and island, New York City)   N:226, 227,
    234; T:175
    picture(s)   I:366
Manhattan (ice breaking oil tanker)   N:339
Manhattan Project (on atomic research)   F:92; N:373, 377
    museum exhibit   N:185
    New Mexico   N:194
    World War II   W:318
Manhattan Transfer (novel by John Dos Passos)   D:287
Mania (symptom of bipolar disorder)   M:221, 225
Manic depression (form of mental illness) see Bipolar disorder
Manifest Destiny (in United States history)   M:239a; P:375;
    T:103; U:183
Manifolds (of an automobile)   A:547
Manigat, Leslie (Haitian president)   H:11
Manila (Philippines)   M:79; P:184, 186, 187; W:76, 314
    picture(s)   M:79; P:187
Manila Bay, Battle of (1898)   D:144; P:188; S:392c
Manila hemp see Abaca
Manioc see Cassava
Manipulative and body-based methods (of alternative medicine)
    A:194e
Man is the measure of all things (belief of ancient Greeks)
    S:95
Manitoba (Canada)   C:84; M:80–86; W:190b
    lakes   L:32, 34
    Riel, Louis   R:232
    map(s)   M:84
    picture(s)
        agriculture   M:82
        Setting Lake   M:81
        Winnipeg   M:83; W:190b
Manitoba, Lake (Manitoba)   L:32; M:80
Manitoba Escarpment   M:80
Manitoulin (island in Lake Huron)   G:327; O:124
Manitowoc (Wisconsin)   W:200
Mankiller, Wilma (Cherokee chief)   O:94–95 profile
    picture(s)   O:95
Manley, Michael (prime minister of Jamaica)   J:18–19
Man-made elements see Transuranium elements
Man-made materials see Synthetic materials

Mann, Horace (American educator)   E:83; M:87
Mann, Thomas (German-born American writer)   F:73; G:181;
    N:361
Manna (kind of food)   M:469
Manned maneuvering units (MMU's) (jet-propelled backpacks
    used by astronauts)   S:349
Manned Spacecraft Center (Houston, Texas) see Lyndon B.
    Johnson Space Center
Mannerheim Line (fortification line in World War II)   W:312
Mannerism (in art and architecture)   I:398–99
    France, art and architecture of   F:424
    Renaissance art   R:171
    sculpture   S:100
    Spain, art and architecture of   S:383
    Tintoretto   T:210
Manners see Etiquette
Mannheim (Germany)   C:352
Manning, Henry Edward (English cardinal)   O:191
Manning, Patrick (prime minister of Trinidad and Tobago)
    T:315
Manolete (Spanish bullfighter)   B:451
Manon (opera by Jules Massenet)   O:156
Manoogian, Alex (American businessman)   A:421
Manorialism   F:413
Manors (feudal estates)   A:98; F:102; H:193; M:292; S:193
    picture(s)   H:192
Man o' War (racehorse)   H:235 profile
    picture(s)   H:235
Manrique, Gómez (Spanish poet)   S:387
Manrique, Jorge (Spanish poet)   S:387
Mansa Musa (Mali emperor)   M:62
    picture(s)
        depicted on European map of 1375   A:65
Mansart (Mansard), Nicolas François (French architect)   F:425
    picture(s)
        Maisons-Laffitte, Château de   F:425
Mansfield, Katherine (New Zealand-born English writer)
    E:289; S:162
Mansfield, Michael Joseph (American political figure)   M:441
    profile
Mansfield, Mount (Vermont)   V:308
    picture(s)   V:312
Mansion of Happiness (game)   G:20
Mansions (large imposing houses) see also Arlington House;
    White House
    Delaware places of interest   D:96
    Newport (Rhode Island)   V:277
    Oak Alley Plantation (Louisiana)   L:322
    Sunrise (Charleston, West Virginia)   W:131
    picture(s)
        Nemours (Delaware)   D:89
Mansur, Abdullah al- (Abbasid caliph)   B:15
Manta rays (fish)   S:145
Mantaro River (Peru)   P:162
Mantegna, Andrea (early Renaissance artist)   R:169
Man That Always Rides, The (painting by Paul Kane)
    picture(s)   C:72
Mantis (insect)   I:236
    picture(s)   A:281; I:233, 237
Mantis flies
    picture(s)   I:241
Mantle (covering of a mollusk)   M:405; O:50, 290; S:208
Mantle (of Earth)   E:11, 23; G:112, 113
    earthquakes   E:36
    earth's plate movement   E:11, 12–13
    volcanoes   E:15–16
Mantle (of the moon)   M:453, 455
Mantle, Mickey (American baseball player)   B:89 profile
    picture(s)   B:89
Mantle cavity (of cephalopods)   O:50, 51
Manual alphabet (of the deaf)
    picture(s)   D:48–49
Manual exposure (in cameras)   P:202
Manual-focus cameras   P:200, 213
Manuals (Keyboards) (of the organ)   K:236, 237, 238

Manual training *see* Industrial arts
Manual transmissions (in motor vehicles) **A:**549; **T:**279
Manual typewriters **T:**373
Manuel, Don Juan (Spanish writer) *see* Juan Manuel, Don
Manufactured fibers **F:**108, 109–12
Manufacturing **M:**87–89 *see also* individual country, province, and state articles; the names of manufactured articles
 Africa **A:**64
 automation **A:**533
 automobiles **A:**542–43
 bread **B:**388a
 chemical industry **C:**197
 clothing industry **C:**380–81
 furniture **F:**515, 516
 hazardous wastes **H:**72–73
 industrial design **I:**213–15
 industrial engineers **E:**226
 Industrial Revolution **I:**216–23
 industry **I:**224–25
 North America, producing regions of **N:**301
 Ontario's advantages of location **O:**129
 patents **P:**99
 plastics **P:**324–26
 retailing, importance of **R:**189
 robots, industrial **R:**253
 technology, development of **T:**40–41
 trademarks **T:**266–67
Manumission *see* Emancipation
Manure (organic fertilizer) **A:**98; **F:**97
Manus (one of the Admiralty Islands) **P:**8
Manuscript books **C:**463–64
 authors' originals prized by collectors **A:**527–28
 books in preparation **B:**323–30
 Dead Sea Scrolls **D:**47
 medieval books **B:**321
Manuscripts, illuminated *see* Illuminated manuscripts
Manuscript writing **H:**22–23; **L:**36
Manutius, Aldus (Italian book publisher) **T:**370
Manx cats **C:**138
 picture(s) **C:**138
Man'yoshu (Japanese poetry collection) **J:**52
Manzanares River (Spain) **R:**243
Manzikert, Battle of (1071) **B:**103f
Manzini (Swaziland) **S:**521
Manzoni, Alessandro (Italian novelist and poet) **I:**408
Manzu, Giacomo (Italian sculptor) **I:**403
Mao Dun (Chinese writer) **C:**279
Maori (a people of New Zealand) **N:**235–36, 239, 241, 242; **P:**4
 mythology **M:**573–74
 top spinning **T:**240
 picture(s) **I:**364; **N:**235
  man carving wood **N:**241
Mao Zedong (Mao Tse-tung) (leader of the People's Republic of China) **C:**271–72; **G:**399–400; **J:**108; **M:**90
 picture(s) **C:**272; **N:**262e
"Maoz Tsur" (Hebrew hymn) **H:**29
Maple syrup and maple sugar **M:**91; **T:**306
 picture(s)
  eating maple syrup on ice **N:**296
  gathering sap **V:**307
  Sugaring Off (painting by Grandma Moses) **M:**470
Maple trees **M:**91; **P:**313
 picture(s) **R:**213
  leaf **L:**113; **P:**305
  seeds **P:**307
  sugar maple **N:**211; **T:**303; **V:**307; **W:**127, 193
  uses of the wood and its grain **W:**224
Mapocho River (Chile) **S:**37
Maps and globes **M:**92–99 *see also* individual continent, country, province, state, and city articles
 aerial photography **P:**208
 animals' map sense **H:**202
 be your own map maker **M:**98

cartography as a division of geography **G:**98–99
 Champlain was early map maker **C:**185
 documenting important facts about the world **W:**254
 early geographers and map makers **G:**105
 four-color map problem **T:**238
 latitude and longitude **L:**77–78
 map and globe terms **M:**93
 oceanography **O:**36–37
 photogrammetry used in making **O:**183–84
 seafloor mapping **U:**24
 surveying, use in **S:**519
 underwater archaeology sites, mapping of **U:**19
 Vespucci, Amerigo **V:**321
 weather maps **W:**92–94
 picture(s)
  globe divisions **M:**93
Map turtles **T:**357
Mapuche (Indians of South America) *see* Araucanians
Maputo (capital of Mozambique) **M:**509
 picture(s) **M:**508
Maquis (French underground) **U:**14
Maquis (Mediterranean scrubby underbrush) **E:**350
Marabouts (Muslim holy men) **M:**23
Maracaibo (Venezuela) **V:**297–98
Maracaibo, Lake (Venezuela) **L:**26, 32; **S:**281; **V:**295, 296
 picture(s) **L:**32; **V:**297
Marajoara (early Indians of Brazil) **I:**170
Marañón River (Peru) **P:**161–62
Maraschino cherry **P:**108
Marasmus (nutrition-deficiency disease) **N:**429
Marat, Jean Paul (political figure of the French Revolution) **F:**470 *profile*
 picture(s) **F:**471
Marathon, Battle of (490 B.C.) **B:**103e; **D:**36; **G:**343; **H:**123
 picture(s) **G:**337
Marathon race (in skiing) **S:**184f
Marathon race (track event) **T:**254
 footrace of Olympic Games **O:**105–6
 Koreans as long-distance runners **K:**300
 world records **T:**261
 picture(s)
  New York Marathon **N:**228
  Spokane (Washington) **W:**23
Marbella (Spain)
 picture(s) **S:**375
Marble (metamorphic rock) **R:**271; **S:**91; **V:**312–13
 picture(s) **G:**118; **Q:**6; **R:**269
Marble Arch (London, England) **L:**293
Marble Faun, The (novel by Hawthorne) **H:**65
Marble House (mansion in Newport, Rhode Island) **V:**277
Marbles **G:**18; **M:**99
Marbury v. Madison (case in constitutional law) **M:**111; **S:**507, 509; **U:**179
Marc, Franz (German painter) **G:**172; **M:**392
 picture(s)
  Little Blue Horse (painting) **G:**172
Marcellinus, Saint (pope) **R:**292
Marcellus I, Saint (pope) **R:**292
Marcellus II (pope) **R:**293
March (3rd month of year) **M:**100–101
Marches (band music) **B:**44
Marchetti, Gino (American football player) **F:**363 *profile*
 picture(s) **F:**363
"Marching Through Georgia" (song by Henry Clay Work) **N:**23
March of the Women (in French history) **F:**469
March on Washington (D.C., 1963) **A:**79n; **C:**330
March to the Sea (during the Civil War) **C:**343; **S:**152
Marciano, Rocky (American boxer) **B:**351, 352
Marconi, Guglielmo (Italian inventor of wireless telegraphy) **C:**469; **M:**102; **R:**58; **T:**47, 52
 inventions of communication **I:**284
 Italy's contributions to science **I:**387
 radio waves **L:**220
 picture(s) **M:**102
Marconi Wireless Company **R:**59

Marco Polo (Venetian traveler) *see* Polo, Marco
Marcos, Ferdinand (president of the Philippines)   A:338;
    P:188
    picture(s)   P:188
Marcos, Fray (Italian missionary) *see* Niza, Marcos de
Marcus, Siegfried (Austrian inventor)   A:540
Marcus Aurelius (Roman emperor)   R:316–17, 317
Marcy, Mount (New York)   N:212
Mardi Gras (Shrove Tuesday) (religious holiday)   H:163; R:154
    carnival   C:116
    Latin America   L:55
    New Orleans   L:314; N:195
    pre-Lenten celebrations   E:44
    picture(s)   L:315
Marduk (Babylonian god)   B:5
Marek's disease (disease of chickens)   A:100
Marengo, Battle of (1800)   N:11
Marengo Cave (Indiana)   I:146
Mares (female horses)   H:237
Mare Serenitatis (feature on the moon)
    picture(s)   M:451
Mares' tails (cirrus clouds)   C:385
Mare Tranquilitatis (feature on the moon)
    picture(s)   M:451
Margaret (princess of England)   E:192
    picture(s)   E:254
Margaret Island (Budapest, Hungary)   B:422b
Margaret of Anjou (queen of Henry VI of England)   E:241;
    H:110
Margaret Tudor (queen of Scotland)   S:88
Margarine (butter substitute)   B:474; O:79, 81; P:112
Margarita (island in the Caribbean)   C:114; S:281
Marggraf, Andreas Sigismond (German chemist)   S:484
Margherita Peak (Democratic Republic of Congo–Uganda)
    C:500; U:5
Margin (buying stocks on)   S:458
Margrethe I (queen of Denmark)   D:113
Margrethe II (queen of Denmark)   S:58g
Marguerite (Margarete) (character in Goethe's *Faust*)   F:73
Marguerite de Navarre (queen of Navarre, France)   R:161
    profile
    picture(s)   R:161
Marguerite de Valois (queen of Navarre, France)   H:279
Maria (Latin word meaning seas)
    Mercury   M:228
    moon   M:450, 452, 455
Maria (Russian princess)
    picture(s)   R:371
Mariachi bands
    picture(s)   L:71; T:129
Maria Laach, Abbey Church of (Germany)
    picture(s)   G:168
Mariana Islands (Pacific Ocean)   M:21; U:85; W:313
Marianas, Northern (islands in the Pacific Ocean)   P:9; T:113;
    U:85
Mariana Trench (Pacific Ocean)   O:21, 46; P:2
Mariánské Lázně (Czech Republic)   C:620
Maria Theresa (Austrian monarch)   A:524; H:3 *profile*
    picture(s)   A:524; H:3
Maribor (Slovenia)   S:204
Maricopa (Indians of North America)   I:183
Mariculture *see* Aquaculture
Marie Antoinette (queen of France)   F:415; M:103
    fashion design, history of   C:381
    French Revolution   F:469, 472
    pupil of Gluck   G:242
    picture(s)   F:457, 471; M:103
Marie de France (French fabulist)   F:4
Marie de Médicis (queen of France)   M:202
    picture(s)   M:202
Marie de Médicis, Queen of France, Landing in Marseilles
    (painting by Rubens)
    picture(s)   P:25
Marie-Louise (empress of the French)   J:99; N:11
Marie-Thérèse (queen of France)   L:313

Marietta (Ohio)   O:75
Marignano, Battle of (1515)   S:546
Marigny, Marquis de (French government official)   F:511
Marigolds (flowers)
    picture(s)   G:50
Marijuana (drug)   D:330
Marimba (musical instrument)   L:71
    picture(s)   L:71
Marin, John (American painter)   W:57
    picture(s)
        Boats and Sea, Deer Isle, Maine (painting)   W:57
Marinas (boat basins or docks)   B:266
Marine biology   B:198; O:35, 36
    Antarctica's marine ecosystem   A:293
    coral polyps   C:555–56
    extinction of many species in Paleozoic era   F:387
    fossils   F:381, 383, 385
    jellyfish and other coelenterates   J:72–77
    migrations in the oceans   H:199–200
    mollusks   M:405–8
    ocean life, kinds of   O:23–27
    ocean life's environment   O:17, 18, 19–20
    plankton   P:283–85
    saltwater species of fish   F:182–83, 202
    underwater exploration of life in the sea   U:25–26
    picture(s)
        path of food resources   O:22
Marine Corps, United States *see* United States Marine Corps
Marine engineers   E:226
Marine geology   O:35, 36
Marine ice sheet   G:224
Marine iguanas (lizards)   A:281; L:277
Marineland (Florida)   D:275, 277
Marine Mammal Protection Act (United States, 1972)   D:278
Marine otters   O:252
Marine paints   P:33–34
Mariner (space probes)
    electronic photography, history of   P:216
    Mariner 10 replica   P:274
    Mars   M:107; S:358
    Mercury   M:227; P:276; S:360
    observatories in space   O:10
    space flight data   S:359
    Venus   S:357–58
Marines (maritime soldiers)   U:119
Marines' Hymn ("From the Halls of Montezuma")   N:23; U:122,
    123
Marinetti, Filippo Tommaso (Italian poet)   I:403; M:391
Marine west coast climate (of North America)   C:362
Marine worms   A:83; O:26
Marini, Marino (Italian sculptor)   I:403
Marino, Giambattista (Italian poet)   I:407
Marinus, Saint (founder of San Marino)   S:35
Marinus I (pope)   R:292
Marinus II (pope)   R:292
Marion, Francis (American Revolutionary War commander)
    M:103; R:207
    picture(s)   S:309
Marionettes *see* Puppets and marionettes
Mariposa Grove (California)   Y:363
Maris, Roger (American baseball player)   N:334 *profile*
    picture(s)   B:91; N:335
Marisol (American artist)   M:396b; S:105
Maritime Administration   T:293
Maritime Alps (Italy–France)   A:194d
Maritime Aquarium at Norwalk (Connecticut)   C:514
Maritime law   S:158
Maritime Museum (Vancouver, British Columbia)   B:406b
Maritime Provinces (Canada)   C:54–55, 58, 61, 83 *see also*
    New Brunswick; Newfoundland and Labrador; Nova
    Scotia; Prince Edward Island
Maritsa River valley (Bulgaria)   B:442, 443
Marius, Gaius (Roman general)   R:315
Marivaux, Pierre Carlet de Chamblain (French writer)   F:440
Mark, Saint (Gospel writer)   B:165; S:18d *profile*

Mark, Saint (pope)   R:292
Mark Antony *see* Antony, Mark
"Market basket" (goods and services on which data is collected)
   C:533
Market economy (in economics)   E:59
   China, People's Republic of   C:272, 273
   Czech Republic   C:620–21
   Kaesŏng (North Korea), free-market zone   K:297
   North Korea's free-market zone   K:298
   Organization for Economic Cooperation and Development
      O:220
Marketing (of products and services)   S:20–21
   advertising   A:29–35
   department stores   D:118
   industry requirements   I:224
   mail order   M:34–35
   mass market   M:88
   motion picture distribution   M:486
   motion picture spin-off products   M:497
   retail stores   R:188–89
   supermarkets   S:498
   trade shows   F:15–16
Marketing research   A:32; O:169; S:20; T:69
Markets *see* Food shopping; Sales; Supermarkets
Markham, Edwin (American poet)   O:215 *profile*
Marking gauge (tool)   T:230
Markova, Alicia (English ballerina)   B:30, 31
Mark Twain *see* Twain, Mark
Markups (of prices)   S:21
Marlboro (Vermont)
   chamber music festival   M:556
Marlborough, Duke of (John Churchill) (English general and
      diplomat)   E:248; M:104
Marlowe, Christopher (English poet and dramatist)   D:301;
   E:272–73; F:72; M:104
Marlowe, Philip (fictional character)   M:564
Marmara, Sea of (Turkey)   I:377; T:345
Marmore waterfall (Italy)   W:59
Marmosets (monkeys)   M:420, 421, 422
   picture(s)   M:420; P:457
Marmots (rodents)   H:126, 127; R:275–76
   picture(s)   H:127
Marne, First Battle of the (1914)   B:103f; P:75; W:281–82
Marne, Second Battle of the (1918)   W:289–90
Maronites (Christian sect)   L:119, 122, 123
Maroons (a people of Jamaica)   J:18
Marovic, Svetozar (president of Serbia and Montenegro)
   S:127
Marple, Jane (fictional character)   M:564
Marquesas Islands (Pacific Ocean)   P:9
   picture(s)
      bone carving   P:5
Marquet, Albert (French painter)   M:388
Marquetry (inlaid furniture)   D:78
   picture(s)   D:78
Marquette (Michigan)   M:269
Marquette, Jacques (French Jesuit missionary and explorer)
   E:408; J:127; M:379
   exploration of area now called Chicago   C:220
   Mississippi River   M:364
   Wisconsin   W:204
   picture(s)   A:416; E:408
      early engraving of expedition   I:303
Márquez, Gabriel García (Colombian writer) *see* García Márquez,
   José Gabriel
Marrakech (Marrakesh) (Morocco)   M:460
Marranos (Christianized Jews)   J:104
Marriage
   divorce   D:230–31
   family group   F:37, 39, 40, 42–43
   homosexuals, where they can legally marry   H:204
   intermarriage of ethnic groups   E:336
   Islam   I:349
   Mormons once practiced polygyny   U:255

partners chosen by parents in Southeast Asia   S:331
   Roman Catholic sacrament   C:287; R:285
Marriage à la Mode (paintings by William Hogarth)   H:159a
Marriage customs *see* Wedding customs
Marriage of Figaro, The (opera by Mozart)   M:542; O:156–58
Marriner, Sir Neville (British orchestra conductor)   O:200–201
   profile
Marriott, John W. (American hotel and restaurant owner)
   U:254 *profile*
Marrow (of bones)   B:278; S:184a
   blood cells made in   B:261, 262, 284
   leukemia is cancer of   C:92
   lymphocytes formed   I:96
   radiotherapy's effects on   C:94
   transplantation   D:191; O:227
Mars (planet)   M:105–9; P:278–79
   expected to be the first planet visited by astronauts
      S:363
   geology in the solar system   G:118, 119
   Is there life on Mars?   M:109
   life on other planets   A:476a; M:32; S:354
   observing Mars   P:281
   robots for dangerous situations   R:254
   space probes   O:10; S:358
   Viking space probes   S:362
   volcanoes   V:386
   water on Earth and beyond   W:50
   picture(s)
      artist's concept of future human base   S:356
      Sojourner on Martian surface   R:254
      surface features   M:107; P:278–79
      Valles Marineris   M:105
Mars (Roman god) *see* Ares
Mars (space probe)   S:358
Marsalis, Wynton (American trumpeter)   J:64 *profile*
   picture(s)   A:80; J:64
Marsaxlokk (Malta)   M:64
Mars Climate Orbiter (space probe)   S:358
Marsden, Samuel (English missionary)   N:241
Marseillaise, La (French national anthem)   N:20–21
Marseille (Marseilles) (France)   F:404, 410; L:124
   picture(s)   F:411
Mars Exploration Rovers (space probes)   M:107; O:10; P:279;
   S:358, 359
Mars Express (space probe)   S:339
Mars Global Surveyor (spacecraft)   M:106; S:358
Marshaling (in heraldry)   H:118
Marshall, George C. (American statesman)   E:123; M:110;
   T:326; V:351
Marshall, John (American jurist)   L:170; M:111; S:507; V:360
Marshall, Paule (American writer)   A:219
Marshall, Thomas Riley (vice president, United States)   V:329
   profile
   picture(s)   V:328
Marshall, Thurgood (U.S. Supreme Court justice)   A:79c,
   79m; M:132–33 *profile;* N:26; S:114
   picture(s)   N:25; S:115
Marshallese (Kajin Majol) (language)   M:112
Marshall Field & Co. (department store)   C:221; D:118
Marshall Islands (Pacific Ocean)   M:112–13; T:113; W:308
   map(s)   M:112
   picture(s)
      flags   F:235
      woman preparing coconuts   M:112
Marshall Plan (for assistance to Europe)   M:110; U:197
   Cold War   C:400
   foreign economic aid under Truman   T:326
   OECD, origin of   O:220
   United States aid to Germany   G:154
Marshall Space Flight Center (Huntsville, Alabama)   A:137;
   S:339, 340a; V:391
Marshals Service, United States *see* United States Marshals
   Service
Marshes (low, swampy land)   L:27; N:63; W:145, 147–48
Marsh Harbour (Bahamas)   B:17

Masked booby (bird)
  picture(s) **B:**236
Masks
  Africa, art of   **A:**70, 73–74; **D:**74
  dances of Bali   **D:**25
  Halloween customs   **H:**13
  Inuit   **I:**275
  skin diving   **S:**186
  picture(s)
    Africa, art of   **A:**73; **D:**74; **I:**420
    jade mosaic mask of Maya ruler Pacal   **A:**233
    Japanese No theater   **J:**53
    Mycenaean burial mask   **A:**229; **G:**340; **M:**562
    papier-mâché   **P:**58b
    Peruvian funerary mask   **S:**274
    symbols of drama   **D:**298
    Vanuatu ceremonial mask   **P:**3
Maslow, Abraham (American psychologist)   **P:**511
Mason, Charles (English surveyor)   **M:**135
Mason, George (American statesman)   **V:**359
Mason, John (English settler and founder of New Hampshire)
  N:150; **T:**174
Mason bees   **B:**121
  picture(s) **B:**121
Mason-Dixon line   **M:**135, 381
Mason jar (for canning and bottling)   **B:**346
Masonry   **B:**392–94
  building construction   **B:**432
  cement and concrete   **C:**165
  nails for masonry   **N:**2
  paints for masonry   **P:**32
Masonry dams   **D:**18
Masqat (capital of Oman)   **O:**121
Masque (poetic pageant)   **E:**273; **O:**142
Mass (in music)   **M:**538
  choral music   **C:**283
  Dutch and Flemish music   **D:**371, 372
  France, music of   **F:**444
Mass (in physics)   **M:**172–73, 174
  acceleration and mass   **M:**475
  air has mass   **A:**480–81
  atoms   **A:**484
  change of mass in nuclear reactions   **N:**367–68
  defined   **C:**204
  Earth's   **E:**9
  forces   **F:**365
  gravity and gravitation   **G:**321–22, 324
  mass numbers   **C:**203
  measurement of   **W:**114, 117
  relativity   **P:**231
  stars   **S:**430, 431
Mass (in Roman Catholic Church)   **R:**284–85, 294
Massachuset (Indians of North America)   **I:**177; **M:**136
Massachusetts   **M:**136–50
  Boston   **B:**339–42
  colonial life in America   **C:**409, 411, 415, 418
  colonial sites you can visit today   **C:**422
  Declaration of Independence signers   **D:**66
  first state to establish free public schools   **E:**84
  homosexuals can legally marry   **H:**204
  Horace Mann and education   **M:**87
  Hutchinson, Thomas   **H:**308
  Intolerable (Coercive) Acts (1774)   **D:**59
  Maine, history of   **M:**49
  New Hampshire, history of   **N:**160
  Plymouth Colony   **P:**344–47
  Puritans   **P:**550–51
  thirteen American colonies   **T:**171–73
  witches, persecution of   **W:**209
  map(s) **M:**147
  picture(s)
    Berkshire Music Festival   **M:**555
    Boston   **B:**339, 340; **M:**137, 145
    digging for clams   **M:**137

  Harvard University   **M:**140
  Springfield   **M:**145
Massachusetts, University of   **M:**141
Massachusetts Bay Colony   **M:**136, 146; **T:**172–73; **U:**174
  Hutchinson, Anne   **H:**308
  Hutchinson, Thomas   **H:**308
  Plymouth Colony becomes part of   **P:**347
  Puritans   **P:**550–51
  Williams, Roger   **W:**175
Massachusetts Colored General Association (African-American
  political group)   **A:**79e
Massachusetts 54th (African-American regiment in the Civil
  War)
  picture(s) **U:**116
Massachusetts Historical Society   **M:**141
Massachusetts State College System   **M:**141
Massage therapy   **A:**194e
  picture(s) **A:**194e
Massamba-Débat, Alphonse (president of the Congo)   **C:**506
Mass arrangements (in floral design)   **F:**278
Massasoit (Native American chief)   **I:**177; **M:**149; **P:**346;
  S:25; **T:**153
Massawa (Eritrea)   **E:**317
Mass burials   **F:**493
Mass communication   **C:**471
Mass destruction, weapons of *see also* Biological warfare;
  Chemical warfare; Nuclear weapons
  Iraq War, background of   **I:**316a
Massenet, Jules (French composer)   **O:**156
Mass extinctions (of plants and animals)   **E:**425–26
Massey, William (New Zealand statesman)   **N:**241
Massine, Léonide (Russian choreographer)   **B:**30
Massive-head buttress dams   **D:**19
  picture(s) **D:**19
Mass market (in economics)   **M:**88
Mass media (in communication)   **C:**471
  advertising   **A:**29, 30–32
  American literature   **A:**214
  television   **T:**67–71
Mass numbers (of atoms)   **A:**486; **C:**204; **N:**367
Mass production   **M:**88–89; **T:**40, 41
  automation   **A:**529–33
  automobiles   **A:**543, 553–54
  clothing   **C:**378, 380
  Connecticut, history of   **C:**508, 522
  decorative arts   **D:**78
  Depression, Great, causes of   **D:**119–20
  Ford, Henry   **F:**369
  glassmaking process   **G:**233–34
  industrial design   **I:**213–15
  inventions   **I:**281
  jewelry production   **J:**97
  modern architecture   **A:**375–76
  pottery   **P:**413
  tools   **T:**231, 235
  Whitney, Eli   **W:**168
Mass spectrometer (scientific instrument)   **R:**74, 76
  picture(s) **R:**75
Massys, Quentin (Flemish painter)   **P:**18
  picture(s)
    The Moneylender and His Wife (painting)   **P:**19
Mastabas (tombs of Egyptian noblemen)   **A:**365; **E:**111
Mast cells (in the body)   **A:**190
MasterCard (credit card)   **C:**582
Master cylinder (in a hydraulic system)   **H:**312
  brakes   **A:**551
Master Francis George Hare (painting by Sir Joshua Reynolds)
  picture(s) **R:**210
Master keys   **L:**283
Masters (golf tournament)   **G:**260
Masters (of craft guilds)   **G:**404
Master's degrees (in education)   **U:**221, 223
Mastiffs (dogs)   **D:**247
  picture(s) **D:**242, 247
Mastitis (infection of a cow's mammary gland)   **D:**7

Mastodon (extinct animal)   E:183; I:12, 415–16
  picture(s)   I:11
Masts (supports for boat's sails)   S:8, 157
Masurian Lakes, Battle of the (1914)   W:283
Masuria region (Poland)   P:358
Matabele (a people of Africa) see Ndebele
Matabeleland (region of Zimbabwe)   Z:381
Matadors (bullfighters)   B:450–51
  picture(s)   S:371
Mata Hari (dancer and spy for Germany during World War I)
  S:408 profile
  picture(s)   S:408
Matanuska River and Valley (Alaska)   A:151
Matapan Trench (Ionian Sea)   M:211
Matches (for starting fires)   F:143, 147
Matchlock guns (early trigger guns)   G:416–17
  picture(s)   G:416, 417
Match play (in golf)   G:256
Match races (in sailing)   S:12
Maté (Yerba maté) (herb tea)   B:374; P:63
  picture(s)   B:374
Materialism   R:293–94
Materiality (in law)   C:575
Materials engineering   M:151
Materials science   M:151–55
Mat foundation (in construction)   B:437
Mathematical logic   L:290; M:159
Mathematical time   T:204
Mathematics   M:156–61
  abacus   A:2–3
  algebra   A:182–84
  aptitude test questions   T:121–22
  arithmetic   A:388–91
  decimal system   D:56
  Descartes' analytic geometry   D:124
  ecological research   E:55
  geometry   G:120–28
  graphs   G:309–13
  history see Mathematics, history of
  Kepler's laws of planetary motion   K:234
  learning disorders   L:107, 108
  metric system of measurement   W:109–12
  number patterns   N:380–88
  numbers and number systems   N:396–402
  numerals and numeration systems   N:403–9
  percentage   P:144–46
  ratio and proportion   R:107
  Roman numerals   R:301
  sets   S:128–28a
  statistics   S:440–41
  Sumerian mathematics based on the number sixty   S:487
  topology   T:236–39
  trigonometry   T:312–13
  picture(s)
    student solving problem   E:85
Mathematics, history of   M:162–70
  American Indians' contributions to world cultures   I:166
  Bernoulli family   B:153
  Gauss, Carl Friedrich   G:64
  Greece, ancient   G:343
  Huygens, Christiaan   H:310
  Newton, Isaac   N:206–7
  Pythagoras   P:559
  Who invented mathematical signs?   M:165
Mather, Cotton (American writer)   A:203; C:411; M:148–49
  profile; P:550
Mather, Increase (American minister and author)   M:148
  profile; P:550
Mather, Richard (English clergyman)   P:550
Mather, Stephen T. (National Park Service director)   N:45, 47
Mathewson, Christy (American baseball player)   B:89 profile
  picture(s)   B:89
Mathias, Bob (American athlete)   O:107 profile, 113; T:263
  picture(s)   T:263
Matilda (Maud) (queen of England)   H:108

Matisse, Henri (French painter)   F:431; M:171
  drawing, history of   D:318
  modern art   M:388, 390
  picture(s)
    page from hand-written book Jazz   F:431
    The Red Studio (painting)   M:389
    Woman with the Hat (painting)   M:171
Matoaka (Native American princess) see Pocahontas
Matolo (Mozambique)   M:509
Matonabbee (Chipewyan chief)   N:413
Matos, Gregorio de (Brazilian writer)   L:67
Mátra Mountains (Hungary)   H:296
Matriarchal family   F:42
Matrimony (Roman Catholic sacrament)   R:285
Matronymic method (of name giving)   N:5
Matsu (island off China's mainland)   T:8
Matta, Roberto (Chilean painter)   L:64
Mattamuskeet National Wildlife Refuge
  picture(s)   N:308
Matte paintings (for motion picture special effects)   M:484
Matter   M:172–78
  atoms   A:483
  black holes   B:252
  changes in physical properties near speed of light   R:142
  definition of the term   C:204
  electricity and matter   E:135–36
  gases   G:56–61
  gravity and gravitation   G:321–22, 324
  heat and changes of state   H:86, 89–92
  instruments for analyzing   O:184–85
  liquids   L:254–55
  magnetism and matter   M:31–32
  nuclear energy   N:366–73
  physics, history of   P:234
  physics is the study of   P:228
  radiation and matter   R:42–47
  relativity   R:139–44
  solids   S:250
  vacuum   V:262–65
Matterhorn (mountain, Switzerland)   A:194d; S:543
  picture(s)   S:543
Matthew, Saint (one of the 12 Apostles)   A:329
  Gospel of   B:165
Matthews, Drummond (British scientist)   G:111
Matthias, Saint (one of the 12 Apostles)   A:329
Matthias Corvinus (king of Hungary)   B:422b; H:298
Matute, Ana María (Spanish novelist)   S:392
Matzeliger, Jan Ernest (American inventor)   A:79i
Matzo (unleavened bread)   B:385; J:146b; P:95, 96
Mauchly, John (American inventor)   C:490
Maud (queen of England) see Matilda
Maugham, W. Somerset (English writer)   E:289
Maui (one of the Hawaiian Islands)   H:51, 52, 53, 60
  picture(s)
    Haleakala National Park   H:50; N:48
Mau Mau (Kikuyu movement to oust Europeans from Kenya)
  K:233
Maumee, Lake (ancient glacial lake)   O:64
Mauna Kea (volcano, Hawaii)   H:51; U:82
  observatories   O:8
  telescopes   T:58–59
Mauna Loa (volcano, Hawaii)   H:48, 51, 52; M:502; V:380
  picture(s)   V:381
Maunder Minimum (period of sunspot inactivity)   S:494
Maupassant, Guy de (French author)   F:441; S:162
Maupeou, René (French chancellor)   L:311
Maurer, Robert (American scientist)   F:107
Mauretania (ocean liner)   O:33
Mauriac, François (French novelist)   F:442
Maurice, Saint, and the Theban Legion   S:18d profile
Mauritania   M:179–80; W:124
  map(s)   M:179
  picture(s)
    flag   F:235
    women learning to read   M:179

Mauritius M:181
　map(s) M:181
　picture(s)
　　flag F:235
Mauritius parakeets (birds) P:86
Maury, Matthew (American oceanographer) O:41
Maurya Dynasty A:453; I:135–36
Maus: A Survivor's Tale (graphic novel by Art Spiegelman)
　C:454
　picture(s) C:454
Mauser, Paul (German gunsmith) G:421
Mauser rifle G:421
　picture(s) G:421
Mausoleum at Halicarnassus (Asia Minor) W:218–19
Mausoleums (burial places) F:493
Mauve (Mauveine) (synthetic dye) D:378; T:142
Mauve and Orange (painting by Mark Rothko)
　picture(s) U:135
Mavica (magnetic video camera) P:218
Mawlid al-nabi (Muslim holiday) I:349
Mawson, Douglas (English explorer) E:415
Maxam, Alan (American biochemist) B:189
Maxentius (Roman emperor) C:528
Maxillofacial surgeon (in dentistry) D:115
Maxim, Hiram Percy (American inventor and industrialist)
　R:63
Maxim, Hiram S. (American-English inventor) G:423
Maximilian (emperor of Mexico) J:142; M:249–50
Maximilian I (Kaiser Max) (Holy Roman emperor) A:523; H:2,
　3 profile; N:120d
　picture(s) H:3
Maxim machine guns G:423
Maxims (sayings) F:439
Maximum Employment Act (United States, 1946) T:326
Maximum security prisons
　picture(s) P:480
Max Schmitt in a Single Scull (painting by Eakins)
　picture(s) E:3
Maxwell, James Clerk (Scottish physicist) P:229, 230, 237
　　profile; S:73
　electromagnetic waves E:141–42; L:218–20; M:31;
　　P:235; R:47
　predicted radio waves R:58
　picture(s) P:237
Maxwell Montes (mountain on Venus) V:303a–303b
May (5th month of year) M:182–83
Maya (Indians of North America) I:167; M:184–87
　ancient civilizations A:243–44
　archaeological specialties A:350
　architecture A:367
　beekeeping H:212
　calendar C:14
　Central America C:174
　Cival artifacts G:398
　decorative arts D:75
　El Salvador E:198
　Guatemala G:394, 395, 397, 398
　hieroglyphic writing systems H:131
　Honduras H:208
　Indians since 1500 I:194
　Milky Way in mythology U:211
　music A:237
　mythology M:571
　numeration system N:405–6
　Pacal A:229
　pyramids P:558
　radar used to detect swamp gardens A:352
　picture(s)
　　burial site I:167
　　Chichén Itzá M:248; N:283
　　Copán H:208; I:169
　　hieroglyphs H:130
　　jade mosaic mask of Lord Pacal A:233
　　limestone lintel A:244

　Maya Indian woman C:172
　photograph of painted vase M:187
　Pyramid of the Magician (Uxmal, Mexico) I:171
　sculpture E:198
　terra cotta figurine I:170
　Tikal temple G:397
Mayagüez (Puerto Rico) P:531
Mayagüez incident (1975) F:368
Mayakovski, Vladimir (Russian poet) R:383
May Day (International Labor Day) H:169
　picture(s)
　　Korea, North K:298
　　maypole H:169
　　Soviet celebrations U:35, 41
Mayer, Louis B. (American film producer) L:308 profile
　picture(s) L:308
Mayer, Maria Goeppert (American physicist) see
　Goeppert-Mayer, Maria
Mayfair (London, England) L:294
Mayflower (flower) see Trailing arbutus
Mayflower (Pilgrims' ship) M:188; P:345; T:170–71
　picture(s) U:175; W:266
Mayflower II (ship) M:188
Mayflower Compact (1620) P:345; T:171
Mayfly
　picture(s) I:248; L:197
Mayo (Indians of North America) I:183
Mayo, Charles Horace (American physician) M:339 profile
Mayo, William James (American physician) M:339 profile
Mayo, William Worrall (English-American physician) M:339
　　profile
Mayo Clinic (Rochester, Minnesota) M:331, 334, 339
Mayo family (American doctors) M:334
Mayombé Escarpment (Congo) C:505
Mayon, Mount (volcano, Philippines) P:185
Mayonnaise F:343; O:81
Mayor-council form (of city government) M:516
Mayotte (island, Indian Ocean) C:475
Mayow, John (English scientist) M:208a
Maypole dances F:300
　picture(s) F:300–301; H:169
Mayreau (island, Saint Vincent and the Grenadines) S:19
Mays, Willie (American baseball player) B:89 profile
　picture(s) B:89
Ma Yuan (Chinese artist) C:275
Mazama, Mount (ancient volcano, Oregon) L:26
Mazār-e Sharīf (Afghanistan) T:117
　picture(s) A:42
Mazarin, Jules, Cardinal (French statesman) F:414, 425;
　L:312
Mazdak (Persian religious leader) P:157
Maze (network of paths enclosed by hedges) P:76–77
　Jordan theorem in topology T:239
Mazowiecki, Tadeusz (Polish prime minister) P:362
Mazzini, Giuseppe (Italian patriot) G:56; I:389; M:189
mb see Millibar
Mbabane (capital of Swaziland) S:521
Mbandzeni (king of Swaziland) S:522
Mbeki, Thabo (president of South Africa) M:78; S:273
Mbira (African musical instrument) A:79; M:542–43
M'Bochi (a people of Africa) C:504
Mboya, Tom (Kenyan statesman) K:233
Mc (contraction of Mac) N:5 see also the names beginning
　with Mac and Mc in alphabetical order as they are
　spelled
McAdam, John Loudon (Scottish engineer) R:249, 250
McAleese, Mary (president of Ireland) I:324
McAuliffe, Christa (American astronaut) N:163 profile; S:352
　Christa McAuliffe Planetarium (Concord, New Hampshire)
　　N:158
　picture(s) N:163
McBey, James (British artist)
　picture(s)
　　Camel Corps: A Night March to Beersheba W:285

Measurement
  barometer measures air pressure   **B:**62
  chemistry, history of   **C:**207
  of energy in foot-pounds   **E:**212
  experiments and other science activities   **E:**382–83
  intelligence   **I:**254
  ocean, mapping and measuring of   **O:**36–37
  with optical instruments   **O:**182–84
  precipitation   **R:**96–97
  surveying   **S:**519–20
  tests and test taking   **T:**118–23
  tools for measuring   **T:**230
  trigonometry, uses of   **T:**313
  weights and measures   **W:**108–17
Measures *see* Weights and measures
Meat and meat packing   **M:**195–98
  automated meat slicers   **A:**530
  beef cattle   **C:**151–53
  cold storage   **F:**341
  cooking, methods of   **C:**543
  curing by salting and smoking   **F:**344
  food regulations and laws   **F:**345
  food shopping   **F:**349
  food supply   **F:**350
  grades of meat   **M:**198
  important agricultural products   **A:**90
  Inuit diet   **I:**274
  Jewish dietary laws   **J:**146b
  Jungle, The (book by Sinclair)   **A:**214
  livestock   **L:**271, 272
  organic foods   **H:**79
  outdoor cooking and picnics   **O:**262
  pemmican   **I:**190
  preservation   **F:**336
  safety of refrigerated foods   **F:**343
  spoilage   **F:**339
  trichinosis (illness from undercooked pork)   **D:**207
  Variant Creutzfeldt-Jakob disease caused by contaminated meat   **D:**208–9
  vegetarianism is the avoidance of meat   **V:**293
  picture(s)
    meat inspection   **F:**345
Mecca (holy city of Islam)   **M:**199
  Arab history and civilization   **A:**344
  Islam   **I:**348, 349, 350; **S:**58b
  Mohammed's birthplace   **M:**401
  pilgrimages   **R:**148
  picture(s)   **R:**145; **S:**58d
    Great Mosque   **I:**346
Mechanical (in printing)
  books   **B:**329
  commercial art   **C:**458
  magazine production   **M:**17
Mechanical advantage (MA) (force-saving feature of simple machines)   **H:**312–13; **W:**247–48
Mechanical clocks   **C:**369–70, 371–72
Mechanical dolls   **D:**269–70
Mechanical drawing   **M:**200
Mechanical energy   **E:**213; **H:**88–89
Mechanical engineers   **E:**226
Mechanical pencils   **P:**144
Mechanical television (early broadcasting system)   **I:**285
Mechanics (branch of physics)   **P:**228, 234
  Archimedes   **A:**363
  falling bodies, laws of   **F:**34; **G:**5–6
  motion   **M:**474–76
  work, power, and machines   **W:**243–52
Mechanics (workers who maintain machinery)   **A:**571
  automobile-related careers   **A:**556
Mechanism of action (of drugs)   **D:**334–35
Mechanization *see* Machines and machinery
Mečiar, Vladimír (prime minister of Slovakia)   **S:**202
Meck, Nadezhda von (patron of Tchaikovsky)   **T:**33

Meckenem, Israel van (Flemish artist)
  picture(s)
    Lute Player and Woman Playing the Harp (painting)   **D:**372
Mecklenburg (West Virginia)   **W:**136
Medallions *see* Medals
Medal of Freedom *see* Presidential Medal of Freedom
Medal of Honor   **D:**69, 71; **U:**101
  picture(s)   **D:**70
Medal play (in golf)   **G:**256
Medals   **D:**69–71
  children's book awards   **C:**239–40
  Olympic medals   **O:**110
  What is the Congressional Medal of Honor?   **U:**101
  picture(s)
    Olympic medals   **O:**110
Medea (in Greek mythology)   **G:**368
Medea (remotely operated vehicle)   **U:**24
Mededovic, Avdo (Slavic poet)   **F:**310
Medellín (Colombia)   **C:**406
Medes (a people of ancient Iran)   **A:**233; **I:**308; **K:**307; **P:**154
Medfly *see* Fruit flies
Medgyessy, Peter (prime minister of Hungary)   **H:**299
Media (of communication)
  advertising   **A:**29, 30–32
  communicating by electricity   **T:**46
  computers and society   **C:**494
  elections, impact on   **E:**129
  journalism   **J:**135–36
  propaganda   **P:**488–89
Media buyers (in advertising agencies)   **A:**32
Media centers (school libraries)   **L:**177–78
Median (average of a set of numbers)   **S:**441
Media planners (in advertising agencies)   **A:**32, 33
Mediation (in international relations)   **I:**269–70
Mediators (in divorce cases)   **D:**230
Medicaid (medical care program)   **H:**78; **W:**120
  disabilities, people with   **D:**180
  legal immigrants ineligible for   **I:**93
  poverty reduction   **P:**420
Medical alert tag
  picture(s)   **F:**156
Medical anthropology   **A:**302
Medical Care Act (Canada, 1968)   **S:**226
Medical directors (doctors who oversee emergency medical systems)   **A:**199
Medical education   **D:**238; **P:**513–14; **S:**513
  continuing medical education   **D:**236–37
  Osler, Sir William   **O:**238
Medical ethics (set of rules for doctors)   **A:**8; **D:**237; **E:**328
Medical examiners (in criminal investigations)   **D:**236
Medical geography   **G:**103
Medical history (of a patient)   **D:**200–202, 237
Medical laboratory tests   **M:**204
Medical records (of patients)   **H:**249
Medical subspecialties (narrow fields of medicine)   **M:**205
Medicare (insurance program)   **S:**226
  disabilities, people with   **D:**180
  Health and Human Services, United States Department of   **H:**78
  part of "Great Society" program   **J:**122
  poverty reduction   **P:**420
  prescription-drug coverage   **B:**468
  Saskatchewan was the first Canadian province to have   **S:**45
Medicare and Medicaid Services, Centers for (United States)   **H:**78
Medici (Italian family)   **M:**201–2
  Botticelli supported by   **B:**345
  Florence (Italy)   **F:**259
  Renaissance   **R:**158
  Renaissance art   **I:**395
  Uffizi Gallery   **U:**2
Medici, Alessandro de' (duke of Florence)   **M:**202
Medici, Anna Maria   **M:**202

Medici, Cosimo (1389–1464)   **M:**201
Medici, Cosimo I de' (1519–1574; grand duke of Tuscany)
   M:202; **R:**161
   picture(s)   **M:**202
Medici, Giovanni di Bicci (1360–1429)   **M:**201
Medici, Lorenzo de' (Lorenzo the Magnificent) (Italian statesman
      and art patron)   **I:**406; **M:**201–2; **R:**158
   Florence, history of   **F:**259
   Michelangelo's patron   **M:**255–56
   Uffizi Gallery   **M:**528
Medicinal plants *see* Plants, medicinal
Medicine   **M:**203–10 *see also* Diseases; First aid; Health
   allergy treatments   **A:**191
   alternative medicine   **A:**194e
   ambulances   **A:**199
   American Indians' contributions to world cultures   **I:**166
   anesthesia   **A:**254–57
   antibiotics   **A:**306–12
   Beaumont's research on the human stomach   **B:**109
   biological clock   **B:**194
   biology, history of   **B:**200–201
   biomedical engineers   **E:**225
   biotechnology   **G:**83–85
   blood transfusion by the Incas   **B:**262
   cancer research   **C:**93–95
   computers used in   **C:**485–86
   cultural anthropology   **A:**302
   deafness, treatment of   **D:**49
   dentistry   **D:**114–16
   dermatology   **D:**123–24
   disabilities, rehabilitation of people with   **D:**179
   disaster relief   **D:**185
   disease, types of   **D:**186–99
   disinfectants and antiseptics   **D:**214
   doctors   **D:**234–39
   drug abuse   **D:**329–33
   drugs   **D:**333–36
   dwarfism   **D:**374–75
   Egypt, ancient   **S:**68
   electronics   **E:**161
   fiber optics   **F:**106, 107
   fire throughout history   **F:**142
   geriatrics   **O:**99
   health care in rural India   **I:**122
   health insurance   **I:**252
   herbs and spices, medicinal use of   **H:**119, 120, 121
   hibernation studied for clues to medical treatments
         H:128
   holistic medicine   **H:**171
   honey, healing properties of   **H:**212
   hospitals   **H:**247–53
   humoral theory in Greek medicine   **S:**68
   hypnotism   **H:**327–29
   imaging, diagnostic   **I:**85–86
   infrared photography   **P:**209
   insulin   **B:**59
   inventions   **I:**286
   laser beams   **L:**46c
   marijuana, medical use of   **D:**330
   mathematics in careers   **M:**161
   Mayo Clinic   **M:**339
   medical education, aid to   **P:**513–14
   medicines from plants   **F:**281; **L:**118; **P:**297; **R:**100
   mummies, study of   **M:**513
   Muslim role in medieval education   **E:**80
   Nobel prizes   **N:**263–65
   nurses and nursing   **N:**417–22
   occupational health and safety   **O:**13
   opium, early use of   **N:**15
   organ transplants   **O:**226–27
   pioneer life   **P:**255
   plastics, uses of   **P:**329
   poisons   **P:**355–56
   poverty reduction through basic health care   **P:**420
   preventing diseases   **H:**76–77
   public health   **P:**512–16
   Renaissance   **R:**162
   robots, medical   **R:**255
   science, milestones in   **S:**75
   science, modern   **S:**73–74
   Shipp, Ellis Reynolds   **U:**255
   snakebite treatment   **S:**215
   statistics, uses of   **S:**439
   surgery   **S:**512–13, 512–15
   Taussig, Helen Brooke   **T:**24
   tobacco, medical uses of   **T:**215
   ultrasonography   **E:**49; **R:**41; **S:**265
   vaccination and immunization   **V:**260–61
   veterinarians   **V:**323
   X-rays   **P:**208; **X:**350
Medicine Bow Range (Colorado–Wyoming)   **W:**336
Medicine Hat (Alberta)   **A:**166, 170
Médicis, Catherine de *see* Catherine de Médicis
Médicis, Marie de *see* Marie de Médicis
Medieval architecture *see* Middle Ages, architecture of
Medieval art *see* Middle Ages, art of the
Medieval history *see* Middle Ages
Medieval manuscripts *see* Manuscript books
Medieval music *see* Middle Ages, music of the
Medieval Tool Period (stage in tool use)   **T:**234
   picture(s)   **T:**235
Medina (Saudi Arabia)   **A:**344; **I:**350; **M:**401; **S:**58b
Medinet Habu (Egyptian temple)   **E:**114
Meditation (method of attaining greater spiritual awareness or
      calm)   **A:**194e; **H:**139–40; **P:**430; **R:**150
Mediterranean climate   **C:**362; **E:**349; **S:**373
Mediterranean fruit fly *see* Fruit flies
Mediterranean scrub forest *see* Maquis
Mediterranean Sea   **M:**211–12
   ancient civilizations   **A:**236–39
   environmental issues   **E:**351
   Europe's southern boundary   **E:**345
   food customs in bordering countries   **F:**330–31
   Gibraltar (British military fortress)   **G:**204
   Malta   **M:**63–64
   Venice was chief sea power during the Renaissance
         V:301
   map(s)   **M:**211
Medium (carrier of sound)   **S:**256
Medium (for artists' paints) *see* Vehicle (medium)
Medium (of communication) *see* Media
Medium (person believed to communicate with spirits of the
      dead)   **G:**200
Medium of exchange (in economics)   **M:**412–15
Medulla (part of the brain)   **B:**288, 289, 365–66; **N:**116
Medulla (part of the kidney)   **K:**242
Medusa (one of the Gorgons in Greek mythology)   **G:**365
Medusae (forms of jellyfish and other coelenterates)   **J:**73,
      75, 76–77
   picture(s)   **J:**74
Meech Lake Accord (in Canadian history)   **C:**85; **M:**511; **Q:**17
Meerkats (animals related to mongooses)   **M:**419
   picture(s)   **M:**419
Meeting, The (painting by Jean Fragonard)
   picture(s)   **F:**402
Meeting at the Golden Gate (painting by Giotto di Bondone)
   picture(s)   **R:**163
Meet the Press (television program)   **T:**70
Megabytes (of computer-stored information)   **C:**481, 491
Megahertz (MHz) (used to measure very-high-frequency radio
      waves)   **R:**53
Megakaryocytes (giant cells in bone marrow)   **B:**260
Megaliths (large stones in prehistoric monuments)
   picture(s)
      Stonehenge   **E:**236
Megalopolis (a supercity)   **C:**321; **M:**120
Megalosaurus (dinosaur)   **D:**168
Megatons (yield of nuclear weapons)   **N:**375
Megawati Sukarnoputri (president of Indonesia)   **I:**212

Megiddo, Battle of (1469 B.C.) B:103e
Mehemet Ali (governor of Egypt) E:104
Mehinacú (Indians of South America) I:197
Mehmed II (Ottoman sultan) O:259
    picture(s) O:261
Mehmed VI (sultan of Turkey) T:349
Meier, Richard (American architect) U:136
Meighen, Arthur (Canadian prime minister) C:77 profile
Meiji (emperor of Japan) J:45
Meiji Shrine (Tokyo) T:219
Mein Kampf (book by Adolf Hitler) H:173; N:79
Meiosis (formation of reproductive cells) C:162; G:79
Meir, Golda (Israeli political leader) M:212
    picture(s) I:375; P:459
Meissen (Germany) G:156
Meissen chinaware see Dresden porcelain
Meistersingers (German singers) G:177, 183
Meistersinger von Nürnberg, Die (opera by Richard Wagner)
        O:159
    picture(s) O:158
Meitner, Lise (Austrian physicist and mathematician) F:222;
        N:373
Meitnerium (element) E:174
Mejdani, Rexhep (Albanian president) A:162
Mejía, Rafael Hipólito (president of Dominican Republic)
        D:283
    picture(s) D:283
Meknes (Morocco) M:460
Mekong River (Asia) R:243
    ancient civilizations A:242
    Cambodia C:36
    Laos L:41, 42
    Southeast Asia S:331, 333, 336
    Tonle Sap L:34
    Vietnam V:334a–334b
    picture(s) R:237; S:331
        fishing A:441
        floating markets V:334b
Melanesia (Pacific islands) P:3, 4 see also the names of
        islands
Melanesians (Pacific islanders) P:4, 5
    New Guinea N:148
    Papua New Guinea P:58d
    Solomon Islands S:252
    Vanuatu V:279
    picture(s) P:9, 10
Melanin (body pigment) B:277; D:129; H:5–6
Melanocytes (pigment-producing cells) B:277; D:123
Melanoma (type of skin cancer) D:123, 124
Melatonin (hormone) B:194; G:228
Melbourne (capital of Victoria, Australia) A:506, 511; M:213
    arts center A:503
    Olympic Games (1956) O:111
    world's fair (1880) F:16
    picture(s) A:513
Melbourne Cup (horse race) M:213
Meles Zenawi (president of Ethiopia) E:334
Melgarejo, Mariano (Bolivian general and dictator) B:310
Méliès, Georges (French film producer) M:487; S:83
Melilla (Spanish city, enclave in Morocco) S:375
Melle see Mali
Mellon, Andrew William (American banker and industrialist)
        N:36; P:140 profile
Mellon, Paul (American banker and philanthropist) N:38
Mellon Collection (of art) N:36
Mellorine (frozen dessert) I:22
Mélodie (French song with piano accompaniment) M:543
Melodrama (form of drama) D:297; M:492
Melody (in music) M:532, 537
    African A:78, 79
    jazz J:56, 57
    orchestra conducting O:199
    ragtime J:57
Melon (fatty deposit on whale's forehead) W:149
Melons (fruits) G:51; M:214; V:290, 291

Melos (Milo) (island between Greece and Crete) I:366
Meltdown (nuclear reactor accident) N:372
Melting (Fusion) (changing from a solid to a liquid) H:90; I:4
    how icebergs melt I:18
Melting point H:90
    ice I:4
    metals M:233
    solids S:250
    picture(s) H:90
"Melting pot" (cultural concept) U:73
Meltwater (water from melted snow and ice) I:6
Meltzer, Milton (American author) C:234 profile
Melville, Herman (American novelist) M:215–16
    American literature A:210–11
    Moby Dick, excerpt from M:215
    novels F:115; N:360
    picture(s) A:206
Melville, Thomas (Scottish scientist) K:268
Membranes
    biochemistry B:187
    body cells B:273
    cell membranes C:160, 161, 162; K:254; L:200; P:495
    microbes M:274
    osmosis process O:240, 241
Memling (Memlinc), Hans (German-Flemish painter)
        D:359–60
Memorial Day H:164, 168; U:121
    picture(s) H:167
Memorial paintings F:293
Memorial University of Newfoundland (Saint John's) N:143
Memory L:100–105
    Alzheimer's disease A:196
    brain function B:365, 367
    emotions E:203
    hypnotism H:329
    mental illnesses affecting memory M:222–23
    remembering dreams D:319, 320
    sleep, importance of S:198
    spelling S:399
    study, methods of S:471
Memory (Storage elements) (of computers) C:481–82
    memory cards of digital cameras P:201, 203, 209
    telephones with automatic dialers T:55
Memory chip (type of integrated circuit) T:277
Memory T cells (in the immune system) I:97
Memphis (capital of ancient Egypt) E:110; M:512
Memphis (Tennessee) M:217; T:74, 79, 81, 83, 87
    picture(s) M:217; T:75, 78
        Graceland T:82
Memphremagog, Lake (Vermont–Quebec) V:309
    picture(s) Q:11
Men (in biology) see Men's health
Mena al Ahmadi (Kuwait) K:310
Menaechmus (Greek mathematician) G:122–23
Menageries see Zoos
Menam River see Chao Phraya
Menander (Greek author) G:357
Menard, John Willis (American political leader) A:79c
    picture(s) R:118; U:187
Menchú, Rigoberta (Guatemalan author) G:398
Mencken, Henry L. (American writer and critic) M:133 profile
Mende (a people of Africa) A:221; S:171
Mendel, Gregor Johann (Austrian priest and botanist) M:218;
        S:72
    genetics, history of G:90
    piecing together the theory of evolution E:375
    start of modern biology B:203
    picture(s) B:202; P:299
Mendeleev, Dmitri Ivanovich (Russian chemist) C:210; E:168;
        S:73
Mendele Mocher Sefarim (Mendele Moykher Sforim) (Hebrew
        and Yiddish author) H:101; Y:360
Mendelevium (element) E:174
Mendelian Laws (of heredity) M:218

Mendelssohn, Felix (German composer) **M:**219
  choral music **C:**284
  A Midsummer Night's Dream (overture) **G:**187
  orchestra-conducting tradition **O:**197, 198
  romantic concert overtures **R:**304
Mendelssohn, Moses (Jewish philosopher) **H:**100
Mendenhall Glacier (Alaska)
  picture(s) **A:**148
Menderes, Adnan (prime minister of Turkey) **T:**349
Menelaus (in Greek mythology) **G:**368; **T:**316
Menelik I (legendary ancestor of Ethiopian kings) **E:**333
Menelik II (ruler of Ethiopia) **E:**333
Menem, Carlos Saúl (Argentine political leader) **A:**386d
  picture(s) **A:**386d
Menéndez de Avilés, Pedro (Spanish naval officer) **F:**271–72
Menes (Narmer) (king of ancient Egypt, united Upper and
    Lower kingdoms) **A:**229, 234–35; **E:**109, 110
Menezes, Fradique de (president of São Tomé and Príncipe)
    S:41
Mengistu Haile Mariam (Ethiopian political leader) **E:**334
Menhaden (fish) **O:**79
Meninas, Las (The Maids of Honor) (painting by Velázquez)
    B:66; **P:**424; **S:**384; **V:**294
  picture(s) **P:**424; **S:**383
Meninges (coverings of the brain) **B:**364
Meningitis (disease) **R:**191
Meniscus (caused by adhesion) **L:**254
  picture(s) **L:**254
Menkure (king of ancient Egypt) *see* Mycerinus
Mennonites (German religious sect) **P:**134; **R:**132
  abolition movement **A:**6
  Manitoba (Canada) **M:**81, 85
  Paraguay **P:**62, 64
  Protestantism in colonial America **P:**493
  Protestant political activism **P:**494
Menominee Indians **W:**206
Menopause (in women) **M:**220
Menora (traditional Malay drama) **M:**58
Menorah (candleholder used for Hanukkah) **H:**28, 29; **J:**146a
  picture(s) **H:**28; **J:**146
Menorca (island) *see* Minorca
Menotti, Gian-Carlo (Italian-born American composer) **M:**555,
    556; **O:**149
  Amahl and the Night Visitors (opera) **O:**150
  Spoleto Festival, U.S.A. **S:**301
  picture(s)
    Amahl and the Night Visitors (opera) **O:**151
Men's health
  heart disease, risk factors for **H:**84
Mensheviks (in Russian history) **U:**40
Menstruation (in human reproduction) **B:**250a, 287;
    M:219–20; **R:**179
Mensuration *see* Measurement
Mental ability tests (intelligence tests) **I:**253, 254; **P:**508;
    T:118
  What is an IQ test? **L:**106
Mental health **H:**77 *see also* Mental illness
  adolescence, emotional changes in **A:**24–26
  astronauts in space exploration and travel **S:**344
  child abuse **C:**222
Mental illness **M:**221–26
  Alzheimer's disease **A:**196
  brain disorders **B:**368, 369
  child abuse **C:**222
  disabilities, people with **D:**178
  diseases **D:**187
  Dix, Dorothea, improves conditions for the insane **D:**231
  emotions **E:**204
  Freud's theories **F:**473–75
  homelessness **H:**183
  Pinel, Philippe, was first in field of psychiatry **M:**208f
  What does it mean to be mentally ill? **P:**509
  picture(s)
    early 1800's treatment of **M:**226
Mental retardation *see* Retardation, mental

Mental suggestion **H:**327–29
Mental tests *see* Tests and test taking
Mentor (a person who gives useful advice) **S:**76, 78
Mentuhotep II (king of ancient Egypt) **E:**112
Menus
  outdoor cooking and picnics **O:**262
  party refreshments **P:**89, 91
  restaurants **R:**187
Meo (Hmong) (a people of Asia) **L:**41
  anthropological studies of **A:**305
  Minnesota, population of **M:**331
  Wisconsin, immigration to **W:**207
Mephistopheles (devil in Faust legends) **F:**72
Mephitids (family of animals) **O:**251
Mequeda (Ethiopian princess) *see* Sheba, Queen of
Mercalli Intensity Scale (to measure earthquakes) **E:**38–39
Mercantile law **L:**85
Mercantilism (economic policy) **C:**103
Mercator, Gerhardus (Flemish geographer) **M:**97, 98
Mercator projection (of maps) **M:**97
Mercedes Benz 280 SEL (automobile)
  picture(s) **A:**545
Merced River (California) **Y:**362
Mercenaries (hired soldiers) **K:**277
  Hessians in Revolutionary War **R:**201, 202, 204
Mercersburg Academy (Pennsylvania)
  picture(s)
    birthplace of James Buchanan **B:**418
Merchandising *see* Advertising; Marketing; Sales
Merchant Adventurers (joint-stock company) **P:**345
Merchant guilds **G:**403
Merchant marine
  Maritime Administration **T:**293
  ships and shipping **S:**154–55
  United States Merchant Marine **U:**126
Merchant of Venice, The (play by Shakespeare) **S:**137
  picture(s) **S:**132
Merchant ships **S:**154–55, 158, 159
Mercier, Philippe (French painter)
  picture(s)
    The Music Party (painting) **E:**291
Mercosur (Mercosul; Southern Common Market) **A:**386a;
    B:380; **L:**59; **U:**240
Mercury (element) **E:**174
  air-pressure measurement **W:**80
  amalgamation **M:**233
  autism link not supported by evidence **A:**527
  barometer **B:**62
  batteries **B:**103b
  fish, concentration in **F:**221
  fluorescent lamps and mercury lamps **L:**236
  gold extracted from ores by **G:**249
  melting point **M:**233
  superconductivity, property of **H:**92
  thermometers **H:**87; **T:**163
  water pollution **W:**64–65
  picture(s)
    cohesive forces as a liquid **L:**254
  table(s) **M:**235
Mercury (planet) **M:**227–30; **P:**276
  observing Mercury **P:**278
  orbit **R:**143
  seen from Earth both morning and evening **S:**246
  space probes **S:**360
  diagram(s)
    orbit **R:**144
  picture(s) **P:**275
    transit **M:**230
Mercury (Roman god) *see* Hermes
Mercury (series of manned United States space flights)
    P:274; **S:**338, 346, 350
Mercury barometer **B:**62
Mercury-vapor lamps **E:**151
Mercury-vapor turbines **T:**343
Meredith, George (English novelist and poet) **E:**286

Meredith, James Howard (American lawyer) **A:**79n
Merengue (Latin-American dance) **L:**72
Merganser (duck) **D:**346
Mergenthaler, Ottmar (American inventor) **T:**371
Meri, Lennart (president of Estonia) **E:**325
Meridian (Mississippi) **M:**359
Meridians (of longitude) **L:**78
  great circles on maps and globes **M:**96
  Greenwich meridian **G:**374b
  international date line **I:**266
  time **T:**202–3
Mérimée, Prosper (French novelist) **F:**441
Merina (a people of Madagascar) **M:**8, 9
Merino (breed of sheep) **A:**509, 516; **N:**239; **W:**234, 235
  picture(s) **A:**92
Merisi, Michelangelo (Italian painter) *see* Caravaggio,
  Michelangelo Merisi da
Merit badges (Boy Scouts) **B:**357
  picture(s) **B:**358–59
Merit system (in civil service) **A:**436, 437; **C:**331
Merit Systems Protection Board (United States) **C:**331
Merkel, Angela (German chancellor) **G:**166
Merle coats (of dogs) **D:**242
MERLIN (interferometer) *see* Multi-Element Radio Linked
  Interferometer Network
Merlin (magician in tales of King Arthur) **A:**438, 438a;
  S:462
Merlons (part of a battlement) **C:**131
Mermaids
  manatees mistaken for **M:**77
Meroë (ancient African kingdom) **S:**479
Merovingian period (in French history) **F:**412, 421
Merriam, Eve (American author) **C:**234–35 *profile*
Merrie Monarch Hula Festival (Hilo, Hawaii) **H:**58, 61
Merrimack (ironclad ship) **C:**338
  picture(s) **C:**338
Merrimack River (Massachusetts–New Hampshire) **M:**138;
  N:152
Merry Christmas, Strega Nona (book by Tomie dePaola)
  picture(s) **C:**236
Merry-go-round (amusement park ride) *see* Carousel
Merry Mount (early settlement in Massachusetts) **P:**347
Merry Widow, The (operetta by Lehár) **M:**553; **O:**168
Merry Wives of Windsor, The (play by Shakespeare) **S:**137
Mersenne primes (type of prime number) **N:**386
Mersey River (England) **U:**52
Merzbild mit Regenbogen (collage by Kurt Schwitters)
  picture(s) **M:**396a
Mesa (Arizona) **A:**401
Mesa, Carlos (president of Bolivia) **B:**310
Mesabi Range (Minnesota) **M:**326, 333, 338
Mesas (small, high plateaus) **A:**394; **C:**432; **D:**127
Mesa Verde (Colorado) **C:**432, 438
  picture(s) **C:**436
Mescaline (drug obtained from peyote cactus) **C:**5
Meseta (tableland section of Spain) **S:**372
Meseta Central (Costa Rica) **C:**564, 565
Meshed (Iran) **I:**307
Mesic, Stipe (president of Croatia) **C:**589
Mesmer, Franz Anton (German physician) **H:**329
Mesoamerica (archaeological name for region from central
  Mexico to northwest Costa Rica) **A:**243–44
Mesons (subatomic particles) **C:**563
Mesophyll (leaf tissue) **L:**114
Mesopotamia (historic region in southwestern Asia) **I:**311;
  M:231–32 *see also* Assyria; Babylonia; Sumer
  ancient civilizations **A:**228, 230–31; **W:**258
  architecture **A:**364–65
  art as a record **A:**429
  Assyria **A:**462
  calendars **C:**14
  ceramics and mosaics **P:**15
  cities, history of **C:**314–15
  cuneiform **H:**131

  dams, history of **D:**20
  decorative arts **D:**72
  early agriculture **A:**97–98
  early cities **U:**235
  glassmaking, history of **G:**232
  Harappan civilization, trade with **A:**240
  homes and housing, history of **H:**191
  irrigation systems **A:**229
  law and law enforcement **L:**84
  pottery **P:**409
  sculpture **S:**93–94
  ships, history of **S:**155
  Sumer **S:**487
  Tigris and Euphrates rivers **R:**241, 246
  wheel, invention of the **I:**280; **W:**159
  World War I **W:**285
  zodiac, origin of **Z:**387
  picture(s)
    clay pot **D:**72
Mesopotamia (region of Argentina) **A:**385, 386
Mesosphere (layer of the atmosphere) **A:**482; **E:**21
Mesozoic era (in geology) **E:**28–29; **F:**387–88; **P:**433
  table(s) **E:**25; **F:**384
Mesquakie (Fox) Indians **I:**179, 204
  Illinois **I:**74–75
  Iowa **I:**294, 302, 303
  Wisconsin **W:**204
Messenger dogs (used by the armed forces) **U:**114
MESSENGER (*ME*rcury *S*urface, *S*pace *EN*vironment,
  *GE*ochemistry, and *R*anging) mission **M:**230
Messenger RNA (nucleic acid) **B:**299; **V:**366
Messerschmitt Bf 109 (German fighter plane) **A:**565
Messerschmitt Me 262 (German fighter plane) **A:**566, 567
Messiaen, Olivier (French composer) **F:**448
Messiah (oratorio by Handel) **C:**283; **E:**292; **G:**185; **H:**21
  picture(s)
    score **M:**540
Messiah (to the Jewish people) **J:**86, 144
Messiah War (1890) **S:**326
Messier, Charles (French astronomer) **A:**476a *profile*
Mestiços (Angolans of mixed ancestry) **A:**259
Mestizos (Latin Americans of mixed Indian and European
  ancestry) **I:**193; **L:**48, 49, 58; **R:**33; **S:**285 *see also*
  the people section of Latin-American countries
  picture(s) **C:**403
Mestral, George de (Swiss inventor) **I:**278
Metabolic diseases **D:**187, 193, 194–95
  dwarfism **D:**374–75
Metabolism (in body chemistry) **B:**298
  biochemistry **B:**187
  birds **B:**223
  body, human **B:**274
  hibernation **H:**126–28
  life process **L:**195
  organisms need energy **B:**196
  vitamins and minerals **V:**370a, 370c
Metacarpals (bones of the hand) **S:**183
Metacognition (thinking about learning) **L:**105–6
Metacomet (Native American chief) *see* Philip (Metacomet)
Metal halide lamps **E:**151
Metallic bonds (in chemistry) **M:**152
Metallic soap **L:**335
Metallogenetic provinces (areas rich in metallic ores) **M:**318
Metalloids (Semimetals) (borderline elements) **E:**169, 170
Metallurgy *see* Metals and metallurgy
Metal resistance thermometers **T:**164
Metals and metallurgy **M:**233–36 *see also* Alloys; Precious
  metals; Soldering; the names of metals
  acid rain **A:**10
  alchemy **C:**207
  alloys **A:**192–93
  aluminum **A:**194f–195
  bronze and brass **B:**409–10
  chemical classification **E:**168–69

Métis (Canadians of mixed Indian and European ancestry) **C:**52, 84
   Northwest Territories **N:**341
   Prairie Provinces **M:**81, 86; **S:**45, 51
   Riel, Louis **R:**232
Metlakatla (Alaska) **A:**156
Metonymy (figure of speech) **F:**123
Metric system (of measures) **W:**109–17
   recipe equivalents **C:**542
   table(s)
      metric conversion **W:**112, 113
Metric ton (unit of weight) **W:**114
Metro-Goldwyn-Mayer (film studio) **A:**291; **L:**308; **M:**492
Metro-Manila (Philippines) **M:**79; **P:**187
Metronome (device for keeping time) **M:**537; **O:**199
Metropolis (motion picture, 1926) **S:**83
   picture(s)
      poster **B:**147
Metropolitan area
   the Standard Metropolitan Statistical Area **U:**96
   Virginia **V:**355
Metropolitan Cathedral (Mexico City) **M:**253
Metropolitan Museum of Art (New York City) **M:**239–39a, 525
   Morgan, John Pierpont **M:**456
   picture(s) **N:**214
Metropolitan Opera House (Lincoln Center for the Performing Arts, New York City) **L:**248
Metropolitan police **P:**366
Metternich, Prince Klemens Wenzel Nepomulk Lothar von (Austrian statesman) **A:**524; **H:**4
Meuse, Battle of the (1940) **B:**103f
Meuse River (Europe) **N:**120a; **R:**236, 243
Mexican American Legal Defense and Educational Fund **C:**326
Mexican Americans (ethnic group) **H:**144, 148
   picture(s) **A:**397; **F:**321; **H:**144
Mexican bean beetle
   picture(s) **B:**127
Mexican burrowing toads **F:**477
Mexican hairless (toy dog) **D:**242
Mexican War (1846–1848) **M:**239a–239b, 249
   Armed Forces history, important dates in **U:**116
   boundary changes **T:**109
   California **C:**18, 30
   Carson, Kit **C:**121
   Grant, Ulysses S. **G:**294
   Mexico City National Cemetery **N:**29
   New Mexico **N:**193
   Perry, Matthew C. **P:**152
   Pierce, Franklin **P:**246
   Polk's administration **P:**376–77
   Scott, Winfield **S:**89
   Taylor, Zachary **T:**31–32
   territory gained and the slavery question **C:**479
   United States, history of the **U:**183–84
   United States Marine Corps **U:**123
   veterans' organizations **U:**121
   picture(s) **P:**377; **T:**108
Mexico M:240–52
   agriculture **N:**300
   Aztecs **A:**575–78; **I:**172–73
   ballads **F:**309
   boundary settlements with United States **T:**109
   Chapala, Lake **L:**29
   Christmas customs **C:**301
   climate **N:**290–91
   Cortés, Hernando **C:**559
   emigration to the United States **I:**92–93
   folk music **F:**324
   food **F:**333
   guerrilla warfare **G:**399
   hat dance **F:**303
   homes and housing **H:**194
   immigration to the United States **H:**148 *see also* Mexican Americans

Indians, American **I:**193–94, 195
Juárez, Benito **J:**142
Latin America **L:**47, 48, 49, 50, 51, 55, 56, 59
Latin-American architecture **L:**61
Latin-American art **L:**63
limes, leading producer and exporter of **L:**139
manufacturing **N:**301
Mexican War **M:**239a–239b
Mexico City **M:**253
Montezuma II **M:**443
North American Free Trade Agreement **N:**305
Olmec civilization **A:**243; **I:**167
Orozco, José **O:**231
political systems, development of **A:**302
population **N:**294, 295, 298
pre-Columbian art **P:**412
pyramids **P:**557–58
Rivera, Diego **R:**235
slavery in recent times **S:**197
Teotihuacán **A:**244; **I:**169
Texas, history of **T:**137–39
Villa, Pancho **O:**264
water supply **N:**293
World War II **W:**303
map(s) **M:**246
picture(s)
   Acapulco **M:**245
   Aztec pyramid **A:**578
   bullfighting **M:**242
   Chichén Itzá **M:**248
   costume, traditional **C:**373
   desert **M:**244
   flag **F:**235
   folk dance **F:**300
   folk musician **F:**324
   guerrillas **G:**399
   hurricane damage **W:**81
   Mayan ruins **N:**283
   Mexico City **C:**319; **L:**52–53; **M:**245, 253; **N:**298
   opal mine **G:**71
   Patzcuaro, Lake **N:**287
   people **M:**240, 241; **N:**294
   Popocatepetl **M:**243
   pre-Columbian art **P:**412
   pyramids **P:**558
   rain forest **M:**244
Mexico, Gulf of
   Alabama coastline **A:**132
   rivers flowing into **U:**82, 84
   Texas shoreline **T:**127
   picture(s)
      oil rigs **N:**303; **P:**167
      oil spill **O:**29
Mexico, National Autonomous University of **L:**65; **M:**241, 253
Mexico City (capital of Mexico) **M:**241, 245, 249, **253**
   Aztec sites uncovered by subway excavation **A:**351
   Mexican War **M:**239b
   Olympic Games (1968) **O:**111
   picture(s) **C:**319; **L:**52–53; **M:**253
      bullring **M:**242
      earthquake (1985) **E:**33
      Independence Monument **N:**298
      shantytown **M:**245
Mey, Cornelius (Dutch explorer) **N:**176
Mey, Uwe-Jens (German speed skater)
   picture(s) **I:**42
Meyerbeer, Giacomo (German opera composer) **F:**447
Meyerhof, Otto Fritz (German biochemist) **B:**186
Meyerson, Goldie (Israeli political leader) *see* Meir, Golda
Mez (Libyan festival) **L:**188
Mezuzah (Jewish religious symbol) **J:**148
Mezzanine (first level above orchestra in theaters) **T:**157
Mezzo-soprano (female voice) **V:**377
Mezzotint (printmaking technique) **G:**307

Micronesia, Federated States of (Pacific Ocean)   M:280; T:113
  Chuuk   P:8
  Kosrae   P:9
  Pohnpei   P:10
  Yap   P:10
  picture(s)
    flags   F:235
Micronesians (Pacific Islanders)   M:112; P:4, 5
  picture(s)   P:9
Micronutrients *see* Trace elements
Micro-organisms *see* Microbes
Microphones (used in transmitting sound)   P:195; R:53, 122
Microphotography   O:59
Microprocessor (computer processor on a single chip)   T:277
Micropropagation (of plants)   P:310
Microscopes   M:281–86; O:179–80
  archaeological laboratory work   A:355
  atoms, evidence of   A:484
  development as aid to biologists   B:201
  electronic microscope   E:163–64
  Galileo perfected compound microscope   G:6
  Leeuwenhoek's new world   L:128; M:277
  lenses   L:146–47
  materials science   M:155
  medicine, history of   M:208a–208b
  photomicrography   P:209
  science, milestones in   S:71
  picture(s)
    Leeuwenhoek's microscopes   L:128
Microsoft Corporation   W:27
Microstructure (atomic arrangement of a substance)   M:151–55
Microsurgery (operations performed under a microscope)   D:179; S:515
Microtome (machine for slicing specimens to be viewed through a microscope)   M:282
Microtone (in music)   M:537, 544
Microwave ovens   C:542; F:149; M:288
  picture(s)   I:279; R:42
Microwave radio relay systems   M:288; T:54–55
Microwaves   M:287–88; R:44–45
  experimental aircraft powered by   A:572
  masers   L:46d
  radio waves   L:221
  telecommunications through space   T:48
  telescopes   T:59
  television   T:63
  Why do foods cook faster in a microwave oven?   M:288
  diagram(s)
    electromagnetic spectrum, place on   R:44
Midas (in Greek mythology)   G:366
Mid-Atlantic Ridge (underwater mountains in the Atlantic Ocean)   A:478; E:18; M:504; O:21; V:386
Midbrain (part of the brain)   B:365–66
Middle Ages   M:289–95; W:262–63 *see also* Feudalism
  advertising, history of   A:34
  agriculture   A:98
  alchemy and the beginnings of the chemical industry   C:196
  architecture *see* Middle Ages, architecture of the
  armor   A:423–24
  art *see* Middle Ages, art of the
  beekeeping   H:212
  beer and brewing   B:114
  bread   B:388b
  castles   F:378–79
  Charlemagne   C:188
  Christianity, history of   C:290–91
  cities   C:315–17; U:235–36
  citizenship idea replaced by feudal system   C:324
  clocks   C:371–72
  clothing, history of   C:375–76
  court jesters   J:125
  craft-guild labor system   G:403–4

  Crusades   C:598–600
  drama   D:299–300
  dueling tournaments   D:349
  education   E:79, 80–81
  Eleanor of Aquitaine   E:126
  England   E:238–42
  exploration and discovery   E:401–2
  fairs and expositions   F:18
  feudalism   F:99–103
  geology, history of   G:108–9
  glassmaking, history of   G:232–33
  Greece, literature of   G:359
  guilds   G:403–5
  heraldry   H:116–18
  Holy Grail   H:175
  Holy Roman Empire   H:175–79
  homes   H:192
  Hundred Years' War   H:292–93
  inventions   I:280
  Italy   I:388
  Jews persecuted in Europe   J:104–5
  knights, knighthood, and chivalry   K:272–77
  knives, forks, and spoons   K:284–85
  labor movement: how it began   L:11
  law and law enforcement   L:85
  leather through the ages   L:111
  libraries   L:172–73
  magic as entertainment   M:22
  medical knowledge   M:208
  medieval engineering   E:228
  museums, history of   M:527
  music *see* Middle Ages, music of the
  mystery, miracle, and morality plays   D:26
  novel, beginning of the   N:358
  public health   P:512
  puppets and marionettes   P:548
  Renaissance grew out of changes in   R:157
  Roman Catholic Church   R:288–90
  sailing ships   S:157
  science, milestones in   S:69–70
  serfdom was a kind of slavery   S:193
  shoes showed social rank   S:160
  teachers and teaching   T:38
  tool use   T:234
  toys, history of   T:251
  trade shows, origins of   F:15
  writing preserved by monks   C:463
  picture(s)
    hairstyling   H:7
    vegetable market   F:336
Middle Ages, architecture of the
  art as a record   A:430
  building construction   B:440
  castles   C:131–32; F:378–79
  cathedrals   C:133–35
  cities   C:316; U:235–36
  German architecture   G:167–68
  Gothic architecture   G:264–71
  homes   H:192
  Italian architecture   I:391–94
  Romanesque architecture   R:295
Middle Ages, art of the   A:428, 430
  bookmaking, art of   B:321
  Cloisters of the Metropolitan Museum of Art   M:239a
  decorative arts   D:76–77
  drawing, history of   D:315–16
  enameling   E:205
  France   F:421–22
  furniture   F:508–9
  German art   G:167–68
  Giotto di Bondone   G:211
  illuminated manuscripts   I:77–78
  illustration of books   I:79
  interior design   I:257

Middle Ages, art of the (cont.)
    Italian art and architecture **I:**391–94
    jewelry **J:**98
    needlecraft **N:**97
    painting **P:**17–20
    realism **R:**115
    Romanesque art **R:**295
    stained-glass windows **S:**417–18
    picture(s)
        clasp with scene from Bible **J:**98
Middle Ages, music of the **M:296–97**
    bell music **B:**141–42
    France **F:**444
    history of Western musical forms **M:**538
    Italy, music of **I:**410
    minstrels and ballads **C:**463
    scale names, origin of **A:**237
    picture(s)
        church choir **M:**539
Middlebury College (Vermont) **V:**311
    picture(s) **V:**311
Middle classes (of people) **M:**293; **R:**157; **U:**125
Middle Comedy (period in Greek literature) **G:**356–57
Middle ear (of the body) **E:**4, 6
    picture(s) **E:**5
Middle East **M:298–305** *see also* the names of countries
    ancient civilizations **A:**230–36
    Arab-Israeli wars **E:**105; **I:**375–76; **J:**107, 132;
        P:41–42; **S:**2
    Arabs **A:**343–47
    breadmaking, history of **B:**388a
    date palm's many uses **D:**41
    dragons in mythology **D:**295
    food **F:**331
    food in North America, influence on **F:**332–33
    geology, history of **G:**108
    Hittites **H:**155
    homes and housing, history of **H:**193
    Kurds **K:**307
    Mesopotamia **M:**231–32
    music **M:**544–45
    Palestine **P:**40c–43
    Persia, ancient **P:**154–57
    Persian Gulf War **P:**158
    population density **A:**444
    refugees **R:**136
    southwestern region of Asia **A:**438g, 440
    terrorism **T:**115
    What is the Fertile Crescent? **M:**301
    World War I **W:**285
    World War II **W:**299–300
Middle English (language) **E:**266, 269–71
Middle High German (language) **G:**174; **Y:**360
Middle Kingdom (2040–1782 B.C., ancient Egypt) **E:**109
Middle latitudes *see* Mid-latitudes
Middle Low German (language) **G:**174
Middlemarch (novel by George Eliot) **E:**190; **N:**359; **R:**114
Middle names **N:**7
Middle Passage (Atlantic crossing of slave ships) **A:**79e;
    S:194
Middle schools **E:**76; **G:**401; **N:**42; **S:**61
Middleton, Arthur (American political figure) **D:**68 *profile*
Middleton Place (near Charleston, South Carolina) **S:**304
    picture(s) **S:**304
Middle Way (in Buddhism) **B:**424; **R:**149
Middleweight (in boxing) **B:**351
Middle West (United States) *see* Midwest, The
Middlings (by-product of flour milling) **F:**277
Midgard (home of humans in Norse mythology) **N:**279
Midgard serpent (in Scandinavian mythology) **G:**201; **N:**280,
    281
Midges (gnats) **H:**261
Midget-auto racing **A:**537
MIDI *see* Musical Instrument Digital Interface
Midlands (region of England) **E:**233

Mid-latitudes (temperate zones)
    climate **C:**362
    deserts **D:**126, 127
    fruits of **F:**481–82
    prairies **P:**426–29
    rain forests **R:**99
Midnight Sun, Land of the *see* Land of the Midnight Sun
Mid-oceanic ridges (of mountains) **G:**111, 113; **I:**161
Midrash (body of Jewish literature) **H:**99
Midribs (of leaves) **L:**112, 113
Midshipmen (at U.S. Naval Academy) **U:**118
Midsummer Night's Dream, A (play by Shakespeare) **S:**138
    fairies **F:**9, 12
    picture(s) **F:**9
Midway (amusement area of fairs) **F:**14–15; **P:**79
    picture(s) **F:**15
Midway (islands in the Pacific Ocean) **H:**50; **I:**366; **P:**9; **U:**85
    occupied by United States **T:**110, 113
Midway, Battle of (1942) **B:**103f; **W:**306
    picture(s) **W:**306
Midway, U.S.A. (nickname for Kansas) **K:**177
Midwest, The (United States)
    flood of 1993 **F:**256
Midwest City (Oklahoma) **O:**91
Midwives (nurses) **N:**417
Miers, Harriet (American jurist) **B:**469
Mies van der Rohe, Ludwig (German-American architect)
    A:375; **M:306**
    international style **G:**173
    modern architecture **A:**374
    modern furniture **F:**517
    United States, architecture of the **U:**136
    picture(s)
        Barcelona chair **F:**515
        Seagram Building **U:**136
Mieszko I (Polish ruler) **P:**361
"Mighty Fortress Is Our God, A" (hymn) **H:**322; **L:**346
Mighty Handful (Russian group of musicians) **R:**385
Mighty line (kind of unrhymed verse) **M:**104
Mignone, Francisco (Brazilian composer) **L:**73
Migrant farm workers **C:**227; **F:**484; **H:**148
Migrant Mother, Nipomo, California (photograph by Dorothea
    Lange)
    picture(s) **D:**120; **W:**273
Migration (of animals) *see* Homing and migration
Migration (of people) **P:**385 *see also* Immigration
    anthropologists' study of **A:**305
    Indians, American **I:**88, 164
    North America **N:**295
    overland trails (United States) **O:**268–82
    pioneer "movers" to western United States **P:**250–51
    refugees **R:**136–37
Migratory agriculture **J:**158; **S:**330; **Z:**377
    picture(s) **F:**144; **R:**100
Migratory legends (found throughout the world) **L:**129,
    130–31
Mihajlović, Draža (Yugoslav general) **T:**213; **Y:**368
Mikado, The (operetta by Gilbert and Sullivan) **G:**209; **M:**553
Mikan, George (American basketball player) **B:**95j *profile*
    picture(s) **B:**95j
Mikhalkov, Sergey (Russian poet) **N:**18
Mikoyan, Anastas Ivanovich (Soviet administrator) **A:**421
Milan (Italy) **I:**382, 385, 387, 388
    cathedral **I:**393
    Renaissance city-states **R:**158
    theater **T:**161
Milan, Edict of (A.D. 313) **R:**286, 317
Milankovitch, Milutin (Yugoslavian scientist) **I:**16
Mildew (fungi) **P:**288–89
Mile (measure of length) **W:**112, 115
    nautical mile **W:**115
Mile High City (nickname for Denver, Colorado) **D:**116
Miles, Miska (American author) **C:**238
Milford Sound (New Zealand)
    picture(s) **N:**235

Milhaud, Darius (French composer)   **F:**448
Military alliances (in international relations)   **I:**269
   North Atlantic Treaty Organization (NATO)   **N:**305
Military assistance   **F:**370
Military engineers   **E:**225
Military Intelligence (of the United States Army)   **U:**102
Military intelligence (spy networks)   **S:**407
   aerial photography   **P:**209, 216
   balloons in war   **B:**36
   kites, spy-carrying   **K:**270
   military satellites   **S:**54
Military parks, national see National military parks
Military Police Corps (of the United States Army)   **U:**102
Military Sealift Command (of the United States Navy)   **U:**111
Military Selective Service Act (United States)   **W:**306
Military service
   comic books used to train soldiers   **C:**453
   Defense, United States Department of   **D:**83–84
   draft (conscription)   **D:**293
   electronics, uses of   **E:**162
   feudalism   **F:**100
   military etiquette   **E:**337
   nurses, where they work   **N:**419
   radar, uses of   **R:**39–40
   ships   **S:**153–54
   sonar, history of   **R:**41
   Texas military bases   **T:**131
   United States, Armed Forces of the   **U:**100–126
   violence and society   **V:**344
Military Working Dogs (dogs used by the armed forces)   **U:**114
Militia (local army)   **D:**293; **N:**41–42
Milk   **M:306–7**
   baby's food   **B:**3
   bread, basic ingredients of   **B:**387
   butter from milk of different animals   **B:**474
   cheese from milk of different animals   **C:**195
   condensed milk used in candy making   **C:**98
   dairy cattle   **C:**153–54
   dairying and dairy products   **D:**3–11
   food shopping   **F:**349
   growth hormone   **H:**228
   mammals   **M:**65
   pasteurization   **D:**212; **F:**342
   Pasteur's experiments   **P:**98
   processing   **D:**7–8, 11
   spoilage   **F:**339
   uses in cooking   **C:**542–43
   vitamin D fortified milk   **V:**370d
   What is "Grade A" milk?   **D:**9
   picture(s)
      bottling   **D:**8
      pasteurization   **D:**8; **F:**342
Milk, Harvey (American political official)   **S:**32
Milk bottle   **B:**346
Milk chocolate   **C:**281
Milking (of dairy cattle)   **D:**6–7, 11
   picture(s)   **D:**7
"Milking" (of venom from snakes)   **S:**215
Milking parlors (for dairy cattle)   **D:**7
Milking Shorthorn (breed of dual-purpose cattle)   **C:**154
   picture(s)   **D:**4
Milk of magnesia (laxative)   **M:**27
Milk River (Montana–Alberta)   **A:**165
Milkweed (plant)   **B:**478; **G:**84; **P:**313
   picture(s)   **F:**285; **P:**313
      seeds   **P:**307
Milky spore disease   **P:**287, 290
Milky Way (galaxy)   **M:308–9;** **U:**211–13, 214
   astronomy, history of   **A:**474
   radio astronomy   **R:**71, 72, 73
   picture(s)   **M:**308
      radiograph   **R:**67
      solar system in relation to   **S:**245
Mill, John Stuart (English philosopher)   **C:**325; **E:**284
Millais, Sir John Everett (English painter)   **E:**263

Millay, Edna Saint Vincent (American poet)   **M:**48 *profile*
Millennium Challenge Account   **F:**370
Millennium Development Goals   **D:**143; **F:**370
Millennium Dome (building, London, England)   **L:**298
Millennium Summit (New York City, 2000)   **F:**370; **P:**420
Miller, Arthur (American playwright)   **A:**218; **D:**306; **N:**225
   profile
   picture(s)
      Death of a Salesman, scene from   **D:**306
Miller, Bode (American athlete)   **O:**118
Miller, Reggie (American basketball player)
   picture(s)   **B:**95g
Miller, Shannon (American gymnast)   **O:**95 *profile*
Miller, Stanley (American scientist)   **L:**210
Millers (moths)   **H:**261
Milles, Carl (Swedish sculptor)
   picture(s)
      angel sculpture   **S:**528
Millet (cereal grass)   **F:**332; **G:**284, 285, 286, 318
   picture(s)   **G:**283
Millet, Jean François (French painter)   **F:**429; **R:**115
Millibar (unit of air pressure)   **W:**80
Millikan, Robert Andrews (American physicist)   **L:**223; **M:**310
Millimeter (measure of length)   **W:**111–12
Milliners (makers of women's hats)   **H:**45
Milliner's Model (type of doll)   **D:**267
Milling machines   **T:**232
Million Man March (Washington, D.C., 1995)   **A:**79p
Millipedes (many-legged animals)   **C:168, 169**
   picture(s)   **I:**231
Mill on the Floss, The (novel by George Eliot)   **E:**190
Mills (in industry)
   flour milling   **F:**276–77; **W:**158
   Industrial Revolution   **I:**219, 222
   inventions   **I:**280
   steel rolling and finishing   **I:**335–37
   water mills   **D:**16, 21; **W:**69–70
   picture(s)
      flour milling   **F:**277
      Glade Creek Grist Mill (West Virginia)   **W:**127
Mills, Robert (American architect and engineer)   **S:**304; **W:**32
Millstones (used in grinding grain)   **F:**277; **W:**69
Mill villages (in Industrial Revolution)   **I:**222
Milne, A. A. (English author)   **M:310–11**
   "Missing" (poem)   **M:**311
   picture(s)   **M:**311
Milo (island between Greece and Crete) see Melos
Milo of Croton (Greek athlete)   **O:**103
Milošević, Slobodan (president of Yugoslavia)   **C:**369; **Y:**366, 369
   Belgrade   **B:**136
   genocide   **G:**97
   Serbia and Montenegro   **S:**127
   picture(s)   **Y:**369
Milt (fluid containing fish's sperm)   **F:**191
Miltiades, Saint (pope)   **R:**292
Milton, John (English poet)   **E:**275; **M:312**
   figures of speech   **F:**122
   freedom of the press upheld in his *Areopagitica*   **E:**275
   L'Allegro, excerpt from   **M:**312
   Paradise Lost   **P:**353
Milton Bradley (game company)   **G:**21
Milwaukee (Wisconsin)   **M:313; W:**192, 198, 200, 201, 205
   picture(s)   **M:**313
      Mitchell Park Conservatory   **W:**200
      Riverwalk area   **W:**201
Milwaukee Art Museum (Wisconsin)   **A:**377
   picture(s)   **A:**377
Mimas (moon of Saturn)   **S:**57, 58
   picture(s)   **S:**58
Mime (acting without using words)   **B:**28, 29
Mimeograph (duplicating machine)   **O:**59
   former trademark   **T:**267
Mimicry (humor)   **H:**291

Mimicry (insect protective device)   **I:**243
  picture(s)   **I:**242
Mimir (Norse god)   **N:**279, 280
Mimosa (tree)   **L:**111, 197
Mina (people of Togo)   **T:**216
Minamoto Yoritomo (first Japanese shogun) *see* Yoritomo
Minarets (towers of mosques)   **A:**370; **I:**356
  Taj Mahal   **A:**367; **T:**14
  picture(s)   **B:**489
Mince pie (Christmas dessert)   **C:**299
Mind   **P:**499 *see also* Brain
  dreaming   **D:**319–20
  extrasensory perception   **E:**427–28
  hypnotism   **H:**327–29
  intelligence   **I:**253–54
  memory   **L:**100–105
  mental illness   **M:**221–26
  physical health, effects on   **D:**187
  sleep   **S:**198
Mindanao (Philippines)   **P:**184, 185, 186
Mindaugas (king of Lithuania)   **L:**263
Mind-body interventions (alternative therapy)   **A:**194e
Mind reading *see* Telepathy
Mind-reading tricks   **M:**25
Mine countermeasure ships   **U:**115
Mine dogs (used by the armed forces)   **U:**114
Mineral dressing *see* Concentration
Mineral oils   **C:**561; **O:**79
Mineral Point (Wisconsin)   **W:**200
Minerals (in geology)   **M:314–17** *see also* the natural
    resources section of continent, country, province,
    and state articles
  Africa   **A:**49
  Arctic region   **A:**380
  Asia's resources   **A:**441–42
  Australia   **A:**506, 509–10
  conservation of   **C:**526
  deserts rich in   **D:**130
  Europe   **E:**351
  gems   **G:**69–75
  hot springs   **G:**192
  magnesium, sources of   **M:**27
  metals   **M:**233
  mineral fibers   **N:**437
  mines and mining   **M:**318–24
  mountain resources   **M:**507
  North America   **N:**292–93
  ocean, uses of the   **O:**28
  ores   **O:**217
  rocks   **R:**265
  Russia   **R:**363
  soils   **S:**234
  South America   **S:**283–84
Minerals (in nutrition)   **F:**330; **N:**425–26; **V:370a, 370b,**
    371–73
  Are natural vitamin or mineral supplements better than
    synthetic supplements?   **V:**370d
  bones contain mineral salts   **S:**184a
  deficiency diseases   **D:**197
  table(s)
    food sources and DRI's   **V:**372
Minerals Management Service (United States)   **I:**256
Minerva (Roman goddess) *see* Athena
Mines (explosives)   **F:**378
  Korean demilitarized buffer zone   **K:**298
  Military Working Dogs used to detect   **U:**114
  mine warfare ships of U.S. Navy   **U:**115
  tanks can be disabled by   **T:**14
Mine Safety and Health Administration (MSHA) (United States)
    L:2; **O:**13
Mines and mining   **M:318–24** *see also* individual country,
    province, and state articles; the names of specific types
    of mines and mining, as Coal and coal mining
  Africa   **A:**64

Asia   **A:**441–42
  Beckley Exhibition Coal Mine (West Virginia)   **W:**134
  Canada   **C:**61, 64–65
  coal mining   **C:**389–90
  Colorado School of Mines   **C:**435
  diamonds   **D:**146–47
  dredges used in   **D:**321, 322
  explosives used in   **E:**423
  gold   **G:**249
  iron ore   **I:**330
  minerals   **M:**317
  miner's safety fuse   **E:**420
  mining engineers   **E:**226
  occupational health and safety   **O:**13
  prairies   **P:**428
  railroads, history of   **L:**287; **R:**86
  rocks   **R:**271
  safety lamp invented by Davy   **D:**44
  salt   **S:**22
  silver   **S:**177–78
  South America   **S:**284, 291
  West Virginia   **W:**133
  picture(s)
    Australian gold mine   **A:**511
    Bolivian tin mine   **B:**309; **T:**209
    early mining railroad   **R:**87
    explosives used in   **E:**421, 422
    Mexican opal mine   **G:**71
    Montana copper mine   **M:**440
    open-pit copper mine   **C:**501; **M:**317; **P:**4
    South African garnet mine   **M:**317
    South African gold mine   **S:**271
    Utah copper mine   **N:**293; **U:**249
    West Virginian coal mine   **W:**133
    Zambian copper mine   **A:**64
Mineta, Norman Yoshio (American political figure)   **A:**459
Ming dynasty (in Chinese history)   **C:**269
  China, art of   **C:**275, 277
  furniture   **F:**507
  Great Wall of China   **A:**241
  jade carving   **D:**74
  libraries and museums   **C:**259
  porcelain   **P:**410
  picture(s)
    vase   **W:**265
Mingus, Charles (American jazz bassist)
  picture(s)   **J:**62
Miniature cameras   **P:**214
Miniature horses   **H:**237, 244
Miniatures (illustrations in illuminated manuscripts)   **F:**422;
    I:78; **P:**17–18
Miniatures (objects reduced to a very small scale) *see*
    Dollhouses; Models and model making
Miniature Synthetic Aperture Radar (MSAR)   **R:**40
Minicomputers   **O:**55
MiniDisc (MD) (recordable compact disc)   **H:**133; **S:**267b
MiniDV camcorders   **V:**332g
Minié, Claude Étienne (French officer)   **G:**418
Minié ball (bullet)   **G:**418–19
Minimal art   **M:**396b; **U:**135
Minimalism (in modern music)   **M:**399, 544
Minimal processing (of vegetables)   **V:**290
Minimata disease (mercury poisoning)   **W:**65
Minimum-security prisons   **P:**481
  picture(s)   **P:**480
Minimum till (agricultural practice)   **A:**95, 100
Minimum wages   **L:**8
Mining *see* Mines and mining
Mining Act (United States, 1866)   **P:**517
Miniseries (television programs)   **T:**70
Miniskirt (in fashion)
  picture(s)   **C:**380
Ministers (of Protestant churches)   **P:**550, 551

Mink (animals of mustelid family)   O:255–56
  furs   F:502, 503, 504
  picture(s)   F:503; O:255
Mink, Patsy Takemoto (American political figure)   H:61 profile
Minke whales   N:347; W:153
Minneapolis (Minnesota)   M:325, 326, 329, 331, 332, 335, 338
  Southdale shopping center   A:376
  picture(s)   M:327, 335
    Aquatennial festival   M:330, 331
Minnehaha Falls (Minneapolis, Minnesota)   M:334
Minnelli, Liza (American singer and actress)   M:488
Minnesingers (medieval German singers)   G:183; M:297
Minnesota   M:326–39
  lakes   L:34
  Minneapolis-Saint Paul   M:325
  Northwest Angle   T:104
  map(s)   M:337
  picture(s)
    boat on lake   M:327
    Minneapolis   M:327, 335
    Saint Paul   M:330
Minnesota, University of   M:331
Minnesota Multiphasic Personality Inventory (test)   T:119
Minnesota River (Minnesota)   M:328
Minnow (fish)   E:208
Minoan civilization (of ancient Crete)   A:236
  art   A:429; G:345; P:15–16
  clothing, history of   C:374
  Greece, ancient   G:340
  plumbing, history of   P:340
  sculpture   S:94–95
  picture(s)
    terra-cotta disc with written script   A:232
    wall painting in Knossos palace   A:236
Minorca (island, Spain)   I:362
Minority Business Development Agency (MBDA)   C:455
Minority groups see Ethnic groups
Minority leaders (in Congress)   U:168, 169
Minor leagues (in baseball)   B:84
Minor scale (in music)   M:532, 537
Minos (in Greek mythology, king of Crete)   G:366, 368; P:340
Minot (North Dakota)   N:330
Minotaur (monster in Greek myth)   G:364, 368
Minsk (capital of Belarus)   B:128; C:460
Minstrels (Jongleurs) (medieval entertainers)   A:76b; C:463; M:297; S:463
Minstrel shows   U:206
Mint (herb)   H:121
Mint (place where coins are made)   M:340
Mint, United States   T:294
  picture(s)   T:295
Minton, Thomas (English porcelain maker)   A:316a
Mint stamps (those not canceled)   S:421
Minuend (in subtraction)   A:389
Minuet (dance)   D:28
  picture(s)   D:28
Minuet (musical form)   M:540
Minuet-trio (musical form)   C:350
Minuit, Peter (Dutch official in America)   N:234; T:175
Minute (measure of time)   W:115
Minuteman (missile)   M:345, 347
Minutemen (American colonial militia)   M:144; R:193, 198
Minyan (group necessary to conduct a Jewish worship service)   J:146, 146b
Miocene epoch (in geology)   E:29
Miquelet (flintlock gun)   G:417
Miquelon (island) see Saint Pierre and Miquelon
Mir (Soviet space station)   S:54, 350, 352, 355, 366
  Polyakov, Valery, record time spent in space   S:349
  space shuttles   S:365
  U.S. astronaut on Mir   S:348
  picture(s)   S:355
Mira Bai (Indian poet)   H:142

Mirabeau, Comte de (French revolutionary leader)   F:468, 471
  profile
Miracle plays (medieval drama)   D:26, 300; E:270–71
Miracles (of Jesus Christ)   J:87, 89
Miracle Worker, The (play by William Gibson)   K:202
Miraculous Draught of Fishes, The (tapestry from a drawing by Raphael)
  picture(s)   J:87
Miraflores (Spain)   S:382
Mirage   M:341–42
Miramichi Bay (New Brunswick)   N:138
Miramichi River (New Brunswick)   N:138a
Miranda (moon of Uranus)   U:233
  picture(s)   U:233
Miranda, Francisco de (Venezuelan patriot)   B:305; V:298
Miranda rights (in United States law)   L:89
Miranda v. Arizona (1966)   S:509
Miribai (Indian poet-saint)   I:142
Miró, Joan (Spanish artist)   M:343, 394; S:385
  picture(s)
    Woman Before the Eclipse (painting)   M:343
Mirror-image twins   T:364
Mirrors
  dolphins' self-recognition in mirror   D:278
  heliostats in solar thermal power plants   S:240
  Hubble Space Telescope   S:367
  Jewish funeral custom   F:494
  kaleidoscope   K:172
  laser mirror left on moon   S:340h
  light reflection   L:213, 214, 215
  obsidian mirrors, legend about   G:232
  optical instruments   O:180, 181, 183
  silver is the best backing material   S:177
  single-lens reflex cameras   P:202
  stone mirrors of Oaxaca   I:167
  superstition about   S:504
  telescopes   T:57, 58–59, 60
  visual signals   C:466
  picture(s)   L:214
    Keck telescopes   O:8; T:59
Mirror-Shadow VII (sculpture by Louise Nevelson)
  picture(s)   S:105
Mirror skating (in pair figure skating)   I:41
Mirror writing (used by Leonardo da Vinci)   L:154
MIRV (Multiple independently targeted re-entry vehicle) system (missile system)   M:348
Miscarriage (natural early ending of pregnancy)   A:8
Misdemeanors (in law)   C:575, 584, 586; J:163
Misdirection, art of (in magic)   M:23–24
Misérables, Les (musical by Schönberg)   M:555
Misérables, Les (novel by Victor Hugo)
  excerpt from   H:277–78
  picture(s)
    film version (1935)   H:277
Misery, Mount (Saint Kitts and Nevis)   S:13
Mishnah (ancient Hebrew laws)   H:98; J:144; R:147; T:13
Miskito (Mosquito) Indians (of Nicaragua)   I:195; N:244
Miskolc (Hungary)   H:297
Miss (form of address)   A:21
Missiles   M:343–49
  Cuban missile crisis   C:611
  electronics, uses of   E:162
  guns and ammunition   G:425
  gyroscopes   G:437
  jet propulsion   J:90–92
  liquid gases   L:253
  rocket power   R:257–62
  tanks   T:14
  United States Air Force   U:110
  United States Army   U:102, 106
  United States Navy   U:115
  picture(s)
    Peacekeeper missile   U:110
    Tomahawk cruise missile   E:162
"Missing" (poem by A. A. Milne)   M:311

Mitterrand, François (president of France) F:420; M:383
  picture(s) M:383
Mixed-breed dogs D:258
Mixed marriages F:40
Mixed media drawings D:313
Mixed metaphor (figure of speech) F:122
Mixed numbers (combining whole numbers and fractions)
    F:397
Mixtec Indians (of Mexico) I:173
  picture(s)
    ancient writing H:22
Mizrachim (Jews of Asian or African origin) I:369
Mizzenmast (on a sailboat or sailing ship) S:8, 157
Mjollnir (hammer of Thor, Norse god) N:279
Mkapa, Benjamin (president of Tanzania) T:19
MLS see Multiple Listing Service
Mnemonics (memory-improving technique) L:104–5
  poem to remember how many days in each month C:14
Moapa dace (fish) E:208
Moas (extinct birds) N:241
  picture(s) O:244
Moat (of a castle) C:132; F:378
  picture(s) H:192
Moawad, René (Lebanese president) L:123
Mobile (Alabama) A:130, 132, 137, 139
  picture(s) A:137
Mobile Bay (Alabama) A:132
  naval battle in Civil War C:343; F:62
Mobile homes (movable houses) C:44, 46; H:189
Mobile phones C:470
Mobile River (Alabama) A:132
Mobile robots R:253, 254, 255
Mobiles (sculpture made of movable parts) D:136
  Calder, Alexander M:396b; S:104
  modern American sculpture U:135
  picture(s)
    Calder, Alexander N:38
Möbius, August F. (German mathematician) T:238
Möbius strip (in topology) T:238
  picture(s) T:238
Mobs (of kangaroos) K:175
Mobutu Sese Seko (president of Zaïre) C:503; M:383
  picture(s) C:503
Moby-Dick (novel by Melville) F:115; N:360
  American literature, place in A:211
  excerpt from M:215–16
  picture(s)
    illustration by Rockwell Kent M:216
Moccasin flower see Lady's slipper
Moccasin snakes see Cottonmouths
Mocha (Yemen) C:397
Moche (Mochica) (early Indian culture of Peru) A:229, 245,
    354; I:109, 170; P:164
Mock-heroic poetry E:277
Mockingbirds B:246
  picture(s) A:407; F:261; M:351; T:75, 125
Mock-ups (design models) I:215
Modacrylic fiber F:112
Modal jazz J:63
Mode (kind of average of a set of numbers) S:441
Model A (automobile) F:369
  picture(s) A:541
Model Cities Program C:321
Modeling (in drawing) D:311
Modeling (in sculpture) S:90
Modeling, fashion M:384–85
Modeling clay (plasticine) C:354
"Model minority" (perception of Asian Americans) A:461
Models and model making
  airplane models A:104–7
  automobile A:534–35
  motion picture special effects M:484
  railroads, model R:91–92
  taxidermy T:26

Model T (automobile) A:543; F:369; M:88–89; T:286
  picture(s) A:541; F:369; I:281
Modem (computer system peripheral) C:470, 481, 491,
    494; T:50
Moderato (musical term) M:537
Moderator (of a discussion) D:52
Moderator (of a nuclear reactor) N:370–71
Modern architecture A:373–77
  cathedrals C:135
  Johnson, Philip J:123
  Le Corbusier L:124
  Mies van der Rohe, Ludwig M:306
  Pei, I. M. P:118
  Sullivan, Louis S:486
  United States U:136
  Wright, Frank Lloyd W:326
Modern art M:386–96b
  art, the meanings of A:428
  art of the artist A:433
  Canada C:73
  Cézanne's influence C:179
  Chagall, Marc C:182
  collage C:402
  cubism C:612
  Escher, M. C. E:320
  expressionism E:424
  French art, 20th-century F:431–32
  furniture design F:516–17
  Germany G:171–73
  impressionism I:103–6
  Johns, Jasper J:114
  Klee, Paul K:271
  Klimt, Gustav K:271
  Latin America L:63–65
  Léger, Fernand L:136
  Modigliani, Amedeo M:400
  Mondrian, Piet M:410
  painting P:29–32
  Picasso, Pablo P:243–44
  Pollock, Jackson P:378
  Pop and Op art P:31–32
  sculpture of the 20th century S:103–5
  surrealism S:518
  tapestry T:22
  United States U:132, 134–35
  Utrillo, Maurice U:256
Modern dance D:31–33
  Duncan, Isadora D:353
  Dunham, Katherine I:74
  gestures D:24
  music D:24–25
  picture(s) D:23
Modernism
  American literature A:214a–214b
  decorative arts D:79
  Latin America, art of L:63
  Latin America, literature of L:69
Modernity (in society) R:293–94
Modern Jazz Quartet (American musicians)
  picture(s) J:56
Modern moral subject (type of painting) H:159a
Modern music M:397–99 see also the names of composers
  France, music of F:447–48
  tempered tuning S:262
  Western musical forms, history of M:543–44
Modified American plan (of hotel rates) H:256
Modigliani, Amedeo (Italian painter and sculptor) M:400
  picture(s)
    Woman with Red Hair (painting) M:400
Modoc (Indians of North America) I:187
Modoc Plateau (California) C:20
Modred (knight of King Arthur's court) A:438
Modulation (in broadcasting) R:54; T:63
Modulation (in music) M:537
Module (of a spacecraft) S:340d

Moeritherium (prehistoric ancestor of the elephant) **E**:183
Moffat Tunnel (Colorado) **D**:117
Mogadishu (capital of Somalia) **S**:255
Mogilny, Alexander (Russian hockey player) **I**:32
Mogollon (early people of North America) **A**:402
Mogollon Rim (Arizona) **A**:394, 396
  picture(s) **A**:394
Mogotón, Pico (highest point in Nicaragua) **N**:245
Mogul (dynasty of Mongol rulers of India) **I**:131–32, 137
Mogul runs (in skiing) **S**:184d
Mohács, Battle of (1526) **H**:298
Mohair goats **F**:109
Mohammad Ali Mosque (Cairo, Egypt)
  picture(s) **C**:8
Mohammed (Muhammad) (Arab prophet, founder of Islam)
      I:346–50; **M**:401; **R**:148
  Arab history and civilization **A**:344
  Arabic education spread by Muslim followers **E**:79–80
  Jerusalem **J**:82
  Jews and Mohammed disliked each other **J**:104
  Koran **K**:292
  Mecca **M**:199
  picture(s) **I**:347
Mohammed, Khalid Shaikh (Kuwait-born terrorist) **T**:117
Mohammed V (king of Morocco) **M**:461
Mohammed VI (king of Morocco) **M**:461
Mohammed Ali (governor of Egypt) *see* Mehemet Ali
Mohammedans *see* Islam
Mohammed Reza Pahlavi (shah of Iran) **I**:309; **K**:240
  picture(s) **I**:308
Mohave (Indians of North America) **I**:183
Mohave, Lake (Nevada) **N**:125
Mohave Desert (California–Arizona) *see* Mojave Desert
Mohawk (Indians of North America) **B**:370–71; **I**:175, 204
Mohawk River (New York) **N**:213
Mohawk Trail (New York) **O**:269
  map(s) **O**:273
Mohawk Valley (New York) **N**:213, 215
Mohegan (Indians of North America) **C**:512; **I**:177
Mohel (Jewish official who performs circumcisions) **J**:146b
Mohenjo-Daro (ancient Harappan city) **A**:240; **I**:131; **P**:40
  picture(s) **A**:453; **P**:40
Moher, Cliffs of (Ireland)
  picture(s) **I**:319
Moho (Mohorovičić discontinuity) (boundary between Earth's
      crust and mantle) **E**:11, 14
Mohr, Joseph (Austrian pastor, author of "Silent Night, Holy
      Night") **C**:118
Mohs, Friedrich (German mineralogist) **G**:70
Mohs' scale (measure for hardness) **G**:70; **M**:315–16
Moi, Daniel arap (president of Kenya) **K**:233
Moisiu, Alfred (Albanian president) **A**:162
Moissac (France) **F**:422
Mojave Desert (California–Arizona) **C**:18; **D**:127
Mojo (Indians of South America) **I**:197
Mokapu (Hawaii) **H**:58
Moksha (Hindu belief in release from cycle of rebirth) **H**:140;
      R:149
Molars (teeth) **T**:43
Molasses **H**:79; **S**:482, 483
  Sugar Act (1764) **R**:195
Moldau River (Czech Republic) *see* Vltava River
Moldavia (former Soviet republic) *see* Moldova
Moldavia (region of Romania) **R**:297, 299
  picture(s) **R**:296, 299
Moldboard plows **F**:54
Molders (tools) **F**:515
Molding (industrial process)
  plastics **P**:322, 325, 326
  rubber **R**:347
  picture(s)
    plastics **P**:325
Moldova **M**:402–3; **U**:34
  picture(s)
    flag **F**:236

Molds (for shaping materials) **D**:158–59
  candles **C**:96
  candy and candy making **C**:98
  ceramics **C**:177
  glass **G**:230, 231
  pottery making **P**:407
  sculpture casting **S**:92
  type **P**:472
Molds (fossils) **F**:381
Molds (fungi) **F**:496, 498–99
  allergies **A**:190
  antibiotics **A**:306, 310, 334
  bioluminescence **B**:205
  cheese making **D**:10
  food spoilage **F**:339, 340, 341
  picture(s) **A**:307; **E**:163; **F**:339; **K**:257
Mole, mechanical (tunnel boring machine) **T**:337
  picture(s) **T**:340
Molecular biology **B**:199; **S**:66
Molecular weight **C**:204
Molecules (combinations of atoms) **A**:483, 485; **C**:198,
      201, 204; **L**:199
  crystals **C**:603–4
  detergents and soaps **D**:139
  gases **G**:56, 58–59
  macromolecules in body chemistry **B**:295–96
  matter and molecules **M**:176, 177
  osmosis **O**:239
  Pauling, Linus **P**:102
  plastics **P**:323
  polymers and polymerization **P**:323
  solids, particles in **S**:250
  temperature of molecules in motion **H**:86
  virus spikes **V**:363
  water molecule **W**:47–50
  diagram(s) **A**:486
  picture(s)
    water molecule **W**:48
Molenaer, Jan Miense (Dutch painter)
  picture(s)
    Family Group (painting) **D**:373
Moles (animals of insectivore group) **M**:67, **404**
  picture(s) **M**:67
Moles (on the skin) **D**:123
Moles, marsupial **M**:115
Molière (French actor-manager and dramatist) **D**:301–2;
      F:438; **M**:405
  picture(s) **D**:301
Molina, Tirso de (Spanish dramatist) *see* Tirso de Molina
Mollusks (group of animals) **A**:267; **M**:405–8
  benthic ocean life **O**:26
  bivalves **O**:290–91
  cephalopods **O**:50–51
  fishing industry **F**:217
  pearls **P**:114–16
  prehistoric animals **P**:432
  shells **S**:149–51
  snails and slugs **S**:208
  zooplankton **P**:284–85
Mollweide projection (of maps) **M**:97
Molly Maguires (secret society) **P**:141
Molly Pitcher (American heroine of Revolutionary War) *see*
      Pitcher, Molly
Molokai (one of the Hawaiian Islands) **H**:50–51, 52, 60
Molotov, Vyacheslav Mikhailovich (Soviet official) **U**:36–37
  profile
Molten rock *see* Magma
Molting (of animals)
  beetles **B**:127
  birds **B**:217–18
  crustaceans **C**:601
  glands control molting **G**:226
  horseshoe crab **H**:245
  lizards **L**:276

lobsters **L:**280
shrimps **S:**168
silkworms **S:**175
snakes **S:**209
spiders **S:**406
ticks **T:**192
waterfowl **D:**346
Moltke, Helmuth Johannes Ludwig, Graf von (Prussian soldier) **M:**408
Moltke, Helmuth von (German general) **F:**452; **M:**408; **W:**280, 282
Moluccas (Maluku; Spice Islands) (Indonesia) **H:**120; **I:**209; **M:**21
Molybdenum (element) **C:**437; **E:**174
picture(s) **M:**152
table(s) **M:**235
Mombacho (volcano, Nicaragua)
picture(s) **N:**245
Mombasa (Kenya) **K:**232
Moment of truth (in bullfighting) **B:**451
Momoh, Joseph Saidu (president of Sierra Leone) **S:**172
Mon (a people of Myanmar) **M:**557
Monaco (principality) **M:409–10**
map(s) **M:**409
picture(s)
flag **F:**236
Grand Prix race **A:**536
Monaco-Ville **M:**409
Monaco-Ville (capital of Monaco) **M:**409
picture(s) **M:**409
Monadnock Mountain (Vermont) **V:**308
Monadnocks (hills or mountains rising above eroded land surface) **N:**150; **O:**202; **S:**298
Monaldeschi, Giovanni, Marquis (Italian nobleman) **C:**295
Mona Lisa (painting by Leonardo da Vinci) **L:**154, 332
picture(s) **I:**397; **L:**153, 332
Monarch butterflies **B:**478
eating habits **I:**237
migration **H:**198–99
milkweed and pollen from genetically engineered corn **G:**84
Viceroy butterfly resembles **I:**243
picture(s) **A:**286; **B:**194; **I:**245
adult life begins **B:**477
chrysalis **I:**233
larva **I:**244
metamorphosis **M:**237
migration **H:**198, 201
stages of life **L:**196
Monarchy (government by single person) **G:**273
constitutional monarchy of the United Kingdom **U:**60
Monasteries **C:**290; **M:**294 *see also* Monks and monasticism
Bhutan **B:**155, 155a
centers of learning for Europe **R:**287
decorative arts of the Middle Ages **D:**77
Greece's Mount Athos **G:**332
Kiev's cave monastery **K:**245
libraries **L:**173
medieval books **B:**321
schools of the Middle Ages **E:**79
picture(s) **C:**290
Rila Monastery (Bulgaria) **B:**445
Moncton (New Brunswick) **N:**138d, 138f
Mondale, Walter Frederick (vice president of the United States) **C:**123; **F:**95; **V:**331 *profile*
picture(s) **C:**124
Monday (day of the week) **D:**46
Mondrian, Piet (Dutch painter) **D:**370; **M:**393, **410**
picture(s)
Composition (paintings) **D:**132, 370
Composition with Red, Blue, and Yellow (painting) **M:**410
Opposition of Lines: Red and Yellow (painting) **M:**392
Moneda, Palacio de la (Santiago, Chile) **S:**37

Monégasques (people of Monaco) **M:**409
Monera (kingdom of living things) **B:**12; **K:**253, 258–59; **L:**208, 209; **T:**27
Monet, Claude (French painter) **M:411**
French art **F:**430
impressionism **I:**103, 104; **P:**29
modern art **M:**387
Orangerie Museum (Paris) **P:**70
picture(s)
Boats at Argenteuil (painting) **M:**411
Impression: Sunrise (painting) **M:**386
Pool of Water Lilies (painting) **F:**430
two paintings of poplars **I:**104
Moneta (Roman goddess) **M:**412
Monetary policy (of a government) **I:**227
Monetary units (of countries) *see* individual country articles
Money **M:412–15**
banks and banking **B:**52–59
budgets, family **B:**427–28
coins and coin collecting **C:**398–400
credit cards **C:**582
currency table of values for representative countries **M:**414
decimal monetary system suggested by Gouverneur Morris **M:**462
dollar **D:**261–63
free silver coinage was Bryan's political issue **B:**416
gold standard for official currencies **G:**247
How can you tell if a bill is counterfeit? **D:**262
inflation and deflation **I:**226–27
mint is place where money is coined **M:**340
monetary economy of trade and commerce **T:**265
monetary units *see* the facts and figures section of country articles
Persia, ancient **P:**155
silver **S:**177–78
silver money under Cleveland **C:**360
Treasury, United States Department of the **T:**294–95
wealth redistribution through income tax **I:**111
picture(s)
currency around the world **M:**414
Moneylender and His Wife, The (painting by Massys) **P:**18
picture(s) **P:**19
Money orders **P:**399
Mongkut (king of Thailand) **T:**152
Mongo (a people of Africa) **A:**76c; **C:**499
Mongol Empire **I:**100; **M:**418
Mongolia **B:**424, 427; **C:**261–62; **M:416–18**
map(s) **M:**417
picture(s)
flag **F:**236
nomads **N:**272
people **M:**416
Ulaanbaatar **M:**416
yurt **H:**189
Mongolism *see* Down syndrome
Mongoloid race **A:**444; **I:**273
Mongols (nomadic tribes of central Asia) *see also* Tatars
China, conquest of **C:**269
Genghis Khan **G:**94
Ivan (rulers of Russia) **I:**413
Korea, history of **K:**298
Mongolia **C:**258; **M:**416–18
Russia invaded by **R:**357, 368–69
yurt homes **H:**189
picture(s) **C:**256; **M:**416; **N:**272
Mongooses (mammals) **M:419**
picture(s) **M:**419
Monhegan Island (Maine)
picture(s) **M:**40
Monica, Saint **A:**494
Monitor, Christian Science see Christian Science Monitor
Monitor and Merrimack (ironclad warships) **C:**338; **U:**20
picture(s) **C:**338
Monitoring (long-term watch on ocean conditions) **O:**40

Monitoring systems (in hospitals)   **H:**248
Monitor lizard   **L:**275
Monitors (computer peripherals)   **C:**481
  picture(s)   **C:**482
Monk, Thelonious (American jazz pianist and composer)   **J:**62
    profile
  picture(s)   **J:**62
Monkey fists (knots)   **K:**287
Monkeys   **M:**420–22
    breeding problems in zoos   **Z:**391
    colobus monkeys eat leaves   **A:**281
    have four hands   **F:**83
    human food source   **P:**457
    play   **P:**334
    rain-forest loss   **R:**100
  picture(s)   **M:**420
      mother and baby   **R:**175
      red howler monkey   **S:**282
Monkey trial (in United States history) *see* Scopes trial
Mon-Khmer (language)   **L:**41
Monks and monasticism   **M:**294–95
    Buddhism   **B:**425, 426
    Christianity, history of   **C:**290
    early Christianization of Europe   **R:**287–88
    Eastern Orthodox Churches   **E:**45
    founding of Dominicans and Franciscans   **R:**289
    illuminated manuscripts   **I:**77–78
    Jesuits   **L:**334; **R:**291
    libraries   **L:**173
    Roman Catholic Church   **R:**284
    Tibet   **T:**189, 190
    writing preserved by medieval monks   **C:**463
  picture(s)
      Buddhism   **A:**448; **B:**425; **L:**42; **M:**557; **R:**150; **S:**328
      Christianity, history of   **C:**290
Monk seals (animals)
  picture(s)   **S:**107
Monmouth, Battle of (1778)   **R:**204, 207
Monocacy National Battlefield (Maryland)   **M:**128
Monochord (ancient instrument)   **K:**237
Monoclinic crystal system (in chemistry)
  picture(s)   **C:**603
Monoclonal antibodies (in cancer treatment)   **C:**95; **I:**98
Monocoque (type of airplane fuselage)   **A:**110
  picture(s)   **A:**111
Monocotyledons (Monocots) (seed plants)   **F:**283; **P:**302
    leaves   **L:**113
  picture(s)   **P:**307
Monocytes (white blood cells)   **B:**260, 261
Monody (in music)   **B:**69
Monoecious plants (with male and female flowers)   **F:**283
Monofil (a single filament)   **N:**438
Monofilament fishing lines   **F:**210, 214
Monofilament yarns   **F:**112
Monogamy (form of marriage)   **F:**42
Monokutuba language   **C:**504
Mono Lake (California)   **C:**21
Monomers (simple one-part molecules)   **P:**323
Monona Terrace (Madison, Wisconsin)   **W:**200
Monongahela National Forest (West Virginia)   **W:**129
Monongahela River (Pennsylvania–West Virginia)   **O:**78;
    P:128, 266; **W:**128, 133
Mononucleosis, infectious *see* Infectious mononucleosis
Monophonic music   **C:**283; **G:**183; **I:**410; **M:**537, 538
Monophonic reproduction (of sound)   **S:**267
Monoplacophores (mollusks)   **M:**406
Monopolies and trusts   **E:**59
    capitalism   **C:**103
    foundations   **F:**391
    guilds   **G:**403–5
    public utilities   **P:**520–23
    Roosevelt, Theodore: "trustbuster"   **R:**330
    Tarbell, Ida, and muckrakers   **T:**23
Monopoly (board game)   **G:**14
Monopropellant (rocket fuel)   **R:**259

Monorail (rapid transit system)   **M:**331
  picture(s)   **A:**513
Mono River (Togo–Benin)   **T:**216
Monotheism (belief in one god)   **R:**146
    Egypt, ancient, in reign of Akhenaten   **E:**109
    Islam   **I:**346, 348
    Judaism   **J:**143
    Sikhism   **R:**150–51
    Zoroastrianism   **Z:**394
Monotone (expressionless voice)   **S:**398
Monotremes (kind of mammal)   **M:**68–69; **P:**331–32
  picture(s)
      platypus as example   **M:**75
Monotype (machine for typesetting and casting)   **T:**371
Monounsaturated fats   **N:**425; **O:**80
Monroe, Bill (American musician)   **C:**571; **K:**225 *profile*
Monroe, Elizabeth Kortright (wife of James Monroe)
    F:166–67; **M:**424
  picture(s)   **F:**166; **M:**424
Monroe, Harriet (American editor)   **A:**214b
Monroe, James (5th president of the United States)
    M:423–26
    Liberia's capital named for him   **L:**167
    Louisiana Purchase   **L:**327, 330
    Monroe Doctrine   **M:**427
    White House   **W:**165
  picture(s)   **M:**423, 425; **P:**445
      grave memorial   **M:**426
Monroe, Marilyn (American film actress)   **M:**490 *profile*
  picture(s)
      silk-screen portrait by Andy Warhol   **W:**7
Monroe Doctrine (American foreign policy)   **M:**427
    Adams, John Quincy, helped write   **A:**17
    foreign affairs of Monroe's administration   **M:**426
    isolationism in U.S. history   **U:**180
    Polk Doctrine was an extension of   **P:**377
    Roosevelt Corollary   **R:**331
  picture(s)
      political cartoon   **M:**427
Monroe Lake (Indiana)   **I:**146
Monrovia (capital of Liberia)   **L:**167–68
  picture(s)   **L:**167
Mons, Battle of (1914)   **W:**281
Monsieur Verdoux (motion picture, 1947)   **C:**186
Monsoons (seasonal winds)   **W:**188
    Asia   **A:**443
    Australia   **A:**505
    Bangladesh   **B:**49
    China   **C:**262
    India   **I:**125
    Indian Ocean   **I:**161
    jet streams   **J:**93
    Malaysia   **M:**57
    Myanmar   **M:**559
    Southeast Asia   **S:**331–32
    Sri Lanka   **S:**415
    tropical climates   **C:**362
Monsters (in Greek mythology)   **G:**364
Mont (geographic term) *see* the names of mountains, as Blanc,
    Mont
Montage (film editing technique)   **M:**490
Montagnais (Indians of North America)   **I:**190
Montaigne, Michel de (French essayist)   **E:**321; **F:**437; **R:**161
    profile
  picture(s)   **E:**321
Montalvo, Garcí Ordóñez de (Spanish author)   **C:**18
Montalvo, Garcí Rodríguez de (Spanish writer)   **S:**388
Montana   **G:**220; **M:**428–41
  map(s)   **M:**438
  picture(s)
      Absaroka Range   **M:**430
      agriculture and industry   **M:**434
      Billings   **M:**435
      Butte   **M:**429

C. M. Russell Museum   **M:**433
copper mine   **M:**440
Devils Canyon   **M:**430
Glacier National Park   **G:**220; **M:**429
Helena   **M:**437
Little Bighorn Battlefield National Monument   **M:**436
National Bison Range   **M:**436
Nevada City   **M:**436
people   **M:**432
prairies and buttes   **M:**430
rodeo   **M:**429
University of Montana   **M:**433
Montaña (region of Peru)   **P:**161
Montana, Joe (American football player)   **F:**363 *profile*
picture(s)   **F:**363
Montana, University of (Missoula)   **M:**433
picture(s)   **M:**433
Montanari (Italian family of doll makers)   **D:**266–67
Montana State University (Bozeman)   **M:**433
Montan wax   **W:**78
Montauk (Indians of North America)   **I:**177
Montauk Point (Long Island, New York)
picture(s)   **N:**212
Montcalm, Louis Joseph, Marquis de (French general)   **F:**464, 465
Mont Cenis Pass (through the Alps)   **A:**194d
Monte Albán (capital of ancient Oaxaca)   **I:**167
Monte Carlo (Monaco)   **M:**409, 410
Monte Cassino (abbey, Cassino, Italy)   **W:**309
Montego Bay (resort, Jamaica)   **J:**18
Montejo, Francisco de (Spanish soldier)   **M:**187
Montemayor, Jorge de (Spanish writer)   **S:**388
Montenegro (former Yugoslav republic) *see* Serbia and Montenegro
Monterey (California)   **A:**337; **C:**28
picture(s)
aquarium   **A:**337
Monterey Park (California)   **L:**304
Monterrey (Mexico)   **M:**241, 247
Monterrey, Battle of (1846)   **M:**239b
Montesquieu, Charles de Secondat, Baron de (French philosopher)   **C:**293; **E:**297 *profile;* **F:**439
picture(s)   **E:**296
Montessori, Maria (Italian educator and physician)   **K:**249
Monte Verde (Chile)   **L:**48
picture(s)   **L:**57
Monteverdi, Claudio (Italian composer)   **B:**70; **C:**283; **I:**412; **O:**140, 195
Montevideo (capital of Uruguay)   **M:**442; **U:**237, 238, 240
picture(s)   **L:**48; **M:**442; **U:**237, 240
Montez, Pedro (Spanish planter in Cuba)   **A:**221
Montezuma II (Aztec ruler of Mexico)   **A:**578; **M:**248, **443**
Cortés' conquest of the Aztecs   **C:**559; **I:**172–73
picture(s)   **M:**249, 443; **W:**264
Montfort, Simon de (English baron)   **E:**239; **H:**109
Montgenèvre Pass (through the Alps)   **A:**194d
Montgolfier, Jacques Étienne and Joseph Michel (French inventors)   **A:**560; **B:**34; **T:**287
Montgomery (capital of Alabama)   **A:**130, 135, 137, 140, 143
bus segregation case   **A:**79m; **K:**251; **P:**76; **S:**115
civil rights march (1965)   **A:**79o; **C:**330
first Confederate capital   **C:**336
picture(s)
state capitol   **A:**139
Montgomery, Bernard Law (British field marshal)   **M:443;** **W:**307, 308, 316
picture(s)   **W:**292
Montgomery, John J. (American aviation pioneer)   **G:**237
Montgomery, Lucy Maud (Canadian author)   **C:**86–87; **P:**465
Montgomery, Richard (American military commander)   **R:**201
Montgomery Ward and Company   **M:**35
Month in the Country, A (play by Ivan Turgenev)   **D:**303

Months (of the year) *see also* the names of months
calendar   **C:**13–17
in French   **F:**434
in Italian   **I:**405
in Spanish   **S:**391
Monticello (Virginia home of Thomas Jefferson)   **A:**373; **J:**66; **V:**354
picture(s)   **J:**67; **U:**179
Montini, Giovanni Battista *see* Paul VI (pope)
Montmartre (Paris)   **P:**69, 73; **T:**245–46
picture(s)   **P:**73
Montmorency cherry   **P:**109
Montmorency Falls (Quebec)   **W:**59
Montpelier (capital of Vermont)   **V:**306, 311, 315
picture(s)   **V:**315
Montpelier (home of James Madison in Virginia)   **M:**10; **V:**354
picture(s)   **M:**13
Montreal (Quebec)   **C:**67; **M:444–45;** **Q:**10, 10b–11, 16
Cartier, Jacques   **C:**126
Expo '67   **F:**17
jazz festival   **M:**556
Jewish community   **C:**52
Olympic Games (1976)   **O:**111
places of interest   **Q:**13
picture(s)   **M:**444, 445; **Q:**10b, 14
Expo '67 site   **F:**13
McGill University   **Q:**13
Montréal, Université de (Quebec)   **C:**52; **M:**445; **Q:**11
Montreal Canadiens (ice hockey team)   **I:**31
Montreux (Switzerland)   **M:**555
Monts, Pierre du Guast, Sieur de (French colonizer)   **N:**356
Mont Sainte-Victoire (painting by Cézanne)
picture(s)   **I:**106
Montserrat   **C:**114
Monument Rocks National Landmark (Kansas)
picture(s)   **K:**178
Monuments   **A:**429 *see also* National monuments; Wonders of the world
Liberty, Statue of   **L:**169
Mount Rushmore (South Dakota)   **S:**312
obelisks   **O:**5
pyramids   **P:**556–58
sculpture   **S:**90–105
Washington Monument   **W:**32
picture(s)
Mount Rushmore (South Dakota)   **S:**313
Monument to Balzac (statue by Rodin)
picture(s)   **M:**387
Monument Valley (Arizona)   **A:**394
picture(s)   **M:**493
Mood (a person's overall emotional state)   **E:**203; **M:**221
Mood disorders (type of mental illness)   **M:**221, 224
Moodie, Susanna (Canadian writer)   **C:**86
picture(s)
illustration from *Roughing It in the Bush*   **C:**87
Moody, Dwight Lyman (American evangelist)   **H:**326; **O:**191
Moody, Helen Wills (American tennis player)   **T:**97 *profile*
picture(s)   **T:**97
Moog, Robert (American composer)   **E:**156
Moog synthesizer (for electronic music)   **E:**156
Moon (of Earth)   **A:**471; **M:446–55**
age estimated with radiometric dating   **R:**75
Armstrong, Neil A.   **A:**426
eclipses of *see* Lunar eclipses
experiments and other science activities   **E:**389
geology in the solar system   **G:**118
gravity and gravitation   **G:**320
Is there water on the moon?   **M:**454
lunar bases   **S:**354, 356
lunar landing   **E:**417; **S:**340e, 340f–340j, 342, 347
lunar tides   **O:**19
lunar time   **T:**200
months of the calendar   **C:**13, 14
orbiting space colony   **S:**356

Moon (cont.)
    satellites of planets **P:**278; **S:**52
    space probes **S:**357
    tides **T:**193–97
    picture(s)
        Galileo space probe photographs **S:**52
        lunar eclipses **E:**52
        lunar landing **E:**417; **U:**201; **W:**275
        orbit **G:**321
Moon, Keith (British rock musician) **R:**263
Moon, Mountains of the (ancient name for Ruwenzori
    Mountains) **A:**61
Moon jellyfish **J:**76
Moonlight **L:**237; **M:**447
Moons (of planets) *see* Moon (of Earth); Satellites
Moonstone (gemstone) **G:**73
Moonstone, The (novel by Collins) **M:**566
Moon worship **A:**245
Moorcock, Michael (English author) **S:**82
Moore, Clement Clarke (American scholar)
    "A Visit from Saint Nicholas" (poem) **C:**299
Moore, Colleen (American film actress) **D:**265
Moore, Douglas (American composer) **O:**149
Moore, Henry (English sculptor) **E:**264; **S:**105; **T:**244
    picture(s)
        Family Group (sculpture) **S:**104
        Reclining Figure No. 4 (sculpture) **E:**264
        Rocking Chair II (sculpture) **D:**137
Moore, James (colonial governor of South Carolina) **S:**309
Moore, Marianne (American poet) **A:**215; **F:**4
Moorer, Michael (American boxer) **B:**351
Moore's Creek Bridge, Battle of (1776) **N:**318
Moore's Law (in computer technology) **T:**278
Moorish art and architecture *see* Islamic art and architecture
Moorish novels **S:**388
Moors (Muslims of northern Africa)
    driven from Spain by Ferdinand and Isabella **F:**88
    fountains **F:**393
    Mauritania **M:**179
    sour orange introduced to Europe **O:**187
    Spain, history of **S:**370, 375–76, 380–81
Moose (hoofed mammals) **A:**274; **D:**80; **E:193**; **H:**216, 218
    picture(s) **D:**80; **M:**37
Moosehead Lake (Maine) **M:**38
    picture(s) **M:**39
Moosehorn National Wildlife Refuge (Maine) **M:**44
Moose Jaw (Saskatchewan) **S:**49
Mopeds **M:**499
Moraine Lake (Alberta)
    picture(s) **B:**46; **C:**56
Moraines (glacial deposits) **G:**116, 225; **I:**8, 14
    picture(s) **I:**9
Morales, Melesio (Mexican composer) **L:**73
Morales, Pablo (American swimmer) **S:**538 *profile*
    picture(s) **S:**538
Morality plays (of the Middle Ages) **D:**26, 300; **E:**271; **P:**12
Moral philosophy *see* Ethics
Moran, Rolando (Guatemalan guerrilla leader)
    picture(s) **G:**398
Morandi, Giorgio (Italian painter) **I:**403
Morante, Elsa (Italian author) **I:**409
Morava River (Europe) **C:**619
Moravia (province of Czech Republic) **C:**619
Moravia, Alberto (Italian author) **I:**409
Moravians **N:**314; **O:**70; **P:**493
Moray eels **A:**276; **E:**93, 94; **F:**199
Morazán, Francisco (Honduran statesman) **H:**209
Morceli, Noureddine (Algerian runner) **T:**259 *profile*
    picture(s) **T:**259
Mordant (substance used to fix dyes) **D:**376, 377, 378, 380,
    381
Mordant dyes **D:**380
Mordecai (character in the Bible) **P:**549
Moré (language) **B:**453

More, Sir Thomas (English statesman and author) **E:**271;
    H:114, 284; **M:456**; **S:**79
Moreau, Pierre (French printer) **T:**370
Morelos y Pavón, José María (Mexican priest and patriot)
    M:248
Morels (mushrooms) **M:**529
    picture(s) **F:**496
Moreno, Luisa (American civil rights leader) **H:**148
Morenz, Howie (Canadian hockey player) **I:**31 *profile*
Morgan, Daniel (American military commander) **R:**208
Morgan, Sir Henry (English buccaneer) **P:**263 *profile*
    picture(s) **P:**263
Morgan, John Hunt (American Confederate general) **O:**76
Morgan, John Pierpont (American banker) **M:**456
Morgan, Morgan (American colonist) **W:**136
Morgan, Thomas Hunt (American zoologist) **K:**225 *profile*
Morgan horses **H:**240; **V:**312
Morganite (beryl gemstone) **G:**73
Morgan le Fay (sorceress in legends of King Arthur) **A:**438
Morgantown (West Virginia) **W:**131
Morgan v. *Virginia* (United States, 1946) **A:**79L
Morgentaler v. *The Queen* (Canada, 1987) **S:**506
Morin (coloring matter from fustic wood) **D:**377
Morisot, Berthe (French painter) **I:**103
    picture(s)
        portrait by Édouard Manet **W:**55
Morley, Edward W. (American physicist) **R:**140–41
Mormons (religious sect) **M:**457
    colonization of Utah **U:**242, 246, 247, 254
    genealogical research **G:**76c
    Nevada, history of **N:**131, 135
    overland trails **O:**281
    Protestantism **P:**493
    Salt Lake City **S:**24
    Smith, Joseph **S:**205
    westward movement displaced Indians **I:**186
    Woodruff, Wilford **U:**255
    Young, Brigham **Y:**363
Mormon Tabernacle Choir **S:**24; **U:**247
    picture(s) **U:**247
Mormon Trail **O:**281
    map(s) **O:**273
Morne Gimie (volcano, Saint Lucia) **S:**17
"Morning after pills" (for emergency birth control) **B:**250b
Morning glory (plant)
    picture(s) **L:**203
Morning rounds (of doctors) **D:**236
Morning Star (name for Mercury or Venus) **P:**278; **V:**303
Morocco **M:458–61**
    New Year **N:**208, 209
    Spanish enclaves of Ceuta and Melilla **S:**375
    Western Sahara **W:**124
    picture(s)
        Atlas Mountains **M:**459
        Berber boy with Koran **A:**54
        Casablanca **M:**460
        flag **F:**236
        oasis **A:**50
        people **A:**345; **M:**458
Moroni (capital of the Comoros) **C:**475
Moros (a people of the Philippines) **P:**153, 184
Morotai Island (Indonesia) **W:**309
Morphine (narcotic drug) **D:**334, 335; **N:**15; **P:**297
Morphing (computer graphics technique) **C:**484
    picture(s) **C:**484
Morrill, Justin Smith (American legislator) **A:**96
Morrill Act (United States, 1862) **P:**517; **U:**220
Morrill Land Grant Act (United States, 1890) **A:**79h
Morris, Esther Hobart (American women's rights advocate)
    W:347 *profile*
Morris, Gouverneur (American statesman and diplomat)
    M:462; **U:**146
Morris, Lewis (American statesman) **D:**67 *profile;* **N:**176
Morris, Mark (American dancer) **D:**33 *profile*
    picture(s) **D:**23

Morris, Robert (American statesman)   **D:**67 *profile;* **F:**392
  picture(s)   **D:**67
Morris, William (English poet and artist)   **E:**285
  decorative arts   **D:**78
  influence on illustration   **I:**81
  reform of furniture design   **F:**514
  tapestry   **T:**22
  Victorian age in English art   **E:**263
  picture(s)
    page from illustrated works of Chaucer   **E:**263
Morris dances   **F:**300, 302–3
  picture(s)   **F:**300
Morris games *see* Nine Men's Morris
Morrison, Philip (American physicist)   **R:**70
Morrison, Toni (American novelist)   **A:**79c, 219; **F:**116;
  M:462; N:363
  picture(s)   **A:**80; **F:**116
Morristown National Historical Park (New Jersey)   **N:**172
Morrisville (Pennsylvania)   **C:**422
Morrow, Anne (American author) *see* Lindbergh, Anne Spencer
  Morrow
Morse, Samuel F. B. (American artist and inventor)   **C:**467;
  I:282–83; **M:463; T:**46, 51
  picture(s)   **M:**463
Morse Code, International   **C:**467; **M:**463; **R:**62; **T:**46, 51
Mortality (number of deaths in a population)   **P:**385, 386,
  387
  countries' infant mortality rates, list of   **P:**387
  first mortality table   **S:**443
  life insurance rates based on force of mortality   **A:**82
Mortal sin (doctrine of the Roman Catholic Church)   **R:**283
Mortar (mixture of cement, sand, and water)   **B:**392–93;
  C:165
Mortarboard cap (part of academic dress)   **H:**46; **U:**223
Mortars (guns)   **G:**425
Mortars (vessels used for grinding or crushing substances)
  L:52
Morte Darthur (book by Thomas Malory)   **A:**438a–438b;
  E:269; **H:**175
Mortgages   **B:**57; **R:**113
Mortise-and-tenon construction (of furniture)   **F:**506, 515
Morton, Ferdinand "Jelly Roll" (American jazz musician)   **J:**59
  profile
  picture(s)   **J:**59
Morton, John (American political figure)   **D:**67 *profile*
Morton, Julius Sterling (American originator of Arbor Day)
  N:82
Morton, Levi Parsons (vice president, United States)   **V:**328
  profile
  picture(s)   **V:**327
Morton, Thomas (English adventurer)   **P:**347
Morton, William T. G. (American doctor)   **A:**255; **M:**208a
  picture(s)   **A:**254; **M:**208a; **S:**512
Mosaic (art form)   **M:**464
  ancient Greece   **G:**351, 352; **H:**191
  Byzantine   **B:**488, 489–90, 492–93
  early Christian and Byzantine artistry   **P:**17
  early Eastern European clothing influenced by   **C:**375
  Islamic decoration of mosques   **I:**358
  Italian art   **I:**392
  Rome, art of   **D:**76
  Saint Sophia Cathedral (Kiev)   **R:**374
  picture(s)
    ancient Greece   **G:**351
    Justinian and His Court   **B:**495; **P:**16
    Roman mosaics   **D:**76; **O:**53
Mosaic (Web browser)   **C:**493
Moscone, George (mayor of San Francisco)   **S:**32
Moscoso, Mireya (president of Panama)   **P:**49
Moscow (capital of Russia)   **M:465–68; R:**359, 364; **U:**34,
  35
  became capital in 1918   **U:**41
  Chechen theater seizure (2002)   **R:**373
  early state of Russia   **R:**369

Ivan (rulers of Russia)   **I:**413
  Muscovite period in architecture   **R:**375–76
  Napoleon's invasion and retreat   **N:**13; **R:**370
  Olympic Games (1980)   **O:**111–12
  World War II   **W:**300
  picture(s)
    Dormition, Cathedral of the   **R:**376
    Kremlin   **C:**313
    Lenin at 1918 May Day gathering   **U:**41
    Saint Basil, Cathedral of   **C:**133; **R:**357
Moscow, Treaty of (2002)   **D:**182
Moscow Art Theater   **T:**161–62
Moseley, Henry Gwyn-Jeffreys (English physicist)   **C:**211;
  E:168
Moselle River (Germany)
  picture(s)   **G:**153
Moser, Lukas (German artist)   **G:**168
Moses (Hebrew leader)   **M:469** *see also* Joshua
  Bible (Old Testament)   **B:**158, 159
  Islamic beliefs   **I:**346
  Judaism, beliefs of   **J:**144
  leader and lawgiver of the Jews   **J:**101–2
  Passover   **P:**95
  received the Ten Commandments   **T:**72
  religions of the world   **R:**147
  picture(s)   **J:**148; **R:**147
    destroying the tablets   **B:**161
    Michelangelo's *Moses* (statue)   **S:**101
    received the Ten Commandments   **J:**102
Moses, Edwin (American hurdler)   **T:**259–60 *profile*
  picture(s)   **T:**260
Moses, Grandma (American artist)   **M:470**
  picture(s)
    Sugaring Off (painting)   **M:**470
Moses, Law of   **H:**155; **M:**469
Moses, Robert (American public official)   **N:**232 *profile*
  picture(s)   **N:**233
Moses ibn Ezra *see* Ibn Ezra, Moses
Moses Saved from the Waters (painting by Poussin)
  picture(s)   **F:**425
Moshavim (Israeli co-operative settlements)   **I:**372
Moshoeshoe I (Basotho chief)   **L:**157
Moshoeshoe II (king of Lesotho)   **L:**157
Mosisile, Pakalitha (Lesotho prime minister)   **L:**157
Moslems *see* Islam
Mosley, Sir Oswald Ernald (British fascist leader)   **F:**64
Mosques (Islamic places of worship)   **I:**352, 355–56
  architecture   **A:**370
  Córdoba (Spain)   **S:**380–81
  decorative arts   **I:**358
  Delhi's Jama Masjid   **D:**103
  India, art and architecture of   **I:**139
  Istanbul   **I:**378
  Jerusalem's Dome of the Rock   **J:**82
  mud mosques in Mali   **A:**76
  Royal Mosque (Isfahan, Iran)   **A:**438d
  picture(s)
    Albania   **A:**160
    Bobo-Dioulasso (Burkina Faso)   **B:**454
    Cairo (Egypt)   **C:**8
    Córdoba (Spain)   **I:**351; **S:**380
    Great Mosque (Mecca)   **I:**346
    Iran   **I:**305
    Iraq   **I:**311
    Islamabad (Pakistan)   **P:**39
    Mazār-e Sharīf (Afghanistan)   **A:**42
    Nigeria   **A:**57
    Pakistani Id al-Fitr celebration   **R:**155
    Sultan Ahmed Mosque (Istanbul)   **T:**348
    wall decorations   **I:**354
Mosquito Coast (Honduras)   **H:**206
Mosquito Coast (Nicaragua)   **N:**244
Mosquitoes (insects)   **I:**237; **M:**471
  household pests   **H:**260

Mosquitoes (cont.)

malaria spread by   **M:**51, 52; **T:**17
mosquito netting for tents   **C:**46
Reed discovers disease carrier   **R:**128
vectors of disease   **D:**189; **V:**282, 283, 284, 285
World Health Organization campaigns against   **P:**515
picture(s)   **I:**245; **V:**282
   fossil   **I:**230
   larva   **I:**244
Mosquito ferns   **F:**94
Moss, Spanish *see* Spanish moss
Moss agate (gem quartz)   **Q:**8
Mosses   **M:**472–73; **P:**302
When is a moss not a moss?   **M:**473
Mossi (a people of Africa)   **B:**453, 454
"Most favored nation" principle   **G:**76d
Mosul (Iraq)   **I:**314
Motagua River (Guatemala)   **G:**396
Motecuhzoma (Aztec rulers) *see* Montezuma
Motels   **H:**256–59
Motet (in music)   **C:**283; **D:**371, 372; **F:**444; **M:**296, 538
"Moth and the Star, The" (fable by James Thurber)   **F:**6
Mother about to Wash Her Sleepy Child (painting by Mary
   Cassatt)
picture(s)   **U:**130
Motherboard (computer component)   **C:**480–81
picture(s)   **C:**482
Mother Goose rhymes   **C:**229, 232; **N:**414–16
picture(s)   **C:**229
Mothering Sunday (in England)   **H:**170
Mother-of-pearl (Nacre)   **J:**96; **O:**290; **P:**114; **S:**149
Mother of Presidents (nickname for Virginia)   **V:**346
Mother of Rivers (nickname for Colorado)   **C:**430
Mother of States (nickname for Virginia)   **V:**346
Mothers Against Drunk Driving (MADD)   **A:**173
Mother's Day   **H:**170; **R:**155; **W:**138–39
Mothers of the Plaza de Mayo (human rights group)
picture(s)   **H:**285
Motherwell, Robert (American painter)   **W:**27 *profile*
Moths   **B:**475–76, 478 *see also* the names of moths, such as
   Gypsy moth
clothes moth   **H:**261
How can you tell a butterfly from a moth?   **B:**475
metamorphosis   **M:**238
peppered moths, genetic changes in   **G:**82
plant pollination   **F:**285; **P:**308
silk moth, life cycle of the   **S:**174–75
picture(s)   **B:**482–83
Motif (in music)   **M:**537
Motion (in physics)   **M:**474–76
Brownian motion   **A:**484
energy   **E:**212–17
forces   **F:**365–66b
Galileo   **S:**70
heat, theory of   **H:**88–89
jet propulsion principle   **J:**90
lift in airplane flight   **A:**109
Newton's laws of   **M:**474–76; **N:**207; **P:**228
optical illusions   **M:**478; **O:**176
physics, history of   **P:**234
principle of the seismograph   **E:**37
reaction engine explained by Newton's third law   **E:**229
relativity   **R:**140, 141–42
rockets explained by Newton's laws   **R:**258
Motion picture directors   **M:**479, 483, 493–94, 497
Motion Picture Experts Group (MPEG)   **V:**332f
Motion picture photography   **C:**466
Motion picture producers   **M:**479
Mayer, Louis B.   **L:**308
Motion Picture Producers and Distributors of America   **M:**491
Motion pictures   **M:**477–97
Africa, literature of   **A:**76d
animation   **A:**288–91
arts of the United States   **U:**99

Australia   **A:**503–4
Barrymore family   **B:**74
Cairo's Hollywood on the Nile   **C:**7
California   **C:**25; **L:**307
Canada   **C:**69
comic books, based on   **C:**454
copyright protection   **C:**555
country music, rise of   **C:**572
Cousteau, Jacques-Yves, films of   **C:**577
cowboy folklore   **C:**579
Crosby, Bing   **W:**27
Dean, James   **I:**156
Edison built world's first studio   **E:**73
feature films on videocassette   **T:**66
Hispanic Americans   **H:**147
journalism   **J:**140
Los Angeles   **L:**306
Mexico   **M:**247
myth in the modern world   **M:**577
New Zealand industry   **N:**240
Robinson, Bill "Bojangles"   **D:**32
Rogers, Will   **O:**95
science fiction   **S:**83
sound tracks   **S:**267a, 267b
Swanson, Gloria   **C:**221
Tracy, Spencer   **W:**207
violence and society   **V:**344
Motions (in parliamentary procedure)   **P:**82
Motion sickness   **E:**6; **S:**342
Motive *see* Motif
Motley, Constance Baker (American jurist and public official)
   A:79c
Motley, John Lothrop (American historian)   **H:**152
Motley, Marion (American football player)
picture(s)   **F:**361
Motor behavior (of animals)   **B:**366–67
Motorboats   **B:**266–69
Motor Carrier Act (United States, 1980)   **T:**321
Motorcycle gangs   **O:**223
Motorcycles   **H:**46; **M:**498–99
picture(s)   **S:**330
French worker assembling motorbike parts   **F:**409
Motor development (of children)   **C:**225
Motor disorders (learning disorders)   **L:**107, 108
Motor neurons (Motor nerves)   **B:**362; **N:**116, 117
Motors *see* Engines
Motors, electric *see* Electric motors
Motors, hydraulic *see* Hydraulic motors
Motor trucks *see* Trucks and trucking
Motor vehicles *see* Automobiles; Buses; Motorcycles; Tractors;
   Trucks and trucking
Motown Recording Corporation   **M:**273
Mott, Lucretia Coffin (American preacher and reformer)
   W:212, 214 *profile*
Motto, Olympic   **O:**108, 112
Mottoes, provincial *see* individual province articles
Mottoes, state *see* individual state articles
Mouflon (hoofed mammal)   **S:**147
Moulmein (Myanmar)   **M:**560
Mouloud (Muslim holiday)   **R:**155
Moultrie, William (American soldier)   **S:**296, 304
Mound Builders (Indians of North America)   **I:**168, 171; **O:**70,
   74
Illinois   **I:**74
Indiana   **I:**156
Iowa   **I:**298, 302
Missouri   **M:**378
Wisconsin   **W:**204
picture(s)
Great Serpent Mound (Ohio)   **O:**63
Moundou (Chad)   **C:**181
Mounds (at archaeological sites)
Grave Creek Mound (West Virginia)   **W:**134
Mound Builder Indians   **O:**70

Mozart, Wolfgang Amadeus (Austrian composer) **M:**510
chamber music **C:**184
choral music **C:**284
clarinet was one of his favorite instruments **C:**348
classical age in music **C:**349, 351, 352; **O:**196
Cosi Fan Tutte (opera) **O:**153
Don Giovanni (opera) **O:**153
German music **G:**186
harp, use of **H:**36
Haydn and Mozart **H:**67
influenced by Italian music **I:**412
The Magic Flute (opera) **O:**156
The Marriage of Figaro (opera) **M:**542; **O:**156–58
opera **C:**351; **O:**144
piano, first great composer for **P:**242
Salzburg Festival **M:**555
picture(s)
child prodigy **A:**522; **G:**185
The Magic Flute (opera) **O:**157
Mozzarella (Italian cheese) **D:**10
MP3 (audio format) **R:**124
Mphahlele, Ezekiel (South African writer) **A:**76d
Mr. (form of address) **A:**21
Mr. America (bodybuilding competition) **B:**293–94
Mr. Olympia contest (bodybuilding competition) **B:**294
Mr. Prejudice (painting by Horace Pippin)
picture(s) **A:**79m
Mr. Sammler's Planet (book by Saul Bellow) **B:**141
Mr. Universe (bodybuilding competition) **B:**294
MRI see Magnetic resonance imaging
Mrs. (form of address) **A:**21
Mrs. N's Place (sculpture by Louise Nevelson)
picture(s) **U:**135
Ms. (form of address) **A:**21
Ms. (magazine) **S:**447
picture(s) **W:**213
MSAR see Miniature Synthetic Aperture Radar
Mswati III (king of Swaziland) **S:**522
Mu'awiyah (Muslim caliph) **I:**351
Mubarak, Muhammad Hosni (Egyptian political and military leader) **E:**105
Much Ado About Nothing (play by Shakespeare) **S:**138
Mucilage (type of adhesive) **G:**243
Mucking (in tunnel building) **T:**337
Muckrakers (crusading reporters) **A:**214; **J:**140; **T:**23
Mucosa (layer of the stomach wall) **S:**460
Mucus (body substance)
bronchitis **D:**189
cystic fibrosis **D:**191
eel's body mucus **E:**93
exocrine glands **G:**226
fish's body mucus **F:**187
lungs **L:**344, 345
stomach **S:**461
Mud, dredging of **D:**321–22
Mudd, Samuel (American doctor) **B:**335
Mud daubers (wasps) **I:**247
Mudejar style (in art and architecture) **S:**381
Mudflows (volcanic) **V:**384
Mudge, Isadore Gilbert (American librarian) **L:**180
Mud houses **A:**76, 364; **H:**191
Mud-mill (dredging machine) **D:**322
Mudpots (pools of boiling mud) **G:**192–93
Mud shows (circus shows that travel by truck) **C:**308
Mud shrimps (crustaceans) **S:**167
Mudskippers (fish) **F:**188
picture(s) **F:**189
Mudslides see Landslides
Mud snakes **S:**212, 216
Mud turtles **T:**356, 357
Mufflers (engine silencers) **A:**547; **I:**265
Mugabe, Robert Gabriel (Zimbabwean political leader) **Z:**384
picture(s) **Z:**384
Mugwumps (reform Republicans) **C:**359
Muhammad (Arab prophet) see Mohammed

Muhammad, Elijah (leader of the Nation of Islam) **A:**79o
Malcolm X **M:**59
Muhammad Ali (American boxer) see Ali, Muhammad
Muharraq, Al (Bahrain) **B:**19
Muir, John (American naturalist and conservationist) **C:**526; **M:**511; **N:**70; **Y:**363
picture(s) **N:**50, 70
Mujahideen (Afghan resistance forces) **A:**45; **G:**400
Mujibur Rahman (Mujib) (president of Bangladesh) **B:**51
Mukden (China) see Shenyang
Mukden Incident (1931) **J:**46; **S:**152
Mukherjee, Bharati (Indian author) **I:**142
Mukhina, Vera (Russian sculptor)
picture(s)
Worker and Collective Farm Woman (sculpture) **R:**379
Mukluks (boots worn by the Inuit) **I:**275
Mulanje Mountains (Malawi) **M:**52, 53
Mulattoes (people of mixed racial ancestry) **L:**48, 49, 50
Mulberry trees **S:**174, 175
Mulch (materials to retain soil moistures) **G:**41–42; **V:**287
Mule deer **D:**80
picture(s) **A:**269
Mules **H:**235, 243
picture(s) **G:**292
carrying sightseers into Grand Canyon **A:**393
Mulhacén (mountain, Spain) **S:**372
Mulholland, William (American civil engineer) **L:**308 profile
picture(s) **L:**308
Mullahs (Shi'ite Muslim leaders) **I:**347
picture(s) **M:**298
Mullan Trail (Montana) **M:**435
Mullins, Priscilla (Pilgrim settler) **P:**345
Mullis, Kary B. (American scientist) **B:**187; **G:**91
picture(s) **B:**187
Mulroney, Martin Brian (Canadian prime minister) **C:**85; **M:**511
picture(s) **C:**77
Multan (Pakistan) **P:**39
Multi-Element Radio Linked Interferometer Network (MERLIN) **R:**68
Multifilament yarns **F:**112
Multilateral treaties (among many countries) **T:**296, 297
Multimedia (technology combining text, sound, and images) **J:**141
Multi-mode fibers (fiber optics) **F:**107
Multinational corporations **O:**220
Multiple-arch dams **D:**19
picture(s) **D:**17, 19
Multiple births **T:**363–64
Multiple-choice tests **T:**118–23
Multiple independently targeted re-entry vehicle system see MIRV system
Multiple Launch Rocket System (MLRS) **U:**106
Multiple Listing Service (MLS) (real estate database) **R:**113
Multiple-point perspective (in art) **H:**159a
Multiple proportions, law of (in chemistry) **A:**483
Multiple-purpose dams **D:**17; **D:**21
Multiples (in mathematics) **N:**380, 381
Multiple sclerosis **D:**197
picture(s) **D:**197
Multiple stars **S:**430
Multiple use (of national forest land) **N:**32–33
Multiplex telegraphy **T:**46, 51
Multiplicand (in multiplication) **A:**390
Multiplication (in mathematics) **A:**390
abacus **A:**2
algebra **A:**182, 183
decimal fractions **F:**401
fractions **F:**399
number systems **N:**398, 399
Multiplicative inverse property (of numbers) **N:**401
Multiplicative systems (type of numeration systems) **N:**405
Multiplier (in multiplication) **A:**390
Multistage rockets **G:**245; **R:**261

Multnomah Falls (Oregon)   **O:**210; **W:**59
picture(s)   **O:**210; **W:**59
Muluzi, Bakili (president of Malawi)   **M:**53
Mumbai (India) *see* Bombay
Mummers (in medieval drama)   **D:**299
Mummies (dead bodies preserved from decay)   **M:512–13**
　Chimu civilization   **A:**245
　Egyptian   **E:**107, 110; **F:**495
　how fossils form   **F:**381–82
　Iceman   **A:**357
　Inca religion   **I:**109
　mummy portraits   **P:**17
　Tutankhamen   **A:**352
　picture(s)
　　Egyptian funeral custom   **E:**106; **F:**495
　　Iceman   **A:**357
　　Inca child   **M:**513
　　Ramses II   **M:**512
Mumps (virus disease)   **D:**188, 197; **G:**228; **L:**350
Munch, Edvard (Norwegian painter)   **N:**348
　The Scream (lithograph)   **G:**307
　picture(s)
　　The Scream (lithograph)   **E:**424
　　The Sick Child   **A:**306
Mundo (painting by Xul Solar)
　picture(s)   **L:**64
Mundurucú (Indians of South America)   **I:**197
Munich (Germany)   **G:**157; **H:**163; **O:**112–13
Munich Pact (1938)   **C:**183; **H:**154; **W:**295
Municipal government   **M:514–17**
　Canada   **C:**78
　cities, problems of   **C:**320, 321; **U:**236
　civil service   **C:**331
　elections   **E:**128, 130
　income tax   **I:**111
　noise control   **N:**271
　police   **P:**366
　public utilities   **P:**520–23
　taxation for levels of government   **T:**25
　Tokyo   **T:**218
　Toronto   **T:**243
Municipal water supply   **D:**16; **W:**76
Munif, Abd al-Rahman (Saudi Arabian writer)   **A:**342
Muñoz Marín, Luis (Puerto Rican political leader)   **P:**532 *see also* Operation Bootstrap
　picture(s)   **P:**532
Mun River (Thailand)   **T:**149–50
Munro, Alice (Canadian writer)   **C:**87
Munsee (Indians of North America)   **I:**177
Muntjacs (deer)   **D:**80–81
Muon (subatomic particle)   **A:**489
Muppets (puppets designed for television)   **M:**362; **P:**548
Muralism (in modern art)   **L:**63–64
Mural painting
　ancient Rome   **I:**257; **P:**17; **R:**319
　Benton, Thomas Hart   **B:**144a
　cave art in India   **I:**136
　cave painting of early man   **P:**14–15
　Egypt, ancient   **I:**257; **P:**15
　fresco technique popular during Renaissance   **P:**20
　Greece, art of   **G:**352
　Hispanic Americans   **H:**147
　Klimt, Gustav   **K:**271
　Leonardo da Vinci's *Last Supper* damaged because of damp wall   **P:**21
　Oregon's capitol building   **O:**211
　Orozco, José   **O:**231
　Rivera, Diego   **R:**235
　Romanesque art   **R:**295
　Venezuela   **V:**298
　picture(s)   **A:**236; **H:**146; **I:**257
Murano glass   **G:**233
Murasaki, Lady (Japanese writer)   **J:**52–53
Murchison Falls (Uganda) *see* Kabalega (Murchison) Falls

Murder (crime)
　capital punishment as sentence for   **C:**104
　forensic science   **F:**373
　Holocaust   **H:**173–74
　juvenile crime   **J:**168
"Murders in the Rue Morgue, The" (story by Poe)   **M:**566
Murdoch, Iris (English writer)   **E:**290
Murex (sea snail)   **D:**377
　picture(s)   **D:**377
Murillo, Bartolomé (Spanish artist)   **S:**384
Murmansk (Russia)   **R:**364
Murnau, F. W. (German film director)   **M:**490
Murphy, Audie Leon (American soldier and movie actor)   **T:**139
　profile; **U:**101
Murray, Joseph (American surgeon)   **M:**208d, 208h; **O:**227
Murray, Philip (American labor leader)   **L:**16–17 *profile*
Murray Harbor (Prince Edward Island)   **P:**466
Murray River (Australia)   **A:**504; **R:**244
Murre (birds of the auk family)   **B:**230–31
Murrow, Edward R. (American news commentator)   **J:**138
　profile; **N:**321 *profile*
　picture(s)   **J:**138
Musala Peak (Bulgaria)   **B:**443
Muscat and Oman *see* Oman
Muscat (capital of Oman) *see* Masqat
Muscle fiber   **M:**518, 520
Muscles *see* Muscular system
Muscular dystrophy (disease)   **D:**197; **M:**521
Muscular system   **M:518–21**
　birds   **B:**222
　body, human   **B:**279–80
　bodybuilding   **B:**293–94
　calcium essential for muscle contraction   **V:**371
　cerebral palsy   **D:**190
　child development   **C:**225
　electrical messages in the nervous system   **E:**138
　first aid for strains   **F:**160
　fish   **F:**190
　hibernating animals   **H:**128
　insects   **I:**241–42
　multiple sclerosis   **D:**197
　muscle cells responsible for movement   **L:**196
　muscular dystrophy   **D:**197
　physical fitness   **P:**224–27
　reflex actions   **N:**118
　sodium, potassium, and chloride needed for muscle contraction   **V:**372
　tetanus makes muscles stiff   **D:**206–7
　tissues of the body   **B:**275
　trichinosis   **D:**207
　weightlessness, effects of   **S:**342
　weight lifting   **W:**107
　What is the levator labii superioris alaeque nasi?   **M:**520
Musée d'Orsay (Paris, France)   **P:**70
　picture(s)   **P:**70
Museo del Prado (Madrid, Spain) *see* Prado
Muses (in Greek mythology)   **M:**530, 570 *see also* the names of the Muses
Museum of Fine Arts (Boston, Massachusetts)   **M:**525
Museum of Jewish Heritage (New York City)   **H:**174
Museum of Modern Art (New York City)   **A:**375; **M:**395
Museum of Science and Industry (Chicago, Illinois)   **I:**67
　picture(s)   **C:**219; **I:**70
Museums   **M:522–28** *see also* Presidential libraries; the education section of country, province, and state articles
　"Agassiz" museum at Harvard   **A:**81
　botanical gardens   **B:**342–43
　Charleston Museum is country's oldest public museum   **S:**301, 306
　comic and cartoon art   **C:**454
　doll collections   **D:**271
　Eisenhower Museum (Abilene, Kansas)   **K:**184
　Hermitage Museum (Saint Petersburg)   **H:**122

Music Party, The (painting by Philippe Mercier)
    picture(s) **E:**291
Musil, Robert (Austrian novelist) **G:**182
Musique concrète (in modern music) **F:**448; **M:**537
Musk (substance from special glands of animals) **M:**419
    perfume **P:**150, 151
    skunks **S:**189
    turtles **T:**356, 357
Musk deer **D:**80–81, 82
Muskegs (swamps) **A:**149; **N:**286
Muskets (guns) **G:**418
    picture(s) **G:**416
Muskie, Edmund Sixtus (American political leader) **M:**49
    profile
    picture(s) **M:**49
Muskmelons (summer melons) **M:**214; **V:**290
    picture(s) **M:**214
Muskogee (Indians of North America) **I:**178
Musk oxen (large mammals) **O:**286; **T:**331
    picture(s) **A:**282
Muskrats (rodents) **F:**504; **R:**277
Musk turtles **T:**356, 357
Musky (Muskellunge) (fish) **W:**195
Muslims (followers of Islam) *see* Arabs; Islam; Moors
Muspell (fiery realm in Norse mythology) **N:**278
Mussels (mollusks) **M:**406; **O:**290, 291; **S:**150
    table(s)
        United States aquaculture production **F:**208
Musset, Alfred de (French writer) **F:**440; **R:**303
Mussolini, Benito (Italian premier) **M:**556
    fall of **W:**316
    Fascism in Italy **F:**63, 64; **I:**390; **V:**332
    rise of dictators before World War II **W:**294, 295
    Rome **R:**308
    World War II **W:**299, 308
    picture(s) **I:**390
Mussorgsky, Modest (Russian composer) **O:**146, 151; **R:**385
Mustangs (wild horses of Spanish stock) **C:**578; **H:**242
    picture(s) **N:**123
Mustard (vegetable) **H:**121; **V:**290
Mustelids (family of animals) **O:**251–57
Mustique (island, Saint Vincent and the Grenadines) **S:**19
Mutations (of genes) **B:**203; **G:**80–81, 82, 87
    bacteria **A:**312
    evolution **E:**376–77
    furs, colors of **F:**502
Mutesa I (king of Buganda) **U:**7
Mutesa II (Sir Edward Mutesa) (king, then president, of Uganda) **U:**7
Mute swans (birds) **D:**348
Mutharika, Bingu wa (president of Malawi) **M:**53
Muths, Guts (German writer) **P:**223
Mutiny on the *Bounty* *see* Bounty, Mutiny on the
Mutombo, Dikembe (American basketball player)
    picture(s) **B:**95h
Mutt and Jeff (comic strip) **C:**128
    picture(s) **C:**128
Mutton (meat from older sheep) **M:**196
Mutual assured destruction theory (in nuclear strategy) **N:**378
Mutual Broadcasting System **R:**60
Mutual funds (investments) **S:**459
Mutualism (a way some different organisms live together)
    L:206; **P:**317
Muzorewa, Abel (prime minister of Zimbabwe-Rhodesia)
    Z:384
Muzzle-loading weapons **G:**416; **H:**300
    picture(s) **G:**415
Muzzles (of dogs) **D:**242
Mwanawasa, Levy (president of Zambia) **Z:**378
Mwanza (Tanzania) **T:**19
Mwinyi, Ali Hassan (president of Tanzania) **T:**19
Myanmar (Burma) **M:**557–61
    Buddhism **B:**424
    economy **S:**332

    gems found in **G:**71
    New Year customs **N:**209
    rice consumption **F:**332
    Thant, U **T:**155
    World War II **W:**303, 304, 315
    Yangon **S:**334
    map(s) **M:**558
    picture(s)
        elephant hauling teak **M:**559
        flag **F:**236
        house on stilts **M:**558
        monk **M:**557
        mountains and forests **M:**559
        rice growing **M:**558
        Shwe Dagon pagoda **M:**557
        woman selling produce **M:**557
        Yangon **M:**560
Myasthenia gravis (disease) **M:**521
Mycelium (of fungi) **F:**497; **K:**257
Mycenae (ancient city of Greece) **S:**59
    picture(s)
        fortress gateway **A:**238
Mycenaean culture **A:**236–37; **G:**345; **M:**562
    art as a record **A:**429
    masonry **B:**394
    sculpture **S:**95
    picture(s)
        Mask of Agamemnon **M:**562
Mycerinus (king of ancient Egypt) **E:**111
Mycobacteria **T:**328, 329
Mycology (study of fungi) **F:**498
Mycorrhizal fungi **P:**313
Myelin (outer covering of neurons) **N:**117
Myers, Walter Dean (American poet)
    picture(s)
        illustration for *Brown Angels* **C:**248
        Lawrence illustration for *The Great Migration* **C:**247
My Fair Lady (musical by Loewe and Lerner) **M:**554
"My Heart Leaps Up When I Behold" (poem by William Wordsworth) **W:**242
"My Kinsman, Major Molineux" (short story by Hawthorne) **H:**65
Mykonos (Greek island)
    picture(s) **G:**331; **M:**211
Mynah (bird) **B:**249–50; **P:**179
Myocardial infarction *see* Heart attack
Myocarditis (heart disease) **H:**84
Myocardium (middle layer of the wall of the heart) **H:**80
Myofibrils (strands of tissue in muscle fibers)
    picture(s) **M:**521
"My Old Kentucky Home" (song by Stephen Foster) **K:**220
Myopia *see* Nearsightedness
Myosin (protein in muscle cells) **M:**521
MyPyramid (nutritional graphic) **F:**348; **N:**428
    picture(s) **F:**349; **N:**428
Myrmecologists (biologists who study ants) **A:**318
Myron of Thebes (Greek sculptor) **G:**349
Myrrh (resin used in incense) **R:**184
Myrtle Beach (South Carolina)
    picture(s) **S:**298, 302
"My Shadow" (poem by Robert Louis Stevenson) **S:**450
Mysore (India) **I:**122
Mysteries of Udolpho, The (novel by Radcliffe) **M:**563
Mystery and detective stories **F:**114; **M:**563–67
    codes and ciphers in **C:**394
    detective story invented by Poe **A:**209
    Sherlock Holmes **D:**291–92
Mystery of Edwin Drood, The (novel by Dickens) **D:**152
Mystery plays (medieval drama) **D:**26, 300
Mysticetes *see* Baleen whales
Mystic Seaport and Marinelife Aquarium (Connecticut) **C:**422, 514
    picture(s) **C:**423, 509, 514

PHOTO CREDITS

The following list credits the sources of photos used in THE NEW BOOK OF KNOWLEDGE. Credits are listed, by page, photo by photo—left to right, top to bottom. Wherever appropriate, the name of the photographer has been listed with the source, the two being separated by a dash. When two or more photos by different photographers appear on one page, their credits are separated by semicolons.

M

Cover © David Schmidt—Masterfile
8 © E. Streichan—SuperStock
10 The Granger Collection; The Bettmann Archive; The Granger Collection; Corbis-Bettmann.
11 The Granger Collection
12 Collection of the New York Historical Society; The Granger Collection.
13 © Skip Brown—Folio, Inc.
14 © David Wells—The Image Works
15 © Paolo Koch—Photo Researchers
16 © Warren Ogden—Art Resource
18 © BP & V Photographic Associates (all photos on page).
20 Culver Pictures
21 The Granger Collection
22 © Martha Swope
26 The Granger Collection
28 © Lyle Leduc—Liaison Agency
29 © Martyn F. Chillmaid—Science Photo Library—Photo Researchers; © David R. Frazier Photolibrary.
30 © Kennan Ward—The Stock Market
32 NASA; © Tim Davis—Stone.
33 © Dale E. Boyer—Photo Researchers
35 Courtesy of Lillian Vernon Corp.
37 © Bill Silliker, Jr.; © Bill Silliker, Jr.; © Joseph Sohm—The Stock Market.
38 © Michael P. Gadomski—Photo Researchers
39 © Jeff Greenberg—Photo Researchers
40 © Voscar—The Maine Photographer (all photos on page).
41 © Randy Ury—The Stock Market; © Voscar—The Maine Photographer.
42 © Jeff Greenberg—Photo Researchers; © Chuck Campbell.
43 © Jeff Greenberg—Photo Researchers; © Voscar—The Maine Photographer.
44 © Voscar—The Maine Photographer; © Gary Stanley; © Voscar—The Maine Photographer; © Voscar—The Maine Photographer.
45 © Voscar—The Maine Photographer (all photos on page).
46 © Chuck Campbell
48 The Bettmann Archive; The Granger Collection; © Chuck Campbell.
49 © George Tames—Globe Photos; Globe Photos.
51 © Sean Sprague—Lineair/Peter Arnold, Inc.
54 © R. Ian Lloyd—Masterfile; © Wood—Zefa Collection/Masterfile; © Ellerbrock & Schafft—Bilderberg/Peter Arnold, Inc.; © Neil Montanus—Houserstock.
55 © R. Ian Lloyd—Masterfile
56 © R. Ian Lloyd—Masterfile
57 © R. Ian Lloyd—Masterfile
58 © ROTA/Camera Press/Retna Ltd.
59 © Eddie Adams—AP/Wide World Photos
61 © Ariadne Van Zandbergen—Lonely Planet Images
62 © Hector Acebes—Photo Researchers
63 © Jose Fuste Raga—eStock Photo
65 © Gary W. Griffen—Animals Animals; © Debra P. Hershkowitz—Bruce Coleman Inc.; Mark Newman—Bruce Coleman Inc.; © Martin Harvey—The Wildlife Collection; © Erwin and Peggy Bauer—Bruce Coleman Inc.
67 © John Shaw—Bruce Coleman Inc.; © Michael and Barbara Reed—Animals Animals;

© Alan D. Carey—Photo Researchers.
68 © Henry Holdsworth—The Wildlife Collection; © Martin Harvey—The Wildlife Collection.
69 © William Munoz—Photo Researchers; © John Canalosi—Peter Arnold, Inc.
70 © Martin Harvey—The Wildlife Collection; © Dan Guravich—Photo Researchers.
71 © F. Stuart Westmorland—Photo Researchers; © Gunter Ziesler—Peter Arnold, Inc.
72 © Leonard Lee Rue—Photo Researchers; © S. R. Maglione—Photo Researchers; © Ted Levin—Animals Animals.
73 © Gerald C. Kelley—Photo Researchers; © Runk/Schoenberger—Grant Heilman Photography.
74 © Brian Milne—Animals Animals
75 © Breck P. Kent—Animals Animals
76 © Gregory G. Dimijian—Photo Researchers
77 © Douglas Faulkner—Photo Researchers; David B. Fleetham—Oxford Scientific Films/ Animals Animals.
79 © Mike Yamashita—Woodfin Camp & Associates
81 © Brian S. Sytnyk—VIS-U-TEL; © Grandmaison—First Light.
82 © Brian Milne—First Light; © Brian S. Sytnyk—VIS-U-TEL; © Brian S. Sytnyk— VIS-U-TEL.
83 © Ken Straiton—First Light; © Brian S. Sytnyk—VIS-U-TEL.
88 Chrysler Corporation
89 Chrysler Corporation
90 © Harry Redel—Black Star
91 © Kevin Fleming—Corbis
92 Los Alamos National Laboratory
98 *Vallard Atlas* by Rand McNally & Co. 1982 Permission of Henry E. Huntington Library, San Marino
99 Great American Marble Factory
102 *Radio Times*—Hulton Picture Library
103 Giraudon/Art Resource
104 The Bridgeman/Art Resource
105 JPL
107 JPL; © Frank Rossotto—Stocktrek.
108 JPL; © Frank Rossotto—Stocktrek.
109 JPL/NASA (all photos on page).
110 U.S. Army Photograph
111 The Granger Collection
112 © Cameramann International, Ltd.
113 © Cameramann International Ltd.
114 © Tom McHugh—Photo Researchers; © Kenneth W. Fink—National Audubon Society/ Photo Researchers; © Peter B. Kaplan—Photo Researchers.
115 © Stouffer Production/Animals Animals; © Fritz Prenzel—Animals Animals.
116 © Capital Features/The Image Works
117 Mansell/TimePix
118 The Granger Collection
119 Scala/Art Resource; The Granger Collection.
121 © Bill Howe—Photri; © Joe Clark; © J. Blank—H. Armstrong Roberts.
122 © Kevin Fleming; © Photri.
125 © Martin Rogers—Uniphoto Picture Agency; © Lucian Nienmeyer—LNS Arts; © Photri.
126 © Ed Drifmeer—Photri; © Cameramann International Ltd.
127 © Photri
128 © Lee Battaglia—Photo Researchers; © S. Barth—H. Armstrong Roberts; © Lani—Photri.

© Kenneth Garrett—Woodfin Camp & Associates.
129 © Cameramann International Ltd.; © Photri.
130 © M. E. Warren—Photo Researchers
132 North Wind Picture Archives; © Arthur Grace—Corbis-Sygma; The Granger Collection.
133 The Granger Collection
137 © Susan Lapides—Woodfin Camp & Associates; © Candace Cochrane—Positive Images; © Joseph Sohm—The Image Works.
138 © Mark D. Phillips—Photo Researchers; © Lionel Deleviogne—Stock, Boston.
140 © Robert E. Murowchick—Photo Researchers
141 © Susan Lapides—Woodfin Camp & Associates; © Bob Kramer—Stock, Boston.
142 © John M. Roberts—The Stock Market
143 © Bob O'Shaughnessy—The Stock Market; © Ulrike Welsch.
144 © J. Blank—H. Armstrong Roberts; © Ivan Massar—Positive Images; © R. Kork—H. Armstrong Roberts.
145 © Grace Schaub—Leo de Wys; © G. Ahrens— H. Armstrong Roberts.
146 The Granger Collection
148 The Granger Collection; The Bettmann Archive.
149 The Bettmann Archive
150 North Wind Picture Archives
152 © O. K. Riegger
154 IBM—Fishkill, N.Y.
155 Courtesy, UMA Chowdhry, E.I. DuPont de Nemours and Co.; IBM Almaden Research Center.
156 © Cameramann International Ltd.
158 © Henry Groskinsky—Peter Arnold
159 © Steve Gerard—Photo Researchers
161 © R. Michael Stuckney—Comstock
162 The British Museum
165 Courtesy, The Science Museum, London
166 The Granger Collection; The Granger Collection; Mary Evans Picture Library.
167 The Granger Collection
170 David Hobill, Michael Welge, Daniel Simkins, Principal Investigators—NCSA; Jeffrey Yost, Visualization—NCSA.
171 © Lee Boltin
179 © Clive Shirley—Panos Pictures
184 Field Museum of Natural History; Copyright © President and Fellows of Harvard College 1982. All Rights Reserved. "Peabody Museum-Harvard University-Photograph by Hillell Burger."
185 © Justin Kerr
187 © Justin Kerr
189 UPI/Bettmann Newsphotos
190 Chicago Historical Society
191 The Granger Collection (all photos on page).
192 The Granger Collection
194 Culver Pictures; The White House Collection, © copyright White House Historical Association.
195 © Ken Heyman
196 © McCarten—PhotoEdit
197 © FPG International
199 Saudi Arabian Information Service
201 The Granger Collection
202 Alinari/Art Resource; Art Resource.
203 © David Schmidt—Masterfile; © SuperStock; © David Job—Stone/Getty Images.
205 Parke Davis & Company, Detroit

396a Mr. and Mrs. Charles B. Benenson—Robert S. Crandall; Ellison Manufacturing Co.—Robert S. Crandall; Collection: Myron Orlovsky—Eric Pollitzer photo—Leo Castelli Gallery.

of Modern Art, Purchase.

397 AP/Wide World Photos; © Pictorial Parade.

399 © Francis Apesteguy—Liaison Agency.

400 © Francis G. Mayer.

402 © Novosti.

404 © James F. Parnell.

406 © Jane Burton—Bruce Coleman Inc.; © James Carmichael—Bruce Coleman Inc.

407 © G. R. Williamson—Bruce Coleman Inc.; © Kjell B. Sandved—Photo Researchers; © Gilbert Grant—Photo Researchers.

408 © Norbert Wu.

409 © Steve Vidler—eStock.

410 The Museum of Modern Art, New York.

411 Scala, New York.

412 Chase Manhattan Archives.

414 © Comstock.

416 © Xinhua-Chine Nouvelle—Liaison Agency; © George Holton—Photo Researchers; © Paul Harris—Stone.

418 Art Resource.

419 © Norman Myers—Bruce Coleman Inc.; © Nigel J. Dennis—Photo Researchers.

420 © Michael Freeman—Bruce Coleman Inc.; © Jean-Claude Carton—Bruce Coleman Inc.; © Kevin Schafer; © G. C. Kelley—Photo Researchers.

421 © Rod Williams—Bruce Coleman Inc.; © Rod Williams—Bruce Coleman Inc.; © Daniel J. Cox—Stone; © Andrew L. Young—Photo Researchers; © Jack Swenson—The Wildlife Collection.

422 © Tom McHugh—Photo Researchers; © Karl & Kay Ammann—Bruce Coleman Inc.; © Diana Rogers—Bruce Coleman Inc.

423 National Portrait Gallery, Smithsonian Institution/Art Resource; The Granger Collection; The Granger Collection.

424 The Granger Collection.

425 The Bettmann Archive.

426 © Ted Hooper—Folio, Inc.

427 Corbis-Bettmann.

429 © John Reddy Photographics; © John Reddy Photographics; © Phil Farnes—Photo Researchers.

430 © Rob Outlaw; © L. Burton—H. Armstrong Roberts; © David Muench—H. Armstrong Roberts.

431 © John Reddy Photographics; © Buddy Mays—Travel Stock.

432 © Tom Dietrich; © Chris Roberts.

433 © John Reddy Photographics; © Wayne Mumford.

434 © John Reddy Photographics; © Wayne Mumford; © Tom Dietrich; © Larry Mayer.

435 © Tom Dietrich.

436 © M. Schneiders—H. Armstrong Roberts; © Jim Brown—The Stock Market; © François Gohier—Photo Researchers.

437 © W. J. Scott—H. Armstrong Roberts.

440 The Bettmann Archive; © SuperStock; © Allan C. Hooper—World Museum of Mining.

441 North Wind Picture Archives.

442 © Kurt Scholz—SuperStock.

443 North Wind Picture Archives.

444 © Perry Mastrovito—Reflexion.

445 © Perry Mastrovito—Reflexion.

446 © John Eastcott/Yva Momatiuk—Woodfin Camp & Associates.

447 NASA—Courtesy of Walt Frerck.

448 © Yerkes Observatory (all photos on page).

449 © Yerkes Observatory (all photos on page).

450 NASA—Courtesy of Walt Frerck; © Hale Observatories—Science Source—Photo Researchers.

453 NASA.

454 Ames Research Center/NASA.

455 Johnson Space Center.

456 The Granger Collection.

457 © Nelson Bohart & Associates.

458 © Penny Tweedie—Stone; © Batt Johnson—Unicorn Stock Photos.

459 © Nicholas DeVore—Stone.

460 © Phyllis Picardi—Photo Network.

461 AFP/Corbis-Bettmann.

462 © Danny Hoffman—Corbis-Sygma.

463 The Bettmann Archive.

464 Scala/Art Resource.

465 © Travelpix—FPG International.

466 © Steve Vidler—Leo de Wys; © Wally McNamee—Woodfin Camp & Associates.

467 © Robert Kalfus—Liaison Agency.

468 © Novosti Press Agency from Sovfoto.

469 Art Resource.

470 Copyright © 1982, Grandma Moses Properties Co., New York.

471 © John Shaw—Bruce Coleman Inc.

472 © E. R. Degginger; © E. R. Degginger; © Michael P. Gadomski—Photo Researchers Inc.

473 © Ed Reschke—Peter Arnold, Inc.

477 © MGM—Courtesy, Kobal; Movie Still Archives; Movie Still Archives; © Frances M. Roberts; © James Wilson—Woodfin Camp & Associates.

478 Photofest.

479 © The Stock Market.

480 Movie Still Archives (all photos on page).

481 © Patricio Estay—GLMR—Liaison Agency; Photofest.

483 © James Hackett—Leo de Wys; © Eddie Adams—Corbis-Sygma.

484 True Lies © Twentieth Century Fox Film Corporation. All Rights Reserved.

485 © Joseph Sohm—The Stock Market; © Jean-Marc Giboux—Liaison Agency.

486 © David Frazier; Photofest.

487 The Kobal Collection; The Bettmann Archive.

488 The Bettmann Archive; Photofest; Photofest.

489 The Bettmann Archive; Courtesy, The Kobal Collection; © Sunset Boulevard—Corbis-Sygma.

490 Courtesy, Kobal; Everett Collection, Inc.; © Bernard of Hollywood—Corbis-Sygma.

491 © Archive Photos; Photofest.

492 Photofest; © Christian Simonpietri—Corbis-Sygma.

493 Movie Still Archives; © Terry O'Neill—Corbis-Sygma.

494 Photofest; © Archive Photos—Archive France.

495 Movie Still Archives; © Richard Falco—Black Star.

496 Photofest; Movie Still Archives; © Everett Collection, Inc.; © Martin H. Simon—SABA; © Douglas Kirkland—Corbis-Sygma.

497 Photofest; © David James—Corbis-Sygma.

498 Jean P. Bonnier—Holmes—Lebel; © Paolo Koch—Rapho Guillumette.

500 © John Cancalosi—Peter Arnold, Inc.; © Keith Gunnar—Bruce Coleman Inc.

501 © Chris Noble.

502 © John M. Burnley—Photo Researchers.

503 © Nicholas DeVore—Bruce Coleman Inc.; © Spencer Swanger—Tom Stack & Associates.

506 © Arthur M. Greene—Bruce Coleman Inc.; Bob & Clara Calhoun—Bruce Coleman Inc.

507 © John Mead—Science Photo Library—Photo Researchers

508 © Robert Semeniuk—Corbis Stock Market

510 The British Museum

512 © Scala/Art Resource

513 © Rickey Rogers—Reuters/Getty Images

514 © Larry Lefever—Grant Heilman Photography; © Richard B. Levine; © Bob Daemmrich—Uniphoto Picture Agency.

516 © Bob Daemmrich—The Image Works

517 © Alfred Bernheim

518 © Rich Meyer—The Stock Market

519 © Lennart Nilsson, Behold Man, Little, Brown and Company

520 © Lennart Nilsson, Behold Man, Little, Brown and Company; © Lennart Nilsson, Behold Man, Little, Brown and Company; © N. Tiffany—Globe Photos.

522 © Paul Conklin—PhotoEdit

523 © Mickey Krakowski—AP/Wide World Photos

524 Courtesy, The Franklin Institute Science Museum; © Jeff Greenberg—PhotoEdit.

525 © Spencer Grant—PhotoEdit

526 © Seth Rossman—AP/Wide World Photos

527 © Picture Finders Ltd./eStock Photo

528 © Cynthia Johnson—Liaison/Getty Images

529 © Michael Lustbader—Photo Researchers; © Larry West—Photo Researchers.

530 © Claudia Parks—The Stock Market; © Jan Lukas—Photo Researchers; © Gabe Palmer—The Stock Market.

531 UPI/Bettmann Newsphotos; © Pedro Coll—The Stock Market; © Mark Gibson—The Stock Market.

538 Art Resource; The Granger Collection.

539 The Granger Collection (all photos on page).

540 The Bettmann Archive; The Granger Collection; Art Resource; The Granger Collection.

541 © ARCHIV—Photo Researchers; The Bridgeman Art Library.

542 © Stock Montage, Inc.; The Granger Collection; The Bridgeman Art Library; North Wind Picture Archives.

543 North Wind Picture Archives; © ARCHIV—Photo Researchers; © ARCHIV—Photo Researchers.

544 Stock Montage, Inc.; The Granger Collection; © John Abbott.

545 © Brownie Harris—The Stock Market; © Marc & Evelyne Bernheim—Woodfin Camp & Associates; Courtesy Air India.

546 © Fabrice Coffrini—AP/Wide World Photos; Michael Newman—PhotoEdit; © Dennis MacDonald—PhotoEdit.

547 PhotoDisc (all photos on page).

548 PhotoDisc (all photos on page).

549 PhotoDisc (all photos on page).

550 PhotoDisc (all photos on page).

551 PhotoDisc (all photos on page).

552 © Jack Vartoogian

553 Scala/Art Resource

554 © Carol Rosegg; Gjon Mili, Life magazine © Time, Inc.

555 © Steve Liss—Boston Symphony Orchestra at Tanglewood

557 © Monika Abraityte—Network Aspen; © Jeffrey Aaronson—Network Aspen; © Dave Bartruff—Danita Delimont, Agent.

558 © Venetia Dearden—Still Pictures/Peter Arnold, Inc.; © Jean-Leo Dugast—Panos Pictures.

559 © Charlyn Zlotnik—Woodfin Camp & Associates; © David Longstreath—AP/Wide World Photos.

560 © Richard I'Anson—Lonely Planet Images

561 © Jeffrey Aaronson—Network Aspen

562 © Erich Lessing—National Archaeological Museum, Athens, Greece/Art Resource, NY

563 The Granger Collection

564 The Granger Collection; UPI/Bettmann.

565 UPI/Bettmann; © Dominick Abel Literary Agency, Inc.

566 The Granger Collection

567 Library of Congress/Rare Books Collection

568 Giraudon/Art Resource; © Erich Lessing—Art Resource; © Nimatallah—Art Resource; The Granger Collection.

569 The Granger Collection; © Erich Lessing—Art Resource; Giraudon/Art Resource; © Ivar Brynjolfsson—National Museum of Iceland.

570 © Erich Lessing—Art Resource

574 Giraudon/Art Resource

575 The Granger Collection